MANAGEMENT

Leading & Collaborating in a Competitive World

13e

©zlikovec/Shutterstock.com RF

Thomas S. Bateman
McIntire School of Commerce
University of Virginia

Scott A. Snell
Darden Graduate School of Business
University of Virginia

Robert Konopaske
McCoy College of Business
Texas State University

Mc Graw Hill Education

MANAGEMENT: LEADING & COLLABORATING IN A COMPETITIVE WORLD, THIRTEENTH
EDITION
Published by McGraw-Hill Education, 2 Penn Plaza, New York, NY 10121. Copyright © 2019 by McGraw-Hill
Education. All rights reserved. Printed in the United States of America. Previous editions © 2017, 2015, and
2013. No part of this publication may be reproduced or distributed in any form or by any means, or stored in
a database or retrieval system, without the prior written consent of McGraw-Hill Education, including, but not
limited to, in any network or other electronic storage or transmission, or broadcast for distance learning.
Some ancillaries, including electronic and print components, may not be available to customers outside the
United States.

This book is printed on acid-free paper.

1 2 3 4 5 6 7 8 9 LWI 21 20 19 18

ISBN 978-1-259-92764-5
MHID 1-259-92764-4

Director: *Michael Ablassmeir*
Product Developer: *Kelsey Darin*
Executive Marketing Manager: *Debbie Clare*
Lead Content Project Manager: *Christine Vaughan*
Content Project Manager: *Keri Johnson*
Senior Buyer: *Laura Fuller*
Lead Designer: *David Hash*
Lead Content Licensing Specialist: *Carrie Burger*
Cover Image: *©zlikovec/Shutterstock.com RF*
Compositor: *SPi Global*

All credits appearing on page or at the end of the book are considered to be an extension of the copyright page.

Library of Congress Cataloging-in-Publication Data

Names: Bateman, Thomas S., author. | Snell, Scott, 1958- author. | Konopaske,
  Robert, author.
Title: Management: leading & collaborating in a competitive world/Thomas
  S. Bateman, McIntire School of Commerce, University of Virginia, Scott A.
  Snell, Darden Graduate School of Business, University of Virginia, Robert
  Konopaske, McCoy College of Business, Texas State University.
Description: Thirteenth edition. | New York, NY: McGraw-Hill Education, [2019]
Identifiers: LCCN 2017048278 | ISBN 9781259927645 (alk. paper)
Subjects: LCSH: Management.
Classification: LCC HD31.2 .B36 2019 | DDC 658-dc23
LC record available at https://lccn.loc.gov/2017048278

The Internet addresses listed in the text were accurate at the time of publication. The inclusion of a website does
not indicate an endorsement by the authors or McGraw-Hill Education, and McGraw-Hill Education does not
guarantee the accuracy of the information presented at these sites.

mheducation.com/highered

For my parents, Tom and Jeanine Bateman,
and Mary Jo, Lauren, T.J., and James

and

My parents, John and Clara Snell,
and Marybeth, Sara, Jack, and Emily

and

My parents, Art and Rose Konopaske,
and Vania, Nick, and Isabella

About the Authors

THOMAS S. BATEMAN

Thomas S. Bateman is Bank of America professor in the McIntire School of Commerce at the University of Virginia, teaching leadership and organizational behavior at undergraduate and graduate levels. For many years prior to joining the University of Virginia, he taught organizational behavior at the Kenan-Flagler Business School of the University of North Carolina to undergraduates, MBA students, PhD students, and practicing managers. He taught for two years in Europe as a visiting professor at the Institute for Management Development (IMD), one of the world's leaders in the design and delivery of executive education. Professor Bateman earned his doctorate in business administration at Indiana University, and his BA from Miami University.

Professor Bateman is an active management researcher, writer, and consultant. He serves on the editorial boards of the *Academy of Management Review*, the *Academy of Management Journal*, and the *Asia Pacific Journal of Business and Management*. His articles appear in professional journals such as the *Academy of Management Journal, Academy of Management Review, Journal of Applied Psychology, Organizational Behavior and Human Decision Processes, Journal of Organizational Behavior, Human Relations, Journal of Macromarketing*, and *Proceedings of the National Academy of Sciences*. His recent work on leadership and psychology in the domain of climate change appears in *Nature Climate Change, Global Environmental Change*, and *The Conversation*.

Tom's long-time research interests center on proactive behavior (including leadership) by employees at all levels, with a recent turn toward scientists and public leadership. His consulting work has included a variety of organizations including Singapore Airlines, the Brookings Institution, the U.S. Chamber of Commerce, the Nature Conservancy, LexisNexis, Weber Shandwick, the Association of Climate Change Officers, and Chicago's Field Museum of Natural History.

SCOTT A. SNELL

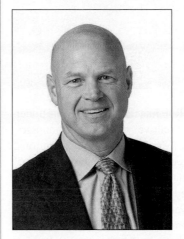

Scott Snell is professor of business administration at the University of Virginia's Darden Graduate School of Business. He teaches courses in leadership, organizational capability development, and human capital consulting. His research focuses on human resources and the mechanisms by which organizations generate, transfer, and integrate new knowledge for competitive advantage. He is co-author of four books: *Managing People and Knowledge in Professional Service Firms, Management: Leading & Collaborating in a Competitive World, M: Management*, and *Managing Human Resources*. His work has been published in a number of journals such as the *Academy of Management Journal, Academy of Management Review, Strategic Management Journal, Journal of Management, Journal of Management Studies*, and *Human Resource Management*, and he was recently listed among the top 100 most-cited authors in scholarly journals of management. He has served on the boards of the Strategic Management Society's human capital group, the Society for Human Resource Management Foundation, the Academy of Management's human resource division, the *Human Resource Management Journal*, the *Academy of Management Journal*, and the *Academy of Management Review*. Professor Snell has worked with companies such as AstraZeneca, Deutsche Telekom, Shell, and United Technologies to align strategy, capability, and investments in talent. Prior to joining the Darden faculty in 2007, he was professor and director of executive education at Cornell University's Center for Advanced Human Resource Studies and a professor of management in the Smeal College of Business at Pennsylvania State University. He received a BA in psychology from Miami University, as well as MBA and PhD degrees in business administration from Michigan State University.

ROBERT KONOPASKE

Rob Konopaske is an associate professor of management and principles of management course coordinator in the McCoy College of Business at Texas State University. At the College, he also serves as the Director of the Institute for Global Business. A passionate educator who cares deeply about providing students with an exceptional learning experience, Rob has taught numerous undergraduate, graduate, and executive management courses, including Introduction to Management, Organizational Behavior, Human Resource Management, International Human Resources Management, and International Business. He has received numerous teaching honors while at Texas State University, most recently the 2016 Presidential Distinction Award, 2014 Gregg Master Teacher Award, and 2012–2013 Namesake for the PAWS Preview new student socialization program (an honor bestowed annually upon eight out of approximately 2,000 faculty and staff). Rob earned his doctoral degree in business administration (management) at the University of Houston, a master in international business studies (MIBS) degree from the University of South Carolina, and a bachelor of arts degree (Phi Beta Kappa) from Rutgers University. He has taught at the University of Houston, the University of North Carolina at Wilmington, and Florida Atlantic University.

Rob is co-author of several recent editions of six books: *Management: Leading & Collaborating in a Competitive World, M: Management, Organizational Behavior and Management, Human Resource Management, Global Management and Organizational Behavior*, and *Organizations: Behavior, Structure, Processes*. The eleventh edition of *Organizations* won a McGuffey Award (for longevity of textbooks and learning materials whose excellence has been demonstrated over time) from the national Text and Academic Authors' Association.

Rob's research has been published in such outlets as the *Journal of Applied Psychology, Academy of Management Executive, Management International Review, Business Horizons, Human Resource Management, Journal of Business Research, Journal of Management Education, Nonprofit Management and Leadership, Journal of Managerial Psychology*, and *Human Resource Management Review*. Dr. Konopaske currently serves on the editorial board of the *International Journal of Human Resource Management*.

Rob has lived and worked internationally, speaks three languages, and has held management positions with a large nonprofit organization and a Fortune 500 multinational firm. He consults, trains, and conducts research projects for a wide range of companies and industries. Current or former clients include Credit Suisse, PricewaterhouseCoopers, Buffalo Wings & Rings, KPMG, New Braunfels Utilities, and Johnson & Johnson.

Preface

Welcome to our 13th edition! Thank you to everyone who has used and learned from previous editions. We are proud to present to you our best-ever edition.

Our Goals

Our mission with this text is to inform, instruct, and inspire. We hope to *inform* by providing descriptions of the important concepts and practices of modern management. We hope to *instruct* by describing how you can identify options, make decisions, and take effective action. We hope to *inspire* not only by writing in an interesting way but also by providing a real sense of the challenges and fascinating opportunities ahead of you. Whether your goal is starting your own company, leading a team to greatness, building a strong organization, delighting your customers, or generally forging a positive and sustainable future, we want to inspire you to take meaningful action.

We hope to inspire you to be both a thinker and a doer. We want you to know the important issues, consider the consequences of your actions, and think before you act. But good thinking is not enough; management is a world of action. It is a world for those who commit to high performance.

Competitive Advantage

The world of management is competitive, while also rich with important collaborative opportunities. Never before has it been so imperative to your career that you learn the skills of management. Never before have people had so many opportunities and challenges with so many potential risks and rewards.

You will compete with other people for jobs, resources, and promotions. Your employer will compete with others for contracts, clients, and customers. To survive the competition, and to thrive, you must perform in ways that give you an edge that makes others want to hire you, buy from you, and do repeat business with you. Now and over time, you will want them to choose you, not the competition.

By this standard, managers and organizations must *perform.* Six essential performance dimensions are *cost, quality, speed, innovation, service,* and *sustainability.* When managed well, these performance dimensions deliver value to your customer and competitive advantage to you and your organization. Lacking performance on one or more of them puts you at a disadvantage. We elaborate on them all, throughout the book.

Our goal is to keep you focused on delivering important "bottom line" results—to make sure you think continually about delivering the goods that make both you and your organization successful. Good management practices and processes are the keys to delivering the results that you want and your employer wants. This results-oriented focus of *Management,* 13th edition, is a unique highlight you will take away from this book.

Leading & Collaborating

Yes, business is competitive. But it's not that simple. In fact, to think strictly in terms of competition is overly cynical, and such cynicism can sabotage your performance. Along with a realistic perspective on competitive realities, important action elements in managerial success are *collaboration* and *leadership.* To succeed, teams and organizations need people to work *with* rather than against one another. Put another way, you can't perform alone—the world is too complex, and business is too challenging.

You need to work with your teammates. Leaders and followers need to work as collaborators more than as adversaries. Work groups throughout your organization need to cooperate with one another. Business and government, often viewed as antagonists, can work productively together. And today more than ever, companies that traditionally were competitors engage in joint ventures and find other ways to collaborate on some things even as they compete in others. Leadership is needed to make these collaborations work.

How does an organization create competitive advantage through collaboration? It's all about the people, and it derives from good leadership.

Three stereotypes of leadership are that it comes from the top of the company, that it comes from one's immediate boss, and that it means being decisive and issuing commands. These stereotypes contain some truth, but realities are much more complex and challenging.

First, the person at the top may or may not provide effective leadership—in fact, truly good leadership is far too rare. Second, organizations need leaders at all levels, in every team and work unit. This includes you, beginning early in your career, and this is why leadership is a vital theme in this book. Third, leaders should be capable of decisiveness and of giving commands, but relying too much on this traditional approach isn't enough. Great leadership is far more inspirational than that, and helps people both to think differently and to work differently—including working collaboratively toward outstanding results.

True leadership—from your boss as well as from you—inspires collaboration, which in turn generates results that are good for you, your employer, your customer, and all the people involved.

As Always, Currency and Variety in the 13th Edition

It goes without saying that this textbook, in its 13th edition, remains on the cutting edge of topical coverage, updated throughout with both current business examples and recent management research. We continue to emphasize real results, sustainability, and diversity, themes on which we were early and remain current leaders.

While still organizing the chapters around the classic management functions, we modernize those functions with a far more dynamic orientation. Looking constantly at change and the future, we describe the management functions as Delivering Strategic Value (for Planning), Building a Dynamic Organization (for Organizing), Mobilizing People (for Leading), and last but hardly least, Learning and Changing (for Controlling).

Special Features

Every chapter offers a fascinating and useful portfolio of special boxed features that bring the subject matter to life in real time:

1. Management in Action, a hallmark feature, presents unfolding contemporary three-part cases about today's business leaders and companies. The first part, "Manager's Brief," encourages students at the start of each chapter to begin thinking about one or more of that chapter's major themes in the context of the current business scene. For example, Chapter 1 introduces Facebook's Mark Zuckerberg and some of the challenges his company faces. The second Management in Action element, "Progress Report," appears about halfway through each chapter and incorporates additional chapter themes into the narrative. At each stage of this unfolding feature, we offer suggestions or questions for classroom discussion, in-class group work, or simply reflection. Closing out the Management in Action three-part series is "Onward," at the end of each chapter, which distills key aspects of the chapter and challenges students with questions for further consideration. Chapter 1's closing "Onward" segment reflects on what it might be like to work at Facebook.

2. Social Enterprise boxes offer examples illustrating chapter themes from outside the private sector. Many students are deeply interested in social entrepreneurs and enterprises, inherently and for future employment possibilities. Examples include: "Ashoka's Bill Drayton, Pioneer of Social Entrepreneurship" (Chapter 1), "Are Business School Graduates Willing to Work for Social Enterprises?" (Chapter 10), and "Piramal Sarvajal Provides Clean Water via 'Water ATMs,'" (Chapter 17).

3. Multiple Generations at Work boxes discuss chapter themes from multigenerational perspectives, based on data rather than stereotypes, with a goal of strengthening what too often are difficult workplace relationships. Examples include: "Are 'Portfolio Careers' the New Normal?" (Chapter 2), "Crowdsourcing: An Inexpensive Source of Creative Ideas" (Chapter 3), and "Tech-Savvy Gen Z Is Entering the Workforce" (Chapter 17).

4. The Digital World feature offers unique examples of how companies and other users employ digital/social media in ways that capitalize on various ideas in each chapter. Students of course will relate to the social media but also learn of interesting examples and practice that most did not know before. Instructors will learn a lot as well!

That's the big picture. We believe the management stories in the boxed features light up the discussion and connect the major themes of the new edition with the many real worlds students will enter soon.

Up next is just a sampling of specific changes, updates, and new highlights in the 13th edition—enough to convey the wide variety of people, organizations, issues, and management challenges represented throughout the text.

Chapter 1

- New Management in Action about Mark Zuckerberg of Facebook.
- New Social Enterprise about Bill Drayton of Ashoka.
- New example of Yum! Brands having 43,000 restaurants in 135 countries.
- New Exhibit 1.1: "Staying Ahead of the Competition."
- New example of entrepreneurial college students pitching sustainable business ideas.
- New passage about artificial intelligence simplifying human-technology interfaces.
- New example of Quicken Loans Rocket Mortgage applications taking minutes to complete.
- New passage about Facebook entering the job posting space to compete against LinkedIn.

Chapter 2

- New Management in Action about Jeff Bezos creating Amazon's organizational environment.
- New Multiple Generations at Work about "portfolio careers" becoming the new normal.
- New Social Enterprise about the Paris Agreement and combating climate change.
- New example of Microsoft's HoloLens teaching medical students about human anatomy.

- Revised Exhibit 2.5: "Potential Substitutes and Complements."

- New example of AstraZeneca losing patent protection of its $5 billion product, Crestor.

- New passage on organizational challenges associated with acquisitions.

- New example of Target investing in "green chemistry innovation."

Chapter 3

- New Management in Action about Uber's questionable decision making.

- New example of General Electric using data analytics to improve efficiencies of digital wind farms.

- Updated Exhibit 3.2: "Comparison of Types of Decisions."

- New passage about *National Geographic*'s "Wanderlust" social media photo competition.

- New Exhibit 3.3: "The Phases of Decision Making."

- New example about IDEO suggesting ways to encourage employee creativity.

- New Exhibit 3.8: "Managing Group Decision Making."

- New example about Havenly crowdsourcing feedback on its pricing and new product ideas.

Chapter 4

- Updated Management in Action about Walt Disney scripting its own success.

- Revised Exhibit 4.1: "Decision-Making Stages and Formal Planning Steps."

- New passage about General Motors and Lyft forming an alliance to create a fleet of on-demand autonomous vehicles.

- Revised Exhibit 4.3: "Hierarchy of Goals and Plans."

- New passage about Chipotle's challenges with recent food-safety events.

- New Exhibit 4.5: "The Strategic Management Process."

- New passage about Elon Musk committing to enable human travel to Mars.

- New example of the U.S. Environmental Protection Agency's methane-to-energy projects.

Chapter 5

- New Multiple Generations at Work about Millennials being bullish on business.

- New Social Enterprise about India's Barefoot College, a college for the poor by the poor.

- New passage about Wells Fargo's incentive system leading to a major corporate scandal.

- New example about Amazon suing companies that sell false positive reviews on its site.

- Revised Exhibit 5.2: "Examples of Decisions Made under Different Ethical Systems."

- New example about Nabisco's utilitarian decision to lay off 1,200 workers at a Chicago plant.

- Updated Exhibit 5.3: "Current Ethical Issues in Business."

- New Exhibit 5.6: "A Process for Ethical Decision Making."

- New example about Starbucks building Leadership Energy and Environmental Design (LEED) stores in 20 countries.

Chapter 6

- New Management in Action about Alibaba's evolution to a global brand.

- New example of Harley-Davidson's marketing of motorcycles to riders in international markets.

- New example of Chinese companies purchasing U.S. firms and divisions like Starwood Hotels, Smithfield Foods, and GE's appliance business.

- Updated Exhibit 6.1: "Top 10 Global Firms."

- New example of a small business, AppIt, expanding internationally by acquiring a software development company in India.

- New example about the Philippines becoming a popular location for outsourcing.

- New passage about McDonald's collaborating with an Indian entrepreneur to adapt its menu (e.g., "Chicken Maharajah Mac") to the vegetarian country.

Chapter 7

- New Management in Action about Starbucks' entrepreneurial beginnings.

- New example about 28 million small businesses generating over half of all jobs in the U.S.

- Updated Exhibit 7.2: "Successful Entrepreneurs Who Started in Their 20s."

- New examples of franchises including Jimmy John's and Jazzercise.

- Updated Multiple Generations at Work: "Millennial Entrepreneurs Can Learn from Others with More Experience."

- New passage about Barbara Nascimento, founder of The Traveller Tours in Portugal, describing how to start a business.

- New example of Gordon Logan, CEO of Sports Clips, leveraging the skills of a top management team.

Chapter 8

- Updated Management in Action about leadership and structural changes at General Motors.
- Updated Social Enterprise about Kiva's approach to organizing.
- Updated Multiple Generations at Work about online networks replacing traditional hierarchies.
- New examples of Shake Shack, Microsoft, and Sanofi using top management teams.
- New Exhibit 8.2: "Examples of Differentiation."
- New Exhibit 8.13: "A Network Organization."
- New examples of how Southwest Airlines, MasterCard, SAP, and Target are integrating marketing and communications functions.
- New example of how the Internal Revenue Service is organized around customer groups.

Chapter 9

- New passages about organizing around ordinary and dynamic capabilities.
- New example of Canon's core capability in innovative image technology.
- New example about Dr Pepper Snapple Group, Coca-Cola, and PepsiCo forming an alliance to cut by 25 percent the amount of sugar in their soft drinks by 2025.
- Revised Exhibit 9.2: "How I's Can Become We's."
- New example of Walmart's CEO trying to reduce bureaucracy while encouraging employees to take more initiative.
- New example of Capital One using predictive analytics to make credit card offers to customers.
- New examples of small and large batch technologies.

Chapter 10

- Updated Management in Action about Google's ability to hire top talent.
- Updated Social Enterprise about business school graduates working for social enterprises.
- Updated Multiple Generations at Work about college students needing soft skills.
- New example about Kayak, Etsy, and W. L. Gore creating unique organization cultures.
- New Exhibit 10.1: "An Overview of the HR Planning Process."
- New examples about John Deere and Siemens Energy finding creative ways to train young employees through a combination of academic and hands-on training.

- New example of the U.S. government considering major changes to the H-1B temporary visa program.
- New passage on companies settling discrimination lawsuits brought by employees.

Chapter 11

- New Management in Action about diversity and inclusion at Apple.
- Updated Social Enterprise about managing diversity at Change.org.
- Updated example about changing workforce demographics.
- Updated Exhibit 11.3: "Top Ten Most Powerful Women Executives."
- New example of Kaiser Permanente, AT&T, and MasterCard continuing their strong commitment to diversity.
- Updated example of the number of women in leadership positions in S&P 500 companies.
- New example of percentage of individuals with disabilities who are employed.
- Updated Exhibit 11.6: "Some Top Executives of Color."

Chapter 12

- Updated Management in Action about Indra Nooyi's leading PepsiCo to perform with purpose.
- New Social Enterprise about Elizabeth Hausler's engineering of disaster-proof homes.
- New example of Richard Branson, CEO of Virgin Group, envisioning a world powered by renewable energy by 2050.
- New Exhibit 12.4: "Sources of Leader Power."
- Updated example of famous leaders including Margaret Thatcher, Nelson Mandela, Julius Caesar, and George Washington.
- New example of servant leadership philosophies at Zappos, Whole Foods Market, and the Container Store.
- New example of how Cheryl Bachelder, CEO of Popeye's Louisiana Kitchen, used active listening to increase store sales by 25 percent.
- New passages about lateral, intergroup, and shared leadership.

Chapter 13

- Updated Management in Action about what makes software company, SAS, such a great place to work.
- Updated Multiple Generations at Work about Millennials wanting to fulfill higher-order needs.
- Updated Social Enterprise about giving veterans a renewed sense of purpose.

- New example of the U.S. Department of Homeland Security setting cyber security goals.
- New example of Colorado-based New Belgium Brewery engaging in environmental and sustainability initiatives.
- New passage about how Ryan LLC rewards its employees with 12 weeks of paid pregnancy leave and paid 4-week sabbaticals.
- New passage about Menlo Innovations offering employees creative nonmonetary rewards.
- Updated passages about extrinsic rewards, empowerment, and quality of work life.

Chapter 14

- Updated Management in Action about self-managed teams working at Whole Foods Market.
- New Social Enterprise about co-working becoming more popular.
- Updated Multiple Generations at Work about preparing for global virtual teamwork.
- New passage about Cisco Systems relying on employee teams to remain competitive.
- New Exhibit 14.6: "A Four-Stage Model of Dispute Resolution."
- New example of parallel teams and team-based rewards being used by organizations.

Chapter 15

- New Management in Action about music-sharing platform SoundCloud encouraging the free flow of information among employees.
- Updated Social Enterprise about when the message is the story.
- New example of company review sites like Glassdoor.com and Salary.com attracting negative posts from employees.
- Updated passage about digital communication and social media.
- Updated passage about communication flowing through all parts of organizations.
- New example of Hilcorp, an oil and gas exploration company, using open book management.
- Updated passage about upward communication and open-door policies.

Chapter 16

- New Management in Action about electronic monitoring of employees' health to control costs.
- Updated Social Enterprise about using multiple ways to measure social impact.

- Updated Multiple Generations at Work about companies shifting to more frequent performance reviews.
- New passage about Chipotle Mexican Grill trying to correct its food-safety challenges.
- New example of Home Depot using six sigma to improve customer checkout processes.
- New passage about the role of board members in relation to governance of companies.
- New passage about feedback control and its relationship to employee performance.
- New example of Toyota asking "Why?" to identify root causes of problems.

Chapter 17

- New Management in Action about Elon Musk being an innovator extraordinaire.
- New Social Enterprise about India-based Piramal Sarvajal providing clean water via "Water ATMs."
- New Multiple Generations at Work about tech-savvy Gen Z entering the workforce
- New Exhibit 17.1: "Innovation Types with Examples."
- New passage about retailers like Macy's in New York attracting young shoppers to stores.
- New example of virtual health care for annual patient visits reducing costs.
- New example of biosensor patches being applied to patients' skin to monitor vital signs.
- New passage about Google's FaceNet research team winning a facial recognition competition.

Chapter 18

- Updated Management in Action about Shell Oil's leaders facing off with investors over climate change.
- Updated Multiple Generations at Work about Millennials being ready for the future of work.
- New example of Sears losing its dominance in retail.
- New example of world-class centers in San Francisco, London, Munich, Warsaw, and Shenzen.
- New Exhibit 18.3: "Reasons for Resistance to Change."
- New example of a manager at John Deere implementing change in a gradual manner.
- New Exhibit 18.8: "Opportunity Is Finding Ways to Meet Customers' Needs."
- New passage about big data, Internet of Things, and artificial intelligence combining to make cities smarter.
- New Exhibit 18.9: "Learning Cycle: Explore, Discover, Act."

A Team Effort

This book is the product of a fantastic McGraw-Hill team. Moreover, we wrote this book believing that we are part of a team with the course instructor and with students. The entire team is responsible for the learning process.

Our goal, and that of your instructor, is to create a positive learning environment in which you can excel. But in the end, the raw material of this course is just words. It is up to you to use them as a basis for further reflection, deep learning, and constructive action.

What you do with the things you learn from this course, and with the opportunities the future holds, *counts*. As a manager, you can make a dramatic difference for yourself and for other people. What managers do matters *tremendously*.

Acknowledgments

This book could not have been written and published without the valuable contributions of many individuals.

Special thanks to Lily Bowles, Taylor Gray, and Meg Nexsen for contributing their knowledge, insights, and research. Thanks to Michael Dutch for his contributions to the Instructor's Manual and PowerPoint Presentations, as well as providing insights whenever we call upon him.

Our reviewers over the last 12 editions contributed time, expertise, and terrific ideas that significantly enhanced the quality of the text. The reviewers of the 13th edition are

Germaine Albuquerque *Essex County College*

Derek B. Bardell *Delgado Community College*

Andrew A. Bennett *Old Dominion University*

Harry Bernstein *Essex County College*

Jennifer Blahnik *Lorain County Community College*

Karen Bridgett *Essex County College*

Angela Bruns *Baton Rouge Community College*

John Ephraim Butt *University of North Carolina–Charlotte*

Holly A. Caldwell *Bridgewater College*

Frank Carothers *Somerset Community College*

Robert Cote *Lindenwood University*

Darrell Cousert *University of Indianapolis*

Tony Daniel *Shorter University*

John T. Finley *Columbus State University*

Roy Lynn Godkin *Lamar University*

Dan Hallock *University of North Alabama*

Anne Kelly Hoel *University of Wisconsin–Stout*

Carrie S. Hurst *Tennessee State University*

Sridharan Krishnaswami *Old Dominion University*

Debra D. Kuhl *Pensacola State College*

Thomas Norman *California State University*

Shane Spiller *Western Kentucky University*

Many individuals contributed directly to our development as textbook authors. Dennis Organ provided one of the authors with an initial opportunity and guidance in textbook writing. Jack Ivancevich did the same for one of the other authors. John Weimeister has been a friend and adviser from the very beginning. Thanks also to Christine Scheid for so much good work on previous editions and for continued friendship.

Enthusiastic gratitude to the entire McGraw-Hill Education team, starting with director Mike Ablassmeir, who—and this is more than an aside—spontaneously and impressively knew *Rolling Stone*'s top three drummers of all time. Mike has long provided deep expertise and an informed perspective, not to mention friendship and managerial cool in everything we do. Not technically an author, Mike is most certainly an educator for us and for the instructors and students who learn from the products he leads.

Special thanks to teammates without whom the book would not exist, let alone be such a prideworthy product:

Jamie Koch: so helpful, resourceful, enthusiastic, fast, and on top of everything;

Christine Vaughan: knowledgeable, tech-savvy, patient, always available to help us navigate the online authoring platform;

Debbie Clare: so creative, energetic, always thinking of unique ideas, and encouraging us to engage in new ways of sharing how much the 13th edition means to us;

Claire Hunter: positive, patient, easily amused (thankfully), amazingly effective at keeping us on track and focused;

Kerrie Carfagno: great depth and breadth, in both experience and knowledge, thanks for teaching even more students about our digital world;

Elisa Adams: eloquent, passionate, expressive, and remarkably good at meeting (or beating) deadlines.

Thanks to you all for getting some of our jokes, for being polite about the others, and for being fun as well as talented and dedicated throughout the project.

Finally, we thank our families. Our parents, Jeanine and Tom Bateman, Clara and John Snell, and Rose and Art Konopaske, provided us with the foundation on which we have built our careers. They continue to be a source of great support. Our wives, Mary Jo, Marybeth, and Vania, were encouraging, insightful, and understanding throughout the process. Our children, Lauren, T.J., and James Bateman; Sara, Jack, and Emily Snell; and Nick and Isabella Konopaske, provided an unending source of inspiration for our work and our nonwork. Thank you.

Thomas S. Bateman
Charlottesville, VA

Scott A. Snell
Charlottesville, VA

Robert Konopaske
San Marcos, TX

Bottom Line

In this ever more competitive environment, there are six essential types of performance on which the organization beats, equals, or loses to the competition: cost, quality, speed, innovation, service, and sustainability. These six performance dimensions, when done well, deliver value to the customer and competitive advantage to you and your organization.

Throughout the text, Bateman, Snell, and Konopaske remind students of these six dimensions and their impact on the bottom line with marginal icons. This results-oriented approach is a unique hallmark of this textbook.

New questions in this edition further emphasize the bottom line. The Instructor's Manual has answers to these questions.

Bottom Line

In all businesses—services as well as manufacturing—strategies that emphasize good customer service provide a critical competitive advantage. *Identify some excellent and poor customer service that you have received.*

Bottom Line

In all businesses—services as well as manufacturing—strategies that emphasize good customer service provide a critical competitive advantage. *Identify some excellent and poor customer service that you have received.*

Bottom Line

In all businesses—services as well as manufacturing—strategies that emphasize good customer service provide a critical competitive advantage. *Identify some excellent and poor customer service that you have received.*

Bottom Line

In all businesses—services as well as manufacturing—strategies that emphasize good customer service provide a critical competitive advantage. *Identify some excellent and poor customer service that you have received.*

Bottom Line

In all businesses—services as well as manufacturing strategies that emphasize good customer service provide a critical competitive advantage. *Identify some excellent and poor customer service that you have received.*

Bottom Line

In all businesses—services as well as manufacturing—strategies that emphasize good customer service provide a critical competitive advantage. *Identify some excellent and poor customer service that you have received.*

In CASE You Haven't Noticed . . .

Bateman, Snell, and Konopaske have put together an outstanding selection of case studies of various lengths that highlight companies' ups and downs, stimulate learning and understanding, and challenge students to respond.

Instructors will find a wealth of relevant and updated cases in every chapter, using companies—big and small—that students will enjoy learning about.

CHAPTER UNFOLDING CASES

Each chapter begins with a "Management in Action: Manager's Brief" section that describes an actual organizational situation, leader, or company. The "Manager's Brief" is referred to again within the chapter in the "Progress Report" section, showing the student how the chapter material relates back to the company, situation, or leader highlighted in the chapter opener. At the end of the chapter, the "Onward" section ties up loose ends and brings the material full circle for the student. Answers to Management in Action section questions can be found in the Instructor's Manual.

SOCIAL ENTERPRISE

Social Enterprise boxes have been updated in each chapter to familiarize students with this fast-growing sector. Answers to Social Enterprise questions are included in the Instructor's Manual.

MULTIPLE GENERATIONS AT WORK

In each chapter, a Multiple Generations at Work box has been updated added to highlight some of the intergenerational challenges faced by managers and employees today.

THE DIGITAL WORLD

The Digital World feature offers unique examples of how companies and other users employ digital/social media in ways that capitalize on various ideas in each chapter.

CONCLUDING CASES

Each chapter ends with a case based on disguised but real companies and people that reinforces key chapter elements and themes.

SUPPLEMENTARY CASES

At the end of each part, an additional case is provided for professors who want students to delve further into part topics.

Outstanding Pedagogy

Management: Leading & Collaborating in a Competitive World is pedagogically stimulating and is intended to maximize student learning. With this in mind, we used a wide array of pedagogical features—some tried and true, others new and novel:

END-OF-CHAPTER ELEMENTS

- **Key terms** are page-referenced to the text and are part of the vocabulary-building emphasis. These terms are defined again in the glossary at the end of the book.

- **Retaining What You Learned** provides clear, concise responses to the learning objectives, giving students a quick reference for reviewing the important concepts in the chapter.

- **Discussion Questions**, which follow, are thought-provoking questions on concepts covered in the chapter and ask for opinions on controversial issues.

- **Experiential Exercises** in each chapter bring key concepts to life so students can experience them firsthand.

Assurance of Learning

This 13th edition contains revised learning objectives and learning objectives are called out within the chapter where the content begins. The Retaining What You Learned for each chapter ties the learning objectives back together as well. And, finally, our test bank provides tagging for the learning objective that the question covers, so instructors will be able to test material covering all learning objectives, thus ensuring that students have mastered the important topics.

Comprehensive Supplements

INSTRUCTOR'S MANUAL

The Instructor's Manual was revised and updated to include thorough coverage of each chapter as well as time-saving features such as an outline, key student questions, class prep work assignments, guidance for using the unfolding cases, video supplements, and, finally, PowerPoint slides.

TEST BANK

The Test Bank includes more than 100 questions per chapter in a variety of formats. It has been revised for accuracy and expanded to include a greater variety of comprehension and application (scenario-based) questions as well as tagged with Bloom's Taxonomy levels and AACSB requirements.

POWERPOINT PRESENTATION SLIDES

The PowerPoint presentation collection contains an easy-to-follow outline including figures downloaded from the text. In addition to providing lecture notes, the slides also include questions for class discussion as well as company examples not found in the textbook. This versatility allows you to create a custom presentation suitable for your own classroom experience.

McGraw-Hill Customer Experience

At McGraw-Hill, we understand that getting the most from new technology can be challenging. That's why our services don't stop after you purchase our products. You can e-mail our product specialists 24 hours a day to get product training online. Or you can search our knowledge bank of frequently asked questions on our support website. For customer support, call **800-331-5094**, submit a support request using our contact us form, **http://mpss.mhhe.com/contact.php**, or visit **www.mhhe.com/support**. One of our technical support analysts will be able to assist you in a timely fashion.

MANAGER'S HOT SEAT

This interactive, video-based application puts students in the manager's hot seat, building critical thinking and decision-making skills and allowing students to apply concepts to real managerial challenges. Students watch as 21 real managers apply their years of experience when confronting unscripted issues such as bullying in the workplace, cyber loafing, globalization, intergenerational work conflicts, workplace violence, and leadership versus management. In addition, Manager's Hot Seat interactive applications, featuring video cases and accompanying quizzes, can be found in Connect.

CREATE

 Instructors can now tailor their teaching resources to match the way they teach! With McGraw-Hill Create, **www.mcgrawhillcreate. com**, instructors can easily rearrange chapters, combine material from other content sources, and quickly upload and integrate their own content, such as course syllabi or teaching notes. Find the right content in Create by searching through thousands of leading McGraw-Hill textbooks. Arrange the material to fit your teaching style. Order a Create book and receive a complimentary print review copy in three to five business days or a complimentary electronic review copy via e-mail within one hour. Go to **www.mcgrawhillcreate.com** today and register.

TEGRITY CAMPUS

 Tegrity makes class time available 24/7 by automatically capturing every lecture in a searchable format for students to review when they study and complete assignments. With a simple one-click start-and-stop process, you capture all computer screens and corresponding audio. Students can replay any part of any class with easy-to-use browser-based viewing on a PC or Mac. Educators know that the more students can see, hear, and experience class resources, the better they learn. In fact, studies prove it. With patented Tegrity "search anything" technology, students instantly recall key class moments for replay online or on iPods and mobile devices. Instructors can help turn all their students' study time into learning moments immediately supported by their lecture. To learn more about Tegrity, watch a twominute Flash demo at **http://tegritycampus.mhhe.com.**

BLACKBOARD® PARTNERSHIP

McGraw-Hill Education and Blackboard have teamed up to simplify your life. Now you and your students can access Connect and Create right from within your Blackboard course—all with one single sign-on. The grade books are seamless, so when a student completes an integrated Connect assignment, the grade for that assignment automatically (and instantly) feeds your Blackboard grade center. Learn more at **www.domorenow.com.**

McGRAW-HILL CAMPUS™

 McGraw-Hill Campus is a new one-stop teaching and learning experience available to users of any learning management system. This institutional service allows faculty and students to enjoy single sign-on (SSO) access to all McGraw-Hill Higher Education materials, including the award-winning McGraw-Hill Connect platform, from directly within the institution's website. With McGraw-Hill Campus, faculty receive instant access to teaching materials (e.g., eTextbooks, test banks, PowerPoint slides, animations, learning objectives, etc.), allowing them to browse, search, and use any instructor ancillary content in our vast library at no additional cost to instructor or students. In addition, students enjoy SSO access to a variety of free content (e.g., quizzes, flash cards, narrated presentations, etc.) and subscription-based products (e.g., McGraw-Hill Connect). With McGraw-Hill Campus enabled, faculty and students will never need to create another account to access McGraw-Hill products and services. Learn more at **www.mhcampus.com.**

ASSURANCE OF LEARNING READY

Many educational institutions today focus on the notion of assurance of learning, an important element of some accreditation standards. *Management: Leading & Collaborating in a Competitive World* is designed specifically to support instructors' assurance of learning initiatives with a simple yet powerful solution. Each test bank question for *Management: Leading & Collaborating in a Competitive World* maps to a specific chapter learning objective listed in the text. Instructors can use our test bank software, EZ Test, to easily query for learning objectives that directly relate to the learning outcomes for their course. Instructors can then use the reporting features of EZ Test to aggregate student results in similar fashion, making the collection and presentation of assurance of learning data simple and easy.

AACSB TAGGING

 McGraw-Hill Education is a proud corporate member of AACSB International. Understanding the importance and value of AACSB accreditation, *Management: Leading & Collaborating in a Competitive World* recognizes the curricula guidelines detailed in the AACSB standards for business

accreditation by connecting selected questions in the text and the test bank to the eight general knowledge and skill guidelines in the AACSB standards. The statements contained in *Management: Leading & Collaborating in a Competitive World* are provided only as a guide for the users of this product. The AACSB leaves content coverage and assessment within the purview of individual schools, the mission of the school, and the faculty. While the *Management: Leading & Collaborating in a Competitive World* teaching package makes no claim of any specific AACSB qualification or evaluation, we have within *Management: Leading & Collaborating in a Competitive World* labeled selected questions according to the eight general knowledge and skills areas.

McGRAW-HILL CUSTOMER EXPERIENCE GROUP CONTACT INFORMATION

At McGraw-Hill Education, we understand that getting the most from new technology can be challenging. That's why our services don't stop after you purchase our products. You can e-mail our Product Specialists 24 hours a day to get product training online. Or you can search our knowledge bank of Frequently Asked Questions on our support website. For Customer Support, call **800-331-5094** or visit **www.mhhe.com/support**. One of our Technical Support Analysts will be able to assist you in a timely fashion.

 **McGraw-Hill Connect®** is a highly reliable, easy-to-use homework and learning management solution that utilizes learning science and award-winning adaptive tools to improve student results.

Homework and Adaptive Learning

- Connect's assignments help students contextualize what they've learned through application, so they can better understand the material and think critically.

- Connect will create a personalized study path customized to individual student needs through SmartBook®.

- SmartBook helps students study more efficiently by delivering an interactive reading experience through adaptive highlighting and review.

Over **7 billion questions** have been answered, making McGraw-Hill Education products more intelligent, reliable, and precise.

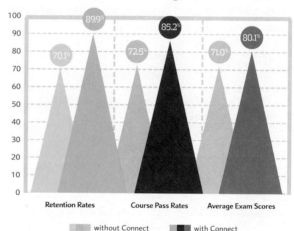

Connect's Impact on Retention Rates, Pass Rates, and Average Exam Scores

	Retention Rates	Course Pass Rates	Average Exam Scores
without Connect	70.1%	72.5%	71.0%
with Connect	89.9%	85.2%	80.1%

Using **Connect** improves retention rates by **19.8%**, passing rates by **12.7%**, and exam scores by **9.1%**.

Quality Content and Learning Resources

73% of instructors who use **Connect** require it; instructor satisfaction **increases** by 28% when **Connect** is required.

- Connect content is authored by the world's best subject matter experts, and is available to your class through a simple and intuitive interface.

- The Connect eBook makes it easy for students to access their reading material on smartphones and tablets. They can study on the go and don't need internet access to use the eBook as a reference, with full functionality.

- Multimedia content such as videos, simulations, and games drive student engagement and critical thinking skills.

Robust Analytics and Reporting

- Connect Insight® generates easy-to-read reports on individual students, the class as a whole, and on specific assignments.

- The Connect Insight dashboard delivers data on performance, study behavior, and effort. Instructors can quickly identify students who struggle and focus on material that the class has yet to master.

- Connect automatically grades assignments and quizzes, providing easy-to-read reports on individual and class performance.

©Hero Images/Getty Images

Impact on Final Course Grade Distribution

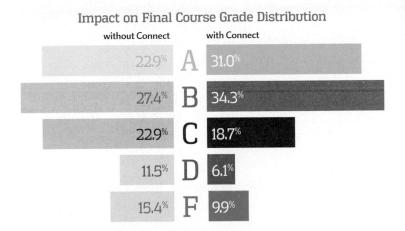

without Connect		with Connect
22.9%	A	31.0%
27.4%	B	34.3%
22.9%	C	18.7%
11.5%	D	6.1%
15.4%	F	9.9%

More students earn **As** and **Bs** when they use **Connect**.

Trusted Service and Support

- Connect integrates with your LMS to provide single sign-on and automatic syncing of grades. Integration with Blackboard®, D2L®, and Canvas also provides automatic syncing of the course calendar and assignment-level linking.

- Connect offers comprehensive service, support, and training throughout every phase of your implementation.

- If you're looking for some guidance on how to use Connect, or want to learn tips and tricks from super users, you can find tutorials as you work. Our Digital Faculty Consultants and Student Ambassadors offer insight into how to achieve the results you want with Connect.

www.mheducation.com/connect

Brief Contents

PREFACE VII

PART ONE FOUNDATIONS OF MANAGEMENT 2

1. Managing and Performing 2
2. The External and Internal Environments 38
3. Managerial Decision Making 72

PART TWO PLANNING: DELIVERING STRATEGIC VALUE 102

4. Planning and Strategic Management 102
5. Ethics, Corporate Responsibility, and Sustainability 130
6. International Management 158
7. Entrepreneurship 188

PART THREE ORGANIZING: BUILDING A DYNAMIC ORGANIZATION 222

8. Organization Structure 222
9. Organizational Agility 250

10. Human Resources Management 276
11. Managing the Diverse Workforce 310

PART FOUR LEADING: MOBILIZING PEOPLE 340

12. Leadership 340
13. Motivating for Performance 370
14. Teamwork 402
15. Communicating 428

PART FIVE CONTROLLING: LEARNING AND CHANGING 458

16. Managerial Control 458
17. Managing Technology and Innovation 488
18. Creating and Leading Change 516

Notes 547

Glossary/Subject Index 594

Name Index 620

Contents

PART ONE FOUNDATIONS OF MANAGEMENT

CHAPTER 1

Managing and Performing 2

MANAGEMENT IN ACTION MANAGER'S BRIEF 3

Managing in a Competitive World 4
  Globalization 4
  Technological Change 5
  Knowledge Management 6
  Collaboration across Boundaries 6

MULTIPLE GENERATIONS AT WORK 7

THE DIGITAL WORLD 7

Managing for Competitive Advantage 8
  Innovation 8
  Quality 8
  Service 9
  Speed 9
  Cost Competitiveness 10
  Sustainability 11
  Delivering All Types of Performance 11
The Functions of Management 12
  Planning: Delivering Strategic Value 12
  Organizing: Building a Dynamic Organization 12

SOCIAL ENTERPRISE 13

  Leading: Mobilizing People 13
  Controlling: Learning and Changing 14
  Performing All Four Management Functions 14

MANAGEMENT IN ACTION PROGRESS REPORT 15

Management Levels and Skills 15
  Top-Level Managers 15
  Middle-Level Managers 16
  Frontline Managers 16
  Working Leaders with Broad Responsibilities 16
  Must-Have Management Skills 17
You and Your Career 18
  Be Both a Specialist and a Generalist 19
  Be Self-Reliant 19
  Connect with People 20

  Actively Manage Your Relationship with Your Organization 20
  Survive and Thrive 21

MANAGEMENT IN ACTION ONWARD 22

  Key Terms 23
  Retaining What You Learned 23
  Discussion Questions 24
  Experiential Exercises 25

CONCLUDING CASE 27

APPENDIX A 28

KEY TERMS 34

DISCUSSION QUESTIONS 35

CHAPTER 2

The External and Internal Environments 38

MANAGEMENT IN ACTION MANAGER'S BRIEF 39

The Macroenvironment 41
  The Economy 41
  Technology 42
  Laws and Regulations 43

MULTIPLE GENERATIONS AT WORK 44

  Demographics 44
  Social Issues 45
  Sustainability and the Natural Environment 45

SOCIAL ENTERPRISE 46

The Competitive Environment 46
  Competitors 47
  New Entrants 48
  Substitutes and Complements 49
  Suppliers 50
  Customers 50

MANAGEMENT IN ACTION PROGRESS REPORT 52

Environmental Analysis 52

Environmental Scanning 53
Scenario Development 53
Forecasting 54
Benchmarking 54

Actively Managing the External Environment 55
Changing the Environment You Are In 55
Influencing Your Environment 55
Adapting to the Environment: Changing the
Organization 56
Choosing an Approach 58

The Internal Environment of Organizations: Culture and
Climate 58
Organization Culture 58

THE DIGITAL WORLD 60

MANAGEMENT IN ACTION ONWARD 61
Organizational Climate 61
Key Terms 62
Retaining What You Learned 62
Discussion Questions 64
Experiential Exercises 64

CONCLUDING CASE 67

APPENDIX B 68

KEY TERMS 70

CHAPTER 3

Managerial Decision Making 72

MANAGEMENT IN ACTION MANAGER'S BRIEF 73
Characteristics of Managerial Decisions 74
Lack of Structure 74
Uncertainty and Risk 75

SOCIAL ENTERPRISE 76
Conflict 76
The Phases of Decision Making 77

Identifying and Diagnosing the Problem 77
Generating Alternative Solutions 77
Evaluating Alternatives 78
Making the Choice 80
Implementing the Decision 80

MANAGEMENT IN ACTION PROGRESS REPORT 81
Evaluating the Decision 82
The Best Decision 82
Barriers to Effective Decision Making 83
Psychological Biases 83
Time Pressures 84

THE DIGITAL WORLD 85
Social Realities 85
Decision Making in Groups 85
Potential Advantages of Using a Group 85
Potential Problems of Using a Group 86
Managing Group Decision Making 87
Leadership Style 87
Constructive Conflict 87
Encouraging Creativity 89
Brainstorming 90

MULTIPLE GENERATIONS AT WORK 91
Organizational Decision Making 91
Constraints on Decision Makers 91
Organizational Decision Processes 92
Decision Making in a Crisis 92

MANAGEMENT IN ACTION ONWARD 94
Key Terms 95
Retaining What You Learned 95
Discussion Questions 96
Experiential Exercises 96

CONCLUDING CASE 98

PART ONE SUPPORTING CASE 99

PART TWO PLANNING: DELIVERING STRATEGIC VALUE

CHAPTER 4

Planning and Strategic
Management 102

MANAGEMENT IN ACTION MANAGER'S BRIEF 103
An Overview of Planning Fundamentals 104
The Basic Planning Process 104

SOCIAL ENTERPRISE 107

Levels of Planning 108
Strategic Planning 108
Tactical and Operational Planning 109
Aligning Tactical, Operational, and Strategic Planning 110
Strategic Planning 111

MANAGEMENT IN ACTION PROGRESS REPORT 112
Step 1: Establishing Mission, Vision, and Goals 113
Step 2: Analyzing External Opportunities and Threats 114

THE DIGITAL WORLD   116
Step 3: Analyzing Internal Strengths and Weaknesses   116
Step 4: SWOT Analysis and Strategy Formulation   118

MULTIPLE GENERATIONS AT WORK   120
Step 5: Strategy Implementation   123
Step 6: Strategic Control   124

MANAGEMENT IN ACTION ONWARD   125
Key Terms   126
Retaining What You Learned   126
Discussion Questions   127
Experiential Exercises   128

CONCLUDING CASE   129

CHAPTER 5

Ethics, Corporate Responsibility, and Sustainability   130

MANAGEMENT IN ACTION MANAGER'S BRIEF   131
It's a Big Issue   132
It's a Personal Issue   133

MULTIPLE GENERATIONS AT WORK   134
Ethics   135
Ethical Systems   135
Business Ethics   137
The Ethics Environment   137

THE DIGITAL WORLD   140
Ethical Decision Making   141
Courage   142

MANAGEMENT IN ACTION PROGRESS REPORT 143
Corporate Social Responsibility   144
Contrasting Views   146
Reconciliation   146
The Natural Environment and Sustainability   147
A Risk Society   147

SOCIAL ENTERPRISE   148
Ecocentric Management   149
Environmental Agendas for the Future   150

MANAGEMENT IN ACTION ONWARD   151
Key Terms   151
Retaining What You Learned   152
Discussion Questions   153
Experiential Exercises   154

CONCLUDING CASE   155

CHAPTER 6

International Management   158

MANAGEMENT IN ACTION MANAGER'S BRIEF   159
Managing in Today's (Global) Economy   160
International Challenges and Opportunities   160
Outsourcing and Jobs   162

The Geography of Business   163
Western Europe   164
Asia: China and India   165
The Americas   166

SOCIAL ENTERPRISE   167
Africa and the Middle East   167
Global Strategy   168
Pressures for Global Integration   168
Pressures for Local Responsiveness   169
Choosing a Global Strategy   170

MANAGEMENT IN ACTION PROGRESS REPORT   172
Entry Mode   173
Exporting   173
Licensing   174
Franchising   174
Joint Ventures   175
Wholly Owned Subsidiaries   175
Working Overseas   176
Skills of the Global Manager   177
Understanding Cultural Issues   177

MULTIPLE GENERATIONS AT WORK   180
Ethical Issues in International Management   181

THE DIGITAL WORLD   182

MANAGEMENT IN ACTION ONWARD   182
Key Terms   183
Retaining What You Learned   183
Discussion Questions   184
Experiential Exercises   185

CONCLUDING CASE   186

CHAPTER 7

Entrepreneurship   188

MANAGEMENT IN ACTION MANAGER'S BRIEF   189
Entrepreneurship   192
Why Become an Entrepreneur?   192
What Does It Take to Succeed?   193
What Business Should You Start?   194

SOCIAL ENTERPRISE   197
What Does It Take, Personally?   199
Success and Failure   200

MANAGEMENT IN ACTION PROGRESS REPORT   201

THE DIGITAL WORLD   202
Common Management Challenges   202
Increasing Your Chances of Success   204

MULTIPLE GENERATIONS AT WORK   209
Corporate Entrepreneurship   209
Building Support for Your Idea   210
Building Intrapreneurship   210
Management Challenges   210
Entrepreneurial Orientation   211

MANAGEMENT IN ACTION ONWARD   212

Key Terms *212*
Retaining What You Learned *212*
Discussion Questions *214*
Experiential Exercises *214*

CONCLUDING CASE   217
PART TWO SUPPORTING CASE   217
APPENDIX C   219

PART THREE ORGANIZING: BUILDING A DYNAMIC ORGANIZATION

CHAPTER 8

Organization Structure   222

MANAGEMENT IN ACTION MANAGER'S BRIEF   223
Fundamentals of Organizing   224
   Differentiation   224
   Integration   225
The Vertical Structure   226
   Authority in Organizations   226
   Hierarchical Levels   227
   Span of Control   228
   Delegation   229
   Decentralization   230
The Horizontal Structure   232
   The Functional Organization   232
SOCIAL ENTERPRISE   234
   The Divisional Organization   234
   The Matrix Organization   236
MANAGEMENT IN ACTION PROGRESS REPORT   237
   The Network Organization   239
MULTIPLE GENERATIONS AT WORK   241
Organizational Integration   241
THE DIGITAL WORLD   242
   Coordination by Standardization   242
   Coordination by Plan   242
   Coordination by Mutual Adjustment   243
   Coordination and Communication   243
Looking Ahead   245
MANAGEMENT IN ACTION ONWARD   245
   Key Terms *246*
   Retaining What You Learned *246*
   Discussion Questions *247*
   Experiential Exercises *247*
CONCLUDING CASE   249

CHAPTER 9

Organizational Agility   250

MANAGEMENT IN ACTION MANAGER'S BRIEF   251
The Responsive Organization   252
Strategy and Organizational Agility   253
MULTIPLE GENERATIONS AT WORK   254
   Organizing around Core Capabilities   254
   Strategic Alliances   255
   The Learning Organization   256
   The High-Involvement Organization   256
Organizational Size and Agility   257
   The Case for Big   257
   The Case for Small   257
   Being Big and Small   258
SOCIAL ENTERPRISE   259
MANAGEMENT IN ACTION PROGRESS REPORT   260
Customers and the Responsive Organization   260
   Customer Relationship Management   260
THE DIGITAL WORLD   262
   Quality Initiatives   262
   Reengineering   264
Technology and Organizational Agility   265
   Types of Technology Configurations   265
   Organizing for Flexible Manufacturing   266
   Organizing for Speed:
   Time-Based Competition   268
Final Thoughts on Organizational Agility   270
MANAGEMENT IN ACTION ONWARD   271
   Key Terms *271*
   Retaining What You Learned *272*
   Discussion Questions *272*
   Experiential Exercises *273*
CONCLUDING CASE   274

CHAPTER 10

Human Resources Management 276

MANAGEMENT IN ACTION MANAGER'S BRIEF 277

Strategic Human Resources Management 278
The HR Planning Process 279

SOCIAL ENTERPRISE 280

Staffing 282
Recruitment 282
Selection 283

THE DIGITAL WORLD 284
Workforce Reductions 286

Developing the Workforce 290
Training and Development 290

MULTIPLE GENERATIONS AT WORK 291

MANAGEMENT IN ACTION PROGRESS REPORT 292

Performance Appraisal 292
What Do You Appraise? 293
Who Should Do the Appraisal? 294
How Do You Give Employees Feedback? 295

Designing Reward Systems 296
Pay Decisions 296
Incentive Systems and Variable Pay 297
Executive Pay and Stock Options 298
Employee Benefits 299
Legal Issues in Compensation and Benefits 299
Health and Safety 300

Labor Relations 300
Labor Laws 301
Unionization 301
Collective Bargaining 302
What Does the Future Hold? 303

MANAGEMENT IN ACTION ONWARD 304
Key Terms 304
Retaining What You Learned 305

Discussion Questions 306
Experiential Exercises 306
CONCLUDING CASE 308

CHAPTER 11

Managing the Diverse Workforce 310

MANAGEMENT IN ACTION MANAGER'S BRIEF 311

Diversity: A Brief History 312

Diversity Today 313
The Changing Workforce 314

MULTIPLE GENERATIONS AT WORK 316
The Age of the Workforce 320

Managing Diversity and Affirmative Action 321
Advantage through Diversity and Inclusion 321
Challenges of Diversity and Inclusion 322

MANAGEMENT IN ACTION PROGRESS REPORT 325

Multicultural Organizations 325

How to Cultivate a Diverse Workforce 326
Top Management's Leadership and Commitment 326

SOCIAL ENTERPRISE 327
Organizational Assessment 327
Attracting Employees 328
Training Employees 329
Retaining Employees 329

THE DIGITAL WORLD 330

MANAGEMENT IN ACTION ONWARD 332
Key Terms 332
Retaining What You Learned 332
Discussion Questions 334
Experiential Exercises 334

CONCLUDING CASE 336

PART THREE SUPPORTING CASE 337

PART FOUR LEADING: MOBILIZING PEOPLE

CHAPTER 12

Leadership 340

MANAGEMENT IN ACTION MANAGER'S BRIEF 341

What Do We Want from Our Leaders? 342
MULTIPLE GENERATIONS AT WORK 343
Vision 343
Leading and Managing 345

Leading and Following   346

Power and Leadership   346
   Sources of Power   346

Traditional Approaches to Understanding Leadership   348
   Leader Traits   348
   Leader Behaviors   349
   The Effects of Leader Behavior   351
   Situational Approaches to Leadership   353

MANAGEMENT IN ACTION PROGRESS REPORT   357

Contemporary Perspectives on Leadership   358
   Charismatic Leadership   358
   Transformational Leadership   359
   Authenticity   360
   Opportunities for Leaders   361

SOCIAL ENTERPRISE   362
   A Note on Courage   362

Developing Your Leadership Skills   363
   How Do I Start?   363

THE DIGITAL WORLD   364
   What Are the Keys?   364

MANAGEMENT IN ACTION ONWARD   364
   Key Terms   365
   Retaining What You Learned   365
   Discussion Questions   367
   Experiential Exercises   367

CONCLUDING CASE   368

CHAPTER 13

Motivating for Performance   370

MANAGEMENT IN ACTION MANAGER'S BRIEF   371

Motivating for Performance   372

Setting Goals   373
   Goals That Motivate   373
   Stretch Goals   374
   Limitations of Goal Setting   374
   Set Your Own Goals   375

Reinforcing Performance   375
   (Mis)Managing Rewards and Punishments   376
   Managing Mistakes   378
   Providing Feedback   378

Performance-Related Beliefs   378
   The Effort-to-Performance Link   379
   The Performance-to-Outcome Link   379
   Impact on Motivation   380
   Managerial Implications of Expectancy Theory   380

MANAGEMENT IN ACTION PROGRESS REPORT   381
   Maslow's Need Hierarchy   381

Understanding People's Needs   381

MULTIPLE GENERATIONS AT WORK   383

Alderfer's ERG Theory   383
McClelland's Needs   384
   Need Theories: International Perspectives   384

Designing Motivating Jobs   385
   Job Rotation, Enlargement, and Enrichment   385

SOCIAL ENTERPRISE   386
   Herzberg's Two-Factor Theory   387
   The Hackman and Oldham Model of Job Design   387
   Empowerment   388

Achieving Fairness   390
   Assessing Equity   390
   Restoring Equity   391
   Procedural Justice   391

Employee Satisfaction and Well-Being   392

THE DIGITAL WORLD   393
   Quality of Work Life   393

MANAGEMENT IN ACTION ONWARD   394
   Psychological Contracts   394
   Key Terms   395
   Retaining What You Learned   395
   Discussion Questions   396
   Experiential Exercises   397

CONCLUDING CASE   399

CHAPTER 14

Teamwork   402

MANAGEMENT IN ACTION MANAGER'S BRIEF   403

The Contributions of Teams   404

Types of Teams   404

MULTIPLE GENERATIONS AT WORK   406
   Self-Managed Teams   406

MANAGEMENT IN ACTION PROGRESS REPORT   407

How Groups Become Real Teams   408
   Group Processes   408
   Critical Periods   409

THE DIGITAL WORLD   410
   Teaming Challenges   410
   Why Groups Sometimes Fail   410

Building Effective Teams   411
   Performance Focus   411
   Motivating Teamwork   412
   Member Contributions   412

SOCIAL ENTERPRISE   413
   Norms   413
   Roles   414
   Cohesiveness   414
   Building Cohesiveness and High-Performance Norms   416

Managing Lateral Relationships   417
   Managing Outward   417

Lateral Role Relationships   418
Managing Conflict   418
Conflict Styles   419
Being a Mediator   420
Electronic and Virtual Conflict   421

MANAGEMENT IN ACTION ONWARD   422
Key Terms   422
Retaining What You Learned   423
Discussion Questions   424
Experiential Exercises   424

CONCLUDING CASE   425

CHAPTER 15

Communicating   428

MANAGEMENT IN ACTION MANAGER'S BRIEF   429
Interpersonal Communication   430
One-Way versus Two-Way Communication   430
Communication Pitfalls   431
Mixed Signals and Misperception   432
Oral and Written Channels   433
Digital Communication and Social Media   433

MULTIPLE GENERATIONS AT WORK   436
THE DIGITAL WORLD   437
Media Richness   437
MANAGEMENT IN ACTION PROGRESS REPORT   438
Improving Communication Skills   438
Improving Sender Skills   438
SOCIAL ENTERPRISE   442
Improving Receiver Skills   442
Organizational Communication   444
Downward Communication   445
Upward Communication   447
Horizontal Communication   448
Informal Communication   448
Boundarylessness   449

MANAGEMENT IN ACTION ONWARD   450
Key Terms   450
Retaining What You Learned   450
Discussion Questions   451
Experiential Exercises   452

CONCLUDING CASE   454
PART FOUR SUPPORTING CASE   455

PART FIVE   CONTROLLING: LEARNING AND CHANGING

CHAPTER 16

Managerial Control   458

MANAGEMENT IN ACTION MANAGER'S BRIEF   459
Bureaucratic Control Systems   461
The Control Cycle   461
SOCIAL ENTERPRISE   463
Approaches to Bureaucratic Control   465
MULTIPLE GENERATIONS AT WORK   467
Management Audits   468
Budgetary Controls   469
Financial Controls   471
Problems with Bureaucratic Control   474
MANAGEMENT IN ACTION PROGRESS REPORT   475
Designing Effective Control Systems   476
The Other Controls: Markets and Clans   480
Market Control   480

Clan Control: The Role of Empowerment and Culture   482
MANAGEMENT IN ACTION ONWARD   483
Key Terms   483
Retaining What You Learned   483
Discussion Questions   485
Experiential Exercises   485
CONCLUDING CASE   487

CHAPTER 17

Managing Technology and Innovation   488

MANAGEMENT IN ACTION MANAGER'S BRIEF   489
Technology and Innovation   490
Technology Life Cycle   491
Diffusion of Technological Innovations   492

MULTIPLE GENERATIONS AT WORK   493

SOCIAL ENTERPRISE   494

Technology Leadership and Followership   495
 Technology Leadership   495
 Technology Followership   497
Assessing Technology Needs   498
 Measuring Current Technologies   498
 Assessing External Technological Trends   499
Making Technology Decisions   499
 Anticipated Market Receptiveness   499
 Technological Feasibility   500
 Economic Viability   501
 Anticipated Capability Development   501
 Organizational Suitability   502

MANAGEMENT IN ACTION PROGRESS
REPORT   503

Sourcing and Acquiring New Technologies   504
 Internal Development   504
 Purchase   504
 Contracted Development   504
 Licensing   504

THE DIGITAL WORLD   505

 Technology Trading   505
 Research Partnerships and Joint Ventures   505
 Acquiring a Technology Owner   505
Technology and Managerial Roles   506
Organizing for Innovation   507
 Unleashing Creativity   508
 Bureaucracy Busting   509
 Design Thinking   509
 Implementing Development Projects   510
 Technology, Job Design, and Human Resources   511

MANAGEMENT IN ACTION ONWARD   511

 Key Terms   512
 Retaining What You Learned   512
 Discussion Questions   513
 Experiential Exercises   514

CONCLUDING CASE   514

CHAPTER 18

Creating and Leading Change   516

MANAGEMENT IN ACTION   517

Becoming World Class   518
 Sustainable, Great Futures   518
 The Tyranny of the *Or*   519
 The Genius of the *And*   520
 Achieving Sustained Greatness   520
 Organization Development   521
Managing Change   522
 Motivating People to Change   522

MULTIPLE GENERATIONS AT WORK   524

 A General Model for Managing Resistance   524
 Enlisting Cooperation   526
 Harmonizing Multiple Changes   528

MANAGEMENT IN ACTION PROGRESS REPORT   529

 Leading Change   529
Shaping the Future   532
 Thinking about the Future   532
 Creating the Future   532

THE DIGITAL WORLD   533

SOCIAL ENTERPRISE   534

 Shaping Your Own Future   535
 Learning and Leading   536

MANAGEMENT IN ACTION ONWARD   538

 A Collaborative, Sustainable Future?   539
 Key Terms   539
 Retaining What You Learned   539
 Discussion Questions   540
 Experiential Exercises   540

CONCLUDING CASE   542

PART FIVE SUPPORTING CASE   543

CASE INCIDENTS

Notes   547

Glossary/Subject Index   594

Name Index   620

Photo on pages xxiii, xxiv, xxvi, xxvii, and xxix: ©zlikovec/Shutterstock.com RF.

The Management Process

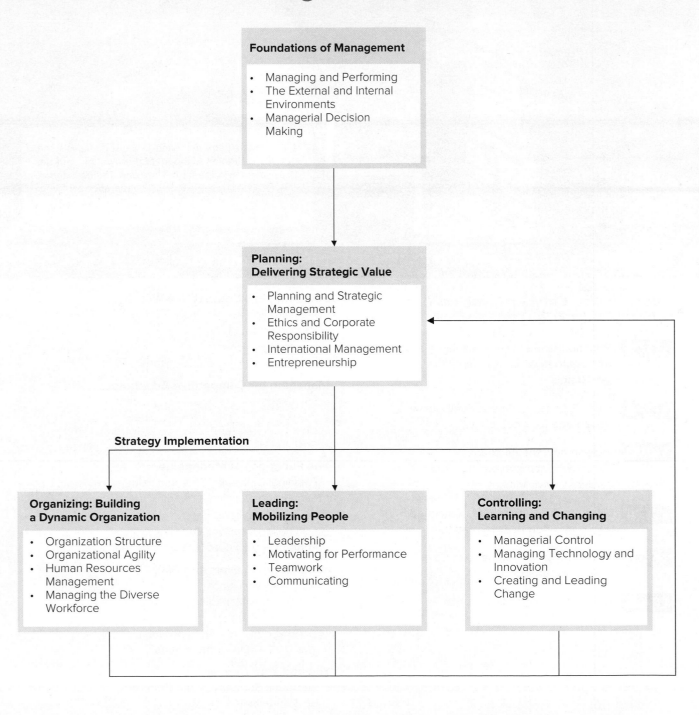

Foundations of Management

- Managing and Performing
- The External and Internal Environments
- Managerial Decision Making

Planning: Delivering Strategic Value

- Planning and Strategic Management
- Ethics and Corporate Responsibility
- International Management
- Entrepreneurship

Strategy Implementation

Organizing: Building a Dynamic Organization

- Organization Structure
- Organizational Agility
- Human Resources Management
- Managing the Diverse Workforce

Leading: Mobilizing People

- Leadership
- Motivating for Performance
- Teamwork
- Communicating

Controlling: Learning and Changing

- Managerial Control
- Managing Technology and Innovation
- Creating and Leading Change

CHAPTER 1
Managing and Performing

Management means, in the last analysis, the substitution of thought for brawn and muscle, of knowledge for folklore and tradition, and of cooperation for force.

—PETER DRUCKER

©Jirsak/Shutterstock.com RF

LEARNING OBJECTIVES

After studying Chapter 1, you will be able to:

LO 1 Summarize the major challenges of managing in the new competitive landscape.

LO 2 Describe the sources of competitive advantage for a company.

LO 3 Explain how the functions of management are evolving in today's business environment.

LO 4 Compare how the nature of management varies at different organizational levels.

LO 5 Define the skills you need to be an effective manager.

LO 6 Understand the principles that will help you manage your career.

CHAPTER OUTLINE

Managing in a Competitive World
Globalization
Technological Change
Knowledge Management
Collaboration across Boundaries

Managing for Competitive Advantage
Innovation
Service
Cost Competitiveness
Sustainability
Quality
Speed
Delivering All Types of Performance

The Functions of Management
Planning: Delivering Strategic Value
Organizing: Building a Dynamic Organization
Leading: Mobilizing People
Controlling: Learning and Changing
Performing All Four Management Functions

Management Levels and Skills
Top-Level Managers
Middle-Level Managers
Frontline Managers
Working Leaders with Broad Responsibilities
Must-Have Management Skills

You and Your Career
Be Both a Specialist and a Generalist
Be Self-Reliant
Connect with People
Actively Manage Your Relationship with Your Organization
Survive and Thrive

Management in Action

ONE WELL-KNOWN MANAGER: FACEBOOK'S MARK ZUCKERBERG

What does a manager do? Dream up a bold new mission for the company? Build a corporate structure that ensures success? Lead and inspire others? Keep the company on track toward its goals?

Most managers perform all these basic functions to some degree, perhaps none more publicly or successfully than Mark Zuckerberg, founder and CEO of Facebook Inc. Zuckerberg has seen his company grow into a unique worldwide phenomenon with almost 2 billion active users, more than 600 times as many people as the average daily viewership of CNN, Fox, and MSNBC combined. Given that the company reported $8.8 billion in revenue in 2016, it seems Zuckerberg's passion for connecting people with one another has more than paid off. Facebook's unparalleled success does not mean Zuckerberg has no management challenges left, however.

Past hurdles that Zuckerberg had to deal with included the need for cash to fund Facebook's rapid growth. In 2012 he announced an initial public offering of stock to attract that cash, and then saw the company go through a damaging initial drop in its stock price. Next came the soaring popularity of smartphones, encouraging Facebook users to go mobile in droves. Facebook was forced to quickly develop its capability to carry advertising on its mobile app. Those mobile ads now bring in 80 percent of the company's revenue, up from zero in 2012.

More recent hurdles include charges that Facebook aided the spread of fake news during the 2016 U.S. presidential election campaign. Zuckerberg responded by developing partnerships with outside fact-checking groups to flag stories of questionable reliability. He

©Frederic Legrand - COMEO/Shutterstock.com RF

directed upgrades of Facebook's user data tracking to counter problems of misreporting results to advertisers, and he wants to focus on artificial intelligence to prevent the sharing of inappropriate content. That story continues to unfold. Meanwhile Facebook teams are working to keep up with newer competitors like Snapchat by adding to the video capabilities of its Instagram platform.

While he is organizing and leading the company and refining its operations, Zuckerberg, ranked #1 in 2017 among the top 50 business people by *Fortune* magazine, is also still shaping plans for what he hopes Facebook can be. He recently released a bold statement of his views on its next big goal: to bring all of humanity together in a safe and informed "global community."[1]

Management challenges are ever-changing. What is going on now for Facebook and Mark Zuckerberg? As you read this chapter, notice the wide variety of skills that Zuckerberg needs to help Facebook meet its goals. Also, think about how managing people, money, and other resources enables Facebook and other organizations to accomplish far more than individuals acting independently could ever achieve.

Facebook's CEO, Mark Zuckerberg, is one of the most interesting leaders in business today. He is an innovator who combines technological know-how with a vision for the future and an obsessive drive to please customers. Together, those qualities have helped him build a business idea into a major corporation that continues to transform how people connect with one another.[2]

Zuckerberg is a standout among other top business leaders. Named 2016 Businessperson of the Year by *Fortune* magazine, he has successfully navigated the $350 billion media company through challenging times, as when Facebook was slow to respond to the shift to mobile, and the clumsy handling of its initial public offering.[3]

Consider the department store Macy's as a contrasting example. Following weaker than expected 2016 holiday sales, Macy's announced that it would close 63 stores and cut 10,000 jobs.[4] Terry Lungren, who stepped down as CEO in February 2017, was replaced by Jeff Gennette, who has the daunting task of turning around seven straight quarters of sales declines.[5] Time will tell whether Macy's can compete effectively against changing shopping habits driven by online retail giants like Amazon.

In business, there is no alternative to managing well. Companies may fly high for a while, but they cannot do well for very long without good management. It's the same for individuals: the best performers succeed by focusing on fundamentals, knowing what's important, and managing well. The aim of this book is to help you succeed in those pursuits.

Managing in a Competitive World

When the economy is soaring, business seems easy. Starting an Internet company looked easy in the 1990s, and ventures related to the real estate boom looked like a sure thing just a few years ago. But investors grew wary of dot-com start-ups, and the demand for new homes dropped off the table when the economy crashed in late 2008. At such times, it becomes evident that management is a challenge requiring knowledge and skills to adapt to new circumstances.

> Management is a challenge requiring knowledge and skills to adapt to new circumstances.

What defines the competitive landscape of today's business? You will be reading about many relevant issues in the coming chapters, but we begin here by highlighting four ongoing challenges that characterize the business landscape: globalization, technological change, the importance of knowledge and ideas, and collaboration across organizational boundaries.

Globalization

Far more than in the past, today's enterprises are global, with offices and production facilities in countries all over the world. Corporations operate worldwide, transcending national borders. Companies that want to grow often need to tap international markets. The change from a local to a global marketplace is irreversible.[6]

Fortune magazine annually publishes a list of the world's most admired companies. Whereas U.S. companies used to dominate, Switzerland-based Nestlé was the most admired maker of consumer food products in 2016, Germany's BMW was the most admired producer of motor vehicles, and Singapore Airlines was the most admired airlines company.[7] According to *Fortune*'s 2016 Global 500 list, the five largest firms are Walmart (U.S.), State Grid (China), China National Petroleum (China), Sinopec Group (China), and Royal Dutch Shell (British-Dutch).[8]

Globalization also means that a company's talent and competition can come from anywhere. As with its sales, more than half (60 percent) of GE's 333,000 employees live outside the United States.[9] Kentucky-based Yum! Brands (KFC, Pizza Hut, and Taco Bell) has over 43,000 restaurants in more than 135 countries. In 2016, about half of its profits came from outside the United States. On average, Yum! Brands opens six stores per day in international locations.[10]

PepsiCo's chief executive, Indra Nooyi, brought a much-needed global viewpoint to a company whose international business was growing three times faster than sales in the United States. Nooyi, who was raised in India and educated there and in the United States, steered the company toward more "better for you" and "good for you" snacks such as a Quaker beverage in China, Natural Balance snack bar in Mexico, and KeVita probiotic drinks in the United States.[11]

Globalization affects small companies as well as large. Many small companies export their goods. Many domestic firms assemble their products in other countries. And companies are under pressure to improve their products in the face of intense competition from foreign manufacturers. Firms today must ask themselves, "How can we be the best in the world?"

For students, it's not too early to think globally. Participating in the Global Business Institute program at Indiana University, one hundred students from North Africa, South Asia, and the Middle East came to the United States to pitch entrepreneurial business ideas to a panel of experts. The panel consisted of officials from Coca-Cola and the U.S. Department of State. The most recent winner was Team Pakistan, who proposed a business model that reduces waste by reselling used clothing.[12]

Globalization has changed the face of the workforce. Managers in this competitive environment needs to attract and effectively manage a talent pool from all over the globe.

©geopaul/E+/Getty Images RF

Technological Change

The Internet of Things, artificial intelligence, mobile applications, Big Data analytics, and cloud computing are only some of the ways that technology is vitally important in the business world. Technology both complicates things and creates new opportunities. The challenges come from the rapid rate at which communication, transportation, information, and other technologies change.[13] For example, after just a couple of decades of widespread desktop use, customers switched to laptop models, which require different accessories. Then, users turned to mini-laptops, tablets, smartphones, and smartwatches to meet their mobility technology needs.[14] Any company that served desktop users had to rethink its customers' wants and needs.

Later chapters discuss technology further, but here we highlight the rise of the Internet and its effects. How is the Internet so critical to business?[15] It is a digital marketplace, a means for manufacturing goods and services, a distribution channel, an information service, an arena for social activism,[16] and more. It drives down costs and speeds up globalization. It improves efficiency of decision making. Managers can watch and learn what companies around the world are doing in real time.

Although these advantages create business opportunities, they create threats, not just from hackers but from competitors as they capitalize sooner on developments than you do.

Things continue to change at breakneck exciting new wave of social networking About years ago, tech guru Tim O'Reilly coined the term "Web 2.0" to Web 2.0 redefined the ways in which customers start-ups that allow users to publish and knowledge. But most failed or stalled; very few, other than Facebook, made "read-write-execute" web where applications, search and sellers, employees and tailored, integrated, and relevant to users.[18] Think

Next came Web 3.0. natives. or a product on Amazon and a list of related products findings, and online thermostats, weight scales, wearable fitness trackers, and so about the last tips and communicate this information wirelessly through networks appeared on tys (regulate home temperature, check body weight, and tally miles where sma forth se to b

What's next for the digital frontier? It's hard to predict with precision, but as billions of people and businesses worldwide demand more personalized and connected experiences, artificial intelligence will simplify the interfaces between humans and technology. Instead of people adapting to new technologies as in the past, technology will adapt to people's preferences.[20]

Knowledge Management

Companies and managers need good new ideas. Because companies in advanced economies have become so efficient at producing physical goods, most workers have been freed up to provide services or "abstract goods" such as software, entertainment, data, and advertising. These workers, whose primary contributions are ideas and problem-solving expertise, are often referred to as *knowledge workers*. Managing these workers poses some particular challenges,[21] which we examine throughout this book.

Because the success of modern businesses so often depends on the knowledge used for innovation and the delivery of services, organizations need to manage that knowledge.[22] **Knowledge management** is the set of practices aimed at discovering and harnessing an organization's intellectual resources—fully using the intellects of the organization's people. Knowledge management is about finding, unlocking, sharing, and capitalizing on the most precious resources of an organization: people's expertise, skills, wisdom, and relationships. The nearby "Multiple Generations at Work" box explores how important knowledge transfer is to organizational survival.

Knowledge managers find these human assets, help people collaborate and learn, generate new ideas, and harness those ideas into successful innovations.

knowledge management

Practices aimed at discovering and harnessing an organization's intellectual resources.

Collaboration across Boundaries

One of the most important processes of knowledge management is to ensure that people in different parts of the organization collaborate effectively with one another. This requires productive communications among different departments, divisions, or other subunits of the organization. For example, "T-shaped" managers break out of the traditional corporate hierarchy to share knowledge freely across the organization (the horizontal part of the T) while remaining committed to the bottom-line performance of their individual business units (the vertical part).[23] Consulting firm McKinsey originally developed this T-shaped concept as a way for its employees to view clients' problems from both broad and deep perspectives.[24]

Toyota keeps its product development process efficient by bringing together design engineers and manufacturing employees from the very beginning. Often, manufacturing employees see ways to simplify a design so that it is easier to make without defects or unnecessary costs. Toyota expects its employees to listen to input from all areas of the organization, so this type of collaboration is a natural part of the organization's culture. Employees use some type of collaboration to share their knowledge—best practices they have developed for design and manufacturing.[25] Thus, at Toyota, knowledge management supports collaboration and vice versa.

Collaboration across boundaries even beyond the boundaries of the organization itself. Companies today must capitalize on the ideas of people outside the organization. Customers, for instance, collaborators. Companies must realize that the need to serve the customer drives.

In this digitally connected era, customers collaborate with their customers by actively their ideas and be heard. Companies L.L.Bean tracks customer comments and reviews continuously listening and responding. fewer than three stars out of five, the company resolve the problem.[26] Businesses pay attention to website; if any product averages Yelp, TripAdvisor, Facebook, Twitter, and many more the product manager to software can search these and other sites and generate Amazon, Zappos, respond to negative online reviews with the goal of winning feedback management Companies can[27]

Multiple Generations at Work

Move over Boomers, Here Comes the Next Generation of Leaders

The workforce is changing rapidly. A large number of Baby Boomers (born 1946–1964) will be exiting the workforce over the next 15 years. According to the Pew Research Center, approximately 10,000 Boomers turn 65 each day in the United States. Though some Boomers work into their later years, others step out of the workforce to enjoy hobbies, travel opportunities, and family time.

The talent exodus of top-level executives, managers, and leaders will translate into career opportunities for younger generations. Gen Xers (born 1965–1979) occupy many middle-level jobs, but there are not enough of them to fill all of the soon-to-be-vacant senior positions. Enter the Millennial generation (born 1980–2000), who make up the largest demographic cohort on record.[28] These early 30- and 20-somethings are flooding into the job market and will be needed to move quickly from team leader and frontline managerial positions to even higher responsibility.

Before Gen Xers and Millennials can assume higher-level positions in businesses, schools, government agencies, and nonprofits, organizational knowledge must be transferred from senior management to the less experienced Gen Xers and Millennial employees. Senior managers and leaders possess "know-how" and "know-who"

©Bike_Maverick/Getty Images RF

that are critical to the long-term success of their organizations. Prior to retirement, senior talent will look to transfer their knowledge to younger employees.

Complicating this need is the fact that generations, like individuals, sometimes differ in their attitudes, personalities, and behaviors. This can affect everything from communication, customer service, teamwork, job satisfaction, morale, and retention to overall organizational performance.

The Digital World

Collaboration across boundaries now includes instant communication with stakeholders around the world. Humanitarian organizations are at the forefront of this collaboration. You can sign up online as a Red Cross digital advocate (redcross.org/volunteer/volunteer-opportunities/be-a-digital-advocate). Volunteers go online and monitor social media for tweets, Facebook posts, and other social media communication that can provide useful information to Red Cross workers. Volunteers also provide direct support by responding on social media with information about basic first aid and shelter locations, and for emotional support. One example was reminding a young teen who had tweeted she was home alone as a tornado was touching down that she needed to get in the bathtub if she didn't have a basement.

Online collaboration allows managers to manage many demands in a brief amount of time during crises. The United Nations (OCHA) uses trained volunteers called the Stand By Task Force (SBTF). They collaborate online from all over the world. When one group sleeps, another group in another part of the world is waking up and ready to help. This provides 24-hour support to leadership in the crucial hours of a crisis.

Businesses are learning from humanitarian organizations and are using online collaboration or crowdsourcing. GlaxoSmithKline (GSK) is crowdsourcing its malaria research by sharing its data online and allowing the public to collaborate. You will learn details of how GSK and others are using technology to support and accelerate management goals later in the text.

Managing for Competitive Advantage

Bottom Line

Because it's easy for managers to be so busy that they lose sight of what really drives performance, you will periodically see icons as bottom-line reminders of the need for innovation, quality, service, speed, cost competitiveness, and sustainability. *Which two or more of these advantages do you think would be hardest to deliver at the same time?*

innovation

The introduction of new goods and services; a change in method or technology; a positive, useful departure from previous ways of doing things.

quality

The excellence of your product (goods or services).

The early Internet years turned careers (and lives) upside down. Students dropped out of school to join Internet start-ups or start their own. Managers in big corporations quit their jobs to do the same. Investors salivated, and invested heavily. The risks were often ignored or downplayed—sometimes tragically as the boom went bust in 2000.

And consider an earlier industry with similar transforming power: automobiles. There have been at least 2,000 carmakers—how many remain?

What is the lesson to be learned from the failures in these important transformational industries? A key to understanding the success of a company is the competitive advantage it holds and how well it can sustain that advantage.

To survive and win over time, you have to gain and sustain advantages over your competitors. You gain competitive advantage by being better than your competitors at doing valuable things for your customers. But what does this mean, specifically? To succeed, managers must deliver performance. The fundamental success drivers of performance are innovation, quality, service, speed, cost competitiveness, and sustainability.

Innovation

Companies must continually innovate. **Innovation** is the introduction of new goods and services. Your firm must adapt to changes in consumer demands and to new competitors.

Products don't sell forever; in fact, they don't sell for nearly as long as they used to because competitors are continuously introducing new products. Your firm must innovate, or it will die.

In 2000, Blockbuster was the market leader of the video rental industry. It didn't see the need to offer customers an alternative to driving to their retail stores to rent a movie, nor did the company eliminate late charges because they were a major source of revenue. Reed Hastings, founder of Netflix, displaced Blockbuster by allowing customers to order videos that would be delivered by mail. Customers could watch a video for as long as they wanted, then mail it back to Netflix. In 2010, Blockbuster filed for bankruptcy. Netflix has become a successful $8.8 billion company.[29]

The need for innovation is driven in part by globalization. One important reason is that facilities in other countries can manufacture appliances or write software code at a lower cost than facilities in the United States; U.S. facilities thus operate at a disadvantage. Therefore, they must provide something their foreign competitors can't—and often that requires delivering something new.

Nevertheless, as labor and other costs rise overseas, and as U.S. companies find ways to improve efficiency at home, the future for North American facilities may brighten. Nissan has expanded production in Smyrna, Tennessee, including assembly of its Infiniti JX luxury car and Leaf electric car. Other companies like BMW have announced plans to expand manufacturing operations in the United States. In 2016, the German auto maker completed its $1 billion expansion to its Spartanburg, South Carolina, plant, bringing annual production capacity to 450,000 vehicles.[30]

Innovation is today's holy grail (2017's number-one most-admired company in *Fortune's* innovativeness category was Starbucks).[31] Like the other sources of competitive advantage, innovation comes from people, it must be a strategic goal, and it must be managed properly. Later chapters show you how great companies innovate.

Quality

Most companies claim that they are committed to quality. In general, **quality** is the excellence of your product. Customers expect high-quality goods and services, and often they will accept nothing less.

©Trevor Lush/Purestock/Superstock RF

Historically, quality pertained primarily to the physical goods that customers bought; it referred to attractiveness, lack of defects, and dependability. The traditional approach to quality was to check work after it was completed and then eliminate defects, using inspection and statistical data to determine whether products were up to standards. But then W. Edwards Deming, J. M. Juran, and other quality gurus convinced managers to take a more complete approach to achieving *total* quality. This includes *preventing* defects before they occur, *achieving zero defects* in manufacturing, and *designing* products for quality. The goal is to solve and eradicate from the beginning all quality-related problems and to live a philosophy of *continuous improvement* in the way the company operates.[32]

Quality is further provided when companies customize goods and services to the wishes of the individual consumer. Choices at Starbucks give consumers thousands of variations on the drinks they can order. NikeID allows customers to customize their athletic shoes, Coca-Cola's Freestyle vending machines empower thirsty consumers to create over 100 soft-drink mixes, and Panera Breads permits visitors to its restaurants to enter custom orders via self-service kiosks.[33]

Providing world-class quality requires a thorough understanding of what quality really is.[34] Quality can be measured in terms of product performance, customer service, reliability (avoidance of failure or breakdowns), conformance to standards, durability, and aesthetics. Only when you move beyond broad, generic concepts such as "quality" and identify specific quality requirements can you identify problems, target needs, set precise performance standards, and deliver world-class value.

By the way, *Fortune* magazine's 2017 number-one company for quality of products and services was also Starbucks.

> The result of long-term relationships is better and better quality, and lower and lower costs.
>
> —*W. Edwards Deming*

Service

Important quality measures often pertain to the service customers receive. This dimension of quality is particularly important because the service sector has come to dominate the U.S. economy. In recent years, the fastest-growing job categories have been almost entirely health care services, and the jobs with the greatest declines are primarily in mining, logging, and manufacturing (although some manufacturing returns to the United States).[35] Services include intangible products such as insurance, hotel accommodations, medical care, and haircuts.

Service means giving customers what they want or need, when they want it. So, service is focused on continually meeting the needs of customers to establish mutually beneficial long-term relationships. Thus cloud computing companies, in addition to providing online access to software, applications, and other computer services, also help their customers store and analyze large amounts of customer and employee data.

service

The speed and dependability with which an organization delivers what customers want.

An important dimension of service quality is making it easy and enjoyable for customers to experience a service or to buy and use products. The Detroit Institute of Arts hired a manager formerly with the Ritz-Carlton hotel chain, noted for its exceptional level of service, to be vice president of museum operations. As the art museum prepared for a grand reopening following a major renovation, the manager analyzed the types of customer interactions that occur in a museum, identifying ways to make the experience more pleasant. He also worked with his staff to identify ways to customize services, such as offering tours tailored to the interests of particular groups.[36]

Speed

Google constantly improves its search product at a rapid rate. In fact, its entire culture is based on rapid innovation. Sheryl Sandberg, chief operating officer of Facebook, made a mistake early in her previous position as vice president of Google because she was moving too fast to plan carefully. Although the mistake cost the company a few million dollars, Google cofounder Larry Page responded to her explanation and apology by saying he was actually glad she had made the mistake. It showed that she appreciated the company's values. Page told Sandberg, "I want to run a company where we are moving too quickly and doing too much, not being too cautious and doing too little. If we don't have any of these mistakes, we're just not taking enough risks."[37]

Although it's unlikely that Google actually favors mistakes over moneymaking ideas, Page's statement expressed an appreciation that in the modern business environment, **speed**—rapid execution, response, and delivery—often separates the winners from the losers. How fast can you develop and get a new product to market? How quickly can you respond to customer requests? You are far better off if you are faster than the competition—and if you can respond quickly to your competitors' actions.

speed

Fast and timely execution, response, and delivery of products.

Quicken Loans became quicker than before and quicker than many others when it introduced Rocket Mortgage.

©dpa picture alliance/Alamy Stock Photo

Speed isn't everything—you can't get sloppy in your quest to be first. But other things being equal, faster companies are more likely to be the winners, slow ones the losers. Even pre-Internet, companies were getting products to market and in the hands of customers faster than ever. Now the speed requirement has increased exponentially. Everything, it seems, is on fast-forward.

Speed is no longer just a goal of some companies; it is a strategic imperative. Quicken Loans (owned by Intuit) is currently the second-largest provider of mortgage loans in the United States, with Wells Fargo being the top issuer.[38] In an ad during the 2016 Superbowl, Quicken announced its new mortgage service, Rocket Mortgage.[39] The online, self-service mortgage application is marketed as cutting the approval time from days to minutes.[40]

Cost Competitiveness

Walmart keeps driving hard to find new ways to cut billions of dollars from its already very low distribution costs. It leads the industry in efficient distribution, but competitors are copying Walmart's methods, so the efficiency no longer gives it as much of an advantage.[41]

cost competitiveness

Keeping costs low to achieve profits and be able to offer prices that are attractive to consumers.

Walmart's efforts are aimed at **cost competitiveness**, which means keeping costs low enough so that the company can realize profits and price its products (goods or services) at levels that are attractive to consumers. Needless to say, if you can offer a desirable product at a lower price, it is more likely to sell.

Singapore Airlines, one of the world's most admired companies, kept profiting during the economic recession while the global airline industry lost money. It did so by cutting costs more strategically than the competition. SA slashed flights, parked planes, and reduced salaries, including the CEO's.[42]

In contrast to the high-quality, even luxurious flying experience offered by Singapore Airlines, Ryanair is a European low-cost airline. CEO Michael O'Leary launched the "no frills" airline with the sole goal of flying people to their destination cheaply and with their luggage intact.[43] His vision is for profits to come from in-flight sales, high luggage fees, low-cost secondary airports, and commissions on travel products sold through the airline's website.[44] O'Leary's no-frills business model appears to be working. In 2016, Ryanair reported a 43 percent increase in net profit to $1.4 billion by carrying over 106 million passengers.[45]

One reason every company must worry about cost is that consumers can use the Internet to easily compare prices from thousands of competitors. Consumers looking to buy popular items, such as cameras, printers, and plane fares, can go online to research the best models and the best deals. If you can't cut costs and offer attractive prices, you can't compete.

Sustainability

Avoiding wasteful use of energy can bolster a company's financial performance while being kind to the environment. Efforts to cut energy waste are just one way to achieve an important form of competitive advantage: **sustainability**, which at its most basic is the effort to minimize the use and loss of resources, especially those that are polluting and nonrenewable.

Although sustainability means different things to different people,[46] in this text we emphasize a long-term perspective on sustaining the natural environment and building tomorrow's business opportunities while effectively managing today's business.[47]

In the United States, corporate efforts aimed at sustainability have fluctuated as environmental laws are strengthened or loosened; overall, the worldwide trend has been in the direction of greater concern for sustainability. Many companies have discovered that addressing sustainability issues often produces bottom-line benefits. Companies with strong sustainability performance that have also become financial winners include athletic-shoe maker Adidas, Spanish fashion group Inditex, French luxury-goods maker Hermès International, and Eaton, a power management company.[48]

Patagonia Sur is a for-profit company that has created the first private land trust in Patagonia to protect the company's land permanently; it plans to create up to 10 profitable, environmentally sustained businesses on that land.[49] The goals are to apply free-market forces to develop the land for profit, do no harm, and spread this radically different land management model to developing nations around the world.

Sustainability is about protecting our options.[50] Done properly, sustainability allows people to live and work in ways that can be maintained over the long term (generations) without depleting or harming our environmental, social, and economic resources.

Delivering All Types of Performance

Don't assume that you can settle for delivering just one of the six competitive advantages: low cost alone, or quality alone, for example. As illustrated in Exhibit 1.1, the best managers and companies deliver on all of these performance dimensions.

Some trade-offs will occur among the six sources of competitive advantage, but this doesn't need to be a zero-sum game in which improving one requires weakening another. The best managers try to optimize among multiple performance dimensions over time.

sustainability
Minimizing the use of resources, especially those that are polluting and nonrenewable.

EXHIBIT 1.1
Staying Ahead of the Competition

Bottom Line
Don't focus on one aspect of performance and neglect the others. You might be better at or more interested in one than the others, but you should strive for all six. *Imagine you're in your first management job, supervising a team. What would be your natural tendency? Which performance measures would you focus on, and why? How can you be sure to pay attention to all of them?*

The Functions of Management

management

The process of working with people and resources to accomplish organizational goals.

Management is the process of working with people and resources to accomplish organizational goals. Good managers do those things both effectively and efficiently. To be *effective* is to achieve organizational goals. To be *efficient* is to achieve goals with minimal waste of resources—that is, to make the best possible use of money, time, materials, and people. Some managers fail on both criteria, or focus on one at the expense of another. The best managers achieve high performance by focusing on both effectiveness *and* efficiency.

These definitions have been around for a long time. But as you know, business is changing radically. The real issue is how to *do* these things.[51]

Although the context of business and the specifics of doing business are changing, there are still plenty of timeless principles that make great managers, and great companies, great. While fresh thinking and new approaches are required now more than ever, much of what has already been learned about successful management practices remains relevant, useful, and adaptable, with fresh thinking, to the 21st-century business environment.

In the business world today, great executives not only adapt to changing conditions but also apply—fanatically, rigorously, consistently, and with discipline—the fundamental management principles.

These fundamentals include the four traditional functions of management: *planning, organizing, leading,* and *controlling.* These are used in organizations of every type (see the nearby "Social Enterprise" feature). They remain as relevant as ever, and they are needed in start-ups as much as in established corporations. But their form has evolved.

Planning: Delivering Strategic Value

planning

The management function of systematically making decisions about the goals and activities that an individual, a group, a work unit, or the overall organization will pursue; see also *strategic planning.*

Planning is specifying the goals to be achieved and deciding in advance the appropriate actions needed to achieve those goals. Planning activities include analyzing current situations, anticipating futures, determining objectives, deciding the types of activities in which the company will engage, choosing corporate and business strategies, and determining the resources needed to achieve the organization's goals. Plans set the stage for action and for major achievements.

The planning function for the new business environment, as discussed in Part 2 of this book, is more dynamically described as *delivering strategic value.* **Value** is an important concept.[52] Fundamentally, it describes the monetary amount associated with how well a job, task, good, or service meets users' needs. Those users might be business owners, customers, employees, society, and even nations.[53] The better you meet those needs (in terms of quality, speed, efficiency, and so on), the more value you deliver.

value

The monetary amount associated with how well a job, task, good, or service meets users' needs.

That value is strategic when it contributes to meeting the organization's goals. On a more personal level, you will do well to periodically ask yourself and your boss, "How can I add value?" Answering that question will enhance your contributions, your job performance, and your career.

> You will do well to periodically ask yourself and your boss, "How can I add value?"

Delivering strategic value is a continual process of identifying opportunities to create, seize, strengthen, and sustain competitive advantage. Effectively creating value requires fully considering a new and changing set of stakeholders and issues, including the government, the natural environment, globalization, and the dynamic economy in which ideas are king and entrepreneurs are both formidable competitors and potential collaborators. You learn about these and related topics in Chapter 4 (planning and strategic management), Chapter 5 (ethics, corporate responsibility, and sustainability), Chapter 6 (international management), and Chapter 7 (entrepreneurship).

Organizing: Building a Dynamic Organization

organizing

The management function of assembling and coordinating human, financial, physical, informational, and other resources needed to achieve goals.

Organizing is assembling and coordinating the human, financial, physical, informational, and other resources needed to achieve goals. Organizing activities include attracting people

Social Enterprise

Ashoka's Bill Drayton, Pioneer of Social Entrepreneurship

Can a company do well and do good at the same time? The idea that business success and positive social change can and indeed should happen together is the driving force behind *social enterprise,* or social entrepreneurship. Think of social entrepreneurs as change agents, managers who commit themselves and their organizations to creating not only private value in the form of profit, but also social value in various forms including innovation, sustainability, and accountability. In fact, social entrepreneurs use the same management functions to achieve business excellence and to advance positive social goals.

A leading force behind the growing strength of social enterprise is Ashoka, founded by Bill Drayton in 1980 as a group of Fellows, or social entrepreneurs, then mostly in developing countries. Since its founding, the group has grown to include more than 3,000 social entrepreneurs around the world. Thanks to its efforts, by the late 1990s social enterprise programs were available in business schools and public policy schools around the world.

Ashoka works worldwide to enable everyone to be a "changemaker" by identifying and supporting Fellows, creating communities for them, and helping build business, social, and financial systems to encourage even more social innovation. (Ashoka was an Indian emperor of the third century BC who renounced violence. His name means "the absence of sorrow.")

Fellows in the United States work on problems in education, women's health, the environment, justice, obesity, mental health, and human trafficking, among many others. In addition, there are almost 30 designated "changemaker campuses" in the United States, where "social innovation [is] an embedded core value." You can check https://www.ashoka.org/en/our-network to see whether your college or university is among them.

In Drayton's view, anyone can be a social entrepreneur. All it takes, he says, is the ability to see a problem, put others' skepticism aside, and allow yourself the time to inch your way first toward a vision and then to a solution that works. You'll read about social entrepreneurs in every chapter of this book.[54]

Questions:

- Do you think every manager should have the responsibility to do good and do well? Why or why not?

- What other means to create social innovation besides efforts like Ashoka's do you think can be effective?

---

to the organization, specifying job responsibilities, grouping jobs into work units, marshaling and allocating resources, and creating conditions so that people and things work together to achieve maximum success.

Part 3 of the book describes the organizing function as *building a dynamic organization.* Historically, organizing involved creating an organization chart by identifying business functions, establishing reporting relationships, and having a human resources department that administered plans, programs, and paperwork. Now and in the future, effective managers will be using new forms of organizing and viewing their people as their most valuable resources.

Rosalind Brewer, former president and CEO of Sam's Club, focused on building a dynamic organization. She was recently appointed COO and group president of Starbucks.

©Sarah Bentham/AP Images

They will build organizations that are flexible and adaptive, particularly in response to competitive threats and customer needs. Progressive human resource practices that attract and retain the very best of a highly diverse population will be essential aspects of the successful company. You will learn about these topics in Chapter 8 (organization structure), Chapter 9 (organizational agility), Chapter 10 (human resources management), and Chapter 11 (managing the diverse workforce).

Leading: Mobilizing People

Leading is stimulating people to be high performers. It includes motivating and communicating with employees, individually and in groups. Leading involves connecting directly with people, helping to guide and inspire them toward achieving team and organizational goals.

leading

The management function that involves the manager's efforts to stimulate high performance by employees.

Leading takes place in teams, departments, and divisions as well as at the tops of large organizations.

In earlier textbooks, the leading function described how managers motivate workers to come to work and execute top management's plans by doing their jobs. Today and in the future, managers must be good at mobilizing people to contribute their ideas—to use their brains in ways never needed or dreamed of in the past.

As described in Part 4, managers must rely on a very different kind of leadership (Chapter 12) that empowers and motivates people (Chapter 13). More now than ever, great work must be done via great teamwork (Chapter 14), both within work groups and across group boundaries. Ideally, underlying these processes will be effective interpersonal and organizational communication (Chapter 15).

Controlling: Learning and Changing

controlling

The management function of monitoring performance and making needed changes.

Planning, organizing, and leading do not guarantee success. The fourth function, **controlling**, monitors performance and implements necessary changes. By controlling, managers make sure the organization's resources are being used properly and that the organization is meeting its goals such as quality and worker safety.

When managers implement their plans, they often find that things are not working out as planned. The controlling function makes sure that goals are met. It asks and answers the question, "Are our actual outcomes consistent with our goals?" It then makes adjustments as needed.

Successful organizations, large and small, pay close attention to the controlling function. But Part 5 of the book makes it clear that today and for the future, the key managerial challenges are far more dynamic than in the past; they involve continually *learning and changing*. Controls must still be in place, as described in Chapter 16. But new technologies and other innovations (Chapter 17) make it possible to control more effectively and to help people use their brains, learn, make a variety of new contributions, and help the organization change in ways that forge a successful future (Chapter 18).

The four management functions apply to you personally as well. You must find ways to create value; organize for your own personal effectiveness; mobilize your own talents and skills as well as those of others; monitor performance; and constantly learn, develop, and change for the future. As you proceed through this book and this course, we encourage you not merely to read as if management were an impersonal course subject but to reflect on it from a personal perspective as well, using the ideas for your own personal and professional development.

Performing All Four Management Functions

As a manager, your typical day will not be neatly divided into the four functions. You will be doing many things more or less simultaneously.[55] Your days will be busy and fractionated, spent dealing with interruptions, meetings, and firefighting. There will be plenty to do that you wish you could be doing but can't seem to get to. These activities will include all four management functions.

Some managers are particularly interested in, devoted to, or skilled in one or two of the four functions but not in the others. But you should devote adequate attention and resources to *all four* functions. You can be a skilled planner and controller, but if you organize your people improperly or fail to inspire them to perform at high levels, you will not be realizing your potential as a manager. Likewise, it does no good to be the kind of manager who loves to organize and lead, but who doesn't really understand where to go or how to determine whether you are on the right track. Good managers don't neglect any of the four management functions. Knowing what they are, you can periodically ask yourself whether you are devoting adequate attention to *all* of them.

Management in Action

CONTROL SYSTEMS AT FACEBOOK

Controlling performance at Facebook takes many forms. One is Mark Zuckerberg's creation of new partnerships with third-party companies like Nielsen and comScore to ensure that his company reports accurate data about users' responses to advertising, such as the average time they spend looking at videos. These data help advertisers decide where and how to spend their ad dollars, based on the ads' measured effectiveness. Some data reported in the fall of 2016 were inaccurate, and advertisers have asked Facebook to be more accountable.

Another means of control is Facebook's new partnerships with outside fact checkers, who are empowered to flag questionable stories as "disputed" to alert readers to possible hoaxes and false reports. This move is in response to charges that Facebook's hands-off editorial policy allowed fake news stories to go viral during the 2016 presidential campaign. The company also promotes greater media literacy with its new Journalism Project, which, among other goals, offers both practical and ethical advice for eyewitnesses uploading breaking news and videos.

Zuckerberg also is betting on artificial intelligence (AI) to help Facebook filter content users don't want to see. "I'm really focused on making sure that our company gets faster at taking the bad stuff down," Zuckerberg said. "The best thing we can do is create AI systems that watch a video and understand that it's problematic and not show it to people."[56]

- Mark Zuckerberg's original vision of Facebook was an interactive message board to help his Harvard classmates keep in touch with each other. Do you think he had to consider many control mechanisms at that time? Why does the site need them now?

- What other aspects of Facebook's performance probably have control mechanisms in place?

Management Levels and Skills

Organizations—particularly large organizations—have many levels. In this section, you learn about the types of managers found at three broad organizational levels: top level, middle level, and frontline.

Top-Level Managers

Top-level managers are the senior executives of an organization and are responsible for its overall management. Top-level managers, often referred to as *strategic managers,* are supposed to focus on long-term issues and emphasize the survival, growth, and overall effectiveness of the organization.

Top managers are concerned not only with the organization as a whole but also with the interaction between the organization and its external environment. This interaction often requires managers to work extensively with outside individuals and organizations.

The chief executive officer (CEO) is the key top-level manager found in large corporations. This individual is the primary strategic manager of the firm and has authority over everyone else. Others include the chief operating officer (COO), company presidents, and other members of the top management team (TMT).

In the 1970s, finance was by far the most common single function represented in the TMT. The top team now typically includes the chief executive officer (CEO), Chief Operating Officer (COO), chief information (or technology, or knowledge) officer, and other chiefs in the C-suite, including ethics, strategy (or corporate development), human resources, and marketing (or branding). Functional chiefs sometimes have the title of senior vice president (SVP).[57] A likely role for the modern C-suite could well be chief sustainability officer or even climate change officer.[58]

top-level managers

Senior executives responsible for the overall management and effectiveness of the organization.

Top managers are increasingly called upon to be not only strategic architects but also true organizational leaders.

Traditionally, the role of top-level managers has been to set overall direction by formulating strategy and controlling resources. But now top managers are increasingly called upon to be not only strategic architects but also true organizational leaders. As leaders, they must create and articulate a broader corporate purpose with which people can identify—and one to which people will enthusiastically commit.

Middle-Level Managers

middle-level managers

Managers located in the middle layers of the organizational hierarchy, reporting to top-level executives.

Middle-level managers are located in the organization's hierarchy below top-level management and above the frontline managers. Sometimes called *tactical managers,* they are responsible for translating the general goals and plans developed by strategic managers into more specific objectives and activities.

Traditionally, the role of the middle manager is to be an administrator who bridges the gap between higher and lower levels. Middle-level managers break down corporate objectives into business unit targets; put together separate business unit plans from the units below them for higher-level corporate review; and serve as translators of internal communication, interpreting and broadcasting top management's priorities downward and channeling and translating information from the front lines upward.

Not long ago the stereotype of the middle manager connoted mediocrity: unimaginative people behaving like bureaucrats and defending the status quo. But middle managers are closer than top managers to day-to-day operations, customers, frontline managers, and employees—so they know the problems and opportunities. They also have many creative ideas—often better than their bosses'. Middle managers can play crucial roles in determining which entrepreneurial ideas are blocked and which are supported,[59] and how well they integrate with top management is crucial to formulating and implementing strategy.[60] Good middle managers provide the operating skills and practical problem solving that keep the company working.[61]

Frontline Managers

frontline managers

Lower-level managers who supervise the operational activities of the organization.

Frontline managers, or *operational managers,* are lower-level managers who supervise the operations of the organization. These managers often have titles such as *supervisor, team leader,* or *assistant manager.* They are directly involved with nonmanagement employees, implementing the specific plans developed with middle managers. This role is critical in the organization because operational managers are the link between management and nonmanagement personnel. Your first management position probably will fit into this category.

Traditionally, frontline managers have been directed and controlled from above to make sure that they successfully implement operations in support of company strategy. But in leading companies, their roles have expanded. Whereas the operational execution aspect of the role remains vital, in leading companies frontline managers are increasingly called on to be innovative and entrepreneurial, managing for growth and new business development.

Managers on the front line are crucial to creating and sustaining quality, innovation, and other drivers of financial performance.[62] In outstanding organizations, talented frontline managers are not only *allowed* to initiate new activities but are *expected* to by their top- and middle-level managers. And they are given freedom, incentives, and support to find ways to do so.[63]

Working Leaders with Broad Responsibilities

In small firms—and in those large companies that have adapted to the times—managers have strategic, tactical, *and* operational responsibilities. They are *complete* business people; they have knowledge of all business functions, are accountable for results, and focus on serving customers both inside and outside their firms. All of this requires the ability to think strategically, translate strategies into specific objectives, coordinate resources, and do real work with lower-level people.

EXHIBIT 1.2
Managerial Roles: What
Managers Do

Decisional Roles	Informational Roles	Interpersonal Roles
Entrepreneur: Searching for new business opportunities and initiating new projects to create change.	*Monitor:* Seeking information to understand the organization and its environment; serving as the center of communication.	*Leader:* Staffing, developing, and motivating people.
Disturbance handler: Taking corrective action during crises and other conflicts.	*Disseminator:* Transmitting information from source to source, sometimes interpreting and integrating diverse perspectives.	*Liaison:* Maintaining a network of outside contacts that provide information and favors.
Resource allocator: Providing funding and other resources to units or people; includes making significant organizational decisions.	*Spokesperson:* Speaking on behalf of the organization about plans, policies, actions, and results.	*Figurehead:* Performing symbolic duties (for example, ceremonies) and serving other social and legal demands.
Negotiator: Engaging in negotiations with parties outside the organization as well as inside (for example, resource exchanges).	n/a	n/a

SOURCE: Adapted from Mintzberg, H., *The Nature of Managerial Work.* New York: Harper & Row, 1973, pp. 92–93.

In short, today's best managers can do it all; they are working leaders.[64] They focus on relationships with other people and on achieving results. They don't just make decisions, give orders, wait for others to produce, and then evaluate results. They get dirty, do hard work themselves, solve problems, and produce value.

What does all of this mean in practice? How do managers spend their time—what do they actually do? A classic study of top executives found that they spend their time engaging in 10 key activities or roles, falling into three categories: interpersonal, informational, and decisional.[65] Exhibit 1.2 summarizes these roles. Even though the study was done decades ago, it remains highly relevant as a description of what executives do. And even though the study focused on top executives, managers at all levels engage in all these activities. As you study the table, you might ask yourself, "Which of these activities do I enjoy most (and least)? Where do I excel (and not excel)? Which would I like to improve?" Whatever your answers, you will be learning more about these activities throughout this course.

Must-Have Management Skills

LO 5

Performing management functions and roles, and achieving competitive advantage, are the cornerstones of a manager's job. However, understanding this does not ensure success. Managers need a variety of skills to do these things well. Skills are specific abilities that result from knowledge, information, practice, and aptitude. Although managers need many individual skills, which you will learn about throughout this textbook, there are three broad, essential categories: technical skills, conceptual and decision skills, and interpersonal and communication skills.[66]

First-timers can underestimate the challenges of management and the many skills required.[67] But when managers apply these three critical management skills to the four management functions, the result is high performance.

Technical   A **technical skill** is the ability to perform a specialized task that involves a certain method or process. The technical skills you learn in school will provide you with the opportunity to get an entry-level position; they will also help you as a manager. For

technical skill

The ability to perform a specialized task involving a particular method or process.

example, your accounting and finance courses will develop the technical skills you need to understand and manage the financial resources of an organization.

conceptual and decision skills

Skills pertaining to abilities that help to identify and resolve problems for the benefit of the organization and its members.

interpersonal and communication skills

People skills; the ability to lead, motivate, and communicate effectively with others.

Conceptual and Decision   **Conceptual and decision skills** involve the ability to identify and resolve problems for the benefit of the organization and everyone concerned. Managers use these skills when they consider the overall strategy of the firm, the interactions among different parts of the organization, and the role of the business in its external environment. As you acquire greater responsibility, you must exercise your conceptual and decision skills with increasing frequency. Much of this book is devoted to enhancing your conceptual and decision skills, but experience also plays an important part in their development.

Interpersonal and Communication   **Interpersonal and communication skills** influence the manager's ability to work well with people. These skills are often called *people skills.* Managers spend the great majority of their time interacting with people,[68] and they must develop their abilities to lead, motivate, and communicate effectively with those around them.

The importance of these skills varies by managerial level. Technical skills are most important early in your career. Conceptual and decision skills become more important than technical skills as you rise higher in the company. But interpersonal skills such as communicating effectively with customers and being a good team player are important throughout your career, at every level of management.

An example of a manager with these skills is Mark Bertolini, chief executive of Aetna, which provides health insurance and related services. As a young man doing assembly work for Ford Motor Company, Bertolini acquired an interest in union management, so he decided to study business and earned a degree in accounting and then a master's degree in finance. Those two specialties involve valuable technical skills, but Bertolini rose through the management ranks at a series of insurance companies because he also has a passion for people. He is constantly engaged in learning about people and forging networks with them. He sees tapping into networks and learning about how to lead people as the key skills that allow managers to get results. At Aetna, Bertolini is not only an expert at insurance matters, but also a promoter of employee health, yoga, and meditation. Furthermore, challenges in his personal life—he survived a spinal cord injury and donated a kidney to his son—help him to empathize with others, including clients.[69]

You and Your Career

LO 6   At the beginning of your career, your contribution to your employer depends on your own performance; often that's all you're responsible for. But on becoming a manager, you are responsible for a group. To use an orchestra analogy, instead of playing an instrument, you're a conductor, coordinating others' efforts.[70] The challenge is much greater than most first-time managers expect it to be.

©Dmytro Sidelnikov/Alamy Stock Photo RF

Throughout your career, you'll need to lead teams effectively as well as influence people over whom you have no authority; thus the human skills are especially important. Business people often talk about **emotional intelligence**,[71] or EQ—the skills of understanding yourself (including strengths and limitations), managing yourself (dealing with emotions, making good decisions, seeking and using feedback, exercising self-control), and dealing effectively with others (listening, showing empathy, motivating, leading, and so on).

Executives who score low on EQ are less likely to be rated as excellent on their performance reviews, and their divisions tend not to perform as well.[72] But please take note: the common phrase "emotional intelligence" is controversial.[73] You should *not* consider EQ to be a type of intelligence but as a set of skills that you can learn and develop. The issue is not lack of ability to change (you can), but the lack of motivation to learn and apply such skills.[74]

A common complaint about leaders, especially newly promoted ones who had been outstanding individual performers, is that they lack what is perhaps the most fundamental of EQ skills: empathy with other people. William George, former chair and CEO of Medtronic, says some people can go a long way in their careers based on sheer determination and aggressiveness, but personal development—including EQ—ultimately becomes essential.[75]

What should you do to forge a successful, gratifying career? You are well advised to be both a specialist and a generalist, to be self-reliant and connected, to actively manage your relationship with your organization, and to know what is required not only to survive but also to thrive in today's world.

Be Both a Specialist and a Generalist

If you think your career will be as a specialist, think again. Chances are, you will not want to stay forever in strictly technical jobs with no managerial responsibilities. Accountants are promoted to team leaders and accounting department heads, sales representatives become sales managers, writers become editors, and nurses become nursing directors. As your responsibilities increase, you must deal with more people, understand more about other aspects of the organization, and make bigger and more complex decisions. Beginning to learn now about these managerial challenges will yield benefits sooner than you think.

So, it will help if you can become both a specialist and a generalist.[76] Seek to become a *specialist:* you should be an expert in something useful. This will give you specific skills that help you provide concrete, identifiable value to your organization and to customers. And over time, you should learn to be a *generalist,* knowing enough about a variety of subject matters so that you can think strategically and work with different perspectives. Exhibit 1.3 gives you more career advice from experts.

Putting this another way, exploit (use, apply, take advantage of) what you know, and explore (search) for new experiences, ideas, knowledge, and perspectives. To both exploit and explore is to be ambidextrous;[77] organizations should do this, and so should we all.[78]

Be Self-Reliant

To be self-reliant means to take full responsibility for yourself and your actions. You cannot count on your boss or your company to take care of you. A useful metaphor is to think of yourself as a business, with you as president and sole employee.

emotional intelligence
Skills of understanding yourself, managing yourself, and dealing effectively with others.

Escape the industry-specific silo.	*Develop a skill set that transcends a single function, industry, or career path.*
Know what you know.	*And find ways to apply it.*
Keep learning throughout your life.	*No one can rest on what they already know.*
Manage your online presence.	*Expand your network, and post about your industry and functional expertise.*
Never compromise your integrity.	*Succumbing to temptations can destroy a career.*
Take a long view.	*Look at your career as a whole, and stay true to yourself.*
Prevent obsolescence.	*Job security comes from transportable skills.*
Zig-zag strategically.	*Job changing can be high-risk but not if you have measurable accomplishments.*
Be willing to take on tough jobs.	*Continually challenge yourself.*

EXHIBIT 1.3
Career Advice from the Experts

SOURCES: "Need a New Year's Resolution? 10 Ideas for a Stronger Career in 2017," *American Recruiters,* January 2, 2017, www.americanrecruiters.com; Kennedy, Joyce Lain, "Best Career Advice for 2013," *Chicago Tribune,* December 23, 2012, http://www.chicagotribune.com; Sanders, Lorraine, "Hilary Novelle Hahn's Zig-Zag Career Guide," *Fast Company,* November 13, 2012, http://www.fastcompany.com; Kadlec, Dan, "Graduation Day Advice: 5 Steps to a Great Career," *Time,* May 9, 2012, http://business.time.com.

To be self-reliant, find new ways to make your overall performance better. Take responsibility for change; be an innovator.[79] Don't just do your work and wait for orders; look for opportunities to contribute in new ways, to develop new products and processes, and to generate constructive change that strengthens the company and benefits customers and colleagues.

Success requires more than talent; you also have to be willing to work hard. The elite, world-class performers in many fields (including managers and leaders) reach the top tier only after 10 years or more of hard work and skillful coaching.[80] The key is to engage in consistent practice, looking at the results and identifying where to improve.

It's easy to see how this works for violinists or basketball players, but what about business managers? The answer is to focus on getting better results each time you try any business task, whether it's writing a report, chairing a meeting, or interpreting a financial statement. To know whether you're getting better, make a point of asking for feedback from customers, colleagues, and bosses.

> Don't just do your work and wait for instructions; look for opportunities to contribute in new ways.

To develop your full potential, assess yourself, including your interests, aptitudes, and personal character strengths. Think about it, ask others who know you well, conduct a formal exercise in which you learn what others consider to be your "best self,"[81] and use recent advances in psychology to identify your signature strengths.[82] Consider the professional image and reputation you would like to develop,[83] and continue building your capabilities. Consider the suggestions found throughout this book, and your other coursework, as you pursue these objectives.

Connect with People

Being connected means having many good working relationships and interpersonal contacts. For example, those who want to become partners in professional service organizations, such as social media marketing, accounting, advertising, and consulting firms, strive constantly to build a network of contacts. Their connectedness goal is to work not only with multiple clients but also with a half dozen or more senior partners, including several from outside their home offices and some from outside their country. Social relationships improve newcomers' knowledge of the organization and their jobs, their social integration into the firm, and their commitment to the organization.[84] Networks of diverse individuals can make huge contributions to your professional development no matter what your career—even if you hope to be inducted into the Major League Baseball Hall of Fame on the first ballot.[85]

social capital

Goodwill stemming from your social relationships; a competitive advantage in the form of relationships with other people and the image other people have of you.

Social capital is the goodwill stemming from your social relationships, and you can mobilize it on your behalf. It aids career success, compensation, employment, team effectiveness, the success of new ventures, entrepreneurship, and relationships with suppliers and other outsiders.[86] Today much of that social capital can be tapped online at social networking websites. Besides the social sites such as Facebook, some of these sites are aimed at helping people tap business networks. For example, LinkedIn has more than 467 million registered members worldwide, with total revenue from premium subscriptions, and marketing and talent solutions of $960 million.[87]

LinkedIn is not the only large player in the online job market space. In early 2017, Facebook announced that it would be providing a free service to enable companies to post job openings on their pages and applicants (FB members) to apply for those positions. The social media giant is hoping that companies and applicants will use Messenger to communicate during the recruitment process.[88]

All business is a function of human relationships.[89] Building competitive advantage depends not only on you but on other people. Management is personal. Commercial dealings are personal. Purchase decisions, repurchase decisions, and contracts all hinge on relationships. Even the biggest business deals—takeovers—are intensely personal and emotional. Without good work relationships, you will not achieve your potential as a manager and leader.

Actively Manage Your Relationship with Your Organization

We have noted the importance of taking responsibility for your own actions and your own career. Unless you are self-employed and your own boss, one way to do this is to think about

#1
You as a passive employee

Employer

↓

You

#2
You as an active contributor in a productive relationship

You ⇄ Your organization

EXHIBIT 1.4
Two Relationships: Which Will You Choose?

the nature of the relationship between you and your employer. Exhibit 1.4 shows two possible relationships—and you have some control over which relationship develops.

Relationship #1 is one in which you view yourself as an employee and passively expect your employer to tell you what to do and give you pay and benefits. Your employer is in charge, and you are a passive recipient of its actions. Your contributions are likely to be adequate but minimal—you won't make the added contributions that strengthen your organization, and if all organizational members take this perspective, the organization is not likely to be strong for the long run. Personally, you may lose your job, or keep your job in a declining organization, or receive few positive benefits from working there and either quit or become cynical and unhappy in your work.

In contrast, relationship #2 is a two-way relationship in which you and your organization both benefit from one another. The mind-set is different: Instead of doing what you are told, you think about how you can contribute—and you act accordingly. To the extent that your organization values your contributions, you are likely to benefit in return by receiving full and fair rewards, support for further personal development, and a more gratifying work environment. If you think in broad terms about how you can help your company, and if others think like this as well, there is likely to be continuous improvement in the company's ability to innovate, cut costs, and deliver quality products quickly to an expanding customer base. As the company's bottom line strengthens, benefits accrue to shareholders as well as to you and other employees.

What contributions can you make? You can do your basic work. But you can, and should, go further. You can figure out new ways to add value—by thinking of and implementing new ideas that improve processes and results. You can do this by using your technical knowledge and skills, as in developing a better information system, accounting technique, or sales strategy.

You also can contribute with your conceptual and human skills and your managerial actions (see Exhibit 1.5). You can execute the essential management functions and deliver competitive advantage. You can deliver strategic value (Part 2 of this book). You can take actions that help build a more dynamic organization (Part 3). You can mobilize people to contribute to their fullest potential (Part 4). And you can learn and change—and help your colleagues and company learn and change—to adapt to changing realities and forge a successful future (Part 5).

Survive and Thrive

You will be accountable for your actions and for results. In the past, people at many companies could show up, do an OK job, get a decent evaluation, and get a raise equal to the cost of living and maybe higher. Today, managers must do more, better. Eminent management scholar Peter Drucker, in considering what makes managers effective, noted that some are charismatic whereas some are not, and some are visionary whereas others are more numbers-oriented.[90] But successful executives do share some common practices:

- They ask "What needs to be done?" not just "What do I want to do?"
- They write an action plan. They don't just think, they do, based on a sound, ethical plan.
- They take responsibility for decisions. This requires checking up, revisiting, and changing if necessary.

Management in Action

WORKING FOR FACEBOOK'S MARK ZUCKERBERG

Said to be forward-looking, disciplined, inquisitive, consistent, and good at communicating, Mark Zuckerberg recently earned a 99.3 approval rating from Facebook employees. That's a little less surprising when you consider that he says he is most strongly influenced by the colleagues with whom he has day-to-day contact, rather than by any outside mentors. His office has glass walls, and he's been known to invite new employees to present their own ideas at meetings.

Zuckerberg believes "[employees] need the ability to fully exercise all their creativity and all their capacity, or else they're not going to be having the biggest impact that they can have on the world, and they're going to want to go do something else." He's also famous for saying, "I will only hire someone to work directly for me if I would work for that person."

Zuckerberg has delegated the commercial side of Facebook's operations to chief operating officer Sheryl Sandberg. This leaves him free to stay focused on the technical aspects that led him to start the social media giant as a simple site he once ran from his Harvard dorm room. Matt Cohler, an early employee and now a venture capitalist, describes Zuckerberg as "a learn-it-all person, to a level that is sometimes maddening. . . . He maintains a relentless focus on innovation, but at the same time he's an applied-science and engineering guy."

Mike Vernal, a former engineering employee, says of Zuckerberg, "Most people think day to day or week to week. Mark thinks century to century."

In his spare time, Zuckerberg is learning Mandarin and programming an AI personal assistant for his home. With his wife, he recently began a tour with the goal of visiting all 50 of the United States.[91]

- As an early career employee at Facebook, what steps could you take to get noticed and position yourself for promotion to frontline manager?
- Most of Facebook's core top employees have been with the company for much of its 13-year life. What do you think accounts for their commitment?

- They focus on opportunities, not just problems. Problems have to be solved, and problem solving prevents more damage. But capturing opportunities is what creates great results.

Career success is most likely if you are flexible, creative, and motivated. You need to learn how to think strategically, make decisions, and work in teams. You will learn more about these and other topics, essential to your successful career, in the upcoming chapters.

EXHIBIT 1.5

Managerial Action Is Your
Opportunity to Contribute

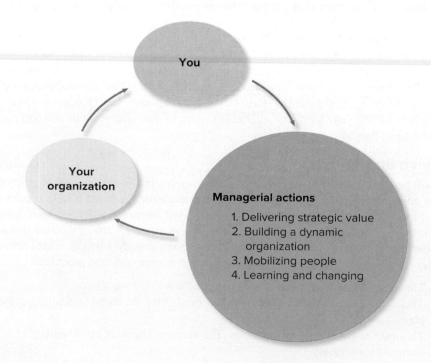

You

Your organization

Managerial actions
1. Delivering strategic value
2. Building a dynamic organization
3. Mobilizing people
4. Learning and changing

KEY TERMS

conceptual and decision skills, p. 18

controlling, p. 14

cost competitiveness, p. 10

emotional intelligence, p. 19

frontline managers, p. 16

innovation, p. 8

interpersonal and communication skills, p. 18

knowledge management, p. 6

leading, p. 13

management, p. 12

middle-level managers, p. 16

organizing, p. 12

planning, p. 12

quality, p. 8

service, p. 9

social capital, p. 20

speed, p. 10

sustainability, p. 11

technical skill, p. 17

top-level managers, p. 15

value, p. 12

RETAINING WHAT YOU LEARNED

You learned that change is the only constant for managers in today's business world. You also learned that high-performance managers seek to deliver superior value to customers by providing high-quality, innovative services or products in a timely, cost-effective, and sustainable manner. The fundamental functions and activities of management are just as important as they were "back in the day." However, their forms have evolved greatly and their strategies and tactics continue to change. Depending on your organizational level, you'll be expected to engage in certain roles and master a variety of managerial skills. Your career, and your professional and personal development along the way, are primarily in your hands.

LO 1   Summarize the major challenges of managing in the new competitive landscape.

- In business, there is no alternative to managing well. The best managers succeed by focusing on the fundamentals and knowing what's important.
- The goal of this book is to help you become an effective, high-performance manager.
- Managers today must deal with dynamic forces that create greater change than ever before, including globalization, technological change (including the continuing development and new applications of the Internet), knowledge management, and collaboration across organizational boundaries.

LO 2   Describe the sources of competitive advantage for a company.

- Because business is a competitive arena, you need to deliver value to customers in ways that are superior to what your competitors do.
- Competitive advantages result from innovation, quality, service, speed, cost competitiveness, and sustainability.

LO 3   Explain how the functions of management are evolving in today's business environment.

- Despite massive change, management retains certain functions that will not disappear.

- The primary functions of management are planning, organizing, leading, and controlling.
- Planning is analyzing a situation, determining the goals that will be pursued, and deciding in advance the actions needed to pursue these goals.
- Organizing is assembling the resources needed to complete the job and coordinating employees and tasks for maximum success.
- Leading is motivating people and stimulating high performance.
- Controlling is monitoring the progress of the organization or the work unit toward goals and then taking corrective action as needed.
- In the modern business environment, these functions require creating strategic value, building a dynamic organization, mobilizing people, and learning and changing.

LO 4   Compare how the nature of management varies at different organizational levels.

- Top-level, strategic managers are the senior executives responsible for the organization's overall management.
- Middle-level, tactical managers translate general goals and plans into more specific objectives and activities.
- Frontline, operational managers are lower-level managers who supervise operations.
- Managers at all levels must perform a variety of interpersonal, informational, and decisional roles.
- Even at the operational level, the best managers think strategically and operate like complete business people.

LO 5   Define the skills you need to be an effective manager.

- To execute management functions successfully, managers need technical skills, conceptual and decision skills, and interpersonal and communication skills.

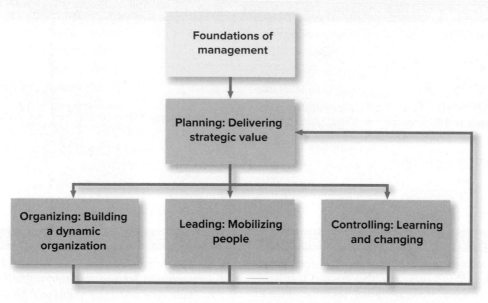

The Management Process

- A technical skill is the ability to perform a specialized task involving certain methods or processes.
- Conceptual and decision skills help the manager recognize complex and dynamic issues, analyze the factors that influence those issues or problems, and make appropriate decisions.
- Interpersonal and communication skills enable the manager to interact and work well with people.
- As you rise to higher organizational levels, technical skills tend to become less important and conceptual skills become more important, whereas interpersonal and communication skills remain extremely important at every level.

LO 6   Understand the principles that will help you manage your career.

- You are more likely to succeed in your career if you become both a specialist and a generalist. You should be self-reliant but also connected.
- You should actively manage your relationship with your organization and continuously improve your skills so you can perform as needed in the changing work environment.

DISCUSSION QUESTIONS

1. Identify and describe a great manager. What makes him or her stand out from the crowd?

2. Have you ever seen or worked for an ineffective manager? Describe the causes and the consequences of the ineffectiveness.

3. Describe in as much detail as possible how the Internet and globalization affect your daily life.

4. Identify some examples of how different organizations collaborate across boundaries.

5. Name a great organization. How do you think management contributes to making it great?

6. Name an ineffective organization. What can management do to improve it?

7. Give examples you have seen of firms that are outstanding and weak on each of the six pillars of competitive advantage. Why do you choose the firms you do?

8. Describe your use of the four management functions in the management of your daily life.

9. Discuss the importance of technical, conceptual, and interpersonal skills at school and in jobs you have held.

10. What are your strengths and weaknesses as you contemplate your career? How do they relate with the skills and behaviors identified in the chapter?

11. Devise a plan for developing yourself and making yourself attractive to potential employers. How would you go about improving your managerial skills?

12. Consider the managers and companies discussed in the chapter. Have they been in the news lately, and what is the latest? If their image, performance, or fortunes have gone up or down, what has changed to affect how they have fared?

EXPERIENTIAL EXERCISES

1.1   YOUR PERSONAL NETWORK

1. See the nearby figure showing primary and secondary connections. Working on your own, write down all of your primary contacts—individuals you know personally who can support you in attaining your professional goals. Then begin to explore their secondary connections. Make assumptions about possible secondary connections that can be made for you by contacting your primary connections. For example, through one of your teachers (primary), you might be able to obtain some names of potential employers (secondary). (10–15 min.)

2. Then meet with your partner or small group to exchange information about your primary and secondary networks and to exchange advice and information on how best to use these connections as well as how you could be helpful to them. (about 5 min. per person; 10–30 min. total, depending on group size)

3. Add names or types of names to your list based on ideas you get by talking with others in your group. (2–5 min.)

4. Discuss with your large group or class, using the following discussion questions. (10 min.)

QUESTIONS

1. What were some of the best primary sources identified by your group?

2. What were some of the best sources for secondary contacts identified by your group?

3. What are some suggestions for approaching primary contacts?

4. What are some suggestions for approaching secondary contacts, and how is contacting secondary sources different from contacting primary contacts?

5. What did you learn about yourself and others from this exercise?

SOURCE: de Janasz, Suzanne C., Dowd, Karen O. and Schneider, Beth Z., *Interpersonal Skills in Organizations.* New York: McGraw-Hill, 2002, p. 211.

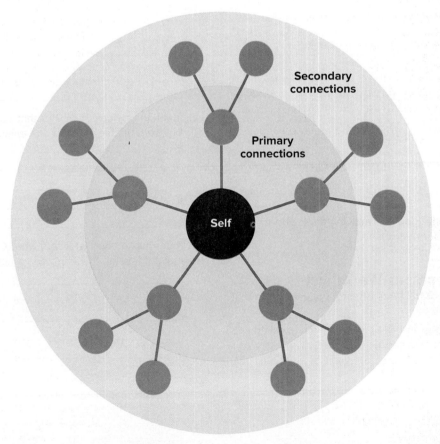

Primary and Secondary Connections

SOURCE: Excerpted from Jauch, Lawrence R., Bedeian, Arthur G., Coltrin, Sally A. and Glueck, William F., *The Managerial Experience: Cases, Exercises, and Readings,* 5th ed. Chicago: South-Western, 1989.

1.2   ARE YOU AN EFFECTIVE MANAGER?

OBJECTIVES

1. To recognize what behaviors contribute to being a successful manager.
2. To develop a ranking of critical behaviors that you personally believe are important for becoming an effective manager.

INSTRUCTIONS

1. Following is a partial list of behaviors in which managers may engage. Rank these items in terms of their importance for effective performance as a manager. Put a 1 next to the item that you think is most important, 2 for the next most important, down to 10 for the least important.
2. Bring your rankings to class. Be prepared to justify your results and rationale. If you can add any behaviors to this list that might lead to success or greater management effectiveness, write them in.

Managerial Behaviors Worksheet

_____ Collaborates with people from different parts of the organization.

_____ Looks for ways to incorporate technology into the operation.

_____ Ensures that services/products are of a high quality and delivered on time.

_____ Keeps costs down and looks for ways to be more efficient.

_____ Makes decisions to help achieve the goals of the organization.

_____ Is organized and effectively allocates resources.

_____ Motivates others to perform at a high level.

_____ Makes sure goals are met and implements changes when necessary.

_____ Exhibits good interpersonal and communication skills.

_____ Is skilled at identifying and resolving problems.

SOURCE: Adapted from Jauch, Lawrence R., Bedeian, Arthur G., Coltrin, Sally A. and Glueck, William F., _The Managerial Experience: Cases, Exercises, and Readings,_ 5th ed. Chicago: South-Western, 1989.

1.3   CAREER SKILLS DEVELOPMENT

OBJECTIVES

1. To develop an understanding of your career-related strengths.
2. To identify career-related skills and behaviors requiring development.
3. To increase confidence in your marketability.

INSTRUCTIONS

Read the instructions for each activity, think about them, and then provide your response.

Career Development Worksheet

Think about a part- or full-time job, or a volunteer role that you've held.

1. Describe <u>activities</u> and <u>skills</u> at which you excelled and which helped you succeed:
   a. _____
   b. _____
   c. _____
   d. _____
   e. _____

2. Identify <u>activities</u> and <u>skills</u> that you wanted to master but were unable to do so due to lack of training or time:
   a. _____
   b. _____
   c. _____
   d. _____
   e. _____

3. Referring to your list in #2, what steps could you take now to develop these important <u>activities</u> and <u>skills:</u>
   a. _____
   b. _____
   c. _____
   d. _____
   e. _____

SOURCE: Adapted from Gordon, Judith R., _Diagnostic Approach to Organizational Behavior._ Upper Saddle River, NJ: Pearson Education, 1983.

Concluding Case

A NEW MANAGER AT USA HOSPITAL SUPPLY

As Charlie Greer drove to work, he smiled, recalling the meeting at the end of the previous day. Inez Rodriguez, the owner of the company where he worked, USA Hospital Supply, had summoned him to her office, where she warmly shook his hand and exclaimed, "Congratulations!" As they settled into chairs, Inez reviewed the conversation she'd had with the company's board of directors that morning: USA Hospital had been growing steadily for the past 10 years despite the economy's ups and downs. As the company's founder, Inez had always been an insightful and enthusiastic leader of the five-person sales team, but the level of activity was becoming too much of a distraction. Inez needed to think about the long-range vision of the company, so she needed a leader who could focus on sales. She had interviewed several candidates outside the firm as well as Charlie and two of the other sales representatives. In the end, Inez told Charlie, the choice was obvious: Charlie was far and away the best sales rep on the team, he had extensive knowledge of the company's product mix, and if anyone could help the sales team achieve its goals, it was Charlie. She offered him the job as the company's first sales manager. He eagerly accepted. When he left work that evening, his head was full of ideas, and his heart was full of confidence.

Now Charlie pulled into the office park where USA Hospital Supply was located and easily found a parking space in the lot outside the one-story office and warehouse facility. As usual, he was one of the first employees to arrive. By habit, he strode toward his cubicle, but after a second, he recalled that Inez had arranged for the small firm's accountant and computer systems manager to share an office so he could have an office of his own. Charlie entered his new domain and settled into the swivel chair behind his desk.

At that instant, the eagerness to enjoy his new status and responsibility began to give way to nervousness. Charlie realized that although he knew a lot about selling supplies to hospitals and doctor's offices, he had never given much thought to managing. Obviously, he mused, his job was to see that his department met or exceeded its sales targets. But how?

Charlie started his computer and then opened his e-mail and his word-processing software, intending to get some ideas into writing. He typed out a list of the four sales reps: Cindy, Paula, John, and Doreen. Cindy handled the large corporate accounts, Paula covered the East Coast, John called on accounts in the South, and Doreen handled the Midwest. Until today, Charlie had been building a fast-growing territory west of the Mississippi. Now who was going to do that? Charlie was tempted to keep that work for himself; he knew he could build a base of loyal clients better than anyone else. Still, he wondered whether he could excel as a manager and as a sales rep at the same time.

While he was pondering that challenge, Cindy walked past the office door and, without stopping, politely called, "Congratulations!" through the doorway. Charlie's heart sank as he realized that Cindy had also wanted this job. They had always enjoyed a friendly rivalry as talented salespeople; now what would happen to the fun of being team members? It was easier to think about the other representatives at the moment. Charlie scanned his e-mail inbox and saw status reports from John and Doreen, both of them out of the office to call on clients. What about Paula? Charlie wasn't quite sure he remembered her plans for this week. Obviously he needed to catch up on what everyone was doing, and that gave him a new idea. He could build on his strengths by traveling with each of the sales reps and coaching them. That way, he could show them all his proven methods for closing a sale, and they could learn to sell as well as he did. Charlie thought, "That's what a good manager does: shows employees how to do the job right." He was starting to feel less nervous as he began to compose an e-mail to Paula.

DISCUSSION QUESTIONS

1. How will Charlie's approach to quality and service affect his company's performance?

2. Which of the basic functions of management has Charlie considered? How well is he preparing to carry out these functions?

3. Which management skills does Charlie have? In what areas do you think he has the greatest need to develop skills? How can he actively manage his development as a manager?

The Evolution of Management

For thousands of years, managers have wrestled with the same issues and problems confronting executives today. Around 1100 BC, the Chinese practiced the four management functions—planning, organizing, leading, and controlling—discussed in Chapter 1. Between 400 BC and 350 BC, the Greeks recognized management as a separate art and advocated a scientific approach to work. The Romans decentralized the management of their vast empire before the birth of Christ. During medieval times, the Venetians standardized production through the use of an assembly line, building warehouses and using an inventory system to monitor the contents.[1]

But throughout history, most managers operated strictly on a trial-and-error basis. The challenges of the Industrial Revolution changed that. Management emerged as a formal discipline at the turn of the century. The first university programs to offer management and business education, the Wharton School at the University of Pennsylvania and the Amos Tuck School at Dartmouth, were founded in the late 19th century. By 1914, 25 business schools existed.[2]

Thus, the management profession as we know it today is relatively new. This appendix explores the roots of modern management theory. Understanding the origins of management thought will help you grasp the underlying contexts of the ideas and concepts presented in the chapters ahead.

Although this appendix is titled "The Evolution of Management," it might be more appropriately called "The Revolutions of Management" because it documents the wide swings in management approaches over the past 100+ years. Out of the great variety of ideas about how to improve management, parts of each approach have survived and been incorporated into modern perspectives on management. Thus, the legacy of past efforts, triumphs, and failures has become our guide to future management practice.[3]

EARLY MANAGEMENT CONCEPTS AND INFLUENCES

Communication and transportation constraints hindered the growth of earlier businesses. Therefore, improvements in management techniques did not substantially improve performance. However, the Industrial Revolution changed that. As companies grew and became more complex, minor improvements in management tactics produced impressive increases in production quantity and quality.[4]

The emergence of **economies of scale**—reductions in the average cost of a unit of production as the total volume produced increases—drove managers to strive for further growth. The opportunities for mass production created by the Industrial Revolution spawned intense and systematic thought about management problems and issues—particularly efficiency, production processes, and cost savings.[5]

Exhibit A.1 provides a time line depicting the evolution of management thought through the decades. This historical perspective is divided into two major sections: classical approaches and contemporary approaches. Many of these approaches overlapped as they developed, and they often had a significant impact on one another. Some approaches were a direct reaction to the perceived deficiencies of previous approaches. Others developed as the needs and issues confronting managers changed over the years. All the approaches attempted to explain the real issues facing managers and provide them with tools to solve future problems.

Exhibit A.1 will reinforce your understanding of the key relationships among the approaches and place each perspective in its historical context.

CLASSICAL APPROACHES

The classical period extended from the mid-19th century through the early 1950s. The major approaches that

EXHIBIT A.1 The Evolution of Management Thought

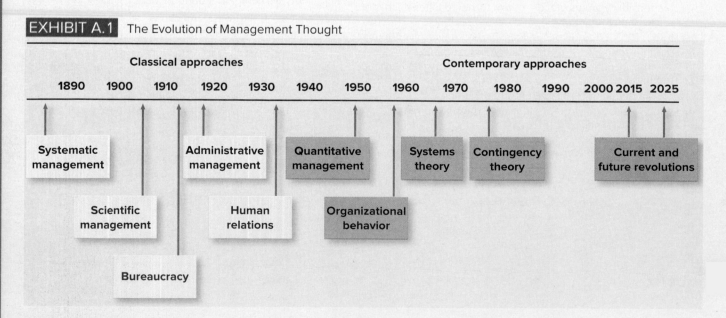

emerged during this period were systematic management, scientific management, administrative management, human relations, and bureaucracy.

Systematic Management

During the 19th century, growth in U.S. business centered on manufacturing.[6] Early writers such as Adam Smith believed the management of these firms was chaotic, and their ideas helped to systematize it. Most organizational tasks were subdivided and performed by specialized labor. However, poor coordination caused frequent problems and breakdowns of the manufacturing process.

The **systematic management** approach attempted to build specific procedures and processes into operations to ensure coordination of effort. Systematic management emphasized economical operations, adequate staffing, maintenance of inventories to meet consumer demand, and organizational control. These goals were achieved through

- Careful definition of duties and responsibilities.
- Standardized techniques for performing these duties.
- Specific means of gathering, handling, transmitting, and analyzing information.
- Cost accounting, wage, and production control systems to facilitate internal coordination and communications.

An Early Labor Contract

The following rules, taken from the records of Cocheco Company, were typical of labor contract provisions in the 1850s.

1. The hours of work shall be from sunrise to sunset, from the 21st of March to the 20th of September inclusively; and from sunrise until eight o'clock, p.m., during the remainder of the year. One hour shall be allowed for dinner, and half an hour for breakfast during the first mentioned six months, and one hour for dinner during the other half of the year; on Saturdays, the mill shall be stopped one hour before sunset, for the purpose of cleaning the machinery.

2. Every hand coming to work a quarter of an hour after the mill has been started shall be docked a quarter of a day; and every hand absenting him or herself, without absolute necessity, shall be docked in a sum double the amount of the wages such hand shall have earned during the time of such absence. No more than one hand is allowed to leave any one of the rooms at the same time—a quarter of a day shall be deducted for every breach of this rule.

3. No smoking or spiritous liquors shall be allowed in the factory under any pretense whatsoever. It is also forbidden to carry into the factory, nuts, fruits, etc. books, or papers during the hours of work.

SOURCE: Sullivan, W., "The Industrial Revolution and the Factory Operative in Pennsylvania," *The Pennsylvania Magazine of History and Biography* 78 (1954), pp. 478–79.

Systematic management emphasized internal operations because managers were concerned primarily with meeting the explosive growth in demand brought about by the Industrial Revolution. In addition, managers were free to focus on internal issues of efficiency, in part because the government did not constrain business practices significantly. Finally, labor was poorly organized. As a result, many managers were oriented more toward things than toward people.

Systematic management did not address all the issues 19th-century managers faced, but it tried to raise managers' awareness about the most pressing concerns of their job.

Scientific Management

Systematic management failed to lead to widespread production efficiency. This shortcoming became apparent to a young engineer named Frederick Taylor, who was hired by Midvale Steel Company in 1878. Taylor discovered that production and pay were poor, inefficiency and waste were prevalent, and most companies had tremendous unused potential. He concluded that management decisions were unsystematic and that no research to determine the best means of production existed.

In response, Taylor introduced a second approach to management, known as **scientific management**.[7] This approach advocated the application of scientific methods to analyze work and to determine how to complete production tasks efficiently. For example, U.S. Steel's contract with the United Steel Workers of America specified that sand shovelers should move 12.5 shovelfuls per minute; shovelfuls should average 15 pounds of river sand composed of 5.5 percent moisture.[8]

Taylor identified four principles of scientific management:

1. Management should develop a precise, scientific approach for each element of one's work to replace general guidelines.

2. Management should scientifically select, train, teach, and develop each worker so that the right person has the right job

3. Management should cooperate with workers to ensure that jobs match plans and principles.

4. Management should ensure an appropriate division of work and responsibility between managers and workers.

To implement this approach, Taylor used techniques such as time-and-motion studies. With this technique, a task was divided into its basic movements, and different motions were timed to determine the most efficient way to complete the task.

After the "one best way" to perform the job was identified, Taylor stressed the importance of hiring and training the proper worker to do that job. Taylor advocated the standardization of tools, the use of instruction cards to help workers, and breaks to eliminate fatigue.

Another key element of Taylor's approach was the use of the differential piecerate system. Taylor assumed workers were motivated by receiving money. Therefore, he implemented a pay system in which workers were paid additional

Frederick Taylor (left) and
Dr. Lillian Gilbreth (right) were
early experts in management
efficiency.

©Bettmann/Getty Images   ©George Rinhart/Getty Images

Scientific Management and the Model T

At the turn of the century, automobiles were a luxury that only the wealthy could afford. They were assembled by craftspeople who put an entire car together at one spot on the factory floor. These workers were not specialized, and Henry Ford believed they wasted time and energy bringing the needed parts to the car. Ford took a revolutionary approach to automobile manufacturing by using scientific management principles.

After much study, machines and workers in Ford's new factory were placed in sequence so that an automobile could be assembled without interruption along a moving production line. Mechanical energy and a conveyor belt were used to take the work to the workers.

The manufacture of parts likewise was revolutionized. For example, formerly it had taken one worker 20 minutes to assemble a flywheel magneto. By splitting the job into 29 operations, putting the product on a mechanical conveyor, and changing the height of the conveyor, Ford cut production time to 5 minutes.

By 1914, chassis assembly time had been trimmed from almost 13 hours to 1½ hours. The new methods of production required complete standardization, new machines, and an adaptable labor force. Costs dropped significantly, the Model T became the first car accessible to the majority of Americans, and Ford dominated the industry for many years.

SOURCE: Kroos, H. and Gilbert, C., *The Principles of Scientific Management.* New York: Harper & Row, 1911.

wages when they exceeded a standard level of output for each job. Taylor concluded that both workers and management would benefit from such an approach.

Scientific management principles were widely embraced. Other proponents, including Henry Gantt and Frank and Lillian Gilbreth, introduced many refinements and techniques for applying scientific management on the factory floor. One of the most famous examples of the application of scientific management is the factory Henry Ford built to produce the Model T.[9] The legacy of Taylor's scientific management approach is broad and pervasive. Most important, productivity and efficiency in manufacturing improved dramatically. The concepts of scientific methods and research were introduced to manufacturing. The piecerate system gained wide acceptance because it more closely aligned effort and reward. Taylor also emphasized the need for cooperation between management and workers. And the concept of a management specialist gained prominence.

Despite these gains, not everyone was convinced that scientific management was the best solution to all business problems. First, critics claimed that Taylor ignored many job-related social and psychological factors by emphasizing only money as a worker incentive. Second, production tasks were reduced to a set of routine, machinelike procedures that led to boredom, apathy, and quality control problems. Third, unions strongly opposed scientific management techniques because they believed management might abuse its power to set the standards and the piecerates, thus exploiting workers and diminishing their importance. Finally, although scientific management resulted in intense scrutiny of the internal efficiency of organizations, it did not help managers deal with broader external issues such as competitors and government regulations, especially at the senior management level.

Administrative Management

The **administrative management** approach emphasized the perspective of senior managers within the organization and argued that management was a profession and could be taught.

An explicit and broad framework for administrative management emerged in 1916, when Henri Fayol, a French mining engineer and executive, published a book summarizing his management experiences. Fayol identified five functions and 14 principles of management. The five functions, which are very similar to the four functions discussed in Chapter 1, are planning, organizing, commanding, coordinating, and controlling. Exhibit A.2 lists and defines the 14 principles. Although some critics claim Fayol treated the principles as universal truths for management, he actually wanted them applied flexibly.[10]

A host of other executives contributed to the administrative management literature. These writers discussed a broad spectrum of management topics, including the social responsibilities of management, the philosophy of management, clarification of business terms and concepts, and organizational principles. Chester Barnard's and Mary Parker Follet's contributions have become classic works in this area.[11]

Barnard, former president of New Jersey Bell Telephone Company, published his landmark book *The Functions of the Executive* in 1938. He outlined the role of the senior executive: formulating the purpose of the organization, hiring key individuals, and maintaining organizational communications.[12] Mary Parker Follet's 1942 book *Dynamic Organization* extended Barnard's work by emphasizing the continually changing situations that managers face.[13] Two of her key contributions—the notion that managers desire flexibility and the differences between motivating groups and individuals—laid the groundwork for the modern contingency approach discussed later in this appendix.

All the writings in the administrative management area emphasize management as a profession along with fields such as law and medicine. In addition, these authors offered many recommendations based on their personal experiences, which often included managing large corporations. Although these perspectives and recommendations were considered sound, critics noted that they might not work in all settings. Different types of personnel, industry conditions, and technologies may affect the appropriateness of these principles.

EXHIBIT A.2
Fayol's 14 Principles of Management

1. *Division of work*—divide work into specialized tasks and assign responsibilities to specific individuals.

2. *Authority*—delegate authority along with responsibility.

3. *Discipline*—make expectations clear and punish violations.

4. *Unity of command*—each employee should be assigned to only one supervisor.

5. *Unity of direction*—employees' efforts should be focused on achieving organizational objectives.

6. *Subordination of individual interest to the general interest*—the general interest must predominate.

7. *Remuneration*—systematically reward efforts that support the organization's direction.

8. *Centralization*—determine the relative importance of superior and subordinate roles.

9. *Scalar chain*—keep communications within the chain of command.

10. *Order*—order jobs and material so they support the organization's direction.

11. *Equity*—fair discipline and order enhance employee commitment.

12. *Stability and tenure of personnel*—promote employee loyalty and longevity.

13. *Initiative*—encourage employees to act on their own in support of the organization's direction.

14. *Esprit de corps*—promote a unity of interests between employees and management.

Human Relations

A fourth approach to management, **human relations**, developed during the 1930s. This approach aimed at understanding how psychological and social processes interact with the work situation to influence performance. Human relations was the first major approach to emphasize informal work relationships and worker satisfaction.

This approach owes much to other major schools of thought. For example, many of the ideas of the Gilbreths (scientific management) and Barnard and Follet (administrative management) influenced the development of human relations from 1930 to 1955. In fact, human relations emerged from a research project that began as a scientific management study.

Western Electric Company, a manufacturer of communications equipment, hired a team of Harvard researchers led by Elton Mayo and Fritz Roethlisberger. They were to investigate the influence of physical working conditions on workers' productivity and efficiency in one of the company's factories outside Chicago. This research project, known as the *Hawthorne Studies,* provided some of the most interesting and controversial results in the history of management.[14]

The Hawthorne Studies were a series of experiments conducted from 1924 to 1932. During the first stage of the project (the illumination experiments), various working conditions, particularly the lighting in the factory, were altered to determine the effects of those changes on productivity. The researchers found no systematic relationship between the factory lighting and production levels. In some cases, productivity continued to increase even when the illumination was reduced to the level of moonlight. The researchers concluded that the workers performed and reacted differently because the researchers were observing them. This reaction is known as the **Hawthorne Effect**.

This conclusion led the researchers to believe productivity may be affected more by psychological and social factors than by physical or objective influences. With this thought in mind, they initiated the other four stages of the project. During these stages, the researchers performed various work group experiments and had extensive interviews with employees. Mayo and his team eventually concluded that productivity and employee behavior were influenced by the informal work group.

Human relations proponents argued that managers should stress primarily employee welfare, motivation, and communication. They believed social needs had precedence over economic needs. Therefore, management must gain the cooperation of the group and promote job satisfaction and group norms consistent with the goals of the organization.

Another noted contributor to the field of human relations was Abraham Maslow.[15] In 1943, Maslow suggested that humans have five levels of needs. The most basic needs are the physical needs for food, water, and shelter; the most advanced need is for self-actualization, or personal fulfillment. Maslow argued that people try to satisfy their lower-level needs and then progress upward to the higher-level needs. Managers can facilitate this process and achieve organizational goals by removing obstacles and encouraging behaviors that satisfy people's needs and organizational goals simultaneously.

Although the human relations approach generated research into leadership, job attitudes, and group dynamics, it drew heavy criticism.[16] Critics believed that one result of human relations—a belief that a happy worker was a productive worker—was too simplistic. Whereas scientific management overemphasized the economic and formal aspects of the workplace, human relations ignored the more rational side of the worker and the important characteristics of the formal organization. However, human relations was a significant step in the development of management thought because it prompted managers and researchers to consider the psychological and social factors that influence performance.

Bureaucracy

Max Weber, a German sociologist, lawyer, and social historian, showed how management itself could be more efficient and consistent in his book *The Theory of Social and Economic Organizations*.[17] The ideal model for management, according to Weber, is the **bureaucracy** approach.

Weber believed bureaucratic structures can eliminate the variability that results when managers in the same organization have different skills, experiences, and goals. Weber advocated that the jobs themselves be standardized so that personnel changes would not disrupt the organization. He emphasized a structured, formal network of relationships among specialized positions in an organization. Rules and regulations standardize behavior, and authority resides in positions rather than in individuals. As a result, the organization need not rely on a particular individual but will realize efficiency and success by following the rules in a routine and unbiased manner.

A Human Relations Pioneer
In 1837, William Procter, a ruined English retailer, and James Gamble, son of a Methodist minister, formed a partnership in Cincinnati to make soap and candles. Both were known for their integrity, and soon their business was thriving.
By 1883, the business had grown substantially. When William Cooper Procter, grandson of the founder, left Princeton University to work for the firm, he wanted to learn the business from the ground up. He started working on the factory floor. "He did every menial job from shoveling rosin and soap to pouring fatty mixtures into crutchers. He brought his lunch in a paper bag . . . and sat on the floor [with the other workers] and ate with them, learning their feelings about work."
By 1884, Cooper Procter believed, from his own experience, that increasing workers' psychological commitment to the company would lead to higher productivity. His passion to increase employee commitment to the firm led him to propose a scandalous plan: share profits with workers to increase their sense of responsibility and job satisfaction. The surprise was audible on the first dividend day, when workers held checks equivalent to seven weeks' pay.
Still, the plan was not complete. Workers saw the profit sharing as extra pay rather than as an incentive to improve. In addition, Cooper Procter recognized that a fundamental issue for the workers, some of whom continued to be his good friends, was the insecurity of old age. Public incorporation in 1890 gave Procter a new idea. After trying several versions, by 1903 he had discovered a way to meet all his goals for labor: a stock purchase plan. For every dollar a worker invested in P&G stock, the company would contribute four dollars' worth of stock.
Finally, Cooper Procter had resolved some key issues for labor that paid off in worker loyalty, improved productivity, and an increasing corporate reputation for caring and integrity. He went on to become CEO of the firm, and P&G today remains one of the most admired corporations in the United States.

SOURCES: Schisgall, O., *Eyes on Tomorrow.* Chicago: Ferguson, J.G., 1981; Welsh, T., "Best and Worst Corporate Reputations," *Fortune,* February 7, 1994, pp. 58–66.

According to Weber, bureaucracies are especially important because they allow large organizations to perform the many routine activities necessary for their survival. Also, bureaucratic positions foster specialized skills, eliminating many subjective judgments by managers. In addition, if the rules and controls are established properly, bureaucracies should be unbiased in their treatment of people—both customers and employees.

Many organizations today are bureaucratic. Bureaucracy can be efficient and productive. However, bureaucracy is not the appropriate model for every organization. Organizations or departments that need rapid decision making and flexibility may suffer under a bureaucratic approach. Some people may not perform their best with excessive bureaucratic rules and procedures.

Other shortcomings stem from a faulty execution of bureaucratic principles rather than from the approach itself. Too much authority may be vested in too few people; the procedures may become the ends rather than the means; or managers may ignore appropriate rules and regulations. Finally, one advantage of a bureaucracy—its permanence—can also be a problem. Once a bureaucracy is established, dismantling it is difficult.

CONTEMPORARY APPROACHES

The contemporary approaches to management include quantitative management, organizational behavior, systems theory, and the contingency perspective. The contemporary approaches have developed at various times since World War II, and they continue to represent the cornerstones of modern management thought.

Quantitative Management

Although Taylor introduced the use of science as a management tool early in the 20th century, most organizations did not adopt the use of quantitative techniques for management problems until the 1940s and 1950s.[18] During World War II, military planners began to apply mathematical techniques to defense and logistics problems. After the war, private corporations began assembling teams of quantitative experts to tackle many of the complex issues confronting large organizations. This approach, referred to as **quantitative management**, emphasizes the application of quantitative analysis to management decisions and problems.

Quantitative management helps a manager make a decision by developing formal mathematical models of the problem. Computers facilitated the development of specific quantitative methods. These include such techniques as statistical decision theory, linear programming, queuing theory, simulation, forecasting, inventory modeling, network modeling, and break-even analysis. Organizations apply these techniques in many areas, including production, quality control, marketing, human resources, finance, distribution, planning, and research and development.

Despite the promise quantitative management holds, managers do not rely on these methods as the primary approach to decision making. Typically, they use these techniques as a supplement or tool in the decision process. Many managers will use results that are consistent with their experience, intuition, and judgment, but they often reject results that contradict their beliefs. Also, managers may use the process to compare alternatives and eliminate weaker options.

Several explanations account for the limited use of quantitative management. Many managers have not been trained in using these techniques. Also, many aspects of a management decision cannot be expressed through mathematical symbols and formulas. Finally, many of the decisions managers face are nonroutine and unpredictable.

Organizational Behavior

During the 1950s, a transition took place in the human relations approach. Scholars began to recognize that worker productivity and organizational success are based on more than the satisfaction of economic or social needs. The revised perspective, known as **organizational behavior**, studies and identifies management activities that promote employee effectiveness through an understanding of the complex nature of individual, group, and organizational processes. Organizational behavior draws from a variety of disciplines, including psychology and sociology, to explain the behavior of people on the job.

During the 1960s, organizational behaviorists heavily influenced the field of management. Douglas McGregor's Theory X and Theory Y marked the transition from human relations.[19] According to McGregor, Theory X managers assume workers are lazy and irresponsible and require constant supervision and external motivation to achieve organizational goals. Theory Y managers assume employees *want* to work and can direct and control themselves. McGregor advocated a Theory Y perspective, suggesting that managers who encourage participation and allow opportunities for individual challenge and initiative would achieve superior performance.

Other major organizational behaviorists include Chris Argyris, who recommended greater autonomy and better jobs for workers,[20] and Rensis Likert, who stressed the value of participative management.[21] Through the years, organizational behavior has consistently emphasized development of the organization's human resources to achieve individual and organizational goals. Like other approaches, it has been criticized for its limited perspective, although more recent contributions have a broader and more situational viewpoint. In the past few years, many of the primary issues addressed by organizational behavior have experienced a rebirth with a greater interest in leadership, employee involvement, and self-management.

Systems Theory

The classical approaches as a whole were criticized because they (1) ignored the relationship between the organization and its external environment, and (2) usually stressed one aspect of the organization or its employees at the expense of other considerations. In response to these criticisms, management scholars during the 1950s stepped back from the details of the organization to attempt to understand it as a whole system. These efforts were based on a general scientific approach called **systems theory**.[22] Organizations are open systems, dependent on inputs from the outside world, such as raw materials, human resources, and capital. They transform these inputs into outputs that (ideally) meet the market's needs for goods and services. The environment reacts to the outputs through a feedback loop; this feedback provides input for the next cycle of the system. The process repeats itself for the life of the system, as illustrated in Exhibit A.3.

Systems theory also emphasizes that an organization is one system in a series of subsystems. For instance, Southwest Airlines is a subsystem of the airline industry, and

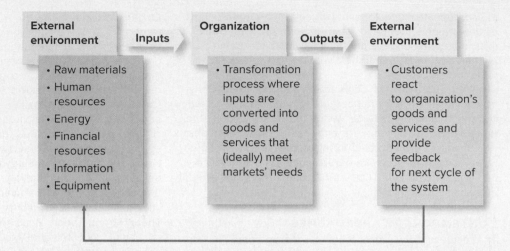

EXHIBIT A.3
Open-System Perspective of an Organization

External environment — Inputs —
- Raw materials
- Human resources
- Energy
- Financial resources
- Information
- Equipment

Organization — Outputs —
- Transformation process where inputs are converted into goods and services that (ideally) meet markets' needs

External environment
- Customers react to organization's goods and services and provide feedback for next cycle of the system

the flight crews are a subsystem of Southwest. Systems theory points out that each subsystem is a component of the whole and is interdependent with other subsystems.

Contingency Perspective

Building on systems theory ideas, the **contingency perspective** refutes universal principles of management by stating that a variety of factors, both internal and external to the firm, may affect the organization's performance.[23] Therefore, there is no one best way to manage and organize because circumstances vary.

Situational characteristics are called **contingencies**. Understanding contingencies helps a manager know which sets of circumstances dictate which management actions. You will learn recommendations for the major contingencies throughout this text. The contingencies include

1. Circumstances in the organization's external environment.

2. The internal strengths and weaknesses of the organization.

3. The values, goals, skills, and attitudes of managers and workers in the organization.

4. The types of tasks, resources, and technologies the organization uses.

With an eye to these contingencies, a manager may categorize the situation and then choose the proper competitive strategy, organization structure, or management process for the circumstances.

Researchers continue to identify key contingency variables and their effects on management issues. As you read the topics covered in each chapter, you will notice similarities and differences among management situations and the appropriate responses. This perspective should represent a cornerstone of your own approach to management. Many of the things you will learn about throughout this course apply a contingency perspective.

CURRENT EVENTS AND AN EYE ON THE FUTURE

Recent years have brought us a shrinking middle class, a struggling Eurozone, "Brexit," cyber security breeches, Alibaba's IP, and President Donald J. Trump. These now-historic events will continue having effects into the future. What are the most important current events unfolding as you read this? What can you learn from them, and how might they affect the future?

This appendix has summarized the major schools of management thought. Some schools offer more general courses in business history, and the subject is well worth knowing. What goes on today derives from what went on yesterday, which stemmed from what began years, decades, even centuries ago. It is reasonable to believe that if decision makers paid more attention to history, the subprime mortgage crisis of 2007 and the more general financial panic of 2008 could have been avoided.[24] Regardless of era and whether economies are rising or falling, it helps to examine the past for help in making good decisions today and in the future.

Knowledge of history could help with economic recoveries and mitigate or prevent future fiascos. Knowing history *could*—if used properly—have a positive impact on *the* future, and on *your* future.[25]

KEY TERMS

administrative management A classical management approach that attempted to identify major principles and functions that managers could use to achieve superior organizational performance, p 31.

bureaucracy A classical management approach emphasizing a structured, formal network of relationships among specialized positions in the organization, p 32.

contingencies Factors that determine the appropriateness of managerial actions, p 34.

contingency perspective An approach to the study of management proposing that the managerial strategies, structures, and processes that result in high performance depend on the characteristics, or important contingencies, of the situation in which they are applied, p 34.

economies of scale Reductions in the average cost of a unit of production as the total volume produced increases, p 28.

Hawthorne Effect People's reactions to being observed or studied resulting in superficial rather than meaningful changes in behavior, p 32.

human relations A classical management approach that attempted to understand and explain how human psychological and social processes interact with the formal aspects of the work situation to influence performance, p 31.

organizational behavior A contemporary management approach that studies and identifies management activities that promote employee effectiveness by examining the complex and dynamic nature of individual, group, and organizational processes, p 33.

quantitative management A contemporary management approach that emphasizes the application of quantitative analysis to managerial decisions and problems, p 33.

scientific management A classical management approach that applied scientific methods to analyze and determine the one best way to complete production tasks, p 29.

systematic management A classical management approach that attempted to build into operations the specific procedures and processes that would ensure coordination of effort to achieve established goals and plans, p 29.

systems theory A theory stating that an organization is a managed system that changes inputs into outputs, p 33.

DISCUSSION QUESTIONS

1. How does today's business world compare with the one of 40 years ago? What is different about today, and what is not so different?

2. What is scientific management? How might today's organizations use it?

3. Exhibit A.2 lists Fayol's 14 principles of management, first published in 1916. Are they as useful today as they were then? Why or why not? *When* are they most, and least, useful?

4. What are the advantages and disadvantages of a bureaucratic organization?

5. In what situations are quantitative management concepts and tools applicable?

6. Choose any organization and describe its system of inputs and outputs.

7. Why did the contingency perspective become such an important approach to management? Generate a list of contingencies that might affect the decisions you make in your life or as a manager.

8. For each of the management approaches discussed in the appendix, give examples you have seen. How effective or ineffective were they?

Experiential Exercises

A.1 APPROACHES TO MANAGEMENT

OBJECTIVES

1. To help you conceive a wide variety of management approaches.

2. To clarify the appropriateness of different management approaches in different situations.

INSTRUCTIONS

Your instructor will divide your class randomly into groups of four to six people. Acting as a team, with everyone offering ideas and one person serving as official recorder, each group will be responsible for writing a one-page memo to your present class. The subject matter of your group's memo will be "My advice for managing people today is . . ." The fun part of this exercise (and its creative element) involves writing the memo from the viewpoint of the person assigned to your group by your instructor.

Among the memo viewpoints your instructor may assign are

- An ancient Egyptian slave master (building the great pyramids).
- Henri Fayol.
- Frederick Taylor.
- Mary Parker Follet.
- Douglas McGregor.
- A contingency management theorist.
- A Japanese auto company executive.
- The chief executive officer of IBM in the year 2030.
- Commander of the Starship *Enterprise* II in the year 3001.
- Others as assigned by your instructor.

Use your imagination, make sure everyone participates, and try to be true to any historical facts you've encountered. Attempt to be as specific and realistic as possible. Remember, the idea is to provide advice about managing people from another point in time (or from a particular point of view at the present time).

Make sure you manage your 20-minute time limit carefully. A recommended approach is to spend 2 to 3 minutes putting the exercise into proper perspective. Next, take about 10 to 12 minutes brainstorming ideas for your memo, with your recorder jotting down key ideas and phrases. Have your recorder use the remaining time to write your group's one-page memo, with constructive comments and help from the others. Pick a spokesperson to read your group's memo to the class.

SOURCE: Krietner, R. and Kinicki, A., *Organization Behavior*, 3rd ed. New York: Richard D. Irwin, 1994, pp. 30–31.

OBJECTIVES

1. To learn to identify the components of a complex system.
2. To understand better how organizations function as systems.

INSTRUCTIONS

1. Think about your university from the perspective of being an open system.
2. Answer the questions on the University System Analysis Worksheet individually, or in small groups, as directed by your instructor.

University System Analysis Worksheet

1. Referring back to Exhibit A.3, what subsystems compose your university system? Diagram the system.

_____

_____

_____

2. Identify the following in your university system: inputs, transformations, outputs, and goods or services.

_____

_____

_____

3. What are the strengths of the current system? What are the weaknesses? (Is it a system failure when a student fails to graduate?)

_____

_____

_____

4. What changes (if any) would you make to the transformation process?

_____

_____

_____

SOURCE: Adapted from Gordon, J., *A Diagnostic Approach to Organizational Behavior.* Englewood Cliffs, NJ: Prentice Hall, 1983, p. 38.

CHAPTER 2
The External and Internal Environments

©Kay/Getty Images RF

> The essence of a business is outside itself.
> — PETER DRUCKER

LEARNING OBJECTIVES

After studying Chapter 2, you will be able to:

LO 1 Describe how environmental forces influence organizations and how organizations can influence their environments.

LO 2 Distinguish between the macroenvironment and the competitive environment.

LO 3 Explain why managers and organizations should attend to economic and social developments.

LO 4 Identify elements of the competitive environment.

LO 5 Summarize how organizations respond to environmental uncertainty.

LO 6 Define elements of an organization's culture.

LO 7 Discuss how an organization's culture and climate affect its response to its external environment.

CHAPTER OUTLINE

The Macroenvironment
  The Economy
  Technology
  Laws and Regulations
  Demographics
  Social Issues
  Sustainability and the Natural Environment

The Competitive Environment
  Competitors
  New Entrants
  Substitutes and Complements
  Suppliers
  Customers

Environmental Analysis
  Environmental Scanning
  Scenario Development
  Forecasting
  Benchmarking

Actively Managing the External Environment
  Changing the Environment You Are In
  Influencing Your Environment
  Adapting to the Environment: Changing the Organization
  Choosing an Approach

The Internal Environment of Organizations: Culture and Climate
  Organization Culture
  Organizational Climate

Management in Action

HOW JEFF BEZOS CREATES AMAZON'S ENVIRONMENT

Most managers strive to cope with their organization's environment, but Jeff Bezos, CEO of the e-commerce and cloud computing giant Amazon.com, is busy *creating* one.

The company Bezos founded in 1994 as an online discount bookseller is now in the business of selling virtually everything, to the tune of $100 billion in sales a year. The fourth-most valuable firm in the United States, Amazon is a pioneer in cloud computing, counting the CIA and Netflix among its customers. Under Bezos, the company has developed a successful e-reader, introduced the Echo as an AI voice service to compete with Google Home, patented its revolutionary 1-Click ordering technology, and explored the use of drones to facilitate same-day delivery. Its Blue Origin company is working with NASA on space travel, and in addition to winning an Emmy and a Golden Globe, Amazon recently made history by winning three of the first Academy Awards ever given for streaming services. Bezos himself owns a major daily newspaper, the multiple Pulitzer Prize–winning *Washington Post*. In a very real sense, he is constantly creating and recreating his company's environment.

Amazon's success was hard-won; when it finally posted a profit in 2003, the *Wall Street Journal* called it "one of the most powerful survivors on the Internet." Since then it has surpassed expectations, launching customer friendly innovations like 1-Click ordering and Prime membership for speedier delivery and enabling the growth of an active third-party marketplace and a vibrant customer community. Many other companies now offer one or more of the services Amazon provides, but none does so with the kind of market power

©Leah Puttkammer/Getty Images Entertainment/Getty Images

that has made Bezos's company a constant threat to competitors in so many industries.

Bezos seems to possess an uncanny ability to make use of environmental forces that others can only react to. His intuition about the unrealized potential of the Internet is what led him to found an online bookstore in the first place, and he has been quick to capitalize on other tech trends like e-readers, cloud computing, streaming, and drones. Although his attempt to develop a smartphone a few years ago failed, it seems likely that his company will continue to dominate its present environment and move into still more new ones. Amazon is opening a handful of bookstores, has launched several private fashion labels, and has begun quietly testing pop-up stores in malls across the United States.[1]

Technology and global competition are just two of the forces shaping the environment in which Amazon operates. As you study this chapter, consider what other forces Amazon's managers should be monitoring and engaging with.

EXHIBIT 2.1
Open-System Perspective of an Organization

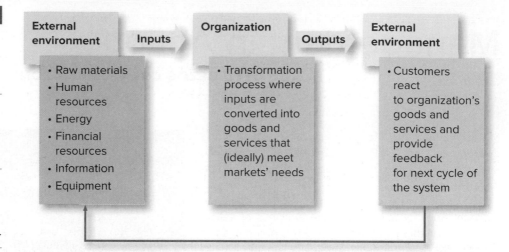

open systems

Organizations that are affected by, and that affect, their environment.

inputs

Goods and services organizations take in and use to create products or services.

outputs

The products and services organizations create.

external environment

All relevant forces outside a firm's boundaries, such as competitors, customers, the government, and the economy.

competitive environment

The immediate environment surrounding a firm; includes suppliers, customers, rivals, and the like.

In this chapter, we discuss in detail how pressures from outside the organization help create the context in which managers and their companies must operate.

Organizations are **open systems**—that is, they are affected by and in turn affect their external environments. For example, they take in **inputs** such as goods or services from their environment and use them to create products and services that are **outputs** to their environment, as shown in Exhibit 2.1. But when we use the term **external environment** here, we mean more than an organization's clients or customers; the external environment includes *all* relevant forces outside the organization's boundaries.

Many of these factors are uncontrollable. Companies large and small are buffeted by recessions, government regulations, competitors' actions, and other factors. But their lack of control does not mean that managers can ignore such forces, use them as excuses for poor performance, and try to just get by. Managers must stay abreast of external developments and respond effectively. Moreover, sometimes managers can influence components of the external environment. We will examine ways in which organizations can do just that.

Exhibit 2.2 shows the external and internal environments of a business organization. The organization exists in its **competitive environment**, which is composed of the firm and its rivals, suppliers, customers (buyers), new entrants, and substitute or complementary

EXHIBIT 2.2
The External and Internal Environments of Organizations

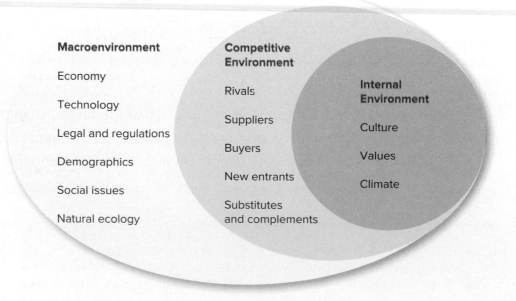

products. At the more general level is the **macroenvironment**, which includes legal, political, economic, technological, demographic, and social and natural factors that generally affect all organizations.

This chapter discusses the basic characteristics of an organization's environment and the importance of that environment for strategic management. We also examine the *internal environment,* or *culture,* of the organization and the ways that culture may influence the organization's response to its environment.

Later chapters delve more deeply into many of the basic environmental forces introduced here. For example, technology receives deeper treatment in Chapter 17. The global environment gets a thorough treatment in Chapter 6. Other chapters focus on ethics, social responsibility, and the natural environment. Chapter 18 reiterates the theme that recurs throughout this text: Organizations must change continually because environments change continually.

macroenvironment

The general environment; includes governments, economic conditions, and other fundamental factors that generally affect all organizations.

The Macroenvironment

All organizations operate in a macroenvironment, which is defined by the most general elements in the external environment that can influence strategic decisions. Top management teams must consider external factors before taking action.

The Economy

Although most Americans think in terms of the U.S. economy, the economic environment for organizations is much larger—created by complex interconnections among the economies of different countries. Wall Street investment analysts begin their workday thinking not just about what the New York Stock Exchange did yesterday but also about how the London and Tokyo exchanges did overnight. Growth and recessions occur worldwide as well as domestically.

The economic environment dramatically affects managers' ability to function effectively and influences their strategic choices. Interest and inflation rates affect the availability and cost of capital, growth opportunities, prices, costs, and consumer demand for products. Steeply rising energy and health care costs greatly affect companies' hiring and cost of doing business. Changes in the value of the dollar on world exchanges make American products cheaper or more expensive than their foreign competitors. Unemployment rates affect labor availability, the wages the firm must pay, and product demand.

During boom times, hiring accelerates, and unemployment rates fall. During the Great Recession of 2007–2009, the drop-off in employment was especially severe. Six and one-half years after the start of the Great Recession, employment levels returned to the pre-recession level.[2] That is two and one-half years longer than with previous recessions.

Long periods of slow hiring pose difficult challenges for societies and their governments. In contrast, the participation rate or percentage of eligible individuals who could be working has not returned to pre-recession levels; it dropped from 66 percent in 2008 to just below 63 percent during the first quarter of 2017.[3]

Governments are an important economic influence. In the United States, the federal government is a major employer and customer for business and military goods and services. When it spends more money than it is receiving, it also is a major borrower in the financial markets (adding to the national debt). These government activities can increase or decrease a nation's economic activity. To be effective, managers educate themselves about the impact of the government on the societies in which they work.

The stock market is another important economic influence. When investors bid up stock prices, the companies have more capital to fuel their strategies. Stock market observers watch trends in major indexes such as the Dow Jones Industrial Average, Standard and Poor's 500, and NASDAQ Composite, which combine many companies' performance into a single measure. Stock indexes tell managers about overall expectations for business value.

Bottom Line

With increased competition from foreign and domestic companies, managers must pay particular attention to cost. *Does low cost mean low quality? Why or why not?*

Economic conditions change over time and are difficult to predict.

The stock market may have a profound effect on the behavior of individual managers. In publicly held companies, managers throughout the organization feel required to meet Wall Street's earnings expectations. Such external pressures usually have a positive effect—they help make many firms more efficient and profitable. But failure to meet those expectations can cause a company's stock price to drop, making it more difficult for the firm to raise additional capital for investment. Managers' compensation also may be affected, particularly if they have been issued stock options. The net effect of these pressures often is that managers focus on short-term results at the expense of the long-term success of their organizations. Even worse, a few managers may be tempted to engage in unethical or unlawful behavior that misleads investors.[4] We will discuss managerial ethics in Chapter 5 and stock options in Chapter 10.

Economic conditions change over time and are difficult to predict. Bull and bear markets come and go. Periods of dramatic growth may be followed by recessions. Every trend undoubtedly will end—but when? Even when times seem good, budget deficits or other considerations create concern about the future.

Technology

Today a company cannot succeed without incorporating into its strategy the astonishing technologies that continually evolve. Technological advances create new products, advanced production techniques, and better ways of managing and communicating. In addition, as technologies evolve, new industries, markets, and competitive niches develop.

For example, early entrants in driverless car technology or 3D printing tried to establish dominant positions, and later entrants worked on technological advances that would give them a competitive niche. Advances in technology also permit companies to enter markets that otherwise would be unavailable to them. Advances in augmented reality led to the creation of Microsoft's HoloLens, which allows wearers of a headset to see 3D objects as if they were part of the real world.[5]

Augmented reality, popularized when millions of people played Pokemon Go in the summer of 2016, now is used for more serious purposes. Case Western Reserve University Medical School and the Cleveland Clinic use HoloLens to teach their medical students about human anatomy. Instead of relying on a cadaver lab to learn the fundamentals of anatomy, students in a classroom setting observe upright human holograms complete with beating hearts, organs, and digital bodies.[6]

The 3D printing process has revolutionized design.

©Maciej Frolow/The Image Bank/ Getty Images

Bottom Line

Managers with ready access to information gain a significant competitive edge. *What are some technologies that have given managers fast access to information?*

New technologies also provide new production techniques. In manufacturing, sophisticated robots perform jobs without suffering fatigue, requiring vacations or weekends off, or demanding wage increases. New methods, such as injecting steam into oil fields at high pressure (known as fracking), are enabling Occidental Petroleum, ExxonMobil, Shell, and other companies to extract oil from locations that had once been considered depleted. In this case, technological and economic forces overlap: the rising price of oil made it worthwhile for companies to develop the new technology.[7]

In addition, new technologies provide new ways to manage and communicate. Computerized management information systems (MISs) make information available when needed, and networking via the Internet makes that information available where it is needed. Computers monitor productivity and note performance deficiencies. Telecommunications allow conferences to take place without requiring people to travel to the same location. Strategies developed around new technological advances create a competitive advantage;

strategies that ignore or lag behind competitors' technologies lead to obsolescence and extinction. This issue is so important that we devote an entire chapter (Chapter 17) to it.

Laws and Regulations

U.S. government policies impose strategic constraints on organizations but may also provide opportunities.[8] In the United States, the Patient Protection and Affordable Care Act, which requires businesses with 50 or more full-time employees to offer health insurance, contains such a variety of provisions that some managers see mainly the costs of compliance, whereas others see opportunities for their companies.[9] This requirement is likely to increase an employers' labor costs, but it also can be used more strategically than competitors when recruiting and retaining talent.[10]

Giving employees more generous benefits could add to the cost of compensating them. At this writing, Congress is debating alternative health care laws. What is happening now with this vital issue?

Other provisions, such as insurance exchanges and tax credits for small businesses, may help smaller firms compete in the market for talent. Some consequences of the law will differ by industry: a retailer that needs to add an insurance benefit would see a new expense, whereas hospitals hope that broader insurance coverage will reduce the cost of providing services to patients who cannot pay. As business people, managers need to sort through the details, plan how to limit any harm, and build on any opportunities.

The government can affect business opportunities through tax laws, economic policies, and international trade rulings. For example, in some countries bribes and kickbacks are common and expected ways of doing business, but for U.S. firms, they are illegal practices. Some U.S. businesses have been fined for using bribery when competing internationally. But laws can also assist organizations. U.S. federal and state governments protect property rights, including copyrights, trademarks, and patents, making it more attractive economically to start businesses in the United States than in countries where laws and law enforcement offer less protection.

As described in Exhibit 2.3, *regulators* are government agencies that have the power to investigate company practices and take legal action to ensure compliance with laws.

Agency Name	Purpose
Securities & Exchange Commission (SEC)	Protects investors and maintains fair, honest, and efficient markets.
Food & Drug Administration (FDA)	Protects the public health by ensuring the safety and efficacy of drugs, products, and food.
Environmental Protection Agency (EPA)	Protects human health and the environment.
Occupational Safety & Health Administration (OSHA)	Enforces workplace safety and health standards.
Federal Aviation Administration (FAA)	Regulates civil aviation to promote safety.
Equal Employment Opportunity Commission (EEOC)	Enforces federal laws that prohibit discrimination in the workplace.
National Labor Relations Board (NLRB)	Safeguards employees' rights to organize and to determine whether to have unions as their bargaining representative.
Office of Federal Contract Compliance Programs (OFCCP)	Monitors federal contractors to make sure they take affirmative action to ensure equal employment opportunities.

EXHIBIT 2.3
Governmental Agencies That Regulate Businesses

Multiple Generations at Work

Are "Portfolio Careers" the New Normal?

Only a decade or two ago, people who changed jobs frequently or took a few months off from work to travel were often perceived as unreliable or lacking dedication. The career model back then was to begin a career immediately after graduating from college, do similar work for two or three different employers, take a couple of weeks of vacation during the summer, and try to retire with a pension. Now, this traditional career model is increasingly being replaced by the portfolio career.

Someone pursuing a portfolio career works multiple jobs (full-time, part-time, freelance, or contract) at a time and over the course of a lifetime. Instead of climbing a traditional career ladder, portfolio careerists seek flexible, engaging, and meaningful work that allows them to take frequent breaks to care for children, pursue hobbies, volunteer, or travel. Such flexible careers appeal to many Millennials. In a recent national survey, 38 percent of this generational cohort is doing freelance work, the highest percentage of any generation.

Are portfolio careers with occasional breaks just a fad? Data suggest otherwise. In a Manpower staffing survey of 19,000 Millennials across 25 countries, about half reported interest in nontraditional types of employment such as working part-time, freelancing, doing contract work, or being self-employed. For women, the most common reasons for wanting flexibility related to caring for children and aging relatives. Men reported wanting time to travel and vacation, and pursue dreams and hobbies.

Millennials aren't the only ones who like portfolio work. Some organizations are turning to seasoned Boomers who want to continue working on a part-time, flexible basis to coach and mentor the next generation of leaders.[11]

Often, the corporate community sees government as an adversary. However, many organizations realize that government can be a source of competitive advantages for an individual company or an entire industry. Public policy may prevent or limit new foreign or domestic competitors from entering an industry. Government may subsidize failing companies or provide tax breaks to some. Federal patents protect innovative products or production process technologies. Legislation may be passed to support industry prices, thereby guaranteeing profits or survival. The government may even intervene to ensure the survival of certain key industries or companies, as it has done to help auto companies, airlines, and agricultural businesses.

Demographics

demographics

Measures of various characteristics of the people who make up groups or other social units.

Demographics are measures of various characteristics of the people who make up groups or other social units. Managers must consider workforce demographics in formulating their human resource strategies. Population growth influences the size and composition of the labor force. Young workers are declining in numbers and the fastest-growing age group will be workers who are 55 and older, who are expected to represent over one-fourth of the labor force in 2022.

The education and skill levels of the workforce are another crucial demographic factor that managers must consider. The share of the U.S. labor force with at least some college education has been increasing steadily over the past several decades.[12] Even so, many companies find that they must invest heavily in training their entry-level workers, who may not have been adequately prepared for some of the more complex tasks the modern workplace requires. Employers also are finding it difficult to recruit employees for jobs that require knowledge of a skilled trade, such as machinists, electricians, and toolmakers, especially in areas where the cost of living is so high that most residents are professionals.[13] However, as education levels increase around the globe, managers can send even technical tasks to lower-priced but highly trained workers overseas. We discuss this further in Chapter 6.

Immigration is another important factor affecting the U.S. population and labor force.[14] Immigrants are frequently of working age but have different educational and occupational backgrounds from the rest of the labor force. Immigration is one reason the labor force continues to become more ethnically diverse. The biggest percentage employment increases will be by Hispanics and Asian Americans, followed by African Americans.

A more diverse workforce has many advantages, but managers have to make certain they provide equality for women and minorities with respect to employment, advancement opportunities, and compensation. They must make strategic plans to recruit, retain, train, motivate, and effectively use people of diverse demographic backgrounds who have the skills to achieve the company's mission. We discuss the issue of managing the diverse workforce in greater depth in Chapter 11.

Social Issues

Societal trends regarding how people think and behave have major implications for management of the labor force, corporate social actions, and strategic decisions about products and markets. For example, during the 1980s and 1990s, women in the workforce often chose to delay having children as they focused on their careers, but today more women are having children and then returning to the workforce. As a result, companies have introduced more supportive policies, including family leave, flexible working hours, and child care assistance.

As the number of people in the workforce with a college education increases, managers must consider how this affects work and careers.

©Visage/Stockbyte/Getty Images RF

Deloitte LLP has earned numerous awards for helping working parents balance life and work demands.[15] The consulting and taxation firm sponsors a Parents Network for members to discuss topics such as child-rearing, marriage, and special needs. Employees then can customize their schedules to help achieve both work and life balance.[16]

Many firms extend such benefits to all employees or allow them to design their own benefits packages, where they can choose from a menu of available benefits. Domestic partners, whether they are in a marital relationship or not, are covered by many employee benefit programs. Firms provide these benefits as a source of competitive advantage: attracting and retaining an experienced workforce.

How companies respond to social issues can affect their reputations in the marketplace, which in turn can help or hinder their competitiveness. For companies in the soft-drink industry, one issue demanding a response is the epidemic of obesity and associated health problems such as diabetes. The New York City Board of Health banned sales of sweetened drinks in containers larger than 16 ounces at restaurants and other establishments inspected by the agency. In this social environment, Coke ran ads pointing out that soft drinks aren't the only source of the problem and encouraging consumers to engage in calorie-burning exercise. All the major soft-drink makers have introduced reduced-calorie sodas, including Coca-Cola's Life and PepsiCo's Pepsi True, which they hope will appeal to consumers who dislike diet drinks.[17]

Sustainability and the Natural Environment

Organizations depend on the natural environment to provide them with resources. Depending on their products and processes, they may need trees for paper, steel for manufacturing goods, petroleum to fuel transportation or make plastics, and adequate air and water quality to maintain a healthy workforce. In addition, the ways in which organizations operate will have some impact on the quantity and quality of natural resources available. When the quantity is depleted or the quality is damaged, costs for resources skyrocket. Furthermore, the impact on natural resources—whether negatively by poisoning wells or positively by restoring forests—affects the quality of life for citizens in the areas where companies operate. Decisions that affect the natural environment therefore shape the climate of social issues and the political and legal environments.

Social Enterprise

Combating Climate Change

Despite its far-reaching impact, the problem of climate change has struggled to gain center stage in the United States. A landmark multination pact called the Paris Agreement took effect around the world in November 2016, calling on all participating countries, including the United States, to curb their emissions of the greenhouse gases that contribute to planet-wide warming temperatures. Left unchecked, warming trends can speed the melting of polar ice and the heating of the Earth's oceans, bringing severe weather disruptions that could herald long-term droughts, floods, and storms; threaten crops and water supplies; and disrupt the lives and habitats of many species. Massive human migration could result if lands are made uninhabitable by drought or flood.

Arguing that controlling climate change is good for business, hundreds of U.S. companies petitioned President Trump's White House to hold to former President Obama's commitment to the Paris Agreement. The companies included Dannon, eBay, Gap, General Mills, Intel, Kellogg, Mars, Monsanto, Nike, Patagonia, Staples, Starbucks, and many smaller firms. Their open letter to the president said, in part, "Failure to build a low-carbon economy puts American prosperity at risk. But the right action now will create jobs and boost US

competitiveness. Implementing the Paris Agreement will enable and encourage businesses and investors to turn the billions of dollars in existing low-carbon investments into the trillions of dollars the world needs to bring clean energy and prosperity to all."

While many countries have yet to figure out how much carbon they are producing and how to reduce that amount, one innovation that holds some promise is the electric car. Electric cars are less dependent on carbon fuels and can use renewable solar energy to recharge. Sales have increased worldwide—to 11 times what they were only five years ago—but they still represent less than 1 percent of car sales around the world. Some industry experts say it could take up to 20 years for electric cars to rise to 30 percent of all the cars on the world's roads, and climate scientists fear that by then the pace of climate warming will be beyond human control.[18]

Questions

- Can most organizations really be profitable while making a positive impact on the environment and society? What challenges do they face?

- Can you envision a world that doesn't produce waste? What changes are needed before that can happen?

Tragically, the explosion of BP's Deepwater Horizon drilling rig in the Gulf of Mexico killed 11 workers and caused millions of barrels of oil to gush into the Gulf and spread toward the coastlands of Mississippi and Louisiana. During the weeks that followed, fisheries closed, and tourists vacationed elsewhere. BP was forced to set aside tens of billions of dollars to cover all costs of the spill and its cleanup. In addition, the U.S. government fined the company billions of dollars. To prevent similar accidents in the future, it imposed additional regulations on any oil companies that want to drill in the Gulf.[19]

The natural environment is so important to managerial decision making that we devote Appendix B following this chapter to that subject.

The Competitive Environment

 LO 4 All managers are affected by the components of the macroenvironment we've just discussed. But each organization also interacts directly with others in a closer, more immediate competitive environment. As shown in Exhibit 2.4, the competitive environment includes rivalries among current competitors and the impact of new entrants, substitute and complementary products, suppliers, and customers.

The model shown in the exhibit originally was developed by Harvard professor Michael Porter, a noted authority on strategic management. According to Porter, successful managers do more than simply react to the environment; they act in ways that actually shape or

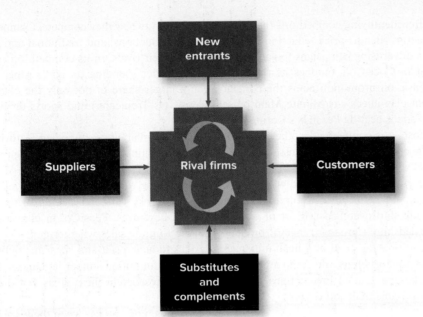

EXHIBIT 2.4
The Competitive
Environment

change the organization's environment. In strategic decision making, Porter's model is an excellent method to help managers analyze the competitive environment and adapt to or influence the nature of their competition.

Competitors

Competitors within an industry must deal with one another. When organizations compete for the same customers and try to win market share at the others' expense, all must react to and anticipate their competitors' actions.

The first question to consider is this: Who is the competition? Sometimes the answer is obvious. The major competitors in the market for soft drinks are Coca-Cola and PepsiCo. But consumer tastes have shifted away from soda to bottled water and other beverages. Young people, who in the past were the main consumers of soft drinks, increasingly prefer to buy water, coffee, or energy drinks, so sales of soda have declined for years. Adding to this decline, a number of cities have applied new taxes to soda purchases. Therefore, Coca-Cola and PepsiCo now compete in introducing new, less sugary products, not just in winning consumers over to their brand of cola.[20]

Thus, as a first step in understanding their competitive environment, organizations must identify their competitors. Competitors may include (1) small domestic firms, especially in tiny, premium markets; (2) strong regional competitors; (3) big new domestic companies exploring new markets; (4) overseas firms, especially those that try to solidify their position in small niches (a traditional Japanese tactic) or draw on an inexpensive labor force on a large scale (as in China); and (5) newer entries, such as firms offering their products on the web.

The competition between Coke and Pepsi products is intense. Often, the products are found side by side, as with these vending machines.

©Alpha and Omega Collection/ Alamy Stock Photo

The growth in competition from other countries has been especially significant with the worldwide reduction in international trade barriers. For example, the North American Free Trade Agreement (NAFTA) sharply reduced tariffs on trade between the United States, Canada, and Mexico. Managers today confront a particular challenge from low-cost producers abroad (see Chapter 6).

After identifying competitors, the next step is to analyze *how* they compete. Competitors use tactics such as price reductions, new-product introductions, and traditional and social media advertising campaigns to gain advantage over their rivals. In its competition against PepsiCo, Coca-Cola outdoes its rival with much heavier spending on advertising.[21] The emphasis on promotion helps the company win a larger share of not only the cola market but also juices (its Minute Maid outsells PepsiCo's Tropicana) and sports drinks (its Powerade is beating PepsiCo's Gatorade).

PepsiCo is competing in other ways. It launched a global emoji campaign featuring 70 unique emojis on PepsiCo cans, bottles, and cups.[22] The innovative emoji campaign is supported with digital and traditional advertising.[23]

It's essential to understand what competitors are doing when you are honing your own strategy. If soft-drink consumption continues to fall, Coke cannot be complacent about its leadership over Pepsi. Most of Coke's sales are beverages. PepsiCo, in contrast, has expanded into a broader range of products, hoping to grow sales whether consumers are looking for a fun treat or a healthful snack. Besides reducing salt and sugar in traditional snacks such as chips, the company is expanding healthful options under its Quaker brand (for example, Gluten Free oatmeal).[24] Coke lacks a presence in these areas, but they are less profitable than soft drinks.[25]

> It's essential to understand what competitors are doing when you are honing your own strategy.

Competition is most intense when there are many direct competitors (including foreign contenders), when industry growth is slow, and when the product or service cannot be differentiated in some way. New, high-growth industries offer enormous opportunities for profits. When an industry matures and growth slows, profits drop. Then intense competition causes an industry shakeout: weaker companies are eliminated, and the strong companies survive.[26]

New Entrants

New entrants into an industry compete with established companies. New entrants in the market for entertainment come from unexpected quarters as increasing broadband speeds and more powerful microprocessors enable many different ways to enjoy movies, TV shows, sports, videos, and games online. Cable and satellite television saw viewers flock to Hulu, Blockbuster lost movie sales to Netflix, and the makers of video game consoles have watched sales dry up as consumers switched to playing games on apps for their smartphones.

When there are many factors that prevent new companies from entering an industry, the threat to established firms is less serious. But if there are few such **barriers to entry**, the threat of new entrants is more serious. Some major barriers to entry are government policy, capital requirements, brand identification, cost disadvantages, and distribution channels.

The government can limit or prevent entry, as occurs when the FDA forbids a new drug to enter the market. On the other hand, when a firm's patent expires, other companies can enter the market and threaten once-dominant pharmaceutical companies–for example when AstraZeneca lost patent protection for its best-selling drug, Crestor. The cholesterol-lowering drug had brought in over $5 billion for the company.[27] In the face of the new stiff competition from generic drug makers, AstraZeneca cut hundreds of positions to offset expected lower revenues in 2017.[28]

Other barriers are less formal but can have the same effect. Capital requirements may be so high that companies won't risk such large amounts of money. Brand identification forces new entrants to spend heavily to overcome customer loyalty. Imagine the costs involved in trying to launch a new cola against Coke or Pepsi. The cost advantages that established companies hold—due to large size, favorable locations, existing assets, and so forth—can be formidable entry barriers.

Finally, existing competitors may have such tight distribution channels that new entrants have difficulty getting their goods or services to customers. For example, established food products already have supermarket shelf space. New entrants must displace existing products with promotions, price breaks, intensive selling, and other tactics.

Substitutes and Complements

Besides products that directly compete, other products can affect a company's performance by being substitutes for or complements of the company's offerings. A *substitute* is a potential threat; customers use it as an alternative, buying less of one kind of product but more of another. A *complement* is a potential opportunity because customers buy more of a given product if they also demand more of the complementary product. Exhibit 2.5 lists a dozen products and their potential substitutes and complements.

Technological advances and economic efficiencies enable firms to develop substitutes for existing products. After Amazon introduced the Kindle e-reader and Barnes & Noble introduced the competing Nook—and even more so as the companies were able to lower the price of these devices—consumers began treating e-books as an attractive substitute for printed books. But even as consumers were still gravitating toward e-readers, Apple launched the iPad tablet computer. Because it is lightweight and versatile, consumers treated it as a substitute not only for e-readers but also in some cases as a substitute for a basic laptop computer.

Companies don't have to be at the mercy of customers switching to a substitute. To avoid losing out when others create a new substitute, some companies try to create their own substitute products. PepsiCo's investment in development of new sweeteners for drinks and a line of more healthful snacks offers substitutes for consumers avoiding the calories, fat, and sugar of its "fun for you" products. Anticipating that a growing share of consumers will care about healthful snacking, PepsiCo CEO Nooyi believes the company's products should include many choices that can aid health and well-being.[29]

Besides identifying and planning for substitutes, companies must consider taking advantage of complements for their products. When people are buying new homes, they are also buying appliances and landscaping products. When customers purchase new smartphones, they may also buy new cases, screen protectors, selfie sticks, car kits, extra batteries, and insurance. And when consumers munch on Lays, Doritos, or Cheetos snacks, they are bound to get thirsty and need a complementary product—say, an ice-cold Pepsi or Sierra Mist. PepsiCo owns all these food and drink brands; thus the company sells products that are complements as well as substitutes. If PepsiCo meets its goal to shift more of its product line to healthier fare, it may become known for its complementary products, too—say, some Tropicana juice with your Quaker oatmeal.[30]

As with substitutes, a company needs to watch for new complements that can change the competitive landscape. Publishers that originally saw e-readers and tablet computers as a threat—as substitutes for their print publications—worked on complements for their print products such as electronic books and magazines plus apps for reading content online. Textbook and cookbook publishers teamed up with software company Inkling to prepare e-book versions that support the use of multimedia and interactive features. These books offer capabilities that would be impossible in the print versions and therefore sell at higher prices.[31]

If the Product Is . . .	The Substitute Might Be . . .
Panera soup and salad	Subway sandwich
Sony laptop computer	iPad tablet computer
Face-to-face college course	Online course
ScanDisk USB flash drive	Dropbox

If the Product Is . . .	The Complement Might Be . . .
Starbucks beverage	Starbucks coffee cake
Netflix streaming video	Orville Redenbacher's popcorn
Evernote app	Evernote scanner
Apartment rental	IKEA furniture

EXHIBIT 2.5
Potential Substitutes and Complements

Suppliers

Recall from our discussion at the start of the chapter that organizations are open systems that acquire resources (inputs) from their environments and convert those resources into products or services (outputs) that they sell. Suppliers provide the resources needed for production. Those resources include people (supplied by trade schools and universities), raw materials (from producers, wholesalers, and distributors), information (supplied by researchers and consulting firms), and financial capital (from banks and other sources).

> Organizations are at a disadvantage if they become overly dependent on a single powerful supplier.

Suppliers are important beyond the mere provision of resources. The resources they supply may be outstanding or defective. They can provide excellent or poor-quality service. Suppliers can raise their prices. Powerful suppliers' price increases can reduce an organization's profits, particularly if the organization cannot pass them on to its customers.

Organizations are at a disadvantage if they become overly dependent on any powerful supplier. A supplier is powerful if the buyer has few other sources of supply or if the supplier has many other buyers. Dependence also results from high **switching costs**—the fixed costs buyers face if they change suppliers. For example, once a buyer learns how to operate a supplier's equipment, such as computer software, the buyer faces both economic and psychological costs in changing to a new supplier.

Of course, close supplier relationships can be an advantage. Food and beverage companies work closely with the makers of the flavorings and additives that make their products appealing to consumers. With companies such as PepsiCo and Coca-Cola looking to offer more healthful and natural soft drinks, suppliers such as Archer Daniels Midland answered the call. ADM bought food-ingredients maker Wild Flavors for $3 billion to supply unique blends of vitamins and minerals, sweeteners based on the stevia plant, energy boosters extracted from coffee beans, and new flavors such as ginger and chili.[32]

Supply chain management is a vital contributor to a company's competitiveness and profitability. By **supply chain management**, also known as the *extended enterprise,* we mean the managing of the entire network of facilities and people that obtain raw materials from outside the organization, transform them into products, and distribute them to customers.[33]

Increasing competition requires managers to pay ever-closer attention to their costs. They can no longer afford to hold large and costly inventories, waiting for orders to come in; once orders do come in, some products still sitting in inventory might be outdated. Customers today look for products built to their specific needs and preferences—and they want them delivered quickly at the lowest available price. This requires the supply chain to be not only efficient but also *flexible,* so that the organization's output can quickly respond to changes in demand.

Choosing the right supplier is an important strategic decision. Suppliers can affect manufacturing time, product quality, and inventory levels. The relationship between suppliers and the organization is changing in many companies. The close supplier relationship has become a new model for organizations using a just-in-time manufacturing approach (discussed in Chapters 16 and 17). And in some companies, innovative managers form strategic partnerships with their key suppliers in developing new products or new production techniques. We describe this kind of strategic partnership in more detail in Chapter 9.

Customers

Without customers to purchase its goods or services, a company won't survive. Customers can be intermediate (wholesalers and retailers) or final (end users), depending on where they are in the value chain. You are a **final consumer** when you buy a pair of Nike running shoes or lunch at Panera Bread. **Intermediate consumers** buy raw materials or wholesale products and then sell to final consumers, as when Lenovo, Dell, and Hewlett-Packard buy processors from Intel to use in their laptop computers.

Intermediate customers make more purchases than individual final consumers do. Types of intermediate customers include retailers, who buy clothes from wholesalers and manufacturers'

switching costs

Fixed costs buyers face when they change suppliers.

Bottom Line

The ability to manufacture customized products quickly became a competitive requirement. *To meet this requirement, what behaviors would a company need from its employees?*

supply chain management

The managing of the network of facilities and people that obtain materials from outside the organization, transform them into products, and distribute them to customers.

final consumer

A customer who purchases products in their finished form.

intermediate consumer

A customer who purchases raw materials or wholesale products before selling them to final customers.

representatives before selling them to their customers, and industrial buyers, who buy raw materials (such as chemicals) before converting them into final products. Selling to intermediate customers is often called *business-to-business* (B2B) selling. Notice in these B2B examples that the intermediate customer eventually goes on to become a seller.

Like suppliers, customers are important to organizations for reasons other than the money they provide for goods and services. Customers can demand lower prices, higher quality, unique product specifications, or better service. They also can play competitors against one another, as occurs when a car buyer (or a purchasing agent) collects different offers and negotiates for the best price. Customers want to be actively involved with their products, as when the buyer of an iPhone customizes it with ring tones, wallpaper, and a variety of apps.

FedEx partners with many health care companies to provide logistics of all types from factory floor to a patient's front door.

©Bloomberg/Bloomberg/Getty Images

Dell Inc. took customer input a step further by asking customers what they want the company to develop next. At Dell's IdeaStorm website (www.ideastorm.com), visitors can post ideas and comments about products. One of IdeaStorm's most enthusiastic customer-users became so involved with the community that he was hired as the project's manager and helped expand the site's customer interactions.[34]

The Internet empowers customers. It provides easy information about product features and pricing. In addition, Internet users informally create and share messages about a product, providing flattering free "advertising" at best or embarrassing and even erroneous bad publicity at worst. Companies try to use this to their advantage by creating opportunities for consumers and the brand to interact.

Another way companies connect with customers is through social media sites like LinkedIn *Company Pages,* which allows companies to invite individuals to join company-related groups. Online retailer Zappos uses LinkedIn to answer questions about its products and the company's culture. Similarly, Google+ *Communities* offers companies a way to interact with individuals who might be interested in their products or services while increasing its visibility and brand awareness.[35]

As we discussed in Chapter 1, customer service means giving customers what they want or need, the way they want it, the first time. This usually depends on the speed and dependability with which an organization can deliver its products. Exhibit 2.6 shows several actions and attitudes that contribute to excellent customer service.

Bottom Line

In all businesses—services as well as manufacturing—strategies that emphasize good customer service provide a critical competitive advantage. *Identify some excellent and poor customer service that you have received.*

EXHIBIT 2.6
Actions and Attitudes = Excellent Customer Service

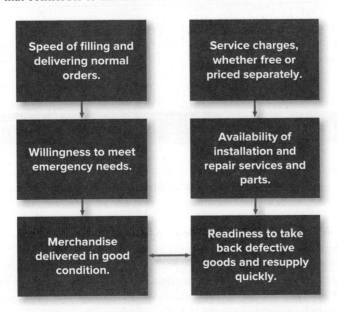

- Speed of filling and delivering normal orders.
- Service charges, whether free or priced separately.
- Willingness to meet emergency needs.
- Availability of installation and repair services and parts.
- Merchandise delivered in good condition.
- Readiness to take back defective goods and resupply quickly.

SOURCE: Adapted from Kotler, P., *Marketing Management: Analysis, Planning, Implementation and Control,* 9th ed. Englewood Cliffs, NJ: Prentice Hall, 1990.

Management in Action

AMAZON REINVENTS THE COMPETITIVE ENVIRONMENT

Amazon.com is known for its focus on the customer, and it's easy to see that focus in its online retail operations. Its famous 1-Click ordering system, its Prime memberships (offering two-day delivery of unlimited purchases plus unlimited music and video streaming services for a one-time annual fee), its enormous product range, and its frequently discounted prices all attest to its commitment to make online shopping as rewarding and easy as possible.

But Amazon's view of its "customer set" is much broader than just consumers who buy things. It also includes about 2 million individuals and small companies that sell a huge array of new and used products in Amazon's famous third-party Marketplace. Rather than competing with these sellers, Amazon has made them part of the family. In exchange for a cut of their proceeds, the online giant provides selling space on its site, handles warehousing and logistics for many sellers, and even offers business coaching for some. The Marketplace brings in an increasingly large share of Amazon's revenues—a record-breaking 50 percent in 2016. With the help of this core business, Amazon, already the largest online retailer in the world, is poised to soon

become the world's second-largest retailer of any kind (trailing only Walmart).

Founder and CEO Jeff Bezos proudly credits Amazon's success in large part to the contribution these third-party sellers make to the vast number and variety of products it can offer. Thanks in part to them, its nearly 340 million separate stock-keeping units (SKUs) far surpass Walmart's 8 million and are a big reason more online shoppers go to Amazon's site than to any other. The company has also designed Amazon Web Services (AWS), the cloud-computing software that powers the site, to supply unbeatable speed and capacity even during the peak holiday shopping season.[36]

- It's likely that no individual member of Amazon's Marketplace could by itself pose a serious competitive threat to the company's retail business. Why do you think Jeff Bezos still thought it important to absorb these potential competitors into his own business?
- Identify as many of Amazon's external competitors as you can in the market for retail consumer goods. What effect do you think the Marketplace has on these competitors?

A company is at a disadvantage if it depends too heavily on powerful customers. Customers are powerful if they make large purchases or if they can easily find alternative places to buy. If you are the largest customer of a firm and you can buy from others, you have power over that firm, and you likely can negotiate with it successfully. Your firm's biggest customers—especially if they can buy from other sources—will have the greatest negotiating power over you.

Customer relationship management is discussed more fully in Chapter 9. As you read "Management in Action: Progress Report," consider how Amazon distinguishes itself with customers by seeking advantages in its relationships with other parties in the competitive environment.

Environmental Analysis

LO 5

environmental uncertainty

When managers do not have enough information about the environment to understand or predict the future.

Failing to understand key environmental influences, or to identify important opportunities and threats, severely undermines managers' ability to make decisions and execute plans. For example, if they know little about customer likes and dislikes, they cannot effectively design new products, schedule production, or develop marketing plans. Timely and accurate environmental information is crucial for running a business.

But information about the environment is not always readily available. Managers find it difficult to forecast how well their own products will sell, let alone how a competitor might respond. In other words, managers often operate under conditions of uncertainty. **Environmental uncertainty** means that managers do not have enough information about the environment to understand it or predict the future.

Uncertainty arises from two related factors: complexity and dynamism. Environmental *complexity* is the number of issues to which a manager must attend and their interconnectedness. For example, industries with many firms competing in vastly different ways are more complex—and uncertain—than industries with only a few key firms competing in fewer ways. Environmental *dynamism* is the degree of discontinuous change occurring within the industry. High-growth industries with products and technologies that change rapidly are more uncertain than stable industries where changes are less dramatic and more predictable.[37]

By analyzing environmental forces—in both the macroenvironment and the competitive environment—managers can identify opportunities and threats that might affect the organization. As environmental uncertainty increases, managers must develop methods like the following for collecting and interpreting information.

> Managers must make important decisions under conditions of uncertainty.

Environmental Scanning

Managers cope with environmental uncertainty by trying to identify what might be important. Frequently, organizations and individuals act out of ignorance, only to regret those actions later. IBM had an opportunity to purchase the technology behind xerography, but turned it down. Xerox saw the potential, and the rest is history. On the other hand, Xerox researchers later developed the technology for the original computer mouse, but executives did not see the potential and the company missed a huge opportunity.

To understand and predict environmental changes, opportunities, and threats, companies such as Amazon, Starbucks, and Citibank spend time and money monitoring events. **Environmental scanning** means both searching for useful information and interpreting what is important and what is not. Managers can ask questions such as these:

Who are our current competitors?
Are there few or many entry barriers to our industry?
What substitutes exist for our product or service?
Is the company too dependent on powerful suppliers?
Is the company too dependent on powerful customers?[38]

Answers to these questions help managers develop **competitive intelligence**, the information necessary to decide how best to manage in their competitive environments. You can see how Porter's competitive analysis, discussed earlier, can guide environmental scanning. Exhibit 2.7 describes two environments: an attractive environment, which provides competitive advantage and high potential, and an unattractive environment, which puts a firm at a competitive disadvantage and offers low potential.[39]

environmental scanning

Searching for and sorting through information about the environment.

competitive intelligence

Information that helps managers determine how to compete better.

©Cathy Yeulet/123RF RF

Scenario Development

As managers attempt to determine the effects of environmental forces on their organizations, they can develop **scenarios** depicting possible futures. Scenarios combine different

scenario

A narrative that describes a particular set of future conditions.

Environmental Factor	Unattractive	Attractive
Competitors	Many; low industry growth; equal size; commodity	Few; high industry growth; unequal size; differentiated
Threat of entry	High threat; few entry barriers	Low threat; many entry barriers
Substitutes	Many	Few
Suppliers	Few; high bargaining power	Many; low bargaining power
Customers	Few; high bargaining power	Many; low bargaining power

EXHIBIT 2.7
Attractive and Unattractive Environments

factors into alternative pictures of future environments and the firm. For example, when Congress and the president forecast the size of the federal budget deficit, they develop several scenarios about what the economy is likely to do in the coming years. Managers often develop a *best-case scenario* (the occurrence of events favorable to the firm), a *worst-case scenario* (the occurrence of unfavorable events), and at least one middle-ground alternative. The formal practice of scenario development was pioneered by Royal Dutch Shell.

Scenario development helps managers develop contingency plans for what they should do given different future situations.[40] For example, as a manager you will be involved in budgeting for your area. You likely will be asked to list initiatives that you would eliminate in case of an economic downturn, and new investments you would make if your firm does better than expected.

Effective managers regard the scenarios they develop as living documents: rather than preparing them once and forgetting them, they update them with relevant new factors as things change over time.

Forecasting

forecasting

Method for predicting how variables will change the future.

Whereas environmental scanning identifies important influences, and scenario development generates alternative pictures of the future, a **forecast** is a single prediction about the future. For example, in making capital investments, firms make forecasts about future interest rates. In deciding to expand or downsize a business, firms predict the demand for goods and services or the supply and demand of required labor. Publications such as the *Economist*'s *Global Forecasting Service,* PricewaterhouseCoopers's *Trendsetter Barometer Business Outlook,* Kiplinger's *Economic Outlook,* and the Conference Board's economic reports provide forecasts to businesses.

Although forecasts are designed to help executives predict the future, their accuracies vary greatly. Because they extrapolate from the past to project the future, forecasts are most accurate when the future proves to look a lot like the past. Forecasts are *potentially* most useful when the future will look radically different from the past, but unfortunately that is when forecasts tend to be less accurate.

The more things might change, the less confidence we have in our forecasts. The best advice for using forecasts includes the following:

Use multiple forecasts, and perhaps average their predictions.
Remember that accuracy decreases the farther into the future you are trying to predict.
Forecasts are no better than the assumptions made and the data used to construct them.
Use simple forecasts (rather than complicated ones) when possible.
Keep in mind that important events often are surprises and represent a departure from predictions.[41]

Benchmarking

benchmarking

The process of comparing an organization's practices and technologies with those of other companies.

In addition to trying to predict environment changes, firms can undertake intensive study of other firms' best practices to understand their sources of competitive advantage. **Benchmarking** means identifying the best-in-class performance by a company in a given area, say, product development or customer service, and then comparing your processes to theirs. To accomplish this, a benchmarking team collects information on its own company's operations and those of the other firm to determine gaps. These gaps serve as a point of entry to learn the underlying causes of performance differences. Ultimately, the team maps out a set of best practices that lead to world-class performance. We will discuss benchmarking further in Chapter 4 .

Actively Managing the External Environment

It is essential to manage the external environment effectively. Clothing retailers who pay no attention to changes in the public's style preferences, or manufacturers who don't make sure they have reliable supply sources, are soon out of business. In managing their environments, managers and companies have several primary options: (1) selecting a new environment, (2) influencing the environment, and (3) adapting to the environment. This section describes the options briefly; we will elaborate on them in Chapter 4.

Changing the Environment You Are In

Organizations need not be stuck within some given environment; they have options for defining where they operate. We refer to this as **strategic maneuvering**. By making a conscious effort to change the boundaries of its competitive environment, a firm can maneuver around potential threats and capitalize on arising opportunities.[42] Managers can use several strategic maneuvers, including domain selection, diversification, merger and acquisition, and divestiture.[43]

Domain selection is the entrance by a company into another suitable market or industry. For example, a market may have limited competition or regulation, ample suppliers and customers, or high growth. PepsiCo's decision to begin selling yogurt was based on the company's goal of selling more healthful snacks coupled with the recent growing popularity of yogurt in the United States.[44]

Diversification occurs when a firm invests in different types of businesses or products or when it expands geographically to reduce its dependence on a single technology or market. Apple successfully diversified its product line when it added the iPod, iTouch, iPad, and iPhone to its offerings of personal computers. As the popularity of the devices spread, Apple identified an opportunity to further diversify in order to tap the fast-growing mobile app market. In 2016, Apple's App Store revenues jumped 40 percent from the previous year fueled by downloads of games like Pokemon Go, Super Mario Run, and Monster Strike. The store offered about 2 million apps and reported 130 billion downloads. This part of Apple's empire generated over $20 billion for app developers, of which Apple retained 30 percent of the revenues.[45]

A **merger** or **acquisition** takes place when two or more firms combine, or one firm buys another, to form a single company. Mergers and acquisitions can offer greater efficiency from combined operations or can give companies relatively quick access to new markets or industries. Acquisitions also can quickly give a company access to a business, technology, or existing customer bases in different geographic markets.[46] The largest deal announced in 2016 was AT&T's plan to purchase Time Warner for over $85 billion, pending formal approval by the U.S. government.[47]

Divestiture occurs when a company sells one or more businesses. At Ford Motor Company, operating losses and the costs of restructuring its workforce brought about a cash shortage. To address anti-monopoly concerns over its proposed merger with U.S. Foods, Sysco sold 11 distribution centers worth $4.6 billion in revenue to a competitor, Performance Food Group.[48]

Some companies, called **defenders**, stay within a limited, stable product domain. In contrast, **prospectors**, are more likely to engage in strategic maneuvering.[49] Aggressive companies continuously change the boundaries of their competitive environments by seeking new products and markets, diversifying, and merging or acquiring new enterprises. In these and other ways, corporations put their competitors on the defensive and force them to react.

Influencing Your Environment

In addition to redefining the boundaries of their environment, managers and organizations can develop proactive responses aimed at changing the environment. Two general types of proactive responses are independent action and cooperative action.

strategic maneuvering

An organization's conscious efforts to change the boundaries of its task environment.

domain selection

Entering a new market or industry using an existing expertise.

diversification

A firm's investment in a different product, business, or geographic area.

merger

One or more companies combining with another.

acquisition

One firm buying another.

divestiture

A firm selling one or more businesses.

defenders

Companies that stay within a stable product domain as a strategic maneuver.

prospectors

Companies that continuously change the boundaries for their task environments by seeking new products and markets, diversifying and merging, or acquiring new enterprises.

EXHIBIT 2.8   Independent Action

Strategy	Definition	Examples
Competitive aggression	Exploiting a distinctive competence or improving internal efficiency for competitive advantage	Aggressive pricing, comparative advertising (McDonald's)
Competitive pacification	Independent action to improve relations with competitors	Helping competitors find raw materials
Public relations	Establishing and maintaining favorable images in the minds of those making up the environment	Nike sponsoring a global sporting event
Voluntary action	Voluntary commitment to various interest groups, causes, and social problems	Johnson & Johnson donating supplies to tsunami victims
Legal action	Engaging company in private legal battle	Warner Music lawsuits against illegal music copying
Political action	Efforts to influence elected representatives to create a more favorable business environment or limit competition	Issue advertising; lobbying at state and national levels

SOURCE: Adapted from Zeithami, C. and Zeithami, V., "Environmental Management: Revising the Marketing Perspective," *Journal of Marketing*, Spring 1984.

independent strategies

Strategies that an organization acting on its own uses to change some aspect of its current environment.

Independent Action   A company uses **independent strategies** when it acts on its own to change some aspect of its current environment.[50] Exhibit 2.8 shows the definitions and uses of these strategies. For example, Southwest Airlines demonstrates competitive aggression by cutting fares when it enters a new market, and Apple uses competitive aggression whenever it launches a new product such as the iPhone or iTunes to establish its dominance as a technological leader.

When Kellogg Company promotes the cereal industry as a whole, it demonstrates competitive pacification. Weyerhaeuser Company advertises its reforestation efforts (public relations). Bank of America, Salesforce, Beats, and other companies have signed on to Product Red, a program in which they market special Red-themed products and donate a percentage of the profits to the Global Fund, a project to help end AIDS in Africa (voluntary action).[51] Viacom sued Google for allowing users to post copyrighted video clips on the Google-owned YouTube website (legal action). In 2015, the pharmaceutical industry spent $240 million to lobby members of Congress (political action).[52] Each of these examples shows how single organizations can have an impact on their environments.

cooperative strategies

Strategies used by two or more organizations working together to manage the external environment.

Cooperative Action   In some situations, two or more organizations work together using **cooperative strategies** to influence the environment.[53] Exhibit 2.9 shows several examples. Contracting occurs when suppliers and customers, or managers and labor unions, sign formal agreements about the terms and conditions of their future relationships. Contracts are explicit attempts to make a future relationship predictable. An example of cooptation might occur when universities invite wealthy alumni to join their boards of directors.

Finally, examples of coalition formation are when businesses band together to curb the rise of employee health care costs and when organizations in the same industry form industry associations and special interest groups. You may have seen cooperative advertising strategies, such as when dairy producers, beef producers, orange growers, and the like jointly pay for television commercials.

Adapting to the Environment: Changing the Organization

To cope with environmental uncertainty, organizations frequently make adjustments in their structures and work processes. A common way to adapt is by decentralizing decision making. For example, if a company faces a growing number of competitors in various markets,

EXHIBIT 2.9
Cooperative Action

Strategy	Definition	Examples
Contraction	Negotiating an agreement between the organization and another group to exchange goods, services, information, patents, and so on	Contractual marketing systems
Cooptation	Absorbing new elements into the organization's leadership structure to avert threats to its stability or existence	Consumer and labor representatives and bankers on boards of directors
Coalition	Two or more group coalesce and act jointly with respect to some set of issues for some period of time	Industry associations; political initiatives of the Business Roundtable and the U.S. Chamber of Commerce

SOURCE: Adapted from Zeithami, C. and Zeithami, V., "Environmental Management: Revising the Marketing Perspective," *Journal of Marketing,* Spring 1984.

if different customers want different things, and if production facilities are being built in different regions of the world, it becomes impossible for the chief executive (or a small group of top executives) to keep abreast of all activities and understand all operating details. The top management team then gives authority to lower-level managers to make decisions that will benefit the firm. The term **empowerment** is used frequently today to talk about this type of decentralized authority. We will address empowerment and decision making in more detail in Chapters 3 and 9.

To cope with uncertainties caused by environmental change (dynamism), organizations can establish more flexible structures. In today's business world, the term *bureaucracy* generally has a bad connotation. Most of us recognize that bureaucratic organizations tend to be formal and stable; frequently they are unable to adjust to changes or exceptional circumstances that don't "fit the rules." Although bureaucratic organizations can be efficient if the environment is stable, they tend to be slow-moving and plodding. When products, technologies, customers, or competitors are changing, *organic* structures give organizations the flexibility to adjust to change. We will discuss organic structures in more detail in Chapter 9.

Adapting at the Boundaries   Because they are open systems, organizations are exposed to uncertainties from both their inputs and outputs. To compete, they can create buffers on both the input and output boundaries with the environment. **Buffering** creates supplies of excess resources to meet unpredictable needs.

On the input side, organizations establish relationships with employment agencies to hire part-time and temporary help during rush periods when labor demand is difficult to predict. In the U.S. these workers, known as *contingent workers,* buffer labor input uncertainties.[54]

Contingency work opportunities are growing. According to Adecco, a firm that places workers in temporary assignments, the demand for temporary workers in finance, administrative support, health care, engineering, and information technology is strong.[55]

On the output side of the system, most organizations use inventories that allow them to keep merchandise on hand in case a rush of customers decide to buy their products. Auto dealers are a common example of this use of buffers, but we see buffer inventories in fast-food restaurants, bookstores, clothing stores, and even real estate agencies.[56]

Organizations also may try **smoothing,** or leveling normal fluctuations at environmental boundaries. For example, during winter months in the north, when automobile sales drop off, dealers cut the price of their in-stock vehicles to increase demand. At the end of each clothing season, retailers discount their merchandise to make room for incoming inventories. Such smoothing helps to level off fluctuations in demand.

empowerment

The process of sharing power with employees, thereby enhancing their confidence in their ability to perform their jobs and their belief that they are influential contributors to the organization.

buffering

Creating supplies of excess resources in case of unpredictable needs.

smoothing

Leveling normal fluctuations at the boundaries of the environment.

In today's business world, the term *bureaucracy* generally has a bad connotation.

flexible processes

Methods for adapting the technical core to changes in the environment.

Bottom Line

The Internet lets customers quickly find products with the cost and quality features they want. *What might "flexible processes" mean for a groceries home delivery company?*

Adapting at the Core   Buffering and smoothing manage uncertainties at system boundaries, firms also can establish **flexible processes** that allow for adaptation in their technical core. For example, firms customize their goods and services to meet the varied and changing demands of customers. Even in manufacturing, where it is difficult to change basic core processes, firms adopt techniques of mass customization that help them create flexible factories. Instead of mass-producing large quantities of a "one-size-fits-all" product, organizations use mass customization to produce individually customized products at low cost.

Whereas Henry Ford used to claim that "you could have a Model T in any color you wanted, as long as it was black," auto companies now offer a wide array of colors, trim lines, options, and accessories. Mass customization uses a network of independent operating units in which each performs a specific process or task such as making a dashboard assembly on an automobile. When an order comes in, different modules join forces to deliver the product or service as specified by the customer.[57] We will discuss mass customization and flexible factories in more depth in Chapter 9.

Choosing an Approach

In choosing your approach to managing the external environment, three general considerations provide guidance. First, environmental actions are most useful when aimed at elements of the environment that (1) cause the company problems, (2) provide it with opportunities, and (3) allow the company to change successfully. Thus, public concern about the obesity epidemic and its impact on health could be a problem for the sales and reputation of a company that makes snacks and soft drinks. PepsiCo CEO Nooyi believed it would be irresponsible to try to change that concern, so she focused on what the company could do to address it: change its product mix to include more healthful alternatives without abandoning the idea that it's fine to enjoy an occasional fun snack.

Second, organizations should choose responses that fit the environmental component of interest. Competitive actions help manage the competitive environment, political action influences the legal environment,[58] and contracting helps manage customers and suppliers.

Third, companies should choose actions that offer the most benefit at the lowest cost. Return-on-investment calculations should incorporate short-term financial considerations as well as long-term impact. Strategic managers who consider these factors carefully will more effectively guide their organizations to competitive advantage.

The Internal Environment of Organizations: Culture and Climate

 We have discussed the external environment, both the macroenvironment and the competitive environment. Managers' actions are shaped also by forces inside the organization. These forces, creating an internal culture and climate, are conditions, routines, and beliefs that influence the decisions and behavior of employees at all organizational levels.

At Nordstrom, the fashion retailer, new employees receive a five-by-eight-inch card with one rule on it, along with a full handbook containing policies and legal regulations.

Organization Culture

organization culture

The set of important assumptions about the organization and its goals and practices that members of the company share.

An organization's culture is like an individual's personality. **Organization culture** is the set of important assumptions about the organization and its goals and practices that members of the company share. It is a system of shared values about what is important and beliefs about how the world works.

A company's culture provides a framework that guides people's behavior on the job.[59] For example, the way people dress and behave, the way they interact with each other and with

©Nordstrom, Inc.   ©Nordstrom, Inc.

customers, and the work habits that managers value are usually quite different at a bank than they are at a rock music company, and different again at a law firm or an advertising agency.

Cultures can be strong or weak. Strong cultures can have great influence on how people think and behave. A strong culture is one in which people understand and strongly believe in the firm's goals, priorities, and practices. A strong culture can be a real advantage to the organization if the behaviors it encourages and facilitates are appropriate and effective ones. As examples, the Walt Disney Company's culture encourages extraordinary devotion to customer service, and the culture at design firm IDEO encourages world-class innovation.

But a strong culture can be counterproductive when changes become necessary. Ideas and practices that have "worked" for years can become ineffective or detrimental or when the external environment changes, as new competitors appear or new customer demands arise. Strong cultures can breed overconfidence and thoughtlessly inspire wrong-headed efforts, as recently at Wells Fargo when strong productivity incentives prompted hard-striving employees to create new accounts that customers never requested.

When a merger or acquisition brings together organizations with strong cultures, long-standing habits and ingrained beliefs are likely to clash. After Cisco Systems acquired Linksys, integration of the two cultures was harder than expected. Linksys employees, accustomed to working in a smaller and less formal company, were used to bringing their new product ideas directly to the owners, a husband-and-wife team. In contrast, Cisco employees needed to obtain formal approval for new product ideas from several layers of management.[60] Eventually, Cisco sold its home networking division (including the Linksys brand) to Belkin.[61]

In contrast, weak organizational cultures lack strong shared values and breed confusion about corporate goals. It is not clear what principles should or really do guide decisions. Some managers may pay lip service to an important behavior ("we would never cheat a customer") but behave very differently ("don't tell him about the bug in the software, we'll take care of it later"). Weak and confused cultures foster poor performance and sometimes worse.

Most managers would agree that they want to create and maintain a strong culture that will make their company more effective. They encourage high values, laudable goals, and useful behaviors. They want to create a culture that is appropriate in every sense for the organization's competitive environment.[62]

LO 7

The Digital World

As new technologies provide new ways to manage and communicate, we see some organizations provide internal communication applications (apps) like Slack. Slack is a cloud-based application for team collaboration. It was originally designed for internal use at a company that was developing an online game.

Slack is a business-oriented chat app that, just over a year after product launch, was valued at $1.12 billion. The app allows small and medium-sized teams to create group chats, send direct messages, and create private groups that branch off the main group. There are many apps, like WhatsApp and Basecamp, that help people communicate within their organizations as teams, sub-teams and project-specific groups. These apps allow managers to support efficient and productive communication.

Diagnosing Culture   You will find it helpful to understand organization culture. Perhaps you are thinking about working there and you want a good fit, or maybe you are working there now and want to deepen your understanding of how your employer operates and what it expects of you. How would you go about making the diagnosis? A variety of things will give you useful insights:

Corporate mission statements and official goals are a starting point because they tell you what the firm's desired public image is. Most companies have a mission statement. Your school has one, and you can probably find it online. But are these statements a true expression of culture? Many employees are not aware of their companies' mission.[63] So, even after reading mission statements or taking note of official goals, you need to figure out whether these reflect reality and how the firm actually conducts its business.

Its important business practices–how a company responds to problems and challenges, makes strategic decisions, and actually treats employees and customers–say a lot about what top management really values. Target recently announced a new strategy to invest $5 million by 2022 in "green chemistry innovation." Working with multiple stakeholders, the retailer wants to identify and reduce the number and types of potentially harmful chemicals in the products it sells.[64] You can use such decisions to assess corporate values and desired action*s.*

Symbols, rites, and ceremonies give further clues about culture. Status symbols, from reserved parking spaces to large corner offices, can tell you about the hierarchy and how power operates. Who is hired and fired and why, and the activities that are most rewarded, indicate the firm's real values.

The stories people tell carry a lot of information about the company's culture. Every company has its myths, legends, and true stories about important past decisions and actions that convey what managers respect, admire, and don't tolerate. The stories often feature the company's heroes, once or still active, who brought to life what the organization especially wants and depends on. A famous business hero and icon, Sam Walton, showed his frugality by driving an old pickup truck when visiting his stores; he provided a powerful role model for Walmart's low-cost culture.

Cultural assessments can make the difference between business and personal successes and failures. As noted earlier, when two companies are considering a merger, acquisition, or joint venture, failing to consider cultural differences can sink the new arrangements.[65] You are likely to be better off in a culture that (1) suits your preferences and (2) you understand well rather than poorly.

Bottom Line

A culture aligned with its environment helps the organization succeed. *To be aligned with its environment, what values should an organic grocery store chain company have?*

Managing Culture   The best managers take several approaches to managing culture. First, they articulate clearly the ideals and visions to strive for. They state these often until they become a known presence throughout the organization.

Second, executives can give constant attention to the telling details of daily affairs, such as communicating with employees regularly, being visible and active, and setting the right

Management in Action

THE CULTURE AT AMAZON

In his 2016 annual letter to shareholders, Amazon's CEO Jeff Bezos noted correctly that corporate cultures are "enduring, stable, hard to change." A recent *New York Times* investigation had publicly revealed Amazon's culture to be ruthlessly competitive and intensely stressful, often bringing white-collar employees at its Seattle headquarters to tears at their desks. Distribution-center workers had grievances too, as evidenced by a 2014 Supreme Court ruling that they did not have to be paid for the time it took to screen them for stolen goods every day.

As a result of the *Times* story, Bezos launched his own investigation into the company culture, and firmly and publicly refuted the newspaper's report. In a further response, his shareholder letter went on to say, "We never claim that our approach is the right one—just that it's ours."

It's hard to argue with a related observation in Bezos's letter about culture and performance: that people work best in a culture that suits them. Clearly, some people thrive on internal competition, others prefer camaraderie and teamwork, and still others do best when they pursue their goals alone. Bezos believes people "self-select,"

choosing to leave employers whose climates don't suit or inspire them.

The *New York Times* story reported a culture that ranked employees by productivity so the lowest performing could be culled, and survivors were "incentivized" to promote themselves at the expense of their colleagues. Perhaps in response, Amazon recently announced changes. It eased some policies that rewarded such competitive behavior, and will launch a retraining program to assign coaching and support to poor performers. Those employees can either appeal the assignment, accept and try to improve, or resign with severance.[66]

- Jeff Bezos's shareholder letter called Amazon a good place to fail, since "failure and invention are inseparable twins." What do you think is the relationship between failure and invention? What do you think, does Amazon's culture tolerate failures?
- Is it possible for a company to be as innovative and successful as Amazon without having a particular type of culture? What would the most appropriate type of culture be?

examples. Executives should not only talk about the vision, but also embody it day in and day out. This makes executive pronouncements credible, creates personal examples others can emulate, and builds trust that progress will continue over time.

Moments of truth are decision dilemmas in which hard choices must be made. Imagine top management trumpeting a culture that emphasizes quality products, but in a moment of truth a manager makes a decision that harms quality. Perhaps a part used in a batch of assembled products is found to be defective. Whether the manager decides to replace the costly part or to ship it in order to save time and money will go a long way toward reinforcing or destroying a quality-oriented culture.

To reinforce a desired culture, managers should celebrate and reward those who exemplify it. By hiring judiciously, teaching newcomers, and rewarding and promoting people on the basis of desired actions, management can ensure that the culture will strengthen and persist.

Managing culture requires time and effort, but the best managers understand its importance. The potential payoffs include the performance benefits of a strong and appropriate culture, plus the avoidance of the many costs of a weak or inappropriate one.

Organizational Climate

An organization's *climate* is the practical, day-to-day aspect of its culture. **Organizational climate** consists of the patterns of attitudes and behaviors that shape people's experience of an organization.[67] Like the weather, is it sunny or dark, stormy or calm? Many tests and surveys measure organizational climate in terms of morale, employees' relationships with managers and co-workers, handling of conflicts, openness and effectiveness of communication,

organizational climate

The patterns of attitudes and behavior that shape people's experience of an organization.

61

methods for measuring and rewarding performance, and how clearly people understand their work roles.

Both climate and deeper culture influence the internal work environment, how people experience their work, and organizational effectiveness. Because organizational climate is easier to measure, managers often find that dimensions of organizational climate are more manageable levers to pull. Later chapters explore a variety of management responsibilities that shape organizational climate, including maintaining ethical conduct (Chapter 5), appraising and rewarding performance (Chapter 10), valuing diversity (Chapter 11), leading (Chapter 12), motivating employees (Chapter 13), fostering teamwork (Chapter 14), communicating (Chapter 15), and leading change (Chapter 18).

Capably and continually addressing key aspects of an organization's climate enables managers to strengthen competitive advantages and develop new ones as needed. What is required is a climate that motivates and enables workers to achieve the organization's strategy. As you read "Management in Action: Onward," consider what the climate at Amazon is like under the leadership of Jeff Bezos.

KEY TERMS

acquisition, p. 55

barriers to entry, p. 48

benchmarking, p. 54

buffering, p. 57

competitive environment, p. 40

competitive intelligence, p. 53

cooperative strategies, p. 56

defenders, p. 55

demographics, p. 44

diversification, p. 55

divestiture, p. 55

domain selection, p. 55

empowerment, p. 57

environmental scanning, p. 53

environmental uncertainty, p. 52

external environment, p. 40

final consumer, p. 50

flexible processes, p. 58

forecasting, p. 54

independent strategies, p. 56

inputs, p. 40

intermediate consumer, p. 50

macroenvironment, p. 41

merger, p. 55

open systems, p. 40

organization culture, p. 58

organizational climate, p. 61

outputs, p. 40

prospectors, p. 55

scenario, p. 53

smoothing, p. 57

strategic maneuvering, p. 55

supply chain management, p. 50

switching costs, p. 50

RETAINING WHAT YOU LEARNED

You learned how pressures from outside the organization create the context in which managers must function. The macroenvironment includes broad forces like the economy, laws, and technology. The competitive environment is closer to the organization and includes forces like competitors, suppliers, and customers. Effective managers need to stay aware of labor force and other trends that can affect their businesses. An organization's competitive environment can range from favorable to unfavorable. Proactive managers attempt to manage environmental uncertainty through a variety of strategies. Organization culture provides an internal values framework that guides people's behavior at work. Organizational climate is people's day-to-day experience of a company's business practices.

LO 1 Describe how environmental forces influence organizations and how organizations can influence their environments.

- Organizations are open systems that are affected by, and in turn affect, their external environments.

- Organizations receive financial, human, material, and information resources from the environment; transform those resources into finished goods and services; and then send those outputs back into the environment to meet market needs.

LO 2 Distinguish between the macroenviroment and the competitive environment.

- The macroenvironment is the economic, legal and political, technological, demographic, social, and natural environment forces that influence strategic decisions.

- The competitive environment is composed of forces closer to the organization, such as current competitors, new entrants, substitute and complementary products, suppliers, and customers.

- A key distinction between the macroenvironment and the competitive environment is the amount of control a firm can exert on external forces.

- Macroenvironmental forces such as the economy and social trends are much less controllable than are

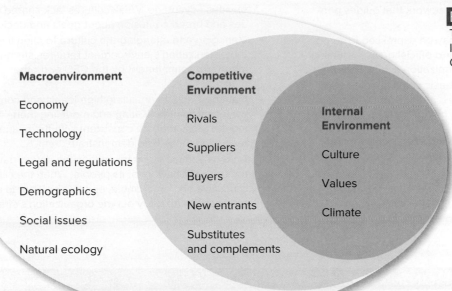

EXHIBIT 2.2 (revisited)
The External and
Internal Environments of
Organizations

forces in the competitive environment such as suppliers and customers.

LO 3 **Explain why managers and organizations should attend to economic and social developments.**

- Developments outside the organization can have profound effects on how managers and their companies operate. For example, higher energy costs or increased spending on security may make it harder for managers to keep their prices low.
- The growing diversity of the labor force gives managers access to a much broader range of talent but also requires them to make sure different types of employees are treated equally.
- Effective managers stay aware of important trends and respond to them appropriately.

LO 4 **Identify elements of the competitive environment.**

- Elements in the competitive environment can be favorable or unfavorable. To determine how favorable a competitive environment is, managers should consider the nature of the competitors, potential new entrants, threat of substitutes, opportunities from complements, and relationships with suppliers and customers.
- Analyzing how these forces influence the organization provides an indication of potential threats and opportunities.
- Effective management of the firm's supply chain is one way to achieve a competitive advantage.
- Attractive environments tend to be those with high industry growth, few competitors, products that can

be differentiated, few potential entrants, many barriers to entry, few substitutes, many suppliers (none with much power), and many customers.
- After identifying and analyzing competitive forces, managers formulate strategies that minimize the power external forces have over the organization.

LO 5 **Summarize how organizations respond to environmental uncertainty.**

- Responding effectively to the environment often requires devising proactive strategies to change the environment.
- Strategic maneuvering involves changing the boundaries of the competitive environment through domain selection, diversification, mergers, and the like.
- Independent strategies require not moving into a new environment but rather changing some aspect of the current environment through competitive aggression, public relations, legal action, and others.
- Cooperative strategies, such as contracting, cooptation, and coalition building, are those in which two or more organizations work together.
- Organizations can become better able to handle environmental change by decentralizing authority, buffering or smoothing, and establishing flexible processes.

LO 6 **Define elements of an organization's culture.**

- An organization's culture is its set of shared values and practices related to what is most important and how the world works.

- The culture provides a framework that guides people's behavior at work.
- Elements of the culture may be expressed in corporate mission statements and official goals, assuming these reflect how the organization actually operates.
- Business practices are a basic cultural indicator. Symbols, rites, ceremonies, and the stories people tell express and reinforce cultural values.

LO 7 Discuss how an organization's culture and climate affect its response to its external environment.

- A culture can be strong or weak. A strong culture with appropriate values and best practices is an obvious advantage. Weak cultures lack shared values and breed confusion about goals and decisions.
- Managing and changing the culture to align it with the organization's environment requires strong, long-term commitment by the CEO and other managers.
- Managers should articulate high ideals and convey values by communicating and modeling them, making decisions that are consistent with them, and rewarding those who demonstrate them.
- An organization's climate shapes the day-to-day attitudes and behaviors of its people. When the climate is positive and predictable, employees want to and are best able to carry out the organization's strategy.

DISCUSSION QUESTIONS

1. This chapter's opening quote by Peter Drucker said, "The essence of a business is outside itself." What do you think this means? Do you agree?

2. What are the most important forces in the macroenvironment facing companies today?

3. What are the main differences between the macroenvironment and the competitive environment?

4. What kinds of changes do companies make in response to environmental uncertainty?

5. We outlined several proactive responses that organizations can make to the environment. What examples have you seen recently of an organization's responding effectively to its environment? Did the effectiveness of the response depend on whether the organization was facing a threat or an opportunity?

6. Select two organizations that interest you. Do some research and talk with an employee or two, if possible. How would you characterize the cultures they have? Write a paragraph that describes each culture.

7. When you visited colleges to select one to attend, were there cultural differences in the campuses that made a difference in your choice? Did these differences help you decide which college to attend?

EXPERIENTIAL EXERCISES

2.1   EXTERNAL ENVIRONMENT ANALYSIS

OBJECTIVE

To give you the experience of performing an analysis of a company's external environment

INSTRUCTIONS

Select a company you want to learn more about. Using online and/or library resources, including websites on the company's industry and its website and annual report, fill out the following External Environment Worksheet for that company:

External Environment Worksheet

Laws and regulations

What are some key laws and regulations under which this company and industry must operate?

_____

_____

The economy

How does the state of the economy influence the sales of this company's products?

_____

_____

Technology
What new technologies strongly affect the company you have selected?

_____
_____

Demographics
What changes in the population might affect the company's customer base?

_____
_____

Social issues
What changes in society affect the market for your company's products?

_____
_____

Suppliers
How does your company's relationship with suppliers affect its profitability?

_____
_____

Competitors
What companies compete with the firm you have selected? Do they compete on price, on quality, or on other factors?

_____
_____

New entrants
Are new competitors to the company likely? Possible?

_____
_____

Substitutes and complements
Is there a threat of substitutes for the industry's existing products? Are there complementary products that suggest an opportunity for collaboration?

_____
_____

Customers
What characteristics of the company's customer base influence the company's competitiveness?

_____
_____

DISCUSSION QUESTIONS

1. What has the company done to adapt to its environment?

2. How does the company attempt to influence its environment?

SOURCE: McShane, Steven L. and Von Glinow, Mary Ann, _Organizational Behavior,_ 3rd ed. New York: McGraw-Hill, 2005, p. 499.

2.2   CORPORATE CULTURE PREFERENCE SCALE

OBJECTIVE
This self-assessment is designed to help you identify a corporate culture that fits most closely with your personal values and assumptions.

INSTRUCTIONS
Read each pair of the statements in the Corporate Culture Preference Scale and circle the statement that describes the organization you would prefer to work in. This exercise is completed alone so students assess themselves honestly without concerns of social comparison. However, class discussion will focus on the importance of matching job applicants to the organization's dominant values.

Corporate Culture Preference Scale

I would prefer to work in an organization:

1a.	Where employees work well together in teams.	**OR**	1b. That produces highly respected products or services.
2a.	Where top management maintains a sense of order in the workplace.	**OR**	2b. Where the organization listens to customers and responds quickly to their needs.
3a.	Where employees are treated fairly.	**OR**	3b. Where employees continuously search for ways to work more efficiently.
4a.	Where employees adapt quickly to new work requirements.	**OR**	4b. Where corporate leaders work hard to keep employees happy.
5a.	Where senior executives receive special benefits not available to other employees.	**OR**	5b. Where employees are proud when the organization achieves its performance goals.
6a.	Where employees who perform the best get paid the most.	**OR**	6b. Where senior executives are respected.
7a.	Where everyone gets his or her job done like clockwork.	**OR**	7b. That is on top of new innovations in the industry.
8a.	Where employees receive assistance to overcome any personal problems.	**OR**	8b. Where employees abide by company rules.
9a.	That is always experimenting with new ideas in the marketplace.	**OR**	9b. That expects everyone to put in 110 percent for peak performance.
10a.	That quickly benefits from market opportunities.	**OR**	10b. Where employees are always kept informed of what's happening in the organization.
11a.	That can quickly respond to competitive threats.	**OR**	11b. Where most decisions are made by the top executives.
12a.	Where management keeps everything under control.	**OR**	12b. Where employees care for each other.

McShane, Steven L. and Von Glinow, Mary Ann, *Organizational Behavior,* 3rd ed. New York: McGraw-Hill, 2005, p. 499. Copyright ©2005 McGraw-Hill Global Education Holdings LLC. All rights reserved. Used with permission.

Scoring Key for the Corporate Culture Preference Scale

Scoring instructions: In each space, write in a "1" if you circled the statement and "0" if you did not. Then add up the scores for each subscale.

Control culture   ___ + ___ + ___ + ___ + ___ + ___ = ___
                    (2a)   (5a)   (6b)   (8b)   (11b)   (12a)

Performance culture   ___ + ___ + ___ + ___ + ___ + ___ = ___
                    (1b)   (3b)   (5b)   (6a)   (7a)   (9a)

Relationship culture   ___ + ___ + ___ + ___ + ___ + ___ = ___
                    (1a)   (3a)   (4b)   (8a)   (10b)   (12b)

Responsive culture   ___ + ___ + ___ + ___ + ___ + ___ = ___
                    (2b)   (4a)   (7b)   (9a)   (10a)   (11a)

Interpreting your score: These corporate cultures may be found in many organizations, but they represent only four of many possible organization cultures. Also, keep in mind none of these subscales is inherently good or bad. Each is effective in different situations. The four corporate cultures are defined here, along with the range of scores for high, medium, and low levels of each dimension based on a sample of MBA students:

Corporate Culture Dimension and Definition	Score Interpretation
Control culture: This culture values the role of senior executives to lead the organization. Its goal is to keep everyone aligned and under control.	High: 3 to 6 Medium: 1 to 2 Low: 0

Performance culture: This culture values individual and organizational performance and strives for effectiveness and efficiency.

High: 5 to 6

Medium: 3 to 4

Low: 0 to 2

Relationship culture: This culture values nurturing and well-being. It considers open communication, fairness, teamwork, and sharing a vital part of organizational life.

High: 6

Medium: 4 to 5

Low: 0 to 3

Responsive culture: This culture values its ability to keep in tune with the external environment, including being competitive and realizing new opportunities.

High: 6

Medium: 4 to 5

Low: 0 to 3

Concluding Case

TATA MOTORS: FROM CHEAP TO AWESOME?

The barriers to entry are so high in the automotive industry that it is rare to see a new entrant. A notable exception has been India's Tata Motors, the country's largest maker of commercial vehicles, which about five years ago promised to become a leading carmaker in the fast-growing economies of the developing world. Comparing its ambitious plan to the iconic Volkswagen Beetle and Ford Model T, Tata launched the Nano in 2009. Branded a "people's car," the Nano was priced at $2,000 to $2,500 (or 1 lakh in Indian currency). Tata Motors marketed the stripped-down minicar to first-time automobile customers in rural areas. The goal was to make the Nano the standard transportation for Indian families working their way up to the middle class.

The promised launch was so ambitious that Tata could not realistically meet expectations. Production was postponed for about a year and a half, and then the company determined it couldn't afford to sell the Nano profitably at the promised price. The first Nanos to roll off assembly lines were priced just $800 below Suzuki's competing Alto, which offered more storage space and a more powerful engine. The Nano's safety performance also ran into embarrassing problems; some reportedly caught fire.

Sales of the Nano have been disappointing. After reaching its maximum sales of 10,000 in April 2012, recent reports of the "people's car" indicate 2,500 units are sold each month. It has been suggested that the low sales were a result of the unacceptably low level of quality and features built into the vehicle, including an underpowered and noisy motor, no stereo or air conditioning, and wires visible in the driver's compartment. Another reason for the Nano's demise was a missed target market, namely young urban drivers. The cheap and unsafe image associated with the Nano turned off many of these would-be buyers.

The Nano's failure was frustrating to Tata Motors that had invested $400 million to develop the Nano and "hundreds of millions more building a factory capable of manufacturing 15,000 to 20,000 of the tiny cars a month." If it were to be successful in the long run, Tata Motors would need to adjust its strategy to overcome the myriad barriers to success in the Indian automotive industry.

Tata Motors has changed both its marketing and manufacturing strategies. Shifting its focus from first-time rural buyers to young urban customers, the company recently launched the Nano Twist and Nano LX. It is trying to rebrand the Nano from "cheapest car in the world" to an "awesome" car that is also affordable. Priced as high as $3,578, these improved Nano models can include several upgrades like power steering, music system with Blue-tooth connectivity, and enhanced interior and exterior features.

Also, Tata has responded with maintenance contracts, test drives, and safety improvements. It has revenues from its commercial vehicles and its Jaguar Land Rover operations to stay afloat. Perhaps the Nano will still become the people's car. Start-ups often make mistakes, and some of them recover brilliantly. What made Tata's stumble remarkable was its grand scale.

DISCUSSION QUESTIONS

1. Which barriers to entry contributed most to Tata Motors' lack of success with the original Nano?
2. Which macroenvironmental factors did Tata Motors consider when adjusting the marketing and manufacturing strategies to achieve success with the more recent Twist and LX models?
3. To what degree do you believe Tata Motors will succeed in delivering a successful low-cost vehicle to consumers in India and other developing economies?

SOURCES: Mahendra, A., "Tata Nano Twist Review," *Auto Tech Review (online)*, http://www.automotechreview.com, accessed February 26, 2015; Able, V., "Tata Nano: The Car That Was Just Too Cheap," *The Guardian (online)*, February 3, 2014, http://www.theguardian.com; McClain, S., "Why the World's Cheapest Car Flopped," *The Wall Street Journal (online)*, October 14, 2013; Eyring, M., "Learning from Tata Motors' Nano Mistakes," *Bloomberg Businessweek*, January 11, 2011, http://www.businessweek.com; and Philip, S., "Tata Motors Profit Rises 100-Fold on Jaguar Land Rover Sales," *Bloomberg Businessweek*, November 10, 2010, http://www.businessweek.com.

Managing in Our Natural Environment

BUSINESS AND THE ENVIRONMENT: CONFLICTING VIEWS

Some people believe everyone wins when business tackles environmental issues.[1] Others disagree.

Business used to look at environmental issues as a no-win situation; you either help the environment and hurt your business or help your business only at a cost to the environment. Fortunately, things have changed. "When Americans first demanded a cleanup of the environment during the early 1970s, corporations threw a tantrum. Their response ran the psychological gamut from denial to hostility, defiance, obstinacy, and fear. But today, when it comes to green issues, many U.S. companies have turned from rebellious underachievers to active problem solvers."[2] This appendix gives examples of things U.S. corporations are doing to help solve environmental problems.

Johan Piet said, "Only win–win companies will survive, but that does not mean that all win–win ideas will be successful."[3] In other words, rigorous analysis is essential. Thus some companies maintain continuous improvement in environmental performance but fund only projects that meet financial objectives.

Most people understand that business has the resources and the competence to bring about constructive change and that this creates great opportunity—if well managed—for both business and the environment.

WHY MANAGE WITH THE ENVIRONMENT IN MIND?

Business is turning its full attention to environmental issues for many reasons, including legal compliance, cost-effectiveness, competitive advantage, public opinion, and long-term thinking.

Legal Compliance Government regulations and liability for damages provide strong economic incentives to comply with environmental guidelines. Most industries already have made environmental protection regulation and liability an integral part of their business planning.[4] The U.S. Justice Department has handed out tough prison sentences to executives whose companies violate hazardous waste requirements.

Cost-Effectiveness Environmentally conscious strategies can be cost-effective.[5] In the short run, company after company is realizing cost savings from repackaging, recycling, and other approaches.

Environmentally conscious strategies offer long-run cost advantages as well. Companies that are functioning barely within legal limits today may incur big costs—being forced to pay damages or upgrade technologies and practices—when laws change down the road.

A few of the other cost savings include fines, cleanups, and litigation; lower raw materials costs; reduced energy use; less expensive waste handling and disposal; lower insurance rates; and possibly higher interest rates.

Competitive Advantage Corporations gain a competitive advantage by channeling their environmental concerns into entrepreneurial opportunities and by producing higher-quality products that meet consumer demand.

Companies that fail to innovate in this area will be at a competitive disadvantage. Competitive advantage can be gained by maintaining market share with old customers and by creating new products for new market opportunities. And if you are an environmental leader, you may set the standards for future regulations—regulations that you are prepared to meet while your competitors are not.

Public Opinion The majority of the U.S. population believes business must clean up; few people think it is doing its job well. Many consumers consider environmentalism in making purchases. Consumers routinely expect companies to come up with environmentally friendly alternatives to current products and practices.[6]

Companies also receive pressure from local communities and from their own employees. Sometimes the pressure is informal and low-key, but much pressure is exerted by environmental organizations; aroused citizen groups, societies and associations; international codes of conduct; and environmentally conscious investors.[7]

Another important reason for paying attention to environmental impact is TRI, the Toxic Release Inventory.[8] The EPA requires all the plants of approximately 10,000 U.S. manufacturers to report annual releases of 650 toxic chemicals into the air, ground, and water. The substances include Freon, PCBs, asbestos, and lead compounds. Hundreds of others have been added to the list. The releases are not necessarily illegal, but they provide the public with an annual environmental benchmark. TRI continues to provide a powerful incentive to reduce emissions.

Finally, it is useful to remember that companies recover very slowly in public opinion from the impact of an environmental disaster. Adverse public opinion may affect sales as well as the firm's ability to attract and retain talented people. You can see why companies such as P&G consider concern for the environment a consumer need, making it a basic and critical business issue.

Long-Term Thinking Long-term thinking about resources helps business leaders understand the nature of their responsibilities with regard to environmental concerns. For example, in Chapter 5 you will read about sustainable growth.[9] Seventh Generation is named after, and operates under, the ideals set by the Iroquois Indians—every decision must consider the impact it will have on the next (seven) generations. Economic arguments and the tragedy of the commons highlight the need for long-term thinking.

Economic Arguments In Chapter 3, we will discuss long-term versus short-term decision making. We state that it is common for managers to succumb to short-term pressure for profits and to avoid spending now when the potential payoff is years down the road. In addition, some economists maintain that it is the responsibility of management to maximize returns for shareholders, implying the preeminence of the short-term profit goal.

But other economists argue that such a strategy caters to immediate profit maximization for stock speculators and neglects serious investors who are with the company for the long haul. Attention to environmental issues enhances the organization's long-term viability because the goal is the long-term creation of wealth for the patient, serious investors in the company[10]—not to mention the future state of our planet and the new generations of humans and other species who will inhabit it.

The Tragedy of the Commons

In a classic article in *Science,* Garrett Hardin described a situation that applies to all business decisions and social concerns regarding scarce resources such as clean water, air, and land.[11] Throughout human history, a commons was a tract of community land on which people grazed their animals. A commons has limited **carrying capacity**, or the ability to sustain a population, because it is a finite resource. For individual herders, short-term interest lies in adding as many animals to the commons as they can. But problems develop as more herders add more animals to graze the commons. This leads to tragedy: As each herder acts in his short-term interest, the long-run impact is the destruction of the commons. The solution is to make choices according to long-run rather than short-run consequences.

In many ways, we are witnessing this **tragedy of the commons**. Carrying capacities are shrinking as precious resources, water chief among them, become scarcer. Inevitably, conflict arises—and solutions are urgently needed.

The Environmental Movement

The 1990s were labeled the earth decade, when a new environmentalism with new features emerged.[12] For example, proponents of the new environmentalism asked companies to reduce their wastes, use resources prudently, market safe products, and take responsibility for past damages. These requests are updated and formalized in the CERES Roadmap for Sustainability.

The new environmentalism combined many diverse viewpoints, but initially it did not blend easily with traditional business values. Some of the key aspects of this philosophy are noted in the following discussion of the history of the movement.[13]

Conservation and Environmentalism

A strand of environmental philosophy that is not at odds with business management is **conservation**. The conservation movement is anthropocentric (human centered), technologically optimistic, and concerned chiefly with the efficient use of resources. The movement seeks to avoid waste, promote the rational and efficient use of natural resources, and maximize long-term yields, especially of renewable resources.

The **environmental movement**, in contrast, historically has posed dilemmas for business management. Following the lead of early thinkers such as George Perkins Marsh (1801–1882), it has shown that the unintended negative effects of human economic activities on the environment often are greater than the benefits. For example, there are links between forest cutting and soil erosion and between the draining of marshes and lakes and the decline of animal life.

Other early environmentalists, such as John Muir (1838–1914) and Aldo Leopold (1886–1948), argued that humans are not above nature but a part of it. Nature is not for humans to subdue but is sacred and should be preserved not simply for economic use but for its own sake—and for what people can learn from it.

Science and the Environment

Rachel Carson's 1962 best-selling book *Silent Spring* helped ignite the modern environmental movement by alerting the public to the dangers of unrestricted pesticide use.[14] Carson brought together the findings of toxicology, ecology, and epidemiology in a form accessible to the public. Blending scientific, moral, and political arguments, she connected environmental politics and values with scientific knowledge.

Barry Commoner's *Science and Survival* (1963) continued in this vein. Commoner expanded the scope of ecology to include everything in the physical, chemical, biological, social, political, economic, and philosophical worlds.[15] He argued that all of these elements fit together and have to be understood as a whole. According to Commoner, the symptoms of environmental problems are in the biological world, but their source lies in economic and political organizations.

Economics and the Environment

Economists promote growth for many reasons: to restore the balance of payments, to make nations more competitive, to create jobs, to reduce the deficit, to provide for the elderly and the sick, and to reduce poverty. Environmentalists criticize economics for its notions of efficiency and its emphasis on economic growth.[16] For example, environmentalists argue that economists do not adequately consider the unintended side effects of efficiency such as negative production externalities, which occur when a firm's production harms the environment or reduces the well-being of others who receive no benefit. Environmentalists hold that economists need to supplement estimates of the economic costs and benefits of growth with estimates of other factors that historically were not measured in economic terms.[17]

Economists and public policy analysts argue that the benefits of eliminating risk to the environment and to people must be balanced against the costs. Reducing risk involves determining how effective the proposed methods of reduction are likely to be and how much they will cost. There are many ways to consider cost factors. Analysts can perform cost-effectiveness analyses, in which they attempt to figure out how to achieve a given goal with limited resources, or they can conduct more formal risk–benefit and cost–benefit analyses, in which they quantify both the benefits and the costs of risk reduction.[18]

Qualitative Judgments in Cost–Benefit Analysis

Formal, quantitative approaches to balancing costs and benefits do not eliminate the need for qualitative judgments. For example, how does one assess the value of a magnificent vista obscured by air pollution? What is the loss to society if a particular genetic strain of grass or animal species becomes extinct? How does one assess the lost opportunity costs of spending vast amounts of money on air pollution that could have been spent on productivity enhancement and global competitiveness?

Fairness cannot be ignored when doing cost–benefit analysis.[19] For example, the costs of air pollution reduction may have to be borne disproportionately by the poor in the form of higher gasoline and automobile prices. Intergenerational fairness also plays a role.[20] Future generations have no representatives in the current market and political processes. To what extent should the current generation hold back on its own consumption for the sake of posterity? This question is particularly poignant because few people in the world today are well off. To ask the poor to reduce their life's chances for the sake of a generation yet to come is asking for a great sacrifice.

International Perspectives Environmental problems present a different face in various countries and regions of the world. Early on, the United States and Great Britain lagged behind Germany and Japan in mandated emissions standards.[21] The United States took more action on climate change during President Obama's administration. In Europe, the Dutch, the Germans, and the Danes have been among the most environmentally conscious. But public sentiment and legalities change over time, and at this writing there is some pushback against progressive legislation in the United States and some western European countries, as well as elsewhere.

Environmentalists in Europe have long been active and sometimes successful in halting environmentally harmful business projects, and consumers generally have been much more resistant to genetically modified foods than in the United States.[22] China has paid a high ecological price for its rapid economic growth. In addition to widespread thick smog in many Chinese cities, it is estimated that a fifth of the country's agricultural land and 60 percent of its groundwater are polluted. In 2014, China's Environmental Protection Law was strengthened to more effectively address these problems.[23]

KEY TERMS

carrying capacity The ability of a finite resource to sustain a population, p. 69.

conservation An environmental philosophy that seeks to avoid waste, promote the rational and efficient use of natural resources, and maximize long-term yields, especially of renewable resources, p. 69.

environmental movement An environmental philosophy postulating that the unintended negative effects of human economic activities on the environment are often greater than the benefits, and that nature should be preserved, p. 69.

tragedy of the commons The environmental destruction that results as individuals and businesses consume finite resources (the commons) to serve their short-term interests without regard for the long-term consequences, p. 69.

CHAPTER 3
Managerial Decision Making

©Cultura/Image Source RF

> The business executive is by profession a decision maker. Uncertainty is his opponent. Overcoming it is his mission.
>
> — JOHN McDONALD

LEARNING OBJECTIVES

After studying Chapter 3, you will be able to:

LO 1 Describe the kinds of decisions you will face as a manager.

LO 2 Summarize the steps in making "rational" decisions.

LO 3 Recognize the pitfalls you should avoid when making decisions.

LO 4 Evaluate the pros and cons of using a group to make decisions.

LO 5 Identify procedures to use in leading a decision-making group.

LO 6 Explain how to encourage creative decisions.

LO 7 Discuss the processes by which decisions are made in organizations.

LO 8 Describe how to make decisions in a crisis.

CHAPTER OUTLINE

Characteristics of Managerial Decisions
Lack of Structure
Uncertainty and Risk
Conflict

The Phases of Decision Making
Identifying and Diagnosing the Problem
Generating Alternative Solutions
Evaluating Alternatives
Making the Choice
Implementing the Decision
Evaluating the Decision

The Best Decision

Barriers to Effective Decision Making
Psychological Biases
Time Pressures
Social Realities

Decision Making in Groups
Potential Advantages of Using a Group
Potential Problems of Using a Group

Managing Group Decision Making
Leadership Style
Constructive Conflict
Encouraging Creativity
Brainstorming

Organizational Decision Making
Constraints on Decision Makers
Organizational Decision Processes
Decision Making in a Crisis

Management in Action

CAN UBER OVERCOME ITS POOR DECISIONS?

Uber Technologies, Inc., the app-based ride-hailing service launched in San Francisco in 2010, claimed to be "changing the logistical fabric of cities around the world" by allowing users to hail a ride via their smartphone. Since going global in 2013, the game-changing company has provided fast access to two billion reliable rides for passengers in more than 540 cities in 70 countries around the world and enabled thousands of independent drivers to earn a share of the fees.

Valued in early 2017 at $70 billion, Uber appears to have made some smart decisions. Its managers' aggressive business strategy put some competitors like Sidecar out of business and put costly pressure on others like Lyft. The company took market share from many cities' venerable public transportation and traditional taxi services, often driving down the high price of taxi medallions in the process. It introduced ride-sharing options, started a delivery service, and began exploring the possibility of building a fleet of self-driving cars.

However, Uber has also made decisions that damaged its reputation and may threaten its future growth and profits. By insisting its drivers are independent contractors rather than employees, the company adopted a risky business model whose legality was questioned. It came under scrutiny in countries around the world for conducting flawed background checks on drivers, which put some riders' safety at risk. Protests by taxi drivers forced it from some markets, such as Hungary.

In the United States, the company was charged with "fraudulent and arguably criminal conduct" for investigating a lawyer and plaintiff who were suing the company. Uber wrongly blamed human error when a self-driving test car ran a red light in San Francisco.

©Al Seib/Los Angeles Times/Getty Images

When local taxi drivers protested President Trump's first immigration order and Uber appeared to capitalize by keeping its airport service rolling, criticism on social media was scathing. The backlash also forced Travis Kalanick, the company's founder and CEO, to resign from the president's Economic Advisory Council.

Meanwhile, allegations by a female software engineer at Uber about a heedless company culture rife with sexism and harassment forced the company to investigate. A report surfaced alleging that for years the company misused a data-collecting tool to engage in systematic deception intended to evade authorities in Boston, Las Vegas, Paris, and other cities. And a video of founder and CEO Travis Kalanick dealing angrily with an Uber driver's complaint went viral, forcing Kalanick to apologize publicly.

It appears that Uber may need to reexamine its management decision-making processes.[1]

Uber has transformed the ride-hailing and ride-sharing industries and perhaps is not done innovating yet, but its management decisions have not always made friends for the company. As you read this chapter, consider what makes decision making difficult, and how managers can overcome those difficulties and make the right choices.

The best managers make decisions constantly. Some are difficult and strategic, while others are smaller decisions that affect day-to-day actions. Marie Robinson, the former chief logistics officer at Toys "R" Us, had to make sure toys arrived at the retailer's 600 U.S. stores and to online customers' homes efficiently and on schedule. For routine decisions, toys are shipped from either warehouses or stores based on which locations are most economical and have enough of the item in stock. Other decisions must be made in crisis mode. When superstorm Sandy shut down transportation systems in the New York City region in October 2012, Robinson learned that a ship loaded with merchandise for the holidays was being rerouted from New Jersey to the Bahamas. She worked with the shipper, so that the toys could still reach stores in time for Black Friday.[2] Robinson's managerial led to fashion retailer Michael Kors hiring her (without any experience in the fashion industry) in 2014 as its new senior vice president of global operations.[3]

The typical organization has the potential to more than double its decision effectiveness in terms of impact on financial results.[4] If you can't make good decisions, you won't be an effective manager. This chapter discusses what kinds of decisions managers face, how they often make them, and how they *should* make them.

Characteristics of Managerial Decisions

LO 1

Managers face problems and opportunities constantly. Some situations that require a decision are relatively simple; others seem overwhelming. Some demand immediate action; others take months or even years to unfold.

Actually, managers often ignore challenges.[5] For several reasons, they avoid taking action.[6] First, managers can't be sure how much time, energy, and trouble lie ahead once they start working on an issue. Second, getting involved is risky; tackling a problem but failing to solve it successfully can hurt a manager's track record. Third, because problems can be so perplexing, it is easier to procrastinate or to get busy with less demanding activities. Managers may lack the insight, courage, or will to decide.

It is important to understand why decision making can be so challenging. Exhibit 3.1 illustrates several characteristics of managerial decisions that contribute to their difficulty and pressure. Most managerial decisions lack structure and entail risk, uncertainty, and conflict.

Lack of Structure

Lack of structure is the usual state of affairs in managerial decision making.[7] Although some decisions are routine and clear-cut, for most there is no automatic procedure to follow. Problems are novel and unstructured, leaving the decision maker uncertain about how to proceed.

An important distinction illustrating this point is between programmed and nonprogrammed decisions. **Programmed decisions** have been encountered and made before. They have objectively correct answers and can be solved by using simple rules, policies, or numerical computations. If you face a programmed decision, a clear procedure or structure exists for arriving at the right decision. For example, if you are a small-business owner and must decide the amounts for your employees' paychecks, you can use a formula—and if the amounts are wrong, your employees will prove it to you. Exhibit 3.2 gives some other examples.

If most important decisions were programmed, managerial life would be much easier. But managers typically face **nonprogrammed decisions**: new, novel, complex decisions having no certain outcomes. They have a variety of possible solutions, all of which have merits and drawbacks. The decision maker must create or impose a method for

programmed decisions

Decisions encountered and made before, having objectively correct answers, and solvable by using simple rules, policies, or numerical computations.

nonprogrammed decisions

New, novel, complex decisions having no proven answers.

 **EXHIBIT 3.1**

Characteristics of Managerial Decisions

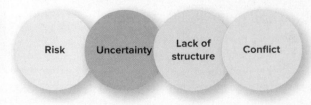

EXHIBIT 3.2
Comparison of Types of Decisions

	Programmed Decisions	Nonprogrammed Decisions
Problem	Frequent, repetitive, routine. Much certainty regarding cause-and-effect relationships.	Novel, unstructured. Much uncertainty regarding cause-and-effect relationships.
Procedure	Dependence on policies, rules, and definite procedures.	Necessity for creativity, intuition, tolerance for ambiguity, creative problem solving.
Examples		
Business firm	Policies to follow when posting about the company on social media.	Developing a new service for different market.
University	Number of course credits that must be accumulated to graduate.	Raising funds to add new technology to classrooms.
Health care	Procedure for admitting patients.	Purchase of experimental equipment.
Government	Merit system for promotion of state employees.	Reorganization of state government agencies.

SOURCE: Adapted from Gibson, J., Ivancevich, J., Donnelly, J., Jr., and Konopaske, R., *Organizations: Behavior, Structure, Processes,* 14th ed. New York: McGraw-Hill, 2011.

making the decision; there is no predetermined structure on which to rely. As Exhibit 3.1 suggests, important, difficult decisions tend to be nonprogrammed, and they demand creative approaches.

Uncertainty and Risk

If you have all the information you need and can predict precisely the consequences of your actions, you are operating under a condition of **certainty**.[8] Managers are expressing their preference for certainty when they are not satisfied hearing about what might have happened or may happen and insist on hearing what did or will happen.[9] But perfect certainty is rare. For important, nonprogrammed managerial decisions, uncertainty is the rule.

Uncertainty means the manager has insufficient information to know the consequences of different actions. Business people do not like uncertainty; it can hold them back from taking action. For example, uncertainty about the strength and timing of the economic recovery made businesses slow to start hiring.[10] But economies don't strengthen until consumer demand picks up, which doesn't happen until employment rises.

When you can estimate the likelihood of various consequences but still do not know with certainty what will happen, you are facing **risk**. Risk exists when the probability of an action being successful is less than 100 percent and losses may occur. If the decision is the wrong one, you may lose money, time, reputation, or other important assets.

Risk, like uncertainty, is a fact of life in managerial decision making. But this is not the same as taking a risk. Although it sometimes seems as though risk takers are admired and entrepreneurs and investors thrive on taking risks, the reality is that good decision makers prefer to *manage* risk. They accept the fact that decisions have consequences entailing risk, but they do everything they can to anticipate the risk, minimize it, and control it.

The stories detailed in "The Greatest Business Decisions of All Time" are creative approaches to managing risk. A classic example is how Henry Ford, when facing high levels of employee turnover and discontent, doubled workers' pay and switched from two 9-hour shifts to three 8-hour shifts per day. These improvements cost Ford $10 million but his gamble paid off with higher retention rates and productivity levels.[11] Ford could not have known with certainty that his changes would work, but he assessed his options and took a calculated risk.

certainty

The state that exists when decision makers have accurate and comprehensive information.

uncertainty

The state that exists when decision makers have insufficient information.

risk

The state that exists when the probability of success is less than 100 percent and losses may occur.

Social Enterprise

Saul Garlick's Social Enterprise: Nonprofit or For-Profit?

When visiting Mpumalanga, South Africa, as a boy, Saul Garlick was shocked at the village's lack of basic resources: "The small rural village had nothing—no classrooms, no electricity, no water." He decided he wanted to help. While still in high school, Garlick founded Student Movement for Real Change (SMRC), a nonprofit whose mission was to fight poverty by encouraging entrepreneurship in villages in Africa. The organization recruited students to "live with local families, hunt for water sources, farm alongside villages and absorb day-to-day nuances of life in a developing country with the goal of building social businesses along with the local residents."

As a nonprofit, the organization was funded through an intermittent stream of donations from friends, family members, and donors. SMRC started to grow. As a 23-year-old who was working full time for the organization, Garlick began to draw a salary and hired a recent graduate to run the daily operations. Even with the extra help, Garlick was under constant pressure to raise enough funds to keep the operation functioning when in fact he wanted to spend more time doing the core work of the organization.

If he wanted to have a high-impact social enterprise, Garlick needed a business model that could sustain itself.

He believed that a market-based solution was his best hope to help him reduce poverty in Africa, resulting in his decision to buy out his nonprofit, SMRC, and launch a for-profit social enterprise, ThinkImpact.

By borrowing an initial $450,000 from friends, family, and angel investors, Garlick developed a growth strategy to set Denver-based ThinkImpact on a profitable course. The for-profit social enterprise developed an eight-week program that brings students and entrepreneurs together from universities and communities around the globe to work with locals in villages in Rwanda, Panama, South Africa, Kenya, and Ghana. The curriculum is designed to spark the creative talents of individuals while developing their social problem-solving skills. ThinkImpact has expanded into funding, supporting, and launching new social enterprises. Since its inception, ThinkImpact's entrepreneurs and scholars have formed 192 social enterprises in such areas as sustainable agriculture, basic health, and engineering and tech businesses.

The belief that continues to inspire Saul Garlick and those involved in ThinkImpact is that social enterprises and the experience of building them together can change lives forever.[12]

A more recent example is how *National Geographic* launched a contest over social media to gather user-generated travel content. Named the "Wanderlust" contest, over 52,000 people shared photos and videos of their travels. In exchange for this content, *National Geographic* offered a chance to win a photo expedition to Yosemite National Park. By involving users in this contest, the organization reduced risk by learning firsthand about current travelers' passions with regard to memorable moments. This information will help *National Geographic* align more precisely its content with users' interests.[13]

Conflict

conflict

Opposing pressures from different sources, occurring on the level of psychological conflict or conflict between individuals or groups.

Important decisions are even more difficult because of the conflicts managers face. **Conflict,** which exists when a manager must consider opposing pressures from different sources, occurs at two levels.

First, individual decision makers experience psychological conflict when several options are attractive or when none of the options is attractive. For instance, a manager may have to decide whom to lay off when she doesn't want to lay off anyone. Or she may have three promising job applicants for one position—but choosing one means she has to reject the other two.

Second, conflict arises between people. A chief financial officer argues in favor of increasing long-term debt to finance an acquisition. The chief executive officer, however, prefers to minimize such debt and find the funds elsewhere. A marketing department wants more product lines to sell, and the engineers want higher-quality products. But the production people want to lower costs by having longer production runs of fewer products with no changes. Few decisions are without conflict.

In the "Social Enterprise" feature, how much "structure" and how many programmed decisions do you see? Try to identify and describe the uncertainties, risks, and potential conflicts in the major unprogrammed decisions.

The Phases of Decision Making

Faced with these challenges, how can you make good decisions? The ideal decision-making process includes six phases. As Exhibit 3.3 illustrates, decision makers should (1) identify and diagnose the problem, (2) generate alternative solutions, (3) evaluate alternatives, (4) make the choice, (5) implement the decision, and (6) evaluate the decision.

LO 2

Identifying and Diagnosing the Problem

The first phase in the decision-making process is to recognize that a problem exists and must be solved. Typically, a manager realizes some discrepancy between the current state (the way things are) and a desired state (the way things ought to be). Such discrepancies— say, in organizational or unit performance—may be detected by comparing current performance against (1) *past* performance, (2) the *current* performance of *other* organizations or units, or (3) *future* expected performance as determined by plans and forecasts.[14]

The "problem" may be an opportunity that can be exploited with appropriate action. In that case, decisions involve choosing how to seize the opportunity. To recognize important opportunities as a manager, you will need to understand your company's macro- and competitive environments (described in Chapter 2).

Recognizing that a problem (or opportunity) exists is only the beginning of this phase. The decision maker must dig in deeper and attempt to analyze its possible causes. For example, a sales manager knows that sales have dropped drastically. If he is leaving the company soon or believes the decreased sales volume is due to the economy (which he can't do anything about), he won't take action. But if he does try to solve the problem, he should not automatically reprimand his sales staff, add new people, or increase the advertising budget. He must analyze *why* sales are down and then develop a solution appropriate to his analysis. Asking why, of yourself and others, is essential to understanding the real problem.

Michael Ortner and Rakesh Chilakapati cofounded a company called Capterra, which created an online directory of companies that sell business software. Their problem was that they wanted to bring more traffic to their website; more listings would make the site more valuable to buyers, and more buyers would make the site more attractive to vendors.[15]

The company asked *why* traffic was low by surveying the directory's users. Buyers wanted to see reviews of vendors; the underlying problem was that the website lacked a key feature that buyers would find helpful.[16]

Exhibit 3.4 lists some useful questions to ask and answer in this phase.[17]

Generating Alternative Solutions

The second phase of decision making links problem diagnosis to the development of alternative courses of action aimed at solving the problem. Managers generate at least some alternative solutions based on past experiences.[18]

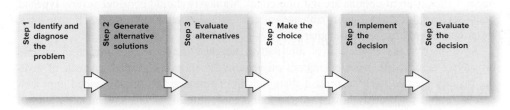

EXHIBIT 3.3
The Phases of Decision Making

EXHIBIT 3.4

Questions for Problem
Identification and
Diagnosis

How can you best describe the difference between what is actually happening and what should be happening?

What is/are the cause(s) of the deviation?

What short- and long-term goals need to be met?

Which goals are absolutely critical to the success of the decision?

ready-made solutions

Ideas that have been seen
or tried before.

custom-made solutions

New, creative solutions
designed specifically for the
problem.

Solutions range from ready-made to custom-made.[19] Decision makers who employ **ready-made solutions** use ideas they have tried before or follow the advice of others who have faced similar problems. **Custom-made solutions**, by contrast, must be designed for specific problems. This technique often combines ideas into new, creative solutions.

For example, IDEO, a design and innovation firm, helped its start-up-in-residence, PillPack, to change how customers of advanced age, of limited mobility, or with serious illnesses interact with their pharmacy. PillPack launched a simple, fast home-delivery service that sorts patients' multiple prescriptions and over-the-counter medicines into packets that are organized by the date and time they should be taken. Pills arrive in an organized, recyclable dispenser with a label that includes an image of the pill. Customers can coordinate refills with or ask questions of PillPack's pharmacists via phone or e-mail on a 24/7 basis. There is no charge for the packaging and delivery service.[20]

Potentially, custom-made solutions can be devised for any challenge. Later in the chapter, we will discuss how to generate creative ideas.

Often, many more alternatives are available than managers realize. For example, what would you do if one of your competitors reduced prices? Managers sometimes assume that cutting prices in response to a competitor's price cuts is their only option, but it is not. Alternatives include conveying consumer risks of low-priced products, building awareness of your products' features and overall quality, and communicating your cost advantage to your competitors so they realize that they can't win a price war. If you do decide to cut your price as a last resort, do it fast; if you do it slowly, your competitors will gain sales in the meantime, which may embolden them to employ the same tactic again in the future.[21]

Returning to the example of Capterra, Michael Ortner was eager to launch the product reviews, but Rakesh Chilakapati, the company's technology manager at the time, wanted to proceed cautiously because of the time and expense required to add the feature, along with fear that some vendors would get bad reviews and leave the directory. So to generate alternatives, the two partners studied existing websites with product reviews (for example, Amazon, eBay, and Edmunds.com). They identified a variety of ways to offer reviewing features. They could simply post testimonials from satisfied customers. They could allow or forbid anonymous comments. They could require reviewers to list both positive and negative points. The big question that remained was whether the features attractive to buyers would repel sellers.[22]

> When it comes to generating alternatives, the first one that comes to mind may not be the best one.

Evaluating Alternatives

The third phase of decision making involves determining the value or adequacy of the alternatives that were generated. Which solution will be the best?

Especially when decisions are important, alternatives should be evaluated with careful thought and logic. Fundamental to this process is to predict the consequences that will occur if the different options are put into effect. Managers should consider several types of consequences, including quantifiable measures of success such as lower costs, higher sales, lower employee turnover, and higher profits.

At Capterra, the evaluation of alternatives weighed the expected impact of reviews on buyers against the expected impact on vendors. Posting testimonials instead of inviting reviews seemed likely to protect the goodwill of vendors, but this one-sided approach seemed unlikely to satisfy buyers, so the founders doubted it would have much effect on

Which goals does each alternative meet and fail to meet?
Which alternatives are most acceptable to you and to other important stakeholders?
If several alternatives might solve the problem, which can be implemented at the lowest cost or greatest profit?
If no alternative achieves all your goals, can two or more of the best ones be combined?

EXHIBIT 3.5
Questions for Evaluating Alternatives

traffic overall. Anonymous reviews seemed risky because vendors' competitors could abuse the system, so they dropped that alternative. Requiring both pros and cons in the reviews would encourage balanced information about vendors, an apparent plus. But Ortner knew that many vendors still worried about the risk of negative reviews.[23]

An important technology affecting the analysis of alternatives is the ability to collect and analyze big data. The term refers to massive amounts of structured and unstructured data that exceed the capabilities of a traditional computer database. Businesses today can gather details about Internet usage, consumer behavior, and employee skills and activities, among many other things. Organizations can store the data, search it for patterns or trends, and analyze it to identify alternatives that previously would have gone unnoticed.

Evaluation that would have relied heavily on intuition or experience now can be data-driven. For example, companies are using big data to make more effective decisions about pay. General Electric uses data analytics to help digital wind farms achieve better efficiencies. By using data to optimize the angle of its turbines, GE can produce up to 10 percent more energy off the same amount of wind.[24]

To evaluate alternatives, refer to your original goals, defined in the first phase. Next, you should consider the questions in Exhibit 3.5.

Several additional questions help:[25]

Is our information about alternatives complete and current? If not, can we get more and better information?

Does the alternative meet our primary objectives?

What problems could we have if we implement the alternative?

Of course, results cannot be forecast with perfect accuracy. But sometimes decision makers can build in safeguards against an uncertain future by considering the potential consequences of several scenarios. Then they generate **contingency plans**—alternative courses of action that can be implemented depending on how the future unfolds.

For example, during an economic crisis when it is unclear when a recovery might begin and how strong it will be or what shape it will take, the range of potential outcomes is wide, and many companies will not survive. Firms could consider at least four scenarios:[26]

1. A most optimistic scenario in which trade and capital flows resume, further recession is averted, globalization stays on course, and developed and emerging economies continue to integrate as confidence rebounds quickly.
2. A battered-but-resilient scenario in which the recession continues for a long period, recovery is slow, confidence is shaken but does rebound, and globalization slowly gets back on course.
3. Stalled globalization, in which the global recession is significant, the intensity varies greatly from nation to nation, but overall growth is slow.
4. A long freeze, in which the recession lasts more than five years, economies everywhere stagnate, and globalization goes into reverse.

As you read this, what economic scenario is unfolding? What are the important current events and trends? What scenarios could evolve six or eight years from now? How will *you* prepare?

contingency plans

Alternative courses of action that can be implemented based on how the future unfolds.

Some decisions do not work out. Although this can surprise and frustrate, you should have contingency plans that will help you still achieve your desired goals.
©Yuri Arcurs/Alamy Stock Photo RF

Making the Choice

Once you have considered the possible consequences of your options, it is time to make your decision. The temptation to overanalyze can lead to paralysis by analysis—that is, indecisiveness caused by too much analysis. When it comes time to decide, assertive decision making can help an organization seize new opportunities or thwart challenges.

Indecisiveness became a risk at Capterra because Ortner and Chilakapati had conflicting worries. Ortner continued to see the lack of reviews as a missed opportunity, whereas Chilakapati remained focused on the risks of adding this feature. Ortner further researched the situation by calling vendors who had expressed concerns about reviews; he became convinced that they, too, were simply not seeing the opportunities of this additional feature and would come around when experience showed them the value. Finally, after three months of debate, Ortner was enjoying his regular five-mile run when he concluded that the analysis had to end, and he must make a decision. As president, he made the final call, respecting Chilakapati's concerns but announcing that it was time to try the reviews.[27]

> The process of considering multiple scenarios raises important "what if" questions for decision makers and highlights the need for contingency plans.

As you make your decision, important guiding concepts include maximizing, satisficing, and optimizing.[28]

maximizing

A decision realizing the best possible outcome.

Maximizing is achieving the best possible outcome. The maximizing decision realizes the greatest positive consequences and the fewest negative consequences. In other words, maximizing results in the greatest benefit at the lowest cost, with the largest expected total return. Maximizing requires searching thoroughly for a complete range of alternatives, carefully assessing each alternative, comparing one to another, and then choosing or creating the very best.

satisficing

Choosing an option that is acceptable, although not necessarily the best or perfect.

Satisficing is choosing the first option that is minimally acceptable or adequate. When you satisfice, you compare your choice against your goal, not against other options. Satisficing means that a search for alternatives stops after you find one that is okay. You do not expend the time or energy to gather more information. Instead you make the expedient decision based on readily available information.

Let's say you are purchasing new equipment, and your goal is to avoid spending too much money. You would be maximizing if you checked out all your options and their prices and then bought the cheapest one that met your performance requirements. But you would be satisficing if you bought the first adequate option that was within your budget and failed to look for less expensive options.

Satisficing is sometimes a result of laziness; other times, there is no other known option because time is short, information is unavailable, or other constraints make maximizing impossible. When the consequences are not huge, satisficing can even be the ideal approach. But in other situations, when managers satisfice, they fail to consider options that might be better.

optimizing

Achieving the best possible balance among several goals.

Optimizing means that you achieve the best possible balance among several goals. Perhaps, in purchasing equipment, you are interested in quality and durability as well as price. So instead of buying the cheapest piece of equipment that works, you buy the one with the best combination of attributes, even though there may be options that are better on the price criterion and others that are better on the quality and durability criteria. The same idea applies to achieving business goals: One marketing strategy could maximize sales, whereas a different strategy might maximize profit. An optimizing strategy is the one that achieves the best balance among multiple goals.

Implementing the Decision

The decision-making process does not end once you make a choice. The chosen alternative must be implemented. Sometimes the people involved in making the choice are the same people who put it into effect. At other times, they delegate the responsibility for

Management in Action

A HUGE PROBLEM AT UBER

Susan Fowler kept meticulous records of the year she worked for Uber as a software engineer. During that time she was an exemplary employee but reportedly faced repeated instances of sexism and sexual harassment, only to see the offending managers let off with a reprimand at best. Sometimes her complaints to human resources were denied, sometimes they were belittled and minimized as a "first offense," and at other times, according to the revealing blog post she wrote later, Fowler was told she herself was the problem. When she resigned in December 2016, from what she called "an organization in complete, unrelenting chaos," it was after a transfer she requested was secretly blocked and she was told she could be fired for reporting a manager who discriminated against her.

Such dismissal is illegal. During Fowler's time at the ride-hailing company, she says she saw the percentage of women employees dwindle from 25 percent to about 6 percent.

Fowler's explosive blog post also included allegations that brutally competitive behavior originated with the company's top managers: "It seemed like every manager was fighting their peers and attempting to undermine their direct supervisor so that they could have their direct supervisor's job. . . . They boasted about it in meetings, told their direct reports about it, and the like."

Her accusations sparked an immediate reaction from the company's founder, Travis Kalanick. At a meeting of all employees, Kalanick announced a thorough investigation into the company culture, to be led by former U.S. attorney general Eric Holder and board member Ariana Huffington (founder of *Huffington Post*). "I am authentically and fully dedicated to getting to the bottom of this," Kalanick said.

And in a separate meeting with female employees, Kalanick reportedly said, "There are people in this room who have experienced things that are incredibly unjust. I want to root out the injustice. I want to get at the people who are making this place a bad place. And you have my commitment."[29]

- Why do you think it took so long for Uber's management to recognize that the company had a problematic corporate culture? What indications of the problem did it apparently overlook?
- Assuming the investigation confirms that the problem is an aggressive company culture that discriminates against women, how do you think the company's managers should begin to generate solutions?

---

implementation to others, such as when a top management team changes a policy or operating procedure and has operational managers carry out the change.

At Capterra, implementation of the decision to add customer reviews included 10 months of software development, followed by invitations to vendors to encourage their customers to submit reviews. Notice that the implementation took into account the concerns about negative reviews by giving the vendors some control over who submitted the initial reviews.[30]

Unfortunately, sometimes managers make decisions but don't take action. Implementing may fail to occur when *talking* a lot is mistaken for *doing* a lot; when people forget that merely making a decision changes nothing; when meetings, plans, and reports are seen as actions, even if they have no effect on what people actually do; and if managers don't check to ensure that what was decided was actually done.[31]

Managers should plan implementation carefully. Adequate planning requires several steps:[32]

1. Determine how things will look when the decision is fully operational.
2. Chronologically order, perhaps with a flow diagram, the steps necessary to achieve a fully operational decision.
3. List the resources and activities required to implement each step.
4. Estimate the time needed for each step.
5. Assign responsibility for each step to specific individuals.

Decision makers should assume that things will *not* go smoothly during implementation. It is useful to take a little extra time to identify *potential problems* and *potential opportunities*

Bottom Line

It's easy to become so focused on maximizing one goal that you lose sight of other important goals. You're optimizing if you make sure that no important result is ignored. *What could be the negative consequences of making decisions that maximize only quality?*

EXHIBIT 3.6
Questions for
Implementing Decisions

What problems could this action cause?
What can we do to prevent the problems?
What unintended benefits or opportunities could arise?
How can we make sure they happen?
How can we be ready to act when the opportunities come?

associated with implementation. Then you can take actions to prevent problems and be ready to seize unexpected opportunities. Exhibit 3.6 lists several useful questions that should be asked in the implementation stage of decision making.

> Decision makers should assume that things will *not* go smoothly during implementation.

Many of the chapters in this book are concerned with implementation issues: how to implement strategy, allocate resources, organize for results, lead and motivate people, manage change, and so on. View the chapters from this perspective and learn as much as you can about how to implement properly.

Evaluating the Decision

The final phase in the decision-making process is evaluating the decision. It involves collecting information on how well the decision is working. Quantifiable goals—a 20 percent increase in sales, a 95 percent reduction in accidents, 100 percent on-time deliveries—can be set before implementing the solution. Then objective data can be gathered to determine its success or failure accurately.

Decision evaluation is useful whether the conclusion is positive or negative. Feedback that suggests the solution is working implies that the decision should be continued and perhaps applied elsewhere in the organization. Negative feedback means that either (1) implementation will require more time, resources, effort, or thought; or (2) the solution wasn't good enough.

The feedback for Capterra was positive. In the first year of offering customer reviews, the site gathered about 500 reviews. A year after that, the site had 2,000 reviews, with about 40 percent of them unsolicited. Most reviews were positive. Even though some are less than glowing, traffic to the site grew to 25,000 reviews; vendors see the review feature as a benefit because they are getting more business. Revenues jumped, and the executives concluded that customer reviews were a great idea.[33]

If the decision appears inadequate, it's time to adjust. The process cycles back to the first phase: (re)defining the problem. The decision-making process begins anew, preferably with more information, new suggestions, and an approach that attempts to eliminate the mistakes made the first time around.

The Best Decision

LO 3

vigilance

A process in which a decision maker carefully executes all stages of decision making.

How can managers tell whether they have made the best decision? Although nothing can guarantee a "best" decision, managers should at least be confident that they followed proper *procedures* that will yield the best possible decision under the circumstances. This means that the decision makers were appropriately vigilant in making the decision. **Vigilance** occurs when the decision makers carefully and conscientiously execute all six phases of decision making, including making provisions for implementation and evaluation.[34]

Even if managers reflect on their decision-making activities and conclude that they executed each step conscientiously, they still will not know whether the decision will work; after all, nothing guarantees a good outcome. But they *will* know that they did their best to make the best possible decision.

Barriers to Effective Decision Making

Vigilance and full execution of the six-phase decision-making process are the exception rather than the rule. But when managers use such rational processes, better decisions result.[35] Managers who make sure they engage in these processes are more effective.

But it is easy to neglect or improperly execute these processes. The problem may be improperly defined or goals misidentified. Not enough solutions may be generated, or they may be evaluated incompletely. A satisficing rather than maximizing choice may be made. Implementation may be poorly planned or executed, or evaluation may be inadequate or nonexistent.

And as discussed next, decisions are influenced by subjective psychological biases, time pressures, and social realities.

Psychological Biases

Decision makers are far from objective in the way they gather, evaluate, and apply information in making their choices. People have biases that interfere with objective rationality. The examples that follow represent only a few of the many documented subjective biases.[36]

The **illusion of control** is a belief that one can influence events even when one has no control over what will happen. Gambling is one example: some people believe they have the skill to beat the odds, even though most of the time they cannot. In business, such overconfidence can lead to failure because decision makers ignore risks and fail to evaluate the odds of success objectively.

illusion of control

People's belief that they can influence events even when they have no control over what will happen.

Managers may believe they can do no wrong or hold a general optimism about the future that can lead them to believe they are immune to risk and failure.[37] They may overrate the value of their experience. They may believe that a previous project met its goals because of their decisions alone, so they can succeed by doing everything the same way on the next project.

Framing effects refer to how problems or decision alternatives are phrased or presented and how these subjective influences can override objective facts. In one example, managers indicated a desire to invest more money in a course of action that was reported to have a 70 percent chance of profit than in one said to have a 30 percent chance of loss.[38] The choices were equivalent in their chances of success; it was the way the options were framed that determined the managers' choices.

framing effects

A decision bias influenced by the way in which a problem or decision alternative is phrased or presented.

Managers may be quick to frame a problem as being similar to problems they have already handled, so they don't search for new alternatives. For example, when CEO Richard Fuld tackled financial problems at Lehman Brothers as the mortgage market tumbled, he assumed that the situation was much the same as when he had handled a previous financial crisis in the late 1990s. Unfortunately for Lehman Brothers, the crisis was far worse. In late 2008, the firm declared bankruptcy—the largest in U.S. history—helping to send global financial markets into a tailspin.

Similarly, at Yahoo! people expected Marissa Mayer to turn around the failing Internet pioneer by making major strategy changes when she took over as CEO. Critics said that she made only minor tactical changes, such as changing Yahoo!'s home page layout, to an "outdated success formula."[39] Her actions were not enough to keep the famous company from being sold to Verizon for $4.8 billion in 2017. Mayer resigned from the board of directors and the company was renamed "Altaba."[40]

Often, decision makers **discount the future**. That is, in their evaluation of alternatives, they weigh short-term costs and benefits more heavily than longer-term costs and benefits. Consider your own decision about whether to go for a dental checkup. The choice to go poses short-term financial costs, anxiety, and perhaps physical pain. The choice not to go will inflict even greater costs and more severe pain if dental problems worsen. How do you choose? Many people decide to avoid the short-term costs by not going for regular checkups, but end up facing greater pain in the long run.

discounting the future

A bias weighting short-term costs and benefits more heavily than longer-term costs and benefits.

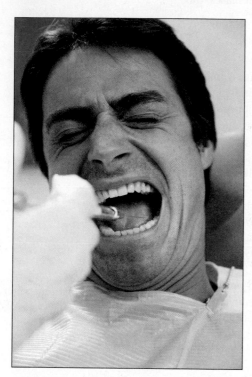

Delaying dental checkups can have a negative impact on the future. It may save money today but lead to larger costs (and more pain) later.

©Ingram Publishing RF

The same bias applies to students who don't study, weight watchers who sneak dessert or skip an exercise routine, and people who take the afternoon off to play golf when they really need to work. It can also affect managers who hesitate to invest funds in research and development programs that may not pay off until far into the future. In all these cases, the avoidance of short-term costs or the seeking of short-term rewards results in negative long-term consequences.

Asian managers tend to think with a longer-term outlook than do American managers, and many believe that this provides competitive advantage for long-term success.[41] Western myopia is driven in part by Wall Street's focus on quarterly earnings, causing managers to make decisions based primarily on short-run considerations and to neglect long-term problems and opportunities. Why is it so hard to make decisions with the long term in mind?

In contrast, when U.S. companies sacrifice present value to invest for the future—such as when Weyerhaeuser incurs enormous costs for its reforestation efforts that won't lead to harvest until 60 years in the future—it seems the exception rather than the rule. Discounting the future partly explains governmental budget deficits, environmental destruction, and decaying infrastructure.[42]

Time Pressures

In today's rapidly changing business environment, the premium is on acting quickly and keeping pace. The most conscientiously made business decisions can become irrelevant or disastrous if managers take too long to make them.

How can managers make decisions quickly? Some natural tendencies, at least for North Americans, might be to skimp on analysis (not be too vigilant), suppress conflict, and make decisions on one's own without consulting others.[43] These strategies may speed up decision making, but they reduce decision quality.

The speed trap can be as dangerous as moving too slowly.[44] In an Internet start-up that went bankrupt, fast decisions initially helped the firm achieve its growth objectives. Early on, the founders did everything they could to create a sense of urgency: They planned a meeting to "light a fire under the company," calling it a "state-of-emergency address" with the purpose of creating "the idea of panic with an emerging deadline." Speed became more important than content. They failed to consider multiple alternatives, used little information, didn't fully acknowledge competing views, and didn't consult outside advisers. They never considered slowing down to be an option.

Can managers under time pressure make decisions that are both timely and high quality? A study of effective decision-making processes in a fast-paced, high-tech industry revealed the tactics that such companies use.[45] First, instead of relying on old data, long-range planning, and futuristic forecasts, they focus on real-time information: current information obtained with little or no time delay. For example, they constantly monitor daily operating measures such as work in process rather than checking periodically the traditional accounting-based indicators such as profitability.

Second, they involve people more effectively and efficiently in the decision-making process. They rely heavily on trusted experts, and this yields both good advice and the confidence to act quickly despite uncertainty. They also take a realistic view of conflict: they value differing opinions, but they know that if disagreements are not resolved, the top executive must make the final choice in the end. Slow-moving firms, in contrast, are stymied by conflict. Like the fast-moving firms, they seek consensus; but when disagreements persist, they fail to decide.

> The speed trap can be as dangerous as moving too slowly.

The Digital World

Even as the volume of information managers have access to increases, we see a decrease in the time they have in which to make decisions. Quickly sorting through so much available information for truly useful data is a challenge. During a crisis, this challenge becomes even bigger.

During natural disasters, organizations use social media as part of their decision-making process. People are asked to tweet and post pictures with descriptions of current situations. Rescue workers get real-time curated data so that rather than wait for reports about blocked routes, they can make decisions that save hours of transportation time.

In Kenya, real-time posts show images and reports from election polling stations. Citizens post which stations are burning the paper ballots, which stations have gangs that intimidate voters not voting for the "right" candidate, and which stations are safe for one or both sides.

Kenyans are then better able to contribute to decisions that matter. They can know that if they walk a greater distance or travel to another town their vote will count, because they choose a safe location based on citizen-provided, real-time data.

Social Realities

Many decisions are made by a group rather than by an individual manager. In slow-moving firms, interpersonal factors decrease decision-making effectiveness. Even the manager acting alone is accountable to the boss and to others and must consider the preferences and reactions of many people. Therefore, many decisions are the result of intensive social interactions, bargaining, and politicking.

The remainder of this chapter focuses on the social context of decisions, including decision making in groups and the realities of decision making in organizations.

Decision Making in Groups

Sometimes managers convene groups of people in order to make important decisions. Some advise that in today's complex business environment, significant problems should *always* be tackled by groups.[46] As a result, managers must understand how groups operate and how to use them to improve decision making.

The basic philosophy behind using a group to make decisions is captured by the adage, "two heads are better than one." But is this statement really valid? Yes, it is—but only potentially, not necessarily.

If enough time is available, groups usually make higher-quality decisions than most individuals acting alone. However, groups often are inferior to the *best* individual.[47]

How well the group performs depends on how effectively it capitalizes on the potential advantages and minimizes the potential problems of using a group. Exhibit 3.7 summarizes these issues.

Potential Advantages of Using a Group

If other people have something to contribute, using groups to make a decision offers at least five potential advantages:[48]

1. More information is available when several people are making the decision. If one member doesn't have all the facts or needed expertise, another member might.
2. A greater number of perspectives on the issues, or different approaches to solving the problem, are available. The problem may be new to one group member but familiar to another. Or the group may need to consider other viewpoints—financial, legal, marketing, human resources, and so on—to achieve an optimal solution.

EXHIBIT 3.7

Pros and Cons of Using Groups to Make Decisions

Potential Advantages	Potential Disadvantages
Larger pool of information.	One person dominates.
More perspectives and approaches.	Satisficing.
Intellectual stimulation.	Groupthink.
People understand the decision.	Goal displacement.
People are committed to the decision.	Social loafing.

Bottom Line

If one person dominates a group discussion, it may feel like you're speeding up the decision making. But one dominant person reduces decision quality, and most of you will have wasted your time. *When you're meeting with a group, how can you help to make sure everyone is contributing?*

3. Group discussion provides an opportunity for intellectual stimulation. It can get people thinking and unleash their creativity to a far greater extent than would be possible with individual decision making.

  Those three potential advantages of using a group improve the odds that a more fully informed, higher-quality decision will result. Thus managers should involve people with different backgrounds, perspectives, and access to information. They should not involve only their colleagues who think the same way they do.

4. People who participate in a group discussion are more likely to understand why the decision was made. They will have heard the relevant arguments both for the chosen alternative and against the rejected alternatives.

5. Group discussion typically leads to a higher level of commitment to the decision. Buying into the proposed solution translates into high motivation to ensure that it is executed well.

  The last two advantages improve the chances that the decision will be implemented successfully. Therefore, managers should involve the people who will be responsible for implementing the decision as early in the deliberations as possible.

Potential Problems of Using a Group

Things can go wrong when groups make decisions. Most of the potential problems concern the processes through which group members interact with one another:[49]

1. Sometimes one group member dominates the discussion. When this occurs—such as when a strong leader makes his or her preferences clear—the result is the same as it would be if the dominant individual made the decision alone. Individual dominance has two disadvantages. First, the dominant person does not necessarily have the most valid opinions—and may even have the most unsound ideas. Second, even if that person's preference leads to a good decision, convening as a group will have been a waste of everyone else's time.

2. Satisficing is more likely with groups. Most people don't like meetings and will do what they can to end them. This may include criticizing members who want to keep exploring new and better alternatives. The result is a satisficing rather than an optimizing or maximizing decision.

3. Pressure to avoid disagreement can lead to a phenomenon called **groupthink**. This occurs when people choose not to disagree or raise objections. Some groups want to think as one, tolerate no dissension, and strive to remain cordial. They can be overconfident, complacent, and perhaps too willing to take risks. Pressure to go along with the group's preferred solution stifles creativity and other positive behaviors characteristic of vigilant decision making.

4. Goal displacement often occurs in groups. The goal of group members should be to come up with the best possible solution to the problem. But when **goal displacement** occurs, new goals emerge to replace the original ones. It is common for two or more group members to have different opinions and present their conflicting cases. Attempts at rational persuasion become heated disagreement. Winning the argument

groupthink

A phenomenon that occurs in decision making when group members avoid disagreement as they strive for consensus.

goal displacement

A decision-making group loses sight of its original goal and a new, less important goal emerges.

becomes the new goal. Saving face and defeating the other person's idea become more important than solving the problem.

5. When members of a group do not feel their contribution is important, they may engage in social loafing by working less hard when in a group.[50] This tendency to not pull one's own weight while working in groups poses many problems. Social loafing reduces cohesiveness between group members, resulting in lower group performance and higher absenteeism.[51] Chapter 14 discusses how managers can address social loafing and other barriers to building effective teams.

Heated arguments can arise when team members have differing opinions and are more concerned with winning the dispute than resolving the initial problem.

©Ingram Publishing RF

Effective managers pay close attention to the group process; they manage it carefully. You have just read about the pros and cons of using a group to make decisions, and you are about to read how to manage the group's decision-making process. Chapter 12, on leadership, helps you decide *when* to use groups to make decisions.

Managing Group Decision Making

As Exhibit 3.8 illustrates, effectively managing group decision making has three major requirements: (1) an appropriate leadership style, (2) the constructive use of disagreement and conflict, and (3) the enhancement of creativity.

Leadership Style

The leader of a decision-making group must attempt to minimize process-related problems. The leader should avoid dominating the discussion or allowing another individual to dominate. Less vocal group members should be encouraged to air their opinions and suggestions, and all members should be asked for dissenting viewpoints.

At the same time, the leader should not allow the group to pressure people into conforming. The leader should be alert to the dangers of groupthink and satisficing. Also, she should be attuned to indications that group members are losing sight of the primary objective: to come up with the best possible solution to the problem.

> First, don't lose sight of the problem and your goals. Second, make a decision! Don't fall prey to analysis paralysis.

These suggestions have two implications. First, don't lose sight of the problem and your goals. Second, make a decision! Slow-moving organizations whose group members can't come to an agreement will be standing still while their competitors move ahead.

Constructive Conflict

Total and consistent agreement among group members can be destructive. It can lead to groupthink, uncreative solutions, and a waste of the knowledge and diverse viewpoints that

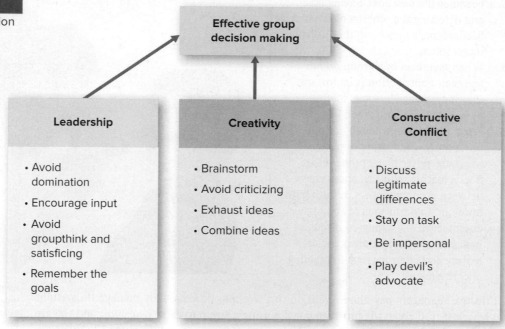

EXHIBIT 3.8
Managing Group Decision Making

people bring to a group. Therefore, a certain amount of constructive conflict should exist.[52] Pixar, which depends on creativity to make its animated films great, encourages constructive conflict with a standard for production meetings: Whenever someone wants to criticize an idea, the critic must attach an idea for improvement. In this way, good ideas can become great, and great ideas can become amazing. The practice is so much a part of Pixar's culture, it even has a name, "plussing."[53]

The most constructive type of conflict is **cognitive conflict**, or differences in perspectives or judgments about issues. In contrast, **affective conflict** is emotional and directed at other people. Affective conflict is likely to be destructive to the group because it can lead to anger, bitterness, goal displacement, and lower-quality decisions. Cognitive conflict can air legitimate differences of opinion and develop better ideas and problem solutions. Conflict, then, should be task-related rather than personal.[54] But even task-related conflict is good only when managed properly.[55]

Managers can generate constructive conflict through structured processes like **devil's advocacy**, in which a group member identifies and states the problems with an idea being considered. The group leader can formally assign people to play this role. Requiring people to point out problems can reduce inhibitions about disagreeing and make the conflict less personal and emotional.

An alternative to devil's advocacy is the dialectic. The **dialectic** goes a step beyond devil's advocacy by requiring a structured debate about two conflicting courses of action.[56] The philosophy of the dialectic stems from Plato and Aristotle, who advocated synthesizing the conflicting views of a thesis and an antithesis. Structured debates between plans and counterplans can be useful prior to making a strategic decision. For example, one team might present the case for acquiring a firm while another team advocates not making the acquisition.

Constructive conflict does not need to be generated on such a formal basis, and is not solely the leader's responsibility. Any team member can introduce cognitive conflict by being honest with opinions, by being unafraid to disagree with others, by pushing the group to action if it is taking too long or making the group slow down if necessary, and by advocating long-term considerations if the group is too focused on short-term results. Introducing

cognitive conflict

Issue-based differences in perspectives or judgments.

affective conflict

Emotional disagreement directed toward other people.

devil's advocate

A person who has the job of criticizing ideas to ensure that their downsides are fully explored.

dialectic

A structured debate comparing two conflicting courses of action.

constructive conflict is a legitimate and necessary responsibility of all group members interested in improving the group's decision-making effectiveness.

Encouraging Creativity

As you've already learned, ready-made solutions to a problem can be inadequate or unavailable. In such cases, custom-made solutions are necessary, so the group must be creative in generating ideas.

Some say that the most fundamental unit of value is ideas. Creativity is more than just an option; it is essential to survival. Allowing people to be creative may be one of the manager's most important and challenging responsibilities.

You might be saying to yourself, "I'm not creative." But even if you are not an artist or a musician, you do have potential to be creative in countless other ways. You don't need to be a genius in school either—Thomas Edison and Albert Einstein were not particularly good students. Nor does something need to change the world to be creative; the little things can always be done in new, creative ways that add value to the product and for the customer. Exhibit 3.9 describes three ways to be creative along with some ideas of college student entrepreneurs who turned their creativity into businesses.[57]

How do you become more creative?[58] Recognize the almost infinite little opportunities to be creative. Assume you can be creative if you give it a try. Escape from work once in a while. Read widely and try new experiences. Take a course or find a good book about creative thought processes; plenty are available. Exchange ideas and seek and give feedback.[59] And be aware that creativity is social;[60] your creativity will be affected by your social relationships at work, including your connections with other people outside your immediate close network.[61] Talk to people, often, about the issues and ideas with which you are wrestling.

How do you get creativity out of other people?[62] Give creative efforts the credit they are due and don't punish creative failures. Avoid extreme time pressure if possible.[63] Stimulate and challenge people intellectually. Listen to employees' ideas and allow enough time to explore different ideas. Put together groups of people with different styles of thinking and behaving. Get your people in touch with customers. Experiment with ways to stimulate fresh modes of thinking. Design company IDEO tells clients to install long communal tables or other spaces for employees to gather. Providing mobile chairs and desks encourages employees to get out of their silos to find new people to collaborate with.[64] And strive to be creative yourself—you'll set a good example.

People are likely to be more creative if they believe they are capable, if they know that their co-workers expect creativity, and if they believe that their employer values creativity.[65]

> **Bottom Line**
>
> Most creative ideas do not come from the lone genius in the basement laboratory, but from people talking and working together. *Why is listening useful in stimulating creativity?*
>
>

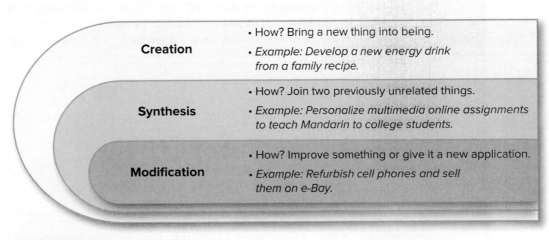

Creation
- How? Bring a new thing into being.
- *Example: Develop a new energy drink from a family recipe.*

Synthesis
- How? Join two previously unrelated things.
- *Example: Personalize multimedia online assignments to teach Mandarin to college students.*

Modification
- How? Improve something or give it a new application.
- *Example: Refurbish cell phones and sell them on e-Bay.*

EXHIBIT 3.9   Creative Actions

Brainstorming is a technique used to generate as many ideas as possible to solve a problem. You have probably engaged in brainstorming sessions for various class or work projects.

©dotshock/123RF RF

brainstorming

A process in which group members generate as many ideas about a problem as they can; criticism is withheld until all ideas have been proposed.

As a manager, you can do much to help employees develop these beliefs by how you listen, what you allow, and what you reward and punish. At a large consumer products company, management signals that it values creativity by inviting managers to post stories on the company's intranet about ideas their employees have suggested and the results of implementing them. The company also awards innovation bonuses linked to how their ideas have benefited the organization.[66]

Brainstorming

A common technique used to elicit creative ideas is brainstorming. In **brainstorming**, group members generate as many ideas about a problem as they can. As the ideas are presented, they are posted so that everyone can read them, and people can use the ideas as building blocks. The group is encouraged to say anything that comes to mind, with one exception: no criticism of other people or their ideas is allowed.

In the proper brainstorming environment—free of criticism—people are less inhibited and more likely to voice their unusual, creative, or even wild ideas. By the time people have exhausted their ideas, a long list of alternatives has been generated. Only then does the group turn to the evaluation stage. At that point, many ideas can be considered, modified, or combined into a creative, custom-made solution to the problem.

Brainstorming isn't necessarily as effective as some people think. Sometimes in a brainstorming session, people are inhibited and anxious, they conform to others' ideas, they set low standards, and they engage in noncreative behaviors including cocktail party–type conversations—complimenting one another, repeating ideas, telling stories—that are nice but don't promote creativity. Exhibit 3.10 shows how McKinsey creates effective brainstorming sessions.[67]

Other techniques that help include brainwriting (taking time to write down ideas silently), using trained facilitators, setting high performance goals, brainstorming electronically so that people aren't competing for air time, and even building a playground with fun elements that can foster creativity.[68] The nearby "Multiple Generations at Work" box discusses an Internet-based approach to soliciting ideas and feedback from customers anywhere in the world.

EXHIBIT 3.10
Improving Brainstorming Effectiveness

1. Choose participants based on their expertise and knowledge of the challenge.
2. Use well-thought-out questions as a platform to spark new ideas.
3. Break up large groups into subgroups of 3–5 people.
4. Ask subgroups to think deeply to generate 2–3 solutions for each key question explored.
5. Do not have the full group evaluate the winning ideas, but rather ask subgroups to identify their top 2 or 3 ideas. Describe next steps (e.g., top management team will evaluate ideas).
6. Act quickly on key ideas and provide feedback to all participants.

Multiple Generations at Work

Crowdsourcing: An Inexpensive Source of Creative Ideas

Remember not to stereotype and that individuals differ within as well as between "generations." But when faced with a difficult work problem to solve, Baby Boomer managers are more likely to seek expert opinions, whereas Millennials are more inclined to *crowdsource:* solicit ideas, opinions, and suggestions from members of large online networks. They may run an online contest to see which fan or customer can create the best tag line, and award them with a modest cash prize or free merchandise. The cost of crowdsourcing is usually much lower than seeking guidance from experts, such as an advertising company.

Anyone from cash-starved entrepreneurial ventures to charities to large companies can use crowdsourcing (and crowdfunding) to help them accomplish a variety of objectives and goals. Here is a sample of how organizations are tapping into the creativity and funding of online crowds:

©McGraw-Hill Education/Roberts Publishing Services

1. Havenly, an interior design website, uses crowdsourcing to get feedback on everything from pricing to new products. According to CEO Lee Mayer: "Crowdsourcing is fast, cheap and scruffy." By sending out fun and brief questionnaires to respondents, Mayer keeps down the cost of product development.
2. PepsiCo turned to the crowd for help naming the newest flavor of Frito-Lay potato chips. After launching the "Do Us a Flavor" online contest, PepsiCo received 3.8 million chip flavor ideas. Celebrity chefs and other experts narrowed the list to three finalists. An online fan vote named the winner, Cheesy Garlic.
3. Chip maker Intel partnered with Zooppa, a company that helps clients collect crowdsourced content, to tap the collective creativity of its 185,000-member online community. Together they ran an online contest to "create a print ad or a video up to 60 seconds long expressing [perceptions] of the technology firm."

Inspired by the Millennial generation, crowdsourcing provides a virtually limitless source of creative ideas for solving problems, building brands, and co-creating products and services with customers around the world.[69]

Organizational Decision Making

Individuals and groups make decisions constantly throughout every organization. To understand decision making in organizations, a manager should consider (1) the constraints decision makers face, (2) organizational decision processes, and (3) decision making during a crisis.

LO 7

Constraints on Decision Makers

Organizations—or, more accurately, the people who make important decisions—cannot do whatever they wish. Resources are scarce,[70] and various constraints—financial, legal, market, human, and organizational—inhibit certain actions. Capital or product markets may make an expensive new venture impossible. Legal restrictions may constrain the kinds of international business activities in which a firm can participate. Labor unions may defeat a contract proposed by management, and managers and investors may block a takeover attempt. In strategic alliances, the allies should pursue rational decisions collaboratively, not separately.[71] Even brilliant ideas must take into account the practical matters of implementation.[72]

Suppose you have a great idea that will provide a revolutionary service for your bank's customers. You won't be able to put your idea into action immediately. You will have to sell it to the people who can give you the go-ahead and to those whose help you will need to carry out the project. You might start by convincing your boss of your idea's merit. Next, the two of you may have to hash it out with a vice president. Then maybe the president has to be sold. At each stage, you must listen to these individuals' opinions and suggestions and often incorporate them into your original concept. Ultimately, you will have to derive a proposal acceptable to others.

In addition, you should carefully think through ethical and legal considerations. Decision makers must consider ethics and the preferences of many constituent groups—the realities of life in organizations. You will have plenty of opportunity to think more about ethical issues in Chapter 5.

Organizational Decision Processes

Just as with individuals and groups, organizational decision making historically was described with rational models like the one depicted earlier, in Exhibit 3.3. But Nobel laureate Herbert Simon challenged the rational model and proposed an important alternative. Due to **bounded rationality**, decision makers cannot be truly rational because (1) they have imperfect, incomplete information about alternatives and consequences; (2) the problems they face are so complex; (3) human beings simply cannot process all the information to which they are exposed; (4) there is not enough time to process all relevant information fully; and (5) people, including managers within the same firm, have conflicting goals.

When these conditions hold—and they do for most consequential managerial decisions—perfect rationality will give way to more biased, subjective, messier decision processes. For example, the **incremental model** of decision making occurs when managers make small decisions, take little steps, move cautiously, and move in piecemeal fashion toward a bigger solution. The classic example is the budget process, which traditionally begins with the budget from the previous period and makes incremental decisions from that starting point.

The **coalition model** of decision making arises when people disagree on goals or compete with one another for resources. The decision process becomes political as groups of individuals band together and try collectively to influence the decision. Two or more coalitions form, each representing a different preference, and each tries to use power and negotiations to sway the decision.

Organizational politics, in which people try to influence organizational decisions so that their own interests will be served, can reduce decision-making effectiveness.[73] One of the best ways to reduce such politics is to create common goals for members of the team—that is, make the decision-making process a collaborative, rather than a competitive, exercise by establishing a goal around which the group can rally. In one study, top management teams with stated goals such as "build the biggest financial war chest" for an upcoming competitive battle, or "create *the* computer firm of the decade," or "build the best damn machine on the market" were less likely to have dysfunctional conflict and politics between members.[74] On a personal level, if you find yourself in a conflict, you and your adversary may be focused on the wrong goals. Work to find common ground in the form of an important goal that you both want to achieve.

The **garbage can model** of decision making occurs when people aren't sure of their goals, or disagree about the goals, and likewise are unsure of or in disagreement about what to do. This situation occurs because some problems are so complex that they are not well understood, and because decision makers move in and out of the decision process due to having so many other things to attend to as well. This model implies that some decisions are chaotic and almost random. You can see that this is a dramatic departure from rationality in decision making.

bounded rationality

A less-than-perfect form of rationality in which decision makers cannot be perfectly rational because decisions are complex and complete information is unavailable or cannot be fully processed.

incremental model

Model of organizational decision making in which major solutions arise through a series of smaller decisions.

coalition model

Model of organizational decision making in which groups with differing preferences use power and negotiation to influence decisions.

garbage can model

Model of organizational decision making depicting a chaotic process and seemingly random decisions.

LO 8   ## Decision Making in a Crisis

In crises, managers must make decisions under a great deal of pressure.[75] You know some of the most famous recent crises: the explosion of BP's oil rig in the Gulf of Mexico, hurricane devastation along the East Coast and elsewhere, the financial crisis that brought turmoil to the housing and banking industries, and the ongoing political crises that have shaken many governments around the world.

Information technology is a new arena for crises. Businesses, homes, government agencies, hospitals, and other organizations send critical information through the Internet and private networks around the clock, and any technical failure—sometimes accidental, sometimes maliciously intentional—could be magnified by the speed and reach of information technology. One vulnerable area is the electrical grid, which links utilities and carries power to each user. Information technology systems allow utility employees to control the grid remotely. Hackers have gained access to the U.S. electrical grid, enabling them to interfere with the grid's operations.[76] It almost feels routine how often hackers gain unethical, illegal, and dangerous access to databases and systems of companies and government agencies.

Superstorm Sandy hit the East Coast with fierce devastation. Managers had to make critical decisions to keep people safe.
©Laura Ballard/123RF RF

The response to IT-related crises must involve senior executives in online communication, both to protect the firm's reputation and to communicate with outside experts, news sources, and key external and internal stakeholders. Managers can use IT to monitor and respond immediately to problems, including scandals, boycotts, rumors, cyberattacks, and other crises.[77]

Although many companies still don't concern themselves with crisis management, this is a recipe for compounding disaster; it is imperative for it to be on management's agenda. As illustrated in Exhibit 3.11, an effective plan for crisis management (CM) should include several elements.[78]

Ultimately, management should be able to answer the following questions:[79]

What kinds of crises could your company face?
Can your company detect a crisis in its early stages?
How will it manage a crisis if one occurs?
How can it benefit from a crisis after it has passed?

Strategic actions such as integrating CM into strategic planning and official policies.

Evaluation and diagnostic actions such as conducting audits of threats, and establishing tracking systems for early warning signals.

Technical and structural actions such as creating a CM team and dedicating a budget to CM.

Communication actions such as providing training for dealing with the media, local communities, and police and government officials.

Psychological and cultural actions such as providing training and psychological support services regarding the human and emotional impacts of crises.

EXHIBIT 3.11
Elements in an Effective Crisis Plan

SOURCES: Meyers, G. with Holusha J., *When It Hits the Fan: Managing the Nine Crises of Business.* Boston: Houghton Mifflin, 1986; Bacharach, S. and Bamberger, P., "9/11 and New York City Firefighters' Post Hoc Unit Support and Control Climates: A Context Theory of the Consequences of Involvement in Traumatic Work-Related Events," *Academy of Management Journal* 50 (2007), pp. 849–68.

Management in Action

UBER IN CRISIS

There is little doubt that Uber's innovative technology disrupted the taxi industry in cities around the world. While its ride-hailing service has been a boon to many a late-night partygoer and stranded office worker, the company recently experienced a series of escalating crises that could imperil its future. In addition to allegations of widespread sexism and sexual harassment, Uber faced accusations from current and former employees that for years it has fraudulently applied a data-sharing program to secretly identify and evade enforcement officials in cities where it had been banned or was not yet authorized to operate.

Intended as a means of identifying potentially problematic riders to protect its drivers, the program, called VTOS (for *violation of terms of service*), employs a software tool called Greyball. Together these technologies reportedly have been used to tag would-be riders Uber suspected might be municipal enforcement officers. These officials might in turn be engaging in a sting operation to locate Uber drivers, who could be issued tickets or have their cars impounded. Once identified by Uber, however, officials would be given false information about whether any cars were available to respond to their hail. If any officer were accidentally picked up, Uber would alert the driver to discharge him or her.

Despite some doubts within the company about whether it was legal or ethical, the Greyballing strategy has been used in the United States and about 12 foreign countries. According to Uber, "This program denies ride requests to fraudulent users who are violating our terms of service—whether that's people aiming to physically harm drivers, competitors looking to disrupt our operations, or opponents who collude with officials on secret 'stings' meant to entrap drivers."

But questions about its legality are now being raised here and in Europe. Said Peter Henning, a law professor at Wayne State University, "With any type of systematic thwarting of the law, you're flirting with disaster. We all take our foot off the gas when we see the police car at the intersection up ahead, and there's nothing wrong with that. But this goes far beyond avoiding a speed trap." Meanwhile, an official in the Netherlands has asked the EU's European Commission whether it plans to investigate.[80]

At this writing, Uber observers are wondering what lies ahead, including for the rest of Silicon Valley regarding sexist culture and sexual harrassment.

- What ideas from this chapter could improve decision making at Uber?
- What's been happening lately? Has there been any evidence of improved decision making?

Crises can harm personal and work relationships and long-term performance. But with effective crisis management, old as well as new problems can be resolved, new strategies and competitive advantages may appear, and positive change can emerge. And if someone steps in and manages the crisis well, a hero is born.

> And if someone steps in and manages the crisis well, a hero is born.

As a leader during a crisis, don't pretend that nothing happened (as did managers at one firm after a visitor died in the hallway despite employees' efforts to save him).[81] Communicate and reinforce the organization's values. Try to find ways for people to support one another and remember that others will take cues from your behavior. You should be optimistic but brutally honest. Show emotion, but not fear. "You have to be cooler than cool," says Gene Krantz of *Apollo 13* ground control fame.

But don't ignore the problems or downplay them and reassure too much; don't create false hopes. Give people the bad news straight—you'll gain credibility, and when the good news comes, it will really mean something.

KEY TERMS

affective conflict, p. 88

bounded rationality, p. 92

brainstorming, p. 90

certainty, p. 75

coalition model, p. 92

cognitive conflict, p. 88

conflict, p. 76

contingency plans, p. 79

custom-made solutions, p. 78

devil's advocate, p. 88

dialectic, p. 88

discounting the future, p. 83

framing effects, p. 83

garbage can model, p. 92

goal displacement, p. 86

groupthink, p. 86

illusion of control, p. 83

incremental model, p. 92

maximizing, p. 80

nonprogrammed decisions, p. 74

optimizing, p. 80

programmed decisions, p. 74

ready-made solutions, p. 78

risk, p. 75

satisficing, p. 80

uncertainty, p. 75

vigilance, p. 82

RETAINING WHAT YOU LEARNED

In Chapter 3, you learned that most managers make less than perfectly rational decisions because they lack the necessary information, time, or structure. The ideal decision-making process includes six steps (see Exhibit 3.3 recreated below). The best decision hinges on the manager's ability to be vigilant at all stages of the decision-making process. Various barriers can diminish the effectiveness of the decision-making process. While there are advantages and disadvantages of making decisions in groups, a good leader can manage the challenges by using the right leadership style, allowing constructive conflict, encouraging creativity, and brainstorming.

Decision making in organizations is complex and individuals are often bounded by multiple constraints. Decisions can be made incrementally, through coalitions, or in a chaotic garbage can manner. Decision making during organizational crises is particularly challenging; managers should anticipate and plan for it.

LO 1 Describe the kinds of decisions you will face as a manager.

- Most important managerial decisions lack structure and are characterized by uncertainty, risk, and conflict.
- Despite these challenges, managers are expected to make rational decisions in a timely manner.

LO 2 Summarize the steps in making "rational" decisions.

- The ideal decision-making process involves six phases. The first, identifying and diagnosing the problem (or opportunity), requires recognizing a discrepancy between the current state and a desired state and then delving below surface symptoms to identifying underlying causes of the problem.
- The second phase, generating alternative solutions, involves applying ready-made or designing custom-made solutions.
- The third, evaluating alternatives, means predicting the consequences of different alternatives, sometimes through building scenarios of the future.
- Fourth, a solution is chosen; the solution might maximize, satisfice, or optimize.
- Fifth, people implement the decision; this phase requires more careful planning than it often receives.
- Finally, managers should evaluate how well the decision is working. This means gathering objective, valid information about the impact the decision is having. If the evidence suggests the problem is not getting solved, either a better decision or a better implementation plan must be developed.

LO 3 Recognize the pitfalls you should avoid when making decisions.

- Situational and human limitations lead most decision makers to satisfice rather than maximize or optimize.
- Psychological biases, time pressures, and the social realities of organizational life may prevent rational execution of the six phases.
- Vigilance and an understanding of how to manage decision-making groups and organizational constraints will improve the process and result in better decisions.

EXHIBIT 3.3 (revisited)   The Phases of Decision Making

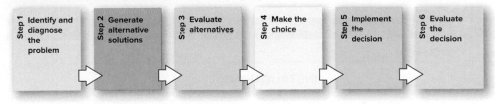

Step 1 Identify and diagnose the problem → Step 2 Generate alternative solutions → Step 3 Evaluate alternatives → Step 4 Make the choice → Step 5 Implement the decision → Step 6 Evaluate the decision

LO 4 Evaluate the pros and cons of using a group to make decisions.

- Advantages of using groups include more information, perspectives, and approaches brought to bear on problem solving; intellectual stimulation; greater understanding of the final decision; and higher commitment to the decision once it is made.
- Potential dangers or disadvantages of using groups include individual domination of discussions, satisficing, groupthink, goal displacement, and social loafing.

LO 5 Identify procedures to use in leading a decision-making group.

- Effective leaders in decision-making teams avoid dominating the discussion; encourage people's input; avoid groupthink and satisficing; and stay focused on the group's goals.
- They encourage constructive conflict via devil's advocacy and the dialectic, posing opposite sides of an issue or solutions to a problem.

LO 6 Explain how to encourage creative decisions.

- When creative ideas are needed, leaders should set a good example by being creative themselves. They should recognize the almost infinite little opportunities for creativity and have confidence in their own creative abilities.

- They can inspire creativity in others by providing creative freedom, rewarding creativity, and not punishing creative failures.
- Leaders should encourage interaction with customers, stimulate discussion, and protect people from managers who might squelch the creative process.
- Brainstorming is one of the most popular techniques for generating creative ideas.

LO 7 Discuss the processes by which decisions are made in organizations.

- Decision making in organizations can be a highly complex process. Individuals and groups are constrained by a variety of factors and constituencies. In practice, decision makers are boundedly rational rather than purely rational.
- Some decisions are made on an incremental basis. Coalitions form to represent different preferences. The process is often chaotic, as depicted in the garbage can model.
- Politics can also enter the process, decisions are negotiated, and crises come and go.

LO 8 Describe how to make decisions in a crisis.

- Crisis conditions make sound, effective decision making more difficult. However, it is possible for crises to be managed well.
- A strategy for crisis management can be developed beforehand, and the mechanisms readied, so that if crises do arise, decision makers are prepared.

DISCUSSION QUESTIONS

1. Discuss Uber's success and crises in terms of risk, uncertainty, and how its managers are handling the company's challenges. What is the current news on this company?

2. Identify some risky decisions you have made. Why did you take the risks? How did they work out? Looking back, what did you learn?

3. Identify a decision you made that had important unexpected consequences. Were the consequences good, bad, or both? Should you, and could you, have done anything differently in making the decision?

4. What effects does time pressure have on your decision making? In what ways do you handle it well and not so well?

5. Recall a recent decision that you had difficulty making. Describe it in terms of the characteristics of managerial decisions.

6. What do you think are some advantages and disadvantages to using computer technologies in decision making?

7. Do you think that when managers make decisions they follow the decision-making steps as presented in this chapter? Which steps are apt to be overlooked or given inadequate attention? What can people do to make sure they do a more thorough job?

8. Discuss the potential advantages and disadvantages of using a group to make decisions. Give examples from your experience.

9. Suppose you are the CEO of a major corporation and one of your company's oil tanks has ruptured, spilling thousands of gallons of oil into a river that empties into the ocean. What do you need to do to handle the crisis?

10. Identify some problems you want to solve. Brainstorm with others a variety of creative solutions.

EXPERIENTIAL EXERCISES

3.1 DECISION MAKING IN ACTION

OBJECTIVE

Learn how to improve your ability to make good decisions.

INSTRUCTIONS

Refer again to Exhibit 3.3. Think back to a recent expensive purchase you made. It could have been a bike, mobile device, suit for interviews, and so forth. In order to evaluate the quality of your decision, please think about your purchase when answering each of the questions below.

Decision Making Worksheet

1. What problem did you hope to solve by making this purchase?

   _____

2. What alternative (or competing) products did you consider?

   _____

3. How did you evaluate the different alternative (or competing) products? Did you identify each product's strengths and weaknesses?

   _____

4. When you made the final choice, was it a maximizing, satisficing, or optimizing outcome?

   _____

5. After purchasing the product, how frequently did you test it out?

   _____

6. Was your decision to make the purchase a positive or negative one? Did it satisfy your original need(s)?

   _____

3.2 GROUP PROBLEM SOLVING AT A SOCIAL ENTERPRISE

OBJECTIVE

To understand the dynamics of group decision making through role-playing a meeting between a president and her employees.

INSTRUCTIONS

1. Identify 5 students to play the roles of the employees. Ask these 5 individuals to read their roles below.

2. Identify 1 student to play the role of the president of the social enterprise (Taylor Johnson). Ask this individual to read his/her role below.

3. Set up a table with 6 chairs at the front of the classroom.

4. Ask the remaining students in the audience to observe how the 6 individuals behave and then answer the discussion questions below.

5. When everyone is ready, Taylor Johnson joins the others at the table in her office, and the scene commences.

6. The meeting continues until there is a successful close unless an argument develops and no progress is made after 10–15 minutes.

DISCUSSION QUESTIONS

1. How did each member frame the problem? What did each member discuss?

2. How effectively did the group generate and evaluate alternatives?

3. What was its final decision?

4. Evaluate the effectiveness of the group's decision making.

5. How could the group's effectiveness be enhanced?

OVERVIEW

The role-play exercise is based on a meeting between a manager of a social enterprise and her 5 employees. Each character's role is designed to re-create a realistic business meeting. Each character brings to the meeting a unique perspective on a major problem confronting the social enterprise as well as some personal views of the other characters developed over several years of knowing them in business and social contexts.

CAST OF CHARACTERS

Taylor Johnson, the president, founded the enterprise 10 years ago as a way to connect outstanding teachers who have recently earned their teaching degrees with students in schools located in economically disadvantaged areas. The new teachers agree to serve in the disadvantaged schools for a 3-year period in exchange for a reasonably good salary and forgiveness of up to $30,000 of their student loans. Taylor is well known for her hard-driving, selfless style of leadership. A charismatic leader, she is highly skilled at bringing diverse stakeholders together. However, Taylor admits that she lacks knowledge related to online classroom and teaching technologies. In the old days, this wouldn't be an issue. However, Taylor's competitors are beginning to overtake the social enterprise by offering new teachers training, mobile devices, and online learning tools (e.g., online homework, interactive videos, eBooks, and so forth) to help them create high-performance classrooms. She doesn't know whether the enterprise should continue doing what it does best (placing new teachers into traditional face-to-face teaching environments) or begin preparing its recruits to teach online and hybrid (combining face-to-face with online modules) classes.

Amit Patel, head of information technology, has worked for the enterprise for 6 months. A recent college graduate,

Amit reports directly to Taylor. She is on a mission to modernize the way the enterprise does its work. She feels strongly that the enterprise should be shifting more of its IT operations to the cloud. Also, Amit feels that a great deal of insight could be mined from 10 years of data currently stored in antiquated servers at the enterprise. Amit believes she could make these changes without spending a lot of funds. Unfortunately, Amit's zeal for rapid change has been a cause of concern for Felipe and Taylor who prefer a more methodical approach to change.

Felipe Rodriguez, director of fund-raising, reports directly to Johnson. He has held this position for 8 years and is a very close friend of Taylor's. Donations and grants for the most recent year are down by 10 percent. Prior to joining the enterprise, he worked as a fund-raiser for a major university in the region. The university offered a wide variety of online and hybrid courses. Felipe would often refer to these innovations when seeking donations from alumni. He was widely viewed as successful at his work.

Mike Clarke, manager in charge of recruiting new teachers, works for Felipe. After working for the enterprise as an entry-level recruiter for two years, Mike was recently promoted to this position. Though a persuasive recruiter of new teachers, he has noticed a recent decline in the number of recruits willing to teach in traditional face-to-face learning environments. He is progressive in his thinking and believes that the enterprise needs to change how it does business in order to keep up with the competitors. Mike and Amit feel they are agents of change and want to modernize the enterprise.

TODAY'S MEETING

Taylor has called the meeting with these three managers to decide whether the social enterprise should begin preparing its new recruits to teach not only traditional face-to-face classes, but also hybrid and online classes. This decision has to be made within 15 minutes because the enterprise's largest client just called and asked to meet with Taylor immediately. Taylor is concerned that the school may be on the verge of discontinuing the contract with the enterprise. If that's the case, Taylor wants the managers to help her decide on a counteroffer to win back the client school. Losing this client school is not an option given that it makes up 40 percent of the enterprise's revenue.

SOURCE: Adapted from Gordon, Judith R., *A Diagnostic Approach to Organizational Behavior* (Upper Saddle River, NJ: Pearson Education, Inc., 1983).

Concluding Case

SOARING EAGLE SKATE COMPANY

As a child, Stan Eagle just knew he loved riding his skateboard and doing tricks. By the time he was a teenager, he was so proficient at the sport that he began entering professional contests and taking home prize money. By his twenties, Eagle was so successful and popular that he could make skateboarding his career. A skateboard maker sponsored him in competitions and demonstrations around the world.

The sponsorship and prize money paid enough to support him for several years. But then interest in the sport waned, and Eagle knew he would have to take his business in new directions. He believed skateboarding would return to popularity, so he decided to launch into designing, building, and selling skateboards under his own brand. To finance Soaring Eagle Skate Company, he pooled his own personal savings with money from a friend, Pete Williams, and came up with $75,000. Sure enough, new young skaters began snapping up the skateboards, attracted in part by the products' association with a star.

As the company prospered, Eagle considered ideas for expansion. Another friend had designed a line of clothing he thought would appeal to Eagle's skateboarding fans, and Eagle's name on the product would lend it credibility. At the friend's urging, Eagle branched out into clothing for skateboarders. However, he discovered that the business of shorts and shirts is far different from the business of sports equipment. The price markups were tiny, and the sales channels were entirely different. Three years into the expansion, Soaring Eagle had invested millions of dollars in the line but was still losing money. Eagle decided to sell off that part of the business to a clothing company and cut his losses.

Soon after that experiment, cofounder Williams proposed another idea: They should begin selling other types of sports equipment—inline roller skates and ice skates. Selling equipment for more kinds of sports would produce more growth than the company could obtain by focusing on just one sport. Eagle was doubtful. He was considered one of the most knowledgeable people in the world about skateboarding. He knew nothing about inline skating and ice skating. Eagle argued that the company would be better off focusing on the sport in which it offered the most expertise. Surely there were ways to seek growth within that sport—or at least to avoid the losses that came from investing in industries in which the company lacked experience.

Williams continued to press Eagle to try his idea. He pointed out that unless the company took some risks and expanded into new areas, there was little hope that Williams and Eagle could continue to earn much of a return on the money they had invested. Eagle was troubled. The attempt at clothing delivered, he thought, a message that they needed to be careful about expansion. But he seemed unable to persuade Williams to accept his point of view. He could go along with Williams and take the chance of losing money again, or he could use money he had earned from his business to buy Williams's ownership share in the company and then continue running Soaring Eagle on his own.

DISCUSSION QUESTIONS

1. How do the characteristics of management decisions—uncertainty, risk, conflict, and lack of structure—affect the decision facing Stan Eagle?
2. What steps can Eagle take to increase the likelihood of making the best decision in this situation?

PART ONE SUPPORTING CASE

Zappos Eliminates All Managers and Titles

Recently, Zappos' CEO Tony Hsieh surprised many observers in the business world by announcing to his 1,500 or so employees that the e-retailer famous for its shoes was doing away with job titles, managers, and other artifacts associated with traditional top-down management and replacing it with a system where employees are expected to act like mini entrepreneurs. This new approach or holacracy encourages employees to self-manage and self-organize, thus eliminating the need for bosses. One of the management system's overarching goals is to "create a dynamic workforce where everyone has a voice and bureaucracy doesn't stifle innovation."

How does a holacracy function? Based on the work of Brian Robertson, who developed the idea while running his start-up, Ternary Software, a holacracy organizes employees into circles of responsibility—similar to functional areas like marketing and customer service, and employee special interest areas like career development and so forth. Though democratic and self-governing, the circles do not operate in a vacuum as they are arranged in a hierarchy (circles report to higher-level circles) and follow detailed procedures for running meetings and making decisions. Employees are free to choose which circles to which they want to belong and on what projects they would like to work. The circles are responsible for achieving a specific set of responsibilities. At meetings, employees are encouraged to address and resolve in a proactive manner "tensions" or problems related to internal (e.g., unfair workloads) or external (e.g., a way to enhance the customer experience) issues. Rather than reporting to a manager with the power to hire or fire, as is the case in hierarchically organized companies, a "lead link" helps employees accomplish the circle's responsibilities and communicates between circles.

Zappos is not the first company in history to experiment with employee self-management. For example, Gore & Associates (maker of Gore-Tex) has no formal chain of command and provides its associates with freedom to self-select work projects and choose associates with relevant expertise to assist in the development of those projects. Semco Partners, a Brazilian industrial machinery manufacturer, engages its 3,000-plus employees through participative management, where employees set their own work hours and pay levels, hire and review their supervisors, and

decide which new businesses in which to enter. Johnsonville Sausage Company eliminated its hierarchy and introduced "self-managed, self-organizing teams throughout the company." Ralph Styer, the CEO who championed this radical change, believed that "helping human beings fulfill their potential is of course a moral responsibility, but it's also good business practice." He believed in the connection between employee happiness and organizational performance: "Learning, striving people are happy people and good workers."

Are the employees at Zappos happy about their expanded responsibilities and freedom to self-govern? How are the managers accepting this change? It's mixed. In a recent e-mail to all staff at the company, Hsieh said that everyone had a choice to make: either embrace the new holacratic system or accept a three-month severance package and resign. Two hundred and ten (or 14 percent) of the staff resigned. Of those who left the company, 20 (or 7 percent) were managers. Does that mean that the 86 percent of staff who decided to stay did so because they believe in the new holacratic approach? Time will tell. One may speculate that the individuals who chose to remain at Zappos did so because they are either "believers" or lack the interest or motivation to switch jobs at the moment.

Some of the employees who are staying have shared concerns about the new management approach like using the complicated new lingo, adjusting to the rapidly changing work roles and expectations, and the "ever-expanding number of circles and the endless meetings" that take employees away from achieving their work goals. On the upside, holacracy promotes employees' ownership and encourages even the lowest-paid employees to add items to meeting agendas that are subsequently discussed and acted upon.

What will become of the 267 ex-managers at Zappos? Though no one knows for sure, the company has created a new circle titled "Reinventing Yourself" to help these individuals find "new roles that might be a good match for their passions, skills, and experience." John Bunch, the employee who is helping Zappos transition to a holacracy, suggests, "most managers will be able to grow into new areas of technical work to replace the time they were doing people management."

There may be an irony in the way that Zappos shifted from a hierarchical management structure to one that is based on democratic, self-organizing circles. The mandate for this change came from Tony Hsieh, the CEO. Those employees and managers who did not agree with the "top-down" change were asked to leave the company. This irony suggests that even for visionary business leaders like Hsieh, radical change may not be easy to accomplish in a consensus-driven manner.

As Zappos and its employees continue to adapt to the new holacratic system of management, Bunch has admitted the company will need to refine salary processes as well as the decision process for assigning projects throughout the company. He is patient and is taking the long view: "We believe that, over time, the ability for people to be empowered and entrepreneurial will make people happy."

1. To what degree do you think that Zappos' new holacratic approach to organizing will enhance its competitive advantage in innovation, quality, service, speed, and cost competitiveness? Explain.

SOURCES: Adapted from Noguchi, Y., "Zappos: A Workplace Where No One and Everyone Is the Boss," *NPR*, July 21, 2015, http://www.npr.org; Gelles, D., "At Zappos, Pushing Shoes and a Vision," *The New York Times*, July 17, 2015, http://www.nytimes.com; Feloni, R., "7% of Zappos' Managers Quit After Recent CEO Ultimatum to Embrace Self-Management or Leave," *Business Insider*, June 9, 2015, http://www.buisnessinsider.com; Silverman, R., "At Zappos, Banishing Bosses Brings Confusion," *The Wall Street Journal*, May 20, 2015, http://www.wsj.com; Petriglieri, G., "Making Sense of Zappos' War on Manager," *Harvard Business Review*, May 19, 2015, http://www.hbr.org; Denning, S., "Zappos Says Goodbye to Bosses," *Forbes*, January 15, 2015, http://www.forbes.com; Fisher, L., "Ricardo Semler Won't Take Control," *Strategy + Business*, November 29, 2005, http://www.strategy-business.com.

CASE INCIDENTS

Employee Raiding

Litson Cotton Yarn Manufacturing Company, located in Murray, New Jersey, decided as a result of increasing labor costs to relocate its plant in Fairlee, a southern community of 4,200. Plant construction was started, and a human resources office was opened in the state employment office, located in Fairlee.

Because of ineffective HR practices in the other three textile mills located within a 50-mile radius of Fairlee, Litson was receiving applications from some of the most highly skilled and trained textile operators in the state. After receiving applications from approximately 500 people, employment was offered to 260 male and female applicants. These employees would be placed immediately on the payroll with instructions to await final installation of machinery, which was expected within the following six weeks.

The managers of the three other textile companies, faced with resignations from their most efficient and best-trained employees, approached the Litson managers with the complaint that their labor force was being "raided." They registered a strong protest to cease such practices and demanded an immediate cancellation of the employment of the 260 people hired by Litson.

Litson managers discussed the ethical and moral considerations involved in offering employment to the 260 people. Litson clearly faced a tight labor market in Fairlee, and management thought that if the 260 employees were discharged, the company would face cancellation of its plans and large construction losses. Litson management also felt obligated to the 260 employees who had resigned from their previous employment in favor of Litson.

The dilemma was compounded when the manager of one community plant reminded Litson that his plant was part of a nationwide chain supplied with cotton yarn from Litson. He implied that Litson's attempts to continue operations in Fairlee could result in cancellation of orders and the possible loss of approximately 18 percent market share. It was also suggested to Litson managers that actions taken by the nationwide textile chain could result in cancellation of orders from other textile companies. Litson's president held an urgent meeting of his top subordinates to (1) decide what to do about the situation in Fairlee, (2) formulate a written policy statement indicating Litson's position regarding employee raiding, and (3) develop a plan for implementing the policy.

How would you prepare for the meeting, and what would you say at the meeting?

SOURCE: Champion, J. and James, J., *Critical Incidents in Management: Decision and Policy Issues*, 6th ed. New York: McGraw-Hill/Irwin, 1989. Copyright © 1989 The McGraw-Hill Companies.

Effective Management

Dr. Sam Perkins, a graduate of the Harvard University College of Medicine, had a private practice in internal medicine for 12 years. Fourteen months ago, he was persuaded by the Massachusetts governor to give up private practice to be director of the State Division of Human Services.

After one year as director, Perkins recognized he had made little progress in reducing the considerable inefficiency in the division. Employee morale and effectiveness seemed even lower than when he had assumed the position. He realized his past training and experiences were of a clinical nature with little exposure to effective management techniques. Perkins decided to research literature on the subject of management available to him at a local university.

Perkins soon realized that management scholars are divided on the question of what constitutes effective management. Some believe people are born with certain identifiable personality traits that make them effective managers. Others believe a manager can learn to be effective by treating subordinates with a personal and considerate approach and by giving particular attention to their need for favorable working conditions. Still others emphasize the importance of developing a management style characterized by an authoritarian, democratic, or laissez-faire approach. Perkins was further confused when he learned that a growing number of scholars advocate that effective management is contingent on the situation.

Because a state university was located nearby, Perkins contacted the dean of its college of business administration. The dean referred him to the director of the college's management center, Professor Joel McCann. Discussions between Perkins and McCann resulted in a tentative agreement that the management center would organize a series of management training sessions for the State Division of Human Services. Before agreeing on the price tag for the management conference, Perkins asked McCann to prepare a proposal reflecting his thoughts on the following questions:

1. How will the question of what constitutes effective management be answered during the conference?

2. What will be the specific subject content of the conference?

3. Who will the instructors be?

4. What will be the conference's duration?

5. How can the conference's effectiveness be evaluated?

6. What policies should the State Division of Human Services adopt regarding who the conference participants should be and how they should be selected? How can these policies be implemented best?

SOURCE: Champion, J. and James, J., *Critical Incidents in Management: Decision and Policy Issues,* 6th ed. New York: McGraw-Hill/Irwin, 1989. Copyright © 1989 The McGraw-Hill Companies.

CHAPTER 4
Planning and Strategic Management

> Manage your destiny, or someone else will.
> —JACK WELCH, FORMER CEO, GENERAL ELECTRIC

©Robert Churchill/Getty Images RF

LEARNING OBJECTIVES

After studying Chapter 4, you will be able to:

LO 1 Summarize the basic steps in any planning process.

LO 2 Describe how to integrate strategic planning with tactical and operational planning.

LO 3 Identify elements of the external environment and internal resources of the firm to analyze before formulating a strategy.

LO 4 Define core capabilities and explain how they provide the foundation for business strategy.

LO 5 Summarize the types of choices available for corporate strategy.

LO 6 Discuss how companies can achieve competitive advantage through business strategy.

LO 7 Describe the keys to effective strategy implementation.

CHAPTER OUTLINE

An Overview of Planning Fundamentals
The Basic Planning Process

Levels of Planning
Strategic Planning
Tactical and Operational Planning
Aligning Tactical, Operational, and Strategic Planning

Strategic Planning
Step 1: Establishing Mission, Vision, and Goals
Step 2: Analyzing External Opportunities and Threats
Step 3: Analyzing Internal Strengths and Weaknesses
Step 4: SWOT Analysis and Strategy Formulation
Step 5: Strategy Implementation
Step 6: Strategic Control

Management in Action

HOW WALT DISNEY COMPANY SCRIPTS ITS OWN SUCCESS

The record-breaking opening weekend for Disney's live-action/digital *Beauty and the Beast* put the movie, starring Emma Watson, on track for becoming the company's latest box-office success, to the tune of an anticipated $1 billion in ticket sales worldwide. Though this "tale as old as time" has no sequels to count on, Disney planned to repeat the formula of remaking its beloved animated classics in the coming years, with digitally enhanced live-action versions of hits including *Dumbo, The Lion King, Aladdin, Mulan,* and *Pinocchio* all in progress.

The company has honed to perfection its ability to appeal to "children from 6 to 60," as founder Walt Disney described his intended audience. Another of Walt Disney's successful strategies, according to Sean Bailey, president of Walt Disney Studios motion picture production, was to take "beautiful, timeless stories he knew had lasting relevance, and he then sort of applied the sensibilities of his times." The company has continued this strategy, even if it has occasionally meant creating a minor dust-up in overseas markets. Because the company refused to delete a few seconds of *Beauty and the Beast* in which a character is revealed to be gay, Russia limited viewers to those 16 and over, and the Malaysian government would not allow the film to be shown at all. The effect of these lost viewers was expected to be minimal for the $56 billion company, one of the largest in the entertainment industry. Walt Disney is not merely huge in terms of sales volume; it has four business divisions, engaged in nearly every kind of commercial entertainment.

It all began with Walt Disney Studios, which today produces movies, music, and stage shows under the banners of Disney, Pixar, Marvel Studios, Lucasfilm,

©Bertrand Guay/AFP/Getty Images

Touchstone Pictures, and Hollywood Records. The Media Networks group covers publishing, radio, and broadcast and cable television, including Disney/ABC Television and ESPN. The Parks and Resorts group encompasses 11 theme parks and 44 resorts around the world as well as a cruise line. Disney's Consumer Products and Interactive Media division offers entertainment on digital platforms, including console games and the Internet, and extends the business value of characters and story lines by operating Disney Stores and licensing its creations for use on toys, clothing, art objects, and a wide variety of other consumer goods.

The man in charge of keeping the magic alive through activities carried out by more than 195,000 employees is Disney's chief executive officer, Robert Iger. Iger and his executive team must define an overall direction and goal for the company and keep an eye on how well each business group is contributing

As you read this chapter, think about the challenge of drawing new revenue from remakes of old properties. What environmental factors would you be tracking to help determine whether this strategy will be financially successful?

to achievement of that goal. Iger does this by spotting opportunities for growth in the industry—hence the expansion into cable television and, more recently, into interactive entertainment and the revitalization of past movie hits. He also looks for characters and brands Disney can make more valuable because of its access to more channels. For example, Disney could afford to pay generously for Pixar and Marvel because those companies' characters generate sales in products as diverse as theme parks, video games, and sweatshirts.

Another coup for Iger was the purchase of ESPN, the most valuable cable channel in terms of revenues. Iger meets weekly with the heads of the business units. Although he keeps an eye on the company's overall direction, he gives each unit's head wide latitude. As the Walt Disney Studios division embarks on a years-long effort to revitalize some of its classic animated features, Iger and the company's management team will be watching closely to see whether this strategy is as effective abroad as it may be at home, or whether new environmental analyses suggest other avenues for the film company to explore.[1]

To imagine Disney—or any organization—navigating into the future without a plan is almost impossible. Planning describes what managers decide to do and how they intend to do it. It provides the framework, focus, and direction for meaningful action. This chapter examines the most important concepts and processes involved in planning and strategic management. By learning these concepts and reviewing the steps outlined, you will be on your way to understanding current approaches to strategic management in today's organizations.

An Overview of Planning Fundamentals

Although management pioneers such as Alfred Sloan of General Motors instituted formal planning processes, planning became a widespread management function only during the past few decades. Initially, larger organizations adopted formal planning, but now even small firms operated by aggressive, opportunistic entrepreneurs engage in formal planning.[2]

As discussed in Chapter 1, planning is the conscious, systematic process of deciding what goals and activities a person, group, work unit, or organization will pursue in the future. Planning is not an informal or haphazard response to a crisis; it is a purposeful effort that is directed and controlled by managers and often draws on the knowledge and experience of employees throughout the organization. Planning provides individuals and work units with a clear map to follow in their future activities; at the same time, this map should be flexible enough to allow for individual circumstances and changing conditions.

The Basic Planning Process

LO 1

Because planning is a decision process—you're deciding what to do and how to go about doing it—the important steps followed during formal planning are similar to the basic decision-making steps we discussed in Chapter 3. Exhibit 4.1 summarizes the similarities between decision making and planning—including the fact that both move not just in one direction but in a cycle. The outcomes of decisions and plans are evaluated, and if necessary, they are revised.

We now describe the basic planning process in more detail. Later in this chapter, we will discuss how managerial decisions and plans fit into the larger purposes of the organization— its strategy, mission, vision, and goals.

situational analysis

A process planners use to gather, interpret, and summarize all information relevant to the planning issue under consideration.

Step 1: Situational Analysis Planning begins with a **situational analysis**. Within their time and resource constraints, planners should gather, interpret, and summarize all information relevant to the planning issue in question. A thorough situational analysis studies past events, examines current conditions, and attempts to forecast future trends. It focuses on the internal forces at work in the organization or work unit and, consistent with the open-systems approach (see Chapter 2), examines influences from the external environment. The outcomes of this step are the identification and diagnosis of planning assumptions, issues, and problems.

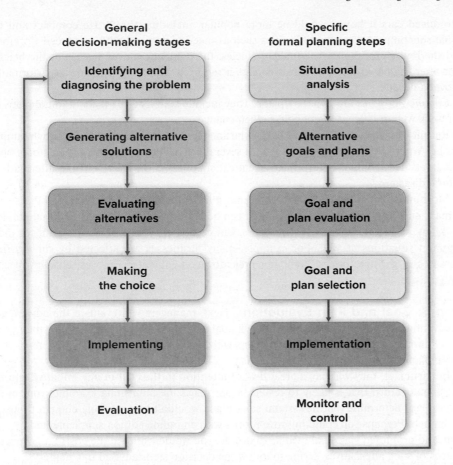

General decision-making stages

- Identifying and diagnosing the problem
- Generating alternative solutions
- Evaluating alternatives
- Making the choice
- Implementing
- Evaluation

Specific formal planning steps

- Situational analysis
- Alternative goals and plans
- Goal and plan evaluation
- Goal and plan selection
- Implementation
- Monitor and control

A thorough situational analysis will help you make important planning decisions. For example, if you are a manager in a magazine company considering the launch of a sports publication for the teen market, you should analyze the number of teens who subscribe to magazines, the appeal of the teen market to advertisers, your firm's ability to serve this market effectively, current economic conditions, the level of teen interest in sports, and any sports magazines already serving this market and their current sales. Such a detailed analysis will help you decide whether to proceed with the next step in your magazine launch.

Step 2: Alternative Goals and Plans   Based on the situational analysis, the planning process should generate alternative goals that could be pursued and the alternative plans that could be used to achieve those goals. This step should stress creativity and encourage managers and employees to think broadly about their work.

Once a range of alternatives has been developed, the merits of these different plans and goals will be evaluated. Continuing with our magazine publishing example, the alternatives you might want to consider include whether the magazine should be targeted at young men, young women, or both, and whether it should be sold mainly online, through subscriptions, or on newsstands.

Goals are the targets or ends the manager wants to reach. **Plans** are the actions or means the manager intends to use to achieve goals. At a minimum, plans should outline alternative actions for attaining each goal, the resources required to reach the goal through those means, and the obstacles that may develop.

After General Motors declared bankruptcy and borrowed billions from the U.S. government in 2009, management made plans for a return to profitability. The plans included reducing costs by producing fewer trucks, eliminating several brands, introducing smaller vehicles, keeping fewer vehicles in inventory, and closing hundreds of dealerships. GM also

goal

A target or end that management desires to reach.

plans

The actions or means managers intend to use to achieve organizational goals.

scenario

A narrative that describes a particular set of future conditions.

Panera Bread officially opened the fifth "Panera Cares Community Cafe" in Boston.

© ZUMA Press, Inc./Alamy Stock Photo

introduced cars it hoped would be more popular, including the Cruze compact and the Sonic subcompact. Despite difficulties such as meeting demand with a reduced workforce and the lower profitability of smaller vehicles, the company moved back into the black a year after the bankruptcy, and in two years it reported its strongest financial performance in over a decade.[3]

Contingency plans are "what if" plans. They include actions to be taken if initial plans do not work well or if events demand a sudden change.

Recent disasters have reminded many businesses how important contingency planning can be. Walmart in the United States has several crisis plans in place to keep stores open and stocked with food, water, pharmaceutical supplies, and so forth in the aftermath of natural disasters.[4]

Most major corporations have contingency plans in place to respond to major disasters—to make sure vital data are backed up and can be recovered, for instance, and that employees know what to do when a crisis occurs. But contingency plans are important for more common situations as well. For example, many businesses are affected by snowstorms, increases in gasoline prices, computer breakdowns, competitors' moves, changes in consumer tastes.

Step 3: Goal and Plan Evaluation   Next, managers will evaluate the advantages, disadvantages, and potential effects of each goal and plan. They must prioritize their goals and eliminate some of them. Also, managers will consider carefully the implications of alternative plans for meeting high-priority goals.

In particular, they will pay a great deal of attention to the cost of any initiative and the investment return that is likely to result. In our magazine publishing example, your evaluation might determine that newsstand sales alone wouldn't be profitable enough to justify the launch. Perhaps you could improve profits with an online edition supplemented by podcasts and promoted via social media. To decide, you would estimate the costs and expected returns of such alternatives, trying to follow the decision steps advised in Chapter 3.

Step 4: Goal and Plan Selection   Once managers have assessed goals and plans, they try to select the best. The evaluation process helps to identify trade-offs and decide what to do. For example, if your plan is to launch a number of new online publications, and you're trying to choose among them, you might weigh the different up-front investment each requires, the size of each market, which one fits best with your existing product line or company image, and so on. Experienced judgment always plays an important role in this process. However, as you will discover later in the chapter, relying on this alone may not be the best way to proceed.

Typically, the planning process leads to a written set of goals and plans that are appropriate and feasible for a particular set of circumstances. In some organizations, the alternative generation, evaluation, and selection steps generate planning **scenarios**, as discussed in Chapter 2. A different contingency plan is attached to each scenario. The manager pursues the goals and implements the plans associated with the most likely scenario. However, the manager will also be prepared to switch to another set of plans if the situation changes and another scenario becomes relevant. This approach helps the firm anticipate and manage problems and allows greater flexibility and responsiveness.

Social Enterprise

Novo Nordisk Monitors Progress with Its Triple Bottom Line

While some companies simply talk about operating in a more socially and environmentally conscious manner, others like Novo Nordisk put this philosophy into action. Headquartered in Denmark, Novo Nordisk is a leading global provider of diabetes care solutions. The firm follows a Triple Bottom Line (TBL: economic, societal, and environmental) strategy, meaning decisions are based on the belief that "a healthy economy, environment, and society are fundamental to long-term business success." Novo Nordisk's goal is to operate its business so that diabetes solutions benefit both the business and patients, while meeting societal expectations in the process. To ensure that the TBL philosophy would stick, Novo Nordisk took the uncommon step of incorporating it into its company bylaws.[5]

In addition to standard financial performance measures, Novo Nordisk monitors multiple short- and long-term goals within the social and environmental areas. The 2014 Integrated Annual Report Emphasizing Long-Term Thinking highlights the company's social and environmental performance:[6]

Novo Nordisk is breaking with traditional profit-only business models by setting and monitoring meaningful social and environmental goals. The TBL model seems to be working. With the diabetes drug market expected to reach $58 billion by 2018, the company is positioned to perform well financially while making a significant, multilevel impact.[7]

Questions

- According to Novo Nordisk, only four companies have incorporated Triple Bottom Line goals into their bylaws. Why do you think so few companies take this step?

- Assume you want your employer to consider adopting a Triple Bottom Line philosophy. How would you pitch the idea? With whom would you speak?

Social impact	• Diabetes care products reached 24.4 million people with the disease. • Over 3,000 new jobs were added in the company.

Environmental impact	• Continued to reduce CO_2 emissions from energy consumption for production (45 percent reduction since 2004). • Decreased energy consumption by 1 percent over previous year.

Step 5: Implementation   Once managers have selected the goals and plans, they must implement the plans designed to achieve the goals. Even the best plans are useless if they are not implemented properly. Managers and employees must understand the plan, have the resources to implement it, and be motivated to do so. As we mentioned earlier, employees usually are better informed, more committed, and more highly motivated when a goal or plan is one they helped develop.

Successful implementation requires a plan to be linked to other systems in the organization, particularly the budget and reward systems. If the manager does not have a budget with financial resources to execute the plan, the plan is probably doomed.

> Even the best strategy won't be effective without a strong focus on implementation.

Similarly, goal achievement must be linked to the organization's reward system. Many organizations use incentive programs to encourage employees to achieve goals and to implement plans properly. Commissions, salaries, promotions, bonuses, and other rewards are based on successful performance.

Lyft, the ride-sharing company, recently entered into a long-term strategic alliance with General Motors to build an "integrated network of on-demand autonomous vehicles in the U.S."[8] As part of the deal, GM bought a $500 million stake in Lyft, currently the second-largest ride-sharing service in the United States. The initial autonomous fleet will likely be comprised of the Chevrolet Bolt electric vehicle.[9]

The ultimate success of this alliance will hinge on the plan's successful implementation. According to GM executive Mike Ableson, success will require "the ability to engineer autonomous systems, to build self-driving vehicles in volume and to deploy them in a ride sharing fleet."[10]

Step 6: Monitor and Control   The sixth step in the formal planning process—monitoring and controlling—is essential. Without it, you will never know whether your plan is succeeding. Remember, planning works in a cycle; it is an ongoing, repetitive process. Managers must continually monitor the actual performance of their work units against the units' goals and plans. They also need to develop control systems to measure that performance and allow them to take corrective action when needed.

The nearby "Social Enterprise" box discusses how Novo Nordisk monitors progress toward achieving important organizational goals. We will discuss the important issue of control systems later in this chapter and in Chapter 16.

Levels of Planning

 In Chapter 1, you learned about the three major types of managers: top-level (strategic managers), middle-level (tactical managers), and frontline (operational managers). Because planning is an important management function, managers at all three levels use it. However, the scope and activities of the planning process often differ at different levels.

Strategic Planning

strategic planning

A set of procedures for making decisions about the organization's long-term goals and strategies; see also *planning*.

strategic goals

Major targets or end results relating to the organization's long-term survival, value, and growth.

strategy

A pattern of actions and resource allocations designed to achieve the organization's goals.

Strategic planning involves making decisions about the organization's long-term goals and strategies. Strategic plans have a strong external orientation and cover major portions of the organization. Senior executives are responsible for the development and execution of the strategic plan, although they usually do not implement the entire plan personally.

Strategic goals are major targets or results that relate to the long-term survival, value, and growth of the organization. Strategic managers—top-level managers—usually establish goals that reflect both effectiveness (providing appropriate outputs) and efficiency (a high ratio of outputs to inputs). Typical strategic goals include achieving growth, increasing market share, improving profitability, boosting return on investment, fostering both quantity and quality of outputs, increasing productivity, improving customer service, and contributing to society.

Organizations usually have a number of mutually reinforcing strategic goals. For example, a computer manufacturer may have as its strategic goals the launch of a specified number of new products in a particular time frame, of higher quality, with a targeted increase in market share. Each of these goals supports and contributes to the others.

A **strategy** is a pattern of actions and resource allocations designed to achieve the goals of the organization. As Exhibit 4.2 illustrates, an effective strategy provides a basis for answering five broad questions about how the organization will meet its objectives.[11] Former Procter & Gamble CEO A. G. Lafley and consultant Roger Martin emphasize that the answers to the "where" and "how" questions should be aimed at winning (question 3), which requires offering a better "value proposition" than the competition. Merely matching the competition, they say, is neither strategic nor a path to success.

For example, P&G gave new life to its Oil of Olay skin care brand by addressing the concerns of middle-aged women and by improving the active ingredients in its product. In addition, P&G used its strength in selling to mass-market retailers to persuade them to set up attractive displays for Oil of Olay. With the value proposition of an affordable, attractive,

EXHIBIT 4.2
Effective Strategies Answer
Five Questions

1. Where will we be active?

2. How will we get there (e.g., by increasing sales or acquiring another company)?

3. How will we win in the market (e.g., by keeping prices low or offering the best service)?

4. How fast will we move and in what sequence will we make changes?

5. How will we obtain financial returns (low costs or premium prices)?

EXHIBIT 4.2
Effective Strategies Answer
Five Questions

widely available product serving a previously ignored market segment, P&G could meet its strategic goal of leadership in the skin care market.[12]

In setting a strategy, managers try to match the organization's skills and resources to the opportunities in the external environment. Every organization has certain strengths and weaknesses; strategies should capitalize and help build on strengths that satisfy consumers and other key factors in the organization's external environment. Organizations also can implement strategies that change or influence the external environment, as discussed in Chapter 2.

Tactical and Operational Planning

Once the organization's strategic goals and plans are identified, they serve as the foundation for planning done by middle-level and frontline managers. As you can see in Exhibit 4.3, goals and plans become more specific and involve shorter periods of time as they move from the strategic level to the tactical level and then to the operational level. A strategic plan will typically have a time horizon of from three to seven years—but sometimes even decades, as with the successful plan to land a probe on Titan, Saturn's moon. Tactical plans may have a time horizon of a year or two, and operational plans may cover a period of months.

Tactical planning translates broad strategic goals and plans into specific goals and plans that are relevant to a particular unit in the organization—often a functional area like marketing or human resources. Tactical plans focus on the major actions a unit must take to fulfill its part of the strategic plan. For example, if the strategy calls for the rollout of a new product line, the tactical plan for the manufacturing unit might involve the design, testing, and installation of the equipment needed to produce the new line.

Operational planning identifies the specific procedures and processes required at lower levels of the organization. Frontline managers usually focus on routine tasks such as production runs, delivery schedules, and the human resources requirements described in later chapters.

The planning model we have been describing is a hierarchical one, with top-level strategies flowing down through the levels of the organization into more specific goals and plans and ever-shorter time frames. But the planning sequence is not as rigid as it sounds so far. As we will see later, managers at all levels may be involved in developing and contributing to the strategic plan.

Furthermore, lower-level managers may be making decisions that shape strategy, whether or not top executives realize it. The fast-casual food chain, Chipotle Mexican Grill, has experienced significant growth since its founding in Denver in 1993.[13] In 2016, however,

tactical planning

A set of procedures for translating broad strategic goals and plans into specific goals and plans that are relevant to a distinct portion of the organization, such as a functional area like marketing.

operational planning

The process of identifying the specific procedures and processes required at lower levels of the organization.

	Managerial Level	Level of Detail	Time Horizon
Strategic	Top	Low	Long (3–7 years)
Tactical	Middle	Medium	Medium (1–2 years)
Operational	Frontline	High	Short (<1 year)

EXHIBIT 4.3
Hierarchy of Goals and Plans

its strategy of "Food With Integrity" was negatively affected by food-related health outbreaks that sickened hundreds of customers.[14] At the store level, inconsistent employee management and food preparation practices contributed to its problems.[15] Steve Ells, CEO of Chipotle, then focused on restoring customer and investor confidence in the restaurant chain by correcting several of these operational-level issues: "The [food-safety] events exposed some weaknesses that our momentum in earlier years may have masked."[16]

The lesson for top managers is to make sure they are communicating strategy to all levels of the organization *and* paying attention to what is happening at all levels in the organization.

Aligning Tactical, Operational, and Strategic Planning

To be fully effective, the organization's strategic, tactical, and operational goals and plans must be aligned—that is, ideally they will be consistent, mutually supportive, and focused on achieving the common purpose and direction. Whole Foods Market, for example, links its tactical and operational planning directly to its strategic planning. The firm describes itself on its website as a mission-driven company that aims to set the standards for excellence for food retailers. The firm measures its success in fulfilling its vision by "customer satisfaction, team member excellence and happiness, return on capital investment, improvement in the state of the environment, and local and larger community support."

Whole Foods has operational goals that focus on high quality, freshness, taste, nutritional value, safety, and appearance.

©Rubberball/Mike Kemp/Getty Images RF

Whole Foods' strategic goal is "to sell the highest-quality products that also offer high value for our customers." Its operational goals focus on ingredients, freshness, taste, nutritional value, safety, and appearance that meet or exceed its customers' expectations, including guaranteeing product satisfaction. Tactical goals include store environments that are "inviting, fun, unique, informal, comfortable, attractive, nurturing, and educational" and are safe and inviting for employees.

One method for aligning the organization's strategic and operational goals is a *strategy map.* A strategy map is a tool for communicating strategic goals and helping employees to understand the parts they will play in helping to achieve them. The map illustrates the four key drivers (or "balanced scorecard") of a firm's long-term success: the skills of its people and their ability to grow and learn; the effectiveness of its internal processes; its ability to deliver value to customers; and ultimately its ability to grow its financial assets. The map shows how specific plans and goals in each area link to the others, and can generate real improvements in an organization's performance.

Exhibit 4.4 shows a strategy map and how the various goals of the organization relate to each other to create long-term value. As an example, let's assume that a company's primary financial goal is "to increase revenues by enhancing the value we offer to existing customers by making our prices the lowest available." (Target and Walmart might be good examples.) The company will have corresponding goals and plans to support that strategy. Its learning and growth goals might include bringing in the most efficient production technologies or work processes and training the staff to use them. These in turn will lead to the internal goals of improved production speed and lower cost, which in turn lead to the customer goal of competitive pricing, making the original financial goal feasible.

As a contrasting example, a financial strategy of revenue growth through new products might lead to people and technology goals that speed up product design, internal processes that lead to innovation, and a customer goal of perceived product leadership. Whatever the strategy, the strategy map can be used to develop the appropriate measures and standards in each operational area and to show how they all are linked.[17]

As you read the nearby "Management in Action: Progress Report," consider how well tactical, operational, and strategic planning are aligned at Walt Disney Company, particularly with regard to its Disney Interactive unit.

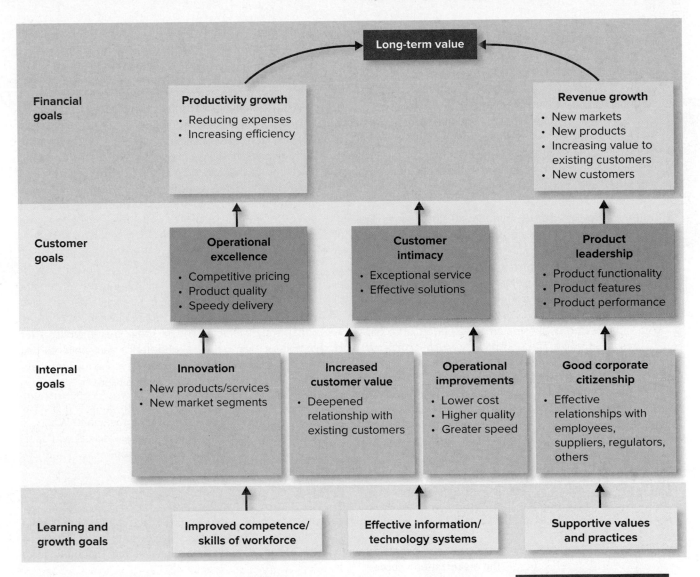

SOURCES: Adapted from Kaplan, R. and Norton, "Plotting Success with Strategy Maps," *Optimize,* February 2004, online; and Kaplan, R. and Norton, "Having Trouble with Your Strategy? Then Map It," *Harvard Business Review,* September–October 2000.

EXHIBIT 4.4

The Strategy Map: Creating Value by Aligning Goals

Strategic Planning

Strategic decision making is one of the most exciting topics in management today. Many organizations are changing the ways they develop and execute their strategic plans.

Traditionally, strategic planning emphasized a top-down approach. Senior executives and specialized planning units developed goals and plans for the entire organization. Tactical and operational managers received those goals and plans, and their own planning activities were limited to specific procedures and budgets for their units.

Over the years, managers and consulting firms created new analytical techniques and planning approaches, many of which have become essential for analyzing complex business challenges and competitive issues. In many instances, however, senior executives spent too much time with their planning specialists to the exclusion of managers in the rest of the organization. A gap often developed between strategic managers and tactical and operational

Management in Action

PLANNING A TURNAROUND FOR DISNEY INTERACTIVE

Walt Disney Company's corporate strategy is to lead in providing entertainment and information. The company's top ranking in the industry and recent profits of $13.5 billion suggest it is succeeding. Despite years of operating at a loss and recent layoffs, Disney Interactive Media is the fastest-growing business segment in the company's portfolio.

Disney Interactive, founded in 2008, has as its ambitious goal to "entertain kids, families, and Disney enthusiasts everywhere with world-class products that push the boundaries of technology and imagination." Its tactical plans include development of games for every digital media platform, including mobile and social media as well as the major gaming consoles.

Measured by those standards, performance has been less than stellar. The slow pace at which it crafts movies is unsuitable for game creation. The six years required to go from concept to release of Epic Mickey, created only for the Nintendo Wii, meant the release came in 2010, after that console's popularity had peaked. At one point, Disney ran six development studios creating games for consoles, which became a problem when players switched to online games and began using mobile devices.

A basic element of Disney's digital strategy has been its entertainment website, Disney.com, successor to the Go.com web portal, which closed in 2001. However, the company has struggled to make it relevant. One challenge is that the brand aims to serve the diverse interests of toddlers and parents as well as game players of all ages in between. Mostly, the site has focused on cross-promoting its entertainment and licensed merchandise.

James A. Pitaro, president of Disney Interactive Media, is pivoting the unit in two significant ways. First, it is focusing more on mobile gaming that can be played on tablets and smartphones. In Japan, the mobile game Tsumu Tsumu is a big hit with over 8 million downloads. And second, Disney Interactive Media seeks brand sponsors for its popular Disney Online website.[18] Pitaro believes that brand sponsors will generate more revenue than the website advertising model currently being used.

- At which steps of the planning process would you say Disney Interactive most needs improvement? Why?
- How can Pitaro ensure that strategic, tactical, and operational management are well aligned?

Bottom Line

New ideas from managers throughout the organization can contribute to a plan's effectiveness.

What experiences might give frontline managers ideas that top-level executives haven't considered?

strategic management

A process that involves managers from all parts of the organization in the formulation and implementation of strategic goals and strategies.

managers, and people throughout the organization became alienated and uncommitted to the organization's success.[19]

Today, however, senior executives increasingly are involving managers throughout the organization in the strategy formation process.[20] The problems just described and the rapidly changing environment of the past few decades years forced executives to look to all levels of the organization for ideas and innovations to make their firms more competitive. Although the CEO and other top managers continue to set the strategic direction, or "vision," for the organization, tactical and operational managers can provide valuable input to the organization's strategic plan. In some cases, these managers also have substantial autonomy to formulate or change their own plans. This authority increases flexibility and responsiveness, critical requirements for success today.

Because of these trends, firms often use the term *strategic management* to describe the process. **Strategic management** involves managers from all parts of the organization in the formulation and implementation of strategic goals and strategies. It integrates strategic planning and management into a single process. Strategic planning becomes an ongoing activity in which all managers are encouraged to think strategically and focus on long-term, externally oriented issues as well as short-term tactical and operational issues.

As shown in Exhibit 4.5, the strategic management process has six major components:

1. Establishing mission, vision, and goals.
2. Analyzing external opportunities and threats.
3. Analyzing internal strengths and weaknesses.

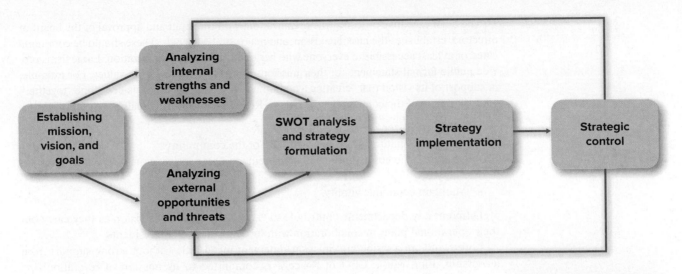

EXHIBIT 4.5
The Strategic Management Process

4. SWOT (strengths, weaknesses, opportunities, and threats) analysis and strategy formulation.
5. Strategy implementation.
6. Strategic control.

Because this process is a planning and decision process, it is similar to the planning framework discussed earlier. Although organizations may use different terms or emphasize different parts of the process, the components and concepts described in this section are found—explicitly or implicitly—in every organization. Even a small entrepreneurial firm can benefit from the kind of planning framework we describe here.

Step 1: Establishing Mission, Vision, and Goals

The first step in strategic planning is establishing a mission, a vision, and goals for the organization. The **mission** is a clear and concise expression of the basic purpose of the organization. It describes what the organization does, for whom it does it, its basic good or service, and its values. Here are some mission statements of firms that you will recognize:[21]

mission

An organization's basic purpose and scope of operations.

CVS: "We will be the easiest pharmacy retailer for customers to use."
Naked Juice: "Making the whole planet feel better. One bottle at a time."
Make-A-Wish: "We grant the wishes of children with life-threatening medical conditions to enrich the human experience with hope, strength and joy."

Smaller organizations, of course, may have missions that aren't as broad as these. For example, the local bar close to most campuses has this implicit mission: "to sell large quantities of inexpensive beer to college students in a noisily enjoyable environment."

While the mission describes the organization's ongoing purpose, the **strategic vision** points to the future—it provides a perspective on where the organization is headed and what it can become. Ideally, the vision statement clarifies the long-term direction of the company and its strategic intent.

strategic vision

The long-term direction and strategic intent of a company.

The most effective vision statements inspire organization members. They offer a worthwhile target for the entire organization to work together to achieve. Often these statements are not strictly financial because financial targets alone may not motivate all organization members. For example, NASA's Armstrong Flight Research Center focuses on the future of flight and exploration. Similarly, Habitat for Humanity envisions "a world where everyone has a decent place to live."

The strategic vision points to the future— where the organization is headed and what it can become.

The chief executive officer of the organization, with the input and approval of the board of directors, establishes the mission, vision, and major strategic goals. These should be communicated or at least accessible to everyone who has contact with the organization. Large firms provide public formal statements of their missions, visions, goals, and even values. For example, in support of its vision that "creating a community of good neighbors" is best done "together" with all sectors of the community, the City of Redmond established goals such as these:

- Enhance citizen engagement in city issues.
- Sustain the natural systems and beauty of the community.
- Sustain a safe community with a coherent, comprehensive, cohesive approach to safety.
- Maintain economic vitality.

Different city departments contribute to various aspects of this vision as they carry out their operational plans in collaboration with local businesses and residents.

Lofty words in a vision and mission statement mean little without strong support from leadership. Elon Musk, CEO of SpaceX, is committed to its mission of revolutionizing space technology to enable individuals to inhabit other planets. Musk, despite significant setbacks (for example, a rocket exploded on the launchpad) and a widely publicized missed deadline, continues to support this goal. Musk wants to help humans become a "spacefaring civilization." By the mid-2020s, Musk believes that humans will be traveling to Mars with the goal of establishing a colony on the Red planet.[22]

Where leadership is strong, statements of visions and goals clarify the organization's purpose to key constituencies outside the organization. They also help employees focus their talent, energy, and commitment in pursuit of organizational goals. When you consider employment with a firm, reviewing its statements of mission, vision, and goals is a good first step in determining whether the firm's purposes and values will be compatible with your own.

stakeholders

Groups and individuals who affect and are affected by the achievement of the organization's mission, goals, and strategies.

Step 2: Analyzing External Opportunities and Threats

The mission and vision drive the second component of the strategic management process: analyzing external environment. Effective strategic management depends on an accurate and thorough evaluation of the competitive environment and macroenvironment (Chapter 2).

The important activities in an environmental analysis include the ones shown in Exhibit 4.6. The analysis begins with an examination of the industry. Next, organizational stakeholders are examined. **Stakeholders** are groups and individuals who affect and are affected by the achievement of the organization's mission, goals, and strategies. These include buyers, suppliers, competitors, government and regulatory agencies, unions and employee groups, the financial community, owners and shareholders, and trade associations. The environmental analysis assesses these stakeholders and the ways they influence the organization.[23]

The environmental analysis also should examine other forces in the environment, such as economic conditions and technological factors. One critical task in environmental analysis is forecasting future trends. As noted in Chapter 2, forecasting techniques range from simple judgment to complex mathematical models that examine systematic relationships among many variables. Even simple quantitative techniques outperform the intuitive assessments of experts. Judgment is susceptible to bias, and managers have a limited ability to process information. Managers should use subjective judgments as inputs to quantitative models or when they confront new situations.

The difference between an opportunity and a threat depends in part on how a company positions itself

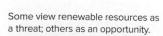

Some view renewable resources as a threat; others as an opportunity.

©Kim Steele/Getty Images RF

EXHIBIT 4.6
Environmental Analysis

Industry and Market Analysis

- **Industry profile:** major product lines and significant market segments in the industry.
- **Industry growth:** growth rates for the entire industry, growth rates for key market segments, projected changes in patterns of growth, and the determinants of growth.
- **Industry forces:** threat of new industry entrants, threat of substitutes, economic power of buyers, economic power of suppliers, and internal industry rivalry (recall Chapter 2).

Competitor Analysis

- **Competitor profile:** major competitors and their market shares.
- **Competitor analysis:** goals, strategies, strengths, and weaknesses of each major competitor.
- **Competitor advantages:** the degree to which industry competitors have differentiated their products or services or achieved cost leadership.

Political and Regulatory Analysis

- **Legislation and regulatory activities** and their effects on the industry.
- **Political activity:** the level of political activity that organizations and associations within the industry undertake (see Chapter 5).

Social Analysis

- **Social issues:** current and potential social issues and their effects on the industry.
- **Social interest groups:** consumer, environmental, and similar activist groups that attempt to influence the industry (see Chapters 5 and 6).

Human Resources Analysis

- **Labor issues:** key labor needs, shortages, opportunities, and problems confronting the industry (see Chapters 10 and 11).

Macroeconomic Analysis

- **Macroeconomic conditions:** economic factors that affect supply, demand, growth, competition, and profitability within the industry.

Technological Analysis

- **Technological factors:** scientific or technical methods that affect the industry, particularly recent and potential innovations (see Chapter 17).

strategically. For example, some states have required electric utilities to get a certain share of their power from renewable sources such as wind and solar energy rather than from fossil fuels, including coal, oil, and natural gas. This requirement poses a threat to utilities because the costs of fossil fuel energy are less, and customers demand low prices.

However, some companies see strategic opportunities in renewable power. Ocean Renewable Power Company (ORPC) has been developing technology that uses "ocean and river currents to produce clean, predictable electricity to power our homes and businesses while protecting the environment." At the Bay of Fundy on the border between Maine and Canada, ORPC operates the first commercial tidal power system in the United States. The system converts ocean energy to electricity that is then delivered to the public electricity grid. ORPC's goal is to increase output to the point where the system will power approximately 2,000 homes and businesses in Maine with clean tidal energy. ORPC has similar renewable energy generation projects under way in Alaska and Nova Scotia.[24]

Similarly, overflowing landfills are an expensive challenge for many municipalities, but a growing number are seeing an opportunity in the form of energy generation. As garbage decomposes, it produces methane gas, which is used as a fuel to power plants and

The Digital World

Corporations must plan their strategies and analyze external opportunities and threats. Yet technology and online communication have changed the picture and complicated this process. Few in their respective industries realized what Netflix would do to Blockbuster, what Amazon would do to bookstores, what Uber would do to taxi services, or what Airbnb would do to the hotel industry.

Online companies can move fast because they often have the ability to scale exponentially compared to brick-and-mortar businesses. Analysts and strategy makers today bear this in mind as they survey the scene. Despite the most thorough industry and market analysis, a business may be surprised to find new online competitors that didn't exist a year ago.

Many companies are closely watching developments in 3D printing. In the automotive field, for example, it will become possible to diagnose an engine problem, send the digital diagnosis to the technician, send specs for the car's make and model, and print the needed part by the time the car has been towed.

Companies must plan for a dynamic digital future in which their inventory, supply-chain, vendors, timing, and infrastructure issues will evolve quickly. For those able to see the strategic value of new business models, there will be many new opportunities.

manufacturing facilities. The United States Environmental Protection Agency (EPA) formed an outreach program that partners with stakeholders—communities, landfill owners, and utilities—which by 2016 had over 650 methane-to-energy conversion projects.[25]

Thinking creatively helps managers see opportunities in the face of serious threats. For Farif Ali Abood, who opened a shop to make commercial signs in his hometown of Najaf, Iraq, the difficulties included sporadic electrical service, lack of funds to borrow, and even occasional sniper fire in the area. Despite these challenges, Abood kept the business running by using a generator when the power goes out. As conditions in the city stabilized, business grew enough for Abood to hire several full-time employees and earn a modest profit.[26] Those who, like Abood, best serve customer needs in difficult times will earn customer loyalty and longer-term business relationships.

Step 3: Analyzing Internal Strengths and Weaknesses

As managers conduct an external analysis, they also assess the strengths and weaknesses of major functional areas inside their organization. Exhibit 4.7 lists some of the major components of this internal resource analysis. For example, is your firm strong enough financially to handle the lengthy and costly investment new projects often require? Can your existing staff carry out its part of the plan, or do you need to provide new training or hire new people? Internal analysis gives strategic decision makers an inventory of the organization's existing functions, skills, and resources as well as its overall performance level. Many of your other business courses will prepare you to conduct a detailed internal analysis.

LO 4

resources

Inputs to a system that can enhance performance.

Resources and Core Capabilities   Strategic planning has been strongly influenced in recent years by a focus on internal resources. **Resources** are inputs to production (recall systems theory) that can be accumulated over time to enhance the performance of a firm.

Resources can take many forms, but they tend to fall into two broad categories: (1) tangible assets such as real estate, production facilities, raw materials, and so on; and (2) intangible assets such as company reputation, culture, technical knowledge, and patents as well as accumulated learning and experience. The Walt Disney Company, for example, has based its strategic plan on combinations of tangible assets (e.g., hotels and theme parks) and intangible assets (brand recognition, talented craftspeople, culture focused on customer service).[27]

Internal analysis provides a clearer understanding of how a company can compete through its resources. Resources provide competitive advantage only under certain circumstances. First, the resource provides advantage if it is instrumental in creating customer value—increasing the benefits customers derive from a good or service relative to the costs they incur.[28] For example, Amazon's powerful search technology, its ability to

EXHIBIT 4.7
Internal Resource Analysis

Financial Analysis
Examines financial strengths and weaknesses through financial statements such as a balance sheet and an income statement, and compares trends to historical and industry figures (see Chapter 18).
Marketing Audit
Examines strengths and weaknesses of major marketing activities and identifies markets, key market segments, and the competitive position (market share) within key markets.
Operations Analysis
Examines the strengths and weaknesses of the manufacturing, production, or service delivery activities of the organization (see Chapters 9, 16, and 17).
Other Internal Resource Analyses
Examines, as necessary and appropriate, the strengths and weaknesses of other organizational activities, such as research and development (product and process), management information systems, engineering, and purchasing.
Human Resources Assessment
Examines strengths and weaknesses of all levels of management and employees and focuses on key human resources activities, including recruitment, selection, placement, training, labor (union) relationships, compensation, promotion, appraisal, quality of work life, and human resources planning (see Chapters 10 and 11).

track customer preferences, its ability to offer personalized recommendations each time its site is accessed, and its quick product delivery system are valuable resources that enhance Amazon's competitiveness.

Second, resources are a source of advantage if they are rare and not equally available to all competitors. Even for extremely valuable resources, if all competitors have equal access, the resource cannot provide competitive advantage. For companies such as W.L. Gore, Intel, Johnson & Johnson, 3M, Dow Chemical, and others, patented formulas are both rare and valuable.

Third, resources provide competitive advantage if they are difficult to imitate. Online retailer Zappos.com seeks competitive advantage via service that makes customers say "Wow!" The company gives new customer service employees seven weeks of training and empowers them to do whatever it takes to delight a customer, from spending hours patiently on the phone, issuing refunds, or sending packages of free cookies. Zappos frees reps from using scripted replies, promotes positive relationships with colleagues through mentoring programs and fun activities, and provides on-site coaching to help employees achieve their career and personal goals.[29] This highly motivating combination of training, socializing, and job design is harder to imitate than just a free return policy.[30]

As shown in Exhibit 4.8, when resources are valuable, rare, inimitable, and organized, they comprise a company's core capabilities. A **core capability** (also referred to as "competence") is something a company does especially well relative to its competitors. BMW has a core competence in high-performance engine design and manufacturing; Chik-fil-A provides a consistently pleasant dining experience for its customers; and Activision Blizzard has a core competence in creating games for video gaming consoles. As in these examples, a core competence typically refers to a set of skills or expertise in some activity rather than physical or financial assets.

Benchmarking   To assess and improve performance, some companies use benchmarking, the process of assessing

Bottom Line

Amazon provides value via speed, low cost, and excellent customer service. *What are some resources Amazon needs to deliver these benefits?*

core capability

A unique skill and/or knowledge an organization possesses that gives it an edge over competitors.

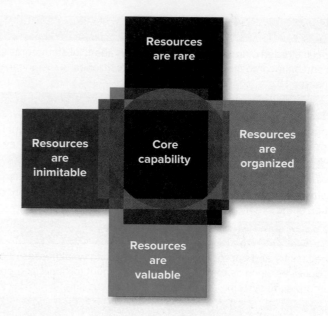

how well one company's basic functions and skills compare with those of another company or set of companies. As introduced in Chapter 2, the goal of benchmarking is to understand the "best practices" of other firms thoroughly and to undertake actions to achieve lower costs and better performance.

According to consulting firm Accenture, benchmarking consists of four stages:[31]

1. Decide what needs to be measured and which metrics will be used.
2. Collect and validate the data; compile initial findings.
3. Assess initial findings to see if additional data need to be collected.
4. Analyze results and make final recommendations to key stakeholders.

Benchmarking programs have helped many companies, such as Ford, Corning, Hewlett-Packard, Xerox, and Anheuser-Busch, make great strides in eliminating inefficiencies and improving competitiveness.

Benchmarking may be of limited help when it only helps a company perform as well as its competitors; strategic management ultimately is about surpassing those companies. Companies can gain additional advantage via *internal* benchmarking: comparing different internal units against one another to disseminate the company's best practices throughout the organization.

AXA Canada, an insurance company, used internal benchmarking to compare results among its regions. However, in a country as vast as Canada, the differences among regions were so great that performance couldn't really be compared. More energy went to arguing about the numbers than looking for ways to close performance gaps. The most success came from gathering performance data from several insurance companies, analyzing it, and reporting on areas of strength and weakness. Using this benchmarking information, AXA Canada found areas where it could operate more efficiently by applying other companies' practices. The company uses the benchmarking data primarily for cutting costs and identifying potential new markets.[32]

Step 4: SWOT Analysis and Strategy Formulation

Once managers have analyzed the external environment and internal organizational resources, they have the information they need to assess the organization's strengths, weaknesses, opportunities, and threats. Such an assessment is called a **SWOT analysis**.

Strengths and weaknesses refer to internal resources. For example, an organization's strengths might include skilled management, positive cash flow, and well-known and highly regarded brands. Weaknesses might be lack of spare production capacity and the absence of reliable suppliers.

Bottom Line

Benchmarking can identify best practices both outside and inside your company. *In some famous benchmarking examples, businesses learned from pit crews for race car teams. What kinds of bottom-line practices could that industry demonstrate?*

SWOT analysis

A comparison of strengths, weaknesses, opportunities, and threats that helps executives formulate strategy.

Opportunities and threats arise in the macroenvironment and competitive environment. Examples of opportunities are a new technology that could make the supply chain more efficient, and an underserved market niche. Threats could include the possibility that competitors will enter the underserved niche if it is shown to be profitable.

SWOT analysis helps managers summarize the relevant, important facts from their external and internal analyses. Based on this summary, they can identify the primary and secondary strategic issues their organization faces. The managers then formulate a strategy that will use the SWOT analysis to pursue opportunities by capitalizing on the organization's strengths, neutralizing its weaknesses, and countering potential threats.

For example, David Handmaker enjoyed several years of unfettered growth since opening his printing company, Next Day Flyers, in Los Angeles. However, over time he noticed that his competitors were more adept at finding and serving online customers. Handmaker needed a plan to restore healthy business growth by migrating parts of his marketing and printing services online before it was too late. But Next Day Flyers originally aimed at local customers, which raised questions about whether the company could serve the needs of geographically dispersed customers.

Handmaker and his team needed to analyze what the firm did well and how it needed to improve relative to the competitive printing marketplace. Exhibit 4.9 summarizes this example in a format commonly used for a basic SWOT analysis. The company developed a strategy calling for it to hire talent with the skills, knowledge, and experience to help Next Day Flyers establish a professional presence on the web, including simple online ordering; free online design services; free printing templates; blog with design and marketing tips; and customer support by phone, e-mail, and live chat.[33]

As a company is formulating strategy, its competitors are, too. Therefore the strategy management process must keep evolving. The more uncertainty that exists in the external environment,

EXHIBIT 4.9

Sample SWOT Analysis: Next Day Flyers

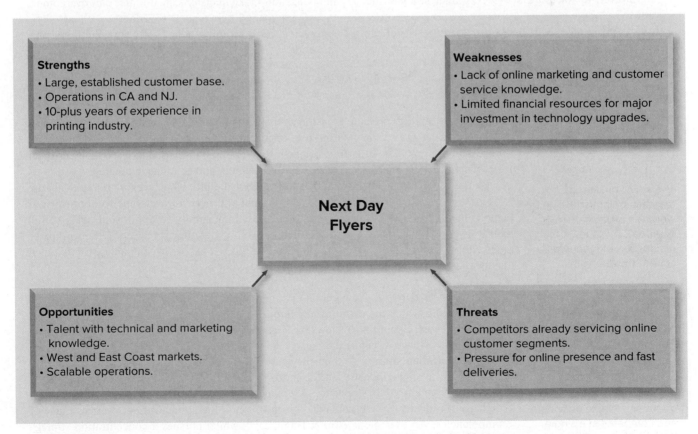

Strengths
- Large, established customer base.
- Operations in CA and NJ.
- 10-plus years of experience in printing industry.

Weaknesses
- Lack of online marketing and customer service knowledge.
- Limited financial resources for major investment in technology upgrades.

Next Day Flyers

Opportunities
- Talent with technical and marketing knowledge.
- West and East Coast markets.
- Scalable operations.

Threats
- Competitors already servicing online customer segments.
- Pressure for online presence and fast deliveries.

SOURCES: Based on information from Myers, R., "That Sounds Like a Plan," *Inc.*, no. 36 (2014), pp. 90–92; and Next Day Flyers company website, "About Next Day Flyers," http://www.nextdayflyers.com.

Multiple Generations at Work

Perceived Strengths and Weaknesses of Each Generation

Ernst & Young, the accounting and consulting firm, recently asked managers and employees across multiple generations and industries to describe the strengths and weaknesses commonly associated with different generational cohorts. The following exhibit includes some of the findings:

Baby Boomers

Strengths
- *Loyal*
- *Mentoring others*
- *Hardworking*

Weaknesses
- *Slower to adapt to change and collaborate with others*

Gen Xers

Strengths
- *Revenue generators*
- *Adaptable*
- *Problem-solvers*

Weaknesses
- *Displaying executive presence and being cost effective*

Millennials

Strengths
- *Tech savvy*
- *Skilled at leveraging social media*
- *Enthusiastic*

Weaknesses
- *Team player and hardworking*

The results show respondents' perceptions of the work-related strengths and weaknesses of different generations. Of course, caution is advised when generalizing to all members of any group, including generational cohorts.

However, if you do a self-SWOT analysis, you may want to compare your self-assessment to the stereotypes this study revealed. This may prove useful for overcoming or leveraging stereotypes. Millennials can think about how to counter the perceived weaknesses of not being hardworking team players. Gen Xers who want to advance into executive positions may want to observe how current executives dress, communicate, plan, work in teams, and make decisions. A Boomer can overcome the stereotype of being slow to adapt to change by embracing and becoming adept with new technologies at work.[34]

---

corporate strategy

The set of businesses, markets, or industries in which an organization competes and the distribution of resources among those entities.

concentration

A strategy employed for an organization that operates a single business and competes in a single industry.

the more the strategy needs to focus on strengthening internal capabilities through practices such as seeking new company expertise, opportunistic knowledge sharing, and continuous process improvement.[35] To keep it competitive, Next Day Flyers identified online customer engagement as the major strategy it needed to commit to and continue to develop.

By the way, you might find a self-SWOT analysis helpful when seeking a job. What are you particularly good at? What weaknesses might you need to overcome to improve your employment chances? What firms offer the best opportunity to apply your skills to full advantage? Who are your competitors? How is your generation perceived in the workplace (see the nearby "Multiple Generations at Work" box)? As with companies, this kind of analysis can lead to a plan of action that improves your own effectiveness.

 Corporate Strategy   A **corporate strategy** identifies the set of businesses, markets, or industries in which the organization competes and the distribution of resources among those businesses. Exhibit 4.10 shows basic alternatives for a corporate strategy that range from very specialized to highly diverse.

A **concentration** strategy (the purple center of the figure) focuses on a single business competing in a single industry. In the food retailing industry, Kroger, Safeway, and A&P all pursue concentration strategies. A company pursues concentration strategies when (perceived) industry growth potential is high or when the company has a narrow range of competencies. An example is Arm & Hammer™, which pursues a concentration strategy by making baking soda for home personal care application; the strategy has enabled the Church & Dwight Company to operate successfully for more than 165 years.

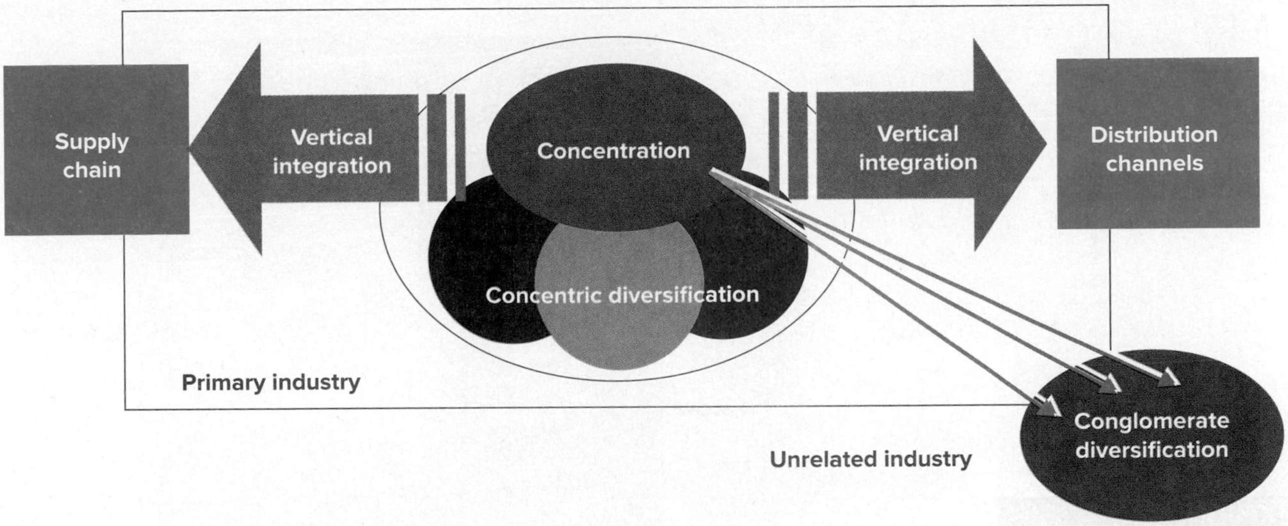

EXHIBIT 4.10
Summary of Corporate Strategies

vertical integration

The acquisition or development of new businesses that produce parts or components of the organization's product.

concentric diversification

A strategy used to add new businesses that produce related products or are involved in related markets and activities.

conglomerate diversification

A strategy used to add new businesses that produce unrelated products or are involved in unrelated markets and activities.

A **vertical integration** strategy (horizontal arrows in the figure) involves expanding the company's domain to include supplier and distributors. At one time, Henry Ford had fully integrated his company from the ore mines needed to make steel all the way to the showrooms where his cars were sold. Vertical integration generally is used to reduce costs associated with suppliers or distributors and to reduce the uncertainties created by unpredictable business relationships.

A strategy of **concentric diversification** (expanded center of the figure) moves into new but related businesses. William Marriott expanded his original restaurant business outside Washington, DC, by moving into airline catering, hotels, and fast food. Each of these businesses within the hospitality industry is related in terms of the services it provides, the skills necessary for success, and the customers it attracts. Often companies such as Marriott pursue a strategy of concentric diversification to take advantage of their strengths in one business to gain advantage in another. Because the businesses are related, the products, markets, technologies, or capabilities used in one business can be transferred to another.

Success in a concentric diversification strategy requires adequate management and other resources for operating more than one business. Guitar maker C. F. Martin once tried expanding through purchases of other instrument companies, but management was stretched too thin to run them well. The company divested the acquisitions and returned to its concentration strategy.[36]

In contrast to concentric diversification, **conglomerate diversification** (multiple arrows pointing outside the primary industry) is a corporate strategy of expansion into unrelated businesses. For example, General Electric Corporation diversified from its original base in electrical and home appliance products into health, finance, insurance, truck and air transportation, and media with its ownership of NBC (now owned with Comcast). Typically, companies pursue a conglomerate diversification strategy to minimize risks due to market fluctuations in one industry.

The diversified businesses of an organization are sometimes called its business *portfolio*. One of the most popular techniques for analyzing a corporation's strategy for managing its portfolio is the BCG matrix, developed by the Boston Consulting Group. Exhibit 4.11 shows the BCG matrix. Each business in the corporation is plotted on the matrix based on the growth rate of its market and the relative strength of its competitive position in that market (market share). To convey additional information visually, each business can be represented by a circle whose size indicates its contribution to corporate revenues.

In the BCG matrix, high-growth, weak-competitive-position businesses are called *question marks*. They require substantial investment to improve their position; otherwise divestiture is recommended. High-growth, strong-competitive-position businesses are the *stars*. These businesses require heavy investment, but their strong position allows them to generate the needed revenues.

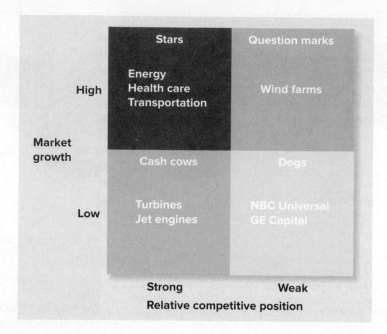

EXHIBIT 4.11

Mapping GE's Business Units and Product Lines to the BCG Matrix

Low-growth, strong-competitive-position businesses are called *cash cows*. These businesses generate revenues in excess of their investment needs and therefore fund other businesses. Finally, low-growth, weak-competitive-position businesses are the *dogs*. Once any remaining revenues from these businesses are realized, the businesses are divested.

The BCG matrix alone is not a substitute for management judgment, creativity, insight, or leadership. But it is a well-known tool that, along with others, can help top corporate executives and the individual business managers understand their business portfolios and strategic options.[37] This approach helps companies like General Electric that need to weigh the relative merits of many business units and product lines.

When GE struggled in some of its widely diversified businesses, the company refocused on its strength as a manufacturer, targeting three industries: energy, health care, and transportation. Not only do these industries offer significant growth potential, but GE already dominates the markets for electric turbines and jet engines. Therefore, besides selling off NBC Universal and GE Capital, GE acquired wind farms and blade manufacturers, and 3D printing companies to manufacture aircraft components.[38]

Trends in Corporate Strategy   Corporate America periodically is swept by waves of mergers and acquisitions (M&As). The targets chosen for mergers and acquisitions depend on the corporate strategy of either concentrating or diversifying the business portfolio.

Many recent deals were aimed at helping companies expand their market share and product offerings within related industries. For example, two telecommunication behemoths, AT&T and Time Warner, merged recently to create a firm with considerable influence in the entertainment space, including cable-TV, broadband Internet, satellite TV, and cellular-data networks.[39]

The value of implementing a more diversified corporate strategy depends on circumstances. Many argue that unrelated diversification hurts a company more often than it helps. Many diversified companies have sold their peripheral businesses so they could concentrate on a more focused portfolio. In contrast, the diversification efforts of an organization competing in a slow-growth, mature, or threatened industry often are applauded.

Business Strategy   Once corporate strategies are determined, managers must determine how they will compete in each business area. **Business strategy** defines the major actions by which an organization builds and strengthens its competitive position. A business can gain competitive advantage using one of two generic business strategies: low cost and differentiation.[40]

Businesses using a **low-cost strategy** attempt to be efficient and to offer standard, no-frills products. Walmart Stores uses the power of its giant size to negotiate favorable prices from

---

Bottom Line

Companies that integrate vertically often do so to reduce their costs.
Why might buying from a division of your company be less costly than buying on the open market?

---

business strategy

The major actions by which a business competes in a particular industry or market.

---

low-cost strategy

A strategy an organization uses to build competitive advantage by being efficient and offering a standard, no-frills product.

suppliers, enabling it to sell at prices below those of most competing retailers. Its size allows it to provide goods and services more efficiently (at lower cost), which leads to higher sales. market share, and profits. Recently, when gasoline prices soared, the company promoted its stores as a place where consumers can save on transportation costs by purchasing everything they need at low prices in one trip.[41]

Companies that succeed with a low-cost strategy often are large and take advantage of economies of scale in production or distribution. An organization using this strategy generally must be the cost leader in its industry or market segment. However, even a cost leader must offer a product that is acceptable to customers compared with competitors' products.

Alternatively, an organization may pursue a **differentiation strategy**. With a differentiation strategy, a company attempts to be unique in its industry or market segment along some dimensions (other than cost) that customers value. This unique or differentiated position within the industry often is based on high product quality, excellent marketing and distribution, or superior service. Nordstrom's well-known commitment to outstanding, personalized customer service in the retail apparel industry is an excellent example of a differentiation strategy.

Whatever strategy managers adopt, the most effective strategy is one that competitors are unwilling or unable to imitate. If the organization's strategic plan is one that can easily be adopted by industry competitors, it will yield only short-term advantage. For example, a strategy to gain market share by being the first to offer an innovative product may or may not succeed, depending in part on competitive responses. In some industries, technologies advance so fast that the first company to provide a new product is quickly challenged by later entrants offering superior products.[42]

Functional Strategy

The final step in strategy formulation is to establish the major functional strategies. **Functional strategies** are implemented by each functional area of the organization to support the business strategy. The typical functional areas include production, human resources, marketing and sales, research and development, finance, and distribution.

For example, Bloomin' Brands, the parent company of restaurant chains Outback Steakhouse, Bonefish Grill, Carrabba's Italian Grill, and Fleming's Prime Steakhouse, set a business strategy with targets for aggressive growth and greater efficiency built on the chains' reputation for offering good food at affordable prices. To achieve this, functional strategies included improving employee retention through enhanced training and development, adding innovative items to menus, and launching a multi-brand loyalty program.[43]

Functional strategies typically are developed by functional managers with input and approval from the executives responsible for business strategy. Senior strategic decision makers review the functional strategies to ensure that each major department is operating consistently with the business strategies. For example, even if they saved money, automated production techniques would not be appropriate for a piano company like Steinway, whose products are strategically positioned (and priced) as high-quality and handcrafted.

At companies that compete based on product innovation, strategies for the research and development functions are especially critical. Based on the previous recession, GE committed itself to an R&D strategy of maintaining high budgets even when sales growth slowed.[44] The company invests over $10 billion each year in R&D expenditures.[45]

Step 5: Strategy Implementation

As with any plan, simply formulating a good strategy is not enough. Strategic managers also must ensure that the new strategies are implemented effectively and efficiently. The best executives and strategy consultants realize that clever planning techniques and a good strategy do not guarantee success.

---

differentiation strategy

A strategy an organization uses to build competitive advantage by being unique in its industry or market segment along one or more dimensions.

Bottom Line
A high-quality strategy is often more difficult for competitors to imitate. *What would be hard about imitating Nordstrom's strategy for top-quality service?*

---

functional strategies

Strategies implemented by each functional area of the organization to support the organization's business strategy.

Employees at Bonefish Grill strive to meet the company's business strategy to provide good food at reasonable cost.

©The Washington Post/Getty Images

Many organizations are extending more participative strategic management process to implementation. Managers at all levels are involved with formulating strategy and identifying and executing ways to implement it. Senior executives still may oversee the implementation process, but they are placing responsibility and authority in the hands of others.

In general, strategy implementation involves these steps:

Step 1: Define strategic tasks. Articulate in simple language what a particular unit must do to create or sustain a competitive advantage. Define strategic tasks to help employees understand how they contribute.

Step 2: Assess organization capabilities. Evaluate the organization's ability to implement the strategic tasks. A task force might interview employees and managers to identify issues that help or hinder implementation. Then the results are summarized for top management.

Step 3: Develop an implementation agenda. Management decides how it will change its own activities and procedures; what skills and individuals are needed in key roles; and what structures, measures, information, and rewards can best support the needed actions.

Step 4: Implement. The top management team, the employee task force, and others develop the implementation plan. The top management team monitors progress. The task force continues its work by providing feedback about how others in the organization are responding to the changes.

strategic control system

A system designed to support managers in evaluating the organization's progress regarding its strategy and, when discrepancies exist, taking corrective action.

This process, though straightforward, does not always go smoothly. Exhibit 4.12 shows six barriers to strategy implementation and provides some key principles for overcoming these silent killers. By paying closer attention to the processes by which strategies are implemented, executives, managers, and employees can make sure that strategic plans are actually carried out.[46]

Step 6: Strategic Control

The final component of the strategic management process is strategic control. A **strategic control system** helps managers evaluate the organization's progress with its strategy and, when

EXHIBIT 4.12   Attacking the Six Barriers to Strategy Implementation

	Change starts with the leader
The Silent Killers	**Beating the Silent Killers**
Top-down or laissez-faire senior management style	The CEO creates a partnership with the top team and lower levels to develop a compelling business direction, create an enabling organizational context, and delegate authority to clearly accountable individuals and teams.
Unclear strategy and conflicting priorities	The top team, as a group, develops a statement of strategy and priorities that members are willing to stand behind.
An ineffective senior management team	Involve the top team in all steps in the change process so that its effectiveness is challenged and developed.
Poor vertical communication	Establish an honest, fact-based dialog with lower levels about the new strategy and the barriers to implementing it.
Poor coordination across functions, businesses, or borders	Define a set of businesswide initiatives and new organizational roles and responsibilities that require "the right people to work together on the right things in the right way to implement the strategy."
Inadequate down-the-line leadership skills and development	Lower-level managers develop skills through newly created opportunities to lead change and drive key business initiatives. They are supported with just-in-time coaching, training, and targeted recruitment. Those who still are not able to make the grade must be replaced.

SOURCE: Beer, M. and Eisenstat, R. A., "The Silent Killers of Strategy Implementation and Learning Barriers," *MIT Sloan Management Review* 4, no. 4 (Summer 2000), pp. 29–40.

discrepancies exist, identify needed corrective actions. The system must encourage efficient operations that are consistent with the plan while allowing flexibility to adapt to changing conditions.

Most strategic control systems include a budget to monitor and control major financial expenditures. As a first-time manager, you are likely to work with your work unit's budget—a key aspect of your organization's strategic plan. Your executive team may give you budget assumptions and targets for your area, reflecting your part in the overall plan, and you may be asked to revise your budget once all the budgets in your organization have been consolidated and reviewed.

The dual responsibilities of a control system—efficiency and flexibility—often seem contradictory with respect to budgets. The budget usually establishes spending limits, but changing conditions or the need for innovation may require different financial commitments during the period. To solve this dilemma, some companies use two budgets: strategic and operational. For example, managers at Texas Instruments control two budgets under the OST (objectives–strategies–tactics) system. The strategic budget creates and maintains long-term effectiveness, and the operational budget is tightly monitored to achieve short-term efficiencies.

The broader topic of control, including budgets in particular, is discussed in more detail in Chapter 16. In "Management in Action: Onward," consider the significance of controls to Disney's decisions about its portfolio of businesses.

> ## Bottom Line
> Firms that follow low-cost strategies exert downward pressure on competitors' prices.
> *How can managers compete against a low-cost strategy so that their firm can continue to charge higher prices for its goods or services?*

Management in Action

WALT DISNEY COMPANY'S STRATEGY UNDER ROBERT IGER

Reportedly, Walt Disney Company's mission statement once was "Make people happy." The corporate website now offers a longer statement: "to be one of the world's leading producers and providers of entertainment and information, using its portfolio of brands to differentiate its content, services and consumer products." The statement adds, "The company's primary financial goals are to maximize earnings and cash flow, and to allocate capital toward growth initiatives that will drive long-term shareholder value."

In pursuit of this two-part objective, Disney has made decisions about its large portfolio of businesses. As it repositions itself for a global marketplace and a social, mobile Internet, it continues making strategic decisions about where to invest and what to divest.

Disney's largest sources of revenues are cable networks and theme parks, with cable providing by far the greatest profits. ESPN alone delivers 45 percent of operating income. Recently, Disney entered into a media rights contract with the NFL and a deal to air NBA games on ESPN and ABC. The company has rolled out apps based on WatchESPN to let cable subscribers watch programming on mobile devices. In the theme park arena, profitability during a sluggish economy lets Disney build when construction costs are low, so it has renovated Disney California Adventure, expanded Hong Kong Disneyland, and added a cruise ship to its fleet. In June 2016, Disney opened a theme park in Shanghai, China.

Disney Interactive is by far the smallest business unit in terms of revenues, and has not been profitable. Still, it matters because children are spending ever more time online, and winning the hearts of children has been the basis for the company's growth. Disney Interactive will continue to engage fans through mobile games like Frozen Free Fall and Disney Tsum Tsum, as well as connect with parents via Disney.com.

Disney's movie studios, though a relatively small unit, are a core business. To increase the brand's appeal with teenage boys, this unit purchased Lucasfilm, producer of *Star Wars*. Disney also signed a deal giving Netflix the right to stream movies soon after release on DVD, when cable channels air movies. Dealing directly with Netflix signals that movie streaming is an important trend for Disney. And Disney created Keychest, which gives buyers of its DVDs and Blu-ray discs automatic access to streamed versions.

China is a huge growth market, so Iger is heavily investing in a new theme park, Shanghai Disney. The venture is risky; Disney's resort in Hong Kong is just breaking even after a 2005 opening. But it offers access to a billion consumers, and the effort is supported by use of the Disney Channel to build consumer relationships in China and 166 other countries.[47]

- How clear is Walt Disney Company's mission? How well does its strategy support the mission?
- In the BCG matrix (see again Exhibit 4.11), where would you place Disney's main businesses? How well is Disney matching its strategic moves to the businesses' positions in the matrix?

MANAGER'S BRIEF

PROGRESS REPORT

ONWARD

KEY TERMS

business strategy, p. 122

concentration, p. 120

concentric diversification, p. 121

conglomerate diversification, p. 121

core capability, p. 117

corporate strategy, p. 120

differentiation strategy, p. 123

functional strategies, p. 123

goal, p. 105

low-cost strategy, p. 122

mission, p. 113

operational planning, p. 109

plans, p. 105

resources, p. 116

scenario, p. 106

situational analysis, p. 104

stakeholders, p. 114

strategic control system, p. 124

strategic goals, p. 108

strategic management, p. 112

strategic planning, p. 108

strategic vision, p. 113

strategy, p. 108

SWOT analysis, p. 118

tactical planning, p. 109

vertical integration, p. 121

RETAINING WHAT YOU LEARNED

In Chapter 4, you learned that managerial planning is a conscious, systematic process of deciding which goals and activities the organization will pursue in the future. Directed and controlled by managers, this purposeful effort should draw on the experience and knowledge of employees throughout the organization. As shown in Exhibit 4.1, the Chapter 3 decision-making model links closely to the formal planning process. Strategic planning should be integrated with tactical and operational planning. Before formulating a strategy, managers should analyze the external environment and internal resources, including core capabilities. A firm can concentrate narrowly or broaden its strategy via related or unrelated diversification. Companies can achieve competitive advantage by being unique and differentiated, or by focusing on cost via efficiency and lower prices. Effective implementation is critical to the success of any strategy.

EXHIBIT 4.1 (revisited)
Decision-Making Stages (Chapter 3) and
Formal Planning Steps (Chapter 4)

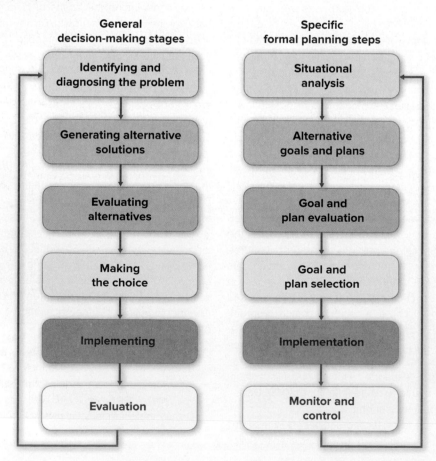

LO 1 Summarize the basic steps in any planning process.

- The planning process begins with a situation analysis of the external and internal forces affecting the organization. This examination helps identify and diagnose issues and problems and can bring to the surface alternative goals and plans for the firm.
- The advantages and disadvantages of these goals and plans should be evaluated and compared against one another.
- Implementing goals and plans involves communicating the plan to employees, allocating resources, and making certain that other systems such as rewards and budgets support the plan.
- Control systems to monitor how implementation is faring: progress toward the goals.

LO 2 Describe how to integrate strategic planning with tactical and operational planning.

- Strategic planning is different from operational planning in that it involves making long-term decisions about the entire organization.
- Tactical planning translates broad goals and strategies into specific actions to be taken within the organization's subunits.
- Operational planning identifies the specific short-term procedures and processes required at lower levels of the organization.

LO 3 Identify elements of the external environment and internal resources of the firm to analyze before formulating a strategy.

- Strategic planning is designed to leverage the strengths of a firm while minimizing the effects of its weaknesses.
- It is difficult to know a firm's potential advantages without a proper internal analysis. Close examine might indicate, for instance, a particularly talented marketing department or a uniquely efficient production system.
- However, managers cannot determine whether internal characteristics are sources of competitive advantage until they learn from external analyses how well competitors compare.

LO 4 Define core capabilities and explain how they provide the foundation for business strategy.

- A core competence is something a company does especially well relative to its competitors.
- When this competence is significantly important to market success, it can be a competitive advantage.
- It can provide a sustainable advantage if it is valuable, rare, difficult to imitate, and well organized.

LO 5 Summarize the types of choices available for corporate strategy.

- Corporate strategy identifies the breadth of a firm's competitive domain.
- Corporate strategy can be kept narrow, as in a concentration strategy, or can move to suppliers and buyers via vertical integration.
- Corporate strategy also can broaden a firm's domain via concentric (related) diversification or conglomerate (unrelated) diversification.

LO 6 Discuss how companies can achieve competitive advantage through business strategy.

- Companies gain competitive advantage in two primary ways. They can attempt to be unique in some way by pursuing a differentiation strategy, or they can focus on efficiency and price by pursuing a low-cost strategy.

LO 7 Describe the keys to effective strategy implementation.

- Many good plans fail due to poor implementation.
- Strategy must be actively supported, for example, by structure, technology, human resources, rewards, information systems, culture, and leadership.
- Ultimately, the success of a plan depends on how well employees at low levels are able and willing to implement it.
- Participative management is one important approach to gaining employees' input and commitment to strategy implementation.

DISCUSSION QUESTIONS

1. This chapter opened with a quote from former CEO of GE Jack Welch: "Manage your destiny, or someone else will." What does "managing your destiny" mean for strategic management? What does it mean when Welch adds, "or someone else will"?

2. List the six steps in the formal planning process. Suppose you manage a local business and you want to launch a new website. What activities you would carry out during each step to create the site?

3. Your friend is frustrated because he's having trouble selecting a career. He says, "I can't plan because the future is too complicated. Anything can happen, and there are too many choices." What would you say to him to change his mind?

4. How do strategic, operational, and tactical planning differ? How might the three levels complement one another in an organization?

5. How might an organization such as Urban Outfitters use a strategy map? With your classmates and using Exhibit 4.4 as a guide, develop a possible strategy map for the company.

6. What accounts for the shift from strategic planning to strategic management? In which industries or companies is this essential? Why?

7. Review Exhibit 4.6, which lists the components of an environmental analysis. Why is this so vitally important to a company's strategic planning process?

8. What are the core capabilities of Harley-Davidson Motor Company motorcycles? How do these capabilities help Harley-Davidson compete against foreign competitors such as Yamaha and Suzuki?

9. How could SWOT analysis help newspaper companies remain competitive in the new media environment?

10. What are the key challenges in strategy implementation? What are some barriers to success, and what can you do about them?

EXPERIENTIAL EXERCISES

4.1 BUSINESS STRATEGIES NEED ADJUSTING

OBJECTIVE

To study why and how a company adjusts its business strategy to adapt to changing external environments.

INSTRUCTIONS

Using an Internet browser or a college's library research portal, identify a recent article from such business news outlets as *The Wall Street Journal, Bloomberg Business, Forbes,* or *Fast Company* that describes a company that is changing its short- and long-term business strategies. Please read the article and provide answers to the following questions:

1. How would you describe the company's former business strategy?

_____

_____

_____

_____

_____

_____

2. Why is the company changing its strategy? What external forces are encouraging it to change?

_____

_____

_____

_____

_____

_____

3. How would you describe the new business strategy?

_____

_____

_____

_____

_____

_____

_____

_____

4. What strategic goals or major targets does the company hope to achieve?

_____

_____

_____

_____

_____

_____

_____

5. How does the company intend to translate its new strategic goals into tactical or operational plans? Which levels of management will carry out these plans?

_____

_____

_____

_____

_____
_____
_____

6. To what extent do you think the new strategy will be successful in addressing or adapting to the external forces? Explain.

_____
_____

_____
_____
_____
_____
_____

SOURCE: Adapted from McGrath, R. R., Jr., _Exercises in Management Fundamentals_, 1st, p. 15. Upper Saddle River, NJ: Pearson Education, 1985.

Concluding Case

WISH YOU WOOD TOY STORE

Wish You Wood is a toy boutique located in the main shopping strip of a resort town near Piney Lake. People who own cabins near the lake or come to visit the local state park enjoy browsing through the town's stores, where they pick up pottery, landscape paintings, and Wish You Wood's beautifully crafted wooden toys. For these shoppers, Wish You Wood is more than a store; it is a destination they associate with family and fun.

The store's owners, Jim and Pam Klein, personally select the toys from craftspeople and toymakers around the world. They enjoy their regular customers but believe selling mostly to vacationers has limited the company's growth. They decided that the lowest-cost way to expand would be to sell toys online. However, after several years, they had to admit that traffic to the store's website was unimpressive. Thanks to e-mail and Facebook reminders, they were luring some of their loyal in-store shoppers to the site to make off-season purchases, but few other people looking for toys ever found Wish You Wood online.

Jim and Pam concluded that the next-best way to sell online would be to partner with Amazon.com. Amazon's Marketplace service lets other retailers sell products on Amazon. The Kleins signed an agreement to list the store's most popular items with Amazon. For example, if a shopper is searching for wooden dollhouses, Wish You Wood's dollhouses will be included in the search results. A customer who chooses to buy from Wish You Wood places the order right on Amazon's website. Under Amazon's participation agreement, the listings must be honest and may not link to Wish You Wood's own website or invite phone calls from customers. In exchange for giving the products exposure on the site, Amazon charges a monthly fee plus a commission on each sale.

Initially, Jim and Pam were thrilled about their decision to partner with Amazon. They tracked each month's sales and compared them with in-store sales. In the first five months, sales jumped 45 percent, mainly because of sales on Amazon. Then, suddenly, sales of popular toy train sets, which were particularly profitable, stopped altogether. Puzzled, Jim visited Amazon to make sure the train sets were still listed. To his surprise, he found that the train set was there, at the usual price of $149, listed right after the same set available directly from Amazon, at $129. He and Pam concluded that shoppers were now buying the product directly from Amazon. It appeared that their store had helped Amazon identify a product consumers value.

The Kleins worried that they needed a new strategy. If they matched Amazon's price, they would lose most of the profit on their most popular items. Wish You Wood was too small of a business to negotiate better prices from its suppliers. If the store didn't match Amazon's price, it would continue to lose sales at the Amazon site. Jim and Pam wondered whether they should pull out of Amazon altogether or find a way to continue working with the partner that had become a competitor. They also considered rethinking which toys to offer on Amazon.

DISCUSSION QUESTIONS

1. Prepare a SWOT analysis for Wish You Wood, based on the information given.
2. Using the SWOT analysis, what general corporate strategy would you recommend for Wish You Wood? Should the store continue or change its current approach?

CHAPTER 5
Ethics, Corporate Responsibility, and Sustainability

> It is truly enough said that a corporation has no conscience; but a corporation of conscientious men is a corporation with a conscience.
>
> —HENRY DAVID THOREAU

©Ingram Publishing RF

LEARNING OBJECTIVES

After studying Chapter 5, *you will be able to:*

LO 1 Describe how different ethical perspectives guide decision making.

LO 2 Explain how companies influence their ethics environment.

LO 3 Outline a process for making ethical decisions.

LO 4 Summarize the important issues surrounding corporate social responsibility.

LO 5 Discuss reasons for businesses' growing interest in the natural environment.

LO 6 Identify actions managers can take to manage with the environment in mind.

CHAPTER OUTLINE

Ethics
    Ethical Systems
    Business Ethics
    The Ethics Environment
    Ethical Decision Making
    Courage

Corporate Social Responsibility
    Contrasting Views
    Reconciliation

The Natural Environment and Sustainability
    A Risk Society
    Ecocentric Management
    Environmental Agendas for the Future

Management in Action

HOW CAN GINNI ROMETTY ENSURE THAT IBM DOES WELL WHILE DOING GOOD?

The standard for principled leadership is set high for IBM's chief executive, Ginni Rometty. She took charge of IBM upon the retirement of the widely admired Sam Palmisano, who saw an opportunity for the company to distinguish itself by applying its data-processing expertise to delivering customized business solutions.

Palmisano, rather than jumping straight into corporate restructuring or marketing campaigns, started with values. He set up a three-day "values jam," during which employees throughout the global company were asked to contribute thoughts about what IBM's values should be. Out of that process came a commitment to helping clients and building relationships based on trust and personal responsibility.

In a further expression of Palmisano's values-based vision, IBM began to use the tagline "Smarter Planet." Employees help companies, cities, and communities around the world make better decisions aimed at improving business results, living conditions, and even the health of planet Earth. This goal was based on the realization that computers have extraordinary power to gather and analyze data, but applying the data also requires creative thinking, productive processes, and open communication. IBM would offer not just computer hardware but also decision-making and analytic expertise to bring all these requirements together.

Palmisano's vision set IBM on course for years of strong growth as businesses, city governments, and nongovernmental organizations saw how the company could help them meet their goals. When he prepared to retire, Palmisano threw his support behind Rometty, who had started as a systems engineer at IBM in the

©AP Images

1980s and worked her way up to senior vice president and group executive for sales, marketing, and strategy. In a recent speech, Rometty signaled that she sees the Smarter Planet strategy as positioning IBM for a future in which data will drive more decisions, cloud computing will transform how industries operate, and mobile and social media will facilitate personalized user engagement.

Rometty's strategy expertise and technical background prepared her to guide IBM through an unprecedented shift away from legacy hardware and services to new business initiatives such as business analytics, cloud computing, and mobile apps. But this change has not been an easy one. IBM's sales revenue declined even as profit margins increased. Change takes time. Rometty believes there is money to be made in caring about the needs of cities, the business community, and the planet.[1]

> For IBM's Sam Palmisano and Ginni Rometty, business success can grow out of values that emphasize focusing on the needs of others. As you read this chapter, think about how well IBM's values-driven approach positions the company to be both ethical and successful.

How would you measure the success of a company such as IBM? By this quarter's profits and its value in the stock market? By the degree of trust people place in its managers and consultants? By the good it does in improving quality of life by helping people make better decisions? Although a company might enjoy high profits in one quarter without these virtues, many argue that in the long run, all these measures of success are interdependent and essential.

This chapter addresses the values and manner of doing business adopted by managers as they carry out their corporate and business strategies. In particular, we will explore ways of applying **ethics**, the system of rules that governs the ordering of values. We do so based on the premise that managers, their organizations, and their communities thrive over the long term when they apply ethical standards that direct them to act with integrity.

ethics

The system of rules that governs the ordering of values; see also *corporate social responsibility.*

We also consider the idea that organizations have a responsibility to meet social obligations beyond earning profits within legal and ethical constraints. As you study this chapter, consider what kind of manager you want to be. What reputation do you hope to have? How would you like others to describe you as a manager?

It's a Big Issue

Scandals periodically engulf company executives, independent auditors, politicians and regulators, and shareholders and employees.[2] In some, executives at public companies make misleading statements to inflate stock prices, undermining the public's trust in the integrity of the financial markets. Often the scandals are perpetrated by a number of people cooperating with one another, and many of the guilty parties had been otherwise upstanding individuals. Lobbyists have been accused—and some convicted—of buying influence with lavish gifts to politicians. Executives have admitted to bribing representatives of foreign governments in order to secure large contracts.

What recent news disturbs you about managers' behavior? Tainted products in the food supply . . . actions that harm the environment . . . Internet hacks and scams . . . employees pressured to meet sales or production targets by any means? The list goes on, and the public becomes cynical. In a 2017 survey by the public relations firm Edelman, only about one-third (down 12 percent over the previous year) of the respondents trusted business leaders to be good stewards of their organizations.[3]

> Temptations exist in every organization and at every level.

When corporations behave badly, it's often not the top executives but the rank-and-file employees who suffer most. For example, Wells Fargo's leaders created a sales incentive system that strongly encouraged cross-selling (example: the bank's employees were expected to convince a customer with only a savings account to open a checking account). Cross-selling is a common practice, but this program was particularly aggressive. The pressure to reach sales quotas was so high that many employees committed fraud by opening over two million phony customer accounts—unbeknownst to the customers.[4]

The scandal came to light after some customers complained of being forced to pay fees on accounts they didn't know existed. Wells Fargo paid over $185 million in government fines, and of course its reputation as a trusted bank was damaged.[5] Other recent corporate scandals include the Samsung Galaxy Note 7 battery debacle and the sexual harassment charges against Roger Ailes, the former chairman and CEO of Fox News.[6]

Simply talking about famous cases as examples of lax company ethics doesn't get at the heart of the problem. Clearly, these cases have culprits, and their ethical lapses are obvious. But this makes it too easy to simply say "Of course I would never do things like that."

The fact is that temptations exist in every type of work and every organization. Many of the decisions you will face will pose ethical dilemmas, and the right thing to do is not always evident or easy.

It's a Personal Issue

"Answer true or false: 'I am an ethical manager.' If you answered 'true,' here's an uncomfortable fact: You're probably not."[7] These sentences are the first in a *Harvard Business Review* article called "How (Un)Ethical Are You?" The point is that most of us think we are good decision makers, ethical, and unbiased. But the fact is, most people have unconscious biases that favor themselves and their own group. For example, managers often hire people who are like them, think they are immune to conflicts of interest, take more credit than they deserve, and blame others when they deserve some blame themselves.

Knowing that you have biases may help you try to overcome them, but usually that's not enough. Consider the act of telling a lie.[8] Many people lie—some more than others, and in part depending on the situation, usually presuming that they will benefit somehow. At a basic level, we all can make ethical arguments against lying and in favor of honesty. Yet it is useful to think thoroughly about the real consequences of lying.[9] Exhibit 5.1 summarizes the possible outcomes of telling the truth or lying in different situations. People often lie or commit other ethical transgressions somewhat mindlessly, without realizing the full array of negative personal consequences.

Ethics issues are not easy, and not just for newsworthy corporate CEOs. For example, people at work use computers with Internet access. If the employer pays for the computer and the time you spend sitting in front of it, is it ethical for you to use the computer to do tasks unrelated to your work?

What if you stream video of games for your own and your co-workers' enjoyment, or take a two-hour lunch to locate the best deal on a flat-panel TV? Besides lost productivity, employers are most concerned about computer users introducing viruses, leaking confidential information, and creating a hostile work environment by downloading inappropriate web content.

Reason for the Lie	Results of Lying	Results of Telling the Truth
Negotiation	• Short-term gain and economically positive. • Harms long-term relationship. • Must rationalize to oneself.	• Supports high-quality, long-term relationship. • Develops reputation of integrity. • Models behavior to others.
Conflicting expectations	• Easier to lie than to address the underlying conflict. • Does not solve underlying problem. • Liar must rationalize the lie to preserve positive self-concept.	• Emotionally more difficult than lying. • May correct underlying problem. • Develops one's reputation as an honest person.
Keeping a confidence (that may require at least a lie of omission)	• Maintains relationship with the party for whom confidence is kept. • May project deceitfulness to the deceived party.	• Violates a trust to the confiding party. • Makes one appear deceitful to all parties in the long run.
Reporting your own performance (within an organization)	• Might advance oneself or one's cause. • Develops dishonest reputation over time.	• Creates a reputation of honesty and integrity. • Performance report may not always be positive.

EXHIBIT 5.1
Possible Outcomes of Lying and Telling the Truth

SOURCE: Adapted from Gover, S. L., "The Truth, the Whole Truth, and Nothing but the Truth: The Causes and Management of Workplace Lying," *The Academy of Management Executive: The Thinking Manager's Source.* Mississippi State, MS: Academy of Management, 2005.

Multiple Generations at Work

Millennials Are Bullish on Business

According to Deloitte's Millennial Survey 2017, Millennials believe that businesses are behaving ethically and that their leaders are committed to improving society.[10] But plenty of room remains for companies to improve continuously on both dimensions.

Organizations can build trust among their Millennial and other employee groups. Leaders and managers can demonstrate ethical behaviors including honesty; strive for high-quality relationships built on respect, trust, and decency; and develop and communicate a clear code of ethics. And, how to consider ethics when making decisions is an excellent topic for training and professional development.[11]

The desire to be ethical in business and make a positive impact on society is growing. In March 2017, Ethisphere hosted the 9th annual "Global Ethics Summit" for leaders from over 200 organizations and companies from around the world. These top executives shared best practices in fostering ethical cultures, increasing value to stockholders, and ensuring sustainable corporate governance.[12]

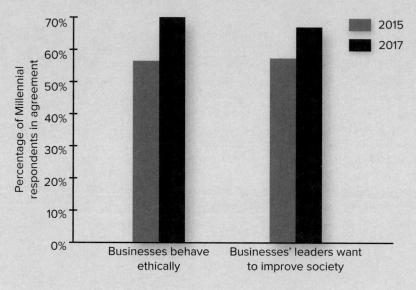

SOURCE: Adapted from "The Deloitte Millennial Survey 2017," www2.deloitte.com.

Sometimes employees write blogs or post comments online about their company and its products. Obviously, companies do not want their employees to say bad things about them, but some companies are concerned about employees who are overly enthusiastic. When employees plug their companies and products on comments or review pages, the practice is spamming at best and deceptive if the employees don't disclose their relationship with their company.

It also is deceptive when companies create fictional blogs as a marketing tactic without disclosing their sponsorship, and when they pay bloggers to write positive comments about them—a practice known as "astroturfing" because the "grassroots" interest it builds is fake. Examples include Bell Canada paying a $1.25 million penalty to the Canadian government for encouraging employees to post positive reviews and ratings regarding its mobile app,[13] and false positive reviews on Amazon paid for via sites including "Buy Amazon Reviews" and "Paid Book Reviews."[14] To protect the integrity of its 5-star product rating system, Amazon sued these and other sites that sell fraudulent online reviews.[15]

Are these examples too small to worry about? No, minor ethical lapses may lead to major problems. This chapter will help you think through decisions with ethical ramifications.

Try to imagine the challenge of leading employees who don't trust you. The nearby "Multiple Generations at Work" box discusses trust in the workplace.

Ethics

The aim of ethics is to identify both the rules that should govern people's behavior and the "goods" that are worth seeking. Ethical decisions are guided by the underlying values of the individual. Values are principles of conduct such as caring, being honest, keeping promises, pursuing excellence, showing loyalty, being fair, acting with integrity, respecting others, and being a responsible citizen.[16]

Most people would agree that all of these values are admirable guidelines for behavior. However, ethics becomes a more complicated issue when a situation dictates that you must chooses one value over others. An **ethical issue** is a situation, problem, or opportunity in which an individual must choose among several actions that must be evaluated as morally right or wrong.[17]

Ethical issues arise in every facet of life; we concern ourselves here with business ethics in particular. **Business ethics** comprise the moral principles and standards that guide behavior in the world of business.[18]

ethical issue

Situation, problem, or opportunity in which an individual must choose among several actions that must be evaluated as morally right or wrong.

Ethical Systems

Moral philosophy refers to the principles, rules, and values people use in deciding what is right or wrong. This is a simple definition in the abstract but often terribly complex and difficult when facing real choices. How do you decide what is right and wrong? Do you know what criteria you apply and how you apply them?

Ethics scholars point to several major ethical systems as potential guides (see Exhibit 5.2).[19] The first, **universalism**, states that all people should uphold certain values, such as honesty, that society needs to function. Universal values are principles

LO 1

> Ethics becomes a more complicated issue when a situation dictates that you must choose one value over others.

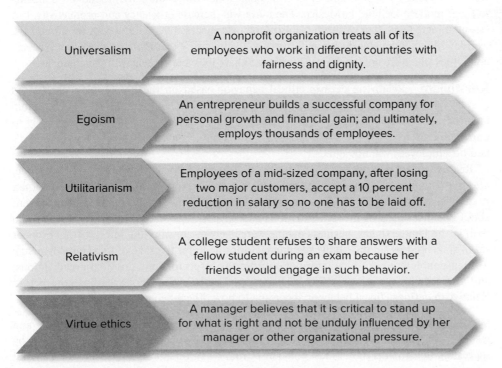

EXHIBIT 5.2
Examples of Decisions Made under Different Ethical Systems

Universalism — A nonprofit organization treats all of its employees who work in different countries with fairness and dignity.

Egoism — An entrepreneur builds a successful company for personal growth and financial gain; and ultimately, employs thousands of employees.

Utilitarianism — Employees of a mid-sized company, after losing two major customers, accept a 10 percent reduction in salary so no one has to be laid off.

Relativism — A college student refuses to share answers with a fellow student during an exam because her friends would engage in such behavior.

Virtue ethics — A manager believes that it is critical to stand up for what is right and not be unduly influenced by her manager or other organizational pressure.

---

business ethics

The moral principles and standards that guide behavior in the world of business. See also *ethics.*

moral philosophy

Principles, rules, and values people use in deciding what is right or wrong.

universalism

The ethical system stating that all people should uphold certain values that society needs to function.

Employees sometimes feel that "borrowing" a few office supplies from their company helps compensate for any perceived inequities in pay or other benefits.

©allesalltag/Alamy Stock Photo

Caux Principles

Ethical principles established by international executives based in Caux, Switzerland, in collaboration with business leaders from Japan, Europe, and the United States.

egoism

An ethical system defining acceptable behavior as that which maximizes consequences for the individual.

so fundamental to human existence that they are important in all societies—for example, rules against murder, deceit, torture, and oppression.

Some efforts have been made to establish global, universal ethical principles for business. The Caux Roundtable, a group of international executives based in Caux, Switzerland, worked with business leaders from Japan, Europe, and the United States to create the **Caux Principles**. Two basic ethical ideals underpin the Caux Principles: *kyosei* and human dignity. *Kyosei* means living and working together for the common good, allowing cooperation and mutual prosperity to coexist with healthy and fair competition. Human dignity concerns the value of each person as an end, not a means to the fulfillment of others' purposes.

Universal principles can be powerful and useful, but what people say, hope, or think they would do is often different from what they *really* do, faced with conflicting demands in real situations. Different individuals in different circumstances apply different moral philosophies. Consider each of the following moral philosophies and the actions to which they might lead.[20]

Egoism and Utilitarianism   According to **egoism**, acceptable behavior is that which maximizes benefits for the individual. "Doing the right thing," the focus of moral philosophy, is defined by egoism as "do the act that promotes the greatest good for oneself." If everyone follows this system, according to its proponents, the well-being of society as a whole should increase. This notion is similar to Adam Smith's concept of the invisible hand in business. Smith argued that if every organization follows its own economic self-interest, the total wealth of society will be maximized.

Unlike egoism, **utilitarianism** directly seeks the greatest good for the greatest number of people. Consider how utilitarianism might justify laying off about half of the 1,200 workers from the Nabisco plant (maker of Oreos, Chips Ahoy, and Ritz Crackers) in Chicago. According to Irene Rosenfeld, CEO of Mondelez International (which owns Nabisco), production is moving to more modern facilities in Mexico. The move will increase efficiency and productivity, two essential ingredients that will help Nabisco compete successfully in 165 countries around the world.[21] Maintaining global competitiveness will help ensure that thousands of other Nabisco employees who were not laid off will continue to have jobs and careers with the company.

Relativism   **Relativism** defines ethical behavior based on the opinions and behaviors of relevant other people. In the Nabisco Oreo layoff example, leaders of other U.S. manufacturers (especially bakers) who are operating aging, less efficient facilities are likely to understand and even support the layoffs. However, city officials in Chicago and the plant's laid off employees will not agree.

Relativism acknowledges the existence of different ethical viewpoints. For example, *norms,* or standards of expected and acceptable behavior, vary from one culture to another. A study of Russian versus U.S. managers found that all followed norms of informed consent about chemical hazards in work situations and paying wages on time. But in Russia more than in the United States, business people were likely to consider the interests of a broader set of stakeholders (in this study, keeping factories open for the sake of local employment), to keep double books to hide information from tax inspectors and criminal organizations, and to make personal payments to government officials in charge of awarding contracts.[22] Relativism defines ethical behavior according to how others behave.

Virtue Ethics   The moral philosophies just described apply different types of rules and reasoning. **Virtue ethics** is a perspective that goes beyond the conventional rules of society by suggesting that what is moral must come also from what a mature person with good "moral

utilitarianism

An ethical system stating that the greatest good for the greatest number should be the overriding concern of decision makers.

relativism

Philosophy that bases ethical behavior on the opinions and behaviors of relevant other people.

virtue ethics

Perspective that what is moral comes from what a mature person with "good" moral character would deem right.

character" would deem right. Society's rules provide a moral minimum, and then moral individuals can transcend rules by applying their personal virtues such as faith, honesty, and integrity.

Individuals differ in this regard. **Kohlberg's model of cognitive moral development** classifies people into categories based on their level of moral judgment.[23] People in the *preconventional* stage make decisions based on rewards and punishments and immediate self-interest. People in the *conventional* stage conform to the expectations of ethical behavior held by groups or institutions such as society, family, or peers. People in the *principled* stage see beyond authority, laws, and norms and follow their self-chosen ethical principles.[24]

Some people forever reside in the preconventional stage, some move into the conventional stage, and some develop further yet into the principled stage. Over time, and through education and experience, people may change their values and ethical behavior.[25]

These major ethical systems underlie personal moral choices and ethical decisions in business.

Kohlberg's model of cognitive moral development

Classification of people based on their level of moral judgment.

Business Ethics

Insider trading, sweatshops and modern slavery,[26] bribery and kickbacks, and other scandals create negative perceptions of business and business leaders. People use illegal and unethical means to beat their rivals,[27] increase profits, or improve their personal positions. Neither young managers nor consumers believe top executives are doing a good job of establishing high ethical standards.[28] Some even joke that *business ethics* is a contradiction in terms.

A recent survey found that about half of the employees in large companies have observed misconduct in the workplace.[29] Many people feel ethically conflicted, stressed, and exhausted as companies sometimes encourage them to behave in ways that differ from their own sense of right and wrong.[30] Many managers must deal frequently with ethical dilemmas, and the issues are becoming increasingly complex. For example, many people seek spiritual renewal in the workplace, in part reflecting a broader religious awakening in the United States, whereas others argue that this trend violates religious freedom and the separation of church and boardroom.[31]

Exhibit 5.3 shows some other important examples of ethical dilemmas in business. Think about how you would address each of these issues as a manager. What ethical principles are you applying?

LO 2

Should pharmaceutical companies be allowed to advertise directly to the consumer if the medicine can be obtained only with a prescription from a doctor? When patients request a particular product, doctors are more likely to prescribe it—even if the patients haven't reported the corresponding symptoms.

©McGraw-Hill Education/John Flournoy

The Ethics Environment

Responding to a series of corporate scandals—particularly the high-profile cases of Enron and WorldCom—Congress passed the **Sarbanes-Oxley Act** in 2002 to improve and maintain investor confidence. The law requires companies to have more independent board directors (not just company insiders), to adhere strictly to accounting rules, and to have senior managers personally sign off on financial results. Violations can result in heavy fines and criminal prosecution. One of the biggest impacts of the law was the requirement for companies and their auditors to provide reports to financial statement users about the effectiveness of internal controls over the financial reporting process.

Companies that make the effort to meet or exceed these requirements can reduce their risks, by lowering the likelihood of misdeeds and the consequences if an employee does break the law.[32] But some executives said Sarbanes-Oxley distracted from their real work and made them more risk-averse. Some complained about the time and money needed to comply with the internal control reporting—millions of dollars at big businesses. But some discovered that the effort helped them avoid mistakes and improve efficiency.

Sarbanes-Oxley created legal requirements intended to improve ethical behavior. After his inauguration, President Donald Trump wanted to ease legal constraints on business including Wall Street. What has happened since then, and what is happening now?

Sarbanes-Oxley Act

An act passed into law by Congress to establish strict accounting and reporting rules in order to make senior managers more accountable and to improve and maintain investor confidence.

EXHIBIT 5.3

Current Ethical Issues in Business

CEO pay	What is a fair level of pay for a top executive? Twenty times, or hundreds of times, what the average company worker earns? Whatever other companies want to pay their top executives?
Climate	What is a company's responsibility for its impact on the climate? For example, if operations in one country contribute to rising global temperatures that lead to greater floods in another country, how should the company respond?
Globalization	When a company operates in countries with lower costs, what are its obligations, if any, to the workers in those countries? What standards should it meet for pay rates?
Health care	With health care costs outpacing inflation, employers struggle to cover the cost of health insurance for workers. Are they ethically obligated to provide this benefit?
Obesity	As an obesity epidemic threatens health and adds to health care costs, what role, if any, should employers play in encouraging healthy employee lifestyles?
Online privacy	What obligations do employers have in protecting the privacy of employee information and information about customers?
Social media	What ethical obligations do employees have in commenting about their employer on social media? What ethical obligations do employers have concerning their employees' privacy on social media?
Wages	When adjusted for inflation, the median wage in the United States has fallen over the past decades. What should employers do to promote a sense that their compensation is fair?

Maintaining a positive ethical climate is always challenging, but it is especially complex for organizations with international activities. Different cultures and countries may have different standards of behavior, and managers have to decide when relativism is more appropriate than adherence to firm standards. Exchange of courtesies is one thing, but a danger is posed for the unwary business person in areas of the world where bribery and graft are commonplace, which is why Congress passed the Foreign Corrupt Practices Act.

(Un)ethical actions are influenced not only by laws and by individual virtue, but also by the company's work environment. Unethical corporate behavior may be the responsibility of an unethical individual, but it often also reveals a company culture that is ethically lax.[33]

ethical climate

In an organization, the processes by which decisions are evaluated and made on the basis of right and wrong.

The **ethical climate** of an organization refers to the processes by which decisions are evaluated and made on the basis of right and wrong.[34] For employees, the right ethical climate can be a source of ethical personal actions plus pride, satisfaction, and commitment to the employer, while the wrong climate will cause unethical behavior or dissatisfaction and quitting.[35]

General Electric's top executives have demonstrated a commitment to promoting high levels of integrity without sacrificing the company's well-known commitment to business results. The measures taken by GE to maintain a positive ethical climate include establishing global standards for behavior to prevent ethical problems. The company's Statement of Integrity reinforces the ethical climate:

> For more than 125 years, GE has demonstrated an unwavering commitment to performance with integrity. At the same time we have expanded into new businesses and new regions and built a great record of sustained growth, we have built a worldwide reputation for lawful and ethical conduct.[36]

As GE managers monitor the external environment, they are expected to consider legal and ethical developments, along with other concerns, so that the company can be prepared for new issues as they arise. Managers at all levels are rewarded for their performance in meeting both integrity and business standards, and when violations occur, even managers

EXHIBIT 5.4

Seven Danger Signs of
Unethical Behavior at Your
Organization

1. Excessive emphasis on **short-term revenues** over longer-term considerations.
2. Failure to establish a **written code of ethics**.
3. A desire for simple, **quick-fix solutions** to ethical problems.
4. An **unwillingness** to take an ethical stand that imposes financial costs.
5. Consideration of ethics solely as a **legal issue** or a public relations tool.
6. **Lack of clear procedures** for handling ethical problems.
7. Responding to the **demands of shareholders** at the expense of other constituencies.

EXHIBIT 5.4

Seven Danger Signs of
Unethical Behavior at Your
Organization

who were otherwise successful are disciplined. This sends a powerful message that ethical behavior truly is valued at GE.[37]

Danger Signs Maintaining consistent ethical behavior by all employees is an ongoing challenge. What are some danger signs that an organization may be allowing or even encouraging unethical behavior? Exhibit 5.4 lists many factors that could create a climate conducive to unethical behavior.[38]

Regardless of your employer's ethical climate, you are responsible for the decisions you make. It's been said that your reputation is your most precious asset. Here's a suggestion: when making decisions, explicitly consider their impact on your personal reputation.

You can have strong personal character, but if you "manage" ethics only by benign neglect, you won't develop a reputation as an ethical leader. Here's another suggestion, if you want to take ethics to the next level: Set a goal for yourself to be seen by others as both a moral person and as a moral manager—someone who influences others to behave ethically. When you are both personally moral and a moral manager, you will truly be an **ethical leader**.[39]

ethical leader

One who is both a moral person and a moral manager influencing others to behave ethically.

Corporate Ethical Standards To create a culture that encourages ethical behavior, managers must be more than ethical people. They also should lead others to behave ethically.[40] At General Electric, longtime (now former) chief executive Jeffrey Immelt demonstrated his concern for ethical leadership by beginning and ending each annual meeting with a statement of the company's integrity principles, emphasizing that "GE's business success is built on our reputation with all stakeholders for lawful and ethical behavior."[41]

> Fear of exposure compels people more strongly in some cultures than in others.

OshKosh provides questions for employees to ask themselves when facing ethical decisions: "Are my actions legal?" "Am I being fair, honest and ethical?" "Will I sleep soundly tonight?" and "What would I tell my child to do?" The implication: if you wouldn't want a decision highlighted in the media, then don't do it.[42] This "light of day" or "sunshine" ethical framework can be a powerful influence.

Such fear of exposure compels people more strongly in some cultures than in others. In some Asian countries, anxiety about losing face often makes executives resign immediately if they are caught in ethical transgressions or if their companies are embarrassed by revelations in the media. By contrast, in the United States, exposed executives might respond with indignation, intransigence, pleading the Fifth Amendment, stonewalling, and mounting an everyone-else-does-it self-defense, or by not admitting wrongdoing and giving no sign that resignation ever crossed their minds. Partly because of legal tradition, the attitude often is never explain, never apologize, don't admit the mistake, and do not resign, even if the entire world knows exactly what happened.[43]

Ethics Codes The Sarbanes-Oxley Act required public companies periodically to disclose whether they have adopted a code of ethics for senior financial officers—and if not, why not. Often such statements are just for show, but when implemented well, they can change a company's ethical climate for the better and truly encourage ethical behavior. Executives say they pay most attention to their company's code of ethics when they feel that

The Digital World

While corporate ethics programs work hard to ensure that employees are behaving ethically, some companies use technology to enforce compliance and limit their liability if a violation occurs. Most companies have a policy that computers, cell phones, and Internet access provided by the company come with the company's legal right to access any content.

Goldman Sachs' compliance department monitors all e-mails and social media with an algorithm that looks for key words, which, when flagged, receive additional scrutiny to determine if there is an issue. Employees sign a document stating that they are aware e-mails are reviewed.

Examples of words and phrases monitored are "worst investment," "I trusted you," and many types of profanity. While the original list of words and phrases was produced in 2008, in 2016 news agencies started publishing words and phrases used by the algorithm that had been obtained from an anonymous inside source.

Digital monitoring tools can affect employee online behavior by their power to catch transgressors, and also by the ease with which stakeholders can post proof online of behavior they think the public should know about. These provide a level of transparency not previously possible, while creating additional ethics challenges. What are your reactions to this?

stakeholders (customers, investors, lenders, and suppliers) try to influence them to do so, to promote a positive image.[44]

Most ethics codes address subjects such as employee conduct, community and environment, shareholders, customers, suppliers and contractors, political activity, and technology. The nonprofit Ethics Resource Center conducts research and assists companies interested in establishing a corporate code of ethics.[45]

Ethics codes must be carefully written and tailored to individual companies' philosophies. Exhibit 5.5 reprints the Commitments section of The Hershey Company's code of ethics.

To make an ethics code effective, do the following: (1) involve those who have to live with it in writing the statement; (2) focus on real-life situations that employees can relate to; (3) keep it short and simple, so it is easy to understand and remember; (4) write about values and shared beliefs that are important and that people can really believe in; and (5) set the tone at the top, having executives talk about and live up to the statement.[46]

When reality differs from the statement—as when a motto says people are our most precious asset or a product is the finest in the world, but in fact people are treated poorly or product quality is weak—the statement becomes a joke to employees rather than a guiding light.

Ethics Programs   Corporate ethics programs commonly include formal ethics codes that articulate the company's expectations: ethics committees that develop policies, evaluate actions, and investigate violations; ethics communication systems that give employees a means of reporting problems or getting guidance; ethics officers or ombudspersons who investigate allegations and provide education; ethics training programs; and disciplinary processes for addressing unethical behavior.[47]

compliance-based ethics programs

Company mechanisms typically designed by corporate counsel to prevent, detect, and punish legal violations.

Ethics programs can range from compliance-based to integrity-based.[48] **Compliance-based ethics programs** are designed by corporate counsel to prevent, detect, and punish legal violations. Program elements include establishing and communicating legal standards and procedures, assigning high-level managers to oversee compliance, auditing and monitoring compliance, reporting criminal misconduct, punishing wrongdoers, and taking steps to prevent offenses in the future.

Such programs can reduce illegal behavior and help a company stay out of court. But as a former chair of the Securities and Exchange Commission said, "It is not an adequate ethical standard to aspire to get through the day without being indicted."

integrity-based ethics programs

Company mechanisms designed to instill in people a personal responsibility for ethical behavior.

Integrity-based ethics programs go beyond the mere avoidance of illegality; they are concerned with the law but also with instilling in people a personal responsibility for ethical

EXHIBIT 5.5

The Hershey Company's
Code of Ethical Business
Conduct: Commitments

We have each made a commitment to operate ethically and to lead with integrity. This commitment is embedded in the Hershey values. Our Code of Ethical Business Conduct ("Code") shows us how to uphold this commitment as we interact with the various groups that have a stake in our Company's success.

OUR COMMITMENT TO FELLOW EMPLOYEES

We treat one another fairly and with respect, valuing the talents, experiences and strengths of our diverse workforce.

OUR COMMITMENT TO CONSUMERS

We maintain the trust consumers place in our brands, providing the best products on the market and adhering to honest marketing practices.

OUR COMMITMENT TO THE MARKETPLACE

We deal fairly with our business partners, competitors and suppliers, acting ethically and upholding the law in everything we do.

OUR COMMITMENT TO STOCKHOLDERS

We act honestly and transparently at all times, maintaining the trust our stockholders have placed in us.

OUR COMMITMENT TO THE GLOBAL COMMUNITY

We comply with all global trade laws, protecting our natural resources and supporting the communities where we live, work and do business.

EXHIBIT 5.5

The Hershey Company's
Code of Ethical Business
Conduct: Commitments

The Hershey Company, "Code of Ethical Business Conduct." Accessed March 20, 2015. http://www. thehersheycompany.com. All rights reserved. Used with permission.

behavior. With such a program, companies and people govern themselves through a set of guiding principles that they embrace.

For example, the Americans with Disabilities Act (amended in 2008) required companies to change the physical work environment so it will allow people with disabilities to function on the job. Mere compliance would involve making the changes necessary to avoid legal problems. Integrity-based programs would go further by training people to understand and perhaps change attitudes toward people with disabilities, and sending clear signals that people with disabilities also have valued abilities. This effort goes far beyond taking action to stay out of trouble with the law.[49]

Ethical Decision Making

We've said it's not easy to make ethical choices. Such decisions are complex.[50] For starters, you may face pressures that are difficult to resist. Furthermore, it's not always clear that a problem has ethical dimensions; they don't hold up signs that say "Hey, I'm an ethical issue, so think about me in moral terms!"[51]

LO 3

Making ethical decisions takes moral *awareness* (realizing the issue has ethical implications), moral *judgment* (knowing what actions are morally defensible), and moral *character* (the strength and persistence to act in accordance with your ethics despite the challenges).[52]

The philosopher John Rawls created a thought experiment based on the "veil of ignorance."[53] Imagine that you are making a decision about a policy that will benefit or disadvantage some groups more than others. For example, a policy might provide extra vacation time for all employees but eliminate flextime, which allows parents of young children to balance their work and family responsibilities. Or you're a university president considering raising tuition or cutting financial support for study abroad.

Now pretend that you belong to one of the affected groups, but you don't know which one—for instance, those who can afford to study abroad or those who can't, or a young parent or a young single person. You won't find out until after the decision is made.

EXHIBIT 5.6   A Process for Ethical Decision Making

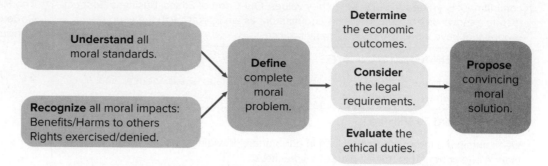

SOURCE: Hosmer, L. T., *The Ethics of Management,* 4th ed. New York: McGraw-Hill/Irwin, 2003, p. 32. Fig. 5.1A.

How would you decide? Would you be willing to risk being in the disadvantaged group? Would your decision be different if you were in a group other than your own? Rawls maintained that only a person ignorant of his own identity can make a truly ethical decision. A decision maker can apply the veil of ignorance to help minimize personal bias.

Thinking before deciding, and having an ethics-oriented conversation with others, can help you and others make more ethical decisions.[54] You can use the process illustrated in Exhibit 5.6. Understand the various moral standards (universalism, relativism, etc.), as described earlier in the chapter. Go through the problem-solving model from Chapter 3 and recognize the impacts of your alternatives: Which people do they benefit and harm, which are able to exercise their rights, and whose rights are denied? You now know the full scope of the moral problem.

Excuses for unethical behavior often are bogus.[55] "I was told to do it" implies a person has no personal thoughts and blindly obeys. "Everybody's doing it" often really means that someone is doing it, but it's rarely everybody; regardless, following convention doesn't mean correctness. "Might equals right" is just a rationalization. "It's not my problem" is sometimes a wise perspective, if it's a battle you can't win, but sometimes it's a cop-out. "I didn't mean for that to happen, it just felt right at the time" can be prevented with more forethought and analysis.

> Excuses are often bogus.

You must also consider legal requirements to ensure full compliance, and the economic outcomes of your options, including costs and potential profits.[56] Some are obvious: fines and penalties. Others, such as corrective actions and lower morale, are less obvious. Ultimately, the effects on customers, employees, and others can be huge. Being fully aware of the potential costs can help prevent people from straying into unethical terrain.

Courage

As stated earlier, behaving ethically requires not just moral awareness and moral judgment but also moral character. It sometimes requires courage to take actions consistent with your ethics when others don't want you to.

Think about how hard it can be to do the right thing.[57] On the job, how hard would it be to walk away from lots of money just to stick to your ethics? To tell colleagues or your boss that you believe they've crossed an ethical line? To disobey a boss's order? To go over your boss's head to someone in senior management with your suspicions about accounting practices? To go outside the company to alert authorities if someone is being hurt and management refuses to correct the problem?

Courage plays a role in the moral awareness involved in identifying an act as unethical, the moral judgment to consider the repercussions fully, and the moral character to take the ethical action. Consider, for example, how difficult it is to deliver unpleasant news, even if you believe that honesty is important and is the way you would want to be treated.

Honesty was a hurdle for some Hilton Worldwide managers as they made staffing decisions for their call centers. Hilton, which operates call centers in five countries and contracts with call centers in the Philippines, reportedly sent employees from its Hemet, California,

Bottom Line

"Costs" aren't exactly synonymous with "ethics." But by considering all costs to all parties, you can make high-quality ethical decisions that you can more effectively sell to others.

What are some costs of treating employees or customers unethically?

center to a new call center in Manila to train those employees in customer service. Only afterward were the California employees told that the company would be closing the Hemet facility and laying off the workers there unless they agreed to relocate to jobs in Texas or Florida. Perhaps the managers feared that telling employees the news earlier would have led to pushback, a poor job of training (intentional or otherwise) in the Philippines, or a refusal to go. Honesty takes courage when it is difficult, and the risks of complete honesty are real.[58]

Even more courage is necessary when you decide that the only ethical course of action is *whistleblowing*—telling others, inside or outside the organization, of wrongdoing. The road for whistleblowers is rocky. When whistleblowers go public, others often see them as acting against the company's interests. Many, perhaps most, whistleblowers suffer consequences such as being ostracized, treated rudely, or given undesirable assignments.

Some organizations offer channels for employees to report ethics problems so they can deal with them internally. Ideally, the reporting method should keep the whistleblower's identity secret, management should investigate and respond quickly, and there should be no retaliation against whistleblowers who use proper channels.

> The road for whistleblowers is rocky.

Management in Action

THE STATE OF ETHICS AT IBM

One advantage IBM has in meeting its standards for trust is that it is part of a relatively trusted industry. In the Edelman Trust Barometer, an annual survey of public attitudes toward various institutions, people from around the world rated the technology industry as the industry they most often trust to do what is right—mainly because they see tech companies as able to benefit society. Ginni Rometty, CEO of IBM, periodically highlights the importance of protecting people's privacy and security.

IBM is tackling this challenge. It has a set of policies aimed at building trust, including a policy for business conduct and ethics and one for protecting data privacy. The ethics policy states, "It is IBM's policy to conduct itself ethically and lawfully in all matters and to maintain IBM's high standards of business integrity." It puts employees on notice that there are consequences for unethical conduct.

IBM's policies explicitly call for fairness, equity, a commitment to quality, and compliance with laws, including employment and anti-corruption laws. Its data privacy laws call for employees to collect only relevant personal information, keep it as accurate as possible, and take measures to keep it secure, among other requirements.

Compliance with ethical standards is most likely when managers and employees at all levels are committed to the standards. Thus, it should help IBM that its strategy and culture changes under Sam Palmisano started with an all-employee values jam. An outcome of that process was a statement of three values:

1. Dedication to every client's success
2. Innovation that matters, for our company and the world
3. Trust and personal responsibility in all relationships

These statements appear on the company's website, where any employee or concerned citizen can be reminded of what IBM is striving to achieve.

Even with formal statements and consequences for behavior, maintaining ethical conduct is a challenge, especially for a global company because employees encounter differences in standards and practices in other countries. Thus, IBM was charged by the Securities and Exchange Commission with bribing government officials in South Korea and China over more than 10 years. As part of its settlement, IBM must file monthly reports with the SEC to demonstrate its efforts to avoid future violations of the Foreign Corrupt Practices Act.

Meanwhile Canadian media reported in 2015 that three IBM employees were arrested there on corruption charges. IBM also says it is cooperating with the SEC as regulators look at IBM's accounting practices in the UK and Ireland, as well as at home in the United States. Living up to its own code of ethics will require continued vigilance at IBM.[59]

- Besides the measures described, how else can IBM promote ethical conduct by its employees?
- In a company operating where bribing government officials is expected, how can employees find the moral courage to forgo bribery at the risk of losing a big sale?

MANAGER'S BRIEF

PROGRESS REPORT

ONWARD

For ethical managers, the goal is to lead employees to maintain high ethical standards, which creates an environment in which whistleblowing is unnecessary. After reading "Management in Action: Progress Report," consider how IBM promotes ethical conduct and how this might reinforce employees' moral courage.

Corporate Social Responsibility

Stewardship means contributing to the long-term welfare of others.[60] Does business ever operate this way? Consider the following examples:

- Unilever structures its production and management processes to reduce negative impact on environments and communities.
- Starbucks has over 1,000 Leadership in Energy and Environmental Design (LEED) certified stores in 20 countries.
- Burt's Bees helped develop the Natural Standard for personal products, which created guidelines for what can be deemed natural.
- Pedigree dog food built its brand by focusing on the need to adopt homeless dogs.
- Whole Foods created Whole Planet Foundation to fight poverty through microlending to microentrepreneurs in rural communities around the world.
- Ford Motor Company fights HIV/AIDS in South Africa.
- Kickboard empowers teachers to use data to improve student performance in high-poverty areas in the United States.
- Bank Boston fosters economic development in communities of moderate income and in the inner city.[61]

Should business be responsible for social concerns beyond its own economic well-being? Do social concerns affect a corporation's financial performance? In the 1960s and 1970s, the political and social environment became more important to U.S. corporations as society turned its attention to issues such as equal opportunity, pollution control, energy and natural resource conservation, and consumer and worker protection.[62] Public debate addressed these issues and the ways business should respond to them. This controversy focused on the concept of corporate social responsibility.

Corporate social responsibility (CSR) is the obligation toward society assumed by business.[63] Corporate social responsibility reflects the social imperatives and the social consequences of business practices; it consists broadly of policies and practices that reflect business responsibility for some wider societal good.[64] This can range from local or small-scale problems to issues of politics, diplomacy, international relations, and peace through commerce.[65] Interesting questions to contemplate include why past corporate irresponsibilities are easily forgotten, and whether and how current managers of an organization should be held responsible for the irresponsible actions of the managers who came before them.[66]

CSR actions and policies take into account stakeholders' expectations and often consider the **triple bottom line** of economic, social, and environmental performance.[67] The precise policies and practices underlying CSR lie at the discretion of the corporation. Some companies refer to their CSR practices in terms of sustainability, on the grounds that these efforts maintain positive long-term relationships with communities, employees, customers, governments, and the natural environment.[68]

Social responsibilities can be categorized[69] as shown in Exhibit 5.7. The **economic responsibilities** of business are to produce goods and services that society wants at a price that perpetuates the business and satisfies its obligations to investors. For Smithfield Foods, the largest pork producer in the United States, this means selling bacon, ham, and other products to customers at prices that maximize Smithfield's profits and keep the company growing over the long term. Economic responsibility may also extend to offering certain products to needy consumers at a reduced price.

stewardship

Contributing to the long-term welfare of others.

corporate social responsibility (CSR)

Obligation toward society assumed by business. See also *ethics*.

triple bottom line

Economic, social, and environmental performance.

economic responsibilities

To produce goods and services that society wants at a price that perpetuates the business and satisfies its obligations to investors.

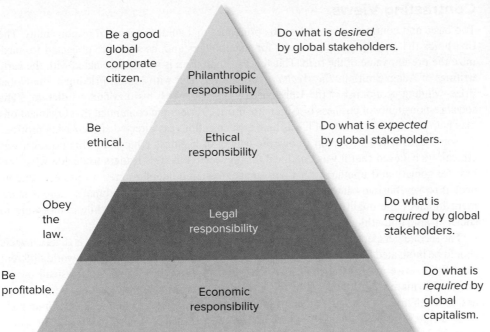

Be a good global corporate citizen.
Philanthropic responsibility
Do what is *desired* by global stakeholders.

Be ethical.
Ethical responsibility
Do what is *expected* by global stakeholders.

Obey the law.
Legal responsibility
Do what is *required* by global stakeholders.

Be profitable.
Economic responsibility
Do what is *required* by global capitalism.

SOURCE: Carroll, A., "Management Ethically with Global Stakeholders: A Present and Future Challenge," *Academy of Management Executive: The Thinking Manager's Source.* Mississippi State, MS: Academy of Management, 2004.

Legal responsibilities are to obey local, state, federal, and relevant international laws. Laws affecting Smithfield cover a wide range of requirements, from filing tax returns to meeting worker safety standards. **Ethical responsibilities** include meeting other societal expectations, not written as law. Smithfield took on this level of responsibility when it responded to requests by major customers, including McDonald's, Walmart, and Safeway, that it discontinue the practice of using gestation crates to house its sows. The customers were reacting to pressure from animal rights advocates who consider it cruel for sows to live in the two-foot by seven-foot crates during their entire gestation period, which means they cannot walk, turn around, or stretch their legs for months at a time.[70] Smithfield was not legally required to make the change (except in two states), and the arrangement was costly, but the company's decision helped its public image—that is, until it backed out of the plan, citing economic woes.

Finally, **philanthropic responsibilities** are additional behaviors and activities that society finds desirable and that the values of the business support. Examples include supporting community projects and making charitable contributions. Philanthropic activities can be more than mere altruism; managed properly, strategic philanthropy can become not an oxymoron but a way to build goodwill in a variety of stakeholders and even add to shareholder wealth.[71]

Many believe that a 21st-century education must help students think about responsibilities beyond self-interest and profitability. Such an education teaches students to leave a legacy that extends beyond the bottom line—a transcendent education.[72] A **transcendent education** has five higher goals that balance self-interest with responsibility to others: *empathy* (feeling your decisions as potential victims might feel them, to gain wisdom); *generativity* (learning how to give as well as take, to others in the present as well as to future generations); *mutuality* (viewing success not merely as personal gain, but a common victory); *civil aspiration* (thinking not just in terms of don'ts [lie, cheat, steal, kill], but also in terms of positive contributions); and *intolerance of inhumanity* (speaking out against unethical actions).

legal responsibilities

To obey local, state, federal, and relevant international laws.

ethical responsibilities

Meeting other social expectations, not written as law.

philanthropic responsibilities

Additional behaviors and activities that society finds desirable and that the values of the business support.

A transcendent education teaches students to leave a legacy that extends beyond the bottom line.

transcendent education

An education with five higher goals that balance self-interest with responsibility to others.

Contrasting Views

Two basic and contrasting views describe principles that guide managerial responsibility. The first holds that managers act as agents for shareholders and, as such, are obligated to maximize the present value of the firm. This tenet of capitalism is widely associated with the early writings of Adam Smith in *The Wealth of Nations* and later with Milton Friedman, the Nobel Prize–winning economist of the University of Chicago. With his now-famous dictum, "The social responsibility of business is to increase profits," Friedman contended that organizations may help improve the quality of life as long as such actions are directed at increasing profits.

Some considered Friedman to be "the enemy of business ethics," but his position was ethical: he believed that it was unethical for unelected business leaders to decide what was best for society and unethical for them to spend shareholders' money on projects unconnected to key business interests.[73] Furthermore, the context of Friedman's famous statement includes the qualifier that business should increase its profits while conforming to society's laws and ethical customs.

The second perspective, different from the profit maximization perspective, is that managers should be motivated by principled moral reasoning. Adam Smith wrote about a world different from the one we are in now, driven in the 18th century by the self-interest of small owner-operated farms and craft shops trying to generate a living income for themselves and their families. This self-interest was quite different from that of top executives of modern corporations.[74]

It is noteworthy that Adam Smith also wrote *A Theory of Moral Sentiments,* in which he argued that "sympathy," defined as a proper regard for others, is the basis of a civilized society.[75] Smith argued further that "the wise and virtuous man is at all times willing that this own private interest should be sacrificed to public interest" if circumstances require it.[76]

Advocates of corporate social responsibility argue that organizations have a wider range of responsibilities that extend beyond the production of goods and services at a profit. As members of society, organizations should actively and responsibly participate in the community and in the larger environment.

From this perspective, many people criticized insurance companies after Hurricane Sandy devastated homes and businesses along the New Jersey and New York coasts. From a social responsibility perspective, it was wrong for companies to watch out for their bottom line and avoid paying claims whereever they could make a case that the damage wasn't covered; the insurers should have been more concerned about their devastated customers.

Reconciliation

Profit maximization and corporate social responsibility used to be regarded as antagonistic, leading to opposing policies. But the two views can converge.[77] The Coca-Cola Company set a goal to improve its water efficiency in manufacturing operations by 25 percent over a ten-year period (ending in 2020).[78] The company is improving water efficiency in the production process and treating its wastewater.[79] From a practical perspective, Coca-Cola's strategic planners have identified water shortages as a strategic risk; from a values perspective, water is, in the words of executive Neville Isdell, "at the very core of our ethos," so "responsible use of that resource is very important to us."[80]

Earlier attention to corporate social responsibility focused on alleged wrongdoing and how to control it. More recently, attention has also centered on the possible competitive advantage of socially responsible actions.

The relationship between corporate social performance and corporate financial performance is complex;[81] socially responsible organizations are not necessarily more or less successful in financial terms.[82] But on net, the accumulated evidence indicates that social responsibility is associated with better financial performance.[83] Companies can avoid unnecessary and costly regulation if they are socially responsible. Such actions also can pay dividends to the

The U.S. Department of Agriculture and Coca-Cola North America are in partnership to restore and protect damaged watersheds on national forests.

©Nature and Science/Alamy Stock Photo

conscience, to the personal reputation, and to the public image of the company as well as in the market response.[84] Plus, society's problems can offer business opportunities, and profits can be made from systematic and vigorous efforts to solve these problems.

Firms can perform cost–benefit analyses to identify actions that will maximize profits while satisfying the demand for corporate social responsibility from multiple stakeholders.[85] In other words, managers can treat corporate social responsibility as they would treat all investment decisions. This has been the case as firms attempt to reconcile their business practices with their effect on the natural environment.

The Natural Environment and Sustainability

Most large corporations developed in an era of abundant raw materials, cheap energy, and unconstrained waste disposal.[86] But many of the technologies developed during this era have contributed to the destruction of ecosystems. Industrial-age systems follow a linear flow of extract, produce, sell, use, and discard—what some call a take–make–waste approach.[87]

At the same time, perhaps no time in history has offered greater possibilities for a change in business thinking than the 21st century. Some maintain that ecological sustainability is now the key driver of innovation.[88] And, whereas some are pessimistic about the planet's future, many are both resolute about creating a healthier planet, and more optimistic now than in recent years. One such optimist is Sanjit Bunker Roy, creator of India's Barefoot College (featured in the nearby "Social Enterprise" box).

> Business used to look at environmental issues as a no-win situation, but now a paradigm shift is taking place.

Business used to look at environmental issues as a no-win situation; you either help the environment and hurt your business or help your business at a cost to the environment. But now a paradigm shift is taking place in corporate environmental management: the deliberate incorporation of environmental values into competitive strategies and into the design and manufacturing of products.[89] In addition to philosophical reasons, companies go green to satisfy consumer demand, to react to a competitor's actions, to meet requests from customers or suppliers, to comply with legal requirements, and to create competitive advantage.

GE used to view environmental rules as a burden and a cost; now it sees environmentally friendly technologies as one of the global economy's most significant business opportunities. Through its Ecomagination program, GE has invested over $17 billion in clean tech R&D that helps solve environmental problems. Its solutions include wind turbines, materials for solar energy cells, and energy-efficient home appliances. These have delivered $232 billion in revenue, a green image for the GE brand, and a leadership position in many rapidly growing markets including high-efficiency jet engines and locomotives.[90]

A Risk Society

We live in a risk society. That is, the creation and distribution of wealth generate by-products that can cause injury, loss, or danger to people and the environment. The fundamental sources of risk in modern society are the excessive production of hazards and ecologically unsustainable consumption of natural resources.[91] Risk has proliferated through population explosion, industrial pollution, and environmental degradation.[92]

Industrial pollution risks include air pollution, smog, global warming, ozone depletion, acid rain, toxic waste sites, nuclear hazards, obsolete weapons arsenals, industrial accidents, and hazardous products. Tens of thousands of uncontrolled toxic waste sites have been documented in the United States alone. The situation is far worse in some other parts of the world. The pattern, for toxic waste and many other risks, is one of accumulating risks and inadequate remedies.

The institutions that create environmental and technological risk (corporations and government agencies) are responsible for controlling and managing the risks.[93] Patagonia admits

Social Enterprise

A College Built by and for the Poor

An extraordinary effort began over 40 years ago. India's Barefoot College is an educational organization working in 1,300 villages across nearly 80 of the world's least developed countries in Asia, Africa, the Pacific islands, and South America. Its mission is to improve rural lives and communities through learning-by-doing training programs in health care, women's empowerment, solar energy, water, and land development that are designed and built by and for the poor.

Barefoot College is based on the guiding principles of service and sustainability espoused by Mahatma Gandhi, along with a commitment to equality, shared decision making, and self-reliance. Its projects have brought artificial light to more than half a million people and provide clean water and solar energy for cooking and heating to thousands of communities. Its Enriche program is dedicated to using simple methods to empower rural women of all ages, even if illiterate, with the scientific and engineering skills they need to undertake environmental stewardship, manage solar energy, and protect women's reproductive health.

Each woman in the program is trained to teach others in turn. Those trained in the six-month solar energy program in Tilonia, India, come from around the world. They receive fellowship grants from the Indian government while enrolled, and leave with a stipend for starting their own business.

Sanjit Bunker Roy, educated in Delhi, was from a wealthy background, but in his 20s he decided to try living on $1 a day. Based on that experience, as a young social worker in 1972 he was inspired to create Barefoot College, which he calls "the only College where the teacher is the learner and the learner the teacher." He has been honored by *Time* magazine for his "grass roots social entrepreneurship" and was *Business Standard*'s 2016 Social Entrepreneur of the Year. Says Roy, "People find

©Ashley Cooper pics/Alamy Stock Photo

something in themselves that they never thought they had. And then go back to the communities they are from and show what they learned — that's how leaders are born."

Among Roy's ambitious plans for Barefoot College's near future include efforts to triple the number of people it trains, reaching 6 million by 2018, by opening more of its simple training centers around the world and making greater use of digital teaching materials and methods. These plans will be supported by an infusion of $11 million, which he hopes to raise from corporate partners.

Questions

- In what ways do you think Barefoot College's mission and goals demonstrate a utilitarian philosophy of ethics?
- Which of Barefoot College's guiding principles have you observed where you have worked or volunteered? Choose a principle you might not have observed and explain how you would go about incorporating it into your current or a recent workplace.[94]

openly that its business activities (its factories use water and release carbon into the air) contribute to climate change. The company uses this factual acknowledgment to do whatever is within its control to "reduce, neutralize, or even reverse the root causes of climate change."[95]

Some of the world's worst environmental problems are in China because of its rapid industrialization and its huge population and size. The smog in Beijing is so unhealthy on certain days that the government closes factories, schools, and bans half the vehicles until the pollution level drops.[96] China's environmental problems affect more than large cities. Hundreds of millions of China's rural population drink unclean water. At least the problem is recognized; the central government is pressuring local authorities to clean up or shut down dirty factories.[97] Still, most cleanup efforts focus on big cities while rural areas worsen.

Developing countries are often seen as sustainability laggards, focused solely on raising people out of poverty. Regulatory agencies can be weak and hesitant to impose restrictions, but visionary individuals the world over can pioneer successful sustainability efforts.[98]

Ecocentric Management

Ecocentric management has as its goal the creation of sustainable economic development and improvement of quality of life worldwide for all organizational stakeholders.[99] **Sustainable growth** is economic growth and development that meet the organization's present needs without harming the ability of future generations to meet their needs.[100] Sustainability is fully compatible with the natural ecosystems that generate and preserve life.[101]

Businesses are both a cause of and a solution to environmental degradation, and clearly have a major role to play in sustainability debates and strategies.[102]

Increasingly, firms are paying attention to their total environmental impact throughout the life cycle of their products.[103] **Life-cycle analysis (LCA)** is a process of analyzing all inputs and outputs, through the entire cradle-to-grave life of a product, to determine the total environmental impact of the production and use of a product. LCA quantifies the total use of resources and the releases into the air, water, and land. Reporting worldwide **carbon footprints** is a big step in environmental reporting in that industry. Previously mentioned apparel maker Patagonia uses LCA to analyze the carbon footprint at each stage of its supply chain from farm to factory.[104]

LCA considers the extraction of raw materials, product packaging, transportation, and disposal. Consider packaging alone. Goods make the journey from manufacturer to wholesaler to retailer to customer; then they are recycled back to the manufacturer. They may be packaged and repackaged several times, from bulk transport, to large crates, to cardboard boxes, to individual consumer sizes. Repackaging not only creates waste but also costs time. The design of initial packaging in sizes and formats adaptable to the final customer can minimize the need for repackaging, cut waste, and realize financial benefits.

Rather than the linear take–make–waste production model described earlier, a fully sustainable model applies a circular borrow–use–return approach.[105] Whereas the former model engages in harmful extraction, generates huge quantities of waste and pollution, and depletes natural resources (a process in which resources move from cradle to grave), the cradle-to-cradle approach is ecologically benign and restorative. In its ideal form, this sustainable approach extracts energy and raw materials without harm, phases out the use of nonrenewable resources, designs processes and products that recirculate so they don't cause environmental or socioeconomic harm, keeps toxic substances in closed-loop industrial cycles, and recirculates biological materials back into nature without harm.[106]

Profitability need not suffer and may be positively affected by ecocentric philosophies and practices. Some, but not all, research has shown a positive relationship between corporate environmental performance and profitability.[107] Of course, whether the relationship is positive, negative, or neutral depends on the strategies chosen and the effectiveness of implementation.

Companies can integrate green practices with strategy in a variety of ways. Certainly they develop and market green products; Toyota's bold move to develop the Prius paid off handsomely with market dominance.[108] Companies also can emphasize green attributes in their marketing but need

LO 6

ecocentric management

Its goal is the creation of sustainable economic development and improvement of quality of life worldwide for all organizational stakeholders.

Timberland has paid particular attention to life-cycle analysis, as implied by what is printed on its recycled material shoe boxes.

©McGraw-Hill Education/Jill Braaten

---

sustainable growth

Economic growth and development that meets present needs without harming the needs of future generations.

life-cycle analysis (LCA)

A process of analyzing all inputs and outputs, through the entire "cradle-to-grave" life of a product, to determine total environmental impact.

carbon footprint

The output of carbon dioxide and other greenhouse gases.

to avoid misleading claims (greenwashing) and public backlash. For instance, previously mentioned Arm & Hammer positioned its baking soda brand as "the number one environmentally sensible alternative for cleaning and deodorizing" and says it's been "committed to the environment since 1846." On the other hand, the company ignored a major problem: it used animal testing. The blogosphere began touting equally green but cruelty-free Bob's Red Mill baking soda.[109]

Companies also can acquire other companies with sustainability (and image) in mind. L'Oréal bought The Body Shop, Colgate-Palmolive bought Tom's of Maine, Unilever bought Ben & Jerry's, and Group Danone bought Stonyfield's.[110] When Clorox bought Burt's Bees, which had decades of leadership and experience with sustainability, it did so for growth and to convince environmental stakeholders that the company's strategic change was genuine, but also to acquire knowledge about the green product space.[111]

If you are interested in learning more, you can check out the Global Reporting Initiative (GRI) list of sustainability performance indicators. This useful resource, at www.globalreporting.org, aims to help companies improve their sustainability practices, including transparent reporting.

Environmental Agendas for the Future

In the past, most companies were oblivious to their negative environmental impact. More recently, many began striving for low impact. Now some strive for positive impact, eager to sell solutions to the world's problems.

Consider climate change and the world's shortage of clean water. By 2025, approximately 3.5 billion people may be living in areas of the world with scarce water resources.[112] When Dow Chemical's Freeport, Texas, site had trouble getting enough water to run its processes during droughts, it installed technology to monitor the water system 24/7 and reduced water consumption by a billion gallons a year.[113] Marriott is pursuing a goal to reduce energy and water consumption by 20 percent per occupied hotel room.[114] Nestlé saves up to 1,375 cubic meters of water per year since improving how it collects and transports milk from farmers.

You don't have to be a manufacturer or a utility to jump on the green bandwagon. Web search giant Google is working hard to reduce its carbon footprint and purchasing offsets—funding projects that reduce greenhouse gas emissions elsewhere.[115]

Collaborative efforts will be essential—for example, the energy industry and environmentalists working with rather than against one another.[116] Networks of companies with a common ecological vision can combine their efforts into high-leverage, highly impactful action.[117] In cities such as San Antonio, Texas, and Columbus, Ohio, federal partner agencies work closely with city governments, utilities, and multiple manufacturers to reduce pollutants and energy consumption and to increase energy savings.

In Kalundborg, Denmark, such a collaborative alliance exists among an electric power generating plant, an oil refiner, a biotech production plant, a plasterboard factory, cement producers, heating utilities, a sulfuric acid producer, and local agriculture and horticulture. Chemicals, energy (for both heating and cooling), water, and organic materials flow among companies. Resources are conserved, waste materials generate revenues, and water, air, and ground pollution all are reduced.

In 2010, the World Bank launched a project to help developing countries arrive at valuations of their natural capital. Then-president Robert Zoellik said, "The natural wealth of nations should be a capital asset, valued in combination with its financial capital, manufactured capital, and human capital."[118] Now, nonprofit organizations and accounting firms offer methodologies that value ecosystems. The for-profit Global Environment Fund currently has invested about $1 billion in firms focused on environmental and natural resources.[119]

Stated Dow CEO Andrew Liveris, "Companies that value and integrate biodiversity and ecosystem services into their strategic plans are best positioned for the future."[120] In addition to the benefits to the world of sustainable practices, many now believe that preparing for and adapting to climate change is a major and fast-growing challenge,[121] and that solving environmental problems is one of the biggest opportunities in the history of commerce.[122]

Management in Action

IBM TAKES RESPONSIBILITY

Because openness builds the kind of trust IBM wants as the basis for its relationships, the company publishes its values and policies online along with an annual Corporate Responsibility Report. IBM's understanding of its role in corporate citizenship includes practices related to the natural environment and the communities it serves. IBM defines its social role this way:

1. We identify and act upon new opportunities to apply our technology and expertise to societal problems.
2. We scale our existing programs and initiatives to achieve maximum benefit.
3. We empower our employees and others to serve their communities.
4. We integrate corporate citizenship and social responsibility into every aspect of our company.

These statements apply IBM's resources as a large global technology company (over 431,000 employees in almost 170 countries) to the communities where it operates.

Especially in its concern for the natural environment, IBM unites a commitment to be responsible with the business opportunities available to a company specializing in data analysis, cloud computing solutions, and planning. In fact, IBM has had policies for protecting the environment and conserving resources since 1967. IBM's product recycling programs are designed to resell, refurbish, or recycle at least 97 percent of its end-of-life products. The company also requires its suppliers to demonstrate that they are taking responsibility for their impact on the environment.

Moreover, environmental protection is now part of IBM's Smarter Planet strategy. IBM's consultants and systems help cities, businesses, and building owners manage the data required to operate as efficiently as possible. For example, IBM is helping San Francisco figure out how to keep all of its waste out of landfills by directing it to recycling and other uses. IBM's Smarter Building initiative installs sensors and building automation software to gather data on building systems and uses, and uses the data to conserve energy and water.

IBM's corporate citizenship also involves supporting selected nonprofit causes, including economic development, education, and health. Its biggest philanthropy is its Smarter Cities challenge, which awards grants to cities to help them improve in a specified area of performance. IBM sends a six-member team of its own experts to each city to help leaders analyze problems and develop solutions. By the end of 2013, IBM had sent teams to 100 cities around the world to address such challenges as improving urban planning, managing traffic, encouraging entrepreneurship, improving energy efficiency, and much more. The company also recently announced plans to add 25,000 U.S. jobs over the next few years, including 2,000 military veterans.[123]

- How is IBM's commitment to corporate social responsibility good for IBM as a business? Explain.
- Improving energy efficiency saves IBM millions of dollars, but recycling its used electronics requires hiring hundreds of people. Is the recycling program justifiable? Why or why not?

KEY TERMS

business ethics, p. 135

carbon footprint, p. 149

Caux Principles, p. 136

compliance-based ethics programs, p. 140

corporate social responsibility (CSR), p. 144

ecocentric management, p. 149

economic responsibilities, p. 144

egoism, p. 136

ethical climate, p. 138

ethical issue, p. 135

ethical leader, p. 139

ethical responsibilities, p. 145

ethics, p. 132

integrity-based ethics programs, p. 140

Kohlberg's model of cognitive moral development, p. 137

legal responsibilities, p. 145

life-cycle analysis (LCA), p. 149

moral philosophy, p. 135

philanthropic responsibilities, p. 145

relativism, p. 136

Sarbanes-Oxley Act, p. 137

stewardship, p. 144

sustainable growth, p. 149

transcendent education, p. 145

triple bottom line, p. 144

universalism, p. 135

utilitarianism, p. 136

virtue ethics, p. 136

RETAINING WHAT YOU LEARNED

In Chapter 5, you learned that ethics is an important and personal issue that affects employee and organizational behavior. Ethical decisions are influenced by personal values and which ethical system people use to frame a given problem. Companies attempt to influence their ethics environment by establishing ethical programs or codes. Codes prescribe guidelines for behavior. Making ethical decisions requires moral awareness, moral judgment, and moral character. A model of ethical decision making is repeated below. Corporate social responsibility suggests that corporations have not only economic but also legal, ethical, and philanthropic responsibilities. While most companies used to view the natural environment as a source of raw materials and profit, now more companies are adopting a greener agenda for business reasons as well as personal commitment to sustainable development. Ecocentric managers attempt to minimize negative environment impact, create sustainable economic development, and improve the quality of life worldwide.

EXHIBIT 5.6 (revisited)

A Process for Ethical Decision Making

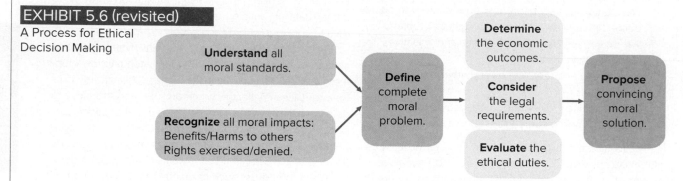

SOURCE: Hosmer, L. T., *The Ethics of Management,* 4th ed. New York: McGraw-Hill/Irwin, 2003, p. 32. Fig. 5.1A.

LO 1 Describe how different ethical perspectives guide decision making.

- The purpose of ethics is to identify the rules that govern human behavior and the "goods" that are worth seeking.
- Ethical decisions are guided by the individual's values or principles of conduct such as honesty, fairness, integrity, respect for others, and responsible citizenship.
- Different ethical systems include universalism, egoism and utilitarianism, relativism, and virtue ethics.
- These philosophical systems, as practiced by different individuals according to their level of cognitive moral development and other factors, underpin the ethical stances of individuals and organizations.

LO 2 Explain how companies influence their ethics environment.

- Different organizations apply different ethical perspectives and standards.
- Ethics codes sometimes are helpful, although they must be implemented properly.
- Ethics programs can range from compliance-based to integrity-based.
- Ethics codes address employee conduct, community and environment, shareholders, customers, suppliers and contractors, political activity, and technology.

LO 3 Outline a process for making ethical decisions.

- Making ethical decisions requires moral awareness, moral judgment, and moral character.
- When faced with ethical dilemmas, the veil of ignorance is a useful metaphor and provides a useful tactic for ethical decision making.
- You can know various moral standards (universalism, relativism, and so on), use the problem-solving model described in Chapter 3, identify the positive and negative effects of your alternatives on different parties, consider legal requirements and the costs of unethical actions, and then evaluate your ethical duties.

LO 4 Summarize the important issues surrounding corporate social responsibility.

- Corporate social responsibility is the extension of the corporate role beyond economic pursuits. It includes not only economic but also legal, ethical, and philanthropic responsibilities.
- Advocates believe managers should consider societal and human needs in their business decisions because corporations are members of society and carry a wide range of responsibilities.
- Critics of corporate responsibility believe managers' first responsibility is to increase profits for the shareholders who own the corporation.

- The two perspectives are potentially reconcilable, especially if managers choose to address areas of social responsibility that contribute to the organization's strategy.

LO 5 Discuss reasons for businesses' growing interest in the natural environment.

- In the past, most companies viewed the natural environment as a resource to be used for raw materials and profit. But consumer, regulatory, competitive, and other pressures arose. Executives often viewed these pressures as burdens, constraints, and costs to be borne.
- Now more companies view the interface between business and the natural environment as a potential win–win opportunity.
- Some are adopting a greener agenda for philosophical reasons and personal commitment to sustainable development.
- Many also are recognizing the potential financial benefits of managing with the environment in mind

and are integrating environmental issues into corporate and business strategy.
- Some see entering businesses that help rather than harm the natural environment as one of the great commercial opportunities in history.

LO 6 Identify actions managers can take to manage with the environment in mind.

- Organizations have contributed risk to society and bear some responsibility for reducing it.
- They also are capable of helping to solve environmental problems.
- Ecocentric management attempts to minimize negative environment impact, create sustainable economic development, and improve the quality of life worldwide.
- Relevant actions are described in the chapter, including strategic initiatives, life-cycle analysis, and inter-organizational alliances.

DISCUSSION QUESTIONS

1. Consider the various ethical systems described early in the chapter. Identify concrete examples from your own past decisions or the decisions of others you have seen or read about.

2. Choose one or more topics from Exhibit 5.3 and discuss their current status and the ethical issues surrounding them.

3. Identify and discuss illegal, unethical, and socially responsible business actions in the current news.

4. Does your school have a code of ethics? If so, what does it say? Is it effective? Why or why not?

5. You have a job you like at which you work 40 to 45 hours per week. How much off-the-job volunteer work would you do? What kinds of volunteer work? How will you react if your boss makes it clear he or she wants you to cut back on the outside activities and devote more hours to your job?

6. What are the arguments for and against the concept of corporate social responsibility? Where do you stand and why? Give your opinions about some of the in-text examples.

7. What do you think of the concept of a transcendent education as described in the chapter? What can be done to implement such a vision for education?

8. What is the current status of the Sarbanes-Oxley Act? What do executives think of it now? What impact has it had?

9. A company in England slaughtered 70,000 baby ostrich chicks each year for their meat. It told a teen

magazine that it would stop if it received enough complaints. Analyze this policy, practice, and public statement using the concepts discussed in the chapter.

10. A Nike ad in the U.S. magazine *Seventeen* showed a picture of a girl, aged perhaps 8 or 9. The ad read,

If you let me play . . .

I will like myself more.

I will have more self-confidence.

I will suffer less depression.

I will be 60 percent less likely to get breast cancer.

I will be more likely to leave a man who beats me.

I will be less likely to get pregnant before I want to.

I will learn what it means to be strong.

If you let me play sports.

Assess this ad in terms of chapter concepts surrounding ethics and social responsibility. What questions would you ask in doing this analysis?

11. Should companies be held accountable for actions of decades past, then legal but since made illegal, as their harmful effects became known? Why or why not?

12. Discuss courage as a requirement for ethical behavior. What personal examples can you offer, either as an actor or as an observer? What examples are in the news?

EXPERIENTIAL EXERCISES

5.1 MEASURING YOUR ETHICAL WORK BEHAVIOR

OBJECTIVES

1. To explore a range of ethically perplexing situations.
2. To understand your own ethical attitudes.

INSTRUCTIONS

Make decisions in the situations described in the Ethical Behavior Worksheet. You will not have all the background information on each situation; instead, you should make whatever assumptions you feel you would make if you were actually confronted with the decision choices described. Select the decision choice that most closely represents the decision you feel you would make personally. You should choose decision options even though you can envision other creative solutions that were not included in the exercise.

Ethical Behavior Worksheet
SITUATION 1

You are taking a very difficult chemistry course, which you must pass to maintain your scholarship and to avoid damaging your application for graduate school. Chemistry is not your strong suit, and, because of a just-below-failing average in the course, you will have to receive a grade of 90 or better on the final exam, which is two days away. A janitor, who is aware of your plight, informs you that he found the master for the chemistry final in a trash barrel and has saved it. He will make it available to you for a price, which is high but which you could afford. What would you do?

_____ (a) I would tell the janitor thanks, but no thanks.

_____ (b) I would report the janitor to the proper officials.

_____ (c) I would buy the exam and keep it to myself.

_____ (d) I would not buy the exam myself, but I would let some of my friends, who are also flunking the course, know that it is available.

SITUATION 2

You have been working on some financial projections manually for two days now. It seems that each time you think you have them completed, your boss shows up with a new assumption or another what-if question. If you only had a copy of a spreadsheet software program for your personal computer, you could plug in the new assumptions and revise the estimates with ease. Then a colleague offers to let you make a copy of some software that is copyrighted. What would you do?

_____ (a) I would accept my friend's generous offer and make a copy of the software.

_____ (b) I would decline to copy it and plug away manually on the numbers.

_____ (c) I would decide to go buy a copy of the software myself, for $300, and hope I would be reimbursed by the company in a month or two.

_____ (d) I would request another extension on an already overdue project date.

SITUATION 3

Your small manufacturing company is in serious financial difficulty. A large order of your products is ready to be delivered to a key customer when you discover that the product is simply not right. It will not meet all performance specifications, will cause problems for your customer, and will require rework in the field; however, this, you know, will not become evident until after the customer has received and paid for the order. If you do not ship the order and receive the payment as expected, your business may be forced into bankruptcy. And if you delay the shipment or inform the customer of these problems, you may lose the order and go bankrupt. What would you do?

_____ (a) I would not ship the order and place my firm in voluntary bankruptcy.

_____ (b) I would inform the customer and declare voluntary bankruptcy.

_____ (c) I would ship the order and inform the customer after I received payment.

_____ (d) I would ship the order and not inform the customer.

SITUATION 4

You are the cofounder and president of a new venture, manufacturing products for the recreational market. Five months after launching the business, one of your suppliers informs you it can no longer supply you with a critical raw material because you are not a large-quantity user. Without the raw material, the business cannot continue. What would you do?

_____ (a) I would grossly overstate my requirements to another supplier to make the supplier think I am a much larger potential customer to secure the raw material from that supplier, even though this would mean the supplier will no longer be able to supply another, noncompeting small manufacturer who may thus be forced out of business.

_____ (b) I would steal raw material from another firm (noncompeting) where I am aware of a sizable stockpile.

_____ (c) I would pay off the supplier because I have reason to believe that the supplier could be persuaded to meet my needs with a sizable under-the-table payoff that my company could afford.

_____ (d) I would declare voluntary bankruptcy.

SITUATION 5

You are on a marketing trip for your new venture for the purpose of calling on the purchasing agent of a major prospective client. Your company is manufacturing an electronic system that you hope the purchasing agent will buy. During your conversation, you notice on the cluttered desk of the purchasing agent several copies of a cost proposal for a system from one of your direct competitors. This purchasing agent has previously reported mislaying several of your own company's proposals and has asked for additional copies. The purchasing agent leaves the room momentarily to get you a cup of coffee, leaving you alone with your competitor's proposals less than an arm's length away. What would you do?

_____ (a) I would do nothing but await the man's return.

_____ (b) I would sneak a quick peek at the proposal, looking for bottom-line numbers.

_____ (c) I would put the copy of the proposal in my briefcase.

_____ (d) I would wait until the man returns and ask his permission to see the copy.

5.2 ETHICAL STANCE

Are the following actions ethical or unethical in your opinion? Why? Consider the actions individually and discuss them in small groups.

- Calling in sick when you really are not
- Taking office supplies home for personal use
- Cheating on a test
- Turning in someone for cheating on a test or paper
- Overcharging on your company expense report
- Trying to flirt your way out of a speeding ticket
- Splicing cable from your neighbor
- Surfing the net on company time
- Cheating on income tax
- Lying (exaggerating) about yourself to influence someone of the opposite sex
- Looking at pornographic sites on the web through the company network
- Lying about your education on a job application
- Lying about experience in a job interview
- Making a copy of a rental DVD before returning it to the store

Concluding Case

MA EARTH SKIN CARE TRIES TO STAY NATURAL

Heather Franklin is a marketing manager for Ma Earth Skin Care. Four years ago, when she was hired to help with the paperwork for promotional campaigns, she was thrilled to become a part of this company because she loved Ma Earth's lotions, soaps, and cosmetics. Besides smelling heavenly and offering exquisite colors for eye shadow and lipstick, the products spoke to Heather's values: Ma Earth promised to use all natural ingredients, sustainably grown or mined, and to operate with minimal adverse impact on the planet. So for Heather, going to work was almost like carrying out a mission, promoting both beauty and concern for the planet's well-being. No doubt, her commitment and enthusiasm helped pave the way when the position of marketing manager opened up.

Currently, Heather and her team are preparing a promotional campaign for a new product line, Oré Essentials, which includes lipsticks, foundation, and eye shadows tinted with a plant extract called orellana. The exciting feature of Oré Essentials is that orellana is harvested deep in the Amazon rain forest, and because of its sustainable practices, Ma Earth will obtain this special ingredient in a socially responsible manner. The company set up a contract with a

tribe living in a remote village. The people of the tribe are supposed to grow and harvest the orellana, which is naturally part of the area's ecosystem, and Ma Earth has promised to pay a fair price to the whole tribe so the people can use the money to maintain their village and their way of life. Consumers will get a beautiful product and the pleasure of knowing that they are helping preserve an endangered ecology—and an endangered way of life for the rain forest people.

But when Heather sat down for a meeting with the photography crew that traveled to the village, some concerns began to surface. She was looking at stunning photos of tribe members arrayed in grass skirts as they stood behind a pile of fruit from the orellana tree. As she was selecting her favorite shots, one of the photographers commented that the translator had made some surprising remarks on the return trip from the village. Apparently the pile of orellana fruit had been gathered just for the photo shoot. The tribe doesn't really bother with growing and harvesting orellana; the people of this area aren't primarily farmers, and there aren't actually many orellana trees within a day's walk of the village. The first year they had tried selling orellana to Ma Earth, they grew only enough to earn a few hundred dollars, not really worth the effort. Heather felt confused by these statements and planned to take a closer look at spending on her product later that day.

Hours later, when the other employees had gone home, Heather finally had a chance to spend some time researching her product on the company's employee website. She found purchasing transactions for "orellana/annatto," and after a little research learned that under either name, the product is just an inexpensive dye. Under the latter name, it is used as a common food coloring. It turns out that Ma Earth made most of its purchases from a mainstream supplier, which is cheaper than persuading remote villagers to provide orellana.

That evening Heather went home feeling betrayed and upset. The next day she asked her boss, the divisional vice president, why the company pretended to care about a remote village if it was just a front for a brand. Heather's boss, Megan McDonough, said, "But we *do* care! We send them tens of thousands of dollars every year. Sure, they don't actually grow that stuff for us, but they could, and we'll buy it if they do. Anyway, our aid has provided a school and a health clinic, not to mention food and clothing. We've helped the tribe members stay healthy and preserve their language and culture."

Heather considered what Megan said. "So," she asked, "does this mean we're using their culture to build an image for our brand, and in exchange, they get money from us to keep that culture alive?" She thought about the traditional designs the marketing department had copied from the tribe as decorations for the Oré Essentials packaging.

Megan nodded encouragingly. "That's exactly what I'm saying. It's a win–win situation." Heather felt relieved but not quite sure that her original idealism would withstand her deeper knowledge of how Ma Earth defined its mission.

DISCUSSION QUESTIONS

1. What ethical issues is Heather facing in this situation? What possible marketing claims about the company's relationship with the Amazonian tribe would cross a line into unethical territory? What claims could it make ethically?

2. How could Ma Earth create an ethical climate that would help managers such as Heather ensure that they are behaving ethically?

3. How effectively do you think Ma Earth is practicing corporate social responsibility in this situation? Explain the reasoning behind your evaluation.

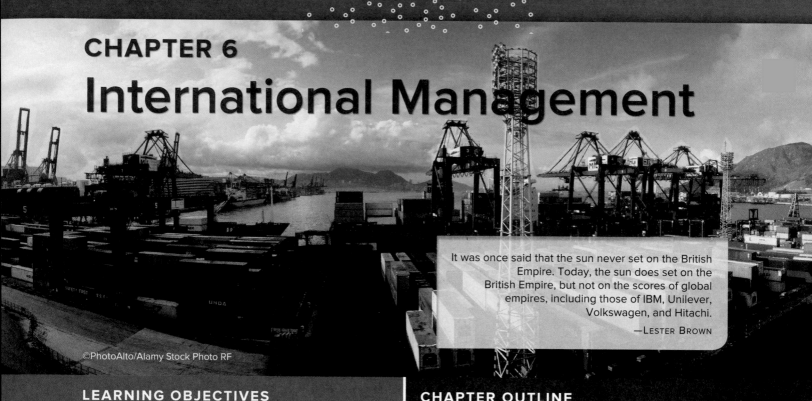

CHAPTER 6
International Management

It was once said that the sun never set on the British Empire. Today, the sun does set on the British Empire, but not on the scores of global empires, including those of IBM, Unilever, Volkswagen, and Hitachi.

—LESTER BROWN

©PhotoAlto/Alamy Stock Photo RF

LEARNING OBJECTIVES

After studying Chapter 6, you will be able to:

LO 1 Discuss what integration of the global economy means for companies and their managers.

LO 2 Describe how the world economy is becoming more integrated than ever before.

LO 3 Define the strategies organizations use to compete in the global marketplace.

LO 4 Compare the various entry modes organizations use to enter overseas markets.

LO 5 Explain how companies can staff overseas operations.

LO 6 Summarize the skills and knowledge managers need to manage globally.

LO 7 Identify ways in which cultural differences between countries influence management.

CHAPTER OUTLINE

Managing in Today's (Global) Economy
International Challenges and Opportunities
Outsourcing and Jobs

The Geography of Business
Western Europe
Asia: China and India
The Americas
Africa and the Middle East

Global Strategy
Pressures for Global Integration
Pressures for Local Responsiveness
Choosing a Global Strategy

Entry Mode
Exporting
Licensing
Franchising
Joint Ventures
Wholly Owned Subsidiaries

Working Overseas
Skills of the Global Manager
Understanding Cultural Issues
Ethical Issues in International Management

Management in Action

HOW ALIBABA IS BECOMING A GLOBAL BRAND

Online shoppers around the world recently spent an astounding $17.7 billion in a record-shattering 24-hour buying spree. That's almost three times as much money as was spent in the United States on Black Friday and Cyber Monday put together.

While some of the more than 40,000 participating brands that day included familiar U.S. retailers like Macy's, Target, Starbucks, Costco, and Gap, the website where this frenzy occurred is one that many U.S. shoppers have yet to hear of—China's e-commerce giant Alibaba, managed by Alibaba Holding Group Ltd.

The occasion was the annual anti–Valentine's Day holiday known as Singles' Day, which unattached Chinese consumers have been celebrating every November 11, mostly quietly, for about 20 years. But since 2009, when Alibaba decided to join the handful of companies then offering shopping discounts on Singles' Day, it has grown into the biggest one-day shopping blitz in the world. Discounts of up to 50 percent are offered on everything from clothing and cosmetics to wine, cars, and chandeliers. Celebrities like Scarlet Johannsen and David Beckham host live events leading up to the midnight opening, and online events run for the entire 24 hours, with virtual-reality gimmicks and special deals for those shopping via their phones (who accounted for 80 percent of sales).

Alibaba has been growing by leaps and bounds, helped by a new generation of young and sophisticated tech-savvy shoppers in China with middle-class tastes and money to spend. They are an attractive market for brands from around the world, including the United States, and for smaller vendors as well, who can sell their wares on Alibaba's third-party market in much the same way they do on Amazon.com.

To fund the growth it seeks at home and abroad, Alibaba raised $25 billion (another record-breaking number) from its IPO, listing itself in the United States. It employs about 45,000 people (far fewer than its nearest rival, Amazon, which holds more than 40 percent of

©VCG/Visual China Group/Getty Images

the U.S. e-commerce market), and posted revenues of over $5 billion in 2016, despite a marked slowing of the Chinese economy. The value of transactions on its site rose to $248 billion, greater than for eBay and Amazon combined.

In addition to its e-commerce site, which has 80 percent market share in China and hundreds of millions of users, Alibaba is in the digital media, entertainment, and cloud computing businesses as well. It has purchased a share of Groupon Inc., of Walmart's e-commerce arm Jet.com, and of Lyft.

Alibaba's founder Jack Ma has promised to expand his company's toehold in the United States. He stresses that his company will remain true to its stated principles, which put customers first, employees second, and shareholders third. "Our philosophy is that we want to be an ecosystem," he says. "Our philosophy is to empower others to sell, empower others to service, making sure the other people are more powerful than us. With our technology, our innovation, our partners—10 million small business sellers—they can compete with Microsoft and IBM. Our philosophy is, using Internet technology we can make every company become Amazon."[1]

How well can Alibaba translate its dedication to elevating the thrill of online shopping to consumers in the United States? As you read this chapter, consider what qualities of the international business environment present threats and opportunities for this company.

The direction of Alibaba's growth resembles that of many successful businesses in recent decades. The company started out by satisfying customers in a local market. As sales increased, the company began serving a larger region. Eventually, it began selling goods to and running operations in other countries. Now it boasts sales and develops managers around the globe.

Today's corporate giants—and many ambitious, creative small businesses—need employees and sales in other countries to meet their objectives. U.S. multinational corporations now employ almost one-third of their workers outside the United States, and the overseas share is growing. Sales of some product categories are growing faster outside the United States. Popular with older riders in the U.S., Harley-Davidson is marketing its motorcycles to first-time, younger riders in international markets. From 2015 to 2016, the company experienced 39 percent growth overseas.[2]

Or consider Walt Disney Company. After years of negotiations, the iconic U.S. company opened a $5.5 billion theme park and resort in Shanghai. The deal was complex because the Chinese government insisted on Chinese ownership, but for Disney it was worth it to bring its brand of entertainment to China's vast population and rapidly developing economy.[3]

Because of such trends, today's managers need to be able to plan how their company will enter markets around the world. That planning begins with understanding the importance of the global economy and the opportunities and threats of the fast-changing global environment.

Managing in Today's (Global) Economy

The global economy matters because our economy *is* global—because your customers, competitors, employees, and suppliers could be located anywhere in the world. For managers, this makes the business environment more complex and exciting than ever: a global economy with threats and opportunities around the world, accompanied by a need to know their customers' specific needs and values, which may vary considerably from place to place.

We will describe how managers can select strategies for this world. But first, let's see how the ever-greater interconnection, or integration, of the world economy is shaping business today.

International Challenges and Opportunities

LO 1

Increasing prosperity and lower trade barriers helped many nations integrate into a now-global economy. This integration has had many important consequences. First, even as the world's economic output grew, the volume of exports grew even (and much) faster. Second, foreign direct investment (FDI) plays an ever-increasing role in the global economy as companies of all sizes invest overseas. Third, imports penetrate more deeply into the world's largest economies. The growth of imports is a natural by-product of the growth of world trade and the trend toward manufacturing component parts, or even entire products, overseas before shipping them back home for final sale.

Finally, the growth of world trade, FDI, and imports means that companies around the globe are finding their home markets under attack from foreign competitors. This is true in the United States, where Chinese companies are purchasing once iconic firms like Starwood Hotels, Smithfield Foods, and GE's appliance business.[4]

What does all this mean for today's managers? Opportunities are greater because many formerly protected national markets are open for business. The potential for export and for making direct investments overseas is greater today than ever before. The environment is more complex due to the challenges of working in radically different cultures and coordinating globally dispersed operations. And the environment is more competitive because of cost-efficient overseas competitors.

Companies both large and small view the world, not just their own country, as their marketplace. As Exhibit 6.1 shows, the United States has no monopoly on international

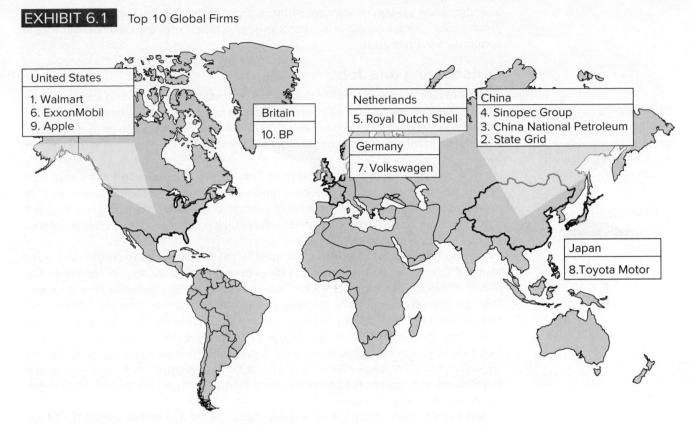

EXHIBIT 6.1   Top 10 Global Firms

United States
1. Walmart
6. ExxonMobil
9. Apple

Britain
10. BP

Netherlands
5. Royal Dutch Shell

Germany
7. Volkswagen

China
4. Sinopec Group
3. China National Petroleum
2. State Grid

Japan
8. Toyota Motor

SOURCE: "Global 500," *Fortune,* March 18, 2017, http://fortune.com/global500/.

business. Of the top 25 corporations in the world, 18 (72 percent) are based in countries outside the United States. Companies have dispersed their manufacturing, marketing, and research facilities to locations around the globe where cost and skill conditions are most favorable. This trend is so pervasive in industries such as automobiles, aerospace, and electronics that it is increasingly irrelevant to talk about "American products" or "Chinese products" or "German products."

> Companies both large and small view the world as their marketplace.

For example, the headquarters of an automaker no longer says much about where a particular car is made. The American-Made Index ranks vehicles based on where they were assembled, whether they have a high percentage of domestic parts, and how popular they are among U.S. consumers. Surprisingly, the "most American" models in 2016 were Toyota Camry, Honda Accord, and Toyota Sienna.[5] A U.S. headquarters doesn't limit a U.S. car company either. General Motors sold 10 million cars in 2016 in China (while sales in the U.S. were lackluster). This all-time record helped GM earn record profits.[6]

This is not just for the largest corporations. Many small companies limit their international involvement to exporting, or sourcing from or setting up production facilities overseas. Others acquire existing small businesses to gain talent and access to new markets. Based in Denver, AppIt Ventures develops custom software apps for client companies. It wasn't long before the company expanded internationally by purchasing a software development company in India. Two years later, AppIt acquired an app development firm in Great Britain. Both acquisitions gave AppIt access to skilled talent and additional markets.[7]

There are other, perhaps less obvious, benefits to collaborating with other countries on trade. Because trade allows each country to obtain more efficiently what it cannot as easily produce on its own, it lowers prices overall and makes more goods more widely available. This in turn raises living standards—and may broaden the market for a manager's own products, both locally and abroad. Trade makes new technologies and methods more widely available, again raising the standard of living. Finally, collaborating with others on trade creates links between people and cultures that, particularly over the long run, can lead to cooperation in other areas.

Outsourcing and Jobs

outsourcing

Contracting with an outside provider to produce one or more of an organization's goods or services.

offshoring

Moving work to other countries.

In recent years, the issues of offshoring and outsourcing became important sources of controversy. **Outsourcing** occurs when an organization contracts with an outside provider to produce one or more of its goods or services. **Offshoring** is a specific type of outsourcing whereby companies move jobs to providers in another country, typically where wages are lower.

Most concerns about offshoring refer to outsourcing because people think that high-paying jobs are being lost to low-cost countries overseas. The concern is prompted by widespread reports of major corporations relocating assembly lines, computer programming, customer service centers, and other parts of their operations to the Philippines, India, Mexico, China, and elsewhere.

The decline in manufacturing employment in the United States is evident, and many blame offshoring. However, considerable evidence suggests that the cause of this job decline is not offshoring but innovation. One important trend is how automation technologies (e.g., machine learning and robotics) are replacing human beings in some jobs.[8] These innovations mean that companies need fewer workers to produce the same quantity of goods or services. The important question, then, is how to prepare the workforce for the types of jobs most needed in the United States of the future—jobs requiring personal interaction with employees and other stakeholders, the use of judgment in physical work (for example, general contractors), and tailored approaches to particular situations (identifying clients' needs rather than following a routine).[9]

Job transfers from offshoring are a small fraction of the 135 million jobs in the United States. Most jobs require workers to be close to their markets; people still shop at their local supermarkets and appliance dealers, visit their doctors, and attend community schools. Importantly, as offshoring increases efficiency, it frees funds for expansion and additional employment. Offshoring is also offset somewhat when foreign companies hire workers in the United States—for example, InBev (owner of Anheuser-Busch), Honda, InfoSys, and Siemens are all large employers.

But people (employees, families) are deeply affected when their jobs are lost. Some organizations decide that they have a social responsibility to retrain their displaced workers to help prepare them for jobs that are less likely to move overseas. Others are less helpful. In this and so many other ways, managers have some latitude, multiple options, and a variety of ways to make decisions that have both positive and negative business and human consequences.

One less positive effect of offshoring is wage stagnation in industries where offshoring is common, because workers in those areas compete with their lower-wage counterparts abroad. On the other hand, wages, energy costs, and other expenses in some other countries have started to rise, reducing the benefits of offshoring.[10] Some firms find lower costs outside India and China in Bangladesh, Vietnam, and Indonesia. In recent years, the Philippines has become a popular location for outsourcing. Over the past decade, the outsourcing sector has generated about 100,000 jobs per year and $23 billion for this developing nation.[11]

Automation reduces labor costs, making it less necessary to move jobs overseas. Also, managers who offshore to save on wages are often surprised by increasing wage rates and the added costs of travel, training, supply chain disruption, quality control, language barriers, and the resistance of some customers who prefer to deal with local personnel.

Many American companies are outsourcing and offshoring to save money. This photo is from a call center in Hyderabad, India.

©Bloomberg/Getty Images

These drawbacks, along with political pressure, have led some companies to engage in **inshoring**, or moving work back to the United States. For example, a large domestic insurer may stop using a call center in Bangalore in favor of one based in the United States. Deloitte Consulting found that one-fourth of companies that outsourced to international locations soon after inshored the operations due to quality and cost concerns.[12]

Using the same example, if the domestic insurer were to create an internal (or in-house) call center staffed with its own employees and managers, that would be an example of **insourcing**.[13]

In deciding whether to offshore, managers should not start out with the assumption that it will be cheaper for them to do so. Instead, here are some factors to take into account:

What competitive advantage do the products offer? If, say, rapid delivery, reliability, and customer contact are paramount, then offshoring is a less attractive option. But if the product is widely available and standardized, like a calculator, and the only competitive advantage is price, the lowest possible production cost is essential and offshoring is beneficial.

Is the business in its early stages? If so, offshoring may well be inappropriate because managers need to stay close to the business and its customers to solve problems and make sure everything is going according to plan. When the business is more mature, managers can afford to consider moving some operations overseas.

Can production savings be achieved locally? Automation can often achieve significant labor cost savings and eliminate the advantage of moving production abroad. Where automation is not feasible, as with computer call centers, then offshoring becomes more attractive.

Can the entire supply chain be improved? As we discussed in Chapter 2, enormous productivity savings are possible when managers develop an efficient supply chain, from suppliers to manufacturing to customers. These improvements permit both lower cost and faster customer service. If the supply chain is already highly efficient or routine, and more savings are needed, then offshoring can achieve efficiencies.[14]

inshoring

Moving work from other countries back to the headquarters country. Work may be done by a domestic provider or in-house.

insourcing

Producing in-house one or more of an organization's goods or services.

The Geography of Business

As we saw in Chapter 2, an organization's external environment includes its economic, technological, legal/regulatory, demographic, social, and natural environments. When today's managers think about the economic potential of a market, the laws that protect their property, and the resources they need for making products, they should be thinking about where the best opportunities lie anywhere in the world. Exhibit 6.2 provides examples of current issues we will consider in each area of this international environment.

LO 2

The global economy is more integrated than ever before. For example, the World Trade Organization (WTO), formed in 1995, now has 164 member countries involved in most of the world's trade. The WTO provides a forum for nations to negotiate trade agreements and procedures for administering the agreements and resolving disputes. Issues that are currently under negotiation include objections to environmental regulations and subsidies to farmers in developed countries, on the grounds that they conflict with free trade. To follow how these and other issues are playing out, you can explore the "Trade Topics" section of the WTO website, http://www.wto.org.

> The global economy is becoming more integrated than ever before.

The global economy is dominated by countries in three regions: North America, western Europe, and Asia. Meanwhile, developing regions and specific countries represent important areas for economic growth.

Economic environment	Foreign investment; growth of developing nations; rising wages in developing nations
Technological environment	Internet and wireless technology
Legal/regulatory environment	Free trade agreements; anticorruption laws
Demographics	Aging population in developed nations; growing population worldwide, especially in the developing world
Social issues	Cultural differences; bribery concerns
Natural environment	Intensifying demand for resources, including oil, water, and food; growing desire for sustainable products and operations; increasingly endangered species; climate change

Western Europe

Following the widespread devastation of World War II, a handful of European countries initiated a bold experiment to bring unification (and avoid future wars) and economic progress. After the Maastricht Treaty, which formally established the European Union (EU), the euro was adopted as a common currency among 19 member countries.[15] The EU allows most goods, services, capital, and human resources to flow freely across its national borders. These efforts helped the EU emerge as an economic superpower. Its 28 members boast a population of more than 508 million and a GDP (gross domestic product) exceeding that of the United States.[16]

The road to European unification has not always been a smooth one. In 2016, British voters surprised many observers during a national referendum by opting to leave the European Union (dubbed "Brexit" or British Exit).[17] What will this departure mean for the future strength of the European Union? It is too early to tell, but there is speculation that it could pave the way for voters in other member nations—like Sweden, Denmark, and Greece—to consider a similar decision.[18]

This divisive sentiment derives partly from recent events including the recent Greek financial crisis and the challenges of heavy migration.[19] Member countries also are reluctant to relinquish control of key aspects of their economies, like the ability to devalue national currencies during an economic downturn (this move boosts exports because they become less expensive). As a result, not all members have adopted the euro.[20]

Despite these difficulties, unification has created a globally more competitive Europe, one that U.S. managers must take into account. Thus in 2017, Priceline purchased UK-based Momondo, a search engine that identifies flights, hotels, and car rentals.[21] Dunkin' Donuts, which has already opened stores in Iceland, Poland, and Denmark, is planning to open more than 1,000 stores in Europe over the next several years.[22]

The EU also presents a regulatory challenge to certain companies from the United States, including large tech firms like Google, Apple, Amazon, and Facebook. Recent complaints levied by EU authorities include "perceived failure to pay local taxes and their collection of reams of personal information."[23]

In late 2017, Europe's top courts will hear an appeal by Apple regarding whether it received $14 billion in preferential tax treatment in Ireland. If Apple loses the appeal (unknown at this writing), it will be required to pay the tax bill in full.[24] As you read this, what related developments have occurred?

Despite these political, economic, and regulatory challenges, Europe will continue to be a hugely important force in global business. At the time of writing, some political developments (for example, the French presidential election) suggest a possible resurgence of optimism about the EU project, Undoubtedly, though, change and uncertainties will continue.

Bottom Line

Globalization requires improvements in all bottom-line practices.
Why might constant innovation be important for a U.S. company in a global market?

Asia: China and India

Japan and its economic success dominated world attention toward the end of the 20th century, particularly so in the United States. Recently the Japanese economy has slowed, but Japanese companies such as Toyota and Sony are a major source of imported goods. As competitors, they are an important influence on how U.S. managers seek quality and efficiency in their operations. Japanese auto makers have a significant presence in the U.S.

Today, China claims the headlines. China has the world's largest population and a fast-growing middle class. The country has industrialized rapidly, and surged ahead of Germany to become the world's largest exporter. It also is the number two importer after the United States.[25] The country is the world's largest consumer of basic raw materials, such as steel and cement, as well as the world's largest cell phone market. China is the largest exporter of goods into the United States, a cause of political concern in the U.S. because of the U.S. trade imbalance with China.

As a consuming nation, China's appeal to managers lies in its huge population of 1.37 billion people and its rapid economic growth. Chinese companies have moved into more complex manufacturing operations such as auto parts, optical devices, and advanced electronics.

Rising incomes in China create a paradox for business expansion: Newly middle-class consumers in China are purchasing more products, both foreign and domestic; at the same time low-cost manufacturers must now look away from China somewhat to set up operations in lower-wage countries.[26] Other companies are staying in China to serve the huge market there. General Motors, for example, is setting up research and design facilities in China so it can introduce innovations aimed at satisfying the demands of Chinese consumers, starting with battery power.[27]

More and more, China's growing consumption makes it a highly attractive market. But China continues to have an even greater global impact as an exporting nation. The enormous size of its labor force, combined with low labor costs, has given it a competitive advantage in manufacturing. This has led many U.S. and European managers to relocate operations to China, and to import an increasing number and variety of Chinese products, instead of continuing to do business with local manufacturers.

Slow economic growth may threaten China's dominance. In 2016, the Chinese economy expanded at a rate of 6.7 percent, the slowest in 26 years.[28] Also, countries that have experienced job loss face growing pressure to restrict Chinese imports, particularly in the EU with its strong labor unions. But for the foreseeable future, China's presence in the world economy, as an importer *and* exporter, is one that you as a manager need to fully appreciate.

This Chevy Volt electric car is charging in the parking lot in Shanghai at General Motors headquarters.

©Peter Parks/Getty Images

India too has become an important player in the global marketplace. The nation is still developing, and its poverty is severe, but its 1.27 billion people (the world's second-largest population), many of them entering the working and professional classes, make India an essential market. For many U.S. companies, India provides online support for computer software, software development, call centers, and other services. In fact, so many companies have set up shop there that the demand for Indian workers with strong technical and English language skills is exceeding the supply. Companies such as Wipro, Infosys, and Tata Group are responding with expanded training programs.[29]

Other rapidly growing countries in the Asia-Pacific region that have strong trade relationships with the United States include South Korea, Taiwan, and Singapore. These countries are important trading partners not merely because of their wage rates, but because many of their companies have competitive advantages in areas such as engineering and technological know-how. South Korea's Samsung has the largest share of the world's market for flat-screen televisions and second-largest share (after Apple) in smartphones.[30] Taiwan's Hon Hai is the leader in contract manufacturing of electronics. You may not have heard of Hon Hai (also known as Foxconn), because it specializes in making components for brand-name products of other companies, including Apple iPhones and Sony PlayStation and Nintendo Wii video game consoles.[31]

These Asian countries and others have joined with the United States, Australia, and Russia to form the 21-member Asia-Pacific Economic Cooperation (APEC) trade group. Combined, APEC members' economies account for more than half of world output (GDP) and 54 percent of world trade.[32] The APEC countries have established policies that reduce trade barriers and encourage international commerce. APEC members address these objectives through dialogue and nonbinding commitments rather than treaties.

Another international organization, the Association of Southeast Asian Nations (ASEAN), brings together 10 developing nations including Indonesia, Malaysia, and Thailand. Economic growth in Vietnam and the Philippines is predicted to remain high at about 6 percent per annum.[33] Along with economic development, ASEAN aims to promote cultural development and political security.

The Americas

North and South America constitute a mix of industrialized countries, such as Canada and the United States, and growing economies such as Argentina, Brazil, Chile, and Mexico. The winter fruit you eat may come from Chile, the coffee you drink from Jamaica, and the shirt you wear from Honduras.

North American Free Trade Agreement (NAFTA)

An economic pact that combined the economies of the United States, Canada, and Mexico into one of the world's largest trading blocs.

The **North American Free Trade Agreement (NAFTA)** combined the economies of the United States, Canada, and Mexico into the world's largest trading bloc with nearly 444 million U.S., Canadian, and Mexican consumers and total trade reaching $1.1 trillion.[34] Although the United States has a long-standing agreement with Canada, after NAFTA Mexico quickly became the United States' third-largest trading partner. U.S. industries that have benefited include capital goods suppliers, manufacturers of consumer durables, grain producers and distributors, construction equipment manufacturers, the auto industry, and the financial industry, which gained privileged access into a previously protected market.

Besides importing and exporting, companies in the NAFTA countries have invested in facilities across national borders. Mexico-based CEMEX, the world's third-largest cement company, is actually the largest cement supplier in the United States. Twenty-two percent of CEMEX's employees and 27 percent of its sales are in the United States, and it conducts management meetings in English because the majority of its employees do not speak Spanish.[35]

After a protracted recession and several political scandals, Brazil's economy may begin growing again.[36] Brazil is the largest economy in South America, and hopes to leverage the $6.2 billion boost it received from tourists attending the 2016 Olympic and Paralympic Games there.[37] Other bright spots in Brazil include increases in private consumption and exports of products like soy beans, iron ore, and raw cane sugar to China, the United States, and Argentina.[38]

As in Asia, South American companies rely on innovation and technology, rather than simply cost advantages, to compete in the global marketplace. "Start-Up Chile," a start-up accelerator for immigrants funded by the Chilean government, helps high-potential entrepreneurs launch their start-up companies. Since its inception in 2010, 4,000 entrepreneurs from 79 countries have participated.[39]

Other agreements have been proposed to promote U.S. trade with Central and South America. The Central America–Dominican Republic–United States Free Trade Agreement (CAFTA-DR) includes Costa Rica, the Dominican Republic, El Salvador, Guatemala, Honduras, and Nicaragua. CAFTA-DR creates the second-largest free trade zone with the United States (NAFTA being the largest). As part of the agreement, Central American nations promised to protect workers' rights in their countries. Complaints that some countries did not deliver on this promise have led the U.S. government to request consultations

Social Enterprise

Student Social Entrepreneurs Compete for $1 Million

The Hult Prize Foundation is a student business competition and start-up accelerator that awards $1 million to talented social entrepreneurs from universities around the world. The annual competition identifies and provides seed funding to promising "start-up social enterprises that tackle grave issues faced by billions of people." Each year, about 1,500 students from 150 countries around the world participate in the Hult Prize and spend over 2.5 million hours on solving the world's most pressing issues. Since its founding in 2009, students from 600 schools have competed for the Hult Prize. Former president Bill Clinton of the Clinton Global Initiative presents the prize money to the student winners.

©Stephanie Keith/Getty Images News/Getty Images

Here are some recent start-ups that were awarded the Hult Prize:

Magic Bus from Indiana's Earnham College came up with a way for bus riders in Nairobi to pre-book their tickets using a text messaging system and a popular mobile pay app, making transportation easier and more reliable.

NanoHealth from the Indian School of Business won for its work in providing affordable, holistic medical services for impoverished "slum-dwellers" who suffer from chronic diseases.

Sweet Bites from the University of Pennsylvania aims to improve the health and quality of life of millions of impoverished people globally who can't afford dental care. Sweet Bites is 100% xylitol chewing gum that stops the progression of tooth decay.

Bee Healthy from HEC Paris uses bees to revolutionize disease detection for underprivileged people around the world. The bees' olfactory system is used to detect signs of diseases such as diabetes, cancer, and tuberculosis on a person's breath.

Are student social entrepreneurs who compete for the Hult Prize making a difference? Yes. According to Muhammad Yunus, Nobel Peace Prize winner for his pioneering work in microlending: "If you can create a real business, the beginning of a prototype, you can change the world."[40]

Questions

- Of the four recent award-winning start-ups mentioned, which do you find most likely to succeed? Why?

- The Hult Prize has been awarded to new social enterprises from all over the world. Why do you think the competition has a global focus?

with Guatemala on "apparent violations of its obligations."[41] Additional trade agreements have been negotiated on a country-by-country basis with Chile, Peru, Colombia, and Panama.

The countries of South America have formed their own trading bloc, called Mercosur, to promote trade within the continent.

Africa and the Middle East

The economy of the Middle East is best known for its export of oil. Although oil exploration and drilling take place in many parts of the world, the oil-rich countries of the Middle East supply by far the most oil to the world's buyers, most of it going to buyers in Asia. The main Middle Eastern supplier of U.S. oil imports is Saudi Arabia,[42] with other major suppliers being Canada, Mexico, and Venezuela.

The United States' dependence on foreign oil has decreased since the shale oil boom in Texas, New Mexico, North Dakota, and Alaska.[43] Nevertheless, U.S. businesses remain concerned about the Middle East because activities there can shape the price of oil, which is important not only for transportation but also for the manufacture of many products including fertilizer and plastic.

Africa has long been seen by managers only as a continent cursed by dire poverty. The continent is still plagued by an epidemic of AIDS, political instability, and ongoing wars. But areas of progress and growth in the middle class in some countries have provided opportunities for businesses willing to learn the needs of the population and make the effort to navigate a challenging environment. For example, the mobile phone industry has leapfrogged the landline phase of communications in Africa.

The nearby "Social Enterprise" box discusses how student social entrepreneurs are tackling some of the world's toughest challenges. As part of its Smarter Planet initiative (described in the "Management in Action" for Chapter 5), IBM learns about Africa's huge potential by sending in teams to help local governments solve problems. As it came to know the region, IBM began selling services, setting up partnerships with local companies, and opening research facilities in Kenya, Senegal, South Africa, and other countries.[44]

Global Strategy

 A crucial task for an international manager is to determine the best strategy for competing in a global marketplace. To determine the most appropriate global strategy—from among global, international, transnational, multinational—managers can plot a company's position on an integration–responsiveness grid (Exhibit 6.3). The vertical axis measures pressures for global integration, and the horizontal axis measures pressures for local responsiveness.

Pressures for Global Integration

Several reasons can cause managers to want or need a common global strategy (high pressures for global integration, on the vertical axis of Exhibit 6.3) rather than one tailored to individual markets (low such pressures): universal customer needs, necessity to reduce costs, or the presence of competitors with a global strategy.

Universal needs exist when consumer tastes and product preferences in different countries are similar. Products that serve universal needs require little adaptation across national markets; thus global strategic integration is facilitated. This is the case in many markets: electronic products such as semiconductor chips, certain basic foodstuffs (such as colas), and appliances (can openers and others).

EXHIBIT 6.3
Organizational Models

SOURCES: Bartlett, C. A. and Ghoshal, S., *Managing across Borders: The Transnational Solution.* Boston, MA: Harvard Business School Press, 1991; and Harzing, A. W., "An Empirical Analysis and Extension of the Bartlett and Ghoshal Typology of Multinational Companies," *Journal of International Business Studies* 31, no. 1 (2000), pp. 101–20.

Competitive pressures to reduce costs may cause managers to integrate manufacturing globally. Costs are particularly important when price is the main competitive weapon and competition is intense (as with smartphones). It is important also if key competitors are based in countries where labor and other operating costs are low. In these cases, products are more likely to be standardized and perhaps produced in few locations to capture economies of scale.

When competitors engage in global strategic coordination, this too creates pressures to integrate globally. A competitor that centrally coordinates the purchase of raw materials worldwide may achieve significant price reductions compared with firms that allow subsidiaries to handle purchases locally. Global competition can create pressures to centralize in corporate headquarters certain decisions being made by different national subsidiaries. Once one multinational company adopts global strategic coordination, its competitors may be forced to do the same.

> Universal needs encourage managers to develop a global strategy.

Bottom Line
The need to lower costs is a key strategy driver.
What is one way in which a global strategy can help reduce costs?

Pressures for Local Responsiveness

The second dimension of the grid, on the horizontal axis of Exhibit 6.3, is the need for responsiveness to local tastes and conditions. In some circumstances, managers must make sure their companies can adapt to different needs or demands in different locations. Strong pressures for local responsiveness emerge when consumer tastes and preferences differ significantly among countries. In such cases, products and/or marketing messages have to be customized. For instance, U.S. consumers' demand for pickup trucks is strong in the South and West, whereas in Europe pickup trucks are viewed as utility vehicles and are purchased primarily by companies rather than by individuals. Automakers must tailor their marketing messages to these differences in consumer demand.

Pressures for local responsiveness also emerge when there are differences in traditional practices among countries. For example, in Great Britain people drive on the left side of the road, creating a demand for right-hand-drive cars, whereas in neighboring France and elsewhere, people drive on the right side of the road. Obviously, automobiles must be customized to accommodate this difference in traditional practices.

For restaurant and fast-food chains, what people like to eat locally creates pressures for local responsiveness. Yum! announced recently that it opened its first Taco Bell restaurant in China.[45] To make the menu more appealing to customers in Shanghai, the company offers a Shrimp and Avocado Burrito made from high-quality ingredients and new sauces.[46] McDonald's faced a bigger challenge when entering India, where most of the population doesn't eat beef. Teaming up with local entrepreneur Amit Jatia, the fast-food giant agreed to not offer any beef or pork items. This decision prompted creative new ideas like the Chicken Maharajah Mac and McVeggie sandwich.[47]

Finally, economic and political demands of host-country governments require local responsiveness. Most important, threats of protectionism, economic nationalism, and local content rules (rules requiring that a certain percentage of a product be manufactured locally) dictate that international companies manufacture locally. Countries may impose tariffs (taxes on imports) or quotas (restrictions on the number of imports allowed into a country) to protect domestic industries from foreign competition perceived to be unfair or not in the nation's interests.

The United States recently imposed high tariffs on steel imported from China.[48] The U.S. government justified the tariffs as a response to complaints that the Chinese companies were selling steel at extremely low prices, presumably because the slowdown in building in China led to a surplus

©Agence France Presse/Douglas E. Curran/Hulton Archive/Getty Images

of steel.[49] Others interpret this and other protectionist actions as being motivated primarily by political objectives.[50] Whatever the reasons for them, tariffs and quotas influence managers' decisions about whether it is economically advantageous, or even possible, to operate locally or rely on exporting.

Choosing a Global Strategy

As Exhibit 6.3 shows, managers can use four approaches to international competition: the international model, the multinational model, the global model, and the transnational model. Organizations using each model compete globally, but they differ in the strategy they use and in the structures and systems that drive their operations.

The International Model   In the **international model**, managers use their firm's core capabilities to expand into foreign markets. As the grid indicates, it is most appropriate when there are few pressures for economies of scale *or* local responsiveness. Komatsu is an example of a company operating with the international model. Its industry doesn't compete on cost, and its earth moving equipment doesn't need to be tailored to local tastes.

The international model uses subsidiaries in each country in which the company does business, under the control exercised by the parent company. Although subsidiaries may have some latitude to adapt products to local conditions, core functions such as research and development are centralized in the parent company. Consequently, subsidiaries' dependence on the parent company for new products, processes, and ideas requires a great deal of coordination and control by the parent company.

The advantage of this model is that it facilitates the transfer of skills and know-how from the parent company to subsidiaries around the globe. IBM and Xerox, among many others, profited from the transfer of their core skills in technology and research and development (R&D) overseas. The overseas successes of Kellogg, Coca-Cola, Heinz, and Procter & Gamble are based more on marketing know-how than on technological expertise. Toyota and Honda successfully penetrated U.S. markets from their base in Japan with their core competencies in manufacturing relative to local competitors. General management skills provided advantages that explain the growth of international hotel chains such as Hilton International, Intercontinental, and Sheraton.

One disadvantage of the international model is that it does not provide much latitude for responding to local conditions. Another is that it does not provide opportunity to achieve a low-cost position via scale economies.

The Multinational Model   Where global efficiency is not required but adapting to local conditions offers advantages, the multinational model is appropriate. The **multinational model**, sometimes referred to as *multidomestic,* uses subsidiaries in each country in which the company does business and allows those offices to respond to local conditions. Each local subsidiary is a self-contained unit with all operating functions in the host market. Thus each has its own manufacturing, marketing, research, and human resources functions. Because of this autonomy, each multinational subsidiary can customize its products and strategies according to the tastes and preferences of local consumers, competitive conditions, and political, legal, and social structures.

A good example of a multinational firm is Heineken, a Netherlands-based brewing company. Heineken has three major global brands—Heineken, Amstel, and Affligem—but it also offers regional and local brands. The company attempts to adapt its products to local attitudes and tastes while maintaining its high quality. The company produces more than 250 brands around the world, from its international brands to local and specialty brews. The localized portfolio includes Red Stripe in Jamaica, Tiger in Asia, and Tecate in Mexico. Countries have considerable autonomy in the beers that they brew locally.[51]

Major disadvantages of the multinational form include higher manufacturing costs and duplication of effort. Although a multinational can transfer core skills among its international operations, it cannot realize scale economies from centralizing manufacturing facilities and offering a standardized product to the global marketplace. Moreover, because a multinational approach tends to decentralize strategy decisions (discussed further in Chapters 8 and 9), launching coordinated global attacks against competitors is difficult. This can be a significant disadvantage when competitors have this ability.

The Global Model   The **global model** is designed to market a standardized product in the global marketplace and to manufacture that product in a limited number of locations having favorable mixes of costs and skills. The global model is adopted by companies that view the world as one market and assume no tangible differences among countries in consumer tastes and preferences.

As part of its effort to improve efficiency while broadening its appeal, Ford launched a line of compact cars under the Ford Focus brand as the company's first truly global product. The Focus models included hybrid, plug-in hybrid, and electric cars, and promotional plans were built around a unified advertising campaign highlighting technology features.[52] Soon after the strategy was launched, the Focus was the best-selling car (by units) in the world for two consecutive years.[53]

Companies adopting the global model construct global-scale manufacturing facilities in a few selected locations. They realize scale economies by spreading the fixed costs of investments in new product development, plants and equipment, and the like over worldwide sales. By using centralized manufacturing facilities and global marketing strategies, Sony was able to push down its unit costs to the point where it became the low-cost player in the global television market. This enabled Sony to take market share away from Philips, RCA, and Zenith, all of which used traditional manufacturing operations based in each major national market (a multinational approach). Because operations are centralized, subsidiaries usually are limited to marketing and service functions.

On the downside, the global model requires a great deal of coordination, with significant management and paperwork costs. Moreover, because a company pursuing a purely global approach tries to standardize its goods and services, it may be less responsive to consumer tastes and demands in different countries. Attempts to lower costs through global product standardization may result in a product that fails to satisfy anyone.

For example, although Procter & Gamble has been quite successful using a global approach, the company experienced problems when it tried to market Cheer laundry detergent in Japan. The product did not suds up as promoted in Japan because the Japanese use a great deal of fabric softener, which suppresses suds. Moreover, the claim that Cheer worked in all water temperatures was irrelevant in Japan, where most washing is done in cold water.

The Transnational Model   Achieving competitive advantage often requires managers to pursue local responsiveness, transfer of know-how, and cost economies simultaneously.[54] The transnational model is designed to help them do just that. It is an approach that enables managers to "think globally but act locally."

In companies that adopt the **transnational model**, functions are centralized where it makes sense to do so, but a great deal of decision making also takes place at the local level. In addition, the experiences of local subsidiaries are shared worldwide to improve the firm's overall knowledge and capabilities. For example, research, training, and the overall development of the corporate strategy and global brand image tend to be centralized at home. Other functions may be centralized as well, but not necessarily in the home country.

To achieve cost economies, companies base global-scale production plants for labor-intensive products in low-wage countries such as Indonesia, Mexico, or Hungary, and locate production plants that require a skilled workforce in high-skill countries such as Germany and Japan. Companies can find locations with an optimal balance of needed skills and relatively low costs. Thus, although wages are rising in India, the technical skills of its workforce make that country an attractive place to locate some knowledge-based operations such as loan approvals, legal research, and biotech R&D. These skilled occupations are growing faster in India than jobs in call centers, the work that once brought India to prominence as an offshoring location.[55]

global model

An organizational model consisting of a company's overseas subsidiaries and characterized by centralized decision making and tight control by the parent company over most aspects of worldwide operations; typically adopted by organizations that base their global competitive strategy on cost considerations.

Bottom Line

The global model of standardization lowers costs. *Could this model apply to a website design company? If so, how? If not, why not?*

transnational model

An organizational model characterized by centralizing certain functions in locations that best achieve cost economies; basing other functions in the company's national subsidiaries to facilitate greater local responsiveness; and fostering communication among subsidiaries to permit transfer of technological expertise and skills.

Management in Action

ALIBABA'S GLOBAL STRATEGY

Alibaba, China's e-commerce giant, shattered sales records during its annual 24-hour discount event and media extravaganza known as Singles' Day. Some U.S. brands participated in the event, such as Starbucks, Target, and Gap. But Alibaba's websites—Taobao and Tmall Global—are not very well known in the United States.

The attraction of China's huge and increasingly profitable market is substantial. Some estimates suggest the new Chinese middle class alone is as big a market as the entire U.S. population. These shoppers are sophisticated and tech-savvy, and despite the risk of counterfeits (a problem Alibaba routinely contends with), they covet—and are willing to pay for—the international brands that make up a fast-growing proportion of the site's Western vendors. There may be no better way for U.S. vendors to reach them, and the $150 billion market they represent, than through e-commerce.

Company founder Jack Ma wants to change that. He plans a major expansion in the United States, which he hopes will not only bring more U.S. shoppers to the site but also attract more American vendors, large and small. Some large companies, including Macy's and Target, made their first appearance in China via Tmall Global. If Jack Ma succeeds in expanding his company's presence in the United States, thousands and possibly millions of other vendors, including the kinds of small operations that thrive in Amazon's third-party marketplace, could follow them.

During his visit with then president-elect Donald Trump, Jack Ma indicated he wants to capitalize on the opportunity to serve U.S. small vendors, and customers too. He announced plans to expand his company's New York City headquarters by leasing several floors in a downtown office building, where he himself will have an office. In fact, Ma's plans for Alibaba in the United States are so aggressive that he has hinted he would like to celebrate the 10th anniversary of Singles' Day, in November 2019, in either New York or Paris. Within the next 15 years, he anticipates the extravagant media and consumer event will be as popular in the United States as it already is in China.[56]

- In what ways do you think Alibaba's Jack Ma is responding to the need for global integration? How does his strategy exemplify local responsiveness?
- Which global strategy (international, multinational, global, or transnational) do you think is most appropriate for Alibaba? Why?

Marketing, service, and final assembly functions tend to be based in the national subsidiaries for greater local responsiveness. Thus major components are manufactured in centralized production plants to realize scale economies and then shipped to local plants, where the final product is assembled and customized to fit local needs.

Panasonic's experience in China has made it more of a transnational company.[57] Panasonic, a Japanese company, initially saw China primarily as a low-cost site for manufacturing its home appliances. In the early years, Panasonic conducted extensive consumer research in Japan but none in China; it served the Chinese market by removing features to make low-cost versions of its appliances. But as China's economy developed, consumers began buying new products from Chinese producers—who were also capturing market share from Panasonic elsewhere. Panasonic's management realized it needed to view China as more than a source of cheap labor. It set up a unit called Panasonic Corporation of China to provide research and development and marketing support, as well as back-office services, to the manufacturing facilities in China. It also set up the China Lifestyle Research Center to learn more about the tastes and lifestyles of Chinese consumers.

The Japanese managers shared their knowledge of technology and production efficiency. Their Chinese colleagues helped Panasonic identify and meet the needs of this huge consumer market. Engineers from different facilities worked together to understand how they could meet the identified needs better. As the efforts helped Panasonic develop better new products, the company began to spread this collaborative approach to other markets—for example, by opening research centers in Germany and India.

Panasonic also set up a global marketing organization to share knowledge about its best practices. Such efforts are critical for Panasonic, whose performance had suffered

Bottom Line

The transnational model tries to deliver on all bottom-line practices.
Does that mean the transnational model is always best? Why or why not?

from efforts to remain profitable in the highly competitive market for electronics such as televisions.

Perhaps the most important distinguishing characteristic of the transnational organization is the fostering of communications among subsidiaries and the ability to integrate the efforts of subsidiaries (when doing so makes sense). Communicating effectively across subsidiaries requires the head office to play an active role, creating formal mechanisms such as transnational committees staffed by people from the various subsidiaries. Equally important is to transfer managers among subsidiaries on a regular basis. This creates a global network of personal contacts in different subsidiaries with whom they can share information as the need arises.

Now that you have seen examples of the need to balance global integration and local responsiveness, consider how those pressures apply to Alibaba's situation as described in "Management in Action: Progress Report."

Entry Mode

 When considering global expansion, international managers must decide on the best means of entering an overseas market. The five basic ways to expand overseas are exporting, licensing, franchising, entering into a joint venture with a host-country company, and setting up a wholly owned subsidiary in the host country.[58] Exhibit 6.4 compares the entry modes.

LO 4

Exporting

Most manufacturing companies begin global expansion as exporters and later switch to one of the other modes for serving an overseas market. The advantages of exporting are that it (1) provides scale economies by avoiding the costs of manufacturing in other countries and (2) is consistent with a pure global strategy. By manufacturing the product in a centralized location and then exporting it to other national markets, the company can realize substantial scale economies from its global sales volume.

However, exporting has a number of drawbacks. First, other countries might offer lower-cost locations for manufacturing the product. An alternative is to manufacture in a location where the mix of costs and skills is most favorable and then export from that location.

Bottom Line
Exporting offers scale economies.
Can services be exported?
Why or why not?

	Exporting	Licensing	Franchising	Joint Venture	Wholly Owned Subsidiary
Advantages					
	Scale economies	Lower development costs	Lower development costs	Local knowledge	Maintains control over technology
	Consistent with pure global strategy	Lower political risk	Lower political risk	Shared costs and risk	Maintains control over operations
				May be the only option	
Disadvantages					
	No low-cost sites	Loss of control over technology	Loss of control over quality	Loss of control over technology	High cost
	High transportation costs			Conflict between partners	High risk
	Tariff barriers				

EXHIBIT 6.4
Comparison of Entry Modes

A second drawback of exporting is that high transportation costs can make it uneconomical, particularly for bulk products. Chemical companies get around this by manufacturing their products on a regional basis, serving several countries in a region from one facility.

A third drawback is that host countries can impose (or threaten to impose) tariff barriers. Trade arrangements described earlier, including the World Trade Organization, NAFTA, and APEC, work to minimize this risk. However, tariffs continue to affect trade between particular countries in various industries. Examples include U.S.-imposed tariffs on sugar imported from Mexico and, as mentioned earlier, steel imported from China. The U.S. government recently ruled that LG and Samsung sold washing machines at prices that are lower than they cost to produce, a practice known as dumping. The government imposed tariffs of between 32 and 52 percent on the two companies.[59]

Licensing

International licensing is an arrangement by which a licensee in another country buys the rights to manufacture a company's product in its own country for a negotiated fee (typically royalty payments on the number of units sold). The licensee then puts up most of the capital necessary to get the overseas operation going. The advantage of licensing is that the company need not bear the costs and risks of opening up an overseas market.

In nine years, Cold Stone Creamery expanded its franchises into 24 countries outside the United States, including Brazil, shown here.

©RosalreneBetancourt 10/Alamy Stock Photo

However, a problem arises when a company licenses its technological expertise to overseas companies. Technological know-how is the basis of the competitive advantage of many multinational companies. But RCA Corporation lost control over its color TV technology by licensing it to a number of Japanese companies. The Japanese companies quickly assimilated RCA's technology and then used it to enter the U.S. market, eventually gaining a bigger share of the U.S. market than RCA held.

Sometimes, licensing is a reasonable alternative when it is not feasible for a firm to operate on its own. Due to a "challenging regulatory, legal and competitive environment," Netflix recently decided to pursue a licensing strategy in China. In lieu of operating on its own, the company will license content to existing online service providers.[60]

Franchising

In many respects, franchising is similar to licensing. However, whereas licensing is a strategy pursued primarily by manufacturing companies, franchising is used primarily by service companies. Anytime Fitness, Bricks 4 Kidz, Subway, and many others have expanded overseas by franchising.[61] 7-Eleven has expanded through franchising to the point where it has 61,000 stores in 18 countries.[62]

In franchising, the company sells limited rights to use its brand name in return for a lump-sum payment and a share of the franchisee's profits. Unlike most licensing agreements, the franchisee has to agree to abide by strict rules regarding how it does business. Thus, McDonald's expects the franchisee to run its restaurants in a manner identical to that used under the McDonald's name elsewhere in the world.

The advantages of franchising as an entry mode are similar to those of licensing. The franchisees put up capital and assume most of the risk. However, local laws can limit this advantage.

The most significant disadvantage of franchising concerns quality control. The company's brand name guarantees consistency in the company's product. Thus a business traveler booking into a Hilton International hotel in Hong Kong can reasonably expect the same quality of room, food, and service that he or she would receive in New York. But if overseas franchisees are less concerned about quality than they should be, the impact can go beyond lost sales in the local market to a decline in the company's reputation worldwide. If

Bottom Line

Franchising is one way to maintain standards globally. *Why does quality control pose a risk in franchising?*

a business traveler has an unpleasant experience at the Hilton in Hong Kong, she or he may decide never to go to another Hilton hotel—and urge colleagues to do likewise.

Joint Ventures

Establishing a joint venture (a formal business agreement discussed in more detail in Chapter 17) with a company in another country has long been a popular means of entering a new market. Joint ventures benefit a company through (1) the local partner's knowledge of the host country's competitive conditions, culture, language, political systems, and business systems; and (2) the sharing of development costs and/or risks with the local partner.

In many countries, political considerations make joint ventures the *only* feasible entry mode. Before China opened its borders to trade, many U.S. companies, including Eastman Kodak, AT&T, Ford, and GM, did business in the country via joint ventures.

In 2014, Duke University and Wuhan University opened a joint venture in China, Duke Kunshan University (DKU). DKU offers programs in global health, medical physics, and management studies. Approved by the Chinese Ministry of Education, DKU joins other high-profile partnerships that have been created between Western and Chinese institutions of higher education. Many of the new ventures focus on "advanced business studies, especially targeting the Chinese MBA market, and most are taught partly or entirely in English."

Fueling this trend in cross-border ventures is China's goal to become a major education hub and the fact that several state-owned enterprises (SOEs) in China want to modernize the way they do business. One way to accomplish both of these goals is by attracting students and scholars from premier learning institutions.[63]

As attractive as they sound, joint ventures have their problems. First, as in the case of licensing, a company runs the risk of losing control over its technology to its venture partner. Japan's Kawasaki Heavy Industries and Germany's Siemens entered into joint ventures with Chinese partners to build China's high-speed rail network, but now those Chinese companies are using some of the technology they learned from the venture to compete with Kawasaki and Siemens for contracts elsewhere.[64]

Second, companies may find themselves at odds with one another. For example, one joint venture partner may want to move production to a country where demand is growing, but the other would prefer to keep its factories at home running at full capacity. Conflict over who controls what within a joint venture is a primary reason many fail.[65]

In fact, many of the early joint ventures American and European companies entered into with companies in China lost money or failed precisely because of conflicts over control. To offset these disadvantages, experienced managers strive to iron out technology, control, and other potential conflicts up front, when they first negotiate the joint venture agreement.

Wholly Owned Subsidiaries

Establishing a wholly owned subsidiary—that is, an independent company owned by the parent corporation—is the most costly method of serving an overseas market. Companies that use this approach must bear the full costs and risks (as opposed to joint ventures, in which the costs and risks are shared, or licensing, in which the licensee bears most of the costs and risks).

Nevertheless, setting up a wholly owned subsidiary offers two clear advantages. First, when a company's competitive advantage is based on technology, a wholly owned subsidiary reduces the risk of losing control over the technology. Wholly owned subsidiaries are thus the preferred mode of entry in the semiconductor, electronics, and pharmaceutical industries.

However, this advantage is limited by the extent to which the government of the country where the subsidiary is located will protect intellectual property such as patents and trademarks. Obviously this is a vital consideration.

Setting up a wholly owned subsidiary offers two clear advantages.

Second, a wholly owned subsidiary gives a company tight control over operations in other countries, which is necessary if the company chooses to pursue a global strategy. Establishing a global manufacturing system requires world headquarters to have a high degree of control over the operations of national affiliates. Unlike licensees or joint venture partners, wholly owned subsidiaries usually accept centrally determined decisions about how to produce, how much to produce, and how to price output for transfer among operations.

Working Overseas

 LO 5

expatriates

Parent-company nationals who are sent to work at a foreign subsidiary.

host-country nationals

Natives of the country where an overseas subsidiary is located.

When establishing operations overseas, headquarters executives can choose to send **expatriates** (individuals from the parent country), use **host-country nationals** (natives of the host country), and deploy **third-country nationals** (natives of a country other than the home country or the host country). Most corporations use all three types of employees, as each has distinctive advantages and disadvantages.

Sending expatriates can cost three to four times as much as employing host-country nationals. Moreover, in many countries—particularly developing countries in which firms are trying to get an economic foothold—the personal security of expatriates is a big issue. Firms therefore may send their expatriates on shorter assignments, or avoid the problem by not sending people to some countries and instead use telecommuting, teleconferencing, and other electronic means to communicate between international divisions.

Working internationally can be highly stressful, even for experienced globetrotters. Exhibit 6.5 shows some of the primary stressors for expatriates at different stages of their assignments. It also shows how managers can cope with the stress, plus some things companies can do to help with the adjustments.

EXHIBIT 6.5   Expatriate Stressors and Coping Responses

Stage	Primary Stressors	Executive Coping Response	Employer Coping Response
Assignment acceptance	Unrealistic evaluation of stressors to come. Hurried time frame.	Think of assignment as a growth opportunity rather than an instrument to vertical promotion.	Do not make hard-to-keep promises. Clarify expectations.
Pre- and postarrival	Ignorance of cultural differences.	Do not make unwarranted assumptions of cultural competence and cultural rules.	Provide pre-, during-, and postassignment training. Encourage support-seeking behavior.
Novice	Cultural blunders or inadequacy of coping responses. Ambiguity owing to inability to decipher meaning of situations.	Observe and study functional value of coping responses among locals. Do not simply replicate responses that worked at home.	Provide follow-up training. Seek advice from locals and expatriate network.
Mastery	Frustration with inability to perform boundary-spanning role. Bothered by living with a cultural paradox.	Internalize and enjoy identification with both cultures and walking between two cultures.	Reinforce rather than punish dual identification by defining common goals.
Repatriation	Disappointment with unfulfilled expectations. Sense of isolation. Loss of autonomy.	Realistically reevaluate assignment as a personal and professional growth opportunity.	Arrange prerepatriation briefings and interviews. Schedule postrepatriation support meetings.

SOURCE: Adapted from Sanchez, J., Spector, P. and Cooper, C., *Academy of Management Executive,* May 2000, pp. 96–106.

Expatriate assignments are valuable for professional and personal development, and having a pool of experienced expatriates is useful. On the other hand, local employees are more available, tend to be familiar with the culture and language, and usually cost less. In addition, local governments often provide incentives to companies that create good jobs for their citizens, or they may place restrictions on the use of expatriates.

Such advantages, coupled with the often-inadequate educational systems of developing nations, create stiff competition for local management talent. The result is that China, India, and Latin America do not have enough qualified talent to fill the demand for local executives. In China, recruiting firm Russell Reynolds finds that local managers offer technical skills but often lack conceptual skills and a strategic perspective. Motorola Mobility meets the challenge in mainland China with a mix of executives—about one-third from mainland China, one-third from other Asian countries, and one-third from the West.[66]

> Estimates are that nearly 15 percent of all employee transfers are to an international location.

Skills of the Global Manager

Estimates are that nearly 15 percent of all employee transfers are to an international location. However, the **failure rate** among expatriates (defined as those who come home early) is considerably higher for American expatriates compared to those international assignees from Europe and Asia.[67] The cost of each of these failed assignments ranges from tens of thousands to hundreds of thousands of dollars.[68]

The causes of failure overseas go beyond technical capability and include personal and social issues. In a recent survey of human resource managers around the globe, two-thirds said the main reason for the failures is family issues, especially dissatisfaction of the employee's spouse or partner.[69] The problem may be compounded for dual-career couples, in which one spouse may have to give up his or her job to join the expatriate manager in the new location. For both the expatriate and the spouse, adjustment requires flexibility, emotional stability, empathy for the culture, communication skills, resourcefulness, initiative, and diplomatic skills.[70]

Companies such as Levi Strauss, Bechtel, Monsanto, Whirlpool, and Dow Chemical have worked to identify the skills that predict expatriate success (Exhibit 6.6). Importantly, in addition to such things as cultural sensitivity, technical expertise, and business knowledge, an individual's success abroad may depend greatly on his or her ability to learn from experience.[71]

Companies such as BPAmoco, Global Hyatt, and others with large international staffs have extensive training programs to prepare employees for international assignments. Exhibit 6.7 suggests ways to improve their likelihood of success. Other companies, such as Coca-Cola, Motorola, Chevron, and Mattel, extend this training to include employees who may be located in the United States but who also deal in international markets. These programs focus on areas such as language, culture, and career development.

Going on overseas assignments affects careers. A manager selected for a post overseas usually is being groomed to become a more effective manager in an era of globalization. In addition, she often will have more responsibility, challenge, and operating leeway than at home. Yet expatriates often worry about being out of the loop on decisions and key developments back home. Good companies and managers address this issue with effective communication between subsidiaries and headquarters and visitations to and from the home office.

Understanding Cultural Issues

In many ways, cultural issues represent the most elusive aspect of international business. In the era of the global village, it is easy to forget how deep and enduring cultural differences can be. The fact that people everywhere drink Coke, wear blue jeans, and drive Toyotas doesn't mean we are all becoming alike. Each country is unique for reasons rooted in history, culture, language, geography, social conditions, race, and religion. These differences complicate any international activity and represent the fundamental issues that inform and guide how a company should conduct business across borders.

LO 6

third-country nationals

Natives of a country other than the home country or the host country of an overseas subsidiary.

failure rate

The number of expatriate managers of an overseas operation who come home early.

LO 7

EXHIBIT 6.6
Identifying International
Executives

End-State Dimensions	Survey Items
1. Sensitivity to cultural differences.	When working with people from other cultures, works hard to understand their perspective.
2. Business knowledge.	Has a solid understanding of the company's products and services.
3. Courage to take a stand.	Is willing to take a stand on issues.
4. Brings out the best in people.	Has a special talent for dealing with people.
5. Acts with integrity.	Can be depended on to tell the truth regardless of circumstances.
6. Is insightful.	Is good at identifying the most important part of a complex problem.
7. Is committed to success.	Clearly demonstrates commitment to seeing the organization succeed.
8. Takes risks.	Takes personal as well as business risks.

Learning-Oriented Dimensions	Survey Items
1. Uses feedback.	Has changed as a result of feedback.
2. Is culturally adventurous.	Enjoys the challenge of working in countries other than his or her own.
3. Seeks opportunities to learn.	Takes advantage of opportunities to do new things.
4. Is open to criticism.	Does not appear brittle—as if criticism might cause him or her to break.
5. Seeks feedback.	Pursues feedback even when others are reluctant to give it.
6. Is flexible.	Doesn't get so invested in things that he or she cannot change when something doesn't work.

SOURCE: Spreitzer, G. M., McCall, M. W. and Mahoney, J. D., "Early Identification of International Executive Potential," *Journal of Applied Psychology* 82, no. 1 (1997), pp. 6–29. ©1997 by American Psychological Association.

Ironically, although most of us would guess that the trick to working abroad is learning about a foreign culture, our problems often stem from being oblivious to our own cultural conditioning. Most of us pay no attention to how our own culture influences our everyday behavior. Because of this, we adapt poorly to situations that are unique or foreign to us.

EXHIBIT 6.7
How to Prevent Failed
Global Assignments

- Structure assignments clearly: Develop clear reporting relationships and job responsibilities.
- Create clear job objectives.
- Develop performance measurements based on objectives.
- Use effective, validated selection and screening criteria (both personal and technical attributes).
- Prepare expatriates and families for assignments (briefings, training, support).
- Create a vehicle for ongoing communication with expatriates.
- Anticipate repatriation to facilitate reentry when they come back home.
- Consider developing a mentor program that will help monitor and intervene in case of trouble.

Without realizing it, some managers may act out of **ethnocentrism**—a tendency to judge foreign people or groups by the standards of one's own culture or group and to see one's own standards as superior. This tendency may be unconscious: "in England, they drive on the *wrong* side of the road" rather than merely on the left. Or people may not recognize the values underlying a local culture—for example, assuming that the culture is backward because it does not air American or European television programming, when actually it is trying to maintain its traditional values and norms.

Such assumptions are one reason people traveling abroad frequently experience **culture shock**—the disorientation and stress associated with being in a foreign environment. Managers are better able to navigate this transition if they are sensitive to their surroundings, including social norms and customs, and adjust their behavior to the new circumstances.[72] Employers can help by conveying cultural norms and suggesting behaviors that contribute to success in the host country.

In this era, when people from all over the globe are collaborating on business issues, it is vital to continue learning about and respecting different cultures.

©Digital Vision/Getty Images RF

A wealth of cross-cultural research has been conducted on the differences and similarities among various countries. Perhaps best known is the work of Geert Hofstede, who identified four types of differences between country cultures within multinational corporations:

> *Power distance:* the extent to which a society accepts the fact that power in organizations is distributed unequally.
> *Individualism/collectivism:* the extent to which people act on their own or as a part of a group.
> *Uncertainty avoidance:* the extent to which people in a society feel threatened by uncertain and ambiguous situations.
> *Masculinity/femininity:* the extent to which a society values quantity of life (e.g., accomplishment, money) over quality of life (e.g., compassion, beauty).

Exhibit 6.8 depicts graphically how 40 nations differ on the dimensions of individualism/collectivism and power distance. Of course, it is easy to stereotype, exaggerate, and overgeneralize differences among countries. Americans often prefer to act as part of a group, just as many Taiwanese enjoy acting individualistically. Globalization by now may have blurred some of Hofstede's distinctions. Still, to suggest that no cultural differences exist is equally simplistic. Clearly, cultures such as the United States which emphasize individualism differ significantly from collectivist cultures such as those of Pakistan, Taiwan, and Colombia.

Cross-cultural management extends beyond U.S. employees going abroad. It includes effective management of **inpatriates**—foreign nationals who are brought in to work at the parent company. These employees bring extensive knowledge about how to operate effectively in their home countries. They also will be better prepared to communicate their organization's products and values when they return. But they often have the same types of problems as American expatriates and may be even more neglected because parent-company managers see the home country as normal—requiring no period of adjustment. Yet the language, customs, expense, and lack of local community support in the United States are at least as daunting to inpatriates as the experience of American nationals abroad.

Thus, culture shock works both ways. Effective managers are sensitive to these issues and consider them when dealing with foreign-national employees. In contrast to American-born employees, co-workers or customers from other countries might tend to communicate less directly, place more emphasis on hierarchy and authority, or make decisions more slowly. In general, managers of international groups can manage misunderstandings by acknowledging cultural differences frankly and participatively establishing behavioral norms to correct and prevent problems that upset group members, or by removing group members who demonstrate they cannot work effectively with others.[73]

Good managers help their employees adjust. Basic issues include the following:

> *Meetings:* Americans tend to have specific views about the purpose of meetings and how much time should be spent. International workers may have different preconceptions

ethnocentrism

The tendency to judge others by the standards of one's own group or culture, which are seen as superior.

culture shock

The disorientation and stress associated with being in a foreign environment.

inpatriate

A foreign national brought in to work at the parent company.

Multiple Generations at Work

Do Millennials Need International Work Experience?

According to the results of a survey of working Millennials from six countries, opinions indicate "yes" but also depend on nationalities. PricewaterhouseCoopers asked early career employees the following question: "Thinking of working outside your home country, do you agree/disagree that you need international experience to further your career?" The percentages of respondents who agreed that they needed international experience are illustrated below.

Large majorities of Millennial respondents from the emerging economies of Brazil, China, and India viewed international experience as important for their careers. In contrast, just over half of respondents from the United States and Germany, both developed economies, thought international experience would benefit their careers.

Given the dramatic increase in globalization and international competition in recent decades, employees of all ages and economies should be looking for opportunities to acquire international business skills. By working with people from different cultures, employees can learn how cultural programming influences their behaviors and attitudes. That is the first step in being able to function effectively in international business situations.[74]

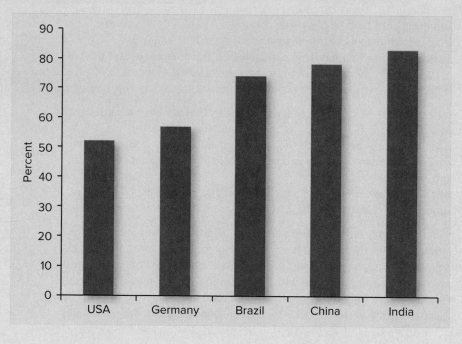

about the nature and length of meetings, and managers should make sure foreign nationals are comfortable with the American approach.

Work(aholic) schedules: Workers from other countries can work long hours, but in countries with strong labor organizations they often get many more weeks of vacation than American workers. Europeans in particular may balk at working on weekends. Matters such as these are most helpfully raised and addressed at the beginning of the work assignment.

E-mail: Not everyone loves e-mail and texting; whether a cultural or an individual preference, many refer to communicate face to face. Particularly when potential language difficulties exist, managers should avoid relying on e-mail for important matters at least at the outset.

Fast-trackers: Although U.S. companies may put a young MBA graduate on the fast track to upper management, most other cultures still see no substitute for the wisdom gained through experience. This is something U.S. managers working abroad should bear in mind.

Feedback: Everyone likes praise, but excessive positive feedback is more prevalent in the United States than in other cultures—a useful fact for (1) American expats receiving

EXHIBIT 6.8
Positions of 40 Countries
on the Power Distance and
Individualism Scales

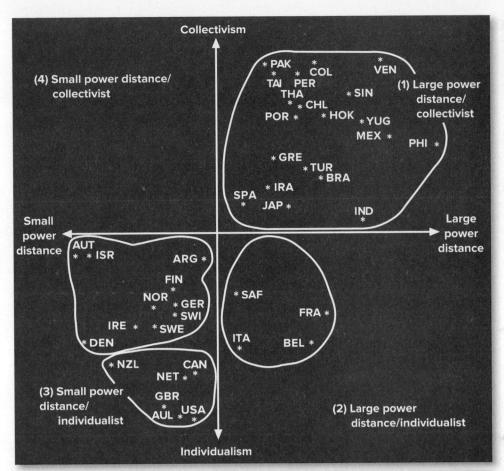

The 40 Countries
(showing abbreviations used above)

ARG Argentina	FRA France	JAP Japan	SIN Singapore
AUL Australia	GBR Great Britain	MEX Mexico	SPA Spain
AUT Austria	GER Germany (West)	NET Netherlands	SWE Sweden
BEL Belgium	GRE Greece	NOR Norway	SWI Switzerland
BRA Brazil	HOK Hong Kong	NZL New Zealand	TAI Taiwan
CAN Canada	IND India	PAK Pakistan	THA Thailand
CHL Chile	IRA Iran	PER Peru	TUR Turkey
COL Colombia	IRE Ireland	PHI Philippines	USA United States
DEN Denmark	ISR Israel	POR Portugal	VEN Venezuela
FIN Finland	ITA Italy	SAF South Africa	YUG Yugoslavia

SOURCE: Hofstede, G., "Motivation, Leadership, and Organization: Do American Theories Apply Abroad?"
Organizational Dynamics 9, no. 1 (Summer 1980), pp. 42–63.

performance reviews overseas, and (2) U.S. managers when they give reviews to foreign nationals.[75]

Ethical Issues in International Management

If managers are to function effectively overseas, they must understand how culture affects both how they are perceived and how others behave. One of the most sensitive issues in this regard is how culture plays out in terms of ethics.[76] Assessments of right and wrong get blurred as we move from one culture to another, as actions that are normal and customary in one setting may be unethical—even illegal—in another. Bribes are a classic example, as they can be an accepted part of commercial transactions in many Asian, African, Latin

The Digital World

International management in the digital age means connecting with people, across the globe at all times of day and night, who have all sorts of different cultural norms and expectations. In the limited context of electronic communication it can be difficult to spot and track subtle cues. For example, straightforward details can seem bare or abrupt via e-mail or text.

The degree of formality in e-mail varies from culture to culture. In many cultures it is expected (and polite) to begin with a personal question about someone's family, but in other cultures, this would be considered prying or rude.

Timing phone calls so they are convenient for all time zones can be a challenge. There are seasonal differences, too. Trying to finalize a deal when the majority of people in some countries go on holiday could indicate a lack of respect for someone's culture.

By the way, don't assume that some countries are technologically less developed than yours. This can result in a social gaffe, and a missed opportunity. In 2016, Senegal, Ghana, Kenya, Tunisia, and Indonesia all had larger percentages of their population using social networking sites on smartphones than the United States.

American, and Middle Eastern cultures. Even companies from cultures that view bribery as a form of corruption sometimes feel they must offer bribes when they think that this is part of the culture they are dealing with.[77]

Consequently, companies with global operations should be at least as active as domestic corporations in identifying, establishing, and enforcing standards for ethical behavior. In Chapter 5, we identified a number of steps organizations can take to clarify and encourage

Management in Action

CONTROLLING ALIBABA'S PROBLEM WITH COUNTERFEITS

Alibaba is China's premier e-commerce site, drawing in hundreds of millions of consumers from China's rising middle class with sophisticated tastes and the money to spend on gratifying them. Willing to pay for high-quality brands, these consumers are growing more savvy about rejecting the counterfeit goods that have long plagued Alibaba's retail platforms, especially Taobao. Black-market sites where counterfeits are rampant are actually experiencing a decline as China's newly wealthy young consumers flex their spending muscle for the first time and choose to shop where they can place their trust.

Problems with counterfeits at Alibaba caused U.S. trade officials to place Taobao on its watchlist of "notorious markets" in 2012. Alibaba responded with efforts to combat fakes—hiring a staff of 2,000 and enlisting 5,000 volunteers to help identify counterfeit goods, setting aside 150 million yuan (almost $22 million) to buy and test suspected fakes, and designing algorithms that help spot fakes by monitoring data such as price. The company invested in a $2.4 million lobbying effort in Washington to seek removal from the list, and a reprieve was finally granted.

In December 2016, however, just a few weeks before company founder Jack Ma met with then president-elect Donald Trump to announce plans for expanding Alibaba in the United States, the United States Trade Representative returned Taobao to its blacklist.

This was an embarrassing setback for the multi-billion-dollar company. The announcement carries no official consequences and is not expected to dent the company's Chinese operations. It could cast a pall over its U.S. expansion plans, however, particularly if the U.S. agency's warning about Alibaba's other retail site, Tmall, does not lead to improvements there also.

Alibaba has responded with a new strategy, taking to Chinese courts to sue two vendors selling fake Swarovski watches on its site. It's the first such suit the company has filed. "We want to mete out to counterfeiters the punishment they deserve in order to protect brand owners," said the company's chief platform governance officer. "We will bring the full force of the law to bear on these counterfeiters so as to deter others from engaging in this crime wherever they are."[78]

- What is Alibaba's ethical responsibility for controlling the sale of counterfeit goods on its websites?
- What cultural issues can you identify in this example?

ethical behavior. The primary difference in the international context is that this must be done with not just domestic employees but also overseas colleagues and partners, who may have their own expectations.

Research has identified five core values that most people embrace regardless of their nationality or religion: compassion, fairness, honesty, responsibility, and respect for others. These values lie at the heart of human experience and human rights, and seem to transcend more superficial differences between countries and regions. Knowing these shared values can help to build more effective partnerships, across as well as within cultures. Perhaps as long as people understand that they share some core values, they can collaborate effectively despite their differences.[79]

To a large extent, the challenge of managing across borders comes down to the practical philosophies and everyday systems developed for working with people. International managers need to develop a portfolio of behaviors and methods adapted to different cultural situations. These adjustments, however, should not compromise the values, integrity, and strengths of their home country cultures.

When managers understand and work effectively across cultures, they can capitalize on the opportunities that our global economy offers. The implications of globalization are evident with Alibaba's emergence as a world player. People around the world are becoming more educated, launching businesses, and enjoying a higher standard of living. The opportunities to responsibly serve their needs are enormous, and even small, local business managers can learn about people's needs and meet them globally. Probably many more will start participating in Alibaba's e-markets.

KEY TERMS

culture shock, p. 179

ethnocentrism, p. 179

expatriates, p. 176

failure rate, p. 177

global model, p. 171

host-country nationals, p. 176

inpatriate, p. 179

inshoring, p. 163

insourcing, p. 163

international model, p. 170

multinational model, p. 170

North American Free Trade
   Agreement (NAFTA), p. 166

offshoring, p. 162

outsourcing, p. 162

third-country nationals, p. 177

transnational model, p. 171

RETAINING WHAT YOU LEARNED

In Chapter 6, you learned how globalization is changing the competitive landscape and influencing the behavior of managers and companies. The lowering of trade barriers is fueling the movement toward increased globalization. Companies use different strategies to compete, including international, multinational, global, and transnational. Each strategy emphasizes a different mix of global integration and local responsiveness. The five methods of entering an overseas market are exporting, licensing, franchising, entering into a joint venture, and setting up a wholly owned subsidiary. When staffing an overseas operation, companies can deploy expatriates from the headquarters' country, host-country nationals, and third-country nationals. To decrease the risk of failure, expatriates should possess not only technical capability but also personal and social skills. By recognizing cultural differences, people can find it easier to work together collaboratively and benefit from the exchange.

LO 1 Discuss what integration of the global economy means for companies and their managers.

- In recent years, rapid growth has occurred in world trade, foreign direct investment, and imports.
- One consequence is that companies around the globe are now finding their home markets under attack from international competitors.
- The global competitive environment is becoming a much tougher place in which to do business. However, companies now have access to markets that previously were denied to them.

LO 1 Describe how the world economy is becoming more integrated than ever before.

- The gradual lowering of barriers to free trade is making the world economy more integrated.

- This means that the modern manager operates in an environment that offers more opportunities but is also more complex and competitive than that faced by the manager of a generation ago.

LO 3   Define the strategies organizations use to compete in the global marketplace.

- The international corporation builds on its existing core capabilities in R&D, marketing, manufacturing, and so on to penetrate overseas markets.
- A multinational is a more complex form that usually has fully autonomous units operating in multiple countries. Subsidiaries have latitude to address local issues such as consumer preferences, political pressures, and economic trends in their own regions of the world.
- The global organization pulls control of overseas operations back into the headquarters and approaches the world market as a unified whole to maximize efficiency on a global scale.
- A transnational attempts to achieve both local responsiveness and global integration by coordinating specialized facilities positioned around the world.

LO 4   Compare the various entry modes organizations use to enter overseas markets.

- Companies can enter overseas markets by exporting, licensing, franchising, entering into a joint venture, and setting up a wholly owned subsidiary.
- Each mode has advantages and disadvantages.

LO 5   Explain how companies can staff overseas operations.

- Most executives use a combination of expatriates, host-country nationals, and third-country nationals.
- Expatriates can establish new country operations quickly, transfer the company's culture, and bring in specific technical skills.

- Host-country nationals have the advantages of being familiar with local customs and culture, costing less, and being viewed more favorably by local governments.
- Third-country nationals often are used as a compromise in politically touchy situations or when home-country expatriates are not available.

LO 6   Summarize the skills and knowledge managers need to manage globally.

- The causes of failure overseas extend beyond technical capability and include personal and social issues.
- Important knowledge permeates the chapter, but in particular see Exhibit 6.6.

LO 7   Identify ways in which cultural differences between countries influence management.

- Culture influences our actions and perceptions as well as the actions and perceptions of others. Unfortunately, we often are unaware of how culture influences us, and this can cause problems.
- Managers must be able to change their behavior to match the needs and customs of people they work with. Hofstede's classic research identified four dimensions of cultural differences; some say those differences are disappearing but this should not be assumed. It is important not to stereotype or overgeneralize, but potential differences deserve attention and mutual accommodation.
- By recognizing cultural differences and discussing behavioral norms for dealing with them, people can find it easier to work together collaboratively and benefit from the exchange.
- Legal and ethical issues create particularly important challenge.

DISCUSSION QUESTIONS

1. Why is the world economy becoming more integrated? What are the implications of this integration for international managers?

2. Imagine you are the CEO of a major company; choose your favorite products or industry. What approach to global competition would you choose for your firm: international, multinational, global, or transnational? Why?

3. Why have franchises been so popular as a method of international expansion in the fast-food industry? Contrast this with high-tech manufacturing, where joint ventures and partnerships have been more popular. What accounts for the differences across industries?

4. What are the pros and cons of using expatriates, host-country nationals, and third-country nationals to run

overseas operations? If you were expanding your business, what approach would you prefer to use?

5. If you had entered into a joint venture with a foreign company but knew that women were not treated fairly in that culture, would you consider sending a female expatriate to handle the start-up? Why or why not?

6. Consider Hofstede's four cultural dimensions. He identified them in a huge global corporation several decades ago. Do you think cultural differences since then have decreased due to globalization? What evidence do you draw from?

7. What are the biggest cultural obstacles that we must overcome if we are to work effectively in Mexico? Are there different obstacles in France? Japan? China?

EXPERIENTIAL EXERCISES

6.1 GLOBAL INTEGRATION—LOCAL RESPONSIVENESS WORKSHEET

OBJECTIVE
To understand how companies compete in the global marketplace.

INSTRUCTIONS
An effective way to learn how companies respond to the competing pressures to be globally integrated and locally responsive is to study them in action. Referring back to Exhibit 6.3, search online for examples of companies that are currently using a global, transnational, international, or multinational organizational model. Please provide answers to the following questions:

PART I: GLOBAL MODEL
Name of company using a *global* organizational model:

URL of website/article describing the company's *global* strategy:

Explain why the company uses a *global* strategy to compete:

PART II: TRANSNATIONAL MODEL
Name of company using a *transnational* organizational model:

URL of website/article describing the company's *transnational* strategy:

Explain why the company uses a *transnational* strategy to compete:

PART III: INTERNATIONAL MODEL
Name of company using an *international* organizational model:

URL of website/article describing the company's *international* strategy:

Explain why the company uses an *international* strategy to compete:

PART IV: MULTINATIONAL MODEL
Name of company using a *multinational* organizational model:

URL of website/article describing the company's *multinational* strategy:

Explain why the company uses a *multinational* strategy to compete:

SOURCE: Adapted from McGrath, R. R., Jr., *Exercises in Management Fundamentals,* 1st, p. 177. Upper Saddle River, NJ: Pearson Education, 1985.

6.2 CROSS-CULTURAL ANTHROPOLOGIST

Assume you are a cross-cultural anthropologist. In this role, please visit multiple public places that are frequented by one or more ethnic or cultural groups. Observe four to five behaviors that strike you as unique or different compared to what you consider to be "normal." After you make your observations, walk to a quiet location and record what you observed in a notebook or mobile device. Think about why these behaviors caught your attention in the first place and then analyze them from the perspective of Hofstede's cultural dimensions (individualism/collectivism, power distance, uncertainty avoidance, and masculinity/femininity).

LEARNING OBJECTIVES

1. To help students interpret nonverbal communication in a more culturally neutral manner.

2. To encourage students to understand their own reactions to different cultural behaviors.

3. To reinforce the importance of observation skills in cross-cultural encounters.

STEPS

1. Visit multiple public places where you can observe the behaviors of one or more ethnic or cultural groups. Examples include major airports, ethnic associations, foreign consulates, religious entities, cultural centers, museums, and cultural or affinity groups at universities.

2. Bring a notebook or mobile device and:

   a. On the *left* side of the page, make a column titled: *"Observation/description."*

      i. In this section, describe what you saw. Any behavior that strikes you as different, frustrating, funny, or confusing is appropriate. Stick to the facts when describing these behaviors. Write down 5–10 observed behaviors.

   b. On the *right* side of the page, make a column titled: ***"How This Observation Relates to Hofstede's Dimensions."***

      i. In this section, interpret the behaviors by using Hofstede's dimensions (individualism/collectivism, uncertainty avoidance, power distance, and masculinity/femininity). How can these dimensions help explain what you observed? Explain.

3. Type and hand in your anthropologist's analysis. This should include:

   a. Your name, date, and the name of each public place you visited.

   b. Include 5–10 observed behaviors (left side of notebook) that you made while visiting the place(s) and describe how these observations relate to Hofstede's cultural dimensions (right side of notebook).

SOURCE: Adapted from Kohls, L. R. and Knight, J. M., *Cross-Cultural Journal in Developing Intercultural Awareness: A Cross-Cultural Training Handbook.* Yarmouth, ME: Intercultural Press, 1994, p. 67.

Concluding Case

A GLOBAL LAUNCH FOR NET-WORK DOCS

Nina Jones and Matt Smith have been raising capital for their start-up, Net-Work Docs. The company will help business clients create and manage their documents electronically. Net-Work Docs will help companies create easily searchable electronic versions of their safety manuals, human resource manuals, training guides, operating instructions, and more. For clients who wish, the company will help in embedding video, audio, and pop-up content along with the basic text and will develop apps for companies that want to make the content available through mobile devices. They also will provide consulting services such as helping clients shop for cloud storage of their documents.

As Nina and Matt developed their business plan, they found themselves expanding their idea of the geographic market they could serve. Initially, they intended to start by working with businesses in their city. But they realized they will be selling a product that can be made anywhere and shipped anywhere. Software and electronic documents can be transported over the Internet at essentially no cost, and a website gives a company an immediate global presence. With that in mind, Nina and Matt have concluded that they are unnecessarily limiting themselves by targeting geographic markets.

Thus, the plan is now to launch Net-Work Docs as a global company, serving clients in any country. After all, reason Nina and Matt, companies everywhere have policies and procedures they need to document. They will describe their services on their website, make initial contacts via e-mail, and set up a PayPal service to handle online payments. They can travel to meet major clients, but routine jobs may not require face-to-face meetings, and cost-conscious clients should appreciate the savings of conducting business online.

One hitch with this plan is that some potential investors have expressed doubts about operating globally before the company has built experience and a reputation serving clients locally. One investor asked Matt and Nina whether they really were prepared to understand the needs of business clients located hundreds or thousands of miles away—and whether they could assess a faraway client's likelihood to pay for services. He asked, "Can you really serve overseas clients without any overseas employees?" The company's founders believe they can because they will start with an English-only website, so they will initially have only English-speaking clients.

DISCUSSION QUESTIONS

1. What are some possible advantages of Net-Work Docs serving a global market?

2. How are the founders balancing pressures for global integration and local responsiveness? Is their global strategy likely to succeed? Why or why not?

3. What skills of a global manager could help Net-Work Docs succeed?

Design elements: Lightbulb icon that indicates innovation: ©McGraw-Hill Education; Money icon that indicates cost: ©McGraw-Hill Education; Recycle icon that indicate sustainability: ©McGraw-Hill Education; Human head with headset that indicate service: ©McGraw-Hill Education; Letter Q icon that indicates quality: ©McGraw-Hill Education; Sand dial that indicates speed: ©McGraw-Hill Education

CHAPTER 7
Entrepreneurship

©kasto/123RF

A (wo)man is known by the company (s)he organizes.

—AMBROSE BIERCE

LEARNING OBJECTIVES

After studying Chapter 7, you will be able to:

LO 1 Describe why people become entrepreneurs and what it takes, personally.

LO 2 Summarize how to assess opportunities to start new businesses.

LO 3 Identify common causes of success and failure.

LO 4 Discuss common management challenges.

LO 5 Explain how to increase your chances of success, including good business planning.

LO 6 Describe how managers of large companies can foster entrepreneurship.

CHAPTER OUTLINE

Entrepreneurship
Why Become an Entrepreneur?
What Does It Take to Succeed?
What Business Should You Start?
What Does It Take, Personally?
Success and Failure
Common Management Challenges
Increasing Your Chances of Success

Corporate Entrepreneurship
Building Support for Your Idea
Building Intrapreneurship
Management Challenges
Entrepreneurial Orientation

Management in Action

STARBUCKS' ENTREPRENEURIAL BEGINNINGS

Shortly after joining Starbucks, a four-store Seattle retailer and wholesaler of fresh-roasted coffee beans, a young employee named Howard Schultz traveled to Italy. He was then the company's director of retail operations and marketing. Deeply impressed by the laid-back culture and popularity of the neighborhood espresso bars and coffeehouses he visited in Italy, Schultz noted how much people enjoyed gathering there, in "a place between work and home," to socialize and enjoy long, leisurely conversations. He returned home to Seattle determined to persuade the owners of Starbucks to let him try the coffeehouse concept in the United States.

The experiment was so successful that within a few short years Schultz had left Starbucks to found his own coffeehouse chain, called Il Giornale, and then purchased Starbucks himself, with capital from local investors. Almost immediately he began opening Starbucks stores outside Seattle, beginning with several in Chicago and Vancouver. By 1992, when the company held its IPO, there were 160 stores, and now the company operates thousands of stores around the world. The feeling of community that so awed Schultz in Italy's neighborhood coffeehouses was the element he was committed to cultivating in all Starbucks stores—along with the finest coffee.

Schultz, who stepped down as Starbucks' CEO in 2017 but remains board chair and active in the company's new ventures, grew up in Brooklyn, New York. He was one of three children in a family living on a marginal income with, as he says, "nothing to fall back on." A football scholarship took him to Northern Michigan University, where he became the first in his family to

©Chip Somodevilla/Getty Images News/Getty Images

earn a college degree. Later he went on to executive-level jobs at Xerox and the U.S. division of a Swedish housewares company before moving to Seattle to join Starbucks.

What drove him to take the inspiration found in his visit to Italy and turn it into a multi-billion-dollar company? Schultz calls Starbucks a "team sport," credits the value of luck, and claims, "I've gotten more credit than I deserve" for the company's many years of success. But he does describe his entrepreneurial ambitions this way: "I willed it to happen," he says. "I took my life in my hands, learned from anyone I could, grabbed what opportunity I could, and molded my success step by step." That spirit still informs his thinking. In his new role within the company, the popular Schultz will be returning to his entrepreneurial roots and focusing on growing the company's new ultra-premium retail stores.[1]

Howard Schultz founded a company on the realization that he could market a familiar product in a coffeehouse environment that was new to U.S. consumers. As you read about the qualities of successful entrepreneurs and the challenges they must overcome, think about which qualities and challenges you see in Schultz and his dream for Starbucks.

entrepreneurship

The pursuit of lucrative opportunities by enterprising individuals.

Bottom Line

Entrepreneurship is inherently about innovation—creating a new venture where one didn't exist before.

How is entrepreneurship different from inventing a new product?

small business

A business having fewer than 100 employees, independently owned and operated, not dominant in its field, and not characterized by many innovative practices.

entrepreneurial venture

A new business having growth and high profitability as primary objectives.

As Howard Schultz and countless others have demonstrated, great opportunity is available to skilled entrepreneurs who are willing to work hard to achieve their dreams. **Entrepreneurship** occurs when an enterprising individual pursues a lucrative opportunity.[2] To be an entrepreneur is to initiate and build an organization rather than being only a passive part of one.[3] The entrepreneurial process involves discovering, evaluating, and capitalizing on opportunities to create new and future goods and services.[4]

Creating value is a central objective of entrepreneurship, just as it is in strategic management. Wealth may be an entrepreneur's ultimate goal, but it won't come without providing value for other individuals, organizations, and/or society.[5]

How does entrepreneurship differ from managing a small business?[6] A **small business** is often defined as having fewer than 500 employees, being independently owned and operated, not dominant in its field, and not characterized by many innovative practices.[7] Small-business owners tend not to manage particularly aggressively, and they expect normal, moderate sales, profits, and growth. In contrast, an **entrepreneurial venture** has growth and high profitability as primary objectives. Entrepreneurs manage aggressively and develop innovative strategies, practices, and products. They and their financial backers usually seek rapid growth, immediate and high profits, and sometimes a quick sellout with large capital gains.

The Excitement of Entrepreneurship   Consider these words from Jeffry Timmons, a leading entrepreneurship scholar and author: "[The] new generation of entrepreneurs has altered permanently the economic and social structure of this nation and the world. . . . It will determine more than any other single impetus how the nation and the world will live, work, learn, and lead in this century and beyond."[8] Timmons had written previously, "We are in the midst of a silent revolution—a triumph of the creative and entrepreneurial spirit of humankind throughout the world. I believe its impact on the 21st century will equal or exceed that of the Industrial Revolution on the 19th and 20th."[9]

Overhype? Well, partly, because the rate of new business formation is slowing down.[10] Given that 99 percent of companies in the United States are small businesses, a slowdown could reduce employment rates.[11] But let's hope the slowdown is temporary, because entrepreneurship has transformed economies all over the world and the global economy in general.[12] The Small Business Administration reports that there are 28 million small businesses in the United States accounting for over half of all jobs.[13]

The self-employed often report the highest levels of pride, satisfaction, and income. Importantly, entrepreneurship is not about the privileged descendants of the Rockefellers and the Vanderbilts—it provides opportunity and upward mobility for anyone who performs well.[14]

Myths about Entrepreneurship   Simply put, entrepreneurs generate new ideas and turn them into business ventures.[15] But entrepreneurship is not simple, and is frequently misunderstood; we need more research and theory,[16] although we do have a lot of useful knowledge. Review Exhibit 7.1 to start thinking about the myths and realities of this important career option.

Another myth, not in the exhibit, is that being an entrepreneur is great because you can get rich quick and enjoy a lot of leisure time while your employees run the company. But the reality is much more difficult. During the start-up period, you are likely to have a lot of bad days. It's exhausting. Even if you don't have employees, you should expect communications breakdowns and other people problems with agents, vendors, distributors, family, subcontractors, lenders, and whomever. Legendary software entrepreneur Dan Bricklin advised that the most important thing to remember is this: "You are not your business. On those darkest days when things aren't going so well—and trust me, you will have them—try to remember that your company's failures don't make you an awful person. Likewise, your company's successes don't make you a genius or superhuman."[17]

As you read this chapter, you will learn about two primary sources of new venture creation: independent entrepreneurship and intrapreneurship. **Entrepreneurs** are individuals

Myth 1—Entrepreneurs are born, not made.

Reality—Adaptive entrepreneurs accumulate the relevant skills, know-how, experiences, and contacts over a period of years. The creative capacity to envision and then pursue an opportunity is earned. . . .

Myth 2—Anyone can start a business.

Reality—Entrepreneurs who recognize the difference between an idea and an opportunity, and who think big enough, start businesses that have a better chance of succeeding. The easiest part is starting. What is hardest is surviving, sustaining, and building a venture so its founders can realize a harvest. Perhaps only 1 in 10 to 20 new businesses that survive five years or more results in a capital gain for the founders.

Myth 3—Entrepreneurs are gamblers.

Reality—Successful entrepreneurs take very careful, calculated risks. They try to influence the odds, often by getting others to share risk with them and by avoiding or minimizing risks if they have the choice. Often they slice up the risk into smaller, digestible pieces; only then do they commit the time or resources to determine whether [each] piece will work.

Myth 4—Entrepreneurs want the whole show to themselves.

Reality—Owning and running the whole show effectively puts a ceiling on growth. It is extremely difficult to grow a higher-potential venture by working single-handedly. Higher-potential entrepreneurs build a team, an organization, and a company.

Myth 5—Entrepreneurs are their own bosses and completely independent.

Reality—Entrepreneurs have to serve many constituencies, including partners, investors, customers, suppliers, creditors, employees, families, and their communities. Entrepreneurs, however, can make free choices about whether, when, and what they respond to.

Myth 6—Entrepreneurs work longer and harder than managers in big companies.

Reality—Some do, some do not. Some actually report that they work less.

Myth 7—Entrepreneurs experience a great deal of stress and pay a high price.

Reality—Being an entrepreneur is stressful. But there is no evidence that it is more so than other highly demanding professional roles, and entrepreneurs find their jobs very satisfying. They have a high sense of accomplishment, are healthier, and are much less likely to retire than those who work for others.

Myth 8—If an entrepreneur is talented, success will happen in a year or two.

Reality—An old maxim among venture capitalists says a lot: The lemons ripen in two and a half years, but the pearls take seven or eight. Rarely is a new business established solidly in less than three or four years.

Myth 9—Entrepreneurs are lone wolves and cannot work with others.

Reality—The most successful entrepreneurs are leaders who build great teams and effective relationships working with peers, directors, investors, key customers, key suppliers, and the like.

EXHIBIT 7.1
Some Myths about Entrepreneurs

Spinelli, S., Jr., and Adams, R. J., *New Venture Creation: Entrepreneurship for the 21st Century,* 9th ed., 2012, pp. 46–47. Copyright ©2012 McGraw-Hill Global Education Holdings LLC. All rights reserved. Used with permission.

who establish a new organization without the benefit of corporate support. **Intrapreneurs** are new venture creators working inside big companies; they are corporate entrepreneurs, using their company's resources to build a profitable line of business based on a fresh new idea.[18] Thus, entrepreneurship is an activity that can and should contribute greatly to mature organizations. Entrepreneurship is vitally important across the entire life cycle of an organization.[19]

entrepreneur

Individual who establishes a new organization without the benefit of corporate sponsorship.

intrapreneurs

New venture creators working inside big companies.

Entrepreneurship

Exhibit 7.2 lists some extraordinary entrepreneurs. The companies they founded are famously successful—and all of the founders started in their 20s. Two young entrepreneurs who started a highly successful business are Tony Hsieh and Nick Swinmurn. About 20 years ago, Swinmurn had the then-new idea to sell shoes online, but he needed money to get started. Hsieh, who at age 24 had already just sold his first start-up, agreed to take a chance on the new venture. It was a smart decision. Ten years later, Amazon purchased Zappos for $1.2 billion.[20]

Swinmurn has moved on, but Hsieh remains at the helm of the company as the CEO of Zappos.com. The real, more complete story of entrepreneurship is not about the famous people in Exhibit 7.2—it's mostly about people you've probably never heard of. Often it's about young people, and definitely it's about people of all demographic groups.[21]

They have built companies, thrived personally, created jobs, and made positive contributions to their communities through their businesses. Or they're just starting out.

Why Become an Entrepreneur?

Jessica Mah was an entrepreneur before she even finished school. At the age of 13, she went into business using eBay to sell computer parts and templates for websites. While in college at the University of California–Berkeley, she and another student, Andy Su, founded InternshipIN, which provided information about internship opportunities.

When she graduated, Mah was ready to launch another venture. With support from Y Combinator, which provides funds and advice to selected start-ups, Mah again partnered with Su, this time founding inDinero, a company that helps small-business owners manage their money and taxes. Basically, inDinero keeps track of transactions, analyzes where their money is going, and provides financial reports. The idea for inDinero came from Mah's own experience: for some people excited about starting a new business, working with customers and products is more exciting and easier to learn than handling money.[22]

Why do Jessica Mah and other entrepreneurs do what they do? Entrepreneurs start their own firms because of the challenge, the profit potential, and the enormous satisfaction they hope lie ahead. People starting their own businesses are seeking a better quality of life than they might have at big companies. They seek independence and a feeling of being part of

EXHIBIT 7.2
Successful Entrepreneurs Who Started in Their 20s

Entrepreneurial Company	Founder(s)
Snapchat	Evan Spiegel
Facebook	Mark Zuckerberg
Suja Juice	Annie Lawless
Google	Sergey Brin and Larry Page
Instagram	Kevin Systrom
Microsoft	Bill Gates and Paul Allen
Pinterest	Ben Silbermann and Evan Sharp
PartPic	Jewel Burks
Spotify	Daniel Ek
Zero Waste Solutions	Shavila Singh
Apple	Steve Jobs and Steve Wozniak

SOURCES: Heath, A. and Stone, M., "The Fabulous Life of Snap CEO Evan Spiegel," *Business Insider,* March 3, 2017, www.businessinsider.com; Howard, C. and Inverso, E., "Forbes 30 Under 30," *Forbes,* www.forbes.com, accessed March 25, 2017; Borison, R., "10 Entrepreneurs Who Can't Be Overshadowed by Men—Even in Silicon Valley," *Inc.* (online), December 18, 2014, http://www.inc.com; Blake, Brock, "Why 20-Somethings Are the Most Successful Entrepreneurs," *Forbes,* November 30, 2012, http://www.forbes.com.

the action. They feel tremendous satisfaction in building something from nothing, seeing it succeed, and watching the market embrace their ideas and products.

People also start their own companies when they see their progress or ideas blocked at big corporations. When people are laid off, they often try to start businesses of their own. And when employed people believe they will not receive a promotion or are frustrated by bureaucracy or other features of corporate life, they may quit and become entrepreneurs. Well worth considering is the hybrid path: starting a business while retaining your "day job."[23]

©The Traveller Tours

For example, Barbara Nascimento was laid off after working for 14 years for a multinational company in sales and marketing, Using this time to reevaluate her career priorities of wanting to be around people and free of an office setting, she founded a tour company, The Traveller Tours. A native of Cascais, a picturesque Portuguese fishing village, Nascimento's strategy is to help tourists travel like locals. The Traveller differentiates itself by blending "informality, local authenticity and a certain gently-funky attitude."[24] While showing customers around Cascais in a Subaru, Nascimento shares stories and information about the village with the flare of a long-time resident, something the Lisbon-based tour guides cannot match. When comparing her entrepreneurial venture to her previous corporate career, Nascimento accepts more financial risk now, but finds running The Traveller to be more fun and rewarding.[25]

When people find conventional paths to economic success closed to them, they may migrate to another location and turn to entrepreneurship.[26] Migration is to move within or across meaningful social or political boundaries, both intra- and internationally.[27] In the late 19th century, mining entrepreneurs moved to the western United States. The Cuban community in Miami has produced many successful entrepreneurs, as has the Vietnamese community throughout the United States. Sometimes the immigrant's experience gives him or her useful knowledge about foreign suppliers or markets that present an attractive business opportunity.

Elon Musk immigrated to the United States from Pretoria, South Africa, to study at the University of Pennsylvania. After graduation, Musk cofounded an online payments company, X.com (renamed PayPal), then he cofounded Tesla Motors, and then SpaceX which shuttles supplies to the International Space Station. What's next for this serial entrepreneur? Famously he has Mars in his sights; he also plans to build a "hyperloop" between Los Angeles and San Francisco in which people travel through tubes at speeds greater than 700 miles per hour.[28]

What Does It Take to Succeed?

What can we learn from the people who start their own companies and succeed? What enables entrepreneurs to succeed? In general terms, Exhibit 7.3 shows that successful

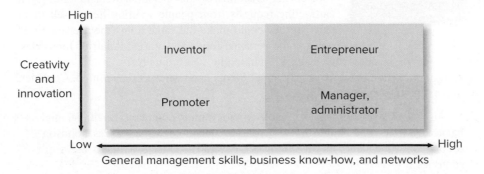

EXHIBIT 7.3
Who Is the Entrepreneur?

entrepreneurs are innovators who also have good knowledge and skills in management, business, and networking.[29] In contrast, inventors may be Highly creative but may lack the skills to turn their ideas into a successful business. Manager-administrators may be great at ensuring efficient operations but aren't necessarily innovators. Promoters have a different set of marketing and selling skills—useful for entrepreneurs, but those skills can be hired, whereas innovativeness and business management skills remain the essential combination for successful entrepreneurship.

What Business Should You Start?

You need a good idea, and you need to find or create the right opportunity. The following discussion offers some general considerations for choosing a type of business.

LO 2

The Idea   Many entrepreneurs and observers say that in contemplating your business, you must start with a great idea. A great product, a viable market, and good timing are essential ingredients.

Many great organizations have been built on a different kind of idea: the founder's desire to build a great organization rather than to offer a particular product.[30] Examples abound. Bill Hewlett and David Packard decided to start a company and then figured out what to make. J. Willard Marriott knew he wanted to be in business for himself but didn't have a product in mind until he opened an A&W root beer stand. Masaru Ibuka had no specific product idea when he founded Sony in 1945. Sony's first product attempt, a rice cooker, didn't work, and its first product (a tape recorder) didn't sell. The company stayed alive by making and selling crude heating pads.

Many now-great companies had early failures. But the founders persisted; they believed in themselves and in their dreams of building great organizations. Be prepared to kill or revise an idea, but never give up on your company—this has been a prescription for success for many great entrepreneurs and business leaders. Think about Sony, Disney, Hewlett-Packard, Procter & Gamble, IBM, and Walmart: their founders' greatest achievements—their greatest ideas—are their organizations.[31]

Limor Fried, Adafruit Industries, combined her academic knowledge and personal interests to prove her capabilities as an entrepreneur.

©Brian Ach/Getty Images

The Opportunity   Entrepreneurs find ways to spot, create, and capture opportunities.[32] Entrepreneurial companies can explore domains that big companies miss or avoid, and introduce goods or services that capture the market because they are simpler, cheaper, more accessible, or more convenient. Limor Fried spotted her opportunity when she got involved with a hobby that flew under the radar of most traditional businesses: building clever do-it-yourself electronic gadgets. When Fried was in school, she relaxed by ordering parts to build homemade MP3 players, programmable jewelry, and other fun gadgets. As she posted her creations on her personal website, she began attracting requests from people wanting her to sell them kits so they could make the same items themselves. Fried took some personal funds and started Adafruit Industries, now a 50-employee business racking up $10 million in sales annually.[33]

To spot opportunities, think carefully about events and trends as they unfold. Consider, for example, the following possibilities:[34]

Technological discoveries. Start-ups in biotechnology, microcomputers, artificial intelligence, robotics, and nanotechnology followed technological advances. Johnson & Johnson will collaborate with Google to develop advanced robots to aid in surgeries.[35]

Demographic changes. Health care organizations of all kinds have sprung up to serve an aging population, from exercise studios to assisted-living facilities. One business that targets the aging American population is fitness center company Welcyon, which provides senior-friendly low-impact cardio machines, background music at lower volumes, and fitness classes that can be taken while seated.[36] The service assists those who are pressed for time or have difficulty getting around.[37]

Lifestyle and taste changes. Start-ups have capitalized on new clothing and music trends, desire for new fast foods, and ever-growing interest in sports. In recent years, more consumers want to help take care of the environment, and more businesses are concerned about showing consumers that they care, too.

Economic dislocations, such as booms or failures. Rising oil prices spurred a variety of developments related to alternative energy or energy efficiency.

Calamities such as wars and natural disasters. The terrorist attacks of September 2001 spurred concern about security, and entrepreneurs still pursue ideas to help government agencies prevent future attacks. Destructive hurricanes, floods, and tornadoes raised awareness of the importance of emergency preparedness.

Government initiatives and rule changes. Deregulation spawned new airlines and trucking companies. Whenever the government changes regulations, tightens energy efficiency requirements, and so forth, opportunities arise for entrepreneurs to think of new ideas for products and processes

Franchises   One important type of opportunity is the franchise. You may know intuitively what franchising is, or you can at least name some prominent franchises: Supercuts, Jimmy John's, Jazzercise—add your favorites here. **Franchising** is an entrepreneurial alliance between two organizations, the franchisor and the franchisee.[38] The franchisor is the innovator who has created at least one successful store and seeks partners to operate the same concept in other local markets. For the franchisee, the opportunity is wealth creation via a proven (but not failureproof!) business concept, with the added advantage of the franchisor's expertise. For the franchisor, the opportunity is wealth creation through growth. The partnership is manifest in a trademark or brand, and together the partners' mission is to maintain and build the

©RosaIreneBetancourt 4/Alamy Stock Photo

brand. For example, the Panera Bread chain of bakery-cafés has expanded rapidly in recent years. In 2014, you could find over 1,900 Panera stores across 45 states.[39]

People often assume that buying a franchise is less risky than starting a business from scratch, but the evidence is mixed.

If you are contemplating a franchise, consider its market presence (local, regional, or national), market share and profit margins, national programs for marketing and purchasing, the nature of the business, including required training and degree of field support, terms of the license agreement (e.g., 20 years with automatic renewal versus less than 10 years or no renewal), capital required, and franchise fees and royalties.[40]

Although some people think success with a franchise is a no-brainer, would-be franchisees have a lot to consider. Luckily, plenty of useful sources exist for learning more, including the International Franchise Association (http://www.franchise.org), the Small Business Administration (http://www.sba.gov), Franchise Chat (http://www.franchise-chat.com), and *Entrepreneur* magazine's online Franchises page (http://www.entrepreneur.com), which includes rankings as well as articles profiling franchisors and franchisees. In addition, the Federal Trade Commission investigates complaints of deceptive claims by franchisors and publishes information about those cases. Take your time in investigating business opportunities, consulting with an accountant or lawyer who has experience.

franchising

An entrepreneurial alliance between a franchisor (an innovator who has created at least one successful store and wants to grow) and a franchisee (a partner who manages a new store of the same type in a new location).

The Next Frontiers   The next frontiers for entrepreneurship—where do they lie? Throughout history, aspiring entrepreneurs have asked this question. The powerful potential of big data to improve decision making is opening up tremendous opportunities for businesses that can help their clients collect, store, manage, and analyze data. Sectors and product categories that have recently enjoyed huge growth are health care, education, and, of course, mobile apps.[41]

One fascinating opportunity for entrepreneurs is outer space. Historically, the space market was driven by the government and was dominated by big defense contractors such as Boeing and Lockheed Martin. But now, with demand for satellite launches and potential profits skyrocketing, smaller entrepreneurs are entering the field. SpaceX has been transporting cargo to the International Space Station for NASA and is developing the capability to transport astronaut crews. NASA also has granted a cargo-shuttling contract to Orbital Sciences Corporation.

More futuristic still is the concept of entrepreneur Robert Bigelow. His company, Bigelow Aerospace, has created a residence module for living in space. The module is made out of a synthetic fiber rather than a metal structure, so it can be compressed for more efficient transportation and then expanded upon its arrival. Bigelow received a $17.8 million contract from NASA to send a module into space for a two-year mission.[42]

transaction fee model

Charging fees for goods and services.

advertising support model

Charging fees to advertise on a site.

The International Space Station is a habitable artificial satellite. Currently the largest artificial body in orbit, it can sometimes be seen with with the naked eye from earth.

SOURCE: NASA

Changes have been coming fast in the health care sector in the United States. Where there is change, smart entrepreneurs spot opportunities. Health care providers have been digitizing their data for patient care, medication management, and treatment outcomes—a trend that yields opportunities for hardware and software businesses that understand the needs of these clients. In addition, rising costs for health care and health insurance create opportunities for entrepreneurs with ideas for restraining those costs. For example, apps that promote fitness or help patients manage chronic conditions can appeal to consumers, insurance companies, and employers. GE's healthymagination program recently partnered with an entrepreneurship support group called Startup Health to fund promising start-ups in the health care field.

The Internet   The Internet is a business frontier that continues to expand. With Internet commerce, as with any start-up, entrepreneurs need sound business models and practices. During the heady days of the Internet rush, many entrepreneurs and investors thought revenues and profits were unimportant and all that mattered was to attract visitors to their websites (to capture eyeballs). But you need to watch costs carefully, and you want to break even and achieve profitability as soon as possible.[43]

At least five successful business models have proven successful in the e-commerce market: transaction fee, advertising support, intermediary, affiliate, and subscription models.[44] In the **transaction fee model**, companies charge a fee for goods or services. Amazon.com and online travel agents are prime examples. In the **advertising support model**, advertisers pay the site operator to gain access to the demographic group that visits the operator's site.

intermediary model

Charging fees to bring buyers and sellers together.

affiliate model

Charging fees to direct site visitors to other companies' sites.

subscription model

Charging fees for site visits.

eBay is a prime example of the **intermediary model**, bringing buyers and sellers together and charging a commission for each sale. With the **affiliate model**, sites pay commissions to other sites to drive business to their own sites. Zazzle.com, Spreadshirt.com, and CafePress.com are variations on this model. They sell custom-decorated gift items such as mugs and T-shirts. Designers are the affiliates; they choose basic, undecorated products (such as a plain shirt) and add their own designs, creating the customized products offered to consumers.[45] Finally, websites using the **subscription model** charge a monthly or annual fee for site visits or access to site content. Newspapers and magazines are good examples.

What about businesses whose primary focus is not e-commerce? Start-ups and established small companies can create attractive websites that add to their professionalism, give them access to more customers, and bring them closer to suppliers, investors, and service

Social Enterprise

Empowering Latina Entrepreneurs

When she was 5 years old, Nely Galan and her family left their native Cuba and began a new life in the United States. As a young person, Galan admired Sherry Lansing, the first female president of Paramount Pictures movie studio. After leaving the entertainment business, Lansing started an "encore career" by pursuing a variety of philanthropic activities.

Galan is following in Lansing's footsteps. Galan became the first Latina president of the Miami-based TV network Telemundo. The "Tropical Tycoon" went on to found her own business, Galan Entertainment, which launched TV channels in Latin America and produced original programming from sitcoms to *telenovelas* (soap operas).

Being an entertainment mogul was not enough. Galan founded Adelante (http://theadelantemovement.com), a movement "designed to empower Latinas in the U.S. economically through inspiration, training, and resources on entrepreneurship." Galan feels that helping Latinas become more financially successful will have a positive impact on their communities and families. The potential ripple effect is significant when considering that the Latina population in the United States is expected to grow to about 13 percent of the United States' population by 2050. In 2013, Latina-owned businesses earned about $66 billion in revenue.

Galan is not working alone. She has joined forces with Coca-Cola's worldwide effort to empower 5 million women entrepreneurs by 2020. Citing a personal goal to train 30,000 Latinas in the United States to became entrepreneurs, Galan sums up her passion this way: "I am a woman that believes in ownership and entrepreneurship as the way for most women to have financial freedom and become actualized."[46]

©Imeh Akpanudosen/Getty Images

Questions

- What motivates Galan to help Latinas become successful entrepreneurs?

- Why do you think Coca-Cola, a global consumer products company, is collaborating with Galan to empower women entrepreneurs?

---

providers. Companies can move much more quickly than in the past and save money on activities including customer service/support, technical support, data retrieval, public relations, investor relations, selling, requests for product literature, and purchasing. Setting up shop online costs less than ever.

Social Entrepreneurship   Social entrepreneurship has been around for decades, but is surging in popularity and impact and as a focus for research.[47] **Social entrepreneurship** has been defined in many ways, but most fundamentally it refers to leveraging resources to address social problems.[48]

It does so by using market-based methods.[49] Organizations that do this are **social enterprises**.[50] Social entrepreneurship creates social value by stimulating social change or meeting social needs.[51]

One of the best-known examples of social entrepreneurship is the Nobel Prize–winning work of Dr. Muhammad Yunus, formerly of Grameen Bank, which began helping women in South Asia obtain microloans.[52] Another is Fabio Rosa's Agroelectric System of Appropriate Technology (STA), which established low-cost electrification and irrigation in rural Brazil.[53] Additional examples include Basic Needs, which provides treatment for people with mental

social entrepreneurship

Leveraging resources to address social problems.

social enterprise

Organization that applies business models and leverages resources in ways that address social problems.

illness across 12 developing countries;[54] Sproxil, which developed a mobile app that enables consumers in Kenya, Ghana, Nigeria, and India to verify the pharmaceutical product they are purchasing is authentic;[55] and Clínicas del Azúcar (Sugar Clinics,) which provides affordable care to low- and middle-income patients who suffer from diabetes.[56]

Social entrepreneurship is not charity, and it is different from corporate social responsibility (CSR),[57] which you read about in Chapter 5. CSR is not necessarily practiced with profit as a guiding principle, and corporations often relegate it to a side activity. As described in the nearby "Social Enterprise" box, social entrepreneurship fully incorporates social as well as economic value into mainstream thinking and decision making. It provides dual, shared value: creating economic value plus social or societal benefit simultaneously.[58] See Exhibit 7.4 for more examples.

Combining social and commercial goals isn't new; consider hospitals, universities, and arts organizations.[59] And not all social problems can be solved by entrepreneurial solutions. But pursuing the dual goal of both economic and social value may be developing as a new norm, with positive social outcomes as key to long-term success.

States Pierre Omidyar, founder of eBay: "you really can make the world better in any sector—in nonprofits, in business, or in government. It's not a question of one sector's

EXHIBIT 7.4

Examples of Social Enterprises

Company Name	Description
40K Plus Education	Sets learning "pods" in rural villages that offer tablet-based after-school tutoring to students of government and low-cost private schools.
Barrier Break	Employs deaf people to provide online services for those who are hearing impaired, utilizing an innovative "Sign-and-Talk" business over video-enabled web connections.
Buy42.com	Promotes sustainable living and resells goods collected from individuals and businesses online with a proportion of the revenue being used to fund charity projects.
Edom Nutritional Solutions	Manufactures organically fortified staple flours cost-effectively and sells them at affordable prices to the malnourished in East Africa.
Healthy-TX	Sells a mobile platform that automates patient education around post, chronic, and preventive care. The physician-designed technology platform and programs greatly improve the quality of care for patients.
Jack and Jake's	Has developed a local/organic wholesale company, sourcing food from within a 100-mile radius of New Orleans to provide healthy food for hospitals and schools.
Kweli	Provides a mobile marketplace for fishermen to access centralized data on market-competitive prices. The goal is to help create a fair marketplace for fishermen.
Not Mass Produced	Is an online marketplace for local, independent businesses in the UK; their flagship site sources local food for UK restaurants, wholesale purchasers, and retail consumers.
PEURegen	Sells a sponge-like scaffold, which is placed inside a deep skin defect to help with wound healing. The product helps patients retain their quality of life through improved healing outcomes after a wound or surgery.
Solidarium	Partners with Walmart and JCPenney to sell ethically produced, fair trade consumer products, selling over 100,000 units and paying its producers 50% more than competitors.

SOURCE: Courtesy of Village Capital.

struggling against another, or of 'giving back' versus 'taking away.' That's old thinking. A true philanthropist will use every tool he can to make an impact. Today business is a key part of the equation, and the sectors are learning to work together."[60]

Opportunities exist to make substantial positive impact on virtually every societal need and to make a profit doing so. Profit is likely to make societal value creation more sustainable over the long run.

What Does It Take, Personally?

Many people assume that there is an entrepreneurial personality. No single personality type predicts entrepreneurial success, but you are more likely to succeed as an entrepreneur if you apply certain perspectives and behaviors:[61]

1. *Commitment and determination:* Successful entrepreneurs are decisive, tenacious, disciplined, willing to sacrifice, and able to immerse themselves in their enterprises. Entrepreneurial passion[62] can play an important role in all of these things.
2. *Leadership:* They are self-starters, team builders, superior learners, and teachers. Communicating a vision for the future of the company—an essential component of leadership that you'll learn more about in Chapter 12—clearly has an impact on venture growth.[63]
3. *Opportunity obsession:* They have an intimate knowledge of customers' needs, are market driven, and are obsessed with value creation and enhancement.
4. *Tolerance of risk, ambiguity, and uncertainty:* They are calculated risk takers and risk managers, tolerant of stress, and able to resolve problems.
5. *Creativity, self-reliance, and ability to adapt:* They are open-minded, restless with the status quo, able to learn quickly, highly adaptable, creative, skilled at conceptualizing, and attentive to details.
6. *Motivation to excel:* They have a strong results orientation, set high but realistic goals, have a strong drive to achieve, know their own weaknesses and strengths, and focus on what can be done rather than on the reasons things can't be done.

Making Good Choices   Success is a function not only of personal approaches but also of making good choices about the business you start. Exhibit 7.5 presents a model for conceptualizing entrepreneurial ventures and making the best possible choices. It depicts ventures along two dimensions: innovation and risk. The new venture may involve high or

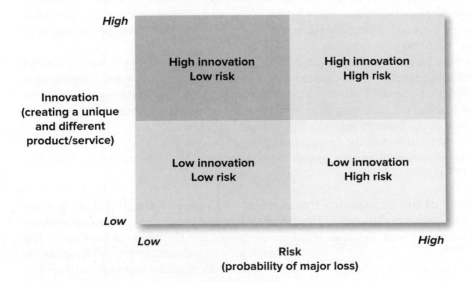

EXHIBIT 7.5
Entrepreneurial Strategy Matrix

SOURCE: Sonfield and Lussier, "Entrepreneurial Strategy Matrix: A Model of New and Ongoing Ventures," *Business Horizons,* May–June 1997.

low levels of innovation or the creation of something new and different. It can also be characterized by low or high risk. Risk refers primarily to the probability of major financial loss. But it also is more than that; it includes psychological risk as perceived by the entrepreneur, including risks to reputation and ego.[64]

The upper-left quadrant, high innovation/low risk, depicts ventures of truly novel ideas with little risk. As examples, the inventors of LEGO building blocks and Velcro fasteners could build their products by hand at little expense. A pioneering product idea from Google might fit here if there are no current competitors and because, for a company of that size, the financial risks of new product investments can seem relatively small.

In the upper-right quadrant, high innovation/high risk, novel product ideas are accompanied by high risk because the financial investments are high and the competition is great. A new drug or a new automobile would likely fall into this category.

Most small-business ventures are in the low innovation/high risk cell (lower right). They are fairly conventional entries in well-established fields. New restaurants, retail shops, and commercial outfits involve high investment for the small-business entrepreneur and face direct competition from similar businesses. Finally, the low innovation/low risk category includes ventures that require minimal investment and/or face minimal competition for strong market demand. Examples are some service businesses having low start-up costs and those involving entry into small towns if there is no competitor and demand is adequate.

How is this matrix useful? It helps entrepreneurs think about their ventures and decide whether they suit their particular objectives. It also helps identify effective and ineffective strategies. You might find one cell more appealing than others. The lower-left cell is likely to have relatively low payoffs but to provide more security. The higher risk/return trade-offs are in other cells, especially the upper right. So you might place your new venture idea in the appropriate cell and determine whether that cell is the one in which you would prefer to operate. If it is, the venture is one that perhaps should be pursued, pending fuller analysis. If it is not, you can reject the idea or take steps to move it toward a different cell.

The matrix also can help entrepreneurs remember a useful point: successful companies do not always require a cutting-edge technology or an exciting new product. Even companies offering the most mundane products—the type that might reside in the lower-left cell—can gain competitive advantage by doing basic things differently from and better than competitors.

Success and Failure

LO 3

Success or failure lies ahead for entrepreneurs starting their own companies as well as for those starting new businesses within bigger corporations. Entrepreneurs succeed or fail in private, public, and not-for-profit sectors; in nations at all stages of development; and in all nations, regardless of their politics.[65]

Start-ups have at least two major liabilities: newness and smallness.[66] New companies are relatively unknown and need to learn how to be better than established competitors at something that customers value. Regarding smallness, the odds of surviving improve if the venture reaches a critical mass of at least 10 or 20 people, has revenues of $2 million or $3 million, and is pursuing opportunities with growth potential.[67]

To understand further the factors that influence success and failure, we'll consider the economic environment, various management-related hazards, and initial public stock offerings (IPOs).

The Role of the Economic Environment   Entrepreneurial activity stems from the economic environment as well as the behavior of individuals. Money is a critical resource for all new businesses. Increases in the money supply and the supply of bank loans, real economic growth, and improved stock market performance lead to both improved prospects and increased sources of capital. In turn, the prospects and the capital increase the rate of business formation. Under

Economic cycles can quickly change favorable conditions into downturns.

Management in Action

STARBUCKS RISKS SUCCESS AND FAILURE

Part of being an entrepreneur is experiencing occasional failures. Despite its worldwide success, which has created hundreds of thousands of jobs and made founder and former CEO Howard Schultz a billionaire, Starbucks has not always succeeded in its attempts to be innovative.

Some of Schultz's bold moves have, of course, been famously successful, including in the areas of social responsibility and sustainability. His company was the first to offer full employment benefits to part-timers and health care coverage to employees' domestic partners, was a pioneer in the use of ethically sourced coffee, and was the first in the industry to use post-consumer recycled fiber in its beverage cups. Highly individualized orders for exotic specialty coffee drinks once unknown to U.S. consumers are now iconic staples in the company's thousands of stores. Prepackaged sandwiches, desserts, and teas and fruit juices are popular items for those who want more than coffee, and some of Starbucks' beverage products are sold in other retail stores and markets for preparation at home. Digital payment and mobile ordering are other innovations for which Starbucks can take credit.

But some product ideas have missed the mark. A product called drinking chocolate, essentially a liquid dessert popular in Europe, was an almost immediate failure. A partnership between Starbucks and PepsiCo yielded a bottled blend of coffee and soda that failed, though it did make way for bottled Frappuccino, a successful extension of the company's iconic blended cold coffee drink. Another dessert, called Sorbetto, failed in its West Coast test market and so didn't go any further. Efforts to build a new Starbucks brand with a line of low-calorie fruit smoothies, billed as a healthy option, failed as well. Smoothies are still offered, but the brand-building effort was abandoned. More recently, the Fizzio line of carbonated drinks, with three flavors rolled out in 16 states, has fizzled.[68]

- How would you categorize Starbucks' decisions to test new products in terms of high or low innovation and risk? Why?
- How is Starbucks' decision making about new products different from that of a start-up company, and how is it similar?
- How would you like to work for a big company (Starbucks, or choose your favorite) and hold the title "entrepreneur in residence"? What would your job entail?

---

favorable conditions, many aspiring entrepreneurs find early success. But economic cycles can quickly change favorable conditions into downturns. To succeed, entrepreneurs must have the foresight and talent to survive when the environment becomes more hostile.

Although good economic times may make it easier to start a company and to survive, bad times can offer an opportunity to expand. Ken Hendricks of ABC Supply found a business opportunity in a grim economic situation: a serious downturn in the manufacturing economy of the Midwest contributed to the shutdown of his town's largest employer, the Beloit Corporation. Hendricks purchased the company's buildings and lured a diverse group of new employers to town despite the economic challenges. In fact, Hendricks turned around struggling suppliers that ABC acquired.[69] Another silver lining in difficult economic times is that it's easier to recruit talent.

Business Incubators and Accelerators

The need to provide a nurturing environment for fledgling enterprises led to the creation of business incubators. **Business incubators**, often located in industrial parks or abandoned factories, are protected environments for new, small businesses. Incubators offer benefits such as low rents and shared costs for up to a 5-year period.[70] Shared staff costs, such as for receptionists and secretaries, avoid the expense of a full-time employee but still provide convenient access to services. The staff manager is usually an experienced businessperson or consultant who advises the new business owners. Incubators often are associated with universities, which provide technical and business services for the new companies.

Whereas a business incubator hatches new businesses in a gradual way in a noncompetitive environment, a **business accelerator** is a 3- to 6-month intensive process designed

business incubators

Protected environments for new, small businesses.

business accelerator

Organization that provides support and advice to help young businesses grow.

The Digital World

One of the main challenges for entrepreneurs is finding funding. Because of the Internet, funding opportunities have grown exponentially. Kickstarter, GoFundMe, and Indiegogo are three examples of sites that raise billions for entrepreneurs via short pitches on their websites.

The same idea applies for social entrepreneurs. Sites like Kiva, DonorsChoose.org, and GiveForward provide funding all over the world for microloans and socially beneficial projects.

Check out these sites to see how entrepreneurs are getting access to funds. While online sites won't replace traditional funding sources like banks and venture capital groups, they do increase opportunities for entrepreneurs to creatively access funds.

to help budding entrepreneurs build and launch rapidly successful ventures. There are at least 2,000 accelerator programs in the world, including Y Combinator, TechStars, and Startupbootcamp.[71] Accelerators pay participants to attend structured learning sessions, and receive in return an equity stake (e.g., 6 or 7 percent). Industry experts, venture capitalists, and fellow cohort members serve as sounding boards and mentors.[72]

Common Management Challenges

As an entrepreneur, you are likely to face several common challenges that you should understand before you face them and then manage effectively when the time comes. Here we discuss several such challenges.

You Might Not Enjoy It

Some managers and employees can specialize in what they love, whether it's selling or accounting. But entrepreneurs usually have to do it all, at least in the beginning. If you love product design, you also have to sell what you create. If you love marketing, get ready to manage the money too. This last challenge was almost a stumbling block for Elizabeth Busch, Anne Frey-Mott, and Beckie Jankiewicz when they launched The Event Studio to run business conferences for their clients. All three women had experience with some aspect of running conferences, but when they started their company, they didn't fully think through all the accounting decisions for measuring their income and cash flow. With some practical advice, they learned some basic accounting lessons that helped them avoid tax troubles later on.[73] If they hadn't been willing to learn new skills, entrepreneurship might not have been the right career path for them.

Survival Is Difficult

Companies without much of a track record tend to have more trouble lining up lenders, investors, and customers. When economic conditions cool or competition heats up, a small start-up serving a niche market may have limited options for survival. Failure can be devastating.

Founders of a start-up must make key decisions in so many areas of business that mistakes are potentially a devastating risk. Several months after starting Zipcar, a car-sharing service, founder Robin Chase evaluated the early financial data and discovered that the company had made a mistake in setting prices. The daily rental fees had been set too low to make the company profitable. Chase concluded that the only way she could keep Zipcar in business was to own up to her error, disclose it to her customers, and explain that the rate would be rising by 25 percent. Only two customers complained, and Zipcar grew into a multimillion-dollar business.[74]

Growth Creates New Challenges

In the beginning, entrepreneurs keep their business afloat with dogged determination to win customers and keep them happy. They work long hours at low pay, deliver great service, get good word-of-mouth advertising, and their business grows. When keeping up with all the work becomes physically impossible, entrepreneurs feel they need to bring in help.

Julie Ladd, founder of CopyShark.net, says she got ready to contract for help after she spent six months doing everything alone: "I was working 70-plus hours a week and wasn't able to get the turnaround time that my clients needed."[75] The challenge, of course, is that you not only have to come up with the money to keep paying people for the long haul, but also have to figure out who will bring enough skills, motivation, and commitment to the company.

Growth seems to be a consuming goal for most entrepreneurs. But some company founders reach the size where they're happy and don't want to grow any further. Reaching a golden mean is possible.[76] Other founders pursue slow growth. Jason Fried, cofounder of Basecamp (formerly known as 37signals), refuses to grow so fast that the workload and stress would push employees to the point of quitting: "I like the people who work here too much. I don't want them to burn out." With a relatively small staff of 43 people, Basecamp is successful with nearly 2.6 million individual and 100,000 company subscribers.[77]

It's Hard to Delegate

As the business grows, entrepreneurs often hesitate to delegate to other people work that they are used to doing themselves. Leadership deteriorates into micromanagement, in which managers monitor too strictly, to the minutest detail. During the early Internet craze, many company founders with great technical knowledge but little experience became instant experts in every phase of business, including branding and advertising.[78] Turns out, they didn't know as much as they thought, and their companies crashed.

Fortunately, many entrepreneurs observe the consequences of their behavior and figure out how to manage more effectively. Kit Hickey and her business partners had a good problem on their hands. Within a month of launching Ministry of Supply, they sold 6,000 shirts and acquired 4,000 customers. The leadership team had to scale production from 300 to 6,000 shirts per month. Their solution was to divide responsibilities and then empower each other to make customers as happy as possible. For example, one partner was in charge of product development and technology, another was the head of customer advocacy, and so forth. These decisions, combined with agile problem solving and transparent communication, helped Ministry of Supply grow rapidly to meet surging customer demand.[79]

Misuse of Funds

Many unsuccessful entrepreneurs blame their failure on inadequate financial resources. Yet failure due to a lack of financial resources doesn't necessarily indicate a real lack of money; it could mean a failure to use the available money properly. A lot of start-up capital may be wasted—on expensive locations, great furniture, and fancy stationery.

Entrepreneurs who fail to use their resources wisely usually make one of two mistakes: They apply financial resources to the wrong uses, or they maintain inadequate control over their resources.

This can be a problem when a lucky entrepreneur gets a big infusion of cash from a venture capital firm or an initial offering of stock. For start-ups, where the money on the line comes from the entrepreneur's own assets, he or she has more incentive to be careful. Tripp Micou, founder of Practical Computer Applications, says, "If all the money you spend is based on what you're bringing in [through sales], you very quickly focus on the right things to spend it on."[80] Micou, an experienced entrepreneur, believes that this financial limitation is actually a management advantage.

Poor Controls

Entrepreneurs, in part because they are very busy, often fail to use formal control systems. One common entrepreneurial malady is an aversion to record keeping. Expenses mount, but records do not keep pace. Pricing decisions are based on intuition without adequate reference to costs. As a result, the company does not earn profit margins adequate to support growth.

Blinded by the light of growing sales, many entrepreneurs fail to maintain vigilance over other aspects of the business. Sometimes, then, an economic slowdown provides a needed alarm, warning business owners to pay attention to controls. When Servatii Pastry Shop and Deli's sales deteriorated even as the prices of ingredients were rising, owner Gary Gottenbusch

set goals and monitored progress. One problem Gottenbusch tackled was the price of baking commodities, such as shortening and flour. He partnered with other local bakeries to form a purchasing association that buys in bulk and passes along the savings. Keeping costs down helped Servatii stay profitable when customers were trimming their budgets for baked goods.[81]

Even in high-growth companies, great numbers can mask brewing problems. In the absence of controls, the business veers out of control. So, don't get overconfident; keep asking critical questions. Is our success based on just one big customer? Is our product just a fad that can fade away? Can other companies easily enter our domain and hurt our business? Are we losing a technology lead? Do we really understand the numbers, know where they come from, and have any hidden causes for concern?

Mortality and Succession

One long-term measure of an entrepreneur's success is the eventual fate of the venture after the founder's retirement or death. Founding entrepreneurs often fail to plan for succession. When death occurs, estate tax problems or the lack of a skilled replacement for the founder can lead to business failure. In the United States and around the world, only one-third of family-owned businesses survive after the second generation takes over.[82]

Family members who are mediocre performers are resented by others. Outsiders can be more objective and contribute expertise the family might not have. Issues of management succession are often the most difficult of all, causing serious conflict and possible breakup of the firm.

Management guru Peter Drucker offered the following advice to help family-managed businesses survive and prosper.[83] Family members working in the business must be at least as capable and hard-working as other employees; at least one key position should be filled by a nonfamily member; and someone outside the family and the business should help plan succession.

Going Public   Many entrepreneurs avoid going public, feeling they'll lose control of their business. But often companies reach a point at which the owners want to go public. **Initial public stock offerings (IPOs)** offer a way to raise capital through federally registered and underwritten sales of shares in the company.[84] You need lawyers and accountants who know current regulations.

The reasons for going public include raising more capital, reducing debt or improving the balance sheet and enhancing net worth, pursuing otherwise unaffordable opportunities, and improving credibility with customers and other stakeholders—you're in the big leagues now. Disadvantages include the expense, time, and effort involved; the tendency to become more interested in the stock price and capital gains than in running the company properly; and the creation of a long-term relationship with an investment banking firm that won't necessarily always be a good one.[85]

Executing IPOs and other approaches to acquiring capital are complex, legalistic, and beyond the scope of this chapter. Sources for more information include the National Venture Capital Association (www.nvca.org), the Small Business Administration's Community page (http://www.sba.gov/community), and the SBA's Small Business Learning Center (http://www.sba.gov/tools/sba-learning-center).

Increasing Your Chances of Success

LO 5

Entrepreneurs need to think through their business idea carefully to help ensure its success. We discuss here the importance of good planning and different types of resources.

Planning   So you think you have identified a business opportunity. And you have the personal drive to make it a success. Now what? Where should you begin?

The Business Plan

Your excitement and intuition may convince you that you are on to something. But they might not convince anyone else. You need more thorough planning and analysis. This effort will help convince other people to get on board and help you avoid costly mistakes.

---

initial public offering (IPO)

Sale to the public, for the first time, of federally registered and underwritten shares of stock in the company.

Opportunity Analysis

What market need does my idea fill?
What personal observations have I experienced or recorded with regard to that market need?
What social condition underlies this market need?
What market research data can be marshaled to describe this market need?
What patents might be available to fulfill this need?
What competition exists in this market? How would I describe the behavior of this competition?
What does the international market look like?
What does the international competition look like?
Where is the money to be made in this activity?

The first formal planning step is to do an opportunity analysis. An **opportunity analysis** includes a description of the good or service, an assessment of the opportunity, an assessment of the entrepreneur (you), a specification of activities and resources needed to translate your idea into a viable business, and your source(s) of capital.[86] Exhibit 7.6 shows the questions you should answer in an opportunity analysis.

The opportunity analysis, or opportunity assessment plan, focuses on the opportunity, not the entire venture. It provides the basis for making a decision on whether to act. Then the **business plan** describes all the elements involved in starting the new venture.[87] The business plan describes the venture and its market, strategies, and future directions. It often has functional plans for marketing, finance, manufacturing, and human resources.

Exhibit 7.7 shows an outline for a typical business plan. The business plan (1) helps determine the viability of your enterprise, (2) guides you as you plan and organize, and (3) helps you obtain financing. It is read by potential investors, suppliers, customers, and others. Get help in writing a sound plan!

Key Planning Elements

The business needs enough cash to cover start-up expenses and keep the company running during slow periods. The initial budget should cover one-time costs, such as the fee to form a corporation, and ongoing expenses such as supplies and rent for the first few months. The company's founders may start the business with their own money, or they may seek financing in the form of debt (taking out a loan from family, friends, or a bank) or equity (taking money in exchange for an ownership share in the company). Typically, start-ups get most of their money from the owners, their families, and loans and credit lines from banks. Other kinds of investors, such as venture capital firms, generate a lot of publicity for splashy deals but provide a very small share of start-up funds.[88]

Raising money to start a business can be one of the entrepreneur's greatest challenges. Peer-to-peer loans are an alternative to using a bank. Using online platforms like Lending Club or Prosper, individual investors loan up to $35,000 to small businesses. For example, Hannah Attwood wanted to raise money to open a cloth diaper supply and cleaning service. After four banks rejected her, Attwood secured from investors a three-year loan to help launch her new business. Combining the loan with her own savings, Attwood was able to purchase industrial washers and dryers.[89]

Just as the Internet has transformed every other aspect of business, it is poised to remake the challenge of raising start-up money. This trend started with the use of social media tools to link would-be entrepreneurs with people who want to make great ideas happen. At crowdfunding websites, such as AngelList, FundersClub, Indiegogo, and Kickstarter, the entrepreneurs post their ideas and anyone can donate to the cause.

opportunity analysis

A description of the good or service, an assessment of the opportunity, an assessment of the entrepreneur, specification of activities and resources needed to translate your idea into a viable business, and your source(s) of capital.

business plan

A formal planning step that focuses on the entire venture and describes all the elements involved in starting it.

EXHIBIT 7.7   Outline of a Business Plan

I.   EXECUTIVE SUMMARY

Description of the Business Concept and the Business

Opportunity and Strategy

Target Market and Projections

Competitive Advantages

Costs

Sustainability

The Team

The Offering

II.   THE INDUSTRY AND THE COMPANY AND ITS PRODUCT(S) OR SERVICE(S)

The Industry

The Company and the Concept

The Product(s) or Service(s)

Entry and Growth Strategy

III.   MARKET RESEARCH AND ANALYSIS

Customers

Market Size and Trends

Competition and Competitive Edges

Estimated Market Share and Sales

Ongoing Market Evaluation

IV.   THE ECONOMICS OF THE BUSINESS

Gross and Operating Margins

Profit Potential and Durability

Fixed, Variable, and Semivariable Costs

Months to Breakeven

Months to Reach Positive Cash Flow

V.   MARKETING PLAN

Overall Marketing Strategy

Pricing

Sales Tactics

Service and Warranty Policies

Advertising and Promotion

Distribution

VI.   DESIGN AND DEVELOPMENT PLANS

Development Status and Tasks

Difficulties and Risks

Product Improvement and New Products

Costs

Proprietary Issues

VII.   MANUFACTURING AND OPERATIONS PLAN

Operating Cycle

Geographical Location

Facilities and Improvements

Strategy and Plans

Regulatory and Legal Issues

VIII.   MANAGEMENT TEAM

Organization

Key Management Personnel

Management Compensation and Ownership

Other Investors

Employment and Other Agreements and Stock Option and Bonus Plans

Board of Directors

Other Shareholders, Rights, and Restrictions

Supporting Professional Advisers and Services

IX.   OVERALL SCHEDULE

X.   CRITICAL RISKS, PROBLEMS, AND ASSUMPTIONS

XI.   THE FINANCIAL PLAN

Actual Income Statements and Balance Sheets

Pro Forma Income Statements

Pro Forma Balance Sheets

Pro Forma Cash Flow Analysis

Breakeven Chart and Calculation

Cost Control

Highlights

XII.   PROPOSED COMPANY OFFERING

Desired Financing

Offering

Capitalization

Use of Funds

Investor's Return

XIII.   APPENDIXES

Until recently, crowdfunding was mostly limited to small contributions from people who gave in exchange for a company-provided experience, discount, or product sample; the funders don't receive equity in the business. The main reason is that the Securities and Exchange Commission, which regulates investing, needs to ensure that investors on these sites have the same protections available to traditional investors. In 2012, however, Congress passed the Jumpstart Our Business Startups Act (JOBS Act), which makes it easier for start-ups to receive funding from online investors (crowdfunding) and to go public. Early results are promising. Two years after the act was passed, the number of IPOs reached a 14-year high.[90]

Most business plans devote so much attention to financial projections that they neglect other important information—information that matters greatly to astute investors. In fact, financial projections tend to be overly optimistic. Investors know this and discount the figures. In addition to the numbers, the best plans convey—and make certain that the entrepreneurs have carefully thought through—five key factors: the people, the opportunity, the competition, the context, and risk and reward.[91]

The *people* should be energetic and have skills and expertise directly relevant to the venture. For many astute investors, the people are the most important variable, more important even than the idea. Arthur Rock, a legendary venture capitalist who helped start Intel, Teledyne, and Apple, stated, "I invest in people, not ideas. If you can find good people, if they're wrong about the product, they'll make a switch."[92]

The *opportunity* should provide a competitive advantage that can be defended. Customers are the focus here: Who is the customer? How does the customer make decisions? How will the product be priced? How will the venture reach all customer segments? How much does it cost to acquire and support a customer and to produce and deliver the product? How easy or difficult is it to retain a customer?

> The opportunity should provide a competitive advantage that can be defended.

It is also essential to fully consider the *competition.* The plan must identify current competitors and their strengths and weaknesses, predict how they will respond to the new venture, indicate how the new venture will respond to the competitors' responses, identify future potential competitors, and consider how to collaborate with or face off against actual or potential competitors.

The original plan for Zappos was for its website to compete with other online shoe retailers by offering a wider selection than they did. However, most people buy shoes in stores, so Zappos cofounders Nick Swinmurn and Tony Hsieh soon realized that they needed a broader view of the competition. They began focusing more on service and planning a distribution method that would make online shopping as successful as visiting a store.[93]

Entrepreneurs should carefully consider the five key factors when developing a business plan: the people, the opportunity, the competition, the context, and risk and reward. Commonly, financial projections dominate the plan while these other important factors are overlooked or undervalued.

©John Lund/Marc Romanelli/Getty Images RF

The *environmental context* should be a favorable one from regulatory and economic perspectives. Such factors as tax policies, rules about raising capital, interest rates, inflation, and exchange rates will affect the viability of the new venture. Importantly, the plan should make clear that you know that the context inevitably will change, should forecast how the changes will affect the business, and should describe how you will deal with the changes.

The *risk* must be understood and addressed as fully as possible. Although you cannot predict the future, you must contemplate head-on the possibilities of key people leaving, interest rates changing, a key customer leaving, or a powerful competitor responding ferociously. Then describe what you will do to prevent, avoid, or cope with such possibilities.

You should also speak to the end of the process: how to get money out of the business eventually. Will you go public? Will you sell or liquidate? What are the various possibilities for investors to realize their ultimate gains?[94]

Selling the Plan

Your goal is to get the right investors to support the plan. You want more than just financial support; you want high-quality partners so that your relationships will continue to be productive.[95] Thus an important decision is whom you try to convince to back your plan.

Many entrepreneurs want passive investors who will give them money and let them do what they want. Doctors and dentists generally fit this image. Professional venture capitalists do not—they demand more control and more of the returns.

But when a business goes wrong—and chances are, it will—nonprofessional investors are less helpful and less likely to advance more (needed) money. Sophisticated investors have seen sinking ships before and know how to help. They are more likely to solve problems, provide more money, and navigate financial and legal waters.[96]

View the plan as a way for you to figure out how to reduce risk, maximize reward, and convince others that you understand the entire new venture process. Don't put together a plan built on naïveté or overconfidence, or one that cleverly hides major flaws. You might not fool others, and you certainly would be fooling yourself.

Nonfinancial Resources   Also crucial to the success of a new business are nonfinancial resources, including legitimacy in the minds of the public and the various ways in which other people can help. The nearby "Multiple Generations at Work" box suggests that start-ups are more likely to gain legitimacy and success by employing multiple generations.

Legitimacy

legitimacy

People's judgment of a company's acceptance, appropriateness, and desirability, generally stemming from company goals and methods that are consistent with societal values.

An important resource for the new venture is **legitimacy**—people's judgment of a company's acceptance, appropriateness, and desirability.[97] When the market confers legitimacy, it helps overcome the liability of newness that creates a high percentage of new venture failure.[98]

Legitimacy helps a firm acquire other resources such as top managers, good employees, financial resources, and government support. In a three-year study of start-ups, the likelihood a company would succeed at selling products, hiring employees, and attracting investors depended most on how skillfully entrepreneurs demonstrated that their business was legitimate.[99]

A business is legitimate if its goals and methods are consistent with societal values. You can generate legitimacy by visibly conforming to rules and expectations created by governments, credentialing associations, and professional organizations; by visibly endorsing widely held values; and by visibly practicing widely held beliefs.[100]

Networks

social capital

Goodwill stemming from your social relationships; a competitive advantage in the form of relationships with other people and the image other people have of you.

The entrepreneur is aided greatly by having a strong network of people. **Social capital**—being part of a social network and having a good reputation—helps entrepreneurs gain access to useful information, gain trust and cooperation from others, recruit employees, form successful business alliances, receive funding from venture capitalists, and become more successful.[101] Social capital provides a lasting source of competitive advantage.[102]

Top Management Teams

The top management team is another crucial resource. Gordon Logan is CEO and founder of Sport Clips, a hair salon franchise specially designed to appeal to male customers of all ages. After experiencing an early setback as an entrepreneur, Logan brought together a top management team to design a plan to help Sport Clips grow at a rapid yet manageable pace. In 2017, Sport Clips had over 1,500 franchises operating in every state of the union. Logan was named 2016 Entrepreneur of the Year by the International Franchise Association.[103]

Advisory Boards

Whether or not the company has a formal board of directors, entrepreneurs can assemble a group of people willing to serve as an advisory board. Board members with business experience can help an entrepreneur learn basics such as how to do cash flow analysis, identify needed strategic changes, and build relationships with bankers, accountants, and attorneys.

Multiple Generations at Work

Millennial Entrepreneurs Can Learn from Others with More Experience

Jerry Jao, CEO and cofounder of Retention Science, enjoys asking older entrepreneurs for advice. Jao reached out to Matt Hulett, CEO of ClickBank, who has decades more experience, and asked him what younger entrepreneurs could learn from more experienced entrepreneurs.

Hulett said that Millennial entrepreneurs should make sure they enjoy and celebrate the small successes and not just the large ones (e.g., getting another round of funding). He added that his younger counterparts shouldn't be afraid to fail; the important thing is to learn from those missteps.

Some Millennial entrepreneurs are tapping into senior wisdom by cofounding firms with older, more seasoned partners or hiring them as consultants. Here are some areas in which Boomers can help start-ups achieve scalability and success:

©ZUMA Press, Inc./Alamy Stock Photo

1. Angel investors and advisers. Boomers can bring funding and advice for business plan development and marketing strategies.
2. Partnership or executive positions. Boomers may be willing to work with founders for an equity stake in the business. This can create a win–win for the cash-starved start-up that needs experienced people.
3. Talent management. Boomers have decades of experience dealing with talent management issues such as hiring, firing, training, compensation, and performance evaluation. This can free up the founders to focus on the core activity of the start-up.

By handling those tasks, Boomers can empower the founders and other employees to focus on developing and improving products, sales, and marketing (traditional and social media) to Millennial and Gen X customers.[104]

Partners

Often two people go into business together as partners. Partners can help one another access capital, spread the workload, share the risk, and share expertise.

But despite the potential advantages of having a compatible partner, partnerships are not always marriages made in heaven. "Mark" talked three of his friends into joining him in starting his own telecommunications company because he didn't want to try it alone. He learned quickly that while he wanted to put money into growing the business, his three partners wanted the company to pay for their cars and meetings in the Bahamas. The company collapsed. "I never thought a business relationship could overpower friendship, but this one did. Where money's involved, people change."

To be successful, partners need to acknowledge one another's talents, let each other do what they do best, communicate honestly, and listen to one another. Partners also must learn to trust each other by making and keeping agreements. If they must break an agreement, it is crucial that they give early notice and clean up after their mistakes.

Corporate Entrepreneurship

Large corporations are more than passive bystanders watching independent entrepreneurs create new businesses. Even established companies try to find and pursue new and profitable ideas—and they need in-house entrepreneurs (sometimes called intrapreneurs)[105] to do so.

Building Support for Your Idea

A manager who has a new idea to capitalize on a market opportunity will need to get others in the organization to buy in or sign on. In other words, you need to build a network of allies who support and will help implement the idea.

If you need to build support for a project idea, the first step involves *clearing the investment* with your immediate boss or bosses.[106] At this stage, you explain the idea and seek approval to look for wider support.

Higher executives often want evidence that the project is backed by your peers before committing to it. This involves *making cheerleaders*—people who will support the manager before formal approval from higher levels.

Next, *horse trading* begins. You can offer promises of payoffs from the project in return for support, time, money, and other resources that peers and others contribute.

Finally, you should *get the blessing* of relevant higher-level officials. This usually involves a formal presentation. You will need to guarantee the project's technical and political feasibility. Higher management's endorsement of the project and promises of resources help convert potential supporters into an enthusiastic team. At this point, you can go back to your boss and make specific plans for going ahead with the project. Along the way, expect some resistance and frustration—and use passion and perseverance, as well as business logic, to persuade others to get on board.

Building Intrapreneurship

Success in fostering a culture in which intrapreneurs flourish comes from making an intentional decision to foster entrepreneurial thinking and behavior, creating new venture teams, and changing the compensation system so that it encourages, supports, and rewards creative and innovative behaviors. In other words, building intrapreneurship derives from careful and deliberate strategy.

Two well-known approaches used to stimulate internal entrepreneurial activity are skunkworks and bootlegging. **Skunkworks** are project teams designated to develop a new product. A team is formed with a specific goal within a specified time frame. A respected person is chosen to manage the skunkworks. In this approach to corporate innovation, risk takers are not punished for taking risks and failing—their former jobs are held for them. The risk takers also have the opportunity to earn large rewards.

Bootlegging refers to informal efforts—as opposed to official job assignments—in which employees work to create new products and processes of their own choosing and initiative. Informal can mean secretive, such as when a bootlegger believes the company or the boss will frown on those activities. But companies should tolerate some bootlegging, and some even encourage it. To a limited extent, they allow people freedom to pursue pet projects without asking what they are or monitoring progress. Bootlegging likely will lead to some lost time but also to learning and some profitable innovations.

W. L. Gore encourages all employees to be intrapreneurs. Employees spend 10 percent of their day (called "dabble time") developing new product ideas. One employee, Dave Myers, learned that the coating from the company's cable product could make guitar strings hold their tone longer and be more comfortable to use. The idea was a success. Gore launched ELIXIR Strings which are now a top-selling product.[107] At Gore, as elsewhere, intrapreneurship derives from deliberate strategic thinking and execution.

Management Challenges

Organizations that encourage intrapreneurship face an obvious risk: the effort can fail. One author noted, "There is considerable history of internal venture development by large firms, and it does not encourage optimism."[108] However, failing to foster intrapreneurship may represent a subtler but greater risk than encouraging it. The organization that resists entrepreneurial initiative may lose its ability to adapt and be creative when needed.

The most dangerous risk in corporate entrepreneurship is overreliance on a single project. Many companies fail while awaiting the completion of one large, innovative project.[109] The

Bottom Line

Recall from Chapter 3 that creativity spawns good new ideas, but innovation requires actually implementing those ideas so they become realities. If you work in an organization and have a good idea, you must convince other people to get on board.

How would you convince people to get behind your new idea?

skunkworks

A project team designated to produce a new, innovative product.

bootlegging

Informal work on projects, other than those officially assigned, of employees' own choosing and initiative.

successful entrepreneurial organization avoids overcommitment to a single project and relies on its entrepreneurial spirit to produce at least one winner from among several projects.

Organizations also court failure when they spread their entrepreneurial efforts over too many projects.[110] If there are many projects, each effort may be too small in scale. Managers will consider the projects unattractive because of their small size. Or those recruited to manage the projects may have difficulty building power and status within the organization.

The hazards in intrapreneurship, then, are related to scale. One large project is a threat, as are too many underresourced projects. But a carefully managed approach to this strategically important process will upgrade an organization's chances for long-term survival and success.

Entrepreneurial Orientation

Earlier in this chapter, we described the characteristics of individual entrepreneurs. To conclude the chapter, we do the same for companies: we describe how highly entrepreneurial companies differ from those that are not. CEOs play a crucial role in promoting entrepreneurship within large corporations.[111]

Entrepreneurial orientation is an organization's tendency to engage in activities designed to identify and capitalize successfully on opportunities to launch new ventures by entering new or established markets with new or existing goods or services.[112] Entrepreneurial orientation is determined by five tendencies: to allow independent action, innovate, take risks, be proactive, and be competitively aggressive. Entrepreneurial orientation should enhance the likelihood of success and may be particularly important for conducting business internationally.[113]

To allow *independent action* is to grant to individuals and teams the freedom to exercise their creativity, champion promising ideas, and carry them through to completion. *Innovativeness* requires the firm to support new ideas, experimentation, and creative processes; it requires a willingness to depart from existing practices and venture beyond the status quo. *Risk taking* comes from a willingness to commit significant resources, and perhaps borrow heavily, to venture into the unknown. The tendency to take risks can be assessed by considering whether people behave boldly or cautiously, whether they require high levels of certainty before taking or allowing action, and whether they tend to stick to tried-and-true paths, reluctant to stray.

To be *proactive* is to act in anticipation of future problems and opportunities. A proactive firm changes the competitive landscape; other firms merely react. Proactive firms are forward thinking and fast to act and are leaders rather than followers. Similarly, some individuals are more likely to be proactive, to shape and create their own environments, than others who more passively cope with the situations in which they find themselves.[114] Proactive firms encourage and allow individuals and teams to be proactive.

Finally, *competitive aggressiveness* is the firm's tendency to challenge competitors directly and intensely to achieve entry or improve its position. In other words, it is a competitive tendency to outperform one's rivals in the marketplace. This might take the form of striking fast to beat competitors to the punch, to take them on head-to-head, and to analyze and target their weaknesses.

Thus, what makes a firm entrepreneurial is its engagement in an effective combination of independent action, innovativeness, risk taking, proactiveness, and competitive aggressiveness.[115] The relationship between these factors and the performance of the firm is a complicated one that depends on many things. Still, you can imagine how the opposite profile—too many constraints on action, business as usual, extreme caution, passivity, and a lack of competitive fire—will inhibit entrepreneurial activity.

Without entrepreneurship, how would firms survive and thrive in a constantly changing environment? If your bosses don't create environments that foster entrepreneurship, consider trying your own experiments.[116] Find and talk with others who share your entrepreneurial bent. What can you learn from them, and teach them?

Sometime it takes individuals and teams of experimenters to show the possibilities to those at the top. Ask yourself and others: Between the bureaucrats and the entrepreneurs, who have a more positive impact? And who have more fun?

entrepreneurial orientation

The tendency of an organization to identify and capitalize successfully on opportunities to launch new ventures by entering new or established markets with new or existing goods or services.

Management in Action

STARBUCKS IS RETAINING ITS ENTREPRENEURIAL SPIRIT

Howard Schultz recently stepped down as CEO of Starbucks, the company he founded, to return to a more entrepreneurial role within the company. The entrepreneurial spirit of innovation is one of the things he has always tried to preserve from the company's earliest days, but now he'll be able to more actively play the pioneering part he once did. Schultz will be in charge of developing two new premium brands. Roasteries is a line of new Starbucks stores that will serve Reserve coffee and food by Princi, a premium Italian bakery. Reserve coffee bars also will roll out in existing Starbucks stores, opening in the United States and internationally at the same time.

There is further evidence of the value Starbucks places on entrepreneurship, even as it has become a worldwide corporate brand in more than 60 countries. The company has its own "entrepreneur in residence." In this position, which reports directly to the CEO, Richard Tait is responsible for "helping the company foster a culture of innovation" and lending an "entrepreneurial lens" to its planning and decision making, with a focus on speed and agility.

Tait, who also is on the steering committee for Starbucks' Innovation Lab, says his role is to maintain the "energy and passion of a start-up inside the rhythm of a large corporation."

Meanwhile, the company continues to innovate as a socially conscious company, with a promise to open stores in low- and middle-income communities in the United States to provide jobs in these communities. In a new expansion strategy, drive-thrus and express stores will help the company expand in the United States without risking the oversaturation it faced some years ago when some stores were forced to close.[117]

- How successfully does Starbucks embody an entrepreneurial orientation? How willing to take risks does it appear to be?
- What evidence do you see that Starbucks supports intrapreneurial behavior? What are some of the risks a large company takes in doing so?

KEY TERMS

advertising support model, p. 196

affiliate model, p. 196

bootlegging, p. 210

business accelerator, p. 201

business incubators, p. 201

business plan, p. 205

entrepreneur, p. 191

entrepreneurial orientation, p. 211

entrepreneurial venture, p. 190

entrepreneurship, p. 190

franchising, p. 195

initial public offering (IPO), p. 204

intermediary model, p. 196

intrapreneurs, p. 191

legitimacy, p. 208

opportunity analysis, p. 205

skunkworks, p. 210

small business, p. 190

social capital, p. 208

social enterprise, p. 197

social entrepreneurship, p. 197

subscription model, p. 196

transaction fee model, p. 196

RETAINING WHAT YOU LEARNED

In Chapter 7, you learned that people become entrepreneurs for a variety of reasons. Successful entrepreneurs are innovators, but also possess management, business, and networking skills. While there is no single entrepreneurial personality, certain characteristics contribute to their success. To start a new business, it is important to monitor the current business environment and other indicators. Choosing a business idea to pursue should be based on planning and trial and error, and fit with risk preferences and personal interests. Effective planning and getting advice from experienced experts are helpful in preventing failure. Common challenges include getting started, warding off competitors, managing growth, and controlling finances. Developing and executing a comprehensive business plan will increase the chances of success. Successful entrepreneurs develop social capital and a network of customers, partners, boards, and other talented people. Managers of large companies can encourage intrapreneurship by using skunkworks and allowing bootlegging. A portfolio of projects should be chosen carefully and funded appropriately. An entrepreneurial orientation in a company comes from encouraging independent action, innovativeness, risk taking, proactive behavior, and competitive aggressiveness.

LO 1 Describe why people become entrepreneurs and what it takes, personally.

- People become entrepreneurs because of the profit potential, the challenge, and the satisfaction they anticipate (and often receive) from participating in the process, and sometimes because they are blocked from more traditional avenues of career advancement.
- As shown in Exhibit 7.3, successful entrepreneurs are innovators, and they have good knowledge and skills in management, business, and networking.
- Although there is no single entrepreneurial personality, certain characteristics are helpful: commitment and determination; leadership skills; opportunity obsession; tolerance of risk, ambiguity, and uncertainty; creativity; self-reliance; the ability to adapt; and motivation to excel.

LO 2 Summarize how to assess opportunities to start new businesses.

- You should always be on the lookout for new ideas, monitoring the current business environment and other indicators of opportunity.
- Trial and error and preparation play important roles. Assessing the business concept on the basis of how innovative and risky it is, combined with your personal interests and tendencies, also will help you make good choices.
- Ideas should be carefully assessed via opportunity analysis and a thorough business plan.

LO 3 Identify common causes of success and failure.

- New ventures are inherently risky. The economic environment plays an important role in the success or failure of the business, and the entrepreneur should anticipate and be prepared to adapt in the face of changing economic conditions.
- How you handle a variety of common management challenges also can mean the difference

between success and failure, as can the effectiveness of your planning and your ability to mobilize nonfinancial resources, including other people who can help.

LO 4 Discuss common management challenges.

- When new businesses fail, the causes often can be traced to some common challenges that entrepreneurs must manage well. You might not enjoy the entrepreneurial process.
- Survival—including getting started and fending off competitors—is difficult.
- Growth creates new challenges, including reluctance to delegate work to others. Funds may be put to improper use, and financial controls may be inadequate.
- Many entrepreneurs fail to plan well for succession.
- When needing or wanting new funds, initial public offerings provide an option, but they represent an important and difficult decision that must be considered carefully.

LO 5 Explain how to increase your chances of success, including good business planning.

- The business plan helps you think through your idea thoroughly and determine its viability. It also convinces (or fails to convince) others to participate.
- The plan describes the venture and its future, provides financial projections, and includes plans for marketing, manufacturing, and other business functions.
- The plan should describe the people involved in the venture, a full assessment of the opportunity (including customers and competitors), the environmental context (including regulatory and economic issues), and the risk (including future risks and how you intend to deal with them).
- Successful entrepreneurs also understand how to develop social capital, which enhances legitimacy and helps develop a network of others including customers, talented people, partners, and boards.

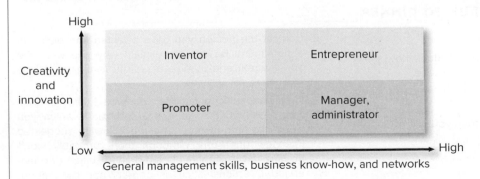

EXHIBIT 7.3 (revisited)
Who Is the Entrepreneur?

Timmons, J. A. and Spinelli, S., Jr., *New Venture Creation: Entrepreneurship for the 21st Century,* 7th ed., 2007, pp. 67–68. Copyright 2007 The McGraw-Hill Companies, Inc. Reprinted with permission.

LO 6 Describe how managers of large companies can foster entrepreneurship.

- Intrapreneurs work within established companies to develop new goods or services that allow the corporation to reap the benefits of innovation.
- To facilitate intrapreneurship, organizations use skunkworks—special project teams designated to develop a new product—and allow bootlegging—informal efforts beyond formal job assignments

in which employees pursue their own pet projects.

- Organizations should select projects carefully, have an ongoing portfolio of projects, and fund them appropriately.
- Ultimately, a true entrepreneurial orientation in a company comes from encouraging independent action, innovativeness, risk taking, proactive behavior, and competitive aggressiveness.

DISCUSSION QUESTIONS

1. On a 1 to 10 scale, what is your level of personal interest in becoming an entrepreneur? Why did you rate yourself as you did?

2. How would you assess your capability of being a successful entrepreneur? What are your strengths and weaknesses? How would you increase your capability?

3. Most entrepreneurs learn the most important skills they need after age 21. How does this affect your outlook and plans?

4. Identify and discuss new ventures that fit each of the four cells in the entrepreneurial strategy matrix.

5. Brainstorm a list of ideas for new business ventures. Where did you get the ideas? Which ones are most and least viable, and why?

6. Identify some businesses that recently opened in your area. What are their chances of survival, and why? How would you advise the owners or managers of those businesses to ensure their success?

7. Assume you are writing a story about what it's really like to be an entrepreneur. To whom would you talk, and what questions would you ask?

8. Conduct interviews with two entrepreneurs, asking whatever questions most interest you. Share your findings with the class. How do the interviews differ from one another, and what do they have in common?

9. Review Exhibit 7.1. Which myths did you believe? Do you still? Why or why not? Interview two entrepreneurs by asking each myth as a true-or-false question. Then

ask them to elaborate on their answers. What did they say? What do you conclude?

10. With your classmates, form small teams of skunkworks. Your charge is to identify an innovation that you think would benefit your school and to outline an action plan for bringing your idea to reality.

11. Identify a business that recently folded. What were the causes of the failure? What could have been done differently to prevent the failure?

12. Does franchising appeal to you? What franchises would most and least interest you, and why?

13. The chapter specified some of the changes in the external environment that can provide business opportunity (technological discoveries, lifestyle and taste changes, and so on). Identify some important recent changes or current trends in the external environment and the business opportunities they might offer.

14. Choose an Internet company with which you are familiar and brainstorm ideas for how its services or approach to business can be improved. How about starting a new Internet company altogether—what would be some possibilities?

15. Find some inspiring examples of social entrepreneurship and describe them to your class.

16. Brainstorm some new ideas for a social enterprise. What challenges do you foresee, and how would you proceed?

EXPERIENTIAL EXERCISES

7.1 TAKE AN ENTREPRENEUR TO DINNER

OBJECTIVES

1. To get to know what an entrepreneur does, how she or he got started, and what it took to succeed.

2. To interview a particular entrepreneur in depth about his or her career and experiences.

3. To acquire a feeling for whether you might find an entrepreneurial career rewarding.

INSTRUCTIONS

1. Identify an entrepreneur in your area you would like to interview.

2. Contact the person you have selected and make an appointment. Be sure to explain why you want the appointment and to give a realistic estimate of how much time you will need.

3. Identify specific questions you would like to have answered and the general areas about which you would like information. (See the following suggested interview questions, although there probably won't be time for all of them.) Using a combination of open-ended questions—such as general questions about how the entrepreneur got started, what happened next, and so forth—and closed-ended questions—such

as specific questions about what his or her goals were, if he or she had to find partners, and so forth—will help keep the interview focused yet allow for unexpected comments and insights.

4. Conduct the interview. If both you and the person you are interviewing are comfortable, using a small voice recorder during the interview can be of great help to you later. Remember, too, that you most likely will learn more if you are an interested listener.

5. Evaluate what you have learned. Write down the information you have gathered in some form that will be helpful to you later on. Be as specific as you can. Jotting down direct quotes is more effective than statements such as "highly motivated individual." Also be sure to make a note of what you did not find out.

6. Write a thank-you note. This is more than a courtesy; it will also help the entrepreneur remember you favorably should you want to follow up on the interview.

Suggested Interview

QUESTIONS FOR GATHERING INFORMATION

- *Would you tell me about yourself before you started your first venture?*
Were your parents, relatives, or close friends entrepreneurial? How so?
Did you have any other role models?
What was your education/military experience? In hindsight, was it helpful? In what specific ways?
What was your previous work experience? Was it helpful? What particular chunks of experience were especially valuable or relevant?
In particular, did you have any sales or marketing experience? How important was this in starting your company?
- *How did you start your venture?*
How did you spot the opportunity? How did it surface?
What were your goals? What were your lifestyle or other personal requirements? How did you fit these factors together?
How did you evaluate the opportunity in terms of the critical elements for success? The competition? The market?
Did you find or have partners? What kind of planning did you do? What kind of financing did you have?
Did you have a start-up business plan of any kind? Please tell me about it.
How much time did it take from conception to the first day of business? How many hours a day did you spend working on it?
How much capital did it take? How long did it take to reach a positive cash flow and break-even sales volume? If you did not have enough money at the time, what were some ways in which you "bootstrapped" the venture (i.e., bartering, borrowing, and the like)? Tell me about the pressures and crises during that early survival period.
What outside help did you get? Did you have experienced advisers? Lawyers? Accountants? Tax experts?

Patent experts? How did you develop these networks and how long did it take?
What was your family situation at the time?
What did you perceive to be your own strengths? Weaknesses?
What did you perceive to be the strengths of your venture? Weaknesses?
What was your most triumphant moment? Your worst moment?
Did you want to have partners or do it solo? Why?
- *Once you got going . . .*
What were the most difficult gaps to fill and problems to solve as you began to grow rapidly?
When you looked for key people as partners, advisers, or managers, were there any personal attributes or attitudes you were especially seeking because you knew they would fit with you and were important to success? How did you find them?
Are there any attributes among partners and advisers that you would definitely try to avoid?
Have things become more predictable? Or less?
Do you spend more/same/less time with your business now than in the early years?
Do you feel more managerial and less entrepreneurial now?
In terms of the future, do you plan to harvest? To maintain? To expand?
Do you plan ever to retire? Would you explain?
Have your goals changed? Have you met them?

QUESTIONS FOR CONCLUDING (CHOOSE ONE)

- What do you consider your most valuable asset—the thing that enabled you to make it?
- If you had it to do over again would you do it again in the same way?
- Looking back, what do you feel are the most critical concepts, skills, attitudes, and know-how you needed to get your company started and grown to where it is today? What will be needed for the next five years? To what extent can any of these be learned?
- Some people say there is a lot of stress being an entrepreneur. What have you experienced? How would you say it compares with other hot-seat jobs, such as the head of a big company or a partner in a large law, consulting, or accounting firm?
- What are the things that you find personally rewarding and satisfying as an entrepreneur? What have been the rewards, risks, and trade-offs?
- Who should try to be an entrepreneur? Can you give me any ideas there?
- What advice would you give an aspiring entrepreneur? Could you suggest the three most important lessons you have learned? How can I learn them while minimizing the tuition?

7.2 STARTING A NEW BUSINESS

OBJECTIVES

1. To introduce you to the complexities of going into business for yourself.

2. To provide hands-on experience in making new business decisions.

INSTRUCTIONS

1. Your instructor will divide the class into teams and assign each team the task of investigating the start-up of one of the following businesses:
   a. Submarine sandwich shop
   b. Day care service
   c. Bookstore
   d. Gasoline service station
   e. Other

2. Each team should research the information necessary to complete the New Business Start-Up Worksheet. The following agencies or organizations might be of assistance:
   a. Small Business Administration
   b. Local county/city administration agencies
   c. Local chamber of commerce
   d. Local small-business development corporation
   e. U.S. Department of Commerce
   f. Farmer's Home Administration
   g. Local realtors
   h. Local business people in the same or a similar business
   i. Banks and S&Ls

3. Each team presents its findings to the class.

New Business Start-Up Worksheet

1. *Product*

   What customer need will we satisfy?

   How can our product be unique?

2. *Customer*

   Who are our customers? What are their profiles?

   Where do they live/work/play?

   What are their buying habits?

   What are their needs?

3. *Competition*

   Who/where is the competition?

   What are their strengths and weaknesses?

   How might they respond to us?

4. *Suppliers*

   Who/where are our suppliers?

   What are their business practices?

   What relationships can we expect?

5. *Location*

   Where are our customers/competitors/suppliers?

   What are the location costs?

   What are the legal limitations to location?

6. *Physical Facilities/Equipment*

   Rent/own/build/refurbish facilities?

   Rent/lease/purchase equipment?

   Maintenance?

7. *Human Resources*

   Availability?

   Training?

   Costs?

8. *Legal/Regulatory Environment*
   Licenses/permits/certifications?   _____
   Government agencies?   _____
   Liability?   _____
9. *Cultural/Social Environment*   _____
   Cultural issues?   _____
   Social issues?   _____
10. *International Environment*   _____
    International issues?   _____
11. *Other*   _____

Concluding Case

ROLLING OUT SCROLLCO

Mandy Toberman had enjoyed her engineering job at Acme Electronics, but she began to grow restless. Most of her work for the past five years had involved designing minor adjustments to existing products. She worried she would lose her edge in a fast-changing industry, and work just didn't engage her imagination or problem-solving skills the way it once did. In the evenings, she found herself pursuing new ideas, researching some of the latest technology, and testing out some possible inventions. As the weeks passed, Mandy became increasingly interested in one idea: an e-reader made with flexible materials that could be rolled up and stuffed into a satchel, backpack, or purse. At first she doubted it could be made, but with some investigation, Mandy began to develop a design for the device, which she called the Scroll.

The more Mandy considered the Scroll, the more she thought it would be an exciting new product for Acme to offer. It would open up a whole new area of sales for the company, which had not seen much growth for the past few years. It would generate tremendous publicity for Acme and excitement in her division. So Mandy collected a few of the drawings she had created, estimated the manufacturing costs, and prepared a proposal. She invited her supervisor, Tom Ringsack, and two of her colleagues to a meeting, saying only that she had an idea she wanted to bring up.

At the meeting, Mandy started her laptop to show her drawings and describe her idea for the Scroll. The other engineers' eyes were wide, and Mandy could sense their eagerness to explore the concept. However, Tom sighed and said, "Mandy, you know our situation, right? In the present economy, we can't get a lot of financing for risky new projects. We have to focus on the product enhancements that will increase our profit margins, and the budget for anything else is tight—well, really, nonexistent." Mandy could tell the discussion was over, so she shut down her computer with a quiet sigh.

That weekend, Mandy spent hours at her desk at home, beginning to plan her escape from Acme Electronics. She perused the Small Business Administration website, looking for advice on writing a business plan, and explored her LinkedIn network, looking for contacts who might give her advice—and possibly funding—for her start-up, which she intended to name ScrollCo. By the end of the weekend, feeling more than a little nervous, Mandy had drafted the outline of a business plan.

DISCUSSION QUESTIONS

1. What actions could Acme Electronics take to foster intrapreneurship? What consequences does it suffer from failing to foster it?
2. What information should Mandy include in her business plan?
3. Describe three nonfinancial resources likely to be important for the future of ScrollCo. How can Mandy ensure that her business has those resources?

PART TWO SUPPORTING CASE

Will Foxconn Remain Apple's Top Supplier of iGadgets?

Apple is famous for its attractive and highly prized electronics, including iPhone and iTouch portable devices, iPod and iTunes for music, and iMac and iPad computers. However, Apple doesn't actually make any of its products. Rather, it develops ideas, designs devices, and promotes the products and its brand. To put the devices together, Apple relies on a set of contractors.

One key contractor is an electronics firm called Foxconn, based in Taiwan. With factories located in China, Foxconn has combined manufacturing expertise with low-cost labor to win deals to make computers and key components such as motherboards. As consumers have slowed their spending on laptop computers in favor of smaller devices such as the iPad tablet computer and smartphones, Foxconn has benefited. Until recently, it was the only company making Apple's iPad and one of just two makers of Apple's iPhone. Workers at Foxconn facilities also produce the Sony PlayStation 3, the Nintendo Wii, and Amazon's Kindle Fire. It also produces TVs for Sony, Sharp, and Toshiba. In China alone, Foxconn employs almost 1.3 million workers, making it one of the largest employers in the world. Many of those workers live in on-site dormitories, eat in company-run dining halls, and relax in bookstores and gyms located right at their workplace.

In recent years, Foxconn has been running into some tragic problems. In 2010, the company drew international media attention when it came to light that several workers at Foxconn's plant in Shenzhen (a city in southern China) had committed suicide. Questions arose about whether working conditions were so horrible as to drive workers to kill themselves. Apple sent executives accompanied by suicide prevention experts to the plant to investigate. Although Apple requires its contract partners to meet specific standards in its code of conduct, and it visits over 100 facilities a year to ensure compliance, it had failed to uncover any problems at Foxconn before the suicides came to light.

In the following year, Foxconn was again in the news about a tragedy when an explosion in its Chengdu, China, plant killed 3 workers and injured 15. Initial investigations suggested that the explosion was the result of a fairly basic manufacturing safety problem: because of improper ventilation, dust collected in the air of a metal-polishing shop, and the dust ignited. If such a problem occurred in the United States, regulators would quickly shut down the facility for violating safety requirements.

Embarrassed by the media and pressured by important customers such as Apple, Foxconn acted to improve working conditions. At the Shenzhen plant, it brought in counselors, improved training of managers and the staff answering calls on the employee hotline, and launched a morale-boosting program called Care–Love, which sponsors employee outings. In the factories in Chengdu and elsewhere, the company took measures to improve ventilation.

Along with these changes, Foxconn began giving out raises. In Shenzhen, workers' wages more than doubled.

Since Foxconn launched the effort to improve morale, employee turnover has fallen, and the suicides seem to have ended. Unfortunately, the payoff for the company is difficult to measure. Higher costs have erased profits, and Foxconn's stock price has tumbled. So now the company is looking for lower-cost locations. It opened facilities in China's interior cities, where wage rates are about one-third below those of Shenzhen. Making matters more challenging for Foxconn is the fact that Apple CEO Tim Cook has shifted some of the production of iPhones and iPad minis to Pegatron, another Taiwan-based electronics manufacturer. Pegatron also makes products for Microsoft, Dell, and Hewlett-Packard.

DISCUSSION QUESTIONS

1. What threats, opportunities, strengths, and weaknesses can you identify at Foxconn? How is it addressing these with its strategy?

2. If Foxconn's management hired you to offer advice on improving its ethical decision making and corporate social responsibility, what measures would you suggest? Why?

3. Why do you think Tim Cook, after years of using Foxconn for most of Apple's production needs, shifted some production to Pegatron?

SOURCES: Gold, M. and Lee, Y., "Apple Supplier Foxconn to Shrink Workforce as Sales Growth Stalls," Reuters, January 27, 2015, http://www.reuters.com; Dou, E., "Apple Shifts Supply Chain Away from Foxconn to Pegatron," The Wall Street Journal (online), May 29, 2013, http://www.wsj.com; Kan, M., "Foxconn Builds Products for Many Vendors, but Its Mud Sticks to Apple," MacWorld (online), October 24, 2012, http://www.macworld.com; Culpan, T., Lifei, Z. and Einhorn, B., "Foxconn: How to Beat the High Cost of Happy Workers," Bloomberg Businessweek, May 5, 2011, http://www.businessweek.com; Nystedt, D., "Apple: Foxconn 'Saved Lives' with Suicide Prevention Efforts," PC World, February 15, 2011, http://www.pcworld.com; Bussey, J., "Measuring the Human Cost of an iPad Made in China," The Wall Street Journal, June 3, 2011, http://online.wsj.com; "Apple Report Details Response to Foxconn Suicides," eWeek, February 15, 2011, Business & Company Resource Center, http://galenet.galegroup.com; and Dalrymple, J., "Apple Reports on Foxconn, Supplier Workplace Standards," CNET News, February 14, 2011, http://news.cnet.com.

APPENDIX C

Information for Entrepreneurs

If you are interested in starting or managing a small business, you have access to many sources of useful information.

PUBLISHED SOURCES

The first step is a complete search of materials in libraries and on the Internet. You can find a huge amount of published information, databases, and other sources about industries, markets, competitors, and personnel. Some of this information will have been uncovered when you searched for ideas. Listed here are additional sources that should help get you started.

Guides and Company Information

Valuable information is available in special issues and on the websites of *Bloomberg Business, Forbes, Inc., The Economist, Fast Company,* and *Fortune,* as well as online in the following:

- Hoovers.com
- ProQuest.com
- Investext.com

Valuable Sites on the Internet

- Entrepreneurship (http://www.kauffman.org/what-we-do/entrepreneurship), the website of the Kauffman Center for Entrepreneurial Leadership, Ewing Marion Kauffman Foundation
- *Fast Company* (http://www.fastcompany.com)
- Ernst & Young (http://www.ey.com)
- *Inc.* magazine (http://www.inc.com)
- Entrepreneur.com and magazine (http://www.entrepreneur.com)
- EDGAR database (http://www.sec.gov)—subscription sources, such as ThomsonResearch (http://www.thomsonfinancial.com), provide images of other filings as well
- Thomson Venture Economics (https://vx.thomsonib.com/VxComponent/vxhelp/VentureXpert_Fact_Sheet.pdf)

Journal Articles via Computerized Indexes

- Factiva with Dow Jones, Reuters, *The Wall Street Journal*
- EBSCOhost
- FirstSearch
- Ethnic News Watch
- LEXIS/NEXIS
- *The New York Times* (http://www.nytimes.com)
- InfoTrac from Gale Group
- ABI/Inform and other ProQuest databases
- RDS Business Reference Suite
- *The Wall Street Journal* (http://www.wsj.com)

Statistics

- Stat-USA (https://www.usa.gov/statistics)—U.S. government subscription site for economic, trade, and business data and market research
- U.S. Bureau of the Census (http://www.census.gov)—the source of many statistical data, including
  - *Statistical Abstract of the United States*
  - *American FactFinder*—population data
  - Economic programs (http://www.census.gov/econ/www/index.html)—data by sector
  - County business patterns
  - Zip code business patterns
- Knight Ridder . . . *CRB Commodity Yearbook*
- Manufacturing USA, Service Industries USA, and other sector compilations from Gale Group
- Economic Statistics Briefing Room (https://www.whitehouse.gov/administration/eop/cea/economic-indicators)
- *Federal Reserve Bulletin*
- Survey of Current Business
- Bureau of Labor Statistics (http://www.bls.gov)
- Global Insight, formerly DRI-WEFA
- International Financial Statistics—International Monetary Fund
- World Development Indicators—World Bank
- Bloomberg Database

Consumer Expenditures

- New Strategist Publications

Projections and Forecasts

- ProQuest
- InfoTech Trends
- Guide to Special Issues and Indexes to Periodicals *(Grey House Directory of Special Issues)*
- RDS Business Reference Suite
- Value Line Investment Survey

Market Studies

- LifeStyle Market Analyst
- MarketResearch.com
- Scarborough Research
- Simmons Market Research Bureau

Consumer Expenditures

- New Strategist Publications
- Consumer Expenditure Survey
- Euromonitor

Other Sources

- Wall Street transcript
- Brokerage house reports from Investext, Multex, and so on
- Company annual reports and websites

OTHER INTELLIGENCE

Everything entrepreneurs need to know will not be found in libraries because this information needs to be highly specific and current. This information is most likely available from people—industry experts, suppliers, and the like. Summarized here are some useful sources of intelligence.

Trade Associations

Trade associations, especially the editors of their publications and information officers, are good sources of information. Trade shows and conferences are prime places to discover the latest activities of competitors.

Employees

Employees who have left a competitor's company often can provide information about the competitor, especially if the employee departed on bad terms. Also, a firm can hire people away from a competitor. Although consideration of ethics in this situation is important, the number of experienced people in any industry is limited, and competitors must prove that a company hired a person intentionally to get specific trade secrets to challenge any hiring legally. Students who have worked for competitors are another source of information.

Consulting Firms

Consulting firms frequently conduct industry studies and then make this information available. Frequently, in such fields as computers or software, competitors use the same design consultants, and these consultants can be sources of information.

Market Research Firms

Firms doing market studies, such as those listed under the previously mentioned published sources, can be sources of intelligence.

Key Customers, Manufacturers, Suppliers, Distributors, and Buyers

These groups are often a prime source of information.

Public Filings

Federal, state, and local filings, such as filings with the Securities and Exchange Commission (SEC), Patent and Trademark Office, or Freedom of Information Act filings, can reveal a surprising amount of information. There are companies that process inquiries of this type.

Reverse Engineering

Reverse engineering can be used to determine costs of production and sometimes even manufacturing methods. An example of this practice is the experience of Advanced Energy Technology, Inc. of Boulder, Colorado, which learned firsthand about such tactics. No sooner had it announced a new product, which was patented, than it received 50 orders, half of which were from competitors asking for only one or two of the items.

Networks

The networks mentioned in this chapter can be sources of new venture ideas and strategies.

Other

Classified ads, buyers' guides, labor unions, real estate agents, courts, local reporters, and so on can all provide clues.

The U.S. government is engaging in new and more extensive outreach efforts so that small-business owners will use government resources more and understand them more easily. In 2009, the U.S. Small Business Administration launched a community forum, the first government-sponsored online community built specifically for small-business owners, on the Business Gateway site of Business.gov. The forum combines discussion threads, blogs, and resource articles. The goals for the SBA and 21 other federal agencies that cosponsor the site are to engage in dialogue with the public, leverage the expertise that exists in both the public and private sectors, and help government serve entrepreneurs better.

SOURCES: Timmons, J. A. and Spinelli, S., Jr., *New Venture Creation,* 7th ed. Burr Ridge, IL: McGraw-Hill/Irwin, 2007,103–4; and Klein, K., "Government Resources for Entrepreneurs," *BusinessWeek,* March 3, 2009.

CHAPTER 8

Organization Structure

> Take my assets—but leave me my organization and in five years I'll have it all back.
>
> —Alfred P. Sloan Jr.

©Chi Ian Chao/Getty Images RF

LEARNING OBJECTIVES

After studying Chapter 8, you will be able to:

LO 1 Explain how differentiation and integration influence an organization's structure.

LO 2 Summarize how authority operates.

LO 3 Define the roles of the board of directors and the chief executive officer.

LO 4 Discuss how span of control affects structure and managerial effectiveness.

LO 5 Explain how to delegate effectively.

LO 6 Distinguish between centralized and decentralized organizations.

LO 7 Summarize ways organizations can be structured.

LO 8 Identify the unique challenges of the matrix organization.

LO 9 Describe important integrative mechanisms.

CHAPTER OUTLINE

Fundamentals of Organizing
Differentiation
Integration

The Vertical Structure
Authority in Organizations
Hierarchical Levels
Span of Control
Delegation
Decentralization

The Horizontal Structure
The Functional Organization
The Divisional Organization
The Matrix Organization
The Network Organization

Organizational Integration
Coordination by Standardization
Coordination by Plan
Coordination by Mutual Adjustment
Coordination and Communication

Looking Ahead

Management in Action

LEADERSHIP AND STRUCTURAL CHANGE AT GENERAL MOTORS

The history of General Motors shows that size and longevity do not guarantee success. GM once dominated the U.S. auto industry with a "price ladder" strategy in which Chevrolet, Pontiac, GMC, Oldsmobile, Buick, and Cadillac catered to specific slices of the consumer market. But after GM's U.S. market share peaked in 1962 at 51 percent, the company steadily began losing share to smaller, more nimble, and more innovative competition. By 2008, GM's U.S. market share was less than half what it was in 1962, and when customer demand and bank lending dried up in the 2008 financial crisis, GM nearly collapsed.

The federal government stepped in with money to keep GM alive through a Chapter 11 managed bankruptcy. In July 2009, after restructuring, the old General Motors Corporation reemerged as General Motors Company. Daniel Akerson, a Navy veteran with experience turning around companies in other industries, was named to the new company's board of directors. In September 2010, Akerson was named Chair and CEO and led the company's initial public offering—the largest in U.S. history—in November of that year.

In 2011, GM posted record earnings and reclaimed its spot as the world's automotive sales leader, but its stock price slid as investors questioned the company's long-term potential. In the years leading up to bankruptcy, GM had become known for a culture in which managers were slow to act, reluctant to speak up, and averse to change. Akerson set out to change that. Among Akerson's challenges was teaching a 213,000-employee multinational company selling millions of vehicles annually to be more nimble, more innovative, and more customer-centric.

Akerson drove change by assembling a management team of seasoned industry insiders. GM also

©Richard Lautens/Getty Images

assembled a diverse board of 14 directors, mostly current and retired executives from other organizations, including representatives from Fortune 100 companies (Walmart, Coca-Cola, Conoco-Phillips, Burlington Northern Santa Fe, etc.), the financial and telecom industries, academia, and a former chair of the U.S. Joint Chiefs of Staff.

The company reported 2016 earnings of $12.5 billion on revenue of more than $166.4 billion, enabling significant reinvestments for growth. GM also boasted the largest market share in China, fueled by record sales of 3.87 million. GM's ability to meet it goals depended on offering attractive new products while continuing to improve vehicle safety, quality, customer service, and global efficiency.[1]

Ex-Chair and CEO Dan Akerson believed that the way employees are organized into departments and divisions played a role in how fast and effectively they could seize new opportunities. As you read this chapter, notice the options available for an organization's structure, and consider whether GM's management has made the right choices to enable continued growth and a more responsive culture.

Since its emergence from bankruptcy, General Motors has been running neck and neck with Toyota and Volkswagen to keep its spot as the world's biggest auto company, even as its U.S. market share slips and it struggles with investor doubts about its ability to operate efficiently. How could the company respond to this situation? The way in which a company organizes itself to address an issue such as declining market share may determine whether its strategy will succeed. GM, like many companies, is working hard to make certain that its strategy and structure are aligned.

This chapter describes the most important components of organization structure. We begin by covering basic principles of differentiation and integration. Next we discuss the vertical structure, which includes issues of authority, hierarchy, delegation, and decentralization. We then describe the horizontal structure, which includes functional, divisional, and matrix forms. Finally, we show how organizations can integrate across multiple units: coordination by standardization, coordination by plan, and coordination by mutual adjustment.

In the chapter following this, we continue with the topic of organization structure but take a different perspective. In that chapter, we focus on the flexibility and responsiveness of an organization—that is, how capable it is of changing its form and adapting to strategy, technology, the environment, and other challenges it confronts.

Fundamentals of Organizing

People often learn about a firm's structure first by looking at its organization chart. The **organization chart** depicts the positions in the firm and the way they are arranged. The chart provides a picture of the reporting structure (who reports to whom) and the various activities that people perform. Most companies have official organization charts that present this information.

Exhibit 8.1 shows a traditional organization chart. It conveys several types of information.

1. The boxes represent different clusters of jobs.
2. The titles in the boxes show the work that each unit performs.
3. The solid lines show reporting and authority relationships: superior–subordinate connections.
4. Each horizontal layer indicates one level of management. A level indicates all persons of the same rank or units of the same rank reporting to someone in the level above.

Not shown in the chart, but just as important in describing an organization's structure, are two additional concepts: differentiation and integration. **Differentiation** means that the organization is composed of many units that work on different kinds of tasks, using different skills and work methods. **Integration** means that the work of these differentiated units is coordinated into an overall product.[2]

Differentiation

Carrying out the many tasks within an organization requires specialization and division of labor. Without these, the totality of work would be too complex—not to mention too much load—for any individual.[3]

Differentiation is created through division of labor and job specialization. **Division of labor** means that the work of the organization is subdivided into smaller tasks. **Specialization** refers to the fact that different people or groups perform those smaller parts of the organization's overall work. As you can see, the two concepts are closely related. Work is divided, and people specialize in certain work tasks.

Differentiation is high when an organization has many subunits and many kinds of specialists. Renowned Harvard professors Lawrence and Lorsch found that organizations in complex, dynamic environments (plastics firms, in their study) developed a high degree of differentiation to cope with the complex challenges. Companies in simple, stable

organization chart

The reporting structure and division of labor in an organization.

differentiation

An aspect of the organization's internal environment created by job specialization and the division of labor.

integration

The degree to which differentiated work units work together and coordinate their efforts.

division of labor

The assignment of different tasks to different people or groups.

specialization

A process in which different individuals and units perform different tasks.

EXHIBIT 8.1
A Conventional
Organization Chart

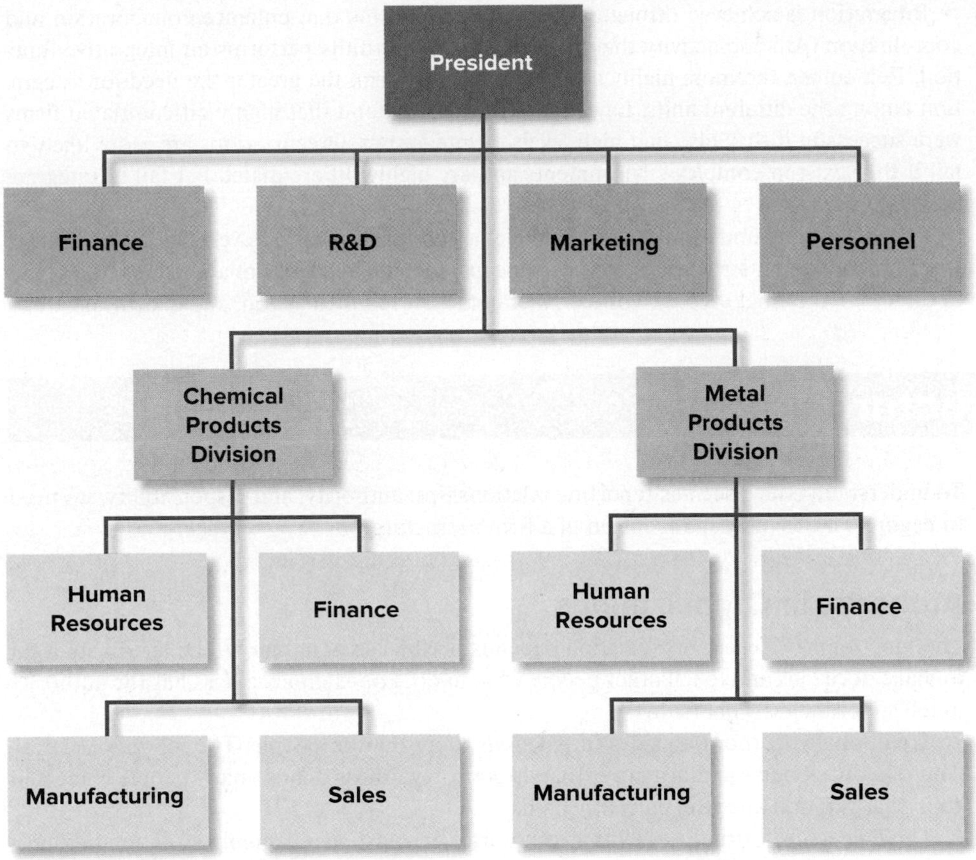

environments (container companies) had low levels of differentiation. Companies in intermediate environments (food companies) showed intermediate differentiation.[4]

As organizations differentiate their structures, managers must simultaneously consider issues of integration.

Integration

As organizations differentiate their structures, managers must consider how best to integrate their different activities. The different units are part of the same organization, and at least some degree of communication and cooperation must occur among them. Integration and its related concept, **coordination**, refer to the procedures that link the parts of the organization to achieve the organization's overall mission.

coordination

The procedures that link the various parts of an organization for the purpose of achieving the organization's overall mission.

FIGURE 8.2
Examples of
Differentiation

Automotive Firms	Fast Food Companies	Cement Companies
• Operate in complex and dynamic environments. • Require high degree of differentiation.	• Operate in intermediate environments. • Require intermediate levels of differentiation.	• Operate in simple, stable environments. • Require low levels of differentiation.

SOURCE: Adapted from Lawrence, P. and Lorsch, J., *Organization and Environment.* Homewood, IL: Richard D. Irwin, 1969.

Integration is achieved through structural mechanisms that enhance collaboration and coordination. Any job activity that links different work units performs an integrative function. Remember, the more highly differentiated your firm, the greater the need for integration among the different units. Lawrence and Lorsch found that highly differentiated firms were successful if they also had high levels of integration. Organizations are more likely to fail if they exist in complex environments and are highly differentiated but fail to integrate adequately.[5]

These concepts underpin the rest of the chapter. First we discuss vertical differentiation within organization structure. Relevant concepts include authority relationships, the board of directors, the chief executive officer, hierarchical levels, delegation, and decentralization.

The Vertical Structure

To understand issues such as reporting relationships, authority, and responsibility, we need to begin with the vertical dimension of a firm's structure.

Authority in Organizations

The functioning of every organization depends on the use of **authority**, the legitimate right to make decisions and to tell other people what to do. For example, a boss has the authority to tell subordinates what to do.

Traditionally, authority resides in positions more than in people. The job of vice president of a division has authority over that division, regardless of how many people come and go in that position and who currently holds it.

The owners of a firm have ultimate authority. In most small, simply structured companies, the owner also acts as manager. Sometimes the owner hires another person to manage the business and its employees. The owner gives this manager some authority to oversee the operations, but the manager is accountable to—that is, reports and defers to—the owner.

Formal position authority is generally the primary means of running an organization. An order that a boss gives to a lower-level employee is usually carried out. As this occurs throughout the organization day after day, the organization can move forward and achieve its goals.[6]

However, power in an organization is not always position-dependent. People with particular expertise, experience, or personal qualities may have considerable *informal* authority—for example, when people carry themselves with confidence, can provide valuable information, or work closely with those who have high positions.[7] We will say more about informal sources of power in the next chapter and Chapter 12. For now, we discuss the formal authority structure of the organization from the top down, beginning with the board of directors.

Board of Directors   In corporations, the owners are the stockholders. But because there are many stockholders, most of whom are busy doing other things and lacking timely information, few are directly involved in managing the company. Instead, stockholders elect a board of directors to oversee the organization.

The board, led by the chair, makes major decisions affecting the organization, subject to corporate charter and bylaw provisions. Boards perform at least three major sets of duties: (1) selecting, assessing, rewarding, and perhaps replacing the CEO; (2) determining the firm's strategic direction and reviewing financial performance; and (3) ensuring ethical, socially responsible, and legal conduct.[8]

The board's membership usually includes some of the company's top executives—called *inside directors*. Outside members of the board tend to be executives at other companies. The trend in recent years has been toward reducing the number of insiders and increasing the number of outsiders. Today, most boards have more outside than inside directors. Boards

authority

The legitimate right to make decisions and to tell other people what to do.

made up of strong, independent outsiders are more likely to provide different information and perspectives and to prevent big mistakes.

The best boards tend to be those who are active, critical participants in determining company strategies. Even so, in the wake of scandals and lawsuits, many boards have shifted their focus to compliance issues, such as audits, financial reporting, and laws against discrimination. These issues are critically important, but a board staffed mainly with legal and regulatory experts cannot always give management the necessary direction on strategy.[9]

The owner and managers of a small business may need the expertise of a board of directors as much as or more than a large company does. Some owners set up a board of advisers, such as owners of noncompeting companies, retired executives, and perhaps their banker or accountant. Others join organizations that facilitate regular meetings of business owners with different areas of expertise.

The job of CEO typically consists of leading the board of directors, motivating employees, and promoting positive change while being accountable for the overall success of the company.
©Tom Merton/AGE Fotostock RF

Members of peer advisory groups, like The Alternative Board, can share problems and exchange solutions with fellow members in a confidential setting.[10] During the last recession, privately owned companies were more profitable if they had a board of directors that included people from outside the company. One important reason was their ability to be more objective about what the company could do during difficult times.[11]

Chief Executive Officer   The authority officially vested in the board of directors is assigned to a chief executive officer (CEO), who occupies the top of the organizational pyramid. The CEO is personally accountable to the board and to the owners for the organization's performance.

In some corporations, one person holds all three positions of CEO, chair of the board of directors, and president.[12] More commonly, however, one person holds two of those positions, with the CEO serving also as either the chair of the board or the president of the organization. When the CEO is president, the chair may be honorary and may do little more than conduct meetings. In other cases, the chair may be the CEO, and the president is second in command.

In recent years, the trend has been to separate the position of CEO and chair of the board. Sometimes this change is related to improved corporate governance; board oversight is easier when the CEO is not so dominant. In other cases, the board acts to reduce an unpopular CEO's power or to help prepare for a successor to the CEO.

Top Management Team   Increasingly, CEOs share their authority with other key members of the top management team or C-suite (the "C" stands for Chief). Top management teams typically are composed of the CEO, president, chief operating officer, chief financial officer, chief information officer, chief human resources officer, and other key executives. Rather than make critical decisions on their own, CEOs at companies such as Shake Shack, Microsoft, and Sanofi regularly meet with their top management teams to make decisions as a unit.[13]

Hierarchical Levels

In Chapter 1, we introduced the organizational pyramid, comprised of multiple levels and commonly called the **hierarchy**. The authority structure is the glue that holds vertical levels together.

hierarchy

The authority levels of the organizational pyramid.

corporate governance

The role of a corporation's executive staff and board of directors in ensuring that the firm's activities meet the goals of the firm's stakeholders.

Bottom Line

A "flat" structure with fewer horizontal layers saves time and money.

Why not eliminate all middle layers to save the most time and money?

subunits

Subdivisions of an organization.

span of control

The number of subordinates who report directly to an executive or supervisor.

The key responsibilities at the top management level include **corporate governance**—a term describing the oversight of the firm by its executive staff and board of directors. The Sarbanes-Oxley Act (Chapter 5). along with requirements of the Securities and Exchange Commission, imposed new, tighter corporate governance rules. For example, company CEOs and CFOs (chief financial officers) now have to personally certify the accuracy of their firm's financial statements.

A powerful trend for U.S. businesses over the past few decades has been to reduce the number of hierarchical levels. General Electric used to have 29 levels; today it has only a handful of levels, and its hierarchical structure is relatively flat. Most executives today believe that fewer layers create a more efficient, fast-acting, and cost-effective organization. This also holds true for the **subunits** of major corporations. A study in a financial services company found that branches with fewer levels tended to have higher operating efficiency than did branches with more.[14]

This trend and research might seem to suggest that hierarchy is a bad thing, but it offers benefits as well. A hierarchy provides management career paths that help organizations retain and develop ambitious, talented people, giving them gradually more challenging experiences as they prepare for executive positions. Where there is little hierarchy, employees who see little chance of promotion may leave to find better opportunities elsewhere. A well-designed hierarchy also can ensure that managers have a reasonable number of people to monitor, as described next.[15]

Span of Control

The number of subordinates who report directly to an executive or supervisor is called the **span of control**. The implications of span of control for the shape of an organization are straightforward. Holding size constant, narrow spans build a tall organization that has many reporting levels. Wide spans create a flat organization with fewer reporting levels.

A span of control can be too narrow or too wide. The optimal span of control maximizes effectiveness because it is (1) narrow enough to permit managers to maintain control over direct reports, but (2) not so narrow that it leads to overcontrol and an excessive number of managers who oversee a small number of people.

What is the optimal number of direct reports? Five, according to Napoleon Bonaparte.[16] Some managers today still consider five a good number. At one Japanese bank, in contrast, several hundred branch managers report to the same boss. In a study by the Corporate Executive Board, the average span of control at large companies increased from 7 direct reports to 12 between 2008 and 2012.

The optimal span of control depends on a number of factors, as shown in Exhibit 8.3.

EXHIBIT 8.3

When Is a Wide Span of Control Better?

Factors	Use a Wide Span of Control When . . .
The nature of the work	Work is clearly defined and unambiguous.
Subordinates' preparation	Subordinates are highly trained and have access to information.
Managers' capabilities	Managers are capable and supportive of subordinates.
Comparability of subordinates' jobs	Subordinates have similar jobs and are rated on comparable performance measures.
Subordinates' supervisory preferences	Subordinates prefer autonomy and independence.
Organizational size	The organization is small.

Note: If the opposite conditions exist, a narrow span of control may be more appropriate.
SOURCES: Adapted from "Span of Control: What Factors Should Determine How Many Direct Reports a Manager Has?" *Society for Human Resource Management,* April 25, 2013, http://www.shrm.org; Jehiel, P., "Information Aggregation and Communication in Organizations," *Management Science* 45, no. 5, May 1999, 659–69; and Altaffer, A., "First-Line Managers: Measuring Their Span of Control," *Nursing Management* 29, no. 7, July 1998, 36–40.

Delegation

As work is spread out over various levels and spans of control, delegating work becomes paramount. A manager **delegates** when she assigns a task to someone at a lower level. It often requires the subordinate to report back to his or her boss about how effectively the assignment was carried out.

Delegation is perhaps the most fundamental process of management because it entails getting work done through others. It is important at all hierarchical levels. The process can occur between any two individuals in any type of structure with regard to any task.

Some managers are comfortable fully delegating an assignment to subordinates; others are not. Consider how the two office managers in the following example gave out the same assignment. Are both of these statements examples of delegation? How are they similar, and how different?

Manager A: "Call Mike Johnson at WorkRite Computer. Ask him to give you the price list on an upgrade for our desktop computers. I want to move up to a 10-core processor with 64 gigs of memory and at least a 2-terabyte hard drive. Ask them to give you a demonstration of the Windows 10 operating system and Microsoft Office 365. I want to be able to establish collaboration capability for the entire group. Invite Cochran and Rodriguez to the demonstration and let them try it out. Have them write up a summary of their needs and the potential applications they see for the new systems. Then prepare me a report with the costs and specifications of the upgrade for the entire department. Oh, yes, be sure to ask for information on service costs."

Manager B: "I'd like to do something about our desktop computers. I've been getting some complaints that the current computers are too slow, can't run the most recent software, and freeze periodically. Could you evaluate our options and give me a recommendation on what we should do? Our budget is around $2,000 per person, but I'd like to stay under that if we can. Feel free to talk to some of the managers to get their input, but we need to have this done as soon as possible."

Responsibility, Authority, and Accountability   When delegating work, it helps to keep in mind the important distinctions among authority, responsibility, and accountability. **Responsibility** means that a person is supposed to carry out an assigned task. When delegating work responsibilities, the manager also can delegate to the subordinate enough authority to get the job done. Authority, recall, means that the person has the power and the right to make decisions, give orders, draw on resources, and do whatever else is necessary to fulfill the responsibility.

Ironically, it is quite common for people to have more responsibility than authority; they must perform as well as they can through informal influence tactics instead of relying purely on authority. More about informal power and how to use it appears in Chapter 12.

As the manager delegates responsibilities, subordinates are accountable for achieving results. **Accountability** means that the subordinate's manager has the right to expect the subordinate to perform the job and the right to take corrective action if the subordinate fails to do so. The subordinate must report upward on the status and quality of his or her task performance.

However, the ultimate responsibility—accountability to higher-ups—lies with the manager doing the delegating. Managers remain responsible and accountable not only for their own actions but also for the actions of their subordinates. Managers should not resort to delegation to others as a means of escaping their own responsibilities.

Advantages of Delegation   Delegating work offers important advantages when done right. Not delegating, or delegating ineffectively, sharply reduces what a manager can achieve, and hurts morale.

Effective delegation leverages the manager's energy and talent and those of his or her subordinates. It allows you to accomplish much more than you would be able to do on your

---

delegation

The assignment of new or additional responsibilities to a subordinate.

responsibility

The assignment of a task that an employee is supposed to carry out.

accountability

The expectation that employees will perform a job, take corrective action when necessary, and report upward on the status and quality of their performance.

 LO 5

own. You also save one of your most valuable assets—time—by giving some of your responsibilities to other people. You then are free to devote energy to important, higher-level activities such as planning, setting objectives, and monitoring performance.

A big advantage of delegation is that it helps managers develop effective subordinates. Delegation essentially gives the subordinate a more important job. The subordinate now has an opportunity to develop new skills and to demonstrate potential for additional responsibilities and perhaps promotion. The subordinate receives a vital form of on-the-job training that could pay off in the future. In addition, for at least some employees, delegation promotes a sense of being an important, contributing member of the organization, so these employees tend to feel a stronger commitment, perform their tasks better, and engage in more innovation.[17]

Bottom Line

Effective delegation raises the quality of subordinates and the service they provide to customers or co-workers. *How might an effort at delegation backfire?*

Look again at the different ways the two office managers gave out the same assignment. The approach that is more likely to empower subordinates and help them develop will be obvious to you. (You might also quickly conclude which of the two managers you would prefer to work for.)

Delegation done well benefits the organization as well as the people. Allowing managers to devote more time to important managerial functions while lower-level employees carry out assignments means that jobs are done more efficiently and cost-effectively. As subordinates develop and grow in their own jobs, their contributions to the organization grow as well.

It is worth noting that not all managers like to delegate. For example, Steve Jobs preferred to micromanage and get involved deeply with each product Apple designed.[18] This approach worked for a guru like Jobs, but many organizations can and do rely heavily on effective delegation.

How Should Managers Delegate?

To reach its potential, delegation must be done properly. As Exhibit 8.4 shows, effective delegation proceeds through several steps.[19]

The first step in the delegation process, defining the goal, requires the manager to have a clear understanding of the outcome he or she wants. Then the manager should select a person who is capable of performing the task. Delegation is especially useful when an employee can benefit from developing new skills through the experience.

The person who gets the assignment should be given authority, time, and resources to carry out the task successfully. Required resources often include people, money, and equipment, plus important information that puts the assignment in context. The manager and the subordinate should work together and communicate periodically about the assignment: progress, problems, and ideas. While the subordinate performs the assignment, the manager is available and stays aware of its current status. These checkups also provide an important opportunity to offer encouragement and praise.

Some tasks, such as disciplining subordinates and conducting performance reviews, should not be delegated. But when managers err, it usually is because they delegated too little rather than too much. The manager who wants to learn how to delegate more effectively should remember this distinction: If you are not delegating, you are merely doing things; but the more you delegate, the more you are truly managing and building an organization.[20]

centralized organization

An organization in which high-level executives make most decisions and pass them down to lower levels for implementation.

decentralized organization

An organization in which lower-level managers make important decisions.

Decentralization

Delegating responsibility and authority *decentralizes* decision making. In a **centralized organization**, important decisions usually are made at the top. In **decentralized organizations**, more decisions are made at lower levels. Ideally, decision making occurs at the level of the people who are most directly affected and have the most relevant knowledge about the work. This is particularly important when the business environment is fast-changing and decisions must be made quickly and well.

The delegation of responsibility and authority decentralizes *decision making. Generally speaking, flat organizations are more decentralized.*

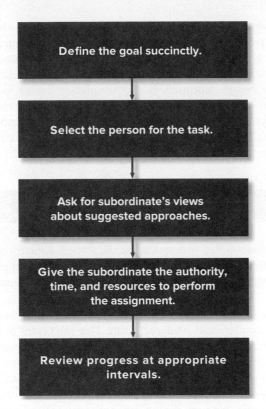

EXHIBIT 8.4
The Steps in Effective
Delegation

Sometimes organizations change their degree of centralization, depending on the particular challenges they face. Tougher times often cause senior management to take charge of decisions, whereas in times of rapid growth, decisions are pushed further down the chain of command.

Time Warner Cable (TWC) tried to decentralize marketing as a way to let regional teams move quickly in response to opportunities in local markets. However, competition for online entertainment and from satellite companies put cable companies such as TWC in a tight spot. In that environment, TWC reversed its decision and returned to a centralized marketing structure.[21] Unfortunately for TWC, decentralizing tends to go more smoothly than trying to centralize.[22]

At times, decentralizing decision making—allowing decisions to be made by middle- and lower-level managers—can be an advantage. These are the managers who deal directly with the problem and are most likely to know the best solutions.

©Cathy Yeulet/123RF RF

Bottom Line
Decentralization often speeds decision making. *What makes centralized decision making slower?*

Most American executives today understand the advantages of pushing decision-making authority down to the point of the action. The level that deals directly with problems and opportunities has the most relevant information and can best foresee the consequences of decisions. Executives also know that the decentralized approach allows people to take faster action.[23]

Global food giant Nestlé decentralizes decision-making power to employees in over 100 countries so they can be responsive to local consumers. The company believes that allowing local employees to make decisions is key to growing the company's global market share. The role of the company's headquarters in Switzerland is to do strategic planning and distribute information."[24]

The Horizontal Structure

Up to this point, we've described structure along the vertical dimension, giving perspective on how managers and employees at different levels relate to one another. But structures are differentiated horizontally as well, and the two structural elements relate to one another in important ways.

As the work of organizations becomes ever more complex, tasks must subdivide—that is, *departmentalize*—into smaller units or departments. One important distinction is between line and staff departments. **Line departments** are those that have responsibility for the principal activities of the firm. Line units deal directly with the organization's primary goods or services; they make things, sell things, or provide customer service. At General Motors, line departments include product design, fabrication, assembly, distribution, and the like.

Line managers typically have much authority and power in the organization. They are responsible for making major operating decisions. They are accountable for the bottom-line results of their units.

Staff departments are those that provide specialized or professional expertise that supports line departments. They include research, legal, accounting, public relations, and human resources departments. Usually, each of these specialized units often has its own vice president. Some are vested with a great deal of authority, as when accounting or finance groups approve and monitor budgetary activities.

In traditionally structured organizations, conflicts often arise between line and staff departments. Career paths and success in many staff functions depend on having a particular functional expertise, whereas success in line functions is based more on knowing the organization's industry. Thus, although line managers might be eager to pursue new products and customers, staff managers might seem to constrain these efforts with a focus on functional requirements and procedures. Line managers might be more willing to take risks for the sake of growth, whereas staff managers might focus more on protecting the company from risks.

But in today's organizations, staff units tend to be focused less on monitoring and controlling performance and more on moving toward new roles providing strategic support and expert advice.[25] For example, managers in human resources—considered back in the day to be a not-very-powerful staff function—have expanded from merely creating procedures that meet legal requirements to helping organizations plan for, recruit, develop, and keep the kinds of employee talent who will provide long-term competitive advantage.[26] Such strategic thinking not only makes staff managers more valuable to their organizations, but also can reduce conflict between line and staff.

As organizations divide work into different units, some common patterns develop in the way departments become clustered and arranged. The three basic approaches to **departmentalization** are functional, divisional, and matrix. We will talk about each and point out some similarities and differences.

The Functional Organization

In a **functional organization**, jobs (and departments) are specialized and grouped according to business functions and the skills they require: production, marketing, human resources,

line departments
Units that deal directly with the organization's primary goods and services.

staff departments
Units that support line departments.

departmentalization
Subdividing an organization into smaller subunits.

functional organization
Departmentalization around specialized activities such as production, marketing, and human resources.

EXHIBIT 8.5 The Functional Organization

research and development, finance, accounting, and so forth. Exhibit 8.5 illustrates a basic functional organization chart.

Functional departmentalization is common in both large and small organizations. Large companies may organize along several functional units, including groupings unique to their businesses. For example, Carmike Cinemas, which operates nearly 3,000 screens in 276 theaters in 41 states, has vice presidents of finance, concessions, film, and digital cinema as well as a general manager of theater operations. Kiva, a nonprofit organization, also uses a functional grouping (see the nearby "Social Enterprise" box).

As shown in Exhibit 8.6, the traditional functional approach to departmentalization has a number of potential advantages.

The functional form does have disadvantages. People may care more about their own function than about the company as a whole, and their attention to functional tasks may make them lose focus on overall product quality and customer satisfaction. Managers develop functional expertise but do not acquire knowledge of the other areas of the business; they become specialists but not generalists. Between functions, conflicts arise, and communication and coordination fall off. In short, although functional differentiation might exist, functional integration might not.

For these reasons, the functional structure is most appropriate in simple, stable environments. If the organization becomes fragmented (or *dis*integrated), it will have difficulty developing and bringing new products to market and responding quickly to customer demands. Particularly when companies are growing and facing changing environments, they need to integrate more effectively. Other forms of departmentalization are more flexible and responsive than the functional structure.

Companies like Southwest Airlines, MasterCard, SAP, and Target are taking steps to integrate their marketing and communications functions.[27] Both functions have experience in capturing, analyzing, and making decisions based on data from interacting with

Bottom Line

When like functions are grouped, savings often result.
Why might a company centralize its information technology (IT) department?

Economies of scale can be realized. When people with similar skills are grouped, the unit can purchase more efficient equipment and make larger, discounted purchases.
People have greater opportunity for specialized training and in-depth skill development.
Performance standards are better maintained. People with similar training and interests may develop a shared concern for high performance.
Technical specialists are relatively free of administrative work.
Environmental monitoring is more effective. Each functional group is more closely attuned to developments in its own field and therefore can adapt more readily.
Decision making and lines of communication are simple and clearly understood.

EXHIBIT 8.6

Advantages of Functional Departmentalization

SOURCES: Adapted from Cross R. and Baird, L., "Technology Is Not Enough: Improving Performance by Building Organizational Memory," *Sloan Management Review* 41, no. 3, Spring 2000, 69–78; and Duncan, R., "What Is the Right Organizational Structure?" *Organizational Dynamics* 7, Winter 1979, 59–80.

Social Enterprise

Kiva Organizes by Function

Imagine having an idea to start a food stand or car cleaning business. Also imagine that you and your family live in poverty and don't have an extra $50 to buy initial supplies to launch the business. Where can you turn? To the local bank? It is unlikely a bank will provide a small, unsecured loan to you.

Kiva, a nonprofit organization, is trying to meet this need. Kiva connects via the Internet a global network of lenders with entrepreneurs in impoverished communities. Individuals can lend as little as $25 to help empower a budding entrepreneur to start a business to feed his or her family. In just 12 years, 1.6 million lenders have made it possible for Kiva to make nearly $694 million in loans to individuals in 82 different countries. With an average repayment rate of just over 97 percent, this social enterprise is making an impact on the lives of countless individuals, their families, and their communities.

While some nonprofits may choose to organize around the clients they serve or the regions they operate in, Kiva takes a different approach. Kiva's organizational structure is unique in how it contributes to the enterprise's efficiency and effectiveness.

Given the global complexity of Kiva's operations, the organization hopes to achieve economies of scale by grouping employees and volunteers with similar training and skills into eight functional areas.[28] Other benefits of functional departmentalization are listed in Exhibit 8.6.

Questions

- Why do you think Kiva is using a functional approach to structuring its organization?
- Referring to the eight areas illustrated, which are considered line activities? Staff activities?

customers on social media. The goal of combining the two functions is to become more customer-centric and efficient. Leaders of these companies want a "data-driven approach to business strategy."[29]

Managers facing tough demands for total quality, customer service, innovation, and speed have learned the shortcomings of the functional form: it is highly differentiated and creates barriers to coordination across functions. Cross-functional coordination is essential for delivering every performance dimension. The functional organization will not disappear, in part because functional specialists will always be needed, but functional managers will make fewer decisions. The more important units will be cross-functional teams that have integrative responsibilities for products, processes, or customers.[30]

The Divisional Organization

divisional organization

Departmentalization that groups units around products, customers, or geographic regions.

The functional structure's weaknesses bring us to an alternative form, the **divisional organization**. As organizations grow and functional departments struggle managing diverse arrays of products, customers, and geographic regions, they can restructure such that *every* division houses *all* functions. Division A in Exhibit 8.7 has its own operations, marketing, and finance departments, Division B also has its own operations, marketing, and finance departments, and so on.

In this structure, separate divisions act almost as separate businesses or profit centers, working autonomously to accomplish the goals of the entire enterprise. Exhibit 8.8 presents examples of how the same work would be organized under functional and divisional structures.

EXHIBIT 8.7   The Divisional Organization

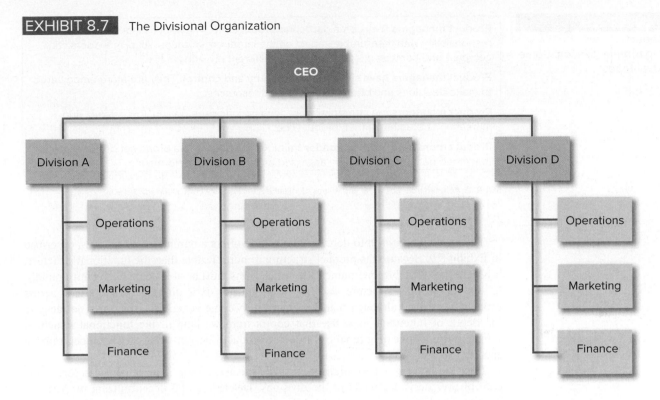

Organizations can create divisions around products, customers, or geographic regions, as described in the following sections.

Product Divisions   In the product organization, all functions that contribute to a product are organized under one product manager. Johnson & Johnson uses this form, organizing into three broad product categories: consumer health care, medical devices, and pharmaceuticals. Within these categories are 250 independent company divisions in 60 countries, many of which are responsible for particular product lines. Ethicon develops and sells surgical equipment, whereas Consumer Products includes Johnson's baby shampoo and Aveeno hair and skin products.[31]

Functional Organization	Divisional Organization
Chain of pharmacies with departments for cosmetics, photos, greetings cards, human resources, operations, and finance, responsible for all store locations.	Chain of pharmacies with one division for each region (e.g., Northeast, Midwest, and Southeast) of the country managing all functions in that region.
Automotive manufacturer with departments for research and development, engineering, purchasing, production, and sales, managing all automotive products.	Automotive manufacturer with product groups (e.g., SUV or truck), each staffed with employees to manage that automobile's development, engineering, purchasing, production, and sales.
One marketing department serving the needs of all the domestic and international subsidiaries of a multinational company, reporting to corporate leadership.	A marketing department at the offices of each subsidiary in which the multinational firm operates, reporting to the leadership in charge of that subsidiary's operations.

EXHIBIT 8.8

Examples of Functional and Divisional Organization

SOURCE: Adapted from Strauss, George and Sayles, Leonard R., *Behavioral Strategies for Managers,* Upper Saddle River, NJ: Prentice Hall, 1980, p.221.

EXHIBIT 8.9
Product
Departmentalization: Some
Advantages

Product managers focus on a particular product line. They have clear bottom-line responsibility with measurable impact on the larger organization. Also, managers can compare and contrast the performance of different divisions.
Product managers have significant autonomy and control. They are more empowered to make decisions and often control needed resources.
Product managers are strategic. They develop long-term design, forecasting, and marketing strategies for their product line.
Product managers receive broader training. They develop a broad set of skills, which they need because they will be assessed on bottom-line performance.

SOURCE: Adapted from Boehm, R. and Phipps, C., "Flatness Forays," *McKinsey Quarterly* 3, 1996,128–43.

The product approach to departmentalization offers a number of advantages, described in Exhibit 8.9. Because the product structure is more flexible than the functional structure, it is better for unstable environments in which firms must be able adapt and change rapidly.

But the product structure also has disadvantages. It is difficult to coordinate across product lines. And although managers learn to become generalists, they may not acquire the depth of functional expertise that comes from working in the functional structure. Furthermore, duplicating functions in every product division, compared with centralizing each function at headquarters, is expensive.

Decision making is decentralized in this structure, so top management can lose some control over decisions made in the divisions. Delegating and decentralizing properly, as discussed earlier, are essential.[32]

Customer and Geographic Divisions

Some companies build divisions around groups of customers or around different geographic areas. A hospital can organize its services around child, adult, intensive, psychiatric, and emergency cases. Banks have different units handling customers with banking (checking and savings) and mortgage needs. The Internal Revenue Service is organized around customer groups such as large business and international, small business and self-employed, and tax-exempt and government agencies.[33]

Divisions also can be structured around geographic regions. Geographic distinctions include district, territory, region, and country. Macy's Group has geographic divisions for its operations including Macy's Northwest, North Central, Northeast, Mid-Atlantic, Southeast, South Central, and Southwest as well as Macys.com for online shoppers.

The primary advantage of both the product and customer/regional approaches to departmentalization is the ability to focus on customer needs and provide faster, better service. But again, duplication of activities across many customer groups and geographic areas is expensive. As you read "Management in Action: Progress Report," consider how well the advantages and drawbacks of these divisional structures might apply to General Motors.

The Matrix Organization

Many structures are more complex than the basic forms that you just read about; often they are hybrids of multiple forms.[34] A **matrix organization** is a hybrid form of organization in which functional and divisional forms overlap. Managers and staff personnel report to two bosses—a functional manager and a divisional manager. Thus matrix organizations have a dual rather than a single line of command.

A large majority of U.S. employees spend at least some of their work time operating in a matrix.[35] In Exhibit 8.10, each project manager draws employees from each functional area to form a group for the project. The employees working on those projects report to the individual project manager as well as to the manager of their functional area.

A good example of the matrix structure can be found at Time Inc., the top magazine publisher in the United States and United Kingdom. At Time Inc. titles such as *Time, Sports Illustrated, Fortune, Travel+Leisure,* and *People,* production managers responsible for

Bottom Line

Customer and geographic divisions often serve customers faster.
Suppose your international company sells scientific equipment to high schools, universities, and businesses. Would you set up customer divisions or geographic divisions? Why?

matrix organization

An organization composed of dual reporting relationships in which some employees report to two superiors—a functional manager and a divisional manager.

Management in Action

GENERAL MOTORS EXPERIENCES A CRISIS AND LEADERSHIP CHANGE

Through 2013, ex-CEO Daniel Akerson's plans to make General Motors more nimble included a corporate reorganization to create more of a functional structure. Over the previous few decades, GM had moved from a structure based on product lines (Chevrolet, Buick, Cadillac, and so on) toward one based on regions (North America, South America, Europe, and International Operations). But the main result was that the company moved from one set of independently operating groups (the brand groups) to another (the geographic groups), and the company still was not operating as a unified whole with a common mission. Efforts to save money by globally applying product designs broke down as regional executives insisted on making their own decisions for their regions.

A functional structure placed more authority in the hands of the functional executives, who could set up companywide systems and identify designs to use for models created to sell in several or all geographic markets.

The effectiveness of Akerson's corporate restructuring at GM was eclipsed by two major events in 2014. In January, Akerson retired earlier than expected for family reasons. Mary Barra, with 33 years of experience at GM, took over as CEO. Barra is known for her candid style and ability to improve efficiencies.

Later in 2014, GM had to recall over 30 million cars and trucks at a cost of $5.9 billion. Nearly 3 million of the recalls were attributed to a faulty ignition switch that has been linked to 124 deaths as of this writing. Evidence suggests that GM managers knew about this problem for over 10 years, but waited until 2014 to address it.[36]

- Review the advantages and drawbacks of functional organizations and geographic divisions. Which ones may have contributed to the decisions to ignore and later to finally address the faulty ignition switch issue?
- What do you think will be the impact of GM's effort to create a more centralized structure based on functional groups?

EXHIBIT 8.10 Matrix Organizational Structure

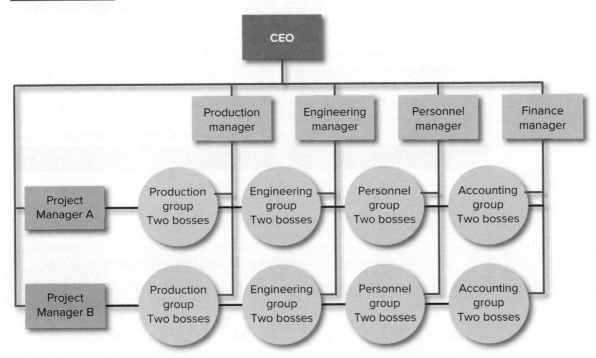

printing the magazines report to the individual publishers and editors of each title *and* to a senior corporate executive in charge of production.

At the corporate level, Time Inc. achieves enormous economies of scale by buying paper and printing in bulk and coordinating production activities across the company. At the same time, each production manager at each title make sure their own magazine's needs and schedules are met. Similar matrix arrangements are in place for other key managers such as circulation and finance. In this way, the company attempts to gain the benefits of both divisional and functional organization structures.

The matrix form originated in the aerospace industry, first with TRW in 1959 and then with NASA. Applications now occur in hospitals and health care agencies, entrepreneurial organizations, government laboratories, financial institutions, and multinational corporations.[37] Other companies that have used or currently use the matrix form include IBM, Boeing, Procter & Gamble, Fujitsu, Cisco, Bechtel, and Dow Corning.

Pros and Cons of the Matrix Form   Like other structures, the matrix has both strengths and weaknesses. Exhibit 8.11 summarizes the advantages and disadvantages of the matrix. Its major potential advantage is a higher degree of flexibility and adaptability.

The same exhibit summarizes the potential shortcomings of the matrix form. Many of the disadvantages stem from the matrix's inherent violation of the **unity-of-command principle**, which states that a person should have only one boss. Reporting to two superiors can create confusion and a difficult interpersonal situation unless steps are taken to prevent these problems.

Matrix Survival Skills   The need to collaborate effectively is particularly high in the matrix, and this can be difficult because people often rotate teams, teammates, and bosses. To a large degree, problems can be avoided if the key managers in the matrix learn the behavioral skills needed in this structure.[38] These skills vary depending on the job in the four-person diamond structure shown in Exhibit 8.12.

The top executive, who heads the matrix, must learn to balance power and emphasis between the product and functional requirements. Product or division managers and

unity-of-command principle

A structure in which each worker reports to one boss, who in turn reports to one boss.

EXHIBIT 8.11
Strengths and Weaknesses of the Matrix Design

Advantages
• Linkage of employees at all levels and in all functions to the company's goals and strategy. • More information shared across functions. • Communication fostered—especially valuable for complex assignments where different groups depend on each other. • Greater responsiveness to customers from bringing together information about customer needs and organizational capabilities. • Creative ideas from cross-functional work. • Loyalty to the organization as a whole rather than to a function or division.

Disadvantages
• Unclear responsibilities and competing priorities. • Violation of the unity-of-command principle. • Accountability difficult to define. • Lower employee engagement. • Possible conflict and stress for employees who must manage a dual reporting role. • Additional time required for meetings and other communications to coordinate work. • Extensive collaboration needed but not always easy to reward.

SOURCES: Based on Bazigos, M. and Harter, J., "Revisting the Matrix Organization," *McKinsey Quarterly,* January 2016, www.mckinsey.com; Krell, E., "Managing the Matrix," *HR Magazine,* April 2011, 69–71; Lash, R., "Cracking the Matrix Code," *Canadian HR Reporter,* March 28, 2011, 16–18.

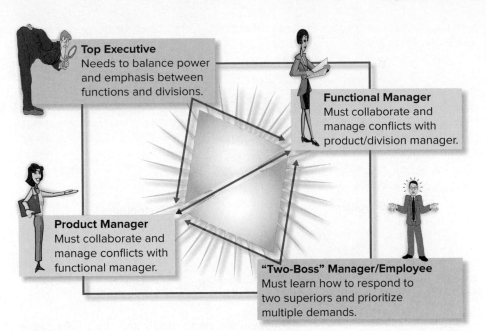

EXHIBIT 8.12
The Matrix Diamond

Top Executive
Needs to balance power and emphasis between functions and divisions.

Functional Manager
Must collaborate and manage conflicts with product/division manager.

Product Manager
Must collaborate and manage conflicts with functional manager.

"Two-Boss" Manager/Employee
Must learn how to respond to two superiors and prioritize multiple demands.

functional managers must learn to collaborate and manage their conflicts constructively. Finally, the two-boss managers or employees at the bottom of the diamond must learn how to be responsible to two superiors. This means prioritizing multiple demands and sometimes even reconciling conflicting orders.

Some people function poorly under these ambiguous, conflictual circumstances; sometimes this signals the end of their careers with the company. Ideally people in the matrix learn to communicate effectively with one another, rise above the difficulties, and manage these work relationships constructively.

> The key to managing in the matrix is to realize that the matrix is a process.

The Matrix Form Today   The popularity of the matrix form waned during the late 1980s, when many companies had difficulty implementing it. But recently it has come back strong. Reasons for this resurgence include pressures to consolidate costs and be faster to market, creating needs for better coordination across functions or across countries for firms with global business strategies. Many of the challenges created by the matrix are particularly acute in an international context, mainly because of the distances involved and the differences in local markets.[39]

The key to managing today's matrix is to realize that the matrix is a process. Managers who have appropriately adopted the matrix structure because of the complexity of the challenges they confront, but have trouble implementing it, often haven't strengthened the interpersonal relationships in ways that make the matrix effective.

It is not enough to create a flexible organization merely by changing its structure. Managers must also attend to the norms, values, and attitudes that shape how people within their organizations behave.[40] We will address these issues in the next chapter and in Part 4 of the book, which focuses on how to lead and manage people.

The Network Organization

Functional, divisional, and matrix structures are variations of the traditional hierarchical organization. In contrast, the **network organization** is a collection of independent, mostly single-function firms that collaborate to produce a good or service. As depicted in Exhibit 8.13, the network organization describes not one organization but the web of relationships among many firms. Network organizations are flexible arrangements among designers, suppliers, producers, distributors, and customers where each firm is able to pursue its own distinctive competence plus work effectively with other members of the network.

Bottom Line
The matrix structure can speed decisions and cut costs.
How might a matrix structure increase speed?

network organization

A collection of independent, mostly single-function firms that collaborate on a good or service.

EXHIBIT 8.13
A Network Organization

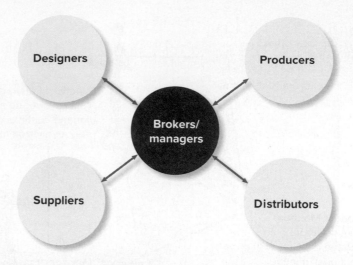

SOURCE: Miles, Raymond E. and Snow, Charles C., "Organizations: New Concepts for New Forms," *California Management Review* 28, no. 3, Spring 1986, 62–73.

dynamic network

Temporary arrangements among partners that can be assembled and reassembled to adapt to the environment.

Bottom Line

Networks can improve cost, quality, service, speed, sustainability, and innovation. *Which functions would you include in a network to improve sustainability?*

Often, members of the network communicate electronically and share information to be able to respond quickly to customer demands. In effect, the normal boundary of a firm becomes blurred or porous as managers within it interact closely with network members outside it. The network as a whole, then, can display the technical specialization of the functional structure, the market responsiveness of the product structure, and the balance and flexibility of the matrix.[41]

A very flexible version of the network organization is the **dynamic network**—also called the *modular* or *virtual* corporation. It is composed of temporary arrangements that can be assembled and reassembled to meet a changing competitive environment. The members of the network are held together by contracts that stipulate results expected—market mechanisms—rather than by hierarchy and authority. Poorly performing firms can be removed and replaced. Such arrangements are common in the electronics, toy, and apparel industries, each of which creates and sells trendy products at a fast pace.

Dynamic networks are suitable when much of the work can be done independently by experts. For example, virtual company SendLove commercialized a software product of the same name: an online communication system that allows co-workers to recognize each other with brief positive messages. Everyone in the company sees a message of appreciation, with the intent that public acknowledgment builds morale.

To create the product, founder Philip Rosedale and his partners launched an online bulletin board where they posted a list of all the tasks they needed done. Freelancers bid on a job by describing how they would carry out the task and what they would charge. To collaborate, the freelancers communicated online at the company's chat room or via e-mail and Skype. Rosedale started this virtual arrangement for programming tasks, and it was so successful in delivering great prices and fast turnaround that the company expanded to support tasks such as recruiting contracts and processing payments.[42]

Networks are flexible, innovative, and quick to respond to threats and opportunities. They reduce costs and risk. But for these arrangements to be successful, several things must happen:

The firm must choose the right specialty. It must be something (good or service) that the market needs and that the firm is better at providing than other firms.

The firm must choose collaborators who are excellent at what they do and that provide complementary strengths.

The firm must make certain that all parties fully understand the strategic goals of the partnership.

Each party must be able to trust all the others with strategic information and trust that each collaborator will deliver quality products even if the business grows quickly and makes heavy demands.

Multiple Generations at Work

Will Online Networks Replace Traditional Hierarchies?

According to journalist and author Malcolm Gladwell, the United States is reaching a "generational tipping point" in which Millennials bring dramatic changes in the structure and function of organizations. Gladwell states that Baby Boomers and other older generations prefer to organize in hierarchies with strong leadership, respect for expertise, a clear strategy, and a guiding ideology.

In comparison, Gladwell points out that Millennials have a different worldview: "[Millennials] take a profoundly different attitude toward authority and toward expertise." As the first generation to grow up with unfettered access to social networking sites, online gaming, and smartphones, these "digital natives" prefer to organize around and seek information from their peers via online social networks.

Because Millennials as children became accustomed to such "open, leaderless platforms," they gravitate naturally toward organizations that are collaborative in nature. In comparison to Boomers, Millennials tend to bristle when working for bosses who exert their authority by micromanaging and imposing too much structure and too many rules on employees. Perhaps this mismatch helps explain why approximately 60 percent of Millennial employees quit their jobs within three years.

©Robert A Tobiansky/Getty Images

What does this generational shift mean for organizations that use hierarchical structures? Managers may want to begin shifting their cultures and designing jobs and teams in a way that encourages collaborative, network-driven engagement. Such adjustments should come soon, because by 2025 approximately 75 percent of workers in the United States will be from the Millennial generation.[43]

The role of managers changes in a network from supervising direct reports to more like that of a **broker**. Broker/managers serve several important boundary roles that aid network integration and coordination:

Designer role: a network architect who envisions a set of groups or firms whose collective expertise can focus on a particular good or service.

Process engineering role: a network co-operator who lays out the flow of resources and relationships and makes certain that everyone shares common goals, standards, payments, and the like.

Nurturing role: a network developer who nurtures and enhances the network (maintains and strengthens the team) to make certain the relationships are healthy and mutually beneficial.[44]

broker

A person who assembles and coordinates participants in a network.

Organizational Integration

At the beginning of this chapter, we said organizations are structured around differentiation and integration. So far, we have focused on *differentiation*. As organizations differentiate their structures, they also need to *integrate* and *coordinate* the work of different parts of the organization. Typically, the more differentiated the organization, the more difficult integration is.

Due to specialization and the division of labor, different groups of managers and employees develop different perspectives. Depending on whether people are in a functional department or a divisional group,

LO 9

Typically, the more differentiated the organization, the more difficult integration is.

The Digital World

Scientists have been increasing information-processing capability for over a decade by involving digital volunteers. As technology progressed, astronomers first used online volunteers, also called citizen scientists, to exponentially increase assessment of images taken of space. This is extremely cost-effective compared with hiring and training additional data collectors and developing new and complex algorithms.

Zooniverse (Zooniverse.org) was one of the first (in 2007) to post images online in batches and ask for amateur astronomers and school classes to view images and rank them to indicate if something might be present. Highly trained scientists could turn their attention to the data with the highest probability of discovery based on how many people identified something in the image.

While astronomers gave up some control, they were able to make substantial progress through an opt-in voluntary supplement to their organizational structure. Biologists now have citizen scientists counting penguins in the Antarctic and wildlife like gazelles on the Serengeti. In 2017, just 48 hours after launching a new project, Zooniverse found four super Earths around a Sun-like star thanks to traditional scientific organizations that embrace a digital division of labor in a decentralized online application.

or are line or staff, they will think and act in ways that are geared toward their own work units. In short, people working in separate functions, divisions, and business units tend to forget and misunderstand one another's perspectives. When this happens, it is difficult for managers to combine their activities into an integrated whole.

Managers have several options for making sure that units doing different work that needs to be coordinated will work together to achieve a common purpose. If employees need to work closely to achieve joint objectives, managers can reward team performance, thus motivating teamwork. In other situations, they might rely more on individuals with unique talents and ideas, so they set up flexible work arrangements and reward individual performance. This inspires strong individual contributions while encouraging people to share knowledge and develop respect for one another's contributions.[45]

You will learn more about how rewards motivate in a later chapter. Additional coordination methods include standardization, plans, and mutual adjustment.[46]

Coordination by Standardization

standardization

Establishing common routines and procedures that apply uniformly to everyone.

Work is standardized when organizations coordinate activities by establishing routines and standard operating procedures that remain in place over time. **Standardization** constrains actions and integrates various units by regulating what people do. People often know how to act, and how to interact, because standard operating procedures determine what they should do. For example, managers may establish standards for which types of computer equipment the organization will use. This simplifies the purchasing and computer-training process—everyone will be on a common platform—and makes it easier for the different parts of the organization to communicate with each other.

formalization

The presence of rules and regulations governing how people in the organization interact.

To improve coordination, organizations also can rely on **formalization**—rules and regulations governing how people interact. Simple, often written, policies regarding attendance, dress, and decorum, for example, may help eliminate a good deal of uncertainty at work.

An important assumption underlying both standardization and formalization is that the rules and procedures should apply to most (if not all) situations. These approaches, therefore, are most appropriate in situations that are relatively stable and unchanging.

When the situation requires flexibility, standardization may not work well. Who hasn't complained about red tape, when rules and procedures—common features of slow bureaucracies—prevented timely action and problem resolution? [47]

coordination by plan

Interdependent units are required to meet deadlines and objectives that contribute to a common goal.

Coordination by Plan

Managers also can establish goals and schedules for interdependent units. **Coordination by plan** does not require the same high degree of stability that standardization does. Units can have some freedom in how they work as long as they meet the deadlines and targets needed by other units as specified in agreed-upon plans.

In writing this textbook, we (the authors) sat down with a publication team that included the editors, the marketing staff, the production group, and support staff. Together, we developed a plan that included dates and deliverables: what was to be accomplished and when it would be forwarded to others in the work flow. The plan allowed flexibility for each subunit as long as each delivered as planned. The agreed-upon plan allowed us to work together smoothly and productively.

Coordination by Mutual Adjustment

The simplest and most flexible approach to coordination may be just to have interdependent parties talk to one another. **Coordination by mutual adjustment** involves discussions to figure out jointly how to approach problems and devise solutions that are agreeable to everyone. Work teams are common in part because they allow flexible coordination; teams can operate under the principle of mutual adjustment.

The flexibility of mutual adjustment as a coordination device does not come without some cost. Hashing out every issue takes time, and may or may not result in clear mutual understanding. Imagine how long it would take to accomplish our work if people had to talk through every task and situation. But mutual adjustment can work when problems are novel and cannot be programmed in advance with rules, procedures, or plans. During crises, in which daily operating procedures don't apply, mutual adjustment is essential.

coordination by mutual adjustment

Units interact with one another to make accommodations to achieve flexible coordination.

Secure information sharing is vital at the National Counterterrorism Center, shown here. Technology enables efficient and safe sharing, but new external developments require unceasing adaptation and better coordination.

©Paul J. Richards/Getty Images

Coordination and Communication

Business environments tend to be complex, dynamic, and therefore uncertain. Huge amounts of information flow from the external environment to the organization and back to the environment. To cope, organizations must acquire, process, and respond to that information. Doing so has direct implications for how firms organize. Organizations need to develop structures for processing a lot of information, effectively.

To cope with high uncertainty and heavy information demands, managers can use the two general strategies shown in Exhibit 8.14. First, management can act to reduce the need for information. Second, it can increase its capacity to handle more information.[48]

Option 1: Reducing the Need for Information   Managers can reduce the need for information in two ways: (a) creating slack resources and (b) creating self-contained tasks. Slack resources are extra resources on which organizations can rely in a pinch so that if they get caught off guard, they can still adjust. Inventory, for example, is a type of slack resource that provides extra stock on hand in case it is needed. With extra inventory, an organization does not need as much information about sales demand, lead times, and so on.

Like slack resources, creating self-contained tasks allows organizations to reduce the need for some information. Creating self-contained tasks refers to changing from a functional organization to a product or project organization and giving each unit the resources it needs to perform its task. Information-processing problems are reduced because each unit has its own full complement of specialties, rather than needing to share functinoal expertise among a number of different product teams. Communications then flow within each team rather than among a complex array of interdependent groups.

Option 2: Increasing Information-Processing Capability   Instead of or in addition to reducing the need for information, managers can attempt to increase the

EXHIBIT 8.14
Managing High
Information-Processing
Demands

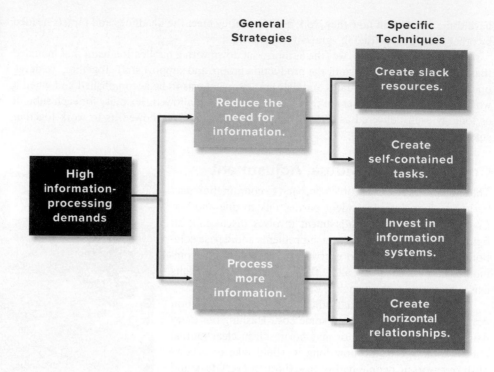

Bottom Line

Cross-unit coordination
can lead to effective
problem solving.
*Why does more shared
information tend to improve
solutions?*

firm's information-processing capability. They can invest in information systems, which usually means employing or expanding computer systems. But increasing an organization's information-processing capability can also mean engaging in better knowledge management (Chapter 1)—capitalizing on the intellect and experience of the organization's human assets to increase collaboration and effectiveness.

One way to do that is by creating horizontal relationships between units to foster coordination and thus integration. The following horizontal processes range from the simplest to the most complex:[49]

1. *Direct contact (mutual adjustment)* among managers who share a problem. In a university, for example, a residence hall adviser might call a meeting to resolve differences between feuding students.

2. *Liaison roles,* or specialized jobs to handle communications between two departments. A fraternity representative is a liaison between the fraternity and the interfraternity council, the university, or the local community.

3. *Task forces,* or groups of representatives from different departments, brought together temporarily to solve a common problem. For example, students, faculty, and administrators may be members of a task force charged with bringing distinguished speakers to campus.

4. *Permanent interdepartmental decision-making groups.* An executive council made up of department heads might meet regularly to make decisions affecting a college of engineering or liberal arts.

5. *Product, program, or project managers* who direct interdisciplinary groups with a common task to perform. In a college of business administration, a faculty administrator might head an executive education program of professors from several disciplines.

6. *Matrix organizations,* composed of dual relationships in which some managers report to two bosses. Your instructors, for example, may report to department heads in their respective disciplines and to a director of undergraduate or graduate programs.

You will learn more about some of these in later chapters covering teams, intergroup relations, and communicating.

Looking Ahead

The organization chart, differentiation, integration, authority, delegation, and coordination convey fundamental information about an organization's structure. However, the information so far provides only a snapshot. The real organization is more like a motion picture—it moves! More flexible and innovative, even virtual, new forms of organizations are evolving continually.

Even if you know departments and authority relationships, you still have much to understand. How do things really get done? Who influences whom, and how? Which managers are the most powerful? How effective is the top leadership? Which groups are most and which are least effective? How do communications flow throughout the organization? The rest of the book discusses these dynamics.

As you read "Management in Action: Onward," consider how the organizing concepts from this chapter help you evaluate the challenges facing General Motors, but also notice where personal relationships and other human factors come into play.

Management in Action

REGROUPING AND CHANGING THE CULTURE AT GENERAL MOTORS

What future changes does Mary Barra have in mind for GE? Her previous position as senior vice president of global product development, whose decisions shaped how fast new products came to market, may provide some clues. Her streamlining of the product development group's structure was an important first step.

Barra, who joined GM as an electrical engineer and worked her way up, also simplified systems. Instead of letting managers constantly tweak their four-year plans, she held twice-yearly meetings for reviewing plans and discussing major changes. Her audit of processes in product development showed that the people in her own group were the ones slowing development due to inefficient processes. Under Barra, such uncoordinated conduct was not tolerated.

Barra has the daunting task of changing the way managers and employees behave at GM. She has made it clear that GM's inward-looking culture and slow responses to major safety issues and product defects will no longer be tolerated. She has pledged to hold people accountable for their actions.

Barra refuses to sweep the tragic events of 2014 under the rug. She wants GM decision makers to remember the pain that the ignition switch problem (and 10-year delay) caused for victims (and the company): "I never want to put this behind us. I want to put this painful experience permanently in our collective memories."

Changing a company's culture is difficult, but some signs indicate that Barra's efforts are paying off. General Motors recently unveiled the Chevy Bolt, which she long championed, as an "affordable all-electric vehicle with over 200 miles per charge." Immediately named *Motor Trend*'s 2017 Car of the Year, the Bolt represents an opportunity for GM to be first in a potentially large and growing market for a new kind of car. It also suggests a once staid and slow company's newfound ability to maneuver quickly and successfully push into uncharted markets.

Industry observers believe that, aided by a new willingness to seek partners among tech companies, GM is correctly foreseeing a future in which cars will be electric, self-driving, and linked to the infrastructure GM also see a future in which drivers will be less willing to own cars outright. The company has already invested $500 million in the ride-sharing company Lyft, has started car-sharing programs in the United States and Germany, and is entering new markets such as India where traditional ideas about car ownership will not apply.[50]

- How might Barra's efforts at changing the culture at GM increase the chances that the structural changes will be effective in the long term?
- What personal, human factors are likely to affect GM's success in achieving greater organizational integration?

MANAGER'S BRIEF

PROGRESS REPORT

ONWARD

KEY TERMS

accountability, p. 229

authority, p. 226

broker, p. 241

centralized organization, p. 230

coordination, p. 225

coordination by mutual adjustment, p. 243

coordination by plan, p. 242

corporate governance, p. 228

decentralized organization, p. 230

delegation, p. 229

departmentalization, p. 232

differentiation, p. 224

division of labor, p. 224

divisional organization, p. 234

dynamic network, p. 240

formalization, p. 242

functional organization, p. 232

hierarchy, p. 227

integration, p. 224

line departments, p. 232

matrix organization, p. 236

network organization, p. 239

organization chart, p. 224

responsibility, p. 229

span of control, p. 228

specialization, p. 224

staff departments, p. 232

standardization, p. 242

subunits, p. 228

unity-of-command principle, p. 238

RETAINING WHAT YOU LEARNED

In Chapter 8, you learned that the structure of organizations is determined fundamentally by their degrees of differentiation and integration. People and groups are assigned specialized tasks, and these tasks are coordinated to achieve the organizations' overall mission. Bosses exercise authority throughout organizations' hierarchies, even though owners or stockholders have ultimate authority. Boards of directors report to stockholders, advise management, consider the firm's legal interests, and protect stockholders' rights. Span of control refers to the number of people who report directly to a manager. Delegation, the assignment of tasks and responsibilities, offers a variety of benefits but must be managed carefully. In centralized organizations, top managers make the most important decisions whereas in decentralized organizations, many decisions are delegated to lower levels. Organizations can be structured in a variety of forms, including function, division (product, customers, or geographic), matrix, and network. Matrix structures allow a company to adapt to changing conditions, but present unique challenges to people working within them. Managers can coordinate interdependent units through standardization, plans, and mutual adjustment.

LO 1 **Explain how differentiation and integration influence an organization's structure.**

- Differentiation means that organizations have many parts. Specialization means that various individuals and units throughout the organization perform different tasks. The assignment of tasks to different people or groups often is the division of labor. But the specialized tasks in an organization cannot all be performed independently of one another.
- Coordination links the various tasks to achieve the organization's overall mission.
- An organization with many specialized tasks and work units is highly differentiated; the more differentiated the organization is, the more integration or coordination is required.

LO 2 **Summarize how authority operates.**

- Authority is the legitimate right to make decisions and tell other people what to do. It is exercised throughout the hierarchy because bosses have the authority to give orders to subordinates.
- Through the day-to-day operation of authority, the organization proceeds toward achieving its goals. Owners or stockholders have ultimate authority.

LO 3 **Define the roles of the board of directors and the chief executive officer.**

- Boards of directors report to stockholders. The board of directors controls or advises management, considers the firm's legal and other interests, and protects stockholders' rights.
- The chief executive officer reports to the board and is accountable for the organization's performance.

LO 4 **Discuss how span of control affects structure and managerial effectiveness.**

- Span of control is the number of people who report directly to a manager. Narrow spans create tall organizations, and wide spans create flat ones.
- No single span of control is always appropriate; the optimal span is determined by characteristics of the work, the subordinates, the manager, and the organization.

LO 5 **Explain how to delegate effectively.**

- Delegation—the assignment of tasks and responsibilities—has many potential advantages for the manager, the subordinate, and the organization.
- But to be effective, the process must be managed carefully. The manager should define the goal, select the person, solicit opinions, provide resources, schedule checkpoints, and discuss progress periodically.

LO 6 Distinguish between centralized and decentralized organizations.

- In centralized organizations, top managers make the most important decisions.
- In decentralized organizations, many decisions are delegated to lower levels.

LO 7 Summarize ways organizations can be structured.

- Organizations can be structured on the basis of function, division (product, customers, or geographic), matrix, and network.
- Each form has advantages and disadvantages.

LO 8 Identify the unique challenges of the matrix organization.

- The matrix is a complex structure with dual authority relationships. A well-managed matrix enables organizations to adapt to change.
- But it can also create confusion and interpersonal difficulties. People in all positions in the matrix—top executives, product and function managers, and two-boss employees—must acquire unique survival skills.

LO 9 Describe important integrative mechanisms.

- Managers can coordinate interdependent units through standardization, plans, and mutual adjustment.
- Standardization stems from work routines and standard operating procedures. They typically are accompanied by formalized rules.
- Coordination by plan is more flexible and allows more freedom in how tasks are carried out but keeps interdependent units focused on joint goals and schedules.
- Mutual adjustment involves feedback and discussions among related parties to accommodate each other's needs. It is the most flexible and simplest to administer, but it is time-consuming.
- Two general ways to deal with high information loads are to reduce the need for information (for example, through creating slack resources and self-contained units) and processing more information (for example, through investing in information systems and creating horizontal relationships).

DISCUSSION QUESTIONS

1. Based on the description of General Motors in this chapter, give some examples of differentiation in that organization. In other words, what specialized tasks have to be performed, and how is labor divided at General Motors? Also, how does General Motors integrate the work of these different units? Based on what you have learned in this chapter, would you say General Motors has an effective structure? Why or why not?

2. What are some advantages and disadvantages of being in the CEO position?

3. Would you like to sit on a board of directors? Why or why not? If you did serve on a board, what kind of organization would you prefer? As a board member, in what kinds of activities do you think you would most actively engage?

4. Interview a member of a board of directors, and discuss that member's perspectives on his or her role.

5. Pick a job you have held and describe it in terms of span of control, delegation, responsibility, authority, and accountability.

6. Why do you think managers have difficulty delegating? What can be done to overcome these difficulties?

7. Consider an organization in which you have worked, draw its organization chart, and describe it by using terms in this chapter. How did you like working there, and why?

8. Would you rather work in a functional or divisional organization? Why?

9. If you learned that a company has a matrix structure, would you be more or less interested in working there? Explain your answer. How would you prepare yourself to work effectively in a matrix?

10. Brainstorm a list of specific ways to integrate interdependent work units. Discuss the activities required and the pros and cons of each approach.

EXPERIENTIAL EXERCISES

8.1 THE BUSINESS SCHOOL ORGANIZATION CHART

OBJECTIVES

1. To clarify the factors that determine organization structure.
2. To provide insight into the workings of an organization.
3. To examine the working relationships within an organization.

INSTRUCTIONS

1. Draw an organization chart for your business school. Be sure to identify all the staff and line positions in the school. Specify the chain of command and the levels of administration. Note the different spans of control. Are there any advisory groups, task forces, or committees to consider?

2. Review the chapter material on organization structure to help identify both strong and weak points in your school's organization. Now draw another organization chart for the school, incorporating any changes you believe would improve the quality of the school. Support the second chart with a list of recommended changes and reasons for their inclusion.

DISCUSSION QUESTIONS

1. Is your business school well organized? Why or why not?

2. In what ways is the school's structure designed to suit the needs of students, faculty, staff, the administration, and the business community?

8.2 DESIGNING A STUDENT-RUN ORGANIZATION THAT PROVIDES CONSULTING SERVICES

OBJECTIVES

1. To appreciate the importance of the total organization on group and individual behavior.

2. To provide a beginning organization design experience that will be familiar to students.

BACKGROUND

The Industry Advisory Council for your school has decided to sponsor a student-run organization that will provide business consulting services to nonprofit groups in your community. The council has donated $20,000 toward start-up costs and has agreed to provide office space, computer equipment, and other materials as needed. The council hopes that the organization will establish its own source of funding after the first year of operation.

TASK 1

The dean of the school wants you to develop alternative designs for the new organization. Your task is to identify the main design dimensions or factors to be dealt with in establishing such an organization and to describe the issues that must be resolved for each factor. For example, you might provide an organization chart to help describe the structural issues involved. Before jumping ahead with your design,

you may also have to think about (1) groups in the community that could use your help and (2) problems they face. Remember, though, your task is to create the organization that will provide services, not to provide an in-depth look at the types of services provided.

You and your team are to brainstorm design dimensions to be dealt with and to develop a one- or two-page outline that can be shared with the entire class. You have one hour to develop the outline. Select two people to present your design. Assume that you will all be involved in the new organization, filling specific positions.

TASK 2

After the brainstorming period, the spokespersons will present the group designs or preferred design and answer questions from the audience.

TASK 3

The instructor will comment on the designs and discuss additional factors that might be important for the success of this organization.

Shani, A. B. (Rami) and Lau, James B., *Behavior in Organizations: An Experimental Approach,* p. 369. Copyright ©2005 McGraw-Hill Global Education Holdings LLC. All rights reserved. Used with permission.

8.3 WHEN SHOULD A COMPANY DECENTRALIZE?

OBJECTIVE

To explore the conditions under which a company should decentralize its structure and decision making.

INSTRUCTIONS

The following scenarios describe situations faced by hypothetical companies that currently have a *centralized* organizational structure. As you review each of the scenarios, provide your opinion as to whether the company should move to a more *decentralized* organizational structure.

1. Company X produces one specialized product line for heart surgeons in the United States.
   - Maintain current centralized organizational structure

   or

   - Move to a more decentralized organizational structure

   Defend your choice:

   _____

   _____

2. Company Y makes over 100 electronic products and has to respond rapidly to the moves of its competitors.
   - Maintain current centralized organizational structure

   or

   - Move to a more decentralized organizational structure

   Defend your choice:

   _____

   _____

3. Company Z's managers are becoming increasingly comfortable with delegating tasks and responsibilities to subordinates in order to develop their decision-making skills.
   - Maintain current centralized organizational structure

   or

   - Move to a more decentralized organizational structure

   Defend your choice:

_____

_____

SOURCE: Adapted from McGrath Jr., R. R., *Exercises in Management Fundamentals.* Englewood Cliffs, NJ: Prentice Hall, 1985, 59–60.

Concluding Case

STANLEY LYNCH INVESTMENT GROUP

The Stanley Lynch Investment Group is a large investment firm headquartered in New York. The firm has 12 major investment funds, each with analysts operating in a separate department. Along with knowledge of the financial markets and the businesses it analyzes, Stanley Lynch's competitive advantage comes from its advanced and reliable computer systems. Thus an effective information technology (IT) division is a strategic necessity, and the company's chief information officer (CIO) holds a key role at the firm.

When the company hired J. T. Kundra as a manager of technology, he learned that the IT division at Stanley Lynch consists of 68 employees, most of whom specialize in serving the needs of a particular fund. The IT employees serving a fund operate as a distinct group, each of them led by a manager who supervises several employees. (Five employees report to J. T.)

He also learned that each group sets up its own computer system to store information about its projects. The problems with that arrangement quickly became evident. As J. T. tried to direct his group's work, he would ask for documentation of one program or another. Sometimes, no one was sure where to find the documentation; it might turn out to be stored in an obscure place such as only on someone's flash drive. Other times, he would quickly get three different responses from three different people with three versions of the documentation. And if he was interested in another group's project or a software program used in another department, getting information was next to impossible. He lacked the authority to ask employees in another group to drop what they were doing to hunt down information he needed.

J. T. concluded that the entire IT division could serve the firm much better if all authorized people had easy access to the work that had already been done and the software that was available. The logical place to store that information was online. From experience at a previous company, he believed that the easiest way to compile the information would be to set up a shared web project called a wiki—an online document created through the collaboration of its users, who can look up or contribute information according to their knowledge and needs. The challenge would be how to get everyone to contribute, given that he had authority over so few of the IT workers.

J. T. started by working with his five employees to build a wiki offering basic information presented in a consistent format. Then he met with two higher-level managers who report to the CIO. He showed them the wiki and explained that fast access to information would improve the IT group's quality and efficiency. He suggested that the managers require all the IT employees to put their documentation on the wiki, and he even persuaded them that this behavior should be measured for performance appraisals. This last tactic was especially significant because at an investment company, bonuses for meeting performance targets are a big part of employees' compensation.

The IT employees quickly came to appreciate that the wiki would help them perform better. When they visited it, they could see from the original information that it would be useful. Adoption of the wiki was swift, and before long, the IT employees came to think of it as one of their most important software systems.

DISCUSSION QUESTIONS

1. Give an example of differentiation in Stanley Lynch's organization structure and an example of integration in this structure.

2. What role did authority play in the adoption of the wiki by the IT division at Stanley Lynch?

3. Describe how the IT division used coordination to achieve greater integration.

CHAPTER 9
Organizational Agility

> I came to the conclusion long ago that limits to innovation have less to do with technology or creativity than organizational agility. Inspired individuals can only do so much.
>
> —RAY STATA, FOUNDER OF ANALOG DEVICES

©John Lund/Blend Images RF

LEARNING OBJECTIVES

After studying Chapter 9, you will be able to:

LO 1   Discuss why it is critical for organizations to be responsive.

LO 2   Describe the qualities of an organic organization structure.

LO 3   Identify strategies and dynamic organizational concepts that can improve an organization's responsiveness.

LO 4   Explain how a firm can be both big and small.

LO 5   Summarize how firms organize to meet customer requirements.

LO 6   Identify ways that firms organize around different types of technology.

CHAPTER OUTLINE

The Responsive Organization

Strategy and Organizational Agility
  Organizing around Core Capabilities
  Strategic Alliances
  The Learning Organization
  The High-Involvement Organization

Organizational Size and Agility
  The Case for Big
  The Case for Small
  Being Big and Small

Customers and the Responsive Organization
  Customer Relationship Management
  Quality Initiatives
  Reengineering

Technology and Organizational Agility
  Types of Technology Configurations
  Organizing for Flexible Manufacturing
  Organizing for Speed: Time-Based Competition

Final Thoughts on Organizational Agility

Management in Action

KEEPING GENERAL ELECTRIC NIMBLE

While he was CEO of General Electric (he stepped down in 2017, after 16 years at the helm), Jeffrey Immelt was asked to identify GE's core capability. Immelt's reply echoed his predecessor, the legendary Jack Welch: "Evaluating people."

Evaluation—needed for identifying, developing, and keeping the best leaders—is a powerful core capability, especially for GE, which requires excellence in so many areas. Unlike specialized or regional companies, GE operated eight large industrial businesses and a financial business, all operating worldwide. It's always had to be able to do *many* things right.

In recent years, some observers started wondering whether GE has been losing its core capability. The recent financial crisis hit GE hard, especially because it had relied heavily on GE Capital's lending and investments for a bit part of its earnings. Although GE Capital managed to turn a profit every year, 2009's profits were less than one-sixth of 2008's, and the numbers climbed back slowly over the next few years.

The recession slowed purchases from GE's business and government customers. Moreover, in the United States, the rising cost of health care hurt demand for GE's imaging equipment such as X-ray machines and MRI scanners. GE's stock price tumbled, and its credit rating slipped.

Immelt responded by focusing the company more on infrastructure, such as transportation and energy systems, and scaling back GE Capital, especially its real estate investments. In 2015 the company launched GE Digital, a software division expected to lead the way in developing the widely anticipated Internet of Things.

Can a behemoth such as GE be nimble enough for our fast-changing business world? Immelt said yes. He viewed GE as a 333,000-employee team, with operations in 175 countries, united by a mission to "build, move, power and cure the world." He was counting on strong growth from its oil and gas and its power and water business units, especially as a result of demand for infrastructure in developing economies.

©Bloomberg/Getty Images

As economies compete for increasingly scarce (and costly) energy resources, Immelt saw potential for GE's energy management business, which helps customers conserve energy. GE executives expected efficiency projects to spur demand in the company's other industrial businesses: aviation, transportation, health care, and home and business solutions.

Few businesses could maintain a lead in so many arenas, but Immelt saw GE as having the resources to do just that. In recessions as well as economic expansions, customers want to save money, so GE invests heavily in research for making jet engines more efficient, cutting waste from energy systems, and upgrading its equipment for the era of big data. It also plans to cut costs by $1 billion by 2018. In his letter to shareholders, Immelt stated, "The challenge for any company is to invest in the future while delivering results. We have challenged ourselves to hit aggressive financial goals as we transform GE."[1]

GE is trying to maintain its position as one of the world's great industrial companies, with an organization that enables innovation and demands high performance. As you read this chapter, consider whether GE can remain competitive in a profoundly changing business world.

Like GE, today's successful companies can't afford to rest on their previous accomplishments. If they do, they easily become vulnerable—to an economic collapse, new competing products, sudden shifts in customer preferences, or countless other environmental shocks and changes. That is, they need to make sure that their structures and systems—and the people within—remain *adaptable*. When structures and systems are designed well, the organization is flexible and agile enough to succeed in a changing world.

Such an organization is ambidextrous. As some people have the gift of writing with either hand, an **ambidextrous organization** is simultaneously good at *exploitation* (using what it knows to efficiently and quickly perform as needed) and *exploration* (seeking and creating new ways to meet future needs).[2] In this chapter, you will see ways to organize people, information, and work that have helped organizations excel at both exploitation and exploration.

The Responsive Organization

The formal structure is put in place to control people, decisions, and actions. But in today's fast-changing business environment, responsiveness—quickness, agility, the ability to adapt to changing demands—is vital to a firm's survival.[3]

Many decades after Max Weber wrote about bureaucracy as a rational way to run large modern organizations, two British management scholars (Burns and Stalker) described what they called the **mechanistic organization**.[4] The mechanistic structure they described was similar to Weber's bureaucracy, but they stated further that the modern corporation has a new option. The **organic structure** is much less rigid and, in fact, emphasizes flexibility.

Compared with the mechanistic structure, in the organic structure:

1. Jobholders have broader responsibilities, and they change as needs arise.
2. Communication occurs through advice and information rather than through orders and instructions.
3. Decision making and influence are more decentralized and informal.
4. Expertise is highly valued.
5. Jobholders rely more heavily on judgment than on rules.
6. Commitment to the organization's goals is more important than obedience to authority.
7. Employees depend more on one another and relate more informally and personally.

Exhibit 9.1 contrasts the formal structure of an organization—epitomized by the organization chart—to the informal structure, which is more organic. As you compare these two charts, what do you notice that should concern this company's managers? Astute managers are keenly aware of the network of interactions among the organization's members, and they work within this network to increase agility. Employees who engage actively in formal and informal networks are likely to perform at higher levels.[5] They find and use diverse and valuable information from different parts of the organization to do their jobs better.[6]

The ideas underlying the organic structure and networks are the foundation for the newer, faster-moving forms of organization described in this chapter. To prepare for and adapt to an uncertain future, managers need to be able to respond to fast-appearing threats and opportunities.

Bottom Line

Speed is vital to an organization's survival. *How can lack of speed kill an organization?*

---

ambidextrous organization

An organization that is simultaneously good at exploitation and exploration.

mechanistic organization

A form of organization that seeks to maximize internal efficiency.

organic structure

An organizational form that emphasizes flexibility.

EXHIBIT 9.1
Formal and Informal
Organizational Structures

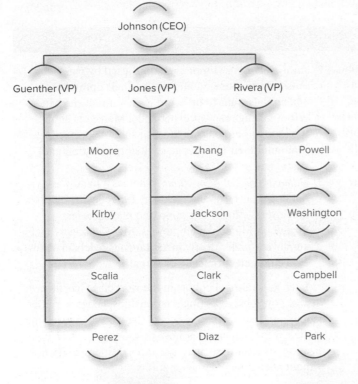

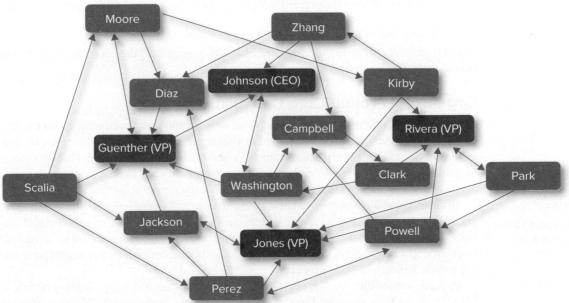

SOURCE: Adapted from Soda, G. and Zaheer, A., "A Network Perspective on Organizational Architecture: Performance Effects of the Interplay of Formal and Informal Organization," *Strategic Management Journal 33 (2012), pp.* 751–71.

Strategy and Organizational Agility

Certain strategies, and the structures, processes, and relationships that accompany them, can help an organization respond quickly and effectively to the challenges it faces. Managers can leverage their people and assets to make the firm more agile and competitive. As described next, these decisions and actions are based on the firm's core capabilities, its

Multiple Generations at Work

Millennials and the Flexible Workplace

Many managers express concerns about the difficulties of finding Millennial talent and then, once hired, of motivating and retaining them. Some estimate that the average length of time these early career employees stay in a professional job, where training is provided, is about three years. About 60 percent of Millennials are "open to a different job opportunity."

The tendency to job-hop is very different from the way older generations approached jobs.

What are some workplace strategies that can help attract and retain Millennial employees?

1. *Flexible work arrangements.* While many Boomers are comfortable being at work Monday–Friday from 9 to 5 p.m., many Millennials find this approach stifling and rigid. Having grown up in a mobile and connected world, Millennials want some flexibility with regard to where and when they do their work. When possible, managers should be flexible but also set clear performance expectations.

2. *Involvement in decision making.* Raised by parents who encouraged and valued their opinions, Millennials want to be heard even without the benefit of having relevant experience. Managers should look for ways to engage them in suitable projects that build their knowledge of the organization and customers.

3. *Different types of recognition.* Whereas a handwritten note may be an effective way to recognize older employees' efforts, this approach may have less impact on Millennial employees. Many younger employees prefer nearly instantaneous feedback delivered either electronically or verbally.

Each generational cohort in the workplace has its own view of how jobs, reporting relationships, co-worker interactions, and so forth should be structured. A pressing challenge for managers is how to modify internal organization structures so they are more Millennial-friendly without alienating older generations.[7]

strategic alliances, its ability to learn, and its ability to engage all the people in the organization in achieving its objectives.

Organizing around Core Capabilities

A different, new, and important perspective on strategy and organization builds on the concept of core capabilities.[8] As you learned in Chapter 4, a core capability is the knowledge, expertise, or skill that underlies a company's ability to be a leader in providing a range of goods or services. Here we add a useful distinction between two types of capabilities—ordinary and dynamic.[9]

ordinary capabilities

Capabilities pertaining to basic administrative and operational functions

Ordinary capabilities pertain to basic administrative and operational functions needed to get tasks done. They involve capable people, facilities and equipment, procedures and routines, and administrative coordination. They can provide temporary competitive advantage in quality, speed, and efficiency, but are easy to imitate as companies hire consultants and implement well-known "best practices."

dynamic capabilities

Higher-level strategic capabilities (compared with ordinary capabilities) that aid rapid adaptation.

Dynamic capabilities are "higher level," strategic activities involving adapting rapidly to (or even proactively shaping) the ever-changing business environment. Whereas ordinary capabilities are about doing basic things right, dynamic capabilities are about doing the right things at the right time, based on new product and process development, unique managerial actions, and a change-oriented organizational culture that spots and seizes opportunities.

Dynamic capabilities focus less on efficiency and more on innovation, allowing the company to compete on the basis of its core strategic strengths and expertise. For example, Canon's core capability is innovative image technology. A core capability gives value to customers, makes the company's products different from—and better than—those of competitors, and help in creating new products.

Developing a world-class core capability opens the door to a variety of future opportunities; failure to develop one means being foreclosed from many markets. Strategically, this means that companies should commit to excellence and leadership in capabilities, and strengthen them, before they commit to winning market share for specific products.

Organizationally, this means that the corporation should be viewed as a portfolio of capabilities, not just a portfolio of specific businesses. Companies should strive for core competence leadership, not just product leadership.

It's not enough to have valuable resources that provide capabilities; those resources have to be managed in a way that provides an advantage over competitors.[10] Managers must do three things. First, they must accumulate the right resources (such as talented people) by determining what resources they need, acquiring and developing those resources, and eliminating resources that don't provide value. Next, they must combine the resources in ways that give the organization capabilities, such as researching new products or resolving customers' problems. These combinations may involve knowledge sharing and alliances between departments or with other organizations.

Third, managers need to leverage or exploit their resources. They do this by identifying opportunities where their competencies deliver value to customers—say, by creating new products or by delivering existing products better than competitors—and then by coordinating and deploying the resources properly. The nearby "Multiple Generations at Work" box discusses further how modifying internal structures can boost the ROI from human capital.

Strategic Alliances

As we discussed in previous chapters, the modern organization has a variety of links with other organizations. These links are more complex than the standard relationships with traditional stakeholders such as suppliers and clients. Today even fierce competitors are working *together* at unprecedented levels to achieve their strategic goals.

For example, Coca-Cola, Dr Pepper Snapple Group, and PepsiCo have come together to cut by 20 percent the amount of sugar-based calories in their soft drinks by 2025.[11] TAG Heuer, Google, and Intel announced recently that they will collaborate to develop a smartwatch.[12] In these and other examples, strategic alliances allow participants to respond to customer demands or environmental threats far faster and less expensively than each would be able to do on its own.

A **strategic alliance** is a formal relationship created with the purpose of joint pursuit of mutual goals. Different organizations share administrative authority, form social links, and accept joint ownership. Alliances occur between companies and their competitors, governments, and universities. As with the TAG Heuer–Google–Intel collaboration, partnering often crosses national and cultural boundaries.

Companies form strategic alliances to develop new technologies, enter new markets, and reduce manufacturing costs. Alliances enable companies to move faster and more efficiently; they also can be the only practical way to bring together a wide variety of needed specialists. Rather than hiring experts who understand the technology and market segments for each new product, companies can form alliances with partners that already have those experts on board.[13]

Managers typically devote plenty of time to screening potential partners in financial terms. For the alliance to work, the partners also must consider one another's areas of expertise and the incentives involved in the structure of the alliance. A comparison of research and development alliances found that the most innovation occurred when the partners were experts in moderately different types of research. If the partners were very different, they shared ideas and innovated more when the alliance was set up through equity (stock) ownership; for similar partners, more innovation came via research contracts rather than equity.[14]

Managers must foster and develop the human relationships in the partnership that facilitate interpersonal cooperation and coordination of activities.[15] Asian companies seem to be the most comfortable with the nonfinancial, people side of alliances; European companies the next so; and U.S. companies the least. Thus U.S. companies may need to pay extra attention to the human side of alliances. Exhibit 9.2 shows some recommendations for how to do this. In fact, most of the ideas apply not only to strategic alliances but to any type of relationship.[16]

strategic alliance
A formal relationship created among independent organizations with the purpose of joint pursuit of mutual goals.

Bottom Line
Core capabilities can be a source of quality and innovation. *Does your school have a core capability? If so, what is it, and why do you identify it as such?*

LO 3

Bottom Line
Alliances can increase speed and innovation and lower costs. *How might an alliance increase innovation?*

Faster Wi-Fi and coffee—a wonderful strategic alliance. Recently, Starbucks switched from AT&T to Google to provide free wireless Internet in its 7,000 U.S. stores. This move allows customers to surf the Internet up to 10 times faster.

©McGraw-Hill Education/John Flournoy, photographer

EXHIBIT 9.2
How I's Can Become We's

The best alliances are true partnerships that meet these criteria:
1. *Relationship:* Both partners work hard on developing a positive working relationship.
2. *Metrics:* The partners measure how they're going to succeed, not just the end result.
3. *Differences:* The partners embrace differences in one another.
4. *Control:* Both partners encourage collaborative behavior with less emphasis on formal systems and structures.
5. *Management:* The partners manage their internal stakeholders who are involved in the alliance.

SOURCE: Adapted from Hughes, J. and Weiss, J., "Simple Rules for Making Alliances Work," *Harvard Business Review*, November 2007, www.hbr.org.

The Learning Organization

Being responsive requires continually learning new ways to act. Some experts maintain that the only sustainable advantage is learning faster than the competition. This has led to a new term that is now part of the vocabulary of most managers: the learning organization.[17] A **learning organization** is an organization skilled at creating, acquiring, and transferring knowledge and at modifying its behavior to reflect new knowledge and insights.[18]

Google, Toyota, and IDEO are good examples. Such organizations are skilled at solving problems, experimenting with new approaches, learning from their own experiences, learning from other organizations, and spreading knowledge quickly and efficiently.

How do firms become true learning organizations? They make sure a few important activities are happening at all levels and in all units:[19]

1. Engaging in disciplined thinking and paying attention to details, so decisions are based on data and evidence rather than guesswork and assumptions.
2. Searching constantly for new knowledge and ways to apply it—looking for broader horizons and opportunities, not just quick fixes for current problems.
3. Valuing and rewarding people who expand their knowledge and skills in areas that benefit the organization.
4. Reviewing successes and failures carefully to find lessons and develop deeper understanding.
5. Benchmarking—identifying and implementing the best business practices of other organizations, stealing ideas shamelessly (that's a metaphor, nothing illegal!).
6. Sharing ideas throughout the organization via reports, information systems, informal discussions, site visits, education, training, and mentoring of less experienced employees by more experienced ones.

Ideally these efforts target domains of ambidexterity mentioned at the beginning of this chapter.[20] The first, exploitation, requires continuously learning ways to operate more efficiently and effectively. We will see ideas for this kind of learning throughout the remainder of this chapter. Future chapters offer more on exploration, or uncovering new areas in which the company can excel.

The High-Involvement Organization

Participative management—involving employees in decision making—can be a good way to create a competitive advantage. In a **high-involvement organization**, top leaders ensure consensus about the direction in which the business is heading by seeking input from their team and middle managers and sometimes from lower levels, depending on the issue. Task forces, study groups, and other

---

learning organization

An organization skilled at creating, acquiring, and transferring knowledge, and at modifying its behavior to reflect new knowledge and insights.

---

high-involvement organization

A type of organization in which top management ensures that there is consensus about the direction in which the business is heading.

Participative management is a good way to create competitive advantage.

techniques foster participation in important decisions. Also fundamental to the high-involvement organization is continual feedback to participants regarding how they are doing compared with the competition and how effectively they are meeting the strategic agenda.

The organizational form is relatively flat and decentralized, built around a customer or product (good or service). Employee involvement is particularly powerful when the environment changes rapidly, work is creative, complex activities require coordination and commitment, and firms need major breakthroughs in innovation and speed. A perfect example is high-technology companies facing stiff international competition.[21]

Organizational Size and Agility

One of the most important characteristics of an organization is its size.[22] Large organizations are typically less organic and more bureaucratic. Retail behemoth Walmart has more than 2 million employees. CEO Doug McMillion is trying to reduce bureaucracy (and revitalize company growth) by encouraging employees to take more initiative. He removed one layer of management from Walmart stores in order to give employees a larger say in how the stores are run.[23]

As firms (and government agencies, and NGOs, and social enterprises) grow, they become more complex structurally. Managers deal with this by introducing more rules, procedures, and paperwork—in short, with bureaucratic controls that increase efficiency but often weaken the ability to innovate.

Let's consider whether and how large companies can be agile, adaptive, and responsive to competitive and consumer demands?

Bottom Line
Large size often leads to scale economies. *How has General Electric's large size affected its ability to compete?*

The Case for Big

Big was best after World War II, when foreign competition was limited and growth seemed limitless. To meet high demand for its products, U.S. industry embraced high-volume, low-cost manufacturing methods. IBM, General Motors (GM), and Sears all grew into behemoths during those decades.

Alfred Chandler, a pioneer in strategic management, noted that big companies were the engine of economic growth throughout the 20th century.[24] Size creates scale economies—that is, lower costs per unit of production. Size can offer specific advantages such as lower operating costs, greater purchasing power, and easier access to capital.

Walmart's size gives it the purchasing power to buy merchandise in larger volumes and sell it at lower prices than its competitors can. Size also creates **economies of scope**; materials and processes employed in one product can be used to make related products. With such advantages, huge companies with lots of money may be the best at taking on large foreign rivals in huge global markets.

economies of scope

Economies in which materials and processes employed in one product can be used to make other, related products.

The Case for Small

But a huge, complex organization can find it hard to manage relationships with customers and among its own units. Too much success can breed complacency, and the resulting inertia hinders change. This is a surefire formula for being left in the dust by hungry competitors.

Giant companies have stumbled as consumers demand a greater diversity of high-quality, customized products supported by excellent service. Some evidence shows that as firms get larger and their market share grows, customers begin to view their products as having lower quality. Also, once a company has captured a big share of the market, future growth is hard because gaining more new customers takes costlier efforts or a fresh approach.

Walmart's low-price strategy helped it become the largest U.S. corporation in terms of sales, but sales growth flattened out. The company's response—cutting labor costs—helped profits in the short term but drove away some shoppers frustrated with unstocked shelves and difficulty finding help. Walmart recently placed last in the American Customer Satisfaction Index for department and discount stores.[25]

Larger companies also are more difficult to coordinate and control. Although size can enhance efficiency by spreading fixed costs over more units, it also may create bureaucratic hassles that constrain performance. Unilever not only has three organizations selling different product lines in each country it serves, but until recently it was run by two chairmen–CEOs, an artifact of a merger that took place decades ago. This cumbersome structure has held back Unilever's efficiency and agility.[26] To describe this problem, a new term has entered the business vocabulary: *diseconomies of scale,* or the costs of being too big. "Small is beautiful" has become a favorite phrase of entrepreneurial business managers.[27]

Nimble small firms frequently outmaneuver big bureaucracies. Smaller companies can move fast, provide quality goods and services to targeted market niches, and inspire greater involvement from their people. They introduce new and better products, and they steal market share. The premium now is on flexibility and responsiveness—the unique potential strengths of the small firm.

An extreme example is Kobold Watch, staffed by founder Michael Kobold and three employees. The small company makes and sells premium mechanical wristwatches priced at thousands of dollars each. Kobold advertises online and through word of mouth generated by sales to celebrities, including former president Bill Clinton, Kiefer Sutherland, and Bruce Springsteen. When sales surge, Kobold calls on two other watchmakers to help out as needed. Kobold intentionally limits production to 2,500 watches a year—not just to maintain the prestige of the brand but also to keep the company small and fast-moving.[28]

downsizing

The planned elimination of positions or jobs.

Being Big and Small

Small *is* beautiful for unleashing energy and speed. But in buying and selling, size offers market power. The challenge, then, is to be both big and small to capitalize on the advantages of each.

When Intuit grew from a software start-up to an established company selling popular accounting software, it brought in a CEO recruited from General Electric, Steve Bennett, to mesh big-company skills with Intuit's entrepreneurial energy. Bennett helped the company reevaluate its strategy to find areas of new growth. After popular Intuit products such as QuickBooks and TurboTax captured most of the market for accounting and tax preparation software, the company expanded into the online banking market with QuickenLoans. In 2017, QuickenLoans was the largest online lender in the United States.[29]

Here's an alternative perspective: companies such as Starbucks and Amazon are very large companies that work hard to act small and maintain a sense of intimacy with employees and customers. Both are considered among the best-managed companies in the world. To avoid problems of growth and size, they decentralize decision making and organize around small, adaptive, team-based work units.

Like many businesses, many social enterprises want to grow, in order to expand their impact. The nearby *"Social Enterprise"* box discusses some unique issues related to scaling SEs.

Bottom Line

Small size may improve speed. *A salesperson learns about a customer's new challenge. Why might a small company be able to react to this information faster?*

The challenge is to be both big and small to capitalize on the advantages of each.

©Paul Sakuma/AP Images

Downsizing   As large companies attempt to gain or regain responsiveness, they sometimes consider downsizing. **Downsizing** is the planned elimination of positions or jobs. Common approaches to downsizing include eliminating functions, hierarchical levels, or even whole units.[30] Another option is to replace full-time employees with less expensive part-time or temporary workers.

Recognizing that people will be unemployed, frightened, and perhaps unable to pay their bills, managers usually opt

Social Enterprise

Increasing Impact: Scaling Social Enterprises

Social enterprises typically begin as small, grassroots efforts whose goal is to create a sustainable organization that helps solve important social problems. For example, Living Goods, a U.S.-based nonprofit, sells essential products such as high-efficiency stoves, fortified foods, and pharmaceuticals "through an Avon-like network of microfranchises in Uganda." Sautil, based in Brazil, uses a web-based platform to provide free health care information to over 100,000 impoverished Brazilians.

What happens when social enterprises want to scale their operations to help more people? How can they expand globally? Here are some unique issues social enterprises face when planning for growth:

1. *Consider alliances with governments.* Governments are the largest consumers of social investment. If a social enterprise's mission aligns with a government's social investment priorities, the two can form a productive alliance. Currently, the G8 governments view social enterprises as a way of "tackling social problems, driving innovation and helping economic growth."

2. *Partner with big businesses.* Big businesses can bring considerable resources to bear on social problems. For this to happen, social enterprises need to develop a viable business model that big businesses are willing to support. Network for Good, an online giving and fund-raising platform, was founded with the help of AOL, the Cisco Foundation, and Yahoo!. Since 2001, the social enterprise has processed over $1 billion for more than 100,000 nonprofits.

3. *Do not lose sight of what matters.* As a social enterprise grows in size and complexity, it risks becoming

©McGraw-Hill Education/Roberts Publishing Services

"detached and unresponsive to the grassroots." Selco Solar, a provider of sustainable energy solutions, manages this risk of becoming too big by "incubating others who can replicate their model in other geographic areas, rather than scaling themselves." Like for-profit companies, social enterprises need to strike the right balance between big and small.[31]

Questions

- As social enterprises try to get larger, what unique challenges do they face?

- What are some of the drawbacks associated with partnering with governments or big businesses? If you ran an SE, which of these options would you pursue?

for downsizing only in response to some kind of pressure. Traditionally, companies have downsized when product demand falls and seems unlikely to rebound in the short run. Laying off workers is a way to avoid paying people who aren't needed to produce goods or services, and reduce costs so that the company remains profitable—or at least viable—until the next upturn in business.

Manufacturing in the United States had been hit hard by layoffs and closings in recent decades. The last recession forced widespread downsizing across many industries, not just manufacturing. Although companies rehired workers during the recovery, tough competition still dictates that they stay as lean as possible.

Done appropriately, with inefficient layers eliminated and resources focused more on adding customer value than on wasteful internal processes, downsizing can indeed lead to a more agile firm. In that case, downsizing can be called **rightsizing**—achieving the size at which the company performs most effectively.

You might refer back to our discussion in Chapter 1 about some of the things you can do to manage your own career successfully in an era where downsizing is a normal occurrence. And for an example of a company that has made downsizing part of its effort to enjoy the advantages of being both big and small, see "Management in Action: Progress Report."

rightsizing

A successful effort to achieve an appropriate size at which the company performs most effectively.

Management in Action

GE HAS BIG ADVANTAGES—AND TRIES TO ACT SMALL

Writing to stakeholders in the company's annual report, GE chief executive Jeffrey Immelt stated: "Positioning GE to win has required change. Every leader talks about change, but most are just managing momentum. This is a luxury we didn't have in GE. We refocused the company to be in businesses where we can lead while investing in new capability to capture future growth. We want GE to be essential to our customers, investors, and the world."

Immelt is referring to the reduction in its financial business and renewed focus on what it does best, developing industrial solutions for customers around the globe. The company operates in several industries, and when it wants to launch new products, it has the resources to do so. Thanks to its 50,000 engineers and scientists, GE ranks in the top 10 companies for U.S. patent applications. In terms of the total value of its stock, GE is one of the world's largest companies.

Consider GE's response to the role big data has begun to play. Companies are analyzing detailed data about customers, employees, and operations so they can identify how to make significant improvements in efficiency and quality. GE got on board by setting up its GE Global Research in California, near Silicon Valley, and hiring hundreds of software and statistical experts to make GE's equipment and systems part of the big-data revolution. Applications include jet engines that monitor their own performance, sensors on hospital equipment to streamline operations, and systems for automating train traffic.

Another example is GE's creation of an energy-efficient battery for heavy-duty use. Applying technology from more than 30 patents it already owned, GE set up a team Immelt calls "a start-up within the Company." GE staffed the team with its own experts from several industries and consulted with customers around the globe. Potential applications such as powering cell phone towers and electric buses, and storing energy at wind farms, could make the battery a billion-dollar business.

Despite the advantages of bigness, Immelt was concerned about the downside, that people in a giant corporation can be more attuned to its rules and habits than to customers' needs. His solution was to focus on measuring whether GE is delivering on its purpose—its mission to "build, move, power and cure the world." GE sold unrelated businesses, such as NBC Universal, and downsized others, such as GE Capital. It plans to merge its oil and gas business with that of Baker Hughes to create what Immelt called "a broad industry leader" in fuel.

The focused approach is also shaping the way GE develops managers. In the past, high-potential managers moved from one industry to another on their way up GE's hierarchy. Today they are likelier to specialize in an industry. GE's recent split of its energy business into three units (Power and Water, Oil and Gas, and Energy Management) opened up more paths for developing leaders within those related industries, even as it removed layers of management from the former energy unit.[32]

- How does GE benefit from being large?
- How can GE also reap some of the benefits of smallness?

Customers and the Responsive Organization

An organization's strategy and size influence its agility, adaptability, and structure. The point of designing and structuring a responsive, agile organization is to enable it to meet and exceed the expectations of its customers—the people who purchase its good or services and whose continued patronage helps drive sustained success.

Any business unit must take into account at least three core players in the *strategic triangle:* the company itself, the competition, and the customer. Successful organizations use their strengths to create value by meeting customer requirements better than competitors do. In this section, we discuss how organizations maintain and extend a competitive advantage with their customers.

Customer Relationship Management

customer relationship management (CRM)

A multifaceted process focusing on creating two-way exchanges with customers to foster intimate knowledge of their needs, wants, and buying patterns.

Customer relationship management (CRM) is a multifaceted process, typically using information technologies, that fosters two-way exchanges with customers so that firms know "intimately" their needs, wants, and buying patterns. Firms acquire this knowledge by applying predictive analytical techniques to the voluminous data (aka, big data) collected from customers. The goal of this analysis is to identify patterns from current and historical data sets in order to make the best possible business decisions.

Ideally, a company can use predictive analysis to figure out how to deliver exactly what customers want.[33] Capital One analyzes over 100 variables to predict the optimal time to make credit card offers to customers.[34] Companies that use CRM effectively learn to both understand and anticipate the needs of current and potential customers. In that way, CRM is part of a business strategy for managing customers to maximize their long-term value to the enterprise.[35]

As you know, customers want quality goods and services, low cost, innovative products, and speed. Traditional thinking is that trade-offs must be made among these basic customer wants. For instance, customers wanted high quality or low costs passed along in the form of low prices. But world-class companies know that the trade-off mentality no longer applies. Customers want it *all,* and they know that somewhere an organization exists that will provide it all.

If all companies try to satisfy customers, how can one firm realize a competitive advantage? World-class companies know that almost any advantage is temporary because competitors will strive to catch up. Simply stated—although obviously not easily done—a company attains and retains competitive advantage by continuing to improve. This concept—in Japan famously called *kaizen,* or continuous improvement—is a vital part of operations strategy.

> World-class companies know that the trade-off mentality no longer applies.

The traditional meaning of "customer" has grown to include internal customers. The word *customer* now refers to any recipient of work—the next person or unit in the production process, or wherever the work goes next in the sequence.[36] This highlights the interdependence among units, and means that all functions—not just marketing people—have to be concerned with customer satisfaction. Any recipient of a person's work, whether co-worker, boss, subordinate, or external party, should be viewed as the customer.

Professor Michael Porter offered a deeper and now very popular way to understand how organizations can add customer value to their products. A **value chain** is the sequence of activities that flow from raw materials to the delivery of a good or service, with additional value created at each step. You can see a generic value chain in Exhibit 9.3. Each step in the chain adds value to the good or service:

Research and development focus on innovation and new products.
Inbound logistics receive and store raw materials and distribute them to operations.

value chain

The sequence of activities that flow from raw materials to the delivery of a good or service, with additional value created at each step.

EXHIBIT 9.3   Generic Value Chain

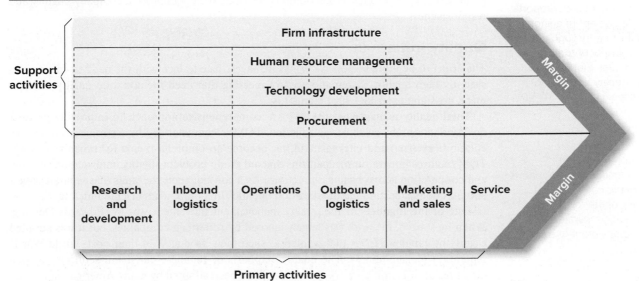

SOURCE: Porter, M., *Competitive Advantage: Creating and Sustaining Superior Performance.* New York: Free Press, 1985.

The Digital World

In the realm of customer relations, continuous improvement includes continually changing to connect with customers, even without waiting for customers to make the first move. Coca-Cola, Philips, the American Red Cross, and other organizations have adopted Salesforce.com's Service Cloud application, which helps companies find customers who take their questions and problems to Facebook, Twitter, or other social networking communities. Customer service agents can locate messages about their products and then offer to help, potentially saving a customer relationship.[37]

Companies know mistakes can go viral at the speed of light with social media. Videos (United forcefully removing a paying customer from a plane due to its overbooking mistake), screengrabs (Abercrombie & Fitch CEO stating they are exclusionary on purpose), and recordings of customer service calls (Comcast's refusal to cancel a customer's service) can be and are posted easily. Being able to directly address a customer with a complaint, or quickly realize and then address an issue, is critical to effective customer relationship management.

Operations transform the raw materials into final product.

Outbound logistics warehouse the product and handle its distribution.

Marketing and sales identify customer requirements and get customers to purchase the product.

Service offers customer support, such as repair, after the item has been bought.

When the total value created—that is, what customers are willing to pay—exceeds the cost of providing the good or service, the result is the profit margin.[38]

Managers can add customer value and build competitive advantage by paying close attention to the value chain—each step in it, plus the ways in which each step interacts with the others. For example, Walmart adds customer value via economies of scale, reducing its materials and operations costs, and Amazon adds customer value by developing innovative distribution channels.

An excellent way to leverage the value chain is for different elements of the chain to collaborate in finding and creating new sources of value. Nike shares its business plans and strategies with its suppliers—what it calls its strategic partners—to encourage collaborative thinking. Sales staff communicate with operations staff, before the manufacturing process even starts, to develop new products jointly. Service managers constantly report back to operations about defects and work with operations and suppliers to reduce and eliminate them. Creating productive collaborations can dramatically improve a company's agility and responsiveness.

Quality Initiatives

The effort to be more responsive brings managers face to face with the need to ensure consistently high quality. Systematic ways of meeting that need include total quality management, six sigma, and ISO 9001 standards.

Total quality management (TQM) is a comprehensive approach to improving product quality and thereby customer satisfaction. TQM is characterized by a strong customer orientation (external and internal) and has become an umbrella theme for organizing work. TQM requires integrative mechanisms that aid group problem solving, information sharing, and cooperation across business functions. As a consequence, the walls that separate stages and functions fade, and the organization operates in a more team-oriented manner.[39]

One of the founders of the quality management movement was W. Edwards Deming. When he started, his work was largely ignored by American companies, but it was adopted eagerly by Japanese firms that wanted to shed their productss of their post–World War II reputation for shoddiness. The quality emphasis of Japanese car manufacturing was one direct result of Deming's work, which has since been adopted by many American and other companies worldwide. As listed in Exhibit 9.4, Deming's "14 points" of quality emphasized

---

total quality management (TQM)

An integrative approach to management that supports the attainment of customer satisfaction through a wide variety of tools and techniques that result in high-quality goods and services.

Bottom Line

High quality requires organization-wide commitment. *What happens when the commitment to quality at the top of the company is weaker than the commitment to saving money?*

1.	Create constancy of purpose—strive for long-term improvement rather than short-term profit.
2.	Adopt the new philosophy—don't tolerate delays and mistakes.
3.	Cease dependence on mass inspection—build quality into the process on the front end.
4.	End the practice of awarding business on price tag alone—build long-term relationships.
5.	Improve constantly and forever the system of production and service—at each stage.
6.	Institute training and retraining—continually update methods and thinking.
7.	Institute leadership—provide the resources needed for effectiveness.
8.	Drive out fear—people must believe it is safe to report problems or ask for help.
9.	Break down barriers among departments—promote teamwork.
10.	Eliminate slogans, exhortations, and arbitrary targets—supply methods, not buzzwords.
11.	Eliminate numerical quotas—they are contrary to the idea of continuous improvement.
12.	Remove barriers to pride in workmanship—allow autonomy and spontaneity.
13.	Institute a vigorous program of education and retraining—people are assets, not commodities.
14.	Take action to accomplish the transformation—provide a structure that enables quality.

EXHIBIT 9.4
Deming's 14 Points of Quality

a holistic approach to management that demands intimate understanding of the process—the delicate interaction of materials, machines, and people that determines productivity, quality, and competitive advantage.

> At six sigma, a product or process is defect-free 99.99966 percent of the time.

Six Sigma   An approach called **six sigma quality** is one of the most important contributors to total quality management: a set of statistical tools to analyze the causes of product defects. Sigma is the Greek letter used to designate the estimated standard deviation or variation in a process. (The higher the sigma level, the lower the amount of variation and the higher the quality.) The product defects analyzed can include anything that results in customer dissatisfaction—for example, late delivery, wrong shipment, or poor customer service as well as problems with the product itself.

Once the defect is identified, managers then engage the organization in a determined, comprehensive effort to eliminate its causes and reduce it to the lowest practicable level. At six sigma, a product or process is defect-free 99.99966 percent of the time—fewer than 3.4 defects or mistakes per million. Reaching that goal almost always requires a fundamental restructuring of internal processes and relationships with suppliers and customers.

Managers may create teams from all parts of the organization to implement the process improvements that will prevent defects from arising. Motorola, where six sigma was developed, and General Electric, whose success with six sigma helped to make the technique famous, credit the method with helping them improve efficiency and quality. Today many companies are combining six sigma's drive to improve quality with a method of improving efficiency known as lean manufacturing, described later in this chapter. This hybrid effort, often called *lean six sigma,* is a powerful driver of responsiveness and agility.

Commitment to total quality requires a thorough, extensive, integrated approach to organizing. To encourage American companies to make that commitment and achieve

six sigma quality

A method of systematically analyzing work processes to identify and eliminate virtually all causes of defects, standardizing the processes to reach the lowest practicable level of any cause of customer dissatisfaction.

excellence, the Malcolm Baldrige National Quality Award was established in 1987. Recent winners include Don Chalmers Ford in Rio Rancho, New Mexico, Kindred Nursing and Rehabilitation Center in Kellogg, Idaho, and Memorial Hermann Hospital in Sugar Land, Texas.[40]

A company can improve its responsiveness to customers and convey to them clearly that it has done so via certifications from the International Organization for Standardization (known globally as ISO), which sets a wide variety of exacting standards for parts, materials, products, and organizational processes and practices.

ISO 9001

A series of quality standards developed by a committee working under the International Organization for Standardization to improve total quality in all businesses for the benefit of producers and consumers.

ISO 9001   The requirements for a quality management system that will ensure such best practices are spelled out in **ISO 9001**. Any type or size of organization can improve its total quality by successfully meeting specific standards set out in eight principles:[41]

1. *Customer focus*—learning and addressing customer needs and expectations.
2. *Leadership*—establishing a vision and goals, establishing trust, and providing employees with the resources and inspiration to meet goals.
3. *Involvement of people*—establishing an environment in which employees understand their contribution, engage in problem solving, and acquire and share knowledge.
4. *Process approach*—defining the tasks needed to carry out each process successfully and assigning responsibility for them.
5. *System approach to management*—putting processes together into efficient systems that work together effectively.
6. *Continual improvement*—teaching people how to identify areas for improvement and rewarding them for making improvements.
7. *Factual approach to decision making*—gathering accurate performance data, sharing the data with employees, and using the data to make decisions.
8. *Mutually beneficial supplier relationships*—working in a cooperative way with suppliers.

U.S. companies first became interested in ISO 9001 because overseas customers, particularly those in the European Union, embraced it. Companies that comply with the quality guidelines of ISO 9001 can apply for official certification. Some countries and companies demand certification as an acknowledgment of compliance before they will do business. Some U.S. customers are making the same demand.

Pursuing certification is not the end of the quality effort, but an initial step. Rather than defining how to operate perfectly, ISO 9001 standards establish practices that enable the organization to keep improving—assuming that it continues to follow these best practices.

Bottom Line

Effective reengineering can cut costs significantly. *What other success drivers can reengineering improve?*

Reengineering

Building from TQM and organizing around customer needs, companies embraced reengineering (introduced in Chapter 1). The goal of reengineering is to revolutionize key organizational systems and processes by answering this question: "If you were the customer, how would you like us to operate?" The answer forms a vision for how the organization should run, and then managers make decisions and take actions accordingly. Processes including product development, order fulfillment, customer service, inventory management, billing, and production are redesigned from scratch as if the organization were brand new and just starting out.

In an early example of this, Procter & Gamble used reengineering to make its products more competitive. The company learned that the average family buying its products rather than private-label or lower-price brands paid an extra $725 per year. That figure was far too high and seemed to warn that high prices could drive the company to extinction.

Additional data also signaled the need for P&G to change. Market shares of famous brands such as Comet, Mr. Clean, and Ivory had been dropping for 25 years. P&G was making 55 price changes *daily* on about 80 brands, and inaccurate billings were common. Its plants were inefficient, and overhead was the highest in the business. P&G had to cut prices, and to do that, it had to cut costs.

In response to this self-examination, P&G reengineered. It tore down and rebuilt nearly every activity that contributed to high costs. It redesigned the way it develops, manufactures, distributes, prices, markets, and sells products. After the reengineering, price changes became rare, factories became far more efficient, inventory levels fell, and sales and profits rose. P&G was able to price its brands nearer to the prices of store brands. P&G reinvented itself as a leader in the industry once again and created for itself a long-term competitive advantage.[42]

Such massive reengineering requires much more than a directive from the top, a change in the formal organization structure, the introduction of new technology, and a well-communicated strategic change. Rather, reengineering requires those things plus a fundamental transformation in the way the parts of the organization work together. They need to see each other as partners in a common effort more than as members of a particular unit or subunit. Teams throughout the organization must share information on problems and possible solutions, and some teams should ask customers and other stakeholders for feedback. When useful information is gathered widely from within and outside the organization, the solutions will enjoy wider acceptance, motivation is higher, and implementation is faster.

You can see that reengineering is not about making minor changes here and there. It is about completely overhauling the operation, in revolutionary ways, to achieve the greatest possible benefits for both the customer and the company.

> Reengineering often requires a fundamental change in the way the parts of the organization work together.

Technology and Organizational Agility

We have discussed strategy, size, and customers as influences on organizational design and agility. We now turn to one more critical factor affecting an organization's structure and responsiveness: its technology.

Broadly, **technology** is the methods, processes, systems, and skills used to transform resources (inputs) into products (outputs). We will discuss technology and innovation more fully in Chapter 17 , but here we highlight how technology affects organizational design.

LO 6

technology
The systematic application of scientific knowledge to a new product, process, or service.

Types of Technology Configurations

Research by Joan Woodward laid the foundation for understanding technology and structure. According to Woodward, three basic technologies characterize how work is done: small batch, large batch, and continuous process. These classifications are equally useful for describing either service or manufacturing technologies. Each differs in terms of volume produced and variety of goods/services offered. Each also has a different influence on how managers organize and structure the work of their organizations.[43]

Small Batch Technologies   When a company provides goods or services in very low volume or **small batches**, it is called a *job shop*. A fairly typical example of a job shop is PMF Industries, a small custom metalworking company in Williamsport, Pennsylvania, that produces aluminum, stainless steel, and titanium assemblies for medical and other uses. In the service industry, restaurants or doctors' offices are job shops because they provide a high variety of low-volume, customized services.

In a small batch organization, structure tends to be organic: not a lot of rules and formal procedures, and (often) decentralized decision making. People engage heavily in mutual adjustment.

small batch
Technologies that produce goods and services in low volume.

Large Batch Technologies   As volume increases, product variety usually decreases. Companies with higher volumes and lower varieties than a job shop use **large batch**, or mass production, technologies. Examples include the auto assembly operations of General Motors, Ford, and Chrysler. In the service sector, Subway and Chipotle are good examples.

large batch
Technologies that produce goods and services in high volume.

Dell revolutionized the concept of mass customization. The production process from order to delivery is managed electronically, which allows Dell to build servers efficiently and its customers to know where their server is during each step of the process.

©PAUL SAKUMA/AP Images

Their production runs are highly standardized, and all customers receive similar (if not identical) products. Machines and robotics tend to replace people in the physical execution of work. People run the machines.

With large batch technology, structure tends to be more mechanistic: more rules and formal procedures, more centralized decision making, and higher spans of control.

Continuous Process Technologies Companies at the very-high-volume end of the scale use **continuous process** technologies—normally they do not stop and start. International Paper and Occidental Chemicals use continuous process technologies to produce a very limited number of products. People are removed from the physical work itself, which is done entirely by machines and/or computers. In some cases, people run the computers that run the machines. Continuous process technology requires less monitoring and supervision, so structure can be more organic: fewer rules and regulations and more informal communication.

Organizing for Flexible Manufacturing

Although volume and variety traditionally required trade-offs, companies today try to produce both high-volume and high-variety products at the same time. This is **mass customization**.[44] Automobiles, clothes, computers, and other products are manufactured to match each customer's taste, specifications, and budget. Although this seemed only a fantasy a few years ago, mass customization quickly became prevalent among leading firms. You now can buy clothes cut to your proportions, supplements with the exact blend of the vitamins and minerals you like, and textbooks with chapters chosen by your professor.

Companies want to deliver mass customization at low cost. They organize (see Exhibit 9.5) around a dynamic network of relatively independent operating units.[45] Each unit performs a specific process or task—called a *module*—such as making a component, performing a credit check, or using a particular welding method. Outside suppliers or vendors may perform some modules.

Different modules join forces to make the good or provide a service. The unique requests of each customer determine when and how the various modules interact with one another. The manager's responsibility is to make it easier and less costly for modules to come together, complete their tasks, and then recombine to meet the next customer demand.

Mass customization is a never-ending campaign to expand the number of ways a company can satisfy customers.

Computer-Integrated Manufacturing Mass customization is made possible by **computer-integrated manufacturing (CIM)**, which links computerized production efforts. Two major elements of CIM, computer-aided design and computer-aided manufacturing, share data for product design, testing, manufacturing, and quality control.

These systems can produce high-variety and high-volume products at the same time.[46] They may also offer greater control and predictability of production processes, reduced waste, faster throughput times, and higher quality. But managers cannot buy their way out of

Bottom Line

Today's technologies offer customization at low cost. *Give an example of a product you'd like to have customized for your personal preferences. Have you found a customized version yet? If not, you may someday.*

---

continuous process

A process that is highly automated and has a continuous production flow.

mass customization

The production of varied, individually customized products at the low cost of standardized, mass-produced products.

computer-integrated manufacturing (CIM)

The use of computer-aided design and computer-aided manufacturing to sequence and optimize a number of production processes.

EXHIBIT 9.5
Key Features in Mass
Customization

Area	High Variety and Customization
Product design	Collaborative design; significant input from customers.
	Short product development cycles.
	Constant innovation.
Operations and processes	Flexible processes.
	Business process reengineering (BPR).
	Use of modules.
	Continuous improvement (CI).
	Reduced setup and changeover times.
	Reduced lead times.
	JIT delivery and processing of materials and components.
	Production to order.
	Shorter cycle times.
Quality management	Quality measured in customer delight.
	Defects treated as capability failures.
Organizational structure	Dynamic network of relatively autonomous operating units.
	Learning relationships.
	Integration of the value chain.
	Team-based structure.
Workforce management	Empowerment of employees.
	High value on knowledge, information, and diversity of employee capabilities.
	New product teams.
	Broad job descriptions.
Emphasis	Low-cost production of high-quality, customized products.

Reprinted with permission of APICS—The Educational Society for Resource Management, *Production and Inventory Management* 41, no. 1 (2000) pp.56–65.

competitive trouble simply by investing in superior technology alone. They also must ensure that their organization has the necessary strategic and people strengths.

Flexible Factories   CIM enables **flexible factories**, which serve customers needing fast turnaround on relatively small orders. In contrast to traditional factories, flexible factories have short production runs, organize work flow around products, and use decentralized scheduling.[47] Instead of moving large orders of standard products through assembly lines, flexible factories have work cells or teams focus on one product at a time. The people on the shop floor doing the work make scheduling decisions, so they can adapt schedules as needed.

Lean Manufacturing   Another organizing approach, **lean manufacturing**, strives for the highest possible productivity and total quality, cost-effectively, by eliminating unnecessary steps in the production process and continually striving for improvement. Rejects are unacceptable, and underused staff, overhead, and inventory are considered wasteful. Well-managed lean production allows a company to develop, produce, and distribute products with half or less of the human effort, space, tools, time, and overall cost.[48]

flexible factories

Manufacturing plants that have short production runs, are organized around products, and use decentralized scheduling.

lean manufacturing

An operation that strives to achieve the highest possible productivity and total quality, cost-effectively, by eliminating unnecessary steps in the production process and continually striving for improvement.

EXHIBIT 9.6
Conditions That Support
Lean Manufacturing

People are broadly trained rather than specialized.
Communication is informal and horizontal among line workers.
Equipment is general-purpose.
Work is organized in teams, or cells, that produce a group of similar products.
Supplier relationships are long-term and cooperative.
Product development is concurrent, not sequential, and is done by cross-functional teams.

SOURCES: Sahin, F., "Manufacturing Competitiveness: Different Systems to Achieve the Same Results," *Production and Inventory Management Journal* 41, no. 1 (First Quarter 2000), pp.56–65; and Vasilash, G. S., "Flexible Thinking: How Need, Innovation, Teamwork a Whole Bunch of Machining Centers Have Transformed TRW Tillsonburg into a Model of Lean Manufacturing," *Automotive Manufacturing & Production* 111, no. 10 (October 1999), pp.64–65.

Some hospitals use lean principles to reduce costs and patient waiting times while improving safety.

©Ariel Skelley/Getty Images RF

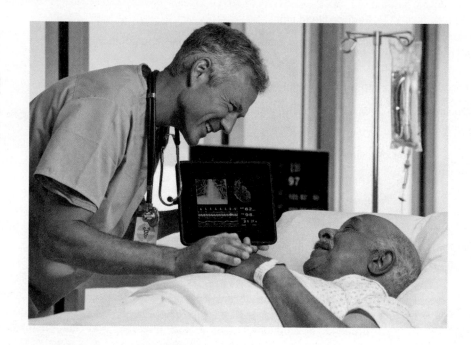

The emphasis is on quality, speed, and flexibility more than on cost, efficiency, and hierarchy. A well-known example is small in detail but large in symbolism: Line workers sometimes have authority to immediately halt the operation and signal for help if they spot a problem. That's a lot of delegated power and discretion, given up by management to operative-level workers in the interest of flexibility, quality, and speedy problem solving.

The lean approach is used for services as well as manufacturing. Banks use lean principles to support their growth strategies, energy companies to lower costs, and retailers to improve customer service.[49] Wipro, an Indian software developer, uses lean methods to "deliver projects that perform better and with lower variation."[50]

Many companies have tried to become leaner by cutting overhead costs, laying off operative-level workers, eliminating layers of management, and using capital equipment more efficiently. But if the move to lean manufacturing is simply a harsh, haphazard cost-cutting approach, the result will be chaos, overworked people, and low morale.

Meeting the conditions specified in Exhibit 9.6 helps to ensure the that the lean approach works well.

Bottom Line
Lean manufacturing strives for high quality, speed, sustainability, and low cost. *Which of the quality improvement approaches could be combined with lean manufacturing?*

Organizing for Speed: Time-Based Competition

Companies worldwide have devoted so much energy to improving product quality that high quality is now the prevailing standard in many industries. Competition has driven quality to such heights—although less lofty when firms operate primarily on a low-cost basis—that quality alone is no longer enough to differentiate one competitor from another. Time is an additional advantage that can separate market leaders from also-rans.[51]

Companies must learn what the customer needs and meet those needs as quickly as possible. **Time-based competition (TBC)** refers to strategies that reduce the total time needed to deliver the good or service. TBC has several key organizational elements: logistics, just-in-time (JIT), and concurrent engineering.

Logistics   The movement of resources into the organization (inbound) and products from the organization to its customers (outbound) is called **logistics**. Like the supply chain (Chapter 2), logistics can become a vital advantage when managed well.

The world of logistics includes the great mass of parts, materials, and products moving via trucks, trains, planes, and ships from and to every region of the globe. Depending on the product, duplication and inefficiency in distribution can cost far more than making the product itself, and slowdowns can cause products to go out of stock so that consumers choose alternatives.

One technology that helps some companies improve logistics efficiency and speed is radio frequency identification (RFID) tags. When manufacturers label their products with RFID tags, automated readers track where each product is in the distribution system, including which items are selling in each store. Macy's uses RFID tags on apparel and shoes for inventory tracking; this ensures that items are replenished and in front of customers during peak selling periods.

Walmart is trying to keep its well-known leadership role in distribution by asking suppliers to use RFID. However, many of them cannot afford to institute the new system while also meeting Walmart's demands to keep prices at a minimum.[52]

Just-in-Time Operations   An additional element of TBC is **just-in-time (JIT)** operations. JIT manufactures subassemblies and components in very small lots and delivers them to the next stage in the process precisely at the time needed (just in time). A customer order triggers a factory order and the production process. The supplying work centers do not produce the next lot of product until the consuming work center requires it. Even external suppliers deliver to the company just in time.

Just-in-time is a companywide philosophy oriented toward eliminating waste and improving materials throughout all operations. It reduces excess inventory and costs. The ultimate goal of JIT is to serve the customer better by providing higher levels of quality and service.

Dell was an early and effective just-in-time operation. Production of a customized computer begins upon receiving a consumer's order with specifications. Contrast this approach with traditional production methods, which require extremely costly warehousing of inventory and parts, uncertain production runs, considerable waste, no customizing capability, and lengthy delivery times.

JIT represents a number of key production and organizational concepts, including:

Elimination of waste. Eliminate all waste of time, people, machinery, space, and materials.

Perfect quality. Produce perfect parts and produce products exactly when needed in the exact quantities needed.

Reduced cycle times. Reduce setup times for equipment, move parts only short distances (machinery is placed in closer proximity), and eliminate all delays.

Employee involvement. The workers make production decisions. Managers and supervisors are coaches. Top management pledges that there will never be layoffs due to employees finding new efficiencies.

time-based competition (TBC)

Strategies aimed at reducing the total time needed to deliver a good or service.

logistics

The movement of the right goods in the right amount to the right place at the right time.

just-in-time (JIT)

A system that calls for subassemblies and components to be manufactured in very small lots and delivered to the next stage of the production process just as they are needed.

concurrent engineering

A design approach in which all relevant functions cooperate jointly and continually in a maximum effort aimed at producing high-quality products that meet customers' needs.

Bottom Line

Time-based competition brings speed to all organization processes.
Give an example of a situation in which speed would be important for a book publisher.

When relevant functions interact with each other regularly, the greater the opportunity to improve processes, maximize efficiency, and reduce cost.

©Glowimages RF

Value-added manufacturing. Do only those things that add value to the finished product. If it doesn't add value, don't do it. For example, inspection does not add value to the finished product, so make the product correctly the first time so inspection is no longer necessary.

Discovery of problems and prevention of recurrence. Foolproofing, or fail-safing, is a key component of JIT. People try to find the weak link in the chain by forcing problem areas to the surface in order to take preventive measures.

JIT has limits. It's not the most efficient choice when the costs of delivery exceed the costs of storage. And if suppliers have trouble fulfilling orders, the whole system breaks down. JIT requires close ties with suppliers, so finding ready replacements can be difficult.

Concurrent Engineering   JIT is a vital component of TBC, but JIT traditionally concentrates on reducing time in only one function: manufacturing. TBC attempts to deliver speed in *all* functions—product development, manufacturing, logistics, and services. Customers will not be impressed if you manufacture quickly but it takes weeks for them to receive their products or get a problem solved.

Many companies use concurrent (sometimes called simultaneous) engineering as a cornerstone of their TBC strategy. **Concurrent engineering**—also an important component of total quality management—is a major departure from the old development process that did various functional tasks sequentially. When R&D completed its part of the project, the work was passed over the wall to engineering, which completed its task and passed it over the wall to manufacturing, and so on. This process was highly inefficient, and errors took a long time to correct.

In contrast, concurrent engineering uses a team-based approach to incorporate the perspectives of all functions—and customers and suppliers—from the beginning of the process. This results in a higher-quality product that is designed for efficient manufacturing *and* meeting customer needs.[53] R. A. Jones & Co., which makes machines used for packaging, moved the engineers' work stations to the factory floor so the engineers and production employees would interact routinely. With more communication during the design process, they coordinated and performed far more effectively.[54]

Some managers resist the idea of concurrent engineering. Why should marketing, product planning and design, and R&D allow manufacturing to get involved in their work? First, decisions made during the early, product concept stage determine most of the manufacturing cost and quality. Second, manufacturing can offer ideas about the product because of its experience with the prior generation of the product and with direct customer feedback. Third, the other functions can learn early on what manufacturing can and cannot do. Fourth, when manufacturing is involved from the start, it is a full and true partner and will be more committed to decisions it helped make.

Final Thoughts on Organizational Agility

You know now that each major approach to organizing has strengths and limitations. Know also that the advantages of even innovative, leading-edge structures and systems are likely to be short-lived if they become fixed rather than remain flexible. Smart managers and smart competitors soon catch up.

Today's advantages are tomorrow's table stakes: the minimum requirements that need to be met if an organization expects to be a major player. To retain or gain a competitive

Management in Action

GE'S PURSUIT OF HIGH QUALITY AND LEANNESS

GE tries to be responsive to customers in multiple ways. To improve quality, GE applies six sigma. To improve efficiency by eliminating waste, it uses lean initiative methods. These methods are not just for manufacturing, either; the company has used six sigma for finance, human resources, and other key service activities.

GE considers six sigma part of its culture, not just a process tacked on. Employees must apply the concepts of six sigma to all GE's processes and in the design of its products. Six sigma is the latest initiative in a series of efforts beginning in the 1980s. Then it launched a program called Work-Out to empower employees, hear ideas from employees at all levels, and eliminate bureaucracy and boundaries that got in the way of making improvements.

The Work-Out initiative continues to create a learning environment in which quality improvement can proceed more effectively. GE trains all its employees in the six sigma practices, with the most basic training being quality overview seminars. Employees also learn to participate on six sigma teams, and some learn the statistical and quality-control techniques needed to become six sigma Green Belts, Black Belts, and Master Black Belts.

Lean gets credit for enabling GE to move some of its appliance manufacturing back to the United States from China and Mexico, according to Chip Blankenship, chief executive of GE Appliances and Lighting. GE seeks input from employees at all levels about how to make its processes more efficient. At the GE Appliances facility in Louisville, Kentucky, one outcome of the lean initiative is that all functions related to manufacturing—design, product development, engineering, production, and quality control—are located at the same facility. When an employee learns of customer concerns or a production problem, everyone is at hand to respond.

GE continues experimenting with methods for becoming more responsive. For example, GE Aviation used a concurrent engineering process, working with its suppliers, to develop wing components for the Airbus A350 XWB. And a few years ago, GE software developers began trying out a technique known as Agile software development. This method entails developing new software with customers by creating a minimally viable product and making adjustments as they work. In one project for GE Healthcare, the Agile process cut development time by about half. [55]

In June 2017, GE announced that Jeff Immelt would be stepping down, consistent with a time frame determined several years earlier. John Flannery, president and CEO of GE Healthcare, became GE CEO on August 1.

- Based on the information in the three parts of this "Management in Action" case, how would you rate GE's organizational agility? Summarize your reasons for this rating.
- How is GE doing now, and what is it doing in terms of the management ideas you have learned here?

edge, managers should remember the principle with which we opened this chapter: The best organizations—and this includes the best managers within them—do not sit still. They keep thinking strategically, and continually improve their operations.

KEY TERMS

ambidextrous organization, p. 252

computer-integrated manufacturing (CIM), p. 266

concurrent engineering, p. 270

continuous process, p. 266

customer relationship management (CRM), p. 260

downsizing, p. 258

dynamic capabilities, p. 254

economies of scope, p. 257

flexible factories, p. 267

high-involvement organization, p. 256

ISO 9001, p. 264

just-in-time (JIT), p. 269

large batch, p. 265

lean manufacturing, p. 267

learning organization, p. 256

logistics, p. 269

mass customization, p. 266

mechanistic organization, p. 252

ordinary capabilities, p. 254

organic structure, p. 252

rightsizing, p. 259

six sigma quality, p. 263

small batch, p. 265

strategic alliance, p. 255

technology, p. 265

time-based competition (TBC), p. 269

total quality management (TQM), p. 262

value chain, p. 261

RETAINING WHAT YOU LEARNED

In Chapter 9, you learned that organizations exert control internally through formal structures and must respond to fast-changing demands in their environments. Organic structures, which are flexible in nature, are decentralized, informal, and guided by the actions of people with broad responsibilities. Certain strategies and organizational forms improve responsiveness, including core capabilities, strategic alliances, learning organizations, and high-involvement organizations. Small firms have certain advantages over their larger counterparts, including the ability to act quickly, respond to customer demands, and serve small niches. The ideal organization today harnesses the power of large firms while staying flexible. Driven to meet customer needs, firms adopt the principles of continuous improvement, total quality management, and six sigma quality (often combined with lean manufacturing). Reengineering efforts completely overhaul processes with the goal of providing world-class customer service. To organize for flexible manufacturing, organizations pursue mass customization via computer-integrated manufacturing and lean manufacturing. To organize for time-based competition, firms strengthen their logistics operations, consider just-in-time operations, and use concurrent engineering.

LO 1 **Discuss why it is critical for organizations to be responsive.**

- Organizations have a formal structure to help control what goes on within them.
- But to survive today, firms need more than control—they need responsiveness. They must act quickly and adapt to fast-changing demands.

LO 2 **Describe the qualities of an organic organization structure.**

- The organic form emphasizes flexibility. Organic organizations are decentralized, informal, and dependent on the judgment and expertise of people with broad responsibilities.
- The organic form is not a single formal structure but a concept that underlies all the new forms discussed in this chapter.

LO 3 **Identify strategies and dynamic organizational concepts that can improve an organization's responsiveness.**

- New and emerging organizational concepts and forms include core capabilities, strategic alliances, learning organizations, and high-involvement organizations.

LO 4 **Explain how a firm can be both big and small.**

- Historically, large organizations have had important advantages over small organizations. Today small size has advantages, including the ability to act quickly, respond to customer demands, and serve small niches.
- The ideal firm today combines the advantages of both large and small. It creates many small, flexible units, while corporate levels add value by taking advantage of size and power.

LO 5 **Summarize how firms organize to meet customer requirements.**

- Firms have embraced principles of continuous improvement, total quality management, and six sigma quality (often combined with lean manufacturing) to respond to customer needs.
- Baldrige criteria and ISO 9001 standards help firms organize to meet high quality specifications.
- Extending these, reengineering efforts are directed at completely overhauling processes to provide world-class customer service.

LO 6 **Identify ways that firms organize around different types of technology.**

- Organizations tend to move from organic structures to mechanistic structures and back to organic structures as they transition from small batch to large batch and continuous process technologies.
- For flexible manufacturing, organizations pursue mass customization via computer-integrated manufacturing and lean manufacturing.
- To organize for time-based competition, firms strengthen their logistics operations, consider just-in-time operations, and use concurrent engineering.

DISCUSSION QUESTIONS

1. Discuss evidence you have seen of the imperatives for change, flexibility, and responsiveness faced by today's firms.

2. Describe large, bureaucratic organizations with which you have had contact that have not responded flexibly to customer demands. Also describe examples of satisfactory responsiveness. What do you think accounts for the differences between the responsive and nonresponsive organizations?

3. Considering the potential advantages of large and small size, would you describe the feel of your college or university as big, small, or small within big? Why? What might make it feel different?

4. What is a core capability? What would you say are the core capabilities of Toyota, Walmart, and Apple? Brainstorm some creative new products and markets to which these capabilities could be applied.

5. If you were going into business for yourself, what would be your personal core capabilities? What capabilities do you have now, and what capabilities will you develop? Describe what your role would be in a network organization and the capabilities

and roles of other firms you would want in your network.

6. Using an Internet search engine, search for "strategic alliance" and identify three recently formed alliances. For each alliance, identify whether the companies' other products are generally competitors or complementary products. What are the goals of each alliance? What brought them together? Discuss how you think a

strategic alliance is or is not an effective way for these organizations to meet their goals.

7. What skills will you need to work effectively in (a) a learning organization, and (b) a high-involvement organization? Be specific, generating long lists. Would you enjoy working in these environments? Why or why not? What can you do to prepare yourself for these eventualities?

EXPERIENTIAL EXERCISES

9.1 MECHANISTIC AND ORGANIC STRUCTURES

OBJECTIVES

1. To think about your own preferences when it comes to working in a particular organizational structure.

2. To examine aspects of organizations by using as an example this class you are a member of.

INSTRUCTIONS

1. Complete the Mechanistic and Organic Worksheet here.

2. Meet in groups of four to six persons. Share your data from the worksheet. Discuss the reasons for your responses and analyze the factors that probably encouraged your instructor to choose the type of structure that now exists.

Mechanistic and Organic Worksheet

1. Indicate your general preference for working in one of these two organizational structures by circling the appropriate response:

| **Mechanistic** | 1 | 2 | 3 | 4 | 5 | 6 | 7 | 8 | 9 | 10 | **Organic** |

2. Indicate your perception of the form of organization that is used in this class by circling the appropriate response for each item:

A. **Task role definition**

| **Rigid** | 1 | 2 | 3 | 4 | 5 | 6 | 7 | 8 | 9 | 10 | **Flexible** |

B. **Communication**

| **Vertical** | 1 | 2 | 3 | 4 | 5 | 6 | 7 | 8 | 9 | 10 | **Multidirectional** |

C. **Decision making**

| **Centralized** | 1 | 2 | 3 | 4 | 5 | 6 | 7 | 8 | 9 | 10 | **Decentralized** |

D. **Sensitivity to the environment**

| **Closed** | 1 | 2 | 3 | 4 | 5 | 6 | 7 | 8 | 9 | 10 | **Open** |

SOURCE: From Davis, Keith and Newstrom, John W., *Human Behavior at Work,* p. 346. Copyright ©1993 McGraw-Hill Global Education Holdings LLC. All rights reserved. Used with permission.

9.2 THE WOODY MANUFACTURING COMPANY

OBJECTIVE
To apply the concepts learned about structure and agility at the individual, group, and organizational levels in designing the Woody Manufacturing Company.

TASK 1 (INDIVIDUAL ASSIGNMENT)

a. Read the following case study of the Woody Manufacturing Company.

b. Review the chapter carefully and choose the organizational design orientation that you feel can best guide you in developing the design for Mr. Woody.

c. Write down your thoughts on alternative management structures, pay systems, and allocation of work to individuals and groups.

TASK 2 (TEAM ASSIGNMENT)

a. Get together with your team and develop a proposal for Mr. Woody that, if followed, would help him fulfill his vision.

b. Prepare a five-minute presentation. Your typewritten team proposal is due prior to your team presentation in Mr. Woody's conference room.

Designing a New Furniture Company

Mr. Woody, the owner/operator of a small furniture company specializing in the manufacture of high-quality bar stools, has experienced a tremendous growth in demand for his products. He has standing orders for $750,000. Consequently, Mr. Woody has decided to expand his organization and attack the market aggressively. His stated mission is "to manufacture world-class products that are competitive in the world market in quality, reliability, performance, and profitability." He would like to create a culture where "pride, ownership, employment security, and trust" are a way of life. He just finished a set of interviews, and he has hired 32 new workers with the following skills:

Four skilled craftspeople.

Ten people with some woodworking experience.

Twelve people with no previous woodworking experience or other skills.

One nurse.

One schoolteacher.

One bookkeeper.

Three people with some managerial experience in nonmanufacturing settings.

Mr. Woody (with your help) must now decide how to design his new organization. This design will include the management structure, pay system, and the allocation of work to individuals and groups. The bar stool–making process has 15 steps:

1. Wood is selected.
2. Wood is cut to size.
3. Defects are removed.
4. Wood is planed to exact specifications.
5. Joints are cut.
6. Tops are glued and assembled.
7. Legs/bases are prepared.
8. Legs/bases are attached to tops.
9. Bar stools are sanded.
10. Stain is applied.
11. Varnish is applied.
12. Bar stools are sanded.
13. Varnish is reapplied.
14. Bar stools are packaged.
15. Bar stools are delivered to the customer.

Mr. Woody currently manufactures three kinds of bar stools (pedestal, four-legged corner, and four-legged recessed). There is no difference in the difficulty of making the three types of bar stools. Major cost variations have been associated with defective wood, imprecise cuts, and late deliveries to customers. Mr. Woody must decide how to organize his company to maintain high quality and profits.

He has thought about several options. He could have some individuals perform the first step for all types of bar stools; he could have an individual perform several steps for one type of bar stool; or he could have a team perform some combination of steps for one or more bar stools. He wonders whether how he organized would affect quality or costs. He's also aware that although the demand for all types of bar stools has been roughly equal over the long run, there were short periods where one type of bar stool was in greater demand than the others. Because Mr. Woody wants to use his people effectively, he has committed an expert in work design to help him set up an optimal organization.

Concluding Case

DIY STORES

DIY Stores is a nationwide chain that offers every tool and supply for repairing and maintaining a home. Shoppers at DIY can find paints and paintbrushes, screwdrivers and lumber, pliers and electrical conduit, spades and shrubs, and much more. Besides the wide variety under one roof, what sets DIY apart is its sales associates. The company hires avid do-it-yourselfers and retired trade workers, assigns them to work in departments where their know-how is relevant, provides training in new products and creative methods, and pays them a little more than they could earn by working for another retailer. The company also makes available fact sheets and lists of tips and building ideas. Together these efforts make DIY Stores a place where shoppers can go to get ideas and advice, so they get more than supplies for a project—they get all the ingredients they need for their project to succeed.

Over the past couple of decades, however, consumers have found an alternative to getting advice in a store: many prefer to do their research online, comfortably seated at a computer. If consumers can use a search engine or chat in an online community to figure out the best way to fix a leaky toilet or make a small bedroom look airy and bright, why would they trek into a store to ask? The answer, DIY's management feared, was that they wouldn't bother. If true, that trend placed DIY's competitive advantage at risk. The retailer needed to change with the times.

DIY's solution was to go where the consumers were: online. Management decided the company needed to supplement its in-store experts with online experts, employees who shared the same kinds of information on the Internet as they did in the stores. The company's corporate communications department was charged with developing a plan for this effort.

The department's people were used to thinking of corporate communications as something that originates at headquarters, so they initially thought the most efficient approach would be to hire a team of writers to work in offices at headquarters, blogging about new products and maintenance tips. But when they presented this plan to top management, one of the vice presidents raised a question: The company's salespeople were its base of knowledge. Why bring in new people? Why not figure out a way to use the human assets the company already had?

The corporate communications people went back to work on the plan. Probably some of the sales associates already were using the Internet themselves and knew how to write a blog and participate in social networking. Probably some of them had the necessary combination of helpfulness and writing skills. So they considered identifying those employees and inviting them to take jobs at headquarters. But as the group discussed this idea, they realized it had a flaw. If employees left the stores, they would no longer be seeing, selling, and watching customers' reactions to products. They would lose the hands-on and face-to-face experiences that kept them up to date and in touch with consumers. Also, consumers would quickly figure out that the online exchanges were not with a real DIY sales associate but with someone who had become a call center employee or professional communicator.

So the team arrived at an unusual plan. The company would identify Internet-savvy sales associates, but it wouldn't remove them from the stores. Rather, the associates who accepted the new position would work three days a week in a store and two days a week in an office, with their schedules staggered so that the online community would be active seven days a week. The company's executives were enthusiastic about this plan.

DIY contacted store managers in cities where it has regional offices. The store managers recommended employees they thought would deliver effective help online, and a team of recruiters interviewed these candidates and selected two dozen to provide an online presence. The typical employee selected had eight years of experience with DIY and submitted an excellent writing sample. Meanwhile, the company built an online "Do It with Us" web page where customers can submit questions, read tips, share ideas, and find links to information about new products available at DIY's stores.

After a three-day training program, the sales associates started the online conversation with DIY. Within months, they and the site's visitors had started thousands of conversation threads. And in an unexpected development, the sales associates have also become a valued source of knowledge for DIY's other employees. In stores, at headquarters, and in the regional offices, if someone wants product or project information, they often start their search at the "Do It with Us" web page.

DISCUSSION QUESTIONS

1. As DIY Stores built its online presence, how well did it organize around its core capabilities?
2. DIY Stores is a large national chain. What impact did its size have on its agility?
3. How could DIY increase its agility in responding to the importance of the Internet?

CHAPTER 10
Human Resources Management

©iStockphoto/Getty Images RF

> You can get capital and erect buildings, but it takes people to build a business.
>
> — Thomas J. Watson, founder, IBM

LEARNING OBJECTIVES

After studying Chapter 10, you will be able to:

LO 1 Discuss how companies use human resources management to gain competitive advantage.

LO 2 Give reasons companies recruit both internally and externally for new hires.

LO 3 Identify various methods for selecting new employees.

LO 4 Evaluate the importance of spending on training and development.

LO 5 Discuss options for who appraises an employee's performance.

LO 6 Describe the fundamental aspects of reward systems.

LO 7 Summarize how unions and labor laws influence human resources management.

CHAPTER OUTLINE

Strategic Human Resources Management
The HR Planning Process

Staffing
Recruitment
Selection
Workforce Reductions

Developing the Workforce
Training and Development

Performance Appraisal
What Do You Appraise?
Who Should Do the Appraisal?
How Do You Give Employees Feedback?

Designing Reward Systems
Pay Decisions
Incentive Systems and Variable Pay
Executive Pay and Stock Options
Employee Benefits
Legal Issues in Compensation and Benefits
Health and Safety

Labor Relations
Labor Laws
Unionization
Collective Bargaining
What Does the Future Hold?

Management in Action

HOW GOOGLE LANDS THE BEST EMPLOYEES IN A TOUGH JOB MARKET

Year after year, we hear that U.S. schools are not preparing enough engineers and software developers to meet employers' demand for skilled technology workers. Yet Google, the software company known for its popular search engine, gets about 2 million job applicants a year and hires the cream of the crop.

How does Google win the competition for talent? An obvious place to find answers is in the way the company treats its nearly 60,000 workers. It pays them well, and knowing they hold demanding jobs, it makes the workplace exceptionally comfortable. Benefits include on-site exercise facilities, extended time off to pursue passions, permission to bring pets to work, a popular stress-reducing mindfulness training program, and free food in all company cafeterias. Google also offers work–life flexibility, with on-site child care and arrangements for job sharing and telecommuting. These qualities help Google land at the top of *Fortune*'s list of the 100 Best Companies to Work For.

Perhaps even more significant is the excitement of being part of something meaningful. At least since the name Google became synonymous with searching the web, people with a passion for technology have considered the company a cool place to work, both because its software is advanced and because it makes the Internet a powerful tool. In a survey of young professionals, Google was by far the top choice as an ideal employer. Universum, which conducted the

©Bloomberg/Getty Images

survey, noted that young professionals value working for companies they already like as consumers.

Because Google is an attractive employer, it can be picky about whom it hires. The company selects people who are excited about what computers can do and who value intellectual excellence. It deliberately seeks people who will fit with its fun-loving corporate culture, and it tries to do a better job of identifying such people by including candidates' potential peers and direct reports in the interview process. "You don't just want to assess the candidate," says Laszlo Bock, the company's human resources executive, whose official title is chief people officer. "You want them to fall in love with you."

In receiving roughly 2 million job applications each year, Google has a huge challenge as well as an opportunity. It has to figure out which of these people to hire, how to bring out the best in them, and how to keep them around. As you read this chapter, think about how the strategic use of people drives Google's and every company's strengths and weaknesses.

Google's decisions about hiring, training, and employee benefits are far from random. Rather, under Bock's leadership, Google applies its prowess in analyzing data to figure out how to acquire, develop, and keep talented people. Every year, Google conducts its Googlegeist employee survey to measure employee attitudes about work, and the company carefully tracks all kinds of people-related measures such as managers' effectiveness.

Prasad Setty, who as the director of people analytics reports to Bock, adds another angle: Google tries to "bring the same level of rigor to people decisions that we do to engineering decisions," so all decisions are based on hard data. Does this contradict, or coexist nicely, with Google's fun-loving, let's-fall-in-love image?

The result has long been a positive image, a popular place, and a high-performing company. Over the years, however, Google has developed a workforce that is predominately male, with a disproportionate number of whites and Asian Americans. The company is now addressing this.[1]

Google's practice of wooing bright people with exciting challenges and generous perks has distinguished the company in important ways. The opening quote by Thomas Watson, founder of IBM, summarizes our view of the importance of people to any organization.

human resources management (HRM)

Formal systems for the management of people within an organization.

Human resources management (HRM), historically known as personnel management, deals with formal systems for managing people at work. It is a pervasive aspect of organizational and managerial life. When you look for a job, your first formal interactions with employers will likely involve the human resources function. You will continue interacting with this important function throughout your career.

We begin this chapter by describing HRM as it relates to strategic management, and then discuss more of the nuts and bolts of HRM: legal issues, staffing, training, performance appraisal, rewards, and labor relations. In the chapter following this one, we describe in depth the importance and challenges of the diverse modern workforce.

Strategic Human Resources Management

 LO 1

HRM plays a vital strategic role as organizations attempt to compete through people. Recall (Chapter 4) that firms hold a competitive advantage when they possess or develop resources that are valuable, rare, inimitable, and organized. We can use the same criteria to talk about the strategic impact of human resources when it:

1. *Creates value.* People can increase value through their efforts to decrease costs or provide something unique to customers. Companies such as Corning and Xerox use empowerment programs, total quality initiatives, and continuous improvement efforts designed to increase the value that employees bring to the bottom line.

2. *Is rare.* People provide competitive advantage when their skills, knowledge, and abilities are better than competitors' and hard to find. Top companies invest a great deal to hire talented people and train them well. Google and top consulting firms hire top students in a wide variety of majors, and the recruits develop new skills with training, work assignments, and other methods.

3. *Is difficult to imitate.* People provide advantage when their capabilities and contributions cannot be copied by others. Kayak, Etsy, and W. L. Gore are known for creating unique cultures that get the most from employees (through teamwork and motivation) and are difficult to imitate.

4. *Is organized.* People provide advantage when organizations know how to deploy them as needed based on their experience, skills, and potential. Johnson & Johnson, Colgate, and other companies have formal systems for developing high-potential employees so the company can promote from within. This way, they fill openings with people who are well acquainted with the company's culture, customers, and industry.

People provide competitive advantage when their skills, knowledge, and abilities are better than competitors'.

These four criteria highlight the importance of people and show how integral HRM is to strategic management.[2] At a growing number of companies, HR managers participate in high-level strategy meetings to identify key issues and propose new methods of acquiring, training, and keeping talent will help the company meet its goals.[3]

This strategic focus for HRM brings positive business results.[4] Effective human resources practices relate to higher corporate valuations in the stock market.[5] Innovation—useful new ideas that emerge from the focused creativity of the organization's people—is ever more critical to gaining and maintaining competitive advantage. Employee skills, knowledge, and abilities are among the most distinctive and renewable resources on which a company can draw.

Etsy is known for creating a unique culture that gets the most from employees.
©Bloomberg/Getty Images

human capital

The knowledge, skills, and abilities of employees that have economic value.

Thus, firms recognize that success depends on what people know. The term **human capital** (or, more broadly, *intellectual capital*) is used today to describe the strategic value of employee knowledge and abilities.[6]

Because the HR function is so important, HR managers must know their company's business and line managers must know how to hire well and motivate their people. HR managers also must deal with tough ethical challenges. Historically, as a specialized staff function, HR could focus on technical issues like the legal requirements for hiring decisions. But now, with broader responsibilities as members of the top management team, HR managers may have to downsize the workforce while still retaining top executives through salaries or bonuses, or they may fail to investigate and challenge corrupt practices of colleagues. Such dilemmas are complex and challenging.

In the long run, organizations are best served when HR leaders are strong advocates for at least four sets of values: strategic, ethical, legal, and financial.[7] But on a day-to-day basis, HR managers also have many other concerns regarding people and the overall personnel puzzle. Which HR activities require the most attention depends in part on whether the organization is growing, declining, or standing still. This leads to the practical issues involved in HR planning.

The HR Planning Process

"Get me the right kind and the right number of people at the right time." It sounds simple enough, but it requires HR planning based on knowing your firm's strategic purpose.

The HR planning process occurs in three stages: planning, programming, and evaluating. First, to ensure that the right number and types of people are available, HR managers need to know the organization's business plans: where the company is headed, the mix of businesses and the industries they will compete in, expected future growth, and so forth.

Few actions are more damaging to morale than laying off recently hired college graduates because of inadequate planning. Hiring enough employees to scale an organization can be challenging, too (see the nearby "Social Enterprise" box).

The second element of the HR planning process is to choose and implement specific human resources activities, such as recruitment, training, and performance appraisals. In this stage, the company's plans are implemented. Third, human resources activities are evaluated to determine whether they are producing the results needed to contribute to the organization's business plans.

Social Enterprise

Are Business School Graduates Willing to Work for Social Enterprises?

According to a recent study, many social enterprises in the United States are operating at a suboptimal level where "approximately 40 percent of these businesses have fewer than five employees." About half of social enterprises' revenues do not exceed $250,000.

Scaling is an important goal for many social enterprises. A larger organization with more resources and employees generally makes more progress toward fulfilling the enterprise's mission. For example, Mason Arnold had a burning desire to improve the food system by delivering fresh, nutritious food to consumers in a way that did not damage the environment. His Austin, Texas–based social enterprise, Greenling, purchased food from farms that use chemical-free land in order to have sustainable food for generations. Greenling's efforts to expand the business faltered, however, and it is now part of a larger company with similar goals called Farmhouse Delivery.

The social enterprise industry in the United States is larger than one might imagine. One estimate suggests that it employs over 10 million people and generates annual revenues of $500 billion. To fuel additional growth, more individuals will be needed to work for organizations that use commercial strategies to support social initiatives. There is good news on this front. A study of MBA students found that over 97 percent of them were "willing to forgo financial benefits to work for an organization with a better reputation for corporate social responsibility and

©Arina P Habich/Shutterstock.com RF

ethics." On average, the MBAs were willing to give up 14 percent of their expected income.

Taken together, it appears that many business school graduates are willing to work for organizations that are socially responsible and managed in an ethical manner.[8]

Questions

- Assume you are the manager of a social enterprise. How would you go about attracting people to work for your organization?

- To what degree would you or your fellow students consider working for a social enterprise?

Exhibit 10.1 illustrates the components of the human resources planning process. In this chapter, we focus on human resources planning and programming. You will learn much more about these processes in later chapters.

Demand Forecasts   Perhaps the most difficult part of human resources planning is conducting demand forecasts—that is, determining how many and what types of people are needed.

Demand forecasts for people needs stem from organizational plans. Companies consider current sales and projected future sales growth as they estimate the plant capacity needed to meet future demand, the sales force required, the support staff needed, and so forth. They calculate the number of labor-hours required to operate a plant, sell the product, distribute it, serve customers, and so forth. These estimates determine the demand for different types of workers.

Labor Supply Forecasts   Managers also forecast the supply of labor—how many and what types of employees are available to do the work. In performing a supply analysis, managers estimate the number and quality of current employees as well as the available external supply of workers. To estimate internal supply, managers typically rely on their experiences with (and ideally data about) turnover, terminations, retirements, promotions, and transfers.

EXHIBIT 10.1   An Overview of the HR Planning Process

Planning	Programming	Evaluating
HR environmental scanning • Labor markets • Technology • Legislation • Competition • Economy **HR Planning** • Demand forecast • Internal labor supply • External labor supply • Job analysis	**HR Activities** • Recruitment • Selection • Diversity and inclusion • Training and development • Performance appraisal • Reward systems • Labor relations	**Results** • Productivity • Quality • Innovation • Satisfaction • Turnover • Absenteeism • Health

Externally, organizations have to look at workforce trends to make projections. In the United States, demographic trends have contributed to a shortage of workers with appropriate skills and education level. Jobs in technical, financial, and customized goods and service industries often require much more training and schooling than the traditional labor-intensive jobs that they replaced. Demand for highly qualified employees continues to outpace supply; this is one reason some jobs are being transferred overseas. A recent survey of IT managers revealed that 82 percent lack employees with adequate cyber-security skills to protect their organizations from cyber attacks.[9]

Some demographic trends we discussed in Chapter 2 may worsen this situation. Baby Boomer retirements are removing large numbers of educated and trained employees from the workforce.[10] And in math, science, and engineering graduate schools, fewer than half of the students receiving graduate degrees are American-born. To fill U.S. jobs, companies must hire U.S. citizens or immigrants with permission to work in the United States.

One response to a skills shortage is to automate routine and repetitive tasks.[11] However, technology advances are cannot fill the jobs gap in low and middle-skilled jobs. So, many companies partner with community colleges to provide students with academic and hands-on training. John Deere designed a curriculum and donated tractors to prepare students to become technicians at dealerships.[12] Siemens Energy, in order to staff its high-tech production plant in Charlotte, North Carolina, launched an apprenticeship program for high school seniors. Selected graduating seniors enter into a four-year on-the-job training program while completing an associates degree at Central Piedmont Community College.[13]

Companies also increase the labor supply by recruiting workers from other countries. The supply of legal immigrant labor is restricted by various laws and regulations. For example, each year the U.S. government awards H-1B (temporary) visas to college-educated people in such high-skilled, highly demanded areas as engineering and teaching. Managers at high-tech companies (Microsoft and Alphabet) and consulting firms (Deloitte and Ernst & Young) rely on H-1B employees to fill key positions.[14] At this writing, the U.S. government was considering major changes to the H-1B program.[15]

Earlier forecasts of a diverse workforce have become fact, adding greatly to the pool of available talent. The next chapter is devoted entirely to this topic.

Reconciling Supply and Demand   Once managers have a good idea of the supply of and the demand for various types of employees, they can start developing ways to reconcile the two. In some cases, they need more people than they currently have (a labor deficit). Then, organizations can hire new employees, promote current employees to new positions, or outsource work to contractors. In other cases, organizations have more people than they need (a labor surplus). If this is known far enough in advance, attrition—the normal turnover of employees—can reduce the surplus. In other instances, the organization may lay off employees or transfer them to other areas.

When managers do need to hire, one tool they can use is their organization's compensation policy. Large companies in particular spend a lot of time gathering information about pay scales for the various jobs they have available and making sure their compensation system is fair and competitive. We discuss pay issues later in this chapter.

job analysis

A tool for determining what is done on a given job and what should be done on that job.

Job Analysis   Issues of supply and demand are fairly "macro" activities—conducted at an organizational level. HR planning also has a more detailed micro side called **job analysis** that does two things.[16] First, it tells the HR manager about each job's specific and essential tasks, duties, and responsibilities. This information is the *job description*. The job description for an accounting manager might specify that the position will be responsible for preparing monthly, quarterly, and annual financial reports; issuing and paying bills; preparing budgets; ensuring the company's compliance with laws and regulations; working closely with line managers on financial issues; and supervising an accounting department.

Second, job analysis describes the skills, knowledge, abilities, and other characteristics needed to perform the job. This is called the *job specification*. For our accounting manager, the job requirements might include a degree in accounting or business, knowledge of computerized accounting systems, prior managerial experience, and excellent communication skills.

Job analysis provides the information needed for virtually every human resources activity: recruitment, training, selection, appraisal, and reward systems. It can help organizations defend themselves in lawsuits over employment practices—for example, by clearly specifying what a job requires if someone claims unfair dismissal.[17] Ultimately, job analysis helps increase the value that employees add because it clarifies what is really required to perform effectively.

> Job analysis provides the information needed for virtually every human resources activity.

Staffing

 Once HR planning is completed, managers can focus on staffing the organization. The staffing function consists of three related activities: recruitment, selection, and outplacement.

Recruitment

recruitment

The development of a pool of applicants for jobs in an organization.

Recruitment activities increase the pool of candidates who can be hired. Recruitment may be internal to the organization (considering current employees for promotions and transfers) or external. Each approach has advantages and disadvantages.[18]

Internal Recruiting   The advantages of internal recruiting are that employers know their employees, and employees know their organization; external candidates may find they don't like working there. A big advantage is that opportunities for promotions can encourage employees to remain with the company, work hard, and perform well. Recruiting from outside the company can be demoralizing to employees. Many companies, such as Booz & Company, H-E-B, and CareerBuilder, prefer internal to external recruiting for these reasons.

Internal staffing has some drawbacks. If employees lack needed skills, internal recruitment yields a limited applicant pool, leading to poor selections. An internal recruitment policy can inhibit a company that wants to change the nature or goals of the business if current employees don't want to change. In changing from a rapidly growing, entrepreneurial organization to a mature business with more stable growth, Dell went outside the organization to hire managers who better fit those needs.

Internal recruiting often uses a job-posting system: a mechanism for advertising open positions, typically on the company's intranet. The posted job description includes a list of duties and the minimum skills and experience required. Employees complete a request form indicating interest in a posted job.

External Recruiting
External recruiting brings in new blood and can inspire innovation. Among the most frequently used sources of outside applicants are Internet job boards, company websites, employee referrals, newspaper advertisements, and college campus recruiting.

Employers prefer referrals by current employees and online job boards.[19] Some companies encourage employees to refer their friends by offering cash rewards. In fact, word-of-mouth recommendations are the way most job positions get filled. Not only is this recruitment method relatively inexpensive, but employees tend to know who will be a good fit with the company. Web job boards such as Snagajob, Indeed, SimplyHired, CareerBuilder, Monster, and Glassdoor easily reach a large pool of job seekers.

For specialized positions, more companies use networking sites such as LinkedIn, Facebook, and Twitter because the job boards generate many unqualified leads that are overwhelming to process. Many companies accept applications and post job openings at their corporate websites. Employers may use employment agencies or, for important management positions, an executive search firm. Campus recruiting is effective, but relying heavily on campus recruiting and employee referrals can result in biased discrimination, even unintentionally.[20]

©littleny/Shutterstock.com RF

Selection

Selection builds on recruiting and is a decision about whom to hire. As important as these decisions are, they sometimes are made in careless or cavalier ways. Here we describe a number of selection practices to which you may soon be exposed, if you haven't been already.

Applications and Résumés
Applications and résumés provide basic information to employers. To make a first cut, employers review the profiles and backgrounds of many job applicants. Applications and résumés typically include the applicant's name, educational background, citizenship, work experiences, certifications, and the like. Their appearance and accuracy say something about the applicant; spelling mistakes, for example, are almost always immediately disqualifying (something to keep in mind when preparing your own). Although a useful starting point, applications and résumés tend not to be extremely useful for making final selection decisions.

Interviews
The most popular selection tool is interviewing, and virtually every company does this. Interviewers must be careful about what they ask and how they ask it. Federal law requires employers to avoid discriminating against people based on criteria such as sex and race; questions that distinguish candidates according to protected categories can be evidence of discrimination.

In a **structured interview**, the interviewer conducts the same interview with each applicant. One type—the *situational interview*—uses hypothetical situations. Here is a sample question used by a restaurant hiring manager to assess applicants for a server position: "Assume a customer became upset because you accidentally overcharged him for his meal. How would you handle the situation?" An answer that said "I would refer the customer to

LO 3

selection
Choosing from among qualified applicants to hire.

structured interview
Selection technique that involves asking all applicants the same questions and comparing their responses to a standardized set of answers.

The Digital World

While organizations spend time and effort to check the references of prospective employees as well as pay for background checks, another type of background check involves checking social media accounts. Many employers will check the social media presence of people being considered for a job or internship.

Anything that has been posted to a public profile can be considered in a hiring decision but some states have made social media searches illegal. Many states have banned employers from requesting access to applicants'

or employees' social media posts; then again, many have not.

Many organizations have policies that discourage viewing social media accounts, due to the risk of tainting hiring decisions with information from the wrong people with the same name. Companies are still weighing the pros and cons of going online to glean information about their potential employees, but in the meantime, people seeking jobs are well advised to evaluate and clean up their social media presence.

During an interview, employers can conduct unstructured interviews, where they ask each potential employee different questions, or structured interviews in which the employer asks everyone the same questions.

©Chris Ryan/Getty Images RF

my supervisor" has some logic to it, but might suggest that the applicant felt incapable of handling the situation on his or her own, or unwilling to try.

The second type of structured interview—the *behavioral description interview*—explores what candidates have actually done in the past. Applicants for a position at Citigroup might be asked: "Tell me about a time when your performance let someone down. Why do you think that happened? What did you learn from that experience? What would you do differently now, knowing what you know?"[21] Because behavioral questions are based on real events, they can provide useful information about how the candidate will actually perform in the future.

Reference Checks   Résumés, applications, and interviews rely on the honesty of the applicant. To make an accurate selection decision, employers have to be able to trust each candidate's words. Unfortunately, some candidates exaggerate their qualifications or hide criminal backgrounds. Scott Thompson was removed as CEO of Yahoo! after it was discovered that he listed a nonexistent computer science degree on his résumé.[22] Once lost, a reputation is hard to regain.

Because of these and more ambiguous ethical gray areas, employers supplement candidate-provided information with reference checks. Virtually all organizations contact references or former employers and educational institutions. Although checking references makes sense, reference information can be difficult to obtain because people have won costly lawsuits against former employers who spoke negatively about them.

> Many interviewers use more than one technique during the same interview.

Nevertheless, employers should make a practice of checking references.[23] Occasionally they raise a red flag: past employers usually just verify basic employment facts, but sometimes they will advise caution.

Background Checks   A higher level of scrutiny comes from background investigations. Some state courts have ruled that companies can be held liable for negligent hiring if they fail to do adequate background checks. Checks include Social Security verification, past employment and education verification, and a criminal records check. A number of other checks can be conducted if they pertain to the job being hired for, including a motor vehicle record check (for jobs involving driving) and a credit check (for money-handling jobs).

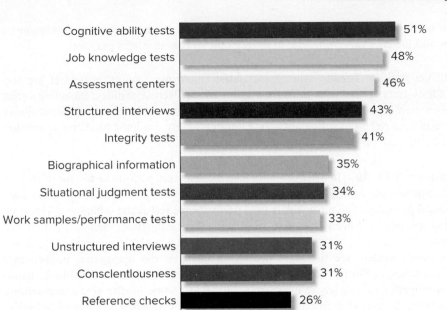

EXHIBIT 10.2
Online Tools Used to
Screen Job Applicants

Tool	Percentage
Cognitive ability tests	51%
Job knowledge tests	48%
Assessment centers	46%
Structured interviews	43%
Integrity tests	41%
Biographical information	35%
Situational judgment tests	34%
Work samples/performance tests	33%
Unstructured interviews	31%
Conscientlousness	31%
Reference checks	26%

SOURCE: http://answers.mheducation.com/management/human-resource-management/personnel-selection.

Basic background checks are fast and easy to perform. Roughly 60 percent of hiring managers use social networking sites, especially Facebook, Twitter, and LinkedIn, to learn about job candidates.[24] Many companies do not make offers to candidates based on content they find online. Anything that carries your name online can become information for potential employers, even years down the road.

Exhibit 10.2 shows which screening tools are used most often.

Personality Tests   Using tests to measure candidates' personalities is on the upswing.[25] Companies that use personality tests include Delaware North Companies, Amtrak, and Target.[26] Some personality types have been associated with greater job satisfaction and performance when the organization builds groups of people with similar positive traits.[27] However, personality tests can be discriminatory and often do not accurately predict job performance.

A number of well-known inventories measure personality traits such as conscientiousness, extraversion, sociability, adjustment, and energy. Typical questions are "Do you like to socialize with people?" and "Do you enjoy working hard?" Some personality tests try to determine the types of working conditions that the candidate prefers, to see whether he would be motivated and productive in the particular job. For example, if a candidate prefers making decisions on her own but the job requires gaining the cooperation of others, another candidate might be a better fit.

Drug Testing   Drug testing is a common screening instrument. Since the passage of the Drug-Free Workplace Act of 1988, applicants and employees of federal contractors and Department of Defense contractors and those under Department of Transportation regulations have been tested for illegal drugs. To avoid discrimination against individuals with disabilities, companies wait to conduct drug testing until after they have made a conditional job offer. Currently, about half of U.S. employers screen for drugs.[28] About 1 in 10 workers test positive for illegal drugs, the highest level in 30 years.[29]

Drug testing became more complicated when some states legalized marijuana use.[30] Companies that fire a worker for failing a drug test because of medical marijuana could be found guilty of discriminating. For many jobs, however, it is critical that workers not be under the influence of any substance, legal or illegal. So far, most state medical marijuana laws do not include employment protections for workers, but because these developments are new and the laws vary from state to state, employers are in a legal gray area.

Cognitive Ability Tests   Among the oldest employment selection devices are cognitive ability tests. These tests measure a range of intellectual abilities, including verbal comprehension (vocabulary, reading) and numerical aptitude (mathematical calculations). These tests have right and wrong answers. Cognitive ability is a good predictor of employees' ability to learn on the job, which helps them perform well.[31]

Performance Tests   In a performance test, the test taker performs a sample of the job. Most companies use some type of performance test, typically for administrative assistant and clerical positions. The most widely used performance test is the typing test. However, performance tests have been developed for almost every occupation, including managerial positions.

Assessment centers are the most notable offshoot of the managerial performance test.[32] Originating in World War II, a typical **assessment center** consists of 10 to 12 candidates participating in a variety of exercises or situations. Some involve group interactions, and others are performed individually. The exercises allow displays of managerial behaviors and skills such as leadership, decision making, and communicating. Assessors, generally line managers, observe and record information about the candidates' performance.

assessment center

A managerial performance test in which candidates participate in a variety of exercises and situations.

Integrity Tests   Sometimes employers administer integrity tests to assess candidates' honesty. Polygraphs, or lie detector tests, have been banned for most employment purposes.[33] Paper-and-pencil tests include questions such as whether a person has ever thought about stealing and whether he or she believes other people steal ("What percentage of people take more than $1 from their employer?"). Some companies, including Payless ShoeSource, have reported that theft decreased when they started using such tests; however the accuracy of these tests is debatable.[34]

reliability

The consistency of test scores over time and across alternative measurements.

Reliability and Validity   For all selection methods, two crucial issues need to be addressed: reliability and validity. **Reliability** is the consistency of test scores over time and across alternative measurements. If three interviewers talked to the same job candidate but drew very different conclusions about his abilities, the interview procedures have questionable reliability.

Validity is the accuracy of the selection test. The most common form of validity, *criterion-related validity,* refers to the degree to which a test actually predicts or correlates with job performance. *Content validity* concerns the degree to which selection tests measure a representative sample of the knowledge, skills, and abilities required for the job. Both types of validity are useful and important, particularly when defending employment decisions in court.

validity

The degree to which a selection test predicts or correlates with job performance.

Workforce Reductions

Hiring is not the only type of staffing decision. Unfortunately, managers sometimes must make difficult decisions to terminate people's employment.

Layoffs   Over two recent decades, three companies alone—IBM, Citigroup, and Sears Roebuck—laid off a combined 160,000 employees.[35] Dismissing anyone is tough, but laying off a substantial portion of the workforce is devastating.[36] The victims of restructuring face all the difficulties of being fired—loss of self-esteem, demoralizing job searches, and the stigma of being out of work.

Even under the best circumstances, downsizing can be traumatic for an organization and its employees. What can be done to manage downsizing as well as possible?

First, firms should avoid excessive hiring to avoid needing major or multiple downsizings. Other common mistakes are making slow, small, frequent layoffs; implementing voluntary early retirement programs that entice the best people to leave; and laying off so many

Use downsizing only as a last resort, when other methods of improving performance by innovating or changing procedures have been exhausted.
Give special attention and help to those who have lost their jobs.
Identify and protect talented people.
Choose positions to be eliminated by engaging in analysis and strategic thinking.
Train people to cope with the new situation.
Communicate constantly with people about the process and invite ideas for alternative ways to operate more efficiently.
Identify how the organization will operate more effectively in the future; emphasize this positive future and remaining employees' new roles in attaining it.

EXHIBIT 10.3
Best Practices When
Downsizing

SOURCES: Adapted from Cascio, W. F., "Strategies for Responsible Restructuring," *Academy of Management Executive* 19, no. 4 (2005), pp. 39–50; Cascio, W. F., "Downsizing: What Do We Know? What Have We Learned?" *Academy of Management Executive* 7 (February 1993); Freeman, S. J., "The Gestalt of Organizational Downsizing: Downsizing Strategies as Package of Change," *Human Relations* 52, no. 12 (December 1999); and Hitt, M. B. et al., "Rightsizing: Building and Maintaining Strategic Leadership and Long-Term Competitiveness," *Organizational Dynamics*, Fall 1994, pp.18–31.

people that the company's work can no longer be performed. Instead, firms can engage in a number of positive practices to ease the pain and increase the effectiveness of downsizing (see Exhibit 10.3).

Employers can offer **outplacement**: helping dismissed people regain employment elsewhere. Even then, the impact of layoffs goes further than the employees who leave. For many of the employees who remain with the company, disenchantment, distrust, and lethargy overshadow the comfort of still having a job. In many respects, how management deals with dismissals will affect the productivity and satisfaction of those who remain.

outplacement

The process of helping people who have been dismissed from the company regain employment elsewhere.

A thoughtful and fair dismissal process can ease tensions somewhat and help remaining employees adjust to the new work situation. It helps if care is taken during the actual layoff process—if workers receive fair notice, severance pay, and help in finding a new job. The people who did not lose their jobs can be comforted somewhat if they know that the employer does what it can to help when bad times arrive.

Termination   People sometimes get fired for poor performance. **Employment-at-will** or *termination-at-will* means that an employee may be fired for *any* reason. A Tennessee court established this in 1884 and the Supreme Court upheld it in 1908.[37] The logic is that if an employee can quit at any time, the employer can dismiss at any time.

employment-at-will

The legal concept that an employer can terminate an employee for any reason.

Courts in most states have made exceptions to this doctrine. Employees cannot be fired for refusing to break the law, taking time off for jury duty, or whistleblowing to report illegal company behavior. For example, if a worker reports an environmental violation to a regulatory agency and the company fires her, the courts may argue that the firing was unfair because the employee acted for the good of the community. Union contracts that limit an employer's ability to fire without cause are another major exception to the employment-at-will doctrine.

How management deals with terminations will affect the productivity, morale, and satisfaction of those who remain.

Employers can avoid the pitfalls of dismissals by developing progressive and positive disciplinary procedures.[38] In this context, *progressive* means that a manager takes graduated steps in attempting to correct unwanted behaviors. For example, an employee who has been absent receives a verbal reprimand for the first offense. A second offense invokes a written reprimand. A third offense results in employee counseling and probation, and a fourth results in a paid leave day to think over the consequences of future rule infractions. The employer is signaling that this is the last straw. Arbitrators are more likely to side with an employer that fires someone when they believe it has tried to help the person correct his behavior.

EXHIBIT 10.4
Advice on Termination

Do's	Don'ts
• Make termination the last step in a clear and fair process, being certain you have the facts.	• Don't spring a termination on an employee as a total surprise.
• Be sure the person terminating the employee is the employee's direct supervisor.	• Don't start a meeting unprepared, causing the terminated employee to wait awkwardly while you find answers or call in an HR representative.
• Be prepared with answers to basic questions such as the official end date and any severance benefits.	• Don't beat around the bush; state the termination simply and briefly.
• Consult with the human resource department to identify any benefits available; give the employee a written list of information about benefits and policies.	• Don't get caught up in responding to the employee's emotions or views about fairness; focus on practical realities including the need to move on.
• Invite a trained HR representative to attend the meeting.	• Don't argue with the employee or apologize.
• Listen respectfully.	• Don't offer to help the employee find another job, if you cannot honestly give a good reference.

SOURCES: Ashkenas, Ron, "If You Have to Fire an Employee—Here's How to Do It Right," *Forbes,* March 11, 2013, http://www.forbes.com; Haden, Jeff, "The Best Way to Fire an Employee," *Inc.,* March 19, 2012, http://www.inc.com; Korn, Melissa, "The Best Ways to Fire Somebody," *The Wall Street Journal,* October 26, 2012, http://online.wsj.com.

termination interview

A discussion between a manager and an employee about the employee's dismissal.

The **termination interview**, in which the manager discusses the dismissal with the employee, is stressful for both parties. The immediate superior should be the one to deliver the bad news to employee. However, it is wise to have a third party, such as an HR manager, present to provide guidance and take notes on the meeting. Terminations can lead to lawsuits, so the manager should prepare carefully by knowing all the facts of the situation and reviewing any documents to make sure they justify the termination.

Ethics and common sense dictate that the manager should be truthful but respectful, and state the facts.[39] Exhibit 10.4 provides some other guidelines for conducting a termination interview.

Legal Issues and Equal Employment Opportunity
Many laws govern employment decisions and practices. They will directly affect your day-to-day work as a manager as well as your employer's human resource function. Exhibit 10.5 shows many of the most important U.S. employment laws.

Failure to comply with these laws exposes the organization to charges of unfair practices, expensive lawsuits, and civil and even criminal penalties. Texas Roadhouse agreed to a $12 million settlement in an age discrimination lawsuit accusing it of not hiring applicants over 40 for front-of-the-house server, host, and bartender positions.[40] In another case, Nestlé Waters North America was hit with a $300,000 fine for sex discrimination.[41] The suit charged that Dawn Bowers-Ferrara, a female manager who had been with the company for 20 years, was denied a promotion due to her gender. Instead, the company promoted a male manager who lacked the minimum requirements for the position.[42]

adverse impact

When a seemingly neutral employment practice has a disproportionately negative effect on a protected group.

One common reason employers are sued is **adverse impact**—when an employment practice has a disproportionately negative effect on a group protected by the Civil Rights Act.[43] For example, if equal numbers of qualified men and women apply for jobs but a particular

EXHIBIT 10.5   U.S. Equal Employment Laws

Act	Major Provisions	Enforcement and Remedies
Fair Labor Standards Act (1938)	Creates exempt (salaried) and nonexempt (hourly) employee categories, governing overtime and other rules; sets minimum wage, child labor laws.	Enforced by Department of Labor, private action to recover lost wages; civil and criminal penalties also possible.
Equal Pay Act (1963)	Prohibits gender-based pay discrimination between two jobs substantially similar in skill, effort, responsibility, and working conditions.	Fines up to $10,000, imprisonment up to 6 months, or both; enforced by Equal Employment Opportunity Commission (EEOC); private actions for double damages up to 3 years' wages, liquidated damages, reinstatement, or promotion.
Title VII of Civil Rights Act (1964)	Prohibits discrimination based on race, sex, color, religion, or national origin in employment decisions: hiring, pay, working conditions, promotion, discipline, or discharge.	Enforced by EEOC; private actions, back pay, front pay, reinstatement, restoration of seniority and pension benefits, attorneys' fees and costs.
Executive Orders 11246 and 11375 (1965)	Requires equal opportunity clauses in federal contracts; prohibits employment discrimination by federal contractors based on race, color, religion, sex, or national origin.	Established Office of Federal Contract Compliance Programs (OFCCP) to investigate violations; empowered to terminate violator's federal contracts.
Age Discrimination in Employment Act (1967)	Prohibits employment discrimination based on age for persons over 40 years; restricts mandatory retirement.	EEOC enforcement; private actions for reinstatement, back pay, front pay, restoration of seniority and pension benefits; double unpaid wages for willful violations; attorneys' fees and costs.
Vocational Rehabilitation Act (1973)	Requires affirmative action by all federal contractors for persons with disabilities; defines disabilities as physical or mental impairments that substantially limit life activities.	Federal contractors must consider hiring persons with disabilities capable of performance after reasonable accommodations.
Americans with Disabilities Act Amendments Act (2008)	Extends affirmative action provisions of Vocational Rehabilitation Act to private employers; requires workplace modifications to facilitate employees with disabilities; prohibits discrimination against persons with disabilities.	EEOC enforcement; private actions for Title VII remedies.
Civil Rights Act (1991)	Clarifies Title VII requirements: disparate treatment impact suits, business necessity, job relatedness; shifts burden of proof to employer; permits punitive damages and jury trials.	Punitive damages limited to sliding scale only in intentional discrimination based on sex, religion, and disabilities.
Family and Medical Leave Act (1991)	Requires 12 weeks' unpaid leave for medical or family needs: paternity, family member illness.	Private actions for lost wages and other expenses, reinstatement.

employment test results in far fewer women being hired, the test had an adverse impact and can be challenged legally on that basis.

Most companies have procedures to ensure compliance with labor and equal opportunity laws. They monitor and compare salaries by race, gender, length of service, and other categories. Smart and effective management practices treat employees as fairly as possible to motivate employees to do their best work and provide legal protection as well.

Developing the Workforce

Bottom Line

Training improves employee skills. *How might you measure the costs and benefits of training salespeople?*

Competitive environments require managers to upgrade continually the skills and performance of employees—as well as their own. Constant improvement increases both personal and organizational effectiveness. It makes organization members more useful in their current jobs and prepares them to take on new responsibilities. It helps the organization meet new challenges and take advantage of new methods and technologies. It also requires appraising employees' performance and giving them effective feedback so they will be motivated to perform at high levels. We will discuss each of these activities in turn.

Training and Development

U.S. businesses spend more than $70 billion annually on employee training. The greatest share goes to training that the organization itself delivers to its employees. The remainder goes to external training companies and technologies.[44]

The average amount spent per employee on training is around $800, and this has remained flat over several years.[45] This lack of investment is a great concern because today's jobs require more education while the education level of U.S. workers has not kept pace.

Although we use the general term *training* here, training sometimes is distinguished from development. **Training** usually refers to teaching lower-level employees how to perform their current jobs, whereas **development** involves teaching managers and professional employees broader skills needed for their current and future jobs.

Cold Stone Creamery spends a portion of its training budget to develop computerized simulations that show how employee actions affect store performance. The company uses computer games because they are familiar and appealing to its young employees.
©Raleigh News & Observer/Getty Images

training

Teaching lower-level employees how to perform their present jobs.

Overview of the Training Process   Training usually starts with a **needs assessment**. Managers conduct an analysis to identify who and what needs training. Job analysis and performance measurements are useful for this purpose. Then it's time to design the training content and methods and decide whether a program will be provided on or off the job. Common methods include lectures, role-playing, business simulation, behavior modeling (watching a video and imitating what is observed), conferences, vestibule training (practicing in a simulated work environment) and job environment), and apprenticeships.

Finally, managers should evaluate program effectiveness. Measures of effectiveness include employee reactions (surveys), learning (tests), improved behavior on the job, and bottom-line results such as an increase in sales or reduction in defect rates following the training.

Types of Training   **Orientation training** is used to familiarize new employees with their new jobs, work units, and the organization in general. Done well, orientation training has a number of benefits, including lower employee turnover, increased morale, better productivity, and lower recruiting and training costs. The need for soft skills training, especially among early career employees, is discussed in the nearby "Multiple Generations at Work" box.

---

development

Helping managers and professional employees learn the broad skills needed for their present and future jobs.

needs assessment

An analysis identifying the jobs, people, and departments for which training is necessary.

orientation training

Training designed to introduce new employees to the company and familiarize them with policies, procedures, culture, and the like.

Multiple Generations at Work

College Students Need Soft Skills, Too

Many college students expect their newly acquired hard skills, like designing a budget, financing a new project, developing an impactful social media advertising campaign, or using the latest accounting software, to be enough to achieve success with employers. While these hard skills are essential, two-thirds of respondents (corporate recruiters, business leaders, college students, and so forth) believe that soft skills are as important as hard skills for success in the workplace.

As illustrated below, business leaders rank integrity, professionalism, and positive attitude as the top three attributes desired in new hires. Strong oral communication and teamwork skills are important as well.

College students can take actions to acquire or refine their soft skills. Internships provide exposure to professional organizational settings. Student organizations or clubs afford chances to learn how to motivate and lead others. Universities' career services offer career fairs, etiquette dinners, and dress for success seminars. Students who display excellent soft skills, combined with the requisite hard skills, increase the chances of promising and satisfying careers.[46]

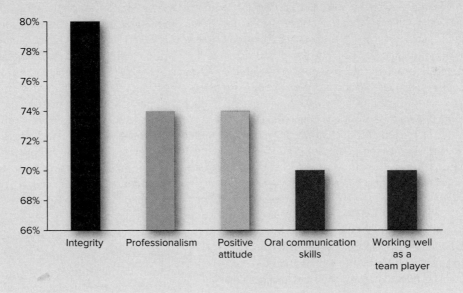

Team training teaches people the skills they need to work together and stimulates interaction among team members. Before the start of the 2016 holiday season, Target set out to hire 70,000 part-time workers. Because some new hires would be new to retailing, Target promised them plenty of training with its experienced teams. The new seasonal hires learned key retail skills plus how to work productively with full-time team members.[47]

Diversity training builds awareness of diversity's advantages and challenges, and teaches skills for strengthening work relationships—the kinds of things you will learn in the next chapter.

Management training programs often seek to improve managers' people skills—their ability to delegate effectively, motivate their subordinates or direct reports, and communicate and inspire high performance. Coaching—receiving customized personal training from a boss or consultant—can be one of the most effective management development tools.

Managers also can learn a lot in programs used for all employees such as job rotation, or by attending special seminars. As you read "Management in Action: Progress Report," consider how Google's management training and coaching complement its hiring methods.

team training

Training that provides employees with the skills and perspectives they need to collaborate with others.

diversity training

Programs that focus on identifying and reducing hidden biases against people with differences and developing the skills needed to manage a diversified workforce.

Management in Action

HOW GOOGLE HIRES AND TRAINS

Google's hiring strategy is to position the company as a highly attractive place to work, receive a flood of applications, and make collaborative decisions about which applicants will fit best with Google's demanding and creative culture.

Now streamlined to take about six weeks, the selection process is demanding and occasionally quirky. Candidates undergo up to four structured interviews and meet with several Google employees, including potential future peers and direct reports, and may complete work sample tests as well. The interviewers compile an extensive file of information to use in making a group decision.

According to Laszlo Bock, chief people officer, they look for the following attributes: (1) ability to learn and apply knowledge to solve problems; (2) willingness to lead and follow others; (3) humility when faced with new or opposing information; and (4) desire to take ownership and defend ideas. Bock urges interviewers to focus on the top two reasons people stay on the job: "Make clear why the work you are doing matters, and let the candidate experience the astounding people they will get to work with."

Google now has an added consideration after discovering it lags the industry in creating a diverse workforce. Men still make up the overwhelming majority of its employees and managers; more than half of all employees are white, and Asian Americans account for about a third. Only 5 percent are Latino; less than 3 percent are black. A companywide diversity effort includes anti-bias training, new hiring practices, the formation of identity groups within the company, benchmarking of other companies' diversity initiatives, and efforts to cast a much wider net when recruiting.

Google expects the changes to show results over time. "Google is in this for the long haul," says VP of engineering Anna Patterson. "Diversity makes all tech better, and our products better."

With regard to training, data-driven decisions match topics to particular employees for whom the training will deliver meaningful results. For management training, Laszlo Bock's People Operations group studied data from employee surveys, managers' performance appraisals, and nominations for best-manager awards. The group identified eight management behaviors associated with success in leading teams and retaining employees and developed training programs for each; programs are recommended to individual managers based on their performance. Management training courses also are recommended based on data showing the skills that are relevant in particular functions or at particular stages of a manager's career. Formal training sessions are backed up with customized reminders and recommendations related to events in the manager's department.[48]

- Discuss why you think Google decided to select people by emphasizing the four attributes mentioned above.
- How could Google's approach to management training address the needs of its nonmanagement employees?

Performance Appraisal

LO 5

performance appraisal (PA)

Assessment of an employee's job performance.

One of the most important responsibilities you will have as a manager is **performance appraisal (PA)**, the assessment of employees' job performance. Done well, it can help employees improve their performance, pay, and chances for promotion; foster communication between managers and employees; and increase individual, team, and organization effectiveness. Done poorly, it has negative effects—resentment, a drop in motivation, lower performance, and sometimes lawsuits.

Performance appraisal serves two basic purposes. First, it generates information managers need to judge the past. They use those judgments to make salary, promotion, and dismissal decisions; help employees understand and accept the basis of those decisions; and create documentation that can support their decisions in court.

Second, and at least as important, appraisal serves a developmental purpose. The information can be used to identify and plan the additional training, learning, and experience employees need. The feedback and coaching people receive help them improve their performance and prepare them for greater future responsibilities.

What Do You Appraise?

Performance appraisals assess three basic categories of employee performance: traits, behaviors, and results. Trait appraisals involve subjective judgments about employee characteristics related to performance. They include dimensions such as initiative, leadership, and attitude. Usually the manager will use a numerical scale to indicate the extent to which an employee "possesses" each trait. For example, if the measured trait is attitude, the employee might be rated anywhere from 1 (very negative attitude) to 5 (very positive attitude).

Trait scales are common because they are simple to use and provide a standard measure for all employees. But often they are not valid as performance measures. Because they tend to be ambiguous as well as highly subjective—does the employee really have a bad attitude, or is he or she just shy?—they tend to have low validity and can be unsuitable for feedback purposes.

Behavioral appraisals, although still subjective, focus on more observable aspects of performance. They were developed in response to the problems of trait appraisals. These scales focus on specific, prescribed behaviors that can help ensure that all parties understand what the ratings are really measuring. Because they are less ambiguous, they can provide useful feedback. Exhibit 10.6 contains an example of a behaviorally anchored rating scale (BARS) for evaluating quality.

Another behaviorally focused approach is the critical incident technique. The manager keeps a regular log and records each significant behavior by the subordinate that reflects the quality of his or her performance. ("Anna impressed the client with her effective presentation today." "Brian was late with his report.") This approach can be subjective and

EXHIBIT 10.6
Example of BARS Used for Evaluating Quality

Performance dimension: total quality management. This area of performance concerns the extent to which a person is aware of, endorses, and develops proactive procedures to enhance product quality, ensure early disclosure of discrepancies, and integrate quality assessments with cost and schedule performance measurement reports to maximize clients' satisfaction with overall performance.

OUTSTANDING 7 — Uses measures of quality and well-defined processes to achieve project goals. Defines quality from the client's perspective.

6 — Looks for/identifies ways to continually improve the process.

5 — Clearly communicates quality management to others. Develops a plan that defines how the team will participate in quality.

Appreciates TQM as an investment.

AVERAGE 4 — Has measures of quality that define tolerance levels.

3 — Views quality as costly. Legislates quality.

2 — Focuses his/her concerns only on outputs and deliverables, ignoring the underlying processes.

POOR 1 — Blames others for absence of quality. Gives lip service only to quality concerns.

time-consuming, and it may give some employees the feeling that everything they do is being recorded. But it does have the advantage of creating records and reminders of things the employee actually did or did not do.

Results appraisals are more objective, focusing on production data such as sales volume (for a salesperson), units produced (for a line worker), or profits (for a manager). One approach to results appraisals—**management by objectives (MBO)**—involves a subordinate and a supervisor agreeing in advance on specific performance goals (objectives). They then develop a plan that describes the time frame and criteria for determining whether the objectives have been reached. The aim is to agree on a set of objectives that are clear, specific, and reachable. For example, an objective for a salesperson might be "Add three big new customers during the following year."

MBO has several important advantages. First, it avoids the biases and measurement difficulties of trait and behavioral appraisals. At the end of the review period, employees are judged on actual job performance as compared against objectives. Second, because the employee and manager have agreed on objectives, the employee is likely to understand and be more committed to reaching them. Third, MBO allows employees to adapt their approach as needed (within limits, for instance legal and ethical), to achieve the desired results.

But the approach has disadvantages as well. It can result in unrealistic objectives being set, frustrating the employee and the manager. The objectives can be too rigid, leaving the employee with insufficient flexibility should circumstances change. Finally, MBO often focuses too much on short-term achievement at the expense of longer-term goals.

None of these systems is easy to do properly, and all have drawbacks that must be guarded against. In choosing an appraisal method, the following guidelines can help:

1. Base performance standards on job analysis.
2. Communicate performance standards to employees.
3. Evaluate employees on specific performance-related behaviors rather than on a single global or overall measure.
4. Document the PA process carefully.
5. If possible, use more than one rater (discussed in the next section).
6. Have a formal and fair appeal process.
7. Always take legal considerations into account.[49]

Who Should Do the Appraisal?

Just as multiple methods can gather performance appraisal information, multiple people can provide it. Managers and supervisors are the traditional sources, because they often are in the best position to observe an employee's performance. However, companies also can use peers, team members, and customers to provide input. These sources often have different perspectives and often are best at identifying leadership potential and interpersonal skills.

One increasingly popular source of appraisal is a manager's subordinates. Managers then receive feedback on how their employees view them. Often this information is given in confidence to the manager and not shared with superiors. Even so, this approach can make managers (and their direct reports) uncomfortable, but the feedback they get can be extremely useful and help them improve their management style. Because this process gives employees power over their bosses, usually it is used for development purposes only, not for salary or promotion decisions.

Internal and external customers also can provide performance appraisal information, particularly for companies like Ford and Honda that emphasize total quality management. Internal customers can be anyone inside the organization who depends on an employee's work output.

Usually it's a good idea to ask employees to evaluate their own performance. Although self-appraisals may be biased upward, self-evaluation increases employees' involvement in the review process and is a good starting point for establishing performance and developmental goals.

---

management by objectives (MBO)

A process in which objectives set by a subordinate and a supervisor must be reached within a given time period.

Because each source of PA information has limitations, and because different people see different aspects of performance, Shell, PepsiCo, and many other companies ask more than one source for appraisal information. In **360-degree appraisal**, people obtain feedback from every direction: subordinates, peers, outsiders (customers, vendors), and superiors.[50] Often the person being rated can select the appraisers, subject to a manager's approval, with the understanding that the individual appraisals are kept confidential; results are consolidated for each group of appraisers.

360-degree appraisal

Process of using multiple sources of appraisal to gain a comprehensive perspective on one's performance.

The 360-degree appraisal offers many advantages. It provides a much fuller picture of a person's strengths and weaknesses, and it often captures information that other methods miss. For example, an employee may have a difficult relationship with his or her supervisor yet be highly regarded by peers and subordinates. The approach can lead to significant improvement, as people often are very motivated to improve their ratings. The 360-degree method has improved managers' performance in many countries, but cultural differences can affect its impact. [51]

On the downside, employees are not always willing to rate their colleagues harshly, so a certain uniformity of ratings may result. Importantly, the 360-degree appraisal does not measure actual job performance, so objective criteria such as sales and cost targets should be used as well. Therefore the objective of this method usually is personal development rather than a basis for administrative decisions such as raises. For those, appraisal methods like MBO are more appropriate.[52]

How Do You Give Employees Feedback?

Appraisals are most effective when they stem from a familiar work relationship rather than being just a top-down formal judgment issued only once a year. Managers of sports teams do not wait until the season is over to appraise their players; they work together throughout the season to improve individual and team performance. In high-functioning companies, informal appraisal and feedback are always taking place. Managers communicate with their employees frequently, praising or coaching as appropriate and together assessing progress toward goals. When managers and employees have good relationships and open communication, the annual formal feedback should rarely be a surprise.

Giving and receiving PA feedback are stressful tasks for both managers and subordinates. The purposes of PA conflict to some degree. Providing developmental feedback requires understanding and support, but the manager must also be objective and be able to make tough decisions. Employees want to know how they are doing, but typically they are uncomfortable about getting feedback. And the organization's need to make HR decisions conflicts with the individual employee's need to maintain a positive image.[53] These conflicts often make PA interviews difficult.

> In high-functioning organizations, informal appraisal and feedback are taking place constantly.

There is no one best way to do a PA interview. Appraisal feedback generally works best when it is specific and constructive—related to clear goals or behaviors and clearly intended to help the employee rather than simply criticize. Managers have an interest not just in rating performance but in raising it, and effective appraisals take that into account. In addition, the appraisal is likely to be more meaningful and satisfying when the manager gives the employee an opportunity to discuss and respond to the appraisal.

One of the most difficult conversations comes when an employee is performing poorly. Exhibit 10.7 contains a PA interview format to use when an employee is performing below acceptable levels.

Here are some guidelines for giving feedback to employees performing at average levels:

1. Summarize the employee's performance and be specific.
2. Explain why the employee's work is important to the organization.
3. Thank the employee for doing the job.
4. Raise any relevant issues, such as areas for improvement.
5. Express confidence in the employee's future good performance.

Bottom Line
Effective feedback raises employee performance.
What kind of feedback is most likely to be effective?

EXHIBIT 10.7

A PA Interview Format for Underperforming Employees

1. **Summarize** the employee's performance as specifically as possible. Describe the performance in behavioral or outcome terms, such as sales or absenteeism. Don't say the employee has a poor attitude; rather, explain which employee behaviors indicate a poor attitude.
2. **Describe** the expectations and standards, again being specific.
3. **Determine** the causes for the low performance; get the employee's input.
4. **Discuss** solutions to the problem with the employee playing a major role.
5. **Agree** to a solution. As a supervisor, you have input into the solution. Raise issues and questions but also provide support.
6. **Agree** to a timetable for improvement.
7. **Document** the meeting.
8. **Follow-up** meetings may be needed.

Designing Reward Systems

 LO 6

Giving people appropriate rewards—most obviously, pay and benefits—is a vital HR activity. Traditionally pay has been the primary monetary reward, but benefits receive a great deal of attention today.[54] The typical employer now pays about 32 percent of payroll costs in benefits.[55] Benefits costs have risen faster than wages and salaries, fueled by the rapidly rising cost of medical care. Accordingly, employers attempt to reduce benefits costs, even as their value to employees is rising.

The typical employer today pays about 32 percent of payroll costs in benefits.

Benefits are more complex than they used to be. Many new types are available, and tax laws affect myriad benefits such as health insurance and pension plans.

Pay Decisions

Reward systems serve the strategic purposes of attracting, motivating, and retaining people. Wages are based on a complex set of forces. Exhibit 10.8 shows some of the factors that influence the wage mix.

Three types of decisions are crucial for designing an effective pay plan: pay level, pay structure, and individual pay.

Pay level refers to the choice of whether to be a high-, average-, or low-paying employer. Compensation is a major cost for any organization, so low wages can be justified on a short-term financial basis. But being the high-wage employer—the highest-paying company in the region—ensures that the company will attract many applicants. Being a wage leader may be important during times of low unemployment or intense competition.

The *pay structure* decision is how to price different jobs within the organization. Jobs similar in worth usually are grouped into job families. Each job family has a pay grade with a floor and a ceiling. Exhibit 10.9 illustrates a hypothetical pay structure.

EXHIBIT 10.8

Factors Affecting the Wage Mix

Internal Factors	External Factors
Compensation policy of organization	Conditions of labor market
Worth of job	Cost of living
Employee's relative worth	Collective bargaining
Employer's ability to pay	Legal requirements

SOURCE: Snell, S.A., and Bohlander, G.W., *Managing Human Resources,* 16th ed. Boston, MA: Cengage Learning, 2012.

EXHIBIT 10.9
Pay Structure

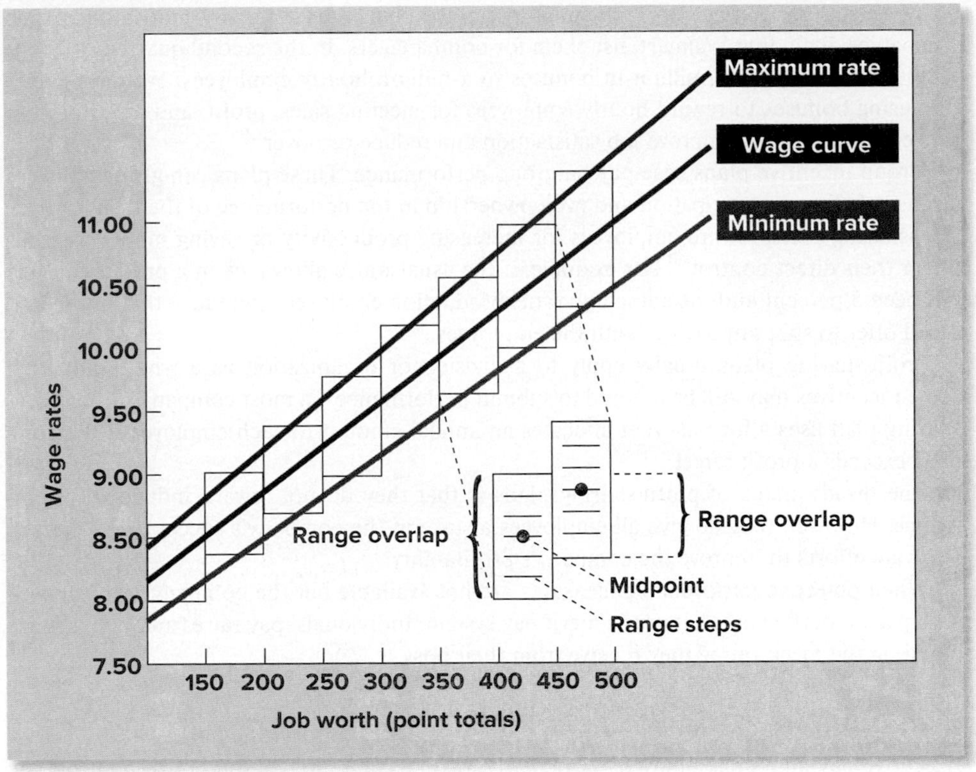

SOURCE: Sherman, Arthur, Bohlander, George and Snell, Scott, *Managing Human Resources,* 11th ed. Boston, MA: South-Western, 1998.

Finally, *individual pay decisions* determine different pay rates for different people holding jobs of similar worth within the same job family. These pay differences are decided in two ways. First, some individuals in the same job family have more seniority than others. Second, some are better performers than others and therefore deserve higher pay. These decisions may become more difficult as more employees use online resources such as Glassdoor.com and Salary.com to check whether their pay is above or below the average for similar job titles.[56]

Decisions about pay often are kept confidential. Surprisingly, there is little recent evidence about the effects of pay secrecy even though it affects almost every private sector employee.[57] The organization may benefit from pay secrecy by protecting people's privacy, avoiding conflicts, and reducing the likelihood that low-paid employees will quit. On the other hand, if people don't see a link between their performance and their pay, they may suspect that the system or the boss is unfair and that working hard to perform well does not pay off.

Moreover, younger people are used to living in a world where most data are readily retrievable online (including pay data on websites such as Glassdoor.com). Many ignore it when their employer requests that pay remain confidential.

Given these possible pros and cons of pay secrecy, do you think this practice is wise? Is it ethical? And what about you—do you want to know how much your co-workers earn?

Incentive Systems and Variable Pay

Various incentive systems have been devised to encourage and motivate employees to be more productive.[58] The most common type of incentive system is the individual incentive plan. An individual incentive system uses an objective standard against which a worker's performance is compared. Pay for each person is determined accordingly. Sales jobs commonly use such plans—for example, a salesperson will receive extra compensation for exceeding a sales target. Another widely used individual incentive is management bonuses.

When designed effectively, individual incentive plans can be highly motivating. Some companies, including Walmart, use them for nonmanagers. In the second quarter 2016, the retailer paid over $200 million in bonuses to a million hourly employees. Walmart hopes that using bonuses to reward hourly employees for meeting sales, profit, and inventory targets each quarter will improve job satisfaction and reduce turnover.[59]

Group incentive plans base pay on group performance. These plans can give employees a sense of shared participation and even ownership in the performance of the team or unit. Gainsharing plans reward employees for increasing productivity or saving money in areas under their direct control.[60] For example, if the usual waste allowance in a production line has been 5 percent and the company wants production employees to reduce that number, it could offer to split any savings with the employees.

Profit-sharing plans usually apply to a division or organization as a whole, although some incentives may still be tailored to subunit performance. In most companies, the profit-sharing plan uses a formula that allocates an annual amount to each employee if the company exceeds a profit target.

One disadvantage of profit-sharing plans is that they do not reward individual performance. However, they do give all employees a stake in the company's success, and thereby motivate efforts to improve the company's profitability.

When objective performance measures are not available but the company still wants to base pay on performance, it uses a merit pay system. Individuals' pay raises and bonuses are based on the merit rating they receive from their boss.

Executive Pay and Stock Options

Executive pay and stock options, particularly for CEOs, are major sources of controversy. One reason is that the gap between the pay of top executives and the average pay of employees has widened considerably. In the mid-1960s in the United States, the average company paid its CEO roughly 20 times as much as it paid its average nonmanagement worker. Since then, the ratio of CEO pay to average-worker pay soared to a peak of around 400-to-1 in 2000 and more recently has been around 340-to-1.[61]

The fastest-growing part of executive compensation comes from stock options and grants. Stock options give the holder the right to purchase shares of stock at a specified price. If the company's stock price is $8 a share, the company may award a manager the right to purchase a specific number of shares of company stock at that price. If the price of the stock rises to, say, $10 a share after a specified holding period—usually three years or more—the manager can exercise the option. She pays $8 per share, sells the shares on the stock market at $10, and keeps the difference. (Of course, if the stock price never rises above $8, the options will be worthless.) For many top managers, large option grants have become a major source of additional compensation.

Adding to the scrutiny over this practice is the striking number of situations in which options were dated just before the company's stock price rose, increasing their value. People suspected that at least some of these options were backdated unethically. These more valuable options give executives less incentive to improve the company's performance in the stock market.[62]

Companies issue options to managers to align their interests with those of the company's owners, the shareholders. The assumption is that managers will become even more focused on making the company successful, delivering stock price increases. Assuming that the executives continue to own stock year after year, the amount of their wealth tied to the company's performance—and their incentive to work hard for the company—should continually increase.[63]

Many critics say that excessive use of options encourages executives to focus on short-term results to drive up the price of their stock at the expense of their firm's long-run competitiveness. Others say that lucrative options have motivated questionable or even unethical behavior. A plunging stock market highlights another problem with stock options: many options become essentially worthless, so they provide no reward.[64]

However, corporations readily adjust executives' total compensation packages when needed or desired. A review of compensation to the five highest-paid executives at 3,000 companies found that after the financial crisis, performance-based pay continued to rise, becoming a majority of the pay package, but shifted away from options toward stock grants and bonuses.

Traditionally, companies incurred no expense when they issued stock options. This was another reason options were an attractive incentive tool and sometimes were issued even to nonmanagers. However, due to corporate scandals and to curb excessive use of options, the rules were changed in 2004 so that options have to be treated as an expense by companies that issue them. This means that compensation committees have to consider more carefully how options motivate executives.

Employee Benefits

Like pay systems, employee benefit plans are subject to regulation. Some benefits are required by law, and some are optional for employers.

The three basic required benefits are workers' compensation, Social Security, and unemployment insurance. *Workers' compensation* provides financial support to employees suffering a work-related injury or illness. *Social Security,* as established in the Social Security Act of 1935, provides financial support to retirees; in subsequent amendments, the act was expanded to cover employees with disabilities. The funds come from payments made by employers, employees, and self-employed workers. *Unemployment insurance* provides financial support to employees who are laid off for reasons they cannot control. Companies that terminate fewer employees pay less into the unemployment insurance fund; thus organizations have an incentive to keep terminations at a minimum.

Many benefits are not required to be employer-provided. The most common are pension plans and medical and hospital insurance, and they are undergoing major changes. For decades, most Americans under the retirement age were covered by health insurance plans provided by their employers. But as the cost of providing this benefit has soared far faster than other compensation costs, employers started dropping it or providing very limited policies.

In 2010 the federal government responded to concern about the rising number of uninsured people and the high cost of care by passing the Patient Protection and Affordable Care Act. What's going on in this area as you read this?

At the same time, retirement benefits have shifted away from guaranteed pension payments. Whereas a promised monthly payout used to be the norm, now only about 7 percent of companies offer this to new employees.[65] Instead, employers, and perhaps their employees, may contribute to an individual retirement account or 401(k) plan, which is invested. When the employee retires, he gets the total amount accumulated in the account.

Because of the wide variety of possible benefits and considerable differences in employee preferences and needs, companies often use **cafeteria** or **flexible benefit programs**. Employees receive credits that they spend on benefits they most desire. They use their credits toward customized packages of benefits—medical and dental insurance, dependent care, life insurance, and so on.

Legal Issues in Compensation and Benefits

Several laws affect employee compensation and benefits. The Fair Labor Standards Act sets minimum wage, maximum hour, and child labor provisions.[66] The Equal Pay Act (EPA) of 1963 prohibits unequal pay for men and women who perform equal work. Equal work means jobs that require equal skill, effort, and responsibility and are performed under similar working conditions. The law does permit exceptions in which the difference in pay is

cafeteria benefit program
An employee benefit program in which employees choose from a menu of options to create a benefit package tailored to their needs.

flexible benefit programs
Benefit programs in which employees are given credits to spend on benefits that fit their unique needs.

Bottom Line
Organizations today seek new ways to reduce benefits costs. *What benefits have you received from an employer? Did you ever consider the cost of those benefits?*

Employee benefits include those required by law, such as workers' compensation, Social Security, and unemployment insurance, and those chosen by the employer. Retirement plans and paid vacation time are examples of employer-provided, nonrequired benefits.

©Triangle Images/Getty Images RF

due to a seniority system, a merit system, an incentive system based on quantity or quality of production, or any other factor other than sex (such as market demand). Although equal pay for equal work may sound like common sense, many employers have fallen victim to this law by rationalizing that men, traditionally the breadwinners, deserve more pay than women or by giving equal jobs different titles (senior assistant versus office manager) as the sole basis for pay differences.

comparable worth

Principle of equal pay for different jobs of equal worth.

The **comparable worth** doctrine implies that women who perform *different* jobs of *equal* worth as those performed by men in the same company should be paid the same wage.[67] In contrast to equal-pay-for-equal-work, comparable worth means that the jobs need *not* be the same to require the same pay. For example, nurses (predominantly female) were paid considerably less than skilled craftworkers (predominantly male), even though the two jobs were found to be of equal value or worth.[68] Under the Equal Pay Act, this would not constitute pay discrimination because the jobs are very different. But under the comparable worth concept, these findings indicate discrimination because the jobs are of equal worth.

To date, no federal law requires comparable worth, and the Supreme Court has made no decisive rulings about it. However, some states, including Iowa, Minnesota, and Washington, have comparable worth laws for public sector employees.

Some laws pertain mostly to benefit practices. The Pregnancy Discrimination Act of 1978 states that pregnancy is a disability and qualifies a woman to receive the same benefits that she would with any other disability. The Employee Retirement Income Security Act (ERISA) of 1974 protects private pension programs from mismanagement. ERISA requires that retirement benefits be paid to those who vest or earn a right to draw benefits. It ensures retirement benefits for employees whose companies go bankrupt or who otherwise cannot meet their pension obligations.

Health and Safety

The Occupational Safety and Health Act (OSHA) of 1970 requires employers to pursue workplace safety. Employers must maintain records of injuries and deaths caused by workplace accidents and submit to on-site inspections. Large-scale industrial accidents and nuclear power plant disasters worldwide have focused attention on the importance of workplace safety.

Coal mining is one of many industries that benefit from safety laws. Mining is one of the five most dangerous jobs to perform, according to the U.S. Bureau of Labor Statistics. Nearly every coal miner can name a friend or family member who has been killed, maimed, or stricken with black lung disease. "You die quick or you die slow," states one mine worker. Mine safety tragically returned to American consciousness in April 2010, when a coal mine explosion at the Massey Energy Company's Upper Big Branch Mine killed 29 workers. An independent investigation found that the accident could have been prevented and was attributable to safety system failures.[69]

Yet, according to the Mine Safety and Health Administration, mines have become safer. In the 1960s, hundreds of coal miners died in mine accidents every year. During the past decade, even in the year of the Massey disaster, the number of annual fatalities was less than 50.[70]

labor relations

The system of relations between workers and management.

Another area of concern is the safety of young immigrant workers. A recent study found that Latino immigrants have a 50 percent higher workplace fatality rate than all other workers. Reasons include lack of safety training, and language and cultural barriers.[71]

Labor Relations

LO 7 **Labor relations** is the system of relations between workers and management. When workers organize for the purpose of negotiating with management to improve their wages, hours, or working conditions, two processes are involved: unionization and collective bargaining. Labor unions recruit members, collect dues, and negotiate to ensure that employees are treated fairly regarding pay, safety, and other issues. Although fewer people than before belong to labor unions, these processes have evolved since the 1930s in the United States to provide important employee rights.[72]

Labor Laws

Try to imagine what life would be like with unemployment at 25 percent. Pretty grim, you would say. Legislators in 1935 felt that way too. Therefore, organized labor received its Magna Carta with the passage of the National Labor Relations Act.

The National Labor Relations Act (also called the Wagner Act after its legislative sponsor) ushered in an era of rapid unionization by (1) declaring labor organizations legal, (2) establishing five unfair employer labor practices, and (3) creating the National Labor Relations Board (NLRB). Prior to the act, employers could fire workers who favored unions, and federal troops often put down strikes. Today the NLRB conducts unionization elections, hears complaints of unfair labor practices, and issues injunctions against offending employers.

The Wagner Act boosted union growth by enabling workers to use the law and the courts to organize and collectively bargain for better wages, hours, and working conditions. Many workplace improvements that now are taken for granted, including minimum wages, health benefits, maternity leave, the 35-hour workweek, and worker protections in general were largely the result of collective bargaining over many years by unions.

Public policy began on the side of organized labor in 1935, but over the next 25 years the pendulum swung toward management's side. The Labor-Management Relations Act, or Taft-Hartley Act (1947), protected employers' free speech rights, defined unfair labor practices by unions, and permitted workers to decertify (reject) a union as their representative.

For years, the Service Employees International Union has aggressively tried to organize workers at McDonald's, the largest fast-food chain in the world. So far, the company remains union-free. For a manager, what would be the pros and cons of a union?

©Tribune Content Agency LLC/ Alamy Stock Photo

Finally, the Labor-Management Reporting and Disclosure Act, or Landrum-Griffin Act (1959), swung the public policy pendulum midway between organized labor and management. By declaring a bill of rights for union members, establishing control over union dues increases, and imposing reporting requirements for unions, Landrum-Griffin focused on curbing abuses by union leadership and ridding unions of corruption.

Unionization

How do workers join unions? Through a union organizer or local union representative, workers learn what benefits they receive by joining.[73] The National Labor Relations Board will conduct a certification election if at least 30 percent of the employees sign authorization cards. Management has several choices at this stage: to recognize the union without an election, to consent to an election, or to contest the number of cards signed and resist an election.

If an election is warranted, an NLRB representative will conduct one by secret ballot. A simple majority of those voting determines the winner. If the union wins the election, it is certified as the bargaining unit representative.

During the campaign preceding the election, management and the union each try to convince the workers how to vote. Most workers, though, are somewhat resistant to campaign efforts, having made up their minds well before the NLRB appears on the scene. If the union wins the election, management and the union are legally required to bargain in good faith to obtain a collective bargaining agreement or contract.

EXHIBIT 10.10
Determinants of Union
Voting Behavior

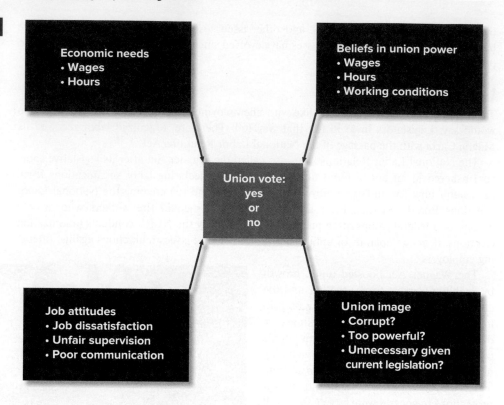

Exhibit 10.10 shows the major influences on union votes.[74] First, economic factors: unions attempt to raise the average wage rate for their members. Second, job dissatisfaction: specific triggers include poor supervisory practices, favoritism, and perceived unfair or arbitrary discipline and discharge. Third is the belief that the union can obtain desired benefits. Finally, the image of the union: for instance, stories of union corruption and dishonesty can discourage workers from unionizing.

Collective Bargaining

In the United States, management and unions engage in a periodic ritual (typically every three years) of negotiating an agreement over wages, benefits, hours, and working conditions. Two types of disputes can arise during this process. First, before an agreement is reached, the workers may go on strike to compel agreement on their terms. This is an *economic strike* and is permitted by law.

Strikes today are not common, although they sometimes occur as a last resort. Strikers are not paid if they are on strike, and few workers want to undertake this hardship unnecessarily. In addition, managers may legally hire replacement workers during a strike, offsetting some of the strike's effect. Finally, workers are as aware as managers of the tough competition companies face today, and if treated fairly they usually will share management's interest in reaching an agreement.

Once an agreement is signed, management and the union sometimes disagree over interpretation of the agreement. Usually they settle their disputes through arbitration. **Arbitration** is the use of a neutral third party, typically jointly selected, to resolve the dispute. U.S. companies use arbitration while an agreement is in effect to avoid *wildcat strikes* (in which workers walk off the job in violation of the contract) or unannounced work stoppages.

What does a collective bargaining agreement contain? In a **union shop**, a union security clause specifies that workers after a while must join the union. **Right-to-work** states, through restrictive legislation, do not permit union shops; that is, workers have the right

---

arbitration

The use of a neutral third party to resolve a labor dispute.

---

union shop

An organization with a union and a union security clause specifying that workers must join the union after a set period of time.

---

right-to-work

Legislation that allows employees to work without having to join a union.

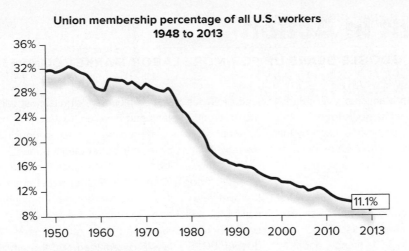

**Union membership percentage of all U.S. workers
1948 to 2013**

11.1%

EXHIBIT 10.11

Decline in Union
Membership—1948 to
2013

SOURCE: Data adapted from the Bureau of Labor Statistics, "Union Members Summary," press release, January 23, 2015, http://www.bls.gov/news.release/union2.nr0.htm.

to work without being forced to join a union. The southern United States has many right-to-work states.

The wage component of the contract spells out pay rates, including premium pay for overtime and paid holidays. Individual rights usually specify how seniority is considered in decisions such as pay, job bidding, and layoffs.

The grievance procedure is a feature of any contract. Through the grievance procedure, unions perform a vital service for their members by giving them a voice in what goes on during contract negotiations and contract administration.[75] In about 50 percent of discharge cases that go to arbitration, the arbitrator overturns management's decision and reinstates the worker.[76]

Unions have a legal duty to provide fair representation, which means they must represent and protect the rights of all workers in the bargaining unit.

What Does the Future Hold?

In recent years, union membership has declined to about 11 percent of the U.S. labor force—down from a peak of more than 33 percent at the end of World War II (see Exhibit 10.11). Automation eliminated many of the manufacturing jobs that used to be union strongholds. Employees in most office jobs are less interested in joining unions and are more difficult to organize. Tough global competition has made managers less willing to give in to union demands, and therefore the benefits of unionization are less apparent to many workers—particularly to young, skilled workers who no longer expect to stay with one company all their lives.

Some people applaud unions' decline. Others hope for a reemergence. Unions are adapting to changing workforce demographics; they are paying more attention to women, older workers, government employees, and people who work at home.

> In recent years, union membership has declined to about 11 percent of the U.S. labor force.

When companies recognize that their success depends on the talents and energies of employees, the interests of unions and managers can converge. Rather than one side exploiting or fighting the other, unions and managers can find common ground in developing, valuing, and involving employees. Whether or not employees belong to a union, they, not companies, own their own human capital. And these employees are free to leave the organization, taking their human capital with them.

This leaves organizations in a particularly vulnerable position if they manage poorly. To establish a strong competitive capability, organizations search for ways to obtain, retain, and

Management in Action

GOOGLE GEARS UP FOR MORE LABOR MARKET COMPETITION

Google's recruiting and selection practices have contributed to its mystique, helping it meet its goals for hiring the best talent. But that HR strategy has been shaken by the appeal of up-and-coming high-tech firms. Thus, even as Google is adding thousands to its ranks, it must keep current employees from leaving.

One way to keep people is to hire well in the first place. Google prides itself on being selective, encouraging employee referrals from current employees, and working to increase the objectivity of its hiring standards. It also offers the opportunity to work with outstanding peers as an inducement for new hires. And while pay isn't everything, Google has increased its budget for compensation. For Google, this is an investment: to enter new, growing areas of the high-tech industry, it needs talented people.

But money aside, one reason tech workers leave for start-ups is that they want to enjoy the excitement of building something new. Google therefore tries to be worker-friendly in its own data-driven way. Its effort to measure and improve management effectiveness was conceived partly as a way to create a more positive work environment. It helps that managers' performance is measured both by the manager's boss and by his or her employees.

The same goal and approach apply to decisions about employee benefits. For example, Google determines what kind of advice helps employees get the most value from their retirement plans and how to structure pay increases so employees will appreciate it most. It concluded, for example, that a pay raise is better than a bonus.

Or consider the case of the disappearing women. Google's People Operations (POPS) department tracked turnover rates and noticed that female employees were leaving at a high rate—an expensive problem, given the costs to recruit, hire, and train replacements. Digging deeper, POPS analysts determined that the attrition was led by women quitting after giving birth.

Google's parental-leave policy was standard for its industry, but the evidence showed that was not enough. So Google began offering mothers 18 months off at full pay—time they may schedule however they want. Turnover among new mothers dropped by half, matching the rate of all employees. That improvement lowered the expense of replacing employees enough to make up for the cost of the new benefit.[78]

- How is Google's approach to employee benefits more effective than a simple decision to offer the biggest benefits package?
- Do you think Google's HR strategy will enable it to maintain a competitive advantage? Why or why not? What will it have to do to sustain advantage?

engage their most valuable resources: human resources. "Management in Action: Onward" explores why and how this is a critical issue for Google. The practices outlined in this chapter form the context for how people behave in organizations,[77] as addressed in the following chapters.

KEY TERMS

adverse impact, p. 288
arbitration, p. 302
assessment center, p. 286
cafeteria benefit program, p. 299
comparable worth, p. 300
development, p. 290
diversity training, p. 291
employment-at-will, p. 287
flexible benefit programs, p. 299
human capital, p. 279
human resources management (HRM), p. 278

job analysis, p. 282
labor relations, p. 300
management by objectives (MBO), p. 294
needs assessment, p. 290
orientation training, p. 290
outplacement, p. 287
performance appraisal (PA), p. 292
recruitment, p. 282
reliability, p. 286
right-to-work, p. 302
selection, p. 283

structured interview, p. 283
team training, p. 291
termination interview, p. 288
360-degree appraisal, p. 295
training, p. 290
union shop, p. 302
validity, p. 286

RETAINING WHAT YOU LEARNED

In Chapter 10, you learned that by aligning their human resources and strategies, organizations can achieve a competitive advantage. Hiring the right number and types of employees requires effective planning. Organizations should design their HR systems to reinforce key employee behaviors. Internal and external recruitment each has advantages and disadvantages. Companies use a variety of selection methods when choosing whom to hire, including interviews and cognitive ability tests. It is important that organizations use methods that are valid and reliable. In order to maintain a competitive edge, companies need talented, flexible workers who engage in continuous training and development. While supervisors typically provide performance appraisals for their subordinates, organizations may seek this information from multiple sources. An organization's reward system consists of pay and benefits. Labor relations involve the interactions between workers and management. In addition to negotiating agreements with management, unions develop grievance procedures to protect member rights. Labor laws seek to protect the rights of operative-level employees and managers.

LO 1 **Discuss how companies use human resources management to gain competitive advantage.**

- To succeed, companies must align their human resources to their strategies. Effective planning is necessary to make certain that the right number and types of employees are available to implement a company's strategic plan.
- Companies that compete on cost, quality, service, and so on also should use their staffing, training, appraisal, and reward systems to elicit and reinforce the kinds of behaviors that underlie their strategies.

LO 2 **Give reasons companies recruit both internally and externally for new hires.**

- Sometimes companies prefer to recruit internally to make certain that employees are familiar with organizational policies and values.

- In other instances, companies prefer to recruit externally, such as through employee referrals, job boards, newspaper advertising, and campus visits, to find people with new ideas and fresh perspectives.
- External recruiting is also necessary to fill positions when the organization is growing or needs skills that do not exist among its current employees.

LO 3 **Identify various methods for selecting new employees.**

- There are myriad selection techniques from which to choose. Interviews and reference checks are the most common. Personality tests and cognitive ability tests measure an individual's aptitude and potential to do well on the job. Other selection techniques include assessment centers and integrity tests. Background and reference checks verify that the information supplied by employees is accurate.
- Regardless of the approach used, any test should be able to demonstrate reliability (consistency across time and different interview situations) and validity (accuracy in predicting job performance).
- In addition, selection methods must comply with equal opportunity laws, which are intended to ensure that companies do not discriminate in any employment practices.

LO 4 **Evaluate the importance of spending on training and development.**

- People cannot depend on a single set of skills for all of their working lives. In today's changing, highly competitive world, old skills quickly become obsolete, and new ones become essential for success.
- Refreshing or updating an individual's skills requires continuous training, designed with measurable goals and methods that will achieve those goals.
- Gaining a competitive edge depends on having the most talented, flexible workers in the industry.

Planning	Programming	Evaluating
HR environmental scanning • Labor markets • Technology • Legislation • Competition • Economy **HR Planning** • Demand forecast • Internal labor supply • External labor supply • Job analysis	**HR Activities** • Recruitment • Selection • Diversity and inclusion • Training and development • Performance appraisal • Reward systems • Labor relations	**Results** • Productivity • Quality • Innovation • Satisfaction • Turnover • Absenteeism • Health

EXHIBIT 10.1 (revisited)

An Overview of the HR Planning Process

LO 5   Discuss options for who appraises an employee's performance.

- Many companies use multiple sources for appraisals because different people see different sides of an employee's performance. Typically, a superior evaluates an employee, but peers and team members are often well positioned to see aspects of performance that a superior misses. Even an manager's subordinates can provide input to get yet another perspective on the evaluation.
- Particularly in companies concerned about quality, internal and external customers can be surveyed.
- Employees should evaluate their own performance, to engage them in the process and get them thinking about future goals.

LO 6   Describe the fundamental aspects of reward systems.

- Rewards systems include pay and benefits.
- Pay systems have three basic components: pay level, pay structure, and individual pay determination. To achieve an advantage over competitors, executives can pay generally higher wages, but this decision must be weighed against the need to control costs.
- To achieve internal equity (paying people what they are worth relative to their peers within the company), managers must look at the pay structure, making certain that pay differentials are based on valid and fair criteria.

- Individual pay determination is often based on merit and contributions. Importantly, men and women should receive equal pay for equal work, and managers may wish to base pay decisions on the idea of comparable worth (equal pay for an equal contribution).

LO 7   Summarize how unions and labor laws influence human resources management.

- Labor relations involve the interactions between workers and management. Unions provide one mechanism by which this relationship is conducted.
- Unions seek to present a collective voice for workers, to make their needs and wishes known to management. Also, they negotiate agreements with management regarding a range of issues such as wages, hours, working conditions, job security, and health care.
- One important tool that unions can use is the grievance procedure, established through collective bargaining. This mechanism gives employees a way to seek redress for wrongful action by management. In this way, unions protect the rights of all employees.
- Labor laws seek to protect the rights of both employees and managers so that their relationship can be productive and agreeable.

DISCUSSION QUESTIONS

1. How will changes in the labor force affect HRM practices for the next decade?
2. Describe the major regulations governing HRM practices. Which, if any, have benefited you? Which ones could have benefited you but were not applied?
3. How could job analysis be relevant to each of the six key HRM activities discussed in the chapter (i.e., planning, staffing, training, performance appraisal, reward systems, labor relations)?
4. What are the various methods for recruiting employees? Why are some better than others? In what sense are they better? Describe some of your personal experiences.
5. What is a test? Give some examples of tests used by employers that you have seen or heard about.

6. What purposes do performance appraisals serve? Why are there so many appraisal methods? Which have you experienced, and what do you think of how they were used?
7. What are some key ideas to remember when conducting a performance appraisal? What mistakes and best practices have you seen?
8. How would you define an effective reward system? What role do benefits serve in a reward system?
9. Why do workers join unions? What implications would this have for an organization that wishes to remain nonunion?
10. Discuss the advantages and disadvantages of collective bargaining for the employer and the employee.

EXPERIENTIAL EXERCISES

10.1 THE LEGAL INTERVIEW

OBJECTIVES

1. To introduce you to the complexities of employment law.
2. To identify interview practices that might lead to discrimination in employment.

INSTRUCTIONS

1. Working alone, review the text material on interviewing and discrimination in employment.
2. In small groups, complete the Legal Interview Worksheet.

3. After the class reconvenes, group spokespersons present group findings.

Legal Interview Worksheet

The employment interview is one of the most critical steps in the employment selection process. It also may be an occasion for discriminating against individual employment candidates. The following represents questions that interviewers often ask job applicants. Identify the legality of each question by circling L (legal) or I (illegal) and briefly explain your decision.

Interview Question	Legality	Explanation
1. Could you provide us with a photo for our files?	L I	_____
2. Have you ever used another name (previous married name or alias)?	L I	_____
3. What was your maiden name?	L I	_____
4. What was your wife's maiden name?	L I	_____
5. What was your mother's maiden name?	L I	_____
6. What is your current address?	L I	_____
7. What was your previous address?	L I	_____
8. What is your Social Security number?	L I	_____
9. Where was your place of birth?	L I	_____
10. Where were your parents born?	L I	_____
11. What is your national origin?	L I	_____
12. Are you a naturalized citizen?	L I	_____
13. What languages do you speak?	L I	_____
14. What is your religious/church affiliation?	L I	_____
15. What is your racial classification?	L I	_____
16. How many dependents do you have?	L I	_____
17. What are the ages of your dependent children?	L I	_____
18. What is your marital status?	L I	_____
19. How old are you?	L I	_____
20. Do you have proof of your age (birth certificate or baptismal record)?	L I	_____
21. Whom do we notify in case of an emergency?	L I	_____
22. What are your height and weight?	L I	_____
23. Have you ever been arrested?	L I	_____
24. Do you own your own car?	L I	_____
25. Do you own your own house?	L I	_____
26. Do you have any charge accounts?	L I	_____
27. Have you ever had your salary garnished?	L I	_____
28. To what organizations do you belong?	L I	_____
29. Are you available to work on Saturdays and Sundays?	L I	_____
30. Do you have any form of disability?	L I	_____

10.2 THE PAY RAISE

OBJECTIVES

1. To further your understanding of salary administration.
2. To examine the many facets of performance criteria, performance criteria weighting, performance evaluation, and rewards.

INSTRUCTIONS

1. Working in small groups, complete the Pay Raise Worksheet.
2. After the class reconvenes, group spokespersons present group findings.

Pay Raise Worksheet

April Knepper is the new supervisor of an assembly team. It is time for her to make pay raise allocations for her subordinates. She has been budgeted $30,000 to allocate among her seven subordinates as pay raises. There have been some ugly grievances in other work teams over past allocations, so Knepper has been advised to base the allocations on objective criteria that can be quantified, weighted, and computed in numerical terms. After she makes her allocations, Knepper must be prepared to justify her decisions. All of the evaluative criteria available to Knepper are summarized as follows:

Employee	Seniority	Output Rating*	Absent Rate	Supervisory Ratings				Personal
				Skills	Initiative	Attitude		
David Bruce	15 yrs.	0.58	0.5%	Good	Poor	Poor		Nearing retirement. Wife just passed away. Having adjustment problems.
Eric Cattalini	12 yrs.	0.86	2.0	Excellent	Good	Excellent		Going to night school to finish his BA degree.
Chua Li	7 yrs.	0.80	3.5	Good	Excellent	Excellent		Legally deaf.
Marilee Miller	1 yr.	0.50	10.0	Poor	Poor	Poor		Single parent with three children.
Victor Munoz	3 yrs.	0.62	2.5	Poor	Average	Good		Has six dependents. Speaks little English.
Derek Thompson	11 yrs.	0.64	8.0	Excellent	Average	Average		Married to rich wife. Personal problems.
Sarah Vickers	8 yrs.	0.76	7.0	Good	Poor	Poor		Women's activist. Wants to create a union.

*Output rating determined by production rate less errors and quality problems.

Concluding Case

INVINCIBILITY SYSTEMS

The 17,000 employees of Invincibility Systems design and make aerospace and defense equipment such as rockets, spacecraft propulsion systems, and missile propulsion systems. Along with cutting-edge engineering, the company stands out for its cutting-edge human resource management. Invincibility has hired quantitative experts to analyze HR data with the same care it uses to analyze rocket trajectories.

A few years ago, the company hired a statistician and an HR planner to join a team that would collect and analyze data, looking for factors that would predict human resource needs. The team started by looking for ways to improve recruiting. They collected data on the various sources of candidates that the company was using and the candidates actually selected. Then they used a statistical method called regression analysis to identify which sources of candidates generated the most hires—as well as the sources that generated hires who went on to perform well. Using the results of the analysis, Invincibility made its recruiting effort more efficient. By focusing on the most productive sources of top employees, it saves time and money that formerly had gone toward recruiting through channels that were less fruitful.

Next the HR team turned its efforts toward workforce planning. For each department of Invincibility, the team collects data describing the workforce—for example, job categories, years with the company, and labor force projections. It runs regression analysis to predict the likelihood that employees will leave the company in the coming year. The results, coupled with sales forecasts, enable the company to predict how many new employees will need to be hired in each department.

Other companies do this kind of planning, but the extent of the analysis at Invincibility is unusual. For one thing, the analysis is conducted on the level of individual employees. Thus it shows not only that turnover may rise or fall, but also which employees are most likely to leave. That level of analysis is important to Invincibility because unlike organizations where many people perform the same type of work and can step in when someone leaves, employees at Invincibility typically fill highly specialized, highly skilled roles. If an engineer with years of experience in developing high-caliber ammunition suddenly departs, there may be no one else on the team with that person's knowledge and skill set.

Another unusual quality of Invincibility's HR planning is the variety of factors that the planners consider when they run their regression analyses. For example, the company has run regressions to determine whether turnover is related to changes in employee benefits and even the month of the year. If the analysis shows that a factor has been significant in the past, the planners take it into account in their forecasts. In one situation, the planners found that retirements in a department rose after the company announced that it would be phasing out health insurance benefits for retirees. More experienced workers left before the phase-out took effect. When the company prepared to phase out similar benefits in another division, the planners knew they would need to step up recruiting efforts there in preparation for an uptick in retirements.

Some of the data Invincibility uses for planning are unsuitable for other kinds of HR decisions. For example, the company has found that employees' ages and marital status are relevant for predicting whether they are likely to leave the company. Turnover rates are higher among unmarried employees and recently hired employees (who tend to be younger). Thus the company plans greater recruiting efforts in departments where it has higher levels of young and unmarried employees. It also may consider stepping up its efforts to mentor and train employees in these departments. However, it does not make employment decisions such as hiring and promotion based on these factors.

DISCUSSION QUESTIONS

1. Besides the factors identified, what other factors should Invincibility Systems take into account in its HR planning?

2. What legal concerns does the data analysis at Invincibility raise? How should the company address those issues?

3. Besides its use for HR planning and recruiting, how might Invincibility's data analysis be applied to improving the company's training programs?

CHAPTER 11
Managing the Diverse Workforce

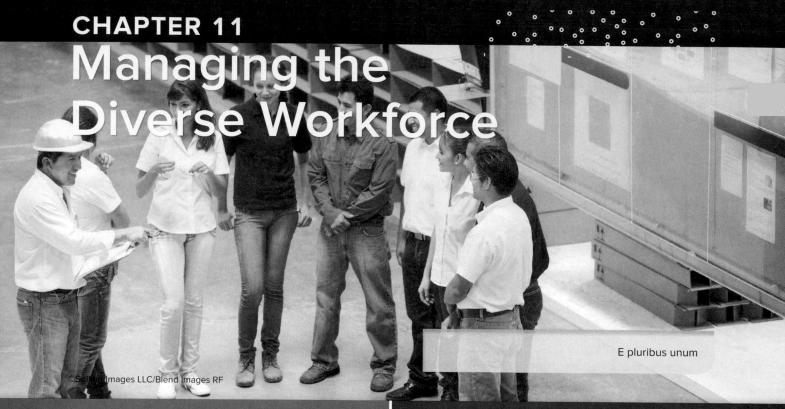

E pluribus unum

©Solinie Images LLC/Blend Images RF

LEARNING OBJECTIVES

After studying Chapter 11, you will be able to:

LO 1 Describe how changes in the U.S. workforce make diversity a critical organizational and managerial issue.

LO 2 Distinguish between affirmative action and managing diversity.

LO 3 Explain how diversity, if well managed, can give organizations a competitive edge.

LO 4 Identify challenges associated with managing a diverse workforce.

LO 5 Define monolithic, pluralistic, and multicultural organizations.

LO 6 List actions managers and their organizations can take to cultivate diversity.

CHAPTER OUTLINE

Diversity: A Brief History

Diversity Today
The Changing Workforce
The Age of the Workforce

Managing Diversity and Affirmative Action
Advantage through Diversity and Inclusion
Challenges of Diversity and Inclusion

Multicultural Organizations

How to Cultivate a Diverse Workforce
Top Management's Leadership and Commitment
Organizational Assessment
Attracting Employees
Training Employees
Retaining Employees

Management in Action

DIVERSITY AND INCLUSION AT APPLE

Silicon Valley has a problem. For all their progress in creating successful new products that forever change the way we live and work, tech companies lag far behind many other industries in creating even a minimally diverse workforce. Blacks and Latinos, who together make up about 30 percent of the U.S. population, account for only about 5 percent of employees in the technology industry, while women, fully half the population, are only 24 percent of the tech workforce.

When it comes to the executive suite, those numbers drop even lower. At Cisco, for instance, women make up about half the administrative staff but hold only about 20 percent of the highest managerial positions. Dell's numbers are about the same.

While some, including Facebook, have blamed a dearth of minority applicants for the lack of diversity, others disagree strongly. "It's not even remotely a pipeline issue," says Andrea Hoffman of Culture Shift Labs, a sourcing company that helps managers meet diversity goals. "For anybody to tell me the talent isn't out there, I know emphatically that's not true." As proof, her company recently accepted a waiting list of 200 people for a sold-out event it hosted to attract minorities looking for jobs in technology and finance.

An African American engineer with two master's degrees and an outstanding management track record agrees with Hoffman. After being turned down for a job at Facebook, he told *Inc.* magazine, "To say there is not enough talent out there is like a slap in the face. There are plenty of diverse people in my network alone who have the aptitude and the competitive edge and innovative mentality necessary to be successful at a tech company."

Other causes for the disproportionately high numbers of white males in tech jobs include unconscious racial and gender bias and companies' tendency to consider only applicants with specific majors. Some employees also believe the extensive media coverage

©Gary Gershoff/WireImage/Getty Images

of sexual harassment complaints at companies like Uber has drawn attention away from underlying industry problems, like entrenched hiring practices that favor white men. Many believe the tech industry, which a few years ago began releasing data about the diversity of its workforce, has succeeded only in raising awareness without taking sufficiently active steps to really solve the problem.

Apple is among the tech companies trying to increase the diversity of its workforce, aiming to make itself "a reflection of the world around us." The company has undertaken a conscious effort to increase the number of women and "underrepresented minorities" among its new hires in several ways over the last few years, and the numbers are ticking slowly upward. CEO Tim Cook takes the definition of diversity farther than most. "One of the reasons Apple products work really great," he says, "is that the people working on them are not only engineers and computer scientists, but artists and musicians. It's this intersection of the liberal arts and humanities with technology that makes products that are magical."[1]

Tim Cook's outlook on diversity may seem surprisingly broad, but that might be just what Silicon Valley needs. As you read this chapter, think about how bringing together a diverse group and leading it toward a common purpose can be challenging but also a source of opportunity

diverse workforce

One in which there are both similarities and differences among employees in terms of age, cultural background, physical abilities and disabilities, race, religion, sex, and sexual orientation.

managing diversity

Managing a culturally diverse workforce by recognizing the characteristics common to specific groups of employees while dealing with employees as individuals and supporting, nurturing, and utilizing their differences to the organization's advantage; see also *diversity*.

Until recently, white American-born males dominated the U.S. workforce, and businesses catered to their needs. Chapter 10 discussed equal opportunity and fair treatment in the workplace. In this chapter, we discuss why a proactive approach to developing and managing a **diverse workforce** has become not only a legal or moral obligation but a fundamental business requirement as well.

Managers need to be highly aware of, and sensitive to, group and cultural differences to succeed in the modern economy. In the United States, the number of racial and ethnic minorities is increasing at a far faster rate than the growth in the white, nonminority population. Women make up a larger share of the workforce than in decades past, and businesses are increasingly global. Workers, customers, and markets are already highly diverse, and are becoming even more so every day.

We have discussed how vital creativity and innovation have become for success. These require different perspectives and talented people from all walks of life. Few societies have access to the range of talents available in the United States, with its immigrant tradition and racially and ethnically diverse population.

Yet getting people from widely divergent backgrounds to work together effectively is not easy. For this reason, managing diversity is both a big challenge and big opportunity.

Managing diversity involves, first, such basic activities as recruiting, training, promoting, and engaging fully people with different backgrounds and perspectives. This means more than just hiring women and minorities and making sure they are treated fairly and encouraged to succeed. It also means understanding and deeply valuing employee differences in ways that build a more effective and profitable organization.

Diversity: A Brief History

Managing diversity is not a new management issue. From the late 1800s to the early 1900s, most of the groups immigrating to the United States were from Italy, Poland, Ireland, and Russia. Many considered them outsiders because most did not speak English and had different customs and work styles. They struggled to gain acceptance in industries such as steel, coal, automobile manufacturing, insurance, and finance.

In the 1800s, it was considered poor business practice for white Protestant–dominated insurance companies to hire Irish, Italians, Catholics, or Jews. As late as the 1940s, and in some cases later yet, colleges routinely discriminated against immigrants, Catholics, blacks, and Jews, and established strict quotas if admitting any at all. Discrimination severely diminished the employment prospects of many groups, and it wasn't until the 1960s that the struggle for acceptance by successful white ethnic and religious groups made notable progress.

Women's struggle for acceptance in the workplace was in some ways even more difficult. When the women's rights movement was launched in Seneca Falls in 1848, most occupations were off-limits to women, and colleges and professional schools were totally closed to them. Women could not vote and lost all property rights once they were married.

In the first part of the 20th century, a widespread, persistent assumption held that certain jobs were done only by men, and other jobs only by women. When women began entering professional schools, they were subject to severe quotas. As recently as the 1970s, classified ad sections in newspapers listed different jobs by sex, with sections headed "Help Wanted–Males" and "Help Wanted–Females." Women who wanted a bank loan needed a male cosigner, and married women could not get credit cards in their own name.[2]

Only when the Civil Rights Act of 1964 and other legislation arrived was this kind of sex discrimination gradually

Many of the rights all of us take for granted today—equal opportunity, fair treatment in housing, the illegality of religious, racial, and sex discrimination—received their greatest impetus from the civil rights movement.

©Francis Miller/The LIFE Picture Collection/Getty Images

eliminated. Women still are underrepresented at the most senior levels of corporate life, and major disparities still exist in other areas such as pay. But now increasing numbers of women occupy most jobs once considered the exclusive province of men, including front-line military units as well as the executive suite.

The most difficult and wrenching struggle for equality involved America's nonwhite minorities. Rigid racial segregation remained a fact of American life for 100 years after the end of the Civil War. Black voting rights, particularly in the South, often were viciously suppressed, and racial discrimination in education, employment.

Years of difficult, courageous protest and struggle gradually began to eat away at both legal and social barriers to equality. Organizations such as the NAACP, formed by a group of blacks and whites, began to use America's court system and the Constitution to bring equality to African Americans and other people of color. The unanimous *Brown v. Board of Education* Supreme Court decision in 1954 declared segregation unconstitutional, setting the stage for other legislation including the Civil Rights Act of 1964.

Consequences of America's bitter racial legacy are still with us; the struggle for equality is far from complete. But many of the rights most of us take for granted today—equal opportunity, fair treatment in housing, the illegality of religious, racial, and sex discrimination—received their greatest impetus from the civil rights movement.

Today nearly half of the U.S. workforce consists of women, 17 percent of U.S. workers identify themselves as Hispanic or Latino, and 12 percent African American. Women own one-third of all businesses in the United States, employing about 20 percent of America's workers.[3]

The traditional American image of diversity has been one of **assimilation**. The United States has long been praised as the world's melting pot, a country in which ethnic and racial differences blended ideally into an American purée. In real life, many see not a melting pot but a mixing bowl. Progress, setbacks, and periods of strain appear, fade, and reappear; progress comes not naturally but only with concerted and sustained effort.

> The traditional American image of diversity has been one of assimilation.

assimilation

The absorption into the cultural tradition of a population or group.

Diversity Today

Diversity refers to far more than skin color and gender. It is a broad term used to refer to all kinds of differences, as summarized in Exhibit 11.1. These differences include education, political belief, religion, and income in addition to gender, race, ethnicity, and nationality.[4]

Members of a demographic group or people who have been through similar important experiences share some common values, attitudes, and perspectives. At the same time, much diversity exists within each category. Every group is made up of individuals, each unique in personality, education, and opinions. There may be more differences among, say, three Asian Americans from Thailand, Hong Kong, and Korea than among a white, an African American, and an Asian American all born in Chicago. And not all white males behave alike, nor do people from the same hometown share the same personal or professional goals and values.

Therefore managing diversity requires awareness of aspects common to a group of employees while also working with each employee as an individual. Managing diversity means not just tolerating or accommodating all sorts of differences, but supporting, nurturing, integrating, and using these differences to the organization's advantage. Knowing that U.S. companies must learn to manage a diverse workforce better than their competitors, Ernst & Young has a program called "EY Unplugged" that connects ethnically diverse new hires from all around the U.S. with executive mentors.[5]

Although many companies initially instituted diversity programs to prevent discrimination, more now see these programs as a crucial way to expand their pool of talent and customer bases worldwide. These potential benefits are making diversity initiatives standard

LO 1

diversity

A broad term used to refer to all kinds of differences. These differences include education, political belief, religion, and income in addition to gender, race, ethnicity, and nationality

EXHIBIT 11.1

Components of a
Diversified Workforce

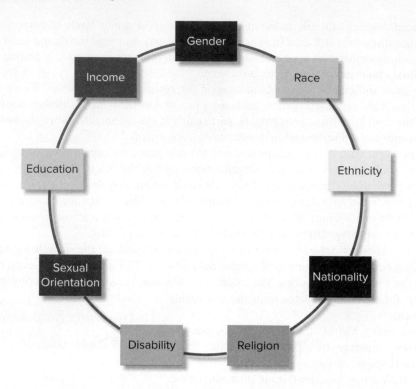

practice among industry-leading companies. A huge majority of large multinational companies have at least one diversity initiative. Exhibit 11.2 shows some additional data.

The Changing Workforce

Although white, American-born males still constitute the largest percentage of workers—about 80 percent of U.S. workers are white, and more than half of them are male—their share of the labor force is declining. The number of white male workers will continue growing, but the numbers of Asian American, African American, and Hispanic American workers will grow faster.[6] This parallels trends in the overall U.S. population.

About one in three U.S. residents is a racial or ethnic minority. The largest and fastest-growing minority group is Hispanics, closely followed by Asian Americans. In several

EXHIBIT 11.2

Examples of Diversity
Programs in S&P 100
Companies

*Refers to corporate structures that govern inclusion strategies across all operations, including board oversight of diversity programs, an established diversity council, CEO and/or chair involvement in inclusion initiatives, and compensation plans tied to diversity objectives.
SOURCE: Based on data in DeGroot, Christine et al., "Examining the Cracks in the Ceiling: A Survey of Corporate Diversity Practices of the S&P 100," *Calvert Investments*, March 2015 Supplement, http://www.calvert.com.

states—California, Hawaii, New Mexico, and Texas—and the District of Columbia, these minority groups plus Native Americans and Pacific Islanders combine to make a population that is "majority minority."[7]

The United States Census Bureau projects that by 2044 these one-time minority groups will collectively represent a majority of the U.S. population.[8]

Gender Issues   Social changes during the 1960s and 1970s, coupled with financial necessity, greatly increased the number of women entering the workforce. Consider:

- Women make up about 47 percent of the workforce.
- Approximately 53 percent of marriages are dual-earner marriages.
- Nearly one of every three married women in two-income households earns more than her husband does.
- The percentage of women in the labor force earning college degrees has nearly quadrupled over the past 45 years.[9]

For anyone holding dual responsibilities, balancing work and family presents an enormous challenge. Although men's roles in our society have been changing, women still adopt the bulk of family responsibilities, including household responsibilities, child care, and care of elderly parents. Yet some companies still expect their employees, particularly at the managerial level or in certain professions, to put in long hours and sacrifice their personal lives for the sake of their work. Not only can these expectations put many women at a career disadvantage, but they also cause companies to lose valuable talent.

glass ceiling

An invisible barrier that makes it difficult for women and minorities to move beyond a certain hierarchical level.

Companies that offer their employees the opportunity to balance work and family are better able to recruit and retain women and sometimes men. These companies offer family-friendly benefits such as onsite child care, in-home care for elderly family members, increased maternity leave, job sharing, and flexible work schedules, and they permit more work from home. The nearby "Multiple Generations at Work" box discusses such work arrangements.

> The average full-time working woman earns about 83 percent as much as men in the same job.

The average full-time working woman earns about 83 percent as much as men in the same job. A long-standing, persistent gap exists between male and female workers' earnings, even after adjusting for age, marital status, geographic region, college major and GPA, type and selectivity of undergraduate school, type of occupation, economic sector, number of hours worked, and months between graduation and starting work. Importantly, differences in performance evaluations do not explain the pay differences.[10]

While career interruptions to care for family reduce women's long-term earnings,[11] another possible explanation for the wage gap is that women are not negotiating pay as effectively as men. This hurdle is complicated by evidence that some negotiation tactics that work for men can backfire when women use them, but women benefit by doing more research into pay scales and expressing their pay requirements in a pleasant tone, backed up with evidence of their worth.[12]

Another concern is the low representation of women in top jobs. As women and minorities move up the corporate ladder, they encounter a **glass ceiling**: an invisible barrier that makes it difficult for women and minorities to move beyond a certain hierarchical level. At this writing, just 29 women are chief executives of S&P 500 companies—that's 29 out of 500. Among all board members of those companies, about 20 percent are women.[13] Still, one positive trend is that women's leadership is beginning to be seen at companies in a broader range of industries. Exhibit 11.3 lists top women executives and their companies.

Irene Rosenfeld has broken through the glass ceiling as CEO of Mondelez International, overseeing the company with revenues of over $30 billion.

©Bloomberg/Bloomberg/Getty Images

Multiple Generations at Work

Flexibility and Work–Life Balance

In addition to offering family-friendly benefits, many companies provide flexible working arrangements to recruit and retain Millennial employees. A recent survey indicates that these early career employees value work flexibility and work–life balance more than compensation growth or skill development.

Additional factors driving the trend toward flexible work arrangements include technology and Millennial employees' affinity for using it. Mobile technology, cloud computing services, and high-speed Internet enable employees to collaborate in teams and with clients from non-office locations. As the first generation to come of age as "digital natives," Millennials are comfortable working in this virtual, flexible environment. The traditional Monday–Friday, 9–5 p.m. work schedule can be perceived as too restrictive for this generation that is used to integrating work and leisure during "off hours."

Here are some tips for making your job more flexible:[14]

1. **Identify** which type of flexible work arrangement you desire. Is it telecommuting, job sharing, flexible work hours . . . ?

2. **Review** your company's existing policies about flexible work arrangements. This information can help you shape your negotiation strategy.

3. **Research** whether your organization has the technology to support virtual workers. For example, does it have shared file folders and documents, videoconferencing software, cloud-based computing, and instant messaging?

4. **Make** a compelling case for why adding flexibility to your work is good for business and productivity. It could be that you have a long commute each day and that you could better spend your time working on projects.

5. **Be prepared** for pushback. Your manager may resist granting a flexible schedule for fear that you will use the time outside the office for nonwork activities. A counterpoint may be that you'll likely put in longer hours (and be more productive) and that your online work and e-communication time stamps will provide consistent evidence of time worked.

sexual harassment

Unwelcome sexual conduct that is a term or condition of employment.

To help break through the glass ceiling, Accenture sponsors monthly networking events and offers flexible schedules and part-time arrangements. Employers sometimes match employees with mentors to help them navigate the corporate environment. Whatever the source of career obstacles, empowerment programs can help. Exhibit 11.4 lists eight companies where women are thriving as a result of proactive leadership, mentoring programs, and hiring initiatives.

As women have gained more presence and power in the workforce, more are drawing attention publicly to the serious problem of **sexual harassment**: unwelcome sexual conduct

EXHIBIT 11.3

Top Ten Most Powerful Women Executives

Rank	Name	Company	Title
1	Mary Barra	General Motors	CEO
2	Indra Nooyi	PepsiCo	Chairman and CEO
3	Marillyn Hewson	Lockheed Martin	Chairman, CEO, and president
4	Ginni Rometty	IBM	Chairman, CEO, and president
5	Abigail Johnson	Fidelity Investments	CEO and president
6	Sheryl Sandberg	Facebook	COO
7	Meg Whitman	Hewlett Packard Enterprises	CEO and president
8	Phebe Novakovic	General Dynamics	CEO and Chairman
9	Irene Rosenfeld	Mondelez International	Chairman and CEO
10	Safra Catz	Oracle	Co-CEO

SOURCE: "The Most Powerful Women in Business," *Fortune,* 2016. http://www.fortune.com.

AT Kearney	Johnson & Johnson
Deloitte	McKinsey & Company
EY (Ernst & Young)	PWC
IBM	Prudential

SOURCE: Adapted from "2016 Working Mother 100 Best Companies," *Working Mother*, www.workingmother.com.

EXHIBIT 11.4
Top Companies for Women

that is a term or condition of employment. Sexual harassment falls into two categories. The first, *quid pro quo harassment,* occurs when submission to or rejection of sexual conduct is used as a basis for employment decisions.

The second type, *hostile environment,* occurs when unwelcome sexual conduct "has the purpose or effect of unreasonably interfering with job performance or creating an intimidating, hostile, or offensive working environment." Behaviors that can cause a hostile work environment include persistent or pervasive displays of pornography, lewd or suggestive remarks, or demeaning taunts or jokes. Both categories of harassment violate Title VII of the Civil Rights Act of 1964.

Regardless of the sex of the harasser and the victim—in a recent year, more than 15 percent of complaints filed with the federal government came from males—if an employee files a complaint of sexual harassment with the Equal Employment Opportunity Commission (EEOC), the commission may investigate. If it finds evidence for the complaint, it may request mediation, seek a settlement, or file a lawsuit. Companies fear these lawsuits, with stiff potential fines and negative publicity that can damage the company's reputation and ability to recruit the best employees.

Harassment via a hostile work environment is now more common than quid pro quo harassment. The former may involve more subjective standards, but managers must maintain an appropriate work environment by ensuring everyone knows what conduct is and is not appropriate and that misconduct has serious consequences. Even when managers do not themselves engage in harassment, they and their employers can be held liable if a lawsuit is filed and they have failed to prevent harassment or to take appropriate action after receiving legitimate complaints. Also important to know is that the "hostile work environment" standard applies to same-sex harassment as well as to non-gender-related cases, such as a pattern of racial or ethnic slurs.

Teenage employees are particularly vulnerable because they are inexperienced, hold lower-status jobs, and often feel hesitant or embarrassed to speak up. A teenager who spoke up recently about being sexually harassed by a manager of a Houston-based Chipotle Mexican was awarded $7.7 million.[15]

The federal EEOC has made this concern a priority and launched a teen-focused page called "Youth at Work" on its website (http://www.youth.eeoc.gov). The National Restaurant Association and National Retail Federation also have stepped up efforts to protect teens from harassment.[16]

A strong commitment to valuing diversity leads to fewer problems with sexual harassment.

One way managers can help their companies prevent harassment, or avoid punitive damages if an unfounded lawsuit is filed, is to make sure their organizations have an effective and comprehensive policy on harassment. Exhibit 11.5 shows the basic components of such a policy. Companies such as Kaiser Permanente, AT&T, and MasterCard know that a strong commitment to valuing diversity leads to fewer problems with sexual harassment.[17]

Gender issues do not apply only to women. In some ways, the changing status of women has given men the opportunity to redefine their roles, expectations, and lifestyles. Some men are deciding that there is more to life than corporate success and choosing to scale back work hours to spend more time with their families. Men as well as women want to achieve a balance between career and family.

EXHIBIT 11.5

Components of Effective
Sexual Harassment
Policies

1. **Develop a comprehensive organizationwide policy** on sexual harassment and present it to all current and new employees. Stress that sexual harassment will not be tolerated under any circumstances. Emphasize how strongly top management believes in the policy.
2. **Hold training sessions with supervisors** to explain Title VII requirements, their role in providing an environment free of sexual harassment, and investigative procedures.
3. **Establish a formal complaint procedure** in which employees can discuss problems without fear of retaliation. Spell out how charges will be investigated and resolved.
4. **Investigate immediately when employees complain of sexual harassment.** Convey clearly that investigations will be conducted objectively and with appreciation for the sensitivity of the issue.
5. When an investigation supports the charges, **discipline the offender at once.** For serious offenses, discipline should include penalties up to and including discharge. Discipline should be applied consistently across similar cases and among managers and hourly employees alike.
6. **Follow up on all cases** to ensure a satisfactory resolution of the problem.

SOURCE: Snell, S. A., and Bohlander, G. W., *Managing Human Resources,* 16th ed. Boston, MA: Cengage Learning, 2012.

Employees who are lesbian, gay, bisexual, or transgender (LGBT) are affected by the same issues. They want to avoid discrimination and harassment too, of course, to obtain benefits for a same-sex spouse or domestic partner, or to feel free not to be secretive about this aspect of who they are. Treatment of LGBT employees is an area of ongoing change, both in societal attitudes and in the law. For example, a few years ago, couples in a same-sex relationship would be categorized legally as single, but now some states have laws allowing them to marry or register as domestic partners and to adopt children together.

Over 90 percent of Fortune 500 companies have policies protecting employees on the basis of sexual orientation, and former president Obama signed an executive order prohibiting federal contractors from discriminating against LGBT workers.[18] In situations where laws, policies, and social norms are in a state of flux, employers must be especially attentive to what is required and how employees, customers, and other stakeholders are affected by company policies and practices.

Minorities and Immigrants   Organizations that do not take full advantage of the skills and capabilities of minorities and immigrants are severely limiting their potential talent pools and their ability to understand and capture diverse markets. As minority shares of the population grow, so do these groups' purchasing power. And if you sell to businesses, you probably deal with minority-owned companies because the number of businesses started by Asian American, African American, and Hispanic entrepreneurs is growing much faster than the overall growth in new companies. Immigrants founded more than half of the companies that started in California's high-tech Silicon Valley; in a recent year, half of patent applications in the United States identified an immigrant as the inventor or a co-inventor.[19]

In many urban areas with large Asian, Hispanic, or African American populations, banks have deliberately increased the diversity of their managers and tellers to reflect the population mix in the community and attract additional business. If they did not, customers would notice and switch to other banks where they would feel more welcome and comfortable.

Such diversity—and effective collaboration among diverse employees—creates better customer service that helps banks compete successfully. For example, tellers approached by new immigrants who do not yet speak English immediately call on their bilingual colleagues for help. The bilingual colleagues also are better able to assist bank customers with special problems such as income transfers from abroad.

Exhibit 11.6 gives signs of progress in the top ranks. Even so, evidence shows some troubling racial disparities in employment and earnings. Unemployment rates are higher for black

EXHIBIT 11.6   Some Top Executives of Color

Name	Company	Title
Ajay Banga	MasterCard	President and CEO
Denice Torres	Johnson & Johnson Medical Devices	Chief strategy and business transformation officer
David P. Bozeman	Caterpillar	Senior vice president, Caterpillar Enterprise System Group
Jin Sook and Do Won Chang	Forever 21	Cofounders and owners
Kenneth Chenault	American Express	Chair and CEO
Gisel Ruiz	Sam's Club	Executive vice president of operations
John Thompson	Microsoft	Chair
Marvin Ellison	JCPenney	President and CEO
Kenneth Frazier	Merck	CEO and chair
Oprah Winfrey	Harpo	Chair and CEO

SOURCES: Company website, "Gisel Ruiz: Executive Vice President of Operations, Sam's Club," www.walmart.com; "Diversity Leadership: Kenneth Frazier, Merck & Co.," *DiversityInc.,* www.diversityinc.com; Kezar, C., "J.C. Penney CEO among Retail Leaders Meeting with Trump over Import Tax," *Biz Journals,* February 15, 2017, www.bizjournals.com; Garcia, A., "MasterCard CEO: Every Woman in Our Company Makes the Same as a Man," *CNNMoney,* April 9, 2016, www.moneycnn.com; "Microsoft Chairman Feels Need for Speed," *Fortune,* June 3, 2016, www.fortune.com; "Kenneth Chenault: Why I Came to American Express," *Bloomberg,* November 9, 2016, www.bloomberg.com.

and Hispanic workers than for whites—twice as high in the case of black men. Earnings of black and Hispanic workers consistently trail those of white and Asian workers, and African Americans and Hispanic Americans are underrepresented in management and professional occupations.[20] This underrepresentation perpetuates the problem because it leaves aspiring young minorities with fewer role models or mentors that are so important to people's careers.

Discrimination accounts for at least some of the disparities in employment and earnings. In one recent study—and there are other such findings—fictitious résumés were used to respond to help-wanted ads in Boston and Chicago newspapers. Résumés with white-sounding names were 50 percent more likely to get a callback for an interview than the same résumés with African American names. Despite equivalence in credentials, the often unconscious assumptions about different racial groups are very difficult to overcome.[21]

Virtually every large organization has policies and programs dedicated to increasing minority representation, including compensation systems that reward managers for increasing diversity. Major companies such as FedEx, Xerox, Shell, PNC Financial, and Sun Microsystems have corporate diversity officers who help managers to attract, retain, and promote minority and women executives. Many organizations support minority internships and MBA programs. Microsoft sponsors summer internship programs for minority undergraduate students pursuing computer science or software engineering degrees. Lockheed Martin partners with the American Management Association's Operation Enterprise on two-week paid summer internship programs for high school and college students. Ideally these internships turn into full-time employment.

Mental and Physical Disabilities   The largest unemployed minority population in the United States is people with disabilities. It includes people of all ethnic backgrounds, cultures, and ages. The share of the population with a disability is growing as the average worker gets older and heavier.[22] According to U.S. government statistics, about 17 percent of people with

Ernst & Young has been named as one of the best companies for valuing diversity, based on how it ranked in four key areas—CEO commitment, human capital, corporate and organizational communications, and supplier diversity.

©Lars Niki RF

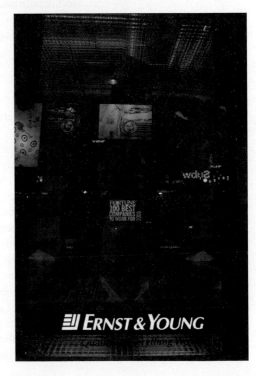

disabilities are employed compared to 65 percent of people without.[23] One-third are employed on a part-time basis.[24] People with a disability are more likely to have jobs if they have higher education levels, and more likely than workers without disabilities to have a part-time job because they can't find full-time work.[25]

The Americans with Disabilities Act Amendments Act (ADAAA) defines a disability as a physical or mental impairment that substantially limits one or more major life activities. Examples of such physical or mental impairments include those resulting from orthopedic, visual, speech, and hearing impairments; cerebral palsy; epilepsy; multiple sclerosis; HIV infections; cancer; heart disease; diabetes; mental retardation; psychological illness; particular learning disabilities; drug addiction; and alcoholism.[26]

New assistive technologies are making it easier for companies to comply with the ADA and for those with disabilities to be productive on the job. In many cases, state governments pay for special equipment or other accommodations. Accommodations can result in unanticipated fringe benefits, too. The National Industries for the Blind (NIB), a Wisconsin company that markets products under the Skilcraft brand name, is a case in point. Seventy-five percent of NIB employees are visually impaired. Because the company's warehouse pickers have trouble reading instructions on paper, NIB installed a voice technology system that conveys instructions to workers through headsets. An added benefit is that the technology has raised the productivity of the entire operation. Accuracy has improved, and workers—both blind and sighted—are able to pick and ship orders faster using the headsets.

For most businesses, people with disabilities represent an unexplored but productive labor market. Employers frequently find that employees with disabilities are more dependable than other employees, miss fewer days of work, and exhibit lower turnover. Companies receive tax credits for hiring workers with disabilities. And such practices send important signals to other employees and outside stakeholders of a strong desire for an inclusive organization.

Education Levels   When the United States was an industrial economy, many jobs required physical strength, stamina, and skill in a trade, rather than college degrees. In today's service and technology economy, more positions require a college education and even a graduate or professional degree, and prospective employees have responded by applying to college in record numbers. One result is rising shares of African American, Hispanic, and female graduates.

The share of workers with a bachelor's degree has more than doubled since 1970.

People with degrees in science and technology are in especially high demand. Employers often expand their search for scientists and computer professionals overseas, but visa requirements limit that supply. On the other side of the spectrum, in the current labor pool almost 25 percent of foreign-born workers have not completed high school, compared with just 5 percent of native-born workers.[27]

The Age of the Workforce

Approximately 10,000 Boomers (those born between 1946 and 1964) are retiring each day in the United States.[28] Industries most at risk of losing this talent include health care (hospitals and nursing facilities), transportation, social assistance, and mining and construction.[29] At the same time, the Bureau of Labor Statistics projects that entry-level workers will be in short supply.

On the plus side, almost 70 percent of workers between the ages of 45 and 74 say that they intend to work in retirement. Retirees often return to the workforce at the behest of their employers, who don't want to lose the knowledge accumulated by longtime employees, their willingness to work nontraditional shifts, and their reliable work habits, which have a positive effect on the entire work group.

To prevent an exodus of talent, employers need strategies to help retain, attract, and motivate skilled and knowledgeable older workers.[30] Phased retirement plans allow older employees to work fewer hours per week. Other strategies include workplace adaptations to help older workers cope with physical problems such as poor vision, hearing, and mobility. This is quite different from previous practice when companies gave older workers incentives to leave in order to reduce overhead and perhaps hire less expensive replacements. Now, a strong majority of employers view their older workers as valuable resources for training, mentoring, and sharing knowledge.[31]

At the same time, companies need to compete hard for the smaller pool of young talent, who know the job market and expect the working conditions they value. Bruce Tulgan, founder of Rainmaker Thinking, which specializes in researching generational differences, says that today's young workers tend to be "high-maintenance" but also "high-performing," having learned information technologies so thoroughly.[32]

Therefore top employers scramble to design work arrangements that are stimulating, involve teamwork, keep work hours reasonable, and provide plenty of positive feedback. Employers also are updating their recruiting tactics to reach young workers where they are—through social media. Most recruiters post job opportunities on Facebook, Instagram, LinkedIn, and Twitter.[33]

affirmative action

Special efforts to recruit and hire qualified members of groups that have been discriminated against in the past.

Managing Diversity and Affirmative Action

For many organizations, the original impetus to diversify their workforces was a combination of social responsibility and legal necessity. Companies introduced **affirmative action**—special efforts to recruit and hire qualified members of groups that were discriminated against in the past. The intent was not to prefer these group members to the exclusion of others, but to correct for the long history of discriminatory practices and exclusion. Viewed from this perspective, amending these wrongs is moral and ethical as well as a legal necessity.

Nevertheless, the legislated approach created fragmented efforts that have not fully achieved the integrative goals of diversity. Employment discrimination persists; even after decades of government legislation, equal employment opportunity (EEO) and affirmative action laws have not adequately improved the upward mobility of women and minorities. To move beyond correcting past wrongs and create truly inclusive organizations requires a change in organization culture to one in which diversity contributes directly to the attainment of organization goals.

Affirmative action and managing diversity are not the same thing. Managing diversity means moving beyond legislated mandates to embrace a proactive business philosophy that values differences positively. *All* employees are different, adding in many ways to the richness of talents and perspectives that organizations can draw upon.

Thus managing diversity is not just about getting more minorities and women into the organization. Managing diversity requires managers to recognize and value the uniqueness of each employee and to see the variety of differences as a potential source of competitive advantage. It is about coming together to benefit the whole, leading many companies to refer now not just to diversity but also *inclusion* as their objectives.

LO 2

Managing diversity involves making changes to remove obstacles that keep people from reaching their full potential.
©Rawpixel.com/Shutterstock.com RF

Affirmative action and managing diversity are not the same thing.

Advantage through Diversity and Inclusion

Diversity in an organization's upper ranks relates to superior financial performance, as shown by a number of studies. Investors' preferences for organizations with a policy of inclusion may play a stronger role than does superior diversity management. Whether and

LO 3

how women on boards of directors relate to firm financial performance is complex and difficult to discern, but the findings sometimes are positive.[34] One recent study shows that female board members can help to deter securities fraud.[35] Diversity can provide an organizational strength, especially if managers know how to leverage it.[36]

Attracting, Motivating, and Retaining Employees   Companies with a reputation for providing opportunities for diverse employees will have an advantage in the labor market, and will be sought out by the most qualified employees. When employees believe their differences are not merely tolerated but valued, they may become more loyal, productive, and committed.

Understanding Differentiated Markets   Companies such as Ford, General Mills, IBM, Target, and Kroger are committed to diversity because as the workforce changes, so does their customer base. Just as diverse groups prefer to work for employers that value diversity, they may prefer to patronize such organizations.

A diverse workforce can provide a company with greater knowledge of the preferences and consuming habits of a diversified marketplace. This knowledge helps in designing products and developing marketing campaigns to meet consumers' needs. In addition, for at least some goods and services, a multicultural sales force can help sell to diverse groups. A diverse workforce also can give a company an edge in a global economy by helping to understand other customs, cultures, and market needs.

Creative Problem Solving   Work team diversity promotes creativity and innovation because people from different backgrounds bring different perspectives. Diverse groups have a broader base of experience from which to approach a problem; when effectively managed, they invent more options and create more solutions than homogeneous groups do. In addition, diverse groups are freer to deviate from traditional approaches and practices. Diversity also can help minimize groupthink (recall Chapter 3).[37]

Many law firms routinely have diverse legal teams working together on cases. Complex cases often require fresh "out of the box" ideas, and a group of lawyers from the same background who all think alike may not be as innovative as a more diverse team. In jury trials, the impression that a legal team makes on a jury can help or badly hurt the client, and a visibly diverse legal team is likely to impress a diverse jury.

Bottom Line
A diverse workforce can lead to greater responsiveness. *Why might a customer who wants something new get a faster response from a company that tolerates different styles?*

Organizational Flexibility   Managing diversity well requires a corporate culture that tolerates many styles and approaches. Less restrictive policies and less standardized operating methods enable greater flexibility and thus quicker response to environmental changes. Procter & Gamble values diversity as key to fulfilling its strategy: "Everyone valued, everyone included, everyone performing at their peak."[38]

Challenges of Diversity and Inclusion

Every year, thousands of lawsuits are filed over issues of discrimination and unfair treatment, some involving the largest and most respected firms.[39] Recently settled governmental EEOC lawsuits include Walgreens for firing a longtime diabetic employee for eating a bag of chips during a diabetes-related episode; Qualcomm paying $19.5 million to settle claims that it did not provide equal pay and job opportunities to its female employees; and DSW for unfairly firing employees over 40 years old in a workforce reduction effort.[40]

Even when there is no overt discrimination in hiring, pay, and firing, managing diversity can be challenging. Minorities and women often find themselves in an environment that does not give them the opportunity to do their best work. And managers with all the goodwill in the world find it harder than they expected to get people from different backgrounds to work together for a common goal.[41]

Managers of the diverse organization need to identify and overcome difficulties including unexamined assumptions, lower cohesiveness, miscommunications, mistrust and tension, and stereotyping.

Unexamined Assumptions   For most of us, seeing the world from someone else's perspective is difficult because our own assumptions and viewpoints seem so normal and familiar. For example, heterosexuals may not even think about whether to put a photo of their loved ones on their desks; it is a routine, even automatic decision, repeated in a million workplaces across the country. But for many gay employees in some environments, displaying (or even considering) such photos can cause considerable anxiety.

Other unexamined assumptions involve the roles of women and men. For example, many people assume that women will shoulder the burden of caring for children, even if it conflicts with the demands of work. In a recent experiment, employers were less likely to invite the fictional candidate for an interview when the résumé implied the candidate was a parent—but only if the name was female.[42] Because the résumés were otherwise identical, the results suggest that people make assumptions about mothers that do not apply to fathers or to childless women.

In organizations that are oblivious to such assumptions and do not actively help people feel welcome and valued, managers will find it more difficult to develop an enthusiastically shared sense of purpose.

Lower Cohesiveness   Diversity can create a lack of cohesiveness. *Cohesiveness* refers to how tightly knit the group is and the degree to which group members perceive things and behave in similar or mutually agreed-upon ways. Because of differences, diverse groups typically are less cohesive than homogeneous groups. Mistrust, miscommunication, stress, and attitudinal differences reduce cohesiveness, which in turn can diminish productivity.

This may be one explanation for the results of a study that showed greater turnover among store employees who feel they are greatly outnumbered by co-workers from other racial or ethnic groups.[43] In a diverse group, managers should take the lead in building cohesiveness by establishing common goals and values. Group cohesiveness will be discussed in greater detail in Chapter 14.

Communication Problems   Communication difficulties include misunderstandings, inaccuracies, inefficiencies, and slowness. Speed is lost when not all group members are fluent in the same language or when additional time is required to explain things. Sometimes diversity decreases communication, as when white male managers feel less comfortable giving feedback to women or minorities for fear of how criticism may be received. If managers don't deliver helpful feedback, employees will not know how to improve their performance.

Diversity also can lead to errors and misunderstandings. Group members may assume they interpret things similarly when in fact they do not, or they may disagree because of their different frames of reference.[44] For example, if managers do not actively encourage and accept the expression of different points of view, some employees may be afraid to speak up at meetings, leaving the manager with a false impression that consensus has been reached. We discuss communication in depth in Chapter 15.

Mistrust and Tension   People prefer to associate with others who are like themselves. This is a normal, understandable tendency. Feeling excluded from joining colleagues at business lunches or after-hour gatherings is isolating and frustrating, and can lead to misunderstandings, mistrust, and ineffective work relationships. Tensions may develop between people of different ages; what one generation might see as a tasteless tattoo is for others a creative example of body art. Such disagreements can cause stress, tension, and resentment, making it more difficult to agree on work issues.

Stereotyping   We learn to see the world in a certain way based on our backgrounds and experiences. Our interests, values, and cultures act as filters and distort, block, and select what we see and hear. We see and hear what we expect to see and hear. Group members often inappropriately stereotype colleagues rather than accurately perceiving their contributions, capabilities, aspirations, and motivations.

Such stereotypes usually are negative or condescending. Women may be stereotyped as not dedicated to their careers, and older workers as incapable and unwilling to learn new skills. But even so-called positive stereotypes can be burdensome. The common stereotype that Asian Americans are good at math may leave unrecognized other positive attributes. Many people dislike being stereotyped at all, even positively, preferring to be understood and treated as individuals.

Stereotypes may lead organizations to miss the opportunity to hire qualified candidates,[45] and can cost the organization dearly by stifling employees' motivation so that they don't contribute fully. Managers want their employees to perform to their full ability, but stereotypes that dampen individual employees' ambition and performance detract from the organization's success.

Managers unaware of stereotyping—by themselves or others—may not recognize its effects on how people are treated. Employees stereotyped negatively will be given work assignments that are less important than those given to co-workers. Those assignments will underuse people's skills, frustrate them, perhaps reduce their commitment, and cause higher turnover.[46]

Leveraging Differences   For all these reasons, and more, managing diversity is not easy. Managers are not immune to the biases, stereotypes, inexperience, and tensions that make communication, teamwork, and leadership in a diverse workforce challenging. But they do need to confront these issues and develop the necessary strategies and skills if they and their organizations are to succeed in our multicultural environment.

One constructive way to begin is with what Professor Martin Davidson calls "leveraging difference." This approach sees diversity not as a problem to be tolerated or solved but as a resource the organization can capitalize on, even though doing so can be difficult. Leveraging difference starts with recognizing that we all bring something different, contributing different strengths, values, and ways of thinking and problem solving. To capitalize on these differences, Exhibit 11.7 offers suggestions applicable to the whole spectrum of organizational activities such as innovating, learning, working as a team, and interacting with customers.[47]

EXHIBIT 11.7   Leveraging Employee Differences

	Key Individual Practices	Key Organizational Practices
Seeing	• Adopt a stance that relevant differences are ubiquitous. • Attend to points of conflict. • Observe silence.	• Attend to intergroup tension. • Reduce the climate of secrecy.

Understanding	• Build skill in acquiring data.
	  – Listen.
	  – Ask questions.
	  – Learn and share your own story.
	• Include people who are different in your inner circle or network.
		• Acquire information via survey and other data gathering.
		• Create and institutionalize inclusive structures.

Valuing	• Lower the levels of unnecessary carefulness when dealing with differences. • Be willing to persist in the midst of conflict and its accompanying discomfort. • Incorporate data into your worldview.	• Reward and hold employees accountable for engaging in difference-related activities. • Recruit and develop people who add diversity to the organization.

SOURCE: Davidson, M. N., *The End of Diversity as We Know It: Why Diversity Efforts Fail and How Leveraging Difference Can Succeed.* San Francisco: Berrett-Kohler Press, 2011.

Management in Action

APPLE'S DRIVE TOWARD DIVERSITY

With the number of women and minorities lagging in the tech industry's workforce, many companies are thinking and talking about ways to remedy the situation. People within and outside the industry are concerned that results have been slow in coming; Facebook's global director of diversity recently drew widespread criticism for saying progress on diversity would take years because there are not enough qualified minority applicants coming through the nation's school system—a statement many deny.

Apple, on the other hand, has moved out in front of many other tech companies, increasing and broadening its recruitment process (including at college campuses), fostering an inclusive workplace climate, cultivating a pool of diverse leaders, addressing current employees' unconscious biases, supporting veterans and people with disabilities, and advocating for the rights of the LGBTQ community. Its Diversity Network Associations are "groups where employees can make connections that create trust and a feeling of belonging," whether they want to identify as and associate with fellow Christians, Jews, Muslims, women, Asian Americans, African Americans, agnostics, or others.

The company has improved some of the diversity statistics it releases in its annual diversity and inclusion report, even if only by a small amount. Change, while slow, is taking place.

Apple says it takes a "holistic view" of diversity, "a view that includes the varied perspectives of our employees as well as app developers, suppliers, and anyone who aspires to a future in tech. Because we know new ideas come from diverse ways of seeing things." The company's efforts to be more diverse extend to pay equity as well as racial, ethnic, and gender diversity. According to the company's website, "We've achieved pay equity in the United States for similar roles and performance. Women earn one dollar for every dollar male employees earn. And underrepresented minorities earn one dollar for every dollar white employees earn." That's a remarkable achievement in a nation where women in general still do not earn what men earn for the same work.[48]

- Do you agree that the achievement of diversity in the tech workforce will take a long time? Why or why not?
- What challenges to achieving diversity has Apple overcome? Which could it work harder to resolve?

Multicultural Organizations

To capitalize on the benefits and minimize the costs of a diverse workforce, one of the first things managers need to do is examine prevailing assumptions about people and cultures. Exhibit 11.8 shows some assumptions that might exist. Based on these assumptions, we can classify organizations as one of three types and describe their implications for managers.

Some organizations are **monolithic**, having very little diversity or inclusiveness. For example, a firm might favor hiring alumni of the same school. In monolithic organizations, groups other than the norm (if represented) work primarily in low-status jobs. Minority group members must adopt the norms of the majority to survive. This fact, coupled with small numbers, keeps conflicts among groups low. Discrimination and prejudice can prevail, integration between groups is almost nonexistent, and minority group members do not identify strongly with the company.

Most large U.S. companies made the transition from monolithic to pluralistic organizations in the 1960s and 1970s because of changing demographics and societal forces such as the civil rights and women's movements. **Pluralistic organizations** have a more diverse employee population and use an affirmative action approach to managing diversity: They actively try to hire and train a diverse workforce and to avoid discrimination. They integrate groups more fully than do monolithic organizations, but like monolithic organizations they often have minority group members clustered at certain levels or in particular functions within the organization.

Because of training programs and greater cultural integration, the pluralistic organization shows less prejudice and some acceptance of minority group members into the informal network. Improved employment opportunities help group members identify more strongly with

monolithic organization

An organization that has a low degree of structural integration—employing few women, minorities, or other groups that differ from the majority—and thus has a highly homogeneous employee population.

pluralistic organization

An organization that has a relatively diverse employee population and makes an effort to involve employees from different gender, racial, or cultural backgrounds.

EXHIBIT 11.8   Diversity Assumptions and Implications

Common and Misleading Assumptions		More Appropriate Assumptions	
Homogeneity	*Melting pot myth:* We are all the same.	**Heterogeneity**	*Image of cultural pluralism:* We are not all the same; groups within society differ across cultures.
Similarity	*Similarity myth:* "They" are all just like me.	**Similarity and difference**	*They are not just like me:* Many people differ from me culturally. Most people exhibit both cultural similarities and differences when compared with me.
Parochialism	*Only-one-way myth:* Our way is the only way. We do not recognize any other way of living or working.	**Equifinality**	*Our way is not the only way:* There are many culturally distinct ways of reaching the same goal, of working, and of living one's life.
Ethnocentrism	*One-best-way myth:* Our way is the best way. All other approaches are inferior versions of our way.	**Culture contingency**	*Our way is one possible way:* There are many and equally good ways to reach the same goal. The best way depends on the culture of the people involved.

SOURCE: Adler, Nancy J., "Diversity Assumptions and Their Implications for Management," *Handbook of Organization,* 1996.

the organization. Sometimes some majority group members' resentments toward women and minorities create more conflict than exists in the monolithic organization.

The pluralistic organization does not adequately address the cultural aspects of integration. In contrast, **multicultural organizations** both are diverse and value differences. These organizations fully integrate gender, racial, and minority group members, both formally and informally. Rather, managers value and leverage the varieties of experiences and knowledge employees bring to help the company achieve agreed-upon strategies and goals.[49]

The truly multicultural organization is marked by an absence of prejudice and discrimination and by low levels of intergroup conflict. It forges a synergistic environment in which all members contribute to their maximum potential, and fully realizes diversity advantages.[50]

multicultural organization

An organization that values cultural diversity and seeks to utilize and encourage it.

How to Cultivate a Diverse Workforce

LO 6   Plans for becoming multicultural and making the most of a diverse workforce should include (1) securing top management's leadership and commitment, (2) assessing the organization's progress toward goals, (3) attracting employees, (4) training employees in diversity, and (5) retaining employees.

Top Management's Leadership and Commitment

If top management is not visibly committed to diversity programs, others in the organization will not take the effort seriously. One way to communicate this commitment to all employees—as well as to the external environment—is to incorporate diversity values into the corporate mission statement and into strategic plans and objectives. Managerial compensation can be linked directly to accomplishing diversity goals. Adequate funding must be allocated to the diversity effort to ensure its success. Also, top management can set an example by participating personally in diversity programs and making participation mandatory for all managers. The "Social Enterprise" box discusses how Change.org manages diversity.

As mentioned earlier, some organizations have corporate offices or committees to coordinate the companywide diversity effort. Among many examples, the City of Boston has a chief diversity officer, and Avon has a director of multicultural planning and design. Other companies prefer to incorporate diversity management into the function of director of affirmative action or EEO.

Social Enterprise

Managing Diversity at Change.org

When Jen Dulski took over as chief operating officer of the online petition platform Change.org, there was only one female employee in the engineering department. For an organization that serves diverse stakeholders in 196 countries, this lack of diversity did not align with the organization's mission.

Change.org's mission is to "empower people everywhere to create the change they want to see." The company helps 150 million global users and 100,000 organizations launch tens of thousands of online petitions per day. While contributing to so many success stories, the company is broadening its mission and revising its revenue model. It recently began a shift toward crowdsourcing that lets U.S. users sign a petition plus donate to the cause it represents; Change.org collects a 5 percent fee from all donations.

Dulski and other leaders have realigned the company's internal culture and employee composition to match those of its customers. The leaders are "embracing openness," which means working toward gender equality while also embracing employees with different perspectives—international workers, older employees, and individuals with different career experiences.

Dulski suggests the following steps to embrace employee diversity and inclusiveness:

1. *Make everyone part of the mission.* Make diversity a part of your firm's core values and celebrate those employees who embody those values.
2. *Improve the hiring process.* Cast a wider recruitment net to find qualified, diverse applicants.

©The Washington Post/Getty Images

3. *Create the right culture.* Encourage open communication between managers and employees and provide rewards that employees value.

Have these initiatives helped increase diversity at Change.org? The company's engineering team is 27 percent female and over half of its employees are women. Women hold 40 percent and non-Americans occupy 43 percent of the leadership positions.[51]

Questions

- What internal and external forces drove Jen Dulski and other managers at Change.org to reexamine their commitment to diversity?

- Why, specifically, was it so important for the company to hire more female and international employees?

The work of managing diversity cannot be done by top management or diversity directors alone. Many rely on minority advisory groups or task forces to monitor organizational policies, practices, and attitudes; assess their impact on the diverse groups within the organization; and provide feedback and suggestions.

At Equitable Life Assurance Society, employee groups meet regularly with the CEO to discuss diversity issues and make recommendations. At Honeywell, employees with disabilities formed a council to discuss their needs. They proposed, and the company accepted, an accessibility program that went beyond federal regulations to accommodate disabilities.

As you can see, progressive companies are moving from asking managers what they think minority employees need and toward asking the employees themselves what they need.

Organizational Assessment

The next step in managing diversity is to establish an ongoing assessment of the organization's workforce, culture, policies, and practices in areas such as recruitment,

Michael Jordan, Basketball Hall of Fame inductee, is one of the high-profile minority team owners in the NBA.

©Streeter Lecka/Getty Images

promotions, benefits, and compensation. Managers evaluate whether they are attracting their share of diverse candidates from the labor pool and whether the current workforce composition is meeting customer needs. The objective is to identify areas with problems or opportunities and to make recommendations. Etsy, the social commerce website for hand-crafted and vintage items, determined that 80 percent of its customers were women but only about 3 percent of its engineers were women. Marc Hedlund, former senior vice president of engineering, determined—easily, with the data—that Etsy needed to bring in more female engineers and develop their customer skills.[52]

Women and Asian Americans can be at a disadvantage when an organization values aggressiveness. Such a culture might exclude—from hiring, or full inclusion—those who do not exhibit high levels of aggressiveness. Managers could then decide that the organization's "values" need to change so that other personal styles are equally acceptable.

Managers can change their own behaviors to reflect such a change; for example, by asking everyone in meetings for their thoughts instead of letting more assertive participants dominate. Corporate norms should be identified and evaluated regarding their real value and their impact on people.

Attracting Employees

Companies can attract a diverse, qualified workforce by using effective recruiting practices, accommodating employees' work and family needs, and offering alternative work arrangements.

Recruiting   Developing a reputation for hiring and promoting all types of people can be a strong recruiting tool. Xerox gives prospective employees an article that rates the company as one of the best places for African Americans to work. Hewlett-Packard ensures that its female candidates are familiar with its high rating by *Working Woman* magazine.

Some employers work hard to attract female applicants, ensure that their talents are used to full advantage, and to keep (avoid losing) their most capable employees. With over 80 percent of its customers female, Etsy's solution was to position itself as a company that values women. It offered female engineers $5,000 scholarships to a programming course, bringing a flood of Etsy-appreciating women to learn the skills Etsy needs. Etsy also shifted its focus from hiring senior engineers to hiring junior engineers and training them to lead. The focus on diversity not only increased the share of female engineers at Etsy, but also has attracted male engineers who value the company's culture and work well in teams. In less than two years, the number of women in engineering positions grew from 4 to 20.[53]

Many minority group members, people with disabilities, and those who are economically disadvantaged are physically isolated from job opportunities. Companies can bring information about job opportunities to the source of labor, or they can transport the labor to the jobs. Polycast Technology in Stamford, Connecticut, contracts with a private van company to transport workers from the Bronx in New York City to jobs in Stamford. Days Inn recruits homeless workers in Atlanta and houses them in a motel within walking distance of their jobs. Burger King has done a lot to recruit and hire immigrants in its fast-food restaurants.

Accommodating Work and Family Needs   Many job seekers put family needs first. Corporate work and family policies have a big impact on recruiting success and failure. SAS, the business analytics software company in North Carolina, keeps turnover to less than 3 percent by providing free "work-life" counseling, helping employees effectively manage the stresses of everyday life. Employees burn stress by working out in a large gym, taking yoga classes, swimming laps in a heated pool, and taking advantage of deeply discounted child care.[54]

Employers offering onsite child care report lower turnover and absenteeism and higher morale. Many companies assist with care for elderly dependents, care for sick family members, parental leaves of absence, and benefits tailored to individual family needs. Some companies accommodate dual-career couples by limiting relocation requirements or providing job search assistance to relocated spouses.

Alternative Work Arrangements   Many employers offer flexible work schedules and arrangements. General Electric Aviation invites its engineers to develop and submit a plan to reduce onsite work hours and work offsite. Approval of the flexible work plan depends on each engineer's job duties and the company's ability to accommodate the request.[55] Other creative work arrangements include compressed workweeks (e.g., four 10-hour days) and job sharing, in which two part-time workers share one full-time job.

Training Employees

Traditionally, most management training was based on the unstated assumption of a homogeneous, often white-male, full-time workforce. But diversity creates an additional layer of complexity.[56] Diversity training programs attempt to identify and reduce hidden biases and develop the skills needed to manage effectively in a diversified workforce.

Most U.S. organizations sponsor some sort of diversity training, typically having two components: awareness building and skill building.

Awareness Building   Diversity training must increase awareness of the meaning and importance of valuing diversity.[57] The aim is to sensitize employees to the assumptions they make about others and the way those assumptions affect their behaviors, decisions, and judgments. For example, a male employee who has never reported to a female manager may feel awkward the first time he is required to do so. Awareness building can reveal this concern in advance and help people address it.

To build awareness, trainers teach people about myths, stereotypes, and cultural differences as well as the organizational barriers that inhibit the full contributions of all employees. They offer a better understanding of corporate culture, requirements for success, and important behaviors that affect opportunities for advancement.

In most companies, the rules for success are ambiguous, unwritten, and perhaps inconsistent with written policy. A common problem for women, minorities, immigrants, and young employees is that they are unaware of unofficial rules that are obvious to people in the mainstream. For example, organizations often have informal networks and power structures that may not be apparent or readily available to all. As a result, some are less likely than others to know where to go when they need approvals, support, and allies.

Skill Building   Diversity training that merely identifies problems without giving participants the tools they need to act is not good enough. Skill building helps people deal more effectively with one another and with diverse customers. Most of the skills taught are interpersonal, such as active listening, coaching, and giving feedback.

Ideally, organizational assessment determines the skills taught; the training is tailored to needs. Tying the training to business goals increases its usefulness and allows managers to assess whether it is working.

The best training relates to the actual challenges employees encounter in the workplace. For example, employees in a hospital diversity training program might practice how to handle a white patient who asks to be treated only by a white doctor and a male patient who wants to be treated only by a male doctor. Training ABC and American Training Resources are among the companies that offer such products. Exhibit 11.9 provides guidelines for designing effective diversity training.

Retaining Employees

As replacing qualified and experienced workers becomes more difficult and costly, retaining good people becomes vitally important. Most executives know that a "lack of attention to

The Digital World

Diversity in the workplace is achieved successfully when people believe in it and support it, and managers hold them accountable when they don't. One development of managing in a digital world is the transparency. If people are disrespectful it is much easier these days to document behavior on video or on audio with smartphones.

Public discussions of "toxic cultures" force organizations that have not embraced diversity workforce to publicly deal with their shortcomings. Hearsay about sexism in Silicon Valley is very different from detailed corroboration, as when in 2017 a former engineer from Uber publicly posted details of systemic sexual harassment and HR complicity. Posting online not only sheds light on an issue, but in many cases it provides impetus for others to come forward and corroborate allegations.

Many employees with diverse backgrounds also find support from within their companies and industries with online special interest groups, and digital mentoring helps retain and attract wide cross-sections of many groups.

Bottom Line

Managers should assume that everyone likes to feel valued.

What makes you feel that your employer values who you are and what you contribute?

diversity and inclusion contributes to employee turnover."[58] Strategies such as the following can improve employee retention.[59]

Support Groups   Support groups, sometimes called affinity groups, provide emotional and career support for members who traditionally have not been included in the majority's informal groups. They also can help diverse employees understand work norms and the corporate culture.

At Apple headquarters in Cupertino, California, support groups include a Jewish cultural group, a gay/lesbian group, an African American group, and a technical women's group. Avon encourages employees to organize into African American, Hispanic American,

EXHIBIT 11.9

Guidelines for Diversity Training

1.	**Position training in your broad diversity strategy.** Training is one important element of managing diversity, but on its own it will probably fail. Culture change means altering underlying assumptions and systems that guide organizational behavior. Training programs must be internally consistent with, and complement, other initiatives focused on culture change.
2.	**Do a thorough needs analysis.** Do not start training prematurely. As with any training program, eagerness to "do something" may backfire unless you assess what specific aspects of diversity need attention first. Focus groups help identify what employees view as priority issues.
3.	**Distinguish between education and training.** Education helps build awareness and understanding but does not teach usable skills. Training involves activities that enhance skills in areas such as coaching, conducting performance appraisals, and adapting communication styles. Education and training are both important, but they're not the same.
4.	**Use a participative design process.** Involve multiple parties to ensure that the content and tone of the program are suitable to all. Outside consultants can provide fresh perspectives and credibility. Insiders have specific company knowledge, sensitivity to local issues, and long-standing relationships with company members. Balance these various sources.
5.	**Test the training before rollout.** Given the sensitivity, even volatility, of diversity issues, use diversity councils and advocacy groups to pilot the programs. Build in ample feedback time to allow these groups to address sensitive concerns and refine the training.
6.	**Incorporate diversity programs into the core training curriculum.** One-time programs do not have a lasting impact. Blend the program's content into other training programs.

SOURCE: *Training: The Human Side of Business,* 1993.

and Asian American networks by granting them official recognition and assigning a senior manager to provide advice. These groups help new employees adjust and provide direct feedback to management about particular concerns.

Mentoring   Many people are puzzled by the apparent inability of women and minorities to move up beyond a certain point on the corporate ladder (the glass ceiling). To help these groups enter the informal network that provides exposure to top management and access to information, many companies use formal mentoring programs. **Mentors** are higher-level managers who coach, advise, and help people meet top managers and learn the norms and values of the organization.

In Canada, EY (formerly Ernst & Young) established several mentoring programs for women, minorities, and immigrants. Mentors work with employees to help them gain relevant experience, new skills, and connections with senior leaders. EY sees these mentorships as ways not only to strengthen employees' contributions but also to fill its talent pipeline with future leaders. In a related but distinct effort, EY identifies high-potential employees and then company leaders sponsor them. Sponsorship is similar to mentorship except that the sponsor is more actively involved in the employee's development.

In an unusual twist on mentorship, EY also has a reverse mentoring program in which women and minority employees discuss with leaders issues related to diversity at the company.[60]

mentors

Higher-level managers who help ensure that high-potential people are introduced to top management and socialized into the norms and values of the organization.

Career Development and Promotions   Because they hit a glass ceiling, many talented people leave their employers for better opportunities elsewhere. Firms such as Deloitte & Touche and Honeywell use teams to evaluate the career progress of women, minorities, and employees with disabilities and to find promotion opportunities. One important step is to make sure deserving employees can work in line positions. Women in particular often work in staff positions, such as human resources, with less bottom-line opportunity to show they can earn money for their employers. Career development programs that give exposure and experience in line jobs can make senior management positions more attainable.

Systems Accommodation   Managers can support diversity by recognizing cultural and religious holidays, differing modes of dress, and dietary restrictions as well as accommodating the needs of people with disabilities. One important disabling condition is AIDS. Under the ADA Amendments Act (ADAAA), organizations must accommodate employees with AIDS as they would persons with any other disability, permitting and even encouraging them to continue working for as long as they are able and, if warranted, allowing flexible scheduling.

Accommodations for disability likely will become increasingly important as the median age of the workforce continues to rise. In addition, the average weight of U.S. workers is increasing, and relates not only to health consequences such as heart disease, joint problems, and diabetes, but also to workplace injury claims and absences related to injuries.[61] Managers should do what they can to maintain safe workplaces and offer benefits that encourage healthy lifestyles.

Accountability   Performance appraisal and reward systems should reinforce effective diversity management. At PepsiCo, each executive reporting to the CEO is responsible for employee development of a particular group. The executive must identify leadership talent, learn group members' concerns, identify areas where support is needed, and create plans for addressing these issues.[62] Now (at this writing), 36 percent of senior executives at the company are people of color and 27 percent are women.[63] PepsiCo has earned several recent awards for its diversity management efforts.[64]

For decades, U.S. corporations strove to integrate their workforces because of regulatory and social responsibility pressures. Today globalization, changing demographics, and the expansion of ethnic markets at home have made managing a diverse workforce a bottom-line issue. Managers at organizations such as Apple realize that to be competitive, they will have to make managing diversity a strategic priority so as to attract, develop, keep, and apply the knowledge of the best talent.

Management in Action

APPLE STILL HAS A LONG WAY TO GO

Recently many companies in the technology industry, following the examples of Intel and Google, began publishing annual statistics describing the demographics of their workforces and their efforts to improve it. Not everyone is impressed. In 2016 the Equal Employment Opportunity Commission (EEOC) published its own report on the subject, concluding that Silicon Valley still employs fewer women and minorities than any other private-sector industry.

The gap is particularly wide at management and executive levels. "Standing still is not an option," said Jenny Yang, the chair of the EEOC. "Expanding diversity and inclusion is critical to unlocking the full potential of tomorrow's economy."

Among the skeptics about Apple's progress is shareholder Tony Maldonado, who has twice presented a proposal to tie the compensation of Apple's board members to the company's progress in creating a more diverse workforce. The rest of the company's shareholders voted the proposal down both times, by a wide margin. One former employee who spoke against Maldonado's proposal at the shareholders' meeting said he preferred slow progress to tokenism. A current employee who favored the proposal pointed to the difference between the diversity on view among the staff in Apple's retail stores and the much narrower range of gender, racial, and other differences among the company's top executives.

The company stands by its efforts. "We are focused on human rights and diversity, [and are] advocating for it around the world and increasing it in our own community," Apple CEO Tim Cook told attendees at the meeting. Even the Rev. Jesse Jackson, who has been an outspoken critic of the tech industry's lack of diversity, found Apple's results, though slight, to be worthy of praise. When CEO Tim Cook asked him for a comment, Jackson lauded Apple for "tearing down walls of division and building bridges between races, religions, cultures."

Apple has demonstrated its support for diversity by becoming a corporate advocate for the LGBTQ community and the country's immigrant population, and by its many internal diversity initiatives. These include the Diversity Network Associations for employees, increased support for employees with disabilities, pay equity for women, and improved recruitment and hiring practices. Apple's efforts appear to be slowly yielding results. But for now the company remains 68 percent male and 56 percent white.[65]

- Suppose you were charged with increasing the diversity of Apple's workforce by reducing turnover among the company's existing female and minority employees. What specific recommendations would you make?
- What factors do you think might be slowing the company's progress toward a more diverse workforce? What more could Apple do to overcome these difficulties?

KEY TERMS

affirmative action, p. 321

assimilation, p. 313

diversity, p. 313

diverse workforce, p. 312

glass ceiling, p. 315

managing diversity, p. 312

mentors, p. 331

monolithic organization, p. 325

multicultural organization, p. 326

pluralistic organization, p. 325

sexual harassment, p. 316

RETAINING WHAT YOU LEARNED

In Chapter 11, you learned that the U.S. workforce is becoming more diverse. A skills gap exists because typical workers often lack the skills to fill jobs that are being created. To fill this gap and achieve competitive advantage, managers need to recruit, develop, motivate, and retain a diverse workforce. Affirmative action is used to correct past exclusion of women and minorities from organizations. Managing diversity takes a broader approach aimed at supporting, nurturing, and using employee differences to the organization's advantage. Managing diversity can result in enhanced talent management practices, marketing strategies

to reach diverse consumers, innovation and problem solving, and organizational flexibility. Challenges associated with managing a diverse workforce include decreased group cohesiveness, communication problems, mistrust and tension, and stereotyping. Based on prevailing assumptions about people and cultures, organizations take one of the following forms: (1) monolithic, (2) pluralistic, or (3) multicultural. In order to cultivate diversity, managers and organizations need to support and commit to it. A thorough assessment needs to be completed before programs can be designed to attract, develop, motivate, and retain diverse talent.

1 Describe how changes in the U.S. workforce make diversity a critical organizational and managerial issue.

- The labor force is getting older and more racially and ethnically diverse, with a higher proportion of women. Exhibit 11.1 (reproduced below) illustrates the components of a diversified workforce.
- The jobs that are being created frequently require higher skills than the typical worker can provide; thus we are seeing a growing skills gap.
- To be competitive, organizations can no longer take the traditional approach of depending on white males to form the core of the workforce.
- Today managers must search widely to make use of talent wherever it can be found. As the labor market changes, organizations that recruit, develop, motivate, and retain a diverse workforce will have a competitive advantage.

LO 2 Distinguish between affirmative action and managing diversity.

- Affirmative action is designed to correct past exclusion of women and minorities from U.S. organizations.
- Despite the accomplishments of affirmative action, it has not eliminated barriers that prevent people from reaching their full potential.
- Managing diversity goes beyond hiring people who are different from the norm, and seeks to support, nurture, and capitalize on employee differences to the organization's advantage.

LO 3 Explain how diversity, if well managed, can give organizations a competitive edge.

- Managing diversity is a bottom-line issue. If managers are effective at managing diversity, they will have an easier time attracting, retaining, and motivating the best employees.
- Diverse workforces will more effectively market to and serve diverse consumer groups in the United States and globally; they will be more creative, more innovative, and better able to solve problems.
- In addition, they potentially increase their employers' flexibility and responsiveness to environmental change.

LO 4 Identify challenges associated with managing a diverse workforce.

- Diversity challenges for managers include decreased group cohesiveness, communication and teamwork problems, mistrust and tension, and stereotyping.
- These challenges can be turned into advantages by means of training and many other management strategies and tactics.

LO 5 Define monolithic, pluralistic, and multicultural organizations.

- These categories are based on the organization's prevailing assumptions about people and cultures.
- Monolithic organizations have a low intergroup integration and relatively homogeneous workforces.
- Pluralistic organizations have a more diverse employee population and try to more fully involve different employee groups (for example, engaging in affirmative action and avoiding discrimination).

EXHIBIT 11.1 (revisited)   Components of a Diversified Workforce

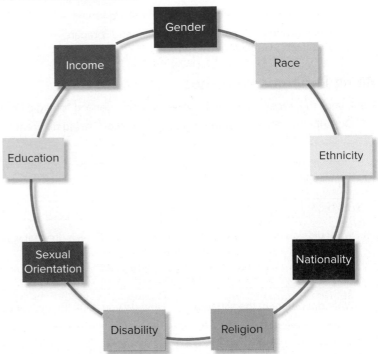

- Multicultural organizations not only have diversity but value it. They fully integrate men and women of various racial and ethnic groups as well as people with different types of experience and expertise.
- Conflict is greatest (all else equal) in pluralistic organizations.

LO 6 List actions managers and their organizations can take to cultivate diversity.

- To be successful, efforts to manage diversity must have top management support and commitment.

- Organizations should first undertake a thorough assessment of their cultures, policies, and practices, as well as the demographics of their labor pools and customer bases.
- Only after this diagnosis has been completed is a company in position to initiate programs designed to attract, develop, motivate, and retain the most talented and diverse workforce possible.

DISCUSSION QUESTIONS

1. What opportunities do you see as a result of changes in our nation's workforce?
2. Is prejudice declining in our society? In our organizations? Why or why not?
3. What distinctions can you make between affirmative action and managing diversity?
4. How can managers overcome obstacles to diversity such as mistrust and tension, stereotyping, and communication problems?
5. How can organizations meet the special needs of different groups (e.g., work and family issues) without appearing to show favoritism?
6. How can diversity give a company a competitive edge? Can diversity really make a difference in the bottom line? How?
7. Why are these issues sometimes difficult to talk about? What could make conversations both more comfortable and productive?

EXPERIENTIAL EXERCISES

11.1 BEING DIFFERENT

OBJECTIVES

1. To increase your awareness of the feeling of being different.
2. To understand better the context of being different.

INSTRUCTIONS

1. Working alone, complete the Being Different Worksheet.
2. In small groups, compare worksheets and prepare answers to the discussion questions.

3. When the class reconvenes, group spokespersons present group findings.

DISCUSSION QUESTIONS

1. Were there students who experienced being different in situations that surprised you?
2. How would you define "being different"?
3. How can this exercise be used to good advantage?

Being Different Worksheet

Think back to a recent situation in which you experienced "being different" and answer the following questions:

1. Describe the situation in which you experienced "being different."

   _____

   _____

2. Explain how you felt.

   _____

   _____

3. What did you do as a result of "being different"? (That is, in what way was your behavior changed by the feeling of "being different"?)

   _____

   _____

4. What did others in the situation do? How do you think they felt about the situation?

   _____

   _____

5. How did the situation turn out in the end?

_____

6. As a result of that event, how will you probably behave differently in the future? In what way has the situation changed you?

_____

_____

11.2 GENDER STEREOTYPES

PART I

Your instructor will divide the group into smaller groups based on gender, resulting in male-only and female-only groups. Groups are to brainstorm a list in response to the following statements. It is not necessary for all members to agree with everything the group generates. Add all inputs to the list.

FEMALE GROUPS COMPLETE THE FOLLOWING:

- All men are _____

- Men think all women are _____

MALE GROUPS COMPLETE THE FOLLOWING:

- All women are _____

- Women think all men are _____

PART II

After generating your lists, your groups will present a role-play to the class based on the following scenarios by switching gender roles (females portray males, and males portray females):

Two friends (of the same gender) meeting each other back at school for the first time this year.

A person flirting with a member of the opposite sex at a party. (Females play a male flirting with a female; males play a female flirting with a male.)

QUESTIONS

1. What aspects of the role-plays were accurate, distorted, or inaccurate?
2. How did you feel portraying the opposite gender, and how did it feel to see your gender portrayed?
3. On what stereotypes or experiences were these role-plays based?

PART III

Your group will now write its brainstorm lists on the board for discussion. Remember that these lists are a product of a group effort and are generally based on stereotypes and not necessarily the view of any one individual.

Analyze the lists for positive and negative results in both personal and professional settings. Generate a list of ways to dispel, reduce, or counter negative stereotypes.

QUESTIONS

1. What similarities, patterns, or trends developed from the groups?
2. How do you feel about the thoughts presented about your gender?
3. What implications do these thoughts have on actions and situations in the work environment?
4. What can you do to reduce the negative effects of these stereotypes? What can you do to help dispel these stereotypes? (Brainstorm with your group or class.)

SOURCES: Portions of this exercise were adapted from concepts in Fritz, S. F. et al., *Interpersonal Skills for Leadership.* Englewood Cliffs, NJ: Prentice Hall, 1999; and Shani A. B. and Lau, J. B., *Behavior in Organizations: An Experiential Approach,* 6th ed. New York: Irwin, 1996.

11.3 HE WORKS, SHE WORKS

INSTRUCTIONS

1. Complete the He Works, She Works Worksheet. In the appropriate spaces, write what you think the stereotyped responses would be. Do not spend too much time considering any one item. Rather, respond quickly and let your first impression or thought guide your answer.

2. Compare your individual responses with those of other class members or participants. It is interesting to identify and discuss the most frequently used stereotypes.

He Works, She Works Worksheet

The family picture is on *his* desk: *He's a solid, responsible family man.*

His desk is cluttered: _____

He's talking with coworkers: _____

He's not at his desk: _____

He's not in the office: _____

The family picture is on *her* desk: *Her family will come before her career.*

Her desk is cluttered: _____

She's talking with coworkers: _____

She's not at her desk: _____

She's not in the office: _____

The family picture is on *his* desk: *He's a solid, responsible family man.*

He's having lunch with the boss: _____

The boss criticized *him:* _____

He got an unfair deal: _____

He's getting married: _____

He's going on a business trip: _____

He's leaving for a better job: _____

The family picture is on *her* desk: *Her family will come before her career.*

She's having lunch with the boss: _____

The boss criticized *her:* _____

She got an unfair deal: _____

She's getting married: _____

She's going on a business trip: _____

She's leaving for a better job: _____

SOURCE: Luthans, F., *Organizational Behavior.* New York: McGraw-Hill, 1989.

Concluding Case

NICHE HOTEL GROUP

Monique Johnson was thrilled about her new position as vice president of human resources for Niche Hotel Group (NHG). The hotel chain has distinctive properties in major cities throughout the United States, attracting a young, international clientele with super-fast Wi-Fi, casual but elegant surroundings, and popular sushi bars. Besides the chance to stay at these establishments as she toured the country, Monique would have opportunities to meet the members of NHG's enthusiastic, talented, and racially diverse workforce.

In addition, she was proud to advance NHG's practice of valuing employees' and customers' diversity, including respect for all people regardless of age, sex, race, ethnicity, nationality, disability status, and sexual orientation. She felt sure those values would be upheld because the commitment came from the top. In fact, NHG's chief executive, Mike Jepsen, had asked Monique to meet with him every Thursday to review the company's performance in attracting and developing talent.

For several weeks, Monique's work progressed much as she had expected. Then she heard some disturbing news. One of the hotel's managers, April Lee, called her to say she had received complaints that an assistant manager in the hotel's sushi bar had been embarrassing some of the male servers. When April met with the servers to investigate, they described being teased because they were gay, but said they had not bothered to complain. Two of the servers admitted that they believed complaining would be futile. As white, male employees, they said, they doubted they would be taken seriously, because NHG's management tended to favor its female and minority employees. April worried that the servers might quit, take legal action, or both before the situation could be sorted out. Meanwhile, she wondered how top management would help her deal with the situation. Monique reviewed with April the basic legal requirements and company policy for handling this type of problem, and she offered to fly out to April's hotel with one of her staff members after her Thursday meeting with the CEO.

That Thursday, Monique briefed Mike about the situation at April's hotel. Mike sighed, "Here we go again." In response to Monique's puzzled look, he explained, "We've had mandatory diversity training three times for every single NHG employee. But it's never enough. Sooner or later, someone hurts someone else's feelings, and we have to bring back the trainers. I guess we just have to keep doing it until everyone respects everyone else's differences."

"You've done diversity training three times without creating a positive climate for diversity?" replied Monique. Mike nodded his head ruefully and then asked if she had a better idea. "Maybe. Hmm, maybe it's time to stop focusing so much on categorizing people and start thinking about how each of us individually is working as part of a team, how each of us is contributing to our mission. Maybe we need to train in something else—say, communication—how we talk and how well we listen."

DISCUSSION QUESTIONS

1. How can promoting a diverse workforce help Niche Hotel Group succeed as a business?
2. Why do you think diversity training has not always prevented problems at NHG?
3. What should NHG do to improve its climate for diversity?

PART THREE SUPPORTING CASE

Zappos

At the turn of the millennium, Zappos, a Las Vegas–based Internet retailer, was a start-up struggling to survive. The company wanted to be *the* online destination for buying shoes, but customers hesitated to pick out shoes online. The company hired a 27-year-old business consultant named Tony Hsieh to figure out what would save Zappos.

Hsieh, a first-generation Taiwanese American with a degree in computer science, already had a couple of successful business start-ups under his belt. Undeterred by Zappos's weak performance, he set an ambitious goal: Zappos would become the largest shoe retailer on the Internet. How? Not by focusing on mainly price or even selection, but by enhancing a company culture designed to make employees happy. Happy employees, Hsieh believed, would deliver superior service. And when customers take a chance on picking out shoes from a website, they want to trust that the seller will ensure they are satisfied with everything about the purchase, from shoe style and fit to fast delivery and an easy returns policy.

The approach quickly began to stimulate sales, and just a year after he started advising Zappos, Hsieh was named chief executive. He works for the startlingly small salary of $36,000. That arrangement doesn't bother Hsieh because he is more motivated by creating a great organization than by earning money. After all, his previous business, LinkExchange, brought him $265 million when he sold it to Microsoft.

The Zappos culture is built on 10 core values:

1. Deliver WOW (an emotional impact and powerful story to tell) through service.
2. Embrace and drive change.
3. Create fun and a little weirdness.
4. Be adventurous, creative, and open-minded.
5. Pursue growth and learning.
6. Build open and honest relationships with communication.
7. Build a positive team and family spirit. ("Family" refers to Zappos co-workers.)
8. Do more with less.
9. Be passionate and determined.
10. Be humble.

These somewhat unconventional values are essential hiring criteria, and the company's career website directs potential applicants to read the values—which are described in whimsical terms—and apply for a job only if they want to be part of this "best thing about the Zappos family." In fact, at the end of the orientation process, employees are offered $3,000 to quit if they feel they aren't a good fit with the company values, and displaying a lack of the values is grounds for being discharged. According to Hsieh, hiring people who share the core values makes it easy to form real friendships, and those relationships, in turn, create an environment in which people think creatively.

The Zappos human resources department, under the leadership of Hollie Delaney, a Salt Lake City native, ensures that job candidates start to experience and participate in this unconventional, fun culture during the application and selection process. An online application invites them to submit video cover letters with their applications, and interviews are conducted in a room that looks like the set of a TV talk show, where candidates might answer a question such as "What's your theme song?" Employees evaluating candidates consider not only work history but also the way candidates interact during lunch. They even take into account the observations of the shuttle drivers who take visiting job candidates back to their hotel. Once on board, employees might discover that fun and a little weirdness at the company includes an opportunity to dye Hsieh's or another manager's hair blue or shave his or her head at the annual Bald & Blue Day. And the commitment to wowing customers spills over into work relationships: Given a chance to reward colleagues' good behavior with a $50 monthly bonus, many employees held off, waiting to see exceptional behavior.

Recently performance appraisals also were brought into line with the focus on values. Employees are rated not just on task accomplishment but also on how well they represent the core values. Managers are expected to describe specific instances of employees demonstrating the values at work, and employees who score low on a measure have the chance to receive training in that value. Outside the formal appraisal process, employees also continue to receive regular feedback on task-related measures such as percentage of hours spent talking to customers.

Delaney acknowledges that the company's values result in a work environment that is loud, hardworking, and full of change—conditions that aren't for everyone. Pay also isn't necessarily high, especially for call center workers. But for those who share the values, this kind of workplace is exhilarating. There also are plenty of rewards and perks, including profit sharing, a nap room, and access to a life coach who counsels employees as they sit on a velvet throne.

With this approach to human resources management, Hsieh helped Zappos grow into a billion-dollar company, which was eventually acquired by Amazon for $1.2 billion. Hsieh negotiated a deal in which Amazon promised to let Zappos continue operating independently, in accordance with its distinctive culture.

Unfortunately, although the 2008 financial crisis didn't keep sales at Zappos from rising, the ongoing economic slowdown eventually hurt, and Zappos laid off some of its workers, letting them down as gently as it could with generous severance packages. Even so, Zappos, unlike many businesses, hasn't outsourced its call center, located in Kentucky, because those employees need to be a part of the company culture. After all, they are the ones who talk directly with customers, and they're trained to wow customers—for example, encouraging them to try multiple sizes because shipping is free in both directions. What's next for this innovative e-retailer? Several reports are emerging that Zappos is moving away from using a hierarchical, traditional management approach with titles and detailed employee job descriptions. Instead, a holacracy approach will likely be implemented which will organize employees into "functional self-organizing circles." Zappos hopes this innovative approach to empowering its diverse employees will keep it at the forefront of employees' minds as a great place to work.

QUESTIONS

1. Evaluate whether you think Zappos is a responsive organization. How do you expect its recent downsizing to affect its responsiveness?

2. How does human resources management reinforce Zappos' core values?

3. How well do you think Zappos' human resource strategy supports the valuing of employee diversity? What diversity issues does Zappos need to address?

SOURCES: Greenfield, R., "Zappos CEO Tony Hsieh: Adopt Holacracy or Leave," *Fast Company* (online), March 30, 2015, http://www.fastcompany.com; Rodriguez, G., "The Great Zappos 'Circles' Experiment and Why It Really Matters," *Forbes* (online), January 15, 2014, http://www.forbes.com; Blodget, H., "Zappos CEO Tony Hsieh Making $36,000 a Year Working for Amazon," *Yahoo Finance,* September 10, 2010, http://finance.yahoo.com; Zappos, Jobs webpage, http://about.zappos.com/jobs/; Gurchiek, K., "Delivering HR at Zappos," *HR Magazine,* June 2011, http://www.shrm.org; O'Brien, J. M., "Zappos Knows How to Kick It," *Fortune,* January 22, 2009, http://money.cnn.com; and Pyrillis, R., "The Reviews Are In," *Workforce Management,* May 1, 2011, Business & Company Resource Center, http://galenet.galegroup.com.

CHAPTER 12
Leadership

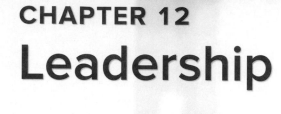

©Matej Kastelic/Alamy Stock Photo RF

> Every soldier has a right to competent command.
>
> — JULIUS CAESAR

LEARNING OBJECTIVES

After studying Chapter 12, you will be able to:

LO 1 Discuss what it means to be a leader.

LO 2 Summarize what people want and organizations need from their leaders.

LO 3 Explain how a good vision helps you be a better leader.

LO 4 Identify sources of power in organizations.

LO 5 List personal characteristics that contribute to leader effectiveness.

LO 6 Describe behaviors that will make you a better leader, and know when situations call for them.

LO 7 Distinguish between charismatic and transformational leadership.

LO 8 Describe types of opportunities to lead.

LO 9 Discover how to further your own leadership development.

CHAPTER OUTLINE

What Do We Want from Our Leaders?

Vision

Leading and Managing
Leading and Following

Power and Leadership
Sources of Power

Traditional Approaches to Understanding Leadership
Leader Traits
Leader Behaviors

The Effects of Leader Behavior
Situational Approaches to Leadership

Contemporary Perspectives on Leadership
Charismatic Leadership
Transformational Leadership
Authenticity
Opportunities for Leaders
A Note on Courage

Developing Your Leadership Skills
How Do I Start?
What Are the Keys?

Management in Action

INDRA NOOYI LEADS PEPSICO TO PERFORMANCE WITH PURPOSE

Indra Nooyi belongs to a very small and select group. As CEO of PepsiCo, maker of Quaker, Tropicana, Frito-Lay, and Pepsi products, she is 1 of only 29 female CEOs of an S&P 500 company. Born in India and educated in Calcutta and at Yale, she joined the company in 1994 and has also served as president and chief financial officer. Nooyi was named chief executive in 2006 and chairperson of the board in 2007. PepsiCo's growth and success owe a great deal to her vision and leadership.

For example, Nooyi devised the company's long-term strategy for growth, called Performance with Purpose. This strategy is designed to generate profit while finding sustainable ways to serve the communities in which PepsiCo products are sold. It commits the company to marketing nourishing food and beverage products, reducing its environmental footprint, and maintaining an inclusive culture that supports diverse and creative people.

To implement Performance with Purpose, Nooyi is trying to focus on healthier items and to reduce the sugar content of many products. "When it comes to transforming our portfolio we are making considerable progress," she says. "What we refer to as 'everyday nutrition products' account for approximately 25 percent of our portfolio by net revenue. These are products that include positive nutrients like grains, fruits and vegetables or protein, plus those that are naturally nutritious like water and unsweetened tea." In total, "guilt-free products" now account for nearly half the company's revenue, while soft drinks account for only 12 percent. And even those will have less sugar by 2025.

©REUTERS/Alamy Stock Photo

The second part of the strategy is about sustainability. As one example, says Nooyi, "in many parts of the world that are water-distressed, we have facilities. So one of the pillars of our environmental sustainability is reducing the water use in our plants and figuring out how to make the whole community water-positive."

Finally, says Nooyi, for the third pillar of the strategy, "We want to create an environment in PepsiCo where every employee can bring their whole self to work and not just make a living but also have a life." For this reason the company offers maternity and paternity leave as well as flextime and on-site day care. Of special importance to Nooyi, and to the company, is the education—and employment—of women and girls around the world.[1]

Indra Nooyi is having a profound effect on PepsiCo's management strategy and objectives, as well as on its performance. The company has been outperforming its rivals even as it tries to reshape the snack and beverage industries. As you read this chapter, compare Nooyi's approach with the kinds of practices recommended for successful leadership.

People get excited about the topic of leadership. They want to know what makes a great leader. Managers in all industries are interested in this question. They believe the answer will bring improved organizational performance and personal career success. They hope to acquire the skills that will transform an average manager into a true leader.

Based on the idea that leadership can be learned, many large organizations such as Verizon, Union Pacific, USAA, and PwC actively recruit retired military personnel in the belief that military training and experience prepare people to lead.[2] Of course you don't have to join the armed services to acquire leadership skills. According to one source, "Leadership seems to be the marshaling of skills possessed by a majority but used by a minority. But it's something that can be learned by anyone, taught to everyone, denied to no one."[3]

LO 1

What is leadership? To start, a leader is one who influences others to attain goals. The greater the number of followers, the greater the influence. And the more successful the attainment of worthy goals, the more evident the leadership. But we must explore beyond this bare definition to capture the excitement and intrigue that devoted followers and students of leadership feel when they see a great leader in action, to understand what organizational leaders really do, and to learn what it takes to become a truly outstanding leader.

Outstanding leaders combine good strategic substance and effective interpersonal processes to formulate and implement strategies that produce results and sustainable competitive advantage.[4] They may launch enterprises, build organization cultures, win wars, or otherwise change the course of events.[5] They are strategists who seize opportunities others overlook, but "they are also passionately concerned with detail—all the small, fundamental realities that can make or mar the grandest of plans."[6]

What Do We Want from Our Leaders?

LO 2

What do people want from their leaders? Broadly speaking, people want their leaders to help them (and not hinder them) as they pursue their goals.[7] These goals include not just more pay and promotions but support for their personal development; clearing obstacles so they can perform at high levels; and treatment that is respectful, fair, and ethical. Leaders serve people best when they help them develop their own initiative and good judgment, enable them to grow, and help them become better contributors. People want competence and proper management—the kinds of things you will read about in this chapter and that are found in other chapters in this book. The "Multiple Generations at Work" box discusses expectations Millennials have of their leaders.

Organizations need people at all levels to be leaders.

What do organizations need? Organizations need people at all levels to be leaders. They need leaders throughout the organization to do the things that their people want, but also to help create and implement strategic direction. Thus organizations place people in formal leadership positions so these leaders will achieve not just their personal goals, but the organization's goals.

At Illinois Tool Works (ITW), general counsel Maria Green learned to create a listening environment so members of the legal staff contribute ideas. In the past, she would have provided answers showcasing her own extensive legal and business knowledge. However, a mentor helped her understand that ITW needs Green, as a leader, to draw out the full potential of the entire group.[8]

These two perspectives—what people want and what organizations need—are neatly combined in a set of five key behaviors identified by James Kouzes and Barry Posner, two well-known authors and consultants (see Exhibit 12.1).

You will read about these and other aspects of leadership in this and the following chapters. The topics we discuss will help you become a better leader, and give you benchmarks you can use to assess the competence and fairness with which your boss manages you.

Multiple Generations at Work

Leadership, Millennial style

Approximately two-thirds of Millennials want to be leaders in the next five years. This generational cohort defines a good leader as one who "mentors others to reach their personal achievements, achieves his/her goals, and affects change in the community." This view of leadership is very different from viewing a leader as someone who takes charge, issues orders, and gets the job done.

Parents, teachers, coaches, and other influencers empowered Millennials to think for themselves, ask questions, challenge conventional wisdom, and take leadership roles. As employees, they expect the same type of mentoring and coaching from their bosses. Millennials also want to have a positive impact on their communities and social causes. As seen in the "Social Enterprise" boxes throughout this textbook, Millennials are applying their leadership skills to help people and communities around the world.

As a generation, Millennials share some common leadership characteristics, including:

1. *Transparency.* As leaders, Millennials tend to be relatively open, and share information more willingly than prior generations with their bosses, team members, and clients.
2. *Authenticity.* Millennials prefer to lead in ways that are personally real and genuine.
3. *Relevancy.* Millennials want to make meaningful contributions to their organizations and communities.
4. *Autonomy and flexibility.* Millennials want choice over when and where they get their work done. As leaders, this generational cohort are more willing to encourage and trust their employees to use creative work arrangements.[9]

---

1. **Challenge the process.** They challenge conventional beliefs and practices, and they create constructive change.

2. **Inspire a shared vision.** They appeal to people's values and motivate them to care about an important mission.

3. **Enable others to act.** They give people access to information and give them the power to perform to their full potential.

4. **Model the way.** They don't just tell people what to do—they are living examples of the ideals they believe in.

5. **Encourage the heart.** They show appreciation, provide rewards, and use various approaches to motivate people in positive ways.

EXHIBIT 12.1
What Do the Best Leaders Do?

SOURCE: Adapted from Kouzes, J. and Posner, B., *The Leadership Challenge,* 2nd ed. San Francisco: Jossey-Bass, 1995.

Vision

"The leader's job is to create a vision," stated Robert L. Swiggett, former chair of Kollmorgen Corporation.[10] Having a vision for the future and communicating that vision to others are known to be essential components of great leadership. Tony Hsieh, CEO of Zappos, is "more of an architect; he designs the big vision and then gets out of the way so that everyone can make things happen."[11] Sir Richard Branson, CEO of the Virgin Group, envisions that by 2050 the entire world will be powered by renewable energy."[12] Practicing business people are not alone in this belief; academic research shows that a clear vision and communication of that vision lead to higher organizational performance.[13]

A **vision** is a mental image of a possible and desirable future state of the organization. It expresses the leader's ambitions for the organization.[14] A leader can create a vision that describes high performance aspirations, the nature of corporate or business strategy, or even the kind of workplace worth building. The best visions are both ideal and unique.[15]

LO 3

vision

A mental image of a possible and desirable future state of the organization.

Imagine trying to complete a challenging jigsaw puzzle without the vision of what you're working toward.

©Tetra Images/Getty Images RF

Bottom Line

You can't perform in the long run if you don't have a vision of what you want to accomplish.

Do you have to be a top-level executive to have a vision?

Not just any vision will do.

Bottom Line

Imagine a world with clean air, clean water, and enough food for all. In many businesses around the world, managers with vision are working toward making parts of that fantasy a reality.

What is your vision for a better future?

If a vision conveys an *ideal,* it communicates a standard of excellence and a clear choice of positive values. If the vision is also *unique,* it communicates and inspires pride in being different from other organizations. The choice of language is important; the words should imply a combination of realism and optimism, an action orientation, and resolution and confidence that the vision will be attained.[16]

Visions can be small or large, and can exist at any organizational level as well as at the very top. The important points are that (1) a vision is necessary for effective leadership; (2) a manager or team can develop a vision for any job, work unit, or organization; and (3) many people, including managers who do not develop into effective leaders, do not develop a clear vision—instead they focus on performing or surviving on a day-by-day basis.

Put another way, leaders must know what they want.[17] And other people must understand what that is. The leader must be able to articulate the vision, clearly and often. Other people throughout the organization should understand the vision and be able to state it clearly themselves. That's a start. But the vision means nothing until the leader and followers take action to turn the vision into reality.[18]

One leader who articulated and modeled a clear vision was George Buckley, former chief executive of 3M Company, the innovative manufacturer best known for its Scotch tape, Post-it Notes, and sandpaper. When the economy turned sour, other manufacturers slashed spending on research and development (R&D), but Buckley wanted to retain 3M's commitment to innovation. So even as he tied R&D spending to revenues (R&D spending fell, but not faster than revenues), he challenged his R&D staff to make products cheaper to produce.

Buckley even convinced them that the effort could be satisfying. He accomplished this by recognizing that what drives researchers is a belief that what they do is intellectually stimulating and significant. For example, when Buckley asked the leader of 3M's abrasives business what innovations were in the pipeline, the unit's head commented that abrasives were "not considered sexy." Buckley replied, "Why not? I think abrasives are sexy. Why can't abrasives be sexy?" Eventually, as researchers saw how their innovations were helping the company serve its markets, they grew enthusiastic about Buckley's vision.[19]

A metaphor reinforces the important concept of vision.[20] Putting a jigsaw puzzle together is much easier if you have the picture on the box cover in front of you. Without the picture, or vision, the lack of direction is likely to result in frustration and failure. That is what communicating a vision is all about: making clear where you are heading.

Not just any vision will do. Visions can be inappropriate, or fail, for a variety of reasons (see Exhibit 12.2).[21] First, an inappropriate vision may reflect merely the leader's personal needs. Such a vision can be unethical, or it may fail because of lack of acceptance by the market or by those who must implement it. Second (and related to the first), an inappropriate vision may ignore stakeholder needs. Third, the leader must stay abreast of environmental changes. Although effective leaders maintain confidence and persevere despite obstacles, the time may come when the facts dictate that the vision must change. You will learn more about change and how to manage it later in the book.

Where do visions come from?[22] Leaders should be sensitive to emerging opportunities, develop the right capabilities or worldviews, and not be overly invested in the status quo. You can capitalize on networks of insightful people who have ideas about the future. Some visions are accidental; a company may stumble into an opportunity, and the leader may get credit for foresight. Some leaders and companies launch many new initiatives and, through trial and error, occasionally hit home runs. If the company learns from these successes, the vision emerges.

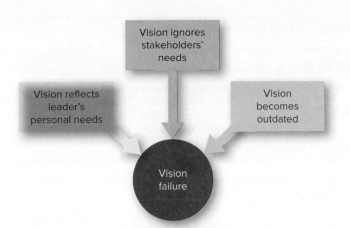

EXHIBIT 12.2
Reasons Why
Visions Fail

SOURCE: Adapted from Conger, J. A., "The Dark Side of Leadership," *Organizational Dynamics* 19, Autumn 1990, 44–55.

Leading and Managing

Effective managers are not necessarily true leaders. Many administrators, supervisors, and even top executives perform their responsibilities successfully without being great leaders. But these positions afford an opportunity for leadership. The ability to lead effectively, then, will set the excellent managers apart from the rest.

Whereas management must deal with the ongoing, day-to-day complexities of organizations, true leadership includes effectively orchestrating important change.[23] Managing requires planning and budgeting routines; leading includes setting the direction (creating a vision) for the firm. Management requires structuring the organization, staffing it with capable people, and monitoring results; leadership goes beyond these functions by inspiring people to accomplish a great vision. Great leaders keep people focused on moving the organization toward its ideal future, motivating them to overcome whatever obstacles lie in the way.

> Good leadership, unfortunately, is all too rare.

Good leadership, unfortunately, is all too rare. Managers may focus on the activities that earn them praise and rewards, such as actions that increase the company's stock price, rather than making tough ethical choices or investing in long-term projects. Some new managers, learning that quick wins will help them establish their credibility as leaders, push a pet project while neglecting the negative impact on the people they were assigned to lead. This approach tends to backfire because employees distrust this type of manager and lose any commitment they might have had to the team's long-term success. Successful leaders, in contrast, enlist the team in scoring collective wins that result from working together toward a shared vision.[24]

It is important to be clear here about several things. First, management and leadership are both vitally important. To highlight the need for more leadership is not to minimize the importance of management or managers. But leadership involves unique processes that are distinguishable from basic management processes.[25] Moreover, just because they involve different processes does not mean that they require different, separate people. The same individual can exemplify effective managerial processes, leadership processes, both, or neither.

Some people dislike the idea of distinguishing between management and leadership, maintaining that it is artificial or derogatory toward the managers and the management processes that make organizations run. An alternative distinction is between supervisory and strategic leadership.[26] **Supervisory leadership** is behavior that provides guidance, support, and corrective feedback for day-to-day activities. **Strategic leadership** gives purpose and meaning to organizations.

supervisory leadership

Behavior that provides guidance, support, and corrective feedback for day-to-day activities.

strategic leadership

Behavior that gives purpose and meaning to organizations, envisioning and creating a positive future.

EXHIBIT 12.3
Behaviors of Effective
Followers

1. **Volunteering** to handle tasks or help accomplish goals.

2. **Accepting** assignments in a willing manner.

3. **Exhibiting** loyalty to the group.

4. **Voicing** differences of opinion, but supporting the group's decisions.

5. **Offering** suggestions.

6. **Maintaining** a positive attitude, even in confusing or trying times.

7. **Working** effectively as a team member.

SOURCE: Adapted from Holden Leadership Center, University of Oregon, http://leadership.uoregon.edu/resources/exercises_tips/skills/followership.

Strategic leadership involves anticipating and envisioning a viable future for the organization and working with others to initiate changes that create that future.[27] For example, Indian business leaders prioritize their top responsibilities[28] as providing input for business strategy (which you studied thoroughly in Part 1 of this book); being keepers of the organizational culture (introduced in Chapter 2); and guiding, teaching, and serving as role models for employees (employees being the focus of this part of the book).

Leading and Following

Organizations succeed or fail not only because of how well they are led, but because of how well followers follow. Just as managers are not necessarily good leaders, people are not always good followers. One leadership scholar stated, "Executives are given subordinates; they have to earn followers."[29] But it's also true that good followers help produce good leadership.

As a manager, you will be asked to play the roles of both leader and follower. As you lead the people who report to you, you will report to your boss. You will be a member of some teams and task forces, and you may head others. Although the official leadership roles get the glamour and therefore are the roles that many people covet, followers must perform their responsibilities conscientiously and well.

Good followership doesn't mean merely obeying orders, although some bosses may view it that way. The most effective followers are capable of independent thinking and at the same time are actively committed to organizational goals.[30] Exhibit 12.3 lists additional behaviors of effective followers. Robert Townsend, who led a legendary turnaround at Avis, said that the most important characteristic of a follower may be the willingness to tell the truth.[31]

The best followers master skills that are useful to their organizations, and they hold performance standards that are higher than required. Effective followers may not get the glory, but they know their contributions to the organization are valuable. And as they make those contributions, they study leaders in preparation for their own leadership roles.[32]

Effective followers also distinguish themselves from ineffective ones by their enthusiasm and commitment to the organization and to a person or purpose—an idea, a product—other than themselves or their own interests.

Power and Leadership

Central to effective leadership is **power**—the ability to influence other people.[33] In organizations, this influence often means the ability to get things done or accomplish one's goals despite resistance from others.

power

The ability to influence others.

Sources of Power

One of the earliest and still most useful approaches to understanding power identifies five important potential sources of power.[34] Exhibit 12.4 shows those power sources.

EXHIBIT 12.4
Sources of Leader Power

SOURCE: Adapted from French, J. R. P. and Raven, B., "The Bases of Social Power," *Studies in Social Power,* ed. D. Cartwright. Ann Arbor, MI: Institute for Social Research, 1959.

Legitimate Power   The leader with *legitimate power* has the right, or the authority, to tell others what to do; employees are obligated to comply with legitimate orders. For example, a supervisor tells an employee to remove a safety hazard, and the employee removes the hazard because he has to obey the authority of his boss. In contrast, when a staff person lacks the authority to give an order to a line manager, the staff person has no legitimate power over the manager. As you might guess, managers have more legitimate power over their direct reports than they do over their peers, bosses, and others inside or outside their organizations.[35]

Reward Power   The leader who has *reward power* influences others because she controls valued rewards; people comply with the leader's wishes in order to receive those rewards. For example, a manager works hard to achieve her performance goals to get a positive performance review and a big pay raise from her boss. On the other hand, if a company directive dictates that everyone receive the same salary increase, a leader's reward power decreases because he or she is unable to give higher raises.

Coercive Power   The leader with *coercive power* has control over punishments; people comply to avoid those punishments. For instance, a manager implements an absenteeism policy that administers disciplinary actions to offending employees. A manager has less coercive power if, say, a union contract limits her ability to punish. In general, lower-level managers have less legitimate, coercive, and reward power than do middle and higher-level managers.[36]

Referent Power   The leader with *referent power* has personal characteristics that appeal to others; people comply because of admiration, personal liking, a desire for approval, or a desire to be like the leader. For example, young, ambitious managers emulate the work habits and personal style of a successful, charismatic executive. An executive who is incompetent, disliked, and less respected has little referent power.

Expert Power   The leader who has *expert power* has certain expertise or knowledge; people comply because they believe in, can learn from, or can otherwise gain from that expertise. For example, a seasoned sales manager gives her salespeople some tips on how to close a deal. The salespeople then alter their sales techniques because they respect the manager's expertise. However, this manager may lack expert power in other areas, such as finance; thus her salespeople may ignore her advice concerning financial matters.

People who are in a position that gives them the right to tell others what to do, who can reward and punish, who are well liked and admired, and who have expertise on which other people can draw will be powerful members of the organization.

All of these sources of power are potentially important. Although it is easy to assume that the most powerful bosses are those who have high legitimate power and control major rewards and punishments, it is important not to underestimate the more personal sources such as expert and referent powers. Additional personal sources of power that do not necessarily stem from one's position or level within an organization include access to information and the strength of one's informal network.[37]

Traditional Approaches to Understanding Leadership

 LO 5   Three traditional approaches to studying leadership are the trait approach, the behavioral approach, and the situational approach.

Leader Traits

trait approach

A leadership perspective that attempts to determine the personal characteristics that great leaders share.

The **trait approach** is the oldest leadership perspective; it focuses on individual leaders and attempts to determine the personal characteristics (traits) that great leaders share. What set Margaret Thatcher, Nelson Mandela, Julius Caesar, and George Washington apart from the crowd? The trait approach assumes the existence of a leadership personality and assumes that leaders are born, not made.

From 1904 to 1948, researchers conducted more than 100 leadership trait studies.[38] At the end of that period, management scholars concluded that no particular set of traits is necessary for a person to become a successful leader. Enthusiasm for the trait approach diminished, but some research on traits continued. By the mid-1970s, a more balanced view emerged: Although no traits ensure leadership success, certain characteristics are potentially useful. The current perspective is that some some personal characteristics—many of which a person need not be born with but can strive to acquire—contribute to leader effectiveness (see Exhibit 12.5).[39]

1. *Drive.* Drive refers to a set of characteristics that reflect a high level of effort. Drive includes high need for achievement, constant striving for improvement, ambition,

EXHIBIT 12.5
Personal Attributes That Aid Leader Effectiveness

energy, tenacity (persistence in the face of obstacles), and initiative. In several countries, the achievement needs of top executives were shown to relate to the growth rates of their organizations.[40] But the need to achieve can be a drawback if leaders focus on personal achievement and get so personally involved with the work that they do not delegate enough work to others.

2. *Leadership motivation.* Great leaders have more than drive; they *want to lead.* In this regard, it helps to be extroverted—extroversion is related to both leader emergence and leader effectiveness.[41] However—and this is a huge point—introverts have great strengths that can contribute to effective leadership, and extroversion can backfire. For example, the assertiveness of extroverted leaders can quash the contributions of group members. Extroverts sometimes should adopt a more reserved, quiet style.[42]

   If you consider yourself to be introverted, as so many of us do, you might want to heed the words of Mahatma Gandhi: "In a gentle way, you can shake the world." And listen to author Susan Cain, who writes that introverts are underrated as leaders and are the people who can help us "think deeply, strategize, solve complex problems, and spot canaries in your coal mine."

   Also important is a high need for power, a preference to be in leadership rather than follower positions.[43] A high power need induces people to want to influence others, and sustains interest and satisfaction in the leadership process. When the power need is exercised in moral and socially constructive ways, rather than to the detriment of others, leaders inspire more trust, respect, and commitment to their vision.

3. *Integrity.* Integrity is the correspondence between actions and words. Honesty and credibility, in addition to being desirable characteristics in their own right, are especially important for leaders because these traits inspire trust in others.

4. *Self-confidence.* Self-confidence is important for a number of reasons. The leadership role is challenging, and setbacks are inevitable. Self-confidence allows a leader to overcome obstacles, make decisions despite uncertainty, and instill confidence in others. Of course you don't want to overdo this; arrogance and cockiness have triggered more than one leader's downfall.

5. *Knowledge of the business.* Effective leaders have a high level of knowledge about their industries, companies, and technical matters. Leaders must be able to interpret vast quantities of information. Advanced degrees are useful in a career, but ultimately less important than acquired expertise in matters relevant to the organization.[44]

Finally, one personal skill may be the most important: the ability to perceive the needs and goals of others and to adjust one's personal leadership approach accordingly.[45] Effective leaders do not rely on one leadership style; rather, they are capable of using different styles as the situation warrants.[46] This quality—flexibility—is the cornerstone of the situational approaches to leadership, which you will read about shortly.

> **behavioral approach**
>
> A leadership perspective that attempts to identify what good leaders do—that is, what behaviors they exhibit.

> **task performance behaviors**
>
> Actions taken to ensure that the work group or organization reaches its goals.

> Arrogance and cockiness have triggered more than one leader's downfall.

Leader Behaviors

The **behavioral approach** to leadership attempts to identify what good leaders do. Should leaders focus on getting the job done, or on keeping their followers happy? Should they make decisions autocratically or democratically? In the behavioral approach, personal characteristics are considered less important than the actual behaviors that leaders exhibit.

Three general categories of leadership behavior have received particular attention: behaviors related to task performance, group maintenance, and employee participation in decision making.

Task Performance   Leadership requires getting the job done. **Task performance behaviors** are the leader's efforts to ensure that the work unit or organization reaches its goals. This dimension is variously referred to as *concern for production, directive leadership,*

LO 6

Bottom Line
Task performance behaviors focus on achieving work goals. *What shows you that a manager cares about task performance?*

initiating structure, or *closeness of supervision.* It includes a focus on work speed, quality and accuracy, quantity of output, and rule following.[47] This type of leader behavior improves leader performance and group and organizational performance.[48]

group maintenance behaviors

Actions taken to ensure the satisfaction of group members, develop and maintain harmonious work relationships, and preserve the social stability of the group.

Group Maintenance   Leadership is inherently an interpersonal, group activity.[49] In exhibiting **group maintenance behaviors**, leaders take action to ensure the satisfaction of group members, develop and maintain harmonious work relationships, and preserve the social stability of the group. This dimension is sometimes referred to as *concern for people, supportive leadership,* or *consideration.* It includes a focus on people's feelings and comfort, appreciation of them, and stress reduction.[50] This type of leader behavior has a strong positive impact on follower satisfaction, motivation, and leader effectiveness.[51]

What specific behaviors do performance- and maintenance-oriented leadership imply? To help answer this question, assume you are asked to rate your boss on these two dimensions. If a leadership study were conducted in your organization, you would be asked to fill out a questionnaire similar to the one in Exhibit 12.6. The behaviors indicated in the first set of questions represent performance-oriented leadership; those indicated in the second set represent maintenance-oriented leadership.

leader—member exchange (LMX) theory

Highlights the importance of leader behaviors not just toward the group as a whole but toward individuals on a personal basis.

Leader–member exchange (LMX) theory highlights the importance of leader behaviors not just toward the group as a whole but toward individuals on a personal basis.[52] The focus in the original formulation, which has since been expanded, is primarily on the leader behaviors historically considered group maintenance.[53] According to LMX theory, and as supported by research evidence, maintenance behaviors such as trust, open communication, mutual respect, mutual obligation, and mutual loyalty form the cornerstone of relationships that are satisfying and perhaps more productive.[54]

EXHIBIT 12.6

Questions Assessing Task Performance and Group Maintenance Leadership

Task Performance Leadership
1.   Is your superior strict about observing regulations?
2.   To what extent does your superior give you instructions and orders?
3.   Is your superior strict about the amount of work you do?
4.   Does your superior urge you to complete your work by a specified time?
5.   Does your superior try to make you work to your maximum capacity?
6.   When you do an inadequate job, does your superior focus on the inadequate way the job is done?
7.   Does your superior ask you for reports about the progress of your work?
8.   How precisely does your superior work out plans for goal achievement each month?

Group Maintenance Leadership
1.   Can you talk freely with your superior about your work?
2.   Does your superior generally support you?
3.   Is your superior concerned about your personal problems?
4.   Do you think your superior trusts you?
5.   Does your superior give you recognition when you do your job well?
6.   When a problem arises in your workplace, does your superior ask your opinion about how to solve it?
7.   Is your superior concerned about your future benefits, such as promotions and pay raises?
8.   Does your superior treat you fairly?

SOURCE: Misumi J. and Peterson, M., "The Performance-Maintenance (PM) Theory of Leadership: Review of a Japanese Research Program," *Administrative Science Quarterly* 30, no. 2 (June 1985).

Remember, though, the potential for cross-cultural differences. Maintenance behaviors are important everywhere, but the specific behaviors can differ from one culture to another.[55] For example, in the United States, maintenance behaviors include dealing with people face to face; in Japan, written memos are preferred over giving directions face to face, thus avoiding confrontation and permitting face-saving in the event of disagreement.[56]

Participation in Decision Making   How should a leader make decisions? More specifically, to what extent should leaders involve their people in making decisions?[57] As a dimension of leadership behavior, **participation in decision making** can range from autocratic to democratic. **Autocratic leadership** makes decisions and then announces them to the group. **Democratic leadership** solicits input from others. Democratic leadership seeks information, opinions, and preferences, sometimes to the point of meeting with the group, leading discussions, and using consensus or majority vote to make the final choice.

The Effects of Leader Behavior

How the leader behaves influences people's attitudes and performance. Studies of these effects focus on autocratic versus democratic decision styles or on performance- versus maintenance-oriented behaviors.

Decision Styles   The classic study comparing autocratic and democratic styles found that a democratic approach resulted in the most positive attitudes, whereas an autocratic approach resulted in somewhat higher performance.[58] A **laissez-faire** style, in which the leader essentially made no decisions, led to more negative attitudes and lower performance. These results seem logical, and probably represent the prevalent beliefs among managers about the general effects of these approaches.

Democratic styles, appealing though they may seem to some, are not always the most appropriate. When speed is of the essence, democratic decision making may be too slow, or people may want decisiveness from their leader.[59] Whether a decision should be made autocratically or democratically depends on the characteristics of the leader, the followers, and the situation.[60] Thus a situational approach to leader decision styles, discussed later in the chapter, is appropriate.

Performance and Maintenance Behaviors   The performance and maintenance dimensions of leadership are independent of each other. In other words, a leader can behave in ways that emphasize one, both, or neither of these dimensions.

A team of Ohio State University researchers investigated the effects of leader behaviors in a truck manufacturing plant of International Harvester.[61] Generally, supervisors who were high on maintenance behaviors (which the researchers termed *consideration*) had fewer grievances and less turnover in

> A leader can behave in ways that emphasize one, both, or neither of these dimensions.

their work units than supervisors who were low on this dimension. The opposite held for task performance behaviors (which the research team called *initiating structure*). Supervisors high on this dimension had more grievances and higher turnover rates.

When maintenance and performance leadership behaviors were considered together, the results were more complex. But one conclusion was clear: when a leader is high on performance-oriented behaviors, he or she should also be maintenance oriented. Otherwise, the leader will face high rates of employee turnover and grievances.

At about the same time the Ohio State studies were conducted, a research program at the University of Michigan was studying the impact of the same leader behaviors on groups' job performance.[62] Among other things, the researchers concluded that the most effective managers engaged in what they called task-oriented behavior: planning, scheduling, coordinating, providing resources, and setting performance goals. Effective managers also exhibited more relationship-oriented behavior: demonstrating trust and confidence, being friendly and considerate, showing appreciation, keeping people informed, and so on. As you can

participation in decision making

Leader behaviors that managers perform in involving their employees in making decisions.

autocratic leadership

A form of leadership in which the leader makes decisions on his or her own and then announces those decisions to the group.

democratic leadership

A form of leadership in which the leader solicits input from subordinates.

laissez-faire

A leadership philosophy characterized by an absence of managerial decision making.

see, these dimensions of leader behavior are essentially the task performance and group maintenance dimensions.

After publication of the Ohio State and Michigan findings, it became popular to talk about the ideal leader as one who is always both performance and maintenance oriented. The best-known leadership training model to follow this style is Blake and Mouton's Leadership Grid.[63] In grid training, managers are rated on their performance-oriented behavior (called *concern for production*) and maintenance-oriented behavior (*concern for people*). Then their scores are plotted on the grid shown in Exhibit 12.7. The highest score is a 9 on both dimensions.

As the figure shows, joint scores can fall at any point on the grid. Managers who did not score a 9,9—for example, those who were high on concern for people but low on concern for production—would then receive training on how to become a 9,9 leader.

For a long time, grid training was warmly received by U.S. business and industry. Later, however, it was criticized for embracing a simplistic, one-best-way style of leadership and ignoring the possibility that 9,9 is not best under all circumstances. For example, even 1,1 can be appropriate if employees know their jobs (and therefore don't need to receive directions). Also, they may enjoy their jobs and their co-workers enough that whether the boss shows personal concern for them is not very important. Nonetheless, if the manager is uncertain how to behave, it probably is best to exhibit behaviors that relate to both task performance and group maintenance.[64]

In fact, a wide range of effective leadership styles exists. Organizations that understand the need for diverse leadership styles will have a competitive advantage in the modern business environment over those that believe there is only one best way.

EXHIBIT 12.7

The Leadership Grid

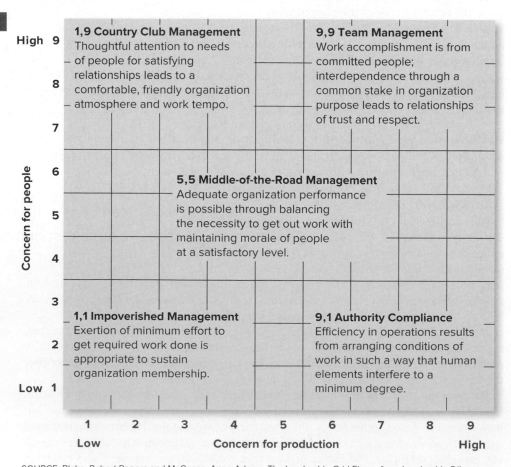

SOURCE: Blake, Robert Rogers and McCanse, Anne Adams, The Leadership Grid Figure from *Leadership Dilemmas—Grid Solutions.* Houston, TX: Gulf Publishing Company, 1991, p. 29.

Situational Approaches to Leadership

According to proponents of the **situational approach** to leadership, universally important traits and behaviors don't exist. They believe effective leader behaviors vary from situation to situation. The leader should first analyze the situation and then decide what to do. In other words, look before you lead.

A head nurse in a hospital described her situational approach to leadership:

> My leadership style is a mix of all styles. In this environment I normally let people participate. But in a code blue situation where a patient is dying I automatically become very autocratic: "You do this; you do that; you, out of the room; you all better be quiet; you, get Dr. Mansfield." The staff tell me that's the only time they see me like that. In an emergency like that, you don't have time to vote, talk a lot, or yell at each other. It's time for someone to set up the order.
>
> I remember one time, one person saying, "Wait a minute, I want to do this." He wanted to do the mouth-to-mouth resuscitation. I knew the person behind him did it better, so I said, "No, he does it." This fellow told me later that I hurt him so badly to yell that in front of all the staff and doctors. It was like he wasn't good enough. So I explained it to him: "That's the way it is. A life was on the line. I couldn't give you warm fuzzies. I couldn't make you look good because you didn't have the skills to give the very best to that patient who wasn't breathing anymore."[65]

> ## Look before you lead.

This nurse has her own intuitive situational approach to leadership. She knows the potential advantages of the participatory approach to decision making, but she also knows that in some circumstances she must make decisions herself.

The first situational model of leadership—still highly useful—was proposed in 1958 by Tannenbaum and Schmidt. In their classic *Harvard Business Review* article, these authors described how managers should consider three factors before deciding how to lead: forces in the manager, forces in the subordinate, and forces in the situation.[66]

Forces in the manager include the manager's personal values, inclinations, feelings of security, and confidence in subordinates. Forces in the subordinate include his or her knowledge and experience, readiness to assume responsibility for decision making, interest in the task or problem, and understanding and acceptance of the organization's goals. Forces in the situation include the type of leadership style the organization values, the degree to which the group works effectively as a unit, the problem itself and the type of information needed to solve it, and the amount of time the leader has to make the decision.

Consider which of these forces makes an autocratic style most appropriate and which dictates a democratic, participative style. By engaging in this exercise, you are constructing a situational theory of leadership.

Although the Tannenbaum and Schmidt article was published more than a half century ago, most of its arguments remain valid. Since that time, other situational models have emerged. We will focus here on four: the Vroom model for decision making, Fiedler's contingency model, Hersey and Blanchard's situational theory, and path–goal theory.

The Vroom Model of Leadership This situational model follows in the tradition of Tannenbaum and Schmidt. The **Vroom model** emphasizes the participative dimension of leadership: how leaders go about making decisions. The model uses the basic situational approach of assessing the situation before determining the best leadership style.[67]

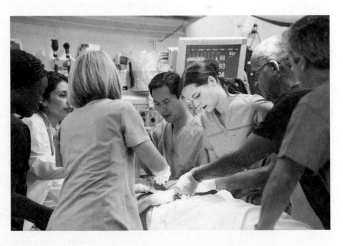

Nurses experience situational leadership on a daily basis. How would you handle a leadership role under pressure?

©monkeybusinessimages/Getty Images RF

The Vroom model operates as a decision tree in which you answer a series of questions one at a time, choosing high or low for each; the specifics are not important here. Eventually you reach 1 of 14 possible endpoints. For each endpoint, the model states which of five decision styles is most appropriate. Several decision styles may work, but the style recommended is the one that takes the least amount of time.

The five leader decision styles—decide alone, consult individuals, consult multiple group members, facilitate a whole-group decision, and delegate to others—indicate that there are several shades of participation, not just autocratic or democratic.

Of course not every managerial decision warrants this complicated analysis. But the model becomes less complex after you work through it a couple of times. Also, using the model for major decisions ensures that you consider the important situational factors and alerts you to the most appropriate style to use.

Fiedler's contingency model of leadership effectiveness

A situational approach to leadership postulating that effectiveness depends on the personal style of the leader and the degree to which the situation gives the leader power, control, and influence over the situation.

Fiedler's Contingency Model According to **Fiedler's contingency model of leadership effectiveness**, effectiveness depends on two factors: the personal style of the leader and the degree to which the situation gives the leader power, control, and influence over the situation.[68] Exhibit 12.8 illustrates the contingency model. The upper half of the figure shows the situational analysis, and the lower half indicates the appropriate style. In the upper portion, three questions are used to analyze the situation:

1. Are leader–member relations good or poor? (To what extent is the leader accepted and supported by group members?)
2. Is the task structured or unstructured? (To what extent do group members know what their goals are and how to accomplish them?)
3. Is the leader's position power strong or weak (high or low)? (To what extent does the leader have the authority to reward and punish?)

These three sequential questions create a decision tree (from top to bottom in the figure) in which a situation is classified into one of eight categories. The lower the category number,

EXHIBIT 12.8 Fiedler's Analysis of Situations in Which the Task- or Relationship-Motivated Leader Is More Effective

Leader–member relations	Good				Poor			
Task structure	Structured		Unstructured		Structured		Unstructured	
Leader position power	High	Low	High	Low	High	Low	High	Low
Favorable for leader → Unfavorable for leader								
Type of leader most effective in the situation	1 Task-motivated	2 Task-motivated	3 Task-motivated	4 Relationship-motivated	5 Relationship-motivated	6 Relationship-motivated	7 Relationship-motivated	8 Task-motivated

SOURCE: Organ, Dennis and Bateman, Thomas, *Organizational Behavior,* 4th ed. New York: McGraw-Hill, 1990.

the more favorable the situation is for the leader; the higher the number, the less favorable the situation. Fiedler originally called this variable "situational favorableness," and later "situational control." Situation 1 is the best: relations are good, task structure is high, and power is high. In the least favorable situation (8), in which the leader has very little situational control, relations are poor, tasks lack structure, and the leader's power is weak.

Different situations dictate different leadership styles. Fiedler measured leadership styles with an instrument assessing the leader's least preferred co-worker (LPC); that is, the attitude toward the follower the leader liked the least. This was considered an indication more generally of leaders' attitudes toward people. If a leader can single out the person she likes the least, but her attitude is not all that negative, she would receive a high score on the LPC scale. Leaders with more negative attitudes toward others would receive low LPC scores.

Based on the LPC score, Fiedler considered two leadership styles. **Task-motivated leadership** places primary emphasis on completing the task and is more likely exhibited by leaders with low LPC scores. **Relationship-motivated leadership** emphasizes maintaining good interpersonal relationships and is more likely from high-LPC leaders. These leadership styles correspond to task performance and group maintenance leader behaviors, respectively.

The lower part of Exhibit 12.8 indicates which style is situationally appropriate. For situations 1, 2, 3, and 8, a task-motivated leadership style is more effective. For situations 4 through 7, relationship-motivated leadership is more appropriate.

Fiedler's theory was not always supported by research. It is better supported if three broad rather than eight specific levels of situational control are assumed: low, medium, and high. The theory was quite controversial in academic circles; among other arguable things, it assumed that leaders cannot change their styles but must be assigned to situations that suit their styles. However, the model has withstood the test of time and still receives attention. Most important, it initiated and continues to emphasize the importance of finding a fit between the situation and the leader's style.

Hersey and Blanchard's Situational Theory

Hersey and Blanchard developed a situational model that added another factor the leader should take into account before deciding whether task performance or maintenance behaviors are more important. Originally called the *life-cycle theory of leadership*, **Hersey and Blanchard's situational theory** highlights the maturity of the followers as the key situational factor.[69] **Job maturity** is the level of the follower's skills and technical knowledge relative to the task being performed; **psychological maturity** is the follower's self-confidence and self-respect. High-maturity followers have both the ability and the confidence to do a good job.

The theory proposes that the more mature the followers, the less the leader needs to engage in task performance behaviors. The required amount of maintenance behavior is a bit more complex; maintenance behaviors are not important with followers of low or high levels of maturity but are important for followers of moderate maturity. For low-maturity followers, the emphasis should be on performance-related leadership; for moderate-maturity followers, performance leadership is somewhat less important and maintenance behaviors become more important; and for high-maturity followers, neither dimension of leadership behavior is important.

Little academic research has been done on this situational theory, but the model is well-known and popular in management training seminars. Regardless of its scientific validity, Hersey and Blanchard's model provides a reminder that it is important to treat different people differently. Moreover, it suggests the importance of treating the same individual differently from time to time as he or she changes jobs or acquires more maturity in his or her particular job.[70]

Path–Goal Theory

Perhaps the most comprehensive and generally useful situational model of leadership effectiveness is path–goal theory. Developed by Robert House, **path–goal theory** gets its name from its concern with how leaders influence followers' perceptions of their work goals and the paths they follow toward goal attainment.[71]

---

task-motivated leadership

Leadership that places primary emphasis on completing a task.

relationship-motivated leadership

Leadership that places primary emphasis on maintaining good interpersonal relationships.

Hersey and Blanchard's situational theory

A life-cycle theory of leadership postulating that a manager should consider an employee's psychological and job maturity before deciding whether task performance or maintenance behaviors are more important.

job maturity

The level of the employee's skills and technical knowledge relative to the task being performed.

psychological maturity

An employee's self-confidence and self-respect.

path—goal theory

A theory that concerns how leaders influence subordinates' perceptions of their work goals and the paths they follow toward attainment of those goals.

EXHIBIT 12.9
The Path–Goal Framework

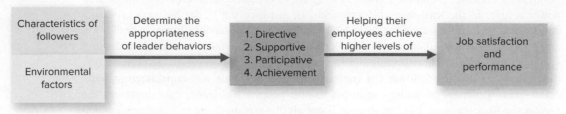

The key situational factors in path–goal theory are (1) personal characteristics of followers and (2) environmental pressures and demands with which followers must cope to attain their work goals. These factors determine which leadership behaviors are most appropriate. The four pertinent leadership behaviors are as follows:

1. *Directive leadership,* a form of task performance-oriented behavior.
2. *Supportive leadership,* a form of group maintenance-oriented behavior.
3. *Participative leadership,* or decision style.
4. *Achievement-oriented leadership,* or behaviors geared toward motivating people, such as setting challenging goals and rewarding good performance.

These situational factors and leader behaviors are merged in Exhibit 12.9. As you can see, appropriate leader behaviors—as determined by characteristics of followers and the work environment—lead to effective performance.

The theory also specifies which follower and environmental characteristics are important. There are three key follower characteristics. *Authoritarianism* is the degree to which individuals respect, admire, and defer to authority. *Locus of control* is the extent to which individuals see the environment as responsive to their own behavior. People with an *internal* locus of control believe that what happens to them is their own doing; people with an *external* locus of control believe that it is just luck or fate. Finally, *ability* is people's beliefs about their own abilities to do their assigned jobs.

Path–goal theory states that these personal characteristics determine the appropriateness of various leadership styles. For example, the theory makes the following propositions:

- A directive leadership style is more appropriate for highly authoritarian people because such people respect authority.
- A participative leadership style is more appropriate for people who have an internal locus of control because these individuals prefer to have more influence over their own work (and lives).
- A directive style is more appropriate when subordinates' ability is low. The directive style helps people understand what has to be done.

Appropriate leadership style is also determined by three important environmental factors: people's tasks, the formal authority system of the organization, and the primary work group:

- Directive leadership is inappropriate if tasks already are well structured.
- If the task and the authority or rule system are dissatisfying, directive leadership will create greater dissatisfaction.
- If the task or authority system is dissatisfying, supportive leadership is especially appropriate because it offers one positive source of gratification in an otherwise negative situation.
- If the primary work group provides social support to its members, supportive leadership is less important.

Path–goal theory offers many more propositions. In general, the theory suggests that the functions of the leader are to (1) make the path to work goals easier to travel by providing coaching and direction, (2) reduce frustrating barriers to goal attainment, and (3) increase opportunities for personal satisfaction by increasing payoffs to people for achieving performance goals. The best way to do these things depends on your people and on the work situation. Again, analyze and then adapt your style accordingly.

Substitutes for Leadership   Sometimes leaders don't have to lead, or situations constrain their ability to lead effectively. The situation may be one in which leadership is unnecessary or has little impact. **Substitutes for leadership** can provide the same influence on people that leaders otherwise would have.

Certain follower, task, and organizational factors are substitutes for task performance and group maintenance leader behaviors.[72] For example, group maintenance behaviors are less important and have less impact if people already have a closely knit group, they have a professional orientation, the job is inherently satisfying, or there is great physical distance between leader and followers. Thus physicians who are strongly concerned with professional conduct, enjoy their work, and work independently do not need social support from hospital administrators.

Task performance leadership is less important and will have less of a positive effect if people have a lot of experience and ability, feedback is supplied to them directly from the task or by computer, or the rules and procedures are rigid. If these factors are operating, the leader does not have to tell people what to do or how well they are performing.

substitutes for leadership

Factors in the workplace that can exert the same influence on employees as leaders would provide.

Management in Action

PEPSICO SHIFTS TO HEALTHIER PRODUCTS

Under CEO Indra Nooyi, PepsiCo has pledged to reduce the sugar content and calorie count of two-thirds of its beverage products by 2025. That's an ambitious change to a category that supplies nearly half the company's annual revenue. But Nooyi is up for the challenge of innovation. As she says, "Every year, if we want to maintain or gain [share] in the world, we have to grow our revenues somewhere between $2.5 billion and $3 billion—just to stay flat. . . . That is a big challenge. So I have to innovate the hell out of the company."

Nooyi is also helping the company expand its healthier food and beverage offerings, introducing Tropicana Essentials Probiotics, salsa from the hummus brand Sabra, Quaker Breakfast Flats, and a premium bottled water called LIFEWTR. And PepsiCo will begin reducing saturated fat and salt in its snack foods.

In line with Nooyi's Performance with Purpose strategy, the company will "increase positive nutrition," specifically by promoting its "Everyday Nutrition" products, which include whole grains, fruits, vegetables, and dairy, and by deploying the PepsiCo Foundation to increase access to these foods and beverages among underserved and food-insecure customers. The company will seek to relieve the problem of chronic hunger and rely on locally sourced and sustainably produced ingredients while also fighting obesity. Nooyi sees the latter as "one of the world's biggest public health challenges, a challenge fundamentally linked to our industry."

Other goals Nooyi hopes to achieve by 2025 are reducing waste in food production by half, and achieving 100 percent recoverable or recyclable packaging. In addition, she wants the company to improve the efficiency of its water use around the world and promote respect for water access as a human right. Working with the PepsiCo Foundation, she wants to provide 25 million at-risk people with access to a safe water supply by 2025.

Described as a perfectionist who believes in "pushing the boundaries to get to flawless execution," Nooyi also says, "I wouldn't ask anyone to do anything I wouldn't do myself." And she is a lifelong learner. "Just because you are CEO, don't think you have landed. You must continually increase your learning, the way you think, and the way you approach the organization. I've never forgotten that."[73]

- What leadership traits and behaviors describe Indra Nooyi? How might they be effective (or not)?
- "Responsible Leadership" is a label sometimes used to describe leaders who care about and act on behalf of social issues. You learned in Chapter 5 about ethics, CSR, and sustainability; how does Indra Nooyi exhibit responsible leadership?

MANAGER'S BRIEF

PROGRESS REPORT

ONWARD

The concept of substitutes for leadership does more than indicate when a leader's attempts at influence will and will not work. It provides useful and practical prescriptions for how to manage more efficiently.[74] If the manager can develop the work situation to the point that a number of these substitutes for leadership are operating, she does not need to spend as much time in direct attempts to influence people. The leader will be free to spend more time on other important activities.

Research indicates that substitutes for leadership may be better predictors of commitment and satisfaction than of performance.[75] These substitutes are helpful, but you can't put substitutes in place and think you've completed your job as leader. Consider, for example, whether these substitutes alone would be enough at PepsiCo (see "Management in Action: Progress Report").

And as a follower, consider this: if you're not getting good leadership, and if these substitutes are not in place, create your own substitute for leadership—self-leadership. Take the initiative to motivate yourself, lead yourself, create positive change, and lead others.

charismatic leader

A person who is dominant, self-confident, convinced of the moral righteousness of his or her beliefs, and able to arouse a sense of excitement and adventure in followers.

Contemporary Perspectives on Leadership

LO 7

So far you have learned the major classic approaches to understanding leadership, all of which remain useful today. Now we will discuss some newer developments that are revolutionizing our understanding of this vital aspect of management.

Charismatic Leadership

Like many great leaders, Ronald Reagan had charisma. So did John F. Kennedy. Thomas Watson, Richard Branson, Oprah Winfrey, Steve Jobs, and Mark Cuban are good examples of charismatic leaders in business.

Martin Luther King was a brilliant, charismatic leader who had a compelling vision, a dream for a better world.

©Trinity Mirror/Mirrorpix/Alamy Stock Photo

Charisma is an elusive concept; it is easy to spot but hard to define, and scholars continue to debate it.[76] What *is* charisma, and how does one acquire it? According to one definition, "Charisma packs an emotional wallop for followers above and beyond ordinary esteem, affection, admiration, and trust. . . . The charismatic is an idolized hero, a messiah, and a savior."[77]

As you can see from this quotation, many people, particularly North Americans, value charisma in their leaders. But some people don't like the term *charisma;* it can be associated with the negative charisma of evil leaders whom people follow blindly.[78] Nevertheless, charismatic leaders who display appropriate values and use their charisma for appropriate purposes serve as ethical role models for others.[79]

Charismatic leaders are dominant and exceptionally self-confident, and have a strong conviction in the moral righteousness of their beliefs.[80] They strive to create an aura of competence and success and communicate high expectations for and confidence in followers. Ultimately, charismatic leaders somehow satisfy other peoples' needs and help reduce their stress.[81] Even people who have no direct contact with a leader can perceive him or her as charismatic, because other followers spread the word.[82]

And guess what: People can learn to be more charismatic.[83]

The charismatic leader articulates ideological goals and makes sacrifices in pursuit of those goals.[84] Martin Luther King Jr. had a dream for a better world, and John F. Kennedy spoke of landing a human on the moon. In other words, such leaders have a compelling vision. The charismatic leader also arouses a sense of excitement and adventure. He or she is an eloquent speaker who exhibits superior verbal skills, which help communicate the vision and motivate followers. Steve Jobs inspired extraordinary performance from employees, had the fortitude to take innovative risks, and was exceptionally skilled at envisioning and designing products.[85]

Leaders who do these things inspire in their followers trust, confidence, acceptance, obedience, emotional involvement, affection, admiration, and higher performance.[86] A study of firefighters found them to be happier when working for charismatic officers who expressed positive attitudes.[87] Having charisma not only helps CEOs inspire employees but also may inspire them to influence external stakeholders, including customers and investors.[88] Evidence for the positive effects of charismatic leadership has been found in a wide variety of groups, organizations, and management levels, and in countries including India, Singapore, the Netherlands, China, Japan, and Canada.[89]

Charisma has been shown to improve corporate financial performance, particularly under conditions of uncertainty—that is, in risky circumstances or when environments are changing and people have difficulty understanding what they should do.[90] Uncertainty is stressful, and it makes people more receptive to the ideas and actions of charismatic leaders. By the way, as an organization's performance improves under a person's leadership, that person becomes seen as more charismatic as a result of the higher performance.[91]

Transformational Leadership

Charisma contributes to transformational leadership. **Transformational leaders** motivate people to transcend their personal interests for the sake of the larger community.[92] They generate excitement and revitalize organizations. At Amazon, chief executive Jeff Bezos generates excitement with his zeal to create a great customer experience coupled with determination to focus on the long term, no matter how hard investors press for quick profits. His vision keeps employees innovating and gives them a sense of purpose greater than quarterly financial performance.[93]

The transformational process moves beyond the more traditional *transactional* approach to leadership. **Transactional leaders** view management as a series of transactions in which they use their legitimate, reward, and coercive powers to give commands and exchange rewards for services rendered. Unlike transformational leadership, transactional leadership is dispassionate; it does not excite, transform, empower, or inspire people to focus on the interests of the group or organization. Transactional approaches may be more effective for individualists than for collectivists (recall Chapter 6).[94]

Generating Excitement   Transformational leaders generate excitement in several ways.[95] First, they are charismatic, as described earlier. Second, they give their followers individualized attention. Transformational leaders delegate challenging work to deserving people, keep lines of communication open, and provide one-on-one mentoring to develop their people. They do not treat everyone alike because not everyone *is* alike.

Third, transformational leaders are intellectually stimulating. They arouse in their followers an awareness of problems and potential solutions. They articulate the organization's opportunities, threats, strengths, and weaknesses. They stir the imagination and generate insights. Therefore, problems are recognized, and high-quality solutions are identified and implemented with the full commitment of followers.

Additional Strategies   At least four additional strategies contribute to transformational leadership.[96] First, transformational leaders have a vision—a goal, an agenda, or a results orientation that grabs people's attention. Second, they communicate their vision; through words, manner, or symbolism, they convey a compelling image of the ultimate goal. Transformational leadership is most effective in motivating followers when they can see directly the meaningful consequences of the leader's vision, such as by interacting with those who benefit from their work.[97]

Third, transformational leaders build trust by being consistent, dependable, and persistent. They position themselves clearly by choosing a direction and staying with it, thus projecting integrity. Finally, they have positive self-regard. They do not feel self-important or complacent; rather, they recognize their personal strengths, compensate for their weaknesses, nurture and continually develop their talents, and know how to learn from failure. They strive for success rather than merely try to avoid failure.

---

transformational leader

A leader who motivates people to transcend their personal interests for the good of the group.

---

transactional leaders

Leaders who manage through transactions, using their legitimate, reward, and coercive powers to give commands and exchange rewards for services rendered.

Transformational leaders strive for success rather than merely try to avoid failure.

Transformational leadership has been identified in industry, the military, and politics.[98] Besides Amazon's Jeff Bezos, transformational leaders in business include Indra Nooyi (CEO of PepsiCo), Richard Branson (founder and CEO of Virgin Group), Meg Whitman (HP), and Brad Smith (CEO of Intuit).[99] Transformational leadership exhibited by CEOs predicts firm performance, at least for small and midsized firms.[100]

As with charisma, transformational leadership and its positive impact on follower satisfaction and performance have been demonstrated in countries the world over, including Egypt, Germany, China, England, and Japan.[101] A study in mainland China found that transformational leadership predicted employee creativity.[102] Under transformational leadership, people view their jobs as more intrinsically motivating (see Chapter 13 for more on this) and are more strongly committed to work goals.[103] And top management teams agree more clearly about important organizational goals, which translates into higher organizational performance.[104]

Transforming Leaders   Importantly, transformational leadership is not the exclusive domain of presidents and chief executives. In the military, leaders who received transformational leadership training had a positive impact on followers' personal development. They also were successful as indirect leaders: military recruits under the transformational leaders' direct reports were stronger performers.[105] Don't forget, though: the best leaders are those who can display both transformational and transactional behaviors.[106]

Ford Motor Company, in collaboration with the University of Michigan School of Business, put thousands of middle managers through a program designed to stimulate transformational leadership.[107] The training included analysis of the changing business environment, company strategy, and personal reflection and discussion about the need to change. Participants assessed their own leadership styles and developed a specific change initiative to implement after the training—a change that would make a needed and lasting difference for the company.

Over the next six months, the managers implemented change on the job. Almost half of the initiatives resulted in transformational changes in the organization or work unit; the rest of the changes were smaller, more incremental, or more personal. Whether managers made small or transformational changes depended on their attitude going into the training, their level of self-esteem, and the amount of support they received from others on the job for their efforts. Thus some managers did not respond to the training as hoped. But almost half embraced the training, acquired a more transformational perspective, and tackled significant transformational changes for the company.

Level 5 leadership, a term well known among executives, is considered by some to be the ultimate leadership style. Level 5 leadership is a combination of strong professional will (determination) and personal humility that builds enduring greatness.[108] A Level 5 leader is relentlessly focused on the organization's long-term success while behaving modestly, directing attention toward the organization rather than him- or herself. Examples include Tim Cook, CEO of Apple, John Chambers, CEO of Cisco Systems, and IBM's former chief executive Louis Gerstner.

Gerstner is widely credited for turning around a stodgy IBM by shifting its focus from computer hardware to business solutions. Following his retirement, Gerstner wrote a memoir that details what happened at the company but says little about himself. Level 5 leadership is seen as a way to transform organizations to make them great, and requires the leader to exhibit a combination of transactional and transformational styles.[109]

Authenticity

Consider **authentic leadership** to be rooted in the ancient Greek philosophy "To thine own self be true."[110] In your own leadership, strive to be self-aware and authentic by being genuine, open with others, and trustworthy. Authentic transformational leaders care about public interests (community, organizational, or group), not just their own.[111] They are willing to sacrifice their own interests for others, and they can be trusted. They are ethically mature; people view leaders who exhibit moral reasoning as more transformational than

leaders who do not.[112] Importantly, these leader behaviors flow down from one organizational level to the next[113] —your actions as a leader have an impact beyond your immediate, direct reports.

Pseudotransformational leaders are the opposite: they talk a good game, but they ignore followers' real needs as their own self-interests (power, prestige, control, wealth, fame) take precedence.[114]

Opportunities for Leaders

A common view of leaders is that they are superheroes acting alone, swooping in to save the day. But especially in these complex times, leaders cannot and need not act alone. Effective leadership must permeate the organization, not reside in one or two superstars at the top. The leader's job becomes one of spreading leadership abilities throughout the firm.[115]

Make people responsible for their own performance. Create an environment in which each person can figure out what needs to be done and then do it well. Point the way and clear the path so that people can succeed. Give them the credit they deserve. Make heroes out of *them*.

Thus what is now required of leaders is less the efficient management of resources and more the effective unleashing of people and their intellectual capital.

This perspective uncovers a variety of nontraditional leadership roles that are emerging as vitally important.[116] The term **servant–leader** was coined by Robert Greenleaf, a retired AT&T executive. The term is paradoxical in the sense that "leader" and "servant" are usually opposites.

The servant–leader's relationship with employees is more like that of serving customers. Leaders at Zappos, Whole Foods, and Container Store adhere to this philosophy.[117] Servant–leaders strive to be self-aware, genuine, open with others, and ethical, and care about their followers' personal well-being and their local communities. For those who want to both lead and serve others, servant–leadership is a way to relate to others and serve their needs, while motivating performance and strengthening the organization.[118]

Cheryl Bachelder provides a good example. When she became CEO of Popeyes Louisiana Kitchen, she knew things had to change in order to reverse the company's sliding stock price. Through active listening, Bachelder learned how best to serve the needs of franchise owners. The turnaround was dramatic as average store sales increased by 25 percent and the company's stock price rose from $13 per share when she took over in 2007 to around $80 per share ten years later.[119]

The nearby "Social Enterprise" box describes how Elizabeth Hausler serves others by harnessing the energies of multiple organizations and individuals to build affordable, disaster-proof homes.

Additional opportunities abound for leadership that is not classically top-down. **Lateral leadership** does not involve a hierarchical, superior–subordinate relationship but instead invites colleagues at the same level to solve problems together.[120] You alone can't provide a solution to every problem, but you can create processes through which people work collaboratively. It's not about you as a leader solving problems; it's about creating better interpersonal processes for finding solutions. Similarly, **intergroup leaders** lead collaborative performance between different groups or organizations.[121] Examples are interdepartmental cooperation, joint ventures, public/private partnerships, and collaborations that cross national, cultural, and religious boundaries.

With work often being team-based (see Chapter 14), **shared leadership** occurs when leadership rotates to the person with the key knowledge, skills, and abilities for the issue facing the team at a particular time.[122] Shared leadership is most important when tasks are interdependent, are complex, and require creativity. High-performing teams engaged in such work exhibit more shared leadership than poorly performing teams.[123] In consulting teams, the higher the shared leadership, the higher their clients rated the teams' performance.[124]

The role of hierarchical leader remains important—the formal leader still designs the team, manages its external boundaries, provides task direction, emphasizes the importance of the shared leadership approach, and engages in the transactional and transformational

---

pseudotransformational leaders

Leaders who talk about positive change but allow their self-interest to take precedence over followers' needs.

servant–leader

A leader who serves others' needs while strengthening the organization.

lateral leadership

Style in which colleagues at the same hierarchical level are invited to collaborate and facilitate joint problem solving.

intergroup leader

A leader who leads collaborative performance between groups or organizations.

shared leadership

Rotating leadership, in which people rotate through the leadership role based on which person has the most relevant skills at a particular time.

Social Enterprise

Elizabeth Hausler Engineers Disaster-Proof Homes

Elizabeth Hausler grew up in Plano, Illinois, where she spent formative summers working as a bricklayer in her father's business. Inspired by the experience, she became an engineer. In 2001, she was moved by news of a severe earthquake in Gujarat, India, that killed thousands and injured many more. In that moment Hausler came to a realization about natural disasters: "In the developed world, the dollar losses may be high, but the death toll tends to be low." What made the difference between homes that could withstand a disaster and those that could not was architectural engineering.

On a trip to Gujarat a few years later, Hausler learned that "if we want people to engage with us about how to build a safe house that will withstand the next earthquake or typhoon, we have to get the architecture right. We have to work with homeowners." Energized to put her engineering skills to use to reduce the scale of loss from unsafe buildings, Hausler founded a nonprofit called Build Change. Its goal is to marshal the efforts of relief agencies, government, and local architects, engineers, and builders to design and build safe, affordable, and appropriate housing to withstand disasters.

Build Change's first test came when a devastating tsunami in the Indian Ocean struck Southeast Asia in late 2004, killing 280,000 people and leaving 1.7 million homeless. In Sumatra to support relief efforts, Hausler found a partner in the Mercy Corps, a humanitarian relief agency based in Oregon. After building several homes designed by local architects and engineers, Build Change was off and running. It has now built nearly 50,000 disaster-resilient buildings for nearly a quarter million people in China, Haiti, Nepal, and the Philippines—and created 12,000 new jobs.

"Elizabeth Hausler's expertise in and passion for prevention of disaster-related deaths runs throughout the Build Change organization," says Shivani Garg Patel of the Skoll Foundation, which recently gave Hausler its Award for Social Entrepreneurship. "The team aims to change the status quo at all levels of the local system—from the homeowner, to builder, to aid agency and government leader—and they dig in to ensure safe houses and schools for the most vulnerable."

Hausler's use of her engineering talent and her unique vision for Build Change exemplify transformational leadership. Her organization is succeeding in many ways, not only saving lives and homes but also nurturing new talent. "We've hired and trained hundreds of our own engineers," she says, "and we've also worked with partner agencies—governments, NGOs, technical training institutions—to train their engineers and construction workers as well."

And, local communities benefit financially. "For every dollar invested in prevention," says Hausler, "we can save $7 in rebuilding and reconstruction costs."[125]

Questions

- What makes Elizabeth Hausler such an effective leader?
- To what degree is Hausler a servant-leader? A Level 5 leader?

---

activities described in this chapter. But at the same time, the metaphor of geese in V-formation adds strength to the group; the lead goose periodically drops to the back, and another goose steps up and takes its place at the forefront.

A Note on Courage

To be a good leader, you need the courage[126] to create a vision of greatness for your unit; identify and manage allies, adversaries, and fence sitters; and execute your vision, often against opposition. This does not mean you should commit career suicide by alienating too many powerful people; it does mean taking reasonable risks, with the good of the firm at heart, to produce constructive change.

Alan Mulally needed courage when he left Boeing to take charge of Ford Motor Company in 2006, a point at which a series of poor decisions had made Ford a money-losing company. Many of Ford's managers were skeptical of Mulally as their new CEO because he came from outside the automobile industry. Nevertheless, Mulally plunged ahead with decisions that were controversial at the time. He borrowed heavily and determined that the company would go forward with greater focus by offering fewer brands and models, with each being the best in its class. A few years later, Mulally's courageous efforts looked brilliant; Ford's borrowing gave the company resources to draw on when other automakers were accepting government loans to survive a financial crisis, and within a few years, Ford was recording record profits.[127]

Fulfilling your vision will require some of the following acts of courage:[128] (1) seeing things as they are and facing them head-on, making no excuses and harboring no wishful illusions; (2) saying what needs to be said to those who need to hear it; and (3) persisting despite resistance, criticism, abuse, and setbacks. Courage includes stating the realities, even when they are harsh, and publicly stating what you will do to help and what you want from others. This means laying the cards on the table honestly: Here is what I want from you . . . what do you want from me?[129]

Developing Your Leadership Skills

As with other things, you must work at developing your leadership abilities. Great musicians and great athletes don't become great on natural gifts alone. They pay their dues by practicing, learning, and sacrificing. Leaders in a variety of fields, when asked how they became the best leader possible, offered the following comments:[130]

- "I've observed methods and skills of my bosses that I respected."
- "By taking risks, trying, and learning from my mistakes."
- "Reading autobiographies of leaders I admire to try to understand how they think."
- "Lots of practice."
- "By making mistakes myself and trying a different approach."
- "By being put in positions of responsibility that other people counted on."

How Do I Start?

How do you go about developing your leadership abilities? You don't have to wait until you land a management job or even finish your education. You can begin establishing credibility by behaving with integrity, learning from your mistakes, and becoming competent in your chosen field. You should look for—and then seize—opportunities to take actions that will help the groups you already belong to. Even before you are a supervisor, you can practice empowering others by listening carefully when you are in a group and by sharing what you know so that the whole group will be better informed. Begin building a network of personal contacts by reaching out to others to offer help, not just to request it.[131]

When you are searching for your next job, look for a position with an employer that is committed to developing leadership talent. Ideally, leadership development is connected to opportunities to practice the skills you are learning about here, so ask about chances to lead a project or a team, even for short periods of time.[132] Companies that excel at leadership development include General Electric, EMC Insurance, Hitachi Data Systems, IBM, and Johnson Controls.[133]

More specifically, here are some developmental experiences you should seek:[134]

Challenges expand knowledge and experiences. Being open to new ideas allows managers to learn, grow, and succeed even though the challenge may be out of their comfort zone.

©Karl Weatherly/Getty Images RF

- *Assignments:* Building something from nothing; fixing or turning around a failing operation; taking on project or task force responsibilities; accepting international assignments.
- *Other people:* Having exposure to positive role models; increasing visibility to others; working with people of diverse backgrounds.
- *Hardships:* Overcoming ideas that fail and deals that collapse; confronting others' performance problems; breaking out of a career rut.
- *Other events:* Formal courses; challenging job experiences; supervision of others; experiences outside work.

The Digital World

Ed Schein, Professor Emeritus at the MIT Sloan School of Management, is one of the most respected scholars of organizational culture and leadership. In 2012, he asserted that how leaders address technology will be the greatest challenge before us.

To lead any organization involves effective communication both online and in person. It also involves understanding what kind of leadership approaches work best when interactions are digital and when small but vocal online groups may want to undermine leadership. Social media have the ability to be catalysts for change, like during the Green Revolution in Iran.

They also have the ability to weaken a leader's control. When is digital dissent useful, and when destructive? What are a leader's options in dealing with it? What examples have you seen?

What Are the Keys?

The most effective developmental experiences have three components: assessment, challenge, and support.[135] *Assessment* includes information that gives you an understanding of where you are now, what your strengths are, your current levels of performance and leadership effectiveness, and your primary development needs. You can think about what your past feedback has been, what previous successes and failures you have had, how people have reacted to your ideas and actions, what your personal goals are, and what strategies you should implement to make progress. You can seek answers from your peers at work, bosses, family, friends, customers, and anyone else who knows you and how you work. The information you collect will help clarify what you need to learn, improve, or change.[136]

MANAGER'S BRIEF

PROGRESS REPORT

ONWARD

Management in Action

NOOYI HAS THE RIGHT STUFF TO HELP PEPSICO EVOLVE AND PROSPER

PepsiCo is a global food and beverage giant, with operations in 200 countries and more than a quarter million employees around the world. An aggressive competitor, it leads its industry in sales growth as it continually innovates, introducing new products and revamping customer favorites to make them healthier and their production more sustainable.

The person who manages such a company might not be expected to have much time for the personal touch. But Indra Nooyi, a longtime top executive who has been PepsiCo's CEO since 2006, has not forgotten how much people appreciate others' respect for their family ties. Every year she writes to the parents of her senior executives to thank them for the contributions their children are making to the company.

Nooyi vividly recalls her first visit home to see her mother in India after being named CEO. As visitors streamed into the house, they complimented Nooyi's mother enthusiastically on bringing up such a successful daughter. For Nooyi they had only a few words of greeting before they left. All the praise lavished on her mother (and her late father) while she herself was overlooked brought home to Nooyi how much her parents had done to make her the success she is. "It occurred to me," she says, "that I had never thanked the parents of my executives for the gift of their child to PepsiCo."

That was the beginning of her custom of writing not only to her direct reports to express gratitude but also to their parents. Many wrote back, and some company executives said Nooyi's letter was "the best thing that's happened to my parents."[137]

- Nooyi enjoys a 75 percent approval rating among employees. What evidence, if any, do you see that she is a charismatic leader? A transformational leader? An authentic leader? A servant–leader?
- Look up recent business news to learn how well PepsiCo is performing today and whether Nooyi remains CEO. Has she been a successful leader of the company? Why or why not?

The most potent developmental experiences provide *challenge*—they stretch you. We all think and behave in habitual, comfortable ways. This is natural and perhaps sufficient to survive. But you've probably heard people say how important it can be to get out of your comfort zone—to tackle situations that require new skills and abilities, that are confusing or ambiguous, or that you simply would rather not deal with. Sometimes the challenge comes from lack of experience; other times, it requires changing old habits.

It may be uncomfortable, but this is how great managers learn. Remember, some people don't bother to learn, or outright refuse to learn. Make sure you think about your experiences along the way and reflect on them afterward, introspectively and in discussion with others.

You receive *support* when others send the message that your efforts to learn and grow are valued. Without support, challenging developmental experiences can be overwhelming. With support, it is easier to handle the struggle, stay on course, open up to learning, and actually learn from experiences. Support can come informally from other people; more formally through the procedures of the organization; and through learning resources in the forms of training, constructive feedback, talking with others, and so on.

What develops in leadership development? Through such experiences, you can acquire more self-awareness and self-confidence, a broader perspective on the organizational system, creative thinking, the ability to work more effectively in complex social systems, and the ability to learn, grow, and make an impact.

KEY TERMS

authentic leadership, p. 360

autocratic leadership, p. 351

behavioral approach, p. 349

charismatic leader, p. 358

democratic leadership, p. 351

Fiedler's contingency model of leadership effectiveness, p. 354

group maintenance behaviors, p. 350

Hersey and Blanchard's situational theory, p. 355

intergroup leader, p. 361

job maturity, p. 355

laissez-faire, p. 351

lateral leadership, p. 361

leader–member exchange (LMX) theory, p. 350

Level 5 leadership, p. 360

participation in decision making, p. 351

path–goal theory, p. 355

power, p. 346

pseudotransformational leaders, p. 361

psychological maturity, p. 355

relationship-motivated leadership, p. 355

servant–leader, p. 361

shared leadership, p. 361

situational approach, p. 353

strategic leadership, p. 345

substitutes for leadership, p. 357

supervisory leadership, p. 345

task-motivated leadership, p. 355

task performance behaviors, p. 349

trait approach, p. 348

transactional leaders, p. 359

transformational leader, p. 359

vision, p. 343

Vroom model, p. 353

RETAINING WHAT YOU LEARNED

In Chapter 12, you learned what it means to be a leader. You also learned that leaders are needed at all levels of organizations and that people want leaders to help them achieve their goals. The best leaders have and share effectively a compelling vision that motivates others to achieve more than they thought was possible. Having and using power are important tools for any leader. Leaders can draw on five types of power—legitimate, reward, coercive, referent, and expert—to influence others. While there are several personal characteristics associated with leaders, the most important skill is the ability to perceive the situation accurately and then change behavior accordingly. Several leadership theories describe the interaction of leaders and the situation at hand, including Vroom's model, Fiedler's contingency model, Hersey and Blanchard's situation theory, and House's path–goal theory. Charismatic leaders are dominant and self-confident, and communicate high expectations for and confidence in their followers. Transformational leaders translate vision into reality by inspiring followers to transcend their individual interests for the good of the larger community. Many nontraditional opportunities to lead include servant, intergroup, shared, or lateral leadership. Furthermore, you can ask for developmental assignments or activities that include assessment, challenge, and support.

LO 1 Discuss what it means to be a leader.

- A leader is one who influences others to attain goals.
- Leaders orchestrate change, set direction, and motivate people to overcome obstacles and move the organization toward its ideal future.

LO 2 Summarize what people want and organizations need from their leaders.

- People want help in achieving their goals, and organizations need leaders at all levels.
- Exemplary leaders challenge the process, inspire a shared vision, enable others to act, model the way, and encourage the heart.

LO 3 Explain how a good vision helps you be a better leader.

- Outstanding leaders have vision. A vision is a mental image of an appealing, attainable future that goes beyond the ordinary and perhaps beyond what others thought possible.
- The vision provides the direction in which the leader wants the organization to move and inspiration for people to pursue it.

LO 4 Identify sources of power in organizations.

- Having power and using it appropriately are essential to effective leadership. Managers at all levels of the organization have five potential sources of power.
- Legitimate power is the company-granted authority to direct others.
- Reward power is control over rewards valued by others in the organization.
- Coercive power is control over punishments that others want to avoid.
- Referent power consists of personal characteristics that appeal to others, who model their behavior on the leader's and seek the leader's approval.
- Expert power is expertise or knowledge that can benefit others.

LO 5 List personal characteristics that contribute to leader effectiveness.

- Useful leader characteristics include drive, leadership, motivation, integrity, self-confidence, and knowledge of the business.
- Perhaps the most important skill is flexibility: the ability to perceive the situation accurately and then change behavior accordingly.

LO 6 Describe behaviors that will make you a better leader, and know when situations call for them.

- Important leader behaviors include task performance behaviors, group maintenance behaviors, and decision making.

- According to the Vroom model, decision making options include deciding alone, consulting individuals, consulting multiple group members, facilitating a whole-group process, or delegating to others, depending on factors such as the significance of the decision and the importance of followers' commitment.
- Fiedler's contingency model says that a task-motivated leader is more successful when leader–member relations are good and the task is highly structured, or with an unstructured task but low position power for the leader, or with poor leader–member relations when the task structure and leader's position power are both low. In other situations, a relationship-oriented leader will perform better.
- Hersey and Blanchard's situational theory says that task performance behaviors become less important as the follower's job maturity and psychological maturity increase.
- Path–goal theory assesses characteristics of the followers, the leader, and the situation; it then indicates the appropriateness of directive, supportive, participative, or achievement-oriented leadership behaviors.

LO 7 Distinguish between charismatic and transformational leadership.

- To have charisma is to be dominant and self-confident, to have a strong conviction of the righteousness of your beliefs, to create an aura of competence and success, and to communicate high expectations for and confidence in your followers. Charisma is one component of transformational leadership.
- Transformational leaders translate a vision into reality by inspiring people to transcend their individual interests for the good of the larger community.
- They do this through charisma, individualized attention to followers, intellectual stimulation, formation and communication of their vision, building of trust, and positive self-regard.

LO 8 Describe types of opportunities to lead.

- There's plenty of opportunity to be a leader; being a manager of others who report to you is just the traditional one.
- You also can find or create opportunities to be a servant–leader or intergroup leader, and engage in shared leadership and lateral leadership. A servant–leader serves others' needs while strengthening the organization.
- Intergroup leaders facilitate collaborative performance between different groups or organizations.
- Shared leadership involves taking on a leadership role when your skills are most relevant to a particular situation.
- Lateral leadership is inspiring people to work collaboratively and solve problems together.

LO 9 **Discover how to further your own leadership development.**

- You can develop your own leadership skills not only by understanding what effective leadership is all about, but also by seeking challenging developmental experiences.
- Such important life experiences come from taking challenging assignments, through exposure to working with other people, by overcoming hardships and failures, by taking formal courses, and via many other actions.
- The most important elements of a good developmental experience are assessment, challenge, and support.

DISCUSSION QUESTIONS

1. What do you want from your leader?
2. Is there a difference between effective management and effective leadership? Explain your views and learn from others' views.
3. Identify someone you think is an effective leader. What makes him or her effective?
4. Do you think most managers can be transformational leaders? Why or why not?
5. In your own words, define courage. What is the role of courage in leadership? Give examples of acts of leadership you consider courageous.
6. Do you think men and women differ in their leadership styles? If so, how? Do men and/or women prefer different styles in their bosses? What evidence do you have for your answers?
7. Who are your heroes? What makes them heroes, and what can you learn from them?
8. Assess yourself as a leader based on what you have read in this chapter. What are your strengths and weaknesses?
9. Identify the developmental experiences you have had that may have strengthened your ability to lead. What did those experiences teach you? Also identify some developmental experiences you need to acquire and how you will seek them. Be specific.
10. Consider a job you hold or held in the past. Consider how your boss managed you. How would you describe him or her as a leader? What substitutes for leadership would you have enjoyed seeing put into place?
11. Consider a group or an organization in which you are a leader or a member. What could great transformational leadership accomplish?
12. Name some prominent leaders whom you would describe as authentic and inauthentic and discuss.
13. Name some leaders you consider servant–leaders and discuss.
14. Identify some opportunities for you to exhibit shared, lateral, and other forms of leadership that are not "top-down."

EXPERIENTIAL EXERCISES

12.1 USING THE FIVE SOURCES OF POWER AT WORK

OBJECTIVE
To explore how power can be applied to organizational challenges to create positive outcomes.

INSTRUCTIONS
Read each of the scenarios (below) and choose one of the five sources of power to resolve the challenge in each scenario.

Five Sources of Power Worksheet
Five Sources of power:

1. Authority
2. Rewards
3. Punishments
4. Appealing personal characteristics
5. Expertise

Scenario #1:
Assume you are a supervisor of an IT department at a website hosting company. You want your staff to complete a large project within the next two months. Usually, such a project would take about three months to accomplish. To persuade your staff to rise to this challenge, you offer each of them three additional paid vacation days. Your staff enjoys taking three-day weekends, so the incentive should motivate them to finish the project within the shorter time frame.

As the supervisor, you are using _____ power to motivate your staff.

Scenario #2:
Assume you work at a local retail store. As a part-time employee working your way through college, you are not interested in becoming a manager. Even so, sometimes you wish you were in charge. Just yesterday, your boss asked if

you would be willing to work two extra days per week for a month. After you explained that you could work only your usual three days per week due to college and other commitments, your boss threatened to cut your hours indefinitely. Given how much you need the money, you grudgingly agreed to work the two extra days per week.

Your manager is using _____ power to persuade you to work the two extra days per week.

Scenario #3:

Assume you were recently promoted to assistant manager of the bank in your hometown. You are friends with the employees who now report to you. You notice that they still treat you like a buddy and do not seem to respect you in your new role. You decide that it will be in everyone's best interest if you assert yourself by reminding them that you are now their manager (and not their buddy). This is a challenging transition, but you feel the need to have their respect now that you are the manager.

You are using _____ power to encourage employees to respect you in your new role as assistant manager.

Scenario #4:

Assume you are an experienced marketer of outdoor adventure trips. You recently changed jobs. While working for your previous employer, Outdoor Adventures, you created several successful marketing programs that resulted in a 30 percent increase in sales over a three-year period. Now that you recently joined Eco Tours & Adventures, none of your co-workers knows the extent of your marketing knowledge. Your goal is to increase your power within the company. You decide to develop a really impactful and creative marketing campaign unlike any used by Eco Tours & Adventures in the past.

You are using _____ power to increase your influence at Eco Tours & Adventures.

Scenario #5:

Assume you are a salesperson and just found out that your organization's largest client is thinking about moving its business to one of your competitors. If this happens, you will lose about 30 percent of your commission this year, not to mention the loss of revenue to your company. You decide to rush over to see your contact at the client company. You spend two hours listening to why the client might leave and ask repeatedly what your company can do to make things right. You are nervous, but still use your charm and sense of humor to convince your contact that you and your company deserve one more chance. Your contact agrees to get you a meeting with the CEO and to put in a good word for your company. She says she is doing this because she likes you (professionally) and doesn't want to see you lose the business.

You are using _____ power to convince your contact that you and your company deserve another chance.

Concluding Case

BREITT, STARR & DIAMOND LLC

Josh Breitt, Rachel Starr, and Justin Diamond started an advertising agency to serve the needs of small businesses selling in and around their metropolitan area. Breitt contributed clever ideas and a talent for writing scripts and wooing clients. Starr brought a wealth of media contacts, and Diamond handled the artwork. Their quirky ad campaigns soon attracted a stream of projects from car dealers, community banks, and a carpet store. Since the agency's first year, these clients have kept the bills paid while the three win contracts from other companies. Breitt, Starr & Diamond (BS&D) prospered by helping clients keep up with the times, and the agency grew to meet the demand, adding a bookkeeper, a graphic artist, a web designer, two salespeople, a social media expert, and a retired human resource manager, who works 10 hours per week.

As the firm grew, the three partners felt they were constantly being pulled away from their areas of expertise to answer questions and solve problems about how to coordinate work, define jobs, and set priorities. They realized that none of them had any management training—and none of them had ever wanted to be a manager. They decided to hire a manager for a position they would call general manager of operations. That person would be responsible for supervising the employees, making sure expenses didn't go over budget, and planning the resources (including people) needed for further growth.

The partners interviewed several candidates and hired Brad Howser, a longtime administrator for a four-physician medical office. Howser spent the first few weeks quietly studying BS&D's financial data and observing employees at work. Then he became more outspoken and assertive. Although the partners had never cared to monitor what time employees came or left, Howser began requiring all employees to start by 9:00 each morning. The graphic artist and one of the salespeople complained that flexible hours were necessary for their child care arrangements, but Howser was unyielding. He also questioned whether the employees had been shopping carefully for supplies, indicating that from then on, he would be making all purchases, and only after the employees submitted their requests on a form of his design. Finally, to promote what he called team spirit, Howser began scheduling weekly Monday-morning staff meetings. He would offer motivational thoughts based on his experience at his previous job and invite the employees to share any work-related concerns or ideas they might have. Generally, the employees chose not to share.

Initially, the partners were impressed with Howser's vigorous approach to his job. They felt more productive than they had been in years because Howser was handling employee concerns himself. Then the top salesperson quit, followed by the social media expert. The bookkeeper asked if she might meet with the partners. "Is it something you should be discussing with Brad?" Rachel asked her. The bookkeeper replied that, no, it was *about* Brad. All the employees were unhappy with him, and more were likely to leave.

DISCUSSION QUESTIONS

1. Assume that hiring a general manager of operations was a good idea. What leadership style would be most effective in this position? Why?

2. What leader behaviors did Brad Howser exhibit? How well did they fit the needs of the ad agency?

3. Consider your own leadership style. What are some of your tendencies, and how might you change your perspective?

CHAPTER 13

Motivating for Performance

©Jacob Wackerhausen/Getty Images RF

> The worst mistake a boss can make is not to say well done.
> — John Ashcroft, business executive
>
> The reward of a thing well done is to have done it.
> — Ralph Waldo Emerson

LEARNING OBJECTIVES

After studying Chapter 13, you will be able to:

LO 1 Identify the kinds of behaviors managers need to motivate in people.

LO 2 List principles for setting goals that motivate employees.

LO 3 Summarize how to reward good performance effectively.

LO 4 Describe the key beliefs that affect people's motivation.

LO 5 Discuss ways in which people's individual needs affect their behavior.

LO 6 Define ways to create jobs that motivate.

LO 7 Summarize how people assess fairness and how to achieve fairness.

LO 8 Identify causes and consequences of a (dis)satisfied workforce.

CHAPTER OUTLINE

Motivating for Performance
Setting Goals
  Goals That Motivate
  Stretch Goals
  Limitations of Goal Setting
  Set Your Own Goals

Reinforcing Performance
  (Mis)Managing Rewards and Punishments
  Managing Mistakes
  Providing Feedback

Performance-Related Beliefs
  The Effort-to-Performance Link
  The Performance-to-Outcome Link
  Impact on Motivation
  Managerial Implications of Expectancy Theory

Understanding People's Needs
  Maslow's Need Hierarchy
  Alderfer's ERG Theory
  McClelland's Needs
  Need Theories: International Perspectives

Designing Motivating Jobs
  Job Rotation, Enlargement, and Enrichment
  Herzberg's Two-Factor Theory
  The Hackman and Oldham Model of Job Design
  Empowerment

Achieving Fairness
  Assessing Equity
  Restoring Equity
  Procedural Justice

Employee Satisfaction and Well-being
  Quality of Work Life
  Psychological Contracts

Management in Action

WHAT MAKES SAS A GREAT PLACE TO WORK?

SAS (named after its first product, Statistical Analysis Software) has grown since its 1976 founding into the world's leader in data analytics software—a $3.1 billion company with more than 14,000 employees in 45 countries. Along the way, SAS has ranked as one of the 100 Best Companies to Work For in America every year since the Great Place to Work Institute began handing out that recognition in *Fortune* magazine—and in the top five every year since 2010.

In 2012, the institute created its first list of the World's Best Multinational Workplaces, and SAS took the number one spot that year. It has been second only to Google ever since. Both rankings are based on a combination of employee surveys and an analysis by the institute.

What does SAS do to earn such prestigious recognition? The company is famous for the perks it offers its employees. Along with medical insurance, vacation time, profit sharing, and retirement savings accounts, SAS employees have access to adoption assistance, parental leave, and a college scholarship program for their children. At the Cary, North Carolina, headquarters, employees can use the on-site fitness center, health clinic, and day care center. Stress management programs include yoga, massage, and exercise programs. Those seeking to juggle home and work responsibilities can seek flexibility through options such as telecommuting, job sharing, or unpaid sabbaticals.

An employee summed up his appreciation of the company this way: "SAS does so much for the employees. I always feel this is my second home. I want to give my best to this company and would like to help in any way possible to make this company more successful."

However, if you talk to SAS's leaders, you hear less about benefits and more about the company's values,

©SAS Software Co.

which shape its work environment. As Jack Poll, SAS's director of recreation and employee services, told a reporter for *Fast Company,* "When people are treated as if they're important and truly make a difference, their loyalty and engagement soar." The kind of treatment Poll is referring to emphasizes appreciating what workers contribute, building their trust, and empowering them to make decisions in their area of responsibility.

Poll and SAS's founder and chief executive, James Goodnight, believe this treatment is the primary way SAS unleashes creativity. "Ninety-five percent of my assets drive out of the gate every evening," says Goodnight. "It's my job to maintain a work environment that keeps those people coming back every morning." That SAS gets it right is evident in the company's sales, which have risen every year of the company's existence. In 2015 it celebrated its 40th year of record revenue.[1]

SAS stands out as a company that offers generous benefits to its workers. As you read this chapter, consider whether generosity is enough to bring out employees' best work, aimed at the company's goals and priorities. If not, what other efforts should managers make?

This chapter tackles an age-old question: How can a manager motivate people to work hard and perform at their best levels? SAS demonstrates that treating employees as valued contributors to the organization can be a key part of motivating them.

A sales manager in one company had a different approach to this question. Each month, the person with the worst sales performance took home a live goat for the weekend. The manager hoped the goat-of-the-month employee would be so embarrassed that he or she would work harder the next month to increase sales.[2]

This sales manager may get high marks for creativity. But if he is graded by results, as he grades his salespeople, he will fail. He may succeed in motivating a few of his people to increase sales, but some good people will be motivated to quit the company.

Motivating for Performance

Understanding why people do the things they do on the job can be a difficult task. Predicting their response to management's latest productivity program is harder yet. Fortunately, enough is known about motivation to give the thoughtful manager practical, effective techniques for increasing people's effort and performance.

motivation

Forces that energize, direct, and sustain a person's efforts.

Motivation refers to forces that energize, direct, and sustain a person's efforts. All behavior, except involuntary reflexes such as eye blinks (which have little to do with management), is motivated. A highly motivated person will work hard toward achieving performance goals. With adequate ability, understanding of the job, and access to necessary resources, someone who is motivated will be a strong performer.

Managers must know what behaviors they want people to exhibit. Although productive people appear to do a seemingly limitless number of things, most of the important activities can be grouped into five general categories.[3] As shown in Exhibit 13.1, managers must motivate people to (1) join the organization, (2) remain in the organization, and (3) come to work regularly. On these points, you should reject the common notion that loyalty is dead and accept the challenge of creating an environment that will attract and energize people so that they commit to the organization.[4]

Of course, companies also want people to (4) perform—that is, once employees are at work, they should work hard to contribute high output and high quality. Finally, managers

EXHIBIT 13.1

Managers Must Motivate People to Engage in Key Behaviors

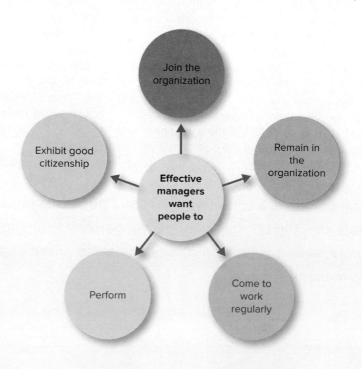

want employees to (5) exhibit good citizenship. Good citizens contribute above and beyond the call of duty by doing extra things that help the company. The importance of citizenship behaviors may be less obvious than sheer productive output, but these behaviors help the organization function smoothly. They also make managers' lives easier.

Setting Goals

LO 2

Setting work-related goals is an extremely effective way to stimulate motivation. In fact, it is perhaps the most important, valid, and useful single approach to motivating performance.

Goal-setting theory states that people have conscious goals that energize them and direct their thoughts and behaviors toward a particular end.[5] Keeping in mind the principle that goals motivate, managers set goals for employees or collaborate with employees to set goals together. For example, in order to keep the United States safe, the Department of Homeland Security (DHS) sets goals to prevent cyber and all other types of terrorist attacks.[6]

Goal setting works for any job in which people have control over their performance.[7] You can set goals for performance quality and quantity, and behavioral goals such as cooperation or teamwork.[8] In fact, you can set goals for whatever is important.[9]

Goals That Motivate

The most powerful goals are meaningful; important purposes that appeal to people's higher values add extra motivating power.[10] Brazilian beauty care maker Natura cares deeply about the environment. New Belgium Brewery is dedicated to continuously improving its sustainability initiatives. Whole Foods sells organic and natural food products but also wants to improve people's health and well-being. ServiceMaster, the cleaning and maintenance company, and Chick-fil-A have religious commitments that appeal to their employees, and Huntsman Corporation has goals of paying off corporate debt but also relieving human suffering—it sponsors cancer research and a number of charities.

Meaningful goals also can be based on data about competitors; exceeding competitors' performance can stoke people's competitive spirit and desire to succeed in the marketplace.[11] This point is not just about the values companies espouse and the lofty goals they pursue; it's also about leadership at a more personal level. Followers of transformational leaders view their work as more important and as highly congruent with their personal goals compared with followers of transactional leaders[12] (recall Chapter 12).

More specifically, much is known about how to manage goals in ways that motivate high job performance. Goals should be acceptable to employees. This means, among other things, that they should not conflict with people's personal values and that people have reasons to pursue the goals. Allowing people to participate in setting their work goals—as opposed to the boss setting their goals for them—is often a great way to generate goals that people accept and pursue willingly.

Acceptable, maximally motivating goals are challenging but attainable. They should be high enough to inspire better performance but not so high that people can never reach them. For instance, setting challenging sales goals for district business units results in higher unit sales performance unless employees don't trust their manager.[13]

Ideal goals are not merely general prompts to improve performance, do one's best, increase productivity, or reduce the time customers must wait to receive service. Rather, the goals should be specific regarding target and time frame. At the Quick Lane Tire & Auto Center that serves Olathe Ford near Kansas City, Missouri, each service adviser has a monthly goal for revenues from service orders and receives daily feedback about sales to see what categories of products need extra attention.

In addition, whenever a customer chooses to postpone needed repairs, these are assigned a red or yellow code. The service center's receptionist has specific goals of calling each red-code customer within seven days and sending a letter within 90 days to each customer who has a yellow code.[14] Such deadlines and measurable performance goals are specific,

Bottom Line

You can set goals related to cost, quality, speed, service, innovation, sustainability— anything that's important. *What is one goal you have set for yourself as a student? If you haven't set any goals, you could start by setting one now for this course.*

goal-setting theory

A motivation theory stating that people have conscious goals that energize them and direct their thoughts and behaviors toward a particular end.

EXHIBIT 13.2
SMART Goals Motivate

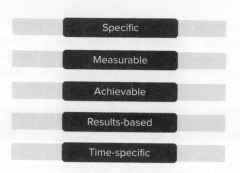

Specific

Measurable

Achievable

Results-based

Time-specific

SOURCE: Adapted from Shaw, K. N., "Changing the Goal-Setting Process at Microsoft," *Academy of Management Executive* 4 (November 2004), pp. 139–43.

quantifiable goals that employees are motivated to achieve. Microsoft and others use the acronym SMART (see Exhibit 13.2) to create motivating goals: specific, measurable, achievable, results-based, and time-specific.[15]

Stretch Goals

stretch goals

Targets that are particularly demanding, sometimes even thought to be impossible.

Some firms and bosses set **stretch goals**—targets that are exceptionally demanding and that some people would never even think of. There are two types of stretch goals: vertical stretch goals, aligned with current activities including productivity and financial results, and horizontal stretch goals, which involve people's professional development such as attempting and learning new, difficult things.[16] Impossible though stretch goals may seem to some, they sometimes are in fact attainable.

Stretch goals can generate a major shift away from mediocrity and toward tremendous achievement. But if someone tries in good faith but doesn't meet their stretch goals, don't punish them—remember how difficult their goals are! Base your assessment on how much performance has improved, how the performance compares with others, and how much progress has been made.[17]

Goals can generate manipulative game-playing and unethical behavior.

Limitations of Goal Setting

Goal setting is an extraordinarily powerful management technique. But even specific, challenging, attainable goals work better under some conditions than others. If people lack relevant ability and knowledge, a better course might be simply to urge them to do their best or to set a goal to learn rather than a goal to achieve a specific performance level.[18]

Individual performance goals can be dysfunctional if people work in a group and cooperation among team members is essential to group performance.[19] Goals aimed at maximizing individual performance can create competition and reduce cooperation, thereby hurting group performance. On the other hand, groupcentric goals aimed at maximizing the individual's contributions to the group's performance have a positive effect.[20] If cooperation is important, performance goals should be established for the team.

Goals can generate manipulative game-playing and unethical behavior. For example, people can sometimes find ingenious ways to set easy goals and convince their bosses that they are difficult.[21] Or they may find ways to meet goals simply to receive a reward, without necessarily performing in other desirable ways. In big law firms it's common for lawyers to keep detailed records of their time and to be rewarded for billing, say, 2,000 hours per year. This system invites inefficient work and creates a dismal, demotivating environment for any lawyer who chose the profession out of concern for clients or love of the law.[22]

In addition, people who aren't on track to meet their goals are more likely to act unethically than are people who are trying to do their best but have no specific performance goals.[23] This is true regardless of whether they have financial incentives, and it is particularly true when people fall just short of reaching their goals.[24]

Another familiar example comes from the pages of financial reports. Some executives have mastered the art of earnings management—precisely meeting Wall Street analysts' earnings estimates or beating them by a single penny.[25] The media trumpet, and investors reward, the company that meets or beats the estimates. People sometimes meet this goal by either manipulating the numbers or initiating whispering campaigns to persuade analysts to lower their estimates, making them more attainable. The marketplace wants short-term, quarterly performance, but long-term viability is ultimately more important to a company's success.

It is important *not* to establish a single productivity goal if there are other important dimensions of performance.[26] If acquiring knowledge and skills is important, you can add a specific and challenging learning goal such as "identify 10 ways to develop relationships with end users of our products." Productivity goals will likely enhance productivity, but they may also cause employees to neglect other areas, such as learning, tackling new projects, or developing creative solutions to job-related problems. A manager who wants to motivate creativity can establish creativity goals along with productivity goals for individuals or for brainstorming teams.[27]

Set Your Own Goals

Goal setting works for yourself as well—it's a powerful tool for self-management. Set goals for yourself; don't just try hard or hope for the best. Create a statement of purpose for yourself comprising three elements: an inspiring distant vision, a mid-distant goal along the way (worthy in its own right), and near-term objectives to start working on immediately.[28] So if you are going into business, you might articulate your goal for the type of businessperson you want to be in five years, the types of jobs that could create the opportunities and teach you what you need to know to become that businessperson, and the specific schoolwork and job search activities that can get you moving in those directions. On the job, apply SMART and other goal-setting advice for yourself.

Setting unprecedented goals can push a person to reach a higher level of achievement.

©photobac/123RF RF

Reinforcing Performance

Goals are universal motivators. So are the processes of reinforcement described in this section. In 1911, psychologist Edward Thorndike formulated the **law of effect**: behavior that is followed by positive consequences probably will be repeated.[29] This powerful law of behavior laid the foundation for countless investigations into the effects of the positive consequences, called **reinforcers**, that motivate behavior. **Organizational behavior modification** (or **OB mod**) attempts to influence people's behavior, and improve performance,[30] by systematically managing work conditions and the consequences of people's actions.

Four key consequences of behavior either encourage or discourage people's behavior (see Exhibit 13.3):

1. **Positive reinforcement**—applying a positive consequence that increases the likelihood that the person will repeat the behavior that led to it. Examples of positive reinforcers include a boss thanking an employee, letters of commendation, favorable performance evaluations, and pay raises.[31]

law of effect

A law formulated by Edward Thorndike in 1911 stating that behavior that is followed by positive consequences will likely be repeated.

---

reinforcers

Positive consequences that motivate behavior.

organizational behavior modification (OB mod)

The application of reinforcement theory in organizational settings.

positive reinforcement

Applying consequences that increase the likelihood that a person will repeat the behavior that led to it.

EXHIBIT 13.3
Behavior, Consequences, and Effects

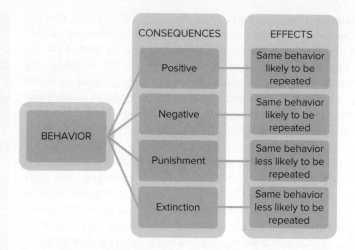

negative reinforcement

Removing or withholding an undesirable consequence.

punishment

Administering an aversive consequence.

extinction

Withdrawing or failing to provide a reinforcing consequence.

2. **Negative reinforcement**—removing or withholding an undesirable consequence. For example, a manager takes an employee (or a school takes a student) off probation because of improved performance.

3. **Punishment**—administering an aversive consequence. Examples include criticizing or shouting at an employee, assigning an unappealing task, and sending a worker home without pay.

   Managers use punishment when they think it is warranted or when they believe others expect them to, and they usually concern themselves with following company policy and procedure.[32] Managers who catch employees behaving badly punish more severely when the managers have a lot of power and have strong opinions about right and wrong.[33] Whereas negative reinforcement can involve the *threat* of punishment and then not delivering the punishment when employees perform satisfactorily, punishment is the actual delivery of the aversive consequence.

4. **Extinction**—withdrawing or failing to provide a reinforcing consequence. When this occurs, motivation is reduced and the behavior is *extinguished,* or eliminated. Ways that managers may unintentionally extinguish desired behaviors include not giving a compliment for a job well done, forgetting to say thanks for a favor, and setting impossible performance goals so a person never experiences success.

   Extinction can be used intentionally on undesirable behaviors, too. The manager might ignore long-winded opining during a meeting or fail to acknowledge unimportant e-mails in the hope that they will discourage the employee from continuing.

The first two consequences, positive and negative reinforcement, are positive for the person receiving them—the person either gains something or avoids something negative. Therefore, the person who experiences them will be motivated to behave in the ways that led to the reinforcement. The last two consequences, punishment and extinction, are negative for the person receiving them: motivation to repeat the behavior that led to the undesirable results will drop.

Managers should be careful to match consequences to what employees will actually find desirable or undesirable. When a supervisor punished an employee for tardiness by suspending him for three days, the employee was delighted. It was fishing season.[34]

(Mis)Managing Rewards and Punishments

You've learned about the positive effects of a transformational leadership style, but giving rewards (a transaction) to high-performing people also is essential.[35] Unfortunately, sometimes organizations and managers reinforce the wrong behaviors.[36] As discussed in Chapter 10, stock options are intended to reinforce behaviors that add to the company's value, but stock options also can motivate decisions that artificially deliver short-term gains in stock prices but hurt the company in the long run. Likewise, programs that punish employees for absenteeism beyond a certain limit may actually encourage them to be absent. People may use up all their allowable absences and fail to come to work regularly until they reach the point at which their next absence will result in punishment.

Sometimes employees are reinforced with admiration for multitasking. This behavior may look efficient and send a signal that the employee is busy and valuable, but multitasking slows down the brain's efficiency and causes mistakes.[37] Scans of brain activity show that the brain is not able to concentrate on two tasks at once; it needs time to switch among the multitasker's activities. As a result, managers who praise the hard work of multitaskers may be unintentionally reinforcing inefficiency and failure to think deeply about problems.

To use reinforcement effectively, managers must identify which kinds of behaviors they reinforce and which they discourage (see Exhibit 13.4). The reward system should support the firm's strategy, defining people's performance in ways that pursue strategic objectives.[38] Reward employees for developing themselves in strategically important ways—for building new skills that are critical to strengthening core competencies and creating value.

Managers can be creative in their use of reinforcers. Ryan LLC, an international tax services company, took several steps to reward its employees. The firm is flexible about when and where employees do their work. Ryan also offers 12 weeks of paid pregnancy leave, paid 4-week sabbaticals every five years, and subsidies for employee health club memberships.[39]

Innovative managers use nonmonetary rewards, including intellectual challenge, meaningful responsibilities, autonomy, recognition, and greater influence over decisions. These and other rewards for high-performing employees, when creatively devised and applied, can continue to motivate when pay and promotions are scarce. Employees at Menlo Innovations, a custom software design firm, are empowered to call for companywide meetings by shouting, "Hey, Menlo!" All employees (who work in the same large room) stop what they're doing, listen to their colleague, respond (if needed), and then get back to work. These impromptu meetings are effective and may last only about one or two minutes.

Another reward of working at Menlo is the ability to work in pairs. CEO Richard Sheridan believes strongly that paired employees who can ask one another, "Hey, what about this?" while writing software can increase quality and creativity. By creating such a rewarding organizational culture, Sheridan hopes that all of Menlo's employees will experience joy.[40]

> **Sometimes organizations and managers reinforce the wrong behaviors.**

At 10:30 every morning, when Richard Sheridan, CEO, passes the Viking helmet, Menlo Innovations employees must talk about their day.

©Andre J. Jackson/Newscom/ Tribune News Service/Ann Arbor/ MI/USA

EXHIBIT 13.4
The Greatest Management Principle in the World

"The things that get rewarded get done" is what Michael LeBoeuf called The Greatest Management Principle in the World. Companies, and individual managers, should reward the following:

1. *Solid solutions* instead of quick fixes.
2. *Risk taking* instead of risk avoiding.
3. *Applied creativity* instead of mindless conformity.
4. *Decisive action* instead of paralysis by analysis.
5. *Smart work* instead of busywork.
6. *Simplification* instead of needless complication.
7. *Quietly effective behavior* instead of squeaky wheels.
8. *Quality work* instead of fast work.
9. *Loyalty* instead of turnover.
10. *Working together* instead of working against.

SOURCE: LeBoeuf, Michael, *The Greatest Management Principle in the World,* 1985.

Managers who inappropriately yell at their staff or overuse punishment often create a climate of fear and anxiety in the workplace. How would you deal with a situation like this?

©Image Source RF

Managing Mistakes

How a manager reacts to people's mistakes has a big impact on motivation. Punishment is sometimes appropriate, as when people violate the law, ethical standards, safety rules, or standards of interpersonal treatment, or when they perform like a slacker. But sometimes managers punish people when they shouldn't—when poor performance isn't the person's fault or when managers take out their frustrations on the wrong people.

Managers who overuse punishment or use it inappropriately create a climate of fear in the workplace.[41] Fear causes people to focus on the short term, sometimes creating problems in the longer run. Fear also creates a focus on oneself rather than on the group and the organization.

B. Joseph White, president emeritus of the University of Illinois, recalls consulting for a high-tech entrepreneur who heard a manager present a proposal and responded with brutal criticism: "That's the . . . stupidest idea I ever heard in my life. I'm disappointed in you." According to White, this talented manager was so upset she never again felt fully able to contribute.[42] To avoid such damage, managers should think about how they handle mistakes.

Recognize that everyone makes mistakes, and that mistakes can be dealt with constructively by discussing and learning from them. Don't punish, but appreciate, people for honestly delivering bad news to their bosses. Treat failure to act responsibly as a failure but don't punish unsuccessful, good-faith efforts. If you're a leader, talk about your mistakes with your people and show how you learned from them. Give people second chances and maybe third chances. Encourage people to try new things and don't punish them if what they try in good faith just doesn't work out.

Providing Feedback

Most managers don't provide enough useful feedback, and most people don't ask for feedback enough.[43] As a manager, you should consider all potential causes of poor performance, pay full attention when employees ask for feedback or want to discuss performance issues, and provide constructive feedback.

Feedback can be offered in many ways.[44] Customers sometimes give feedback directly; you also can request customer feedback and give it to the employee. You can provide statistics on work that the person has directly influenced. A manufacturing firm—high tech or otherwise—can put the phone number or website of the production team on the product so customers can contact the team directly. Performance reviews should be conducted regularly, as discussed in Chapter 10. And bosses should give more regular, ongoing feedback—it helps correct problems immediately, provides immediate reinforcement for good work, and prevents surprises when the formal review comes.

For yourself, try not to be afraid of receiving feedback; in fact, you should actively seek it. But whether or not you seek the feedback, when you get it, don't ignore it. Try to avoid negative emotions such as anger, hurt, defensiveness, or resignation. Think, It's up to me to get the feedback I need; I need to know these things about my performance and my behavior; learning what I need to know about myself will help me identify needs and create new opportunities; it serves my interest best to know rather than not know; taking initiative on this gives me more power and influence over my career.[45]

expectancy theory

A theory proposing that people will behave based on their perceived likelihood that their effort will lead to a certain outcome and on how highly they value that outcome.

> Try not to be afraid of receiving feedback; in fact, you should actively seek it.

Bottom Line

Make sure that you reward the right things, not the wrong things. Sound obvious? You'd be surprised how often this principle is violated!
What is rewarding, and not rewarding, about feedback from your manager?

Performance-Related Beliefs

LO 4   In contrast to reinforcement theory, which describes the processes by which factors in the work environment affect people's behavior, expectancy theory considers some of the cognitive processes that go on in people's heads. According to **expectancy theory**, the person's

EXHIBIT 13.5
Basic Concepts of
Expectancy Theory

Expectancy	Instrumentality
How confident am I that my effort will lead to good performance?	Will my good performance be rewarded with desired outcomes?

Effort → Performance → Outcome Valence

work efforts lead to some level of performance.[46] Then, performance leads to one or more outcomes for the person. This process is shown in Exhibit 13.5. People develop two important beliefs linking these events: expectancy, which links effort to performance, and instrumentality, which links performance to outcomes.

The Effort-to-Performance Link

The first belief, **expectancy**, is people's perceived likelihood that their efforts will enable them to attain their performance goals. An expectancy can be high (up to 100 percent), such as when a student is confident that if she studies hard, she will get a good grade on the final. An expectancy can also be low (down to a 0 percent likelihood), such as when a suitor is convinced that his dream date will never go out with him.

All else equal, high expectancies create higher motivation than do low expectancies. In the preceding examples, the student is more likely to study hard for the exam than the suitor is to pursue the dream date, even though both want their respective outcomes.

Expectancies can vary among individuals, even in the same situation. For example, a sales manager might initiate a competition in which the top salesperson wins a free trip to Hawaii. In such cases, the few top people, who have performed well in the past, will be more motivated by the contest than will the historically average and below-average performers. The top people will have higher expectancies—stronger beliefs that their efforts can help them win the competition.

The Performance-to-Outcome Link

The example of the sales contest illustrates how performance results in some kind of **outcome**, or consequence, for the person. Actually, it often results in several outcomes. For example, turning in the best sales performance could lead to (1) a competitive victory, (2) the free trip to Hawaii, (3) feelings of achievement, (4) recognition from the boss, (5) status throughout the company, and (6) resentment from other salespeople.

But how certain is it that performance will result in all of those outcomes? Will winning the contest really lead to resentment? Will it really lead to increased status?

These questions address the second key belief described by expectancy theory: instrumentality.[47] **Instrumentality** is the perceived likelihood that performance will be followed by a particular outcome. Like expectancies, instrumentalities can be high (up to 100 percent) or low (approaching 0 percent). For example,

expectancy

Employees' perception of the likelihood that their efforts will enable them to attain their performance goals.

outcome

A consequence a person receives for his or her performance.

instrumentality

The perceived likelihood that performance will be followed by a particular outcome.

Winning a competition for a free trip to Hawaii would be great, but what about all the losers?
©Ruth Peterkin/123RF RF

you can be fully confident that if you do a good job, you'll get a promotion; or you can feel that no matter how well you do, the promotion will go to someone else.

valence

The value an outcome holds for the person contemplating it.

Each outcome has an associated valence. **Valence** is the value the person places on the outcome. Valences can be positive, as a Hawaiian vacation would be for most people, or negative, as in the case of the other salespeople's resentment.

Impact on Motivation

For motivation to be high, expectancy, instrumentalities, and total valence of all outcomes must all be high. A person will not be highly motivated if any of the following conditions exist:

1. He believes he can't perform well enough to achieve the positive outcomes that he knows the company provides to good performers (high valence and high instrumentality but low expectancy).
2. He knows he can do the job and is fairly certain what the ultimate outcomes will be (say, a promotion and a transfer). However, he doesn't want those outcomes or believes other, negative outcomes outweigh the positive (high expectancy and high instrumentality but low valence).
3. He knows he can do the job and wants several important outcomes (a favorable performance review, a raise, and a promotion). But he believes that no matter how well he performs, the outcomes will not be forthcoming (high expectancy and positive valences but low instrumentality).

Managerial Implications of Expectancy Theory

Expectancy theory helps the manager zero in on key leverage points for influencing motivation. Three implications are crucial:

1. *Increase expectancies.* Provide a work environment that facilitates good performance and set realistically attainable performance goals. Provide training, support, required resources, and encouragement so that people are confident they can perform at the levels expected of them. Recall from Chapter 12 that some leaders excel at boosting their followers' confidence.
2. *Identify positively valent outcomes.* Understand what people want to get out of work. Think about what their jobs provide them and what is not, but could be, provided. Consider how people may differ in the valences they assign to outcomes. Know the need theories of motivation, described in the next section, and their implications for identifying important outcomes.
3. *Make performance instrumental toward positive outcomes.* Make sure that good performance is followed by personal recognition and praise, favorable performance reviews, pay increases, and other positive results. Also, make sure that working hard and doing things well will have as few negative results as possible. It is useful to realize, too, that bosses usually control rewards and punishments, but others do so as well. Peers, direct reports, customers, and others tend to provide outcomes in the form of compliments, help, criticism, and other social punishments.

Organizations set up formal reward systems as well. Founded in 2012, Austin-based YouEarnedIt created an app designed to increase employee happiness and engagement at work. The app empowers employees to recognize one another's contributions and hard work. The idea of having employees provide one another with real-time, meaningful recognition on a daily basis is catching on. YouEarnedIt's clients include Conde Nast, Tempur-Pedic, and Rent-2-Own.[48] As you read "Management in Action: Progress Report," consider whether similar ideas would motivate employees at SAS.

Management in Action

GETTING EMPLOYEES TO BACK THE SAS MISSION

James Goodnight, a statistician, founded SAS with colleagues from North Carolina State University. Since his first experiences of programming a computer while in college, Goodnight had recognized the joy of creating something that would benefit others. Goodnight expected that his employees too would feel rewarded by their accomplishments. On SAS's website, Goodnight describes SAS's culture as one that "rewards innovation, encourages employees to try new things and yet doesn't penalize them for taking chances."

To see how this works, consider how SAS has recently innovated in a couple of important areas of computing. One is the rapid switch of the computer industry to cloud computing. SAS grew up when big organizations invested in large, powerful computers, and its software was written for those systems. With the rise of the Internet, data have streamed in from many sources in real time, and computing systems are being reworked to process the data in parallel on multiple computers that do not necessarily reside at the organization using the data.

Some observers wondered whether SAS could rewrite its software for this new era of computing. But because SAS attracts the best people (thanks to its reputation for treating employees well), hires for creativity, and makes it easy to stay on the job (thanks to corporate perks such as subsidized cafeterias and on-site haircuts), SAS has no trouble convincing employees to push hard toward reaching ambitious goals. SAS impressed observers by announcing new, cloud-ready software with graphics that even nonexperts can view on their laptop or tablet computers. Sales revenues from cloud services have grown rapidly.

SAS also has smoothly entered the social media era by introducing a networking site for its employees. While managers get a monthly newsletter called "To the Point," company employees, especially the younger ones, were sharing work information with each other on sites such as Facebook. Although some companies were cracking down on social media use, SAS got busy creating software that would be so useful and easy to learn that employees wouldn't be able to resist.

The result was the Hub, which enrolled more than 1,400 employees even before its official launch. Jenn Mann, vice president of human resources, calls it "like Facebook for SAS employees." Rather than micromanaging how the Hub would be used, SAS's information systems division showed off some relevant features, gently pointed out advantages to nonusers, and trusted them to behave professionally. Before long, about two-thirds of SAS employees were trading information on the Hub, and 94 percent feel their company has "great communication."[49]

- What kinds of reinforcement and feedback do you think would be most useful and productive with SAS employees?
- How should SAS's managers apply the implications of expectancy theory to keep the company innovative?

Understanding People's Needs

The manager who appropriately applies goal-setting, reinforcement, and expectancy theories is creating essential motivating elements in the *work environment*. But motivation also is affected by characteristics of the *person*. Several important theories describe the kinds of needs that people want to satisfy. The extent to which and the ways in which a person's needs are met or not met at work affect his or her behavior on the job.

The most important theories describing the content of people's needs are Maslow's need hierarchy, Alderfer's ERG theory, and McClelland's needs.

Maslow's Need Hierarchy

Abraham Maslow organized five major types of human needs into a hierarchy, as shown in Exhibit 13.6.[50] **Maslow's need hierarchy** illustrates his conception of people satisfying their needs in a specified order, from bottom to top. The needs are

Maslow's need hierarchy

A conception of human needs organizing needs into a hierarchy of five major types.

EXHIBIT 13.6
Maslow's Need Hierarchy

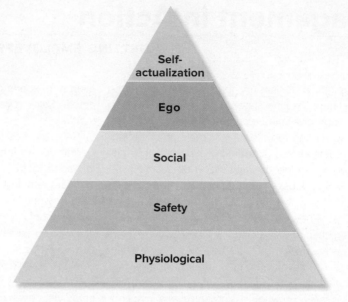

SOURCE: Organ D., and Bateman, T., *Organizational Behavior,* 4th ed., New York: McGraw-Hill, 1991.

1. *Physiological* (food, water, sex, and shelter).
2. *Safety or security* (protection against threat and deprivation).
3. *Social* (friendship, affection, belonging, and love).
4. *Ego* (independence, achievement, freedom, status, recognition, and self-esteem).
5. *Self-actualization* (realizing one's full potential, becoming everything one is capable of being).

> Safety issues are still very important in manufacturing, mining, health care, and other work environments.

According to Maslow, people are motivated to satisfy the lower needs before they try to satisfy the higher needs. In the modern workplace, physiological and safety needs generally are well satisfied, making social, ego, and self-actualization needs important. But safety issues are still very important in manufacturing, mining, health care, and other work environments. To deal with such safety issues, managers can show what the employer does to improve security and manage employee risk.

Once a need is satisfied, it is no longer a powerful motivator. For example, labor unions negotiate for higher wages, benefits, safety standards, and job security. These bargaining issues relate directly to the satisfaction of Maslow's lower-level needs. After these needs are reasonably satisfied, the higher-level needs—social, ego, and self-actualization—become dominant concerns.

Maslow's hierarchy, however, is a simplistic and not altogether accurate theory of human motivation.[51] For example, not everyone progresses through the five needs in hierarchical order. But Maslow made three important contributions. First, he identified important need categories, which can help managers create effective positive outcomes. Second, it is helpful to think of two general levels of needs, in which lower-level needs must be satisfied before higher-level needs become important. Third, Maslow alerted managers to the importance of personal growth and self-actualization.

Self-actualization is the best-known concept from this theory. According to Maslow, the average person is only 10 percent self-actualized. In other words, most of us are living our lives and working at our jobs with a large untapped reservoir of potential. The implication is clear: Managers should create work environments that provide training, resources, autonomy, responsibilities, and challenging assignments. This type of environment gives people a

Multiple Generations at Work

Millennials Want to Fulfill Higher-Order Needs

A recent survey found that 60 percent of Millennials leave their organizations in less than three years. Turnover has both direct (e.g., lost productivity) and indirect (e.g., lower morale) costs. Many companies are trying to attract, motivate, and retain this generation of employees by offering flexible work arrangements, additional vacation time, and relaxed dress codes. For some firms, these measures may not be enough to motivate and retain high performers.

David Glickman, CEO of mobile carrier Ultra Mobile, believes that Millennials are motivated by jobs that fulfill their higher-order needs. Eighty percent of Ultra Mobile's 300-plus employees and contractors are Millennials. Over the past four years, the company has grown rapidly to about $120 million in sales revenue with a high level of retention.

Glickman believes that many Baby Boomers at younger ages were willing to accept jobs that fulfilled basic needs like a constant paycheck, health care, and a modest home. Glickman states that Millennials are "less interested in job promotion than in becoming an entrepreneur and [they] will quit if they feel they do not have freedom" to grow and develop. A recent survey confirms his observation: 87 percent of Millennials reported that development is an important component in a job.[52]

He offers the following tips for motivating and retaining Millennials:[53]

©Ryan Miller/Getty Images

1. *Focus on results, not time in the office.* After they have proven themselves, provide Millennial employees with the freedom and trust to do at least some of their work offsite.
2. *Make your organization a cool place to work.* Do fun things (e.g., invite a pet shelter to bring in kittens and puppies for an hour for possible adoption) for employees so they have something to brag about on social media.
3. *Leverage their passions.* Get to know what really matters to each employee, and try to design jobs and volunteer opportunities that tap into those passions.

Glickman concludes: "Provide the belonging and self-actualization needs they crave, and Millennials will knock your socks off with astounding performance."

chance to use their skills and abilities in creative ways and allows them to achieve more of their full potential (see "Multiple Generations at Work").

So, treat people not merely as a cost to be controlled but an asset to be developed. Many companies have programs that provide personal growth experiences for their people. For example, associates at W. L. Gore are encouraged to reach their full potential by developing their talents, enjoying their work, and directing their own work activities.[54]

Organizations gain by making full use of their human resources, and employees gain by capitalizing on opportunities to meet their higher-order needs on the job. Wegmans Food Markets, known for its high-quality workforce, invests heavily in training and developing its people. It sends staff around the world to become experts in their products, trains cashiers for 40 hours before allowing them to interact with customers, and doesn't lay off employees.[55] Employees feel secure in their jobs, enjoy friendships with co-workers and customers, and experience a sense of achievement.

Alderfer's ERG Theory

Maslow's theory has general applicability, but Alderfer aimed his ERG theory expressly at understanding people's needs at work.[56]

Alderfer's ERG theory postulates three sets of needs: existence, relatedness, and growth. Existence needs are all material and physiological desires. Relatedness needs involve relationships with other people and are satisfied through the process of mutually sharing

Alderfer's ERG theory

A human needs theory postulating that people have three basic sets of needs that can operate simultaneously.

thoughts and feelings. Growth needs motivate people to change themselves or their environment productively or creatively. Satisfaction of the growth needs comes from fully using personal capacities and developing new capacities.

What similarities do you see between Alderfer's and Maslow's needs? Roughly speaking, existence needs subsume physiological and security needs, relatedness needs are similar to social and esteem needs, and growth needs correspond to self-actualization.

ERG theory proposes that several needs can operate at once. Whereas Maslow said that self-actualization is important to people only after other sets of needs are satisfied, for Alderfer employees can be motivated on the job to satisfy existence, relatedness, and growth needs at the same time.

Maslow's theory is better known to American managers than Alderfer's, but ERG theory has more research support.[57] Both have practical value in that they remind managers of the types of reinforcers or outcomes that can be used to motivate people. Regardless of whether a manager prefers the Maslow or the Alderfer theory, she can motivate people by helping them satisfy their needs, particularly by offering opportunities for self-actualization and growth.

McClelland's Needs

David McClelland also identified a number of basic needs that motivate people. The most important needs for managers, according to McClelland, are the needs for achievement, affiliation, and power.[58] Different needs predominate for different people. As you read about these needs, think about yourself—which ones are most and least important to you?

The need for achievement is characterized by a strong orientation toward accomplishment and an obsession with success and goal attainment. Most managers and entrepreneurs in the United States have high levels of this need and like to see it in their employees.

The need for affiliation reflects a strong desire to interact with and be liked by other people. Individuals who have high levels of this need are oriented toward getting along with others and may be less concerned with achieving at high levels.

The need for power is a desire to influence or control other people. This need can be a negative force—termed *personalized power*—if it is expressed by aggressively manipulating and exploitating others. People high on the personalized power need want power purely for the pursuit of their own goals. But the need for power also can be a positive motive—called *socialized power*—because it can be channeled toward constructively helping people, organizations, and societies.

Low need for affiliation and moderate to high need for power are associated with managerial success for both higher- and lower-level managers.[59] One reason the need for affiliation is not necessary for leadership success is that people high on this need have difficulty making tough but necessary decisions that will make some people unhappy.

Need Theories: International Perspectives

How do the need theories apply abroad?[60] Whereas managers in the United States care most strongly about achievement, esteem, and self-actualization, managers in Greece and Japan are motivated more by security. Social needs are most important in Sweden, Norway, and Denmark. "Doing your own thing"—the phrase from the 1960s that describes an American culture oriented toward self-actualization—is not even translatable into Chinese.

"Achievement," too, is difficult to translate into most other languages. Researchers in France, Japan, and Sweden would have been unlikely even to conceive of McClelland's achievement motive because people of those countries traditionally tend to be more group-oriented (collectivist) than individually oriented.

Clearly, achievement, growth, and self-actualization are profoundly important in the United States, Canada, and Great Britain. But these needs are not universally important. People the world over have some similar basic needs, but what engages people most can vary from culture to culture.[61] Employees in Canada were attracted by competitive pay, work-life balance, and opportunities for advancement; workers in Germany by autonomy;

in Japan by high-quality co-workers; in the Netherlands by a collaborative work environment; and in the United States by competitive health benefits. Generally, no single way is best, and managers can customize their approaches by considering how individuals differ.[62]

Designing Motivating Jobs

Here's an example of a reward that didn't motivate. One of Mary Kay Ash's former employers gave her a sales award: a flounder-fishing light. Unfortunately, she didn't fish. Fortunately, she later was able to design her own organization, Mary Kay Cosmetics, around intrinsic as well as extrinsic motivators that mattered to her people.[63]

Jobs can be rewarding both extrinsically and intrinsically.[64] **Extrinsic rewards** are given to people by the boss, the company, or some other person. In contrast, a person derives an **intrinsic reward** directly from performing the job itself. An interesting project, an intriguing subject that is fun to study, a completed sale, helping a co-worker achieve a difficult task, and the discovery of the perfect solution to a difficult problem all can give people the feeling that they have done something meaningful and well. As an example, the nearby "Social Enterprise" box discusses how one organization is providing intrinsic rewards to veterans in the form of a renewed sense of purpose.

If you have read elsewhere that extrinsic rewards are bad things because they decrease intrinsic motivation, be aware that those findings come from laboratory research done primarily with students. In the world of working adults, the two types of rewards together[65] can motivate powerfully. People expect extrinsic rewards for their work; they will be all the more motivated if their jobs are intrinsically rewarding as well.

Intrinsic rewards are essential to the motivation that drives creativity.[66] A challenging problem, a chance to create something new, and work that is exciting in and of itself can provide intrinsic motivation that inspires people to devote time and energy to the task. So do managers who allow people some freedom to pursue the tasks that interest them most. The opposite situations result in routine, habitual behaviors that interfere with creativity.[67] In manufacturing facilities, researchers found that employees initiated more applications for patents, made more novel and useful suggestions, and were rated by their managers as more creative when their jobs were challenging and their managers did not control their activities closely.[68]

Some managers and organizations create environments that quash creativity and motivation.[69] The classic example of a demotivating job is the highly specialized assembly line job; each worker performs one boring operation before passing the work along to the next worker. Such specialization, the mechanistic approach to job design, was the prevailing practice in the United States through most of the 20th century.[70] But jobs that are too simple and routine result in employee dissatisfaction, absenteeism, and turnover.

Especially in industries that depend on highly motivated knowledge workers, keeping talented employees may require letting them design their own jobs so their work is more interesting than it would be elsewhere.[71] Designing jobs in the following ways can make them more intrinsically motivating.

Job Rotation, Enlargement, and Enrichment

With **job rotation**, workers who otherwise would spend all their time in one routine task can instead move from one task to another. Rather than working in a single section of a department store for an entire month, an employee might be rotated through housewares, shoes, and toys. Job rotation is intended to alleviate boredom by giving people different things to do at different times.

extrinsic reward
Reward given to a person by the boss, the company, or some other person.

intrinsic reward
Reward a worker derives directly from performing the job itself.

Bottom Line
Intrinsic rewards and the freedom to be creative are keys to creativity. *Why might an employee be more creative when a job is intrinsically rewarding?*

> Intrinsic rewards are essential to the motivation underlying creativity.

job rotation
Changing from one task to another to alleviate boredom.

Social Enterprise

Giving Veterans a Renewed Sense of Purpose

Shortly after returning from his deployments in Iraq and Afghanistan, Marine veteran Jake Wood cofounded Team Rubicon. Staffed by veterans, his organization bridges the gap between the moment a natural disaster happens and the time at which conventional aid organizations respond. Wood seeks to solve two problems. The first is that many aid organizations are not equipped or trained to respond rapidly during the "crucial window" of time immediately following a disaster. The second is the inadequate way that many veterans are reintegrated into society after serving in the military. Veterans have a unique set of skills and experiences that are ideal for disaster relief situations.

Team Rubicon provides veterans with three things they lose after leaving the military:

©Justin Sullivan/Getty Images

1. *Purpose:* Doing work with a higher purpose, in this case helping survivors of natural disasters, appeals to veterans.
2. *Community:* Veterans are accustomed to serving with and protecting their team members.
3. *Self-worth:* Helping others in crisis provides veterans with a sense of self-worth and accomplishment.

Since its founding in 2011, Team Rubicon has made a positive impact on survivors immediately following many disasters around the world, including the contaminated water emergency in Flint, Michigan, the surge of refugees in Greece, an outbreak of Ebola in Sierra Leone, a dam failure in Nevada, the devastating wildfire in Gatlinburg, Tennessee, and Hurricane Matthew in Virginia, Georgia, and Florida.

Disaster relief missions are highly motivating for veterans, and their skills bring victims badly needed assistance, medical supplies, and other forms of relief until organizations like the Red Cross arrive. Team Rubicon staff and volunteers know how to get the work done: "When we arrive on site after a disaster in a foreign country, all eyes and hope have turned to us, expecting immediate action and results. Disasters are no-excuse, results-only zones."[72]

Questions

- Of those veterans who would like to work for Team Rubicon, what types of rewards are likely to keep them motivated: extrinsic, intrinsic, or both?
- How and to what degree do you think Team Rubicon will make a positive impact on natural disaster victims? Explain.

As you may guess, however, the person may just be changing from one boring job to another. But job rotation can benefit everyone when done properly, with people's input and career interests in mind. Starbucks hires MBAs straight out of school to join its Rotational Development Program, a full-time, two-year program that focuses on developing future leaders.[73]

job enlargement

Giving people additional tasks at the same time to alleviate boredom.

Job enlargement is similar to job rotation in that people are given different tasks to do. But whereas job rotation involves doing one task at one time and changing to a different task at a different time, job enlargement means that the worker has multiple tasks at the same time. Thus an assembly worker's job is enlarged if he or she is given two tasks rather than one to perform. At a financial services firm, enlarged jobs led to higher job satisfaction, better error detection by clerks, and improved customer service.[74]

job enrichment

Changing a task to make it inherently more rewarding, motivating, and satisfying.

With job enlargement, the person's additional tasks are at the same level of responsibility. **Job enrichment**, however, creates more profound changes by adding higher levels of responsibility. This practice includes giving people not only more tasks but higher-level ones, such as making more important decisions. The first approach to job enrichment was Herzberg's two-factor theory, followed by the Hackman and Oldham model.

Herzberg's Two-Factor Theory

Frederick Herzberg's **two-factor theory** distinguished between two broad categories of factors that affect people in their jobs.[75] The first category, **hygiene factors**, are characteristics of the workplace: company policies, working conditions, pay, co-workers, supervision, and so forth. These factors can make people unhappy if they are poorly managed. If they are well managed and viewed as positive by employees, the employees will no longer be dissatisfied. However, no matter how good these factors are, they will not make people truly satisfied or motivated to do a good job.

According to Herzberg, the key to true job satisfaction and motivation to perform lies in the second category: the motivators. The **motivators** describe the job itself—that is, what people *do* at work. Motivators are the nature of the work itself, the actual job responsibilities, opportunity for personal growth and recognition, and the feelings of achievement the job provides when peoplel perform well. When these factors are present, jobs are both satisfying and motivating for most people.

Herzberg's theory has been criticized by many scholars, and for that reason we will not go into more detail about the theory. But Herzberg was a pioneer in the area of job design and still is a respected name. Furthermore, even if the specifics of his theory do not hold up to scientific scrutiny, he made several important contributions. First, Herzberg's theory highlights the important distinction between extrinsic rewards (hygiene factors) and intrinsic rewards (motivators). Second, it reminds managers not to count solely on extrinsic factors to motivate workers, but to focus on intrinsic rewards as well. Third, it set the stage for later theories, such as the Hackman and Oldham model, that explain more precisely how managers can enrich people's jobs.

two-factor theory
Herzberg's theory describing two factors affecting people's work motivation and satisfaction.

hygiene factors
Characteristics of the workplace, such as company policies, working conditions, pay, and supervision, that can make people dissatisfied.

motivators
Factors that make a job more motivating, such as additional job responsibilities, opportunities for personal growth and recognition, and feelings of achievement.

The Hackman and Oldham Model of Job Design

Following Herzberg's work, Hackman and Oldham proposed a more complete model of job design.[76] Exhibit 13.7 illustrates their model. As you can see, well-designed jobs lead to high motivation, high-quality performance, high satisfaction, and low absenteeism and turnover.

EXHIBIT 13.7
The Hackman and Oldham Model of Job Enrichment

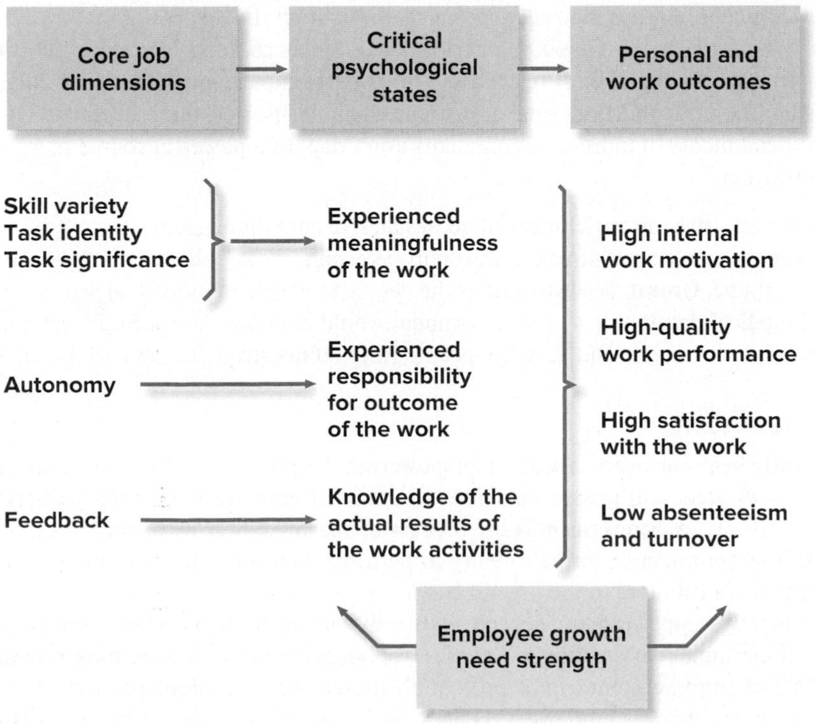

SOURCE: Hackman, J. Richard et al., "A New Strategy for Job Enrichment," *California Management Review* 17, no. 4 (Summer 1975), pp. 57–71.

These outcomes occur when people experience three critical psychological states shown in the middle column of the figure:

1. They believe they are doing something meaningful because their work is important to other people.
2. They feel personally responsible for how the work turns out.
3. They learn how well they perform their jobs.

These psychological states occur when people are working on enriched jobs—that is, jobs that offer the following five core job dimensions:

1. *Skill variety*—different job activities involving several skills and talents. When cleaning employees in hospitals were given some freedom in how they carried out their work, they added skill variety through extra efforts such as engaging patients in small talk and figuring out ways they could make nurses' jobs easier. After adding this skill variety, the employees were more satisfied with their jobs.[77]
2. *Task identity*—the completion of a whole, identifiable piece of work. At State Farm Insurance, agents are independent contractors who sell and provide service for State Farm products exclusively. They have built and invested in their own businesses. As a result, agent retention and productivity are far better than industry norms.[78]
3. *Task significance*—an important, positive impact on the lives of others. A study of lifeguards found dramatic improvements in their performance if they were taught about how lifeguards make a difference by preventing deaths. Lifeguards who were told simply that the job can be personally enriching showed no such improvements.[79] Similarly, James Perry, an expert on motivation of government employees, says public sector employees generally have a strong commitment to serving the public good, including public welfare and stewardship of public resources.[80]
4. *Autonomy*—independence and discretion in making decisions. In China, a GE Healthcare team was given freedom to develop an inexpensive ultrasound device to serve poorly funded health clinics. The device was successful and inspired the development of other innovative products throughout the division.[81]
5. *Feedback*—information about job performance. Many companies provide information on productivity, number of rejects, and other performance indicators. The Parasole restaurant group in Minnesota, as just one example, uses customer feedback on social media—hundreds of comments every day—as a powerful source of motivation.[82]

The most effective job enrichment increases all five core dimensions.

A person's growth need strength will help determine how effective a job enrichment program might be. **Growth need strength** is the degree to which an individual wants personal and psychological development. Job enrichment would be more successful for people with high growth need strength. But very few people respond negatively to job enrichment.[83]

Empowerment

We frequently hear managers talk about empowering their people. Individuals may—or may not—feel empowered, and groups can have a culture of empowerment that predicts work unit performance.[84] **Empowerment** is the process of sharing power with employees, thereby enhancing their confidence in their ability to perform their jobs and their belief that they are influential contributors to the organization.

Unfortunately, empowerment doesn't always live up to its hype. One problem is that managers undermine it by sending mixed messages such as "Do your own thing—the way we tell you."[85] But empowerment can be profoundly motivating when done properly.[86]

Empowerment changes employees' beliefs—from feeling powerless to believing strongly in their own personal effectiveness.[87] When the job fits their values, empowered employees

growth need strength

The degree to which individuals want personal and psychological development.

empowerment

The process of sharing power with employees, thereby enhancing their confidence in their ability to perform their jobs and their belief that they are influential contributors to the organization.

perceive meaning in their work. They feel competent, or capable of performing their jobs with skill. They have a sense of self-determination, of having some choice in regard to the tasks, methods, and pace of their work. And they know they have an impact because they have some influence over important strategic, administrative, or operating decisions or outcomes on the job.

The result is that people are more fully invested and engaged in their work—physically, cognitively, and emotionally.[88] They take more initiative and persevere in achieving their goals and their leader's vision even in the face of obstacles.[89] Ultimately, managed well, they and their units perform at higher levels.[90]

When speaking of times when they felt disempowered, people mentioned the following:[91]

- I had no input into a hiring decision of someone who was to report directly to me. I didn't even get to speak to the candidate.
- They treated us like mushrooms. They fed us and kept us in the dark.
- I worked extremely hard—long hours and late nights—on an urgent project, and then my manager took full credit for it.
- My suggestions, whether good or bad, were either not solicited or, worse, ignored.
- The project was reassigned without my knowledge or input.

In contrast, people felt empowered in the following examples:

- I was able to make a large financial decision on my own. I got to write a large check without being questioned.
- After having received a memo that said, "Cut travel," I made my case about why it was necessary to travel for business reasons, and I was told to go ahead.
- I was five years old, and my dad said, "You'll make a great mechanic one day." He planted the seed. Now I'm an engineer.
- My president supported my idea without question.
- All the financial data were shared with me.

To foster empowerment,[92] management must create an environment in which all the employees feel they have real influence over performance standards and business effectiveness within their areas of responsibility. An empowering work environment provides people with information necessary for them to perform at their best, knowledge about how to use the information and how to do their work, power to make decisions that give them control over their work, and the rewards they deserve for the contributions they make.[93]

Such an environment reduces costs because fewer people are needed to supervise, monitor, and coordinate. It improves quality and service because high performance is inspired at the source—the people who do the work. It also allows quick action because people on the spot see problems, solutions, and opportunities for innovation on which they are empowered to act.

More specific empowering actions include increasing signature authority at all levels; reducing the number of rules and approval steps; assigning nonroutine jobs; allowing independent judgment, flexibility, and creativity; defining jobs more broadly as projects rather than tasks; and providing more access to resources and people throughout the organization.[94]

You should not be surprised when empowerment causes some problems, at least in the short term. This occurs with virtually any change, including changes for the better. It's important to remember that with empowerment comes responsibility, and employees don't necessarily like the extra accountability at first.[95] People may make mistakes at first, especially until they receive training. And because more training is needed, costs are higher.

Furthermore, because people acquire new skills and make greater contributions, they may demand higher wages. But if they are well-trained and truly empowered, they will deserve them—and both they and the company will benefit.

Bottom Line

Job enrichment and empowerment don't work magic overnight; people may resist the new approaches and make mistakes along the way. But done right, their potential to achieve real results is undeniable. *What might be some differences between empowerment "done right" and "done wrong"?*

Achieving Fairness

LO 7   Ultimately, one of the most important issues in motivation is how people view their contributions to the organization and what they receive from the organization. Ideally, they will view their relationship with their employer as a well-balanced, mutually beneficial exchange. People assess (1) the contributions they make in their work, and (2) the positive and negative outcomes they receive—overall, how fairly the organization treats them.[96]

Equity theory suggests that people compare the ratio of their outcomes to inputs against the outcome-to-input ratio of some comparison person. How would you deal with someone you perceive to be a slacker who gets promoted over you?

©imtmphoto/Shutterstock.com RF

equity theory

A theory stating that people assess how fairly they have been treated according to two key factors: outcomes and inputs.

The starting point for understanding how people interpret their contributions and outcomes is equity theory.[97] **Equity theory** proposes that when people assess how fairly they are treated, they consider two key factors: outcomes and inputs. Outcomes, as in expectancy theory, refer to the various things the person receives on the job: recognition, pay, benefits, satisfaction, security, job assignments, punishments, and so forth. Inputs refer to the contributions the person makes to their employer: effort, time, talent, performance, extra commitment, good citizenship, and so forth. People have a general expectation that the outcomes they receive will reflect, or be proportionate to, the inputs they provide—a fair day's pay (and other outcomes) for a fair day's work (broadly defined by how people view all their contributions).

But this comparison of outcomes to inputs is not the whole story. People also pay attention to the outcomes and inputs others receive. At salary review time, for example, most people—from executives on down—try to pick up clues that will tell them who got the highest raises. As described in the following section, they compare ratios, try to restore equity if necessary, and derive more or less satisfaction based on how fairly they believe they have been treated.

Assessing Equity

Equity theory states that people compare the ratio of their own outcomes to inputs against the outcome-to-input ratio of some comparison person. The comparison person can be a fellow student, a co-worker, a boss, or an average industry pay scale. Stated more succinctly, people compare their own outcomes and inputs to those of a comparison person (see Exhibit 13.8). If the ratios are equivalent, people believe the relationship is equitable, or fair. Equity causes people to be satisfied with their treatment. But the person who believes his or her ratio is lower than another's will feel inequitably treated. Inequity causes dissatisfaction and leads to an attempt to restore balance to the relationship.

Inequity and the negative feelings it creates can appear anywhere. As a student, perhaps you have been in the following situation. You stay up all night and get a C on the exam. Meanwhile another student studies a couple of hours, goes out for the rest of the evening, gets a good night's sleep, and gets a B on the exam. You perceive your inputs (time spent studying) as much greater than the other student's, but your outcomes (exam grade) are lower. It doesn't feel fair, and you are not happy.

In business, the same thing can happen with pay raises. One manager puts in long weeks, has a degree from a prestigious university, and believes she is destined for the top. When her archrival—whom she perceives as less deserving ("she never comes into the office on weekends, and all she does when she is here is butter up the boss")—gets the higher raise or the promotion, she feels serious inequity.

Many people feel inequity when they learn about the huge sums paid to high-profile CEOs. Fair pay became a more public issue for U.S. companies because the Dodd-Frank Wall Street Reform and Consumer Protection Act required greater disclosure of performance-based pay details.[98]

EXHIBIT 13.8   Equity Theory

Comparing Your Ratio to Other's Ratio		Your Likely Perception	Actions You May Take to Restore Equity
$\dfrac{\text{Your Outcomes}}{\text{Your Inputs}}$ = $\dfrac{\text{Other's Outcomes}}{\text{Other's Inputs}}$		Equitably treated.	No action necessary.
$\dfrac{\text{Your Outcomes}}{\text{Your Inputs}}$ < $\dfrac{\text{Other's Outcomes}}{\text{Other's Inputs}}$		Inequitably treated. Feel underrewarded.	Reduce your inputs (e.g., exert less effort). Try to increase your outcomes (e.g., ask for a raise). Change your perception of inputs or outcomes (e.g., maybe so-and-so really did deserve the bonus).
$\dfrac{\text{Your Outcomes}}{\text{Your Inputs}}$ > $\dfrac{\text{Other's Outcomes}}{\text{Other's Inputs}}$		Inequitably treated. Feel overrewarded.	Increase your inputs by putting in extra effort. Help other person increase her outcomes (e.g., urge her to ask for a larger bonus).

Assessments of equity are not made objectively. They are subjective perceptions or beliefs. In the preceding examples, the person who got the higher raise probably felt she deserved it. Even if she admits she doesn't put in long workweeks, she may convince herself she doesn't need to because she's so talented. The student who got the higher grade may believe it was a fair, equitable result because (1) she kept up all semester, while the other student did not, and (2) she's extra-smart. (Ability and experience, not just time and effort, can be seen as inputs.)

Restoring Equity

People who feel inequitably treated and dissatisfied are motivated to do something to restore equity. They have a number of options to change the ratios, or reevaluate the situation and decide it is equitable after all.

The equity equation shown earlier indicates a person's options for restoring equity. People who feel inequitably treated can reduce their inputs by giving less effort, performing at lower levels, or quitting. ("Well, if that's the way things work around here, there's no way I'm going to work that hard [or stick around].") Or they can attempt to increase their outcomes. ("My boss [or teacher] is going to hear about this. I deserve more; there must be some way I can get more.")

On the positive side, employees can also put forth extra effort to keep a situation equitable for the group. When employees see their colleagues working hard to meet an important deadline, they may be inclined to work harder themselves.

Other ways of restoring equity focus on changing the other person's ratio. A person can decrease others' outcomes. An employee may sabotage work to create problems for his company or his boss.[99] A person can change her perceptions of inputs or outcomes. ("That promotion isn't as great a deal as he thinks. The pay is not that much better, and the headaches will be unbelievable.") It is also possible to increase others' inputs, particularly by changing perceptions. ("The more I think about it, the more I see he deserved it. He's worked hard all year, he's competent, and it's about time he got a break.")

Thus a person can restore equity in a number of ways by behaviorally or perceptually changing inputs and outcomes.

Procedural Justice

Inevitably, managers make decisions that have outcomes more favorable for some than for others. Those with favorable outcomes will be pleased; those with worse outcomes, all else equal, will be more displeased. But managers desiring to put salve on the wounds—say, of

procedural justice

Using fair processes in decision making and making sure others know that the process was as fair as possible.

people they like or respect or want to keep and motivate—still can take actions to reduce the dissatisfaction. The key is for people to believe that managers provide **procedural justice**—using fair process in decision making. When people perceive procedural fairness, they are more likely to support decisions and decision makers.[100] For example, nurses who perceived their performance evaluations as fair were more likely to remain in their jobs.[101]

Even if people believe that their outcome was inequitable and unfair, they are more likely to view justice as having been served if the process was fair. You can increase people's beliefs that the process was fair by making the process open and visible; stating decision criteria in advance rather than after the fact; making sure that the most appropriate people—those who have valid information and are viewed as trustworthy—make the decisions; giving people a chance to participate in the process; and providing an appeal process that allows people to question decisions safely and receive complete answers.[102] However, the impact of procedural justice can differ by country and culture—for instance, the impact is strongest among nations characterized by individualism, uncertainty avoidance, and low power distance (recall Chapter 6).[103]

At an elevator plant in the United States, an army of consultants arrived one day, unexplained and annoying.[104] The rumor mill kicked in; employees thought the plant was to be shut down or that some of them would be laid off. Three months later, management unveiled its new plan, involving a new method of manufacturing based on teams. As the changes were implemented, management did not adequately answer questions about the purpose of the changes, employees resisted, conflicts arose, and the formerly popular plant manager lost the trust of his people. Costs skyrocketed, and quality plummeted.

Concerned, management conducted a survey. Employees were skeptical that the results would lead to any positive changes and were worried that management would be angry that people had voiced their honest opinions. But management reacted by saying, "We were wrong, we screwed up, we didn't use the right process." They went on to share with employees critical business information, the limited options available, and the dire consequences if the company didn't change.

Employees saw the dilemma and came to view the business problem as theirs as well as management's, but they were scared that some of them would lose their jobs. Management retained the right to lay people off if business conditions grew worse but also made several promises: no layoffs as a result of changes made; cross-training programs for employees; no replacements of departing people until conditions improved; a chance for employees to serve in new roles as consultants on quality issues; and sharing of sales and cost data on a regular basis.

The news was bad, but people understood it and began to accept a greater share of responsibility along with management. Trust and commitment began to return, as did stronger performance.

Employee Satisfaction and Well-Being

LO 8

If people feel fairly treated from the outcomes they receive and the processes used, they will be satisfied. A satisfied worker is not necessarily more productive than a dissatisfied one; sometimes people are happy with their jobs because they don't have to work hard! But job dissatisfaction, aggregated across many individuals, creates a workforce that is more likely to exhibit (1) higher turnover; (2) higher absenteeism; (3) less good citizenship;[105] (4) more grievances and lawsuits; (5) strikes; (6) stealing, sabotage, and vandalism; (7) poorer mental and physical health (which can mean higher job stress, higher insurance costs, and more lawsuits);[106] (8) more injuries;[107] (9) poor customer service;[108] and (10) lower productivity and profits.[109] All of these consequences of dissatisfaction, either directly or indirectly, are costly to organizations.

Sadly, most people are dissatisfied with their jobs, with the greatest dissatisfaction among lower wage earners and workers aged 25 and younger.[110]

The Digital World

A low-cost way to motivate employees is to recognize them on social media sites. Often companies will acknowledge accomplishments on corporate intranets (or internal company-only web portals) so that people are celebrated for successful projects or work milestones.

External articles about employees at the company provide recognition, while also building relationships with stakeholders who can view articles posted on the company website.

Regarding how it affects job performance, job satisfaction is especially important for relationship-oriented service employees such as realtors, hair stylists, and stockbrokers. Customers develop (or don't develop) a commitment to a specific service provider. Satisfied service providers are less likely to quit the company and more likely to provide an enjoyable customer experience.[111]

Quality of Work Life

Quality of work life is a decades-old but still highly useful concept. **Quality of work life (QWL) programs** create a workplace that enhances employee job satisfaction and overall physical and mental well-being.[112] The general goal of QWL programs is to satisfy the full range of employee needs. Promoting QWL is a social and political cause that sprang originally from the establishment of democratic societies and basic human rights.[113]

A good example is Plante Moran, an accounting firm with offices in 18 midwestern cities. Cofounder Frank Moran's goal was for the business to be a "people firm disguised as an accounting firm," and he brought that vision to life by allowing any flexible work arrangement that is satisfactory to the employee's clients. The firm's website, which promises a "jerk-free" workplace, describes challenging jobs with varied assignments and buddies assigned to new employees so they can more wisely navigate their careers. Employees say they appreciate most the interesting assignments that bring them into direct contact with key people at client companies.[114]

Traditionally, QWL has at least eight categories:[115]

1. Adequate and fair compensation
2. A safe and healthy environment
3. Jobs that develop human capacities
4. A chance for personal growth and security
5. A social environment that fosters personal identity, freedom from prejudice, a sense of community, and upward mobility
6. Constitutionalism, or the rights of personal privacy, dissent, and due process
7. A work role that minimizes infringement on personal leisure and family needs
8. Socially responsible organizational actions

Organizations differ drastically in their attention to QWL. Critics claim that QWL programs don't necessarily inspire employees to work harder if the company does not tie rewards directly to individual performance. Advocates of QWL claim that it improves organizational effectiveness and productivity overall. The term *productivity,* as applied by QWL programs, means much more than each person's quantity of work output.[116] It also includes turnover, absenteeism, accidents, theft, sabotage, creativity, innovation, and the quality of work.

Bottom Line

A single satisfied person doesn't necessarily produce well on every performance dimension. But an organization full of people with high job satisfaction will likely perform well in many ways.

In a company with a strategy focused on low cost, how is employee satisfaction important?

Plante Moran promises applicants a "jerk-free" workplace.

Source: Plante & Moran, PLLC

quality of work life (QWL) programs

Programs designed to create a workplace that enhances employee well-being.

Management in Action

HOW SAS MAKES WORK MOTIVATING

Jennifer Mann, SAS's vice president of human resources, says everyone there "is working toward the same vision and inspiring each other to do their best work." Mann sees this as evidence that the company's culture is yielding great results. Other signs of success include employee turnover below 5 percent (versus the industry average of more than 20 percent), tens of thousands of job applicants for hundreds of open positions, and steadily growing revenues.

What convinces employees that SAS values their contributions? We have already talked about employee benefits, but these are mere symbols of company values. The managers rewarded at SAS are those who advocate for and develop their people.

CEO James Goodnight (also an owner of the privately held company) puts his time and money on the line for his people. Each month, he presides at a breakfast meeting where any employee may join in and ask questions or share ideas. In 2008, as financial crisis gave way to Great Recession, other software companies announced major layoffs, and SAS employees became nervous. Goodnight spoke to all of them via webcast, saying there would be no layoffs; they just all needed to be more frugal. Not only did the company weather that economic downturn, it continued growing and developed new products to launch as the economy recovered.

Another quality of the SAS culture is trust in employees. The company's standard workweek is just 35 hours. "I don't expect people to work 60 to 70 hours a week. It's been my experience, much past 40 hours a week and you're writing pretty worthless code, which you spend the next day unraveling," says Goodnight. The company's on-site facilities and beautiful grounds make it easy for employees to take a break to work out, get a haircut or massage, or go for a hike. Managers don't worry that employees will goof off; they find that trust motivates employees to work hard to please customers and help the company succeed. In fact, great subsidized food (some of it grown on an SAS-owned organic farm) and other services can make staying at work easier than going home. A similar attitude of trust applies to sick days at SAS, which are unlimited.

SAS also ensures that work is meaningful. Goodnight reminds employees that SAS software is useful to people all over the world. Programmers' work is designed so they feel ownership of their creations. Even the landscapers at headquarters are assigned to particular plots, so these employees enjoy imparting beauty to that parcel and feel the same identification with the company as any programmer does.[117]

- How does SAS make its jobs motivating? What other principles of job design could enhance motivation at SAS?
- What elements of SAS's approach to motivation do you think would contribute more to job satisfaction than to performance? Why?

All in all, people's satisfaction and well-being have many important consequences, beneficial to both employees and employers.[118] These range from better attitudes and health to work behaviors and performance, and ultimately include firm value[119] and other business outcomes.[120] In a well-managed workplace, win–win solutions are indeed possible.

Psychological Contracts

psychological contract

A set of perceptions of what employees owe their employers, and what their employers owe them.

The relationship between individuals and employing organizations typically is formalized by a written contract. But in employees' minds, there also exists a **psychological contract**—a set of perceptions of what they owe their employers and what their employers owe them.[121] This contract, whether it is seen as being upheld or violated—and whether the parties trust one another or not—has important implications for employee satisfaction and motivation and the effectiveness of the organization. Experiencing significant breach of psychological contract also can adversely affect physical and mental health.[122]

Historically, in big companies, the employment relationship was stable and predictable. But mergers, layoffs, and other disruptions tore apart the old deal.[123] As one executive put it, "The 'used-to-be's' must give way to the realities of 'What is and what will be.'"[124]

The fundamental used-to-be of traditionally managed organizations was that employees were expected to be loyal, and employers would provide secure employment. But now the implicit contract goes something like this:[125] If people stay, do their own jobs plus someone else's (who has been downsized), and do additional things such as participating in task forces, the company will try to provide a job (if it can), provide gestures that it cares, and keep providing more or less the same pay (with periodic small increases).

The likely result of this not-very-satisfying arrangement: uninspired people and a business trying to survive. Career advisors tell disillusioned employees to think of themselves as free agents and to change jobs when a new option beckons.

But a better deal is possible, for both employers and employees.[126] Ideally, your employer will provide continuous skill updating and an invigorating work environment in which you can use your skills and are motivated to stay even if you have other job options.[127] The employer says, in essence, "If you make us more valuable, we'll make you more valuable," and the employee says, "If you help me grow, I'll help the company grow." The company benefits from your contributions, and you thrive in your work while you also become more marketable if and when you decide to look elsewhere. Employment is an alliance—perhaps temporary, perhaps long term—aimed at helping both employer and employee succeed.[128] The results of such a contract are much more likely to be a mutually beneficial and satisfying relationship and a high-performing, successful organization.

Finally, consider how these ideas for motivation apply at SAS. Read the "Management in Action: Onward" feature and ask yourself whether old-fashioned stable employment relationships can—or should—be the norm.

KEY TERMS

Alderfer's ERG theory, p. 383

empowerment, p. 388

equity theory, p. 390

expectancy, p. 379

expectancy theory, p. 378

extinction, p. 376

extrinsic reward, p. 385

goal-setting theory, p. 373

growth need strength, p. 388

hygiene factors, p. 387

instrumentality, p. 379

intrinsic reward, p. 385

job enlargement, p. 386

job enrichment, p. 386

job rotation, p. 385

law of effect, p. 375

Maslow's need hierarchy, p. 381

motivation, p. 372

motivators, p. 387

negative reinforcement, p. 376

organizational behavior modification (OB mod), p. 375

outcome, p. 379

positive reinforcement, p. 375

procedural justice, p. 392

psychological contract, p. 394

punishment, p. 376

quality of work life (QWL) programs, p. 393

reinforcers, p. 375

stretch goals, p. 374

two-factor theory, p. 387

valence, p. 380

RETAINING WHAT YOU LEARNED

In Chapter 13, you learned that managers can motivate employees in a variety of ways. Goals that are specific, quantifiable, and challenging are powerful tools for motivating individuals and teams. Organizations develop programs that use different types of reinforcement to influence employees' behaviors. Managers should reinforce appropriate behaviors, manage mistakes properly, and provide useful feedback. Expectancy theory states that employees are motivated when they believe they can perform a job well and their performance will be rewarded with a valued outcome. People's needs affect their behaviors at work. Maslow and Alderfer offered similar need theories of motivation. McClelland said people vary in the extent to which they need achievement, affiliation, and power. Managers can create motivating jobs by making them intrinsically rewarding. Jobs can be enriched by building in skill variety, task identity, task significance, autonomy, and feedback. Employees with jobs that have the necessary information, knowledge, power, and rewards feel empowered. Equity theory explores how an individual's perceptions of fairness can lead to either feeling satisfied or dissatisfied at work. A satisfied workforce has many advantages for the firm, including lower absenteeism and turnover; fewer grievances, lawsuits, and strikes; lower health costs; and higher-quality work. A psychological contract is a set of perceptions of what employees think they owe their employer and what they think their employer owes them.

LO 1   Identify the kinds of behaviors managers need to motivate in people.

- All important work behaviors are motivated.
- Managers need to motivate employees to join and remain in the organization and to exhibit high attendance, job performance, and citizenship.

LO 2   List principles for setting goals that motivate employees.

- Goal setting is a powerful motivator. Specific, quantifiable, and challenging but attainable goals motivate high effort and performance.
- Goal setting can be used for teams as well as for individuals.
- Care should be taken to avoid setting single goals to the exclusion of other important dimensions of performance.
- Managers also should keep sight of the other potential downsides of goals.

LO 3   Summarize how to reward good performance effectively.

- Organizational behavior modification programs influence work behavior by arranging consequences for people's actions.
- Most programs use positive reinforcement as a consequence, but other important consequences are negative reinforcement, punishment, and extinction.
- Care must be taken to reinforce appropriate, not inappropriate, behavior.
- Innovative managers use a wide variety of rewards for good performance.
- They also understand how to manage mistakes and provide useful feedback.

LO 4   Describe the key beliefs that affect people's motivation.

- Expectancy theory describes three important work-related beliefs.
- Motivation is a function of people's (1) expectancies, or effort-to-performance links; (2) instrumentalities, or performance-to-outcome links; and (3) valences that they attach to the outcomes of performance.

LO 5   Discuss ways in which people's individual needs affect their behavior.

- According to Maslow, important needs arise at five levels of a hierarchy: physiological, safety, social, ego, and self-actualization needs.

- Focusing more on the context of work, Alderfer's ERG theory described three sets of needs: existence, relatedness, and growth.
- McClelland stated that people vary in their needs for achievement, affiliation, and power.
- Because people are inclined to satisfy their own needs, these theories tell managers the kinds of rewards that motivate people.

LO 6   Define ways to create jobs that motivate.

- One approach to motivating people is to create intrinsic motivation through redesigning jobs.
- Jobs can be enriched by building in more skill variety, task identity, task significance, autonomy, and feedback.
- Empowerment includes perceived meaning, competence, self-determination, and impact. These qualities come from an environment in which people have necessary information, knowledge, power, and rewards.

LO 7   Summarize how people assess fairness and how to achieve fairness.

- Equity theory states that people compare their inputs and outcomes to the inputs and outcomes of others.
- Perceptions of equity (fairness) are satisfying; feelings of inequity (unfairness) are dissatisfying and motivate people to change their behavior or their perceptions to restore equity.
- In addition to fairness of outcomes, as described in equity theory, fairness is also appraised and managed through procedural justice.

LO 8   Identify causes and consequences of a (dis)satisfied workforce.

- A satisfied workforce has many advantages for the firm, including: lower absenteeism and turnover; fewer grievances, lawsuits, and strikes; lower health costs; and higher-quality work.
- One general approach to generating higher satisfaction for people is to implement a quality of work life program. QWL seeks to provide a safe and healthy environment, opportunity for personal growth, a positive social environment, fair treatment, and other improvements in people's work lives.
- These and other benefits from the organization, exchanged for contributions from employees, create a psychological contract.
- Over time, how the psychological contract is upheld or violated will influence people's satisfaction and motivation.

DISCUSSION QUESTIONS

1. Think of a significant mistake you've seen someone make on a job. How did the boss handle it, and what was the effect?

2. It is difficult for managers to empower their people successfully, in part because the process is not simple but complex. Discuss in depth.

3. Think of a job you hold or held in the past. How would you describe the psychological contract? How does (did) this affect your attitudes and behaviors on the job?

4. If a famous executive or sports figure were to give a passionate motivational speech, trying to persuade

people to work harder, what do you think the impact would be? Why?

5. Give some examples of situations in which you wanted to do a great job but were prevented from doing so. What was the impact on you, and what would this teach you as you try to motivate other people to perform?

6. Discuss the similarities and differences between setting goals for other people and setting goals for yourself. When does goal setting fail, and when does it succeed?

7. Identify four examples of people inadvertently reinforcing the wrong behaviors or punishing or extinguishing good behaviors.

8. Assess yourself on McClelland's three needs. On which need are you highest, and on which are you lowest? What are the implications for you as a manager?

9. Identify a job you have held and appraise it on Hackman and Oldham's five core job dimensions. Also describe the degree to which it made you feel empowered. As a

class, choose one job and discuss together how it could be changed to be more motivating and empowering.

10. Using expectancy theory, analyze how you have made and will make personal choices, such as a major area of study, a career to pursue, or job interviews to seek.

11. Describe a time when you felt unfairly treated and explain why. How did you respond to the inequity? What other options might you have had?

12. Provide examples of how outcomes perceived as unfair can decrease motivation. Then discuss how procedural justice, or fair process, can help overcome the negative effects.

13. Describe what you expect of your psychological contract with your employer after your graduation. How will you deal if it doesn't meet your expectations?

14. Set some goals for yourself, considering the relevant discussion in the chapter.

EXPERIENTIAL EXERCISES

13.1 ASSESSING YOURSELF

Circle the response that most closely correlates with each of the following items:

	Agree	Neither Agree nor Disagree	Disagree	
1. I have developed a written list of short- and long-term goals I would like to accomplish.	1	2	3	4 5
2. When setting goals for myself, I give consideration to what my capabilities and limits are.	1	2	3	4 5
3. I set goals that are realistic and attainable.	1	2	3	4 5
4. My goals are based on my hopes and beliefs, not on those of my parents, friends, or significant other.	1	2	3	4 5
5. When I fail to achieve a goal, I get back on track.	1	2	3	4 5
6. My goals are based on my personal values.	1	2	3	4 5
7. I have a current mission statement and have involved those closest to me in formulating it.	1	2	3	4 5
8. I regularly check my progress toward achieving the goals I have set.	1	2	3	4 5
9. When setting goals, I strive for performance, not outcomes.	1	2	3	4 5
10. I have a support system in place—friends, family members, and/or colleagues who believe in me and support my goals.	1	2	3	4 5
11. I apply SMART characteristics to my goals.	1	2	3	4 5
12. I prioritize my goals, focusing only on the most important or valuable ones at a particular point in time.	1	2	3	4 5
13. I reward myself when I achieve a goal or even when I reach a particular milestone.	1	2	3	4 5
14. I revisit my goals periodically and add and modify goals as appropriate.	1	2	3	4 5

Sum your circled responses. If your total is 42 or higher, you might want to explore ways to improve your skill in the area of goal setting.

de Janasz, Suzanne C., Dowd, Karen O. and Schneider, Beth Z., *Interpersonal Skills in Organizations,* McGraw-Hill, 2012, p. 56. Copyright ©2012 McGraw-Hill Global Education Holdings LLC. All rights reserved. Used with permission.

13.2 PERSONAL GOAL SETTING

1. In the spaces provided, brainstorm your goals in the following categories. Write down as many as you wish, including goals that are short-, mid-, and long-term.

   Academic, intellectual

   Health, fitness

   Social: family, friends, significant other, community

   Career, job

   Financial

   Other

2. Of the goals you have listed, select from each of the six categories the two most important goals that you would like to pursue in the short term (next 6–12 months). Write these here.

   a. _____

   b. _____

   c. _____

   d. _____

   e. _____

   f. _____

   g. _____

   h. _____

   i. _____

   j. _____

   k. _____

   l. _____

3. From the 12 goals listed, choose the 3 that are the most important to you at this time: the 3 you commit to work on in the next few months. Write a goal statement for each one, using the following guidelines:

   Begin each with the word "To . . ."

   Be specific.

Quantify the goal if possible.

Each goal statement should be realistic, attainable, and within your control.

Each goal statement should reflect your aspirations—not those of others such as parents, roommates, significant others, and the like.

   a. _____
   _____

   b. _____
   _____

   c. _____
   _____

4. On a separate sheet of paper, develop an action plan for each goal statement. For each action plan, list the steps you will take to accomplish the goal.
   Include dates (by when) and initials (who's responsible) for each step.

   Visualize completing the goal and, working backward, specify each step necessary between now and then to reach the goal.

   Identify any potential barriers you might experience in attaining the goal. Problem-solve around these obstacles and convert them into steps in your action plan.

   Identify the resources you will need to accomplish these goals and build in steps to acquire the necessary information into your action plan.

5. Transfer the dates of each step for each goal in your action plan to a daily calendar.

6. Keep an ongoing daily or weekly record of the positive steps you take toward meeting each goal.

13.3 WHAT DO STUDENTS WANT FROM THEIR JOBS?

OBJECTIVES

1. To demonstrate individual differences in job expectations.

2. To illustrate individual differences in need and motivational structures.

3. To examine and compare extrinsic and intrinsic rewards.

INSTRUCTIONS

1. Working alone, complete the "What I Want from My Job" survey.

2. In small groups, compare and analyze differences in the survey results and prepare group responses to the discussion questions.

3. After the class reconvenes, group spokespersons present group findings.

DISCUSSION QUESTIONS

1. Which items received the highest and lowest scores from you? Why?

2. On which items was there most and least agreement among students? What are the implications?

3. Which job rewards are extrinsic, and which are intrinsic?

4. Were more response differences found in intrinsic or in extrinsic rewards?

5. In what ways do you think blue-collar workers' responses would differ from those of college students?

What I Want from My Job

Determine what you want from a job by circling the level of importance of each of the following job rewards:

	Very Important	Important	Indifferent	Unimportant	Very Unimportant
1. Advancement opportunities	5	4	3	2	1
2. Appropriate company policies	5	4	3	2	1
3. Authority	5	4	3	2	1
4. Autonomy and freedom on the job	5	4	3	2	1
5. Challenging work	5	4	3	2	1
6. Company reputation	5	4	3	2	1
7. Fringe benefits	5	4	3	2	1
8. Geographic location	5	4	3	2	1
9. Good co-workers	5	4	3	2	1
10. Good supervision	5	4	3	2	1
11. Job security	5	4	3	2	1
12. Money	5	4	3	2	1
13. Opportunity for self-development	5	4	3	2	1
14. Pleasant office and working conditions	5	4	3	2	1
15. Performance feedback	5	4	3	2	1
16. Prestigious job title	5	4	3	2	1
17. Recognition for doing a good job	5	4	3	2	1
18. Responsibility	5	4	3	2	1
19. Sense of achievement	5	4	3	2	1
20. Training programs	5	4	3	2	1
21. Type of work	5	4	3	2	1
22. Working with people	5	4	3	2	1

Concluding Case

BIG BISON RESORTS: FINDING THE KEY TO WHAT EMPLOYEES VALUE

Frank Schuman, vice president of human resources for Big Bison Resorts, heard laughter as he approached the chief executive's office door. As he stepped into the room, he saw CEO Janette Briggs seated behind her desk, regaling two other executives with a story that the three were obviously enjoying immensely.

"Oh, Frank! Good!" exclaimed Janette when she saw him enter. "I was just telling Pedro and Marlys about my great adventure in TV land." Janette had been away from the office for the past two weeks, taping the popular reality TV show *Executive in Disguise* instead of running her company, a regional chain of indoor water parks.

"How did it go?" asked Frank. "From the laughter I heard outside your door, it must have been hilarious."

"Well, funny, yes," replied Janette. "But mainly it was eye-opening. After spending all that time in our kitchens and

cleaning the guest rooms and pools, I see our people and their jobs in a totally new way."

"Is that why you called me here? I was expecting you wanted to review our plans for the Employee of the Month program we're unrolling next month. That is, until I saw—" He waved his hand toward the other two people seated in the room, Pedro Gutierrez, head of operations, and finance chief Marlys Higgenbotham. "Or at least I was guessing they're not here to nominate the first employee of the month."

"No, see, that's the issue. After working directly with our frontline staff, I'm having my doubts about putting resources into Employee of the Month," replied the CEO. Frank swallowed. Employee of the Month had been a pet idea of Janette's, so he had poured most of his time into developing the program. Each month, a manager at each resort was going to nominate a top-performing employee to be the Employee of the Month and enjoy the glory, not to mention a premium parking space and a framed photo posted in the lobby of the resort where he or she worked. Now it appeared that Janette shared what, he had to admit, were his own doubts about whether the program would really do much to improve performance or lower turnover. Janette continued, "Have a seat, Frank, and let me tell you about what I saw the past two weeks." Frank settled into a chair next to Marlys.

Janette brought Frank up to date: "I've been telling Marlys and Pedro what it was like to work in one of our kitchens. The pace is unbelievable. The workload is unbelievable. And the teamwork is out of this world. Frank, I was amazed, and you would be, too. I know how to make a grilled cheese sandwich, but these folks do a lot more than cook. They're planning and controlling on the fly: How many salads? How many pancakes? How can we make all that without any waste? There's no supervisor on the line; they're *all* thinking like managers—how to please customers, control costs. Honestly, our managers could take lessons from them on teamwork and quality control."

"It sounds like we have a lot of Employees of the Month," Frank said hopefully. Maybe the program wouldn't be canceled after all, and his group's efforts wouldn't have been wasted.

"No, no, no!" broke in Marlys. "The point is, we've tried so many programs to boost productivity. As you know, we were looking at bonuses last year, till the economy got so bad. We simply couldn't justify paying more when occupancy rates were diving. But we have to do something. Now that business is picking up in our market area, other hotels and resorts are going to start recruiting away our best people. The question is, what can we do that will keep employees working as hard as they are now without burning out and leaving us? We thought people would just like a little recognition, but Janette is saying she doubts it now."

"Exactly," said Janette. "And that's why I called you in. We need your expertise about human relations. What do people want? I thought it would be pay, prizes, that sort of thing. And you went along with me. But really, Frank, can that be it? The people I worked with the past two weeks—they have so much skill at what they do, and they're constantly thinking up ways to make our guests happy. They already take pride in what they accomplish. We need to decide what will make their jobs better so they can accomplish more without us getting in their way with, well, Employee of the Month ceremonies."

"OK," replied Frank, "now that you've put it that way, I have to ask if maybe what we *don't* want to do is decide what will make their jobs better."

As Janette and Marlys gazed at Frank quizzically, Pedro spoke up. "That's great, Frank. You're saying we shouldn't make their jobs better? I came up through the ranks at Big Bison, and I can recall that those hourly jobs aren't exactly perfect the way they are."

"What I mean," replied Frank, "is that we need to *listen* before we *decide.*"

DISCUSSION QUESTIONS

1. What kinds of behavior would an Employee of the Month program, as described here, reinforce at Big Bison Resorts? How might the company apply the principles of reinforcement more effectively?

2. How might Big Bison Resorts get input from employees to make the company's jobs more motivating? What impact would this effort have on the company's performance?

3. How would Big Bison's employees perceive the equity of the Employee of the Month program? Compare their reactions to that program with the response you would expect from an effort to involve employees in improving their jobs.

4. Think about a previous job you have held or hold currently. If you had the power to make such decisions, what would you do to make the job more motivating for employees?

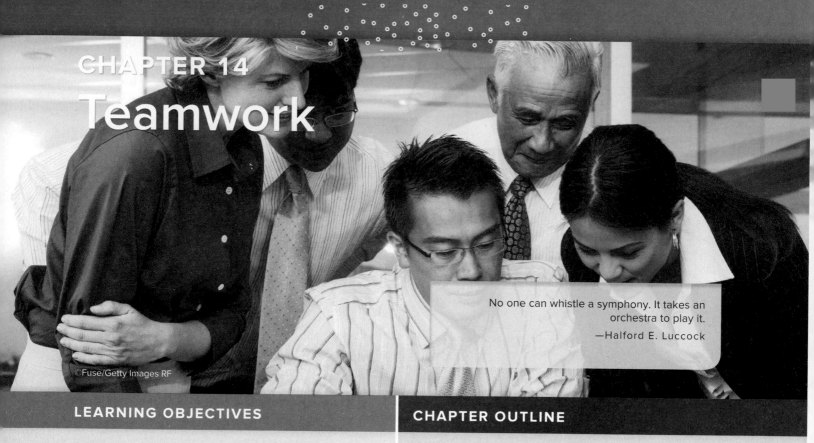

CHAPTER 14
Teamwork

©Fuse/Getty Images RF

No one can whistle a symphony. It takes an orchestra to play it.
—Halford E. Luccock

LEARNING OBJECTIVES

After studying Chapter 14, you will be able to:

LO 1 Discuss how teams can contribute to an organization's effectiveness.

LO 2 Describe different types of teams.

LO 3 Summarize how groups become teams.

LO 4 Explain why groups sometimes fail.

LO 5 Describe how to build an effective team.

LO 6 List methods for managing a team's relationships with other teams.

LO 7 Identify ways to manage conflict.

CHAPTER OUTLINE

The Contributions of Teams

Types of Teams
  Self-Managed Teams

How Groups Become Real Teams
  Group Processes
  Critical Periods
  Teaming Challenges
  Why Groups Sometimes Fail

Building Effective Teams
  Performance Focus
  Motivating Teamwork
  Member Contributions
  Norms
  Roles
  Cohesiveness
  Building Cohesiveness and High-Performance Norms

Managing Lateral Relationships
  Managing Outward
  Lateral Role Relationships
  Managing Conflict
  Conflict Styles
  Being a Mediator
  Electronic and Virtual Conflict

Management in Action

HOW TEAMS WORK AT WHOLE FOODS MARKET

Whole Foods Market has a purpose beyond profits, and even a purpose beyond selling gorgeous vegetables and great cheeses. The chain of more than 400 health-food stores in the United States, Canada, and the United Kingdom seeks to do no less than "contribute to the well-being of people and the planet." This mission shapes the selection of merchandise grown organically and sustainably, including fresh produce, meats and fish, and whole grains, all attractively displayed. It also shapes the way the company treats its 80,000-plus employees.

Managing employees is based on key values: personal responsibility, diversity, and commitment to the organization's purpose. To sustain this combination of values, the company operates as a set of teams, with every employee being a team member. A team may have between 6 and 100 members, with the large teams divided into subteams. The leader of each team in a store is a member of the store's leadership team, and the head of each store leadership team is a member of a regional team. At the top of the Whole Foods hierarchy is an executive team.

Each employee is responsible for participating in decisions related to his or her team's work. Team members have a vote in which employees are part of the team and what benefits will be included in their compensation packages.

Team spirit and empowerment at Whole Foods has laid a strong foundation for business success. CEO John Mackey says living out the store's values creates a climate that frees employees to innovate without fear, and the creative, fear-free environment feels great to shoppers.

©Bloomberg/Getty Images

Whole Foods is one of a handful of companies that has attained a spot on *Fortune*'s list of Best Companies to Work For in every year the list has been compiled (as of this writing). Whole Foods reports employee turnover of just 15 percent per year (the industry average is almost 39 percent). Mark Ehrnstein, global vice president of Team Member Services, attributes the low turnover to the company's ability to foster a strong, team-oriented culture. And after year upon year of strong growth, Whole Foods became the world's largest supermarket chain specializing in natural and organic foods, with far more room to grow when Amazon bought it in 2017.[1]

Whole Foods Market expresses a strong commitment to its employees, empowers them to make decisions, and expects a high level of commitment to serving customers. As you read this chapter, consider additional ingredients that can help ensure truly effective teamwork.

Sometimes teams work, and sometimes they don't. The goal of this chapter is to help make sure that your teams (and you) succeed. Empowerment at Whole Foods Market illustrates one way a company can apply teamwork with extraordinary results.

Teams transform the ways organizations do business.[2] Almost all companies now use teams to produce goods and services, to manage projects, and to make decisions and run the company.[3] For you, this has two vital implications. First, you *will* be working in and sometimes managing teams. Second, the ability to work in and lead teams is valuable to your employer and important to your career. Fortunately, coursework focusing on team training can enhance students' teamwork knowledge and skills.[4]

The Contributions of Teams

LO 1

Bottom Line
Well-managed teams are powerful forces that can deliver all desired results. *What do you think makes a team more powerful than a set of individuals?*

Companies are increasingly using teams to achieve competitive advantage.[5] Used properly, teams can be powerfully effective as a building block for organization structure. Organizations such as Semco, W. L. Gore, and Kollmorgen are structured entirely around teams. 3M's breakthrough products emerge through the use of teams that are small entrepreneurial businesses within the larger corporation.

Teams can increase productivity, improve quality, and reduce costs. At Massachusetts-based manufacturer FLEXcon, teams of employees applying the lean principles described in Chapter 9 significantly increased productivity and decreased energy consumption.[6] At Nucor's steel plant in Decatur, Alabama, the general manager credits teamwork for high productivity and improved safety.[7]

Teams also can enhance speed and be powerful forces for innovation, change, and creativity.[8] Amazon, 3M, Boeing, and many other companies use teams to create new products faster. Cisco relies on teams to keep the firm competitive in the ever-changing field of technology. CEO John Chambers states: "We compete against market transitions, not competitors. Product transitions used to take five to seven years; now they take one to two."[9] To ensure competitiveness of its teams, Cisco is redesigning its talent management practices to optimize team performance, develop team leaders, plan for succession management, and transfer talent between teams.[10]

Teams also provide many benefits for their members.[11] The team is a very useful learning mechanism. Members learn about the company and themselves, and they acquire new skills and performance strategies. The team can satisfy important personal needs, such as affiliation and esteem. Other needs are met as team members receive tangible organizational rewards that they could not have achieved working alone. Moreover, teams help individuals develop their networks.[12]

work teams
Teams that make or do things like manufacture, assemble, sell, or provide service.

Teams can enhance speed in decision making and be powerful forces for innovation, change, and creativity.

Team members can provide one another with feedback; identify opportunities for growth and development; and train, coach, and mentor.[13] A marketing representative can learn about financial modeling from a colleague on a new product development team, and the financial expert can learn about consumer marketing. Experience working together in a team, and developing strong problem-solving capabilities, is a vital supplement to specific job skills or functional expertise. And—a big advantage—you can transfer these skills to new positions.

Types of Teams

LO 2

Your organization may have hundreds of groups and teams, and the variety of different types is vast.[14] Following are a few of the most common.[15] **Work teams** make or do things such as manufacture, assemble, sell, or provide service. They typically are well defined, a clear part of the formal organization structure, and composed of a full-time, stable membership. Work teams are what most people think of when they think of teams in organizations.[16]

Project and development teams work on long-term projects, sometimes over a period of years. They have specific assignments, such as research or new product development, and members usually must contribute expert knowledge and judgment. These teams work toward a one-time product, disbanding once their work is completed. Then new teams are formed for new projects.

Parallel teams operate separately from the regular work structure of the firm on a temporary basis. Members often come from different units or jobs and are asked to do work that is not being done by the standard structure. Their charge is to recommend solutions to specific problems. They usually do not have authority to act, however. Examples include task forces and quality or safety teams formed to study a particular problem. For example, in response to the United States Department of Education and Justice's recent decision to "rescind guidance regarding transgender students," members of Congress relaunched a bipartisan task force to help preserve the rights of transgender students.[17]

Management teams coordinate and provide direction to the subunits under their jurisdiction and integrate work among subunits.[18] The management team is based on authority stemming from hierarchical rank and is responsible for the overall performance of the business unit. At the top of the organization resides the executive management team that establishes strategic direction and manages the firm's overall performance.

Transnational teams are composed of multinational members whose activities span multiple countries.[19] Such teams differ from other work teams by being multicultural and by often being geographically dispersed, being psychologically distant, and working on highly complex projects having considerable impact on company objectives.

Transnational teams tend to be **virtual teams**, communicating electronically more than face to face, although other types of teams may operate virtually as well. Virtual teams face difficult challenges: building trust, cohesion, and team identity, and overcoming the isolation of virtual team members.[20] Exhibit 14.1 suggests ways that managers can improve the effectiveness of virtual teams. As discussed in "Multiple Generations at Work," universities are experimenting with ways to train students to work effectively in global virtual teams.

In today's fast-changing, unpredictable environment, **teaming** is a strategy of teamwork on the fly.[21] In teaming, organizations create many temporary, changing teams, and you might feel like you are in a shifting series of temporary pick-up basketball games, working with different teammates and facing different challenges. You will leave one team when it has achieved (or failed at), its goal and join new teams when new opportunities arise. Because no two projects are alike, people need to get up to speed quickly on brand-new topics again and again. Because solutions can come from anywhere, team members can, too.

project and development teams

Teams that work on long-term projects but disband once the work is completed.

parallel teams

Teams that operate separately from the regular work structure and are temporary.

management teams

Teams that coordinate and provide direction to the subunits under their jurisdiction and integrate work among subunits.

transnational teams

Teams composed of multinational members whose activities span multiple countries. Such teams differ from other work teams by being multicultural and by often being geographically dispersed, being psychologically distant, and working on highly complex projects having considerable impact on company objectives.

virtual teams

Teams that are physically dispersed and communicate electronically more than face-to-face.

teaming

A strategy of teamwork on the fly, creating many temporary, changing teams.

The 29-person product development team at Omnica is responsible for rapidly and efficiently producing medical and high-tech products for their clients.

©Omnica

Multiple Generations at Work

Are You Ready for Global Virtual Teamwork?

Approximately 1.3 billion people worldwide are engaged in virtual work. Cisco reports that over 70,000 employees work remotely, many from dispersed locations. Companies equip their employees for virtual teamwork with advanced videoconferencing software and instant messaging, as well as mobile devices like smartphones and tablets.

Managers need to master the necessary skills to collaborate effectively with team members in virtual settings. According to a recent survey, over half (51 percent) of Millennials believe that remote teams and enhanced communications technology will make meeting face-to-face obsolete in the future.[22]

Virtual teamwork skills fall into two broad areas: (1) using online sharing tools like Google Docs, Slack, Yammer, and Dropbox and communication technology like online chat text; and (2) cross-cultural skills such as adapting to language and value differences, overcoming stereotypes, and coordinating across different time zones.[23]

To prepare students to work effectively in global virtual teams, instructors from several universities in multiple countries engaged in a large-scale collaboration project. Over 6,000 business students were assigned to mostly seven-member, multinational teams. Working together virtually, the teams were tasked with developing a proposal for creating a new product for a client company and analyzing how the product would be brought to market. Instructors graded the projects, and feedback was collected from the students regarding how much they learned. The global virtual team assignments helped students:[24]

1. Improve their understanding of the challenges associated with global virtual teamwork;
2. Change their attitudes toward different cultures (reduction in perceived differences); and
3. Use more effective behaviors with regard to team leadership, coordination, and communication.

Are you ready to be an effective member or leader of a global virtual team?

---

self-managed teams

Autonomous work groups in which workers are trained to do all or most of the jobs in a unit, have no immediate supervisor, and make decisions previously made by frontline supervisors.

autonomous work groups

Groups that control decisions about and execution of a complete range of tasks.

Self-Managed Teams

Traditional work groups have no managerial responsibilities;[25] the frontline manager plans, organizes, staffs, directs, and controls them, and other groups provide support activities, including quality control and maintenance. But one important trend has been to give teams more autonomy so that workers are trained to do all or most of the jobs in the unit, and they make decisions previously made by their bosses.[26] People sometimes resist these **self-managed teams**, in part because they don't want so much responsibility and the change is difficult.[27] Moreover, poorly managed conflict is a particular problem in self-managed teams.[28] But compared with traditionally managed teams, self-managed teams tend to be more productive, have lower costs, provide better customer service, provide higher quality, have better safety records, and are more satisfying for members.

Autonomous work groups control decisions about and execution of a complete range of tasks—acquiring raw materials and performing operations, quality control, maintenance, and shipping. They are fully responsible for an entire product or an entire part of a production

---

EXHIBIT 14.1
Best Practices of Virtual Team Leaders

1. Establish and maintain trust through the use of communication technology.
2. Ensure diversity in the team is understood, appreciated, and leveraged.
3. Manage virtual work cycles and meetings.
4. Monitor team progress through the use of technology.
5. Enhance external visibility of the team and its members.
6. Ensure individuals benefit from participating in virtual teams.

SOURCE: Adapted from Malhotra, A. Majchrzak, A., and Rosen, B., "Leading Virtual Teams," *Academy of Management Perspectives*, February 2007, pp. 60–70.

Management in Action

SELF-MANAGED TEAMS AT WHOLE FOODS MARKET

To spur innovation and strengthen commitment, Whole Foods Market empowers its nearly 60,000 employees to participate in planning and decision making with their teams. Within a store, teams are organized by department such as meat, produce, and dairy. They make decisions about product selection, pricing, promotion and merchandising (the way products are displayed to entice buyers), as well as efforts to improve efficiency. They also contribute to decisions about hiring and compensation.

The company is widely known for team member involvement in hiring decisions, but employees support rather than control the entire hiring process. A human resource employee at each store or other facility screens job applications and selects candidates with the necessary skills and concern for customer service. Candidates who pass the initial screening may be interviewed by one or more store leaders. (Applicants to lead teams generally interview with a group.)

Each employee hired begins an orientation period, during which he or she has probationary status. After the new employee has worked for one to three months, the team meets to decide whether to keep the person on the team, based on whether he or she meets the job requirements, follows company policies and procedures, provides excellent customer service, and works well with the team. Two-thirds must vote in favor of keeping the employee; otherwise, the person can try to join another team or will have to leave the company.

Whole Foods recognizes that for empowerment to succeed, employees need information and other resources to support them in carrying out their responsibilities. Managers share information about the company's financial performance, and everyone can see a list of the gross pay of every team member, including top executives. The company also provides key information for decisions about benefits, starting with the total amount the company will allocate to that expense. Every three years, employees vote on which benefits they want to receive as part of their compensation package. The company provides a list of possible benefits, identifying the cost of each one. Then the employees set priorities within the spending limit.

Rewards, too, are linked to teamwork. Most incentive pay, such as bonuses, is tied to team performance, and teams exist throughout the hierarchy. As CEO John Mackey said, "We have a shared fate. We either succeed together or we fail together."[29]

- What advantages does teamwork offer to Whole Foods Market?
- Why do you think human resource professionals conduct the initial screening process for new hires? What might be the consequences of having the store teams carry out the entire process of hiring and rewarding team members?

---

process. **Self-designing teams** do all of that and go one step further—they also have control over the design of the team. They decide themselves whom to hire, whom to fire, and what tasks the team will perform.

When teams reach the point of being truly self-managed, results have included lower costs and greater levels of team productivity, quality, and customer satisfaction.[30] Autonomous teams are known to improve the organization's financial and overall performance.[31] For example, at Lockheed Martin's Missiles and Fire Control facility in Troy, Alabama, all members of the workforce are assigned to self-directed work teams, and many also participate in performance management teams, which set goals and monitor progress. The teams have achieved 100 percent on-time delivery, 99 percent of first-pass production meeting quality standards, and a 43 percent cut in energy consumption per unit produced.[32]

In trying to take such practices to operations outside the United States, managers need to recognize that cultural differences may affect how employees react to being given decision-making authority. As you learn more about the self-managed teams at Whole Foods Market, described in "Management in Action: Progress Report," consider whether they would continue to be equally effective if the company expanded into other countries with different cultures, and what you might do to help make sure they work well.

self-designing teams

Teams with the responsibilities of autonomous work groups, plus control over hiring, firing, and deciding what tasks members perform.

Teams at Lockheed Martin have achieved success in terms of on-time delivery and high production standards, allowing the company to meet customer demand.

©508 collection/Alamy Stock Photo

How Groups Become Real Teams

LO 3

The words *group* and *team* often are used interchangeably.[33] Modern managers sometimes use the word *teams* to the point that it has become a cliché; often they talk about teams while skeptics believe there is no real teamwork.

Therefore making a distinction between groups and teams can be useful. A *working group* is a collection of people who work in the same area or have been drawn together to undertake a task, but do not necessarily come together as a unit and achieve significant performance improvements. A real **team** is formed of people (usually a small number) with complementary skills who trust one another and are committed to a common purpose, common performance goals, and a common approach for which they hold themselves mutually accountable.[34]

Groups become true teams via basic group processes, critical time periods, and the management practices described throughout this chapter.

Group Processes

Assume you are the leader of a newly formed group—actually just a bunch of people. What will you face as you attempt to develop your group into a high-performing team? If groups are to develop successfully, they will engage in various processes, including the stages detailed in Exhibit 14.2

To be perfectly clear: this is an idealized version, with real teamwork and performance outcomes. But many teams don't make it that far, or do so but only at mediocre levels, or don't do much during forming and disintegrate quickly. Moving from group of co-workers to

team

A small number of people with complementary skills who are committed to a common purpose, set of performance goals, and approach for which they hold themselves mutually accountable; see also *groups.*

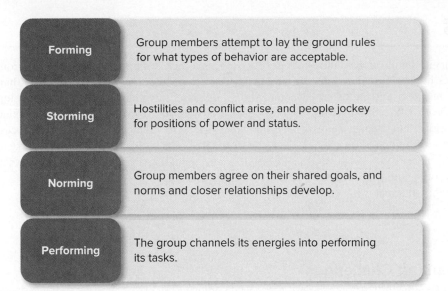

EXHIBIT 14.2
Stages of Team
Development

SOURCE: Adapted from Tuckman, B. W., "Developmental Sequence in Small Groups," *Psychological Bulletin* 63 (1965), pp. 384–99.

high-performing team requires certain strategies and tactics; the process must be managed strategically and well.

Virtual groups, too, can go through these stages of group development.[35] The forming stage is characterized by unbridled optimism: "I believe we have a great team and will work well together. We all understand the importance of the project and intend to take it seriously." Optimism turns into reality shock in the storming stage: "No one has taken a leadership role. We have not made the project the priority that it deserves." The norming stage comes at about the halfway point in the project life cycle, in which people refocus and recommit: "You must make firm commitments to a specific time schedule." The performing stage is the dash to the finish as teammates show the discipline needed to meet the deadline.

This is the most famous of several lifecyle models of team development.[36] Groups don't necessarily go through those processes in that particular sequence, but all the processes are important. From a leadership perspective, it is particularly useful to know the two most fundamental phases of team functioning: a transition phase of planning and establishing the group's mission, goals, and processes, and an action phase in which the team executes the work activities that contribute directly to it performance goals.[37] Think about how often your study or project groups dive into their work without adequately tackling the transition phase and the problems that arise when they neglect that phase.

Critical Periods

Groups pass through critical periods, or times when they are particularly open to formative experiences.[38] The first such critical period is in the forming stage, at the first meeting, when the group establishes rules and roles that set longer-lasting precedents. A second critical period is the midway point between the initial meeting and a deadline (such as completing a project or making a presentation). At this point, the group has enough experience to understand its work; it comes to realize that time is becoming a scarce resource and it must get on with it; and there is enough time left to change its approach if necessary.

In the initial meeting, the group should establish desired norms, roles, and other determinants of effectiveness that are discussed throughout this chapter. At the second critical period (the midpoint), groups should renew or open lines of communication with outside constituencies. The group can use fresh information from its external environment to revise its approach to performing its task and ensure that it meets customer needs. Without these activities, groups may get off on the wrong foot from the beginning, and members may never revise their behavior in a needed direction.[39]

The Digital World

Researchers are using game theory to better understand teamwork. Game theory examines human behavior, and specifically decision making, in business and in social and behavioral sciences. *Game theory* is a blanket term for a number of different applications, but management teams are most interested in the research focused on economics and human behavior.

Game theory analyzes, among other things, independent decisions made by groups that interact with and depend on one another. Companies are learning from game theory how to encourage cooperation rather than competition, increase communication, and develop more effective teamwork. Companies also see value in using game theory to teach teamwork to employees. Gametheory.net is a website that explains game theory in an accessible way, including an entire section on the science of business strategy.

Teaming Challenges

psychological safety

When employees feel they can speak up honestly and freely without fear.

Fast-forming, fast-acting, temporary groups do not have the luxury of time to allow all necessary team processes to develop slowly and naturally. Practices that are particularly helpful in this context[40] include (1) emphasizing the team's purpose, including why it exists, what's at stake, and what its shared values are; (2) building **psychological safety**, making clear that people need to and can freely speak up, be honest, disagree, offer ideas, raise issues, share their knowledge, ask questions, or show fallibility without fear that others will think less of them or criticize them; (3) embracing failure, understanding that mistakes are inevitable, errors should be acknowledged, and learning as we go is a way to create new knowledge while we execute; and (4) putting conflict to work by explaining how we arrive at our views, expressing interest in one another's thinking and analyses, and attempting fully to understand and capitalize on others' diverse perspectives.[41]

The leader, and team members who want to help the team perform well, should ask for, expect, and model these behaviors.

Why Groups Sometimes Fail

LO 4

Team building does not necessarily progress smoothly and culminate in a well-oiled team and superb performance.[42] Some groups never do work out. Such groups can be frustrating for managers and members, who conclude that teams are a waste of time and that the difficulties are not worth the trouble.

It is not easy to build high-performance teams. *Teams* is often just a word management uses to describe merely putting people into groups. "Teams" sometimes are launched with little or no training or support systems. Both managers and group members need new skills to make a group work, including negotiating goals that everyone can get behind, delivering on promises made, speaking up in groups to share ideas and build cooperation, recognizing and getting along with people's different work styles, and finding constructive ways to deal with conflict.[43] Giving up some authority and control is very difficult for managers from traditional systems, but they have to realize they will gain control in the long run by creating stronger, better-performing units.

Teams should be properly empowered,[44] as discussed in Chapter 13. The benefits of teams are reduced when they are not allowed to make important decisions—in other words, when management doesn't trust them with important responsibilities. If teams must acquire permission for every innovative idea, they will revert to making safe, traditional decisions.[45]

Empowerment enhances team performance even among virtual teams. Empowerment for virtual teams includes thorough training in using the technologies and strong technical support from management. Some virtual teams have periodic face-to-face interactions, which help performance; empowerment is particularly helpful for virtual teams that don't often meet face to face.[46]

Empowerment enhances team performance even among virtual teams.

In a fast-moving business environment, the difference between success and failure often lies with whether people can rapidly form and contribute to one team after another as new opportunities and challenges arise. Teamwork fails when individuals have not considered what they bring to a team and how to bring out the best in others. To be successful, team members must apply clear thinking and appropriate practices.[47]

Building Effective Teams

All the processes just described form the building blocks of an effective work team. But what does it really mean for a team to be effective? Team effectiveness is defined by three criteria:[48]

1. *Team productivity.* The output of the team meets or exceeds the standards of quantity and quality expected by the customers, inside and outside the organization, who receive the team's goods or services.
2. *Member satisfaction.* Team members realize satisfaction of their personal needs.
3. *Member commitment.* Team members remain committed to working together again; that is, the group doesn't burn out and disintegrate after a grueling project. Looking back, the members are glad they were involved. In other words, effective teams remain viable and have good prospects for repeated success in the future.[49]

Performance Focus

The key element of effective teamwork is commitment to a common purpose.[50] The best teams are those that have been given an important performance challenge by management and then reach a common understanding and appreciation of their collective purpose. Without, a group will be just a bunch of individuals.

The best teams also work hard at developing a common understanding of how they will work together to achieve their purpose.[51] They discuss and agree on such details as how they will allocate tasks and how they will make decisions. The team should examine its performance strategies and be open to changing them when appropriate. Teams usually standardize at least some processes, but they should be willing to try creative new ideas if the situation calls for them.[52] With a clear, strong, motivating purpose and effective performance strategies, people pull together into a powerful force that has a chance to achieve extraordinary things.

The team's general purpose should be translated into specific, measurable performance goals.[53] You learned in Chapter 13 about how goals motivate individual performance. Performance can be defined by collective end products instead of an accumulation of individual products.[54] Team-based performance goals help define and distinguish the team's product, encourage communication within the team, energize and motivate team members, provide feedback on progress, signal team victories (and defeats), and ensure that people focus clearly on team results. It is not simple in practice, but teams with both difficult goals and incentives to attain them tend to achieve the highest performance levels.[55]

The best team-based measurement systems inform top management of the team's level of performance, and help the team understand its own processes and gauge its own progress. Ideally, the team plays the lead role in designing its own measurement system. This responsibility is a great indicator of whether the team is truly empowered.[56]

Teams, like individuals, need feedback on their performance. Feedback from customers is especially crucial. Some customers for the team's products are inside the organization. Teams should be responsible for satisfying customers and should be given or should seek performance feedback.

Better yet, wherever possible, teams should interact directly with external customers who make the ultimate buying decisions about their goods and services. External customers typically provide the most honest, and most crucial and useful, performance feedback of all.[57]

Bottom Line
Teams, with guidance from internal and external customers, should identify the nature of the results they want to achieve.
What characteristics should a team's goal have?

Motivating Teamwork

Sometimes people work less hard and are less productive when they are members of a group. Such **social loafing** occurs when individuals believe that their contributions are not important, others will do the work for them, their lack of effort will go undetected, or they will be the lone sucker if they work hard but others don't. Perhaps you have seen social loafing in some of your student teams.[58] Conversely, sometimes individuals work harder when they are members of a group than when they are working alone. This **social facilitation effect** occurs because individuals usually are more motivated when others are present, they are concerned with what others think of them, and they want to maintain a positive self-image.

A social facilitation effect is maintained—and a social loafing effect can be avoided—when group members know each other, they can observe and communicate with one another, clear performance goals exist, the task is meaningful to the people working on it, they believe that their efforts matter and others will not take advantage of them, and the culture supports teamwork.[59] Thus, under ideal circumstances, everyone works hard, contributes in concrete ways to the team's work, and is accountable to teammates.

> Accountability to one another, rather than just to the boss, is an essential aspect of good teamwork.

Accountability to one another, rather than just to the boss, is an essential aspect of good teamwork. Accountability inspires mutual commitment and trust.[60] Trust in your teammates—and their trust in you—may be the ultimate key to effectiveness.

Team effort also comes from designing the team's task to be motivating. Techniques for creating motivating tasks appear in the guidelines for job enrichment discussed in Chapter 13. Tasks are motivating when they use a variety of member skills and provide high task variety, identity, significance, autonomy, and performance feedback.

Ultimately, teamwork is motivated by tying rewards to team performance.[61] Further, combining individual and shared rewards can reduce social loafing and increase team performance.[62] If team performance can be measured validly, team-based rewards can be given accordingly.

It is not easy to move from a system of rewards based on individual performance to one based on team performance and cooperation. It also may not be appropriate unless people are truly interdependent and must collaborate to attain true team goals.[63] Team-based rewards, provided by about 30 percent of companies, often are combined with regular salaries and rewards based on individual performance.[64] At Whole Foods Market, members (employees) work in teams and receive bonuses based on labor costs and sales of their section of their store.[65]

If team performance is difficult to measure validly, then desired behaviors, activities, and processes that indicate good teamwork can be rewarded. Individuals in teams can be given differential rewards based on teamwork indicated by each person's active participation, cooperation, leadership, and other contributions to the team.

If team members are to be rewarded differentially, such decisions are better *not* left only to the boss.[66] They should be made by the team itself, through peer ratings or multirater evaluation systems. Why? Team members are in a better position to observe, know, and make valid reward allocations.

Member Contributions

Team members should be selected and trained so that they become effective contributors to the team. The teams themselves often hire their new members. MillerCoors Brewing Company and Eastman Chemical teams select members based on the results of tests designed to predict how well they will contribute to team success in an empowered environment. At website design firm Geonetric, team members are responsible for budgets and revenues, and present companywide project updates each month.[67]

Generally, the skills required by teams include technical or functional expertise, problem-solving and decision-making skills, and interpersonal skills. Some managers and teams mistakenly overemphasize some skills, particularly technical or functional ones, and

Social Enterprise

Co-working Reaches a New Level

Freelancers, entrepreneurs, and remote workers who prefer not to work at home often turn to nontraditional work locations to get their work done. Growing in popularity since the mid-2000s, co-working offers space on a temporary basis (daily, weekly, monthly) in which to work and connect with other people. Such interactions facilitate the exchange of business ideas, advice, and new project opportunities. "Having a place that's relaxed and comfortable is very good for creative type work," says David James, cofounder of Cowork Café. "There's a certain feeling that you get in a place like this you can't get in an office-type building."

One new co-working trend is to use space that is typically empty during the workday, such as high-end restaurants that are open to the public only at dinnertime. A start-up called Spacious offers such space in several New York City restaurants. Another option is to use surplus retail space; a handful of Staples stores in the Boston area offer workspaces for rent in a partnership with a co-working company called Workbar.

Co-working providers that share restaurant or retail space must limit user benefits to avoid disrupting the intended use of the location. Others that offer their own space now offer lockers and storage space, dedicated workspaces (usually for a premium), and a growing list of amenities such as gyms, cafés and bars, and skills classes and workshops.

As office equipment shrinks in size from desktops to tablets and smartphones, and as the product of work becomes digital more than physical, the market for co-working space is growing rapidly, especially with so

©MANDEL NGAN/Getty Images

many freelancers and entrepreneurs making their way in the "gig economy." But even some larger companies like Cisco and KPMG are housing their employee teams in co-working spaces, to take advantage of an atmosphere that can foster communication, innovation, and collaborative working relationships.[68]

Questions

- Do you think co-working can help entrepreneurs or remote workers feel like part of a team? Could this be important? Why or why not?

- What do you think the owners of co-working spaces can do to promote collaboration and information sharing among their clients?

underemphasize the others. In one study, groups in which members shared sad feelings performed better at analytical tasks and difficult decisions, and groups did better at creative tasks if they shared positive emotions.[69] Learning to share emotions appropriately can contribute to team success. For the best team performance, all three types of skills should be represented, and developed, among team members.

The "Social Enterprise" box discusses an innovative way in which individuals contribute to one another's success.

Norms

Norms are shared beliefs about how people should think and behave. For example, some people like to keep information and knowledge to themselves, but teams should try to establish a norm of knowledge sharing because it can improve team performance.[70] Teams perform better when they think and talk about their tasks and about how they interact with and depend on one another.[71]

From the organization's standpoint, norms can be positive or negative. In some teams, everyone works hard; in other groups, employees are anti-management and do as little work as possible. Some groups develop norms of taking risks, others of being conservative.[72]

norms

Shared beliefs about how people should think and behave.

The mission of Cassini Imaging Science Team is to guide the cameras that take photos of the outer reaches of space. Though the team is widely dispersed (members' locations include New York, California, and Belgium), they are united by a shared sense of purpose and a high value placed on scientific knowledge and technical excellence.

Source: NASA, ESA and A. Nota

roles

Different sets of expectations for how different individuals should behave.

task specialist role

An individual who has more advanced job-related skills and abilities than other group members possess.

team maintenance role

Individual who develops and maintains team harmony.

cohesiveness

The degree to which a group is attractive to its members, members are motivated to remain in the group, and members influence one another.

A norm could dictate that employees speak either favorably or critically of the company. Team members may show concern about poor safety practices, drug and alcohol abuse, and employee theft, or they may not care about these issues (or may even condone such practices). Health consciousness is the norm among executives at some companies, but smoking is a norm at tobacco companies. Some groups have norms of distrust and of being closed toward one another; but as you might guess, norms of trust and open discussion about conflict are better for group performance.[73]

A professor described his consulting experiences at two companies that exhibited different norms in their management teams.[74] At Federal Express Corporation, a young manager interrupted the professor's talk by proclaiming that a recent decision by top management ran counter to the professor's point about corporate planning. He was challenging top management to defend its decision. A hot debate ensued, and after an hour everyone went to lunch without a trace of hard feelings. But at another corporation, the professor opened a meeting by asking a group of top managers to describe the company's culture. There was silence. He asked again. More silence. Then someone passed him an unsigned note that read, "Dummy, can't you see that we can't speak our minds? Ask for the input anonymously, in writing." As you can see, norms are important and can vary greatly from one group to another.

Roles

Roles are different sets of expectations for how different individuals should behave. Whereas norms apply generally to all team members, different roles exist for different members within the norm structure.

Two important sets of roles must be performed.[75] **Task specialist roles** are filled by individuals who have particular job-related skills and abilities. These employees keep the team moving toward accomplishment of the objectives. **Team maintenance roles** develop and maintain harmony within the team. They boost morale, give support, provide humor, soothe hurt feelings, and generally exhibit a concern with members' well-being.

Note the similarity between these roles and the important task performance and group maintenance leadership behaviors you learned about in Chapter 12. Some of these roles will be more important than others at different times and under different circumstances. But these behaviors need not be carried out only by one or two leaders; any member of the team can assume them at any time. Both types of roles can be performed by different people at different times to create and maintain an effectively functioning work team.

Beyond what you read about in Chapter 12, what roles should team leaders perform? Superior leaders are better at relating, scouting, persuading, and empowering than are average team leaders.[76] *Relating* includes exhibiting more social and political awareness, caring for team members, and building trust. *Scouting* means seeking information from managers, peers, and specialists, and investigating problems systematically. *Persuading* means not only influencing the team members but also obtaining external support for teams. Empowering includes delegating authority, being flexible regarding team decisions, and coaching. Leaders also should roll up their sleeves and do real work to accomplish team goals, not just supervise.[77]

Finally, recall from Chapter 12 the importance of shared leadership, in which group members rotate or share leadership roles.[78]

Cohesiveness

One of the most important properties of a team is cohesiveness.[79] Expanding the Chapter 13 description, **cohesiveness** refers to how attractive the team is to its members, how motivated members are to remain in the team, and the degree to which team members influence one another. In general, it refers to how tightly knit the team is.

The Importance of Cohesiveness   Cohesiveness is important for two primary reasons. First, it contributes to member satisfaction. In a cohesive team, members communicate and get along well with one another. They feel good about being a part of the team. Even if their jobs are unfulfilling or the organization is oppressive, people gain some satisfaction from enjoying their co-workers.

Second, cohesiveness has a major impact on performance. A study of manufacturing teams showed that performance improvements in both quality and productivity occurred in the most cohesive unit, whereas conflict within another team prevented any quality or productivity improvements.[80] Sports fans read about this all the time. When teams are winning, players talk about the team being close, getting along well, and knowing one another's games. In contrast, players attribute losing to problems between teammates or general lack of teamwork.

Cohesiveness clearly can have a positive effect on performance.[81] But this interpretation is simplistic; exceptions to this intuitive relationship do occur. Tightly knit work groups also can be disruptive to the organization, such as when they sabotage the assembly line, get their boss fired, or enforce low performance norms.

When does high cohesiveness lead to good performance, and when does it result in poor performance? The ultimate outcome depends on the task and on whether the group has high or low performance norms.

The Task   If the task is to make a decision or solve a problem, cohesiveness can lead to poor performance. Groupthink (discussed in Chapter 3) occurs when a tightly knit group is so cooperative that agreeing with one another's opinions and refraining from criticizing others' ideas become norms. For a cohesive group to make good decisions, it should establish a norm of constructive disagreement. This type of debating is important for groups up to the level of boards of directors.[82] In top management teams it improves the companies' financial performance.[83]

But the effect of cohesiveness on performance can be positive, particularly if the task is to produce some tangible production output. In day-to-day work groups for which decision making is not the primary task, cohesiveness can enhance performance. However, that depends on the group's performance norms.[84]

Performance Norms   Some groups are better than others at ensuring that their members behave the way the group prefers. Cohesive groups are more effective than non-cohesive groups at norm enforcement. But the next question is, Do they have norms of high or low performance?

As Exhibit 14.3 shows, the highest performance occurs when a cohesive team has high-performance norms. But if a highly cohesive group has low-performance norms, that group

Bottom Line

Cohesive groups are better than non-cohesive groups at attaining the goals they want to attain; as a manager, you need to ensure that your team's goals represent good business results.
What happens if a team leader builds a cohesive team but fails to set the right goals?

EXHIBIT 14.3
Cohesiveness, Performance Norms, and Group Performance

	Performance norms	
	Low	**High**
Cohesiveness — High	High goal attainment (group's perspective) and lowest task performance (management's perspective)	High goal attainment and task performance
Cohesiveness — Low	Poor goal attainment and task performance	Moderate goal attainment and task performance

will have the worst performance. In the group's eyes, however, it will have succeeded in achieving its goal of poor performance.

Non-cohesive groups with high-performance norms can be effective from the company's standpoint. However, they won't be as productive as they would be if they were more cohesive. Non-cohesive groups with low-performance norms perform poorly, but they will not ruin things for management as effectively as can cohesive groups with low-performance norms.

Building Cohesiveness and High-Performance Norms

So, managers should build teams that are cohesive and have high-performance norms. The following actions can help create such teams:[85]

1. *Recruit members with similar attitudes, values, and backgrounds.* Similar individuals are more likely to get along with one another. Don't do this, though, if the team's task requires heterogeneous skills and inputs. For example, a homogeneous committee or board might make poor decisions because it will lack different information and viewpoints and may succumb to groupthink. Educational diversity and national diversity provide more benefits than limitations to groups' information use and application.[86]

2. *Maintain high entrance and socialization standards.* Teams and organizations that are difficult to get into have more prestige. Individuals who survive a difficult interview, selection, or training process will be proud of their accomplishment and feel more attachment to the team.

3. *Keep the team small* (but large enough to get the job done). The larger the group, the less important members may feel. Small teams make individuals feel like large contributors. Amazon uses a two-pizza rule when deciding how many people should be on a team. If two pizzas can feed the team (usually between 5 and 8 members), then the team is not too big.[87]

4. *Help the team succeed, and publicize its successes.* You can empower teams as well as individuals.[88] Be a path–goal leader who facilitates success; the experience of winning brings teams closer together. Then, if you inform superiors of your team's successes, members will believe they are part of an important, prestigious unit. Teams that get into a good performance track continue to perform well as time goes on; groups that don't often enter a downward spiral in which problems compound over time.[89]

5. *Be a participative leader.* Participation in decisions gets team members more involved with one another and striving toward goal accomplishment. Too much autocratic decision making from above can alienate the group from management.

6. *Present a challenge from outside the team.* Competition with other groups makes team members band together to defeat the enemy (witness what happens to school spirit before a big game against an arch-rival). Some of the greatest teams in business and in science have been focused on winning a competition.[90]

    But don't *you* become the outside threat. If team members dislike you as a boss, they will become more cohesive—but their performance norms will be against you, not with you.

7. *Tie rewards to team performance.* To a large degree, teams are motivated just as individuals are—they do the activities that are rewarded. Make sure that high-performing teams get the rewards they deserve and that poorly performing groups get fewer rewards. Bear in mind that not just monetary rewards but also recognition for good work are powerful motivators. Recognize and celebrate team accomplishments. The team will become more cohesive and perform better to reap more rewards. Performance goals will be high, the organization will benefit from higher team motivation and productivity, and the individual needs of team members will be better satisfied. Ideally, being a member of a high-performing team, recognized as such throughout the organization, becomes a badge of honor.[91]

But don't forget: strong cohesiveness encouraging too much agreeableness can be dysfunctional. For problem solving and decision making, the team should establish norms promoting an open, constructive atmosphere including honest disagreement over issues without personal conflict and animosity.[92]

boundary-spanning

Interacting with people in other groups, thus creating linkages between groups.

Managing Lateral Relationships

Teams do not function in a vacuum; they are interdependent with other teams. For example, **boundary-spanning** teams are responsible for interfacing with other teams to eliminate production bottlenecks, implement new processes, and work with suppliers on quality issues.[93] Boundary-spanning activities[94] are those that entail dealing with people outside the group.

LO 6

Managing Outward

Several vital roles (see Exhibit 14.4) link teams to their external environments—that is, to other individuals and groups both inside and outside the organization. One type of role that spans team boundaries is the **gatekeeper**, a team member who stays abreast of current information in scientific and other fields and informs the group of important developments. Information useful to the group also includes information about resources, trends, and political support throughout the corporation or the industry.[95]

General team strategies include informing, parading, and probing.[96] The **informing** strategy entails making decisions with the team and then telling outsiders of the team's intentions. **Parading** means that the team's strategy is to emphasize internal team building and achieve external visibility simultaneously. **Probing** involves a focus on external relations. This strategy requires team members to interact frequently with outsiders; diagnose the needs of customers, clients, and higher-ups; and experiment with solutions before taking action.

The appropriate balance between an internal and external strategic focus and between internal and external roles depends on the team's strategy and how much members need information, support, and resources from outside. When teams are very dependent on outsiders, probing is the best strategy. Parading teams perform at an intermediate level, and informing teams are likely to fail. They are too isolated from the outside groups on which they depend.

Informing or parading strategies are more effective for teams that are less dependent on outside groups—for example, established teams working on routine tasks in stable environments. But for most important work teams—task forces, new product teams, and strategic decision-making teams tackling unstructured problems in rapidly changing external environments—interfacing effectively with the outside is vital.

gatekeeper

A team member who keeps abreast of current developments and provides the team with relevant information.

informing

A team strategy that entails making decisions with the team and then informing outsiders of its intentions.

parading

A team strategy that entails simultaneously emphasizing internal team building and achieving external visibility.

probing

A team strategy that requires team members to interact frequently with outsiders, diagnose their needs, and experiment with solutions.

EXHIBIT 14.4

Teams Link to the External Environment in Different Ways

SOURCE: Adapted from Ancona, D. G., "Outward Bound: Strategies for Team Survival in an Organization," *Academy of Management Journal* 33 (1990), pp. 334–65.

Lateral Role Relationships

To repeat—teams do not function in a vacuum; they are interdependent with other teams. These interdependencies require coordination and leadership.[97] To understand the process and make it more productive, it helps to know the different types of lateral role relationships.

Different teams, like different individuals, have roles to perform.

Different teams, like different individuals, have roles to perform. As teams carry out their roles, several distinct patterns of working relationships develop:[98]

1. *Workflow relationships* emerge as materials are passed from one group to another. A group commonly receives work from one unit, processes it, and sends it to the next unit in the sequence. Your group, then, will come before some groups and after others in the process.

2. *Service relationships* exist when top management centralizes an activity to which a large number of other units must gain access. Common examples include technology services and administrative staff. Such units assist others to help them accomplish their goals.

3. *Advisory relationships* exist when teams with problems call on centralized sources of expert knowledge. For example, staff members in the human resources or legal department advise work teams when needed.

4. *Audit relationships* develop when people not directly in the chain of command evaluate the methods and performances of other teams. Financial auditors check the books, and technical auditors assess the methods and quality of the work.

5. *Stabilization relationships* involve auditing before the fact. In other words, teams sometimes must obtain clearance from others—for example, for large purchases—before they take action.

6. *Liaison relationships* involve intermediaries between teams. Managers often are called on to mediate conflict between two organizational units. Public relations people, sales managers, purchasing agents, and others who work across organizational boundaries serve in liaison roles as they maintain communications between the organization and the outside world.

By assessing each working relationship with another unit (from whom do we receive work, and to whom do we send work? what permissions do we control, and to whom must we go for authorizations?), teams can better understand whom to contact and when, where, why, and how to do so. Coordination throughout the working system improves, problems are avoided or short-circuited before they get too serious, and performance improves.[99]

Managing Conflict

LO 7

The complex maze of interdependencies provides many opportunities for conflict to arise. Some conflict is constructive for the organization. Typically, conflict can foster creativity when it is about ideas rather than personalities. On the other hand, team members can work to maintain harmony during meetings, but unresolved differences can spill over into nasty remarks outside the office.[100]

Many factors cause great potential for destructive conflict: the sheer number and variety of interpersonal contacts, ambiguities in jurisdiction and responsibility, differences in goals, competition for scarce resources, different perspectives held by members of different units, and varying time horizons in which some units attend to long-term considerations and others focus on short-term need. For many reasons, and very commonly, subgroups form along conflict fault lines.[101]

Both demographic and cross-functional heterogeneity initially lead to problems such as stress, lower cooperation, and lower cohesiveness.[102] Transformational leadership (Chapter 13), effective diversity management (Chapter 11), and constructive conflict management (discussed next) can reduce the problems and help realize the often-untapped potential benefits of groups.[103]

Conflict Styles

People inevitably disagree and have deeper conflicts, and must decide how to manage them. The aim should be to make the conflict productive—that is, to make those involved believe they have benefited rather than lost from the conflict.[104] People believe they have benefited from a conflict when (1) a new solution is implemented, the problem is solved, and it is unlikely to emerge again; and (2) work relationships have been strengthened and people believe they can work together productively in the future.

People handle conflict in different ways. You have your own style; others' styles may be similar or may differ. Styles depend in part on the home country's cultural norms. For example, as you learned in Chapter 6, people from some cultures are more concerned with collective than with individual interests, and they are more likely than managers in the United States to turn to higher authorities to make decisions rather than resolve conflicts themselves.[105]

Culture aside, any team or individual has several options regarding how to deal with conflicts.[106] These personal styles of dealing with conflict, shown in Exhibit 14.5, differ based on how much people strive to satisfy their own concerns (the assertiveness dimension) and how much they focus on satisfying the other party's concerns (the cooperation dimension).

For example, a common reaction to conflict is **avoidance**. Here, people do nothing to satisfy themselves or others. They ignore the problem by doing nothing at all, or address it by merely smoothing over or deemphasizing the disagreement. This, of course, fails to solve the problem or clear the air. In a large retail company, employees in the marketing department were tired of dealing with the limits placed on them by the security team of the company's information technology (IT) department. Marketing wanted more communication with consumers, while IT security was obsessed with protecting the company's data from unauthorized access. Avoiding direct conflict, but feeling good about taking action, the marketing group set up a website without telling anyone in IT security.[107]

Accommodation means cooperating on behalf of the other party but not being assertive about one's own interests. **Compromise** involves moderate attention to both parties' concerns, being neither highly cooperative nor highly assertive. This style results in satisficing

Teams inevitably face conflicts and must decide how to manage them.
©Juice Images/Glow Images RF

avoidance
A reaction to conflict that involves ignoring the problem by doing nothing at all or deemphasizing the disagreement.

accommodation
A style of dealing with conflict involving cooperation on behalf of the other party but not being assertive about one's own interests.

compromise
A style of dealing with conflict involving moderate attention to both parties' concerns.

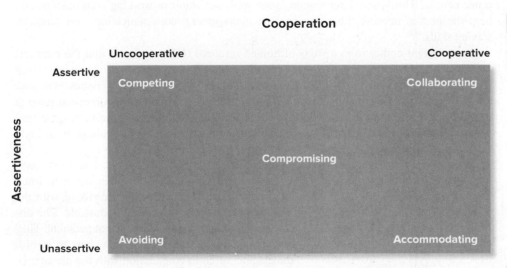

EXHIBIT 14.5
Conflict Management Strategies

SOURCE: Thomas, K., "Conflict and Conflict Management," *Handbook of Industrial and Organizational Psychology,* ed. M. D. Dunnette. Skokie, IL: Rand McNally, 1976.

competing

A style of dealing with conflict involving strong focus on one's own goals and little or no concern for the other person's goals.

collaboration

A style of dealing with conflict emphasizing both cooperation and assertiveness to maximize both parties' satisfaction.

superordinate goals

Higher-level goals taking priority over specific individual or group goals.

mediator

A third party who intervenes to help others manage their conflict.

but not optimizing solutions. **Competing** is when people focus strictly on their own wishes and are unwilling to recognize the other person's concerns. Finally, **collaboration** emphasizes both cooperation and assertiveness. The goal is to maximize satisfaction for both parties.

At the retail company in the previous example, a consulting firm called Solutionary discovered the website secretly created by the marketing group during a routine test of the company's computer network. The consultants hacked into the company's network and altered some information including some store prices. Knowing this would be simple for an outsider to do, the consultants used this to bring together the IT security people and the marketing people to find a solution that would meet marketing goals without compromising the company's data.[108]

Imagine you and a friend want to go to a movie together, and you have different movies in mind. If he insists that you go to his movie, he is showing the competing style. If you agree, even though you prefer another movie, you are accommodating. If one of you mentions a third movie that neither of you is excited about but both of you are willing to live with, you are compromising. If you realize you don't know all the options, do some research, and find another movie that you're both enthusiastic about, you are collaborating.

Different approaches are necessary at different times.[109] For example, *competing* can be necessary for cutting costs or dealing with other scarce resources. *Compromise* may be useful when people are under time pressure, when they need to achieve a temporary solution, or when collaboration fails. People should *accommodate* when they learn they are wrong or to minimize loss when they are outmatched. Even *avoiding* may be appropriate if the issue is trivial or resolving the conflict should be someone else's responsibility.

But when the conflict concerns important issues, when both sets of concerns are valid and important, when a creative solution is needed, and when commitment to the solution is vital to implementation, *collaboration* is the ideal approach. Collaboration is an open-minded discussion aimed at making the conflict constructive rather than destructive,[110] and includes airing feelings and opinions, addressing all concerns, and not letting personal attacks interfere with problem solving.

An important technique is to invoke **superordinate goals**—higher-level organizational goals toward which everyone should be striving and that ultimately need to take precedence over personal or unit preferences.[111] Collaboration offers the best chance of reaching mutually satisfactory solutions based on the ideas and interests of all parties and of maintaining and strengthening work relationships.

Being a Mediator

Managers spend a lot of time trying to resolve conflict between other people. You already may have served as a **mediator**, a third party intervening to help settle a conflict between other people. Third-party intervention, done well, can improve working relationships and help the parties improve their own conflict management, communication, and problem-solving skills.[112]

Some insight comes from a study of human resource (HR) managers and the conflicts with which they deal.[113] HR managers encounter every type of conflict imaginable: interpersonal difficulties from minor irritations to jealousy to fights; operations issues, including union issues, work assignments, overtime, and sick leave; discipline over infractions ranging from drug use and theft to sleeping on the job; sexual harassment and racial bias; pay and promotion issues; and feuds or strategic conflicts among divisions or individuals at the highest organizational levels.

In the study, the HR managers successfully settled most of the disputes. These managers typically follow a four-stage strategy, summarized in Exhibit 14.6. They *investigate* by interviewing the disputants and others and gathering more information. While talking with the disputants, they seek both parties' perspectives, remaining as neutral as possible. The discussion should stay issue oriented, not personal. They *review the findings* to determine how best to resolve the dispute, often in conjunction with the disputants' bosses. They do not assign blame prematurely; at this point they explore solutions.

HR managers encounter every type of conflict imaginable.

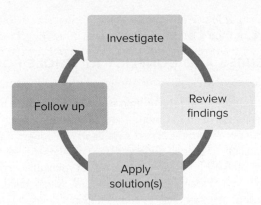

EXHIBIT 14.6
A Four-Stage Model of
Dispute Resolution

SOURCE: Adapted from Blum, M. and Wall Jr., J. A., "HRM: Managing Conflicts in the Firm," *Business Horizons,* May–June 1997, pp. 84–87.

They take action by *applying solutions* and explaining their decisions and the reasoning, and advise or train the disputants to avoid future incidents. And they *follow up* by making sure everyone understands the solution, documenting the conflict and the resolution, and monitoring the results by checking back with the disputants and their bosses. Throughout, the objectives of the HR people are to be fully informed so that they understand the conflict; to be active and assertive in trying to resolve it; to be as objective, neutral, and impartial as humanly possible; and to be flexible by modifying their approaches according to the situation.

Here are some other recommendations for managing conflict well.[114] Don't allow dysfunctional conflict to build, or hope or assume that it will go away. Address it before it escalates. Try to resolve it, and if the first efforts don't work, try others. And remember our earlier discussion of procedural justice (Chapter 13). Even if disputants are not happy with your decisions, it helps to strive for fairness, making a good-faith effort, and giving them a voice in the proceedings. Caring about others' goals as well as your own will help ensure a collaborative process. Remember, too, that you may be able to ask HR specialists to help with difficult conflicts.

Electronic and Virtual Conflict

When teams are geographically dispersed, as with virtual teams, team members tend to experience more conflict and less trust.[115] Conflict management affects the success of virtual teams.[116] In a recent study, avoidance hurt performance. Accommodation—conceding to others to maintain harmony rather than assertively attempting to negotiate integrative solutions—had no effect on performance. Collaboration had a positive effect on performance. The researchers also uncovered two surprises: compromise hurt performance, and competition helped performance. Compromises hurt because they often are watered-down, middle-of-the-road, suboptimal solutions. Competitive behavior was useful because the virtual teams were temporary and under time pressure, so having some individuals behave dominantly and impose decisions to achieve efficiency was more useful than detrimental.

When people have problems in business-to-business e-commerce—for example, costly delays—they tend to behave competitively and defensively rather than collaboratively.[117] Technical problems and recurring problems test people's patience. Conflict will escalate unless people use more cooperative, collaborative styles.

Try to prevent conflicts before they arise; for example, make sure your information system is running smoothly before linking with others. Monitor and reduce or eliminate problems as soon as possible. When problems do appear, express your willingness to cooperate, and then actually be cooperative. Even technical problems require the social skills of good management.

In the end, of course, conflicts in the complex web of human relationships are unavoidable, whether virtually or face to face. As you read "Management in Action: Onward," think about what Whole Foods needs to keep diverse employees working together constructively.

Management in Action

COHESIVENESS AND CONFLICT AT WHOLE FOODS MARKET

What unifies employees at Whole Foods Market is the sense of mission and shared values. Team members develop a sense of purpose, and the team monitors performance, making sure everyone contributes. In addition, unlike many retailers, Whole Foods schedules most of its employees for full-time work; this helps them learn about their jobs, build stronger relationships, and develop a greater commitment to the organization.

A challenge to cohesiveness, however, is one of the very values the company espouses: diversity. Whole Foods stresses its commitment to hiring employees from many different backgrounds. Compared with other supermarkets, its dress code offers wide latitude for personal style. To counteract misunderstandings that can occur when people come from different backgrounds and express themselves differently, the company expects team members to communicate frequently and respectfully and to show appreciation for what others contribute.

CEO John Mackey sees a role for competition as well as collaboration. The company encourages teams to compete with one another to be best at what they do. For example, the produce teams might strive to have the biggest sales increase in their region or among all the company's stores. The glory of being the best Whole Foods produce team is a compelling motivator, with or without a bonus. As team members collaborate in trying to outdo other teams, they build the sense of identity Mackey sees in what he considers the company's strongest teams. "The best part of my job is developing my team members and helping them on the path of success. . . . Nothing makes

me happier than seeing them start to move up the ranks and get more and more excited about Whole Foods and our products," says Leah McFadden, a team leader in the cheese department in Los Altos, California.

Beyond this kind of desirable competition among teams, conflicts do occur within teams. In one incident that recently made national news, two team members at a store in Albuquerque were suspended (with pay) after they became upset during a team meeting. At the meeting, discussion turned to the men's use of Spanish at work. The two men interpreted statements by the team leader to mean they were forbidden from speaking Spanish while on the job, and they became angry. Management saw their anger as "rude and disrespectful both in an office and in the store in front of customers," so the two were suspended.

Through official statements, Whole Foods said it uses English as its "default" language, especially for safety matters, but does not forbid the speaking of other languages. It added that its leadership team would soon review the company's language policy.[118]

- How does Whole Foods promote team cohesiveness? What else can it do?
- How should Whole Foods manage the conflict in its Albuquerque store? What should it do to minimize similar conflicts in the future?
- In 2017, Amazon bought Whole Foods. How is it doing, and how has the culture changed or remained the same?

KEY TERMS

accommodation, p. 419

autonomous work groups, p. 406

avoidance, p. 419

boundary-spanning, p. 417

cohesiveness, p. 414

collaboration, p. 420

competing, p. 420

compromise, p. 419

gatekeeper, p. 417

informing, p. 417

management teams, p. 405

mediator, p. 420

norms, p. 413

parading, p. 417

parallel teams, p. 405

probing, p. 417

project and development teams, p. 405

psychological safety, p. 410

roles, p. 414

self-designing teams, p. 407

self-managed teams, p. 406

social facilitation effect, p. 412

social loafing, p. 412

superordinate goals, p. 420

task specialist role, p. 414

team, p. 408

teaming, p. 405

team maintenance role, p. 414

transnational teams, p. 405

virtual teams, p. 405

work teams, p. 404

RETAINING WHAT YOU LEARNED

In Chapter 14, you learned that teams can help organizations be more effective, productive, and innovative. Compared to the past, teams now have more authority and may be self-managed. Teams come in several shapes and sizes, including work teams, project and development teams, parallel teams, management teams, transnational teams, and virtual teams. Groups that keep developing may go through stages: forming, storming, norming, and performing. A group generally becomes a team when team members commit to a purpose, pursue goals, and hold themselves accountable to one another. Moving from a traditional structure to a team-based approach tends to be challenging for many companies. Ways to build high-performance teams include establishing a common purpose, setting measurable goals, and making sure everyone works hard and contributes in meaningful ways. Team members perform important roles such as gatekeeping, informing, parading, and probing. Inevitably, conflict arises on teams. Five basic interpersonal approaches to managing conflict are avoidance, accommodation, compromise, competition, and collaboration. Techniques for managing conflict between other parties include acting as a mediator.

LO 1 Discuss how teams can contribute to an organization's effectiveness.

- Teams are building blocks for organization structure and forces for productivity, quality, cost savings, speed, change, and innovation.
- They potentially provide many benefits for both the organization and individual members.

LO 2 Describe different types of teams.

- Compared with traditional work groups that were closely supervised, today's teams have more authority and often are self-managed.
- Teams now are used in many more ways, for many more purposes, than in the past. Types of teams include work teams, project and development teams, parallel teams, management teams, transnational teams, and virtual teams.
- Work teams range from traditional groups with low autonomy to self-designing teams with high autonomy.

LO 3 Summarize how groups become teams.

- Groups carry on a variety of important developmental processes, including forming, storming, norming, and performing (see Exhibit 14.2).
- A true team has members who complement one another; who are committed to a common purpose, performance goals, and approach; and who hold themselves accountable to one another.

LO 4 Explain why groups sometimes fail.

- Teams do not always work well. Some companies underestimate the difficulties of moving to a team-based approach.

- Teams require training, empowerment, and a well-managed transition to make them work.
- Groups often fail to become effective teams unless managers and team members commit to the idea, understand what makes teams work, and implement appropriate practices.

LO 5 LO 5 Describe how to build an effective team.

- Create a team with a high-performance focus by establishing a common purpose, translating the purpose into measurable team goals, designing the team's task so it is intrinsically motivating, designing a team-based performance measurement system, and providing team rewards.
- Work to develop a common understanding of how the team will perform its task. Make it clear that everyone has to work hard and contribute in concrete ways.
- Establish mutual accountability and build trust among members.
- Examine the team's strategies periodically and be willing to adapt.
- Make sure members contribute fully by selecting them appropriately, training them, and ensuring that all important roles are carried out.
- Take steps to establish team cohesiveness and high-performance norms.

LO 6 List methods for managing a team's relationships with other teams.

- Don't manage inside the team only. Manage the team's relations with outsiders, too.
- Perform important roles such as gatekeeping, informing, parading, and probing.
- Identify the types of lateral role relationships you have with outsiders. This can help coordinate efforts throughout the work system.

LO 7 Identify ways to manage conflict.

- Managing lateral relationships well can prevent some conflict. But conflict arises because of the sheer number of contacts, ambiguities, goal differences, competition for scarce resources, and different perspectives and time horizons.
- Five basic interpersonal approaches to managing conflict can be used: avoidance, accommodation, compromise, competition, and collaboration. You should be willing and able to use them all, depending on the situation.
- Superordinate goals are higher-level organizational goals that can help generate a collaborative relationship if conflicting parties commit to them.
- As a manager, you undoubtedly will need to act as a mediator between conflicting parties; the chapter offers a number of useful strategies and tactics.

DISCUSSION QUESTIONS

1. Why do you think some people resist the idea of working in teams? How would you deal with their resistance?

2. Consider a job you have held. To what extent did you work in teams, and how effective was the teamwork? What determined your assessment?

3. Experts say that teams are a means, not an end. What do you think they mean? What do you think happens in a company that creates teams just for the sake of having teams because it's a fad or because it sounds good? How can this pitfall be avoided?

4. Choose a sports team with which you are familiar. Assess its effectiveness and discuss the factors that contribute to its successes and failures.

5. Assess the effectiveness, as in Question 4, of a student group with which you have been affiliated. Could anything have been done to make it more effective?

6. Consider the various roles members have to perform for a team to be effective. Which roles would play to your strengths, and which to your weaknesses? How can you become a better team member?

7. Discuss personal examples of virtual conflict and how they were managed, well or poorly.

8. What do you think is your most commonly used style in handling conflict? Least common? What can you do to expand your repertoire and become better at conflict management?

9. Generate real examples of how superordinate goals have helped resolve a conflict. Identify some current conflicts and provide some specific ideas for how superordinate goals could help.

10. Have you ever been part of a group that was self-managed? What was good about it, and what not so good? Why do many managers resist this idea? Why do some people love the idea of being a member of such a team, while others don't?

11. How might self-managed teams operate differently in different cultures? What are the advantages, disadvantages, and implications of homogeneous versus highly diverse self-managed teams?

EXPERIENTIAL EXERCISES

14.1 STUDENT PROJECT GROUP DEVELOPMENT

OBJECTIVE
To explore how students' project groups develop through various stages.

INSTRUCTIONS

1. Think about the last time you were assigned to a student group to complete a course-related project.

2. Next, write down how your group experienced (if at all) each of the four stages of group development: forming, storming, norming, and performing.

3. The instructor assigns students into groups of three and asks team members to share their answers with one another.

Student Project Group Processes Worksheet

Process	To what degree did your student project group experience this stage? Explain.
Forming	
Storming	
Norming	
Performing	

14.2 WHICH STYLE OF CONFLICT RESOLUTION WOULD YOU USE?

OBJECTIVE

To explore which conflict styles students would use in a variety of workplace scenarios.

INSTRUCTIONS

1. Read each of the following workplace scenarios.

2. Next, choose the conflict style being used by the individual in the scenario.

3. Describe why you think the conflict style will (or will not) help resolve the situation.

Conflict Styles

- Avoidance
- Accommodation
- Compromise
- Competing
- Collaboration

CONFLICT STYLE WORKSHEET

Scenario #1: While at work, Maria and her co-worker notice that a laptop is missing from an employee's cubicle (note that the employee is on vacation). Maria's first impulse is to report the missing laptop to the manager. However, her co-worker thinks there may be an innocent reason for the missing laptop. He wants Maria to join him in speaking with employees who are in the office. Maria agrees to team up with her co-worker but insists that if after one hour they haven't found the missing laptop, they would inform the manager.

Maria is using the _____ conflict style.

To what degree will this style help (or not help) resolve the situation?

_____

_____

_____

Scenario #2: Assume Paul is waiting to hear from his boss whether he is finally going to receive the promotion that he has been promised. Paul's boss just found out that the budget for the new position for which Paul was slotted has been cut. Consequently, he will not receive the promotion. His boss thinks she can get Paul a job transfer and promotion in another division in the company. She needs a few days to make it happen and doesn't want to discuss the situation with Paul until it is a done deal. Paul's boss intends to keep him busy with projects over the next few days until she finds out whether Paul receives the alternate promotion.

Paul's boss is using the _____ conflict style until she hears back from her contact in the other division.

To what degree will this style help (or not help) resolve the situation?

_____

_____

_____

Concluding Case

EXCEL PRO DRILLING SYSTEMS

Based in Alabama, Excel Pro Drilling Systems sells drilling equipment around the world. Its factories in Brazil, China, the Czech Republic, India, and South Africa run three shifts to keep up with strong demand in developing nations. Excel Pro enjoys profitability, but environmental groups have expressed concern about its impact on climate change. As executives explored their response, they saw that achieving more sustainable resource use also could make the company more efficient and create a more favorable business environment for the long term.

The executives decided to form a group called the Excel Pro Green Team, made up of representatives in each of its locations. Each facility's managers chose three employees, one each from engineering, production, and finance, with leadership skills, English-language ability, and interest in the topic of environmental sustainability. These 18 employees formed the Green Team.

To save money as well as fuel, the Green Team operates as a virtual team. Its members meet by videoconferencing once a month. Between meetings, they share thoughts via e-mail and in a social media–style page Excel Pro created for this purpose.

Initially, all the Green Team members were enthusiastic. The Czech and Brazilian representatives even came to the first meeting with specific ideas. Other team members were inspired to prepare ideas for the next meeting, but several were concerned that the team needed a plan establishing goals and a time line before the team addressed specific actions. Most of the third meeting was devoted to debating whether to establish an action plan or refine the ideas already submitted. Frustrated, the South African representatives took one idea to their facility's management for approval and began to implement it without telling the rest of the team.

By the fourth meeting, the representatives in India and the Czech Republic were openly complaining that meetings were always scheduled at times convenient for the headquarters employees. The Chinese team members agreed; in fact, one had quietly stopped attending meetings, although she did continue to participate in the exchange of e-mail ideas. The debate about whether headquarters should always schedule meetings lasted for 45 minutes, after which no one was in any mood to discuss sustainability.

Two of the Alabama team representatives took their frustration to their managers. The executive team investigated and decided the team needed to be unified behind a common goal. They directed the team to present three resource-saving ideas by the end of the year, and they offered a reward system to promote teamwork. The team members are each allocated 100 points a month. Whenever one team member appreciates another's actions, he or she gives that person points. All team members' point scores are viewable by the whole team at a shared website. At the end of the year, the points earned by each employee will be exchanged for cash rewards in the local currency. The executives hope the program will motivate greater cooperation.

DISCUSSION QUESTIONS

1. What went wrong in the formation of the Green Team? What should Excel Pro have done differently?

2. What conditions contribute to this team's cohesiveness? What reduces cohesiveness?

3. What do you think of the points plan? How should Excel Pro's management help the Green Team manage its conflict?

CHAPTER 15
Communicating

> The single biggest problem with communication is the illusion that it has taken place.
>
> —G. B. Shaw

©Nattanan Zia/Shutterstock.com RF

LEARNING OBJECTIVES

After studying Chapter 15, you will be able to:

LO 1 Discuss important advantages of two-way communication.

LO 2 Identify communication problems to avoid.

LO 3 Describe when and how to use the various communication channels.

LO 4 Summarize ways to become a better sender and receiver of information.

LO 5 Explain how to improve downward, upward, and horizontal communication.

LO 6 Summarize how to work with the company grapevine.

LO 7 Describe the boundaryless organization and its advantages.

CHAPTER OUTLINE

Interpersonal Communication
One-Way versus Two-Way Communication
Communication Pitfalls
Mixed Signals and Misperception
Oral and Written Channels
Digital Communication and Social Media
Media Richness

Improving Communication Skills
Improving Sender Skills
Improving Receiver Skills

Organizational Communication
Downward Communication
Upward Communication
Horizontal Communication
Informal Communication
Boundarylessness

Management in Action

SOUNDCLOUD PRIORITIZES INFORMATION FLOW

Where do Internet users go to upload and listen to high-quality music and sound and connect with its creators? The answer is SoundCloud, the start-up music- and audio-sharing platform that Alexander Ljung and Eric Wahlforss founded in a Berlin nightclub in 2008.

In a few short years their company has grown into a highly valued resource, not only for established and aspiring musicians but also for their fans, who can connect with them on the site, and for those who enjoy listening to university lectures, comedy acts, radio shows, and arts reviews. SoundCloud currently hosts more than 135 million high-quality tracks accessed by more than 175 million users, and it employs 300 people in four different locations: Berlin (still the headquarters), London, New York, and San Francisco.

Ljung and Wahlforss built the company culture as a collaborative and entrepreneurial environment that minimizes hierarchy and top-down management. "The aim of the organization/process is getting out of the way as much as possible for people to actually get the job done," says Wahlforss. Thus, product teams are responsible for creating their own workflows and communication flows, and product managers are charged with communicating their vision of the product to team members and ensuring that everyone takes ownership of it. "We aim to empower our employees rather than to control them," Wahlforss explains.

SoundCloud's flat organization and hands-off management style depend on a healthy flow of communication within and between the company's functional

©Bloomberg/Bloomberg/Getty Images

groups, as well as across four different time zones. That flow is supported by a company intranet and chat platform, and by regular "All Hands" meetings that everyone is expected to attend (remotely or in person in Berlin).

David Noël, in charge of the company's internal communications, chooses a theme for each meeting, and he or one of his team prepares an agenda, selects the speakers, and serves as host. Planning begins a few weeks in advance, and a run-through ensures that speakers are prepared and polished. Noël surveys all employees after every meeting, asking three brief questions: Was the meeting valuable? What did you like best? How can we improve the meeting?[1]

SoundCloud's All Hands meetings are so popular that some remote employees now meet for breakfast so they can participate in the Berlin event in real time rather than watch taped footage later. As you read this chapter, consider how free-flowing communication among employees can build commitment and empowerment.

Communicating effectively is a fundamental component of work performance and organizational effectiveness.[2] It is a primary means by which managers carry out the responsibilities described throughout this book, such as making group decisions, sharing a vision, interacting with external stakeholders, motivating employees, and leading teams. In this chapter, we present important communication concepts and practical guidelines for improving your own effectiveness. We also discuss communication throughout the organization.

Interpersonal Communication

communication

The transmission of information and meaning from one party to another through the use of shared symbols.

Communication is the transmission of information and meaning from one party to another through the use of shared symbols. Exhibit 15.1 shows a general model of how one person communicates with another.

The sender initiates the process by conveying information to the receiver—the person for whom the message is intended. The sender has a meaning she wishes to convey and encodes the meaning into symbols (chosen words). Then the sender transmits, or sends, the message through some channel, such as a verbal or written medium.

The receiver decodes the message (reads it) and attempts to interpret the sender's meaning. The receiver may provide feedback to the sender by encoding a message in response to the sender's message.

This sounds simple, but noise, or interference in the process, often blocks understanding. Noise could be anything that interferes with accurate communication: poor phone reception, poor listening while distracted by other things, or simple fatigue or stress.

one-way communication

A process in which information flows in only one direction—from the sender to the receiver, with no feedback loop.

The model in Exhibit 15.1 is more than a theoretical treatment of the process: it points out the key ways in which communications can break down. Mistakes can be made at each stage of the model. A manager who is alert to potential problems can perform each step carefully to ensure more effective communication. The model also helps explain the topics discussed next: the differences between one-way and two-way communication, communication pitfalls, mixed signals and misperception, and types of communication channels.

One-Way versus Two-Way Communication

 LO 1

In **one-way communication**, information flows in only one direction—from the sender to the receiver, without the feedback loop show in Exhibit 15.1. A CEO sends an e-mail to all employees without asking for a response. An employee phones the information technology (IT) department and leaves a message requesting repairs for her computer. A supervisor yells at a production worker about defects and then storms away.

two-way communication

A process in which information flows in two directions—the receiver provides feedback, and the sender is receptive to the feedback.

When receivers respond to senders—Person B becomes the sender and Person A the receiver—**two-way communication** has occurred. One-way communication in situations like those just described can become two-way if the manager's e-mail invites the receiver to reply with any questions, the IT department returns the employee's call and asks for details

EXHIBIT 15.1

A General Model of Communication

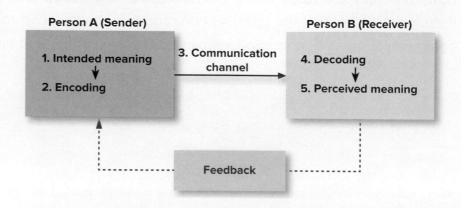

about the computer problem, and the supervisor calms down and listens to the production worker's explanation of what's wrong.

True two-way communication means not only that the receiver provides feedback but also that the sender is receptive to the feedback. In these constructive exchanges, information is shared between both parties, rather than merely delivered from one person to the other.

Because it is faster and easier for the sender, one-way communication is much more common than it should be. A busy executive finds it easier to dash off an e-mail message than to discuss a problem in person with a subordinate. Also, he doesn't have to deal with questions or challenges from someone who disagrees.

Two-way communication is more difficult and time-consuming than one-way communication. However, it is more accurate: fewer mistakes occur, and fewer problems arise later. When receivers have a chance to ask questions, share concerns, and make suggestions or modifications, they understand more precisely what the sender is communicating and what they should do with the information.[3] Effectively sharing information among teammates is a prime contributor to performance.[4]

These advantages of two-way communication are why Cisco manager Randy Pond wants to see and hear the people he is meeting with. If some participants are in remote locations, Pond, who is Cisco's executive vice president of operations, processes, and systems, uses a videoconference. During one such meeting, when Pond made a statement, he watched his colleagues on his computer screen and noticed that one put his head in his hands. Pond reminded the participants that he could see them, adding, "If you disagree, tell me." This prodding opened up a fuller discussion of the ideas under consideration.[5]

Communication Pitfalls

As we know from personal experience, the sender's intended message does not always get across to the receiver. You are operating under an illusion if you think there is a perfect correlation between what you say and what people hear.[6] Errors can occur in every stage of the communication process. In the encoding stage, people misuse words, fail to understand text abbreviations, leave out facts, or write confusing phrases. In the transmission stage, a message may get lost in a cluttered inbox, bullet points on PPT slides could be too small to read from the back of the room, or words might have ambiguous inflections.

Decoding problems arise when the receiver doesn't pay attention or reads too quickly and overlooks a key point. And of course receivers can misinterpret the message: A reader draws the wrong conclusion from an unclear text passage, a listener takes a general statement by the boss too personally, or a sideways glance is taken the wrong way.

More generally, people's perceptual and filtering processes create misinterpretations. **Perception** is the process of receiving and interpreting information. As you know, such processes are not perfectly objective. They are subjective because people's self-interested motives and attitudes create biased interpretations. People often assume that others share their views, and care more about their own views than those of others.[7] But perceptual differences get in the way of shared consensus.

To remedy this, it helps to remember that others' viewpoints are legitimate and to incorporate others' perspectives into your interpretation of issues.[8] Generally, understanding others' viewpoints is fundamental to working collaboratively. And your ability to take others' perspectives—for instance, really to understand the viewpoints of customers or suppliers—can strengthen your job performance.[9]

Filtering is the process of withholding, ignoring, or distorting information. Senders do this when they tell the boss what they think the boss wants to hear, or give unwarranted compliments rather than honest criticism. Receivers also filter information; they may fail to recognize a message's importance, or attend to some aspects of it but not others. Probably you have heard the saying: "So-and-so hears only what he wants to hear (or sees only what he wants to see)."

Sometimes managers, so as not to demotivate, soften or distort the fact that an employee needs to correct a problem behavior. A manager may sugarcoat the feedback by saying

perception

The process of receiving and interpreting information.

filtering

The process of withholding, ignoring, or distorting information.

"That wasn't bad" or "You'll get the hang of it after a while." Honesty, including better ideas or suggestions, works better.[10] You can start by giving a heads-up that something important and useful is coming.[11]

Because of such filtering and perceptual differences, you cannot assume the other person means what you think he means, or understands the meanings you intend. Managers need to interpret signals and adjust their own communication styles and perceptions to the people with whom they interact.[12] The very human tendencies to filter and perceive subjectively underlie much of the need for more effective communication practices that you will read about in the rest of this chapter.

Mixed Signals and Misperception

People inadvertently send mixed signals that can undermine the intended messages. Different people attend to different things, and people interpret the same thing in different ways. All of this creates problems in communication (see the "Social Enterprise" box example later in the chapter).

These problems are magnified if the communication is between people from different cultures.[13] Communication breakdowns often occur when business transactions take place between people from different countries.[14] Chapter 6 introduced you to the importance of such differences.

Any interpersonal situation holds potential for perceptual errors, filtering, and other communication breakdowns.

©Andor Bujdoso/Alamy Stock Photo RF

Here's an example highlighting how mixed signals lead to misperceptions. A bank CEO knew that to be competitive he had to downsize his organization, and the employees who remained would have to commit to better customer service, become more empowered, and really earn customer loyalty.[15] Knowing that his employees would have doubts and concerns about the coming reorganization, he promised that he would do his best to guarantee employment to the layoff survivors.

What signals did the CEO communicate to his people by his promise? One positive signal was that he cared about his people. But he also signaled that *he* would take care of *them,* thus undermining his goal of giving them more responsibility and empowering them. The employees wanted management to take responsibility for the market challenge that *they* needed to face—to handle things for them when in fact *they* needed to learn the new ways of doing business. Inadvertently, the CEO spoke to their backward-looking need for security when he had meant to make them see that the bank's future depended on their efforts.

However, the CEO did avoid one common pitfall at companies that announce plans for downsizing or outsourcing: ignoring the emotional significance of the message.[16] Sometimes managers are so intent on delivering the business rationale for the changes that they fail to acknowledge the human cost of layoffs. When employees hear a message that neglects to address their feelings, they usually interpret the message to mean that managers don't care.

Consider how many problems can be avoided if people take the time to (1) ensure that the receivers attend to the message they are sending, (2) consider the other party's frame of reference and attempt to convey the message with that viewpoint in mind, (3) take concrete steps to minimize perceptual errors and improper signals in both sending and receiving, and (4) send consistent messages.

You should make an effort to predict people's interpretations of your messages and think in terms of how they could misinterpret them. It helps to say not only what you mean but also what you don't mean. Every time you say "I am not saying *X,* I am saying *Y,*" you eliminate a possible misinterpretation.[17]

Oral and Written Channels

Communication can be sent through a variety of channels including oral, written, and digital. Each channel has advantages and disadvantages.

Oral communication includes face-to-face discussions, phone conversations, meetings, and formal presentations and speeches. Its advantages are that questions can be asked and answered, feedback is immediate and direct, the receiver(s) can sense the sender's sincerity (or lack thereof), and oral communication is more persuasive and sometimes less expensive than written. However, oral communication also has disadvantages: it can lead to spontaneous, ill-considered statements (and regret), and there is no permanent record of it (unless an effort is made to record it).

Written communication includes e-mail, memos, letters, reports, speadsheets, and other documents. Advantages to using written messages are that you can revise and perfect them and save them in a permanent record. Your message stays the same even if relayed through many people, and receivers have more time to analyze the message. Disadvantages are that the sender has no control over where, when, or if the message is read; the sender does not receive immediate feedback; the receiver may not understand parts of the message; and the message might not contain all the information others need.[18]

You should weigh these considerations when deciding whether to communicate orally or in writing. Also, sometimes use both channels, such as following up a meeting with a confirming memo, or writing an e-mail to prepare someone for your phone call.

Digital Communication and Social Media

Among other things, digital and social media at the workplace provide employees opportunities to communicate 24/7 from virtually anywhere in the world. Additional means of digital communication include videoconferencing like Skype for Business, Cisco's WebEx, and the newly launched Amazon Chime.[19] And you probably are very familiar with e-mail, instant messaging, text messaging, and selfies and videos.

Employers are catching up with consumers in their use of social media. For example, a recent survey of the Fortune 500 companies found that 70 percent of CEOs engage in at least one major social network (LinkedIn, Facebook, Twitter, Google Plus, YouTube, or Instagram).[20]

E-mail is one of the most convenient forms of communication, but what are some of the pitfalls? How often have you sent an e-mail, whether personal or professional, and found that someone misinterpreted the message?

©Comstock/Getty Images RF

Advantages Advantages of digital communication are numerous and dramatic. Within firms, the advantages include the sharing of more information and speed and efficiency in delivering routine messages to large numbers of people across vast geographic areas. Discussing ideas with colleagues in other cities is much faster and less expensive with teleconferencing or corporate social media than when the colleagues must travel to be at the same location.

For example, Microsoft's SharePoint allows companies to create websites that enable employees to collaborate on web pages, documents, lists, calendars, and data. Hitachi Solutions Europe helps client companies create SharePoint platforms to quickly respond to changing business needs and reduce their training costs.[21] Groupon, IBM, and Blue Cross/Blue Shield use the online platform Candor to gather ideas anonymously before participants meet in person to discuss.[22] This approach tends to yield a wider range of potential solutions.

Some research indicates that more data sharing and critical argumentation occur with a group decision support system than is found in face-to-face meetings, resulting in higher-quality decisions.[23] But anonymity tempts participants to make careless, rude, or ill-advised statements, so employers may require identities to be revealed or limit access to social networking technologies. However, a growing number of companies see services such as LinkedIn, Twitter, and Facebook as necessary for staying in touch with the hundreds of millions of people who use these services—especially younger generations of co-workers and customers who are likelier to check tweets and texts than voice mail and e-mail.[24] Complicating this trend is how employees use their own mobile devices and applications in the workplace (see "Multiple Generations at Work").

Disadvantages   Disadvantages of digital communication include the inability to pick up subtle, nonverbal, or inflectional cues about what the communicator is thinking or conveying, and difficulties in solving complex problems that require extended, face-to-face interactions. Plus, people are more willing to lie online.[25] In online bargaining—even before it begins—negotiators distrust one another more than in face-to-face negotiations. After the negotiation (compared with face-to-face negotiators), people usually are less satisfied with their outcomes, even when the outcomes are economically equivalent.[26]

Although organizations rely heavily on computer-aided communication for group decision making, face-to-face groups generally develop more trust among members, take less time, make higher-quality decisions, and are more satisfying for members.[27] E-mail is most appropriate for routine messages that do not require the exchange of large quantities of complex information. It is less suitable for confidential information, resolving conflicts, or negotiating.[28] Employees sometimes are laid off via e-mail and even text messages.[29] Not only do these more impersonal forms of communication cause hurt feelings, but an upset employee can also easily forward messages, and forwarding often has a snowball effect that can embarrass everyone involved.

Companies worry about leaks and negative portrayals, and may require employees to agree to specific guidelines before they post information on company review sites like Glassdoor.com or Salary.com.

Unisys, Sprint, and Hewlett-Packard provide training programs to help employees use social media in a productive manner. Guidelines for social media use include the following: (1) use reasonable etiquette and treat people respectfully; (2) identify and represent yourself (usually you are not representing your employer); (3) be factual and don't violate company disclosure policies; and (4) review the message before posting it (it will become a permanent record).[30]

Cisco employees in New York (left) and San Jose, California (on screen), meeting via monitor. What are the advantages and disadvantages to using this type of technology to communicate?

©Ariel Skelley/Getty Images RF

Two results of digital communication are a proliferation of negative and nasty messages, and misinterpretations. People hurl insults, vent frustration, snitch on co-workers to the boss, and otherwise breach protocol. The lack of nonverbal cues can result in kidding remarks being taken seriously, causing resentment and regret.[31] People see negative meanings in neutral messages[32] and are more likely to feel justified in lying.[33] Confidential messages—including details about people's personal lives and insulting, embarrassing remarks—can become public knowledge through digital leaks.

Other obstacles to effective digital communication are important to know.[34] Different people and sometimes different business units latch onto different channels as their medium of choice. For example, many Millennial employees and customers (born in 1980 or later) tend to ignore voice mail and infrequently check e-mail because they expect these messages to be mostly spam.[35] Another disadvantage is that digital messages sometimes are seen by those for whom they are not intended. Be careful with whether you click Reply or Reply to All. Most companies save all digital messages, and can use them in court cases to indict individuals or companies. Digital messages sent from work and on company-provided devices are private property—but they are private property of the system's owner, not of the sender.

Here's a golden rule (like the sunshine rule in the ethics chapter): Don't hit Send or post a comment unless you'd be comfortable having the contents become public and read by your mother or a competitor.

> Digital messages like texts and e-mails are private property of the system's owner, not of the sender.

Managing the Digital Load   Digital communication media are essential, but the sheer volume and variety of sources can be overwhelming.[36] Fortunately, a few rules of thumb can help; by one estimate, workers can improve their productivity in e-mail use alone by as much as 30 percent.[37]

With information overload, the challenge is to separate the truly important from the routine. Take control over your time by deciding how often you need to check e-mail, texts, and social media updates, and turn off the notifications when you are doing other things.[38] When you check messages, reply immediately if you can, so you handle each message only once, and use the organizational tools such as file folders. And avoid burdening others by copying them on messages they do not need to see.

Social media offer more efficient communication tools than e-mail. You can post answers to business questions on social media sites where it is far simpler to address the usual follow-up questions and forwards that accompany e-mail discussions.[39]

Management also has a role to play. Employees check messages constantly if they believe (perhaps correctly) that this is what their bosses or customers expect of them. Managers can help employees by establishing a "standard response time" policy that sets acceptable guidelines.[40]

Some companies recognize the downsides of digital media overuse. Atos, a French IT company, banned and replaced internal e-mail with an instant messaging software. Other companies like Reliable PSD and Graystone Industries are experimenting with "going e-mail free" for part of each workday or week.[41] And JPMorgan recently announced that it would be dropping voice-mail service for its retail banking employees. The move is expected to save about $3.2 million annually.[42]

The Virtual Office   Based on the philosophy that management's focus should be on what people do, not on where they are, the **virtual office** is a mobile office in which people can work anywhere—their home, car, airport, coffee houses, customers' offices—as long as they have the tools to communicate with customers and colleagues. Consulting firm Deloitte gives many of its employees the choice to work up to five days a week outside the office. When desired, employees can reserve a workspace at the company for the day.[43]

In the short run, at least, the benefits of virtual offices appear substantial. Saving money on rent and utilities is an obvious advantage. Deloitte saved 30 percent in office rental and

virtual office

A mobile office in which people can work anywhere, as long as they have the tools to communicate with customers and colleagues.

Multiple Generations at Work

Bring Your Own Device to Work (BYOD)

Many employees view their mobile devices as indispensible tools for both fun and work activities. According to Cheryl Tang, a senior manager for Symantec: "Today, work is no longer a place I go to, it's something I do." Organizations are adjusting to the changing times: nearly two-thirds of firms allow employees to use personal smartphones and tablets for work-related activities. VMware, a cloud-computing software company, has taken the next step by requiring all 6,000 employees in the United States to use personal smartphones for work.

As with so many things, both advantages and disadvantages come from allowing employees to use their own devices for work:

Advantages	Disadvantages
1. Reduces a company's equipment costs.	1. Increases risk of security breach and data loss.
2. Reduces training time since employee knows device.	2. Increases cost of supporting various devices.
3. Improves employee job satisfaction and morale.	3. Shifts purchase cost of devices to employees.
4. Boosts innovation as new applications are used.	4. Enables non-work-related activities.

A related trend known as "bring your own app" (BYOA) is when employees use their own applications for work-related purposes. For example, employees may find that transferring large files via Dropbox is faster and easier than using their company e-mail accounts. Though good for employee morale and innovation, unsecured devices and applications are vulnerable to security threats like hacking, lost data, or theft of the device.

Employee attitudes toward security matter, too. A recent study found that 70 percent of Millennials "admitted to bringing outside applications into the enterprise in violation of IT policies, compared to just 31 percent of Baby Boomers."

Mobile devices and boundaryless work are here to stay. A major goal for managers will continue to be how to balance employee independence and innovation with effective security policies.[44]

energy costs.[45] A virtual office gives employees access to whatever information they need from the company, whether they are in a meeting, visiting a client, or working from home.[46] Hiring and retaining talented people is easier because virtual offices support scheduling flexibility and may make it possible to keep an employee who wants to relocate—for example, with a spouse taking a new job in another city.

Web-hosting company Automattic, based in San Francisco, takes the virtual office to an extreme, and its people love it. Employees work at their homes in 28 states and 53 countries. For meetings, participants sign in to the Skype or Google+ Hangouts video chat service. If a topic is sensitive or a misunderstanding occurs, employees place a phone call (the traditional way or using Skype). For an informal chat, they often use the ICQ instant-messaging system.

Automattic has not abandoned face-to-face communication. Teams are encouraged to meet at least once a year in mutually agreed-on locations. And at a different location each year, the company hosts a weeklong grand meetup for everyone to gather, get acquainted, and talk strategy.[47]

But what will be the longer-term impact on productivity and morale? We may be in danger of losing too many human moments, those authentic encounters that happen only when two people are physically together.[48] Some people hate working at home. Some send texts or e-mails in the middle of the night—and others receive and reply to them. Some work around the clock and still feel they are not doing enough. The long hours of being constantly close to the technical tools of work can cause burnout.

The Digital World

Simple things can improve digital communication. When on a video call:

- Know where the camera is and remember to look at the camera instead of the screen to better connect with your audience.

- Choose your background (bookcase is better than bed) and always check what is behind you while on video (roommate, cat, messy piles of papers).

- Spend time practicing with the technology to look more professional and lessen the likelihood of technical issues.

- Move around as little as possible without looking rigid. What may seem like natural energy face-to-face can come across as fidgeting on camera.

- Wear solid colors because when small patterns are digitized they can look pixelated.

- Smiling is a surprisingly powerful way to connect with a digital audience. It indicates that you are happy to be there and increases voice inflection.

And some companies are learning that direct supervision at the office is necessary to maintain the quality of work, especially when employees are inexperienced and need guidance. The virtual office requires changes in how human beings work and interact, and presents technical challenges. So, although it is much hyped and useful, it will not completely replace real offices and face-to-face work.

Media Richness

Some communication channels convey more information than others. The amount of information a medium conveys is called **media richness**.[49] (See Exhibit 15.2 for a comparison.) The more information or cues a medium sends to the receiver, the richer the medium is.[50]

The richest media are more personal than technological, provide quick feedback, allow lots of descriptive language, and send different types of cues. Thus face-to-face communication is the richest medium because it offers a variety of cues in addition to words: tone of voice, facial expression, body language, and other nonverbal signals. It also allows more descriptive language than, say, an e-mail does. In addition, it affords more opportunity for the receiver to give feedback to and ask questions of the sender, turning one-way into two-way communication.

A phone conversation is less rich than face-to-face communication, and e-mail and texts are less rich yet. In general, you should send difficult and unusual messages through richer media, transmit simple and routine messages through less rich media, and use multiple media for important messages that you want to ensure people attend to and understand.[51] You should also consider factors such as which medium your receiver prefers, the preferred communication style in your organization, and cost.[52]

media richness
The degree to which a communication channel conveys information.

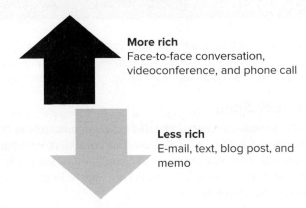

More rich
Face-to-face conversation, videoconference, and phone call

Less rich
E-mail, text, blog post, and memo

EXHIBIT 15.2
Differences in Media Richness

Management in Action

SOUNDCLOUD USES MULTIPLE CHANNELS

SoundCloud, the Internet's growing music and audio platform, takes the quality of its internal communications so seriously that it has put a top manager directly in charge of them. It's David Noël's job to help the company's 300 employees keep effortlessly in touch even though they work in four different cities: Berlin, London, New York, and San Francisco.

SoundCloud's flat structure and minimal organizational hierarchy mean employees carry a great deal of responsibility for communicating with each other, and the company's rapid growth and location in four time zones have raised challenges that called for creative solutions. Fortunately, the company has many communication channels to rely on.

SoundCloud's regular All Hands meeting takes place a few times each quarter and focuses on a theme, such as new products, quarterly objectives, or strategy. All employees are expected to attend, whether remotely in real time or via recorded video or, in Berlin, in person. The IT team helps maintain high production values, checking sound quality and camera angles, to make viewing the meetings as engaging as possible for SoundCloud's remote employees. Says Noël, "We want to make it feel just like everyone is in the same room." Employees can participate in the All Hands Q&A sessions directly or by submitting questions through the company's intranet or chat platform, however they feel comfortable, so the boldest and the shyest can all be heard from.

Other kinds of meetings that occur throughout the company are Town Halls and Open Houses. In Town Halls, team members gather to discuss goals and performance, and to kick off new projects or celebrate completed ones.

Open Houses are small and informal; they can center on new or surprising user research findings, product prototypes, or progress reports on new product launches. These meetings, according to Noël, "provide a way for people to stay informed about all of the things they choose to care about."

SoundCloud's new intranet was adopted as the company grew and people began to encounter difficulties sharing information with each other. Called Opus, it has many more features than the wiki it replaced and always features new content from the internal communications team, which encourages users to visit regularly. There is also a Q&A tool, a blog space, and a separate page for every team in the company to use for posting new information and sharing quarterly priorities.

For real-time communications, SoundCloud relies on Slack, the collaborative messaging platform, as well as Skype to connect the company's four far-flung offices. Noël credits these tools with allowing employees to have conversations they might not have had before, and to interact with people they might not approach in person. Slack also serves a social function, hosting separate discussion groups and channels for special interests and hobbies that bring together people from all over the company.[53]

- What benefits does SoundCloud enjoy from implementing so many different communication channels?
- How well do you think the company is supporting its employees' need to communicate across four different locations? What additional communication channels or tools could it add?

Improving Communication Skills

 Employers are dismayed by college graduates' poor communication skills. A demonstrated ability to communicate effectively will make you a more attractive job candidate. You can do many things to improve your communication skills, both as a sender and as a receiver.

Improving Sender Skills

To start, be aware that honest, direct, straight talk is important but all too rare. CEOs sometimes spin their messages for different audiences—the investment community, employees, government, or the board. This may or may not be straight talk: the focus of the messages can differ, but inconsistencies cause difficulties. People want to be able to identify a leader's perspective, reasoning, and intentions.[54]

EXHIBIT 15.3
Ten Ways to Add Power to
Your Presentations

"All the great speakers were bad speakers at first." Ralph Waldo Emerson

1. *Spend adequate time on the* **content** *of your presentation.* It's easy to get so distracted with PowerPoint slides or concern about delivery skills that the actual content of a presentation is neglected. Know your content inside and out; you'll be able to discuss it conversationally and won't be tempted to memorize. If you believe in what you're saying and *own* the material, you will convey enthusiasm and will be more relaxed.

2. *Clearly understand the* **objective** *of your presentation.* Answer this question with one sentence: "What do I want the audience to believe following this presentation?" Writing down your objective will help you focus on your bottom line. Everything else in a presentation—the structure, the words, the visuals—should support your objective.

3. **Tell** *the audience the* **purpose** *of the presentation.* As the saying goes, "Tell them what you're going to tell them, then tell them, then tell them what you've told them." Use a clear preview statement early on to help the audience know where you're taking them.

4. *Provide* **meaning,** *not just data.* Today information is widely available; you won't impress people by overloading them with data. People have limited attention spans and want presenters to help clarify the meaning of data.

5. **Practice, practice, practice.** Appearing polished and relaxed during a presentation requires rehearsal time. Practice making your points in a variety of ways. Above all, don't memorize a presentation's content.

6. *Remember that a presentation is more like a* **conversation** *than a speech.* Keep your tone conversational, yet professional. Audience members will be much more engaged if they feel you are talking with them rather than at them. Rely on PowerPoint slides or a broad outline to jog your memory.

7. *Remember the incredible power of* **eye contact.** Look at individual people in the audience. Try to have a series of one-on-one conversations with people in the room. This will calm you and help you connect with your audience.

8. **Allow imperfection.** If you forget what you were going to say, simply pause, look at your notes, and go on. Don't break character and effusively apologize or giggle or look mortified. Remember that an audience doesn't know your material nearly as well as you do and won't notice many mistakes.

9. *Be prepared to* **answer tough questions.** Try to anticipate the toughest questions you might receive. Plan your answers in advance. If you don't have an answer, acknowledge the fact and offer to get the information later.

10. *Provide a* **crisp wrap-up** *to a question-and-answer session.* Whenever possible, follow the Q&A period with a brief summary statement. Set up the Q&A session by saying, "We'll take questions for 10 minutes and then have a few closing remarks." This prevents your presentation from just winding down to a weak ending. Also, if you receive hostile or hard-to-answer questions, you'll have a chance to have the final word.

Lynn Hamilton, University of Virginia, class handout. Used with permission.

Beyond this basic point, senders can improve their skills in persuasion, writing, language, and nonverbal signaling. Exhibit 15.3 offers some useful tips on formal presentations; the following discussion focuses more on other keys to persuasion.

Presentation and Persuasion Skills   Throughout your career, you will be called on to state your case on a variety of issues. You will have information and perhaps an opinion or proposal to present to others. Typically, your goal will be to sell your idea. In other words, your challenge will be to persuade others to go along with your personal recommendation. As a leader, you will find that some of your toughest challenges arise when people do not want to do what has to be done. Leaders have to be persuasive to get people on board.[55]

Persuading others is an integral part of communicating effectively.

Persuasion is not what many people think: merely selling an idea or convincing others to see things your way. Don't assume that it takes a "my way or the highway" approach, with a one-shot effort to make a hard sell without compromise.[56] Usually it is more constructive to consider persuasion a process of learning from each other and negotiating a shared solution.

Persuasive speakers are seen as authentic, which happens when speakers are open with the audience, make a connection, demonstrate passion, and show they are listening as well as speaking. As a speaker, you can practice this kind of authenticity by adopting the body language you use when you're around people you're comfortable with, planning how to engage directly with your listeners, identifying the reasons you care about your topic, and watching for nonverbal cues plus fully engaging when you listen to audience comments and questions.[57]

The most powerful and persuasive messages are simple and informative, are told with stories and anecdotes, and convey excitement.[58] People are more likely to remember and buy into your message if you express it as a story that is simple, unexpected, concrete, and credible and that includes emotional content.

For example, the Chicago energy company Exelon wanted to build employee support for its corporate values. To teach about diversity, the company posted videos of its executives making personal statements about what diversity means to them. A finance executive told about being from a working-class family in England and feeling like an outsider when he took a job in a bank where most of the employees came from the upper class. When this manager asserted, "I never want anyone else to feel that way," his openness about his own life made his statement more powerful.[59] Then, to be credible, a communicator backs up the message with actions consistent with the words.

Writing Skills   Effective writing is more than correct spelling, punctuation, and grammar (although these help). Good writing above all requires clear, logical thinking.[60] The act of writing can be a powerful thinking aid, because you have to think about what you really want to say and what the logic is behind your message.[61]

You want people to find your writing readable and interesting. Strive for clarity, organization, readability, and brevity.[62] Brevity is much appreciated by readers who are overloaded with documents, including e-mail. Help e-mail recipients manage the flood of information by providing specific subject lines, putting your main point at the beginning of the message, limiting paragraphs to five lines or less, and avoiding sarcasm or caustic humor (which can be misinterpreted, especially when readers are scanning messages in a hurry).[63]

Your first draft rarely is as good as it could be. If you have time, revise it. Take the reader into consideration. Go through your entire message and delete all unnecessary words, sentences, and paragraphs. Use specific, concrete words rather than abstract phrases. Instead of saying, "A period of unfavorable weather set in," say, "It rained every day for a week."

Language   Word choice can enhance or interfere with communication effectiveness. For example, jargon is a form of shorthand and can make communication more effective when both the sender and the receiver know the buzzwords. But when the receiver is unfamiliar with the jargon, misunderstandings result. This occurs often when people from different functional areas or disciplines communicate with one another. As in writing, simplicity usually helps.

Whether speaking or writing, you should consider the receiver's background—cultural as well as technical—and adjust your language accordingly. When you are receiving, don't assume that your understanding is the same as the speaker's intentions. Cisco CEO John Chambers, whose background is in business, simply asks the engineering managers in his high-tech company to explain any jargon. He says, "They do it remarkably well."[64] At the same time, Chambers shows respect and enhances his credibility by being truly interested in their work. Whenever Chambers travels with or reviews engineers, he asks them to teach him a topic—and he listens.

The meaning of word choices also can vary by culture. Japanese people use the simple word *hai* (yes) to convey that they understand what is being said; it does not necessarily mean that they agree. Asian business people rarely use the direct "no," using more subtle or tangential ways of disagreeing.[65] Similarly, Japanese speakers apologize more often than Americans; the Japanese focus on the potential of an apology to repair damage in relationships, whereas U.S. speakers interpret apologies as admissions of guilt and therefore avoid them.

Global teams fail when members have difficulties communicating because of language, cultural, and geographic barriers. Heterogeneity harms team functioning at first. But when they develop ways to interact and communicate, teams develop a common identity and perform well.[66]

Global teams fail when members have difficulty communicating because of language, cultural, and geographic barriers. What could you do to overcome these barriers?

©Morsa Images/Getty Images RF

When conducting business overseas, try to learn something about the other country's language and customs. Americans are less likely to do this than people from some other cultures; most Americans do not consider a foreign language necessary for doing business abroad, and most U.S. firms do not require employees sent abroad to know the local language.[67] But those who do will have an edge over their competitors who do not.[68] Making the effort to learn the local language builds rapport, sets a proper tone for doing business, aids in adjustment to culture shock, and can help you get inside the other culture.[69] You will learn more about how people think, feel, and behave, both in their lives and in their business dealings.

> Those who learn host country languages and customs will have an edge over their competitors who do not.

Nonverbal Skills People send and interpret signals other than those that are spoken or written. Nonverbal messages can support or undermine the stated message. Often nonverbal cues make a greater impact than other signals. In employees' eyes, managers' actions often speak louder than the words they choose.

In conversation, except when you intend to convey a negative message, you should give nonverbal signals that express warmth, respect, concern, a feeling of equality, and a willingness to listen. Negative nonverbal signals show coolness, disrespect, lack of interest, and a feeling of superiority.[70] The following suggestions can help you send positive nonverbal signals.

First, use time appropriately. Don't keep your employees (or teammates, or bosses!) waiting to see you. Devote sufficient time to your meetings with them and communicate frequently to show your interest in their concerns. Second, make your office arrangement conducive to open communication. A seating arrangement that avoids separation of people helps establish a warm, cooperative atmosphere (in contrast, an arrangement in which you sit behind your desk and your subordinate sits before you creates a more intimidating, authoritative environment).[71] Third, remember your body language. Facial expression and tone of voice can account for much of the communication between two people.[72]

©Sam Edwards/AGE Fotostock RF

Several nonverbal body signals convey a positive attitude toward the other person: assuming a position close to the person; gesturing frequently; maintaining eye contact; smiling; having an open body orientation, such as facing the other person directly; uncrossing the arms; and leaning forward to convey interest in what the other person is saying. To show

Social Enterprise

When the Message Is a Story

Everyone loves a good story, but for social enterprises, storytelling also serves a critical function. More than mere facts, analysis, or numerical data, a well-told story informs stakeholders about the work of the organization, builds their commitment and advocacy, spreads the word about the organization's impact, and can even help secure funding that contributes to its survival. Stories can establish a shared vision with readers or listeners, and motivate them to join the social enterprise's campaign or become part of its community.

Says Summer Edwards, founder of Social Impact Stories, a consulting company, "Knowing your impact and then communicating it to your audience enables you to connect with your donors or customers on a deeply empathetic level. Human beings are social creatures and the power of storytelling transports us into another person's world, creating a sense of connection, and inspiring empathy and action."

From grant and funding applications to case studies, blogs, press releases, social media pages, reports for stakeholders, documentary films, and online photo essays, social enterprises can tell their stories in many creative ways. The goal of the message is to engage the receivers' emotions and imaginations, and motivate them to act.

For example, DoSomething.org, which aims to involve more teens in volunteering, used a visual presentation to tell the story behind some demographic data it uncovered. That led one audience member to an important realization: that there was untapped growth potential for the organization's work among white male college students in the northwestern United States.

Success stories about people whose lives have been changed by a social enterprise are especially powerful, and some firms specialize in helping SEs uncover and communicate these victories. The Sundance Institute's Stories of Change program, for instance, brings independent filmmakers and social entrepreneurs together "to support the creation of compelling films about solutions to urgent social issues that enlighten and inspire audiences."

Another resource is the Social Enterprise Alliance, a membership organization for SEs that helps them spread success stories like that of Tevin, a young New Orleans man. Tevin received training and job placement as a chef from a New Orleans SE called Liberty's Kitchen, but he still cherished the dream of becoming an artist. With the help of a mentor found for him by Liberty's Kitchen, Tevin enrolled in a community college design program, where he is working toward a degree, and he has become a youth mentor himself. Liberty's Kitchen's blog tells his story and those of many others.[73]

Questions

- Why is storytelling a more powerful tool for change than a list of results or facts?
- What do social enterprises need to know about their audiences in order to successfully communicate their stories? Why?

confidence, managers (and employees, too) should make eye contact, use a firm handshake, dress professionally, and speak in an appropriate tone of voice.[74]

Silence is an interesting nonverbal signal. The average American is said to spend about twice as many hours per day in conversation as the average Japanese.[75] North Americans tend to talk to fill silences; Japanese allow long silences to develop, believing they can get to know people better. Japanese believe that two people with good rapport will know each other's thoughts. The need to use words implies a lack of understanding.

Improving Receiver Skills

Once you become effective at sending oral, written, and nonverbal messages, you are halfway toward becoming a complete communicator. However, you must also develop adequate receiving capabilities. Receivers need good listening, reading, and observational skills.

Listening   Managers need good listening skills. Although people often assume that good listening is easy and natural, in fact it is difficult and not nearly as common as needed. Consultant Bernard Ferrari saw this challenge in a meeting of an industrial company's chief marketing officer (CMO) and the team that had introduced a new product that was not selling. The CMO listened carefully as the engineers explained how great the product was. She then asked what customers were saying that might explain the lack of orders. The engineers admitted they had not spoken with any customers; rather, they had been careful not to leak any information while the product was under development and assumed that customers would clearly see its value. Because the CMO took time to listen to the engineers, instead of jumping to conclusions about their product, she and the engineers could devise a plan for them to begin talking to key people at the customer firms, and orders soon began flowing in.[76]

A basic technique called *reflection* helps people listen well.[77] **Reflection** is a process by which a person states what he or she believes the other person is saying. This technique places a greater emphasis on listening than on talking. When the listener reflects to the speaker, who then signals accuracy or corrects misunderstandings, the result is more effective two-way communication.

Besides using reflection, you can improve how well you listen by practicing the techniques described in Exhibit 15.4. (Note the date of the original source; some things don't change!) For managers, the stakes are high; failure to listen not only causes managers to miss good ideas but even drives employees to quit.[78]

Listening begins with personal contact. Staying in the office, keeping the door closed, and eating lunch at your desk are sometimes necessary to get pressing work done, but that is no way to stay on top of what's going on. Better to walk the halls, initiate conversations, and go to lunch even with people outside your area.[79] Reed Hastings, CEO of Netflix, doesn't have an office. He stays connected by talking with employees as he works at empty desks around headquarters.[80]

reflection
Process by which a person states what he or she believes the other person is saying.

1. *Find an area of interest.* Even if you decide the topic is dull, ask yourself, "What is the speaker saying that I can use?"
2. *Judge content, not delivery.* Don't get caught up in the speaker's personality, mannerisms, speaking voice, or clothing. Instead, try to learn what the speaker knows.
3. *Hold your fire.* Rather than getting immediately excited by what the speaker seems to be saying, withhold evaluation until you understand the speaker's message.
4. *Listen for ideas.* Don't get bogged down in all the facts and details; focus on central ideas.
5. *Be flexible.* Have several systems for note taking and use the system best suited to the speaker's style. Don't take too many notes or try to force everything said by a disorganized speaker into a formal outline.
6. *Resist distraction.* Close the door, shut off the radio, move closer to the person talking, or ask him or her to speak louder. Don't look out the window or at papers on your desk.
7. *Exercise your mind.* Some people tune out when the material gets difficult. Develop an appetite for a good mental challenge.
8. *Keep your mind open.* Many people get overly emotional when they hear words referring to their most deeply held convictions—for example, *union, subsidy, import, Republican* or *Democrat,* and *big business.* Try not to let your emotions interfere with comprehension.
9. *Capitalize on thought speed.* Take advantage of the fact that most people talk at a rate of about 125 words per minute, but most of us think at about four times that rate. Use those extra 400 words per minute to think about what the speaker is saying rather than turning your thoughts to something else.
10. *Work at listening.* Spend some energy. Don't just pretend you're paying attention. Show interest. Good listening is hard work, but the benefits outweigh the costs.

EXHIBIT 15.4
Ten Keys to Effective Listening

SOURCE: Nichols, Ralph G., "Listening Is a 10-Part Skill," *Nation's Business* 45 (July 1957), pp. 56–60. Cited in Huseman, R. C., Logue, C. M. and Freshley, D. L. eds., *Readings in Interpersonal and Organizational Communication.* Boston: Allyn & Bacon, 1977.

When a manager takes time to really listen to and get to know people, those same people think, "She's showing an interest in me" or "He's letting me know that I matter" or "She values my ideas and contributions." Trust develops.

Listening and learning from others are even more important for innovation than for routine work. Successful change and innovation come through lots of human contact.

Reading   Illiteracy is a significant problem in the United States as well as in other countries. Even if illiteracy is not a problem in your organization, reading mistakes are common and costly. As a receiver, for your own benefit, read messages as soon as possible, before it's too late to respond. You may skim most of your reading materials, but read important messages, documents, and passages slowly and carefully. Note important points for later referral.

Consider taking courses to increase your reading speed and comprehension skills. And don't limit your reading to items about your particular job skills or technical expertise; read materials that fall outside your immediate concerns. You never know when a creative idea that will help you in your work will be inspired by a novel, a biography, a sports story, or an article about a problem in another business or industry.

Observing   The best communicators are also good at observing and interpreting nonverbal communications. (As Yogi Berra said, "You can observe a lot by watching.") For example, by reading nonverbal cues, a presenter can determine how her talk is going and adjust her approach if necessary. Some companies train their sales forces to interpret the nonverbal signals of potential customers. People can decode nonverbal signals to determine whether a sender is being truthful or deceitful. Deceitful communicators tend to maintain less eye contact, make either more or fewer body movements than usual, and smile either too much or too little. Verbally, they offer fewer specifics than do truthful senders.[81]

A vital source of useful observations comes from personally visiting people, plants, and other sites to get a firsthand view.[82] Many corporate executives rely heavily on reports from the field and don't travel to remote locations to observe firsthand what is going on. Reports are no substitute for actually seeing things happen in practice. Frequent visits to the field and careful observation can help a manager develop deeper understanding of current operations, future prospects, and ideas for how to exploit capabilities fully.[83] Tools like the Rapid Plant Assessment are available for visiting managers to evaluate a plant's performance on such factors as safety, scheduling, teamwork, and inventory.[84]

Of course, you must accurately interpret what you observe. An American employee working at Razorfish in Shanghai was surprised to discover how much he was expected to socialize with his Chinese boss. Beyond attending occasional happy hours and lunches, the employee observed: "In China, it's really expected that you become friends with your boss and you go out and socialize in a way that doesn't happen in the U.S."[85]

Japanese are skilled at interpreting every nuance of voice and gesture, putting most Westerners at a disadvantage.[86] When one is conducting business in other countries, local guides can be invaluable not only to interpret language but to decode behavior at meetings, spot subtle hints and nonverbal cues, identify who the key people are, and tell you how the decision-making process operates.

Organizational Communication

 Communicating poorly or well affects individuals, relationships, groups and teams, and entire organizations.[87] Every minute of every day, countless bits of information are transmitted in small interactions and through every corner of every organization. The flow of information affects performance at every level. Communications travel downward, upward, horizontally, and informally.

Downward Communication

Downward communication refers to the flow of information from higher to lower levels in the organization's hierarchy. Examples include a manager giving an assignment to an assistant, a supervisor making an announcement to his subordinates, and a company president delivering a talk to her management team. Downward communication that provides relevant information can strengthen employee identification with the company, stimulate supportive attitudes, and help motivate decisions consistent with the organization's objectives.[88]

©Fuse/Getty Images RF

People must receive useful information to perform their jobs and become—and remain—loyal members of the organization. But they often lack adequate information.[89] One problem is information overload; they are bombarded with so much information that they fail to absorb it all. Much of it is not very important, but its volume causes some useful information to be lost.

downward communication

Information that flows from higher to lower levels in the organization's hierarchy.

A second problem is a lack of openness between managers and employees. Managers may believe "No news is good news," "I don't have time to keep them informed of everything they want to know," or "It's none of their business, anyway." Some managers withhold information even if sharing it would be useful.

A third problem is filtering, introduced earlier in the chapter. When messages are passed from one person to another, some information is left out. When a message passes through many people, each transmission may cause further information loss. The message also gets distorted as people add their own words or interpretations.

> As messages are communicated downward through successive organizational levels, much information is lost.

Filtering poses serious problems. As messages are communicated downward through successive organizational levels, much information is lost. The data in Exhibit 15.5 suggest that by the time messages reach lower levels, the receivers may get very little useful information. The smaller the number of authority levels through which communications must pass, the less information will be lost or distorted. Flatter organization offers the advantage of less filtering due to fewer hierarchical layers.

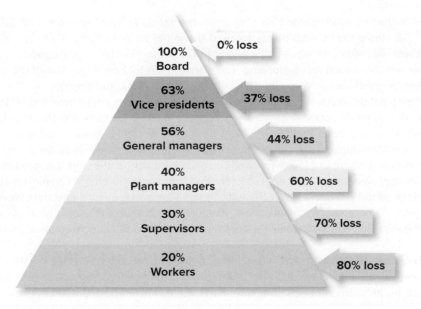

EXHIBIT 15.5

Information Loss in Downward Communication

- 100% Board — 0% loss
- 63% Vice presidents — 37% loss
- 56% General managers — 44% loss
- 40% Plant managers — 60% loss
- 30% Supervisors — 70% loss
- 20% Workers — 80% loss

Coaching   Some of the most important downward communications occur when managers give performance feedback to their direct reports. We discussed earlier the importance of giving feedback and positive reinforcement when it is deserved. It is also important to discuss poor performance explicitly and how to improve.

coaching

Dialogue with a goal of helping another be more effective and achieve his or her full potential on the job.

Coaching is dialogue with a goal of helping someone become more effective and achieve their full potential on the job.[90] When done properly, coaching develops executives and enhances performance.[91] Even CEOs desire coaching, especially in the areas of managing conflict, delegating, building teams, and mentoring.[92]

When people have performance problems or exhibit behaviors that need to be changed, coaching is often the best way to help them change and succeed. And coaching is not just for poor performers; as even the greatest athletes know, it is for anyone who is good and aspires to excellence. Although coaches for executives sometimes are hired from the outside, coaches from outside your organization may not understand fully the context in which you are working.[93] So don't take advice automatically. The best use of coaches is as sounding boards, helping you think through the potential impact of your ideas, generate new options, and learn from experience.

Companies such as Coca-Cola use coaching as an essential part of their executive development process. When done well, coaching is true dialogue between two committed people engaged in joint problem solving. Good coaching requires achieving real understanding of the problem, the person, and the situation; jointly generating ideas for what to do; and encouraging the person to improve. Good coaches ask a lot of questions, listen well, provide input, and encourage others to think for themselves. Effective coaching requires honesty, calmness, and supportiveness—all aided by a sincere desire to help. The ultimate and longest-lasting form of help is to help people think through and solve their own problems.

Downward Communication in Difficult Times   Managers frequently need to deliver bad news,[94] and proper downward communication can be particularly valuable during difficult times. During corporate mergers and acquisitions, people are anxious as they wonder how the changes will affect them. Ideally—and ethically—top management should communicate with employees about the change as early as possible.

But some argue against that approach, maintaining that informing employees about the reorganization might cause them to quit too early. Then too, top management often isolates itself, prompting rumors and anxiety. CEOs and other senior execs are surrounded by lawyers, investment bankers, and so on—people who are paid merely to make the deal happen, not to make it work.

Yet with the people who are affected by the deal, it's important to increase, not decrease, communication.[95]

In a merger of two Fortune 500 companies, two plants received very different information.[96] All employees at both plants received the initial letter from the CEO announcing the merger. But after that, one plant was kept in the dark while the other received continual information about what was happening. Top management told employees about the layoffs, transfers, promotions and demotions, and changes in pay, jobs, and benefits.

Which plant do you think fared better as the difficult transitional months unfolded? In both plants, the merger decreased employees' job satisfaction and commitment to the organization and increased their belief that the company was untrustworthy, dishonest, and uncaring. In the plant where employees got little information, these problems persisted for a long time. But in the plant where employees received complete information, the situation stabilized and attitudes improved toward their normal levels. Full communication helped employees survive an anxious period and offered symbolic value by signaling management's care and concern for employees. Without such communications, employee reactions to a merger or acquisition may be so negative that they undermine the corporate strategy and future performance.

Open-Book Management   Executives often are proud of their newsletters, staff meetings, videos, and other vehicles of downward communication. More often than not, the information provided concerns company sports teams, birthdays, and new copy machines.

But here is a more unconventional philosophy: **Open-book management** is the practice of sharing with employees at all levels of the organization vital information traditionally meant for management's eyes only. This information includes financial goals, income statements, budgets, sales, forecasts, and other relevant data about company performance and prospects. This practice is dramatically different from the usual closed-book approach in which people may or may not have a clue about how the company is doing, may or may not believe the things that management tells them, and may or may not believe that their personal performance makes a difference.

Open-book management is controversial because many managers prefer to keep such information to themselves. Sharing strategic plans and financial information with employees could lead to leaks to competitors or to employee dissatisfaction with compensation. Father of scientific management Frederick Taylor, early in the 20th century, would have considered opening the books to all employees idiotic.[97]

Rob Tolleson at CPO Commerce credits open-book management with saving his company from collapse. Due to a major IT malfunction, the online vendor of power tools struggled to figure out how to fulfill customers' orders. Employees, who had full access to company information, were able to work together for weeks to develop creative solutions until the company could stabilize itself.[98] And Hilcorp, an oil and gas exploration company that uses open book management, is one of the Fortune 100 best companies to work for.

However, the practice remains uncommon; only an estimated 4,000 U.S. firms are true believers.[99] Most firms apparently consider it too risky and/or too difficult. But perhaps managers in every company should consider carefully whether they provide their people with too much information, or too little.

Upward Communication

Upward communication travels from lower to higher ranks in the hierarchy. Good upward communication is important for several reasons.[100] First, managers learn what's going on. Management gains a more accurate picture of subordinates' work, accomplishments, problems, plans, attitudes, and ideas. Second, employees gain from the opportunity to communicate upward. People can relieve some of their frustrations and gain a stronger sense of participation in the enterprise. Third, effective upward communication facilitates downward communication as good listening becomes a two-way street.

The problems common in upward communication are similar to those for downward communication. Managers are bombarded with information and may neglect or miss information from below. Furthermore, some employees are not always open with their bosses; in other words, filtering occurs upward as well as downward. People tend to share only good news with their bosses and suppress bad news because they (1) want to appear competent; (2) mistrust their boss and fear being punished, even if the reported problem is not their fault; or (3) believe they are helping their boss if they shield him or her from problems.

For these and other reasons,[101] managers may not learn about important problems. As one leadership expert put it, "If the messages from below say you are doing a flawless job, send back for a more candid assessment."[102]

Managing Upward Communication   Generating useful information from below requires managers to both facilitate and motivate upward communication. For example, they could have an open-door policy and encourage people to use it, have lunch or coffee with employees, use surveys, institute a suggestion program, or hold town hall meetings. They can ask for advice, make informal plant visits, really think about and respond to employee suggestions, and distribute summaries of new ideas and practices inspired by employee suggestions and actions.[103]

Some executives practice MBWA (management by wandering around). That term refers simply to getting out of the office, walking around, and talking frequently and informally with employees.[104] Over his 40-year career with Marriott Corporation, Bill Marriott would walk through many of the firm's hotels to speak with employees and to ensure they were delivering consistent, high-quality service to customers.[105]

Useful upward communication must be reinforced and not punished. The person who tries to talk to the manager about a problem must not be brushed off repeatedly. An announced open-door policy must truly be open-door. Ideally, people trust their bosses and know that they will not hold a grudge against whoever delivers negative information. Managers should truly listen and learn, not punish the messenger for being honest, and take constructive action on valid comments.

Horizontal Communication

Much information needs to be shared among people on the same hierarchical level. Such **horizontal communication** can take place among people in the same work team or in different departments. For example, a purchasing agent discusses a problem with a production engineer, and a task force of department heads meets to discuss a particular concern. Communicating with others outside the firm, including potential investors, is another vital type of horizontal communication.[106]

Horizontal communication serves several important functions.[107] It shares information, coordinates activities, and allows problem solving among units. Effective dialogue between disagreeing individuals and units helps resolve conflict constructively.[108] By allowing interaction among peers, it provides social and emotional support to people. All these factors contribute to morale and effectiveness.

Managing Horizontal Communication
The need for horizontal communication is similar to the need for integration, discussed in Chapter 8. Particularly in complex environments, in which decisions in one unit affect another, information must be shared horizontally. Google provides space for ongoing horizontal communication in Google Cafés, which are designed to encourage more interaction among employees within and between teams.[109]

Applied Materials, a semiconductor equipment manufacturer in Santa Clara, California, took a sophisticated approach to managing horizontal communication. To improve the caliber and efficiency of its information technology (IT) group, the company outsourced routine tasks, cut the in-house IT workforce, and focused the remaining IT employees on supporting strategy. The IT workers were expected to collaborate with each other (and with customers) to develop and implement creative projects.

Applied Materials surveyed its IT staff to determine their communication patterns. About half of the IT people were communication hubs—that is, many colleagues consulted with them for ideas and questions. Those highly networked employees weren't necessarily managers; they were people at all levels whom others trusted and respected. The company assembled a team of 12 highly networked IT employees to share insights about what affected collaboration in the company. This team identified barriers, and Applied Materials used that information to provide coaching in better communication. A follow-up survey showed that more employees had become highly networked.[110]

Informal Communication

LO 6

Communications differ in their levels of formality. Formal communications are official, management-sanctioned episodes of information transmission. They can move upward, downward, or horizontally and often are preplanned and necessary for performing some task.

Informal communication is more unofficial. People gossip; employees complain about their bosses; friends talk about their favorite sports teams; work teams tell newcomers how to get by.[111]

The **grapevine** is the social network of informal communications. Informal networks provide people with information, help them solve problems, and teach them how to do their work. You should develop a good network of people willing and able to help.[112] However, the grapevine can be destructive when misinformation proliferates and harms people and operations.[113]

What does this mean for you personally? Don't overindulge in gossip, digital or otherwise. But don't avoid the grapevine, either.[114] Listen, but evaluate before believing what you hear. Who is the source, and how credible? Does the rumor make sense? Is it consistent or inconsistent with other things you know or have heard? Seek more information. Don't stir the pot.

Managing Informal Communication   Rumors start over any number of topics, including who's leaving, who's getting a promotion, salaries, job security, and costly mistakes. Rumors can destroy people's faith and trust in the company—and in each other. But the grapevine cannot be eliminated. Therefore, managers need to work with the grapevine.

The grapevine can be managed in several ways.[115] First, the manager who hears a story that could get out of hand should talk to the key people involved to get the facts and their perspectives. Don't allow malicious gossip.

It's hard to know how rumors get started, but we do know they happen.
©Bill Varie/Getty Images

Second, managers can prevent rumors from starting by explaining important events, providing facts, and working to establish open communications and trust over time. These efforts are especially important during times of uncertainty, such as after a merger or layoff or when sales slow down, because rumors increase along with anxiety.

Third, neutralize rumors once they have started. Disregard a rumor if it is ridiculous; confirm parts that are true; make public comments ("no comment" is seen as a confirmation of the rumor); deny the rumor if the denial is based in truth (don't make false denials); make sure communications about the issue are consistent; select a spokesperson of appropriate rank and knowledge; and hold town meetings if needed.[116]

Boundarylessness

Many executives and management scholars today consider open access to information in all directions to be an organizational imperative. Jack Welch, when he was CEO of General Electric, coined the now-famous word *boundarylessness*. A **boundaryless organization** is one that has no barriers to information flow. Instead of metaphorical barriers separating people and places, in "boundarylessness" organizations' ideas, information, and decisions move to where they are most needed.[117]

This free flow does not imply a random free-for-all of unlimited communication and information overload. It implies information available *as needed* moving *quickly and easily* enough that the organization functions far better as a whole than as separate parts.

GE's chief learning officer used the metaphor of the organization as a house having three kinds of boundaries: the floors and ceilings, the walls that separate the rooms, and the outside walls. These barriers correspond in organizations to the boundaries between different organizational levels, different units, and the organization and its external stakeholders—for example, suppliers and customers.[118]

GE's famous Workout program is a series of meetings for people across multiple hierarchical levels, characterized by extremely frank, tough discussions that break down even vertical boundaries. Hundreds of thousands of GE people have been through a Workout program.[119] Customers and suppliers participate in Workout programs as well, breaking down external boundaries.

GE uses plenty of additional techniques to break down boundaries. It relentlessly benchmarks competitors and organizations in other industries to learn best practices all over the world. GE places different functions together physically, such as engineering and manufacturing. It shares services across units. And sometimes it shares physical locations with its customers.

LO 7

boundaryless organization

Organization in which there are no barriers to information flow.

Management in Action

BOUNDARYLESS COMMUNICATION AT SOUNDCLOUD

SoundCloud, the music- and audio-sharing platform, has grown rapidly since its founding in 2008. When the company consisted of only a few dozen employees, it was easy for everyone to keep informed and connected. But although SoundCloud has managed to retain its flat organization and minimal hierarchy as it's grown, it did experience some communications challenges as the number of employees rose to about 300 people and operations expanded from Berlin headquarters to additional offices in London, San Francisco, and New York.

To address those challenges, the format of SoundCloud's regular companywide and team meetings has been honed over time to better serve the now larger employee community. The company's new intranet also helps keep employees in touch, as do Skype and Slack, the commercial messaging platforms. And SoundCloud has one more innovative tool for bringing people together and encouraging the free flow of information—a program it calls Cameos.

Cameos lets any SoundCloud employee request the opportunity to sit in on any other team's meeting or offsite event. For instance, David Noël, the company's director of internal communications, once attended an offsite meeting of engineering managers that was called to discuss the results of a workplace happiness survey. The only requirement for those using Cameos is that they must share at least one interesting fact about their own team, and in turn take one new idea back from the meeting to share with their team.

Even senior management's quarterly offsite meetings have been opened to Cameo appearances. Three employees, chosen at random from a pool of nominees, spent half a day each at a recent top-level meeting held offsite over a day and a half. Noël found that these employees' experiences, which they wrote about on the company blog, created a sense of transparency that helped everyone better understand management's plans for the future and their potential impact. The three employees themselves felt valued and rewarded by being asked to attend, and Cameo participants lined up quickly for the next leadership meeting.[120]

- In what other ways besides Cameos do you think SoundCloud could encourage internal communications that move in all directions?
- David Noël calls effective internal communications the "glue" that holds a thriving workplace together. What does this analogy mean? Do you agree or disagree with this idea?

Boundarylessness facilitates dialogue by turning barriers—physical or psychological—into permeable membranes. As the GE people put it, people from different parts of the organization need to learn "how to talk."[121] They must also learn "how to walk." That is, dialogue is essential, but it must be followed by commensurate action.

KEY TERMS

boundaryless organization, p. 449

coaching, p. 446

communication, p. 430

downward communication, p. 445

filtering, p. 431

grapevine, p. 448

horizontal communication, p. 448

media richness, p. 437

one-way communication, p. 430

open-book management, p. 447

perception, p. 431

reflection, p. 443

two-way communication, p. 430

upward communication, p. 447

virtual office, p. 435

RETAINING WHAT YOU LEARNED

In Chapter 15, you learned that there are key differences between one-way and two-way communication flows. One-way communication is faster and easier than two-way communication, but two-way communication is more accurate and results in better performance. Problems in communication can occur in all stages: encoding, transmission, decoding, and interpreting. Noise can complicate communication. Subjective perceptions and filtering are potential sources of error. Communications are sent through oral, written, and digital channels. People should weigh the advantages and disadvantages of each channel before sending a message. Digital media have a major impact on interpersonal and organizational communications. Media richness is one factor to consider as you decide which channels to use and how to use them. You can improve your writing and speaking skills n many ways. You also can actively manage downward, upward, and horizontal communications. The informal flow of communication (the grapevine) is important as well, and it too needs to be managed actively. Boundaries exist between different organizational levels, units, and organizations and external stakeholders. The boundaryless organization is one without major barriers to the flow of important communications.

LO 1   Discuss important advantages of two-way communication.

- One-way communication flows from the sender to the receiver with no feedback loop.
- In two-way communication, each person is both a sender and a receiver as both parties provide and react to information.
- One-way communication is faster and easier but less accurate than two-way; two-way communication is slower and more difficult but is more accurate and results in better performance.

LO 2   Identify communication problems to avoid.

- The communication process involves a sender who conveys information to a receiver.
- Problems in communication can occur in all stages: encoding, transmission, decoding, and interpreting.
- Noise in the system further complicates communication, creating more distortion. Moreover, feedback may be unavailable or misleading.
- Subjective perceptions and filtering add to the possibility of error.

LO 3   Describe when and how to use the various communication channels.

- Communications are sent through oral, written, and digital channels. All have important advantages and disadvantages that you should consider before choosing a channel.
- Digital media have a huge impact on interpersonal and organizational communications and make possible the virtual office.
- Key advantages of digital media are speed, cost, and efficiency, but the downsides are also significant, including information overload.
- Media richness, or how much and what sort of information a channel conveys, is one factor to consider as you decide which channels to use and how to use them both efficiently and effectively.

LO 4   Summarize ways to become a better sender and receiver of information.

- Practice writing, be critical of your work, and revise.
- Train yourself as a speaker. Use language carefully and well and work to overcome cross-cultural language differences. Be alert to the nonverbal signals that you send, including your use of time as perceived by other people.
- Know the common bad listening habits and work to overcome them. Read widely and engage in careful, firsthand observation and interpretation.

LO 5   Explain how to improve downward, upward, and horizontal communication.

- Actively manage communications in all directions. Engage in two-way communication more than one-way. Make information available to others.
- Useful approaches to downward communication include coaching, special communications during difficult periods, and open-book management.
- You should also both help and motivate people to communicate upward.
- Many mechanisms exist for enhancing horizontal communications.

LO 6   Summarize how to work with the company grapevine.

- The informal flow of information is important, just as formal communication is, to organizational effectiveness and employee morale.
- Managers must understand that the grapevine cannot be eliminated and should be managed actively.
- Many of the suggestions for managing formal communications apply also to managing the grapevine. Moreover, managers can take steps to prevent rumors or neutralize the ones that arise.

LO 7   Describe the boundaryless organization and its advantages.

- Boundaries—psychological if not physical—exist between different organizational levels, units, and organizations and external stakeholders.
- The boundaryless organization has no major barriers to the flow of important communications. Ideas, information, decisions, and actions move to where they are most needed.
- Relevant information should be available as needed so that the organization as a whole functions far better than as separate parts.

DISCUSSION QUESTIONS

1. Think of an occasion when you faced a miscommunication problem. What do you think caused the problem? How do you think it should have been handled better?

2. Have you ever *not* given someone information or opinions that perhaps you should have? Why? Was it the right thing to do? Why or why not? What would cause you to be glad that you provided (or withheld) negative

or difficult information? What would cause you to regret providing/withholding it?

3. Think back to discussions you have heard or participated in. Consider the differences between one-way and two-way communication. How can two one-ways be turned into a true two-way?

4. Share with the class some of your experiences—both good and bad—with digital media.

5. Report examples of mixed signals you have received (or sent). How can you reduce the potential for misunderstanding and misperception as you communicate with others?

6. What makes you want to say to someone, "You're not listening"?

7. What do you think about the practice of open-book management? What would you think about it if you were running your own company?

8. Discuss organizational rumors you have heard: what they were about, how they got started, how accurate they were, and how people reacted to them. What lessons can you learn from these episodes?

9. Refer to the "The Virtual Office" section. What do you think will be the long-term impact of the mobile office

on job satisfaction and performance? If you were a manager, how would you maximize the benefits and minimize the drawbacks? If you worked in this environment, how would you manage yourself to maximize your performance and avoid burnout?

10. Have you ever made or seen mistakes due to people not speaking a common language well? How do you or will you deal with others who do not speak the same language as you?

11. Have you ever tried to coach someone? What did you do well, and what mistakes did you make? How can you become a better coach?

12. Have you ever been coached by someone? What did he or she do well, and what mistakes were made? How was it for you to be on the receiving end of the coaching, and how did you respond? What is required to be successful as the receiver of someone else's coaching attempts?

13. Think about how companies communicate with Wall Street and the media and how analysts on TV communicate with viewers. What concepts from the chapter apply, and how can you become a more astute consumer of such information?

EXPERIENTIAL EXERCISES

15.1 INTERPRETING NONVERBAL COMMUNICATION

OBJECTIVE

To become more skilled at interpreting meanings associated with nonverbal communication.

INSTRUCTIONS

Assume your boss exhibits each of the four behaviors listed below over the course of a month. Read each behavior and then record your interpretation of what it most likely means.

Nonverbal Communication Interpretation Worksheet

Your boss . . .	You interpret this behavior to mean . . .
Arrives to the office earlier than usual and has a worried look on her face.	
Spends more time than any other manager when training new employees.	
Wears the same old jeans, T-shirt, and sneakers to work each day.	
Looks at her phone to read texts and e-mails several times per hour, even during meetings and one-on-one conversations.	

SOURCE: Adapted from Jauch, Laurence R. et al., *The Managerial Experience: Cases, Exercises, and Readings,* 5th ed. Boston: South-Western, 1989.

15.2 LISTENING SKILLS SURVEY

OBJECTIVES

1. To measure your skills as a listener.
2. To gain insight into the factors that determine good listening habits.
3. To demonstrate how you can become a better listener.

INSTRUCTIONS

1. Working alone, complete the Listening Skills Survey.
2. In small groups, compare scores, discuss survey test items, and prepare responses to the discussion questions.

3. After the class reconvenes, group spokespersons present group findings.

DISCUSSION QUESTIONS

1. In what ways did students' responses on the survey agree or disagree?
2. What do you think accounts for the differences?
3. How can the results of this survey be put to practical use?

Listening Skills Survey

To measure your listening skills, complete the following survey by circling the degree to which you agree with each statement.

	Strongly Agree	Agree	Neither Agree nor Disagree	Disagree	Strongly Disagree
1. I tend to be patient with the speaker, making sure she or he is finished speaking before I respond in any fashion.	5	4	3	2	1
2. When listening, I don't doodle or fiddle with papers and things that might distract me from the speaker.	5	4	3	2	1
3. I attempt to understand the speaker's point of view.	5	4	3	2	1
4. I try not to put the speaker on the defensive by arguing or criticizing.	5	4	3	2	1
5. When I listen, I focus on the speaker's feelings.	5	4	3	2	1
6. I let a speaker's annoying mannerisms distract me.	5	4	3	2	1
7. While the speaker is talking, I watch carefully for facial expressions and other types of body language.	5	4	3	2	1
8. I never talk when the other person is trying to say something.	5	4	3	2	1
9. During a conversation, a period of silence seems awkward to me.	5	4	3	2	1
10. I want people to just give me the facts and allow me to make up my own mind.	5	4	3	2	1
11. When the speaker is finished, I respond to his or her feelings.	5	4	3	2	1
12. I don't evaluate the speaker's words until she or he is finished talking.	5	4	3	2	1

15.3 ACTIVE LISTENING

This exercise involves triads. Each triad counts off into threes: 1, 2, 3, 1, 2, 3, and so on. In the first round, all the 1s in their respective triads take the pro position (see the topics given later in exercise), all the 2s take the con position, and all the 3s act as observers. After a topic is given, two individuals representing opposing viewpoints have one minute to collect their thoughts and then five to

seven minutes to arrive at a mutually agreeable position on that topic.

The observer should use the form here to capture actual examples of what the individuals said or did that indicated active and less-than-active listening. When time is called, the pro individuals share their opinion of which listening behaviors they performed well and which ones they'd like to improve. Then the con individuals do the same. Finally, the observers share their observations and insights, using examples to reinforce their feedback.

If additional rounds are used, rotate the roles so that each person plays a speaking role and, if possible, an observing role.

Round 1:
Topic selected: _____
Notes:

Round 2:
Topic selected: _____
Notes:

Listening Feedback Form

Indicators of Active Listening	Pro	Con
1. Asked questions for clarification		
2. Paraphrased the opposing view		
3. Responded to nonverbal cues (e.g., body posture, tone of voice)		
4. Appeared to move toward a mutually satisfying solution		
Indicators of Less-Than-Active Listening		
5. Interrupted before allowing the other person to finish		
6. Was defensive about her or his position		
7. Appeared to dominate the conversation		
8. Ignored nonverbal cue		

Potential topics to be used:

 1. Gun control
 2. Capital punishment
 3. Race as a criterion for college admission
 4. Prison reform
 5. U.S. intervention in wars outside the United States
 6. Legalization of marijuana
 7. Mandatory armed forces draft
 8. Interracial adoption
 9. Premarital and extramarital sex
10. Prayer in schools
11. Diversity in the workplace
12. Pornography on the Internet

QUESTIONS

1. Did you arrive at a mutually agreeable solution? What helped you get there?
2. What were some factors that hindered this process?
3. How comfortable did you feel arguing the position you were given? How did this influence your ability to listen actively?
4. If the position you were given was exactly opposite your values or beliefs, do you see this topic differently now than before the exercise?
5. What steps can you take to improve your ability to listen actively to friends or associates, especially when you don't agree with their viewpoint?

Concluding Case

BEST TRUST BANK

Best Trust Bank attracts accounts from households and businesses based on its broad name recognition and reputation for integrity. In this way, Best Trust has grown to one of the world's top 25 banks. Its 73,000 employees work at headquarters and in facilities located in 47 countries.

One of those employees is Paul Wysinsky, who in the 1970s took an entry-level job as a bank teller. As he developed a track record of satisfying customers, working efficiently, and cooperating well with others on his team, Paul moved up to teller supervisor, branch manager, and operations manager. He took business courses during the

evening, earned a master's degree, and worked his way up through middle management positions. Twenty years later, he was offered a vice president's job in the human resources division, responsible for recruiting and retaining Best Trust's employees in Houston. Eager to learn about a new part of the company, Paul tackled the new responsibilities so well that when there was an opening for a new executive vice president in charge of corporate human resources, Paul was tapped to run all of HR.

The nature of Paul's work communications changed considerably as he rose through the ranks. When Paul was a teller, he looked forward to chatting with his co-workers during breaks; their enjoyment of each other's company made the days pass pleasantly. His supervisor checked in with him regularly to make sure Paul understood his job. His favorite responsibility, though, was greeting customers and listening to them carefully, trying to guess the unspoken needs that Best Trust might be able to meet. When customers were upset about a problem, he used to get nervous; but with experience, he became an expert at listening attentively, helping the customer find the best possible solution, and speaking in a respectful tone that almost always soothed any frayed nerves.

Now that Paul is an executive vice president, he rarely talks with Best Trust's customers, and more of his communications are structured and formal. Although he cares about attracting, motivating, and retaining employees in all positions, he knows he cannot possibly have a dialogue with 73,000 people in dozens of countries. In fact, he can't even have personal conversations with all of the HR employees—Best Trust has more than 800 of them, including several at each facility.

Consequently, Paul looks for a variety of ways to communicate. He meets weekly with all the department and functional heads involved in formulating strategy. The meeting's agenda includes reviewing HR issues such as leadership development, succession planning, diversity management, and employee satisfaction. Paul is well prepared because he meets at least weekly with each of the managers who report directly to him. In these one-on-one meetings, Paul and the manager review progress on the issues handled by that manager. Paul also uses those meetings to learn what challenges the manager is facing so he can offer coaching and encouragement. And Paul looks for ways to meet with as many employees outside HR as he can. For example, he attends an annual employee recognition gathering held to honor the company's 800 top-performing employees. There he talks to as many people as he can. He asks open-ended questions such as "What are you happy about at Best Trust? What could we do better?"

Talking one on one to employees can feel like an escape from one of the chief annoyances of his job: poorly written messages from many of the bank's middle managers. It seems that Best Trust has excelled at finding people with strong analytic and customer service skills, but many of these people stumble at presenting an idea or summarizing their progress in e-mails and reports. Paul feels intense time pressure, and if he gets a suggestion but can't figure out the main idea in the first couple of sentences, he simply passes it to one of his managers for a possible follow-up. Paul suspects that good ideas and real problems are being missed. Rambling reports and presentations loaded with jargon seem to have become a norm at Best Trust, and Paul is thinking about adding a new training program to improve writing skills.

To get out the word about the bank's policies, benefits, and other initiatives, Paul uses a variety of media. He gives presentations at events such as the employee recognition gathering and at branches around the world. Four times a year, he records a video that is posted on the bank's intranet. Topics range from a summary of HR resources to interviews with key leaders at Best Trust. Also on the intranet, Paul leads regular town hall meetings, a live video feed that allows employees to post questions and ideas, which Paul and other executives answer immediately on the video.

Promotions to the executive level are not the only reason communication has changed for Paul at Best Trust. Another source of change is technology. When Paul was a teller, the Internet was just a concept, and transmitting data online was a major undertaking that required computer experts. Now the Internet is a basic tool. On the plus side, it helps Paul deliver information efficiently and keep up with far-flung colleagues. But Paul also has a whole set of policy concerns related to the Internet, such as whether to allow employees to access social networking sites and how closely to monitor blogs and other public information for company-related posts. When Paul thinks about it, he realizes that his communication skills have barely grown as fast as the communication demands of his work.

QUESTIONS

1. How has the media richness of Paul's communications changed since the days when he was a teller?

2. What sender and receiver skills are described in this case? Which ones need improvement? Offer one suggestion for improving the weak skills.

3. How might Paul improve upward communication and the communication culture more generally at Best Trust?

PART FOUR SUPPORTING CASE

Leading and Motivating When Disaster Strikes: Magna Exteriors and Interiors

The name of Magna Exteriors and Interiors Corporation captures its product mix of vehicle components that give each car or truck model its distinctive look. Some of Magna's exterior products are trim, roof systems, body panels, and front and rear end fascia; interior products include trim, cockpit systems, and cargo management systems. Nowadays auto companies don't make all these components but, instead, create the designs and handle the final assembly of components from suppliers such as Magna, delivered to the auto company as needed to meet production plans.

Magna Exteriors and Interiors is a unit of Magna International, which describes itself as "the most diversified automotive supplier in the world." Magna has 263 manufacturing operations plus sales and engineering centers in 26 countries of North America, South America, Africa, Europe, and Asia. These meet the needs of more than two dozen customers, including General Motors, Ford, Chrysler, Toyota, Mack, Harley-Davidson, Freightliner, and Volkswagen. The customers sell very different kinds of vehicles, and it is expensive to build and transport large components, so Magna's factories need to be close to customers both geographically and in their working relationships.

Meeting these requirements suddenly became a problem for Magna's factory in Howell, Michigan, on a recent Wednesday evening in March. A fire started on an assembly line at the facility, which makes interior trim such as rear window trays, door panels, and skins for instrument panels. Fortunately the hundred workers who were finishing up the afternoon shift all escaped safely.

The Howell facility employs about 450 workers. Its customers include 16 GM, Ford, Chrysler, Nissan, and Mazda assembly plants. Forecasting a shortage of parts, some of its customers slowed production and canceled shifts in the days immediately after the fire. Magna's managers knew they needed to scramble, or employees would be out of work and important customers would be lost. Robert Brownlee, president of Magna Exteriors and Interiors North America, decided the Howell facility should be running again within just two days. Meeting that goal would require an all-out effort.

While the firefighters were still battling the blaze, Brownlee conferred by phone with his top managers, figuring out what they should do first. Because they couldn't yet assess the extent of the damages, they had to work with a worst-case scenario: destruction of the entire building. They identified four Magna facilities making similar products, where they could ship the Howell plant's tooling on flatbed trucks if need be. That night, Brownlee directed all four of the plants to increase production and build up their inventories in case they would be needed for the Howell plant's customers.

Next the managers set up a reconstruction team, including electricians, pipe fitters, millwrights, mechanics, toolmakers, and information technology specialists. The team assembled in Howell with a structural engineer, awaiting permission to enter the damaged building. On Thursday night, about 24 hours after the fire, the fire department let the team enter the plant. The structural engineer determined that the fire had been contained in one part of the plant. About 30 percent of the plant, representing one out of four production sectors, was destroyed beyond repair. One of the four remaining production sectors had largely escaped damage.

Now the clock was ticking on Brownlee's two-day recovery goal. On Friday morning, workers pulled damaged tooling out of the rubble and had it moved to Brighton, a city 12 miles away, where they cleaned it and set up a temporary assembly line in a Magna warehouse. Back in Howell,

the reconstruction team was building a temporary wall to seal off the undamaged part of the facility and repairing the roof. The heating and electrical systems were destroyed, so they brought in a dozen diesel generators to power heaters and lighting. Until the roof was repaired, they coped with Michigan's wintry March weather by wearing snowmobile suits while clearing out debris and damaged products, working around the clock.

The next morning, spirits rose when power was restored to the least-damaged sector, and the lights came back on. Workers continued to repair, clean, and rewire the tooling. By Saturday night, workers were able to restart some of the machinery and do test runs. Unfortunately they ran into problems with each attempt. Managers were scrambling to keep on top of the plant reconstruction and the attempts to restart machinery. Brownlee saw that this was too much responsibility. He called together the managers, put each one in charge of relaunching one product line, and directed them to put a subordinate in charge of every other duty, including reconstruction.

The efforts to restart continued as representatives from every customer monitored the progress. Magna gave customers daily updates, and as each assembly line resumed, the relevant customer's representative signed off as part of the quality-control practices. By Sunday, limited production had begun at the Howell plant. Six days after the fire department determined that the fire was extinguished, the Howell plant was running at 80 percent of capacity, and its temporary line in Brighton handled the remaining production.

In a statement to the media, the company publicly thanked "the Magna Howell employees who continue to do whatever it takes to meet customer requirements; the Magna group office employees and Magna employees from numerous other divisions who have come to support the effort," the company's contractors and customers, the community's firefighters, and others who helped after the fire.

QUESTIONS

1. As a leader, what vision did Robert Brownlee offer? What combination of task performance and group maintenance behaviors did he use? Was this the appropriate combination after the fire? Why or why not?

2. What do you think the Magna managers and employees were motivated by most after the fire? Why?

3. Management set up a cross-functional reconstruction team, but there is no evidence that this was a self-managed team. Would a self-managed team have been more effective? Why or why not?

SOURCES: Sedgwick, D., "Five-Alarm Planning," *Crain's Detroit Business*, April 18, 2011, Business & Company Resource Center, http://galenet.galegroup.com; Magna International, "About Magna Exteriors and Interiors," http://www.magna.com; Van Alphen, T., "Magna Plant Resumes Full Deliveries after Fire," *Toronto Star*, March 10, 2011, http://www.thestar.com; and Magna International, "Magna Atreum Howell Plant Back in Business Six Days after Fire," news release, March 9, 2011, http://www.magna.com.

CHAPTER 16
Managerial Control

> More than at any time in the past, companies will not be able to hold themselves together with the traditional methods of control: hierarchy, systems, budgets, and the like. . . . The bonding glue will increasingly become ideological.
>
> —COLLINS AND PORRAS[1]
>
> Use your good judgment in all situations.
>
> —NORDSTROM'S EMPLOYEE MANUAL

©Corbis/age fotostock RF

LEARNING OBJECTIVES

After studying Chapter 16, you will be able to:

LO 1 Explain why companies develop control systems.

LO 2 Summarize how to design a basic bureaucratic control system.

LO 3 Describe the purposes for using budgets as a control device.

LO 4 Define basic types of financial statements and financial ratios used as controls.

LO 5 List procedures for implementing effective control systems.

LO 6 Identify ways in which organizations use market control mechanisms.

LO 7 Discuss the use of clan control in an empowered organization.

CHAPTER OUTLINE

Bureaucratic Control Systems
The Control Cycle
Approaches to Bureaucratic Control
Management Audits
Budgetary Controls
Financial Controls
Problems with Bureaucratic Control
Designing Effective Control Systems

The Other Controls: Markets and Clans
Market Control
Clan Control: The Role of Empowerment and Culture

Management in Action

MONITORING EMPLOYEE HEALTH AND CONTROLLING COSTS

The cost of providing employee health insurance is a major expense for most companies. Health problems caused by employee obesity cost U.S. companies about $73 billion (including the cost of lost productivity) every year. Companies are eager to find ways to reduce this outlay.

One novel solution is to try to keep employees from getting sick or overweight in the first place; health insurance costs would go down and workers would file fewer claims to treat preventable conditions. More than 80 percent of large U.S. companies now have wellness programs to help employees lose weight, stop smoking, eat healthier food, or work more safely and productively. Some run fitness contests or offer financial rewards. On-site gyms and healthy cafeteria offerings encourage and strengthen employee health.

Although their ability to permanently lower costs is unproven, and some kinds of monitoring raise privacy concerns, employee wellness programs are popular. How do employers measure the results of these efforts? One way is to use fitness trackers. Among the corporate giants that have given Fitbit devices to thousands of their employees are Bank of America, IBM, Target, Time Warner, and Barclays. Fitbit has even created a wellness division to train its corporate clients to better monitor and improve their employees' overall health outcomes.

©Mile Atanasov/123RF RF

At IBM, 96 percent of the 40,000 employees who were given Fitbits used them consistently throughout the company's fitness challenge, and an astonishing 63 percent continued using them afterward. For some companies, like the cloud-services start-up Appirio in San Francisco, tracking devices led directly to cost savings. After outfitting about 400 workers with Fitbits, the company shaved more than a quarter of a million dollars from its annual employee health insurance bill.

What do employees think of the wellness programs? Indiana University Health Center ran a weight loss challenge that included discounted Fitbits. Says one employee who lost 30 pounds and lowered his cholesterol during the program, "I racked up enough points for a free exercise ball and a slight discount on my insurance. But by far the biggest reward was my health."[2]

Some companies also monitor employees' use of e-mail, social media, and the Internet, and even their weight loss progress and physical location. As you read this chapter, think about the kinds of control measures and processes that can best help a company manage its costs, including the cost of maintaining a healthy and productive workforce.

At Teco Energy, 170 team members alertly find ways to reduce waste and improve customer services. Teco also assigns improvement projects to teams to *prevent* problems.[3] It assigns a production engineer to design teams to ensure production efficiencies, reducing defects as well as costs.[4]

Spotting and preventing problems are two sides of the same coin: control—a means or mechanism for regulating employee behavior. Left on their own, people may work in ways that they believe to be beneficial to themselves, but hurt overall organizational performance.

Employees simply wasting time online (shopping, watching funny cat videos . . .) cost U.S. employers about $85 billion each year![5] Even well-intentioned people may not know whether they are directing their efforts toward the activities that are most important. Thus control is one of the fundamental forces that keep the organization together and heading in the right direction.

Control is defined as any process that directs activities toward organizational goals. It is how effective managers make sure that activities are going as planned. Some managers don't want to admit it (see Exhibit 16.1), but control problems—the lack of controls or the wrong kinds of controls—frequently cause irreparable damage.

Ineffective control systems result in problems ranging from employee theft to defective products. BP spent billions of dollars to repair damage to the Gulf of Mexico following the Deepwater Horizon disaster; years later, it was still in court, defending charges of negligence. The damage to its reputation could hardly help the company as it more recently responded to safety questions related to oil leaks in Lake Michigan and off the coast of Norway.[6]

control

Any process that directs the activities of individuals toward the achievement of organizational goals.

Bottom Line

Control is essential for the attainment of any management objective. *What happens in the absence of control?*

> Effective managers exert control without micromanaging.

Once managers form plans and strategies, they must ensure that the plans are carried out. They must make sure that people are doing what needs to be done, and are not doing inappropriate things. As problems arise, management must take corrective action. This process is the control function of management.

Effective planning facilitates control, and control facilitates planning. Planning lays out a framework for the future and provides a blueprint for control. Control systems then regulate resource allocation and use and facilitate the next planning cycle. Managers today must control their people, inventories, quality, and costs, to mention just a few of their responsibilities.

Managers can use three broad strategies for achieving organizational control: bureaucratic control, market control, and clan control.[7] **Bureaucratic control** is the use of rules, regulations, and formal authority to guide performance. It includes such items as budgets, statistical reports, and performance appraisals to regulate behavior and results.

bureaucratic control

The use of rules, regulations, and authority to guide performance.

EXHIBIT 16.1

Symptoms of an Out-of-Control Company

- **Lax top management**—senior managers do not emphasize or value the need for controls, or they set a bad example.

- **Absence of policies**—the firm's expectations are not established in writing.

- **Lack of agreed-upon standards**—organization members are uncertain about what needs to be achieved.

- **"Shoot the messenger" management**—employees feel their careers would be at risk if they reported bad news.

- **Lack of periodic reviews**—managers do not assess performance on a regular, timely basis.

- **Bad information systems**—key data are not measured and reported in a timely and easily accessible way.

- **Lack of ethics in the culture**—organization members have not internalized a commitment to integrity.

EXHIBIT 16.2
Characteristics of Controls

Control System	Features and Requirements
Bureaucratic control	Uses formal rules, standards, hierarchy, and legitimate authority. Works best where tasks are clear and workers are independent.
Market control	Uses prices, competition, profit centers, and exchange relationships. Works best where tangible outputs are specified and markets can be established between parties.
Clan control	Uses culture, shared values, beliefs, expectations, and trust. Works best where there is no one best way to do a job, and employees are empowered to make decisions.

SOURCES: Ouchi, W. G., "A Conceptual Framework for the Design of Organizational Control Mechanisms," *Management Science* 25 (1979), pp. 833–48; Ouchi, W. G., "Markets, Bureaucracies, and Clans," *Administrative Science Quarterly* 25 (1980), pp. 129–41; and Robey, R. D. and Sales, C. A., *Designing Organizations*. Burr Ridge, *IL:* Richard D. Irwin, 1994.

Market control uses pricing mechanisms to regulate activities as though they were economic transactions. Business units are profit centers that trade resources (services or goods) with one another via such mechanisms. Managers who run these units are responsible for and evaluated by of profit and loss.

Unlike the first two types, **clan control** (or *cultural control*) does not assume that the interests of the organization and individuals naturally diverge. Instead, clan control is based on the idea that employees share the values, expectations, and goals of the organization and behave and perform accordingly. When organizational members have common values and goals—and trust one another—formal controls are less necessary. Clan control is based on informal interpersonal processes influenced by culture, leaders, and teams (for example, group norms and cohesiveness).

Exhibit 16.2 summarizes the main features of bureaucratic, market, and clan controls. Bureaucratic controls are ubiquitous, and therefore we give them the most attention; we discuss market and clan controls toward the end of the chapter.

market control

Control based on the use of pricing mechanisms and economic information to regulate activities within organizations.

clan control

Control based on the norms, values, shared goals, and trust among group members.

Bureaucratic Control Systems

Bureaucratic (or formal) control systems measure progress toward performance goals and apply corrective measures as needed to ensure that performance achieves managers' objectives. Control systems detect and correct significant variations, or discrepancies, in the results of planned activities.

The Control Cycle

As Exhibit 16.3 shows, a typical control system has four major steps:

1. Setting performance standards.
2. Measuring performance.
3. Comparing performance against the standards and determining deviations.
4. Taking action to correct problems and reinforce successes.

Step 1: Setting Performance Standards Every organization has goals for profitability, customer satisfaction, costs, and so on. A **standard** is the targeted level of performance for a particular goal. Standards establish desired performance levels, motivate performance, and serve as benchmarks against which to assess actual performance. Standards can be set for any activity—financial activities, operating activities, legal compliance, charitable contributions,[8] and social impact (see the nearby "Social Enterprise box").

standard

Expected performance for a given goal: a target that establishes a desired performance level, motivates performance, and serves as a benchmark against which actual performance is assessed.

EXHIBIT 16.3
The Control Process

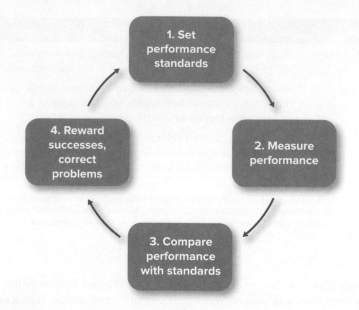

1. Set performance standards

2. Measure performance

3. Compare performance with standards

4. Reward successes, correct problems

Bottom Line
Standards should be set for all bottom-line practices. *Give an example of a standard for sustainability.*

Performance standards can be set with respect to (1) quantity, (2) quality, (3) time used, and (4) cost. Production activities include volume of output (quantity), defects (quality), on-time availability of finished goods (time use), and dollar expenditures for raw materials and direct labor (cost). Customer service can be measured by the same standards—adequate supply and availability of products, quality of service, speed of delivery, and cost.

Step 2: Measuring Performance   The second step in the control process is to measure performance levels. Managers can count units produced, websites viewed, days absent, samples distributed, and dollars earned. Performance data commonly are obtained from three sources: written reports, oral reports, and personal observations.

Written reports include computer-generated reports. Thanks to computers' data-gathering and analysis capabilities and decreasing costs, both large and small companies can gather huge amounts of performance data.

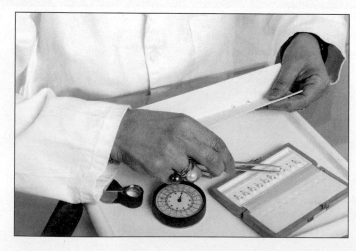

At the Baccarat factory in France, the workers in the quality control area are responsible for the quality and selection of these fine cut crystal glasses.

©Patrizio Martorana/Alamy Stock Photo RF

One common example of oral reports occurs when a salesperson contacts his or her immediate manager at the close of each business day to report the accomplishments, problems, or customers' reactions during the day. The manager can ask questions to gain additional information or clear up any misunderstandings. When necessary, the discussion can generate tentative corrective actions.

Personal observation involves going to the area where activities take place and watching what is occurring. Managers can directly observe work methods, employees' nonverbal signals, and the general operation. Personal observation gives a detailed picture of what is going on, but it has some disadvantages. It does not provide accurate quantitative data; the limited information usually is general and subjective. Employees can misunderstand the purpose of personal observation as mistrust.

Still, many managers believe in the value of firsthand observation. Personal contact can increase leadership visibility and upward communication. It also can provide valuable information to supplement written and oral reports.

It is important to acquire performance data on a timely basis. For example, consumer goods companies such as General Foods carefully track new product sales in selected local

Social Enterprise

Beyond Counting: Alternate Ways to Measure Social Impact

Nobel laureate Mohammed Yunus, founder of Grameen Bank, set a high standard when he declared that "social business" could lead to a "world without poverty." But progress cannot be assessed unless social enterprises know how to measure their impact on social challenges such as poverty. A recent survey found that 95 percent of investors in social enterprises see it as "part of our mission to understand the social/environmental performance of our investments."

Many social enterprises count the number of people who received the enterprise's product or service. TOMS counts the shoes it donates annually to impoverished children (over 70 million pairs in 70 countries as this book goes to press). Root Capital has made loans to 1.1 million small-scale farmers and reached more than 4.5 million family members.

Both organizations are certainly making a social impact, but the questions remain: What impact are they having on their recipients? How many recipients wear the shoes or use the loan money as intended? To what degree did the recipients fare better than comparable individuals who didn't receive free shoes or a loan?

Despite its popularity, counting outcomes is an incomplete measure. More comprehensive assessments of social impact include:

1. *Impact Value Chain (IVC).* Developed by Professor Catherine Clark, the IVC takes a holistic approach to measuring social impact. Social enterprises can measure their impact by evaluating the entire process or value chain, including inputs, outputs, and outcomes.
2. *Progress Out of Poverty Index (PPI).* Created by the Grameen Foundation, the PPI "provides a relatively low-cost and efficient way to evaluate the poverty level of a given community."

©McGraw-Hill Education/Roberts Publishing Services

3. *B Impact Assessment (BIA).* Developed by B-Lab, a nonprofit that certifies benefit corporations, the BIA evaluates an organization's "impact on its workers, community, environment, and customers."

Some argue that we need specific analyses measures customized to each social enterprise's goals. With better measures, we can more truly know when and how a social enterprise changes the world.[9]

Questions

- Can you think of other ways TOMS could assess its social impact?
- Dive a little deeper by doing a bit of research. Which of the three measures (IVC, PPI, or BIA) do you think is the most accurate way to measure social impact? Why?

markets first so they can make adjustments before a national rollout. Unavailable information is useless information.

Step 3: Comparing Performance with the Standard   Now, armed with relevant data, the manager can evaluate the performance. For some activities, small deviations from standard are acceptable, whereas in others a slight deviation may be serious. In many manufacturing processes, a significant deviation in either direction (e.g., drilling a hole that is too small or too large) is utterly unacceptable. In other cases, a deviation in one direction, such as sales or customer satisfaction that fall below the target level, is a problem, but a deviation in the other, exceeding the sales target or customer expectations, means employees are delivering better-than-expected results. Managers who perform the oversight must analyze and evaluate results carefully.

Managers save time and effort by applying the principle of exception.

principle of exception

A managerial principle stating that control is enhanced by concentrating on the exceptions to or significant deviations from the expected result or standard.

The managerial **principle of exception** states that control is enhanced by concentrating on the exceptions to—that is, significant deviations from—the expected result or standard. In comparing performance with the standard, managers need to attend to the exception—for example, a few defective components produced on an assembly line, or the feedback from customers who are upset (or delighted) with a service. When Accurid Pest Solutions installed GPS tracking software on company-issued smartphones, the owner discovered and fired two drivers who were taking time off from work each day without permission.[10]

Applying this principle, only exceptional cases require attention and action. This principle is important in controlling. The manager is not concerned with performance that equals or closely (adequately) approximates the expected results. Managers can save much time and effort by using the principle of exception.

Step 4: Taking Action to Correct Problems and Reinforce Successes The last step in the control process is to take appropriate action on significant deviations. This step ensures that operations are adjusted to better achieve the planned results, or if the performance news is good to keep achieving those exceptional results. When discovering significant variances, managers should take immediate and vigorous action.

McDonald's has an extra challenge in taking corrective action: When it catches problems in a restaurant, it has to persuade the franchise owner to make changes. Most McDonald's restaurants have independent owners (franchisees), so the company cannot simply direct them as it would direct employees.

Recently, McDonald's addressed the problem that its sales had begun to fall after years of solid growth. Customer satisfaction data showed an increase in complaints about service quality and speed. Survey data from the National Restaurant Association showed that customers care almost as much about high-quality service as about value for the price. McDonald's urged franchisees to schedule more employees for peak hours, and it provided equipment and training for its new dual-point ordering system.[11]

The best corrective action depends on the nature of the problem. To solve a systemic problem, such as major delays in work flow, often a team approach is most effective. As you know, teams can bring a greater diversity of resources, ideas, and perspectives to problem solving. Knowledgeable team members can prevent managers from implementing simplistic solutions that don't address a problem's underlying causes. They are more likely to take into account the effects of a proposed solution on other parts of the organization, preventing new problems from arising. And they may develop solutions that managers would have considered on their own. As a result, the corrective action will probably be more effective.

Sometimes managers learn they can get better results if they adjust their own actions. Each year, FedEx surveys employees to learn about their job satisfaction and opinions about management. Managers then hold feedback sessions to discuss the survey findings with employees. The discussions identify problems and action plans to resolve them. This process has become a problem-solving tool that operates both horizontally and vertically throughout the organization.[12]

after-action review

A frank and open-minded discussion of four basic questions aimed at continuous improvement.

After taking corrective action, some managers conduct an **after-action review**, using the four questions shown in Exhibit 16.4 to guide a frank and open-minded discussion aimed at continuous improvement.[13] The U.S. Army developed this process to help soldiers learn from their experiences, and the method applies equally well in business.

Employees at the J. M. Huber Corporation conduct a review after every planned project and major unplanned event, and post lessons learned in an online database. In the public sector as well, emergency response teams improve their performance via after-action reviews. These reviews are most effective when scheduled consistently and when participation is mandatory for everyone involved.

1. What were our intended results?	2. What were our actual results?	3. What caused our results?	4. What will we sustain? Improve?
(What was planned?)	(What really happened?)	(Why did it happen?)	(What can we do better next time?)

EXHIBIT 16.4
Questions for an After-Action Review

Approaches to Bureaucratic Control

Three approaches to bureaucratic control are feedforward, concurrent, and feedback. **Feedforward control** takes place before operations begin and includes policies, procedures, and rules designed to ensure that planned activities are carried out properly. Examples include inspection of raw materials and proper selection and training of employees. **Concurrent control** takes place while plans are being carried out; it includes directing, monitoring, and fine-tuning activities as they occur. **Feedback control** uses information about results to correct deviations after they arise.

Feedforward Control   Feedforward control (sometimes called *preliminary control*) is future oriented; its aim is to prevent problems before they arise. Instead of waiting for results and comparing them with goals, a manager can exert control by limiting activities in advance. Formal rules and procedures prescribe people's actions before they occur.

For example, human resource policies defining what forms of body art are acceptable to display at work can avoid awkward case-by-case conversations about particular people.[14] Or a company might dictate that managers adhere to clear ethical and legal guidelines when making decisions. Legal experts advise companies to establish policies forbidding disclosure of proprietary information or making clear that employees are not speaking for the company when they post messages on blogs, microblogging sites, and social networking sites.

Some firms, concerned about the pitfalls of workplace romance, have sought a solution in feedforward control. Romantic activities between a supervisor and subordinate create a conflict of interest or sexual harassment. Other employees might infer from lack of action that the company allows a culture of harassment or sanctions personal relationships as a path to advancement. And relationship ups and downs can affect everyone's mood and motivation.

Controls aimed at preventing such problems include training in appropriate behavior (including how to avoid sexual harassment) and even requiring executives and their romantic interests to sign "love contracts" stating that the relationship is voluntary and welcome. The company keeps a copy of the contract in case the relationship dissolves and an unhappy employee blames the company for allowing it in the first place.[15]

Concurrent Control   Concurrent control takes place while plans are carried out, and is the heart of any control system. On a manufacturing floor, all efforts are directed toward producing the correct quantity and quality of the right products in the specified amount of time. In an airline terminal, the baggage must get to the right airplanes before flights depart. In factories, materials must be available when and where needed, and breakdowns in the production process must be repaired immediately. Concurrent control also is in effect when supervisors watch employees to ensure they work efficiently and avoid mistakes.

Information technology provides powerful concurrent controls, giving managers immediate access to data from the most remote corners of their companies. For example, managers update budgets instantly based on a continuous flow of performance data. In production facilities, monitoring systems that track errors per hour, machine speeds, and other measures allow managers to correct small production problems before they become disasters.

feedforward control

The control process used before operations begin, including policies, procedures, and rules designed to ensure that planned activities are carried out properly.

concurrent control

The control process used while plans are being carried out, including directing, monitoring, and fine-tuning activities as they are performed.

feedback control

Control that focuses on the use of information about previous results to correct deviations from the acceptable standard.

Point-of-sale terminals in store checkout lines send sales data to a retailer's headquarters to show which products are selling in which locations.

Concurrent control also applies in service settings. As part of its efforts to transform safety, quality, and efficiency, Virginia Mason Medical Center authorized employees to issue personal safety alerts (PSAs). If any employee has a concern or question about a patient's safety, that employee calls an alert. The PSA system has both improved the hospital's safety performance and lowered its costs for professional liability insurance.[16]

Timing is an important aspect of feedback control.

Feedback Control   Feedback control involves gathering performance data, using it to identify performance below standard, and then taking corrective action as needed. When supervisors monitor ongoing behavior, they are exercising concurrent control. When they check results to discover and then correct improper performance, they are using feedback as a means of control.

Timing matters greatly in feedback control. Long time lags often occur between performance and feedback, such as when actual spending is compared with the quarterly budget, or when an employee's annual performance is compared to goals set a year earlier. Performance feedback after shorter time lags allows faster problem identification and corrections, preventing more serious harm.[17] The "Multiple Generations at Work" box discusses the trend toward more frequent, timely performance feedback.

Some feedback processes are under real-time (concurrent) control, as with computer-controlled robots on assembly lines. Such units have sensors that continually determine whether they are in the correct positions to perform their functions. If they are not, a built-in control device makes immediate corrections.

In other situations, feedback processes take more time. Hertz uses feedback including customer ratings of service and car quality. Compliments and complaints help the company reinforce or correct practices at particular facilities. If a customer is upset about something, Hertz wants to know as soon as possible so it can correct the problem.

In the past, gathering and interpreting customer feedback from surveys and online comments could take three weeks. Now, analytic software collects and tallies data as they arrive, and delivers daily reports to local managers. Armed with the information, the managers are expected to respond to any problems within 24 hours. These changes quickly improved customer satisfaction with Hertz.[18]

The Role of Six Sigma   A particularly robust and powerful application of feedback control is six sigma, introduced in Chapter 9. Six sigma is designed to reduce defects in all organization processes—not just product defects but anything that may cause customer dissatisfaction. The system was developed at Motorola in the late 1980s, when the company was being beaten consistently by foreign firms producing higher-quality products at lower cost. Since then, the technique has been adopted and improved by many companies, including GE, AlliedSignal, Ford, and Xerox.

Sigma is the Greek letter used in statistics to designate the estimated standard deviation, or variation, in a process. It indicates how often defects in a process are likely to occur. The higher the sigma number, the lower the level of variation or defects. Exhibit 16.5 shows that a two-sigma-level process has more than 300,000 defects per million opportunities (DPMO)—not a well-controlled process. A three-sigma-level process has 66,807 DPMO, which is roughly a 93 percent level of accuracy. Many organizations operate at this level, which on its face does not sound too bad until we consider its implications—for example, 7 pieces of airline baggage lost for every 100 processed. The additional costs to organizations of such inaccuracy are enormous. As you can see in the exhibit, even at just above a 99 percent defect-free rate, or 6,210 DPMO, the accuracy level can be unacceptable.[19]

Recalling Chapter 9, at a six-sigma level a process produces fewer than 3.4 defects per million, or a 99.99966 percent level of accuracy. Six-sigma companies have close to zero defects plus substantially lower production costs and cycle times, leading to much higher customer

Bottom Line

Six sigma aims for defect-free performance.
How would attempting and achieving six-sigma quality influence costs?

Multiple Generations at Work

Timely Performance Reviews

Companies like Gap, IBM, and SAP are doing away with annual performance evaluations in favor of more frequent coaching and employee development. Some attribute this change to Millennial employees' desire for greater responsibility and a "feedback-rich" culture in which learning is continuous. Others suggest that fast-changing business environments require more frequent dialogue between managers and employees to ensure alignment between employees' actions and the firm's business strategy.

Tata Consulting Services (TCS) of India has a workforce of 240,000 employees of which over 70 percent are Millennials. Ajoy Mukherjee, the director of human resources, has managers provide performance feedback more quickly and give junior employees more responsibility sooner.

Software maker Adobe used to spend over 80,000 hours per year administering traditional performance evaluations. After trying to modify the system, the firm decided "it was inconsistent with Adobe's strong culture of teamwork and collaboration." Now, every three months, a manager or employee requests a "check-in" to discuss performance. Prior to the meeting, fellow employees provide performance feedback. Adobe's goal is to "make

©E. Audras/PhotoAlto RF

coaching and developing a continuous, collaborative process between managers and employees." Since launching the new performance feedback system, Adobe reported a 30 percent reduction in its voluntary employee turnover.

Organizations that want to align their skilled talent with evolving business strategies must provide frequent coaching and developmental feedback.[20]

satisfaction. This methodology isn't just for the factory floor, either. Accountants have used six sigma to improve the quality of their audits investigating risks faced by their clients.[21]

The six-sigma approach begins by defining the outputs and information that flow through each stage of the process and then measuring performance at each stage. Tools for analyzing results include looking for the root causes of problems. Suppose some customers are dissatisfied with a company's customer service. Asking "why?" over and over (famously, thanks to Toyota, asking "why?" five times) could reveal that customers are dissatisfied because phone calls go unanswered, which happens because support staff can't keep up with the call volume, which happens because the department is understaffed, which is the result of a hiring freeze, which is the result of budget cuts.

Sigma Level	DPMO	Is Four Sigma Good Enough?
2σ	308,537	Consider these everyday examples of four-sigma quality . . .
3σ	66,807	• 20,000 lost articles of mail per hour.
4σ	**6,210**	• Unsafe drinking water 15 minutes per day.
5σ	233	• 5,000 incorrect surgical operations per week.
6σ	3.4	• 200,000 wrong prescriptions each year.
		• No electricity for 7 hours each month.

EXHIBIT 16.5
Relationship between Sigma Level and Defects per Million Opportunities

SOURCE: Rancour, Tom and McCracken, Mike, "Applying 6 Sigma Methods for Breakthrough Safety Performance," *Professional Safety* 45, no. 10 (October 2000), pp. 29–32.

A good solution should somehow address the budget restrictions, either by increasing the budget or by learning how a small department can better satisfy customers. After changing and evaluation the new processes, this cycle continues until the desired quality level is achieved. This is how the six-sigma process creates continuous improvement.

Six sigma doesn't automatically and always deliver better business results.[22] It focuses only on how to eliminate defects in a process, not whether the process is the best one for the bottom line. At Home Depot, six sigma improved customer checkout processes and decisions about where to place products in stores, but the effort took store workers away from customers. At 3M, driving efficiency through six sigma slowed down the flow of innovative ideas. One way to apply the strengths of six sigma and minimize its drawbacks is to create goals and control processes for new products that are different from those for mature products.

Management Audits

management audit

An evaluation of the effectiveness and efficiency of various systems within an organization.

Management audits evaluate the effectiveness and efficiency of the organization's various systems, from social responsibility programs to accounting systems. Managers conduct external and internal audits: external audits of other companies and internal audits of their own companies. Some of the same tools and approaches are used for both types.[23]

External Audits   An **external audit** occurs when one organization evaluates another organization. Commonly an external body such as a CPA firm conducts financial and accounting audits. But any company can conduct external audits of competitors or other companies for its own strategic purposes. This type of analysis (1) investigates other organizations for possible merger or acquisition, (2) determines the soundness of a company being considered as a supplier, or (3) discovers the strengths and weaknesses of a competitor to maintain or better exploit the competitive advantages of the investigating organization. Typically firms use publicly available data for these evaluations.[24]

external audit

An evaluation conducted by one organization, such as a CPA firm, on another.

External audits provide essential feedback control when they identify evidence of legal and ethical lapses that could harm the organization and its reputation. They also provide feedforward control because they can prevent problems from occurring in the future. When a company seeking to buy other businesses gathers accurate information about candidates, it is more likely to acquire the best companies and avoid unsound acquisitions.

internal audit

A periodic assessment of a company's own planning, organizing, leading, and controlling processes.

Internal Audits   Your employer might assign a group to conduct an **internal audit** to assess (1) what the company has done for itself, and (2) what it has done for its customers or other recipients of its goods or services. The audit can assess a variety of things including financial stability, production efficiency, sales effectiveness, human resources development, earnings growth, energy use, public relations, civic responsibility, and other effectiveness criteria. The audit reviews the company's past, present, and future, including any risks the organization should be prepared to face.[25]

Stock prices of companies with highly rated audit committees tend to rise faster than shares of companies with lower-rated internal auditors. Strong audit committees do a better job of finding and eliminating undesirable practices.[26]

To perform a management audit, auditors compile a list of desired qualifications and weight each qualification. Management audits uncover common undesirable practices such as unnecessary work, work duplication, poor inventory control, uneconomical use of equipment and machines, procedures that are costlier than necessary, and wasted resources.

In the aftermath of *E. coli* outbreaks at multiple restaurants in 2016, Chipotle Mexican Grill took several steps to prevent further incidents. All regional managers conducted weekly food-safety audits every week, up from every 45 days. The co-COOs e-mailed managers: "Your only job right now is to ensure all new procedures and food-safety practices are being executed 100% of the time in 100% of your restaurants."[27]

Sustainability Audits and the Triple Bottom Line   Companies that are serious about sustainability conduct audits to evaluate how effectively they are serving all stakeholders and protecting the environment. Sustainability audits typically evaluate performance in terms of a triple bottom line—that is, the company's financial performance, environmental impact, and impact on people in the company and the communities where it operates. Adapting a slogan coined by Shell in the 1990s, an easy way to remember the three bottom lines is *profit, planet,* and *people.*[28]

In practice, reporting a triple bottom line is not standardized and regulated the way financial reporting is. A company might report its profitability in the traditional way, its environmental impact in terms of efficiency of resource use, and its human impact in terms of general policies. Specific practices vary, but performing a sustainability audit can serve as a first step toward measuring and reinforcing sustainable business practices.

Budgetary Controls

Budgetary control ties together feedforward control, concurrent control, and feedback control, depending on the point at which it is applied. Budgetary control is the process of finding out what's being done and comparing the results with the corresponding budget data to verify accomplishments or remedy differences. Budgetary control is commonly called **budgeting**.

 LO 3

budgeting
The process of investigating what is being done and comparing the results with the corresponding budget data to verify accomplishments or remedy differences; also called *budgetary controlling.*

Fundamental Budgetary Considerations   In business, budgetary control begins with an estimate of sales and expected income. Exhibit 16.6 shows a budget with a forecast of expected sales (the sales budget) on the top row, followed by several categories of estimated expenses for the first three months of the year. In the bottom row, the profit estimate is determined by subtracting each month's budgeted expenses from the sales in that month's sales budget. Columns next to each month's budget provide space to enter the actual accomplishments so that managers can readily compare expected amounts and actual results.

Although we focus here on the flow of money into and out of the company, budgeting information is not confined to finances. The entire enterprise and any of its units can create budgets for their activities, using units other than dollars as appropriate. For example, many organizations use production budgets forecasting physical units produced and shipped, and labor can be budgeted in skill levels or required work hours.

A primary consideration is the length of the budget period. All budgets are prepared for a specific time period. Many budgets cover one, three, or six months or one year.

The length of time chosen depends on the primary purpose and the normal cycle of activity. For example, seasonal variations should be included for production and for sales. The budget period commonly coincides with other control tools such as managerial reports, balance sheets, and statements of profit and loss. The choice of budget period also should consider how accurately reasonable forecasts can be made.

EXHIBIT 16.6   A Sales Expense Budget

	January		February		March	
	Expectancy	Actual	Expectancy	Actual	Expectancy	Actual
Sales	$1,200,000		$1,350,000		$1,400,000	
Expenses						
General overhead	310,000		310,000		310,000	
Selling	242,000		275,000		288,000	
Producing	327,000		430,500		456,800	
Research	118,400		118,400		115,000	
Office	90,000		91,200		91,500	
Advertising	32,500		27,000		25,800	
Estimated gross profit	80,100		97,900		112,900	

Budgetary control proceeds through several stages. Establishing expectancies starts with the broad plan for the company and the estimate of sales, and it ends with budget approval and publication. Next, the budgetary operations stage deals with comparing results with expectancies. The last stage, as in any control process, involves responding appropriately by reinforcing successes and correcting problems.

In a small company, budgeting responsibility generally rests with the owner. In bigger companies, practices vary, with a member of top management often serving as the chief budget coordinator. Usually the chief financial officer (CFO) has these duties. This executive resolves conflicting interests, recommends adjustments when needed, and gives official sanction to the budgetary procedures.

Types of Budgets   Common types of budgets are:

- *Sales budget.* Usually data for the sales budget include forecasts of sales by month, sales area, and product.
- *Production budget.* The production budget commonly is expressed in physical units. Required information for preparing this budget includes types and capacities of machines, quantities to produce, and availability of materials.
- *Cost budget.* The cost budget is used for areas of the organization that incur expenses but no revenue, such as human resources and other support departments. Cost budgets may also be included in the production budget. Costs may be fixed, or independent of the immediate level of activity (such as rent), or variable, rising or falling with the level of activity (such as raw materials).
- *Cash budget.* The cash budget is essential to every business. It should be prepared after all other budget estimates are completed. The cash budget shows the anticipated receipts and expenditures, the amount of working capital available, the extent to which outside financing may be required, and time periods and amounts of cash available.
- *Capital budget.* The capital budget is used for the cost of fixed assets such as plants and equipment. Such costs are usually treated not as regular expenses but as investments, because of their long-term nature and importance to productivity.
- *Master budget.* The master budget includes all the major activities of the business. It brings together and coordinates all the activities of the other budgets. Think of it as a budget of budgets.

Traditionally, senior management imposed budgets top-down, by setting specific targets for the entire organization at the beginning of the budget process. Now the budget process is likely also to be bottom-up, with top management setting the general direction but with lower-level and middle-level managers developing budget specifics and submitting them for approval. When the budgets are consolidated, senior managers determine whether overall budget objectives are being met. Then they either approve the budget or send it back down the organization for refinements.

accounting audits

Procedures used to verify accounting reports and statements.

Accounting records must be inspected periodically to ensure that they were prepared properly. **Accounting audits**, designed to verify accounting reports and statements, are essential to the control process. This audit is performed by members of an outside firm of public accountants. Knowing that accounting records are accurate, true, and in keeping with generally accepted accounting principles (GAAP) creates confidence that a reliable base exists for sound overall controlling purposes.

activity-based costing (ABC)

A method of cost accounting designed to identify streams of activity and then to allocate costs across particular business processes according to the amount of time employees devote to particular activities.

Activity-Based Costing   Traditional cost accounting methods may be inappropriate today because they are based on outdated methods of rigid hierarchical organizations. Instead of assuming that organizations are bureaucratic machines with separate component functions such as human resources, purchasing, and and marketing, companies such as Hewlett-Packard and GE use **activity-based costing (ABC)** to allocate costs across business *processes* rather than functions.

ABC starts with the assumption that organizations are collections of people performing many different but related activities to satisfy customer needs. The ABC system identifies

Administrative expenses		Laboratory	Radiology	Dr. Kent (240 visits)	Dr. Olson (200 visits)	Dr. Lane (160 visits)
Office salaries						
Direct	1,500			600	500	400
Payroll and personnel	1,000	119	39	337	254	251
Supervision	2,000	238	79	673	508	502
Unutilized*	500					
Advertising	600			200	200	200
Rent	1,000	125	125	250	250	250
Utilities	200	25	25	50	50	50
Office supplies	300			100	100	100
Building insurance	100	12	13	25	25	25
Telephone	600			200	200	200
Depreciation	300			100	100	100
Total	8,100	519	281	2,535	2,187	2,078

Expenses allocated to services provided

*Not allocated.

EXHIBIT 16.7
Activity-Based Costing Example: ABC Medical Clinic

SOURCE: Based on Schuneman, Pam, "Master the 'ABCs' of Activity-Based Costing," *Managed Care,* May 1997. http://www.managedcaremag.com.

those activity streams and then assigns expenses to those areas of activity. In a manufacturing company, a group of employees might process sales orders, buy parts, and request engineering changes. The expenses for their salaries and fringe benefits are divided among these activities according to the amount of time spent on each.

A similar approach, illustrated in Exhibit 16.7, is to allocate costs of providing support services to the business functions served. In this example, a medical clinic, administrative expenses such as office workers' salaries, rent, and utilities are divided among the doctors' practices and the clinic's laboratory and radiology services. Options for allocating these expenses include the number of employees in each group, the number of patients seen, and the square footage each group occupied.

Traditional and ABC systems reach the same bottom line. However, because the ABC method allocates costs across business processes, it provides a more accurate picture of how costs should be charged to products (goods and services).[29]

This greater accuracy can give managers a more realistic picture of how the organization actually is allocating its resources. It can highlight where wasted activities are occurring or whether activities cost too much relative to the benefits provided. Managers can then take corrective action.

Financial Controls

In addition to budgets, businesses commonly use other statements for financial control. Two financial statements that help control overall organizational performance are the balance sheet and the profit and loss statement.

The Balance Sheet   The **balance sheet** shows the financial picture of a company at a given time. This statement itemizes three elements: (1) assets, (2) liabilities, and (3) stockholders' equity. **Assets** are the values of the various items the corporation owns. **Liabilities** are the amounts the corporation owes to various creditors. **Stockholders' equity** is the amount accruing to the corporation's owners. The relationship among these three elements is as follows:

$$\text{Assets} = \text{Liabilities} + \text{Stockholders' equity}$$

Exhibit 16.8 shows an example of a balance sheet. During the year, the company grew because it enlarged its building and acquired more machinery and equipment by means of long-term debt in the form of a first mortgage. Additional stock was sold to help finance the

balance sheet

A report that shows the financial picture of a company at a given time and itemizes assets, liabilities, and stockholders' equity.

assets

The values of the various items the corporation owns.

Bottom Line

Activity-based costing can highlight overspending. *When a certain activity is the most costly, how would you decide whether it's a case of overspending?*

liabilities

The amounts a corporation owes to various creditors.

stockholders' equity

The amount accruing to the corporation's owners.

EXHIBIT 16.8
A Comparative Balance Sheet

Comparative Balance Sheet for the Years Ending December 31	This Year	Last Year
Assets		
Current assets:		
Cash	$161,870	$119,200
U.S. Treasury bills	250,400	30,760
Accounts receivable	825,595	458,762
Inventories:		
Work in process and finished products	429,250	770,800
Raw materials and supplies	251,340	231,010
Total current assets	1,918,455	1,610,532
Other assets:		
Land	157,570	155,250
Building	740,135	91,784
Machinery and equipment	172,688	63,673
Furniture and fixtures	132,494	57,110
Total other assets before depreciation	1,202,887	367,817
Less: Accumulated depreciation and amortization	67,975	63,786
Total other assets	1,134,912	304,031
Total assets	$3,053,367	$1,914,563
Liabilities and stockholders' equity		
Current liabilities:		
Accounts payable	$287,564	$441,685
Payrolls and withholdings from employees	44,055	49,580
Commissions and sundry accruals	83,260	41,362
Federal taxes on income	176,340	50,770
Current installment on long-term debt	85,985	38,624
Total current liabilities	667,204	622,021
Long-term liabilities:		
15-year, 9 percent loan, payable in each of the years 2005–2018	210,000	225,000
5 percent first mortgage	408,600	
Registered 9 percent notes payable		275,000
Total long-term liabilities	618,600	500,000
Stockholders' equity:		
Common stock: authorized 1,000,000 shares, outstanding last year 492,000 shares, outstanding this year 700,000 shares at $1 par value	700,000	492,000
Capital surplus	981,943	248,836
Earned surplus	75,620	51,706
Total stockholders' equity	1,757,563	792,542
Total liabilities and stockholders' equity	$3,053,367	$1,914,563

expansion. At the same time, accounts receivable were increased, and work in process was reduced. Observe that Total assets ($3,053,367) = Total liabilities ($677,204 + $618,600) + Stockholders' equity ($700,000 + $981,943 + $75,620).

Summarizing balance sheet items over time uncovers important trends and gives managers further insight into overall performance and areas in need of adjustments. For example, this company might find it prudent to slow down its expansion plans.

The Profit and Loss Statement   The **profit and loss statement** is an itemized financial statement of the income and expenses of a company's operations. Exhibit 16.9 shows a comparative statement of profit and loss for two consecutive years. In this illustration, the company's operating revenue increased. Expenses also went up but at a lower rate, resulting in a higher net income.

Some managers draw up tentative profit and loss statements and use them as goals. Then performance is measured against these goals or standards. From comparative statements of this type, a manager can identify trouble areas and correct them.

Controlling by profit and loss is commonly used for the entire enterprise and, in the case of a diversified corporation, its divisions. However, if controlling is by departments, as in a decentralized organization in which managers have control over both revenue and expense, each department has a profit and loss statement. Each department's output is measured, and each is charged a cost, including overhead. Expected net income is the standard for measuring departmental performance.

Financial Ratios   An effective approach for monitoring an enterprise's overall performance is to use key financial ratios. Ratios help indicate strengths and weaknesses in a company's operations. Key ratios are calculated from selected items on the profit and loss statement and the balance sheet. We describe three categories of financial ratios: liquidity, leverage, and profitability:

- *Liquidity ratios.* Liquidity ratios indicate a company's ability to pay short-term debts. The most common liquidity ratio is *current assets to current liabilities,* called the

profit and loss statement

An itemized financial statement of the income and expenses of a company's operations.

Comparative Statement of Profit and Loss for the Years Ending June 30			
	This Year	Last Year	Increase or Decrease
Income:			
Net sales	$253,218	$257,636	$4,418*
Dividends from investments	480	430	50
Other	1,741	1,773	32*
Total	255,439	259,839	4,400*
Deductions:			
Cost of goods sold	180,481	178,866	1,615
Selling and administrative expenses	39,218	34,019	5,199
Interest expense	2,483	2,604	121*
Other	1,941	1,139	802
Total	224,123	216,628	7,495
Income before taxes	31,316	43,211	11,895*
Provision for taxes	3,300	9,500	6,200*
Net income	$ 28,016	$ 33,711	$5,695*

EXHIBIT 16.9
A Comparative Statement of Profit and Loss

*Decrease

current ratio

A liquidity ratio that indicates the extent to which short-term assets can decline and still be adequate to pay short-term liabilities.

debt–equity ratio

A leverage ratio that indicates the company's ability to meet its long-term financial obligations.

return on investment (ROI)

A ratio of profit to capital used, or a rate of return from capital.

management myopia

Focusing on short-term earnings and profits at the expense of longer-term strategic obligations.

current ratio or *net working capital ratio.* This ratio indicates the extent to which current assets can decline and still be adequate to pay current liabilities. Some analysts set a ratio of 2 to 1, or 2.00, as the desirable minimum. Referring back to Exhibit 16.8, the liquidity ratio there is about 2.86 ($1,918,455/$667,204). The company's current assets are more than capable of supporting its current liabilities.

- *Leverage ratios.* Leverage ratios show the funds in the business supplied by creditors and shareholders. An important example is the **debt–equity ratio**, which indicates the company's ability to meet its long-term financial obligations. A common rule of thumb is that if this ratio is less than 1.5, the amount of debt is not considered excessive. In Exhibit 16.8, the debt–equity ratio is only 0.35 ($618,600/$1,757,563). The company has financed its expansion almost entirely by issuing stock rather than by incurring long-term debt.

- *Profitability ratios.* Profitability ratios indicate management's ability to generate a financial return on sales or investment. For example, **return on investment (ROI)** is a ratio of profit to capital used, or a rate of return from capital (equity plus long-term debt). This ratio allows managers and shareholders to assess how well the firm is doing compared with other investments. If the net income of the company in Exhibit 16.8 were $300,000 this year, its return on capital would be 12.6 percent [$300,000/($1,757,563/$618,600)]—normally a very reasonable rate of return.

Using Financial Ratios   Although financial ratios provide useful performance standards and indicators, relying on them exclusively is unwise. Because ratios usually are based on short time horizons (monthly, quarterly, or yearly), they often cause **management myopia**—focusing on short-term earnings and profits at the expense of longer-term strategic objectives.[30] Control systems using longer-term performance targets (for example, three to six years) can reduce management myopia and focus attention farther into the future.

A second negative impact of ratios is that they relegate other important considerations to secondary positions. Research and development, management development, progressive human resource practices, and other activities may receive insufficient attention.

Therefore managers should supplement financial ratios with additional control measures. Controls can hold managers accountable for market share, number of patents granted, sales of new products, human resource development, and other performance indicators.

Problems with Bureaucratic Control

> A control system cannot be effective without considering how people will react to it.

People are not machines that automatically fall into line as the designers of control systems intend. In fact, control systems easily can lead to dysfunctional behavior. A control system cannot be effective without considering how people react to it. Managers should know at least three potential behavioral problems: rigid bureaucratic behavior, tactical behavior, and resistance.[31]

Rigid Bureaucratic Behavior   People want to look good on what the control system measures. This focuses them on what management requires, but can result in rigid, inflexible behavior geared toward doing *only* what the system demands. For example, we noted earlier that six sigma emphasizes efficiency over innovation. After 3M began using six sigma extensively, it fell below its goal of having at least one-third of sales come from new products.

So when George Buckley took the CEO post, he relied less on efficiency controls. Buckley explained, "Invention is by its very nature a disorderly process."[32] The control challenge, of course, is for 3M to be both efficient and creative.

Rigid bureaucratic behavior can help employees stay out of trouble by sticking strictly to the rules. Unfortunately, this can make the entire organization slow to act, leading to poor customer service. (Recall the discussion of bureaucracy in Chapter 10).

Probably you have been victimized by rigid bureaucratic behavior. Reflect for a moment on this classic story of a nightmare at a hospital:

> At midnight, a patient with eye pains enters an emergency room at a hospital. At the reception area, he is classified as a non-emergency case and referred to the hospital's eye clinic. Trouble is, the eye clinic doesn't open until the next morning. When he arrives at the clinic, the nurse asks for his referral slip, but the emergency room doctor had forgotten to give it to him. The patient has to return to the emergency room and wait for another physician to screen him. The physician refers him back to the eye clinic and to a social worker to arrange payment. Finally, a third doctor looks into his eye, sees a small piece of metal, and removes it—a 30-second procedure.[33]

Stories like these have given bureaucracy a bad name. Some managers will not even use the term *bureaucratic control* because of its negative connotations. Problems occur when a system is viewed not as a tool that helps run the business, but one that dictates rigid, inflexible behavior.

Tactical Behavior   People sometimes engage in tactics aimed at beating the system. A common type of tactical behavior is to manipulate information or report false performance data. People can provide two kinds of invalid data: about what *has* been done and about what *can* be done.

False reporting about the past is less common because it is easier to spot the discrepancy and identify the culprit, in contrast to someone giving an erroneous prediction or estimate

Management in Action

PRIVACY CONCERNS IN EMPLOYEE TRACKING

While fitness tracking devices and other types of electronic employee monitoring can improve employees' health or productivity, some types raise privacy concerns. Some employees may want to opt out of contests or challenges, for instance, or avoid public shaming when struggling to lose weight or stop smoking.

Some monitoring is useful. Biometric data can prevent sleep-deprived workers from undertaking dangerous tasks. Data showing that a restaurant worker's tables generate lower-than-average checks might suggest the need for training in more assertively suggesting drinks and desserts, and employees at risk for a health problem could be offered counseling and referrals.

Sociometric Solutions is a start-up that uses sensors to record employees' communications, behavior, and body language. The company was able to show a client pharmaceutical company that larger cafeteria tables encouraged more employee communication, leading to higher productivity.

Companies should inform employees about what they monitor and obtain their individual consent, but surveillance can have a dark side. People feel stressed by negative reinforcement tools, like higher insurance premiums for those who fall short of health goals. Even intended positive reinforcement, such as financial and other rewards for meeting difficult challenges, can create pressure.

Federal law requires consulting firms to provide only aggregated data to corporate clients, and not information about individuals. Companies can monitor social media but cannot force current or former employees to disclose their social media passwords. But monitoring practices face few other constraints. Many worry that sophisticated tracking and recording devices can be misused, and lead to discriminatory practices that exceed normal management controls.[34]

- What downsides to employee tracking do you think are possible despite existing safeguards? What additional safeguards, if any, would you suggest?
- Do the potential benefits of biometric monitoring outweigh the potential for privacy violations? Why or why not?

MANAGER'S BRIEF

PROGRESS REPORT

ONWARD

of what might happen in the future. But people do sometimes intentionally feed false information into management information systems to cover up errors or poor performance. In 2014, some employees of the U.S. Department of Veterans Affairs allegedly falsified records regarding how many days it took for veterans to receive medical help.[35] According to guidelines, new patients were entitled to see a physician within 14 days of completing the necessary paperwork. But in Phoenix, 1,700 veterans waited an average of 115 days for their first appointments.[36]

The VA's inspector general discovered that it was medical center officials—not their employees—who falsified the records. Additional evidence of alleged wrongdoing came from other VA medical units in multiple cities.[37] One U.S. senator summed up the scandal: "Poor management is costing the department billions of dollars more and compromising veterans' access to medical care."[38]

More commonly, people falsify their predictions or requests for the future. When asked to give budgetary estimates, they often ask for larger amounts than they need. On the other hand, people sometimes submit unrealistically *low* estimates when they believe that will help them get a budget or a project approved. Budget-setting sessions can become tugs of war between subordinates trying to get slack in the budget and superiors attempting to minimize slack.

Managers use similar tactics when they negotiate low performance goals for themselves so they will have little trouble meeting them; salespeople when they make low sales forecasts so they will look good by exceeding them; and workers when they slow down the work pace while analysts are setting work pace standards. In these sorts of cases, people care about their own performance figures more than the overall performance of their departments or companies.

Resistance to Control   People often resist control systems, for several reasons. First, control systems make employees more accountable for their actions and performance. Control systems decrease people's autonomy, uncover mistakes, and can feel like threats to job security and status.

Second, control systems can change expertise and power structures. Management information systems can more quickly make the costing, purchasing, and production decisions that managers made previously. As a result, people can lose decision-making authority, power, and expertise.

Third, control systems can change the organization's social structure. They can create competition and disrupt social groups and friendships. People may end up competing against those with whom they formerly had comfortable, cooperative relationships. People often resist control systems that reduce their social need satisfaction.

Additionally, control systems can invade privacy, lead to lawsuits, and cause low morale.

Designing Effective Control Systems

LO 5   Effective control systems maximize potential benefits and minimize dysfunctional behaviors. To achieve this, management needs to design control systems that

1. Establish valid performance standards.
2. Provide adequate information to employees.
3. Ensure acceptability to employees.
4. Maintain open communication.
5. Use multiple approaches.

Establish Valid Performance Standards   The most effective standards, as you know, are expressed in quantitative terms; they are objective rather than subjective. Furthermore, the system should incorporate all important aspects of performance, because people often neglect unmeasured behaviors. In addition, the best standards are not readily susceptible to sabotage or cheating.

Management also must defend against another problem: too many measures that create overcontrol and employee resistance. To make multiple controls tolerable, managers can emphasize the most important areas. They can prioritize; for example, purchasing agents might rank performance targets this way: quality, availability, cost, and inventory level. Managers also can set tolerance ranges, for example by specifying optimistic, expected, and minimum levels.

Some companies' budgets set cost targets only. This causes managers to control spending, but to neglect earnings. At Emerson Electric, profit and growth are key measures. If an unanticipated opportunity to increase market share arises, managers can spend what they need to go after it. The phrase "it's not in the budget" is less likely to stifle people at Emerson than it is at most other companies. A company that focused only on sales volume without also looking at profitability might soon go out of business.

This principle applies as well to nonfinancial performance dimensions. At many customer service call centers, control aims to maximize efficiency by focusing on the average time each agent spends handling phone calls. But the business objectives of call centers should also include other measures such as cross-selling products or improving customer satisfaction and repeat business. Customer service agents at TD bank are evaluated by their ability to "achieve first-call issue resolution and receive favorable customer feedback—not by how quickly they can get the customer off the phone."[39]

Business consultant Michael Hammer offered seven "deadly sins" to avoid in performance measurement:[40]

1. *Vanity*—using measures that are sure to make managers and the organization look good. For example, a company might measure order fulfillment in terms of whether products are delivered by the latest date promised by the organization, rather than by the tougher and more meaningful measure of delivery dates requested by customers.

2. *Provincialism*—limiting measures to functional or departmental responsibilities rather than the organization's overall objectives. If a company's transportation department measures only shipping costs, it won't attend enough to shipping reliability (delivery on a given date).

3. *Narcissism*—measuring from the manager's or company's viewpoint rather than the customer's. A maker of computer systems measured on-time shipping of each component; if 90 percent of the system's components arrived at the customer on time, it was 90 percent on time. But from the customer's point of view, the system wasn't on time at all: it needed *all* the components to be on time.

4. *Laziness*—not expending the effort to analyze what is important. An electric power company assumed customers cared about installation speed, but in fact, customers cared most about receiving an accurate installation schedule.

5. *Pettiness*—measuring just one component of what affects business performance. An example would be clothing manufacturers assuming they can consider only manufacturing costs rather than all costs of providing stores with exactly the right products when customers demand them.

6. *Inanity*—failing to consider the way standards will affect real-world human behavior and company performance. A fast-food restaurant implemented a food waste reduction program and was surprised when restaurant managers focused on this goal at the cost of not serving food quickly.

7. *Frivolity*—making excuses for poor performance rather than taking performance standards seriously. In some organizations, more effort goes into blaming other people than into correcting problems.

Provide Adequate Information   Management must communicate to employees the importance and nature of the control system. Then people must receive performance feedback. Feedback enables them to correct their own deviations from performance standards. Allowing people to initiate their own corrective action encourages self-control and reduces the need for outside supervision.

In general, a manager designing a control system should evaluate the information system with the following questions:

1. Does it provide people with data relevant to the decisions they need to make?
2. Does it provide the right amount of information to decision makers throughout the organization?
3. Does it provide enough information to each part of the organization about how other, related parts of the organization are functioning?[41]

Ensure Acceptability to Employees

People will work well within the system if they accept it. They are more likely to accept systems that have reasonable, achievable performance standards but are not overly controlling. Ideally, the control system will emphasize positive behavior rather than focus solely on controlling negative behavior.

In more than two decades, Johnson & Johnson's Ethicon San Lorenzo facility has never had to recall a product. The company makes sutures, meshes, and other supplies for surgery—an industry in which quality must be perfect and recalls are all too common. To achieve these outstanding results, the company created the Do It Right Framework, which includes training, employee involvement in process improvements, and open communication about company objectives.

Importantly, employees should understand how their work matters. Every employee sees a video about Ethicon's work, highlighted by a cardiovascular surgeon describing how he uses the products and why their quality affects patients' recovery. Doing the job right is something employees genuinely care about.[42]

One of the best ways to establish reasonable standards and gain employee acceptance is to set standards participatively. As we discussed in Chapter 4, participation in decision making secures people's understanding and cooperation and results in better decisions. Allowing employees to collaborate in decisions that affect their jobs will help overcome resistance to the system. In addition, employees on the front line are more likely to know which standards are most important and practical, and they can inform their bosses about these issues. Moreover, when deviations from standards occur, it's easier to obtain cooperation in problem solving if standards were established collaboratively.

Maintain Open Communication

Employees should feel willing and able to report deviations so that problems can be addressed. If they feel that their bosses want to hear only good news, or fear reprisal for reporting bad news (even if it is not their fault), then controls become less effective. Problems go unreported and over time become more expensive or difficult to solve. But if managers create an environment of openness and honesty, and appreciate it when employees convey problems in a timely fashion, then the control system is far more likely to work to its potential.

Use Multiple Approaches

No single control system will suffice. Multiple controls are necessary. For example, banks need controls on risk so that they don't lose a lot of money from defaulting borrowers, plus profit controls including sales budgets that aim for growth in accounts and customers.

As you now know, control systems should include both financial and nonfinancial performance targets and incorporate aspects of feedforward, concurrent, and feedback control. Many companies use **strategy maps** to show how they plan to convert their various assets into desired outcomes. Related to these maps is the **balanced scorecard** which holds managers responsible for a combination of four sets of performance measures (see Exhibit 16.10): (1) financial, (2) customer satisfaction, (3) business processes, and (4) learning and growth.[43] The general goal is to broaden management's horizon beyond short-term financial results in order to sustain long-term success.

Michael Boo, chief strategy officer of the National Marrow Donor Program (NMDP), wanted to develop new ways of reaching the nonprofit's vision of 10,000 bone marrow transplants per year. Such transplants can prolong the lives of individuals with leukemia and

strategy map

A depiction of how an organization plans to convert its various assets into desired outcomes

balanced scorecard

Control system combining four sets of performance measures: financial, customer satisfaction, business processes, and learning and growth.

EXHIBIT 16.10   A Strategy Map and Balanced Scorecard for Performance Improvement at a Hospital

Strategy Map

Financial	Steady growth	Return on investor capital	Productivity
Customer Satisfaction	Service leadership	Patient satisfaction	Operational excellence
Business Processes	Improve quality and timeliness of services	Continuously improve staff's skills	Improve patient value
Learning & Growth	Promote culture of quality service	Align employee competencies with strategy	Implement technology to support innovation

Balanced Scorecard

Objectives	Measurement	Target
Grow sales revenue Increase profit	Balance sheet Profit and loss statement	10% annually 5% annually
Increase satisfaction Attract repeat patients	Satisfaction surveys Track in database	90% highly satisfied 80% return rate
Increase expertise of staff Reduce error rates	Completion rate of online training modules Number of incorrect dosages	90% passed with score of 85% or higher 2% or lower
Communicate importance of high quality Develop succession plan	Number of e-mails and mentions during meetings Percentage completed and times updated	One e-mail and mention per week 90% by year-end and one time per month

SOURCES: Adapted from Kaplan, R. S. and Norton, D. P., "Having Trouble with Your Strategy? Then Map It," *Harvard Business Review,* September–October 2000, pp. 167–72; and Kaplan, R. S. and Norton, D. P., *The Balanced Scorecard: Translating Strategy into Action.* Boston: Harvard Business School Press, 1996, p. 76.

other life-threatening diseases. He and colleagues developed a Balanced Scorecard with four perspectives: stakeholder, financial performance, processes, and people/knowledge/technology. In the first year, the NMDP made headway against its ambitious goal, averaging nearly 500 transplants each month.[44]

Effective control requires using many of the other techniques and practices of good management. For example, compensation systems will grant rewards for meeting standards and impose consequences if they are not met. And to gain employee acceptance, managers may also rely on many of the other communication and motivational tools that we discussed in earlier chapters, such as group decision making and positive reinforcement.

The Other Controls: Markets and Clans

Formal bureaucratic control systems are pervasive (and the most talked about in management textbooks), but they alone don't ensure optimal control. Market controls and clan controls offer more flexible, though no less potent, approaches to regulating performance.

Market Control

Unlike bureaucratic controls, market controls use economic forces—and the pricing mechanisms that accompany them—to regulate performance. The system works like this: when a person or unit produces a good or service that others value, a price for it can be negotiated. As a market for these transactions becomes established, two things happen:

- The price indicates the value of the good or service.
- Price competition controls productivity and performance.

The basic principles underlying market controls operate at the corporate level, the business unit (or department) level, and the individual level. Exhibit 16.11 shows a few ways in which organizations use market controls.

Bottom Line

Market controls help maintain low prices.
You manage the tech support unit for your company. How might market controls affect your costs?

Market Controls at the Corporate Level   Large, diversified companies use market controls to regulate independent business units. Conglomerates that act as holding companies treat business units as profit centers that compete with one another. Top executives may place very few bureaucratic controls on business unit managers but use profit and loss data to evaluate their performance. Decision making and power are decentralized to the business units, and market controls help ensure that business unit performance is in line with corporate objectives.

Using market controls is criticized by those who insist that economic measures do not adequately reflect the organization's total value. Employees often suffer as diversified companies are repeatedly bought and sold based on market controls.

EXHIBIT 16.11

Examples of Market Control

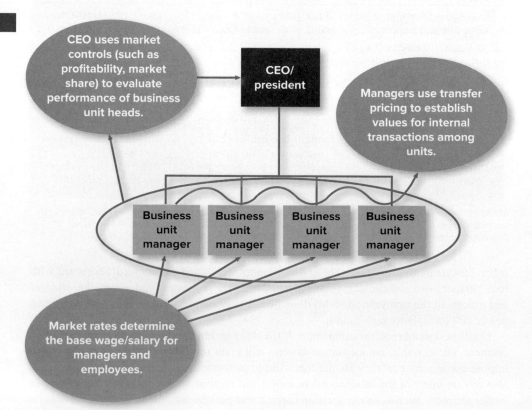

Market Controls at the Business Unit Level   Market control is used within business units to regulate exchanges among departments and functions. Transfer pricing is one method that organizations use to try to reflect market forces for internal transactions. A **transfer price** is the charge by one unit for a good or service that it supplies to another unit of the same organization. For example, in automobile manufacturing, a transfer price is affixed to components and subassemblies before they are shipped to subsequent business units for final assembly. Ideally, the transfer price reflects the price that the receiving business unit would have to pay for that product or service in the external marketplace.

As organizations have options to outsource and get goods and services from external partners, market controls such as transfer prices provide natural incentives to keep costs down and quality up. Managers stay in close touch with prices in the marketplace to make sure their own costs are in line, and they try to improve the service they provide to increase their department's value to the organization.

Consider the situation in which training and development can be done internally by the human resources department or outsourced to a consulting firm. If the human resources department cannot supply quality training at a reasonable price, the department's internal value drops—and managers generally don't want that to happen. To state this more positively: a manager or unit can add value—and benefit accordingly—by competing with outside suppliers and delivering a better product at lower cost.

Market Controls at the Individual Level   Market controls are used also at the individual level. For example, when organizations hire employees, the supply and demand for particular skills influence the wages employees can expect to receive. Employers pay higher wages to people with skills most valued by labor markets. Wages don't perfectly reflect external market rates—internal considerations pertain as well—but the market rate is often the best indicator of an employee's potential worth to a firm.

External market forces apply at executive levels as well. Board members use market controls to manage CEOs. Ironically, CEOs usually are seen as the ones controlling everyone else in the company; but the CEO is accountable to the board of directors, and the board must devise ways to ensure that the CEO acts in its interest.

You read a great deal about CEO compensation packages in Chapter 10. While compensation committees and boards decide the details, what other companies are doing for their CEOs is a major determinant. Compensation fads come and go, trends rise and fall, and top executive behaviors change in accord with these control systems. Examples include stock-based features that motivate longer or shorter time horizons and decisions, and the use (or not) of the balanced scorecard.

transfer price

Price charged by one unit for a good or service provided to another unit within the organization.

It would seem that market controls play an important role in professional athletes' salaries. But do the absurdly high salaries that some players make truly indicate a player's skill—or something else? If the player doesn't live up to expectations, or has a bad year, should the team cut his pay?

©Ilene MacDonald/Alamy Stock Photo RF

The Digital World

Leaders all over the world say that loss of control is the biggest change and challenge of the last 15 years. They feel a loss of control due to the trifecta of the Internet, cell phones, and social media.[45]

Any stakeholder has the ability to post personal opinions online. This can dramatically affect a leader's control over an issue, especially when people can easily find and add images to support their position, or create humorous memes that distract from the real issue. When many people agree, or just complain, it can create momentum and change. Social media have the ability to affect clan control by reinforcing opinions, changing opinions, or bifurcating complex issues.

Clan Control: The Role of Empowerment and Culture

LO 7

Managers are discovering that control systems based solely on bureaucratic and market mechanisms are insufficient for directing today's workforce. There are several reasons for this:

- *Employees' jobs have changed.* The nature of work is changing. More work is knowledge-based and difficult to monitor. There is no one best way to work, and standardizing jobs is difficult. Close supervision is unrealistic in part because it is nearly impossible to supervise activities such as thinking and creative problem solving.
- *Management has changed.* Supervisors used to know more about jobs than employees did. Today many employees know more about their jobs than anyone else does. This is the shift from touch labor to knowledge work. When real expertise in organizations exists at the very lowest levels, hierarchical control is less practical.[46]
- *The employment relationship has changed.* The social contract at work is being renegotiated. It used to be that employees were most concerned about pay, job security, and work hours. Now more employees want to be more fully engaged in their work, taking part in decision making, devising solutions to unique problems, and doing challenging assignments. They want to use their brains.

For these reasons, empowerment is a necessary aspect of a manager's control repertoire. With no one best way to approach a job and no way to scrutinize knowledge activities all day, managers empower employees to make decisions and trust that they will act in the best interests of the firm. But this does not mean giving up control. It means creating a strong culture of high standards and integrity so that employees will exercise effective control on their own.

Recall our discussion of organization culture in Chapter 2. A culture that encourages the wrong behaviors will severely hinder efforts to impose controls. But if managers create a strong culture that encourages correct behavior, one in which everyone understands and accepts management's values and expectations, then clan control can be highly effective.[47] Employees then are working within a guiding framework of values, and use their best judgment.

As an example, Starbucks relies partly on clan control to shape and guide employee behavior.[48] It emphasizes satisfying customers more than pleasing the bosses. Good-faith work that results in a mistake is tolerated as the unavoidable by-product of dealing with uncertainty, and is viewed as an opportunity to learn. And team members learn together.

Clan control can be a double-edged sword. It takes a long time to develop and even longer to change. This provides stability and direction during periods of upheaval. Yet if managers want to establish a new culture—a new version of clan control—they must help employees unlearn the old values and behaviors and embrace the new. We will talk more about this change process in the final chapter of this book.

Bottom Line

Clan control can ensure that employees meet performance standards. *What examples have you seen?*

Management in Action

FUTURE TRENDS IN EMPLOYEE MONITORING

Employers have a growing range of options for tracking, recording, and crunching employee data. For instance, a network of tiny sensors, installed in computers or lighting or heating fixtures, can detect people's motion and energy use in real time. Employees wear badges with RFID (radio frequency identification) technology, infrared detectors, and microphones tracking their speech and physical location at all times while at work (except the restroom, legally off limits).

Some employees might resent the privacy invasion. But one hospital's GPS tracking saved night-shift nurses time and effort by revealing how much extra walking they were doing to find understocked medications. And a recent survey of 1,000 workers produced a surprising result: only 16 percent of people who were not monitored felt positively about this kind of control measure but among those who *were* tracked, 54 percent had positive feelings. Perhaps they valued their employers' ability to locate them in an emergency or prevent unwarranted complaints about their work, and were less concerned that their privacy could be invaded or the monitoring system hacked.

Other workplace monitoring systems can tell when a keyboard has been inactive for 15 minutes or when an employee visits a non-work-related website. The restaurant industry leverages "big data" to mine huge amounts of information from tracking data regarding average serving time, tables turned per hour, and popularity of appetizers. Managers can counsel and train participating wait staff, increasing both tips and profits.

Some companies crunch all kinds of data—not just health or productivity statistics—and identify, for instance, who should be advised about the risk of diabetes or who might value a recommendation for an obstetrician. Credit scores, Internet search data, and even the stores where employees shop can identify healthy employees who keep doctors' appointments and ride bikes to work, as well as those who buy video games and could use counseling about weight loss. "All sorts of monitoring takes place for all sorts of reasons," says Lewis Maltby, president of the National Workrights Institute. "Virtually every company conducts electronic monitoring."[49]

- How much should employers tell their employees about what data they are collecting and what they are using them for? Why?

- What effect do you think employees' consent to monitoring has on their willingness to follow up on recommendations their employer may send them?

KEY TERMS

accounting audits, p. 470

activity-based costing (ABC), p. 470

after-action review, p. 464

assets, p. 471

balance sheet, p. 471

balanced scorecard, p. 478

budgeting, p. 469

bureaucratic control, p. 460

clan control, p. 461

concurrent control, p. 465

control, p. 460

current ratio, p. 474

debt–equity ratio, p. 474

external audit, p. 468

feedback control, p. 465

feedforward control, p. 465

internal audit, p. 468

liabilities, p. 471

management audit, p. 468

management myopia, p. 474

market control, p. 461

principle of exception, p. 464

profit and loss statement, p. 473

return on investment (ROI), p. 474

standard, p. 461

stockholders' equity, p. 471

strategy map, p. 478

transfer price, p. 481

RETAINING WHAT YOU LEARNED

In Chapter 16, you learned that companies develop control systems in order to keep employees focused on achieving organizational goals. The basic bureaucratic control system includes setting performance standards, measuring performance, comparing performance to standards, and eliminating unfavorable deviations. Performance standards should cover issues such as quantity, quality, time, and cost. Budgets are a control mechanism that act as an initial guide for allocating resources and using funds. Many companies are changing how they prepare budgets, with activity-based costing, to eliminate waste and improve business processes. Balance sheets compare the value of company assets to the obligations the company owes to owners and creditors. Profit and loss statements show company income relative to costs incurred. Financial ratios provide goals for managers as well as standards against which to evaluate performance. Managers use a variety of procedures to maximize the effectiveness of control systems. Market controls can be used at the level of the corporation, the business unit or department, and the individual. To be responsive to customers, companies are increasingly using clan control to harness the expertise of employees and give them the freedom to act on their own initiative.

LO 1 Explain why companies develop control systems.

- Left to their own devices, employees may act in ways that do not benefit the organization.
- Control systems are designed to eliminate idiosyncratic behavior and keep employees directed toward achieving the goals of the firm.
- Control systems are a steering mechanism for guiding resources and for guiding each individual to act on behalf of the organization.

LO 2 Summarize how to design a basic bureaucratic control system.

- The design of a basic control system involves four steps: (1) setting performance standards, (2) measuring performance, (3) comparing performance with the standards, and (4) eliminating unfavorable deviations by taking corrective action.
- Performance standards should be valid and should cover issues such as quantity, quality, time, and cost.
- Once performance is compared with standards, the principle of exception suggests that the manager needs to attend to and take action on the exceptional cases of significant deviations. Then the manager should take the action most likely to solve the problem.

LO 3 Describe the purposes for using budgets as a control device.

- Budgets combine the benefits of feedforward, concurrent, and feedback controls. They serve as an initial guide for allocating resources, a reference point for using funds, and a feedback mechanism for comparing actual levels of sales and expenses with their expected levels.
- Recently companies have modified their budgeting processes to allocate costs over basic processes (such as customer service) rather than to functions or departments.

- By changing the way they prepare budgets, many companies have discovered ways to eliminate waste and improve business processes.

LO 4 Define basic types of financial statements and financial ratios used as controls.

- The basic financial statements are the balance sheet and the profit and loss statement.
- The balance sheet compares the value of company assets to the obligations the company owes to owners and creditors.
- The profit and loss statement shows company income relative to costs incurred. In addition to these statements, companies look at liquidity ratios (whether the company can pay its short-term debts), leverage ratios (the extent to which the company is funding operations by going into debt), and profitability ratios (profit relative to investment). These ratios provide goals for managers as well as standards against which to evaluate performance.

LO 5 List procedures for implementing effective control systems.

- To maximize the effectiveness of controls, managers should (1) establish valid performance standards, (2) provide adequate information to employees, (3) ensure acceptability, (4) maintain open communication, and (5) use multiple approaches (such as bureaucratic, market, and clan control).

LO 6 Identify ways in which organizations use market control mechanisms.

- Market controls are useful at the level of the corporation, the business unit or department, or the individual.
- At the corporate level, business units are evaluated against one another based on profitability. At times, less profitable businesses are sold while more profitable businesses receive more resources.
- Within business units, transfer pricing can be used to approximate market mechanisms to control transactions among departments.
- At the individual level, market mechanisms control the wage rate of employees, including top executives.

LO 7 Discuss the use of clan control in an empowered organization.

- Approaching control from a centralized, mechanistic viewpoint is increasingly impractical. In today's organizations, it is difficult to program one best way to approach work, and it is often difficult to monitor performance.
- To be responsive to customers, companies can use clan control to harness the expertise of employees and give them the freedom to act on their own initiative.

DISCUSSION QUESTIONS

1. What controls can you identify in the management of your school or at a company where you have worked? If you can, interview a manager or employee of the organization to learn more about the controls in use there. How might the organization's performance change if those controls were not in place?

2. How are leadership and control different? How are planning and control different? How are structure and control different?

3. Imagine you are the sales manager of a company that sells medical supplies to hospitals nationwide. You have 10 salespeople reporting to you. You are responsible for your department achieving a certain level of sales each year. In general terms, how might you go about taking each step in the control cycle?

4. In the situation described in Question 3, what actions would you need to take if sales fell far below the budgeted level? What, if any, actions would you need to take if sales far exceeded the sales budget? If sales are right on target, does effective controlling require any response from you? (Would your answer differ if the department were on target overall, but some salespeople fell short and others exceeded their targets?)

5. Besides sales and expenses, identify five other important control measures for a business. Include at least one nonfinancial measure.

6. What are the pros and cons of bureaucratic controls such as rules, procedures, and close supervision?

7. Suppose a company at which executives were rewarded for meeting targets based only on profits and stock price switches to a balanced scorecard that adds measures for customer satisfaction, employee engagement, employee diversity, and ethical conduct. How would you expect executives' behaviors and performance to change in response to the new control system? How would you expect the company's performance to change?

8. Google uses Google Apps, such as Gmail, Google Calendar, and Docs & Spreadsheets, as collaboration tools for employees. Describe how the company could use controls to determine whether Google employees will use these software programs or competing software (e.g., Word and Excel).

9. How effective is clan control as a control mechanism? What are its strengths and limitations? When should a manager rely primarily on clan control?

10. Does empowerment imply that management loses control? Why or why not?

11. Some people use the concept of personal control to describe the application of business control principles to individual careers. Thinking about your school performance and career plans, which steps of the control process (Exhibit 16.3) have you been applying effectively? How do you keep track of your performance in meeting your career and life goals? How do you measure your success? Does clan control help you meet your personal and professional goals?

EXPERIENTIAL EXERCISES

16.1 SAFETY PROGRAM

OBJECTIVE

To understand some of the specific activities that fall under the management functions of planning, organizing, controlling and staffing, and directing.

INSTRUCTIONS

Read the following case and then evaluate the likely success of this managerial control effort. Specifically, how well did the manager review the source of the problems? How well designed is the new control system? How effectively is the manager building employee commitment to using the control mechanisms? How could this manager improve the control process? Summarize your findings and recommendations in a paragraph or two.

MANAGING THE VAMP CO. SAFETY PROGRAM

If there are specific things that a manager does, how are they done? What does it look like when one manages? The following describes a typical situation in which a manager performs managerial functions:

As production manager of the Vamp Stamping Company, you've become quite concerned over the metal stamping shop's safety record. Accidents that resulted in operators' missing time on the job have increased quite rapidly in the past year. These more serious accidents have jumped from 3 percent of all accidents reported to a current level of 10 percent.

Because you're concerned about your workers' safety as well as the company's ability to meet its customers' orders, you want to reduce this downtime accident rate to its previous level or lower within the next six months.

You call the accident trend to the attention of your production supervisors, pointing out the seriousness of the situation and their continuing responsibility to enforce the gloves and safety goggles rules. Effective immediately, every supervisor will review his or her accident reports for the past year, file a report summarizing these accidents with you, and state their intended actions to correct recurring causes of the accidents. They will make out weekly safety reports as well as meet with you every Friday to discuss what is being done and any problems they are running into.

You request the union steward's cooperation in helping the safety supervisor set up a short program on shop safety practices.

Because the machine operators are having the accidents, you encourage your supervisors to talk to their workers and find out what they think can be done to reduce the downtime accident rate to its previous level.

While the program is going on, you review the weekly reports, looking for patterns that will tell you how effective the program is and where the trouble spots are. If a supervisor's operators are not decreasing their accident rate, you discuss the matter in considerable detail with the supervisor and his or her key workers.

SOURCE: Herbert, Theodore T., *The New Management: Study Guide,* 4th ed. Upper Saddle River: Prentice Hall, 1987, 41.

16.2 FEEDFORWARD, CONCURRENT, AND FEEDBACK CONTROL

OBJECTIVES

1. To demonstrate the need for control procedures.
2. To gain experience in determining when to use feedforward, concurrent, and feedback controls.

INSTRUCTIONS

1. Read the text materials on feedforward, concurrent, and feedback control.
2. Read the Control Problem Situation and be prepared to resolve those control problems in a group setting.
3. Your instructor will divide the class into small groups. Each group completes the Feedforward, Concurrent, and Feedback Control Worksheet by achieving consensus on the types of control that should be applied in each situation. The group also develops responses to the discussion questions.
4. After the class reconvenes, group spokespersons present group findings.

DISCUSSION QUESTIONS

1. For which control(s) was it easier to determine application? For which was it harder?
2. Would this exercise be better assigned to groups or to individuals?

CONTROL PROBLEM SITUATION

Your management consulting team has just been hired by Technocron International, a rapidly growing producer of electronic surveillance devices that are sold to commercial and government end users. Some sales are made through direct selling, and some through industrial resellers. Direct-sale profits are being hurt by what seem to be exorbitant expenses paid to a few of the salespeople, especially those who fly all over the world in patterns that suggest little planning and control. There is trouble among the resellers because standard contracts have not been established and each reseller has an entirely different contractual relationship. Repayment schedules vary widely from customer to customer. Also, profits are reduced by the need to customize most orders, making mass production almost impossible. However, no effort has been made to create interchangeable components. There are also tremendous inventory problems. Some raw materials and parts are bought in such small quantities that new orders are being placed almost daily. Other orders are so large that there is hardly room to store everything. Many of these purchased components are later found to be defective and unusable, causing production delays. Engineering changes are made that make large numbers of old components still in storage obsolete. Some delays result from designs that are very difficult to assemble, and assemblers complain that their corrective suggestions are ignored by engineering. To save money, untrained workers are hired and assigned to experienced worker-buddies who are expected to train them on the job. However, many of the new people are too poorly educated to understand their assignments, and their worker-buddies wind up doing a great deal of their work. This, along with the low pay and lack of consideration from engineering, is causing a great deal of worker unrest and talk of forming a union. Last week alone nine new worker grievances were filed, and the U.S. Equal Employment Opportunity Commission has just announced intentions to investigate two charges of discrimination on the part of the company. There is also a serious cash flow problem because a number of long-term debts are coming due at the same time. The cash flow problem could be relieved somewhat if some of the accounts payable could be collected.

The CEO manages corporate matters through five functional divisions: operations, engineering, marketing, finance, and human resources management and general administration.

Feedforward, Concurrent, and Feedback Control Worksheet

Technocron International is in need of a variety of controls. Complete the following matrix by noting the feedforward, concurrent, and feedback controls that are needed in each of the five functional divisions.

Divisions	Feedforward, Controls	Concurrent Controls	Feedback Controls
HRM and general administration			
Operations			
Engineering			
Marketing			
Finance			

Concluding Case

THE GRIZZLY BEAR LODGE

Diane and Rudy Conrad own a small lodge outside Yellowstone National Park. Their lodge has 15 rooms that can accommodate up to 40 guests, with some rooms set up for families. Diane and Rudy serve a continental breakfast on weekdays and a full breakfast on weekends, included in the room rates they charge. Their busy season runs from May through September, but they remain open until Thanksgiving and reopen in April for a short spring season. They currently employ one cook and two waitpersons for the breakfasts on weekends, handling the other breakfasts themselves. They also have several housekeeping staff members, a groundskeeper, and a front-desk employee. The Conrads take pride in the efficiency of their operation, including the loyalty of their employees, which they attribute to their own form of clan control. If a guest needs something—whether it's a breakfast catered to a special diet or an extra set of towels—Grizzly Bear workers are empowered to supply it.

The Conrads are considering expanding their business. They have been offered the opportunity to buy the property next door, which would give them the space to build an annex containing an additional 20 rooms. Currently their annual sales total $300,000. With expenses running at $230,000—including mortgage, payroll, maintenance, and so forth—the Conrads' annual income is $70,000. They want to expand and make improvements without cutting back on the personal service they offer to their guests. In

fact, in addition to hiring more staff to handle the larger facility, they are considering collaborating with more local businesses to offer guided rafting, fishing, hiking, and horseback riding trips. They also want to expand their food service to include dinner during the high season, which means renovating the restaurant area of the lodge and hiring more kitchen and wait staff. Ultimately, the Conrads would like the lodge to be open year-round, offering guests opportunities to cross-country ski, ride snowmobiles, or hike in the winter. They hope to offer holiday packages for Thanksgiving, Christmas, and New Year's celebrations in the great outdoors. The Conrads report that their employees are enthusiastic about their plans and want to stay with them through the expansion process. "This is our dream business," says Rudy. "We're only at the beginning."

QUESTIONS

1. Discuss how Rudy and Diane can use feedforward, concurrent, and feedback controls both now and in the future at the Grizzly Bear Lodge to ensure their guests' satisfaction.
2. What might be some of the fundamental budgetary considerations the Conrads would have as they plan the expansion of their lodge?
3. Describe how the Conrads could use market controls to plan and implement their expansion.

CHAPTER 17

Managing Technology and Innovation

©SFIO CRACHO/Shutterstock.com RF

> The imperatives of technology and organization, not the images of ideology, are what determine the shape of economic society.
>
> —JOHN KENNETH GALBRAITH

LEARNING OBJECTIVES

After studying Chapter 17, you will be able to:

LO 1 List the types of processes that spur development of new technologies.

LO 2 Describe how technologies proceed through a life cycle.

LO 3 Discuss ways to manage technology for competitive advantage.

LO 4 Summarize how to assess technology needs.

LO 5 Identify alternative methods of pursuing technological innovation.

LO 6 Define key roles in managing technology.

LO 7 Describe the characteristics of innovative organizations.

LO 8 Describe the characteristics of successful development projects.

CHAPTER OUTLINE

Technology and Innovation
Technology Life Cycle
Diffusion of Technological Innovations

Technology Leadership and Followership
Technology Leadership   Technology Followership

Assessing Technology Needs
Measuring Current Technologies
Assessing External Technological Trends

Making Technology Decisions
Anticipated Market Receptiveness
Technological Feasibility
Economic Viability
Anticipated Capability Development
Organizational Suitability

Sourcing and Acquiring New Technologies
Internal Development
Purchase
Contracted Development
Licensing
Technology Trading
Research Partnerships and Joint Ventures
Acquiring a Technology Owner

**Technology and Managerial Roles
Organizing for Innovation**
Unleashing Creativity   Implementing
Bureaucracy Busting   Development Projects
Design Thinking   Technology, Job Design,
                                  and Human Resources

Management in Action

ELON MUSK: INNOVATOR EXTRAORDINAIRE

Elon Musk's passions are many and varied; many people believe that's the reason he is such a successful innovator and entrepreneur, launching multibillion-dollar ventures in fields as different as digital payment systems and space travel. He is a cofounder of PayPal (later sold to eBay), founder and CEO of the commercial rocket company SpaceX, and chair and CEO of Tesla, the maker of electric and self-driving cars.

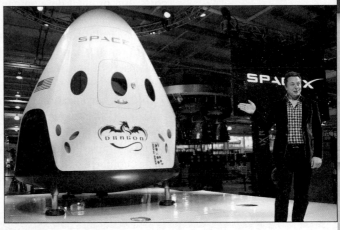

©ROBYN BECK/AFP/Getty Images

These and other industry-changing ventures have made him one of the wealthiest and most influential people in the world. Morgan Stanley calls Tesla "the world's most important car company." Tesla also recently acquired Solar City, a maker of solar panels.

Meanwhile Musk is investing in energy-efficient high-speed rail travel with a new venture called Hyperloop, and running a nonprofit called OpenAI to limit the possible ill effects of artificial intelligence. He even thinks about how to make Mars a habitable Earth-like planet, such as by warming it with nuclear fusion, and envisions a human settlement there. His goal is literally and truly to change the world.

Musk was born in South Africa and earned an undergraduate degree in business and physics from the University of Pennsylvania. In his late 20s, he sold his first company to Compaq Computers for more than $400 million and invested the money in founding PayPal with a few partners. A compulsively hard worker, he often puts in 85-hour weeks, although as the father of five sons (one set each of twins and triplets) he no longer spends nights sleeping at his desk as he did in his younger days.

Musk also is a lifelong voracious reader whose interests span science fiction, philosophy, biography, product design, business, technology, and other disciplines. Musk credits his study of physics with giving him a counterintuitive way of thinking that is "very effective for coming to correct answers that are not obvious." He seems easily able to transfer learned knowledge from one area of interest to another, and to reduce problems to their fundamentals in order to find new ways to address and then solve them.

Musk, who was the inspiration for Robert Downey Jr.'s portrayal of Tony Stark in the Iron Man movies, believes "most people can learn a lot more than they think they can." His advice? "It is important to view knowledge as sort of a semantic tree—make sure you understand the fundamental principles, i.e. the trunk and big branches, before you get into the leaves/details or there is nothing for them to hang onto."[1]

Elon Musk is an extraordinarily innovative thinker who seems able to translate his ideas into action. As you read this chapter, think about how technology and innovation work together to bring about change.

Although some visionaries such as Tesla's Elon Musk seem fearless, technological innovation is daunting in its complexity and pace of change. But it is vital for a firm's competitive advantage—not to mention its survival.[2]

Not long ago, new products took years to plan and develop, were standardized and mass produced, and were pushed onto the market through extensive selling and promotional campaigns. Product sales lives were measured in decades, production processes used equipment dedicated only to those standardized products, and economies of scale minimized costs. But product development now is a race to become the first to introduce innovative products that often live for months rather than years, as they are displaced by ever more technologically sophisticated products. For example, robotics technology used to apply only to repetitive, programmable tasks such as are found in manufacturing. Now it is used in a variety of human–machine contexts, from nursing to customer service roles in big box retailers.[3]

Today's organizations depend on effective technology management to carry out basic tasks but also, even more important, to remain competitive by constantly offering new goods or services. In a marketplace where technology and rapid innovation are critical for success, managers must understand how technologies emerge, develop, and change the ways companies compete and people work. This chapter discusses how to integrate technology into competitive strategy, how to assess technological needs, and how to meet these needs.

Bottom Line
Innovation is a key to competitiveness.
Why does innovation matter for a service business?

Technology and Innovation

 LO 1

We defined **technology** in Chapter 9 as the methods, processes, systems, and skills used to transform resources into products. It is not contradictory to add now that we can view technology as the commercialization of science: the systematic application of scientific knowledge to a new product, process, or service. In this sense, technology is embedded in every product, service, and procedure used or produced.[4]

When technology is used to create a new good or service, or a new way of working, it is a form of innovation. Innovation differs from invention, or turning new ideas into realities, which may or may not add value to an organization. In the context of management, **innovation** is any new way of working that creates value.

Innovations can be of these fundamental types:[5]

technology

The systematic application of scientific knowledge to a new product, process, or service.

innovation

The introduction of new goods and services; a change in method or technology; a positive, useful departure from previous ways of doing things.

1. *Product innovation* is a change in the outputs (goods or services) the organization produces. If BP's research into biofuels results in a new kind of fuel to sell, this would be an example of product innovation.
2. *Process innovation* is a change in the way outputs (goods or services) are produced. If BP's research into biofuels resulted in a more efficient way to produce fuel from sugarcane, it's a process innovation. Other examples of process innovation are flexible manufacturing processes discussed in Chapter 9, including mass customization, just-in-time, and concurrent engineering.
3. *Business model innovation* refers to a change in the way the organization creates and delivers value. The change may affect any component of a company's business model: its customer value proposition (the basic problem it solves, such as ecofriendly fuel for about the same cost as fossil fuels), its profit formula (the financial road map for its success), its key resources (people, technology, facilities, brand), and its key processes. Exhibit 17.1 has additional examples.

These categories cover many creative new ideas (see the nearby "Social Enterprise" box), which can range throughout every business via changes in: product offerings, brand, platforms or processes of product creation, solutions to customer problems, customers served, nature of the customer experience, ways of earning money, process efficiencies, organization structure, supply chain, physical or virtual points of customer interactions, and more.[6]

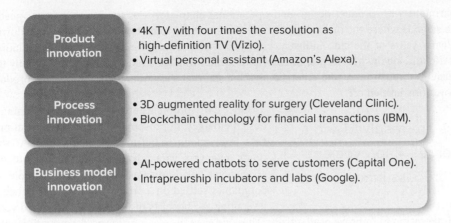

EXHIBIT 17.1
Innovation Types with Examples

Technologies emerge, develop, and are replaced in predictable patterns. Critical forces converge to create new technologies, which then follow well-defined life-cycle patterns. We describe the technology life cycle after noting these driving forces of technological development:

1. There must be a need, or demand, for the technology. Without, there is no reason for technological innovation to occur.
2. Meeting the need must be theoretically possible, and basic science must contain the knowledge that makes it possible.
3. We must be able to convert the scientific knowledge into practice in both engineering and economic terms. If we can theoretically do something but doing it is economically impractical, the technology cannot yet emerge.
4. The funding, skilled labor, time, space, and other resources needed to develop the technology must be available.
5. Entrepreneurial initiative is needed to identify and pull all the necessary elements together.

technology life cycle

A predictable pattern followed by a technological innovation, from its inception and development to market saturation and replacement.

Technology Life Cycle

Technological innovations typically follow a predictable pattern called the **technology life cycle**, shown in Exhibit 17.2. Early progress can be slow as competitors continually

LO 2

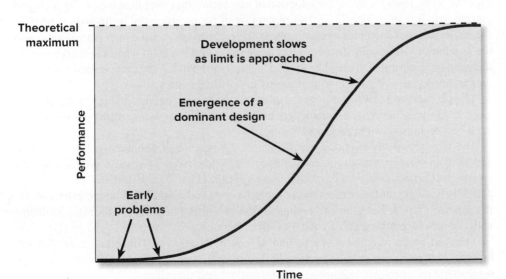

EXHIBIT 17.2
The Technology Life Cycle

experiment with product design and operational characteristics to meet consumer needs. This stage is where the rate of product innovation tends to be highest. For example, during the early years of the auto industry, companies tried a wide range of machines, including electric and steam-driven cars, to determine which would be most effective. Eventually the internal combustion engine emerged as the dominant design, and the number of product innovations leveled off.

> Once early problems are resolved and a dominant design emerges, improvements come more from process innovations.

Once early problems are resolved and a dominant design emerges, improvements come more from process innovations to refine the technology. At this point managers gain advantage by finding process efficiencies and lower cost. In the auto example, as companies settled on a product standard, they began leveraging the benefits of mass production and vertical integration to improve productivity. These process innovations lowered production costs and brought automobile prices in line with consumer budgets.[7]

Eventually the new technology begins to reach the upper limits of both its performance capabilities and the spread of its use. Development slows and becomes increasingly costly, and the market becomes saturated (there are few new customers). The technology can remain in this mature stage for some time—as with autos—or can be replaced quickly by another technology offering superior performance or economic advantage.

Life cycles can take decades or even centuries, as with iron- and steel-making technologies. A more dynamic example of technology evolution is in the recorded music industry, which moved from the relatively primitive device Thomas Edison invented through the vinyl record to the cassette tape to the digitally recorded CD to MP3 files on mobile phones. Currently, the dominant music delivery technology is free and subscription-based streaming services from companies like Apple Music, Pandora, and Spotify.[8] Streamed music can be played from virtually any Internet-enabled device.

As the music example shows, a technology life cycle can be made up of many individual product life cycles. Each product performs a similar task—delivering recorded music to listeners—yet each is an improvement over its predecessors. Significant innovations, often entirely new technologies, are followed by many small, incremental innovations.

Ongoing development of a technology increases the benefits it provides, makes it easier to use, and generates new applications. In the process, the technology spreads to new adopters.

Diffusion of Technological Innovations

Like the technology life cycle, the adoption of new technology over time follows an S-shaped pattern (top line in Exhibit 17.3). The percentage of people using the technology is small in the beginning, but increases dramatically as the technology succeeds and spreads through the population. Eventually the number of users peaks and levels off when the market for the technology is saturated. This pattern, first observed in 1903, has been verified with many new technologies and ideas in a wide variety of industries and settings.[9]

The adopters of a new technology fall into five groups (see the bottom line in Exhibit 17.3). Each group presents different challenges and opportunities to managers who want to market a new technology or product innovation.

The first group, representing approximately 2.5 percent of adopters, is the *innovators*. Typically, innovators are adventurous and willing to take risks. They pay a premium for latest new technology or product and champion it if they like it. The enthusiasm of innovator-adopters is no guarantee of success—for example, the product may still be too expensive for the general market. But a lack of enthusiasm in this group often signals serious problems with the new technology, and a need for further development.

The next group to adopt a new technology are *early adopters*. This group is crucial and includes well-respected opinion leaders. Early adopters often are those whom others look to for leadership, up-to-date technological information, and suggestions.

Multiple Generations at Work

Tech-Savvy Gen Z Is Entering the Workforce

Move over Millennials, a new generation is entering the workforce. Generation Z (a.k.a., Gen Z, Centennials, or iGen) refers to people born in the mid-1990s or later. While much has been written about the Millennial generation, less is known about this younger generation and how its members view technology and work.

Gen Zers were the first truly digital natives who grew up with smartphones. According to Jason Dorsey, co-founder of the Center for Generational Kinetics: "When you come from an age never remembering a time before smartphones, which is true for all Gen Zers in the U.S., it fundamentally changes your learning, communication and workplace expectations." This immersion into smartphone technology enabled Gen Z to become web- and app-savvy.

In contrast to Millennials, this younger generation is weary of posting personal information on platforms that store it. Gen Z shuns e-mail and Facebook for more personal and immediate social media platforms like Snapchat, Whisper, Instagram, and Vine that don't "leave a trail."

When Gen Zers want to learn something new, check the news, or connect with friends, they turn to their phones. According to Dorsey: ". . . as Gen Z enters the

©George Rudy/Shutterstock.com RF

workforce, they expect everything to be mobile first, from communication and collaboration to training, retention and engagement strategies."

To attract members of the Gen Z generation, companies should invest in the "latest tech" for employee collaboration, communication, and productivity.[10]

Marketing managers often spend heavily in promotion to these first two adopter groups. For example, companies are increasingly using gamification to engage their customers and employees (see "Multiple Generations at Work").

The next group to adopt is the *early majority*. These adopters are more deliberate, taking longer to decide to use something new. Often they are important members of a

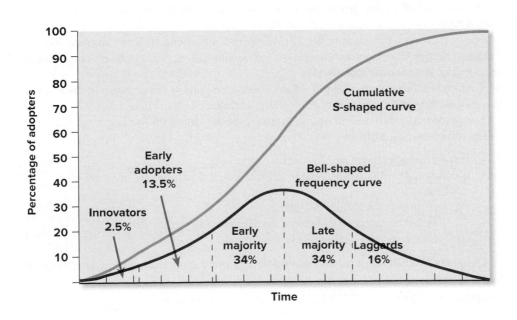

EXHIBIT 17.3
Technology Dissemination Pattern and Adopter Categories

Social Enterprise

Piramal Sarvajal Provides Clean Water via "Water ATMs"

"Problems of poverty are, on most occasions, inextricably linked with those of water—its availability, its proximity, its quantity, and its quality." So said the United Nations in its World Water Report of 2015. As just one example, many of India's more than 1.3 billion people rely on untreated water, and about 75 percent of all diseases in that country, some fatal, can be traced to these contaminated supplies.

Piramal Sarvajal is a social enterprise dedicated to leveraging technology to help remedy this urgent health problem. Founded by Anand Shah in 2008, the organization currently serves 320,000 consumers every day via nearly 600 innovative "water ATMs" installed in 14 of India's 29 states. Centralized water treatment plants are expensive, and pipelines can bring water only so far, meaning the country's more remote populations would still face the problem of carrying heavy containers over long distances to their homes.

This time-consuming daily chore often falls to women and girls. The Sarvajal solution was to build local water-treatment plants and then distribute the clean water through solar-powered vending machines available 24 hours a day.

Customers use their mobile phones to buy prepaid, refillable cards that allow them to purchase a specific amount of water and collect it in their own containers for the relatively short trip home. With training in the purification technology and in maintenance and marketing, local franchisees own and operate the water ATMs and treatment systems. The franchise system ensures that clean water reaches street corners, stores, schools, and other gathering places even in remote villages. The system so far has dispensed more than half a billion liters (154 million gallons) of potable water.

At first Sarvajal dispensed the water free of charge, but people used it for bathing and to water their cattle. So it devised an affordable pricing plan that both sustains the project and encourages customers to use the water only for drinking.

The water more than pays for itself via reduced health care costs. With local doctors' support, Sarvajal spread this cost-benefit message to customers face to face, in posters painted on walls, and via speakers mounted on local trucks. Customers who live below the national poverty line (about 30 percent of the country's population) receive water that is either free or subsidized by Sarvajal.[11]

Questions

- Into which technology types (one or more) would you classify Sarvajal's water ATMs?
- Would you expect the technology that powers water ATMs to follow the typical S-shaped pattern of diffusion? Why or why not?

community or industry, but not the leaders. It may take awhile for the technology or new product to spread to this group, but once it does, use will begin to proliferate into the mainstream.

The next group is the *late majority*. The members of this group are more skeptical of technological change, and approach innovation with great caution, often adopting only because of economic necessity or social pressure.

The final 16 percent are *laggards*. Often isolated and highly conservative in their views, laggards are extremely suspicious of innovation and change.

The speed with which an innovation spreads depends largely on five attributes. An innovation will spread quickly if it

- Has a great advantage over its predecessor.
- Is compatible with existing systems, procedures, infrastructures, and ways of thinking.
- Has less rather than greater complexity.
- Can be tried or tested easily without significant cost or commitment.
- Can be observed and copied easily.

Designing products with these considerations in mind can make a huge contribution to their success.

Technology Leadership and Followership

Discussions about technology life cycles and diffusion patterns can imply that technological change occurs naturally or automatically. But just the opposite is true: Change is neither easy nor natural (we discuss change more fully in our final chapter). Decisions about technology and innovation are highly strategic, and managers need to approach them systematically and thoughtfully.

In Chapter 4, we discussed two generic strategies a company can use to position itself in the market: low cost and differentiation. With low-cost leadership, the company maintains an advantage because it operates at lower cost than its competitors. With a differentiation strategy, the advantage comes from having a unique good or service for which customers are willing to pay a premium price.[12] Technological innovations can support either of these strategies: They gain cost advantage through pioneering lower-cost product designs and creating low-cost ways to operate, and they can support differentiation by pioneering unique goods or services that increase buyer value and thus command premium prices.

As with recorded music, technology can completely change the rules of competition within an industry. Clayton Christensen coined the term **disruptive innovation** to describe situations in which a simple application swiftly takes over the market.[13] Laptop users initially mocked tablet computers because they offer less computing power than a laptop and more bulk than a smartphone. Nevertheless, Apple's iPad (first launched in 2010) quickly helped tablets carve out a big share of the market for portable computers.

Disruptive innovation creates a dilemma for companies: Should they continue on with the superior technology (and possibly lose the advantages of early adoption) or switch over to the new technology (and find themselves with an inferior product that may or may not succeed)?

The usual tendency is to innovate to the point that goods or services become too sophisticated, inconvenient, or expensive for buyers' tastes, creating new opportunities for the next disruptive innovation. To be a disruptive innovator, focus on the users of a product and look for customers whose needs are being ignored—say, because they want something that costs less or is easier to use. For example, Uber disrupted the global taxi industry by giving customers an easier, faster, and less expensive way to hail a ride.[14]

But industries do not transform overnight. Typically, signs of a new technology's impact are visible well in advance, leaving time for companies to respond. Almost every competitor in the telecommunications industry fully understood the value of cellular technology. Often the key issue is not whether to adopt a new technology, but when, plus how to integrate it with the organization's operating practices and strategies.

Technology Leadership

The adage "timing is everything" applies to many things, from financial investments to telling jokes. It applies also to developing and exploiting new technologies. Industry leaders such as 3M, Amazon, Nike, and Merck built and maintain their competitive positions through early development and application of new technologies.

However, technology leadership imposes costs and risks, and is not always the best approach (see Exhibit 17.4).[15] Apple is well known for its technology leadership, beginning with its Macintosh computer, which pioneered the mouse and graphical desktop icons instead of strings of typed computer commands. Not to mention a string of popular innovations ever since.[16]

> Often the key question is not whether to adopt a new technology but when.

Advantages of Technology Leadership Technology leadership is attractive thanks to its potential for high profits and first-mover advantages. If technology leadership increases a firm's efficiency relative to competitors, it achieves a cost advantage. The advantage generates greater profits and can attract more customers through lower prices.

Bottom Line

Innovation can improve any bottom-line practice. *How can innovation support a differentiation strategy?*

disruptive innovation

A process by which a product, service, or business model takes root initially in simple applications at the bottom of a market and then moves "up market," eventually displacing established competitors.

EXHIBIT 17.4

Advantages and
Disadvantages of
Technology Leadership

Advantages	Disadvantages
First-mover advantage	Greater risks
Little or no competition	Cost of technology development
Greater efficiency	Costs of market development and customer education
Higher profit margins	Infrastructure costs
Sustainable advantage	Costs of learning and eliminating defects
Reputation for innovation	Possible cannibalization of existing products
Establishment of entry barriers	
Occupation of best market niches	
Opportunities to learn	

Top pharmaceutical companies depend on patents to allow them several years of selling new drugs without competition before cheaper generic versions of their drugs are released. They must develop new drugs in the meantime to sustain their success.

©Thinkstock/Getty Images RF

And if a company is first to market, it might charge a premium price because it faces no competition. Higher prices and greater profits defray the costs of developing new technologies.

This one-time advantage of being the technology leader can be turned into a sustainable advantage. Sustaining the lead depends on competitors' ability to duplicate the technology and the firm's ability to keep improving quickly enough to outpace competitors.

A firm can do this in several ways. The reputation for being an innovator can create an ongoing advantage and even spill over to the company's other products. For example, 3M's reputation for innovation and quality differentiates some of its standard products, such as adhesive tape, and allows them to command a premium price. A competitor may be able to copy the product but not the reputation. 3M's strong reputation stems partly from how it dedicates about 6 percent of its annual revenue to research and development.[17]

Patents and other institutional barriers can be used to block competitors and maintain leadership. The big players in the pharmaceutical industry invest heavily in research and development; they depend on patents to give them several years to sell their new drugs without competition before generic versions are permitted. For example, erectile dysfunction drug, Viagra, which had recent annual sales of over $1.0 billion, had only one direct competitor (Cialis) until its patent expired in 2017.[18] As additional blockbuster drug patents expire, pharmaceutical companies face a tremendous challenge to develop the next new drugs.

The first mover also can preempt competitors by occupying the best market niches. If it can establish high switching costs (recall Chapter 2) for repeat customers, these positions can be difficult for competitors to capture. Microsoft dominates the software market with its Windows operating system because of the large library of software packaged with it. Although other companies offer more advanced software, their products are not as attractive because they are not bundled as the Windows-based systems is.

Technology leadership can provide an important learning advantage. Competitors may copy or adopt a new technology, but new learning by the technology leader can generate minor improvements that are difficult to imitate. Many Japanese manufacturers use several small, incremental improvements generated with their *kaizen* programs (Chapter 9) to continually upgrade their process and product quality. Competitors cannot easily copy these many small improvements, which collectively provide significant advantage.[19]

> The first mover can preempt competitors by occupying the best market niches.

Disadvantages of Technology Leadership   Being the first to develop or adopt a new technology does not always lead to immediate advantage and high profits. Such potential may exist, but technology leadership does impose high costs and risks that followers do not have to bear. Being the leader thus can be more costly than being the follower; there's good reason the forefront of technology is often called the "bleeding edge." Costs include educating buyers unfamiliar with the new technology, building an infrastructure to support it, and developing complementary products to help achieve its full potential.

When the personal computer was first developed in the 1970s, dozens of computer companies entered the market. Almost all of them failed, usually because they lacked the financial, marketing, and sales ability needed to attract and service customers. Also, many new products require regulatory approval. Developing a new drug, including testing and obtaining FDA approval, can take 10 years or more and cost an average of $2.6 billion or more. After that, developers enjoy a profitable period of patent protection until competitors move in with low-cost generics. Although these followers do not get the benefits of being first to market, they can copy the drug for a fraction of the cost once the original patents expire. This strategy can be highly profitable.[20]

Being a pioneer carries other risks. If raw materials and equipment are new or have unique specifications, a ready supply at a reasonable cost may not be available. Or the technology may not be fully developed, and have problems yet to be resolved. In addition, the unproven market creates uncertainty in demand. Finally, the new technology may have an adverse impact on existing business. It may cannibalize current products or make current investments obsolete.

Technology Followership

Not all organizations are equally prepared to be technology leaders, nor would leadership benefit each organization equally. In deciding whether to be a technology leader or follower, managers consider their company's competitive strategy, the benefits to be gained through the technology, and characteristics of their organization.[21]

Technology followership shares a feature with technology leadership: it too can be used to support both low-cost and differentiation strategies. If the follower learns from the leader's experience, it can avoid the costs and risks of leadership and thereby establish a low-cost position. Generic drug makers use this strategy. Followership also can support differentiation. By learning from the leader, followers can adapt the products or delivery systems to fit buyers' needs more closely.

Microsoft built great success on this type of followership. The company launched many products, including music players, video game consoles, spreadsheet and word-processing software, and web browsers, after technology leaders paved the way. Likewise, Facebook came to dominate social networking only after Friendster and MySpace burned through money introducing the concept. Newer competitors, such as Google, and photo- and video-sharing apps like Instagram, Snapchat, and WhatsApp continue to enter the market hoping they can lure away users with services that improves on Facebook's. This follower strategy is more challenging once an industry leader has established widespread customer loyalty.

Management decisions about when to adopt new technologies depend also on their potential benefits plus their organization's technology skills. As discussed earlier, technologies do not emerge in their final state; rather, they develop continually. This eventually makes them easier to use and more adaptable to various strategies. For example, high-bandwidth communication networks enabled more companies to work with suppliers located abroad.

At the same time, complementary products and technologies can make the main technology more useful. For example, doctors and nurses now use a phone app to track eight vital signs, from heart and respiratory rates to falls.[22] The phone app works with a small biosensor patch applied to the skin of patients.[23] While this technology is not yet replacing traditional monitoring (such as heart rate tracking equipment and manual blood pressure testing), it holds great promise for improving the patient experience during hospital stays.

Bottom Line
Following the technology leader can save development expense.
How can being a follower help reduce costs?

These complementary products and technologies combine with the gradual diffusion of the technology to form a shifting competitive impact. The best time to adopt a technological innovation is when the costs and risks of switching to the technology are outweighed by the benefits. This point will be different for each organization; some will benefit from a leadership (early adopter) role, and others from a followership role, depending on organizational characteristics and strategies.[24]

Assessing Technology Needs

LO 4   The biggest industry sector in the U.S. economy is health care services, where spending is soaring, much to the dismay of the insurers and patients paying the medical bills. One reason U.S. health care costs so much is that the industry has been slower than others to adopt technologies that can make day-to-day operations more efficient. According to an Accenture study: "using virtual healthcare for annual patient visits could save more than $7 billion worth of primary care physician (PCP) time each year."[25] Virtual health care is technology-enabled services that do not have to be performed in a doctor's office or medical facility, including videoconferences with physicians, remote biometric tracking, and mobile apps for managing health. About one in five Americans have tried this novel approach to their annual health care check-ups.[26]

Failure to correctly assess your organization's technology needs can fundamentally impair its effectiveness. A thorough assessment measures current technologies plus external trends affecting the industry.

Measuring Current Technologies

technology audit

Process of clarifying the key technologies on which an organization depends.

Before managers can devise strategies for developing and exploiting technological innovation, they must gain a clear understanding of their current technology base. A **technology audit** helps identify which technologies are most important. The most important thing about a new technology is its competitive value.

One technique for measuring competitive value uses four technology categories:[27]

- *Emerging technologies* are still under development and thus are unproved. They may, however, significantly alter the rules of competition in the future. Managers should monitor emerging technologies but might not invest in them until they are developed more fully.
- *Pacing technologies* have yet to prove their full value but have the potential to alter the rules of competition. When first installed, computer-aided manufacturing was a pacing technology. Its potential was not fully understood, but companies that used it effectively realized major speed and cost advantages.
- *Key technologies* have proved effective, and provide advantage because not everyone uses them. They continue to provide some first-mover advantages. A key technology for Intel is a powerful proprietary processing chip. Eventually, alternatives to key technologies can emerge. Until alternatives merge, key technologies provide a major competitive edge that prevents threats from new entrants.
- *Base technologies* are commonplace in the industry; everyone in the industry must have them. Thus they provide little or no advantage. Managers have to invest merely to ensure their organization's continued competence.

Technologies can evolve rapidly through these categories. Back in the late 1970s, electronic word processing was an emerging technology. By the early 1980s, it was a pacing technology. With continued improvements and more powerful computer chips, it quickly became a key technology. Costs dropped, usage spread, and it enhanced productivity demonstrably. By the late 1980s, electronic word processing was a base technology in most applications. It now is a routine activity in almost every office.

Assessing External Technological Trends

As with any planning, decisions about technology must balance internal capabilities (strengths and weaknesses) with external opportunities and threats. Managers can use several techniques to understand better how technology is changing within an industry.

Benchmarking   Technology benchmarking (Chapter 4) varies across industries. Competitors understandably are reluctant to share their secrets, but trading information for benchmarking purposes can prove highly valuable. For example, Harley-Davidson recovered its reputation for manufacturing quality motorcycles only after company executives toured Honda's plant and witnessed firsthand the weaknesses of Harley's manufacturing technologies and the vast potential for improvement.

Benchmarking against potential competitors in other countries can be useful. Companies may find key or pacing technologies overseas that they can import easily and to significant advantage. Moreover, overseas firms may be more willing to share their knowledge if they are not direct competitors and if they can receive beneficial information in exchange.

Scanning   Whereas benchmarking identifies current practices, scanning uncovers what can be done and what is being developed. In other words, benchmarking examines key and perhaps some pacing technologies, whereas scanning seeks pacing and emerging technologies—those just being introduced and still in development.

For example, IBM's million-neuron TrueNorth chip may be a game changer in the computer industry. Still in development, the neuromorphic chip is hundreds of times more powerful than current chips and likely will empower the next level of artificial intelligence where computers will be designed to "anticipate and learn."[28] The U.S. Air Force Research Lab, the first customer to purchase the experimental chip, uses it to enhance the ability of drones, aircraft, and satellites to identify images on the ground.[29]

Scanning uses some of the same tactics used in benchmarking. However, scanning identifies and monitors potential sources of new technologies for the industry. It often requires reading more cutting-edge research journals and attending research conferences and seminars. How much scanning is done depends largely on how close to the cutting edge of technology an organization decides to operate.

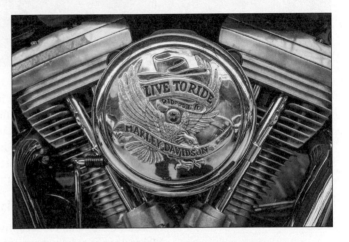

After Harley-Davidson executives toured a Honda plant, they were able to identify the weaknesses within their own company and use that knowledge to improve their products and boost their reputation.

©Sergey Kohl/123RF RF

Making Technology Decisions

Once managers have analyzed their organization's current technological position, they can make decisions about how to develop or exploit emerging innovations. Decision making must balance the many interrelated factors discussed next.

LO 5

Anticipated Market Receptiveness

The first strategic consideration is market potential. Often innovations are stimulated by external demand for new goods and services. A Boston company called Rethink Robotics believes the problem of repetitive-motion injuries will drive demand for robots that can work safely near humans to perform simple tasks like picking, sorting, and arranging items. The company responded by developing its Baxter robot with plastic, padded arms and sensors in the joints so workers can safely stand nearby and program the six-foot-tall robot. To help production workers control the robot, Baxter has a display screen on which expressive eyes signal the robot's status.[30] Since its launch a few years ago, the robot's sales have increased in several markets, including the United States, Spain, China, Israel, and Mexico.[31]

In assessing market receptiveness, executives need to make two determinations:

1. In the short run, the new technology should have an immediate, valuable application.
2. In the long run, the technology must be able to satisfy future market needs.

©Bloomberg/Bloomberg/Getty Images

For example, many brick-and-mortar retailers are looking for innovative ways to increase current and future sales by motivating their tech-friendly customers to visit and make purchases in their physical stores. This priority is especially important for retailers who want to avoid the fate of once-dominant brands like Sears that didn't adapt successfully to technology-enabled retail. According to the U.S. Census Bureau, retail e-commerce sales for the fourth quarter of 2016 totaled $123.6 billion, an increase of 32 percent from the third quarter of the same year.[32] Online shopping continues to increase from mobile phones and other devices.

Retailers are attracting customer visits with "in-store" technology. At its flagship store in New York City, Macy's opened a new floor called "One Below" featuring selfie walls and 3D printing for customizing accessories.[33] The store also hosts dance parties to attract more online shoppers to see, feel, and try on its wares.[34] Nordstrom also is trying to enhance the in-store customer experience. It collaborated with custom women's footwear maker Shoes of Prey to open custom shoe boutiques in six of its brick-and-mortar.[35] "We're focused on what the customer is looking for. They're interested in personalization and customization," says Scott Meden, Nordstrom's Executive Vice President and General Merchandise Manager of shoes.[36]

Technological Feasibility

In addition to market receptiveness, managers must consider an innovation's feasibility. Visions can stay unrealized for a long time. Technical obstacles block progress.

For example, security experts for years have wanted reliable facial recognition systems. Such systems, if they could accurately link a face captured via video or camera to a correct identity in a database, could help locate wanted criminals, reduce fraudulent use of driver's licenses and stolen credit cards, and increase the efficiency of security check processes of businesses, airports, and other organizations that currently require check-in procedures. Several challenges have contributed to error rates associated with facial recognition technology, including the aging of faces, unique poses, lighting distortions, distance from the recording device, and incomplete images of a face.[37] Despite these challenges, the accuracy of facial recognition continues to improve.[38]

Researchers from the University of Washington challenged several research teams from around the world to test the accuracy of their algorithms on 1 million images (nearly 700,000 were unique individuals) obtained from Flickr. Google's FaceNet displayed near perfect accuracy on a smaller subset of the images, but dropped to 75 percent when the program was asked to distinguish all 1 million images.[39] In a different test conducted by the National Institute of Standards and Technology, NEC, a Japanese IT and communications technology company, earned the highest accuracy rating (0.8 percent error rate) in facial recognition as individuals walked past a camera in an airport without stopping or acknowledging the camera.[40]

In the oil industry, technological barriers prevent exploration and drilling in the deepest parts of the ocean. In medicine, scientists and doctors struggle mightily to find causes of and cures for deadly diseases. Makers of electronic devices are constantly challenged by how to keep their processors cool enough to function properly even as they get smaller and more powerful.

GE Global Research developed advanced cooling jets that are quieter and use less energy to keep electronic components from overheating. The jets can be scaled to cool smaller (a laptop) or larger (an aircraft engine) electronic applications.[41] But as time passes, manufacturers will surely be looking for something even smaller. Each of these innovations is slowed by the technical limits of currently available technologies.

Economic Viability

Technological feasibility relates closely to economic viability. Apart from whether a firm can pull off a technological innovation, executives must find enough financial incentive to try. Hydrogen-powered fuel cell technology for automobiles is almost feasible technically, but its costs are still too high. Even with lower costs, lack of supporting societal infrastructure—such as hydrogen refueling stations—remains a barrier to economic viability.

But if a company can find niche markets for a high-priced new technology, it often can advance the technology so that applications become more affordable. Three-dimensional (3D) printers read plans and translate them into physical objects by spraying out extremely thin layers of plastic or other materials to create the physical object. A skilled designer can create a 3D model of a part in a matter of hours and then direct the printer to finish the job. If the design disappoints, changes are easy to make with the software's commands, and no machinery needs to be retooled. A factory might invest in a high-end printer for $100,000 or more, but the price of basic printers has fallen below $1,500, putting them in reach of entrepreneurs and inventors.[42]

> Closely related to technological feasibility is economic viability.

Less futuristic innovations, as well, require a careful assessment of economic viability. New technologies often represent an expensive and long-term commitment of resources. Once an organization commits to an innovation, changing direction is costly and difficult. For these reasons, a careful, objective analysis of technology costs versus benefits is essential.

Of course, benefits as well as costs can be substantial. Spending on health care technology is helping people live longer.[43] While that is a positive, the cost of such life-extending technology is a major contributing factor to the rising costs of health care services and insurance.[44]

The issue of economic viability takes us back to our earlier discussion of adoption timing. Earlier adopters may have first-mover advantages, but must deal with the strategy's costs. The development costs of a particular innovation may be quite high, as in pharmaceuticals, chemicals, and software. Patents and copyrights may help organizations recoup the costs of their investments in technological innovations. Without such protection, the investments in research and development might not be justifiable.

Globalization has created a worldwide market for goods produced by low-cost counterfeiters and pirates, who incur no research and development expense. Furthermore, technology makes it easy to copy software, and download movies and music without paying for it. Ugg boots, Apple iPhones, Pfizer's drug Viagra, Rolex watches, Prada handbags, and LEGO building sets—all these and many more are counterfeited or illegally copied and sold. This exploding growth in piracy and fake pharmaceuticals, footware, and other products adds new barriers to economic viability.[45] According to the International Trademark Association, $460 billion worth of counterfeit goods were bought and sold in 2016.[46]

Anticipated Capability Development

It bears repeating that organizations should (and do) build their strategies based on core capabilities. This advice applies as well to technology and innovation strategies. Merck, Apple, and Intel are prime examples of companies with core capabilities in research and development. But even in these cases, research capabilities are not always a good match with market opportunities. Merck and other firms found that new opportunities for fighting disease are in biotechnology, but their primary expertise was chemistry-based drugs. So they added new capabilities by acquiring or setting up ventures with biotechnology start-ups.

Bottom Line

Innovation requires financial feasibility.

Say an innovation is exciting but unprofitable. What are the pros and cons of pursuing it anyway?

Some innovations are competency enhancing—exploiting or strengthening a core capability—whereas others are competency destroying. Continuing the Merck example, most core capabilities in the industry are in chemistry-based drugs, which continue to play an important role in its success. For example, sales of the cancer-fighting drug Keytruda earned $483 million (a 125 percent increase over the previous year) in the fourth quarter of 2016.[47] Ken Frazier, CEO of Merck, summarized the blended strategy this way: "The performance of Merck's broad and balanced portfolio allows us to remain committed to biomedical innovation that saves and improves lives and delivers long-term value to shareholders."[48]

A firm may not be technology oriented, but it still must pay attention to changing technology because it will need new capabilities to survive. When Amazon.com revolutionized retailing in the 1990s, traditional brick-and-mortar bookstores had to adapt quickly. To regain competitiveness, they had to dramatically overhaul their information technology capabilities.

The upshot: although a new technology may have tremendous market potential, managers must have or develop the internal capabilities needed to execute the new strategy. Without proper implementation skills, the most promising technological advances can prove disastrous.

Organizational Suitability

The final considerations in deciding about technological innovations are your organization's culture, managers' interests, and stakeholders' expectations. Companies such as indoor cycling firm SoulCycle and vacation rental homes provider Airbnb are proactive innovators with outward-looking, opportunistic cultures. Executives in these *prospector* firms give considerable priority to developing and exploiting technological expertise, and decision makers tend to have bold intuitive visions of the future. Technology champions articulate competitively aggressive, first-mover strategies. In many cases, executives are more concerned about the opportunity costs of not taking action than they are about the potential to fail.

By contrast, *defender* firms, such as Kroger and Safeway, hold a more circumspect posture toward innovation. These firms operate in more stable environments, so their strategies employ complementary technologies that extend rather than replace their current ones. Supermarkets in the United States have competed for decades by emphasizing low-cost distribution over large distances. That strategy may have become less viable as a low-cost German supermarket chain, Lidl, opened its first stores in the U.S. market in mid-2017.[49] The European firm operates smaller stores than its American counterparts and offers generic products, keeping prices about 30 percent lower than mainstream grocers.[50] Lidl, which currently operates 10,000 stores in 27 European countries, is expected to compete with Kroger's, Trader Joe's, Walmart, and Whole Foods Market.[51]

A hybrid *analyzer* firm, such as Microsoft, needs to stay technologically competitive but tends to allow others to demonstrate solid demand in new arenas before it responds. Microsoft's Xbox game console, Office software, and Zune music player all contain innovations, but other companies pioneered the original path-breaking product concepts. These firms adopt early follower strategies to grab dominant positions using their strengths in marketing and manufacturing more than through technological innovation.

Early adopters of new technologies tend to be larger, more profitable, and more specialized. Therefore, they are in an economic position to absorb the risks. Managers who adopt early are comfortable dealing with uncertainty and have strong problem-solving capabilities. Thus early adopters manage the difficulties of less fully developed technologies.[52]

One additional consideration is the impact the new technology will have on employees. Their cooperation (or lack thereof) often is a major factor in determining how difficult and costly the introduction of new technology will be. We discuss how to manage such change in our final chapter.

Exhibit 17.5 summarizes all these considerations: market receptiveness, technological feasibility, economic viability, anticipated competence development, and organizational suitability. They all influence managerial decisions about technology innovations.

Considerations	Sample Contexts
Market receptiveness—assess external demand for the technology (short/long run).	Smartphones, MP3s, wearable technology, water conserving washers, HDTVs.
Technological feasibility—evaluate technical barriers to progress.	Deep-sea oil exploration, physical size of PC microprocessors.
Economic viability—examine any cost considerations and forecast profitability.	Solar fusion, fuel cells for automobiles, missile defense systems.
Competence development—determine whether current capabilities are sufficient.	Information technology in health care, digital technology in cameras.
Organizational suitability—assess the fit with culture and managerial systems.	Steel companies focusing on creativity and innovation.

EXHIBIT 17.5
Key Considerations in Technology Decisions

A shortage of just one of them can derail an otherwise promising project. For example, consider how these factors apply to Tesla Motors' introduction of a luxury electric car as you read "Management in Action: Progress Report."

Management in Action

THE CHALLENGING ROAD FOR TESLA MOTORS

For Tesla to continue leading in what founder and CEO Elon Musk sees as the future of driving, it must sell enough electric vehicles at a sufficient profit. Therefore, Tesla is innovating in marketing, distribution, and access to recharging stations.

Initial orders for the Model S sedan arrived faster than Tesla could make them, and the company quickly ramped up production. The Model X sport-utility vehicle soon followed. To broaden its customer base, Tesla now plans to introduce a mass-market vehicle, the Model 3, and has booked orders for almost half a million units. The company hopes to make about 5,000 cars a week, mostly Model 3 units, in its Fremont, California, factory (the former site of a Toyota–GM joint venture). It has added plants in the Netherlands and California as well.

Next, Tesla must persuade more drivers to go electric. The federal government is helping with a tax credit of $7,500 on the purchase of an electric vehicle (it also loaned Tesla $465 million). And, with the help of a new Nevada factory and a partnership with Panasonic, the company will hugely increase its output of lithium ion cells and battery packs.

As a start-up with an innovative product in a mature industry, Tesla needed a plan for getting cars and information to consumers. Instead of approaching auto dealerships, the company opened stores in upscale shopping centers. Each store displays a Tesla car surrounded by exhibits about its features. At touch screens, shoppers learn what they can save on gas, select options, and see an image of their car.

Tesla pays salespeople a flat rate, not commissions, to motivate them to advocate for electric cars and develop customer relationships, not just move merchandise. However, dealer franchises have sued Tesla for violating state franchise laws, so in some states, including Texas, the showrooms display cars and information but orders are placed online.

Another roadblock to adoption of all-electric vehicles is that stations for recharging a car away from home have been few, and fully recharging can take hours. Tesla developed battery technology that takes a car farther—about 240 miles in the case of the Model S. It also is building a network of Supercharger stations, where 30 minutes of charging provides up to 170 miles of range. Today, the company offers more than 2,600 Superchargers at 373 locations in the United States, Canada, and Mexico, including "destination charging" at many hotels, resorts, restaurants, and shopping centers. That number will soon double, the company says. About 800 locations around the world offer more than 5,000 Superchargers.[53]

- What are the advantages and disadvantages to Tesla Motors in being a technology leader?
- How has Tesla Motors addressed market receptiveness, technological feasibility, and economic viability?

MANAGER'S BRIEF   PROGRESS REPORT   ONWARD

Sourcing and Acquiring New Technologies

Developing new technology may conjure up visions of scientists and product developers working in famous research and development (R&D) laboratories like those of Amazon's Lab 126 and Microsoft's Research Lab.[54] However, new technologies come from many other sources including suppliers, manufacturers, users, other industries, universities, the government, and overseas companies. Every source of innovation should be explored, but each industry usually has specific sources for most of its new technologies.

For example, farming innovations most often come from manufacturers, suppliers, and government extension services. Seed manufacturers develop and market superior hybrids; chemical producers improve pesticides and herbicides; and equipment manufacturers design improved farm equipment. Land grant universities develop new farming techniques, and extension agents spread their usage.

In many industries, however, the primary innovators are firms that improve upon the technologies they employ. For example, most scientific instrument innovations come from users who improve and then sell or license them to manufacturers or suppliers.[55]

make-or-buy decision

The question an organization asks itself about whether to acquire new technology from an outside source or develop it itself.

The question of how to acquire a new technology is essentially a **make-or-buy decision**. Should the organization develop the technology itself, or acquire it from an outside source? This decision is not nearly as simple as it sounds; many options exist, and each has advantages and disadvantages as discussed next.

Internal Development

Developing a new technology within the company has the great potential advantage of keeping it proprietary—exclusive to the organization. The disadvantage is that it usually requires staff and funding for an extended period. Even if the development succeeds, considerable time elapses before realizing the benefits. Managers must carefully weigh the potential benefits of proprietary technology against the cost of developing it.

Intel balances risks and benefits by operating research and development laboratories in several locations, including Oregon, Israel, India, and China. Engineers in the various labs come up with breakthrough ideas, and labs in offshore locations can avoid legal restrictions on imports plus save money relative to the cost of hiring talent in the United States.[56]

Purchase

Most technology already in use is available openly for purchase. For example, a bank that needs sophisticated information technology need not develop it itself. It can simply buy it from manufacturers or suppliers. Usually this is the simplest, easiest, and most cost-effective way to acquire new technology. However, the technology itself will not provide competitive advantage.

Contracted Development

If the technology is not available and a company lacks the resources or time to develop it internally, it can contract the development from outside sources. Possible contractors include other companies, independent research laboratories, and university and government institutions. Usually outside contracting involves an agreed-upon series of objectives and timetables, with payments made as each part of the project is tested and achieved.

Licensing

Technologies that are not easily purchased can be licensed for a fee. Companies like Epic Games in North Carolina that develop video games often license technologies including the software that models the physics behind the activities depicted in the game. The artwork, characters, and music for a game may be unique, but the basic laws of physics apply to the action shown in today's sophisticated games, so there is no advantage to programming these aspects of each game. Licensing is more economical.[57]

The Digital World

The University of Washington worked with Foldit.com to have groups compete and collaborate in a gaming format. In three weeks a team was able to determine the enzyme structure of an AIDS retrovirus that had eluded scientists for over 10 years.

GlaxoSmithKline (GSK) is crowdsourcing its malaria, sleeping sickness, and tuberculosis research by sharing its data online and in an industry that usually keeps the R&D process confidential. While pharmaceutical companies are criticized for not prioritizing "diseases of poverty," posting their research online provides a low-cost opportunity that has substantial upside. Anyone can access and use the open source drug discovery (OSDD) database and the electronic lab notebook (ELN) app.

GSK still has the manufacturing and distribution network to do something with any discoveries. If new epidemics emerge it has a system in place, using technology and crowdsourcing to manage a project faster than traditional timeframes and organizational structures could deliver.

This allows innovation at a pace not seen in this industry. Many other industries are evaluating how they can use technology to innovate and how connecting online to stakeholders can strengthen their businesses.

Technology Trading

Another way to gain access to new technologies is with technology trading. Mary Jo Cartwright, a director of plant operations at Batesville Casket Company, adopted Toyota's manufacturing philosophy of lean production and continuous improvement. This decreased manufacturing costs by 25 percent and the number of hours to make a coffin by 40 percent. Prior to adopting the "Toyota way," 20 percent of manufactured coffins needed repair. That rate fell to 1 percent.[58]

Sometimes even rival companies trade technologies. Not all industries or companies are amenable, but technology trading is increasing because of the high cost of developing advanced technologies independently.[59]

Toyota, known for keeping secret its manufacturing techniques, is planning to sell complete powertrain modules (and share the technology) of Prius cars to rivals. This unprecedented decision is driven by the world's largest automaker's desire to defray its research and development costs.[60]

Research Partnerships and Joint Ventures

Research partnerships pursue specific new technology development jointly. Typically each member enters the partnership with different skills or resources. One common and effective combination is an established company and a start-up. Joint ventures are similar in most respects to research partnerships, but they tend to have greater permanence, and they result in entirely new companies.[61]

As we noted in Chapter 9, sometimes even powerful competitors collaborate on projects. Nestlé Health Sciences and Chi-Med, a health care group in China, established Nutrition Science Partners, a joint venture to develop and market "innovative nutritional and medicinal products derived from botanical plants." This venture brings together Nestlé's knowledge of marketing to global customers and Chi-Med's expertise in traditional Chinese medicine plus its collection of more than 50,000 extracts from 1,200 different herbal plants.[62]

> Sometimes even powerful competitors collaborate on projects.

Acquiring a Technology Owner

If a company lacks a needed technology but wishes to acquire proprietary ownership, one option is to purchase the company that owns it. This transaction can take a number of forms, from outright purchase of the entire company to a minority interest sufficient to

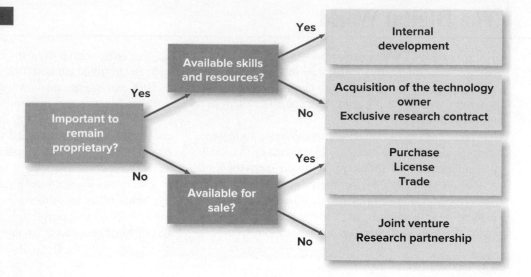

EXHIBIT 17.6
Technology Acquisition
Options

gain access to the technology. Over the past few years, Facebook has purchased several privately owned tech companies to fulfill its growth strategy.[63] Among these acquisitions were Oculus, Snapchat, and FacioMetrics. These moves gave Facebook instant ownership of virtual reality technology, a popular image messaging and multimedia mobile app, and facial recognition developer tools.

Choosing among these alternatives becomes easier by asking these basic questions:

1. Is it important (and possible) in terms of competitive advantage for the technology to remain proprietary?
2. Are the time, skills, and resources for internal development available?
3. Is the technology readily available outside the company?

As Exhibit 17.6 illustrates, the answers to these questions guide the manager to the most appropriate technology acquisition options.

If managers decide to acquire a company, they take additional steps to ensure that the acquisition will make sense for the long term. They try to make sure that key employees will remain with the firm instead of leaving and taking essential technical expertise with them. As with any large investment, managers carefully assess whether the financial benefits of the acquisition justify the purchase price.

Technology and Managerial Roles

**chief information
officer (CIO)**

Executive in charge of
information technology
strategy and development.

Within organizations, technology traditionally was the responsibility of vice presidents for research and development. These executives are responsible for corporate and divisional R&D laboratories; typically their jobs have a functional orientation. But increasingly executives with technology responsibilities hold the prestigious position of **chief information officer (CIO)**, often called the chief technology officer (CTO).

The CIO is a senior position at the corporate level with broad, integrative responsibilities. CIOs help ensure adequate cybersecurity measures are in place; coordinate the technological efforts of the various business units; identify ways that technology can support the company's strategy; supervise new technology development; and assess the technological implications of major strategic initiatives such as acquisitions, new ventures, and strategic alliances. They also lead their organization's information technology (IT) group.[64]

Particularly when organizations value highly the agility resulting from continuous learning, this position is called *chief innovation officer,* another variation of the CIO or CTO.

Whatever the C-level title, this officer ensures that technology advances in line with the company's strategy, and that ideas and knowledge flow freely between R&D, managers, and other employees.[65]

Without the CIO's integrative role, different departments could adopt different technology tools and standards, leading to much higher equipment and maintenance expense and difficulties in connecting the different parts of the organization. And because technologists often have very specialized expertise, managers without such expertise would find it difficult to supervise them effectively. A CIO can help managers ensure that the work technologists do is coordinated and aligned with overall strategic goals.

Sophie Vandebroek, chief technology officer and president of the innovation group of Xerox, took on this role with the goal of making Xerox's systems simpler, speedier, smaller, smarter, more secure, and socially responsible—what she calls the "six S's."

©Boston Globe/Boston Globe/Getty Images

Chief technology officers also perform an important boundary role: they work directly with outside organizations. For example, they work with universities funding research to stay abreast of technical developments, and with regulatory agencies to ensure compliance with regulations, identify trends, and influence the regulatory process.

In addition to the entrepreneurs who invent new products or find new ways to deliver old products, specific key technology roles are the technical innovator, product champion, and executive champion.[66] **Technical innovators** develop the new technology or have the skills needed to install and operate it. They possess the requisite technical skills but not always the time or the managerial skills needed to push the idea forward and secure acceptance in the organization.

This is where the product champion gets involved, because introducing new technology requires someone to promote the idea. The **product champion**—sometimes at some professional risk—promotes the idea seeking support. The champion can be a high-level manager but often is not. If the champion lacks the needed power and financial resources to act independently, she or he must convince people who have such authority to support the innovation. In other words, product champions must get sponsorship.

Sponsorship comes from the **executive champion**, who has the status, authority, and financial resources to support the project and protect the product champion. Without this support and protection, the product champion, and thus the new technology, could not succeed.

technical innovator

A person who develops a new technology or has the key skills to install and operate the technology.

product champion

A person who promotes a new technology throughout the organization in an effort to obtain acceptance of and support for it.

Organizing for Innovation

Successful innovation is much more than a great idea. A Boston Consulting Group study found that lack of good ideas is hardly ever the obstacle to profitable innovation. Far more often, ideas fail to generate financial returns because the organization isn't set up to innovate.

One requirement for innovation is to find new developments from external sources that can bring lasting value. Another is overcoming internal resistance (a "not invented here" mindset) and fear of change (discussed in the final chapter) in order to apply the new technologies to complement or enhance internal processes.[67] In contrast, Exhibit 17.7 shows that innovation has a chance to flourish when constructive values are in place, when the organization integrates internal and external knowledge, and when people are encouraged to solve problems and to experiment continuously.

In Chapter 9 we described learning organizations—companies that excel at solving problems, seeking and finding new approaches, and sharing new

LO 7

executive champion

An executive who supports a new technology and protects the product champion.

Creative ideas can fail to generate financial returns because the organization isn't set up to innovate.

EXHIBIT 17.7
Requirements for
Innovation

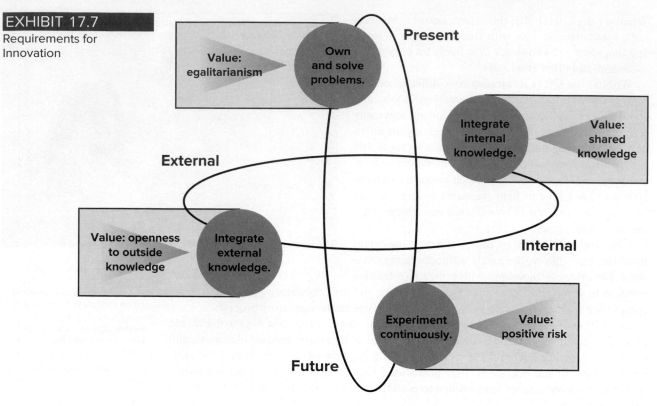

SOURCE: Barton, Dorothy Leonard, "The Factory as Learning Laboratory," *Sloan Management Review,* 1992, p. 34.

knowledge throughout the organization. Learning organizations are well positioned to develop useful innovations.

Some innovations *exploit existing capabilities*—to improve production speed or product quality, for example. Other innovations *explore new knowledge,* seeking to develop new products or services.[68] Both innovation processes—exploitation and exploration—are necessary. Innovative learning organizations use their strengths to improve their operations and thus their bottom lines, plus encourage people to explore new possibilities that will ensure their long-term competitiveness.

Unleashing Creativity

Failure, managed properly, spurs learning,
growth, and future successes.

3M has a strong orientation toward intrapreneurship, and derives a substantial amount of its revenues from new products. 3M, Google, Apple, and IBM have proud histories of producing many great new technologies and products. What sets these and other continuous innovators apart? One thing they have in common is a culture that encourages innovation.[69]

Consider the 3M story from the early 1920s about inventor Francis G. Okie. Okie dreamed up the idea of using sandpaper instead of razor blades for shaving. The aim was to reduce the risk of nicks and avoid sharp instruments. The idea failed, but rather than being punished for the failure, Okie was encouraged to champion other ideas, which included 3M's first blockbuster success: waterproof sandpaper. That's just one example of a culture that permits well-intended efforts that "fail."

As counterintuitive as it may seem at first blush, celebrating good-faith flop can be vital to the innovation process.[70] Failure, managed properly, spurs learning, growth, and future successes. Innovative companies have many balls in the air at all times, with many people trying many new ideas. Most are strikeouts, but through this process a few home runs turn

EXHIBIT 17.8
Elements Essential to
Innovation

- **Experimenting** with new ideas and drawing on data to inform decisions.
- **Removing obstacles** throughout the company so innovation can occur.
- **Keeping up** with changing customer expectations and new technologies.
- **Collaborating** across boundaries to see challenges from multiple perspectives.
- **Implementing** by aligning vision and execution.

SOURCE: Schwab, K., "Ideo Studied Innovation in 100+ Companies—Here's What It Found," *Fast Codesign,* March 3, 2017, www.fastcodesign.com

a company into an innovative star. This management perspective and approach fosters creative thinking and innovative efforts throughout the ranks.

Bureaucracy Busting

Bureaucracy is an enemy of innovation. Although bureaucracy helps maintain orderliness and gain efficiencies, it also can work directly against innovation. Developing new technologies requires a fluid and flexible (organic) structure that does not restrict thought and action.

Although "fluid and flexible" can sometimes feel more like "chaotic and uncertain," companies take this approach because it facilitates rapid change. Elmer's Products, which makes many products as well as the famous white glue, has a policy of open innovation. A cross-functional team of seven employees is responsible for sharing ideas about innovation, and all employees are encouraged to submit ideas. About a dozen employees in another group are assigned to spend 25 to 50 percent of their time exploring ideas from sources outside the organization, including inventors, suppliers, other companies, and university researchers.[71]

To balance innovation with other business goals, companies often establish special temporary project structures that are isolated from the rest of the organization and allowed to operate under different rules. These units go by many names, including skunkworks (Chapter 7), greenhouses, and reserves. At General Motors, chief talent officer Michael Arena launched InnovationXchange Lab. The lab's goal is to "Connect employees and ideas across the business to amplify impact." The ultimate goal of these interactions is to inspire new innovations.[72]

To foster an innovative culture, software maker Intuit created Innovation Lab. The company encourages employees to spend 10 percent of their time working on activities they choose personally—a new product idea they feel passionate about, or simply devoting company time to learning about new technologies. Intuit also sponsors idea jams—one-day events, four times per year, when employees with an idea assemble their own development teams. Intuit provides cash awards for winning ideas, but the excitement of Innovation Lab and idea jams is what really motivates Intuit employees to pursue innovations such as the mobile version of QuickBooks Online, GoPayment, and ViewMyPaycheck.[73]

At steel companies Chaparral and Nucor, employees work in cross-functional teams to find innovative problem solutions. Teams focus on current issues and problems as well as future concerns and opportunities. In addition, teams collaborate with outside partners to bring knowledge into the organization. All the while, teams are supported by values of egalitarianism, information sharing, openness to outside ideas, and positive risk. The aim is to destroy the traditional boundaries between functions and departments to create collaborative, less-bureaucratic learning laboratories.[74]

Design Thinking

Many organizations now use **design thinking**, a human-centered approach to innovation that integrates customer needs, the potential of technology, and the requirements for business success.[75] Championed by the Institute of Design at Stanford University, design thinking relies on "close, almost anthropological observation of people to gain insight into problems that may not be articulated yet."[76]

Bottom Line
Bureaucracy busting encourages innovation. *Name three ways to bust bureaucracy.*

design thinking
A human-centered approach to problem solving and solution finding that is based on nonlinear iterations of inspiration, ideation, and implementation.

Courtesy of IDEO

IDEO, the global design firm that uses design thinking with clients, views the process as a "system of overlapping spaces rather than a sequence of orderly steps."[77] The company defines the three interrelated spaces this way: (1) *inspiration* is the motivating problem or solution; (2) *ideation* is the process of generating, developing, and testing ideas, and (3) *implementation* is the path that leads from the project stage into customers' lives. The problem-solving process is not linear but rather moves iteratively, in and out of these spaces.

Traditionally, when a company wanted to redesign or create a new product, it would use customer focus groups to provide feedback on projects already under development.[78] Design thinking differs by starting with developing a thorough understanding (through direct observation) of current and potential customers. Design teams, consisting of people with diverse expertise (engineering, anthropology, design, marketing, and so forth), work together to identify "what people want and need in their lives and what they like or dislike about the way particular products are made, packaged, marketed, sold, and supported."[79] Experts like Jeanne Liedtka and Tim Ogilvie have developed prominent practical applications.[80]

Health care provider Kaiser Permanente used design thinking to improve the process by which nursing shifts change at its hospitals. A core project team, consisting of a strategist (former nurse), a technology expert, a process designer, designers from IDEO, and others, observed that nurses at four hospitals spent 45 minutes of each shift changeover discussing patient status. Depending on the hospital, nurses used different methods to exchange and record patient information. Some nurses, despite the time spent, missed or failed to relay important patient information.

The project team brainstormed and prototyped potential solutions for improving the changeover process. After evaluating the options, the team decided that (1) the arriving and departing nurses would exchange information in front of their patients (instead of at the nurses' station), and (2) new easy-to-use software would enable nurses to check notes from the previous shifts and enter new notes. This cut in half the average time between a nurse's arrival and first contact with patients, and increased nurses' job satisfaction. Kaiser introduced the new program in all of its health care facilities, and established a new innovation center based on design thinking to continuously improve the quality of patient care.[81]

Implementing Development Projects

LO 8

A powerful tool for managing technology and innovations is the **development project**:[82] a focused organizational effort to create a new product or process via technological advances. When MTV launched channels aimed at various Asian American markets, it used development projects embedded in a culture that valued innovation.

Development projects typically feature a special cross-functional team working together on an overall concept or idea. The development teams interact frequently with suppliers and customers, complicating their work but strengthening the final product. Due to urgency and strategic importance, most development teams work under intense time pressures.

Development projects have multiple benefits. They create new products and processes, plus cultivate skills and knowledge useful for future endeavors. Thus, the capabilities that companies gain from development projects frequently can be turned into a source of competitive advantage. When Ford launched a development project to design an air-conditioning

development project

A focused organizational effort to create a new product or process via technological advances.

compressor to outperform its Japanese rival, executives discovered new processes that Ford could use in the future. Their new capability in integrated design and manufacturing helped Ford reduce costs and lead times for other projects. Thus organizational learning is a useful criterion for evaluating project benefits.

To achieve their full potential benefit, development projects should build on core capabilities; have a guiding vision about what must be accomplished and why; have a committed team; strive for continuous improvement; and ensure integrated, coordinated efforts across all units.

Technology, Job Design, and Human Resources

Adopting a new technology may require changes in job design. Often job redesign forces people to fit into the demands of the technology to maximize operational efficiency. But this often backfires, because it neglects the human part of the productivity equation. Social relationships and the positive human aspects of work may suffer, lowering overall performance.

The **sociotechnical systems** approach to work redesign addresses this problem directly. This approach redesigns tasks to jointly optimize the social and technical efficiencies of work. Beginning in 1949 with studies of new coal-mining technologies, the sociotechnical systems approach to work design used small, self-regulating work groups.[83] Today's trends in bureaucracy bashing, lean and flat organizations, self-managed teams, and an empowered workforce are logical extensions of the sociotechnical philosophy.

sociotechnical systems

An approach to job design that attempts to redesign tasks to optimize operation of a new technology while preserving employees' interpersonal relationships and other human aspects of the work.

Management in Action

ELON MUSK'S SPACEX IS HEADED TO MARS

Have you ever wanted to see Mars up close? Elon Musk, the innovative entrepreneur behind SpaceX, is hoping to land a manned craft on the Red Planet by 2024. His company reached a milestone of spacecraft reusability in 2017 when it made the first successful relaunch of an orbital-class rocket.

Musk founded SpaceX to design, manufacture, and launch rockets and spacecraft. Its mission is simple: to allow humans to live on other planets. Musk sees humanity facing two alternate futures: to stay on Earth forever and face eventual extinction, or "to become a spacefaring civilization and a multi-planetary species." He's determined to make the latter goal achievable "in our lifetimes."

Despite some initial failures, including an unmanned rocket that exploded on the launchpad in 2016, SpaceX has won NASA's applause and praise for undertaking the $10 billion effort to support "a sustainable human presence on Mars." The first ship Musk hopes to send to Mars will carry 100 to 200 passengers and be nearly twice as long as a Boeing 747, with a reusable booster. It will refuel from other ships remaining in Earth's orbit, but it may also be able to synthesize its own fuel for return journeys by transforming water and carbon dioxide on Mars. Reusability and self-fueling capabilities are important to Musk, not only for ensuring the sustainability of the craft but also to help reduce the price of passage.

SpaceX, a private company, currently carries people and supplies to the International Space Station and launches satellites into Earth's orbit, earning revenue from NASA that Musk hopes will help pay for the Mars missions. The U.S. Air Force also has contributed about $34 million to the development of the rocket. But Musk plans to put his own money into the program, too.

"The reason I am personally accruing assets is to fund this," he says. "I really have no other purpose than to make life interplanetary." At some future point, however, SpaceX will try to put a public–private partnership together to help fund continuing missions.

If you are considering a trip to Mars, note that the planet aligns with Earth only every 26 months, and you might have more than one opportunity to sign up. The journey is expected initially to cost about $200,000.

It's estimated that a self-sustaining settlement on Mars would need about a million people, requiring 10,000 trips from Earth and the passage of 40 to 100 years. But your craft, the largest ever built so far, will have movie theaters and restaurants to keep you occupied. Musk promises it will be "really fun to go. You'll have a great time."[84]

- Is SpaceX a prospector, a defender, or an analyzer firm? Why?
- How well is Elon Musk managing the technological and economic viability of SpaceX's Mars mission?

MANAGER'S BRIEF

PROGRESS REPORT

ONWARD

Technology can limit employees' responsibilities and "de-skill" the workforce, thus turning people into servants of the technology. Alternatively, managers can select and train people to master the technology, achieve great things, and improve the quality of work lives. Technology, managed smartly, can empower people as it improves a company's competitiveness.[85]

Taken as a whole, these considerations provide guidelines for managing the strategic and organizational issues associated with technology and innovation. The issues are relevant whether a company is simply automating an activity or, as in the case of Tesla Motors, entering a new high-tech business (see "Management in Action: Onward"). In our final chapter, we expand on these processes by discussing leading change, learning and adapting as we go, and shaping our futures.

KEY TERMS

chief information officer (CIO), p. 506

design thinking, p. 509

development project, p. 510

disruptive innovation, p. 495

executive champion, p. 507

innovation, p. 490

make-or-buy decision, p. 504

product champion, p. 507

sociotechnical systems, p. 511

technical innovator, p. 507

technology, p. 490

technology audit, p. 498

technology life cycle, p. 491

RETAINING WHAT YOU LEARNED

In Chapter 17, you learned that different forces, like scientific knowledge and capital resources, encourage development of new technologies. New technologies follow a predictable life cycle. Companies adopt technology at different times. Some desire to be first movers while others prefer to be followers. Technology can be managed for competitive advantage and used to support a firm's low-cost or differentiation strategy. Selecting an appropriate technology strategy depends on the degree to which the technology supports the organization's competitive requirements. A company assesses its technology needs by benchmarking, or comparing, the technologies it employs with those of both competitors and noncompetitors. New technologies can be acquired through acquisition and other means, or developed internally. People play many roles in managing technology such as chief information officer, entrepreneur, technical innovator, product champion, and executive champion. Innovative organizations establish cultures that support creativity and intrapreneurship. Successful development projects share characteristics like building on core capabilities, having a guiding vision of what needs to be achieved, and having a committed team.

LO 1 List the types of processes that spur development of new technologies.

- Forces that compel the emergence of a new technology include (1) a need for the technology, (2) the requisite scientific knowledge, (3) the technical convertibility of this knowledge, (4) the resources to fund

development, and (5) the entrepreneurial insight and initiative to pull the components together.

LO 2 Describe how technologies proceed through a life cycle.

- New technologies follow a predictable life cycle. First, a workable idea about how to meet a market need is developed into a product innovation. Early progress can be slow.

- Eventually a dominant design emerges as the market accepts the technology, and further refinements to the technology result from process innovations.

- As the technology begins to approach both the theoretical limits to its performance potential and market saturation, growth slows and the technology matures. At this point, the technology can remain stable or be replaced by new technology.

LO 3 Discuss ways to manage technology for competitive advantage.

- Adopters of new technologies are categorized according to the timing of their adoption: innovators, early adopters, the early majority, the late majority, and laggards.

- Technology leadership offers many first-mover advantages but also poses significant disadvantages. The same is true for followership.

- Technology that helps improve efficiency will support a low-cost strategy, whereas technologies that help make products more distinctive or unique support a differentiation strategy.

- Determining an appropriate technology strategy depends on the degree to which the technology supports the organization's competitive requirements. If a technology leadership strategy is preferred, management should consider the company's ability (skills, resources, and commitment) to deal with the risks and uncertainties of leadership.

LO 4   Summarize how to assess technology needs.

- Assessing a company's technology needs begins by benchmarking, or comparing, the technologies it employs with those of both competitors and noncompetitors. Benchmarking should be done on a global basis to understand practices used worldwide.
- Technology scanning helps identify emerging technologies and those still under development in an effort to project their eventual competitive impact.

LO 5   Identify alternative methods of pursuing technological innovation.

- New technologies can be acquired or developed. Options include internal development, purchase, contracted development, licensing, trading, research partnerships and joint ventures, and acquisition.
- The approach used depends on the existing availability of the technology; the skills, resources, and time available; and the importance of keeping the technology proprietary.

LO 6   Define key roles in managing technology.

- Many roles contribute to technology management. The chief information officer can go by other titles as well, and has broad, integrative responsibility for technological innovation.

- The entrepreneur is the person who recognizes and pursues the competitive potential of the technology.
- Technical innovators develop or install and operate the technology.
- A product champion promotes the new idea(s) to gain support within the organization.
- The executive champion is the person providing authority and resources to support the project.

LO 7   Describe the characteristics of innovative organizations.

- Organizing for innovation involves unleashing the creative energies of employees while directing their efforts toward meeting market needs in a timely manner.
- Companies can unleash creativity by establishing a culture that encourages intrapreneurship; accepts failure as a sign of innovation; and reinforces innovation.
- The organization's structure should balance process controls with a flexibility that allows innovation to take place. Development projects provide an opportunity for cross-functional teamwork aimed at innovation.
- Job design should consider and attempt to optimize social relationships as well as technical efficiencies.

LO 8   Describe the characteristics of successful development projects.

- For development projects to achieve fullest benefit, they should: (1) build on core capabilities; (2) have a guiding vision about what must be accomplished and why; (3) have a committed team; (4) instill a philosophy of continuous improvement; and (5) generate integrated, coordinated efforts across all relevant teams and units.

DISCUSSION QUESTIONS

1. According to Francis Bacon, "A wise man will make more opportunities than he finds." What does this have to do with technology and innovation? What does it have to do with competitive advantage?

2. What examples of technological innovation can you identify? What forces led to the commercialization of the science behind those technologies? Did the capability exist before the market demand, or was the demand there before the technology was available?

3. Thomas Edison once said that most innovations are 10 percent inspiration and 90 percent perspiration. How does this match what you know about technology life cycles?

4. Why would a company choose to follow rather than lead technological innovations? Is the potential advantage of technological leadership greater when

innovations are occurring rapidly, or is it better in this case to follow?

5. If you were in the grocery business, whom would you benchmark for technological innovations? What could you possibly learn from companies outside the industry?

6. Think about the key roles in technology management. Which ones appeal to you most, and how can you learn the necessary skills?

7. Among those same roles, how and why might conflicts arise? And how would you deal with them?

8. Think about an employer you are familiar with, or your school. How would you describe it using the concepts in this chapter? Where and how could it become more effective?

EXPERIENTIAL EXERCISES

17.1 TECHNOLOGY LIFE CYCLE

OBJECTIVES
To explore the different stages of the technology life cycle.

INSTRUCTIONS
Refer back to the technology life cycle in Exhibit 17.2. Review each product or technology listed below and indicate whether it is in the first, second, or third stage of the cycle.

STAGES
Stage 1: A new technology is created to address a need. Competitors experiment with operational designs and product characteristics. Progress is slow. The rate of product innovation is high.

Stage 2: As initial problems are resolved and a dominant design emerges, technology is refined through process innovations. Efficiencies and cost competitiveness are pursued.

Stage 3: The technology reaches the limit of its performance capabilities and usage. In this mature stage, development slows and production becomes increasingly costly.

Product or Technology	Stage 1	Stage 2	Stage 3
Apple Watch	_____	_____	_____
Twitter	_____	_____	_____
Microsoft Windows	_____	_____	_____
Google self-driving car	_____	_____	_____
McGraw-Hill Education's e-book	_____	_____	_____

17.2 INNOVATION FOR THE FUTURE

OBJECTIVES
To look ahead into the future.

INSTRUCTIONS
Choose a partner. Together, develop an innovative product or service that will be popular in the year 2025. As you develop your product or service, ask yourselves the following questions:

1. What trends lead you to believe that this product or service will be successful?

2. What current technologies, services, or products will your idea replace?

Present your idea to the class for discussion.

Concluding Case

WORLDWIDE GAMES

Players of video games often purchase their fun from Worldwide Games, which develops and markets game consoles, portable game devices, and software for playing games either on the company's hardware or on personal computers. Game enthusiasts are always on the lookout for game-playing experiences that are more intense, more lifelike, or more complex, so satisfying them drives constant innovation at Worldwide. The company has developed major and minor advances in screen resolution, processor speed, new kinds of controllers, creative story lines, and more. Its console division focuses on hardware technology, and its online division focuses on powerful new gaming software, often involving elaborate story lines played by subscribers around the world, using the Internet to collaborate or compete. Continuous innovation in both divisions essentially keeps Worldwide on a par with its major competitors, who also are constantly on the lookout for the best new idea.

In recent years, two related areas of technology have been essential for the growth of Worldwide and its competitors: social networking and the ability of broadband Internet connections to deliver fast audio and video streams for playing elaborate games online. Worldwide's console division has adopted this technology by inviting purchasers of its latest console to join its Players Network. Those who join the Players Network can use their console to make an Internet connection and play games with other members anywhere in the network. Each player uses his or her controller, console, and television display and sees all the participants' actions on the display. In addition, Worldwide's online division continues to push the limits of online games played with the processing power of the latest personal computers. For the most popular programs, gamers who pay a subscription fee create their own characters, or avatars, to act out the parts in the game. Although the personal data of the players are kept private, players can use the avatars' names to look up other players' track records and invite selected avatars to join their team.

Because a necessary component of both kinds of games—console based and computer based—is for players to register and pay a fee or join the Players Network, Worldwide collects not only money from customers but also information about them. That system came under real risk when hackers recently broke into first the Players Network database and then the registration records of Worldwide Online's subscribers.

As soon as the company detected an intrusion into the Players Network, it shut down the network. When the company's security employees realized they couldn't immediately prevent intrusions within a day or two, Worldwide announced that hackers had obtained the names and possibly the credit card numbers of its tens of millions of network members. Until the problem was fixed, they would be able to play games from disks loaded into their consoles but would not be able to use the network.

While the company was investigating the original security breach, it discovered that the Worldwide Online user database also had been hacked. The company immediately announced that breach, including the fact that some credit card accounts might have been accessed. It shut down that network as well until the security hole could be plugged.

Fixing the problem, which took about a month, included adding firewalls and encryption to the existing security measures. Afterward the company reopened both networks, apologized to consumers, and offered a month of free access to paid services. Returning customers had to download upgraded security software before they could resume play. The entire incident cost the company hundreds of millions of dollars for the investigation, upgrades, and lost sales.

As operations returned to normal, Worldwide tried to minimize the risk of future intrusions by putting an executive in charge of security. The company announced that it had hired a chief information security officer. This manager reports to the company's chief information officer, who reports to the chief transformation officer, who reports to the chief executive officer.

QUESTIONS

1. Is Worldwide Games a technology leader or a technology follower? What are the risks and benefits of staking out this position?

2. What opportunities might Worldwide be missing by not having its chief information officer report directly to the CEO?

3. What makes innovation important for Worldwide? Following the hacking incident, how might bureaucracy be expected to interfere with innovation? How should Worldwide engage in bureaucracy busting?

CHAPTER 18
Creating and Leading Change

> The world hates change, yet that is the only thing that has brought progress.
> —CHARLES KETTERING

> My interest is in the future because I am going to spend the rest of my life there.
> —CHARLES KETTERING

©Darren Greenwood/Design Pics RF

LEARNING OBJECTIVES

After studying Chapter 18, you will be able to:

LO 1 Discuss what it takes to be world class.

LO 2 Describe how to manage and lead change effectively.

LO 3 Describe strategies for creating a successful future.

CHAPTER OUTLINE

Becoming World Class
Sustainable, Great Futures
The Tyranny of the *Or*
The Genius of the *And*
Achieving Sustained Greatness
Organization Development

Managing Change
Motivating People to Change
A General Model for Managing Resistance
Enlisting Cooperation
Harmonizing Multiple Changes
Leading Change

Shaping the Future
Thinking about the Future
Creating the Future
Shaping Your Own Future
Learning and Leading
A Collaborative, Sustainable Future?

Management in Action

SHELL OIL'S MANAGERS FACE OFF WITH INVESTORS OVER CLIMATE CHANGE

Shell Oil Company is a U.S. subsidiary of Royal Dutch Shell, one of the largest oil companies in the world. At a recent annual general meeting of the company, nearly 99 percent of Shell investors voted to support a motion for it to report on whether its activities were consistent with worldwide governments' goals to limit climate change. They angrily questioned executives about the sustainability of Shell's business strategy and its commitment to the environment. There is widespread international support to limit the increase in global warming to 2 degrees Celsius.

Why were investors frustrated with Shell's top management? One reason is that as the more easily accessible oil and natural gas reserves became exhausted, Shell had been taking greater risks by investing in controversial oil drilling projects in the Arctic Ocean and Nigerian Delta. Some investors questioned how much longer the strategy of extracting fossil fuels from environmentally sensitive regions could be sustained. One nonprofit group in the UK warned that big oil companies would meet a "short, brutal end" within a decade if they didn't fundamentally change their business.

Shell responded to these and other concerns about its future and its impact on the environment by creating a New Energies Division, charged with investing in renewable and sustainable power sources, like wind, that rely less heavily on carbon. New Energies has a budget of $1.7 billion, less than 1 percent of the amount the company invests in oil and gas production. But Shell promises the division will grow, if slowly.

Meanwhile, the parent company, Royal Dutch Shell, has sold off some of its biggest fossil-fuel assets (such as large oil sands in Canada), acquired more

©Bloomberg/Bloomberg/Getty Images

natural-gas preserves, and changed executive pay policies to encourage management efforts to reduce and control pollution. As the price and demand for crude oil drop around the world and the focus shifts to low-carbon and sustainable fuels, Shell saw oil profits imperiled.

Ben van Beurden, the chief executive of Royal Dutch Shell, said, "The big challenge, both for society and for a company like Shell, is how to provide much more energy, while at the same time significantly reducing carbon dioxide emissions." The chairperson of the Carbon Tracker Initiative, an energy think tank, sees an even more stark need for change at Shell: "My prediction is there will come a day in that boardroom when it will become clear to a critical mass of directors that their business model has no future in hydrocarbons, including gas."[1]

Changes like the ones faced by, and required of, Shell Oil and other fossil-fuel companies are not easy, do not happen automatically, and often require managers to overcome a host of obstacles. As you study this chapter, think about why the ability to change is both challenging and essential.

An ever-changing world is full of uncertainty and risk.[2] Now and in the foreseeable future, just a sampling of the many disruptive forces in play includes a fragile financial system, breakdowns in global trade, growing income inequality, political upheavals, environmental degradation, declining public health and education, and underperforming institutions.[3] These and other dynamic forces make it essential for organizations (and people) to cope, anticipate, adapt, and change.

Lest the preceding paragraph sound like gloom and doom, one useful perspective is to view problems as opportunities.[4] As but one example, manufacturing was presumed in recent years to be virtually dead in the United States, but global circumstances are changing, and leaders and entrepreneurs are attempting a manufacturing comeback.[5] According to a survey in 2017, 93 percent of American manufacturers, an all-time high, are optimistic about the business climate.[6]

Fun fact: You are reading this months or a year or more after we wrote it. What changes are happening now? Where are the problems and opportunities? How will you deal?

As you can imagine, currently and forevermore, some organizations and people deal with change more effectively than others. The challenge for organizations is not just to produce innovative new products but to create a culture that is innovative and that builds a sustainable business. For individuals, the ability to cope with change affects their job performance, the rewards they receive,[7] their career success, and feelings they hold toward the organization.[8]

But coping with change isn't enough. Managers and their organizations need to create desired changes, and improve constantly, to achieve world-class excellence and competitive advantage into the future. For Shell and its leaders, a changing environment is something they must deal with by creating their own changes.

Becoming World Class

LO 1

Managers want, or *should* want, their organizations to become world class.[9] Being world class requires applying the best and latest knowledge and ideas and having the ability to operate at the highest standards of any place anywhere.[10] Thus becoming world class does not mean merely improving. It means becoming one of the very best in the world at what you do.

To some, striving for world-class excellence seems a lofty, impossible, unnecessary goal. But for every manager and organization, achieving excellence can serve as a stretch goal that helps one survive and succeed in a competitive world.

World-class companies create high-value products and earn superior profits over the long run. They demolish the obsolete methods, systems, and cultures of the past that impeded their progress, and apply more effective strategies, structures, processes, and management of human resources. And as you know, companies are vehicles for accomplishing societal purposes.[11] Great leaders, collaborating with others, build enduring institutions that can compete successfully, and even serve society, on a global basis.[12]

Bottom Line

It's a worthy aspiration: becoming world class at every one of your competitive goals.
What does it mean to be world class at a goal such as quality or sustainability?

Sustainable, Great Futures

Two Stanford professors, James Collins and Jerry Porras, studied 18 corporations that had achieved and maintained greatness for half a century or more.[13] The companies included 3M, American Express, Disney, General Electric, Procter & Gamble, Sony, and Walmart. Over the years, these companies have been widely admired, been considered the premier institutions in their industries, and made a real impact on the world. Although every company goes through periodic downturns—and these firms are no exceptions over their long histories—these companies have consistently prevailed across the decades. They turn in extraordinary performance over the long run, rather than fleeting greatness.

The researchers sought to identify the essential characteristics of enduringly great companies. These companies have strong core values in which they believe deeply, and they express and live the values consistently. They are driven by goals—not just incremental improvements or business-as-usual goals, but stretch goals (Chapter 13). They change continuously, driving for progress via adaptability, experimentation, trial and error, entrepreneurial thinking, and fast action. And they do not focus on beating the competition; they focus primarily on beating themselves. They continually ask, "How can we improve ourselves to do better tomorrow than we did today?"

But underneath the action and the changes, the core values and vision remain steadfast and uncompromised. Exhibit 18.1 displays the core values of several companies that were built to last. Note that the values are not all the same. In fact, no set of common values consistently predicts success. Instead the critical factor is that great companies *have* core values, *know* what they are and what they mean, and *live* by them—year after year.

The Tyranny of the *Or*

Many companies, and individuals, are plagued by the **tyranny of the *or***. This refers to binary thinking, the belief that things must be either A or B and cannot be both. The authors of *Built to Last* provide many common examples: beliefs that you must choose either change or stability; be conservative or bold; have control and consistency or creative freedom; do well in the short term or invest for the future; plan methodically or be opportunistic; create shareholder wealth or do good for the world; be pragmatic or idealistic.[14] Such beliefs, that only one goal but not another can be attained, often are invalid and certainly are constraining—unnecessarily so.

tyranny of the *or*

The belief that things must be either A or B and cannot be both; that only one goal and not another can be attained.

EXHIBIT 18.1

Core Ideologies in Built-to-Last Companies

3M	Innovation—"Thou shalt not kill a new product idea."
	Absolute integrity.
	Respect for individual initiative and personal growth.
	Tolerance for honest mistakes.
	Product quality and reliability.
	"Our real business is solving problems."
Sony	To experience the sheer joy that comes from the advancement, application, and innovation of technology that benefits the general public.
	To elevate the Japanese culture and national status.
	Being pioneers—not following others, but doing the impossible.
	Respecting and encouraging each individual's ability and creativity.
Walmart	"We exist to provide value to our customers"—to make their lives better via lower prices and greater selection; all else is secondary.
	Swim upstream, buck conventional wisdom.
	Be in partnership with employees.
	Work with passion, commitment, and enthusiasm.
	Run lean.
	Pursue ever-higher goals.
Disney	No cynicism allowed.
	Fanatical attention to consistency and detail.
	Continuous progress via creativity, dreams, and imagination.
	Fanatical control and preservation of Disney's "magic" image.
	"To bring happiness to millions" and to celebrate, nurture, and promulgate "wholesome American values."

SOURCE: Collins, James C. and Porras, Jerry I., *Built to Last*. New York: HarperCollins, 1997.

The Genius of the *And*

In contrast to the tyranny of the *or,* the **genius of the *and***—more academically, **organizational ambidexterity**—refers to being able to achieve multiple objectives at the same time.[15] It develops via the actions of many individuals throughout the organization. We discussed earlier in the book the importance of delivering multiple competitive values to customers, performing all the management functions, reconciling hard-nosed business logic with ethics, leading and empowering, and others. Authors Collins and Porras have their own list:[16]

- Purpose beyond profit *and* pragmatic pursuit of profit.
- Relatively fixed core values *and* vigorous change and movement.
- Conservatism with the core values *and* bold business moves.
- Clear vision and direction *and* experimentation.
- Stretch goals *and* incremental progress.
- Control based on values *and* operational freedom.
- Long-term thinking and investment *and* demand for short-term results.
- Visionary, futuristic thinking *and* daily, nuts-and-bolts execution.

Your organization and its managers collectively should not lose sight of any of these—either in your thoughts or in your actions. To achieve them all, ebbing and flowing over time, requires the continuous and effective management of change.

Achieving Sustained Greatness

A Harvard/McKinsey study of 200 management techniques employed by 160 companies over 10 years identified the specific management practices that lead to sustained, superior performance.[17] The authors boiled their findings down to four key factors:

1. *Strategy*—focused on customers, continually fine-tuned based on marketplace changes, and clearly communicated to employees.
2. *Execution*—good people, with decision-making authority on the front lines, doing quality work and cutting costs.
3. *Culture*—one that motivates, empowers people to innovate, rewards people appropriately (psychologically as well as economically), entails strong values, challenges people, and provides a satisfying work environment.
4. *Structure*—making the organization easy to work in and easy to work with, characterized by cooperation and the exchange of information and knowledge throughout the organization.

You have been learning about these concepts throughout this course. Now, looking to the future, it is important to know that companies must continue to change and better themselves.

Even companies that have performed well and had excellent reputations over many years can founder. Consider how Sears was for many years the largest, most dominant retailer in the United States. That all changed when a newcomer to retail, Walmart, overtook the venerable retailer.[18] Sears leadership was faulted for being more concerned about protecting their turf than on "transforming the company in response to changing times."[19]

> Becoming world class doesn't apply only to the private sector.

Becoming world class doesn't apply only to the private sector. People worry about globalization's negative effects on local communities as plants shut down and people lose their jobs. But local communities do have options—not easy ones, but doable.

A locality can strive to become a world-class center of *thinkers, makers,* or *traders.*[20] An analysis of 125 global cities found that San Francisco was the leader in terms of innovation. Boston led the world in terms of the number of top universities. London had the largest number of top global services firms. Munich, Shenzhen, and Houston had the most patents per capita. And Warsaw rated highest for the ease with which companies can conduct business.[21] The keys to creating world-class local communities include visionary leadership, a climate friendly to business, a commitment to training workers, and collaboration among businesses and between business and local government.[22]

Organization Development

How do organizations become more ambidextrous and move in the other positive directions described throughout this book? This chapter discusses several general approaches that will create such positive changes. We begin here with an umbrella concept called organization development.

Probably the single most widely used approach to organizational change in the Western world, applied increasingly on a global scale,[23] is **organization development (OD)**. OD is a systemwide application of behavioral science knowledge to develop, improve, and reinforce the strategies, structures, and processes that lead to organization effectiveness.[24] Throughout this course, you have learned about human behavior and the strategies, structures, and processes that help organizations become more effective.

The systemwide component of the OD definition means that it is not a narrow improvement in technology or operations but a broader approach to changing organizations, units, or people. The behavioral science component means that OD does not *directly* emphasize economic, financial, or technical aspects of the organization—although those aspects should benefit through changes in the people's behavior. The other key part of the definition—to develop, improve, and reinforce—refers to the actual process of changing for the better and for the long term.

Two features of organization development are important to note.[25] First, it aims to increase organizational effectiveness—improving the organization's ability to deal with customers, stockholders, governments, employees, and other stakeholders, which results in better-quality products, higher financial returns, and high quality of work life. Second, OD has an underlying value orientation: It supports human potential, development, and participation in addition to organizational performance and competitive advantage.

Many specific OD techniques fit under this philosophical umbrella (see Exhibit 18.2).[26] Much of you what you have already learned in this course pertains, and this final chapter offers more yet on creating and leading change.

organization development (OD)

The systemwide application of behavioral science knowledge to develop, improve, and reinforce the strategies, structures, and processes that lead to organizational effectiveness.

Trivago is a German multinational technology company specializing in internet-related services and products in the hotel, lodging, and metasearch fields.

©REUTERS/Alamy Stock Photo

Intervention	Goals
Strategic	Helping organizations conduct mergers and acquisitions, change their strategies, and develop alliances.
Techno-structural	Relating to organization structure and design, employee involvement, and work design.
Human process	Improving conflict resolution, team building, communication, and leadership.
Human resource management	Attracting good people, setting goals, and appraising and rewarding performance.

EXHIBIT 18.2
Basic Types of OD Interventions

SOURCE: Cummings, T. and Worley, C., *Organization Development and Change,* 10th ed. Stamford: Cengage, 2015.

Managing Change

 People are the key to successful change.[27] For an organization to be great, or even just to survive, its people have to care about its fate and know how they can contribute. But typically leadership lies with only a few people at the top. Too few take on the burden of change; the number of people who care deeply, and who make innovative contributions, is too small. People throughout the organization need to take a greater interest and a more active role in helping the business as a whole. Ideally, people will identify with and commit to the entire organization, not just with their unit and close colleagues.

In other words, shared leadership is crucial to the success of most change efforts—people must be not just supporters of change but also implementers.[28]

This shared responsibility for change is not unusual in start-ups and very small organizations. But too often it is lost with growth and over time. In large, bureaucratic corporations, it is all too rare. Organizations need to rekindle individual responsibility and creativity. The essential task is to motivate people to keep adapting to new business challenges.

Motivating People to Change

If people are to change, they must be motivated to do so. But often they resist changing. Some people resist change more than others, but managers tend to underestimate the amount of resistance they will encounter.[29]

People at all organizational levels, from entry-level workers to top executives, resist change. For example, many banks and credit unions are switching from specialized roles in branches, such as tellers and personal bankers, to universal agents who process transactions, open accounts, and sell products. When they make this change, the main source of resistance is that the new jobs involve selling—identifying unmet customer needs and suggesting products and services. A typical branch employee is unaccustomed to selling and may even have a negative opinion of a sales role, especially in a bank.[30]

Many people (and organizations) often settle for business-as-usual rather than aspire to excellence. When told by their managers, "We have to become world class," their reactions resemble the following statements:

- "Those world-class performance numbers are ridiculous! I don't believe them, they are impossible! Maybe in some industries, some companies . . . but ours is unique . . ."
- "Sure, maybe some companies achieve those numbers, but there's no hurry . . . We're doing all right. Sales were up 5 percent this year, costs were down 2 percent. And we've got to keep cutting corners . . ."
- "We can't afford to be world class like those big global companies; we don't have the money or staff . . ."
- "We don't need to expand internationally. One of our local competitors tried that a few years ago and lost its shirt."
- "It's not a level playing field . . . the others have unfair advantages . . ."

To deal with such reactions and successfully implement positive change, managers must understand why people often resist changing. Many factors go into people's resistance to, ambivalence toward, and readiness for change.[31] Exhibit 18.3 shows some common reasons for resistance. Some reasons are general and arise in most change efforts. Other reasons for resistance relate to the specifics of a particular change.

Why People Resist Change   Several reasons for resistance arise regardless of the actual content of the change:[32]

- *Inertia.* Usually people don't want to disturb the status quo. The old ways of doing things are comfortable and easy, so people don't want to shake things up and try something new. For example, it is easier to keep living in the same apartment or house than to move to another.

Inertia	Timing	Surprise	Peer pressure
Self-interest	Misunder-standing	Different assessments	Management tactics

EXHIBIT 18.3
Reasons for Resistance to Change

- *Timing.* People often resist change because of poor timing. Maybe you would like to move to a different place to live, but do you want to move this week? If managers or employees are (as usual) busy or under stress, or if relations between management and workers are strained, the change will be difficult. Where possible, managers should introduce change when people are receptive.

- *Surprise.* One common contributor to resistance is surprise. If the change is sudden, unexpected, or extreme, resistance may be the initial—almost reflexive—reaction. Suppose your school announced an increase in tuition, effective at the beginning of next term. Wouldn't you want more time to prepare? Managers or others initiating a change often forget that others haven't given the matter much thought; when possible the change leaders show allow time for people to prepare.

- *Peer pressure.* Often work teams resist new ideas coming from above. Even if individual members do not strongly oppose a change suggested by management, the team may band together in opposition. Peer pressure will cause individuals to resist even reasonable changes, especially if a group is highly cohesive and has anti-management norms (recall Chapter 14). But change leaders who invite—and listen to—ideas from team members may find that peer pressure becomes a positive force that helps drive the change's success.

- *Self-interest.* Most people care less about the organization's best interests than they do about their own best interests. They will resist a change if they think it will cause them to lose something of value. What could people fear to lose? At worst, their jobs, if management is considering closing a plant. A merger, reorganization, or technological change could create the same fear. Other possible fears include losing the feeling of being competent in a familiar job, expectations that the job will become more difficult or time-consuming, and concerns about the organization's future (see "Multiple Generations at Work").

- *Misunderstanding.* People resist change when they do not understand it; perhaps they don't have much information, or see how it fits with the firm's strategy, or see its advantage over current practices.[33] One company met resistance to the idea of introducing flexible working hours, a system in which workers have some say regarding the hours they work. This system can benefit employees, but a false rumor circulated among plant employees that people would have to work evenings, weekends, or whenever their supervisors wanted. The initiative was dropped.

- *Different assessments.* Employees receive different—and usually less—information than management receives. Such discrepancies cause people to develop different assessments of a proposed change. Some may be aware that the benefits outweigh the costs, whereas others may see only the costs and not the benefits. This is a common problem when management announces a change and doesn't explain to employees why it is needed. Management expects benefits, but workers may see the change as another arbitrary, ill-informed management rule that causes headaches for those who must carry it out.

- *Management tactics.* Management may attempt to force the change without addressing people's concerns. Or it may fail to provide the necessary resources, knowledge, or leadership to help the change succeed. Sometimes a change receives so much exposure and glorification that employees resent it and resist. Managers who overpromise what they, or the change, can deliver may discover that the next time they introduce a change, they have lost credibility, so employees resist.

Multiple Generations at Work

Are You Ready for the Future of Work?

A recent study of 10,000 people from five countries found that "Disruptive innovations are creating new industries and business models, and destroying old ones. New technologies, data analytics and social networks are having a huge impact on how people communicate, collaborate and work."

Employees from every generation are well advised to remain flexible with regard to job opportunities and to continually acquire marketable skills and experiences. Expect breakthroughs in technology that will alter the way people work. Try also to work for organizations that fit with your personal values. You might not find this in your first or second job, but with persistence and networking, it is possible to find the right employer for you.

The study predicted that three types of organizations will dominate the economy over the next 5 to 10 years. You can use these general descriptions to judge where you might best fit:

1. *Large global corporations.* Driven by profit and growth, these "mega-corporations" will compete on economies of scale. Employees who are flexible and perform well under pressure will be rewarded with job security and generous pay and benefits.
2. *Social and environmental enterprises.* Motivated by a "powerful social conscience and green sense of responsibility," these organizations pursue goals that

©asiseeit/Getty Images RF

benefit both business and society. Loyal employees appreciate working in ethical environments that support work–life balance.

3. *Small, agile companies.* Operating in a flexible, autonomous manner while minimizing fixed costs, these agile firms seek a variety of specialized projects. People working as short-term contractors will enjoy flexible work arrangements and variety in their job challenges.[34]

Of the three options above, where do you see yourself fitting? Best wishes to you . . .

Employees' assessments can be more accurate than management's; employees may know a change won't work even if management doesn't. In this case, resistance to change is a useful thing—if the bosses pay attention. Thus, even though management typically views resistance as an obstacle that must be overcome, it actually may be an important signal that the proposed change requires further, more open-minded scrutiny.[35]

A General Model for Managing Resistance

Motivating people to change often requires three basic stages, shown in Exhibit 18.4: unfreezing, moving to institute the change, and refreezing.[36]

EXHIBIT 18.4

Motivating People to Change

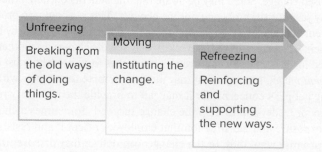

Unfreezing

Breaking from the old ways of doing things.

Moving

Instituting the change.

Refreezing

Reinforcing and supporting the new ways.

Unfreezing In the **unfreezing** stage, management realizes that its current practices are no longer appropriate and the company must break out of (unfreeze) its present mold by doing things differently. People must come to recognize that some of the past ways of thinking and doing things are obsolete.[37] A direct and sometimes effective way to do this is to communicate the negative consequences of the old ways by comparing the organization's performance with that of its competitors. As discussed in Chapter 15, management can share with employees data about costs, quality, and profits.[38]

Sometimes managers can open minds by easing employees into the transition gently and letting the more receptive employees deliver the message favoring change. George Tome, a software engineer and project manager in John Deere's IT group, initiated software changes in a gradual manner. Over time, software development units throughout the company adopted Tome's software solutions.[39]

When managers communicate the need to change, they should take care not to arouse people's defensiveness. Instead of unfreezing resistance, managers make employees feel defensive when they pin the blame for shortcomings on the workers.[40] Similarly, bombarding employees with facts aimed at inducing fear may only add to their resistance. When a problem seems huge, people often decide it is hopeless and don't face it. In these difficult situations, leaders more effectively unfreeze negative behavior with a message of hope and a commitment to collaborate so that together they can change successfully.

> Think about the vital gap between what is and what could be.

Recognizing a performance gap is a gateway to the unfreezing process. A **performance gap** is the difference between actual performance and the performance that should or could exist.[41] As an impetus for change, a performance gap can apply to the organization as a whole; it also can apply to departments, groups, and individuals.

A gap typically implies poor performance; for example, sales, profits, stock price, or other financial indicators are down. This situation attracts management's attention, and management introduces changes to try to correct things.

But another, very important form of performance gap can exist. This type of gap occurs when performance is good but someone realizes that it could be better. Thus the gap is between what is and what could be. Important changes can and should be made even when performance is good.[42]

People are particularly motivated when a sense of urgency that comes from seeing a problem combines with a sense of excitement that comes from spotting an opportunity. Furthermore, managers communicating a performance gap should remember that employees care about things other than market share and revenues. Employees want to know how a change can help them, plus how it might have a positive impact on their work group, customers, company, and community.

A financial services company met resistance when it tried to persuade employees that a change would enhance the company's competitive position. Employees got on board only after the change leaders started talking about how the change would help employees reduce errors, enable teams to avoid duplication of effort, make jobs more interesting, and help the organization fulfill its mission to deliver affordable housing.[43]

Moving The next step, **moving** to institute the change, begins with establishing a vision of the desired future. The desired future state can be achieved through strategic, structural, cultural, and individual change. But opposing forces cause conflict for people; some things make people want to change while other things—including the reasons discussed earlier—make them resist change.

One technique to managing the change process, **force-field analysis**, identifies the specific forces that keep people from changing plus the different forces that drive people toward change.[44] Eliminating the restraining forces helps people unfreeze, and increasing the driving forces helps and motivates people to move forward.

The great social psychologist Kurt Lewin developed force-field analysis and the unfreezing/moving/refreezing model, which for decades served as a foundation for many change

---

unfreezing

Realizing that current practices are inappropriate and that new behavior is necessary.

performance gap

The difference between actual performance and desired performance.

Bottom Line

A useful tactic for innovating toward a positive future is to imagine the difference between what *is* and what *could be.*
Can you think of a personal example?

moving

Instituting the change.

force-field analysis

An approach to implementing the unfreezing/moving/refreezing model by identifying the forces that prevent people from changing and those that will drive people toward change.

Lawrence Ellison, executive chairman and chief technology officer of Oracle, knows what it takes to convey a vision for successful change. Oracle often acquires other companies, creating change that challenges its people and the company.

©David Paul Morris/Getty Images

refreezing

Strengthening the new behaviors that support the change.

management models.[45] Lewin theorized that although driving forces can be easy to change, changing them may increase conflict and opposition, thereby creating new restraining forces. Therefore, to create change, it is crucial to remove restraining forces as well as add driving forces.

Refreezing   Finally, **refreezing** means strengthening the new behaviors that support the change. Refreezing involves implementing control systems that support the change (Chapter 16), applying corrective action when necessary, and reinforcing behaviors and performance (Chapter 13) that support the new agenda. Management should consistently support and reward evidence of movement in the right direction.[46]

Refreezing is not always successful if it creates and rewards new behaviors that are as rigid as the old ones. Refreezing is appropriate when it permanently installs behaviors that focus on important business results and maintains essential core values. But refreezing should not create new rigidities that might become dysfunctional as the business environment continues to change.[47] Managers should refreeze behaviors that promote continued adaptability, flexibility, experimentation, assessment of results, and continuous improvement—in other words, lock in key values, capabilities, and strategic mission but not necessarily specific practices and procedures.

Enlisting Cooperation

You can try to command people to change, but the key to long-term success is to use other approaches.[48] Developing true support is better than simply driving a program forward.[49] How, more specifically, can managers motivate people to change?

Most managers underestimate the variety of influence strategies available for motivating people during a period of change.[50] Several effective approaches to managing resistance and enlisting cooperation are available, as described in Exhibit 18.5 and discussed below.

Education and Communication   Management should educate people about upcoming changes before they occur. It should communicate not only the nature of the change but its logic. This process can include one-on-one discussions, presentations to groups, and reports. And as we discussed in Chapter 15, effective communication includes feedback and listening. That provides an environment in which management can not just explain the rationale for the change, but improve it.

Participation and Involvement   The people who are affected by the change should be involved in its design and implementation. For major, organizationwide change, participation in the process can extend from the highest to the lowest levels.[51] When feasible, management should use the input of people throughout the organization.

As you learned in Chapter 3, people who are involved in decisions understand them more fully and are more committed to them. These are vital ingredients in successful change implementation. Participation also provides an excellent opportunity for education and communication.

Facilitation and Support   Management should make the change as easy as possible for employees and support their efforts. Facilitation involves providing the training and other resources people need to carry out the change and perform their jobs under the new circumstances. This step often includes decentralizing authority and empowering people— that is, giving them the power to make the decisions and changes needed to improve their performance.

EXHIBIT 18.5   Methods for Managing Resistance to Change

Approach	Commonly Used in Situations	Advantage	Drawbacks
Education and communication	When there is a lack of information or inaccurate information and analysis.	Once persuaded, people will often help with the implementation of the change.	Can be very time-consuming if lots of people are involved.
Participation and involvement	When the initiators do not have all the information they need to design the change and when others have considerable power to resist.	People who participate will be committed to implementing change, and any relevant information they have will be integrated into the change plan.	Can be very time-consuming if participators design an inappropriate change.
Facilitation and support	When people are resisting because of adjustment problems.	No other approach works as well with adjustment problems.	Can be time-consuming and expensive and still fail.
Negotiation and rewards	When someone or some group will clearly lose out in a change and when that group has considerable power to resist.	Sometimes it is a relatively easy way to avoid major resistance.	Can be too expensive in many cases if it alerts others to negotiate for compliance.
Manipulation and cooptation	When other tactics will not work or are too expensive.	It can be a relatively quick and inexpensive solution to resistance problems.	Can lead to future problems if people feel manipulated.
Explicit and implicit coercion	When speed is essential, and the change initiators possess considerable power.	It is speedy and can overcome any kind of resistance.	Can be risky if it leaves people angry at the initiators.

SOURCE: Kotter, John P. and Schlesinger, Leonard A., "Choosing Strategies for Change," *Harvard Business Review*, March–April 1979.

Offering support involves listening patiently to problems, being understanding if performance drops temporarily or the change is not perfected immediately, and generally being on the employees' side and showing consideration during a difficult period.

Negotiation and Rewards   When necessary and appropriate, management can offer concrete incentives for cooperation with the change. Perhaps job enrichment is acceptable only with a higher wage rate, or a work rule change is resisted until management agrees to a concession on some other rule (say, regarding taking breaks). Even among higher-level managers, one executive might agree to another's idea for a policy change only in return for support on some other issue of more personal importance. Rewards such as bonuses, wages and salaries, recognition, job assignments, and perks can be examined and perhaps restructured to reinforce the direction of the change.[52]

When people trust one another, change is easier. But change is further facilitated by demonstrating its benefits to people.[53] Describing benefits can take place in the context of negotiation or collaborating to find a mutually acceptable way to implement the change. A Colorado nonprofit agency, Envision, did this when the state government cut its funding by 7.5 percent.

Envision provides services to adults and children with developmental disabilities to enhance their quality of life, and depends on employees' commitment to its mission.[54] Executive director Mary Lu Walton set up a team of employees to figure out how to cut costs, and she encouraged them to focus on eliminating the tasks employees dislike. The team members restructured work, sparing seven of the ten jobs originally targeted for layoffs. Within a few months, Envision was a leaner organization with employees fully committed to the change.[55] Today, the nonprofit continues its mission and enlists the support of many volunteers and sponsors.

Manipulation and Cooptation   Sometimes managers use subtler, more covert tactics to implement change. One form of manipulation is cooptation, which involves giving a resisting individual a desirable role in the change process. For example, management might invite a union leader to become a member of an executive committee or ask a member of an useful outside organization to join the company's board of directors. As a person becomes involved in the change, he or she becomes more familiar with and sometimes even committed to the actions of the coopting group or organization.

Explicit and Implicit Coercion   Some managers apply punishment or the threat of punishment to those who resist change. In other words, managers use force to make people comply with their wishes. For example, a manager might insist that subordinates cooperate with the change and threaten them with job loss, denial of a promotion, or an unattractive work assignment. Sometimes managers rely too heavily on coercion, but sometimes you just have to lay down the law.

Each approach to managing resistance has advantages and drawbacks, and each is useful in different situations. Look back at Exhibit 18.5, which summarizes the advantages, drawbacks, and appropriate circumstances for these various strategies. As the exhibit implies, managers should not use just one or two general approaches, regardless of circumstances. Effective change managers are familiar with the various approaches and know how to apply them all, according to the situation.

Throughout the process, change leaders need to build in some stability. Recall that built-to-last companies have essential core characteristics that they refuse to abandon. In the midst of change, turmoil, and uncertainty, people need anchors onto which they can latch.[56] Making an organization's values and mission constant and visible can serve this stabilizing function.

Strategic principles can be important anchors during change.[57] Maintaining the visibility of key people, continuing key assignments and projects, and making announcements about what will *not* change also can promote stability. Such anchors will reduce anxiety and help overcome resistance.

Harmonizing Multiple Changes

large group interventions (total organization change)

Introducing and sustaining multiple policies, practices, and procedures across multiple units and levels.

There are no silver bullets that always result in successful change. Single shots rarely hit a moving target. Usually many issues need simultaneous attention, and any single, small change will be absorbed by the prevailing culture and disappear.

Large group interventions[58] —those attempting **total organization change**—involve introducing, coordinating, and sustaining multiple policies, practices, and procedures across multiple units and levels.[59] Such change affects the thinking and behavior of everyone in the organization, can enhance the organization's culture and success, and can be sustained over time.

But commonly it's more like this: A survey of about 3,000 executives found that the average attendee's company had five major change efforts going on at once.[60] The problem is, these efforts usually are simultaneous but not coordinated. As a result, changes get muddled; people lose focus.[61] The people involved suffer from confusion, frustration, low morale, and low motivation.

Because companies introduce new changes constantly, many people complain about their companies' "flavor of the month" approach to change. That is, employees often see many change efforts as the company just jumping on the latest bandwagon or fad. The more these change fads come and go, the more cynical people become, and the more difficult it is to get them committed to making the change a success.[62]

> Many people complain about their companies' "flavor of the month" approach to change.

So an important question is, Which change efforts are really worth undertaking? Here are some specific questions to ask before embarking on a change project:[63]

- What is the evidence that the approach really can produce positive results?
- Is the approach relevant to your company's strategies and priorities?
- Can you assess the costs and potential benefits?

Management in Action

SHELL BELIEVES DEMAND FOR FOSSIL FUELS WILL REMAIN STRONG

Even as Shell Oil Company pivots to address investors' concerns about climate change, and to protect its profits from the worldwide decline in supply and demand for oil, it has not abandoned its fossil-fuel business. Shell's managers believe oil and natural gas markets will peak as soon as 10 to 15 years from now but then remain strong for several more decades.

Still, the company knows it must change, and quickly, to compete not only against its fellow oil companies but also against rising threats from wind, solar, and other renewable- and clean-energy providers. As the company's website says, "Today, Shell is still primarily an oil and gas company, but we have a long tradition of innovation. We know that long-term success depends on our ability to anticipate the types of energy and fuels people will need in the future and remain commercially competitive and environmentally relevant."

But the company also says it takes seriously its role in combating climate change, and it is making changes. In a reversal of its earlier skepticism about governments' ability to slow climate change, Shell supports the ground-breaking 2016 United Nations Paris Agreement, which seeks to commit nations to keep warming below 2 degrees Celsius by reducing the emissions that contribute to climate change. It also favors government efforts to reduce carbon emissions through carbon pricing. The company ramped up its investment in natural gas and low-carbon biofuels, and put billions of dollars into offshore wind farms in the North Sea. It's leveraging its considerable marketing expertise to seek contracts to produce and supply wind power throughout Europe, and won two big contracts with the Dutch government. Wind power is appealing to Shell because it also provides hydrogen, which the company hopes will prove a dependable fuel for cleaner-running cars in the future.

Shell's recently announced New Energies Division will explore investments in renewable and sustainable power sources, with a budget of $1.7 billion. The company is also trying to reduce emissions from its fossil-fuel business by working on ways to capture and store carbon so it will not be released into the atmosphere.

Shell Technology Ventures, the company's venture capital division, supports new solar and wind businesses. Still, despite such efforts, Shell believes the effort to give up fossil fuels will need to be a global one "supported by effective policy, a sense of urgency, and long-term vision."[64]

- If you were the CEO of Shell, how would you respond to pressures from shareholders to become a more environmentally friendly company? What changes, if any, would you pursue in the short term? Long term?
- Do you agree with Shell's CEO that fossil fuels will be needed to meet energy demand for several more decades? Explain.

- Does it really help people add value through their work?
- Does it help the company focus better on customers and the things they value?
- Can you go through the decision-making process described in Chapter 3, understand what you're facing, and feel that you are taking the right approach?

Management also needs to connect the dots—that is, integrate the various efforts into a coherent picture that people can see, understand, and get behind.[65] You connect the dots by understanding each change program and its goals, by identifying similarities among the programs and their differences, and by dropping programs that don't meet priority goals or demonstrate clear results.

Most important, you do it by communicating to everyone concerned the common themes among the various programs: their common rationales, objectives, and methods. You show them how the various parts fit the strategic big picture and how the changes will make things better for the company and its people. You should communicate these benefits thoroughly, honestly, and frequently.[66]

Leading Change

Successful change requires managers to lead it actively. The essential activities of leading change are summarized in Exhibit 18.6.

EXHIBIT 18.6
Leading Change

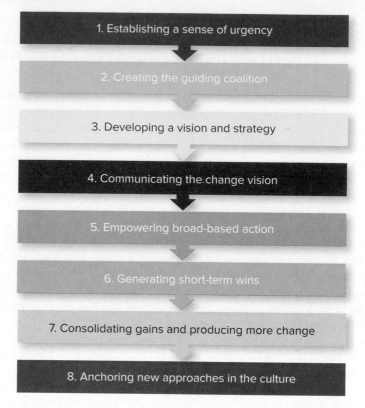

1. Establishing a sense of urgency

2. Creating the guiding coalition

3. Developing a vision and strategy

4. Communicating the change vision

5. Empowering broad-based action

6. Generating short-term wins

7. Consolidating gains and producing more change

8. Anchoring new approaches in the culture

SOURCE: Kotter, John P., *Leading Change*. Brighton, Boston: Harvard Business School Publishing, 1996.

The companies that lead change most effectively *establish a sense of urgency*.[67] To do this, managers can examine current realities and pressures in the marketplace and the competitive arena, identify both crises and opportunities, and be frank and honest about them. In this sense, urgency is a reality-based sense of determination, not just fear-based busyness. The immediacy of the need for change is an important component, in part because so many large companies grow complacent.

Exhibit 18.7 shows some common reasons for complacency. To stop complacency and create urgency, a manager can talk candidly about the organization's weaknesses compared with competitors, making a point to back up statements with data. Other tactics include setting stretch goals, putting employees in direct contact with unhappy customers and

EXHIBIT 18.7
Sources of Complacency

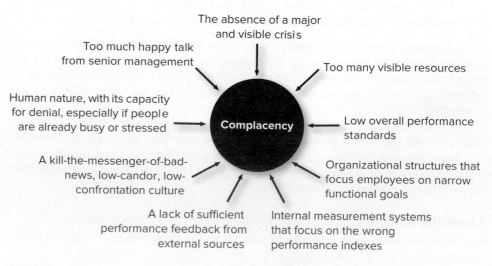

The absence of a major and visible crisis

Too much happy talk from senior management

Too many visible resources

Human nature, with its capacity for denial, especially if people are already busy or stressed

Complacency

Low overall performance standards

A kill-the-messenger-of-bad-news, low-candor, low-confrontation culture

Organizational structures that focus employees on narrow functional goals

A lack of sufficient performance feedback from external sources

Internal measurement systems that focus on the wrong performance indexes

SOURCE: Kotter, John P., *Leading Change*. Brighton, Boston: Harvard Business School Publishing, 1996.

shareholders, distributing worrisome information to all employees instead of merely engaging in management happy talk, eliminating excessive perks, and highlighting to everyone opportunities that the organization so far has failed to pursue.

Ultimately, urgency is driven by time pressure along with compelling business reasons to change. Survival, competition, and winning in the marketplace are compelling; they provide a sense of direction and energy around change. Change becomes not a hobby, a luxury, or something nice to do, but a business necessity.[68]

To *create a guiding coalition* means putting together a group with enough power to lead the change. Change efforts fail without a sufficiently powerful coalition.[69] Major organization change requires leadership from top management, working as a team. But over time, the support must gradually expand outward and downward throughout the organization. Middle managers and supervisors are essential. Groups at all levels are the glue that can hold change efforts together, the medium for communicating about the changes, and the means for supporting new behaviors.[70]

Developing a vision and strategy, as discussed in earlier chapters, directs the change effort. This process involves determining the idealized, expected state of affairs after the change is implemented. Because confusion is common during major organizational change, the clearest possible image of the future state must be developed and conveyed to everyone.[71] This image, or vision, is a target or guideline that can clarify expectations, dispel rumors, and mobilize people's energies.

The portrait of the future also should communicate how the transition will occur, why the change is being implemented, and how people will be affected by the change. The power of a compelling vision is one of the most important aspects of change and should not be underestimated or underused.

Communicating the change vision requires using every possible channel and opportunity to talk up and reinforce the vision and required new behaviors. It is said that aspiring change leaders undercommunicate the vision by a factor of 10, or even 100 or 1,000, seriously undermining the chances of success.[72] In delivering more messages, however, do not forget that communication is a two-way street.

Empowering broad-based action means getting rid of obstacles to success, including systems and structures that constrain rather than facilitate. Encourage risk taking and experimentation and empower people by providing information, knowledge, authority, and rewards, as described in Chapter 13.

Generate short-term wins. Don't wait for the ultimate grand realization of the vision. You need some early progress. As small victories accumulate, you make the transition from an isolated initiative to an integral part of the business.[73] Plan for and create small victories that indicate to everyone that progress is being made. Recognize and reward the people who made the wins possible, doing it visibly so that people notice and the positive message permeates the organization.

Make sure you *consolidate gains and produce more change.* With the well-earned credibility of previous successes, keep changing things in ways that support the vision. Hire, promote, and develop people who will further the vision. Reinvigorate the organization and your change efforts with new projects and change agents.

Finally, *anchor new approaches in the culture.*[74] Highlight positive results, communicate the connections between the new behaviors and the improved results, and keep developing new change agents and leaders. Continually increase the number of people joining you in taking responsibility for change.[75]

The conventional way in which organizations apply these eight steps of leading change has been to use ad hoc teams to conduct annual strategy reviews or launch new projects that might take months or years. But this approach can be too slow for seizing fast-appearing and fast-disappearing opportunities. Therefore John Kotter, who proposed the eight steps, advises companies to become more agile by empowering networks of employees to accelerate change.[76] These networks bring together volunteers from all levels and functions of the organization who are excited about the change vision and have the skills needed to implement it. When someone sees a problem or opportunity, any member of the network can invite others to join a team in developing a solution.

Shaping the Future

reactive change

A response that occurs under pressure; problem-driven change.

proactive change

A response that is initiated before a performance gap has occurred.

Most change is reactive. A better approach is to be proactive. **Reactive change** means responding to pressure after a problem has arisen. It also implies being a follower. **Proactive change** means anticipating and preparing for an uncertain future. It implies being a leader and creating the future you want.

The road to the future includes drivers, passengers, and road kill. Put another way: on the road to the future, who will be the windshield, and who will be the bug?[77] Needless to say, it's best to be a driver.[78]

How do you become a driver? By being proactive more than merely reactive, by really thinking about the future, and by *creating* futures.

Thinking about the Future

If you think only about the present or simply wallow in the uncertainties of the future, your future is just a roll of the dice. It is far better to exercise foresight, set an agenda for the future, and pursue it with everything you've got.

> On the road to the future, who will be the windshield, and who will be the bug?

Before the 20th century, people lived without antibiotics, automobiles, airplanes, tractors, and air conditioning. Imagine how this combination of inventions has revolutionized where and how well people live. And in recent years, we have seen the invention and spread of smartphones, 3D printing, artificial intelligence, machine learning, and the mapping of the human genome. These innovations are still shaping how we learn, communicate, and treat disease.

What will the rest of the 21st century bring? The potential for innovation and growth is unprecedented in areas such as artificial intelligence, smart cities, and renewable energy technologies.[79]

Deep-neural networks, an emerging branch of the artificial intelligence field, is expected to become an invisible part of every organization. Programmers will embed learning algorithms into images, video, and text. Machines learn from these online interactions and will replace many human tasks.[80]

Companies like IBM, Microsoft, and Cisco are using big data and the Internet of Things to help cities around the world become smarter.[81] More than half of the world's population lives in urban environments, and city leaders want to improve their citizens' quality of life. Garbage receptacles with sensors will automatically send garbage through underground tubes to waste pickup areas, reducing the need for noisy and smelly garbage trucks. New apps will help city dwellers find free (available) parking, register vehicles, pay electric bills, and take advantage of other services. By 2021, smart innovations focused on easing traffic congestion alone are projected globally to save cities about $4.2 billion annually.[82]

Renewable energies like wind and solar power continue to grow. Most electricity in the United States now comes from renewables.[83] Worldwide, digital technologies and the Internet of Things improve wind farm efficiency and drive more solar panel use.[84] Development and use of renewable energy sources will accelerate into the foreseeable future.

Just as technologies change, so do other trends rise and fall, recently including a (temporary, most likely) damper on globalization, rising distrust of business, a growing role of government, strains on natural resources, and changing patterns of global consumption.[85] Vast new markets will exist, new kinds of companies will appear, and new business models will emerge.[86] All offer prime opportunity to those who create the future.

adapters

Companies that take the current industry structure and its evolution as givens, and choose where to compete.

Creating the Future

Companies can try different strategic postures in preparing to compete in an uncertain future. **Adapters** take the current industry structure and its future evolution as givens,

The Digital World

"Students are at the center of everything we do." So begins the Ford NGL website, and visitors quickly get the sense that the statement is very true.

Ford Next Generation Learning (Ford NGL), a strategic initiative of the Ford Motor Company Fund, brings students, educators, employers, and community leaders together to collaboratively develop and implement a plan for transforming secondary schools. Using the career academy model, Ford NGL seeks to infuse more career relevance into traditional academics and address unique local and regional workforce needs. Long term, the intentions are to (1) better prepare young people for careers, college, lifelong learning, and leadership; (2) increase community prosperity; (3) strengthen local and regional talent pipelines; (4) build local capacity to sustain change; and (5) promote greater educational equity and justice for all students.

High school career academies have three key components: (1) the small learning community structure, (2) a college preparatory curriculum with a career theme, and (3) partnerships with employers, the community, and local postsecondary institutions. Housed within a larger high school, each academy is a "school-within-a-school."

The typical curriculum is project- and problem-based, relies on inquiry, critical thinking, and teamwork, and is organized around a core career theme such as manufacturing, information technology, or health care. Community partners bring industry expertise and the latest resources to students, collaborate with academy teachers on curriculum, and provide students with work-based learning opportunities such as job shadows and internships.

The Ford NGL community-driven approach and the career academy model help change the conversation around education, and provide an avenue for true transformation from the ground up. The academies allow students to explore programs that interest them and align with regional workforce needs. Because student interests evolve and change, the academies often help students learn what they *don't* want to do as well as what they *do* want to do in the future.

When students, educators, employers, and community partners come together in these ways, students better understand the purpose of school and are more likely to find personal meaning. The process generates a shared community-wide sense of accountability for both student success and for community prosperity. What's more, students leave high school with career-related experience, relationships with employers, and tangible next steps toward their envisioned futures.

"Education is the foundation of individual and community prosperity. It was true in Henry Ford's day and it's still true today," stated Vella, president, Ford Motor Company Fund and Community Services.

To learn more, visit www.fordngl.com.

conduct standard strategic analyses, and then choose where to compete. In contrast, **shapers** try to change the structure of industries, creating future competitive landscapes of their own design.[87] For an example, see the nearby "Social Enterprise" box.

Shapers can be high-tech industry disruptors or innovators in any industry.[88] Purple is changing the mattress industry by selling its products online, directly to customers; by cutting out distributors and retailers, they sell at lower prices. Sourcify saves entrepreneurs search time and lowers their risk by using algorithms to match them with trustworthy manufacturers.[89] Financial service firms are investing aggressively in start-up firms like Circle Internet Financial, Coinbase, and Ripple that use blockchain technology (the distributed ledger technology behind bitcoin).[90] Blockchain technology is expected to disrupt the financial services industry (among others) by increasing the efficiency, transparency, and security of financial transactions.[91]

Not every company can create an idea that is so revolutionary that it disrupts an industry. On the other hand, a strategy that focuses primarily on delivering the same services or products to current customers will not thrive. An ever-growing field of competitors, advancing technology, and changing customer preferences require companies to continuously offer new goods and services that meet or exceed the needs of current and future customers.

Exhibit 18.8 shows four quadrants depicting growth opportunities based on customers' needs. Companies that follow a business-as-usual philosophy meet customers' needs with current product offerings, in the lower left quadrant. An example is a municipal utility serving city residents by purchasing and distributing power from coal-fired power plants.

shapers

Companies that try to change the structure of their industries, creating a future competitive landscape of their own design.

Social Enterprise

Using Co-creation to Build a Better Future

Co-creation is when diverse stakeholders come together to develop new practices. The stakeholders—social enterprises, for-profit companies, nonprofit entities, educational institutions, or government agencies—leverage one another's strengths and resources in order to solve social and environmental challenges.

Stephanie Schmidt, managing director of Ashoka Europe, believes the social sector can learn from what companies do well: ". . . scale, but also efficiency in terms of operations, product development, distribution, as well as innovation." At the same time, for-profit companies can learn how social enterprises are agile with strategies, operate on low budgets, and maintain extreme client focus.

Here are two examples of how co-creation is solving social and environmental problems:

BASF Agricultural Solutions (India) developed a digital platform to exchange information with farmers regarding the correct mix of seeds and chemicals to use when planting crops. The company trained farmers to "optimize their yield and to become better stewards of their land." Within one year, the co-creation effort increased yields by 25 percent. BASF became India's market leader in agricultural products.

The City of Porto Alegre in southern Brazil co-creates by involving citizens in allocating $200 million annually in public funds. Using live in-person and online broadcasts of town hall meetings, nearly 50,000 people participate in the budgeting process. Popular topics include school and sewer construction in the city's most disadvantaged areas. The World Bank "credited Porto Alegre's participatory budgeting process with helping to reduce inequality in the city."

Co-creating is an exciting movement that holds real promise in bringing diverse stakeholders together to fight the world's most pressing problems—poverty, inequality, hunger, illiteracy, climate change, and disease.[92]

Questions

- Can you think of additional examples in which diverse organizations joined forces to address social or environmental problems?

- Do you believe this co-creation movement is sustainable? What will ensure that it's not just a passing fad?

Forward-looking utilities purchase more from natural gas plants and renewable energies like water, wind, and solar.[93] These strategies occupy the lower right quadrant, offering new goods and services to existing customers. Or a company can use new products to attract new customers, thus operating in the upper right quadrant.

For example, because research showed that the hardest problem facing small businesses was "finding the right people to hire," Facebook started allowing companies to post job ads on

EXHIBIT 18.8

Opportunity Is Finding Ways to Meet Customers' Needs

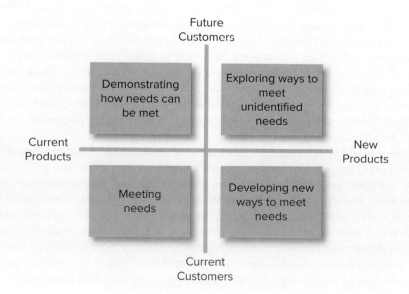

their news feeds. With job seekers applying for more positions more efficiently via Facebook, future business customers will use the new service in recruiting. Meanwhile, in the upper left quadrant, Facebook keeps using current products to attract future customers—for instance, with its e-commerce platform Delivery.com, where business sells directly to customers.[94]

World-class companies are typically the most proactive and can operate successfully in all four quadrants. They meet their current customers' needs by continually updating existing products or launching new goods and services. They try to shape their future by prospecting for new and future customers. They demonstrate how current products and services can solve the needs of new customers, while searching continuously for unidentified needs to address. For example, developed and fast-developing nations present problems in the strain they put on the planet's resources, but proactive firms see opportunities to serve new customers with new products that are made more sustainably or enable consumers to live more sustainable lifestyles.[95]

Other companies hope to meet unidentified needs by developing cutting-edge technologies. The nanometer, one billionth of a meter, is the building block of an emerging industry, nanotechnology. The nanometer is so important because matter at this scale behaves differently—speeding electrons through circuits faster, conducting heat better, or offering qualities such as greater strength.[96] Nano-based technologies are launching new or improve existing products in industries including information technology, homeland security, transportation, health care, cosmetics, energy, and many others.[97] Current applications include diagnosing medical problems at earlier stages, making personal body armor stronger, enhancing the efficiency of fuel production, improving the durability of eyeglass lenses, and decreasing the weight of cars, trucks, and airplanes to reduce fuel costs.[98]

Is nanotech—for that matter, are most industries of the future—being overhyped? Products using nanotech materials have surpassed $1 trillion in global sales.[99] Impressive growth for a technology that is still developing![100] However, the technology may be risky.[101] The particles are so small that they can pass through most manufactured filters and cell walls, and reactions at the atomic level could have negative chemical and biological consequences. Thus the industry must apply this exciting new technology while protecting workers and customers against risks that aren't yet known.[102]

Whatever your industry, all things considered, which should you and your firm do?

- Preserve old advantages or create new advantages?
- Lock in old markets or create new markets?
- Take the path of greatest familiarity or the path of greatest opportunity?
- Be only a benchmarker or a pathbreaker?
- Place priority on short-term financial returns or on making a real, long-term impact?
- Do only what seems doable or what is difficult and worthwhile?
- Change what is or create what isn't?
- Look to the past or live for the future?[103]

Shaping Your Own Future

If you are a manager and your employer operates in traditional ways, perhaps you can help start a revolution, genetically reengineering your company before it becomes a dinosaur of the modern era.[104]

But maybe you are not going to lead a revolution. Maybe you just want a good career and a good life. You still must be able to choose and pursue long-term goals[105] and deal with an economic environment that is highly competitive and fast-moving.[106]

Creating the future you want for yourself requires setting high personal standards. Don't settle for mediocrity; don't assume that good is necessarily good enough—for yourself or for your employer. Think about how not just to meet expectations but to exceed them; not merely to live with apparent constraints but break free of the unimportant, arbitrary, or imagined ones; and to seize opportunities instead of letting them pass by.[107]

Look for positions that stretch you and for bosses who develop their protégés.

The most successful individuals take charge of their own development the way an entrepreneur takes charge of a business.[108] More specific advice from the leading authors on career management:[109] Consciously and actively manage your own career. Develop marketable skills and keep developing more. Make career choices based on personal growth, development, and learning opportunities. Look for positions that stretch you and for bosses who develop their protégés. Seek environments that provide training and the opportunity to experiment and innovate. And know yourself; assess your strengths and weaknesses, your true interests, and ethical standards. If you are not already thinking in these terms and taking commensurate action, you can start now.

Additionally, become indispensable to your organization. Be enthusiastic in your job and committed to doing great work, but don't be blindly loyal to one company. Be prepared to leave if necessary. View your job as an opportunity to prove what you can do and increase what you can do, not as a comfortable niche for the long term.[110] Go out on your own if it meets your skills and temperament to do so.

This points out the need to maintain your options. More and more, contemporary careers can involve leaving behind a large organization and going entrepreneurial, becoming self-employed in the postcorporate world.[111] In such a career, independent individuals are free to make their own choices. They can flexibly and quickly respond to demands and opportunities. Developing start-up ventures, consulting, accepting temporary employment, doing project work for one organization and then another, working in professional partnerships, being a constant deal maker—these can be the elements of a successful career. Ideally, this self-employed model contributes to work-life balance.

This go-it-alone approach can sound ideal, but it also has downsides. Independence can be frightening, the future unpredictable. It can isolate road warriors who are always on the go, working from their cars and airports, and can interfere with social and family life.[112] Effective self-management is essential to keep career and family obligations in perspective and under control.

Don't think taking risks and being fearless is only for companies; think of your own quest for personal advantage in the same way. Ultimately where you go, what you do, who you become are up to you.

©DWD-Media/Alamy Stock Photo

Coping with uncertainty and change is easier if you develop resilience. To become more resilient, practice thinking of the world as complex but full of opportunities; expect change, but view it as interesting and potentially rewarding, even if changing is difficult. Keep a sense of purpose, set priorities for your time, be flexible when facing uncertainty or a need to change, and take an active role in the face of change rather than waiting for change to happen to you.[113]

Learning and Leading

Bottom Line

Continuous learning provides a competitive advantage by helping you and your organization achieve difficult goals.

What are the three phases in the process of continuous learning?

Continuous learning is a vital route to renewable competitive advantage.[114] People in your organization—and you, personally—should constantly explore, discover, and take action, as illustrated in Exhibit 18.9. With this approach, you can learn what is effective and what is not, and adjust and improve accordingly. The philosophy of continuous learning helps your company achieve lower cost, higher quality, better service, superior innovation, greater sustainability, and greater speed—and helps you grow and develop on a personal level.

Commit to lifelong learning. Lifelong learning requires occasionally taking risks, moving outside your comfort zone, honestly assessing the reasons behind your successes and failures, asking for and listening to other people's information and opinions, and being open to new ideas.[115]

In a career, a person inhabits and can move through the hierarchy of stages in Exhibit 18.10 from Jim Collins's book *Good to Great*. The descriptions in the hierarchy suggest not only that you might do these things, but that you should do them well. Your first job may not include managerial responsibilities, but it will require you to be an individual contributor and probably to be part of a team. Level 3 is where

Commit to lifelong learning.

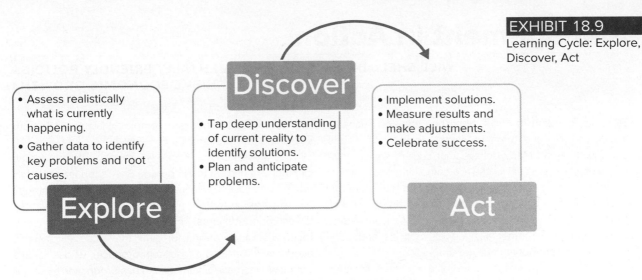

EXHIBIT 18.9
Learning Cycle: Explore, Discover, Act

SOURCE: Adapted from Binney, George and Williams, Collin, *Leaning into the Future: Changing the Way People Change Organizations.* Boston: Nicholas Brealey Publishing Ltd., 1997.

managerial capabilities are required, whereas Level 4 distinguishes true leadership from competent management. Level 5 represents a leadership style that you read about briefly in Chapter 12, combining personal humility with strong will and determination. Level 5 leadership represents a peak achievement, the ultimate contribution of a leader who can turn a good company into a great one.[116]

You might ask yourself, What is my level now (or where will I be after graduation)? What do I aspire to? What have I learned to this point that can help me progress, and what do I need to learn to develop myself further?

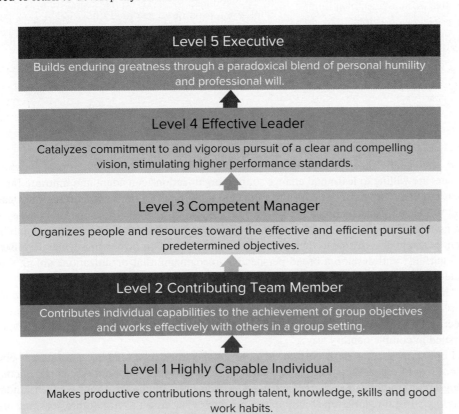

EXHIBIT 18.10
Level 5 Hierarchy

SOURCE: Collins, Jim, *Good to Great.* New York: HarperCollins, 2001.

Management in Action

WILL SHELL DEVELOP ENVIRONMENTALLY FRIENDLY POLICIES *AND* ACHIEVE ECONOMIC GROWTH?

Since its founding in 1907, Shell has adapted successfully to an array of external pressures. Today's challenges may be different. Many believe that current social, environmental, and political forces are combining in a way that will force disruptive change within Shell and the rest of the energy industry. Jeremy Leggett of the Carbon Tracker Initiative, a group that advises energy company investors, argues that "environmentally friendly policies and economic growth are not mutually exclusive."

The Carbon Tracker Initiative joins a chorus of other voices for change. Recently, the Norwegian sovereign wealth fund divested its shares in coal. Students at Edinburgh University convinced officials at the school to divest from three of the largest fossil-fuel energy companies. Over 200 alumni (and parents) from Massachusetts Institute of Technology, Stanford University, Syracuse University, and other schools diverted their post-graduation donations to a Multi-School Fossil Free Divestment Fund. The universities will receive the donations only if they divest their interests from fossil-fuel companies.

The Guardian, an international weekly newspaper, recently started a "Keep It in the Ground" campaign that features 20 journalists who chronicle stories related to climate change. While recently discussing the environment, Pope Francis of the Catholic Church stated: "We are not faced with two separate crises, one environmental and the other social, but rather one complex crisis which is both social and environmental."

Are these forces in the macroenvironment (recall Chapter 2) sufficient to encourage Shell's top managers to move faster toward a more sustainable business strategy? A sharp drop in the price of oil in 2016 left Shell with its lowest reported annual income in 10 years. The company recently stopped drilling for oil in the Arctic and instead acquired British Gas, a fossil-fuel producer, whose record output will increase Shell's oil and gas production by about 20 percent and make it one of the most valuable oil and gas companies in the world.

The company knows the energy business is changing, but as its then-outgoing president Marvin Odum argued in a recent interview, "That transition is much more difficult than most people think it is, not the least because of the scale of the energy system and the trillions and trillions of dollars that have gone into developing that system."[117]

- How much influence do external stakeholders like the ones mentioned above exert on Shell's top management?
- Shell executives need to decide how much, how fast, and *how* to move toward greener energy technologies. Identify specific challenges and discuss how to proceed. What has Shell done recently?

A leader—and this can include you—should be able to create an environment in which "others are willing to learn and change so their organizations can adapt and innovate [and] inspire diverse others to embark on a collective journey of continual learning and leading."[118] Learning leaders exchange knowledge freely; commit to their own continuous learning as well as to others'; examine their own behaviors and defensiveness that may inhibit their learning; devote time to their colleagues, suspending their own beliefs while they listen thoughtfully; and develop a broad perspective, recognizing that organizations are an integrated system of human relationships.[119]

Honored as one of the best management books of the year in Europe, *Leaning into the Future* gets its title from a combination of the words *leading* and *learning*.[120] The two perspectives, on the surface, appear very different. But they are powerful and synergistic when pursued in complementary ways.

Long-term success derives from adapting to the world *and* shaping the future; being responsive to others' perspectives *and* being clear about what you want to change; encouraging others to change *while* recognizing what you need to change about yourself; understanding current realities *and* passionately pursuing your vision for the future; learning *and* leading.

Remember the importance of ambidexterity, and the genius of the *and*.

A Collaborative, Sustainable Future?

As you lead and learn into the future, we urge you to (1) think long term, along with handling the immediate demands you must face, and (2) consider collaboration as a key to sustained success. You've learned about many of today's big challenges. The good news is that new business models and new forms of collaboration are taking root, and others are waiting to be created.[121] Entrepreneurs with societal goals are driving new approaches to commerce. The private sector is tackling social and environmental issues, the public sector is enacting market-based approaches to delivering services, and nonprofits pursue sustainable business models.

Business and tomorrow's leaders in every sector help determine the future. It would be naïve to think that long-term considerations will guide our behavior more than do the short-term pressures for immediate results. ("The Management in Action: Onward" spotlights this dilemma for oil companies like Shell.) And the controversy persists over what the obligations of business really are. But only a long-term perspective, balanced with prudent near-term considerations, will sustain your organization's purpose enduringly over time.

Collaboration will not replace competition. Competition has upsides and downsides, and although new competitors continually appear, former competitors become collaborators when they realize the potential advantages.[122] Certainly at local levels and sometimes at regional and global levels, multisector clusters of businesses, schools, universities, nonprofits, and governments are collaborating in mutually beneficial and effective ways. People are learning how to work more effectively together—not just within but across organizational, industry, and sector boundaries—to produce new models for action that revitalize commerce and will indeed create the future.[123]

KEY TERMS

adapters, p. 532
force-field analysis, p. 525
genius of the *and,* p. 520
large group interventions, p. 528
moving, p. 525

organization development (OD), p. 521
organizational ambidexterity, p. 520
performance gap, p. 525
proactive change, p. 532
reactive change, p. 532

refreezing, p. 526
shapers, p. 533
total organization change, p. 528
tyranny of the *or,* p. 519
unfreezing, p. 525

RETAINING WHAT YOU LEARNED

In Chapter 18, you learned what it takes to achieve world-class excellence. Sustaining greatness requires having strong core values and striving for continuous improvement, among other things. It is crucial to believe that multiple important goals can be achieved simultaneously and synergistically. Effective change management occurs when organizations move from their current state to a desired future state. General reasons that people resist change include inertia, poor timing, surprise, self-interest, and others. Motivating people to change requires a general process of unfreezing, moving, and refreezing. More specific strategies include education and communication, participation and involvement, facilitation and support, negotiation and rewards, manipulation and cooptation, and coercion. Each approach has strengths, weaknesses, and appropriate uses, and multiple approaches can be used. Effective change requires active leadership, including creating a sense of urgency, forming a guiding coalition, developing a vision and strategy, and

taking further actions. You can proactively forge the future by being a shaper more than an adapter, creating new competitive advantages, actively managing your career and your personal development, and becoming an active leader and a lifelong learner.

LO 1 Discuss what it takes to be world class.

- You should strive for world-class excellence, which means using the very best and latest knowledge and ideas to operate at the highest standards of any place anywhere.
- Sustainable greatness comes from, among other things, having strong core values, living those values constantly, striving for continuous improvement, experimenting, and always trying to do better tomorrow than today.
- It is essential not to fall prey to the tyranny of the *or*—that is, the belief that one important goal can be attained only at the expense of another. The genius

of the *and* is that multiple important goals can be achieved simultaneously and synergistically.

LO 2 Describe how to manage and lead change effectively.

- Effective change management occurs when the organization moves from its current state to a desired future state without excessive cost to the organization or its people.
- People resist change for a variety of reasons, including inertia, poor timing, surprise, peer pressure, self-interest, misunderstanding, different information about (and assessments of) the change, and management's tactics.
- Motivating people to change requires a general process of unfreezing, moving, and refreezing, with the caveat that appropriate and not inappropriate behaviors be refrozen.
- More specific techniques to motivate people to change include education and communication, participation and involvement, facilitation and support, negotiation and rewards, manipulation and

cooptation, and coercion. Each approach has strengths, weaknesses, and appropriate uses, and multiple approaches can be used. It is important to harmonize the multiple changes that are occurring throughout the organization.

- Effective change requires active leadership, including creating a sense of urgency, forming a guiding coalition, developing a vision and strategy, communicating the change vision, empowering broad-based action, generating short-term wins, consolidating gains and producing more change, and anchoring the new approaches in the culture.

LO 3 Describe strategies for creating a successful future.

- Preparing for an uncertain future requires a proactive approach.
- You can proactively forge the future by being a shaper more than an adapter, creating new competitive advantages, actively managing your career and your personal development, and becoming an active leader and a lifelong learner.

DISCUSSION QUESTIONS

1. Why do some people resist the goal of becoming world class? How can this resistance be overcome?
2. Generate specific examples of world-class business that you have seen as a consumer. Also, generate examples of poor business practice. Why and how do some companies inspire world-class practices while others do not?
3. How might blogging and other social forms of communication via social media affect the process of managing change? What are the professional and career implications of blogging for you?
4. Generate and discuss examples of problems and opportunities that have inspired change, both in businesses and in you personally.
5. Review the methods for dealing with resistance to change. Generate specific examples of each that you have seen and analyze why they worked or failed to work.
6. Choose some specific types of changes you would like to see happen in groups or organizations with which you are familiar. Imagine that you were to try to bring about these changes. What sources of resistance should you anticipate? How would you manage the resistance?
7. Develop a specific plan for becoming a continuous learner.
8. In your own words, what does the idea of creating the future mean to you? How can you put this concept to good use? Again, generate some specific ideas that you can really use.
9. In what ways do you think the manager's job will be different in 20 years from what it is today? How can you prepare for that future?

EXPERIENTIAL EXERCISES

18.1 OVERCOMING RESISTANCE TO CHANGE

OBJECTIVE
To learn how to overcome resistance to change.

INSTRUCTIONS
Refer back to Exhibit 18.5 and the different ways to manage resistance to change. Next, think about the last time

you tried to introduce a new idea or way of doing things at work, school, or some other organization. Describe the new idea and which approach(es) you used to overcome others' resistance to trying out the new idea.

RESISTANCE TO CHANGE WORKSHEET

Describe a new idea you tried to introduce at work, school, or some other organization:

_____

_____

_____

_____

Which (if any) of the following approaches to overcoming resistance to change did you use? (Please check all that apply)

_____Education and communication   _____Negotiation and rewards

_____Participation and involvement   _____Manipulation and cooptation

_____Facilitation and support   _____Explicit and implicit coercion

What was the outcome? To what degree were you successful in overcoming the resistance to change? Explain.

_____

_____

_____

If you could go back in time, would you use a different approach to overcome the resistance to your new idea? Why or why not?

_____

_____

_____

18.2 NETWORKING SCENARIOS

1. Working on your own, develop a networking strategy for the following three scenarios. (10 min.)

2. Working with your partner or small group, collaborate on identifying the best strategy for dealing with each of the three scenarios. Each group should develop one best strategy for each scenario. (20 min.)

3. Each group reports, sharing its best strategies for each of the three scenarios (or at least one if not enough time is available). (2–3 min. per group per strategy)

4. The large group or class engages in discussion, using the questions at the end. (10 min.)

SCENARIOS

I. You are running for student government president. What steps would you take to make your candidacy a success?

1. _____

2. _____

3. _____

4. _____

5. _____

6. _____

II. You are in an internship and are interested in becoming a permanent full-time employee at the organization. What people would you approach and what steps could you take to obtain an offer?

1. _____

2. _____

3. _____

4. _____

5. _____

6. _____

III. You just moved to a new community, and your company's business growth relies heavily on referrals. How do you make contacts in a place where you don't know anyone? How can you build a client base?

1. _____

2. _____

3. _____

4. _____

5. _____

6. _____

QUESTIONS

1. What was difficult about this exercise?

2. What creative means were devised to build networks of contacts in these scenarios?

3. Which of these ideas would be easy to implement? Which would be difficult? What makes some strategies easier to do than others?

4. What personal qualities are needed actually to use these strategies?

5. How can someone who is shy about approaching new people use (some or all of) these strategies successfully?

6. What did you learn about yourself and others from this exercise?

SOURCE: de Janasz, Suzanne C., Dowd, Karen O. and Schneider, Beth Z., *Interpersonal Skills in Organizations,* McGraw-Hill/Irwin. 2002, p. 212.

Concluding Case

EATWELL TECHNOLOGIES

Cristina Muñoz and P. R. (Pete) Prakash started EatWell Technologies as a result of conversations they held while they were graduate students in bioengineering. Both scientists were interested in how to develop crops offering superior nutrition in developing countries, and both believe that business innovation can and should drive social change. They focused their research on a genetically modified strain of rice that is drought tolerant and high in vitamin A and iron. Upon completing their studies, they wrote a business plan and formed EatWell Technologies to commercialize their new rice. Their aim was to sell first in Africa, where nutrition is an urgent problem and the potential for economic development presents huge opportunities for business. They selected Nigeria as their first target market.

Working through the government and with nongovernmental development organizations and local farmers, Cristina and Pete established a reputation for integrity and a desirable product. As farmers began purchasing their rice, the two owners hired research assistants, office staff, and sales representatives. They began to enjoy modest profits and started paying themselves a monthly salary—far from what they could earn as scientists in a large corporation but

enough to live on. They began discussing what products to offer next. Cristina suggested they develop improved leafy greens to provide variety in local diets; Pete was inclined to add new strains of rice, their area of greatest knowledge.

The two entrepreneurs also realized that as their venture grew, it needed management expertise beyond their skills as scientists. They hired an experienced office manager, and the office staff appreciated her tactful guidance. They also interviewed Bill Jensen, a retired vice president of a community bank. Bill was impressed with the company's mission and thought an interesting retirement project would be to help EatWell become financially stronger. Pete, Cristina, and Bill reached an agreement by which Bill would become a third partner in exchange for investing $450,000. The partners met daily, and Bill helped the scientists track cash flow, choose suppliers, and meet experts who can help the business expand into new markets.

At one of their strategy meetings, Pete and Cristina agreed it is time to settle on the direction for product development: Will EatWell be a rice company, or should it diversify into green vegetables? Bill surprised them with a few PowerPoint slides about his idea. Bill pointed out that rice and leafy greens are commodities, and EatWell will never get much of a return from investing in commodities. Instead, he pointed out the value of the rice as a brand. Imagine where EatWell could go by incorporating the rice into other products, such as energy bars and breakfast cereal. They could go beyond farming into the cities and sell to Africa's rapidly growing middle class, who could pay a premium. They could even start paying themselves salaries in line with their expertise and the risks they took on by forming the company. Pete and Cristina were shocked. From their viewpoint, Bill had lost sight of the company's purpose.

DISCUSSION QUESTIONS

1. Review the first section of the chapter, about becoming world class. How can EatWell Technologies fulfill its social mission and be profitable?
2. In this case, where do you see resistance to change? How can leaders overcome the resistance? How should they?
3. Suppose you are coaching Pete and Cristina. What advice would you give them about shaping their future?

PART FIVE   SUPPORTING CASE

Technology Helps Dollar General Remain Competitive

More and more consumers determined to save money are winding up at deep-discount retailers popularly known as dollar stores. These relatively small stores—including Dollar General, Family Dollar, and Dollar Tree—offer food, clothing, and household items at deep discounts. Discounters such as Target and Walmart offer a wider selection, but more consumers are trading down to find the best possible prices.

Competing with Walmart on price is hardly an easy strategy. When Kathleen Guion took charge of store operations and store development for Dollar General, she got to work initiating a whole host of changes. Many of these were aimed at controlling costs and helping the stores run more efficiently, and many of the changes involved improving the technology used by store employees, bringing it more in line with industry standards.

Guion found that Dollar General used some truly low-tech approaches to activities involved in running the stores. When trucks pulled up with deliveries, for example, store employees pulled cartons out of the truck one by one and carried them into the store for stocking the shelves. And whenever items languished on shelves too long, the same employees would repack them in boxes and carry them into the back room for storage. Not only were these methods slow, but employees hated lugging the boxes around. Calling her change program EZ Store, Guion simplified those jobs. She bought large wheeled bins called rolltainers, which employees use to move products from the trucks to back rooms to the sales floor. And when products don't sell as expected, the EZ Store plan calls for marking down the price low enough that the products do get sold. Not only does EZ Store make working for Dollar General more enjoyable by eliminating undesirable chores, but the greater efficiency gives employees more time to serve customers.

Under Guion's direction, Dollar General also upgraded its computer systems to deliver better information faster. The company introduced handheld scanners connected to an inventory management system so employees can quickly and accurately see which items need to be replenished and when. Computers linked to headquarters have been installed in the back rooms of all the stores. (Surprising as it may sound, until 2009, headquarters sent messages to stores via postal mail.) The company introduced computer-based training programs to improve employees' skills, as well as software for screening job candidates to identify which of them have qualities associated with success. And to reduce thefts in the stores, the company installed closed-circuit television systems.

Managers also have been given better technology. Dollar General bought district managers personal computers with software that monitors performance and flags exceptions to standards. It also gave them BlackBerry handheld devices so they can keep in touch with their people and keep up to date on store performance while they travel. The technology has enabled Dollar General to widen the district managers' span of control because fewer managers can keep up with more stores. More efficient management, in turn, has supported the company's program of rapidly opening new stores. (It now has more than 12,000 in 43 states.)

These efficiency improvements are essential for remaining successful in the changing deep-discount retailing industry. Recently, Dollar General's competitor Dollar Tree surprised industry observers by announcing that it would be purchasing Family Dollar for nearly $9 billion. This new entity (it'll keep both brands) will be larger than Dollar General in both sales and number of stores. In response to the move, Dollar General CEO Richard Dreiling has postponed his retirement to help the retailer adjust to the new competitive landscape. The company plans to open 730 additional stores in the next 12 months. As Dollar General tries to maintain profitability, it will keep looking for ways to change how it does business, and technology will continue to play a role in the solutions. So far, it's a strategy that has fueled tremendous growth at Dollar General even as other retailers are struggling to maintain sales volume.

QUESTIONS

1. What types of control are important at Dollar General? Why are these important?

2. What technological innovations did Kathleen Guion introduce at Dollar General? How did these innovations support the company's strategy?

3. What challenges would you have expected Guion to face in introducing these changes? What principles of managing change would you have suggested she apply?

SOURCES: Based on company website, "Dollar General Opens 12,000th Store," May 30, 2015, http://www.dollargeneral.com; Ziobro, P., "Dollar Tree Wins the Battle for Family Dollar," *The Wall Street Journal (online)*, January 22, 2015, http://www.wsj.com; Townsend, M., "Family Dollar Holders Accept $8.81 Billion Dollar Tree Bid," *Bloomberg Business (online)*, January 22, 2015, http://www.bloomberg.com; "Operational Improvements Benefit Employees, Customers," *MMR*, May 17, 2010, Business & Company Resource Center, http://galenet.galegroup.com; Jannarone, J., "Will Dollar General Lead Retailers into Battle?" *The Wall Street Journal*, June 6, 2011, http://online.wsj.com; Zimmerman, A., "Dollar Stores Find Splurges Drying Up," *The Wall Street Journal*, July 11, 2011, http://online.wsj.com; Burritt, C.,"Dollar Stores: More Brands, More Customers," *Bloomberg Businessweek*, July 29, 2010, http://www.businessweek.com; Jarzemsky, M., "Dollar General's Earnings Gain 15%," *The Wall Street Journal*, June 1, 2011, http://online.wsj.com; Dollar General, "About Us," http://dollargeneral.com; and Dollar General, "Dollar General Announces Kathleen Guion, Division President of Store Operations and Store Development, Will Transition to Retirement," news release, July 25, 2011, http://newscenter.dollargeneral.com.

CASE INCIDENTS

Robot Repercussion

Victor Principal, vice president of industrial relations for General Manufacturing, Inc., sat in his office reviewing the list of benefits the company expected to realize from increasing its use of industrial robots. In a few minutes, he would walk down to the labor management conference room for a meeting with Ralph McIntosh, president of the labor union local representing most of the company's industrial employees. The purpose of this meeting would be to exchange views and positions informally preliminary to the opening for formal contract negotiations later in the month, which would focus on the use of computer-integrated robotics systems and the resulting impact on employment, workers, and jobs.

Experts concluded that the impact of robot installation on employment would be profound, although the extent of the worker replacement was not clear. The inescapable conclusion was that robot usage had the capacity to increase manufacturing performance and decrease manufacturing employment.

Principal walked down to the conference room. Finding McIntosh already there, Principal stated the company's position regarding installation of industrial robots: "The company needs the cooperation of the union and our workers. We don't wish to be perceived as callously exchanging human workers for robots." Then Principal listed the major advantages associated with robots: (1) improved quality of product as a result of the accuracy of robots; (2) reduced operating costs because the per-hour operational cost of robots was about one-third of the per-hour cost of wages and benefits paid to an average employee; (3) reliability improvements because robots work tirelessly and don't require behavioral support; and (4) greater manufacturing flexibility because robots are readily reprogrammable for different jobs. Principal concluded that these advantages would make the company more competitive, which would allow it to grow and increase its workforce.

McIntosh's response was direct and strong: "We aren't Luddites racing around ruining machines. We know it's necessary to increase productivity and that robotic technology is here. But we can't give the company a blank check. We need safeguards and protection." McIntosh continued, "We intend to bargain for the following contract provisions:

1. Establishment of labor–management committees to negotiate in advance about the labor impact of robotics technology and, of equal importance, to have a voice in deciding how and whether it should be used.

2. Rights to advance notice about installation of new technology.

3. Retraining rights for workers displaced, to include retraining for new positions in the plant, the community, or other company plants.

4. Spreading the work among workers by use of a four-day workweek or other acceptable plan as an alternative to reducing the workforce."

McIntosh's final sentence summed up the union's position: "We in the union believe the company is giving our jobs to robots to reduce the labor force."

Their meeting ended amiably, but Principal and McIntosh each knew that much hard bargaining lay ahead. As Principal returned to his office, the two opposing positions were obvious. On his yellow tablet, Principal listed the requirements as he saw them: (1) A clearly stated overall policy was needed to guide negotiation decisions and actions; (2) it was critical to decide on a company position regarding each of the union's announced demands and concerns; and (3) a plan had to be developed.

As Principal considered these challenges, he idly contemplated a robot possessing artificial intelligence and vision capability that could help him in his work. Immediately a danger alarm sounded in his mind. A robot so constructed might be more than helpful and might take over this and other important aspects of his job. Slightly chagrined, Principal returned to his task. He needed help—but not from any smart robot.

Champion, J. and James, J., *Critical Incidents in Management: Decision and Policy Issues*, 6th ed. McGraw-Hill/Irwin, 1989. ©1989 by Dr. John M. Champion and John H. James. All rights reserved. Used with permission.

Implementing Strategic Change

James Fulmer, chief executive officer of Allied Industries, reviewed three notes he had exchanged with Frank Curtis, director of fiscal affairs, now president of a company owned by Allied. The two executives were going to meet in a few minutes to discuss problems that had recently surfaced. During the past decade, Allied had aggressively pursued a growth objective based on a conglomerate strategy of acquiring companies in distress. CEO Fulmer's policy was to appoint a new chief operating officer for each acquisition with instructions to facilitate a turnaround. Fulmer reviewed two of the notes he had written to Curtis.

Date: January 15
Memorandum
To: Frank Curtis, Director of Fiscal Affairs, Allied Industries
From: James Fulmer, Chairman, Allied Industries
Subject: Your Appointment as President, Lee Medical Supplies

You are aware that Allied Industries recently acquired Lee Medical Supplies. Mr. John Lee, founder and president of the company, has agreed to retire, and I am appointing you to replace him. Our acquisitions group will brief you on the company, but I want to warn you that Lee Medical Supplies has a history of mismanagement. As a distributor of medical items, the company's sales last year totaled approximately $300 million, with net earnings of only $12 million. Your job is to make company sales and profits compatible with Allied standards. You are reminded that it is my policy to call for an independent evaluation of company progress and your performance as president after 18 months.

Date: September 10
Memorandum
To: Frank Curtis, President, Lee Medical Supplies
From: James Fulmer, Chairman, Allied Industries
Subject: Serious Problems at Lee Medical Supplies

In accord with corporate policy, consultants recently conducted an evaluation of Lee Medical Supplies. In a relatively short period of time, you have increased sales and profits to meet Allied's standards, but I am alarmed at other aspects of your performance. I am told that during the past 18 months, three of your nine vice presidents have resigned and that you have terminated four others. An opinion survey conducted by the consultants indicates that a low state of morale exists and that your managerial appointees are regarded by their subordinates as hard-nosed perfectionists obsessed with quotas and profits. Employees report that ruthless competition now exists between divisions, regions, and districts. They also note that the collegial, family-oriented atmosphere fostered by Mr. Lee has been replaced by a dog-eat-dog situation characterized by negative management attitudes toward employee feelings and needs. After you have studied the enclosed report from the consultants, we will meet to discuss their findings. I am particularly concerned with their final conclusion that "a form of corporate cancer seems to be spreading throughout Lee Medical Supplies."

As Fulmer prepared to read the third note, written by Frank Curtis, he reflected on his interview with the consultants. Although Fulmer considered Curtis a financial expert and a turnaround specialist, his subordinates characterized Curtis as an autocrat better suited to be a marine boot camp commander.

Date: September 28
Memorandum
To: James Fulmer
From: Frank Curtis
Subject: The So-Called Serious Problems at Lee Medical Supplies

I have received your memorandum dated September 10, and reviewed the consultants' report. When you appointed me to my present position, I was instructed to take over an unprofitable company and make it profitable. I have done so in 18 months, although I inherited a family-owned business that by your own admission had been mismanaged for years. I found a group of managers and salespeople with an average company tenure of 22 years. Mr. Lee had centralized all personnel decisions so that only he could terminate an employee. He tolerated mediocre performance. All employees were paid on a straight salary basis, with seniority the sole criterion for advancement. Some emphasis was given to increasing sales each year, but none was given to reducing costs and increasing profits. Employees did indeed find the company a fun place to work, and the feeling of being a part of a family did permeate the company. Such attitudes were, however, accompanied by mediocrity, incompetence, and poor performance.

I found it necessary to implement immediate strategic changes in five areas: the organization's structure, employee rewards and incentives, management information systems, allocation of resources, and managerial leadership style. As a result, sales areas were reorganized into divisions, regions and districts. Managers who I felt were incompetent and/or lacking in commitment to my objectives and methods were replaced. Unproductive and mediocre employees were encouraged to find jobs elsewhere. Authority for staffing and compensation decisions was decentralized to units at the division, region, and district levels. Managers of those units were informed that along with their authority went responsibility for reducing costs and for increasing sales and profits. Each unit was established as a profit center. A new department was established and charged with reviewing performance of those units. Improved accounting and control systems were implemented. A program was developed to establish standards and monitor performance. Performance appraisals are now required for all employees. To encourage more aggressive action, bonuses and incentives are offered to managers of units showing increased profits. A commission plan based on measurable sales and profit performances has replaced straight salaries. Resources are allocated to units based on their performance.

My own leadership style has probably represented the most traumatic change for employees. Internal competition is a formally mandated policy throughout the company. It has been responsible for much of the progress achieved to date. Progress, however, is never made without costs, and I recognize that employees are not having as much fun as in the past. I was employed to achieve results and not to ensure that employees remain secure and happy in their work. Don't let a few crybabies unable to adjust to changes lead you to believe that problems take precedence over profits. Does it mean that I am not people oriented if I believe it is unlikely that a spirit of aggressiveness and competitiveness can coexist with an atmosphere of cooperativeness and family orientation? Do you feel that we are obligated to employees because of past practices? Frankly, I thought I had your support to do whatever was necessary to get this company turned around. In our meeting, tell me if you think my approaches have been wrong and, if so, tell me what I should have done differently.

Just as Fulmer finished reviewing the third memorandum, his secretary informed him that Curtis had arrived for their scheduled meeting. He realized he was undecided about how to communicate to Curtis his ideas and beliefs regarding how changes in an organization can best be implemented. One thing he did know: He didn't appreciate how Curtis had expressed his views in his memorandum, but he recognized that he probably should set aside emotions and respond to the questions Curtis posed.

NOTES

Chapter 1

1. Sources: Adrienne LaFrance, "Mark Zuckerberg Manifesto Is a Blueprint for Destroying Journalism," *The Atlantic,* February 17, 2017, https://www.theatlantic.com/technology/archive/2017/02/the-mark-zuckerberg-manifesto-is-a-blueprint-for-destroying-journalism/517113/; Ezra Klein, "Mark Zuckerberg's Theory of Human History," Vox.com, February 18, 2017, http://www.vox.com/new-money/2017/2/18/14653542/mark-zuckerberg-facebook-manifesto-sapiens; "#10 Mark Zuckerberg," *Forbes,* http://www.forbes.com/profile/mark-zuckerberg/accessed February 20, 2017; Kathleen Chaykowski, "Facebook Shares Rise on Fourth Quarter Revenue, Earnings That Blow Away Estimates," February 1, 2017, http://www.forbes.com/sites/kathleenchaykowski/2017/02/01/facebook-shares-rise-on-fourth-quarter-revenue-earnings-that-beat-estimates/#3a8a8318223d; Amarendra Bhushan Dhiraj, "Fortune's 50 Top Business Leaders of 2016, Mark Zuckerberg and Jeff Bezos Tops," *CEO World,* November 23, 2016, http://ceoworld.biz/2016/11/23/fortunes-50-top-business-leaders-2016-mark-zuckerberg-jeff-bezos-tops/.

2. J. McGregor, "Why Mark Zuckerberg's New Year's Challenge to Himself Just Might Work," *The Washington Post,* January 4, 2016, www.washingtonpost.com.

3. http://fortune.com/businessperson-of-the-year/mark-zuckerberg-1/, accessed February 21, 2017.

4. P. Wahba, "Macy's Is Closing 63 Stores and Cutting 10,000 Jobs as Sales Plunge Again," *Fortune,* January 4, 2017, www.fortune.com.

5. Ibid.

6. S. Green, F. Hassan, J. Immelt, M. Marks, and D. Meiland, "In Search of Global Leaders," *Harvard Business Review,* August 2003, pp. 38–45.

7. "World's Most Admired Companies," *Fortune* (online), accessed February 21, 2017, http://beta.fortune.com/worlds-most-admired-companies/.

8. "Global 500," *Fortune* (online), accessed February 21, 2017, http://beta.fortune.com/global500/.

9. GE Factsheet, accessed February 21, 2017, https://www.ge.com/about-us/fact-sheet.

10. See company website, http://www.yum.com/company/, accessed February 21, 2017.

11. PepsiCo's 2015 Annual Report, accessed February 21, 2017, https://www.pepsico.com/docs/album/annual-reports/pepsico-2015-annual-report_final_s57dqszgmy22ggn.pdf?sfvrsn=0, J. Kell, "PepsiCo to Acquire Probiotic Drinks Maker," *Fortune,* November 22, 2016, http://fortune.com/2016/11/22/pepsico-acquires-probiotic-kevita/.

12. S. Dollard, "How Coca-Cola Helps Students 'Think Global, Act Local,'" *Share America,* August 6, 2015, www.share.america.gov.

13. D. Hinchcliffe, "How Can Businesses Keep Up with Tech Change Today?" *ZDNet,* May 31, 2016, www.zdnet.com.

14. A. Scroxton, "Deloitte Predicts Major Advances in Mobile Technology in 2017," *Computer Weekly,* January 11, 2017, www.computerweekly.com.

15. A. Meola, "The Critical Role of Infrastructure in the Internet of Things," *Business Insider,* December 21, 2016, www.businessinsider.com; "Industry 4.0: Top 10 Critical Trends for 2017," *Information Age,* December 28, 2016, www.information-age.com.

16. "Mobilization in the Internet Age: Internet Activism and Corporate Response," *Academy of Management Journal* 59, pp. 2045–68.

17. "The Party's Over," *Fortune,* June 1, 2010, http://tech.fortune.cnn.com.

18. "Web 1.0 vs. Web 2.0 vs. Web 3.0 vs. Web 4.0 vs. Web 5.0; A Bird's Eye on the Evolution and Definition," *Flatworld,* www.business.com, accessed January 17, 2015.

19. B. Houghland, "What Is the Internet of Things? And Why Should You Care?" *TED Talk,* December 17, 2014, www.ted.com.

20. "Tech Vision 2017: Technology for People, The Era of the Intelligent Enterprise," *Accenture,* www.accenture.com, accessed February 26, 2017.

21. Robert Austin, "Managing Knowledge Workers," *Science,* July 21, 2006, accessed at ScienceCareers.org, http://sciencecareers.sciencemag.org.

22. D. McIver, C. Lengnick-Hall, and M. Lengnick-Hall, "Understanding Work and Knowledge Management from a Knowledge-in-Practice Perspective," *Academy of Management Review* 38 (2013), pp. 597–620; K. Dekas, T. Bauer, and B. Well, et al., "Organizational Citizenship Behavior, Version 2.0: A Review and Qualitative Investigation of OCBs for Knowledge Workers at Google and Beyond," *Academy of Management Perspectives* 27 (2013), pp. 219–37.

23. I. Wladawsky-Berger, "The Rise of the T-Shaped Organization," *The Wall Street Journal,* December 18, 2015, www.wsj.com; Morten T. Hansen and Bolko von Oetinger, "Introducing T-Shaped Managers: Knowledge Management's Next Generation," *Harvard Business Review,* March 2001, www.hbr.org.

24. "Working with McKinsey," *Blog,* January 12, 2013, www.workingwithmckinsey.blogspot.com.

25. D. Sturdevant, "(Still) Learning from Toyota," *McKinsey Quarterly,* February 2014, www.mckinsey.com.

26. Shelly Banjo, "Firms Take Online Reviews to Heart," *The Wall Street Journal,* July 29, 2012, http://online.wsj.com.

27. S. Vozza, "How to Turn a Bad Review into a Great Opportunity," *Fast Company,* accessed January 17, 2015, http://www.fastcompany.com.

28. R. Fry, "Millennials Overtake Baby Boomers as America's Largest Generation," Pew Research Center, April 25, 2016, www.pewresearch.org.

29. NFLX Company Financials, NASDAQ, www.nasdaq.com, accessed February 26, 2017; G. Satell, "A Look Back at Why Blockbuster Really Failed and Why It Didn't Have To," *Forbes,* September 5, 2014, http://www.forbes.com.

30. D. Kurylko, "Largest BMW Plant Will Expand This Year," *Automotive News,* March 7, 2016, www.autonews.com.

31. "Fortune's Most Admired Companies (Innovation)," http://fortune.com/worlds-mostadmired-companies/, accessed February 26, 2017.

32. O. Port, "The Kings of Quality," *BusinessWeek,* August 30, 2004, p. 20.

33. H. Johnson, "Fast Food Workers Are Becoming Obsolete," *Business Insider,* May 16, 2016, www.businessinsider.com; M. Greenwald, "NikeId, Coca-Cola Freestyle and Other Brands Mastering Infinite Customization," *Forbes,* October 8, 2014, www.forbes.com.

34. W. E. Deming, *Out of the Crisis* (Cambridge, MA: MIT Press, 2000); D. A. Garvin, "Manufacturing Strategic Planning," *California Management Review,* Summer 1993, pp. 85–106.

35. Bureau of Labor Statistics, "Current Employment Statistics Highlights," January 2017, www.bls.gov; "Occupational Employment Projections to 2024," *Occupational Outlook Handbook,* December 2015, http://www.bls.gov.

36. Sherri Begin, "The Art of Service," *Crain's Detroit Business,* February 12, 2007, Business & Company Resource Center, http://galenet.galegroup.com.

37. Adam Lashinsky, "Chaos by Design," *Fortune,* October 2, 2006, http://money.cnn.com.

38. J. Creswell, "Quicken Loans, the New Mortgage Machine," *The New York Times,* January 21, 2017, www.nytimes.com.

39. A. Mason, "Is the Rocket Mortgage a Fast Ride to Trouble?" *CBS News,* February 9, 2016, www.cbsnews.com.

40. K. Graham, "Rocket Mortgage: Your Questions Answered," Quicken Loans website, December 30, 2015, www.quickenloans.com.

41. K. Gustafson, "This Wal-Mart Tactic Should Send Shivers across Retail," *CNBC,* May 19, 2016, www.cnbc.com; P. Wahba, "Who's Eating Walmart's Lunch? Lots of Companies," *Fortune,* May 19, 2015, www.walmart.com.

42. S. Cendrowski, "Singapore Airlines," *Fortune,* June 14, 2010, p. 22.

43. Gulliver, "Flying on a Budget Carrier for Business Is Bad for the Ego, but Necessary," *The Economist,* July 10, 2016, www.theeconomist.com.

44. F. Gillette, "The Duke of Discomfort," *Bloomberg Businessweek,* September 6, 2010, pp. 58–61.

45. S. Pogatchnik, "Ryanair Posts Record 2016 Profit, Sees Lower Summer Fares," *Business Insider,* May 23, 2016, www.businessinsider.com.

46. J. Pfeffer, "Building Sustainable Organizations: The Human Factor," *Academy of Management Perspectives* 24 (2010), pp. 34–45.

47. S. L. Hart, *Capitalism at the Crossroads,* 3rd ed. (Upper Saddle River, NJ: Wharton School Publishing, 2010).

48. Morten T. Hansen, Herminia Ibarra, and Urs Peyer, "The Best-Performing CEOs in the World," *Harvard Business Review,* November 2014, http://hbr.org, p. 90.

49. B. Dumaine, "Searching for Profits in Patagonia," *Fortune,* March 21, 2011, pp. 97–105.

50. B. Doppelt, *Leading Change toward Sustainability* (Sheffield, UK: Greenleaf, 2010).

51. J. W. Cortada, *21st Century Business* (London: Financial Times/Prentice Hall, 2001).

52. D. Lepak, K. Smith, and M. S. Taylor, "Value Creation and Value Capture: A Multilevel Perspective," *Academy of Management Review* 23 (2007), pp. 180–94.

53. A. Kroeger and C. Weber, "Developing a Conceptual Framework for Comparing Social Value Creation," *Academy of Management Review* 39 (2014), pp. 513–40.

54. "About Ashoka," https://www.ashoka.org/en/about-ashoka, accessed February 18, 2017; "Bill Drayton," bteam.org, http://bteam.org/team/bill-drayton/, accessed February 18, 2017; Mee-Hyoe Koo, "Interview with Bill Drayton, Pioneer of Social Entrepreneurship," *Forbes,* September 30, 2013, https://www.forbes.com/sites/meehyoekoo/2013/09/30/interview-with-bill-drayton-pioneer-of-social-entrepreneurship/#79d31973bed4; "Ashoka," Charity Navigator.org, https://www.charitynavigator.org/index.cfm?bay=search.summary&orgid=5389, accessed February 18, 2017.

55. R. Webber, "General Management Past and Future," *Financial Times Mastering Management,* 1997.

56. LaFrance, "Mark Zuckerberg Manifesto Is a Blueprint for Destroying Journalism"; Klein, "Mark Zuckerberg's Theory of Human History" "#10 Mark Zuckerberg,"; Chaykowski, "Facebook Shares Rise on Fourth Quarter Revenue, Earnings That Blow Away Estimates" Bhushan Dhiraj, "Fortune's 50 Top Business Leaders of 2016, Mark Zuckerberg and Jeff Bezos Tops."

57. M. Menz, "Functional Top Management Team Members: A Review, Synthesis, and Research Agenda," *Journal of Management* 38 (2012), pp. 45–80.

58. D. Kreeger, "Is Your Organization Positioned to Meet the Challenge of Climate Change?" *World Climate Change Report,* October 22, 2009, pp. 1–7.

59. C. Ren and C. Guo, "Middle Managers' Strategic Role in the Corporate Entrepreneurial Process: Attention-Based Effects," *Journal of Management* 37 (2011). pp. 1586–1610.

60. A. Raes, M. Heijltjes, U. Glunk, et al., "The Interface of the Top Management Team and Middle Managers: A Process Model," *Academy of Management Review* 36 (2011), pp. 102–26.

61. Q. N. Huy, "In Praise of Middle Managers," *Harvard Business Review,* September 2001, pp. 72–79.

62. L. A. Hill, "New Manager Development for the 21st Century," *Academy of Management Executive,* August 2004, pp. 121–26.

63. C. Bartlett and S. Goshal, "The Myth of the Generic Manager: New Personal Competencies for New Management Roles," *California Management Review* 40, no. 1 (1997), pp. 92–116.

64. L. R. Sayles, "Doing Things Right: A New Imperative for Middle Managers," *Organizational Dynamics,* Spring 1993, pp.5–14.

65. H. Mintzberg, *The Nature of Managerial Work* (New York: Harper & Row, 1973).

66. R. Katz, "Skills of an Effective Administrator," *Harvard Business Review* 52 (September–October), pp. 90–102.

67. Hill, "New Manager Development for the 21st Century."

68. H. Mintzberg, "The Manager's Job: Folklore and Fact," *Harvard Business Review* 53 (July–August 1975), pp. 49–61.

69. D. Gelles, "At Aetna, a C.E.O.'s Management by Mantra," *The New York Times,* February 27, 2015, www.nytimes.com; "Nontraditional Path: From Pre-Med Dropout to Next Aetna CEO," *DiversityInc.,* October 28, 2010, http://diversityinc.com; Aetna, "Executive Biographies: Mark T. Bertolini," About Us: Corporate Profile, http://www.aetna.com, accessed February 25, 2011.

70. Hill, "New Manager Development for the 21st Century."

71. D. Goleman, R. Boyatzis, and A. McKee, *Primal Leadership: Realizing the Power of Emotional Intelligence* (Boston: Harvard Business School Press, 2002); O. Ybarra, E. Kross, and J. Sanchez-Burks, "The 'Big Idea' That Is Yet to Be: Toward a More Motivated, Contextual, and Dynamic Model of Emotional Intelligence," *Academy of Management Perspectives* 28 (2014), pp. 93–107.

72. Ybarra et al., "The 'Big Idea' That Is Yet to Be"; Stephen Xavier, "Control Yourself: What Role Does Emotional Intelligence Play in Executive Leadership?" *US Business Review,* March 2006, Business & Company Resource Center, http://galenet.galegroup.com.

73. J. McClesky, "Emotional Intelligence and Leadership: A Review of the Progress, Controversy, and Criticism," *International Journal of Organizational Analysis* 22, no. 1 (2014), pp. 76–93; J. Antonakis, N. Ashkanasy, and M. Dasborough, "Does Leadership Need Emotional Intelligence?" *Leadership Quarterly* 20 (2009), pp. 247–61; E. A. Locke, "Why Emotional Intelligence Is an Invalid Concept," *Journal of Organizational Behavior* 26 (2005), pp. 425–31.

74. R. Boyatzis, "Get Motivated," *Harvard Business Review,* January 2004, p. 30.

75. W. George, "Find Your Voice," *Harvard Business Review,* January 2004, p. 35.

76. W. Kiechel III, "A Manager's Career in the New Economy," *Fortune,* April 4, 1994, pp. 68–72.

77. M. Benner and M. Tushman, "Reflections on the 2013 Decade Award 'Exploitation, Exploration, and Process Management: The Productivity Dilemma Revisited' Ten Years Later," Academy of *Management Review* 40 (2015), pp. 497–514; P. Junni, R. Sarala, and T. Vas, et al., "Organizational Ambidexterity and Performance: A Meta-analysis," *Academy of Management Perspectives* 27 (2013), pp. 299–312; C. A. O'Reilly III and M. Tushman, "Organizational Ambidexterity: Past, Present, and Future," *Academy of Management Perspectives* 27 (2013), pp. 324–38; J. Birkinshaw and K. Gupta, "Clarifying the Distinctive Contribution of Ambidexterity to the Field of Organization Studies," *Academy of Management Perspectives* 27 (2013).

78. T. Bateman and A. Hess, "Different Personal Propensities among Scientists Predict Deeper vs. Broader Knowledge Contributions." Proceedings of the National Academy of Sciences, March 2, 2015.

79. K. Inkson and M. B. Arther, "How to Be a Successful Career Capitalist," *Organizational Dynamics,* Summer 2001, pp. 48–60.

80. A. Ericsson, M. Prietula, and E. Cokely, "The Making of an Expert," *Harvard Business Review,* July–August, 2007, http://www.hbr.org; Geoffrey Colvin, "What It Takes to Be Great," *Fortune,* October 19, 2006, http://money.cnn.com.

81. L. M. Roberts, J. Dutton, G. Spreitzer, E. Heaphy, and R. Quinn, "Composing the Reflected Best-Self Portrait: Building Pathways for Becoming Extraordinary in Work Organizations," *Academy of Management Review* 30 (2005), pp. 712–36.

82. L. M. Roberts, "Changing Faces: Professional Image Construction in Diverse Organizational Settings," *Academy of Management Review* 30 (2005), pp. 685–711.

83. M. E. P. Seligman, *Authentic Happiness: Using the New Positive Psychology to Realize Your Potential for Lasting Fulfillment* (New York: Free Press, 2002).

84. E. W. Morrison, "Newcomers' Relationships: The Role of Social Network Ties during Socialization," *Academy of Management Journal* 45 (2002), pp. 1149–60.

85. R. Cotton, Y. Shen, and R. Llvne-Tarandach, "On Becoming Extraordinary: The Content and Structure of the Developmental Networks of Major League Baseball Hall of Famers," *Academy of Management Journal* 54 (2011), pp. 15–46.

86. C. Galunic, G. Ertug, and M. Gargiulo, "The Positive Externalities of Social Capital: Benefiting from Senior Brokers," *Academy of Management Journal* 55 (2012), pp. 1213–31; P. Adler and S. Kwon, "Social Capital: Prospects for a New Concept," *Academy of Management Review* 27 (2002), pp. 17–40.

87. Company website, "About Us," press.linkedin.com, accessed February 26, 2017.

88. K. Wagner, "Facebook Is Rolling Out Job Postings and Applications," *Recode,* February 15, 2017, www.recode.net.

89. T. Peters, *Liberation Management* (New York: Alfred A. Knopf, 1992).

90. P. Drucker, "What Makes an Effective Executive?" *Harvard Business Review*, June 2004, pp. 58–63.

91. LaFrance, "Mark Zuckerberg Manifesto Is a Blueprint for Destroying Journalism"; Klein, "Mark Zuckerberg's Theory of Human History"; "#10 Mark Zuckerberg" Chaykowski, "Facebook Shares Rise on Fourth Quarter Revenue, Earnings That Blow Away Estimates"; Bhushan Dhiraj, "Fortune's 50 Top Business Leaders of 2016, Mark Zuckerberg and Jeff Bezos Tops."

Appendix A

1. C. George, *The History of Management Thought* (Englewood Cliffs, NJ: Prentice-Hall, 1972).

2. C. George, *The History of Management Thought* (Englewood Cliffs, NJ: Prentice-Hall, 1972).

3. P. Godfrey, J. Hassard, E. O'Connor et al., "What Is Organizational History? Toward a Creative Synthesis of History and Organization Studies," *Academy of Management Review*, 41 (2016), pp. 590–608.

4. A. D. Chandler, *Scale and Scope: The Dynamic of Industrial Capitalism* (Cambridge, MA: Belknap Press of Harvard University Press, 1990).

5. A. D. Chandler, *Scale and Scope: The Dynamic of Industrial Capitalism* (Cambridge, MA: Belknap Press of Harvard University Press, 1990).

6. J. Baughman, *The History of American Management* (Englewood Cliffs, NJ: Prentice Hall, 1969), chap. 1.

7. C. George, *The History of Management Thought* (Englewood Cliffs, NJ: Prentice-Hall, 1972), chaps. 5–7; F. Taylor, *The Principles of Scientific Management* (New York: Harper & Row, 1911).

8. J. Case, "A Company of Business people," *Inc.*, April 1993, pp. 70–93.

9. J. Schlosser and E. Florian, "Fortune 500 Amazing Facts!" *Fortune*, April 2004.

10. H. Fayol, *General and Industrial Management*, trans. C. Storrs (Marshfield, MA: Pitman Publishing, 1949).

11. C. George, *The History of Management Thought* (Englewood Cliffs, NJ: Prentice-Hall, 1972), chap. 9; J. Massie, "Management Theory," in *Handbook of Organizations*, ed. J. March (Chicago: Rand McNally, 1965), pp. 387–422.

12. C. Barnard, *The Functions of the Executive* (Cambridge, MA: Harvard University Press, 1938).

13. C. George, *The History of Management Thought* (Englewood Cliffs, NJ: Prentice-Hall, 1972); J. Massie, "Management Theory," in *Handbook of Organizations*, ed. J. March (Chicago: Rand McNally, 1965), pp. 387–422.

14. E. Mayo, *The Human Problems of Industrial Civilization* (New York: Macmillan, 1933): F. Roethlisberger and W. Dickson, *Management and the Worker* (Cambridge, MA: Harvard University Press, 1939).

15. A. Maslow, "A Theory of Human Motivation," *Psychological Review* 50 (July 1943), pp. 370–96.

16. A. Carey, "The Hawthorne Studies: A Radical Criticism," *American Sociological Review* 32, no.3 (1967), pp. 403–16.

17. M. Weber, *The Theory of Social and Economic Organizations,* trans. T. Parsons and A. Henderson (New York: Free Press, 1947).

18. C. George, *The History of Management Thought* (Englewood Cliffs, NJ: Prentice-Hall, 1972), chap. 11.

19. D. McGregor, *The Human Side of Enterprise* (New York: McGraw-Hill, 1960).

20. C. Argyris, *Personality and Organization* (New York: Harper & Row, 1957).

21. R. Likert, *The Human Organization* (New York: McGraw-Hill, 1967).

22. L. von Bertalanffy, "The History and Status of General Systems Theory," *Academy of Management Journal* 15 (1972), pp. 407–26; D. Katz and R. Kahn, *The Social Psychology of Organizations,* 2nd ed. (New York: John Wiley & Sons, 1978).

23. J. Thompson, *Organizations in Action* (New York: McGraw-Hill, 1967); J. Galbraith, *Organization Design* (Reading, MA: Addison-Wesley, 1977); D. Miller and P. Friesen, *Organizations: A Quantum View* (Englewood Cliffs, NJ: Prentice-Hall, 1984).

24. R. E. Wright, "Teaching History in Business Schools: An Insider's View," *Academy of Management Learning & Education* 9 (2010), pp. 697–700.

25. S. Cummings and T. Bridgman, "The Relevant Past: Why the History of Management Should Be Critical for Our Future," *Academy of Learning & Education* 10 (2011), pp. 77–93.

Chapter 2

1. "Amazon and Netflix Pick Up Their First Academy Awards," *Fortune,* February 27, 2017, http://fortune.com/2017/02/27/amazon-netflix-moonlight-oscars-academy-awards/; Jillian D'Onfro and Eugene Kim, "The Life and Awesomeness of Amazon Founder and CEO Jeff Bezos," *Business Insider,* February 11, 2016, http://www.businessinsider.com/the-life-of-amazon-founder-ceo-jeff-bezos-2014–7; Daphne Howland, "Amazon Overtakes Exxon as Fourth-Most Valuable U.S. Company," *Retail Dive,* August 2, 2016, http://www.retaildive.com/news/amazon-overtakes-exxon-as-fourth-most-valuable-us-company/423689/; Eugene Kim, "Amazon Is Doubling Down on Retail Stores . . ." *Business Insider,* September 9, 2016, http://www.businessinsider.com/amazon-big-expansion-retail-pop-up-stores-2016–9; Elizabeth Weise, "Amazon Heads Deeper into Brick and Mortar with Books," *USA Today,* January 18, 2017, http://www.usatoday.com/story/tech/news/2017/01/18/amazon-bookstores-brick-and-mortar/96667506/; Alexander Nazaryan, "How Jeff Bezos Is Hurtling toward World Domination," *Newsweek,* July 22, 2016, http://www.newsweek.com/2016/07/22/jeff-bezos-amazon-ceo-world-domination-479508.html.

2. Center on Budget and Policy Priorities, "Chart Book: The Legacy of the Great Recession," Special Series: Economic Recovery Watch, updated February 15, 2015, http://www.cbpp.org.

3. "Charting the Labor Market: Data from the Current Population Survey (CPS)," February 3, 2017, U.S. Bureau of Labor Statistics, www.bls.gov.

4. J. Fuller and M. C. Jensen, "Just Say No to Wall Street," *Journal of Applied Corporate Finance* 14, no. 4 (Winter 2002), pp. 41–46.

5. Company website, Microsoft HoloLens, https://www.microsoft.com/microsoft-hololens/en-us, accessed March 4, 2017; S. Ranger, "Microsoft HoloLens, Hands-on: What It's Like to Wear the Future: Testing Out Microsoft's Mixed-Reality Headset," *ZDNet,* November 2, 2016, www.zdnet.com.

6. "Virtual Reality Check," *Sunday Morning Show,* CBS News, January 8, 2017, www.cbsnews.com; "CWRU Takes the Stage at Microsoft's Build Conference to Show How HoloLens Can Transform Learning," Case Western Reserve University, http://case.edu/hololens/, accessed March 4, 2017.

7. M. Egan, "Oil Milestone: Fracking Fuels Half of U.S. Output," *CNN Money,* March 24, 2016, www.money.cnn.com; L. Laughlin, "Four Stocks That Should Rise as Oil Rebounds," *Fortune,* June 1, 2016, www.fortune.com.

8. Marc Levinson, "Job Creation in the Manufacturing Revival," Congressional Research Service Report for Congress R41898, June 20, 2012, available at http://www.fas.org/sqp/crs/misc/R41898.pdf.

9. U.S. Department of Health and Human Services (DHHS), "Small Employers: Top Five Things to Know," *HealthCare.gov,* http://www.healthcare.gov; Internal Revenue Service (IRS), "Small Business Health Care Tax Credit for Small Employers," http://www.irs.gov; DHHS, "Large Employers: Insurance and Tax Information," *HealthCare.gov,* http://www.healthcare.gov; IRS, "Affordable Care Act Tax Provisions," http://www.irs.gov; DHHS, "About the Law: Provisions of the Affordable Care Act, by Year," *HealthCare.gov,* http://www.healthcare.gov; Jen Wieczner, "Why Your Boss Is Dumping Your Wife," *MarketWatch,* February 22, 2013, http://www.marketwatch.com.

10. "Communicating with Employees about Health Care Benefits under the Affordable Care Act," Society for Human Resource Management, July 25, 2016, www.shrm.org.

11. "Millennial Careers: 2020 Vision," Manpower Group, www.manpower.com, accessed March 4, 2017; S. Lindner, "Millennials with 'Portfolio Careers'—Multiple Jobs—Increasing," *New York Daily News,* June 13, 2016, www.nydailynews.com; S. Horowitz, "Why Millennials Understand the Future of Work Better Than Anyone Else," *Fast Company,* April 1, 2015, www.fastcompany.com.

12. Bureau of Labor Statistics, Table A4: "Employment Status of the Civilian Population 25 Years and over by Educational Attainment," February 6, 2015, http://www.bls.gov/spotlight.
13. See, for example, J. Wright, "America's Skilled Trades Dilemma: Shortages Loom as Most-in-Demand Group of Workers Ages," *Forbes,* March 7, 2013, http://www.forbes.com; B. Arnoldy, "Too Prosperous, Massachusetts Is Losing Its Labor Force," *Christian Science Monitor,* January 9, 2007, http://www.csmonitor.com.
14. Bureau of Labor Statistics, news release, "Foreign-Born Workers: Labor Force Characteristics—2013," May 22, 2014, http://www.bls.gov.
15. "Best Companies—Deloitte," *Working Mother,* November 7, 2016, www.workingmother.com.
16. Ibid.
17. M. Esterl, "PepsiCo Expands Distribution of Stevia-Sweetened Cola," *The Wall Street Journal,* January 26, 2015, http://www.wsj.com; Michael M. Grynbaum, "Health Panel Approves Restriction on Sale of Large Sugary Drinks," *The New York Times,* September 13, 2012, http://www.nytimes.com; Mike Esterl, "Is This the End of the Soft-Drink Era?" *The Wall Street Journal,* January 18, 2013, http://online.wsj.com; Angela Hanson, "Middle of the Road," *Convenience Store News,* October 1, 2012, Business Insights: Essentials, http://bi.galegroup.com; Stephanie Strom, "PepsiCo, Shifting Aim, Sees Promise in Yogurt," *The New York Times,* July 8, 2012, http://www.nytimes.com; Alan Richman, "Refreshing Revival," *International Food Ingredients,* Autumn 2012, Business Insights: Essentials, http://bi.galegroup.com.
18. Company website, http://www.terracycle.com, accessed February 27, 2015; E. Young, "Waste Not, Want Not—Making Money from Rubbish," *BBC News* (online), February 1, 2015, http://www.bbc.com; "Fertilizer Company Grows Profits with Zero Waste," *Yahoo Finance* (online), June 10, 2014, http://finance.yahoo.com.
19. T. Webb, "BP to Cut Production amid Impact of Deepwater Horizon Spill," *The Observer,* January 30, 2011, http://www.guardian.co.uk; "The Shores of Recovery," *The Economist,* April 23, 2011, Business & Company Resource Center, http://galenet.galegroup.com; C. Prentice, "Doing Business on the Gulf Coast, Post-Spill," *Bloomberg Businessweek,* April 19, 2011, http://www.businessweek.com; and Suzanne Goldenberg, "Justice Department Deal Reduces BP's Deepwater Horizon Fine by $3.4 Billion," *Guardian* (London), February 20, 2013, http://www.guardian.co.uk.
20. K. Taylor, "Pepsi Is Laying Off Up to 100 Workers in Philadelphia and Blaming a 2-Month-Old Soda Tax," *Business Insider,* March 1, 2017, www.businessinsider.com; J. Kaplan, "Coca-Cola, PepsiCo Hit with Wave of Soda Taxes," *Bloomberg,* November 9, 2016, www.bloomberg.com;

A. Petroff, "Pepsi Gets Aggressive on Cutting Sugar," *CNN Money,* October 17, 2016, www.money.cnn.com.
21. T. Team, "Coca-Cola's Advertising and Marketing Efforts Are Helping It to Stay on Top," *Forbes,* September 26, 2016, www.forbes.com.
22. E. Schultz and J. Wohl, "Pepsi Preps Global Emoji Can and Bottle Campaign," *Advertising Age,* February 19, 2016, www.adage.com.
23. Ibid.
24. M. Watrous, "Inside PepsiCo's Innovation Agenda," *Food Business News,* April 18, 2016, www.foodbusinessnews.net.
25. Company Annual Report 2015, www.pepsico.com, accessed March 5, 2017.
26. D. J. Collis and C. A. Montgomery, *Corporate Strategy: Resources and Scope of the Firm* (New York: McGraw-Hill/Irwin, 1997).
27. A. Pollack, "Generic Crestor Wins Approval, Dealing a Blow to AstraZeneca," *The New York Times,* July 20, 2016, www.nytimes.com.
28. S. Mukherjee, "Big Pharma Just Had a Terrible, Horrible, No Good, Very Bad Week of Job Cuts," *Fortune,* December 12, 2016, www.fortune.com.
29. R. Safian, "How PepsiCo CEO Indra Nooyi Is Steering the Company toward a Purpose-Driven Future," *Fast Company,* January 9, 2017, www.fastcompany.com.
30. PepsiCo website, http://www.pepsico.com.
31. Danielle Kucera, "Inkling Builds a Better (and Pricier) E-Book," *Bloomberg Businessweek,* February 12, 2013, http://www.businessweek.com.
32. J. Bunge and P. Evans, "ADM to Buy Wild Flavors for $3 Billion," *The Wall Street Journal,* July 7, 2014, www.wsj.com.
33. Adapted from H. L. Lee and C. Billington, "The Evolution of Supply-Chain-Management Models and Practice at Hewlett-Packard," *Interfaces* 25, no. 5 (September–October 1995), pp. 42–63. See also Edward W. Davis and Robert E. Spekman, *The Extended Enterprise: Gaining Competitive Advantage through Collaborative Supply Chains* (Upper Saddle River, NJ: Prentice Hall, 2004).
34. Connie Bensen, "When Brand Advocates Become Employees: IdeaStorm PM Cy Jervis Shares Tips for Businesses," Dell Community: Social Business Connection, January 7, 2013, http://en.community.dell.com.
35. B. McGrath, "7 Ways to Improve Your Social Media Engagement," *Social Media Examiner,* May 2, 2013, http://www.socialmediaexaminer.com.
36. Ovidijus Jurevicius, "Amazon SWOT Analysis 2017," *Strategic Management Insight,* January 8, 2017, https://www.strategicmanagementinsight.com/swot-analyses/amazon-swot-analysis.html; Ángel González, "Third-Party Sellers Giving Amazon a Huge Boost," *Seattle Times,* May 31, 2016, http://www.seattletimes.com/business/amazon/amazon-to-host-forum-for-its-marketplace-merchants/; Amazon's Third-Party Sellers Had Record-Breaking

Sales in 2016," *Fortune,* January 4, 2017, http://fortune.com/2017/01/04/amazon-marketplace-sales/.
37. A. A. Buchko, "Conceptualization and Measurement of Environmental Uncertainty: An Assessment of the Miles and Snow Perceived Environmental Uncertainty Scale," *Academy of Management Journal* 37, no. 2 (April 1994), pp. 410–25.
38. A. F. Hagen, "Corporate Executives and Environmental Scanning Activities: An Empirical Investigation," *SAM Advanced Management Journal* 60, no. 2 (Spring 1995), pp. 41–47; R. L. Daft, "Chief Executive Scanning, Environmental Characteristics, and Company Performance: An Empirical Study," *Strategic Management Journal* 9, no. 2 (March–April 1988), pp. 123–39; and M. Yasai-Ardekani, "Designs for Environmental Scanning Systems: Tests of a Contingency Theory," *Management Science* 42, no. 2 (February 1996), pp. 187–204.
39. S. Ghoshal, "Building Effective Intelligence Systems for Competitive Advantage," *Sloan Management Review* 28, no. 1 (Fall 1986), pp. 49–58; and K. D. Cory, "Can Competitive Intelligence Lead to a Sustainable Competitive Advantage?" *Competitive Intelligence Review* 7, no. 3 (Fall 1996), pp. 45–55.
40. P. J. H. Schoemaker, "Multiple Scenario Development: Its Conceptual and Behavioral Foundation," *Strategic Management Journal* 14, no. 3 (March 1993), pp. 193–213.
41. R. R. Peterson, "An Analysis of Contemporary Forecasting in Small Business," *Journal of Business Forecasting Methods & Systems* 15, no. 2 (Summer 1996), pp. 10–12; and S. Makridakis., "Business Forecasting for Management: Strategic Business Forecasting," *International Journal of Forecasting* 12, no. 3 (September 1996), pp. 435–37.
42. R. A. D'Aveni, *Hypercompetition—Managing the Dynamics of Strategic Maneuvering* (New York: Free Press, 1994); and M. A. Cusumano, "Strategic Maneuvering and Mass-Market Dynamics: The Triumph of VHS over Beta," *Business History Review* 66, no. 1 (Spring 1992), pp. 51–94.
43. Model adapted from C. Zeithaml and V. Zeithaml, "Environmental Management: Revising the Marketing Perspective," *Journal of Marketing* 48 (Spring 1984), pp. 46–53.
44. Stephanie Strom, "PepsiCo, Shifting Aim, Sees Promise in Yogurt," *The New York Times,* July 8, 2012, http://www.nytimes.com.
45. T. Bradshaw, "Apple App Store Sales Leap 40% in 2016," *The Financial Times,* January 5, 2017, www.ft.com; S. Perez, "Apple's App Store Hits 2M Apps, 130B Downloads, $50B Paid to Developers," *TechCrunch,* June 13, 2016, www.techcrunch.com; P. Sikka, "Apple's App Store Earns 60% More Revenues Than Google Play," *Yahoo! Finance* (online), February 19, 2015, http://finance.yahoo.com.
46. R. Thomson, R. Thomas, and M. Garay, "Deloitte M&A Trends: Year End Report

2016," www2.deloitte.com, accessed March 5, 2017.

47. T. Shields, "AT&T Woos Washington over Time Warner Deal, Schmoozes Trump," *Bloomberg,* February 8, 2017, www.bloomberg.com; T. Gryta, K. Hagey, D. Cimilluca, and A. Sharma, "AT&T Reaches Deal to Buy Time Warner for $85.4 Billion," *The Wall Street Journal,* October 22, 2016, www.wsj.com.

48. Company press release, "Sysco Reaches Agreement to Sell 11 US Foods Distribution Centers to Performance Food Group Contingent on Consummation of Sysco-US Foods Merger," February 2, 2015, http://investors.sysco.com, accessed February 20, 2015.

49. R. Miles and C. Snow, *Organizational Strategy, Structure, and Process* (New York: McGraw-Hill, 1978).

50. Zeithaml and Zeithaml, "Environmental Management: Revising the Marketing Perspective."

51. Organization website (RED), http://www.red.org, accessed March 5, 2017.

52. G. Chon, "Drugmakers Get Their $2.3 Bln Worth in Washington," Reuters, September 1, 2016, www.blogs.reuters.com.

53. W. P. Burgers, "Cooperative Strategy in High Technology Industries," *International Journal of Management* 13, no. 2 (June 1996), pp. 127–34; and J. E. McGee, "Cooperative Strategy and New Venture Performance: The Role of Business Strategy and Management Experience," *Strategic Management Journal* 16, no. 7 (October 1995), pp. 565–80.

54. C. Vandlen, "Making 'Cents' of Temps: The Costs and Benefits of Contingent Workers," *Cornell HR Review,* May 16, 2011, www.cornellreview.org.

55. Tammy Erickson, "The Rise of the New Contract Worker," *Harvard Business Review,* September 7, 2012, http://blogs.hbr.org; Adecco, "2012 Job Market Perspectives," http://www.adeccousa.com; "Integrating Contingent Workers," *Baseline,* January 19, 2012, Business Insights: Essentials, http://bi.galegroup.com; and "Tech Talk," *Workforce Management,* August 1, 2012, Business Insights: Essentials, http://bi.galegroup.com.

56. M. B. Meznar, "Buffer or Bridge? Environmental and Organizational Determinants of Public Affairs Activities in American Firms," *Academy of Management Journal* 38, no. 4 (August 1995), pp. 975–96.

57. D. Lei, "Advanced Manufacturing Technology: Organizational Design and Strategic Flexibility," *Organization Studies* 17, no. 3 (1996), pp. 501–23; and J. W. Dean Jr. and S. A. Snell, "The Strategic Use of Integrated Manufacturing: An Empirical Examination," *Strategic Management Journal* 17, no. 6 (June 1996), pp. 459–80.

58. P. Sun, K. Mellahi, and M. Wright, "The Contingent Value of Corporate Political Ties," *Academy of Management Perspectives* 26 (2012), pp. 68–82.

59. S. Giorgi, C. Lockwood, and M. Glynn, "The Many Faces of Culture: Making Sense of 30 Years of Research on Culture in Organization Studies," *Academy of Management Annals* 9 (2015), pp. 1–54; H. Kilmann, M. J. Saxton, and R. Serpa, *Gaining Control of the Corporate Culture* (San Francisco: Jossey-Bass, 1985); and K. S. Cameron and R. E. Quinn, *Diagnosing and Changing Organizational Culture: Based on the Competing Values Framework* (Englewood Cliffs, NJ: Addison-Wesley, 1998).

60. S. Milligan, "Culture Clash," *HR Magazine,* July 21, 2014, www.shrm.org.

61. D. Cai and B. Worthen, "Cisco to Sell Linksys Unit to Belkin," *The Wall Street Journal,* January 24, 2013, www.wsj.com.

62. Cameron and Quinn, *Diagnosing and Changing Organizational Culture.*

63. C. Groscurth, "Why Your Company Must Be Mission-Driven," *Gallup Business Journal,* March 6, 2014, http://www.gallup.com.

64. Company press release, "Target Recently Announced a New Strategy to Invest $5 Million by 2022 in Green Chemistry Innovation," January 25, 2017, www.corporate.target.com.

65. J. Koob, "Early Warnings on Culture Clash," *Mergers & Acquisitions,* July 1, 2006, Business & Company Resource Center, http://galenet.galegroup.com.

66. Nazaryan, "How Jeff Bezos Is Hurtling toward World Domination;" 2016 Shareholder Letter, Amazon.com, https://www.sec.gov/Archives/edgar/data/1018724/000119312516530910/d168744dex991.htm; Jena McGregor, "Amazon CEO Jeff Bezos Shares Thoughts on Corporate Culture, Decision Making and Failure," *Los Angeles Times,* April 10, 2016, http://www.latimes.com/business/la-fi-0410-on-leadership-bezos-20160410-story.html; Jacob Kastrenakes, "Jeff Bezos on Amazon's Culture: 'We Never Claim That Our Approach Is the Right One,'" *The Verge.com,* April 5, 2016, http://www.theverge.com/2016/4/5/11373438/amazon-corporate-culture-comment-jeff-bezos; Daphne Howland, "Amazon Revamps HR Strategies to Aid Underperforming Employees," *Retail Dive.com,* January 23, 2017, http://www.retaildive.com/news/amazon-revamps-hr-strategies-to-aid-underperforming-employees/434526/.

67. The Kennedy Group Ltd., "Culture vs. Climate," Kennedy Group Executive Strategies, http://thekennedygroup.com; R. L. Manning, "Development of the Psychological Climate Scale for Small Business," *Journal of New Business Ideas and Trends* 8, no. 1 (2010), pp. 50–65; OCLC FirstSearch, http://newfirstsearch.org; and Grapevine Solutions, "Job Climate Surveys," http://www.grapevinesurveys.com.

Appendix B

1. P. Hawken, A. Lovins, and L. Hunter Lovins, *Natural Capitalism* (Boston: Little Brown, 1999).

2. F. Rice, "Who Scores Best on the Environment?" *Fortune,* July 26, 1993, p. 114–22.

3. R. Clarke, R. Stavins, J. Greeno, J. Bavaria, F. Cairncross, D. Etsy, B. Smart, J. Piet, R. Wells, R. Gray, K. Fischer, and J. Schot, "The Challenge of Going Green," *Harvard Business Review,* July-August Issue (1994), www.hbr.org.

4. F. B. Cross, "The Weaning of the Green: Environmentalism Comes of Age in the 1990s," *Business Horizons,* September–October 1990, pp. 40–46.

5. J. Singh, "Making Business Sense of Environmental Compliance," *Sloan Management Review,* Spring 2000, pp. 91–100; L. Word, "A Green Museum: Preserving Collections in Sustainable Ways," National Endowment for the Arts, May 6, 2013, http://www.neh.gov.

6. A. Kleiner, "What Does It Mean to Be Green?" *Harvard Business Review,* July-August 1991, pp. 38–47; and "Global Consumers Are Willing to Put Their Money Where Their Heart Is," Nielsen (online), June 17, 2014, http://www.nielsen.com.

7. D. C. Kinlaw, *Competitive and Green: Sustainable Performance in the Environmental Age* (Amsterdam: Pfeiffer & Co., 1993).

8. United States Environmental Protection Agency, "2013 TRI National Analysis: Introduction," http://www2.epa.gov, accessed March 21, 2015.

9. F. Rice, "Who Scores Best on the Environment?" *Fortune,* July 26, 1993, pp. 114–22; J. O'Toole, "Do Good, Do Well: The Business Enterprise Trust Awards," *California Management Review,* Spring 1991, pp. 9–24.

10. J. O'Toole, "Do Good, Do Well: The Business Enterprise Trust Awards," *California Management Review,* Spring 1991, pp. 9–24.

11. G. Hardin, "The Tragedy of the Commons," *Science* 162 (1968), pp. 1243–48.

12. D. Kirkpatrick, "Environmentalism: The New Crusade," *Fortune,* February 12, 1990, pp. 44–55.

13. D. Kirkpatrick, "Environmentalism: The New Crusade," *Fortune,* February 12, 1990, pp. 44–55.

14. R. Carson, *Silent Spring* (Boston: Houghton Mifflin, 1962); R. Paehlke, *Environmentalism and the Future of Progressive Politics* (New Haven, CT: Yale University Press, 1989), pp. 13–41, 76–143; R. Nash, ed., *The American Environment* (Reading, MA: Addison-Wesley, 1968); R. Revelle and H. Landsberg, eds., *America's Changing Environment* (Boston: Beacon Press, 1970); L. Caldwell, *Environment: A Challenge to Modern Society* (Garden City, NY: Anchor Books, 1971); and J. M. Petulla, *Environmental Protection in the United States* (San Francisco: San Francisco Study Center, 1987).

15. B. Commoner, *Science and Survival* (New York: Viking Press, 1963); and B. Commoner, *The Closing Circle: Nature, Man and Technology* (New York: Bantam Books, 1971).

16. R. Paehlke, *Environmentalism and the Future of Progressive Politics* (New Haven: Yale University Press, 1989).

17. P. Shrivastava, "Ecocentric Management for a Risk Society," *Academy of Management Review* 20 (1995), pp. 118–37.

18. B. Commoner, *The Closing Circle: Nature, Man and Technology* (New York: Bantam Books, 1971).

19. R. Paehlke, *Environmentalism and the Future of Progressive Politics* (New Haven: Yale University Press, 1989).

20. R. Paehlke, *Environmentalism and the Future of Progressive Politics* (New Haven: Yale University Press, 1989).

21. R. Paehlke, *Environmentalism and the Future of Progressive Politics* (New Haven: Yale University Press, 1989).

22. M. E. Porter, "America's Green Strategy," *Science,* April 1991, p. 168.

23. "Green Teeth: The Government Amends its Environmental Law," *The Economist,* May 17, 2014.

Chapter 3

1. Avery Harmans and Nathan McAlone, "The Story of How Travis Kalanick Built Uber into the Most Feared and Valuable Startup in the World," *Business Insider,* August 1, 2016, http://www.businessinsider.com/ubers-history; Farhad Manjoo, "Culture Fix at Uber Could Aid Women in Tech," The New York Times March 2, 2017, p. B1, https://www.nytimes.com/2017/03/01/technology/uber-case-could-be-a-watershed-for-women-in-tech.html; Mike Isaac, "Uber Uses Tech to Deceive Authorities Worldwide," *The New York Times*, March 4, 2017, p. 1, https://www.nytimes.com/2017/03/03/technology/uber-greyball-program-evade-authorities.html; Bradley Seth McNew, "Could Uber's Brutal Backlash Derail an IPO This Year?" *The Motley Fool,* February 1, 2017, https://www.fool.com/investing/2017/02/01/could-ubers-brutal-backlash-derail-an-ipo-this-yea.aspx; Madeleine Johnson, "Will Uber Be the Hottest IPO of 2017?" Zacks.com, January 9, 2017, https://www.zacks.com/stock/news/244845/will-uber-be-the-hottest-ipo-of-2017; Elyse Dupre, "How Uber Won the Riseshare Wars and What Comes Next," *DMNews.com,* August 29, 2016, http://www.dmnews.com/marketing-strategy/how-uber-won-the-rideshare-wars-and-what-comes-next/article/518825/; Janet Burns, "Just 3000 Ride-Share Vehicles Could Replace NYC's Whole Taxi Fleet," *Forbes,* January 3, 2017, https://www.forbes.com/sites/janetwburns/2017/01/03/just-3000-ride-share-vehicles-could-replace-nycs-whole-taxi-fleet/#9dfcccb5a012; Kara Swisher, "Uber CEO Travis Kalanick Is Leaving Donald Trump's Advisory Council," Recode.net, February 2, 2017, http://www.recode.net/2017/2/2/14490950/travis-kalanick-uber-ceo-leaves-donald-trump-advisory-council.

2. Ann Zimmerman, "The New Logistics of Christmas," *The Wall Street Journal,* December 13, 2012, http://online.wsj.com.

3. A. Ilyashov, "Michael Kors Taps Cathy Marie Robinson as SVP of Global Operations," *Fashion Week Daily* (online), May 12, 2014, http://fashionweekdaily.com.

4. M. Blenko, M. Mankins, and P. Rogers, "The Decision-Driven Organization," *Harvard Business Review,* June 2010, pp. 54–62.

5. M. Magasin and F. L. Gehlen, "Unwise Decisions and Unanticipated Consequences," *Sloan Management Review* 41 (1999), pp. 47–60.

6. M. McCall and R. Kaplan, *Whatever It Takes: Decision Makers at Work* (Englewood Cliffs, NJ: Prentice-Hall, 1985); and Luda Kopeikina, "The Elements of a Clear Decision," *MIT Sloan Management Review* 47 (Winter 2006), pp. 19–20.

7. B. Bass, *Organizational Decision Making* (Homewood, IL: Richard D. Irwin, 1983).

8. J. March, "Bounded Rationality, Ambiguity, and the Engineering of Choice," *Bell Journal of Economics* 9 (1978), pp. 587–608.

9. D. Messick and M. Bazerman, "Ethical Leadership and the Psychology of Decision Making," *Sloan Management Review* (Winter 1996), pp. 9–22.

10. I. Katz and B. Willis, "A CEO's Dilemma: When Is It Safe to Hire Again?" *Bloomberg Businessweek,* 2011., pp. 22–24.

11. Alex Taylor III, "The Greatest Business Decisions of All Time: Ford," *Fortune,* October 1, 2012, http://money.cnn.com/gallery/news/companies/2012/10/01/greatest-business-decisions.fortune/index.html.

12. Social enterprise website, *ThinkImpact,* www.thinkimpact.com, accessed May 17, 2017; E. Chhabra, "A Social Entrepreneur's Quandary: Nonprofit or For-Profit?" *The New York Times* (online), July 10, 2013, http://www.nytimes.com; E. Chhabra, "A Social Entrepreneur Transforms a Nonprofit into a Profit-Making Enterprise," *The New York Times* (online), July 10, 2013, http://www.nytimes.com; N. Richardson, "Transformative Thinking for Sale," *Inc.* (online), May 28, 2013, http://www.inc.com.

13. D. Fontein, "4 Excellent User Generated Content Contests Using Social Media," January 15, 2016, *Hootsuite blog,* www.blog.hootsuite.com.

14. McCall and Kaplan, *Whatever It Takes: Decision Makers at Work.*

15. Amy Barrett, "The Case for User Reviews," *Inc.,* September 1, 2010, http://www.inc.com.

16. Ibid.

17. Q. Spitzer and R. Evans, *Heads, You Win! How the Best Companies Think* (New York: Simon & Schuster, 1997).

18. C. Gettys and S. Fisher, "Hypothesis Plausibility and Hypotheses Generation," *Organizational Behavior and Human Performance* 24 (1979), pp. 93–110.

19. E. R. Alexander, "The Design of Alternatives in Organizational Contexts: A Pilot Study," *Administrative Science Quarterly* 24 (1979), pp. 382–404.

20. D. Primack, "PillPack Is Raising More Money to Take On Pharmacies," *Fortune,* September 6, 2016, www.fortuned.com; Company website, https://www.pillpack.com; Company website, http://www.ideo.com/work/disrupting-the-drugstore.

21. A. R. Rao, M. E. Bergen, and S. Davis, "How to Fight a Price War," *Harvard Business Review,* March–April 2000, pp. 107–16.

22. Barrett, "The Case for User Reviews."

23. Ibid.

24. M. Buluswar, V. Campisi, A. Gupta, Z. Karu, V. Nilson, and R. Sigala, "How Companies Are Using Big Data and Analytics," McKinsey & Company, April 2016, www.mckinsey.com; Rachel Emma Silverman, "Big Data Upends the Way Workers Are Paid," *The Wall Street Journal,* September 19, 2012, http://online.wsj.com.

25. Spitzer and Evans, *Heads, You Win!*

26. L. Bryan and D. Farrell, "Leading through Uncertainty," *McKinsey Quarterly,* December 2008, http://www.mckinsey.com.

27. Barrett, "The Case for User Reviews."

28. McCall and Kaplan, *Whatever It Takes: Decision Makers at Work.*

29. Madison Malone Kircher, "Gender Discrimination at Uber Is a Reminder of How Hard Women Have to Fight to Be Believed," *NYMag.com,* February 21, 2017, http://nymag.com/selectall/2017/02/susan-fowler-alleges-sexual-discrimination-against-uber.html; Mike Isaac, "Inside Uber's Aggressive, Unrestrained Workplace Culture," *The New York Times,* February 22, 2017, https://www.nytimes.com/2017/02/22/technology/uber-workplace-culture.html; Manjoo, "Culture Fix at Uber Could Aid Women in Tech"; Susan J. Fowler, "Reflecting on One Very Strange Year at Uber," February 9, 2017, https://www.susanjfowler.com/blog/2017/2/19/reflecting-on-one-very-strange-year-at-uber.

30. Barrett, "The Case for User Reviews."

31. J. Pfeffer and R. Sutton, *The Knowing-Doing Gap* (Boston: Harvard Business School Press, 2000).

32. D. Siebold, "Making Meetings More Successful," *Journal of Business Communication* 16 (Summer 1979), pp. 3–20.

33. Barrett, "The Case for User Reviews"; Company website, "Capterra Surpasses 25,000 Software Reviews," press release on September 26, 2015.

34. I. Janis and L. Mann, *Decision Making* (New York: Free Press, 1977); and B. Bass, *Organizational Decision Making.*

35. Daniel Michaels, "Innovation Is Messy Business," *The Wall Street Journal,* January 24, 2013, http://online.wsj.com; Jon Ostrower and Joann S. Lublin, "The Two Men behind the 787," *The Wall Street Journal,* January 24, 2013, http://online.wsj.com.

36. J. W. Dean Jr. and M. Sharfman, "Does Decision Process Matter? A Study of Strategic Decision-Making Effectiveness," *Academy of Management Journal* 39 (1996), pp. 368–96; and R. Nisbett and L. Ross, *Human Inference: Strategies and Shortcomings* (Englewood Cliffs, NJ: Prentice-Hall, 1980).

37. D. Messick and M. Bazerman, "Ethical Leadership and the Psychology of Decision Making," *Sloan Management Review* (Winter 1996), pp. 9–22.

38. T. Bateman and C. Zeithaml, "The Psychological Context of Strategic Decisions: A Model and Convergent Experimental Findings," *Strategic Management Journal* 10 (1989), pp. 59–74.

39. A. Hartung, "How Bad Leadership Doomed Yahoo: CEO Mistakes Are Costly," *Forbes,* December 6, 2015, www.forbes.com.

40. A. Ha, "Verizon Reportedly Closes In on a Yahoo Acquisition with a $250M Discount," *TechCrunch,* February 15, 2007, www.techcrunch.com; J. Swartz and E. Weise, "Big Yahoo Changes: Marissa Mayer to Depart; Company to Be Renamed Altaba," *USA Today,* January 9, 2017, www.usatoday.com.

41. D. Barton, "Capitalism for the Long Term," *Harvard Business Review,* March 2011 pp. 84–91.

42. Messick and Bazerman, "Ethical Leadership and the Psychology of Decision Making"

43. N. Adler, *International Dimensions of Organizational Behavior* (Boston: Kent, 1990).

44. L. Perlow, G. Okhuysen, and N. Repenning, "The Speed Trap: Exploring the Relationship between Decision Making and Temporal Context," *Academy of Management Journal* 45 (2002), pp. 931–55.

45. K. M. Esenhardt, "Speed and Strategic Choice: How Managers Accelerate Decision Making," *California Management Review* 32 (Spring 1990), pp. 39–54.

46. Q. Spitzer and R. Evans, "New Problems in Problem Solving," *Across the Board,* April 1997, pp. 36–40.

47. G. W. Hill, "Group versus Individual Performance: Are N + 1 Heads Better than 1?" *Psychological Bulletin* 91 (1982), pp. 517–39.

48. N. R. F. Maier, "Assets and Liabilities in Group Problem Solving: The Need for an Integrative Function," *Psychological Review* 74 (1967), pp. 239–49.

49. Ibid.

50. B. Latane, K. Williams, and S. Harkins, "Many Hands Make Light the Work: The Causes and Consequences of Social Loafing," *Journal of Personality and Social Psychology* 37 (1979), pp. 822–32; J. George, "Extrinsic and Intrinsic Origins of Perceived Social Loafing in Organizations," *Academy of Management Journal* 35 (1992), pp. 191–206.

51. S. Murphy, S. Wayne, R. Liden, and B. Erdogan, "Understanding Social Loafing: The Role of Justice Perceptions and Exchange Relationships," *Human Relations* 56 (2003), pp. 61–84.

52. D. A. Garvin and M. A. Roberto, "What You Don't Know about Making Decisions," *Harvard Business Review,* September 2001, pp. 108–16.

53. Christopher Borrelli, "'Brave' Co-Director, Producer Take Up Arms to Promote Pixar's Latest," *Chicago Tribune,* June 21, 2012, http://www.chicagotribune.com.

54. A. Amason, "Distinguishing the Effects of Functional and Dysfunctional Conflict on Strategic Decision Making: Resolving a Paradox for Top Management Teams," *Academy of Management Journal* 39 (1996), pp. 123–48; and R. Dooley and G. Fyxell, "Attaining Decision Quality and Commitment from Dissent: The Moderating Effects of Loyalty and Competence in Strategic Decision-Making Teams," *Academy of Management Journal,* August 1999, pp. 389–402.

55. C. De Dreu and L. Weingart, "Task versus Relationship Conflict, Team Performance, and Team Member Satisfaction: A Meta-Analysis," *Journal of Applied Psychology* 88 (2003), pp. 741–49.

56. R. Cosier and C. Schwenk, "Agreement and Thinking Alike," *Academy of Management Executive* 4, no. 1, pp. 69–74.

57. G. Ruhe, "9 Cool College Start-ups," *Inc.* (online), http://www.inc.com, accessed March 1, 2015.

58. S. Harvey, "Creative Synthesis: Exploring the Process of Extraordinary Group Creativity," *Academy of Management Review* 39 (2014), pp. 324–43; J. Perry-Smith and P. Vittorio, "From Creativity to Innovation: The Social Network Drivers of the Four Phases of the Idea Journey," *Academy of Management Review* 42 (2017), pp. 53–79.

59. K. DeStobbeleir, S. Ashford, and D. Buyens, "Self-Regulation of Creativity at Work: The Role of Feedback-Seeking Behavior in Creative Performance," *Academy of Management Journal* 54 (2011), pp. 811–31; and Y. Gong, S. Cheung, M. Wang, and J. Huang, "Unfolding the Proactive Process for Creativity: Integration of the Employee Proactivity, Information Exchange, and Psychological Safety Perspectives," *Journal of Management* 38 (2010), pp. 1611–33.

60. S. Harvey, "Creative Synthesis: Exploring the Process of Extraordinary Group Creativity," *Academy of Management Review* 39 (2014), pp. 324–43; Perry-Smith and Vittorio, "From Creativity to Innovation: The Social Network Drivers of the Four Phases of the Idea Journey."

61. M. Bear, "Putting Creativity to Work: The Implementation of Creative Ideas in Organizations," *Academy of Management Journal* 55 (2012), pp. 1102–19; J. Perry-Smith and C. Shalley, "The Social Side of Creativity: A Static and Dynamic Social Network Perspective," *Academy of Management Review* 28 (2003), pp. 89–106; and J. Perry-Smith, "Social yet Creative: The Role of Social Relationships in Facilitating Individual Creativity," *Academy of Management Journal* 49 (2006), pp. 85–101.

62. "Innovation from the Ground Up," *Industry Week,* March 7, 2007, http://www.industryweek.com (interview of Erika Andersen); T. M. Amabile, "A Model of Creativity and Innovation in Organizations," in *Research in Organizational Behavior,* ed. B. Straw and L. Cummings, vol. 10 (Greenwich, CT: JAI Press, 1988), pp. 123–68.

63. T. Amabile, C. Hadley, and S. Kramer, "Creativity under the Gun," *Harvard Business Review,* August 2002, pp. 52–61.

64. N. Stevenson, "13 Ways to Make Your Workspace More Creative," *IDEO blog,* March 6, 2017, www.ideo.com.

65. S. Farmer, P. Tierney, and K. Kung McIntyre, "Employee Creativity in Taiwan: An Application of Role Identity Theory," *Academy of Management Journal* 46 (2003), pp. 618–30.

66. "Innovation from the Ground Up."

67. K. Coyne and S. Coyne, "Seven Steps to Better Brainstorming," *McKinsey Quarterly,* March 2011, http://www.mckinsey.com.

68. L. Thompson, "Improving the Creativity of Organizational Work Groups," *Academy of Management Executive* 17 (2003), pp. 96–109.

69. C. Gustke, "Crowdsourcing to Get Ideas, and Perhaps Save Money," *The New York Times,* May 11, 2016, www.nytimes.com; "Accenture, Deloitte Name Crowdsourcing as a Key Trend For 2014," http://www.crowdsourcing.org, accessed March 2, 2015; Company website, http://www.weargustin.com, accessed March 2, 2015; K. Wagner, "5 Companies That Let Fans Lend a Hand," *Fortune* (online), June 24, 2013, http://fortune.com.

70. S. Sonenshein, "How Organizations Foster the Creative Use of Resources," *Academy of Management Journal* 57 (2014), pp. 814–48; P. Puranam, N. Stieglitz, M. Osman, et al., "Modeling Bounded Rationality in Organizations: Progress and Prospects," *Academy of Management Annals* 9 (2015), pp. 337–92.

71. J. Walter, F. Fellermanns, and C. Lechner, "Decision Making within and between Organizations: Rationality, Politics, and Alliance Performance," *Journal of Management* 38 (2012), pp. 1582–1610.

72. T. Levitt, "Creativity Is Not Enough," *Harvard Business Review,* August 2002, pp. 137–44.

73. Dean Jr. and Sharfman, "Does Decision Process Matter?"

74. K. Eisenhardt, J. Kahwajy, and L. J. Bourgeois III, "How Management Teams Can Have a Good Fight," *Harvard Management Review,* July–August 1997, pp. 77–85.

75. W. Kahn, M. Barton, and S. Fellows, "Organizational Crises and the Disturbance of Relational Systems," *Academy of Management Review* 38 (2013), pp. 377–96; C. M. Pearson and I. I. Mitroff, "From Crisis Prone to Crisis Prepared: A Framework for Crisis Management," *Academy of Management Executive,* February 1993, pp. 48–59.

76. Jordan Robertson and Eileen Sullivan, "U.S. Power Grid Hacked, Officials Say," *Chicago Tribune,* April 9, 2009, http://www.chicagotribune.com.

77. S. Moore, "Disaster's Future: The Prospects for Corporate Crisis Management and Communication," *Business Horizons,* January–February 2004, pp. 29–36.

78. G. Meyers with J. Holusha, *When It Hits the Fan: Managing the Nine Crises of Business*

(Boston: Houghton Mifflin, 1986); and S. Bacharach and P. Bamberger, "9/11 and New York City Firefighters' Post Hoc Unit Support and Control Climates: A Context Theory of the Consequences of Involvement in Traumatic Work-Related Events," *Academy of Management Journal* 50 (2007), pp. 849–68.

79. McCall and Kaplan, *Whatever It Takes: Decision Makers at Work.*

80. Biz Carson, "Uber's Unraveling: The Stunning, 2-Week String of Blows That Has Upended the World's Most Valuable Startup," *Business Insider,* March 4, 2017, http://www.businessinsider.com/uber-scandal-recap-2017-3; Danielle Muoio, "Uber Has Been Secretively Deceiving Authorities for Years with a Tool Called 'Greyball,'" *Business Insider,* March 3, 2017, http://www.businessinsider.com/uber-greyball-app-vtos-authorities-2017-3; Isaac, "Uber Uses Tech to Deceive Authorities Worldwide."

81. J. Dutton, P. Frost, M. Worline, J. Lilius, and J. Kanov, "Leading in Times of Trauma," *Harvard Business Review,* January 2002, pp. 54–61.

Chapter 4

1. Frank Pallotta, "Disney's Formula for Rebooting Tales as Old as Time," *Clickondetroit.com,* March 17, 2017, http://www.clickondetroit.com/entertainment/disneys-formula-for-rebooting-tales-as-old-as-time; Anders Bylund, "How Walt Disney Co. Has Changed in the Last Ten Years," *Fool.com,* March 15, 2017, https://www.fool.com/investing/2017/03/15/how-walt-disney-co-has-changed-in-the-last-10-year.aspx; Richard C. Paddock, "Disney Says It Won't Edit 'Beauty and the Beast' for Malaysian Censors," *The New York Times,* March 15, 2017, https://www.nytimes.com/2017/03/15/world/asia/beauty-beast-gay-character-malaysia.html?_r=1 ; Brooks Barnes, "'Beauty and the Beast' Clobbers Record with $170 Million Opening," *The New York Times,* March 19, 2017, https://www.nytimes.com/2017/03/19/movies/beauty-and-the-beast-clobbers-record-with-170-million-opening.html.

2. J. Bracker and J. Pearson, "Planning and Financial Performance of Small Mature Firms," *Strategic Management Journal* 7 (1986), pp. 503–22; and P. Waalewijn and P. Segaar, "Strategic Management: The Key to Profitability in Small Companies," *Long Range Planning* 26, no. 2 (April 1993), pp. 24–30.

3. D. Welch, "GM Doubles Profit in North America to Record on Truck Surge," *Bloomberg Business,* July 23, 2015, http://www.bloomberg.com; S. Terlep, "GM Caps Profitable Year," *The Wall Street Journal,* February 24, 2011, http://online.wsj.com; B. Cox, "For Big Three Automakers, an Unlikely Time for a Turnaround," *Fort Worth Star-Telegram,* April 15, 2011, http://www.star-telegram.com; and D. Barkholz, "Dealers: We Want More Cars!" *Automotive News,* August 23, 2010, Business &

Company Resource Center, http://galenet.galegroup.com.

4. "Interview with Mark Cooper: Walmart Takes Collaborative Approach to Disaster Recovery," PricewaterhouseCoopers report, accessed March 8, 2015.

5. Company website, "Triple Bottom Line," http://www.novonordisk-us.com, accessed March 10, 2015.

6. Company website, "Novo Nordisk Publishes 2014 Integrated Annual Report Emphasizing Long-Term Thinking," http://www.novonordisk-us.com, accessed March 10, 2015.

7. A. Torsoli, "Novo Nordisk Fourth-Quarter Net Beats Estimates on Victoza," *Bloomberg Business* (online), January 30, 2015, http://www.bloomberg.com.

8. Company press release, "GM and Lyft to Shape the Future of Mobility," January 4, 2016, www.media.gm.com.

9. "GM and Lyft Plan to Deploy Thousands of Self-Driving Chevy Bolts," *Fortune,* February 17, 2017, www.fortune.com.

10. Ibid.

11. D. C. Hambrick and J. W. Fredrickson, "Are You Sure You Have a Strategy?" *Academy of Management Executive* 19, no. 4 (2005), pp. 51–62.

12. Brendan Byrnes, "Playing to Win: How Procter & Gamble Increased Its Market Cap by $100 Billion," *Motley Fool,* February 27, 2013, http://www.fool.com (interview with Roger Martin); unsigned review of *Playing to Win: How Strategy Really Works,* by A. G. Lafley and Roger Martin, *The Economist,* January 12, 2013, http://www.economist.com; and Dan Schawbel, "A. G. Lafley: Develop a Strategy to Win at Business," *Forbes,* February 5, 2013, http://www.forbes.com (interview with A. G. Lafley).

13. K. Hardy, "How to Prevent Another Chipotle," *QSR Magazine,* May 2016, www.qsrmagazine.com.

14. Carr, "Recovery Efforts Stalled, Chipotle Faces Challenges That Go Well beyond Food Safety." *Fast Company,* December 14, 2016, www.fastcompany.com.

15. Hardy, "How to Prevent Another Chipotle."

16. A. Carr, "Recovery Efforts Stalled, Chipotle Faces Challenges That Go Well beyond Food Safety,"

17. R. Kaplan and D. Norton, "Plotting Success with 'Strategy Maps,'" *Optimize,* February 2004, http://www.optimizemag.com; and R. S. Kaplan and D. P. Norton, "Having Trouble with Your Strategy? Then Map It," *Harvard Business Review,* September–October 2000.

18. B. Barnes, "Interactive Unit at Disney Cuts a Quarter of Its Staff," *The New York Times* (online), March 6, 2014; Walt Disney Company, "Company Overview"; Brooks Barnes, "Disney, Struggling to Find Its Digital Footing, Overhauls Disney.com," *The New York Times,* October 21, 2012, http://www.nytimes.com; Derrik J. Lang, "Disney Closing 'Epic Mickey' Video Game Developer," *Bloomberg Businessweek,* January 29, 2013, http://www.businessweek.com;

Associated Press, "Disney to Shutter Online Movie Store, Website," *Bloomberg Businessweek,* November 19, 2012, http://www.businessweek.com; Jacob Pramuk, "Disney Shares Rise in Choppy Trade after Earnings and Revenues Fall Short," CNBC.com, November 10, 2016, http://www.cnbc.com/2016/11/10/disney-reports-fiscal-fourth-quarter-earnings.html.

19. M. Randall, "Employees Can't Carry Out a Strategy If They Didn't Help Plan It," *Business Insider,* July 1, 2013, www.businessinsider.com; J. L. Bower and C. G. Gilbert, "How Managers' Everyday Decisions Create or Destroy Your Company's Strategy," Harvard Business Review, February 2007, pp. 72–79. and "Business: Fading Fads," *The Economist,* April 22, 2000, pp. 60–61.

20. S. W. Floyd and P. J. Lane, "Strategizing throughout the Organization: Management Role Conflict in Strategic Renewal," *Academy of Management Review* 25, no. 1 (January 2000), pp. 154–77.

21. Mission statements quoted from the organizations' websites: CVS, "Mission and Values," www.cvs.com; Naked Juice, "Mission," www.nakedjuice.com; and Make-A-Wish, "Our Mission" www.wish.org.

22. A. Yuhas, "SpaceX to Send Two People around the Moon Who Paid for a 2018 Private Mission," *The Guardian,* February 28, 2017, www.theguardian.com; Company website, "About SpaceX," www.spacex.com/about; N. Drake, "Elon Musk: A Million Humans Could Live on Mars by the 2060s," *National Geographic,* September 27, 2016, www.nationalgeographic.com.

23. A. A. Thompson and A. J. Strickland III, *Strategic Management: Concepts and Cases,* 8th ed. (New York: Richard D. Irwin, 1995), p. 23; R. Edward Freeman, J. S. Harrison, and A. C. Wicks, *Managing for Stakeholders* (New Haven, CT: Yale University Press, 2007).

24. Quoted from the company's website, "About Us," Ocean Renewable Power Company, http://www.orpc.co.

25. Organizational website, "Landfill Methane Outreach Program (LMOP)," United States Environmental Protection Agency, www.epa.gov, accessed March 12, 2017.

26. A. Loten, "Running a Business in a Disaster Zone," *The Wall Street Journal,* December 30, 2010, http://online.wsj.com.

27. D. J. Collis and C. A. Montgomery, *Corporate Strategy: A Resource-Based Approach,* 2nd ed. (New York, McGraw-Hill/Irwin, 2005).

28. R. L. Priem, "A Consumer Perspective on Value Creation," *Academy of Management Review* 32, no. 1 (2007), pp. 219–35.

29. J. Greathouse, "From Call Center Agent to Zappos' Life Coach: This Woman Is Amazing," *Forbes,* February 4, 2014, www.forbes.com; Jim Edwards, "Check Out the Insane Lengths Zappos Customer Service Reps Will Go To," *Business Insider,* January 9, 2012, http://articles.businessinsider.com; Zappos.com, "About," http://about.zappos.com; Mig Pascual, "Zappos: Five

Out-of-the-Box Ideas for Keeping Employees Engaged," *U.S. News & World Report,* October 30, 2012, http://money.usnews.com.

30. A. Wilcox King, "Disentangling Interfirm and Intrafirm Causal Ambiguity: A Conceptual Model of Causal Ambiguity and Sustainable Competitive Advantage," *Academy of Management Review* 32, no. 1 (2007), pp. 156–78.

31. Accenture company report, "Achieving High Performance: The Value of Benchmarking," http://www.accenture.com, accessed March 8, 2015.

32. "Beware of Benchmarking Pitfalls Warns AXA Chief," *Europe Intelligence Wire,* May 13, 2010, Business & Company Resource Center, http://galenet.galegroup.com.

33. Company website, "About Next Day Flyers," http://www.nextdayflyers.com, accessed March 8, 2015; R. Myers, "That Sounds Like a Plan," *Inc.,* no. 36 (2014), pp. 90–92.

34. L. Rainee and A. Perrin, "Technology Adoption by Baby Boomers (and Everybody Else)," Pew Research, March 22, 2016, www.pewinternet.org; Company website, "Ernst & Young: Younger Managers Rise in the Ranks: Managing the Generational Mix and Preferred Workplace Perks," http://www.ey.com, accessed March 10, 2015; and V. Giang, "Here Are the Strengths and Weaknesses of Millennials, Gen X, and Boomers," *Business Insider* (online), September 9, 2013, http://www.businessinsider.com.

35. D. G. Sirmon, M. A. Hitt, and R. D. Ireland, "Managing Firm Resources in Dynamic Environments to Create Value: Looking inside the Black Box," *Academy of Management Review* 32, no. 1 (2007), pp. 273–92.

36. A. Bluestein, "The Success Gene," *Inc.,* April 2008, pp. 83–94.

37. P. Haspeslagh, "Portfolio Planning: Uses and Limits," *Harvard Business Review* 60, no. 1 (1982), pp. 58–67; R. Hamermesh, *Making Strategy Work* (New York: John Wiley & Sons, 1986); and R. A. Proctor, "Toward a New Model for Product Portfolio Analysis," *Management Decision* 28, no. 3 (1990), pp. 14–17.

38. T. Mann and E. Henning, "GE Doubles Down on 3-D Printing with European Deals," *The Wall Street Journal,* September 6, 2016, www.wsj.com; D. Weston, "GE Acquires LM Wind Power," *Wind Power Monthly,* October 11, 2016, www.windpowermonthly.com; J. Wieczner, "Last Big Chunk of GE Capital Sold to Wells Fargo," *Fortune,* October 13, 2015, www.fortune.com; Associated Press, "GE Energy and Other Firms Buy Wind Farms in France," *Bloomberg Businessweek,* January 2, 2013, http://www.businessweek.com.

39. L. Shen, "Here Are the 5 Biggest M&A Deals of 2016," *Fortune,* December 28, 2016, www.fortune.com.

40. M. Porter, *Competitive Advantage* (New York: Free Press, 1985), pp. 11–14.

41. K. Talley, "Wal-Mart Sees Shoppers' Pain," *The Wall Street Journal,* April 28, 2011, http://online.wsj.com.

42. F. F. Suarez and G. Lanzolla, "The Role of Environmental Dynamics in Building a First Mover Advantage Theory," *Academy of Management Review* 32, no. 2 (2007), pp. 377–92.

43. Company website, Investor Presentation Q3, January 3, 2016, www.investors.bloominbrands.com.

44. G. Norris, "GE Orders Two HondaJets for Supply Chain Flights," *Aviation Week* (online), October 21, 2014, http://aviationweek.com; and J. Scheck and P. Glader, "R&D Spending Holds Steady in Slump," *The Wall Street Journal,* April 6, 2009, http://online.wsj.com.

45. Company website, "GE 2015 Annual Report," www.ge.com.

46. R. A. Eisenstat, "Implementing Strategy: Developing a Partnership for Change," *Planning Review,* September–October 1993, pp. 33–36.

47. Company website, "About Disney Interactive," http://www.disneyinteractive.com/about/, accessed March 9, 2015; T. Huddleston Jr., "'Frozen' Heats Up Disney's Earnings," *Fortune* (online), March 7, 2015, http://fortune.com; Jennifer Reingold, "Bob Iger: Disney's Fun King," *Fortune,* May 9, 2012, http://management.fortune.cnn.com; Brooks Barnes, "Disney, Struggling to Find Its Digital Footing, Overhauls Disney.com," *The New York Times,* October 21, 2012, http://www.nytimes.com; Walt Disney Company, "Investor Relations," http://thewaltdisneycompany.com/investors; Daniel Rasmus, "Defining Your Company's Vision," *Fast Company,* February 28, 2012, http://www.fastcompany.com; Matthew Panzarino, "Disney and Netflix Just Pushed Streaming Video into Its Next Era," *Next Web,* December 4, 2012, http://thenextweb.com; Ethan Smith, "Disney CEO Turns Slump into a Springboard," *The Wall Street Journal,* November 8, 2010, http://online.wsj.com; Ethan Smith and Erica Orden, "Mickey, Darth Vader Join Forces in $4.05 Billion Deal," *The Wall Street Journal,* October 31, 2012, http://online.wsj.com; and Associated Press, "Disney Rolls Out More Live TV Apps with Comcast," *Bloomberg Businessweek,* June 14, 2012, http://www.businessweek.com.

Chapter 5

1. A. Barinka, "IBM's Rometty Takes 2014 Bonus amid Struggles in Cloud Shift," *Bloomberg Business,* January 30, 2015, http://bloomberg.com; J. Bort, "IBM Reports Earnings: It's a Miss on Revenue but a Beat on Profits," *Business Insider,* January 20, 2015, http://www.businessinsider.com; Company website, "IBM Think Forum," October 8, 2014, http://www.ibm.com; Bill George, "How IBM's Sam Palmisano Redefined the Global Corporation," *HBR Blog Network: HBS Faculty,* January 18, 2012, http://blogs.hbr.org; IBM, "What Is a Smarter Planet?" http://www.ibm.com; Ann Bednarz, "IBM's Rometty Nets $16.2 Million in First Year

as CEO," *Network World,* March 13, 2013, http://www.networkworld.com; Steve Lohr, "IBM's Rometty on the Data Challenge to the Culture of Management," *The New York Times,* March 7, 2013, http://bits.blogs.nytimes.com.

2. V. Anand, B. Ashforth, and M. Joshi, "Business as Usual: The Acceptance and Perpetuation of Corruption in Organizations," *Academy of Management Executive* (May 2004), pp. 39–53; and B. Ashforth, D. Gioia, S. Robinson, and L. Trevino, "Re-viewing Organizational Corruption," *Academy of Management Review* 33 (July 2008), 670–84.

3. Edelman Berland, "2017 Edelman Trust Barometer: Executive Summary," http://www.edelman.com.

4. M. Egan, "5,300 Wells Fargo Employees Fired over 2 Million Phony Accounts," *CNN Money,* September 9, 2016, www.money.cnn.com.

5. M. Corkery, "Wells Fargo Struggling in Aftermath of Fraud Scandal," *The New York Times,* January 13, 2017, www.nytimes.com.

6. C. Mathews and M. Heimer, "The 5 Biggest Corporate Scandals of 2016," *Fortune,* December 28, 2016, www.fortune.com.

7. M. Banaji, M. Bazerman, and D. Chugh, "How (Un)Ethical Are You?" *Harvard Business Review,* December 2003, pp. 56–64.

8. K. Leavitt and D. Sluss, "Lying for Who We Are: An Identity-Based Model of Workplace Dishonesty," *Academy of Management Review* 40 (2015), pp. 587–610.

9. S. L. Grover, "The Truth, the Whole Truth, and Nothing but the Truth: The Causes and Management of Workplace Lying," *Academy of Management Executive* 19 (May 2005), pp. 148–57.

10. Company website, "Pro-Business, but Expecting More," The Deloitte Millennial Survey 2017, www2.deloitte.com.

11. V. Lipman, "So You'd Like to Work in a More Ethical Culture?" *Forbes,* July 1, 2015, www.forbes.com; K. Darcy, "Ways to Build Strong Ethical Cultures," *The Wall Street Journal,* April 6, 2015, www.wsj.com.

12. Organization website, "Companies Offer Special Preview of Upcoming Topics at Ethisphere's Global Ethics Summit in New York," Ethisphere, March 1, 2017, www.ethisphere.com.

13. "Bell Agrees to $1.25 Million Fine after Fake Company App Reviews," *Huffington Post,* October 14, 2015, www.huffingtonpost.com.

14. H. Brueck, "Amazon Sues Again to Kill More Fake Product Reviews," *Fortune,* April 26, 2016, www.fortune.com; T. Bishop, "Amazon Sues 'Buy Amazon Reviews' and Four Other Sites in New Crackdown on Bogus Reviews," *GeekWire,* April 25, 2016, www.geekwire.com.

15. B. Rubin, "Amazon Continues Crackdown on Alleged Fake Reviews," *CNET,* April 25, 2016, www.cnet.com.

16. M. E. Guy, *Ethical Decision Making in Everyday Work Situations* (New York: Quorum Books, 1990).

17. O. C. Ferrell and J. Fraedrich, *Business Ethics: Ethical Decision Making and Cases*, 3rd ed. (Boston: Houghton Mifflin, 1997).

18. Ibid.

19. Guy, *Ethical Decision Making in Everyday Work Situations*.

20. Ferrell and Fraedrich, *Business Ethics: Ethical Decision Making and Cases*.

21. T. James, "Nabisco Plant," *Chicago Tribune*, November 2, 2016, www.chicagotribune.com; G. Trotter, "Laid Off Oreo Bakery Workers Question Mondelez CEO on Job Cuts," *Chicago Tribune*, May 19, 2016, www.chicagotribune.com.

22. A. Spicer, T. Dunfee, and W. Biley, "Does National Context Matter in Ethical Decision Making? An Empirical Test of Integrative Social Contracts Theory," *Academy of Management Journal* 47 (2004), pp. 610-20; W. Bailey and A. Spicer, "When Does National Identity Matter? Convergence and Divergence in International Business Ethics," *Academy of Management Journal*, 2007, pp. 1462-80; and K. Martin, J. Cullen, J. Johnson, and K. Parboteeah, "Deciding to Bribe: A Cross-Level Analysis of Firm and Home Country Influences on Bribery Activity," *Academy of Management Journal*, 2007, pp. 1401-22.

23. L. Kohlberg and D. Candee, "The Relationship of Moral Judgment to Moral Action" in *Morality, Moral Behavior, and Moral Development*, ed. W. M. Kurtines and J. L. Gerwitz (New York: John Wiley & Sons, 1984).

24. L. K. Trevino, "Ethical Decision Making in Organizations: A Person–Situation Interactionist Model," *Academy of Management Review*, 1992, pp. 601-17.

25. S. Hannah, B. Avolio, and D. May, "Moral Maturation and Moral Conation: A Capacity Approach to Explaining Moral Thought and Action," *Academy of Management Review* 36 (2011), pp. 663-85.

26. A. Crane, "Modern Slavery as a Management Practice: Exploring the Conditions and Capabilities for Human Exploitation," *Academy of Management Review* 38 (2013), pp. 49-69.

27. G. Kilduff, A. Galinsky, A. Gallo, et al., "Whatever It Takes to Win: Rivalry Increases Unethical Behavior," *Academy of Management Journal* 59 (2016), 1508-34.

28. J. Badarocco Jr. and A. Webb, "Business Ethics: A View from the Trenches," *California Management Review*, Winter 1995, pp. 8-28; and G. Laczniak, M. Berkowitz, R. Brookes, and J. Hale, "The Business of Ethics: Improving or Deteriorating?" *Business Horizons*, January–February 1995, pp. 39-47.

29. "State of Ethics in Large Companies," Ethics & Compliance Initiative, www.ethics.org, accessed March 14, 2017.

30. J. Kammeyer-Mueller, L. Simon, and B. Rich, "The Psychic Cost of Doing Wrong: Ethical Conflict, Divestiture Socialization, and Emotional Exhaustion," *Journal of Management* 38 (2012), pp. 784-808.

31. Anand et al., "Business as Usual."

32. S. Glover, "SOX Compliance Proves Beneficial to Organizations, Fuels Risk Consciousness," *National Underwriter Property & Casualty*, November 15, 2010, pp. 34, 36; and P. Sweeney, "Will New Regulations Deter Corporate Fraud?" *Financial Executive*, January–February 2011, pp. 54-57.

33. R. E. Allinson, "A Call for Ethically Centered Management," *Academy of Management Executive*, February 1995, pp. 73-76.

34. R. T. De George, *Business Ethics*, 3rd ed. (New York: Macmillan, 1990).

35. A. Simha and J. Cullen, "Ethical Climates and Their Effects on Organizational Outcomes: Implications from the Past and Prophecies for the Future," *Academy of Management Perspectives*, 2012, p. 146.

36. Company Code of Conduct, General Electric, www.sec.gov, accessed March 14, 2017.

37. B. W. Heineman Jr., "Avoiding Integrity Land Mines," *Harvard Business Review*, April 2007, pp. 100-8.

38. R. A. Cooke, "Danger Signs of Unethical Behavior: How to Determine If Your Firm Is at Ethical Risk," *Journal of Business Ethics*, April 1991, pp. 249-53.

39. L. K. Trevino and M. Brown, "Managing to Be Ethical: Debunking Five Business Ethics Myths," *Academy of Management Executive*, May 2004, pp. 69-81.

40. Ibid.

41. Heineman Jr., "Avoiding Integrity Land Mines."

42. Company website, "The OshKosh Way: A Corporate Code of Ethics & Standards of Conduct," www.oshkoshcorp.com, accessed March 14, 2017.

43. C. Handy, *Beyond Uncertainty: The Changing Worlds of Organizations* (Boston: Harvard Business School Press, 1996).

44. J. Stevens, H. Steensma, D. Harrison, and P. Cochran, "Symbolic or Substantive Document? The Influence of Ethics Codes on Financial Executives' Decisions," *Strategic Management Journal* 26 (2005), pp. 181-95; and J. Weber, "Does It Take an Economic Village to Raise an Ethical Company?" *Academy of Management Executive* 19 (May 2005), pp. 158-59.

45. Ethics Resource Center website, http://www.ethics.org, accessed March 14, 2017.

46. R. J. Zablow, "Creating and Sustaining an Ethical Workplace: Ethics Resource Center (ERC)," "Code Construction and Content," *The Ethics Resource Center Toolkit*, http://www.ethics.org; and J. Brown, "Ten Writing Tips for Creating an Effective Code of Conduct," Ethics Resource Center, http://www.ethics.org.

47. G. R. Weaver, L. K. Trevino, and P. L. Cochran, "Corporate Ethics Programs as Control Systems: Influences of Executive Commitment and Environmental Factors," *Academy of Management Journal* 42 (1999), pp. 41-57.

48. L. S. Paine, "Managing for Organizational Integrity," *Harvard Business Review*, March–April 1994, pp. 106-17.

49. Government website, "ADA Amendments Act of 2008," http://www.eeoc.gov accessed March 20, 2015; F. Hall and E. Hall, "The ADA: Going beyond the Law," *Academy of Management Executive*, February 1994, pp. 7-13; and A. Farnham, "Brushing Up Your Vision Thing," *Fortune*, May 1, 1995, p. 129.

50. C. Moore and F. Gino, "Approach, Ability, Aftermath: A Psychological Process Framework of Unethical Behavior at Work," *Academy of Management Annals* 9 (2015), pp. 235-89.

51. Trevino and Brown, "Managing to Be Ethical."

52. Ibid.

53. M. Banaji, M. Bazerman, and D. Chugh, "How (Un)Ethical Are You?" *Harvard Business Review*, December 2003, pp. 56-64.

54. Moore and Gino, "Approach, Ability, Aftermath"; B. Gunia, L. Wang, L. Huang, J. Wang, and K. Murnighan, "Contemplation and Conversation: Subtle Influences on Moral Decision Making," *Academy of Management Journal* 55 (2012), pp. 13-33.

55. Anand et al., "Business as Usual"; and Remi Trudel and June Cotte, "Does Being Ethical Pay?" *The Wall Street Journal*, May 12, 2008, http://online.wsj.com.

56. T. Thomas, J. Schermerhorn Jr., and J. Dienhart, "Strategic Leadership of Ethical Behavior in Business," *Academy of Management Executive*, May 2004, pp. 56-66.

57. Trevino and Brown, "Managing to Be Ethical."

58. B. Rokos and J. Katzanek, "325 Could Lose Jobs When Hemet Call Center Closes," *Press-Enterprise* (Riverside, CA), August 5, 2010, Business & Company Resource Center, http://galenet.galegroup.com; and B. Rokos, "Hilton Call Center Employees in Hemet Trained Overseas Workers before Losing Jobs," *Press-Enterprise* (Riverside, CA), August 13, 2010, Business & Company Resource Center, http://galenet.galegroup.com.

59. J. Bort, "IBM Reports Earnings: It's a Miss on Revenue but a Beat on Profits," *Business Insider*, January 20, 2015, http://www.businessinsider.com; Bill George, "How IBM's Sam Palmisano Redefined the Global Corporation," HBR Blog Network: HBS Faculty, January 18, 2012, http://blogs.hbr.org; Leigh Nakanishi, "Technology's Achilles' Heel," Edelman Conversations: Global Practices, January 28, 2013, http://www.edelman.com; IBM, "IBM Policies," About IBM, http://www.ibm.com; IBM, "Our Values," IBM Employment, http://www-03.ibm.com; Christopher M. Matthews, "Judge Limits Requirements to IBM, SEC Settlement," *The Wall Street Journal*, February 4, 2013, http://blogs.wsj.com; Arne Alsin, "The IBM Hall of Shame: A (Semi) Complete List of Bribes, Blunders and Fraud," *Medium.com*, November 26, 2016, https://medium.com/worm-capital/the-ibm-hall-of-shame-a-semi-complete-list-of-bribes-blunders-and-fraud-19e674a5b986#.wg23ud43p; "IBM, Revenue Quebec

Employees Arrested in UPAC Raid," *CBC News*, March 11, 2015, http://www.cbc.ca/news/canada/montreal/ibm-revenue-quebec-employees-arrested-in-upac-raid-1.2990211.

60. M. Hernandez, "Toward an Understanding of the Psychology of Stewardship," *Academy of Management Review* 37, (2012), pp. 172–93.

61. Company website, LEED Certified Stores, www.starbucks.com, accessed March 14, 2017; Company website, Kickboard for Teachers, www.kickboardforteachers, accessed March 21, 2015; J. Smith, "The Companies with the Best CSR Reputations," *Forbes* (online), October 2, 2013, http://www.forbes.com; R. Bies, J. Bartunek, T. Fort, and M. Zald, "Corporations as Social Change Agents: Individual, Interpersonal, Institutional, and Environmental Dynamics," *Academy of Management Review,* 2007, pp. 788–93; and B. Liodice, "10 Companies with Social Responsibility at the Core," *Advertising Age,* April 19, 2010.

62. L. Preston and J. Post, eds., *Private Management and Public Policy* (Englewood Cliffs, NJ: Prentice-Hall, 1975).

63. Ferrell and Fraedrich, *Business Ethics.*

64. M. Nalick, M. Josefy, A. Zardkoohi, et al., "Corporate Sociopolitical Involvement: A Reflection of Whose Preferences?" *Academy of Management Perspectives* 30 (2016), pp. 384–403.

65. M. Westermann-Behaylo, K. Rehbein, and T. Fort, "Enhancing the Concept of Corporate Diplomacy: Encompassing Political Corporate Social Responsibility, International Relations, and Peace through Commerce," *Academy of Management Perspectives* 29 (2015), pp. 387–404; A. Simha and J. Cullen, "Ethical Climates and Their Effects on Organizational Outcomes: Implications from the Past and Prophecies for the Future," *Academy of Management Perspectives* 26 (2012), pp. 20–34.

66. S. Mena, J. Rintamaki, P. Fleming, et al., "On the Forgetting of Corporate Irresponsibility," *Academy of Management Review* 41 (2016), pp. 720–38; J. Schrempf-Stirling, G. Palazzo, and R. Phillips, "Historic Corporate Social Responsibility," *Academy of Management Review* 41 (2016), pp. 700–19.

67. C. Flammer, "Corporate Social Responsibility and Shareholder Reaction: The Environmental Awareness of Investors," *Academy of Management Journal* 56 (2013), pp. 758–81; and H. Aguinis and A. Glavas, "What We Know and Don't Know about Corporate Social Responsibility: A Review and Research Agenda," *Journal of Management,* 2012, pp. 932–68.

68. D. Matten and J. Moon, "'Implicit' and 'Explicit' CSR: A Conceptual Framework for a Comparative Understanding of Corporate Social Responsibility," *Academy of Management Review,* 2008, pp. 404–24.

69. A. Carroll, "Managing Ethically with Global Stakeholders: A Present and Future Challenge," *Academy of Management Executive,* May 2004, pp. 114–20.

70. D. Jackson and G. Marx, "Pork Producers Defend Gestation Crates, but Consumers Demand Change," *Chicago Tribune,* August 3, 2016, www.chicagotribune.com.

71. P. Godfrey, "The Relationship between Corporate Philanthropy and Shareholder Wealth," *The Academy of Management Review* 30 (2005), pp. 777–98; and H. Wang and C. Qian, "Corporate Philanthropy and Corporate Financial Performance: The Roles of Stakeholder Response and Political Access," *Academy of Management Journal* 54 (2011), pp. 1159–81.

72. R. Giacalone, "A Transcendent Business Education for the 21st Century," *Academy of Management Learning & Education,* 2004, pp. 415–20.

73. M. Witzel, "Not for Wealth Alone: The Rise of Business Ethics," *Financial Times Mastering Management Review,* November 1999, pp. 14–19.

74. D. C. Korten, *When Corporations Ruled the World* (San Francisco: Berrett-Koehler, 1995).

75. C. Handy, *Beyond Uncertainty: The Changing Worlds of Organizations* (Boston: Harvard Business School Press, 1996).

76. D. Barton, "Capitalism for the Long Term," *Harvard Business Review,* March 2011, pp. 84–91.

77. D. Quinn and T. Jones, "An Agent Morality View of Business Policy," *Academy of Management Review* 20 (1995), pp. 22–42.

78. Company website, "Improving Our Water Efficiency," www.coca-cola.com, accessed March 14, 2017.

79. Coca-Cola Company, "About Water Stewardship," http://www.coca-colacompany.com; Coca-Cola Company, "Setting a New Goal for Water Efficiency," http://www.coca-colacompany.com; and Coca-Cola Company, "RAIN: The Replenish Africa Initiative," http://www.coca-colacompany.com.

80. B. McKay, "Why Coke Aims to Slake Global Thirst for Safe Water," *The Wall Street Journal,* March 15, 2007, http://online.wsj.com.

81. M. Delmas, D. Etzion, and N. Nairn-Birch, "Triangulating Environmental Performance: What Do Corporate Social Responsibility Ratings Really Capture?" *Academy of Management Perspectives* 27 (2013), pp. 255–67; J. A. Aragon-Correa, A. Marcus, and N. Hurtado-Torres, "The Natural Environmental Strategies of International Firms: Old Controversies and New Evidence on Performance and Disclosure," *Academy of Management Perspectives* 30 (2016), pp. 24–39.

82. D. Schuler and M. Cording, "A Corporate Social Performance–Corporate Financial Performance Behavioral Model for Consumers," *Academy of Management Review* 31 (2006), pp. 540–58.

83. M. Orlitzky, F. Schmidt, and S. Rynes, "Corporate Social and Financial Performance: A Meta-Analysis," *Organization Studies* 24 (2003), pp. 403–41; J. Peloza, "The Challenge of Measuring Financial Impacts from Investments in Corporate Social Performance," *Journal of Management* 35 (2009), pp. 1518–41.

84. D. Turban and D. Greening, "Corporate Social Performance and Organizational Attractiveness to Prospective Employees," *Academy of Management Journal* 40 (1997), pp. 658–72.

85. A. McWilliams and D. Siegel, "Corporate Social Responsibility: A Theory of the Firm Perspective," *Academy of Management Review* 26 (2001), pp. 117–27.

86. S. L. Hart and M. B. Milstein, "Global Sustainability and the Creative Destructions of Industries," *Sloan Management Review,* Fall 1999, pp. 23–33.

87. P. M. Senge and G. Carstedt, "Innovating Our Way to the Next Industrial Revolution," *Sloan Management Review,* Winter 2001, pp. 24–38.

88. C. K. Prahalad and M. R. Rangaswami, "Why Sustainability Is Now the Key Driver of Innovation," *Harvard Business Review,* September 2009, pp. 56–64.

89. C. Holliday, "Sustainable Growth, the DuPont Way," *Harvard Business Review,* September 2001, pp. 129–34; and P. Bansal and K. Roth, "Why Companies Go Green: A Model of Ecological Responsiveness," *Academy of Management Journal* 43 (2000), pp. 717–36.

90. Company website, A Letter from the CEO, www.gesustainability.com, accessed March 14, 2017; D. Lubin and D. Esty, "The Sustainability Imperative," *Harvard Business Review,* May 2010, pp. 42–50; and R. Nidumolu, C. K. Prahalad, and M. R. Rangaswami, "Why Sustainability Is Now the Key Driver of Innovation," *Harvard Business Review,* September 2009, pp. 57–64.

91. P. Shrivastava, "Ecocentric Management for a Risk Society," *Academy of Management Review* 20 (1995), pp. 118–37.

92. Ibid.

93. Ibid.

94. Barefoot College website, https://www.barefootcollege.org/about/, accessed March 23, 2017; Tony Woodcock, "How to Change the World," *Huffington Post.com,* February 24, 2016, http://www.huffingtonpost.com/tony-woodcock/how-to-change-the-world_1_b_9274690.html; Sudipto Day, "Social Entrepreneur of the Year: A Place for Learning and Unlearning," *Business Standard,* March 8, 2017, http://www.business-standard.com/article/companies/social-entrepreneur-of-the-year-a-place-for-learning-unlearning-117030800010_1.html; "Tilonia, India: Barefoot Solar Warriors Take on Gender Injustice and Climate Change," *MenaFN.com,* November 3, 2017, http://menafn.com/1095306304/TILONIA-India-Barefoot-Solar-Warriors-Take-On-Gender-Injustice-and-Climate-Change.

95. Company website, "Our Business and Climate Change," www.patagonia.com, accessed March 14, 2017.

96. "China Pollution: Factories Closed by Beijing Smog," *BBC News,* December 19, 2015, www.bbc.com.

97. "Four-fifths of China's Water from Wells 'Unsafe Because of Pollution,'" *The Guardian,* April 12, 2016, www.theguardian. com; E. Albert, "China's Environmental Crisis," Council on Foreign Relations, January 18, 2016, www.cfr.org.

98. K. Haanaes, D. Michael, J. Jurgens, and S. Rangan, "Making Sustainability Profitable," *Harvard Business Review,* March 2013, pp. 110-14.

99. Shrivastava, "Ecocentric Management for a Risk Society."

100. M. Gunther, "Green Is Good," *Fortune,* March 22, 2007, http://money.cnn.com;

101. S. Waddock, "Leadership Integrity in a Fractured Knowledge World," *Academy of Management Learning & Education,* 2007, pp. 543-57.

102. R. Martin and A. Kemper, "Saving the Planet: A Tale of Two Strategies," *Harvard Business Review,* April 2012, pp. 48-56.

103. J. O'Toole, "Do Good, Do Well: The Business Enterprise Trust Awards," *California Management Review,* Spring 1991, pp. 9-24; and Shrivastava, "Ecocentric Management for a Risk Society."

104. Patagonia, "The Footprint Chronicles," http://www.patagonia.com, accessed March 17, 2017.

105. B. Doppelt, *Leading Change toward Sustainability* (Sheffield, UK: Greenleaf, 2010).

106. Ibid.

107. M. Magali, D. Etzion, and N. Nairn-Birch, "Triangulating Environmental Performance: What Do Corporate Social Responsibility Ratings Really Capture?" *Academy of Management Perspectives* 27 (2013), pp. 255-67; M. Russo and P. Fouts, "A Resource-Based Perspective on Corporate Environmental Performance and Profitability," *Academy of Management Journal* 40 (1997), pp. 534-59; and R. D. Klassen and D. Clay Whybark, "The Impact of Environmental Technologies on Manufacturing Performance," *Academy of Management Journal* 42 (1999), pp. 599-615.

108. Company website, "Worldwide Sales of Toyota Hybrids Surpass 9 Million Units," May 20, 2016, www.corporatenews. pressroom.toyota.com; G. Unruh and R. Etternson, "Growing Green," *Harvard Business Review,* June 2010, pp. 94-100.

109. G. Unruh and R. Etternson, "Growing Green," *Harvard Business Review,* June 2010, pp. 94-100.

110. Ibid.

111. Ibid.

112. R. Anderson, "Companies Get Serious about Water Use," *BBC News,* April 13, 2016, www.bbc.com.

113. G. Colvin, "The King of Water," *Fortune,* July 5, 2010, pp. 52-59.

114. Marriott, "Reducing Our Footprint," http://www.marriott.com, accessed March 21, 2015.

115. J. Ball, "Green Goal of 'Carbon Neutrality' Hits Limit," *The Wall Street Journal,* December 30, 2008, http://online.wsj.com; and Google Inc., "Going Green at Google," Corporate Overview:

Green Initiatives, Google Corporate home page, http://www.google.com/corporate/green/.

116. D. VanderHart, "Environmentalists and Power Companies Reached an Important—and Surprising—Agreement," *Portland Mercury,* January 13, 2016, www.portlandmercury.com.

117. G. Pinchot and E. Pinchot, *The Intelligent Organization* (San Francisco: Berrett-Koehler, 1996); and S. L. Hart, *Capitalism as the Crossroads,* 3rd ed. (Upper Saddle River, NJ: Wharton School Publishing, 2010).

118. Y. Chouinard, J. Ellison, and R. Ridgeway, "The Sustainable Economy," *Harvard Business Review,* October 2011, pp. 52-62.

119. Company website, "About GEF," Global Environment Fund, www.globalenvironmentfund.com, accessed March 17, 2017.

120. B. Walsh, "Nature: A Major Company Puts a Value on the Environment," *Time,* January 24, 2011, www.science.time.com.

121. A. Singh, "How to Help Your Company Prepare for Climate Change in 2016," *The Guardian,* January 1, 2016, www.theguardian.com.

122. S. L. Hart, "Beyond Greening: Strategies for a Sustainable World," *Harvard Business Review,* January–February 1997, pp. 66-76.

123. IBM, "Product Recycling Programs," http://www.ibm.com; A. MacArthur, "IBM's Smarter Cities Challenge Is Transforming Our World," *The New Global Citizen* (online), June 26, 2013, http://newglobalcitizen.com; IBM, "Responsibility at IBM," About IBM, http://www.ibm.com; IBM, "IBM Policies," About IBM, http:// www.ibm.com; Jen Crozier, "Urban Challenges," *Citizen IBM Blog,* November 14, 2012, http://citizenibm.com; IBM, "EPA Recognizes IBM for Climate Change Leadership," news release, March 1, 2013, http://www.ibm.com; IBM, "Sustainability on a Smarter Planet," Smarter Planet: Sustainability, http://www.ibm.com; Nick Zieminski, "IBM's 'Building Whisperer' Sees Retrofit Boom," *Chicago Tribune,* May 8, 2012, http://articles.chicagotribune.com; Verne Kopytoff, "The Complex Business of Recycling E-Waste," *Bloomberg Businessweek,* January 8, 2013, http://www.businessweek.com; IBM, "IBM's Energy Program Saves $43 Million and Avoids 175,000 Metric Tons of CO2 Emissions," news release, July 2, 2012, http://www-03.ibm.com; and Jake Smith, "IBM Plans to Hire 2,000 More Veterans," *Zdnet.com,* March 17, 2017, http://www.zdnet.com/article/ibm-announces-plans-to-hire-2000-more-veterans/.

Chapter 6

1. Anita Balakrishnan, "Jack Ma Explains the Difference between Alibaba and Amazon: 'Amazon Is More Like an Empire,'" *CNBC News,* January 18, 2017, http://www.cnbc.com/2017/01/18/jack-ma-difference-between-alibaba-and-amazon.html; Fahad Saleem, "Amazon.com, Inc. (AMZN)

vs Alibaba Group Holding Ltd (BABA): How Donald Trump's Era Can Change Everything," Library for Smart Investors.com, January 10, 2017, https://www.libraryforsmartinvestors.com/2017/01/amazon-com-inc-amzn-vs-alibaba-group-holding-ltd-baba-donald-trumps-era-can-change-everything/41370011.htm; "What Is Alibaba," http://projects.wsj.com/alibaba/, accessed March 23, 2017; Frank Lavin, "Why Alibaba in America Is the Growth We Need to Support," *Forbes,* January 16, 2017, https://www.forbes.com/sites/franklavin/2017/01/16/why-alibaba-in-america-is-the-growth-we-need-to-support-trump-jack-ma/#143011375678; Haley Petersen, "A Company Many Americans Have Never Heard of Just Shattered Every Shopping Record," *Business Insider,* November 11, 2016, http://www.businessinsider.com/singles-day-alibaba-sales-2016-11; Sherisse Pham, "Alibaba's Singles Day: World's Biggest Shopping Bonanza Sets New Record," *Money.CNN.com,* November 11, 2016, http://money.cnn.com/2016/11/10/technology/alibaba-singles-day-shopping-festival-breaks-records/.

2. B. Tita, "Harley-Davidson Gets Boost from Overseas Sales, Marketing; Motorcycle Maker Tops Sales, Profit Expectations and Backs Projections for Shipments," *The Wall Street Journal,* April 19, 2016, www.wsj.com.

3. J. Mullen, "Is Shanghai Disney's Magic Wearing Off Already?" *CNNMoney,* October 5, 2016, www.cnn.money.com; T. Smith, "First Look: Shanghai Disney Resort Images Revealed," *Disney Parks blog,* February 3, 2015, http://www.disneyparks.com; B. Fritz and J. Areddy, "Shanghai Disneyland Opening Pushed to First Half of 2016," *The Wall Street Journal* (online), February 2, 2015.

4. S. Gandel, "The Biggest American Companies Now Owned by the Chinese," *Fortune,* March 18, 2016, www.fortuned.com.

5. K. Mays, "The 2016 Cars.com American-Made Index," June 28, 2016, www.cars.com.

6. "General Motors Sold 10 Million Cars in a Year for the First Time in Its Century-Plus History," *CNNMoney,* February 7, 2017, www.cnn.money.com.

7. "Colorado Software Company AppIt Ventures Acquires London Software Shop," news release, January 25, 2017, www.businessnewswire.com.

8. M. Chui, J. Manyika, and M. Miremadi, "Where Machines Could Replace Humans—and Where They Can't (Yet)," *McKinsey Quarterly,* July 2016, www.mckinsey.com.

9. Ibid.

10. D. Whitford, "Where in the World Is Cheap Labor?" *Fortune,* March 22, 2011, http://money.cnn.com.

11. "Philippines Outsourcing Firms Hit by Trump and 'Trump East,'" Reuters, December 8, 2016, www.reuters.com.

12. "Home or Abroad? Herd Instinct," *The Economist* (online), January 19, 2013, http://www.economist.com.

13. N. McLernon and J. Walters, "Insourcing Survey 2014," PricewaterhouseCoopers (online), March 2014, http://www.pwc.com; D. Anderson, J. Tweardy, M. Mancher, P. Lowes, J. Montrosse, and S. Chitre, "From Bangalore to Boston: The Trend of Bringing IT Back In-house," Deloitte (online), February 2013, http://www.deloitte.com.

14. C. Lombardi, "Survey: Software Companies Increasing Offshoring Work," C/Net News, January 12, 2007, http://news.com.com; "When Staying Put Trumps Offshoring," McKinsey Quarterly, December 7, 2004, online; and C. Koepfer, "A Look at Total Cost Can Change the View," Production Machining, January 2011, p. 6.

15. A. Rinke, E. Pineau, and A. Macdonald, "EU Founders Speak of Possible 'Multispeed' Future after Brexit," Reuters, February 3, 2017, www.reuters.com.

16. European Union, "About the EU," www.europa.eu; European Union, "Living in the EU," www.europa.eu.

17. S. Erlanger, "Britain Votes to Leave E.U.; Cameron Plans to Step Down," The New York Times, June 23, 2016, www.nytimes.com.

18. R. Noack, "These Countries Could Be Next Now That Britain Has Left the E.U.," The Washington Post, June 24, 2016.

19. Rinke et al., "EU Founders Speak of Possible 'Multispeed' Future after Brexit."

20. European Union, "The Euro," www.europa.eu.

21. "The Priceline Group Agrees to Acquire Momondo Group," press release, The Priceline Group, February 7, 2017, www.prnewswire.com.

22. C. Groden, "Dunkin' Donuts Has Big Plans to Expand in Europe," Fortune, February 11, 2016, www.fortune.com.

23. M. Scott, "What U.S. Tech Giants Face in Europe in 2017," The New York Times, January 1, 2017, www.nytimes.com.

24. Ibid.

25. World Trade Organization, "World Trade Developments," Table 1.7.

26. Alex Frangos, "Behind China's Switch to High-End Exports," The Wall Street Journal, March 24, 2013, http://online.wsj.com; and Yajun Zhang, "China Begins to Lose Edge as World's Factory Floor," The Wall Street Journal, January 16, 2013, http://online.wsj.com.

27. "Three Snapshots of Chinese Innovation," McKinsey Quarterly, February 2012, http://www.mckinseyquarterly.com.

28. N. Gan, "Hard Times ahead for China's Economy, says Alibaba Tycoon," CNBC, January 26, 2017; "China's Economy Grows at 6.7% in 2016," BBC, January 20, 2017, www.bbc.com.

29. J. Mendoca and N. Alawadhi, "IT Firms Are Spending Millions to Train Workforce to Meet Increasing Demand for Digital Services," Economic Times, October 21, 2015, www.tech.economictimes.indiatimes.com.

30. C. Miller, "Latest Gartner Data Shows Apple Edge Out Samsung in Market Share During Q4 2016," 9to5Mac, February 15, 2017, www.9to5mac.com.

31. "How Taiwan's Hon Hai Exemplified a Historic Turn in Asian Tiger Manufacturing," Forbes Asia, March 2017, www.forbes.com.

32. Office of the United States Trade Representative, "U.S.–APEC Trade Facts," http://www.ustr.gov, accessed March 20, 2017.

33. "Economic Outlook for Southeast Asia, China, and India 2017," OECD, January 23, 2017, www.oecd.org.

34. "NAFTA's Impact on the U.S. Economy: What Are the Facts?" Knowledge at Wharton Partners, September 6, 2016, www.knowledge.wharton.upenn.edu.

35. A. van Agtmael, "Industrial Revolution 2.0," Foreign Policy, January–February 2007, Business & Company Company Resource Center, http://galenet.galegroup.com; and CEMEX website, http://www.cemex.com.

36. L. Gerbelli, "Economists Turn Bullish on Brazil 2017 Growth as Interest Rates Fall," Reuters, February 14, 2017, www.reuters.com; "Brazil: Economic Forecast Summary," OECD, November 2016, www.oecd.org.

37. K. Gilchrist, "Brazil's Economy Heats Up for Rio Carnival," February 2, 2017, www.cnbc.com.

38. "Trade Summary for Brazil," World Integrated Trade Solution—World Bank, www.wits.worldbank.org, accessed March 20, 2017.

39. "Start-Up Chile Impact," www.startupchile.org, accessed March 20, 2017.

40. Hult Prize website, "2015 Hult Prize Online Challenge," http://www.hultprize.org, accessed March 26, 2015; Hult Prize website, "2016 Hult Prize Winners Set to Double Income of Urban Slum Dwellers," http://www.hultprize.org, accessed March 27, 2017; D. Thorpe, "President Clinton Presents Hult Prize to Indian Social Entrepreneurs," Forbes (online), October 22, 2014, http://www.hultprize.org, accessed March 26, 2015; and Parija Kavalanz, "Can Magic Bus Double Incomes of Slum Dwellers?" CNNTech.com, September 22, 2016, http://money.cnn.com/2016/09/21/technology/hult-prize-winner-magic-bus/.

41. Office of the United States Trade Representative, "Free Trade Agreements," http://www.ustr.gov.

42. R. Rapier, "Where America Gets Its Oil: The Top 10 Foreign Suppliers of Crude to the U.S.," Forbes, April 11, 2016, www.forbes.com.

43. M. Egan, "Here Comes the Next Wave of the U.S. Oil Boom," CNNMoney, February 17, 2017, www.money.cnn.com; M. Philips, "U.S. Oil Imports from Africa Are Down 90 Percent," Bloomberg Business (online), May 22, 2014, http://www.bloomberg.com; and K. Dhillon, "Why Are U.S. Oil Imports Falling?" Time (online), April 17, 2014, http://www.time.com.

44. F. Aquila, "Africa's Biggest Score: A Thriving Economy," Bloomberg Businessweek, June 28, 2010, http://www.businessweek.com; Sarah Frier, "For IBM, Africa Is Risky and Rife with Opportunity," Bloomberg Businessweek, February 21, 2013, http://www.businessweek.com.

45. H. Hong and Y. Doz, "L'Oréal Masters Multiculturalism," Harvard Business Review, June 2013, http://www.hbr.org.

46. "Yum China Launches Taco Bell Brand in China," Yum China Holdings press release, January 9, 2017, www.prnewswire.com.

47. S. Kannan, "How McDonald's Conquered India," BBC, November 19, 2014, www.bbc.com.

48. C. Riley, "U.S. Hikes Duties on Chinese Steel to More Than 500%," CNNMoney, May 18, 2016, www.money.cnn.com.

49. A. Illmer, "What's behind China's Cheap Steel Exports?" BBC, April 25, 2016, www.bbc.com.

50. J. Perlez and C. Buckley, "Trump Injects High Risk into Relations with China," The New York Times, January 24, 2017, www.nytimes.com.

51. Heineken website, www.theheinekencompany.com, accessed March 20, 2017.

52. S. Elliott, "Ford Tries a Global Campaign for Its Global Car," The New York Times, February 25, 2011, Business & Company Resource Center, http://galenet.galegroup.com.

53. "Ford Focus Tops Global Sales List," The Economist Intelligence Unit, April 10, 2014, http://www.eiu.com.

54. A.-W. Harzing, "An Empirical Analysis and Extension of the Bartlett and Ghoshal Typology of Multinational Companies," Journal of International Business Studies 31, no. 1 (2000), pp. 101–20; Sucheta Nadkarni, Pol Herrmann, and Pedro David Perez, "Domestic Mindsets and Early International Performance: The Moderating Effect of Global Industry Conditions," Strategic Management Journal 32, no. 5 (May 2011), pp. 510–31; S. M. Morris and S. A. Snell, "Intellectual Capital Configurations and Organizational Capability: An Empirical Examination of Human Resource Subunits in the Multinational Enterprise," Journal of International Business Studies 42, no. 6 (2011), pp. 805–27; and Elaine Ferndale, Jaap Paauwe, Shad S. Morris, Günther K. Stahl, Philip Stiles, Jonathan Trevor, and Patrick M. Wright, "Context-Bound Configurations of Corporate HR Functions in Multinational Corporations," Human Resource Management 49, no. 1 (January–February 2010), pp. 45–66.

55. J. Sandberg, "How Long Can India Keep Office Politics out of Outsourcing?" The Wall Street Journal, February 27, 2007, http://online.wsj.com.

56. Sherisse Pham, "Alibaba's Singles Day: World's Biggest Shopping Bonanza Sets New Record," Money.CNN.com, November 11, 2016, http://money.cnn.com/2016/11/10/technology/alibaba-singles-day-shopping-festival-breaks-records/; Lavin, "Why Alibaba in America Is the Growth We Need to Support"; Daniel Geiger, "Chinese E-Commerce Giant Alibaba Expands Downtown Manhattan Headquarters,"

Crain's, December 27, 2016, http://www.crainsnewyork.com/article/20161227/REAL_ESTATE/161229944/chinese-online-retail-giant-alibaba-expands-lower-manhattan-headquarters-as-it-plans-new-york-expansion-known-as-an-alternative-to-amazon-the-hangzhou-based-company-founded-by-billionaire-jack-ma-is-valued-at-200-billion.

57. Toshiro Wakayama, Junjiro Shintaku, and Tomofumi Amano, "What Panasonic Learned in China," *Harvard Business Review,* December 2012, pp. 109–113; and Daisuke Wakabayashi, "Panasonic to Pare Unprofitable Units," *The Wall Street Journal,* March 28, 2013, http://online.wsj.com.

58. C. H. Moon, "The Choice of Entry Modes and Theories of Foreign Direct Investment," *Journal of Global Marketing* 11, no. 2 (1997), pp. 43–64; and I. Maignan and B. A. Lukas, "Entry Mode Decisions: The Role of Managers' Mental Models," *Journal of Global Marketing* 10, no. 4 (1997), pp. 7–22.

59. A. Tangel, "U.S. Trade Officials Back Whirlpool Washer Dumping Complaint," *The Wall Street Journal,* January 10, 2017, www.wsj.com.

60. "Netflix Joins Ranks of U.S. Tech Companies Admitting They Can't Conquer China," *Marketwatch,* October 24, 2016, www.marketwatch.com.

61. "2016 Top Global Franchises," *Entrepreneur,* www.entrepreneur.com, accessed March 20, 2017.

62. "7-Eleven® Tops Entrepreneur's 2017 Franchise 500," company press release, January 10, 2017, www.prnewswire.com.

63. Company website, "About Kunshan University—Overview," www.dukekunshan.edu.cn, accessed March 20, 2017; "Western Universities Expanding Joint Ventures in China," *ICEF Monitor* (online), September 30, 2014, http://monitor.icef.com.

64. S. Oster, N. Shirouzu, and P. Glader, "China Squeezes Foreigners for Share of Global Riches," *The Wall Street Journal,* December 28, 2010, http://online.wsj.com.

65. R. C. Beasley, "Reducing the Risk of Failure in the Formation of Commercial Partnerships," *Licensing Journal* 24, no. 4 (April 2004), p. 71; and Elie Chrysostome, Roli Nigam, and Chaire Stephen Jarilowski, "Revisiting Strategic Learning in International Joint Ventures: A Knowledge Creation Perspective," *International Journal of Management* 30, no. 1 (March 2013), pp. 88–98.

66. K. Hille, "Western Faces Are Vital to China," *Financial Times,* December 9, 2010, Business & Company Resource Center, http://galenet.galegroup.com; and J. S. Lublin, "Finding Top Talent in China, India, Brazil," *The Wall Street Journal,* April 11, 2011, http://online.wsj.com.

67. R. Tung, "Selection and Training of Personnel for Overseas Assignments," *Columbia Journal of World Business* 15 (1981), pp. 68–78; and R. Tung, "Selection and Training Procedures of U.S., European,

and Japanese Multinationals," *California Management Review* 25 (1981), pp. 57–71.

68. A. W. Andreason, "Expatriate Adjustment to Foreign Assignments," *International Journal of Commerce and Management* 13, no. 1 (Spring 2003), pp. 42–61.

69. P. Capell, "Know before You Go: Expats' Advice to Couples," *Career Journal Europe,* May 2, 2006, htp://www.careerjournaleurope.com; and Mila Lazarova, Mina Westman, and Margaret A. Shaffer, "Elucidating the Positive Side of the Work-Family Interface on International Assignments: A Model of Expatriate Work and Family Performance," *Academy of Management Review* 35, no. 1 (January 2010), pp. 93–117.

70. R. A. Swaak, "Expatriate Failures: Too Many, Too Much Cost, Too Little Planning," *Compensation & Benefits Review,* November–December 1995, pp. 50–52.

71. G. M. Sprietzer, M. W. McCall, and J. D. Mahoney, "Early Identification of International Executive Potential," *Journal of Applied Psychology* 82, no. 1 (1997), pp. 6–29; R. Mortensen, "Beyond the Fence Line," *HRMagazine,* November 1997, pp. 100–9; "Expatriate Games," *Journal of Business Strategy,* July–August 1997, pp. 4–5; "Building a Global Workforce Starts with Recruitment," *Personnel Journal* (special supplement), March 1996, pp. 9–11; Ming Li, William H. Mobley, and Aidan Kelly, "When Do Global Leaders Learn Best to Develop Cultural Intelligence? An Investigation of the Moderating Role of Experiential Learning Style," *Academy of Management Learning & Education* 12, no. 1 (March 2013), pp. 32–50; and Nicola M. Pless, Thomas Maak, and Günther K. Stahl, "Developing Responsible Global Leaders through International Service-Learning Programs: The Ulysses Experience," *Academy of Management Learning & Education* 10, no. 2 (June 2011), pp. 237–60.

72. John Slocum, "Coming to America," *Human Resource Executive,* October 2, 2008, http://www.hrexecutive.com.

73. E. Meyer, *The Culture Map* (New York: Public Affairs, 2014); J. Brett, K. Behfar, and M. C. Kern, "Managing Multicultural Teams," *Harvard Business Review,* November 2006, pp. 84–91.

74. PricewaterhouseCoopers website, "Millennials Survey: Millennials at Work: Reshaping the Workplace," http://www.pwc.com, accessed March 26, 2015.

75. Meyer, *The Culture Map*; D. Stamps, "Welcome to America," *Training,* November 1996, pp. 23–30.

76. L. K. Trevino and K. A. Nelson, *Managing Business Ethics: Straight Talk about How to Do It Right* (New York: John Wiley & Sons, 1995).

77. Transparency International, "Leading Exporters Undermine Development with Dirty Business Overseas," news release, October 4, 2006, http://www.transparency.org.

78. Lavin, "Why Alibaba in America Is the Growth We Need to Support"; Cao

Li, "Alibaba Faces Growing Pressure over Counterfeit Goods," *The New York Times,* December 22, 2016, https://www.nytimes.com/2016/12/22/business/alibaba-ustr-taobao-counterfeit.html?_r=0; Arjun Kharpal, "Alibaba Sues Sellers of Counterfeit Goods for the First Time after It Was Blacklisted by the U.S.," CNBC.com, January 4, 2017, http://www.cnbc.com/2017/01/04/alibaba-sues-sellers-of-counterfeit-goods-for-the-first-time-after-it-was-blacklisted-by-the-us.html.

79. A. B. Desai and T. Rittenburg, "Global Ethics: An Integrative Framework for MNEs," *Journal of Business Ethics* 16 (1997), pp. 791–800; and P. Buller, J. Kohls, and K. Anderson, "A Model for Addressing Cross-Cultural Ethical Conflicts," *Business & Society* 36, no. 2 (June 1997), pp. 169–93.

Chapter 7

1. Company website, www.starbucks.com, accessed March 31, 2017; Catherine Clifford, "How Starbucks' Howard Schultz Went from the Projects to Creating 300,000 Jobs and a $3 Billion Fortune," CNBC.com, December 2, 2016, http://www.cnbc.com/2016/12/02/how-starbucks-howard-schultz-went-from-the-projects-to-creating-300000-jobs-and-a-3-billion-fortune.html; Daniel B. Kline, "Wal-Mart and Starbucks Are Trying to Think Like Start-Ups," *Motley Fool,* March 16, 2017, https://www.fool.com/investing/2017/03/16/wal-mart-and-starbucks-are-trying-to-think-like-st.aspx.

2. S. Shane and S. Venkataraman, "The Promise of Entrepreneurship as a Field of Research," *Academy of Management Review* 25 (2000), pp. 217–26.

3. J. A. Timmons, *New Venture Creation* (Burr Ridge, IL: Richard D. Irwin, 1994).

4. Shane and Venkataraman, "The Promise of Entrepreneurship as a Field of Research."

5. M. A. Hitt, R. D. Ireland, D. Sirmon, and C. Trahms, "Strategic Entrepreneurship: Creating Value for Individuals, Organizations, and Society," *Academy of Management Perspectives,* May 2011, pp. 57–75.

6. W. Megginson, M. J. Byrd, S. R. Scott Jr., and L. Megginson, *Small Business Management: An Entrepreneur's Guide to Success,* 2nd ed. (Boston: Irwin McGraw-Hill, 1997).

7. "Summary of Size Standards by Industry Sector," U.S. Small Business Administration, February 26, 2016, www.sba.gov.

8. J. Timmons and S. Spinelli, *New Venture Creation: Entrepreneurship for the 21st Century,* 6th ed. (New York: McGraw-Hill/Irwin, 2004), p. 3.

9. J. A. Timmons, *The Entrepreneurial Mind* (Andover, MA: Brick House, 1989).

10. J. Clifton, "American Entrepreneurship: Dead or Alive?" *Gallup Business Journal,* January 13, 2015, http://www.gallup.com; B. Casselman, "Risk-Averse Culture Infects

U.S. Workers, Entrepreneurs," *The Wall Street Journal,* June 2, 2013, p. A1.

11. J. Hecht, "Are Small Businesses Really the Backbone of the Economy?" *Inc.* (online), December 17, 2014, http://www.inc.com.

12. D. J. Isenberg, "The Global Entrepreneur," *Harvard Business Review,* December 2008, pp. 107–11.

13. "Small Business, Big Impact!" U.S. Small Business Administration, www.sba.gov, accessed March 25, 2017.

14. Timmons and Spinelli, *New Venture Creation.*

15. Ibid.

16. R. Arend, H. Sarooghi, and A. Burkemper, "Effectuation as Ineffectual? Applying the 3E Theory-Assessment Framework to a Proposed New Theory of Entrepreneurship," *Academy of Management Review,* 40(2015), 630–51.

17. D. Bricklin, "Natural-Born Entrepreneur," *Harvard Business Review,* September 2001, pp. 53–59,58.

18. S. Ramoglou and E. W. K. Tsang, "A Realist Perspective of Entrepreneurship: Opportunities as Propensities," *Academy of Management Review,* 41, (2016), pp. 410–34; D. Williams, "The 4 Essential Traits of 'Intrapreneurs,'" *Forbes* (online), October 30, 2013, http://www.forbes.com; and Alexandra Levit, "'Insider' Entrepreneurs," *The Wall Street Journal,* April 6, 2009, http://online.wsj.com.

19. Hitt et al., "Strategic Entrepreneurship: Creating Value for Individuals, Organizations, and Society.

20. T. Hsieh, "Why I Sold Zappos," *Inc.* (online), June 1, 2010, http://www.inc.com.

21. R. Fairlie, "Kaufman Index of Entrepreneurial Activity," Ewing Marion Kauffman Foundation, April 2014, http://www.kaufmann.org; and C. Conner, "Who's Starting America's New Businesses? And Why?" *Forbes,* July 22, 2012.

22. J. Jennings and C. Brush, "Research on Women Entrepreneurs: Challenges to (and from) the Broader Entrepreneurship Literature?" *Academy of Management Annals* 7 (2013), pp. 663–715; inDinero, "About inDinero," http://www.indinero.com, accessed March 25, 2017; "Coolest College Start-Ups: Where Are They Now?" *Inc.,* March 2011, http://www.inc.com; E. Lee, "The Small-Business Numbers Cruncher," *San Francisco Chronicle,* January 3, 2011, Business & Company Resource Center, http://galenet.galegroup.com.

23. J. Raffiee and J. Feng, "Should I Quit My Day Job?" *Academy of Management Journal,* 57 (2014), pp. 936–63.

24. M. Solomon, "How a Laid-Off Corporate Worker Turned a Love of Travel into a Thriving Entrepreneurial Business," *Inc.,* March 28, 2016, www.inc.com.

25. Ibid.

26. H. Aldrich, *Ethnic Entrepreneurs: Immigrant Business in Industrial Societies* (Newbury Park, CA: Sage, 1990).

27. R. Waldinger, "A Cross-Border Perspective on Migration: Beyond the Assimilation/Transnationalism Debate," *Journal of Ethnic and Migration Studies* 43, no. 1 (2016), pp. 3–17.

28. "Billionaire Immigrants," *Forbes* (online), http://www.forbes.com, accessed March 27, 2015; "Elon Musk," Biography (online), http://www.biography.com, accessed March 29, 2015.

29. Jennings and Brush, "Research on Woman Entrepreneurs": Timmons and Spinelli, *New Venture Creation.*

30. J. Collins and J. Porras, *Built to Last* (London: Century, 1996).

31. Ibid.

32. Jennings and Brush, "Research on Women Entrepreneurs": C. Navis and O. V. Ozbek, "The Right People in the Wrong Places: The Paradox of Entrepreneurial Entry and Successful Opportunity Realization," *Academy of Management Review* 41 (2016), pp. 109–29; and K. H. Vesper, *New Venture Mechanics* (Englewood Cliffs, NJ: Prentice Hall, 1993).

33. "Entrepreneur of 2012: Limor Fried," *Entrepreneur,* December 18, 2012, http://www.entrepreneur.com.

34. Vesper, *New Venture Mechanics.*

35. Johnson & Johnson, "Johnson & Johnson Announces Definitive Agreement to Collaborate with Google to Advance Surgical Robotics," press release, March 26, 2015, http://www.jnj.com.

36. D. Internicola, "New Fitness Centers Cater to Aging Baby Boomers," Reuters, January 7, 2013, http://www.reuters.com.

37. Timmons and Spinelli, *New Venture Creation.*

38. P. J. Sauer, "Serving Up Success," *Inc.,* January 2007, http://www.inc.com.

39. Panera, "Our History," http://www.panera.com, accessed March 29, 2015.

40. Timmons and Spinelli, *New Venture Creation.*

41. D. Fenn, "30 Under 30," *Inc.,* July 2, 2012.

42. Bigelow Aerospace, "The First Private Space Habitat Is Here," http://www.bigelowaerospace.com, accessed March 29, 2015; "Innovation: Inside the Space Station," *Inc.,* April 1, 2013, http://www.inc.com; and Andy Pasztor, "Nerve-Wracking Space Drama Swirls around Unmanned Cargo Capsulc," *The Wall Street Journal,* March 1, 2013, http://online.wsj.com.

43. J. J. Colao, "America's Most Promising Company Is Redefining Mobile: Meet 3Cinteractive," *Forbes,* January 23, 2013, http://www.forbes.com; Justine Griffin, "John Duffy, Small Business Leader, Palm Beach County," *South Florida Sun-Sentinel,* April 26, 2012, http://www.sun-sentinel.com; and 3Cinteractive, "About 3Cinteractive," http://www.3cinteractive.com/About/.

44. J. E. Lange, "Entrepreneurs and the Continuing Internet: The Expanding Frontier," in J. Timmons and S. Spinelli, *New Venture Creation: Entrepreneurship for the 21st Century,* 6th ed. (New York: McGraw-Hill/Irwin, 2004), pp. 183–220.

45. Ibid.

46. "Coca-Cola and Nely Galan Honor Latinas on International Women's Day and Beyond," *Yahoo Finance,* March 29, 2015, http://finance.yahoo.com; "Pioneer Studio Executive & Philanthropist," *Makers* (online), http://www.makers.com, accessed March 29, 2015; S. Cole, "Meet the Woman Inspiring Thousands of American Latina Entrepreneurs," *Fast Company* (online), March 16, 2015, http://www.fastcompany.com; D. Parnell, "Media Mogul Nely Galan, on Succeeding through Diversity," *Forbes* (online), March 13, 2015, http://www.forbes.com; and "Inspiring Latina: Businesswoman and Entertainment Mogul Nely Galan," *Latina* (online), June 10, 2014, http://www.latina.com.

47. J. E. Vascellaro, "Selling Your Designs Online," *The Wall Street Journal,* April 5, 2007, http://online.wsj.com.

48. J. Short, T. Moss, and G. Lumpkin, "Research in Social Entrepreneurship: Past, Contributions and Future Opportunities," *Strategic Entrepreneurship Journal* 3 (2009), pp. 161–94; and S. Zahra and M. Wright, "Entrepreneur's Next Act," *Academy of Management Perspectives,* 2011, pp. 67–83.

49. P. Dacin, M. T. Dacin, and M. Matear, "Social Entrepreneurship: Why We Don't Need a New Theory and How We Move Forward from Here," *Academy of Management Perspectives* 24 (2010), pp. 37–57.

50. J. Battilan, M. Sengul, A. C. Pache, and J. Model, "Harnessing Productive Tensions in Hybrid Organizations: The Case of Work Integration Social Enterprises," *Academy of Management Journal* 58 (2015), pp. 1658–85.

51. T. Miller, M. Grimes, J. McMullen, and T. Vogus, "Venturing for Others with Heart and Head: How Compassion Encourages Social Entrepreneurship," *Academy of Management Review* 37 (2012), pp. 616–40.

52. J. Mair and I. Marti, "Social Entrepreneurship Research: A Source of Explanation, Prediction, and Delight," *Journal of World Business* 41 (2006), pp. 36–44.

53. D. Bornstein and S. Davis, *Social Entrepreneurship: What Everyone Needs to Know* (Oxford, UK: Oxford University Press, 2010).

54. Schwab Foundation for Social Entrepreneurship, "Social Entrepreneurs," http://www.schwabfound.org/entrepreneurs, accessed March 29, 2015.

55. Ibid.

56. Ibid.

57. M. Driver, "An Interview with Michael Porter: Social Entrepreneurship and the Transformation of Capitalism," *Academy of Management Learning & Education* 11 (2012), pp. 421–31.

58. M. Porter and M. Kramer, "Creating Shared Value," *Harvard Business Review* (January–February 2011), pp. 62–77.

59. H. Sabeti, "The For-Benefit Enterprise," *Harvard Business Review,* November 2011, pp. 98–194.

60. P. Omidyar, "eBay's Founder on Innovating the Business Model of Social Change," *Harvard Business Review,* September 2011, pp. 41–44.

61. Timmons, *New Venture Creation.*

62. M. Cardon, J. Wincent, J. Singh, and M. Drnovsek, "The Nature and Experience of Entrepreneurial Passion," *Academy of Management Review* 34 (2009), pp. 511–32.

63. J. R. Baum and E. A. Locke, "The Relationship of Entrepreneurial Traits, Skill, and Motivation to Subsequent Venture Growth," *Journal of Applied Psychology* 89 (2004), pp. 587–98.

64. M. Sonfield and R. Lussier, "The Entrepreneurial Strategy Matrix: A Model for New and Ongoing Ventures," *Business Horizons,* May–June 1997, pp. 73–77.

65. Lange, "Entrepreneurs and the Continuing Internet".

66. Rafflee and Feng, "Should I Quit My Day Job?" pp. and S. Venkataraman and M. Low, "On the Nature of Critical Relationships: A Test of the Liabilities and Size Hypothesis," in *Frontiers of Entrepreneurship Research* (Babson Park, MA: Babson College, 1991), p. 97.

67. Timmons and Spinelli, *New Venture Creation.*

68. Company website, www.starbucks.com, accessed March 31, 2017; Clifford, "How Starbucks' Howard Schultz Went from the Projects to Creating 300,000 Jobs and a $3 Billion Fortune"; Kline, "Wal-Mart and Starbucks Are Trying to Think Like Start-Ups"; Daniel B. Kline, "Starbucks' 4 Biggest Product Flops and Failures," *Motley Fool,* January 23, 2016, https://www.fool.com/investing/general/2016/01/23/starbucks-x-biggest-product-flops-and-failures.aspx; Daniel B. Kline, "Starbucks' Fizzio Soda Line Has Gone Flat," *Motley Fool,* October 7, 2016, https://www.fool.com/investing/2016/10/07/starbucks-fizzio-soda-line-has-gone-flat.aspx.

69. L. Buchanan, "Create Jobs, Eliminate Waste, Preserve Value," *Inc.,* December 2006, pp. 94–106.

70. I. Hathaway, "What Startup Accelerators Really Do," *Harvard Business Review,* March 1, 2016. www.hbr.org.

71. Company website, www.techstars.com; Company website, www.ycombinator.com; Company website, www.startupbootcamp.com; "Getting Up to Speed," *The Economist,* January 16, 2014, www.theeconomist.com.

72. Hathaway, "What Startup Accelerators Really Do.

73. Norm Brodsky, "Street Smarts: Our Irrational Fear of Numbers," *Inc.,* January 2009, http://www.inc.com.

74. Jeremy Quittner, "Robin Chase: How I Survived a Huge Screw-Up," *Inc.,* February 28, 2013, http://www.inc.com.

75. S. E. Needleman, "When It's Time to Take On Help," *The Wall Street Journal,* January 16, 2011, http://online.wsj.com.

76. L. Kanter, "The Eco-Advantage," *Inc.,* November 2006, pp. 78–103.

77. Company website, www.basecamp.com, accessed March 25, 2017; and J. Stillman,

"Slow Business: The Case against Fast Growth," *Inc.* (online), September 18, 2012, http://www.inc.com.

78. S. Finkelstein, "The Myth of Managerial Superiority in Internet Startups: An Autopsy," *Organizational Dynamics,* Fall 2001, pp. 172–85.

79. K. Hickey, "5 Lessons from Managing Our Startup's Rapid Growth," *Forbes* (online), April 9, 2013, http://www.forbes.com.

80. R. Weisman, "Bootstrappers Avoid Outside Money Ties," *Boston Globe,* February 5, 2007, Business & Company Resource Center, http://galenet.galegroup.com.

81. A. Cordeiro, "Sweet Returns," *The Wall Street Journal* (online), April 23, 2009, http://www.wsj.com.

82. L. Bolelovic, "Most Companies Don't Last 50 Years, but These Pittsburgh Businesses Have," *Pittsburgh Post-Gazette,* December 19, 2016, www.post-gazette.com; G. Stalk and H. Foley "Avoid the Traps That Can Destroy Family Businesses," *Harvard Business Review,* (January–February, 2012) pp. 25–27.

83. P. F. Drucker, "How to Save the Family Business," *The Wall Street Journal,* August 19, 1994, p. A10.

84. D. Gamer, R. Owen, and R. Conway, *The Ernst & Young Guide to Raising Capital* (New York: John Wiley & Sons, 1991).

85. Ibid.

86. R. D. Hisrich and M. P. Peters, *Entrepreneurship: Starting, Developing, and Managing a New Enterprise* (Burr Ridge, IL: Irwin, 1994).

87. Ibid.

88. Small Business Administration, "Frequently Asked Questions about Small Business Finance," SBA Office of Advocacy, September 2011, http://www.sba.gov; and Ewing Marion Kauffman Foundation, "Six Myths about Venture Capital Offer Dose of Reality to Startups in *Harvard Business Review* Article," news release, April 16, 2013, http://www.kauffman.org.

89. Lending Club, "Business Loans," http://www.lendingclub.com, accessed March 31, 2015; Prosper, "Company Overview," http://www.prosper.com, accessed March 31, 2015; and I. Mount, "When Banks Won't Lend, There Are Alternatives, though Often Expensive," *The New York Times* (online), August 1, 2012, http://www.nytimes.com.

90. M. Zeidel, "The JOBS Act: Did It Accomplish Its Goals?" Corporate Governance and Financial Regulation, Harvard Law School, July 18, 2016, www.corporate.law.harvard.edu; "JOBS Act, One Year Later: Hang Tight, Equity Crowdfunding Is Coming," *Entrepreneur,* April 5, 2013, http://www.entrepreneur.com; "Crowdfunding Industry on Fire: Trends to Watch," *Entrepreneur,* April 8, 2013, http://www.entrepreneur.com; Becky Yerak, "Is Promise Worth Peril?" *Chicago Tribune,* February 24, 2013, sec. 2, pp. 1, 3; and Sarah E. Needleman and Lora Kolodny, "Site Unseen: More 'Angels' Invest via Internet," *The Wall Street Journal,* January 23, 2013, http://online.wsj.com.

91. W. A. Sahlman, "How to Write a Great Business Plan," *Harvard Business Review,* July–August 1997, pp. 98–108.

92. Ibid.

93. M. Copeland, "Start Last, Finish First," *Business 2.0 Magazine* (online), February 2, 2006, http://www.money.cnn.com.

94. Sahlman, "How to Write a Great Business Plan".

95. B. Hallen and E. C. Pahnke, 'When Do Entrepreneurs Accurately Evaluate Venture Capital Firms' Track Records? A Bounded Rationality Perspective," *Academy of Management Journal* 59 (2016), pp. 1535–60; L. Huang and A. Knight, "The Development and Effects of the Entrepreneur-Investor Relationship," *Academy of Management Review* 42 (2017), pp. 80–102.

96. M. Zimmerman and G. Zeitz, "Beyond Survival: Achieving New Venture Growth by Building Legitimacy," *Academy of Management Review* 27 (2002), pp. 414–21.

97. A. L. Stinchcombe, "Social Structure and Organizations," in J. G. March, ed., *Handbook of Organizations* (Chicago: Rand McNally, 1965), pp. 142–193.

98. Ibid.

99. L. Taylor, "Want Your Start-Up to Be Successful? Appearance Is Everything," *Inc.,* February 23, 2007, http://www.inc.com.

100. Ibid.

101. R. A. Baron and G. D. Markman, "Beyond Social Capital: How Social Skills Can Enhance Entrepreneurs' Success," *Academy of Management Executive,* February 2000, pp. 106–16.

102. J. Florin, M. Lubatkin, and W. Schulze, "A Social Capital Model of High-Growth Ventures," *Academy of Management Journal* 46 (2003), pp. 374–84.

103. "M. Ferringer, "Sport Clips Founder & CEO Gordon Logan Named 2016 IFA Entrepreneur of the Year," International Franchise Association website, December 9, 2016, www.ifa.1851franchise.com.

104. J. Jao, "What Can Seasoned Entrepreneurs Teach Millennial Entrepreneurs?" *Forbes,* January 13, 2016, www.forbes.com; N. Fallow, "6 Ways to Keep Control of a Fast-Growing Startup," Fox Small Business Center, May 23, 2014, http://www.foxbusiness.com; and "Baby Boomers, Who Are More Successful as Entrepreneurs, Are Great Startup Assets," *Entrepreneur* (online), October 24, 2014, http://www.entrepreneur.com.

105. A. J. Kacperczyk, "Opportunity Structures in Established Firms: Entrepreneurship versus Intrapreneurship in Mutual Funds," *Administrative Science Quarterly* 57 (2012), pp. 484–521; S. C. Parker, "Intrapreneurship or Entrepreneurship?" *Journal of Business Venturing* 26 (2011), pp. 19–34.

106. R. M. Kanter, *The Change Masters* (New York: Simon & Schuster, 1983).

107. W.L. Gore, "Consumer Products," http://www.gore.com, accessed March 31, 2015; R. Kneece, "10 Inspiring Examples of Successful Intrapreneurship," *Wired*

(online), September 17, 2014, http://www
.wired.com; and R. Safian, "Terri Kelli, the
'Un-CEO' of W.L. Gore, on How to Deal
with Chaos: Grow Up," *Fast Company,*
October 29, 2012, http://www.fastcompany.
com.

108. R. M. Kanter, C. Ingols, E. Morgan, and
T. K. Seggerman, "Driving Corporate
Entrepreneurship," *Management Review* 76
(April 1987), pp. 14–16.

109. J. Argenti, *Corporate Collapse: The Causes
and Symptoms* (New York: John Wiley &
Sons, 1979).

110. Kanter et al., and "Driving Corporate
Entrepreneurship".

111. Y. Ling, Z. Simsek, M. Lubatkin, and J.
Veiga, "Transformational Leadership's Role
in Promoting Corporate Entrepreneurship:
Examining the CEO-TMT Interface,"
Academy of Management Journal, 2008,
pp. 557–76.

112. G. T. Lumpkin and G. G. Dess, "Clarifying
the Entrepreneurial Orientation Construct
and Linking It to Performance," *Academy of
Management Review* 21 (1996), pp. 135–72;
and G. G. Dess and G. T. Lumpkin, "The
Role of Entrepreneurial Orientation
in Stimulating Effective Corporate
Entrepreneurship," *The Academy of
Management Executive* 19 (February 2005),
pp. 147–56.

113. H. J. Sapienza, E. Autio, G. George, and
S. A. Zahra, "A Capabilities Perspective on
the Effects of Early Internationalization
on Firm Survival and Growth," *Academy of
Management Review* 31 (2006), pp. 914–33.

114. T. Bateman and J. M. Crant, "The Proactive
Dimension of Organizational Behavior,"
Journal of Organizational Behavior, 1993,
pp. 103–18.

115. Lumpkin and Dess, "Clarifying the
Entrepreneurial Orientation Construct."

116. C. Pinchot and E. Pinchot, *The Intelligent
Organization* (San Francisco: Barrett-
Koehler, 1996).

117. Company website, www.starbucks.com,
accessed March 31, 2017; Clifford, "How
Starbucks' Howard Schultz Went from
the Projects to Creating 300,000 Jobs and
a $3 Billion Fortune"; Kline, "Wal-Mart
and Starbucks Are Trying to Think Like
Start-Ups"; Trefis Team, "Starbucks Is
Maintaining Its Competitive Edge," *Forbes,*
October 13, 2016, https://www.forbes.
com/sites/greatspeculations/2016/10/13/
how-is-starbucks-maintaining-its-
competitive-edge/#41a3ab1a759c; Janet I.
Tu, "Starbucks' New Reserve Bars Push
High-End Coffee Another Notch Higher,"
Seattle Times, February 27, 2017, http://
www.seattletimes.com/business/retail/
starbucks-new-reserve-bars-push-high-end-
coffee-another-notch-higher/.

Chapter 8

1. "GM Reports Record Full-Year Earnings
per Share," February 7, 2017, https://
www.gm.com/investors/earnings-releases.
html; Melissa Burden, "GM Sells Record
3.87 Million Vehicles in China in 2016,"
Detroit News, January 5, 2017, http://
www.detroitnews.com/story/business/
autos/general-motors/2017/01/05/
china/96200326/.

2. R. N. Ashkenas and S. C. Francis,
"Integration Managers: Special Leaders for
Special Times," *Harvard Business Review*
78, no. 6 (November–December 2000),
pp. 108–16.

3. T. Malone, R. Laubacher, and T.
Johns, "The Big Idea: The Age of
Hyperspecialization," *Harvard Business
Review* (online), July 1, 2011, http://www.
hbr.org; A. West, "The Flute Factory: An
Empirical Measurement of the Effect of
the Division of Labor on Productivity and
Production Cost," *American Economist* 43,
no. 1 (Spring 1999), pp. 82–87.

4. P. Lawrence and J. Lorsch, *Organization
and Environment* (Homewood, IL: Richard
D. Irwin, 1969).

5. Ibid. and B. L. Thompson, *The New
Manager's Handbook* (New York: McGraw-
Hill, 1994). See also S. Sharifi and K. S.
Pawar, "Product Design as a Means of
Integrating Differentiation," *Technovation*
16, no. 5 (May 1996), pp. 255–64; and W.
B. Stevenson and J. M. Bartunek, "Power,
Interaction, Position, and the Generation
of Cultural Agreement in Organizations,"
Human Relations 49, no. 1 (January 1996),
pp. 75–104.

6. A. J. Ali, R. C. Camp, and M. Gibbs, "The
Ten Commandments Perspective on Power
and Authority in Organizations," *Journal of
Business Ethics* 26, no. 4 (August 2000), pp.
351–61; and R. F. Pearse, "Understanding
Organizational Power and Influence
Systems," *Compensation & Benefits
Management* 16, no. 4 (Autumn 2000), pp.
28–38.

7. J. Pfeffer, *Power: Why Some People
Have It—and Others Don't* (New York:
HarperCollins, 2010).

8. S. F. Shultz, *Board Book: Making Your
Corporate Board a Strategic Force in Your
Company's Success* (New York: AMACOM,
2000); and R. D. Ward, *Improving
Corporate Boards: The Boardroom Insider
Guidebook* (New York: John Wiley & Sons,
2000).

9. O. Faleye, R. Hoitash, and U. Hoitash,
"The Trouble with Too Much Board
Oversight," *MIT Sloan Management Review,*
March 19, 2013, http://www.sloanreview.
mit.edu; and T. Perkins, "The 'Compliance
Board,'" *The Wall Street Journal,* March 2,
2007, http://online.wsj.com.

10. The Alternative Board, "About," http://
www.thealternativeboard.com, accessed
March 31, 2017; and J. Aldridge, "The
Alternative Board Expanding to Rapidly
Growing Boerne Area," *San Antonio Biz
Journal* (online), January 6, 2015, http://
www.bizjournals.com.

11. Margaret Heffernan, "You *Really* Need
Outside Directors: Here's Why," *Inc.,*
October 15, 2012, http://www.inc.
com; Kingston Smith LLP, "Lessons
Learned: Surviving the Recession," news
release, February 20, 2009, http://www.
kingstonsmithw1.co.uk; and Karl Stark and
Bill Stewart, "Why You Need an Advisory
Board," *Inc.,* January 24, 2012, http://www.
inc.com.

12. C. M. Daily and D. R. Dalton, "CEO
and Board Chair Roles Held Jointly or
Separately: Much Ado about Nothing?"
Academy of Management Executive 11, no. 3
(August 1997), pp. 11–20.

13. Company website, "Corporate
Management," www.en.sanofi.com,
accessed March 31, 2017; J. Kell, "Shake
Shack Shakes Up Senior Management
Team," *Fortune,* January 5, 2017, www.
fortune.com; S. Lebowitz, "The CEO of
Microsoft Has an 8-Hour Meeting with
His Leadership Team Every Month,"
Business Insider, October 2, 2015, www.
businessinsider.com.

14. S. Vickery, C. Droge, and R. Germain,
"The Relationship between Product
Customization and Organizational
Structure," *Journal of Operations
Management* 17, no. 4 (June 1999), pp.
377–91. See also N. Nohria, W. Joyce,
and B. Roberson, "What Really Works,"
Harvard Business Review (July 2003).

15. Andrew R. McIlvaine, "Flat, Fast and . . .
Risky?" *Human Resource Executive Online,*
March 6, 2012, http://www.hreonline.
com.

16. D. Van Fleet and A. Bedeian, "A History
of the Span of Management," *Academy of
Management Review* 2 (1977), pp. 356–72.
Results of Corporate Executive Board
survey reported in McIlvaine, "Flat, Fast
and . . . Risky?"

17. S. Lloyd, "Managers Must Delegate
Effectively to Develop Employees," Society
for Human Resource Management (online),
February 2, 2012, http://www.shrm.org;
Z. X. Chen and S. Aryee, "Delegation
and Employee Work Outcomes: An
Examination of the Cultural Context of
Mediating Processes in China," *Academy of
Management Journal* 50, no. 1 (2007), pp.
226–38.

18. I. Kalb, "3 Ways Micromanagers Can
Destroy a Company," *Business Insider*
(online), July 7, 2014, http://www.
businessinsider.com; S. Finkelstein,
"In Praise of Micromanagement," *BBC*
(online), October 3, 2013, http://www.bbc.
com.

19. "How to Delegate More Effectively,"
Community Banker, February 2009, p. 14;
B. Nefer, "Don't Be Delegation-Phobic,"
Supervision, December 2008, Business &
Company Resource Center, http://galenet.
galegroup.com; J. Mahoney, "Delegating
Effectively," *Nursing Management* 28,
no. 6 (June 1997), p. 62; and J. Lagges,
"The Role of Delegation in Improving
Productivity," *Personnel Journal,* November
1979, pp. 776–79.

20. G. Matthews, "Run Your Business or Build
an Organization?" *Harvard Management
Review,* March–April 1984, pp. 34–44.

21. "Missing Its Targets," *Delaney Report,*
November 26, 2012, Business Insights:
Essentials, http://bi.galegroup.com.

22. J. R. Hollenbeck, A. P. J. Ellis, S. E. Humphrey, A. S. Garza, and D. R. Ilgen, "Asymmetry in Structural Adaptation: The Differential Impact of Centralizing versus Decentralizing Team Decision-Making Structures," *Organizational Behavior and Human Decision Processes* 114 (2011), pp. 64–74.

23. R. Forrester, "Empowerment: Rejuvenating a Potent Idea," *Academy of Management Executive* 14, no. 3 (August 2000), pp. 67–80; and M. L. Perry, C. L. Pearce, and H. P. Sims Jr., "Empowered Selling Teams: How Shared Leadership Can Contribute to Selling Team Outcomes," *Journal of Personal Selling & Sales Management* 19, no. 3 (Summer 1999), pp. 35–51.

24. T. McDowell, D. Agarwal, D. Miller, T. Okamoto, and T. Page, "Organizational Design: The Rise of Teams," Deloitte University Press, February 29, 2016, www. dupress.deloitte.com; K. Hara, "Nestlé's CEO Sees Decentralization as Key," *Nikkei Asian Review* (online), June 26, 2014, http://www.asia.nikkei.com.

25. E. E. Lawler III, "New Roles for the Staff Function: Strategic Support and Services," in *Organizing for the Future*, J. Galbraith, E. E. Lawler III, & Associates (San Francisco: Jossey-Bass, 1993).

26. L. Barratt-Pugh and S. Bahn, "HR Strategy During Culture Change: Building Change Agency," *Journal of Management & Organization*, February 10, 2015, pp. 1–14; and A. Adams, "Changing Role of HR," *Human Resources*, June 2010, pp. 45–48.

27. Conference Board press release, "More Companies Move to Integrate Marketing and Communications," *PR Newswire*, September 27, 2016, www.prnewswire.com.

28. Kiva, "About Us," http://www.kiva.org, accessed March 31, 2017.

29. Ibid.

30. G. S. Day, "Creating a Market-Driven Organization," *Sloan Management Review* 41, no. 1 (Fall 1999), pp. 11–22.

31. Johnson & Johnson, "Our Products," http://www.jnj.com, accessed March 31, 2017.

32. B. T. Lamont, V. Sambamurthy, K. M. Ellis, and P. G. Simmonds, "The Influence of Organizational Structure on the Information Received by Corporate Strategists of Multinational Enterprises," *Management International Review* 40, no. 3 (2000), pp. 231–52.

33. Organization website, "At-a-Glance: IRS Divisions and Principal Offices," www.irs. gov, accessed March 31, 2017.

34. J. Battilana and M. Lee, "Advancing Research on Hybrid Organizing: Insights from the Study of Social Enterprises," *Academy of Management Annals* 8 (2014), pp. 397–441.

35. B. Rigoni and B. Nelson, "The Matrix: Teams Are Gaining Greater Power in Companies," *Gallup Business Journal*, May 17, 2016, www.gallup.com.

36. "GM Ignition Switch Death Count Rises to 67," *CBS News* (online), March 16, 2015, http://www.cbsnews.com; "GM's Total Recall Cost: $4.1 Billion," *CNNMoney* (online), February 4, 2015, http://money. cnn.com; General Motors, *Annual Report 2014*, www.gm.com; Tim Higgins and Jeff Green, "GM Seen Planning Global Reorganization against `Fiefdoms,'" *Bloomberg*, August 17, 2012, http://www. bloomberg.com; "GM Names Mary Barra Chief Executive, Dan Akerson to Retire," *Los Angeles Times* (online), December 10, 2013, http://www.latimes.com; Paul A. Eisenstein, "Big Management Shake-Up on the Horizon at GM," *NBC News*, August 22, 2012, http://www.nbcnews. com; Ben Klayman, "Car Guy or Bean Counter?" Reuters, July 19, 2012, http:// www.reuters. com; Sharon Terlep, "GM's Chief Labors to Get Rebuilt Car Maker into Gear," *The Wall Street Journal*, June 11, 2012, http://online.wsj.com; "Mary Barra: GM's Next CEO?" *Fortune*, December 17, 2012, http://management.fortune.cnn. com; and Chris Isidore, "Death Toll for GM Ignition Switch: 124," *CNNMoney. com*, December 10, 2015, http://money. cnn.com/2015/12/10/news/companies/ gm-recall-ignition-switch-death-toll/

37. J. Galbraith, "Matrix Is the Ladder to Success," *Bloomberg Business* (online), http://www.businessweek.com, accessed April 5, 2015; W. Bernasco, P. C. de WeerdNederhof, H. Tillema, and H. Boer, "Balanced Matrix Structure and New Product Development Process at Texas Instruments Materials and Controls Division," *R&D Management* 29, no. 2 (April 1999), pp. 121–31; J. K. McCollum, "The Matrix Structure: Bane or Benefit to High Tech Organizations?" *Project Management Journal* 24, no. 2 (June 1993), pp. 23–26; R. C. Ford, "Cross-Functional Structures: A Review and Integration of Matrix," *Journal of Management* 18, no. 2 (June 1992), pp. 267–94; and H. Kolodny, "Managing in a Matrix," *Business Horizons*, March–April 1981, pp. 17–24.

38. D. Cackowski, M. K. Najdawi, and Q. B. Chung, "Object Analysis in Organizational Design: A Solution or Matrix Organizations," *Project Management Journal* 31, no. 3 (September 2000), pp. 44–51; J. Barker, "Conflict Approaches of Effective and Ineffective Project Managers: A Field Study in a Matrix Organization," *Journal of Management Studies* 25, no. 2 (March 1988), pp. 167–78; G. J. Chambers, "The Individual in a Matrix Organization," *Project Management Journal* 20, no. 4 (December 1989), pp. 37–42, 50; and S. Davis and P. Lawrence, "Problems of Matrix Organizations," *Harvard Business Review*, May–June 1978, pp. 131–42.

39. M. Staples, "Perspectives on Global Organizations," McKinsey & Company (2012), http://www.mckinsey.com; A. Ferner, "Being Local Worldwide: ABB and the Challenge of Global Management Relations," *Industrielles* 55, no. 3 (Summer 2000), pp. 527–29; and C. Bartlett and S. Ghoshal, "Matrix Management: Not a Structure, a Frame of Mind," *Harvard Business Review* 68 (July–August 1990), pp. 138–45.

40. J. Tata, S. Prasad, and R. Thorn, "The Influence of Organizational Structure on the Effectiveness of TQM Programs," *Journal of Managerial Issues* 11, no. 4 (Winter 1999), pp. 440–53; and Davis and Lawrence, "Problems of Matrix Organizations."

41. R. E. Miles and C. C. Snow, *Fit, Failure, and the Hall of Fame* (New York: Free Press, 1994); and G. Symon, "Information and Communication Technologies and Network Organization: A Critical Analysis," *Journal of Occupational and Organizational Psychology* 73, no. 4 (December 2000), pp. 389–95.

42. SendLove, "Send-Love—The Cool New Employee Recognition System," http:// www.sendlove.com, accessed April 7, 2015; and D. Dahl, "A Radical Take on the Virtual Company," *Inc.*, March 1, 2011, http://www.inc.com.

43. B. Hay and A. Gowdridge, "As the Traditional Workplace Breaks Down Will Leaders Adapt," *The Guardian* (online), January 21, 2015, http://www.theguardian. com; D. Schwabel, "10 Ways Millennials Are Creating the Future of Work," *Forbes* (online), December 16, 2013, http://www. forbes.com; Millennial Branding, "The Cost of Millennial Retention Strategy," August 6, 2013, http://www.millennialbranding. com; J. Menza, "Malcolm Gladwell: A Generational Tipping Point Is Coming," *CNBC* (online), January 31, 2013, http:// www.cnbc.com; and J. Scorza, "Millennials Usher in New Social Paradigm," June 25, 2012, Society for Human Resource Management, www.shrm.org.

44. R. E. Miles and C. C. Snow, *Fit, Failure, and the Hall of Fame* (New York: Free Press, 1994).

45. S. C. Kang, S. S. Morris, and S. A. Snell, "Relational Archetypes, Organizational Learning, and Value Creation: Extending the Human Resource Architecture," *Academy of Management Review* 32, no. 1 (2007), pp. 236–56.

46. J. G. March and H. A. Simon, *Organizations* (New York: John Wiley & Sons, 1958); and J. D. Thompson, *Organizations in Action* (New York: McGraw-Hill, 1967).

47. deloitte.com; and P. S. Adler, "Building Better Bureaucracies," *Academy of Management Executive* 13, no. 4 (November 1999), pp. 36–49.

48. J. Galbraith, "Organization Design: An Information Processing View," *Interfaces* 4 (Fall 1974), pp. 28–36. See also S. A. Mohrman, "Integrating Roles and Structure in the Lateral Organization," in *Organizing for the Future*, ed. J. Galbraith, E. E. Lawler III, & Associates (San Francisco: Jossey-Bass, 1993); and B. B. Flynn and F. J. Flynn, "Information-Processing Alternatives for Coping with Manufacturing Environment Complexity," *Decision Sciences* 30, no. 4 (Fall 1999), pp. 1021–52.

49. Galbraith, "Organization Design,"; and Mohrman, "Integrating Roles and Structure in the Lateral Organization.

50. "Speaker Information: Michael Arena, Chief Talent Officer, General Motors Corporation," Talent Management Exchange, http://www.talentmanagementexchange.com, accessed May 8, 2015; R. Feloni, "GM CEO Mary Barra Explains How Shrinking the Dress Code to 2 Words Reflects Her Mission for the Company," *Business Insider* (online), March 27, 2015, http://www.businessinsider.com; G. Colvin, "Mary Barra's (Unexpected) Opportunity," *Fortune* (online), September 18, 2014, http://www.fortune.com; General Motors, *Annual Report 2013;* Higgins and Green, "GM Seen Planning Global Reorganization"; Qineqt, "General Motors Reorganization: Will the Glory Days Be Back?" *Seeking Alpha,* September 3, 2012, http:// seekingalpha.com; Eisenstein, "Big Management Shake-Up"; Klayman, "Car Guy or Bean Counter?"; Terlep, "GM's Chief Labors"; *Fortune,* "Mary Barra"; David Shepardson, "U.S. Sells Nearly 20 Percent of Remaining GM Shares," *Detroit News,* April 25, 2013, http://www.detroitnews.com; *CBS News,* "Government in March Sold $621M"; company website, http://www.chevrolet.com/bolt-ev-electric-vehicle, accessed April 3, 2017; and Alex Davies, "Power Play," *Wired,* February 2016, https://www.wired.com/2016/01/gm-electric-car-chevy-bolt-mary-barra/#slide-1.

Chapter 9

1. General Electric 2014 CEO Letter in the *2014 Annual Report,* http://www.ge.com/ar2014/ceo-letter/; A. Sorkin and M. de al Merced, "G.E. to Retreat from Finance in Post-Crisis Reorganization," *The New York Times* (online), April 10, 2015, http://www.nytimes.com; General Electric, "Fact Sheet," http://www.ge.com/company/fact-sheet; Wayne Duggan, "GE Stock May Be Poised to Climb," *U.S. News and World Report,* March 31, 2017, http://money.usnews.com/investing/articles/2017-03-31/analyst-ge-stock-may-be-poised-to-climb; company website, https://www.ge.com/about-us/fact-sheet, accessed April 3, 2017; and company 2016 annual report, "Letter to Shareholders," http://www.ge.com/ar2016/ceo-letter/ accessed April 3, 2017.

2. C. O'Reilly and M. Tushman, "Ambidexterity as a Dynamic Capability: Resolving the Innovator's Dilemma," Research Paper no. 1963, Stanford Graduate School of Business, March 2007, http://ssrn.com/abstract 5978493.

3. P. Sebastian, J. Fourne, J. Jansen, and T. Mom, "Strategic Agility in MNEs," *California Management Review* 56 (2014), pp. 13–38; P. M. Wright, L. Dyer, and M. G. Takla, "What's Next? Key Findings from the 1999 State-of-the-Art and Practice Study," *Human Resource Planning* 22, no. 4 (1999), pp. 12–20; and Donald Sull, "How to Thrive in Turbulent Markets," *Harvard Business Review,* February 2009, pp. 78–88.

4. T. Burns and G. Stalker, *The Management of Innovation* (London: Tavistock, 1961).

5. G. Soda and A. Zaheer, "A Network Perspective on Organizational Architecture: Performance Effects of the Interplay of Formal and Informal Organization," *Strategic Management Journal* 33 (2012), pp. 751–71.

6. Ibid.

7. A. Adkins, "Millennials: The Job-Hopping Generation," *Gallup Business Journal,* May 12, 2016, www.gallup.com; K. Klein, "How to Keep Millennials from Getting Bored and Quitting," *Bloomberg Business* (online), August 22, 2014, http://www.bloomberg.com; R. Ray et al., "The State of Human Capital 2012," Research Report R-1501-12-RR, McKinsey & Company and The Conference Board, accessed April 13, 2015.

8. G. Hamel and C. K. Prahalad, "Competing for the Future," *Harvard Business Review,* July–August 1994, pp. 122–28.

9. D. J. Teece "The Foundations of Enterprise Performance: Dynamic and Ordinary Capabilities in an (Economic) Theory of Firms," *Academy of Management Perspectives* 28 (2014), pp. 328–52.

10. D. G. Sirmon, M. A. Hitt, and R. D. Ireland, "Managing Firm Resources in Dynamic Environments to Create Value: Looking inside the Black Box," *Academy of Management Review* 32, no. 1 (2007), pp. 273–92.

11. S. Strom, "Soda Makers Coca-Cola, PepsiCo and Dr. Pepper Join in Effort to Cut Americans' Drink Calories," *The New York Times,* September 23, 2014, www.nytimes.com.

12. Intel, "TAG Heuer, Google, and Intel Announce Swiss Smartwatch Collaboration," news release, March 19, 2015, http://www.intel.com.

13. G. Slowinski, E. Hummel, A. Gupta, and E. R. Gilmont, "Effective Practices for Sourcing Innovation," *Research-Technology Management,* January–February 2009, pp. 27–34.

14. R. C. Sampson, "R&D Alliances and Firm Performance: The Impact of Technological Diversity and Alliance Organization on Innovation," *Academy of Management Journal* 50, no. 2 (2007), pp. 364–86.

15. R. Gulati, F. Wohlgezogen, and P. Zhelyazkov, "The Two Facets of Collaboration: Cooperation and Coordination in Strategic Alliances," *Academy of Management Annals* 6 (2012), pp. 531–83.

16. R. M. Kanter, "Collaborative Advantage: The Art of Alliances," *Harvard Business Review,* July–August 1999, pp. 96–108; J. B. Cullen, J. L. Johnson, and T. Sakano, "Success through Commitment and Trust: The Soft Side of Strategic Alliance Management," *Journal of World Business* 35, no. 3 (Fall 2000), pp. 223–40; and P. Kale, H. Singh, and H. Perlmutter, "Learning and Protection of Proprietary Assets in Strategic Alliances: Building Relational Capital," *Strategic Management Journal* 21, no. 3 (March 2000), pp. 217–37.

17. P. Senge, *The Fifth Discipline* (New York: Doubleday Currency, 1990).

18. D. A. Garvin, "Building a Learning Organization," *Harvard Business Review,* July–August 1993, pp. 78–91; D. A. Garvin, *Learning in Action: A Guide to Putting the Learning Organization to Work* (Boston: Harvard Business School Press, 2000); and V. J. Marsick and K. E. Watkins, *Facilitating Learning Organizations: Making Learning Count* (Aldershot, Hampshire: Gower, 1999).

19. Garvin, "Building a Learning Organization" Garvin, *Learning in Action;* Marsick and Watkins, *Facilitating Learning Organization;* and N. Anand, H. K. Gardner, and T. Morris, "Knowledge-Based Innovation: Emergence and Embedding of New Practice Areas in Management Consulting Firms," *Academy of Management Journal* 50, no. 2 (2007), pp. 406–28.

20. J. G. March, "Exploration and Exploitation in Organizational Learning," *Organization Science* 2, no. 1 (February 1991), pp. 71–87; and S.-C. Kang and S. A. Snell, "Intellectual Capital Architectures and Ambidextrous Learning: A Framework for Human Resource Management," *Journal of Management Studies* 46, no. 1 (2009), pp. 65–92.

21. M. Marchington and A. Kynighou, "The Dynamics of Employee Involvement and Participation during Turbulent Times," *The International Journal of Human Resource Management* 23 (2012), pp. 3336–54; R. J. Vandenberg, H. A. Richardson, and L. J. Eastman, "The Impact of High Involvement Work Process on Organizational Effectiveness: A Second-Order Latent Variable Approach," *Group & Organization Management* 24, no. 3 (September 1999), pp. 300–39; G. M. Spreitzer and A. K. Mishra, "Giving Up Control without Losing Control: Trust and Its Substitutes Effects on Managers Involving Employees in Decision Making," *Group & Organization Management* 24, no. 2 (June 1999), pp. 155–87; and S. Albers Mohrman, G. E. Ledford, and E. E. Lawler III, *Strategies for High Performance Organizations The CEO Report: Employee Involvement, TQM, and Reengineering Programs in Fortune 1000 Corporations* (San Francisco: Jossey-Bass, 1998).

22. M. Josefy, S. Kuban, R. D. Ireland et al., "All Things Great and Small: Organizational Size, Boundaries of the Firm, and a Changing Environment," *Academy of Management Annals* 8 (2015), pp. 715–802.

23. P. Wahba, "Walmart's CEO Calls on Staff to Be Like Han Solo, Other Star Wars Rebels," *Fortune,* June 5, 2015, www.fortune.com.

24. J. Smothers, M. Novicevic, M. Buckley, S. Carraher, L. Bynum, M. Hayek, and Alfred D. Chandler Jr., "Historical Impact and Historical Scope of His Works," *Journal of Management History* 16 (2010),

pp. 521–26; Alfred Chandler, *The Economist,* May 17, 2007, http://www.economist.com; C. Farrell and Alfred Chandler, "Big Business Big Loss," *Bloomberg Businessweek,* May 14, 2007, http://www.businessweek.com.

25. The American Customer Satisfaction Index, "ACSI: Retail Customer Satisfaction Drops Despite Improvements for Online Shopping," press release, February 18, 2015, http://www.theacsi.org; and Renee Dudley, "Walmart Faces the Cost of Cost-Cutting: Empty Shelves," *Bloomberg Businessweek,* March 28, 2013, http://www.businessweek.com.

26. R. Pagnamenta, "Transformation That Could Rescue Unilever from the Slippery Slope," *The Times* (London), January 3, 2007.

27. L. L. Hellofs and R. Jacobson, "Market Share and Customers' Perceptions of Quality: When Can Firms Grow Their Way to Higher versus Lower Quality?" *Journal of Marketing* 63, no. 1 (January 1999), pp. 16–25.

28. E. Doerr, "Kobolds Spirit of America: Navy Seals, Made in America, and Pandemonium," *Forbes* (online), July 4, 2014, http://www.forbes.com; and J. Dean, "The Greatly Improbable, Highly Enjoyable, Increasingly Profitable Life of Michael Kobold," *Inc.,* May 2007, pp. 126–34.

29. J. Creswell, "Quicken Loans, the New Mortgage Machine," *The New York Times,* January 21, 2017, www.nytimes.com; "Company Fast Facts," http://www.intuit.com, accessed April 11, 2015.

30. D. DeRue, J. Hollenbeck, M. Johnson, D. Ilgen, and D. Jundt, "How Different Team Downsizing Approaches Influence Team-Level Adaptation and Performance," *Academy of Management Journal* 51 (2008), pp. 182–96; W. F. Cascio, "Downsizing: What Do We Know? What Have We Learned?" *Academy of Management Executive* 7 (February 1993), pp. 95–104; and S. J. Freeman, "The Gestalt of Organizational Downsizing: Downsizing Strategies as Package of Change," *Human Relations* 52, no. 12 (December 1999), pp. 1505–41.

31. Network for Good, "About Us," www.networkforgood.org, accessed April 12, 2015; Selco, "About Us," www.selco-india.com, accessed April 12, 2015; E. Howard, "10 Things We Learned about Scaling Global Social Enterprise," *The Guardian,* November 20, 2014, http://www.theguardian.com; R. Murphy and D. Sachs, "The Rise of Social Entrepreneurship Suggests a Possible Future for Global Capitalism," *Forbes,* May 2, 2013, http://www.forbes.com.

32. General Electric, *2014 Annual Report;* General Electric, "Jeff Immelt: A Simpler, More Valuable GE," http://www.ge.com, accessed April 12, 2015; Michal Lev-Ram, "Why GE Is Betting on Software," *Fortune,* April 25, 2013, http://tech.fortune.cnn.com. Kate Linebaugh, "The New GE Way: Go Deep, Not Wide,"

The Wall Street Journal, March 7, 2012, http://online.wsj.com; Beth Kowitt, "How a Top GE Exec Engineered Himself out of a Job," *Fortune,* August 3, 2012, http://management.fortune.cnn.com; Kate Linebaugh, "GE Shake-Up Will Audition New Leaders," *The Wall Street Journal,* July 20, 2012, http://online.wsj.com; Ashlee Vance, "GE Tries to Make Its Machines Cool and Connected," *Bloomberg Businessweek,* http://www.businessweek.com; Peter Coy, "GE Builds a Better Battery," *Bloomberg Businessweek,* July 11, 2012, http://www.businessweek.com; and company 2016 annual report, "Letter to Shareholders," http://www.ge.com/ar2016/ceo-letter/, accessed April 3, 2017.

33. B. Kerschberg, "Five Steps to Master Big Data and Predictive Analytics in 2014," *Forbes* (online), January 3, 2014, http://www.forbes.com; "Predictive Analytics 101: Next-Generation Big Data Intelligence," Intel IT Center (online), March 2013, http://www.intel.com; and "Predicting the Future, Part 1: What Is Predictive Analytics?" IBM Developer Works (online), http://www.ibm.com, accessed May 27, 2015.

34. E. O'Neill, "10 Companies That Are Using Big Data," ICAS, September 23, 2016, www.icas.com.

35. S. Sluis, "Mobile Sales to Represent Half of E-Commerce by 2018," *Customer Relationship Management* 18 (2014), pp. 15–18; T. Wailgum, "CRM Definition and Solutions," *CIO,* March 6, 2007, http://www.cio.com; M. Burns, "CRM Survey 2011," *CA Magazine,* May 2011, http://www.camagazine.com; and M. Burns, "CRM Survey 2010," *CA Magazine,* April 2010, http://www.camagazine.com.

36. K. Ishikawa, *What Is Total Quality Control? The Japanese Way,* trans. D. J. Lu (Englewood Cliffs, NJ: Prentice-Hall, 1985); and J. Seibert and J. Lingle, "Internal Customer Service: Has It Improved?" *Quality Progress* 40, no. 3 (March 2007), OCLC FirstSearch, http://firstsearch.oclc.org.

37. Salesforce, "What Is Salesforce?" http://www.salesforce.com, accessed April 5, 2017.

38. M. Porter, *Competitive Advantage: Creating and Sustaining Superior Performance* (New York: Free Press, 1985); and Internet Center for Management and Business Administration, "The Value Chain," Strategy pages, *NetMBA,* http://www.netmba.com.

39. B. Creech, *The Five Pillars of TQM: How to Make Total Quality Management Work for You* (New York: Plume Publishing, 1995); and J. R. Evans and W. M. Lindsay, *Management and Control of Quality* (Mason, OH: South-Western College Publishing, 1998).

40. National Institute of Standards and Technology, "Four U.S. Organizations Receive Nation's Highest Honor for Performance Excellence," news release, November 17, 2016, http://www.nist.gov.

41. International Organization for Standardization, "ISO 9000 Quality Management," http://www.iso.org.

42. J. Champy, *Reengineering Management* (New York: HarperBusiness, 1995). See also M. Hammer and J. Champy, *Reengineering the Corporation* (New York: HarperCollins, 1992).

43. J. Woodward, *Industrial Organization: Theory and Practice* (London: Oxford University Press, 1965).

44. J. H. Gilmore and B. J. Pine, eds., *Markets of One: Creating Customer-Unique Value through Mass Customization* (Cambridge, MA: Harvard Business Review Press, 2000); and B. J. Pine, *Mass Customization: The New Frontier in Business Competition* (Cambridge, MA: Harvard Business School Press, 1992).

45. M. Zhang, X. Zhao, and Y. Qi, "The Effects of Organizational Flatness, Coordination, and Product Modularity on Mass Customization Capability," *International Journal of Production Economics* 158 (2014), pp.145–55; F. Sahin, "Manufacturing Competitiveness: Different Systems to Achieve the Same Results," *Production and Inventory Management Journal* 41, no. 1 (First Quarter 2000), pp. 56–65.

46. S. Wadhwa and K. S. Rao, "Flexibility: An Emerging Meta-Competence for Managing High Technology," *International Journal of Technology Management* 19, no. 7–8 (2000), pp. 820–45.

47. A. Bozek and M. Wysocki, "Flexible Job Shop with Continuous Material Flow," *International Journal of Production Research* 53 (2015), pp. 1273–90; B. A. Peters and L. F. McGinnis, "Strategic Configuration of Flexible Assembly Systems: A Single Period Approximation," *IIE Transaction* 31, no. 4 (April 1999), pp. 379–90.

48. J. K. Liker and J. M. Morgan, "The Toyota Way in Services: The Case of Lean Product Development," *Academy of Management Perspectives* 20, no. 2 (May 2006), pp. 5–20; "Strategic Reconfiguration: Manufacturing's Key Role in Innovation," *Production and Inventory Management Journal* (Summer–Fall 2001), pp. 9–17; J. Jusko, "Lean Confusion," *Industry Week,* September 2010, pp. 32–34; and Sahin, "Manufacturing Competitiveness."

49. P. Guarraia, G. Carey, A. Corbett, and K. Neuhaus, "Lean Six Sigma for the Services Industry," Bain & Company, May 20, 2008, http://www.bain.comm.

50. S. Silversthorne, "Can Lean Production Methods Work in Services?" *CBS News,* May 21, 2009, http://www.cbsnews.com; J. Hanna, "Bringing Lean Production to Service Industries," Harvard Business School Working Knowledge (online), October 22, 2007, http://www.hbs.edu.

51. W. Yang and K. Meyer, "Competitive Dynamics in an Emerging Economy: Competitive Pressures, Resources, and the Speed of Action," *Journal of Business Research* 68 (2015), pp. 1176–85; C. H. Chung, "Balancing the Two Dimensions of Time for Time-Based Competition,"

Journal of Managerial Issues 11, no. 3 (Fall 1999), pp. 299–314; and D. R. Towill and P. McCullen, "The Impact of Agile Manufacturing on Supply Chain Dynamics," *International Journal of Logistics Management* 10, no. 1 (1999), pp. 83–96. See also G. Stalk and T. M. Hout, *Competing against Time: How Time-Based Competition Is Reshaping Global Markets* (New York: Free Press, 1990).

52. C. Swedberg, "Macy's Expands RFID and Beacon Deployments," *RFID Journal* (online), September 16, 2014, http://www. rfidjournal.com; M. O'Connor, "Can RFID Save Brick-and-Mortar Retailers After All?" *Fortune* (online), April 16, 2014, http:// www.fortune.com.

53. J. E. Ettlie, "Product Development beyond Simultaneous Engineering," *Automative Manufacturing & Production* 112, no. 7 (July 2000), p. 18; U. Roy, J. M. Usher, and H. R. Parsaei, eds., *Simultaneous Engineering: Methodologies and Applications* (Newark, NJ: Gordon and Breach, 1999); and M. M. Helms and L. P. Ettkin, "Time-Based Competitiveness: A Strategic Perspective," *Competitiveness Review* 10, no. 2 (2000), pp. 1–14.

54. Richard J. Schonberger, "DFMA a Potent Lean Methodology," *Assembly,* April 2013, http://www.assemblymag.com.

55. "How GE Is Creating Software and Making Money Faster," *CIO Journal* (online), October 9, 2013, http://www.wsj.com; Guy Boulton, "GE Healthcare Systems CEO Sees Challenges, Opportunities," *Milwaukee Journal-Sentinel,* December 4, 2011, http:// www.jsonline.com; General Electric, "What Is Six Sigma? The Roadmap to Customer Impact," n.d., http://www.ge.com/sixsigma/ SixSigma.pdf; Ed Crooks, "Lean Cuts Fat off GEs Production Line," *Financial Times,* April 2, 2012, http://www.ft.com; Rachel King, "GE Becomes More Agile," *CIO Journal,* May 30, 2012, http://blogs. wsj.com; and General Electric, "GE Aviation Delivers Its First Production Wing Components for the Airbus A350 XWB," news release, March 7, 2013, http://www .businesswire.com.

Chapter 10

1. L. Gellman, "Everyone (Still) Wants to Work for Google," *The Wall Street Journal* (online), March 26, 2015, http://www.wsj. com; "100 Best Companies to Work for 2015," *Fortune,* accessed April 14, 2015; S. Phelps, "Cracking into Google: 15 Reasons Why More Than 2 Million People Apply Each Year," *Forbes* (online), August 5, 2014, http://www.forbes.com; J. D'Onfro and K. Smith, "Google Employees Reveal Their Favorite Perks about Working for the Company," *Business Insider* (online), July 1, 2014, http://www.businessinsider. com; R. Waters, "Google Tries New Angle on Hiring," *Financial Times,* February 7, 2011, Business & Company Resource Center, http://galenet.galegroup.com; M. Liedtke and B. Ortutay, "Google Wants to Be Cool Again," *Houston Chronicle,* January 22, 2011, Business & Company Resource Center, http://galenet.galegroup. com; Farhad Manjoo, "How Google Became Such a Great Place to Work," *Slate,* January 21, 2013, http://www.slate.com; Meghan Casserly, "Here's What Happens to Google Employees When They Die," *Forbes,* August 8, 2012, http://www.forbes.com; "What You Can Learn from Google's Hiring Secrets," *Insurance Business,* February 22, 2017, http://www.insurancebusinessmag. com/ca/business-strategy/what-you-can-learn-from-googles-hiring-secrets-60758. aspx; Claire Cain Miller, "Is Blind Hiring the Best Hiring," *The New York Times,* February 25, 2016, https://www.nytimes. com/2016/02/28/magazine/is-blind-hiring-the-best-hiring.html?_r=1; and https://www. fastcompany.com/3055974/how-google-and-twitter-train-their-employees-to-be-more-mindful.

2. J. Marler "Strategic Human Resource in Context: A Historical and Global Perspective," *Academy of Management Perspectives* 26 (2012), pp. 6–11.

3. N. Gardner, D. McGranahan, and W. Wolf, "Question for Your HR Chief: Are We Using Our 'People Data' to Create Value?" *McKinsey Quarterly,* March 2011, https:// www.mckinseyquarterly.com; D. Ulrich and J. Dulebohn, "Are We There Yet? What's Next for HR?" *Human Resource Management Review* 25 (2015), pp. 188–204.

4. A. Denisi and C. Smith, "Performance Appraisal, Performance Management, and Firm-Level Performance: A Review, a Proposed Model, and New Directions for Future Research," *Academy of Management Annals* 8 (2014), pp. 127–179; G. Saridakis, Y. Lai, and C. Cooper, "Exploring the Relationship between HRM and Firm Performance: A Meta-analysis of Longitudinal Studies," *Human Resource Management Review* 27 (2017), pp. 87–96.

5. A. Cardenal, "Costco vs. Wal-Mart: Higher Wages Mean Superior Returns for Investors," *The Motley Fool,* March 12, 2014, www.fool.com.

6. J. Hollenbeck and B. Jamieson, "Human Capital, Social Capital, and Social Network Analysis: Implications for Strategic Human Resource Management," *Academy of Management Perspectives* 29 (2015), pp. 370–385; D. Kryscynski and D. Ulrich, "Making Strategic Human Capital Relevant: A Time-Sensitive Opportunity", *Academy of Management Perspectives* 29 (2015)pp. 357–69; A. Nyberg and P. Wright," 50 Years of Human Capital Research: Assessing What We Know, Exploring Where We Go," *Academy of Management Perspectives* 29 (2015), pp. 287–95.

7. P. M. Wright and S. A. Snell, "Partner or Guardian? HR's Challenge in Balancing Value and Values," *Human Resource Management* 44, no. 2 (2005), pp. 177–82.

8. "Scaling Up: Catalyzing the Social Enterprise," A.T. Kearney (online), January 2015, http://www.atkearney. com; Greenling, "About Us," http://www. greenling.com, accessed April 18, 2015; M. Paisner, "Is Social Entrepreneurship Transforming Millennial Talent Acquisition," *Forbes* (online), April 17, 2015, http://www.forbes.com; N. Flores, "Austin's Social Entrepreneurs Redefine How to Drive Social Change," *Forefront Austin* (online), August 2011, http://www.forefrontaustin.com; Adam M. Beal, "Funding the Future: Social Enterprise on the Rise," Huffington Post.com, May 3, 2016, http://www. huffingtonpost.com/adam-m-beal/ funding-the-future-social_b_9825656. html; Claudia Grisales, "Austin Farmhouse Delivery Buys Greenling, Urban Acres," *My Statesman,* January 15, 2016, http:// www.mystatesman.com/business/austin-farmhouse-delivery-buys-greenling-urban-acres/4FITV48A6cM11KIuD0mAJL/.

9. K. Sheridan, "Cyber-Security Skills Shortage Leaves Companies Vulnerable," *InformationWeek,* August 1, 2016, www. informationweek.com.

10. E. Siedle, "The Greatest Retirement Crisis in American History," *Forbes* (online), March 20, 2013, http://www.forbes.com.

11. R. Dobbs, J. Manyika, and J. Woetzel, "How U.S. Can Fill the Skills Gap," *Fortune,* May 12, 2015, www.fortune.com.

12. J. Selingo, "Wanted: Factory Workers, Degree Required," *The New York Times,* January 30, 2017, www.nytimes.com.

13. Ibid.

14. A. Elahi, "What Is an H-1B Visa, and Why Are Tech Companies Worried about Them?" *Chicago Tribune,* February 1, 2017, www.chicagotribune.com.

15. J. Brustein and J. Cao, "H-1B Visa Overhaul Could Actually Benefit Big Tech Companies," *Bloomberg,* April 4, 2017, www.bloomberg.com.

16. D. E. Hartley, *Job Analysis at the Speed of Reality* (Amherst, MA: HRD Press, 1999); F. P. Morgeson and M. A. Campion, "Accuracy in Job Analysis: Toward an Inference-Based Model," *Journal of Organizational Behavior* 21, no. 7 (November 2000), pp. 819–27; and J. S. Shippmann, R. A. Ash, L. Carr, and B. Hesketh, "The Practice of Competency Modeling," *Personnel Psychology* 53, no. 3 (Autumn 2000), pp. 703–40.

17. J. S. Schippmann, *Strategic Job Modeling: Working at the Core of Integrated Human Resources* (Mahwah, NJ: Lawrence Erlbaum Associates, 1999).

18. M. Applegate, "Difference between the Internal & External Recruitment Strategies," *Houston Chronicle* (online), http://www.chron.com, accessed April 14, 2015; D. E. Terpstra, "The Search for Effective Methods," *HR Focus,* May 1996, pp. 16–17; H. G. Heneman III and R. A. Berkley, "Applicant Attraction Practices and Outcomes among Small Businesses," *Journal of Small Business Management* 37, no. 1 (January 1999), pp. 53–74; and J.-M. Hiltrop, "The Quest for the Best: Human Resource Practices to Attract and Retain Talent," *European Management Journal* 17, no. 4 (August 1999), pp. 422–30.

19. G. Crispin and M. Mehler, "10th Annual CareerXroads Source of Hire Report: by the Numbers," CareerXroads, March 2011, http://www.careerxroads.com; and J. Light, "Recruiters Rethink Online Playbook," *The Wall Street Journal,* January 18, 2011, http://online.wsj.com.

20. M. Feffer, "Expanding Employee Referrals into the Social Media World," *Society for Human Resource Management* 60 (April 4, 2015), http://www.shrm.org; N. Schwarz, "In Hiring, a Friend in Need Is a Prospect, Indeed," *The New York Times* (online), January 27, 2013, http://www.nytimes.com; and F. Hansen, "Employee Referral Programs, Selective Campus Recruitment Could Touch Off Bias Charges," *Workforce Management* 85 (June 26, 2006), pp. 59–60.

21. J. Scott, "Five Interview Questions That Reveal Top Talent," May 2013, www.online.citi.com.

22. D. Jacobs, "The High Price of Career Lies," *Forbes* (online), May 14, 2012, http://www.forbes.com; and J. Pepitone, "Yahoo Confirms CEO Is Out after Resume Scandal," *CNNMoney* (online), May 14, 2012, http://money.cnn.com.

23. D. Meinert, "Seeing behind the Mask," *HR Magazine,* February 2011, pp. 31–37.

24. CareerBuilder, "Number of Employers Using Social Media to Screen Candidates Has Increased 500 Percent over the Last Decade," April 28, 2016, www.careerbuilder.com.

25. L. Weber and E. Dwoskin, "Are Workplace Personality Tests Fair?" *The Wall Street Journal* (online), September 29, 2014, http://www.wsj.com; Alton Lane, http://www.altonlane.com, accessed May 12, 2015; T. Ackerman, "Does Psych Testing Result in Better Hires?" *Houston Chronicle,* June 21, 2010, Business & Company Resource Center, http://galenet.galegroup.com; Center for Advanced Human Resource Studies, "Should Personality Testing Be Part of the Hiring Process?" CAHRS ResearchLink, no. 12, November 2010, http://digitalcommons.ilr.cornell.edu; and E. Frauenheim, "Personality Tests Adapt to the Times," *Workforce Management,* February 1, 2010, Business & Company Resource Center, http://galenet.galegroup.com.

26. J. LaPlante, "Be Careful What You Ask on Pre-employment Tests to Avoid a Multimillion Dollar EEOC Action," *Employer Lawyer Report,* September 9, 2015, www.employerlawreport; D. Meinert, "What Do Personality Tests Really Reveal?" Society for Human Resource Management, June 1, 2015, www.shrm.org; L. Weber, "To Get a Job, New Hires Are Put to the Test—Applicants Increasingly Face Assessments to Gauge Personality, Performance," *The Wall Street Journal,* April 15, 2015, www.wsj.com.

27. R. E. Ployhart, J. A. Weekley, and K. Baughman, "The Structure and Function of Human Capital Emergence: A Multilevel Examination of the Attraction-Selection-Attrition Model," *Academy of Management Journal* 49, no. 4 (2006), pp. 661–77.

28. R. Zeidner, "Putting Drug Screening to the Test," *HR Magazine,* November 2010, ProQuest, http://proquest.umi.com.

29. D. Lieberman and M. Gannon, "As More Americans Fail Drug Tests, Employers Turn to Refugees," CNN, March 29, 2017, www.cnn.com.

30. K. Steinmetz, "Report Predicts 18 States Will Legalize Pot by 2020," *Fortune* (online), January 26, 2015, http://www.fortune.com; and C. Rubin, "Medical Marijuana Laws Leave Employers Dazed and Confused," *Inc.,* February 12, 2010, http://www.inc.com.

31. H. Heneman III, T. Judge, and J. Kammeyer-Mueller, *Staffing Organizations,* 8th ed. (New York: McGraw-Hill, 2015).

32. W. Arthur Jr., D. J. Woehr, and R. Maldegen, "Convergent and Discriminant Validity of Assessment Center Dimensions: A Conceptual and Empirical Reexamination of the Assessment Center Construct-Related Validity Paradox," *Journal of Management* 26, no. 4 (2000), pp. 813–35; and R. Randall, E. Ferguson, and F. Patterson, "Self-Assessment Accuracy and Assessment Center Decisions," *Journal of Occupational and Organizational Psychology* 73, no. 4 (December 2000), p. 443.

33. L. A. McFarland and A. M. Ryan, "Variance in Faking across Noncognitive Measures," *Journal of Applied Psychology* 85, no. 5 (October 2000), pp. 812–21; and D. E. Terpstra, R. B. Kethley, R. T. Foley, and W. Limpaphayom, "The Nature of Litigation Surrounding Five Screening Devices," *Public Personnel Management* 29, no. 1 (Spring 2000), pp. 43–54.

34. American Psychological Association, "The Truth about Lie Detectors (aka Polygraph Tests)," http://www.apa.org, accessed April 14, 2015; and D. S. Ones, C. Viswesvaran, and F. L. Schmidt, "Comprehensive Meta-analysis of Integrity Test Validities: Findings and Implications for Personnel Selection and Theories of Job Performance," *Journal of Applied Psychology* 78 (August 1993), pp. 679–703.

35. J. McGregor, "The Biggest Mass Layoffs of the Past Two Decades," *The Washington Post* (online), January 28, 2015, http://www.washingtonpost.com.

36. S. Adams, "What to Do as Soon as You Get Laid Off," *Forbes* (online), February 18, 2015, http://www.forbes.com; R.-L. DeWitt, "The Structural Consequences of Downsizing," *Organization Science* 4, no. 1 (February 1993), pp. 30–40; and P. P. Shah, "Network Destruction: The Structural Implications of Downsizing," *Academy of Management Journal* 43, no. 1 (February 2000), pp. 101–12.

37. See *Adair v. United States,* 2078 U.S. 161 (1908); and D. A. Ballam, "Employment-at-Will: The Impending Death of a Doctrine," *American Business Law Journal* 37, no. 4 (Summer 2000), pp. 653–87.

38. L. Petersen, "Is It Less Risky to Terminate an Employee within the First 90 Days of Employment?" *HR Magazine* (online), September 2014, pp. 20–21, http://www.shrm.org; J. A. Segal, "A Warning about Warnings," *HR Magazine,* February 2009, pp. 67–70; International Public Management Association for Human Resources (IPMA-HR), "Progressive Discipline," IPMA-HR website, http://www.ipma-hr.org; U.S. Chamber of Commerce, "Progressive Discipline," http://business.uschamber.com; and D. Grote, "Positive Approach to Employee Discipline," *ManagerNewz,* March 12, 2007, http://archive.managernewz.com.

39. "How to Discipline and Fire Employees," *Entrepreneur* (online), http://www.entrepreneur.com, accessed April 14, 2015; J. W. Bucking, "Employee Terminations: Ten Must-Do Steps When Letting Someone Go," *Supervision,* May 2008, Business & Company Resource Center, http://galenet.galegroup.com; and M. Price, "Employee Termination Process Is Tough for Those on Both Sides," *Journal Record (Oklahoma City, OK),* October 23, 2008, Business & Company Resource Center, http://galenet.galegroup.com.

40. "Texas Roadhouse to Pay $12 Million to Settle EEOC Age Discrimination Lawsuit," EEOC press release, March 31, 2017, www.eeoc.gov.

41. "Nestlé Waters North America to Pay $300,000 to Settle Sex Discrimination Lawsuit," EEOC press release, March 13, 2017, www.eeoc.gov.

42. Ibid.

43. R. Gatewood and H. Field, *Human Resource Selection,* 3rd ed. (Chicago: Dryden Press, 1994), pp. 36–49; and R. A. Baysinger, "Disparate Treatment and Disparate Impact Theories of Discrimination: The Continuing Evolution of Title VII of the 1964 Civil Rights Act," in *Readings in Personnel and Human Resource Management,* ed. R. S. Schuler, S. A. Youngblood, and V. L. Huber (St. Paul, MN: West Publishing, 1987).

44. "2016 Training Industry Report," *Training Magazine,* November/December 2016, www.trainingmag.com.

45. Ibid.

46. K. Vasel, "The Skills Employers Wish College Grads Had," *Fox Business* (online), January 30, 2014, http://www.foxbusiness.com; "The Prepared U Project: An In-Depth Look at Millenial Preparedness for Today's Workforce," Bentley University (online), January 29, 2014, http://www.bentley.edu.

47. Target.com, "Hiring for the Holidays! Target's Looking for More than 70,000 Team Members to Make Shopping Season Magic," September 12, 2016, www.corporate.target.com.

48. T. Friedman, "How to Get a Job at Google," *The New York Times* (online), February 22, 2014, http://www.nytimes.com; J. Light, "Google Is No. 1 on List of Desired Employers," *The Wall Street*

Journal, March 21, 2011, http://online. wsj.com; Waters, "Google Tries New Angle"; Digits, "Want to Work for Google? Here's How," *The Wall Street Journal,* June 8, 2011, http://online.wsj.com (video; interview with Joseph Walker); A. Fisher, "So You Want to Work at Google," *Fortune,* April 7, 2011, http://management. fortune.cnn.com; A. Bryant, "The Quest to Build a Better Boss," *The New York Times,* March 13, 2011, Business & Company Resource Center, http://galenet. galegroup.com; Manjoo, "How Google Became Such a Great Place to Work"; Joseph Walker, "School's in Session at Google," *The Wall Street Journal,* July 5, 2012, http://online.wsj.com; https://www. fastcompany.com/3055974/how-google-and-twitter-train-their-employees-to-be-more-mindful; company website site, http:// careers.google.com/howwehire, accessed April 20, 2017; Jenna Goudreau, "Google HR Boss Explains the Only 2 Ways to Keep Your Best People from Quitting," *Business Insider,* April 8, 2015, http://www. businessinsider.com/google-laszlo-bock-how-to-retain-employees-2015-4;"What You Can Learn from Google's Hiring Secrets"; Ellen McGirt, "Google Searches Its Soul," *Fortune,*February 1, 2017, http://fortune. com/google-diversity/.

49. For more information, see K. Wexley and G. Latham, *Increasing Productivity through Performance Appraisal* (Reading, MA: Addison-Wesley, 1994).

50. H. Bernardin, R. Konopaske, and C. Hagan, "A Comparison of Adverse Impact Levels Based on Top-down, Multisource, and Assessment Center Data: Promoting Diversity and Reducing Legal Challenges," *Human Resource Management* 51 (2012), pp. 313–41; and I. O'Boyle, "Traditional Performance Appraisal versus 360–Degree Feedback," *Training & Management Development Methods* 27 (2013), pp. 201–07.

51. F. Shipper, R. C. Hoffman, and D. M. Rotondo, "Does the 360 Feedback Process Create Actionable Knowledge Equally across Cultures?" *Academy of Management Learning & Education* 6, no. 1 (2007), pp. 33–50.

52. G. Toegel and J. Conger, "360 Degree Assessment: Time for Reinvention," *Academy of Management Learning and Education* 2, no. 3 (September 2003), p. 297; and L. K. Johnson, "Retooling 360s for Better Performance," *Harvard Business School Working Knowledge,* February 23, 2004, online.

53. M. Edwards and A. J. Ewen, "How to Manage Performance and Pay with 360-Degree Feedback," *Compensation and Benefits Review* 28, no. 3 (May/June 1996), pp. 41–46. See also S. Crabtree, "What Your Employees Need to Know," *Gallup Management Journal,* April 13, 2011, Business & Company Resource Center, http://galenet.galegroup.com; and R. S. Schuler, *Personnel and Human Resource Management* (St. Paul, MN: West Publishing, 1984).

54. Bureau of Labor Statistics, "Employer Costs for Employee Compensation—March 2017," news release, March 17, 2017, http:// www.bls.gov.

55. Ibid.

56. C. Gray, "How to Negotiate Your Salary," *Glassdoor,* July 13, 2016, www.glassdoor. com; L. Quast, "Job Seekers: 8 Tips to Negotiation Your Starting Salary," *Forbes* (online), March 31, 2014, http://www. forbes.com.

57. A. Colella, R. L. Paetzold, A. Zardkoohi, and M. J. Wesson, "Exposing Pay Secrecy," *Academy of Management Review* 32, no. 1 (2007), pp. 55–71; Lauren Weber and Rachel Emma Silverman, "Workers Share Their Salary Secrets," *The Wall Street Journal,* April 16, 2013, http:// online.wsj.com; and E. Belogolovsky and P. Bamberger "Signaling in Secret: Pay for Performance and the Incentive and Sorting Effect of Pay Secrecy" *Academy of Management Journal* 57 (2014), pp. 1706–33.

58. S. Gross and J. Bacher, "The New Variable Pay Programs: How Some Succeed, Why Some Don't," *Compensation and Benefits Review* 25, no. 1 (January–February 1993), p. 51; and G. Milkovich, J. Newman, and B. Gerhart, *Compensation,* 11th ed. (New York: McGraw-Hill/Irwin, 2013).

59. "Wal-Mart Pays over $200M in Store Staff Bonuses," *Fox Business,* September 21, 2016, www.foxbusiness.com; J. Dorfman, "Want a Job with Bonuses, 401(k) Match, Health Insurance, and More? Work for Walmart," *Forbes* (online), December 11, 2014, http://www.forbes.com.

60. J. Arthur and C. Huntley, "Ramping Up the Organizational Learning Curve: Assessing the Impact of Deliberate Learning on Organizational Performance under Gainsharing," *Academy of Management Journal* 48 (2005), pp. 1159–70; T. Welbourne and L. Gomez-Mejia, "Gainsharing: A Critical Review and a Future Research Agenda," *Journal of Management* 21, no. 3 (1995), pp. 559–609; L. P. Gomez-Mejia, T. M. Welbourne, and R. M. Wiseman, "The Role of Risk Sharing and Risk Taking under Gainsharing," *Academy of Management Review* 25, no. 3 (July 2000), pp. 492–507; D. Collins, *Gainsharing and Power: Lessons from Six Scanlon Plans* (Ithaca, NY: ILR Press, 1998); and P. K. Zingheim and J. R. Schuster, *Pay People Right!* (San Francisco: Jossey-Bass, 2000).

61. J. Kasperkevic, "America's Top CEOs Pocket 340 Times More Than Average Workers," *The Guardian,* May 17, 2016, www.theguardian.com.

62. C. Forelle and J. Bandler, "The Perfect Payday," *The Wall Street Journal,* March 18, 2006, http://online.wsj.com.

63. M. J. Conyon, "Executive Compensation and Incentives," *Academy of Management Perspectives* 20, no. 1 (February 2006), pp. 25–44.

64. J. D. Glater, "Stock Options Are Adjusted after Many Share Prices Fall," *The New York Times,* March 27, 2009, http:// www.nytimes.com; Carol Bowie, "Post-Crisis Trends in U.S. Executive Pay," Harvard Law School Forum on Corporate Governance and Financial Regulation, February 27, 2012, https://blogs.law. harvard.edu; and Scott Thurm, " 'Pay for Performance' No Longer a Punchline," *The Wall Street Journal,* March 20, 2013, http:// online.wsj.com.

65. J. Marte, "Nearly a Quarter of Fortune 500 Companies Still Offer Pensions to New Hires," *The Washington Post* (online), September 5, 2014, http://www. washingtonpost.com.

66. E. C. Kearns and M. Gallagher, eds., *The Fair Labor Standards Act* (Washington, DC: BNA, 1999).

67. C. Fay and H. W. Risher, "Contractors, Comparable Worth and the New OFCCP: Deja Vu and More," *Compensation and Benefits Review* 32, no. 5 (September/ October 2000), pp. 23–33; and G. Flynn, "Protect Yourself from an Equal-Pay Audit," *Workforce* 78, no. 6 (June 1999), pp. 144–46.

68. G. W. Bohlander, S. A. Snell, and A. W. Sherman Jr., *Managing Human Resources,* 12th ed. (Mason, OH: South-Western Publishing, 2001).

69. "US Mine Disasters Fast Facts," CNN Library, February 22, 2017, www.cnn.com.

70. Mine Safety and Health Administration, "MSHA Issues 2014 Preliminary Safety Data," news release, April 14, 2015, http:// www.msha.gov; and Mine Safety and Health Administration, "Coal Fatalities for 1990 through 2010," Mining Fatality Statistics, http://www.msha.gov/stats/ centurystats/coalstats.asp.

71. M. Flynn, "Safety and Health for Immigrant Workers," Centers for Disease Control and Prevention, December 4, 2014, http://www.blogs.cdc.gov.

72. L. Kahn, *Primer of Labor Relations,* 25th ed. (Washington, DC: Bureau of National Affairs Books, 1994); and A. Sloane and F. Witney, *Labor Relations* (Englewood Cliffs, NJ: Prentice-Hall, 1985).

73. S. Premack and J. E. Hunter; "Individual Unionization Decisions," *Psychological Bulletin* 103 (1988), pp. 223–34; L. Troy, *Beyond Unions and Collective Bargaining* (Armonk, NY: M. E. Sharpe, 1999); and J. A. McClendon, "Members and Nonmembers: Determinants of Dues-Paying Membership in a Bargaining Unit," *Relations Industrielles* 55, no. 2 (Spring 2000), pp. 332–47.

74. R. Sinclair and L. Tetrick, "Social Exchange and Union Commitment: A Comparison of Union Instrumentality and Union Support Perceptions," *Journal of Organizational Behavior* 16, no. 6 (November 1995), pp. 669–79. See also Premack and Hunter, "Individual Unionization Decisions."

75. D. Lewin and Richard B. Peterson, *The Modern Grievance Procedure in the United States* (Westport, CT: Quorum Books, 1998).

76. G. Bohlander and D. Blancero, "A Study of Reversal Determinants in Discipline and

Discharge Arbitration Awards: The Impact of Just Cause Standards," *Labor Studies Journal* 21, no. 3 (Fall 1996), pp. 3–18.

77. R. E. Ployhart, "Strategic Organizational Behavior (STROBE): The Missing Voice in the Strategic Human Capital Conversation," *Academy of Management Perspectives* 29 (2015) 342–56.

78. Light, "Google Is No. 1"; Liedtke and Ortutay, "Google Wants to Be Cool Again"; Bryant, "The Quest to Build a Better Boss"; A. Efrati and P. W. Tam, "Google Battles to Keep Talent," *The Wall Street Journal,* November 11, 2010, http://online.wsj.com; M. Ahmed, "Why Sensible Uncle Is Being Consigned to the Back Seat," *Times (London),* January 22, 2011, Business & Company Resource Center, http://galenet.galegroup.com; C. C. Miller, "New Stage, New Skills," *The New York Times,* January 22, 2011, Business & Company Resource Center, http://galenet.galegroup.com; Manjoo, "How Google Became Such a Great Place to Work"; Casserly, "Here's What Happens to Google Employees"; and Richard Feloni, "Google's HR Boss Explains the Company's 4 Rules for Hiring the Best Employees," *Business Inside,* February 18, 2016, http://www.businessinsider.com/how-google-hires-exceptional-employees-2016-2/#1-set-an-uncompromisable-high-standard-1.

Chapter 11

1. Salvador Rodriguez, "It's Time for Silicon Valley to Stop Making Excuses on Diversity," *Inc.,* July 18, 2016, https://www.inc.com/salvador-rodriguez/silicon-valley-diversity-stop-excuses.html; "How Diverse Is Silicon Valley," *CNN.com,* http://money.cnn.com/interactive/technology/tech-diversity-data/, accessed April 11, 2017; Cecilia Kang and Todd C. Frankel, "Silicon Valley Struggles to Hack Its Diversity Problem," *The Washington Post,* July 16, 2015, https://www.washingtonpost.com/business/economy/silicon-valley-struggles-to-hack-its-diversity-problem/2015/07/16/0b0144be-2053-11e5-84d5-eb37ee8eaa61_story.html?utm_term=.9ddeeb34c9a2; Company website, http://www.apple.com/diversity/, accessed April 11, 2017; Mikey Campbell, "Apple CEO Tim Cook Talks Diversity, Inclusion at Alma Mater Auburn University," *AppleInsider.com,* April 6, 2017, http://appleinsider.com/articles/17/04/06/apple-ceo-tim-cook-talks-diversity-inclusion-at-alma-mater-auburn-university; Dwyer Gunn, "These Five Tech Companies Are Trying to Solve Silicon Valley's Diversity Problem," *The Guardian,* June 6, 2016, https://www.theguardian.com/sustainable-business/2016/jun/06/silicon-valley-diversity-problem-tech-industry-solutions.

2. B. Eisenberg and M. Ruthsdotter, "Living the Legacy: The Women's Rights Movement 1848–1998," National Women's History Project, http://www.legacy98.org/move-hist.html.

3. Ibid.; R. Gladstone, "Women Run 30 Percent of All Businesses, but Only 5 Percent of the Biggest, Study Shows," *The New York Times* (online), January 12, 2015, http://www.nytimes.com; Bureau of Labor Statistics, "2016 Labor Force Statistics from the Current Population Survey," http://www.bls.gov/cps.

4. Shung J. Shin, Tae-Yeol Kim, Jeong-Yeon Lee, and Lin Bian, "Cognitive Team Diversity and Individual Team Member Creativity: A Cross-Level Interaction," *Academy of Management Journal* 55 (February 2012), pp. 197–212; David A. Harrison and Katherine J. Klein, "What's the Difference? Diversity Constructs as Separation, Variety, or Disparity in Organizations," *Academy of Management Review* 32 (October 2007), pp. 1199–1228; and Scott E. Page, "Making the Difference: Applying a Logic of Diversity," *Academy of Management Perspectives* 21 (November 2007), pp. 6–20.

5. "The 2016 DiversityInc. Top 50 Companies for Diversity," *DiversityInc,* www.diversityinc.com, accessed April 10, 2017.

6. Bureau of Labor Statistics, "Table 1: Civilian Labor Force by Age, Sex, Race, and Ethnicity, 1992, 2002, 2012, and Projected 2022," news release, December 19, 2013, http://www.bls.gov.

7. M. Lopez, "In 2014, Latinos Will Surpass Whites as Largest Racial/Ethnic Group in California," Pew Research Center (online), January 24, 2014, http://www.pewresearch.org.

8. E. Horowitz, "When Will Minorities Be the Majority?" *Boston Globe,* February 26, 2016, www.bostonglobe.com.

9. Bureau of Labor Statistics, *Women in the Labor Force: A Databook,* Report 1059, December 2016, https://www.bls.gov/opub/reports/womens-databook/archive/women-in-the-labor-force-a-databook-2015.pdf.

10. A. Joshi, J. Son, and H.Roh "When Can Women Close the Gap? A Meta-analytic Test of Sex Differences in Performance and Rewards" *Academy of Management Journal* 58 (2015) 1516–45.

11. A. Brown and E. Patten, "The Narrowing, but Persistent, Gender Gap in Pay," Pew Research, April 3, 2017, http://www.pewresearch.org.

12. B. Cronin, "Negotiating Tactics Play Role in Gender Pay Gap," *The Wall Street Journal* (online), April 1, 2013, http://www.wsj.com; Bureau of Labor Statistics (BLS), "Labor Force Characteristics by Race and Ethnicity, 2011," Report 1036, August 2012, http://www.bls.gov; AAUW, "The Simple Truth about the Gender Pay Gap," 2013, http://www.aauw.org; and Jessica Bennett, "How to Attack the Gender Wage Gap? Speak Up," *The New York Times,* December 15, 2012, http://www.nytimes.com.

13. Catalyst, "Women CEOs of the S&P 500," http://www.catalyst.org, accessed April 11, 2017.

14. P. Wolfe, "Staying Flexible: 5 Tips for Creating a Millennial-Friendly Workplace," *SHRM Blog,* January 18, 2017, www.shrm.org; N. Wu and A. Donovan, "NextGen Study: How Millennials View and Impact the Workplace," PricewaterhouseCoopers (online), accessed April 28, 2015; T. Meek, "Work/Life Balance: What It Means to Millennials," Coca-Cola website, October 1, 2014, http://www.coca-colacompany.com; R. Ashgar, "What Millennials Want in the Workplace (And Why You Should Start Giving It to Them)," *Forbes* (online), January 13, 2014, http://www.forbes.com.

15. "Teen Wins $8 Million in Sexual Harassment Case against Chipotle Mexican Grill," Fox News, September 30, 2016, www.foxnews.com.

16. "National Restaurant Association Offers Training DVDs on Harassment Prevention, Social Media Use, and Customer Service," National Restaurant Association (online), press release, on April 22, 2014, http://www.restaurant.org.

17. "The 2016 DiversityInc Top 50 Companies for Diversity,"; S. Snell, S. Morris, and G. Bohlander, *Managing Human Resources,* 17th ed. (Mason, OH: South-Western Publishing, 2015).

18. "Presidential Order Protects LGBT Workers at Federal Contractors," *Society for Human Resource Management* (online), July 21, 2014, http://www.shrm.org; D. Wilkie, "More Than Half of LGBT Workers Closeted," *Society for Human Resource Management* (online), May 15, 2014, http://www.shrm.org.

19. J. Quittner, "Not Made in America: Where U.S. Innovation Really Comes From," *Inc.,* April 10, 2014, www.inc.com; "The United States of Entrepreneurs," *The Economist,* March 14, 2009, http://www.economist.com.

20. Bureau of Labor Statistics, "Labor Force Characteristics by Race and Ethnicity, 2015," September 2016, www.bls.gov.

21. M. Bertrand and S. Mullainathan, "Are Emily and Greg More Employable Than Lakisha and Jamal?" NBER Working Paper No. 9873, July 2003, http://www.nber.org.

22. "Persons with a Disability: Labor Force Characteristics Summary," Bureau of Labor Statistics, June 21, 2016, www.bls.gov; Pattison and H. Waldron, "Growth in New Disabled-Worker Entitlements, 1970–2008," *Social Security Administration Bulletin* (online) 73, no. 4 (2013), http://www.ssa.gov.

23. Bureau of Labor Statistics, "Persons with a Disability: Labor Force Characteristics," news release, June 21, 2016, http://www.bls.gov.

24. Ibid.

25. U.S. Bureau of the Census, "Anniversary of Americans with Disabilities Act: July 26," Facts for Features CB11-FF.14, May 31, 2011, http://www.census.gov; and Bureau of Labor Statistics, "Persons with a Disability: Labor Force Characteristics—2009," news release, August 25, 2010, http://www.bls.gov/cps.

26. Equal Employment Opportunity Commission (EEOC), "Disability Discrimination," http://www.eeoc.gov; EEOC, "Notice Concerning the Americans with Disabilities Act (ADA) Amendments Act of 2008," http://www.

eeoc.gov; and EEOC, "ADA Charge Data by Impairments/Bases: Resolutions, FY1997–FY2008," http://www.eeoc.gov.

27. Daniel de Vise, "Number of U.S. Adults with College Degrees Hits Historic High," *The Washington Post,* February 23, 2012, http://articles.washingtonpost.com; Bureau of the Census, "Kurt Bauman, Chief of the Education and Social Stratification Branch, Appeared on C-SPAN's 'Washington Journal' to Discuss Educational Attainment in the United States," newsroom, February 24, 2012, http://www.census.gov/newsroom/cspan/educ/; and BLS, "Foreign-Born Workers: Labor Force Characteristics, 2012," news release, May 22, 2013, http://www.bls. gov;

28. P. Taylor and the Pew Research Center, *The Next America* (New York: Public Affairs, 2014).

29. The Conference Board, "Growing Labor Shortages on the Horizon in Mature Economies," press release, September 2, 2014, http://www.conference-board.org.

30. C. Kulik, S. Perera, and C. Cregan, "Engage Me: The Mature-Age Worker and Stereotype Threat," *Academy of Management Journal* 59 (2016), pp. 2132–56.

31. S. Vernon, "Will Boomers Really Be Able to Work Past 65?" *CBS News* (online), January 6, 2015, http://www.cbsnews.com.

32. P. Shergill, "Managing High-Performing but Demanding Gen Y," *HR Magazine* (online), August 22, 2014, http://www.hrmagazine.co.uk; N. A. Hira, "Attracting the Twenty-Something Worker," *Fortune,* May 15, 2007, http://money.cnn.com.

33. L. Roepe, "Retool Recruiting to Attract Millennials," Society for Human Resource Management, March 21, 2017, www.shrm.org.

34. C. Post and K. Byron, "Women on Boards and Firm Financial Performance: A Meta-Analysis," *Academy of Management Journal* 58 (2015), pp. 1546–71.

35. D. Cumming, T. Y. Leung, and O. Rui, "Gender Diversity and Securities Fraud," *Academy of Management Journal* 58 (2015), pp. 1572–93.

36. See, for example, R. Riccò and M. Guerci, "Diversity Challenge: An Integrated Process to Bridge the 'Implementation Gap,'" *Business Horizons* 57 (2014), pp. 235–45; C. Francoeur, R. Labelle, and B. Sinclair-Desgangnè, "Gender Diversity in Corporate Governance and Top Management," *Journal of Business Ethics* 81, no. 1 (2008), pp. 83–95; A. McMillan-Capehart, J. R. Aaron, and B. N. Cline, "Investor Reactions to Diversity Reputation Signals," *Corporate Reputation Review* 13 (2010), pp. 184–97; P. Wang and J. L. Schwarz, "Stock Price Reactions to GLBT Nondiscrimination Policies," *Human Resource Management* 49, no. 2 (2010), pp. 195–216; R. C. Anderson, D. M. Reeb, A. Upadhyay, and W. Zhao, "The Economics of Director Heterogeneity," *Financial Management* 40, no. 1 (2011), pp. 5–38; M. Davidson, "Leveraging Difference for Organizational Excellence:

Managing Diversity Differently," technical note UVA-OB-0767 (Charlottesville, VA: Darden Business Publishing, 2002); Eric Kearney, Diether Gebert, and Sven C. Voelpel, "When and How Diversity Benefits Teams: The Importance of Team Members' Need for Cognition," *Academy of Management Journal* 52 (June 2009), pp. 581–98.

37. A. Diaz-Uda, C. Medina, and B. Schill, "Diversity's New Frontier: Diversity ofThought and the Future of the Workforce," Deloitte University Press (online), July 23, 2013, http://www.dupress.com; N. Adler, *International Dimensions of Organizational Behavior,* 3rd ed. (Boston: PWS-Kent, 1997); and T. Cox and S. Blake, "Managing Cultural Diversity: Implications for Organizational Competitiveness," *Academy of Management Executives* 5 (August 1991), pp. 45–56.

38. Procter & Gamble, "Fulfilling Our Potential," corporate Purpose & People website, http://www.pg.com/en_US/company/purpose_people/diversity_inclusion.

39. See www.eeco.gov.

40. H. Kelly, "Qualcomm to Pay $19.5 Million to Settle Gender Discrimination Suit," CNN, July 27, 2916, www.money.cnn.com; U.S. Equal Employment Opportunity Commission, http://www.eeoc.gov, accessed April 24, 2015.

41. B. Kreissl, "Managing a Multigenerational Workforce," *Canadian HR Reporter* 28 (2015), pp. 19–20; and R. R. Thomas Jr., "From Affirmative Action to Affirming Diversity," *Harvard Business Review,* March–April 1990.

42. K. Jesella, "Mom's Mad, and She's Organized," *The New York Times,* February 22, 2007, http://www.nytimes.com.

43. G. Avalos, "Study Looks at Diversity, Turnover," *Contra Costa Times (Walnut Creek, CA),* October 13, 2006, Business & Company Resource Center, http://galenet.galegroup.com; Aparna Joshi and Hyuntak Roh, "The Role of Context in Work Team Diversity Research: A Meta-Analytic Review," *Academy of Management Journal* 52 (June 2009), pp. 559–627.

44. Adler, *International Dimensions of Organizational Behavior;* T. Cox and S. Blake, "Managing Cultural Diversity: Implications for Organizational Competitiveness," *Academy of Management Executives* 5 (August 1991), pp. 45–56; Brian Blume, Timothy Baldwin, and Katherine Ryan, "Communication Apprehension: A Barrier to Students' Leadership, Adaptability, and Multicultural Appreciation," *Academy of Management Learning and Education* 12, September 12, 2012, pp. 158–72.

45. J. Nanley, A. Pugh, N. Romero, and A. Seals, "An Examination of Racial Discrimination in the Labor Market for Recent College Graduates: Estimates from the Field," Auburn University Department of Economics Working Paper Series no. 2014-06, http://www.http://cla.auburn.edu/econwp/.

46. Adler, *International Dimensions of Organizational Behavior.*

47. Davidson, "Leveraging Difference for Organizational Excellence:".

48. Company website, http://www.apple.com/diversity/, accessed April 11, 2017; "Apple Reports Improving Racial and Gender Diversity among Employees," *The Guardian,* August 3, 2016, https://www.theguardian.com/technology/2016/aug/03/apple-diversity-report-race-gender-facebook-google; Salvador Rodriguez, "It's Time for Silicon Valley to Stop Making Excuses on Diversity," *Inc.,* July 18, 2016, https://www.inc.com/salvador-rodriguez/silicon-valley-diversity-stop-excuses.html..

49. K. A. Jehn, "Workplace Diversity, Conflict, and Productivity: Managing in the 21st Century," SEI Center for Advanced Studies in Management, Wharton School, University of Pennsylvania, Diversity, http://mktg-sun.wharton.upenn.edu/SEI/diversity.html; and Anne Nederveen Pieterse, Daan van Knippenberg, and Dirk van Dierendonck, "Cultural Diversity and Team Performance: The Role of Team Member Goal Orientation," *Academy of Management Journal* 56 (July 20, 2012), pp. 782–804.

50. A. J. Murrell, F. J. Crosby, and R. J. Ely, *Mentoring Dilemmas: Developmental Relationships within Multicultural Organizations* (Mahwah, NJ: Lawrence Erlbaum Associates, 1999). See a review of this book by M. L. Lengnick-Hall, "Mentoring Dilemmas: Developmental Relationships within Multicultural Organizations," *Personnel Psychology* 53, no. 1 (Spring 2000), pp. 224–27.

51. Change.org, "About," http://www.change.org, accessed April 29, 2015; C. Logorio Chafkin,"4 Smart Ways to Work on Your Diversity Problem," *Inc.* (online), November 7, 2014, http://www.inc.com; A. Bluestein, "How Ben Rattray's Change.org Became a Viral Consumer Watchdog," *Fast Company* (online), September 2014, http://www.fastcompany.com; J. P. Mangalindan, "Change.org Lays Off 30% of Its Staff,"*finance.yahoo.com,* September 1, 2016, http://finance.yahoo.com/news/change-org-lays-off-30-000000994.html; Company website, https://www.change.org/about/, accessed April 11, 2017; Sarah Kessler, "Change.org Dives into Crowdfunding," *Fast Company,* June 30, 2016, https://www.fastcompany.com/3061456/changeorg-dives-into-crowdfunding; and Connie Loizos, "Change.org Introduces Change Politics, Helping Voters Make Informed Choices on Election Day," *Techcrunch.com,* January 14, 2016, https://techcrunch.com/2016/01/14/change-org-introduces-change-politics-helping-voters-make-informed-choices-on-election-day/.

52. Brett Berson, Jack Zenger, Kellan Elliott-McCrea, and Joseph Folkman, "Why Recruiting Women Requires Creativity," *Build,* February 25, 2013, http://thebuildnetwork.com.

53. R. Rosen, "Etsy CTO: Prioritizing Diversity in Our Hiring Fielded Better Women and Men," *The Atlantic* (online), February 7, 2013, http://www.theatlantic.com.

54. K. Jones, "The Most Desirable Employee Benefits," *Harvard Business Review,* February 15, 2017, www.hbr.org.

55. Society of Women Engineers, "Establishing a Flexible Career Arrangement Porgram," February 13, 2014, http://www.societyofwomenengineers.com; and M. D. Lee, S. M. MacDermid, and M. L. Buck, "Organizational Paradigms of Reduced-Load Work: Accommodation, Elaboration, and Transformation," *Academy of Management Journal* 43, no. 6 (December 2000), pp. 1211-34.

56. L. E. Overmyer Day, "The Pitfalls of Diversity Training," *Training and Development* 49, no. 12 (December 1995), pp. 24-29; S. Rynes and B. Rosen, "A Field Survey of Factors Affecting the Adoption and Perceived Success of Diversity Training," *Personnel Psychology* 48, no. 2 (Summer 1995), pp. 247-70; L. Ford, "Diversity: From Cartoons to Confrontations," *Training & Development* 54, no. 8 (August 2000), pp. 70-71; J. M. Ivancevich and J. A. Gilbert, "Diversity Management: Time for a New Approach," *Public Personnel Management* 29, no. 1 (Spring 2000), pp. 75-92; and Katerina Bezrukova, Karen A. Jehn, and Chester S. Spell, "Reviewing Diversity Training: Where We Have Been and Where We Should Go," *Academy of Management Learning and Education* 11 (June 2012), pp. 207-27.

57. "How to Increase Workplace Diversity," *The Wall Street Journal* (online), April 7, 2009, http://www.wsj.com; and M. Burkart, "The Role of Training in Advancing a Diversity Initiative," *Diversity Factor* 8, no. 1 (Fall 1999), pp. 2-5.

58. Korn Ferry, "Executive Survey Finds a Lack of Focus on Diversity and Inclusion Key Factors in Employee Turnover," press release, March 2, 2015, http://www.kornferry.com.

59. D. M. Robinson and T. Reio Jr., "Benefits of Mentoring African-American Men," *Journal of Managerial Psychology* 27 (2012), pp. 406-21; "How Bad Is the Turnover Problem?" *HR Focus,* March 2007, Business & Company Resource Center, http://galenet.galegroup.com; B. Thomas, "Black Entrepreneurs Win, Corporations Lose," *BusinessWeek,* September 20, 2006, General Reference Center Gold, http://find.galegroup.com; and P. Shurn-Hannah, "Solving the Minority Retention Mystery," *The Human Resource Professional* 13, no. 3 (May/June 2000), pp. 22-27.

60. "6 Tips on Working with Much Younger Colleagues," *Forbes,* March 27, 2017, www.forbes.com.

61. K. Van Nuys, D. Globe, D. Ng-Mak, H. Cheung, J. Sullivan, and D. Goldman, "The Association between Employee Obesity and Employer Costs: Evidence from a Panel of U.S. Employers," *American Journal of Health Promotion* 28 (May-June 2014), pp. 277-85.

62. R. Rodriguez, "Diversity Finds Its Place," *HR Magazine,* August 2006, Business & Company Resource Center, http://galenet.galegroup.com.

63. C. Clifford, "PepsiCo CEO: Hiring More Women and People of Color Is a Business Imperative,'" CNBC, October 17, 2016, www.cnbc.com.

64. PepsiCo, "Diversity & Engagement," http://www.pepsic.com, accessed April 11, 2017.

65. Marco della Cava, "Apple Shareholders Reject Bolder Diversity Push, Again," *USA Today,* February 28, 2017, https://www.usatoday.com/story/tech/news/2017/02/28/apple-shareholders-reject-bolder-diversity-push-again/98530788/; Company website, http://www.apple.com/diversity/, accessed April 11, 2017; Dwyer Gunn, "These Five Tech Companies Are Trying to Solve Silicon Valley's Diversity Problem,".

Chapter 12

1. Robert Safian, "How PepsiCo CEO Indra Nooyi Is Steering the Company toward a Purpose-Driven Future," *Fast Company,* January 9, 2017, https://www.fastcompany.com/3066378/how-pepsico-ceo-indra-nooyi-is-steering-the-company-tow; Jackie Wattles, "Pepsi CEO Indra Nooyi Gets Big Pay Bump," *Money.cnn.com,* March 18, 2017, http://money.cnn.com/2017/03/18/news/companies/pepsi-indra-nooyi/; Alana Petroff, "Pepsi Gets Aggressive on Cutting Sugar," *Money.cnn.com,* October 17, 2016, http://money.cnn.com/2016/10/17/news/pepsi-sugar-drinks-soda/index.html?iid=EL; "Indra Nooyi," *Wall Street Journal,* http://topics.wsj.com/person/N/indra-k-nooyi/247, accessed April 11, 2017; Monica Watrous, "Nooyi: PepsiCo Making 'Considerable Progress' in Portfolio Transformation," *Food Business News,* February 1, 2017, http://www.foodbusinessnews.net/articles/news_home/Financial-Performance/2017/02/Nooyi_PepsiCo_making_considera.aspx?ID=%7B31501A45-3203-42FC-8874-3F00E014386D%7D.

2. "Best for Vets: Employers 2016," *Military Times,* www.bestforvets.militarytimes.com, accessed April 14, 2017.

3. W. Bennis and B. Nanus, *Leaders* (New York: Harper & Row, 1985), p. 27.

4. J. Petrick, R. Schere, J. Brodzinski, J. Quinn, and M. Fall Ainina, "Global Leadership Skills and Reputational Capital: Intangible Resources for Sustainable Competitive Advantage," *Academy of Management Executive,* February 1999, pp. 58-69.

5. Bennis and Nanus, *Leaders.*

6. Ibid.,

7. E. E. Lawler III, *Treat People Right! How Organizations and Individuals Can Propel Each Other into a Virtual Spiral of Success* (San Francisco: Jossey-Bass,2003); G. Llopis, "The 6 Most Important Things Employees Need from Their Leaders to Realize High Potential," *Forbes* (online), September 30, 2013, http://www.forbes.com

8. Alejandra Cancino, "Deliberate Change of Pace Works for ITW Attorney," *Chicago Tribune,* May 6, 2013, sec. 2, pp. 1, 4.

9. M. Curtin, "The Top 4 Traits Millennials Look for in Leaders," *Inc.,* March 27, 2017, www.inc.com; L. Pollak, "Millennials: Tomorrow's Leaders, Today," *The Hartford,* April 2014, http://www.thehartford.com; "The Deloitte Millennial Survey Executive Survey," Deloitte, January 2014, http://www2.deloitte.com; L. Stiller Rikleen, Esq., "Creating Tomorrow's Leaders: the Expanding Roles of Millennials in the Workplace," Boston College Center for Work & Family, http://www.bc.edu, accessed May 7, 2015.

10. J. Kouzes and B. Posner, *The Leadership Challenge* (San Francisco: Jossey-Bass, 1987).

11. "5 Influential CEOs Weigh in What Makes a Good Leader," *Entrepreneur* (online), February 25, 2013, http://www.entrepreneur.com.

12. "Branson Outlines World Powered by Wind, Solar Power," *Phys.org,* September 25, 2015, www.phys.org.

13. A. M. Carton, C. Murphy, and J. R. Clark, "A (Blurry) Vision of the Future: How Leader Rhetoric about Ultimate Goals Influences Performance," *Academy of Management Journal* 57 (2014), pp. 1544-70; A. Ruvio, Z. Rosenblatt, and R. Hertz-Lazarowitz, "Entrepreneurial Leadership Vision in Nonprofit vs. For-Profit Organizations," *Leadership Quarterly* 21 (2010), pp. 144-58; J. Baum, E. A. Locke, and S. Kirkpatrick, "A Longitudinal Study of the Relation of Vision and Vision Communication to Venture Growth in Entrepreneurial Firms," *Journal of Applied Psychology* 83 (1998), pp. 43-54.

14. E. C. Shapiro, *Fad Surfing in the Boardroom* (Reading, MA: Addison-Wesley, 1995).

15. J. Kouzes and B. Posner, *The Leadership Challenge* (San Francisco: Jossey-Bass, 1995).

16. Ibid. (1995)

17. W. Bennis and R. Townsend, *Reinventing Leadership* (New York: William Morrow, 1995).

18. Ibid.

19. D. Mattioli and K. Maher, "At 3M, Innovation Comes in Tweaks and Snips," *The Wall Street Journal,* March 1, 2010, http://online.wsj.com.

20. Kouzes and Posner, *The Leadership Challenge* (1987).

21. J. A. Conger, "The Dark Side of Leadership," *Organizational Dynamics* 19 (Autumn 1990), pp. 44-55.

22. J. Conger, "The Vision Thing: Explorations into Visionary Leadership," in *Cutting Edge Leadership 2000,* ed. B. Kellerman and L. Matusak (College Park, MD: James MacGregor Burns Academy of Leadership, 2000).

23. J. P. Kotter, "What Leaders Really Do," *Harvard Business Review* 68 (May-June 1990), pp. 103-11.

24. J. Jensen, "From Me to We," *Leadership Excellence* 31 (2014), pp. 65-66; M. E. Van

Buren and T. Safferstone, "Collective Quick Wins," *Computerworld,* January 26, 2009, pp. 24–25.

25. G. Yukl, *Leadership in Organizations,* 3rd ed. (Englewood Cliffs, NJ: Prentice Hall, 1994).

26. R. House and R. Aditya, "The Social Scientific Study of Leadership: Quo Vadis?" *Journal of Management* 23 (1997), pp. 409–73.

27. K. Boal and P. Schultz, "Storytelling, Time, and Evolution: The Role of Strategic Leadership in Complex Adaptive Systems," *Leadership Quarterly* 18 (2007), pp. 411–28; R. D. Ireland and M. A. Hitt, "Achieving and Maintaining Strategic Competitiveness in the 21st Century: The Role of Strategic Leadership," *Academy of Management Executive,* February 1999, pp. 43–57.

28. P. Cappelli, H. Singh, J. V. Singh, and M. Useem, "Leadership Lessons from India," *Harvard Business Review,* March 2010, pp. 90–97.

29. J. Gardner, "The Heart of the Matter: Leader–Constituent Interaction," in *Leading & Leadership,* ed. T. Fuller (Notre Dame, IN: University of Notre Dame Press, 2000), pp. 239–44, quote at p. 240.

30. R. E. Kelly, "In Praise of Followers," *Harvard Business Review* 66 (November–December 1988), pp. 142–48.

31. Bennis and Townsend, *Reinventing Leadership: Strategies to Empower the Organization.*

32. Kelly, "In Praise of Followers,".

33. C. Manz and D. Gioia, "The Interrelationship of Power and Control," *Human Relations* 36, no. 5 (1983), pp. 459–76.

34. J. R. P. French and B. Raven, "The Bases of Social Power," in *Studies in Social Power,* ed. D. Cartwright (Ann Arbor, MI: Institute for Social Research, 1959).

35. G. Yukl and C. Falbe, "Importance of Different Power Sources in Downward and Lateral Relations," *Journal of Applied Psychology* 76 (1991), pp. 416–23.

36. Ibid.

37. "S. Badal, "For Great Business Builders, Knowledge Is Power," *Gallup Business Journal* (online), September 30, 2014, http://www.gallup.com; L. Bryan, E. Matson, and L. Weiss, "Harnessing the Power of Informal Employee Networks," *The McKinsey Report* 4 (2007), pp. 44–55.

38. R. M. Stogdill, "Personal Factors Associated with Leadership: A Survey of the Literature," *Journal of Psychology* 25 (1948), pp. 35–71.

39. G. Moran, "Leadership: Nature or Nurture?" *Entrepreneur* (online), October 14, 2013, http://www.entrepreneur.com; S. Kirkpatrick and E. Locke, "Leadership: Do Traits Matter?" *The Executive* 5 (May 1991), pp. 48–60.

40. G. A. Yukl, *Leadership in Organizations,* 2nd ed. (Englewood Cliffs, NJ: Prentice-Hall, 1989).

41. T. Judge, J. Bono, R. Ilies, and M. Gerhardt, "Personality and Leadership: A Qualitative and Quantitative Review," *Journal of Applied Psychology* 87 (2002), pp. 765–80.

42. A. Grant, F. Gino, and D. Hofmann, "Reversing the Extroverted Leadership Advantage: The Role of Employee Proactivity," *Academy of Management Journal* 54 (2011), pp. 528–50.

43. R. Foti and N. M. A. Hauenstein, "Pattern and Variable Approaches in Leadership Emergence and Effectiveness," *Journal of Applied Psychology* 92 (2007), pp. 347–55.

44. J. P. Kotter, *The General Managers* (New York: Free Press, 1982).

45. T. Manning, "The Art of Successful Influence: Matching Influence Strategies and Styles to the Context," *Industrial and Commercial Training* 44 (2012), pp. 26–34; S. Zaccaro, R. Foti, and D. Kenny, "Self- Monitoring and Trait-Based Variance in Leadership: An Investigation of Leader Flexibility across Multiple Group Situations," *Journal of Applied Psychology* 76 (1991), pp. 308–15.

46. D. Goleman, "Leadership That Gets Results," *Harvard Business Review,* March–April 2000, pp. 78–90.

47. J. Misumi and M. Peterson, "The Performance-Maintenance (PM) Theory of Leadership: Review of a Japanese Research Program," *Administrative Science Quarterly* 30 (June 1985), pp. 198–223.

48. T. Judge, R. Piccolo, and R. Ilies, "The Forgotten Ones? The Validity of Consideration and Initiating Structure in Leadership Research," *Journal of Applied Psychology* 89 (2004), pp. 36–51.

49. G. Thomas, R. Martin, and R. Riggio, "Leading Groups: Leadership as a Group Process," *Group Processes & Intergroup Relations* 16 (2013), pp. 3–16.

50. Misumi and Peterson, "The Performance-Maintenance (PM) Theory. judge et al.,

51. Judge, Piccolo, and Ilies, "The Forgotten Ones?"

52. G. Graen and M. Uhl-Bien, "Relationship-Based Approach to Leadership: Development of Leader-Member Exchange (LMX) Theory of Leadership over 25 Years: Applying a Multi-Level Multi-Domain Perspective," *Leadership Quarterly* 6, no. 2 (1995), pp. 219–47.

53. R. House and R. Aditya, "The Social Scientific Study of Leadership: Quo Vadis?" *Journal of Management* 23 (1997), pp. 409–73.

54. C. R. Gerstner and D. V. Day, "Meta-Analytic Review of Leader-Member Exchange Theory: Correlates and Construct Issues," *Journal of Applied Psychology* 82 (1997), pp. 827–44.

55. T. Rockstuhl, J. Dulebohn, S. Ang, and L. Shore, "Leader-Member Exchange (LMX) and Culture: A Meta-analysis of Correlates of LMX Across 23 Countries," *Journal of Applied Psychology* 97 (2012), pp. 1097–1130.

56. Misumi and Peterson, "The Performance-Maintenance (PM) Theory".

57. M. Mills and S. Culbertson, "High-Involvement Work Practices: Are They Really Worth It?" The *Academy of Management Perspectives* 23 (2009), pp. 93–95; J. Wagner III, "Participation's Effect on Performance and Satisfaction: A Reconsideration of Research," *Academy of Management Review,* April 1994, pp. 312–30.

58. R. White and R. Lippitt, *Autocracy and Democracy: An Experimental Inquiry* (New York: Harper & Brothers, 1960).

59. R. Charan, "Conquering a Culture of Indecision," *Harvard Business Review* 84 (2006), pp. 108–17; J. Muczyk and R. Steel, "Leadership Style and the Turnaround Executive," *Business Horizons,* March–April 1999, pp. 39–46.

60. A. Tannenbaum and W. Schmidt, "How to Choose a Leadership Pattern," *Harvard Business Review* 36 (March–April 1958), pp. 95–101.

61. E. Fleishman and E. Harris, "Patterns of Leadership Behavior Related to Employee Grievances and Turnover," *Personnel Psychology* 15 (1962), pp. 43–56.

62. R. Likert, *The Human Organization: Its Management and Value* (New York: McGraw-Hill, 1967).

63. R. Blake and J. Mouton, *The Managerial Grid* (Houston: Gulf, 1964).

64. Misumi and Peterson, "The Performance-Maintenance (PM) Theory."

65. J. Wall, *Bosses* (Lexington, MA: Lexington Books, 1986), p. 103.

66. Tannenbaum and Schmidt, "How to Choose a Leadership Pattern,".

67. To practice using the decision tree, please see V. H. Vroom, "Leadership and the Decision-Making Process," *Organizational Dynamics,* Spring 2000, pp. 82–93.

68. F. E. Fiedler, *A Theory of Leadership Effectiveness* (New York: McGraw-Hill, 1967).

69. P. Hersey and K. Blanchard, *The Management of Organizational Behavior* (Englewood Cliffs, NJ: Prentice Hall, 1984).

70. Yukl, *Leadership in Organizations,.*

71. R. J. House, "A Path-Goal Theory of Leader Effectiveness," *Administrative Science Quarterly* 16 (1971), pp. 321–39.

72. J. Howell, D. Bowen, P. Dorfman, S. Kerr, and P. Podsakoff, "Substitutes for Leadership: Effective Alternatives to Ineffective Leadership," *Organizational Dynamics* 19 (Summer 1990), pp. 21–38.

73. Watrous, "Nooyi: PepsiCo Making 'Considerable Progress' in Portfolio Transformation"; John Kell, "PepsiCo's Promise to Get Healthier Is Paying Off," *Fortune,* February 15, 2017, http://fortune.com/2017/02/15/pepsico-healthy-paying-off/; "Leadership Lessons from Pepsi CEO Indra Nooyi," *Business Insider,* March 29, 2016, http://www.businessinsider.in/careers/winning/slidelist/51597475.cms; Benjamin Snyder, "7 Quotes That Prove What Kind of Leader Indra Nooyi Really Is," *Fortune,* June 7, 2015, http://fortune.com/2015/06/07/indra-nooyi/; Safian, "How PepsiCo CEO Indra Nooyi Is Steering the Company Toward a Purpose-Driven Future.

74. R. G. Lord and W. Gradwohl Smith, "Leadership and the Changing Nature of Performance," in *The Changing Nature of Performance,* ed. D. R. Ilgen and E. D. Pulakos (San Francisco: Jossey-Bass, 1999).

75. S. Dionne, F. Yammarino, L. Atwater, and L. James, "Neutralizing Substitutes for Leadership Theory: Leadership Effects and Common-Source Bias," *Journal of Applied Psychology* 87 (2002), pp. 454–64.

76. D. Van Knippenberg and S. Sitkin, "A Critical Assessment of Charismatic Transformational Leadership Research: Back to the Drawing Board?" *Academy of Management Annals* 7 (2013), pp. 1–60.

77. Bass, *Leadership and Performance Beyond Expectations*

78. T. Chamorro-Premuzic, "The Dark Side of Charisma," *Harvard Business Review* (online), November 16, 2012, http://www.hbr.org; Y. A. Nur, "Charisma and Managerial Leadership: The Gift That Never Was," *Business Horizons,* July–August 1998, pp. 19–26; and R. J. House, "A 1976 Theory of Charismatic Leadership," in *Leadership: The Cutting Edge,* ed. J. G. Hunt and L. L. Larson (Carbondale IL: Southern Illinois University Press, 1977).

79. M. Brown and L. Trevino, "Socialized Charismatic Leadership, Values Congruence, and Deviance in Work Groups," *Journal of Applied Psychology* 91 (2006), pp. 954–62.

80. M. Potts and P. Behr, *The Leading Edge* (New York: McGraw-Hill, 1987).

81. M. A. LePine, Y. Zhang, E. R. Crawford, and B. L. Rich, "Turning Their Pain to Gain: Charismatic Leader Influence on Follower Stress Appraisal and Job Performance," *Academy of Management Journal* 59 (2016) pp. 1036–59; J. Howell and B. Shamir, "The Role of Followers in the Charismatic Leadership Process: Relationships and Their Consequences," *Academy of Management Review* 30 (2005), pp. 96–112.

82. B. Galvin, P. Balkundi, and D. Waldman, "Spreading the Word: The Role of Surrogates in Charismatic Leadership Processes," *Academy of Management Review* 35 (2010), pp. 477–94; B. Galvin, P. Balkundi, and D. Waldman, "Can Charisma Be Taught? Tests of Two Interventions," *Academy of Management Review* 35 (2010), pp. 477–94.

83. Galvin, et al., "Can Charisma Be Taught?"; M. Fenley, and S. Liechti, *Academy of Management Learning & Education* 10 (2011), pp. 374–96.

84. S. Yorges, H. Weiss, and O. Strickland, "The Effect of Leader Outcomes on Influence, Attributions, and Perceptions of Charisma," *Journal of Applied Psychology* 84 (1999), pp. 428–36.

85. G. Colony, "Apple = Sony," *Forrester Blogs,* April 25, 2012, http://blogs.forrester.com.

86. D. A. Waldman and F. J. Yammarino, "CEO Charismatic Leadership: Levels-of-Management and Levels-of-Analysis Effects," *Academy of Management Review* 24 (1999), pp. 266–85.

87. A. Erez, V. F. Misangyi, D. E. Johnson, M. A. LePine, and K. C. Halverson, "Stirring the Hearts of Followers: Charismatic Leadership as the Transferral of Affect," *Journal of Applied Psychology* 93 (2008), pp. 602–16.

88. D. Cossin and J. Caballero, "Transformational Leadership Background Literature Review," IMD Global Board Center, June 2013, www.imd.org; A. Fanelli and V. Misangyi, "Bringing Out Charisma: CEO Charisma and External Stakeholders," *Academy of Management Review* 31 (2006), pp. 1049–61.

89. House and Aditya, "The Social Scientific Study of Leadership."

90. D. A. Waldman, G. G. Ramirez, R. J. House, and P. Puranam, "Does Leadership Matter? CEO Leadership Attributes and Profitability under Conditions of Perceived Environmental Uncertainty," *Academy of Management Journal* 44 (2001), pp. 134–43.

91. S. Boehm, D. Dwertmann, H. Bruch, and B. Shamir, "The Missing Link? Investigating Organizational Identity Strength and Transformational Leadership Climate as Mechanisms That Connect CEO Charisma with Firm Performance," *Leadership Quarterly* 26 (2015), pp. 156–71; B. Agle, N. Nagarajan, J. Sonnenfeld, and D. Srinivasan, "Does CEO Charisma Matter? An Empirical Analysis of the Relationships among Organizational Performance, Environmental Uncertainty, and Top Management Team Perceptions of CEO Charisma," *Academy of Management Journal* 49 (2006), pp. 161–74.

92. J. M. Howell and K. E. Hall-Merenda, "The Ties That Bind: The Impact of Leader-Member Exchange, Transformational and Transactional Leadership, and Distance on Predicting Follower Performance," *Journal of Applied Psychology* 84 (1999), pp. 680–94; and B. M. Bass, "Leadership: Good, Better, Best," *Organizational Dynamics,* Winter 1985, pp. 26–40.

93. B. Thompson, "Take a Tip from Bezos: Customers Always Need a Seat at the Table," *Entrepreneur* (online), May 28, 2014, http://www.entrepreneur.com; Adam Lashinsky, "Amazon's Jeff Bezos: The Ultimate Disrupter," *Fortune,* November 16, 2012, http://management.fortune.cnn.com.

94. D. I. Jung and B. J. Avolio, "Effects of Leadership Style and Followers' Cultural Orientation on Performance in Group and Individual Task Conditions," *Academy of Management Journal* 42 (1999), pp. 208–18.

95. Bass, *Leadership and Performance Beyond Expectations.*

96. Bennis and Nanus, *Leaders.*

97. A. M. Grant, "Leading with Meaning: Beneficiary Contact, Prosocial Impact, and the Performance Effects of Transformational Leadership," *Academy of Management Journal* 55 (2012), pp. 458–76.

98. B. Bass, B. Avolio, and L. Goodheim, "Biography and the Assessment of Transformational Leadership at the World-Class Level," *Journal of Management* 13 (1987), pp. 7–20.

99. D. Williams, "Top 10 List: The Greatest Living Business Leaders Today," *Forbes* (online), July 24, 2012, http://www.forbes.com.

100. Y. Ling, Z. Simisek, M. Lubatkin, and J. F. Veiga, "The Impact of Transformational CEOs on the Performance of Small to Medium-Sized Firms: Does Organizational Context Matter?" *Journal of Applied Psychology* 93 (2008), pp. 923–34.

101. T. A. Judge and J. E. Bono, "Five-Factor Model of Personality and Transformational Leadership," *Journal of Applied Psychology* 85 (2000), pp. 751–65; and B. Bass, "Does the Transactional-Transformational Paradigm Transcend Organizational and National Boundaries?" *American Psychologist* 22 (1997), pp. 130–42.

102. C. Li, H. Zhao, and T. M. Begley, "Transformational Leadership Dimensions and Employee Creativity in China: A Cross-level Analysis," *Journal of Business Research* 68, no. 6 (2015), pp. 1149–56.

103. R. Piccolo and J. Colquitt, "Transformational Leadership and Job Behaviors: The Mediating Role of Core Job Characteristics," *Academy of Management Journal* 49 (2006), pp. 327–40.

104. A. Colbert, A. Kristof-Brown, B. Bradley, and M. Barrick, "CEO Transformational Leadership: The Role of Goal Importance Congruence in Top Management Teams," *Academy of Management Journal* 51 (2008), pp. 81–96.

105. T. Dvir, D. Eden, B. Avolio, and B. Shamir, "Impact of Transformational Leadership on Follower Development and Performance: A Field Experiment," *Academy of Management Journal* 45 (2002), pp. 735–44.

106. B. M. Bass, *Transformational Leadership: Industry, Military, and Educational Impact* (Mahwah, NJ: Lawrence Erlbaum Associates, 1998); T. Judge and R. Piccolo, "Transformational and Transactional Leadership: A Meta-analytic Test of Their Relative Validity," *Journal of Applied Psychology* 89 (2004), pp. 755–68.

107. G. Spreitzer and R. Quinn, "Empowering Middle Managers to Be Transformational Leaders," *Journal of Applied Behavioral Science* 32 (1996), pp. 237–61.

108. J. Collins, "Level 5 Leadership," *Harvard Business Review* 1 (2001), pp. 66–76; and J. Kline Harrison and M. William Clough, "Characteristics of 'State of the Art' Leaders: Productive Narcissism versus Emotional Intelligence and Level 5 Capabilities," *Social Science Journal* 43 (2006), pp. 287–92.

109. G. Satell, "Why Tim Cook's 'Level 5 Leadership' Might Not Be Enough to Secure Apple's Future," *Forbes* (online), June 4, 2013, http://www.forbes.com; D. Vera and M. Crossan, "Strategic Leadership and Organizational Learning," *Academy of Management Review* 29 (2004), pp. 222–40.

110. F. Luthans, *Organizational Behavior,* 10th ed. (New York: McGraw-Hill/Irwin, 2005); F. Luthans and B. Avolio,

"Authentic Leadership Development," in *Positive Organizational Scholarship,* eds. K. Cameron, J. Dutton, and R. Quinn (San Francisco: Berrett-Koehler, 2003), pp. 241–58.

111. B. M. Bass, "Thoughts and Plans," in *Cutting Edge Leadership 2000,* ed. B. Kellerman and L. R. Matusak (College Park, MD: James MacGregor Burns Academy of Leadership, 2000), pp. 5–9.

112. N. Turner, J. Barling, O. Epitropaki, V. Butcher, and C. Milner, "Transformational Leadership and Moral Reasoning," *Journal of Applied Psychology* 87 (2002), pp. 304–11.

113. D. M. Mayer, M. Kuenzi, R. Greenbaum, M. Bardes, and R. Salvador, "How Low Does Ethical Leadership Flow? Test of a Trickle-Down Model," *Organizational Behavior and Human Decision Processes* 108 (2009), pp. 1–13.

114. Bass, "Thoughts and Plans,"; J. Spangenburg, "The Effect of a Pseudo-transformational Leader: Whitewater Rafting in a Hurricane," *International Journal of Management & Information Systems* 16 (2012) (online), p. 325.

115. W. Bennis, "The End of Leadership: Exemplary Leadership Is Impossible without Full Inclusion, Initiatives, and Cooperation of Followers," *Organizational Dynamics,* Summer 1999, pp. 71–79.

116. Robert K. Greenleaf Center for Servant Leadership, "What Is Servant Leadership?" https://www.greenleaf.org; Larry W. Boone and Sanya Makhani, "Five Necessary Attitudes of a Servant Leader," *Review of Business* 83, no. 1 (Winter 2012), pp. 83–96.

117. Z. Ilgaz, "How to Retain Employees through 'Servant' Leadership," *Entrepreneur,* March 1, 2017, www.entrepreneur.com.

118. M. Chiniara and K. Bentein, "Linking Servant Leadership to Individual Performance: Differentiating the Mediating Role of Autonomy, Competence and Relatedness Need Satisfaction," *Leadership Quarterly* 27 (2016), pp. 124–41; R. Liden, S. Wayne, C. Liao, and J. Meuser, "Servant Leadership and Serving Culture: Influence on Individual and Unit Performance," *Academy of Management Journal* 57 (2014), pp. 1434–52; D. Parris and J. Peachey, "A Systematic Literature Review of Servant Leadership Theory in Organizational Contexts," *Journal of Business Ethics* 113 (2013), pp. 377–93; D. Van Dierendonck, "Servant Leadership: A Review and Synthesis," *Journal of Management* 37 (2011), pp. 1228–61.

119. Google Finance, "Popeyes Louisiana Kitchen Inc.," March 27, 2017, www.google.com; J. Goudreau, "The CEO of Popeyes Says Becoming a 'Servant Leader' Helped Her Turn Around the Struggling Restaurant Chain," *Business Insider,* March 24, 2015, www.businessinsider.com.

120. Ibid.

121. M. Hogg, D. van Knippenberg, and D. E. Rasst III, "Intergroup Leadership in Organizations: Leading across Group and Organizational Boundaries," *Academy of Management Review* 37 (2012), pp. 232–55; T. Pittinsky (ed.), *Crossing the Divide: Intergroup Leadership in a World of Difference* (Cambridge, MA: Harvard Business Publishing, 2009); T. Pittinsky and S. Simon, "Intergroup Leadership," *Leadership Quarterly* 18 (2007), pp. 586–605.

122. D. Wang, D. Waldman, and Z. Zhang, "A Meta-analysis of Shared Leadership and Team Effectiveness," *Journal of Applied Psychology* 99 (2014), pp. 181–98; Pearce, "The Future of Leadership.":

123. V. Nicolaides, K. LaPort, T. Chen, A. Tomassetti, E. Weis, S. Zaccaro, and J. Cortina, "The Shared Leadership of Teams: A Meta-Analyses of Proximal, Distal, and Moderating Relationships," *Leadership Quarterly* 25 (2014), pp. 923–42.

124. J. Carson, P. Tesluk, and J. Marrone, "Shared Leadership in Teams: An Investigation of Antecedent Conditions and Performance," *Academy of Management Journal* 50 (2007), pp. 1217–34.

125. C. L. Pearce, "The Future of Leadership: Combining Vertical and Shared Leadership to Transform Knowledge Work," *Academy of Management Executive,* February 2004, pp. 47–57.

126. M. M. Koerner, "Courage as Identity Work: Accounts of Workplace Courage," *Academy of Management Journal* 57 (2014), pp. 63–93.

127. S. Caldicott, "Why Ford's Alan Mulally Is an Innovation CEO for the Record Books," *Forbes* (online), June 25, 2014, http://www.forbes.com; J. Reed and B. Simon, "Adroit in Detroit," *Financial Times,* January 25, 2011, Business & Company Resource Center, http://galenet.galegroup.com; "Epiphany in Dearborn: Ford," *The Economist,* December 11, 2010, Business & Company Resource Center, http://galenet.galegroup.com; and J. LaReau, "Ford Slashes Debt, Spends on Operations," *Automotive News,* January 31, 2011, Business & Company Resource Center, http://galenet.galegroup.com.

128. P. Block, *The Empowered Manager* (San Francisco: Jossey-Bass, 1991).

129. Ibid.

130. Kouzes and Posner, *The Leadership Challenge* (1995).

131. L. W. Boone and M. S. Peborde, "Developing Leadership Skills in College and Early Career Positions," *Review of Business,* Spring 2008, Business & Company Resource Center, http://galenet.galegroup.com.

132. A. Gaines, "Straight to the Top," *American Executive,* August 2008, Business & Company Resource Center, http://galenet.galegroup.com; and S. J. Allen and N. S. Hartman, "Leadership Development: An Exploration of Sources of Learning," *SAM Advanced Management Journal,* Winter 2008, pp. 10–19, 62–63.

133. L. Whylly, "Chief Executive Magazine Announces Its 2016 Best Companies for Leaders," *Chief Executive,* January 25, 2016, www.chiefexecutive.net.

134. M. McCall, *High Flyers* (Boston: Harvard Business School Press, 1998).

135. E. Van Velsor, C. D. McCauley, and R. Moxley, "Our View of Leadership Development," in *Center for Creative Leadership Handbook of Leadership Development,* ed. C. D. McCauley, R. Moxley, and E. Van Velsor (San Francisco: Jossey-Bass, 1998), pp. 1–25.

136. D. S. DeRue and N. Wellman, "Developing Leaders via Experience: The Role of Developmental Challenge, Learning Orientation, and Feedback Availability," *Journal of Applied Psychology* 94 (2009), pp. 859–75.

137. Marguerite Ward, "Why PepsiCo CEO Indra Nooyi Writes Letters to Her Employees' Parents," *CNBC.com,* February 1, 2017, http://www.cnbc.com/2017/02/01/why-pepsico-ceo-indra-nooyi-writes-letters-to-her-employees-parents.html; "Leadership Lessons from Pepsi CEO Indra Nooyi"; Snyder, "7 Quotes That Prove What Kind of Leader Indra Nooyi Really Is.

Chapter 13

1. Great Place to Work, "SAS," http://us.greatrated.com/sas, accessed May 8, 2015; SAS, "SAS Achieves Record Revenue in 2014–$3.09 Billion: Cloud Analytics and Data Visualization Offerings Influence 39th Consecutive Year of Growth," press release, January 29, 2015, http://www.sas.com; Mark C. Crowley, "How SAS Became the World's Best Place to Work," *Fast Company,* January 22, 2013, http://www.fastcompany.com; Omar Akhtar, "Best Companies: All-Stars," *Fortune,* January 24, 2013, http://money.cnn.com; "100 Best Companies to Work For 2013," *Fortune,* February 4, 2013, http://money.cnn.com; Great Place to Work, "World's Best Multinational Workplaces 2012," http://www.greatplacetowork.com; SAS, "SAS Ranks No. 1 in the World for Best Workplaces," news release, November 14, 2012, http://www.sas.com; SAS website, http://www.sas.com; Nicola Leske, "SAS Says Spurned IBM and Others for Independence," Reuters, June 21, 2012, http://in.reuters.com; company website, https://www.sas.com/en_us/company-information/great-workplace.html, accessed April 17, 2017; "10 Best Large Workplaces in Tech, 2016," *Fortune,* http://fortune.com/best-large-workplaces-in-technology/sas-10/, accessed April 17, 2017; company website, "2016 Benefits," https://www.sas.com/content/dam/SAS/en_us/doc/other1/fulltime-employee-benefits-program-booklet.pdf, accessed April 17, 2017; company press release, "SAS Celebrates 40th Year of Record Revenue," https://www.sas.com/tr_tr/news/press-releases/2016/february/2015-financials.html, accessed April 17, 2017.

2. R. Kreitner and F. Luthans, "A Social Learning Approach to Behavioral Management: Radical Behaviorists 'Mellowing Out,'" *Organizational Dynamics,* Autumn 1984, pp. 47–65.

3. D. Katz and R. L. Kahn, *The Social Psychology of Organizations* (New York: John Wiley & Sons, 1966).

4. C. A. Bartlett and S. Ghoshal, "Building Competitive Advantage through People," *Sloan Management Review,* Winter 2002, pp. 34–41.

5. E. Locke, "Toward a Theory of Task Motivation and Incentives," *Organizational Behavior and Human Performance* 3 (1968), pp. 157–89.

6. Department of Homeland Security, "Fiscal Years 2014–2018 Strategic Plan," http://www.dhs.gov, accessed April 16, 2017.

7. E. A. Locke, "Guest Editor's Introduction: Goal-Setting Theory and Its Applications to the World of Business," *Academy of Management Executive* 4 (November 2004), pp. 124–25.

8. G. P. Latham, "The Motivational Benefits of Goal-Setting," *Academy of Management Executive* 4 (November 2004), pp. 126–29.

9. E. A. Locke, "Linking Goals to Monetary Incentives," *Academy of Management Executive* 4 (November 2004), pp. 130–33.

10. E. E. Lawler III, *Treat People Right!* (San Francisco: Jossey-Bass, 2003).

11. Ibid.

12. J. Bono and T. Judge, "Self-Concordance at Work: Toward Understanding the Motivational Effects of Transformational Leaders," *Academy of Management Journal* 46 (2003), pp. 554–71.

13. C. Crossley, C. Cooper, and T. Wernsing, "Making Things Happen through Challenging Goals: Leader Proactivity, Trust, and Business-Unit Performance," *Journal of Applied Psychology,* 2013, pp. 540–49.

14. A. Wilson, "Kansas Quick Lane Operation Is Well-Tuned," *Automotive News,* April 5, 2010, Business & Company Resource Center, http://galenet.galegroup.com.

15. K. N. Shaw, "Changing the Goal-Setting Process at Microsoft," *Academy of Management Executive* 4 (November 2004), pp. 139–43.

16. S. Kerr and S. Laundauer, "Using Stretch Goals to Promote Organizational Effectiveness and Personal Growth: General Electric and Goldman Sachs," *Academy of Management Executive* 4 (November 2004), pp. 134–38.

17. Ibid.

18. Latham, "The Motivational Benefits of Goal-Setting."

19. T. Mitchell and W. Silver, "Individual and Group Goals When Workers Are Interdependent: Effects on Task Strategies and Performance," *Journal of Applied Psychology* 75 (1990), pp. 185–93.

20. A. Kleingeld, H. van Mierlo, and L. Arends, "The Effect of Goal Setting on Group Performance: A Meta-Analysis," *Journal of Applied Psychology* 96 (2011), pp. 1289–1304.

21. Latham, "The Motivational Benefits of Goal-Setting".

22. D. H. Pink, *Drive: The Surprising Truth about What Motivates Us* (New York: Riverhead Books, 2009), pp. 98–99.

23. D. Welsh and L. Ordóñez, "The Dark Side of Consecutive High Performance Goals: Linking Goal Setting, Depletion, and Unethical Behavior," *Organizational Behavior and Human Decision Processes* 123 (2014), pp. 79–89.

24. M. Schweitzer, L. Ordonez, and B. Douma, "Goal Setting as a Motivator of Unethical Behavior," *Academy of Management Journal* 47 (2004), pp. 422–32.

25. T. Gryta, S. Ng, and T. Francis, "Companies Routinely Steer Analysts to Deliver Earnings Surprises," *The Wall Street Journal,* August 4, 2016, www.wsj.com; C. Beaudoin, A. Cianci, and G. Tsakumis, "The Impact of CFOs' Incentives and Earnings Management Ethics on Their Financial Reporting Decisions: The Mediating Role of Moral Disengagement," *Journal of Business Ethics* 128 (2015), pp. 505–18.

26. G. Seijts and G. Latham, "Learning versus Performance Goals: When Should Each Be Used?" *Academy of Management Executive* 19 (February 2005), pp. 124–31; P. C. Early, T. Connolly, and G. Ekegren, "Goals, Strategy Development, and Task Performance: Some Limits on the Efficacy of Goal Setting," *Journal of Applied Psychology* 74 (1989), pp. 24–33; and C. E. Shalley, "Effects of Productivity Goals, Creativity Goals, and Personal Discretion on Individual Creativity," *Journal of Applied Psychology* 76 (1991), pp. 179–85.

27. R. C. Litchfield, "Brainstorming Reconsidered: A Goal-Based View," *Academy of Management Review* 33 (2008), pp. 649–68.

28. R. Fisher and A. Sharp, *Getting It Done* (New York: HarperCollins, 1998).

29. E. Thorndike, *Animal Intelligence* (New York: Macmillan, 1911).

30. A. D. Stajkovic and F. Luthans, "Differential Effects of Incentive Motivators on Work Performance," *Academy of Management Journal* 44 (2001), pp. 580–90.

31. B. Sims Jr., "Want Your Team to Perform Better? Try Positive Reinforcement," *Entrepreneur* (online), February 6, 2014, http://www.entrepreneur.com; J. Zaslow, "The Most-Praised Generation Goes to Work," *The Wall Street Journal,* April 20, 2007, http;//online.wsj.com.

32. K. Butterfield, L. K. Trevino, and G. Ball, "Punishment from the Manager's Perspective: A Grounded Investigation and Inductive Model," *Academy of Management Review* 39 (1996), pp. 1479–1512.

33. S. Wiltermuth and F. Flynn, "Power, Moral Clarity, and Punishment in the Workplace," *Academy of Management Journal* 56 (August 2013) pp. 1002–23.

34. Adam Madison, "Positive Results," *Rock Products,* September 1, 2008, Business & Company Resource Center, http://galenet.galegroup.com.

35. T. Judge and R. Piccolo, "Transformational and Transactional Leadership: A Meta-Analytic Test of Their Relative Ability," *Journal of Applied Psychology* 89 (2004), pp. 755–68.

36. S. Kerr, "On the Folly of Rewarding a While Hoping for B," *Academy of Management Journal* 18 (1975), pp. 769–83.

37. D. Levitin, "Why the Modern World Is Bad for Your Brain," *The Guardian* (online), January 18, 2015, http://www.theguardian.com; T. Bradberry, "Multitasking Damages Your Brain and Career, New Studies Suggest," *Forbes* (online), October 8, 2014, http://www.forbes.com; S. Lohr, "Science Finds Advantage in Focusing, Not Multitasking," *Chicago Tribune,* March 25, 2007, sec. 1, p. 10.

38. E. E. Lawler III, *Rewarding Excellence* (San Francisco: Jossey-Bass, 2000).

39. C. Meyer, "Money Isn't Everything: Nonfinancial Rewards That Retain the Best Workers," *Journal of Accountancy,* June 20, 2016, www.journalofaccountancy.com.

40. R. Sheridan, *Joy, Inc.: How We Build a Workplace People Love* (New York: Portfolio/Penguin, 2015); M. May, "Creating a Company Culture of Joy," American Express Open Forum, January 15, 2014, www.americanexpress.com.

41. J. Pfeffer and R. Sutton, *The Knowing-Doing Gap* (Boston: Harvard Business School Press, 2000).

42. J. S. Lublin, "Recall the Mistakes of Your Past Bosses, So You Can Do Better," *The Wall Street Journal,* January 2, 2007, http://online.wsj.com.

43. A. Vaccaro, "The Best Leaders Ask for More Feedback," *Inc.* (online), December 24, 2013, http://www.inc.com; S. Moss and J. Sanchez, "Are Your Employees Avoiding You? Managerial Strategies for Closing the Feedback Gap," *Academy of Management Executive* 18, no. 1 (February 2004), pp. 32–44.

44. Lawler, *Treat People Right!*

45. R. Cheramie, "An Examination of Feedback-Seeking Behaviors: The Feedback Source and Career Success," *Career Development International* 18 (2013), pp. 712–31; S. B. Silverman, C. E. Pogson, and A. B. Cober, "When Employees at Work Don't Get It: A Model for Enhancing Individual Employee Change in Response to Performance Feedback," *Academy of Management Executive* 19, no. 2 (May 2005), pp. 135–47; and J. Jackman and M. Strober, "Fear of Feedback," *Harvard Business Review,* April 2003, pp. 101–7.

46. V. H. Vroom, *Work and Motivation* (New York: John Wiley & Sons, 1964).

47. R. E. Wood, P. W. B. Atkins, and J. E. H. Bright, "Bonuses, Goals, and Instrumentality Effects," *Journal of Applied Psychology* 84 (1999), pp. 703–20.

48. YouEarnedIt, "Company Spotlight," http://www.youearnedit.com, accessed May 11, 2015.

49. D. Ranil, "SAS's 2014 Revenue Rose to $3.09 Billion," *News Observer* (online), January 29, 2015, http://www.newsobserver.com; Crowley, "How SAS Became the World's Best Place to Work"; L. Buchanan, How SAS Continues to Grow," Inc., September 2011, http://www.

inc.com; Steve Lohr, "The Nimble Dance of a Rich Legacy Software Company," *The New York Times,* March 28, 2013, http://bits.blogs.nytimes.com; Kristin Burnham, "Five Tips for Social Business Adoption: How SAS Succeeded," *CIO,* May 21, 2012, http://www.cio.com; Nancy Pardue, "Jenn Mann, Vice President of Human Rresources, SAS," *Cary Magazine,* August 24, 2015, https://www.carymagazine.com/features/jenn-mann-vice-president-of-human-resources-sas/; "SAS Institute Inc.," http://reviews.greatplacetowork.com/sas, accessed April 17, 2017; Karen Lee, "Let's Get' To the Point' of Internal Communications," February 28, 2014, http://blogs.sas.com/content/sascom/2014/02/28/lets-get-to-the-point-of-internal-communications/.

50. A. H. Maslow, "A Theory of Human Motivation," *Psychological Review,* July 1943, pp. 370-96.

51. M. Wahba and L. Birdwell, "Maslow Reconsidered: A Review of Research on the Need Hierarchy Theory," *Organizational Behavior and Human Performance* 15 (1976), pp. 212-40.

52. A Adkins and B. Rigoni, "Millennials Want Jobs to be Developmental Opportunities," Gallup, June 30, 2016, www.gallup.com.

53. "How I Managed Millennials to $100 Million in Sales," CNBC, March 26, 2015, www.cnbc.com; C. Seager, "Generation Y: Why Young Job Seekers Want More than Money," *The Guardian* (online), February 19, 2014, http://www.theguardian.com; M. Rafter, "Best Companies Offer Employees More Flexible Work Options," Great Place to Work, January 22, 2014, http://www.usgreatrated.com.

54. W. L. Gore, "Associates' Standards of Ethical Conduct," http://www.gore.com, accessed May 11, 2015.

55. "Help Wanted: More Jobs for America," *The New York Times,* December 3, 2016, www.nytimes.com; D. Rohde, "The Anti-Walmart: The Secret Sauce of Wegmans Is People," *The Atlantic* (online), March 23, 2012, http://www.theatlantic.com.

56. C. Alderfer, *Existence, Relatedness, and Growth: Human Needs in Organizational Settings* (Glencoe: IL: Free Press, 1972).

57. C. Pinder, *Work Motivation* (Glenview, IL: Scott, Foresman, 1984).

58. D. McClelland, *The Achieving Society* (New York: Van Nostrand Reinhold, 1961).

59. D. McClelland and R. Boyatzis, "Leadership Motive Pattern and Long-Term Success in Management," *Journal of Applied Psychology* 67 (1982), pp. 737-43.

60. N. Adler, *International Dimensions of Organizational Behavior,* 2nd ed. (Boston: Kent, 1991); and G. Hofstede, *Cultures and Organizations* (London: McGraw-Hill, 1991).

61. "2014 Trends in Global Employee Engagement," *AON Hewitt* (online), http://www.aon.com, accessed May 11, 2015; N. R. Lockwood, "Leveraging Employee Engagement for Competitive Advantage: HR's Strategic Role," *HR Magazine,* March 2007, Business & Company Resource Center, http://galenet.galegroup.com.

62. E. E. Lawler III and D. Finegold, "Individualizing the Organization: Past, Present, and Future," *Organizational Dynamics,* Summer 2000, pp. 1-15.

63. Ibid.

64. B. Gerhart and M. Fang, "Pay, Intrinsic Motivation, Extrinsic Motivation, Performance, and Creativity in the Workplace: Revisiting Long-Held Beliefs," *Annual Review of Organizational Psychology and Organizational Behavior* 2 (2015), pp. 489-521.

65. Gerhart and Fang, "Pay, Intrinsic Motivation, Extrinsic Motivation, Performance, and Creativity in the Workplace: C. Cerasoli, J. Nicklin, and M. Ford," Intrinsic Motivation and Extrinsic Incentives Jointly Predict Performance: A 40-Year Meta-Analysis," *Psychological Bulletin* 140 (2014), pp. 980-1008.

66. T. M. Amabile, "A Model of Creativity and Innovation in Organizations," in *Research in Organizational Behavior,* ed. B. M. Staw and L. L. Cummings (Greenwich, CT: JAI Press, 1988), pp. 10, 123-67.

67. N. Madjar, E. Greenberg, and Z. Chen, "Factors for Radical Creativity, Incremental Creativity, and Routine, Noncreative Performance," *Journal of Applied Psychology* 96 (2011), pp. 730-43; C. M. Ford, "A Theory of Individual Creative Action in Multiple Social Domains," *Academy of Management Review* 21 (1996), pp. 1112-42.

68. G. Oldham and A. Cummings, "Employee Creativity: Personal and Contextual Factors at Work," *Academy of Management Journal* 39 (1996), pp. 607-34.

69. A. Fisher, "How Companies Kill Creativity," *Fortune* (online), October 17, 2013, http://www.fortune.com; T. Amabile, R. Conti, H. Coon, J. Lazenby, and M. Herron, "Assessing the Work Environment for Creativity," *Academy of Management Journal* 39 (1996), pp. 1154-84.

70. M. Campion and G. Sanborn, "Job Design," in *Handbook of Industrial Engineering,* ed. G. Salvendy (New York: John Wiley & Sons, 1991).

71. Lawler and Finegold, "Individualizing the Organization."

72. Team Rubicon, "Our Mission," http://www.teamrubiconusa.com, accessed May 16, 2015; *Team Rubicon Blog,* "Deploying Abroad," April 26, 2014, http://www.teamrubiconusa.com; Federal Emergency Management Agency, "Team Rubicon Volunteers Help Disaster Survivors in Vilonia, Arkansas," May 22, 2014, http://www.fema.gov; https://teamrubiconusa.org, accessed April 17, 2017.

73. "2013 List of 15 Top MBA Employers," *CNNMoney,* http://www.money.cnn.com, accessed May 12, 2015.

74. M. Campion and D. McClelland, "Interdisciplinary Examination of the Costs and Benefits of Enlarged Jobs: A Job Design Quasi-Experiment," *Journal of Applied Psychology* 76 (1991), pp. 186-98.

75. F. Herzberg, *Work and the Nature of Men* (Cleveland: World, 1966).

76. J. R. Hackman, G. Oldham, R. Janson, and K. Purdy, "A New Strategy for Job Enrichment," *California Management Review* 16 (Fall 1975), pp. 57-71.

77. Pink, *Drive: The Surprising Truth about What Motivates Us,* p. 119.

78. R. Rechheld, "Loyalty-Based Management" *Harvard Business Review,* March–April 1993, pp. 64-73.

79. "Motivation in Today's Workplace: The Link to Performance," *HR Magazine,* July 2010, pp. 1-9.

80. B. Trahant, "Recruiting and Engaging the Federal Workforce," *Public Manager,* Spring 2008, Business & Company Resource Center, http://galenet.galegroup.com.

81. J. Immelt, V. Govindarajan, and C. Trimble, "How GE Is Disrupting Itself," *Harvard Business Review* 87 (October 2009), pp. 56-65.

82. Ashish Gambhir, "Use Online Feedback to Motivate, Engage Employees," *QSRweb.com,* April 16, 2012, http://www.qsrweb.com; Parasole website, http://www.parasole.com.

83. Campion and Sanborn, "Job Design."

84. S. Seibert, S. Silver, and W. A. Randolph, "Taking Empowerment to the Next Level: A Multiple-Level Model of Empowerment, Performance, and Satisfaction," *Academy of Management Journal* 47 (2004), pp. 332-49.

85. C. Argyris, "Empowerment: The Emperor's New Clothes," *Harvard Business Review,* May–June 1998, pp. 98-105.

86. R. Forrester, "Empowerment: Rejuvenating a Potent Idea," *Academy of Management Executive,* August 2000, pp. 67-80; N. Lorinkova, M. Pearsall, and H. P. Sims Jr., "Examining the Differential Longitudinal Performance of Directive versus Empowering Leadership in Teams," *Academy of Management Journal* 56 (2012), pp. 573-96; D. Liu, S. Zhang, L. Wang, and T. Lee, "The Effects of Autonomy and Empowerment on Employee Turnover: Test of a Multilevel Model in Teams," *Journal of Applied Psychology* 96 (2011), pp. 1305-16; M. T. Maynard, L. Gilson, and J. Mathieu, "Empowerment—Fad or Fab? A Multilevel Review of the Past Two Decades of Research," *Journal of Management* 38 (2012), pp. 1231-81; X. Zhang and K. Bartol, "Linking Empowering Leadership and Employee Creativity: The Influence of Psychological Empowerment, Intrinsic Motivation, and Creative Process Engagement," *Academy of Management Journal* 53 (2010), pp. 107-28.

87. R. C. Liden, S. J. Wayne, and R. T. Sparrowe, "An Examination of the Mediating Role of Psychological Empowerment on the Relations between the Job, Interpersonal Relationships, and Work Outcomes," *Journal of Applied Psychology* 85 (2000), pp. 407-16.

88. M. R. Barrick, G. R. Thurgood, T. A. Smith, and S. H. Courtright, "Collective Organizational Engagement: Linking Motivational Antecedents, Strategic Implementation, and Firm Performance" *Academy of Management Journal* 58 (2015), pp. 111-35; B. L. Rich, J. Lepine, and E.

Crawford, "Job Engagement: Antecedents and Effects on Job Performance," *Academy of Management Journal* 53 (2010), pp. 617–35.

89. T. Peters and N. Austin, *A Passion for Excellence* (New York: Random House, 1985).

90. D'Innocenzo, M. Lucian, J. Mathieu, et al., "Empowered to Perform: A Multilevel Investigation of the Influence of Empowerment on Performance in Hospital Units," *Academy of Management Journal* 58 (2016), pp. 1290–1307.

91. J. Kouzes and B. Posner, *The Leadership Challenge,* 2nd ed. (San Francisco: Jossey-Bass, 1995).

92. M. M. Butts, R. J. Vandenberg, D. M. DeJoy, B. S. Schaffer, and M. G. Wilson, "Individual Reactions to High Involvement Work Processes: Investigating the Role of Empowerment and Perceived Organizational Support," *Journal of Occupational Health Psychology* 14 (2009), pp. 122–36; Price Waterhouse Change Integration Team, Better Change (Burr Ridge, IL: Richard D. Irwin, 1995).

93. E. E. Lawler III, *The Ultimate Advantage: Creating the High Involvement Organization* (San Francisco: Jossey-Bass, 1992).

94. Kouzes and Posner, *The Leadership Challenge.*

95. W. A. Randolph and M. Sashkin, "Can Organizational Empowerment Work in Multinational Settings?" *Academy of Management Executive* 16 (2002), pp. 102–15.

96. J. Colquitt and K. Zipay, "Justice, Fairness, and Employee Reactions," *Annual Review of Organizational Psychology and Organizational Behavior* 2 (2015), pp. 75–99.

97. J. Adams, "Inequality in Social Exchange," in *Advances in Experimental Social Psychology,* ed. L. Berkowitz (New York: Academic Press, 1965).

98. "A Closer Look: The Dodd-Frank Wall Street Reform and Consumer Protection Act," PricewaterhouseCoopers, http://www.pwc.com, accessed May 12, 2015; T. Jackson, "Dodd-Frank Will Only Deepen Corporate Pay Envy," *Financial Times,* March 21, 2011, Business & Company Resource Center, http://galenet.galegroup.com; M. E. Podmolik, "Kraft CEO Sees Bonus Cut as Goals Go Unmet," *Chicago Tribune,* April 1, 2011, sec. 1, pp. 21, 23; Emily Chasan, "Executive Pay Gets New Spin," *The Wall Street Journal,* September 25, 2012, http://online.wsj .com.

99. T. Weiss, "How to Prevent IT Sabotage Inside Your Company," *CIO* (online), August 19, 2011, http://www.cio.com; D. Skarlicki, R. Folger, and P. Tesluk, "Personality as a Moderator in the Relationships between Fairness and Retaliation," *Academy of Management Journal* 42 (1999), pp. 100–08.

100. J. Brockner, "Making Sense of Procedural Fairness: How High Procedural Fairness Can Reduce or Heighten the Influence of Outcome Favorability," *Academy of Management Review* 27 (2002),

pp. 58–76; and D. De Cremer and D. van Knippenberg, "How Do Leaders Promote Cooperation? The Effects of Charisma and Procedural Fairness," *Journal of Applied Psychology* 87 (2002), pp. 858–66.

101. M. Armstrong-Stassen, M. Freeman, S. Cameron, and D. Rajacic, "Nurse Managers' Role in Older Nurses' Intention to Stay," *Journal of Health Organization and Management,* 29 (2015), pp. 55–74.

102. Lawler, *Treat People Right!*

103. R. Shao, D. Rupp, D. Skarlicki, and K. Jones, "Employee Justice across Cultures: A Meta-Analytic Review," *Journal of Management* 39 (2013), pp. 263–301.

104. W. C. Kim and R. Mauborgne, "Fair Process: Managing in the Knowledge Economy," *Harvard Business Review,* July–August 1997, pp. 65–75.

105. T. Bateman and D. Organ, "Job Satisfaction and the Good Sold: The Relationship between Affect and Employee 'Citizenship,'" *Academy of Management Journal,* 1983, pp. 587–95.

106. A. de Castro, G. Gee, and D. Takeuchi, "Relationship between Job Dissatisfaction and Physical and Psychological Health among Filipino Immigrants," *American Association of Occupational Health Nurses Journal* 56 (2008), pp. 33–40; D. Henne and E. Locke, "Job Dissatisfaction: What Are the Consequences?" *International Journal of Psychology* 20 (1985), pp. 221–40.

107. J. Barling, E. K. Kelloway, and R. Iverson, "High-Quality Work, Job Satisfaction, and Occupational Injuries," *Journal of Applied Psychology* 88 (2003), pp. 276–83.

108. D. Bowen, S. Gilliland, and R. Folger, "HRM and Service Fairness: How Being Fair with Employees Spills Over to Customers," *Organizational Dynamics,* Winter 1999, pp. 7–23.

109. J. Harter, F. Schmidt, and T. Hayes, "Business-Unit-Level Relationship between Employee Satisfaction, Employee Engagement, and Business Outcomes: A Meta-Analysis," *Journal of Applied Psychology* 87 (2002), pp. 268–79.

110. S. Adams, "Most Americans Are Unhappy at Work," *Forbes* (online), June 20, 2014, http://www.forbes.com; The Conference Board, "U.S. Workers More Satisfied? Just Barely," press release, June 18, 2014, http://www.conference-board.org.

111. Heiner Evanschitzky, Christopher Groening, Vikas Mittal, and Maren Wunderlich, "How Employer and Employee Satisfaction Affect Customer Satisfaction: An Application to Franchise Services," *Journal of Service Research* 14, no. 2 (May 2011), pp. 136–48; and "Motivation in Today's Workplace," pp. 1–2, 4.

112. G. Grote and D. Guest, "The Case for Reinvigorating Quality of Working Life Research," *Human Relations* 70 (2017), pp. 149–67; S. Sonnentag, "Dynamics of Well-Being," *Annual Review of Organizational Psychology and Organizational Behavior* 2 (2015), pp. 261–93.

113. Grote and d. Guest, "The Case for Reinvigorating Quality of Working Life Research".

114. Erika Fry, "Low Key, High Quirk," *Fortune,* January 17, 2013, http://management.fortune.cnn.com; Plante Moran, "Careers at Plante Moran," http://www.plantemoran.com.

115. R. E. Walton, "Improving the Quality of Work Life," *Harvard Business Review,* May–June 1974, pp. 12, 16, 155. Ibid, Grote & Guest, 2017.

116. E. E. Lawler III, "Strategies for Improving the Quality of Work Life," *American Psychologist* 37 (1982), pp. 486–93; J. L. Suttle, "Improving Life at Work: Problems and Prospects," in *Improving Life at Work,* ed. J. R. Hackman and J. L. Suttle (Santa Monica, CA: Goodyear, 1977); B. Erdogan, T. Bauer, D. Truxillo, et al., "Whistle while You Work: A Review of the Life Satisfaction Literature," *Journal of Management* 38 (2012), pp. 1038–83.

117. Crowley, "How SAS Became the World's Best Place to Work"; Buchanan, "How SAS Continues to Grow"; Great Place to Work, "World's Best Multinational Workplaces 2014"; *Fortune,* "100 Best Places to Work For 2014"; Barber, "What Makes Workers Happy?"; Jenn Mann, "The Best Place to Work . . . in the World!" *SAS Voices,* November 14, 2012, http://blogs.sas .com; Roberta Matuson, "Why Most Recruitment Strategies Are Failing and What You Can Do to Fix This," *Forbes,* March 13, 2013, http://www.forbes.com; company press release, "SAS Ranks No. 4 on Fortune List of Best Companies to Work for in the US," March 5, 2015, https://www.sas.com/en_in/news/press-releases/2015/march/great-workplace-US-Fortune-2015.html; Bruce Rogers, "Tech Titan Jim Goodnight Positions SAS for the Future," *Forbes,* October 31, 2016, https://www.forbes.com/sites/brucerogers/2016/10/31/tech-titan-jim-goodnight-positions-sas-for-the-future/#1591edce4e55.

118. P. B. Warr, "Well-Being and the Workplace," in D. Kahneman, E. Diener, and N. Schwarz, eds., *Well-Being: The Foundations of Hedonic Psychology* (New York: Russell Sage Foundation, 1999); T. A. Wright and R. Cropanzano, "The Role of Psychological Well-Being in Job Performance: A Fresh Look at an Age-Old Quest," *Organizational Dynamics* 33 (2004), pp. 338–51; Grote and Guest, "The Case for Reinvigorating Quality of Working Life Research," *Human Relations* 70 (2017), pp. 149–67.

119. A. Edmans, "The Link between Job Satisfaction and Firm Value, with Implications for Corporate Social Responsibility," *Academy of Management Perspectives* 26 (2012), pp. 1–19.

120. T. Wright and D. Bonett, "Job Satisfaction and Psychological Well-Being as Nonadditive Predictors of Workplace Turnover," *Journal of Management* 33 (2007), 141–60; J. K. Harter, F. L. Schmidt, and C. L. M. Keyes, "Well-Being in the Workplace and Its Relationship to Business

Outcomes: A Review of the Gallup Studies," in C. L. M. Keyes and J. Haidt, eds., *Flourishing: The Positive Person and the Good Life* (Washington DC: American Psychological Association, 2003), pp. 205–24.

121. S. L. Robinson, "Trust and Breach of the Psychological Contract," *Administrative Science Quarterly* 41 (1996), pp. 574–99.

122. J. Robbins, M. Ford, and L. Tetrick, "Perceived Unfairness and Employee Health: A Meta-Analytic Integration," Journal of Applied Psychology 97 (2012), pp. 235–72; M. Dahl, "Organizational Change and Employee Stress," *Management Science* 57 (2011), pp. 240–56.

123. L. Grunberg, S. Moore, E. Greenberg, and P. Sikora, "The Changing Workplace and Its Effects A Longitudinal Examination of Employee Responses at a Large Company," *Journal of Applied Behavioral Science* 44 (2008), pp. 215–36; D. Rousseau, "Changing the Deal While Keeping the People," *Academy of Management Executive* 10 (1996), pp. 50–58.

124. E. Ridolfi, "Executive Commentary," *Academy of Management Executive* 10 (1996), pp. 59–60.

125. E. E. Lawler III, *From the Ground Up* (San Francisco: Jossey-Bass, 1996).

126. Ibid.

127. S. Ghoshal, C. Bartlett, and P. Moran, "Value Creation: The New Management Manifesto," *Financial Times Mastering Management Review,* November 1999, pp. 34–37.

128. R. Hoffman, B. Casnocha, and C. Yen, "Tours of Duty: The New Employer-Employee Contract," *Harvard Business Review,* June 2013, pp. 48–58.

Chapter 14

1. "Whole Foods Market Celebrates 18 Consecutive Years on Fortune's '100 Best Companies to Work For' List," press release on, March 5, 2015, http://www.media.wholefoodsmarket.com; K. Hope, "Are Executive Sleepovers the Best Way for Staff to Bond?" *BBC News* (online), April 8, 2014, http://www.bbc.com; John Mackey and Raj Sisodia, "Want to Hire Great People? Hire Consciously," *Fortune,* January 17, 2013, http://management.fortune.cnn.com; Andrea Davis, "Benefits Democracy: Whole Foods Takes Benefits to a Vote," *Employee Benefit News,* May 2012, p. 11; Jessica Rohman, "Whole Foods Market," *Great Place to Work blog,* March 6, 2013, http://www.greatplacetowork.com; Anne VanderMey, "World's Most Admired Companies 2013: Whole Foods Market," *Fortune,* March 18, 2013, http://money.cnn.com; "Groups Wield Power at Whole Foods," *Executive Leadership,* May 2013, Business Insights: Essentials, http://bi.galegroup.com; Whole Foods Market, "Careers," http://www.wholefoodsmarket.com/careers; "Fast Facts," http://media.wholefoodsmarket.com/fast-facts/; Melanie J. Martin, "Data on Employee Turnover in the Grocery Industry," *Small Business*

Chronicle, http://smallbusiness.chron.com/data-employee-turnover-grocery-industry-18817.html, accessed April 17, 2017; Russ Buchanan, "Employee Turnover in a Grocery," *Small Business Chronicle,* http://smallbusiness.chron.com/employee-turnover-grocery-15810.html, accessed April 17, 2017.

2. J. Martin and K. Eisenhardt, "Rewiring: Cross-Business-Unit Collaborations in Multibusiness Organizations," *Academy of Management Journal* 53 (2010), pp. 265–301; E. C. Wenger and W. M. Snyder, "Communities of Practice: The Organizational Frontier," *Harvard Business Review,* January–February 2000, pp. 139–45.

3. "How Companies Use Teams to Drive Performance," Ernst & Young Insights (online), http://www.ey.com, accessed May 23, 2015; S. Cohen and D. Bailey, "What Makes Teams Work: Group Effectiveness Research from the Shop Floor to the Executive Suite," *Journal of Management* 23 (1997), pp. 239–90.

4. G. Chen, L. Donahue, and R. Klimoski, "Training Undergraduates to Work in Organizational Teams," *Academy of Management Learning and Education* 3 (2004), pp. 27–40.

5. T. McDowell, D. Agarwal, D. Mille, T. Okamoto, and T. Page, "Organization Design: The Rise of Teams," Deloitte, February 29, 2016, www.dupress.deloitte.com.

6. Steve Minter, "Better Together," *Industry Week,* February 2012, Business Insights: Global, http://bi.galegroup.com.

7. E. Fleischauer, "Nucor Manager Says Teamwork Key to Success; Q1 Earnings Up," *Decatur (AL) Daily,* April 20, 2007, http://www.decaturdaily.com.

8. M. Mace, "Google Logic: Why Google Does the Things It Does the Way It Does," *The Guardian* (online), July 9, 2013, http://www.theguardian.com; A. Somech and A. Drach-Zahavy, "Translating Team Creativity to Innovation Implementation: The Role of Team Composition and Climate for Innovation," *Journal of Management* 39 (2013).

9. Mace, "Google Logic"; 2013, Somech and Drach-Zahavy, "Translating Team Creativity to Innovation Implementation."

10. Mace, "Google Logic"; Somech and Drach-Zahavy, "Translating Team Creativity to Innovation Implementation."

11. D. Nadler, J. R. Hackman, and E. E. Lawler III, *Managing Organizational Behavior* (Boston: Little, Brown, 1979).

12. A. C. Edmondson, "Teamwork on the Fly," *Harvard Business Review* April, 2012, pp. 72–80.

13. L. Gratton and T. Erickson, "Eight Ways to Build Collaborative Teams, *Harvard Business Review* (online), November 2007, http://www.hbr.com; M. Cianni and D. Wnuck, "Individual Growth and Team Enhancement: Moving toward a New Model of Career Development," *Academy of Management Executive* 11 (1997), pp. 105–15.

14. J. Hollenbeck, B. Beersma, and M. Schouten, "Beyond Team Types and Taxonomies: A Dimensional Scaling Conceptualization for Team Description," *Academy of Management Review* 37 (2012), pp. 82–106.

15. S. Cohen, "New Approaches to Teams and Teamwork," in J. Galbraith, E. E. Lawler III, and Associates, *Organizing for the Future* (San Francisco: Jossey-Bass, 1993).

16. Cohen and Bailey, "What Makes Teams Work."

17. M. O'Hara, "Congress Relaunches Transgender Equality Task Force," NBC News, March 2, 2017, www.nbc.com.

18. L. Mullins, "Integration Crew for Maryland Bank," *American Banker,* February 13, 2007, General Reference Center Gold, http://find.galegroup.com; P. C. Earley and C. B. Gibson, *Multinational Work Teams* (Mahwah, NJ: Lawrence Erlbaum, 2002), p. 214.

19. K. Lagerstrom and M. Andersson, "Creating and Sharing Knowledge within a Transnational Team—The Development of a Global Business System," *Journal of World Business* 38 (2003), pp. 84–95; C. Snow, S. Snell, S. Davison, and D. Hambrick, "Use Transnational Teams to Globalize Your Company," *Organizational Dynamics,* Spring 1996, pp. 50–67.

20. B. Kirkman, B. Rosen, C. Gibson, P. Tesluk, and S. McPherson, "Five Challenges to Virtual Team Success: Lessons from Sabre, Inc.," *Academy of Management Executive* 16 (2002), pp. 67–80.

21. Edmondson, "Teamwork on the Fly."

22. "Dell and Intel Future Workforce Study Provides Key Insights into Technology Trends Shaping the Modern Global Workplace," Dell, July 18, 2016, www.dell.com.

23. J. Ferri-Reed, "Building Innovative Multi-Generation Teams," *The Journal of Quality and Participation* 37 (October 2014), pp. 20–22; R. Shehadi and D. Karam, "Five Essential Elements of the Digital Workplace," *Forbes* (online), March 31, 2014, http://www.forbes.com; T. Johns and L. Grafton, "The Third Wave of Virtual Work," *Harvard Business Review* (online), January 1, 2013, http://www.hbr.org.

24. V. Taras, D. Caprar, D. Rottig, R. Sarala, N. Zakaria, F. Zhao, et al. "A Global Classroom? Evaluating the Effectiveness of Global Virtual Collaboration as Teaching Tool in Management Education," *Academy of Management Learning & Education* 12 (2013), pp. 414–35.

25. R. Banker, J. Field, R. Schroeder, and K. Sinha, "Impact of Work Teams on Manufacturing Performance: A Longitudinal Field Study," *Academy of Management Journal* 39 (1996), pp. 867–90.

26. M. Muethel and M. Hoegl, "Shared Leadership Effectiveness in Independent Professional Teams," *European Management Journal* 31 (2013), pp. 423–32; D. Yeatts, M. Hipskind, and D. Barnes, "Lessons Learned from Self-Managed Work Teams,"

Business Horizons, July–August 1994, pp. 11–18.

27. B. Kirkman and D. Shapiro, "The Impact of Cultural Values on Job Satisfaction and Organizational Commitment in Self-Managing Work Teams: The Mediating Role of Employee Resistance," *Academy of Management Journal* 44 (2001), pp. 557–69.

28. C. Langfred, "The Downside of Self-Management: A Longitudinal Study of the Effects of Conflict on Trust, Autonomy, and Task Interdependence in Self-Managing Teams," *Academy of Management Journal,* 2007, pp. 885–900.

29. K. Peterson, "At Whole Foods, Paychecks Are Public," *CBS News Moneywatch* (online), March 5, 2014, http://www.cbsnews.com; Mackey and Sisodia, "Want to Hire Great People?"; Davis, "Benefits Democracy"; Rohman, "Whole Foods Market"; Whole Foods Market, "Careers"; *Executive Leadership,* "Groups Wield Power"; David Burkus, "Why Whole Foods Builds Its Entire Business on Teams," *Forbes,* June 8, 2016, https://www.forbes.com/sites/davidburkus/2016/06/08/why-whole-foods-build-their-entire-business-on-teams/#386ddaa03fa1.

30. Kirkman and Shapiro, "The Impact of Cultural Values on Employee Resistance to Teams."

31. M. Johnson, J. Hollenbeck, D. DeRue, C. Barnes, and D. Jundt, "Functional versus Dysfunctional Team Change: Problem Diagnosis and Structural Feedback for Self-Managed Teams," *Organizational Behavior and Human Decision Processes* 122 (2013), pp. 1–11; S. Sarker, S. Sarker, S. Kirkeby, and S. Chakraborty, "Path to 'Stardom' in Globally Distributed Hybrid Teams: An Examination of a Knowledge-centered Perspective Using Social Network Analysis," *Decision Sciences* 42 (2011), 339–70; B. Macy and H. Isumi, "Organizational Change, Design, and Work Innovation: A Meta-Analysis of 131 North American Field Studies—1961–1991," *Research in Organizational Change and Development* 7 (1993), pp. 235–313.

32. Jill Jusko, "2012 IW Best Plants Winner: Engaged Teams Keep Lockheed Martin Delivering on Time, Every Time," *Industry Week,* January 17, 2013, http://www.industryweek.com.

33. Cohen and Bailey, "What Makes Teams Work."

34. J. Katzenbach and D. Smith, "The Discipline of Teams," *Harvard Business Review,* March–April 1993, pp. 111–20.

35. D. Mukherjee, S. Lahiri, D. Mukherjee, and T. Billing, "Leading Virtual Teams: How Do Social, Cognitive, and Behavioral Capabilities Matter?" *Management Decision* 50 (2012), pp. 273–90; S. Furst, M. Reeves, B. Rosen, and R. Blackburn, "Managing the Life Cycle of Virtual Teams," *Academy of Management Executive,* May 2004, pp. 6–20. Quotes in this paragraph are from pp. 11 and 12.

36. S. Humphrey and F. Aime, "Team Microdynamics: Toward an Organizing Approach to Teamwork" *Academy of Management Annals* 8 (2014), pp. 443–503.

37. M. Marks, J. Mathieu, and S. Zaccaro, "A Temporally Based Framework and Taxonomy of Team Processes," *Academy of Management Review* 26 (2011), pp. 356–76; F. Morgeson, D. S. DeRue, and E. Karam, "Leadership in Teams: A Functional Approach to Understanding Leadership Structures and Processes," *Journal of Management* 36 (2010), pp. 5–39.

38. C. J. G. Gersick, "Time and Transition in Work Teams: Toward a New Model of Group Development," *Academy of Management Journal* 31 (1988), pp. 9–41.

39. J. R. Hackman, *Groups That Work (and Those That Don't)* (San Francisco: Jossey-Bass, 1990).

40. Ibid.,

41. I. Hoever, D. van Knippenberg, W. van Ginkel, and H. Barkema, "Fostering Team Creativity: Perspective Taking as Key to Unlocking Diversity's Potential," *Journal of Applied Psychology* 97 (2012), pp. 982–96.

42. R. Cross, "Looking before You Leap: Assessing the Jump to Teams in Knowledge-Based Work," *Business Horizons,* September–October 2000, pp. 29–36.

43. Geoff Colvin, "The Art of the Self-Managing Team," *Fortune,* December 5, 2012, http://management.fortune.cnn.com; Chana R. Schoenberger, "How to Get People to Work Together," *The Wall Street Journal,* September 7, 2012, http://blogs.wsj.com; John Baldoni, "The Secret to Team Collaboration: Individuality," *Inc.,* January 18, 2012, http://www.inc.com.

44. N. Lorinkova, M. Pearsall, and H. P. Sims Jr., "Examining the Differential Longitudinal Performance of Directive versus Empowering Leadership in Teams," *Academy of Management Journal* 56 (2013), pp. 573–96; M. T. Maynard, L. Gilson, and J. Mathieu, "Empowerment—Fad or Fab? A Multilevel Review of the Past Two Decades of Research," *Journal of Management* 38 (2012), pp. 1231–81; S. Seibert, G. Wang, and S. Courtright, "Antecedents and Consequences of Psychological and Team Empowerment in Organizations: A Meta-Analytic Review," *Journal of Applied Psychology* 96 (2011), pp. 981–1003; G. Chen, P. N. Sharma, S. Edinger, D. Shapiro, and J.-L. Farh, "Motivating and Demotivating Forces in Teams: Cross-Level Influences of Empowering Leadership and Relationship Conflict," *Journal of Applied Psychology* 96 (2011), pp. 541–57.

45. A. Nahavandi and E. Aranda, "Restructuring Teams for the Reengineered Organization," *Academy of Management Executive,* November 1994, pp. 58–68.

46. B. Kirkman, B. Rosen, P. Tesluk, and C. Gibson, "The Impact of Team Empowerment on Virtual Team Performance: The Moderating Role of Face-to-Face Interaction," *Academy of Management Journal* 47 (2004), pp. 175–92.

47. J. R. Katzenbach and D. K. Smith, *The Wisdom of Teams* (Boston: Harvard Business School Press, 1993); and Maggie Starvish, "Why Leaders Need to Rethink Teamwork," *Forbes,* December 28, 2012, http://www.forbes.com.

48. D. Nadler, J. R. Hackman, and E. E. Lawler III, *Managing Organizational Behavior* (Boston: Little, Brown, 1979).

49. Ibid.

50. Katzenbach and Smith, "The Discipline of Teams".

51. Ibid.

52. L. Gibson, J. Mathieu, C. Shalley, and T. Ruddy, "Creativity and Standardization: Complementary or Conflicting Drivers of Team Effectiveness?" *Academy of Management Journal* 48 (2005), pp. 521–31.

53. C. Meyer, "How the Right Measures Help Teams Excel," *Harvard Business Review,* May–June 1994, pp. 95–103.

54. J. R. Katzenbach and J. A. Santamaria, "Firing Up the Front Line," *Harvard Business Review,* May–June 1999, pp. 107–17.

55. D. Blumenthal, Z. Song, A. Jena, and T. Ferris, "Guidance for Structuring Team-Based Incentives in Health Care," *American Journal of Managed Care* 19 (2013), pp. 64–70; D. Knight, C. Durham, and E. Locke, "The Relationship of Team Goals, Incentives, and Efficacy to Strategic Risk, Tactical Implementation, and Performance," *Academy of Management Journal* 44 (2001), pp. 326–38; A. Kleingeld, H. van Mierlo, and L. Arends, "The Effect of Goal Setting on Group Performance: A Meta-Analysis," *Journal of Applied Psychology* 96 (2011), pp. 1289–1304; C. Barnes, J. Hollenbeck, D. Jundt, D. S. De Rue, and S. Harmon, "Mixing Individual Incentives and Group Incentives: Best of Both Worlds or Social Dilemma?" *Journal of Management* 37 (2011), pp. 1611–35.

56. B. L. Kirkman and B. Rosen, "Powering Up Teams," *Organizational Dynamics* (Winter 2000), pp. 48–66.

57. E. E. Lawler III, *From the Ground Up* (San Francisco: Jossey-Bass, 1996).

58. M. Schippers, "Social Loafing Tendencies and Team Performance: The Compensating Effect of Agreeableness and Conscientiousness," *Academy of Management Learning & Education,* 13 (2014), pp. 62–81; A. Jassawalla, H. Sashittal, and A. Maishe, "Students' Perceptions of Social Loafing: Its Antecedents and Consequences in Undergraduate Business Classroom Teams," *Academy of Management Learning and Education,* 2009, pp. 42–54.

59. M. Erez, "Is Group Productivity Loss the Rule or the Exception? Effects of Culture and Group-Based Motivation," *Academy of Management Journal* 39 (1996), pp. 1513–37; A. Mas and E. Moretti, "Peers at Work" *The American Economic Review* 99 (2009), pp. 112–145.

60. Katzenbach and Smith, "The Discipline of Teams."

61. Y. Garbers and U. Konradt, "The Effect of Financial Incentives on Performance: A Quantitative Review of Individual and Team-Based Financial Incentives," *Journal of Occupational and Organizational Psychology* 87 (2014), pp. 102–37; and M. Johnson, J. Hollenbeck, S. Humphrey, D. Ilgen, D. Jundt, and C. Meyer, "Cutthroat Cooperation: Asymmetrical Adaptation to Changes in Team Reward Structures," *Academy of Management Journal,* 2006, pp. 103–19.

62. M. J. Pearsall, M. S. Christian, and A. P. J. Ellis, "Motivating Interdependent Teams: Individual Rewards, Shared Rewards, or Something Between?" *Journal of Applied Psychology* 95 (2010), pp. 183–91.

63. R. Wageman, "Interdependence and Group Effectiveness," *Administrative Science Quarterly* 40 (1995), pp. 145–80.

64. S. Grant, "What the Best Companies Get Right about Salaries," *Bloomberg,* March 1, 2016, www.bloomberg.com.

65. M. Sturdevant, "Top Large Employer: Whole Foods Teamwork Is a Natural," *Hartford Courant,* September 21, 2014, www.courant.com.

66. Lawler, *From the Ground Up.*

67. R. Rayasam, "Who's the Boss? In Some Companies, It's Nobody," *BBC* (online), January 7, 2015, http://www.bbc.com.

68. Susan Johnston Taylor, "Are Empty High-End Restaurants the Next Coworking Trend?" *Fast Company,* July 8, 2016, https://www.fastcompany.com/3061602/why-freelancers-are-paying-to-work-in-high-end-restaurants-before-they-op; Ansel Liu, "Five Co-Working Trends to Watch Out For in 2017," *Virgin.com,* January 30, 2017, https://www.virgin.com/entrepreneur/five-co-working-trends-watch-out-2017; Nidhi Singh, "#5 Upcoming Trends in 2017 That Co-Working Spaces Should Prepare For," *Entrepreneur India,* April 12, 2017, https://www.entrepreneur.com/article/292758.

69. R. Preidt, "Work Teams Who Share Negative Emotions Better at Problem Solving," *Bloomberg Businessweek,* November 23, 2010, http://www.businessweek.com.

70. A. Grant, "Givers Take All: The Hidden Dimension of Corporate Culture," *The McKinsey Quarterly* (2013), pp. 52–65; A. Srivastava, K. Bartol, and E. Locke, "Empowering Leadership in Management Teams: Effects on Knowledge Sharing, Efficacy, and Performance," *Academy of Management Journal,* 2006, pp. 1239–51.

71. L. A. DeChurch and J. R. Mesmer-Magnus, "The Cognitive Underpinnings of Effective Teamwork: A Meta-Analysis," *Journal of Applied Psychology* 95 (2010), pp. 32–53.

72. J. M. Levine, E. T. Higgins, and H. Choi, "Development of Strategic Norms in Groups," *Organizational Behavior and Human Decision Processes* 82 (2000), pp. 88–101.

73. M. Duffy, K. Scott, J. Shaw, B. Tepper, and K. Aquino, "A Social Context Model of Envy and Social Undermining," *Academy of Management Journal* 55 (2012), pp. 643–66; K. Jehn and E. Mannix, "The Dynamic Nature of Conflict: A Longitudinal Study of Intragroup Conflict and Group Performance," *Academy of Management Journal* 44 (2001), pp. 238–51.

74. J. O'Toole, *Vanguard Management: Redesigning the Corporate Future* (New York: Doubleday, 1985).

75. R. F. Bales, *Interaction Process Analysis: A Method for the Study of Small Groups* (Reading, MA: Addison-Wesley, 1950).

76. V. U. Druskat and J. Wheeler, "Managing from the Boundary: The Effective Leadership of Self-Managing Work Teams," *Academy of Management Journal* 46 (2003), pp. 435–57.

77. Katzenbach and Smith, *The Wisdom of Teams.*

78. V. Nicolaides, K. LaPort, T. Chen, A. Tomassetti, E. Weis, S. Zaccaro, and J. Cortina, "The Shared Leadership of Teams: A Meta-analysis of Proximal, Distal, and Moderating Relationships," *Leadership Quarterly* 25 (2014), 923–42; J. Carson, P. Tesluk, and J. Marrone, "Shared Leadership in Teams: An Investigation of Antecedent Conditions and Performance," *Academy of Management Journal,* 2007, pp. 1217–34.

79. S. E. Seashore, *Group Cohesiveness in the Industrial Work Group* (Ann Arbor: University of Michigan Press, 1954).

80. Banker et al., "Impact of Work Teams on Manufacturing Performance."

81. S. Wise, "Can a Team Have Too Much Cohesion? The Dark Side to Network Density," *European Management Journal* 32 (2014), pp. 703–11; B. Mullen and C. Cooper, "The Relation between Group Cohesiveness and Performance: An Integration," *Psychological Bulletin* 115 (1994), pp. 210–27.

82. R. Hasson, "How to Resolve Board Disputes More Effectively," *MIT Sloan Management Review 48* (2006), pp. 77–80; D. P. Forbes and F. J. Milliken, "Cognition and Corporate Governance: Understanding Boards of Directors as Strategic Decision-Making Groups," *Academy of Management Review* 24 (1999), pp. 489–505.

83. T. Simons, L. H. Pelled, and K. A. Smith, "Making Use of Difference: Diversity, Debate, and Decision Comprehensiveness in Top Management Teams," *Academy of Management Journal* 42 (1999), pp. 662–73.

84. Seashore, *Group Cohesiveness in the Industrial Work Group.*

85. B. Lott and A. Lott, "Group Cohesiveness as Interpersonal Attraction: A Review of Relationships with Antecedent and Consequent Variables," *Psychological Bulletin,* October 1965, pp. 259–309.

86. K. Dahlin, L. Weingart, and P. Hinds, "Team Diversity and Information Use," *Academy of Management Journal* 48 (2005), pp. 1107–23.

87. R. Gillett, "Productivity Hack of the Week: The Two Pizza Approach to Productive Teamwork," *Fast Company* (online), October 24, 2014, http://www.fastcompany.com.

88. B. L. Kirkman and B. Rosen, "Beyond Self-Management: Antecedents and Consequences of Team Empowerment," *Academy of Management Journal* 42 (1999), pp. 58–74.

89. Hackman, *Groups That Work (and Those That Don't).*

90. W. Bennis, *Organizing Genius* (Reading, MA: Addison-Wesley, 1997).

91. M. Cianni and D. Wnuck, "Individual Growth and Team Enhancement: Moving toward a New Model of Career Development," *Academy of Management Executive* 11 (1997), pp. 105–15.

92. K. Jehn, "A Multimethod Examination of the Benefits and Detriments of Intragroup Conflict," *Administrative Science Quarterly* 40 (1995), pp. 245–82.

93. R. S. Wellins and W. C. Byham, *Inside Teams: How 20 World-Class Organizations Are Winning through Teams.* San Francisco: Jossey-Bass, 1996.

94. J. A. Marrone, "Team Boundary Spanning: A Multilevel Review of Past Research and Proposals for the Future," *Journal of Management* 36 (2010), pp. 911–40.

95. D. G. Ancona, "Outward Bound: Strategies for Team Survival in an Organization," *Academy of Management Journal* 33 (1990), pp. 334–65.

96. Ibid.

97. W. De Vries, F. Walter, G. Van der Vegt, and P. Essens, "Antecedents of Individuals' Interteam Coordination: Broad Functional Experiences as a Mixed Blessing," *Academy of Management Journal* 57 (2014), pp. 1334–59; H. Bruns, "Working Alone Together: Coordination in Collaboration Across Domains of Expertise," *Academy of Management Journal* 56 (2013), pp. 62–83; M. Hogg, D. van Knippenberg, and D. Rast III, "Intergroup Leadership in Organizations: Leading Across Group and Organizational Boundaries," *Academy of Management Review* 37 (2012), pp. 232–55.

98. L. Sayles, *Leadership: What Effective Managers Really Do, and How They Do It* (New York: McGraw-Hill, 1979).

99. Ibid.

100. M. Holt, "Risks of Not Confronting Conflict in the Workplace," *Chron (Houston Chronicle),* http://www.smallbusiness.chron.com, accessed May 25, 2015; M. Myatt, "5 Keys of Dealing with Workplace Conflict," *Forbes* (online), February 22, 2012, http://www.forbes.com; and P. Lencioni, "How to Foster Good Conflict," *The Wall Street Journal,* November 13, 2008, http://online.wsj.com.

101. A. Caron and T. Cummings, "A Theory of Subgroups in Work Teams," *Academy of Management Review* 37 (2012), pp. 441–70.

102. D. Staples and L. Zhao, "The Effects of Cultural Diversity in Virtual Teams versus Face-to-Face Teams," *Group Decision and Negotiation* 15 (2006), pp. 389–406; J. Chatman and F. Flynn, "The Influence of Demographic Heterogeneity on the Emergence and Consequences

of Cooperative Norms in Work Teams," *Academy of Management Journal* 44 (2001), pp. 956–74; and R. T. Keller, "Cross-Functional Project Groups in Research and New Product Development: Diversity, Communications, Job Stress, and Outcomes," *Academy of Management Journal* 44 (2001), pp. 547–55.

103. J.-L. Farh, C. Lee, and C. Farh, "Task Conflict and Team Creativity: A Question of How Much and When," *Journal of Applied Psychology* 2010, pp. 1173–80; J. Shaw, J. Zhu, M. Duffy, K. Scott, H. A. Shih, and E. Susanto, "A Contingency Model of Conflict and Team Effectiveness," *Journal of Applied Psychology* 96 (2011), pp. 391–400; F. R. C. de Wit, L. Greer, and K. Jehn, "The Paradox of Intergroup Conflict: A Meta-Analysis," *Journal of Applied Psychology* 97 (2012), pp. 360–90; S. Thatcher and P. Patel, "Group Faultlines: A Review, Integration, and Guide for Research," *Journal of Management* 38 (2012), pp. 969–1009; "Fostering Team Creativity."

104. D. Tjosvold, *Working Together to Get Things Done* (Lexington, MA: Lexington Books, 1986).

105. T. Kim, C. Wang, M. Kondo, and T. Kim, "Conflict Management Styles: The Differences Among the Chinese, Japanese and Koreans," *International Journal of Conflict Management* 18 (2007), pp. 23–41; C. Tinsley and J. Brett, "Managing Workplace Conflict in the United States and Hong Kong," *Organizational Behavior and Human Decision Processes* 85 (2001), pp. 360–81.

106. K. W. Thomas, "Conflict and Conflict Management," in *Handbook of Industrial and Organizational Psychology,* ed. M. D. Dunnette (Chicago: Rand McNally, 1976).

107. D. Tynan, "IT Turf Wars," *InfoWorld. com,* February 14, 2011, Business & Company Resource Center, http://galenet.galegroup. com.

108. Ibid.

109. K. Conerly and A. Tripathi, "What Is Your Conflict Style? Understanding and Dealing with Your Conflict Style," *The Journal for Quality and Participation* 27 (2004), pp. 16–20; K. W. Thomas, "Toward Multidimensional Values in Teaching: The Example of Conflict Behaviors," *Academy of Management Review,* 1977, pp. 484–89.

110. D. Tjosvold, A. Wong, and N. Chen, "Constructively Managing Conflicts in Organizations," *Annual Review of Organizational Psychology and Organizational Behavior* 1 (2014), pp. 545–68.

111. R. Lau and A. Cobb, "Understanding the Connections between Relationship Conflict and Performance: The Intervening Roles of Trust and Exchange," *Journal of Organizational Behavior* 31 (2010), pp. 898–917; C. O. Longenecker and M. Neubert, "Barriers and Gateways to Management Cooperation and Teamwork," *Business Horizons,* September–October 2000, pp. 37–44.

112. P. S. Nugent, "Managing Conflict: Third-Party Interventions for Managers,"*Academy of Management Executive* 16 (2002), pp. 139–54.

113. M. Blum and J. A. Wall Jr., "HRM: Managing Conflicts in the Firm," *Business Horizons,* May–June 1997, pp. 84–87.

114. J. Leon-Perez, F. Medina, A. Arenas, and L. Munduate, "The Relationship between Interpersonal Conflict and Workplace Bullying," *Journal of Managerial Psychology* 30 (2015), pp. 250–63; J. A. Wall Jr. and R. R. Callister, "Conflict and Its Management,"*Journal of Management* 21 (1995), pp. 515–58.

115. J. Polzer, C. B. Crisp, S. Jarvenpaa, and J. Kim, "Extending the Faultline Model to Geographically Dispersed Teams: How Collocated Subgroups Can Impair Group Functioning," *Academy of Management Journal* 49 (2006), pp. 679–92.

116. F. Siebdrat, M. Hoegl, and H. Ernst, "How to Manage Virtual Teams," *MIT Sloan Management Review* 50 (2009), pp. 63–68; M. Montoya-Weiss, A. Massey, and M. Song, "Getting It Together: Temporal Coordination and Conflict Management in GlobalVirtual Teams," *Academy of Management Journal* 44 (2001), pp. 1251–62.

117. R. Standifer and J. A. Wall Jr., "Managing Conflict in B2B Commerce," *Business Horizons,* March–April 2003, pp. 65–70.

118. Mackey and Sisodia, "Want to Hire Great People?"; Rohman, "Whole Foods Market"; Whole Foods Market, "Careers"; *Executive Leadership,* "Groups Wield Power"; Mike Sunnucks, "Language Dispute Puts Whole Foods in Workplace Spotlight,"*Phoenix Business Journal,* June 6, 2013, http://www.bizjournals.com/ phoenix; Susanna Kim, "Whole Foods Says It Does Not Forbid Employees from Speaking Foreign Languages," *ABC News,* June 7, 2013, http://abcnews.go.com; Jacquelyn Smith, "What It's Really Like to Work at Whole Foods," *Business Insider,* April 9, 2015, http://www.businessinsider. com/what-its-really-like-to-work-at-whole-foods-market-2015-4.

Chapter 15

1. Company website, https://soundcloud. com/, accessed April 19, 2017; Lucy England, "The Fabulous Life of SoundCloud Cofounder and CEO Alexander Ljung," *Business Insider,* August 27, 2015, http://www.businessinsider.com/ life-of-soundcloud-founder-ceo-alexander-ljung-2015-8/#ljungs-relationship-with-soundcloud-cofounder-eric-wahlforss-started-when-they-were-both-studying-at-kth-royal-institute-of-technology-in-sweden-they-bonded-over-a-shared-love-of-music–and-because-they-were-the-only-two-guys-in-class-with-a-mac-1; Ariston Anderson, "SoundCloud: On Startup Culture, Entrepreneurial Employees & Hackdays," *99u.com,* [no date], http://99u. com/articles/7191/soundcloud-on-startup-

culture-entrepreneurial-employees-hackdays, accessed April 19, 2017; "How SoundCloud Keeps Communication Flowing across Four Offices in 4 Time Zones," *FirstRound. com,* [no date], http://firstround. com/review/how-soundcloud-keeps-communication-flowing-across-4-offices-in-4-time-zones/, accessed April 19, 2017.

2. M. Venus, D. Stam, and D. van Knippenberg, "Leader Emotion as a Catalyst of Effective Leader Communication of Visions, Value-Laden Messages, and Goals," *Organizational Behavior and Human Decision Processes* 122 (2013), pp. 53–68; L. Penley, E. Alexander, I. E. Jernigan, and C. Henwood, "Communication Abilities of Managers: The Relationship to Performance," *Journal of Management* 17 (1991), pp. 57–76.

3. W. V. Haney, "A Comparative Study of Unilateral and Bilateral Communication," *Academy of Management Journal* 7 (1964), pp. 128–36.

4. J. R. Mesmer-Magnus and L. A. DeChurch, "Information Sharing and Team Performance: A Meta-Analysis," *Journal of Applied Psychology* 94 (2009), pp. 535–46.

5. Boris Groysberg and Michael Slind, "Leadership Is a Conversation," *Harvard Business Review,* June 2012, pp. 76–84.

6. I. Wickelgren, "Speaking Science: Why People Don't Hear What You Say," *Scientific American* (online), November 8, 2012, http://www.scientificamerican. com; M. McCormack, "The Illusion of Communication," *Financial Times Mastering Management Review,* July 1999, pp. 8–9.

7. F. Flynn and S. Wiltermuth, "Who's with Me? False Consensus, Brokerage, and Ethical Decision Making in Organizations," *Academy of Management Journal* 53 (2010), pp. 1074–89; R. Cross and S. Brodt, "How Assumptions of Consensus Undermine Decision Making," *Sloan Management Review* 42 (2001), pp. 86–94.

8. S. Mohammed and E. Ringseis, "Cognitive Diversity and Consensus in Group Decision Making: The Role of Inputs, Processes, and Outcomes," *Organizational Behavior and Human Decision Processes* 85 (2001), pp. 310–35.

9. S. Parker and C. Axtell, "Seeing Another Viewpoint: Antecedents and Outcomes of Employee Perspective Taking," *Academy of Management Journal* 44 (2001), pp. 1085–100.

10. C. Folz, "How to Deliver Bad News," Society for Human Resource Management, August 25, 2016, www.shrm.org.

11. Ibid.

12. Novo Nordisk website, "Our Triple Bottom Line," http://www.novonordisk.com, accessed June 8, 2015; J. Ochs, "Defining 'Social Enterprise,'" *Minnesota Business Magazine* (online), December 17, 2014, http://www.minnesotabusiness.com; J. Jervis, "Social Enterprises: Popular but Confusing, Says Study," *The Guardian* (online), January 8, 2013, http://www. theguardian.com; A. Field, "Salesforce.

com's Thwarted Efforts to Trademark Social Enterprise Should Be a Wake Up Call," *Forbes* (online), September 11, 2012, http://www.forbes.com.

13. R. Merkin, V. Taras, and P. Steel, "State of the Art Themes in Cross-Cultural Communication Research: A Systematic and Meta-Analytic Review," *International Journal of Intercultural Relations* 38 (2014), pp. 1–23; C. Cramton and P. Hinds, "An Embedded Model of Cultural Adaptation in Global Teams," *Organization Science* 25 (2014), pp. 1056–81; L. K. Larkey, "Toward a Theory of Communicative Interactions in Culturally Diverse Workgroups," *Academy of Management Review,* April 1996, pp. 463–91.

14. L. A. Liu, C. H. Chua, and G. Stahl, "Quality of Communication Experience: Definition, Measurement, and Implications for Intercultural Negotiations," *Journal of Applied Psychology* 95 (2010), pp. 469–87.

15. C. Argyris, "Good Communication That Blocks Learning," *Harvard Business Review,* July–August 1994, pp. 77–85.

16. H. Peterson, "Here's the Email Sears' CEO Just Sent to the Company Announcing Layoffs," *Business Insider,* February 23, 2017, www.businessinsider.com; T. Donnelly, "How to Deliver Bad News to Employees," *Inc.* (online), January 14, 2011, http://www.inc.com.

17. C. Deutsch, "The Multimedia Benefits Kit," *The New York Times,* October 14, 1990, sec. 3, p. 25.

18. T. W. Comstock, *Communicating in Business and Industry* (Albany, NY: Delmar, 1985).

19. C. Osborne, "Amazon Launches Video Conference Call Service Chime, Takes on Rivals WebEx, Skype for Business," *ZDNet,* February 14, 2017, www.zdnet.com.

20. A. Nusca, "Social Media Use By CEOs Is Increasing—Slowly," *Fortune,* January 25, 2016, www.fortune.com.

21. Microsoft Support, https://support.office.com, accessed on June 2, 2015; Hitachi Solutions Europe, Ltd., http://uk.hitachi-solutions.com, accessed on June 2, 2015.

22. Candor, http://www.usecandor.com, accessed on June 2, 2015; R. Greenfield, "Brainstorming Doesn't Work: Try This Technique Instead," *Fast Company* (online), July 29, 2014, http://www.fastcompany.com.

23. S. S. K. Lam and J. Schaubroeck, "Improving Group Decisions by Better Pooling Information: A Comparative Advantage of Group Decision Support Systems," *Journal of Applied Psychology* 85 (2000), pp. 565–73.

24. J. Goudreau, "How to Communicate in the New Multigenerational Office," *Forbes* (online), February 14, 2013, http://www.forbes.com; M. Schmulen, "Memo to the Boss: Twitter's Not a Time Suck," *Fortune,* January 19, 2010, http://tech.fortune.cnn.com; D. Lindorff, "Facing Up to Facebook," *Treasury & Risk,* April 2011, Business & Company; J. Goudreau, "How to Communicate in the New Multigenerational Office," *Forbes* (online),

February 14, 2013, http://www.forbes.com; M. Schmulen, "Memo to the Boss," Resource Center, http://galenet.galegroup.com; and S. Ali, "Why No One under 30 Answers Your Voicemail," *DiversityInc,* August 27, 2010, http://www.diversityinc.com.

25. M. Drouin, D. Miller, S. Wehle, and E. Hernandez , "Why Do People Lie Online? 'Because Everyone Lies on the Internet,'" *Computers in Human Behavior,* 64 (2016), pp. 134–142; S. Aral, "The Problem with Online Ratings," *MIT Sloan Management Review* 55 (2014), pp. 47–52; C. Naquin, T. Kurtzberg, and L. Belkin, "The Finer Points of Lying Online: E-Mail versus Pen and Paper," *Journal of Applied Psychology* 95 (2010), pp. 387–94.

26. C. Naquin and G. Paulson, "Online Bargaining and Interpersonal Trust," *Journal of Applied Psychology* 88 (2003), pp. 113–20.

27. N. Hill, K. Bartol, P. Tesluk, and G. Langa, "Organizational Context and Face-to-Face Interaction: Influences on the Development of Trust and Collaborative Behaviors in Computer-Mediated Groups," *Organizational Behavior and Human Decision Processes,* 108 (2009), pp. 187–201; B. Baltes, M. Dickson, M. Sherman, C. Bauer, and J. LaGanke, "Computer-Mediated Communication and Group Decision Making: A Meta-Analysis," *Organizational Behavior and Human Decision Processes* 87 (2002), pp. 156–79.

28. E. Martínez-Moreno, P. González-Navarro, A. Zornoza, and P. Ripoll, "Relationship, Task and Process Conflicts and Team Performance: The Moderating Role of Communication Media," *International Journal of Conflict Management* 20 (2009), pp. 251–68; R. Rice and D. Case, "Electronic Message Systems in the University: A Description of Use and Utility," *Journal of Communication* 33 (1983), pp. 131–52; and C. Steinfield, "Dimensions of Electronic Mail Use in an Organizational Setting," *Proceedings of the Academy of Management,* San Diego, 1985.

29. A. Farnham, "Kicked to Curb by Text: New, Awful Way to Be Fired," *ABC News* (online), July 16, 2013, http://www.abcnews.com; M. Gardner, "You've Got Mail: 'We're Letting You Go,' " *Christian Science Monitor,* September 18, 2006, http://www.csmonitor.com; and Linton Weeks, "Read the Blog: You're Fired," *National Public Radio,* December 8, 2008, http://www.npr.org.

30. J. Meister, "To Do: Update Company's Social Media Policy ASAP," *Forbes* (online), February 7, 2013, http://www.forbes.com.

31 J. DeMers, "Communication in 2015: Text, Voice, Video or In-Person?" *Inc.* January 29, 2015, www.inc.com; K. Ferrazzi, "How to Avoid Virtual Communication," *Harvard Business Review* (online), April 12, 2013, http://www.hbr.org.

32. K. Byron, "Carrying Too Heavy a Load? The Communication and Miscommunication of Emotion by Email,"

Academy of Management Review 33 (2008), pp. 309–27.

33. Naquin et al., "The Finer Points of Lying Online."

34. T. Bradley, "Email vs. IM vs. SMS: Choosing the Right One," *PC World* (online), January 13, 2012, http://www.pcworld.com; B. Glassberg, W. Kettinger, and J. Logan, "Electronic Communication: An Ounce of Policy Is Worth a Pound of Cure," *Business Horizons,* July–August 1996, pp. 74–80; Ali, "Why No One under 30 Answers Your Voicemail."

35. Ali, "Why No One under 30 Answers Your Voicemail."

36. G. Moran, "6 Ways to Tame Your Email Overload," *Fast Company,* March 2, 2016, www.fastcompany.com; A. Hopp, "Overwhelming Communication," *Training Journal* (online), April 23, 2014, http://www.trainingjournal.com.

37. Chui et al., "The Social Economy," p. 47.

38. N. Fallon, "12 Easy Ways to Be More Productive at Work," *Business News Daily,* April 20, 2017, www.businessnewsdaily.com; Robby Macdonell, "Can We Talk for a Minute about Why Email Sucks So Much?" *RescueTime Blog,* February 16, 2013, http://blog.rescuetime.com.

39. Chui et al., "The Social Economy," p. 29.

40. L. Vanderkam, "What Is an Appropriate Response Time to Email?" *Fast Company,* March 29, 2016, www.fastcompany.com; C. Conner, "Why Every Organization Needs a Standard Response Time Policy," *Forbes* (online), August 16, 2013, http://www.forbes.com.

41. S. Vozza, "Why Your Company Should Consider Banning Email," *Fast Company* (online), February 20, 2015, http://www.fastcompany.com; E. Horng, "No E-mail Fridays Transform Office," *ABC News,* March 10, 2007, http://abcnews.go.com.

42. K. Tausche, "JPMorgan Cuts the Cord on Voicemail," *CNBC* (online), May 2, 2015, http://www.cnbc.com.

43. D. Meinert, "Make Telecommuting Pay Off," *HR Magazine* 56 (online), June 11, 2011, http://www.shrm.org.

44. "Millennials Don't Care about Mobile Security, and Here's What to Do about It," *Wired,* September 2014, http://www.wired.com; E. Weise, "Bring Your Own Dilemmas: Dealing with BYOD and Security," *USA Today* (online), August 26, 2014, http://www.usatoday.com; T. Kaneshige, "12 Big BYOD Predictions for 2014," *CIO* (online), January 8, 2014, http://www.cio.com; "BYOD/BYOA: A Growing, Applicable Trend," *Comcast Business* (2014), http://www.inc.com; Gartner, "Gartner Predicts by 2017, Half of Employers Will Require Employees to Supply Their Own Device for Work Purposes," press release on, May 1, 2013, http://www.gartner.com.

45. Ibid.

46. P. Economy, "5 Ways to Get the Most from Virtual Employees," *Inc.* (online), June 13, 2014, http://www.inc.com; T. Mackintosh, "Is This the Year You Move to a Virtual Office?" *Accounting Technology,* May 2007,

General Reference Center Gold, http://find.galegroup.com.

47. Company website, "Work with Us," http://automattic.com/work-with-us/, accessed on May 3, 2015; Rachel Emma Silverman, "Step into the Office-less Company," *The Wall Street Journal,* September 4, 2012, http://online.wsj.com; Verne Kopytoff, "Why Some Company Offices Are Virtual," *Bloomberg Businessweek,* September 10, 2012, *EBSCOhost,* http://web.ebscohost.com; Automattic, "Work with Us," http://automattic.com.

48. E. Hallowel, "The Human Moment at Work," *Harvard Business Review* (online), January–February 1999, http://www.hbr.org.

49. R. Lengel and R. Daft, "The Selection of Communication Media as an Executive Skill," *Academy of Management Executive* 2 (1988), pp. 225-32.

50. J. R. Carlson and R. W. Zmud, "Channel Expansion Theory and the Experiential Nature of Media Richness Perceptions," *Academy of Management Journal* 42 (1999), pp. 153-70.

51. J. Fulk and B. Boyd, "Emerging Theories of Communication in Organizations," *Journal of Management* 17 (1991), pp. 407-46.

52. Ibid.

53. Company website, https://soundcloud.com/, accessed April 19, 2017; "How SoundCloud Keeps Communication Flowing across Four Offices in 4 Time Zones,"; "How SoundCloud's All Hands Meetings Keep Its Four Offices Aligned," *Future of Work,* http://futureofwork.nobl.io/future-of-work/how-soundclouds-all-hands-meetings-keep-its-four-offices-aligned, accessed April 19, 2017.

54. L. Bossidy and R. Charan, *Confronting Reality: Doing What Matters to Get Things Right* (New York: Crown Business, 2004).

55. C. Beers, "Leading through the Power of Persuasion," *Fast Company* (online), November 8, 2012, http://www.fastcompany.com; M. McCall, M. Lombardo, and A. Morrison, *The Lessons of Experience: How Successful Executives Develop on the Job* (Lexington, MA: Lexington, 1988).

56. J. A. Conger, "The Necessary Art of Persuasion," *Harvard Business Review,* May–June 1998, pp. 84-95.

57. N. Morgan, "How to Become an Authentic Speaker," *Harvard Business Review,* November 2008, pp. 115-19.

58. N. Nohria and B. Harrington, *Six Principles of Successful Persuasion* (Boston: Harvard Business School Publishing Division, 1993).

59. Boris Groysberg and Michael Slind, "Leadership Is a Conversation," *Harvard Business Review,* June 2012, pp. 79-80.

60. H. K. Mintz, "Business Writing Styles for the 70's," *Business Horizons,* August 1972, cited in *Readings in Interpersonal and Organizational Communication,* ed. R. C. Huseman, C. M. Logue, and D. L. Freshley (Boston: Allyn & Bacon, 1977).

61. C. D. Decker, "Writing to Teach Thinking," *Across the Board,* March 1996, pp. 19-20.

62. M. Forbes, "Exorcising Demons from Important Business Letters," *Marketing Times,* March–April 1981, pp. 36-38.

63. R. Gillett, "Here's Why No One Gets Your Sarcastic Emails," *Fast Company* (online), May 30, 2014, http://www.fastcompany.com; T. Flood, "Top Ten Mistakes Managers Make with Email," *The Wall Street Journal,* February 3, 2010, http://online.wsj.com.

64. D. Jones, "Cisco CEO Sees Tech as Integral to Success," *USA Today,* March 19, 2007, p. 4B (interview with John Chambers).

65. G. Ferraro, "The Need for Linguistic Proficiency in Global Business," *Business Horizons,* May–June 1996, pp. 39-46; William W. Maddux, Peter H. Kim, Tetsushi Okumura, and Jeanne M. Brett, "Why 'I'm Sorry' Doesn't Always Translate," *Harvard Business Review,* June 2012, p. 26.

66. P. C. Early and E. Mosakowski, "Creating Hybrid Team Cultures: An Empirical Test of Transnational Team Functioning," *Academy of Management Journal* 43 (2000), pp. 26-49.

67. Ferraro, "The Need for Linguistic Proficiency."

68. C. Chu, *The Asian Mind Game* (New York: Rawson Associates, 1991).

69. Ferraro, "The Need for Linguistic Proficiency."

70. T. W. Comstock, *Communicating in Business and Industry* (Albany, NY: Delmar, 1985).

71. M. Korda, *Power: How to Get It, How to Use It* (New York: Random House, 1975).

72. A. Mehrabian, "Communication without Words," *Psychology Today,* September 1968, p. 52. Cited in M. B. McCaskey, "The Hidden Message Managers Send," *Harvard Business Review,* November–December 1979, pp. 135-48.

73. Social Impact Stories, http://www.social-impact-stories.com/about, accessed April 21, 2017; Renyung Ho, "The Power of Storytelling for Social Business," *Conscious* magazine, [no date], http://consciousmagazine.co/the-power-of-storytelling-for-social-businesses/, accessed April 21, 2017; "Stories of Change," http://www.sundance.org/support/storiesofchange, accessed April 21, 2017; Jeff Bladt and Bob Filbin, "A Data Scientist's Real Job: Storytelling," March 27, 2013, https://hbr.org/2013/03/a-data-scientists-real-job-sto; "Social Enterprise Stories," https://socialenterprise.us/story-telling/, accessed April 21, 2017; organization website, Liberty's Kitchen, http://www.libertyskitchen.org/blog/, accessed April 21, 2017.

74. J. Smith, "10 Nonverbal Cues That Convey Confidence at Work," *Forbes* (online), March 11, 2013, http://www.forbes.com.

75. Ferraro, "The Need for Linguistic Proficiency."

76. Bernard T. Ferrari, "The Executive's Guide to Better Listening," *McKinsey Quarterly,* February 2012, https://www.mckinseyquarterly.com.

77. A. Athos and J. Gabarro, *Interpersonal Behavior* (Englewood Cliffs, NJ: Prentice-Hall, 1978).

78. M. K. Pratt, "Five Ways to Drive Your Best Workers out the Door," *Computerworld,* August 25, 2008, pp. 26-27, 30.

79. J. Kouzes and B. Posner, *The Leadership Challenge* (San Francisco: Jossey-Bass, 1995).

80. A. Vance, "Netflix, Reed Hastings Survive Missteps to Join Silicon Valley's Elite," *Bloomberg Business* (online), May 9, 2013, http://www.bloomberg.com.

81. G. Graham, J. Unruh, and P. Jennings, "The Impact of Nonverbal Communication in Organizations: A Survey of Perceptions," *Journal of Business Communications* 28 (1991), pp. 45-62.

82. Ibid.

83. E. Goodson, "Read a Plant—Fast," *Harvard Business Review,* May 2002, pp. 105-13; D. Upton and S. Macadam, "Why (and How) to Take a Plant Tour," *Harvard Business Review,* May–June 1997, pp. 97-106.

84. Goodson, "Read a Plant—Fast."

85. H. Seligson, "For American Workers in China, a Culture Clash," *The New York Times* (online), December 23, 2009, http://www.nytimes.com.

86. Chu, *The Asian Mind Game.*

87. J. Keyton, "Communication in Organizations," *Annual Review of Organizational Psychology and Organizational Behavior* 4 (2017), pp. 501-26.

88. A. Smidts, A. T. H. Pruyn, and C. B. M. van Riel, "The Impact of Employee Communication and Perceived External Prestige on Organizational Identification," *Academy of Management Journal* 49 (2001), pp. 1051-62.

89. X. Qin, R. Ren, Z. Zhang, and R. Johnson, "Fairness Heuristics and Substitutability Effects: Inferring the Fairness of Outcomes, Procedures, and Interpersonal Treatment When Employees Lack Clear Information," *Journal of Applied Psychology* 100 (2015), pp. 749-66; J. Koehler, K. Anatol, and R. Applebaum, *Organizational Communication: Behavioral Perspectives* (Orlando, FL: Holt, Rinehart & Winston, 1981).

90. J. Waldroop and T. Butler, "The Executive as Coach," *Harvard Business Review,* November–December 1996, pp. 111-17; S. Toye, "Coaching Comes of Age," *Training Journal* (2015), pp. 21-24.

91. D. T. Hall, K. L. Otazo, and G. P. Hollenbeck, "Behind Closed Doors: What Really Happens in Executive Coaching," *Organizational Dynamics,* Winter 1999, pp. 39-53; D. O'Neil, M. Hopkins, and D. Bilimoria, "A Framework for Developing Women Leaders: Applications to Executive Coaching," *The Journal of Applied Behavioral Science* 51 (2015), pp. 253-76.

92. D. Larcker, S. Miles, B. Tayan, and M. Gutman, "2013 Executive Coaching Survey," The Miles Group and Stanford University, August 2013, http://www.gsb.stanford.edu/faculty-research/

publications/2013-executive-coachingsurvey.

93. T. Judge and J. Cowell, "The Brave New World of Coaching," *Business Horizons,* July–August 1997, pp. 71–77; E. E. Lawler III, *Treat People Right!* (San Francisco: Jossey-Bass, 2003); and L. A. Hill, "New Manager Development for the 21st Century," *Academy of Management Executive,* August 2004, pp. 121–26.

94. R. J. Bies, "The Delivery of Bad News in Organizations: A Framework for Analysis," *Journal of Management* 39 (2013), pp. 136–62.

95. J. Gutknecht and J. B. Keys, "Mergers, Acquisitions, and Takeovers: Maintaining Morale of Survivors and Protecting Employees," *Academy of Management Executive,* August 1993, pp. 26–36.

96. D. Schweiger and A. DeNisi, "Communication with Employees Following a Merger: A Longitudinal Field Experiment," *Academy of Management Journal* 34 (1991), pp. 110–35.

97. J. Case, "Opening the Books," *Harvard Business Review,* March–April 1997, pp. 118–27.

98. "How Total Transparency Saved My Company," *Inc.* (online), March 2014, http://www.inc.com.

99. S. Stevenson, "We Spent *What* on Paper Clips?" *Slate,* May 19, 2014, http://www.slate.com; "Hilcorp Hits #15 on Fortune's 100 Best Companies to Work For List," press release on, January 23, 2014, http://www.hilcorp.com; P. Patel, "Houston's Top Workplaces 2010: No. 1 Midsize Company, Hilcorp Energy Company," *Houston Chronicle,* November 7, 2010, www.houstonchronicle.com.

100. W. V. Ruch, *Corporate Communications* (Westport, CT: Quorum, 1984).

101. L. Tost, F. Gino, and R. Larrick, "When Power Makes Others Speechless: The Negative Impact of Leader Power on Team Performance," *Academy of Management Journal* 56 (2013), pp. 1465–86.

102. J. Gardner, "The Heart of the Matter: Leader-Constituent Interaction," in *Leading & Leadership,* ed. T. Fuller (Notre Dame, IN: Notre Dame University Press, 2000), pp. 239–44.

103. R. Ashkenas, D. Ulrich, T. Jick, and S. Kerr, *The Boundaryless Organization* (San Francisco: Jossey-Bass, 1995).

104. Ruch, *Corporate Communications.*

105. H. Touryalai, "Marriott's Upgrade: New CEO Arne Sorenson Freshens Up the Brand for Millennials," *Forbes* (online), June 26, 2013, http://www.forbes.com.

106. A. Hutton, "Four Rules for Taking Your Message to Wall Street," *Harvard Business Review,* May 2001, pp. 125–32.

107. Koehler et al., *Organizational Communication.*

108. Tjosvold, A. S. H.Wong, and N. Y. F. Chen, "Constructively Managing Conflicts in Organizations" *Annual Review of Organizational Psychology and Organizational Behavior* 1 (2014), pp. 545–68.

109. L. He, "Google's Secrets of Innovation: Empowering Its Employees," *Forbes*

110. T. Harbert, "Teamwork for Techies," *Computerworld,* December 20, 2010, pp. 24–27.

111. N. B. Kurland and L. H. Pelled, "Passing the Word: Toward a Model of Gossip and Power in the Workplace," *Academy of Management Review* 25 (2000), pp. 428–38.

112. T. Grosser, V. Lopez-Kidwell, G. Labianca, and L. Ellwardt, "Hearing It through the Grapevine: Positive and Negative Workplace Gossip," *Organizational Dynamics* 41 (2012), 52–61; L. Abrams, R. Cross, E. Lesser, and D. Levin, "Nurturing Interpersonal Trust in Knowledge-Sharing Networks," *Academy of Management Executive* 17 (November 2003), pp. 64–77.

113. R. L. Rosnow, "Rumor as Communication: A Contextual Approach," *Journal of Communication* 38 (1988), pp. 12–28.

114. L. Burke and J. M. Wise, "The Effective Care, Handling, and Pruning of the Office Grapevine," *Business Horizons,* May–June 2003, pp. 71–76.

115. K. Davis, "The Care and Cultivation of the Corporate Grapevine," *Dun's Review,* July 1973, pp. 44–47.

116. N. Difonzo, P. Bordia, and R. Rosnow, "Reining in Rumors," *Organizational Dynamics,* Summer 1994, pp. 47–62.

117. R. Ashkenas, D. Ulrich, T. Jick, and S. Kerr, *The Boundaryless Organization, Breaking the Chains of Organizational Structure* (San Francisco: Jossey-Bass, 1995).

118. R. M. Hodgetts, "A Conversation with Steve Kerr," *Organizational Dynamics,* Spring 1996, pp. 68–79.

119. R. M. Fulmer, "The Evolving Paradigm of Leadership Development," *Organizational Dynamics,* Spring 1997, pp. 59–72; R. Gagnon, "GE Workout: Physical Fitness for Your Organization," *Huffington Post* (online), October 11, 2013, http://www.huffingtonpost.com.

120. Company website, https://soundcloud.com/, accessed April 19, 2017; https://soundcloud.com/bell-pottinger/the-importance-of-the-employee-engagement podcast, accessed April 19, 2017; "How SoundCloud Keeps Communication Flowing across Four Offices in 4 Time Zones"; "How SoundCloud's All Hands Meetings Keep Its Four Offices Aligned,".

121. Ashkenas et al., *The Boundaryless Organization.*

Chapter 16

1. J. C. Collins and J. I. Porras, *Built to Last: Successful Habits of Visionary Companies* (New York: Harper Business, 1994).

2. Stephen T. Watson, "Insurers Turn to Wellness Programs in Bid to Cut Costs," *Buffalo News,* February 2, 2017, http://buffalonews.com/2017/02/02/insurers-promote-wellness-programs-employees-members/; Christina Farr, "How Fitbit Became the Next Big Thing in Corporate Wellness," *Fast Company,* April 18, 2016, https://www.fastcompany.com/3058462/

how-fitbit-became-the-next-big-thing-in-corporate-wellness; company website, http://www.fitbit.com/en-ca/product/corporate-solutions, accessed May 1, 2017.

3. Company website, "Continuous Improvement," Teco Energy, www.tecoenergy.com, accessed April 30, 2017.

4. Ibid.

5. C. Zakrzewski, "The Key to Getting Workers to Stop Wasting Time Online," *The Wall Street Journal,* March 13, 2016, www.wsj.com.

6. "BP Refinery Leaks Oil into Lake Michigan Near Chicago," *BBC News,* March 26, 2014, http://www.bbcnews.com; Tom Fowler, "BP Promotes a New Approach to Safety," *The Wall Street Journal,* February 13, 2013, http://blogs.wsj.com; Kjetil Malkenes Hovland, "Norway Orders BP Safety Review after Leak," *The Wall Street Journal,* April 29, 2013, http://online.wsj.com.

7. W. G. Ouchi, "Markets, Bureaucracies, and Clans," *Administrative Science Quarterly* 25 (1980), pp. 129–41; R. Simons, A. Davila, and R. S. Kaplan, *Performance Measurement & Control Systems for Implementing Strategy* (Englewood Cliffs, NJ: Prentice Hall, 2000).

8. E. D. Pulakos, S. Arad, M. A. Donovan, and K. E. Plamondon, "Adaptability in the Workplace: Development of a Taxonomy of Adaptive Performance," *Journal of Applied Psychology* 85, no. 4 (August 2000), pp. 12–24; and K. A. Merchant and T. Sandino, "Four Options for Measuring Value Creation: Strategies for Managers to Avoid Potential Flaws in Accounting Measures of Performance," *Journal of Accountancy* 208, no. 2 (2009), pp. 34–38.

9. "Why Measure What Matters?" *B Corporation* (online), May 22, 2015, http://www.bcorporation.net; Global Impact Investing Network, IRIS Metrics, https://iris.thegiin.org/metrics, accessed June 14, 2015; J. Anner, "Jessica Alba and the Impact of Social Enterprise," *Stanford Social Innovation Review* (online), September 26, 2014, http://www.ssireview.org; "When Measuring Social Impact, We Need to Move Beyond Counting," *Forbes* (online), July 15, 2013, http://www.forbes.com; Anne Field, "Why Measuring Impact Is Good for Business," *Forbes,* August 28, 2016, https://www.forbes.com/sites/annefield/2016/08/28/why-measuring-impact-is-good-for-business/#6925d68c7ddf; Kate Ruff and Sara Olsen, "The Next Frontier in Social Impact Measurement Isn't Measurement At All," *Stanford Social Innovation Review,* May 10, 2016, https://ssir.org/articles/entry/the_next_frontier_in_social_impact_measurement_isnt_measurement_at_all; company website, http://www.toms.com/what-we-give-shoes, accessed May 2, 2017.

10. S. Ante and L. Weber, "Memo to Workers: The Boss Is Watching," *The Wall Street Journal,* October 22, 2013, www.wsj.com.

11. Julie Jargon, "McDonald's Tackles Repair of 'Broken' Service," *The Wall Street Journal,* April 10, 2013, http://online.wsj.com; Julie Jargon, "Your McDonald's

Ordering Ritual Is about to Change," *The Wall Street Journal,* April 10, 2013, http://blogs.wsj.com; Martha C. White, "McDonald's Executive Says 'Service Is Broken,'" *NBC News,* April 12, 2013, http://www.nbcnews.com.

12. FedEx website, "Attributes Success to People-First Philosophy," http://www.fedex.com, accessed June 11, 2015.

13. Todd Henshaw, "Nano Tools for Leaders: After Action Reviews," *Wharton@Work,* April 2012, http://executiveeducation.wharton.upenn.edu; John Kello, "Upon Further Review: Benefits of Brief Post-Shift Huddles," *Industrial Safety & Hygiene News,* August 2012, p. 30; Stephen C. Harper, "Survival of the Swiftest," *Industrial Management,* January 2012, pp. 16–20.

14. "Dress & Appearance: Tattoos/Piercings: May Employers Have Dress Code Requirements That Prohibit All Visible Tattoos and Piercings?" Society for Human Resource Management, May 25, 2015, www.shrm.org; B. Miller, K. Nicols, and J. Eure, "Body Art in the Workplace: Piercing the Prejudice?" *Personnel Review,* 38. no. 6 (2009), pp. 621–40.

15. M. Berman-Gorvine, "Let Love Bloom at Work, but Very Carefully," *Bloomberg BNA,* January 30, 2017, www.bna.com; "Office Romances and 'Love' Contract'?," *National Law Review,* February 2, 2016, www.natlawreview.com; L. Howell, "Happy Valentine's Day! Please Sign This Love Contract Before You Go to Lunch . . . ." *Austin HR,* February 17, 2014, http:/www.austinhr.com.

16. Gary S. Kaplan, "Pursuing the Perfect Patient Experience," *Frontiers of Health Services Management,* Spring 2013, pp. 16–27. For an additional example in another type of organization, see David T. Goomas, Stuart M. Smith, and Timothy D. Ludwig, "Business Activity Monitoring: Real-Time Group Goals and Feedback Using an Overhead Scoreboard in a Distribution Center," *Journal of Organizational Behavior Management* 31 no. 3 (2011), pp. 196–209.

17. M. Kownatzki, J. Walter, S. Floyd, and C. Lechner, "Corporate Control and the Speed of Strategic Business Unit Decision Making," *Academy of Management Journal* 56 (2013), pp. 1295–1324; V. U. Druskat, "Effects and Timing of Developmental Peer Appraisals in Self-Managing Work Groups," *Journal of Applied Psychology* 84, no. 1 (February 1999), p. 58; Baard Kuvaas, "The Interactive Role of Performance Appraisal Reactions and Regular Feedback," *Journal of Managerial Psychology* 26 no. 2 (2011), pp. 123–37.

18. PricewaterhouseCoopers, "2014 State of the Internal Audit Profession Study," March 2014, http://www.pwc.com; "Business Analytics: Numbers and Nuance," *CIO Insight,* January 12, 2011, Business & Company Resource Center, http://galenet.galegroup.com.

19. S. Waddock and N. Smith, "Corporate Responsibility Audits: Doing Well by Doing Good," *Sloan Management Review* 41, no. 2

(Winter 2000), pp. 75–83; L. L. Bergeson, "OSHA Gives Incentives for Voluntary Self-Audits," *Pollution Engineering* 32, no. 10 (October 2000), pp. 33–34; Scott M. Shafer and Sara B. Moeller, "The Effects of Six Sigma on Corporate Performance: An Empirical Investigation," *Journal of Operations Management* 30, no. 7–8 (November 1, 2012), pp. 521–32.

20. "SAP, Maker of Performance Review Software, Ditches Performance Reviews," *Fortune,* August 12, 2016, www.fortune.com; C. Zillman, "IBM Is Blowing Up Its Annual Performance Review," *Fortune,* February 1, 2016, www.fortune.com; B. Miller, "Banish 'Annual' from Your Performance Review Vocabulary," *Entrepreneur* (online), October 10, 2014, http://www.entrepreneur.com; L. Barry, A. Erhardt-Lewis, S. Garr, and A. Liakopoulos, "Performance Management Is Broken: Replace 'Rank and Yank' with Coaching and Development," Deloitte University Press, March 4, 2014, http://dupress.com/articles/hc-trends-2014-performance-management/; Deloitte, "Performance Management Is Broken," Global Human Capital Trends 2014: Engaging the 21st Century Workforce, http://www2.deloitte.com.

21. S. Aghili, "A Six Sigma Approach to Internal Audits," *Strategic Finance,* February 2009, Business & Company Resource Center, http://galenet. galegroup.com.

22. See, for example, Ryan Huang, "Six Sigma 'Killed' Innovation in 3M," *ZD Net* (online), March 14, 2013, http://www.zdnet.com; S. Chakravorty, "Where Process-Improvement Projects Go Wrong," *The Wall Street Journal* (online), January 25, 2010, http://www.wsj.com.

23. "Unlocking the Strategic Value of Internal Audit," Ernst & Young/Forbes Insight (2010), http://www.forbes.com; T. Rancour and M. McCracken, "Applying 6 Sigma Methods for Breakthrough Safety Performance," *Professional Safety* 45, no. 10 (October 2000), pp. 29–32; and G. Eckes, "Making Six Sigma Last," *Ivey Business Journal,* January–February 2002, p. 77.

24. J. L. Colbert, "The Impact of the New External Auditing Standards," *Internal Auditor* 5, no. 6 (December 2000), pp. 46–50.

25. Aghili, "A Six Sigma Approach"; Y. Giard and Y. Nadeau, "Improving the Processes," *CA Magazine,* December 2008, Business & Company Resource Center, http://galenet.galegroup.com; and G. Cheney, "Connecting the Dots to the Next Crisis," *Financial Executive,* April 2009, pp. 30–33.

26. J. D. Glater, "The Better the Audit Panel, the Higher the Stock Price," *The New York Times,* April 8, 2005, p. C4; and M. Alic and B. Rusjan, "Contribution of the ISO 9001 Internal Audit to Business Performance," *International Journal of Quality and Reliability Management* 27, no. 8 (2010), pp. 916–37.

27. A. Carr, "Chipotle Eats Itself," *Fast Company,* October 16, 2016, www.fastcompany.com.

28. Jan Tullberg, "Triple Bottom Line—a Vaulting Ambition?" *Business Ethics: A European Review* 21 no. 3 (June 2012), pp. 310–24; Grant Davis, "The Triple Bottom Line Goal of Sustainable Businesses," *Entrepreneur,* April 24, 2013, http://www.entrepreneur.com; Rebecca Coons, "Corporate Social Responsibility: Pursuing the Triple Bottom Line," *IHS Chemical Week,* May 27–June 3, 2013, pp. 21–23.

29. Pam Schuneman, "Master the 'ABCs' of Activity-Based Costing," *Managed Care,* May 1997, http://www.managedcaremag.com; Ivana Drazic Lutilsky and Martina Dragija, "Activity Based Costing as a Means to Full Costing: Possibilities and Constraints for European Universities," *Management* 17 no. 1 (June 2012), pp. 33–57.

30. J. Farre-Mensa, "Managerial Myopia: Why Public Companies Underinvest in the Future," *Forbes* (online), February 3, 2013, http://www.forbes.com; K. Merchant, *Control in Business Organizations* (Boston: Pitman, 1985); and C. W. Chow, Y. Kato, and K. A. Merchant, "The Use of Organizational Controls and Their Effects on Data Manipulation and Management Myopia," *Accounting, Organizations, and Society* 21, nos. 2/3 (February/April 1996), pp. 175–92.

31. E. E. Lawler III and J. Rhode, *Information and Control in Organizations* (Pacific Palisades, CA: Goodyear, 1976); A. Ferner, "The Underpinnings of 'Bureaucratic' Control Systems: HRM in European Multinationals," *Journal of Management Studies* 37, no. 4 (June 2000), pp. 521–39; and M. S. Fenwick, "Cultural and Bureaucratic Control in MNEs: The Role of Expatriate Performance Management," *Management International Review* 39 (1999), pp. 107–25.

32. Hindo, "At 3M, a Struggle between Efficiency and Creativity." See also Jason J. Dahling, Samantha L. Chau, and Alison O'Malley, "Correlates and Consequences of Feedback Orientation in Organizations," *Journal of Management* 38 no. 2 (2012), pp. 531–46.

33. J. Veiga and J. Yanouzas, *The Dynamics of Organization Theory,* 2nd ed. (St. Paul, MN: West, 1984).

34. Steve Lohr, "Unblinking Eyes Track Employees," *The New York Times,* June 21, 2014, https://www.nytimes.com/2014/06/22/technology/workplace-surveillance-sees-good-and-bad.html?_r=0; Farr, "How Fitbit Became the Next Big Thing"; Justine Hoffher, Can Your Boss Really Use 'Workplace Wellness' data to Track Your Birth Control Habits? "Boston.com, February 18, 2016, https://www.boston.com/jobs/jobs-news/2016/02/18/are-employers-really-using-data-to-monitor-workers-health; Mark Feffer, "Should You Track the Social Media of Fired Employees?" Society for Human Resource Management, SHRM.org, January 30, 2017, https://www.shrm.org/resourcesandtools/hr-topics/employee-relations/pages/social-media-tracking.aspx

35. K. Zezima, "Everything You Need to Know about the VA—and the Scandals Engulfing It," *The Washington Post* (online), May 30, 2014, http://www.washingtonpost.com.
36. Ibid.
37. Ibid.
38. C. Devine, "Bad VA Care May Have Killed More Than 1,000 Veterans, Senator's Report Says," *CNN* (online), June 24, 2014, http://www.cnn.com.
39. D. Vater, Y. Cho, and P. Sidebottom, "The Digital Challenge to Retail Banks," Bain & Company, 2012, http://www.bain.com.
40. M. Hammer, "The Seven Deadly Sins of Performance Measurement and How to Avoid Them," *MIT Sloan Management Review* 48, no. 3 (Spring 2007), pp. 19–28.
41. Lawler and Rhode, *Information and Control in Organizations;* and J. A. Gowan Jr. and R. G. Mathieu, "Critical Factors in Information System Development for a Flexible Manufacturing System," *Computers in Industry* 28, no. 3 (June 1996), pp. 173–83.
42. Adrienne Selko, "Ethicon: Employee Engagement Results in Zero Product Recalls," *Industry Week,* January 17, 2013, http://www.industryweek.com.
43. R. S. Kaplan and D. P. Norton, *The Balanced Scorecard: Translating Strategy into Action* (Boston: Harvard Business School Press, 1996); and Z. Hoque, "20 Years of Studies on the Balanced Scorecard: Trends, Accomplishments, Gaps and Opportunities for Future Research," *The British Accounting Review,* March 2014, pp. 33–59.
44. "National Marrow Donor Program (NMDP) Case Study," Balanced Scorecard Institute, http://www.theinstitutepress.com, accessed June 12, 2015; National Marrow Donor Program and Be The Match, "Key Messages, Facts & Figures," http://www.bethematch.org, accessed June 12, 2015.
45. A Ross, "How Connective Tech Boosts Political Change," *CNN,* 2012, http://www.cnn.com/2012/06/20/opinion/opinion-alec-ross-tech-politics/index.html;
46. K. Moores and J. Mula, "The Salience of Market, Bureaucratic, and Clan Controls in the Management of Family Firm Transitions: Some Tentative Australian Evidence," *Family Business Review* 13, no. 2 (June 2000), pp. 91–106; and A. Walker and R. Newcombe, "The Positive Use of Power on a Major Construction Project," *Construction Management and Economics* 18, no. 1 (January/February 2000), pp. 37–44.
47. P. H. Fuchs, K. E. Mifflin, D. Miller, and J. O. Whitney, "Strategic Integration: Competing in the Age of Capabilities," *California Management Review* 42, no. 3 (Spring 2000), pp. 118–47; M. A. Lando, "Making Compliance Part of Your Organization's Culture," *Healthcare Executive* 15, no. 5 (September/October 1999), pp. 18–22; K. A. Frank and K. Fahrbach, "Organization Culture as a Complex System: Balance and Information in Models of Influence and Selection," *Organization Science* 10, no. 3 (May/June

1999), pp. 253–77; Serge A. Rijsdijk and Jan van den Ende, "Control Combinations in New Product Development Projects," *Journal of Product Innovation Management* 28, no. 6 (November 2011), pp. 868–80.
48. Starbucks website, "Control," www.starbucks.com, accessed May 2, 2017.
49. Lohr, "Unblinking Eyes Track Employees," Hoffher, "Can Your Boss Really Use 'Workplace Wellness' Data?"; Clayton Moore, "The Workplace of the Future Tracks Your Every Move, Whether You Like It or Not," *DigitalTrends.com,* February 15, 2017, http://www.digitaltrends.com/home/smart-sensors-in-the-workplace/; Rachel Emma Silverman, "Bosses Tap Outside Firms to Predict Which Workers Might Get Sick," *The Wall Street Journal,* February 17, 2016, https://www.wsj.com/articles/bosses-harness-big-data-to-predict-which-workers-might-get-sick-1455664940; Lee Michael Katz, "Monitoring Employee Productivity: Proceed with Caution," Society for Human Resource Management, SHRM.org, June 1, 2015, https://www.shrm.org/hr-today/news/hr-magazine/pages/0615-employee-monitoring.aspx

Chapter 17

1. Tanner Christensen, "How Elon Musk Comes Up with Epic Ideas? A Simple Strategy, Actually," *Inc.,* February 8, 2016, https://www.inc.com/tanner-christensen/how-people-like-elon-musk-achieve-epic-innovation.html; Umair Ahmed, "7 Takeaways in the Success of Elon Musk for Young Entrepreneurs," *Entrepreneur,* June 17, 2016, https://www.entrepreneur.com/article/276386; Lydia Belanger, "19 Weird Things We've Learned about Elon Musk," *Entrepreneur,* March 22, 2017, https://www.entrepreneur.com/article/288010; Michael Simmons and Ian Chew, "How to Think Like Elon Musk," *Fortune,* August 11, 2016, http://fortune.com/2016/08/11/how-to-think-like-elon-musk/; and Drake Baer, "Here's How Studying Physics Has Helped Elon Musk Find Insights Everybody Else Misses," *Business Insider,* January 23, 2015, http://www.businessinsider.com/elon-musk-physics-leadership-2015-1.
2. W. McKinley, S. Latham, and M. Braun, "Organizational Decline and Innovation: Turnarounds and Downward Spirals," *Academy of Management Review* 39 (2014), pp. 88–110.
3. B. Meyerson, "Top 10 Emerging Technologies of 2015," *Scientific American* (online), March 4, 2015, http://www.scientificamerican.com; "Customer Service Robots to Roam the Aisles at Lowe's," *CBS News* (online), October 28, 2014, http://www.cbsnews.com.
4. R. A. Burgelman, M. A. Maidique, and S. C. Wheelwright, *Strategic Management of Technology and Innovation* (New York: McGraw-Hill, 2000); Panagiotis Ganotakis and James H. Love, "The Innovation Value Chain in New Technology-Based Firms," *Journal of Product Innovation Management* 29, no. 5 (September 2012), pp. 839–60.

5. D. C. L. Prestwood and P. A. Schumann Jr., "Revitalize Your Organization," *Executive Excellence* 15, no. 2 (February 1998), p. 16; C. Y. Baldwin and K. B. Clark, "Managing in an Age of Modularity," *Harvard Business Review* 75, no. 5 (September–October 1997), pp. 84–93; S. Gopalakrishnan, P. Bierly, and E. H. Kessler, "A Reexamination of Product and Process Innovations Using a Knowledge-Based View," *Journal of High Technology Management Research* 10, no. 1 (Spring 1999), pp. 147–66; J. Pullin, "Bombardier Commands Top Marks," *Professional Engineering* 13, no. 3 (July 5, 2000), pp. 40–46; M. Johnson, C. Christensen, and H. Kagermann, "Reinventing Your Business Model," *Harvard Business Review* (December 2008), pp. 50–59; C. M. Christensen, *The Innovator's Dilemma* (Boston: Harvard Business Publishing, 1997); and C. M. Christensen, S. D. Anthony, and E. A. Roth, *Seeing What's Next* (Boston: Harvard Business Publishing, 2004).
6. M. Sawhney, R. C. Wolcott, and I. Arroniz, "The 12 Different Ways for Companies to Innovate," *MIT Sloan Management Review* 47, no. 3 (Spring 2006), pp. 75–81; Julian Birkinshaw, Gary Hamel, and Michael J. Mol, "Management Innovation," *Academy of Management Review* 33 (October 2008), pp. 825–45.
7. G. P. Pisano, *The Development Factory: Unlocking the Potential of Process Innovation* (Boston: Harvard Business School Press, 1996); and R. Leifer, C. M. McDermott, G. C. O'Connor, L. S. Peters, M. Rice, and R. W. Veryzer, *Radical Innovation: How Mature Companies Can Outsmart Upstarts* (Cambridge MA: Harvard Business School Press, 2000).
8. P. Seitz, "Pandora Joins On-Demand Streaming Music Fray, Takes On Spotify, Apple," *Investors,* March 14, 2017, www.investors.com; R. Levine, "Inside Pandora's Quest to Take on Spotify, Apple Music & Amazon," *Billboard,* January 19, 2017, www.billboard.com.
9. H. M. O'Neill, R. W. Pounder, and A. K. Buchholtz, "Patterns in the Diffusion of Strategies across Organizations: Insights from the Innovation, Diffusion Literature," *Academy of Management Review* 23, no. 1 (January 1998), pp. 98–114; E. M. Rogers, *Diffusion of Innovations* (New York: Free Press, 1995); and B. Guilhon, ed., *Technology and Markets for Knowledge: Knowledge Creation, Diffusion and Exchange within a Growing Economy,* Economics of Science, Technology and Innovation 22 (Dordrecht, Netherlands: Kluwer Academic Publishing, 2000).
10. "Gen Z and Millennials Collide at Work," *Randstad USA,* www.randstad.com, accessed May 17, 2017; "Generation Z Will Be Welcomed: The Deloitte Millennial Survey 2017," Deloitte, www2.deloitte.com; M. Ward, "Gen Z Is about to Hit the Workforce—Here's What They Want in a Job," CNBC, August 30, 2016, www.cnbc.com; B. Mastroianni, "How Generation Z Is Changing the Tech World," CBS News,

March 10, 2016, www.cbsnews.com; Aliah Wright, "Generation Z's Tech Habits May Surprise HR," Society for Human Resource Management, February 29, 2016, www.shrm.org; J. Boitnott, "Generation Z and the Workplace: What You Need to Know," *Inc.,* January 27, 2016 www.inc.com; Dan Schwabel, "Gen Y and Gen Z Global Workplace Expectations Study," *Millennial Branding,* September 2, 2014, www.millennialbranding.com.

11. Organization website, http://www.sarvajal.com, accessed May 2, 2017; Alessandra Kortenhorst, organization blog, http://piramalsarvajal.blogspot.com, accessed May 2, 2017; Lisa Goldapple, "Water ATMs Making a Splash in India," *Project Breakthrough,* February 5, 2017, http://breakthrough.unglobalcompact.org/briefs/piramal-sarvajal-water-atms-making-a-splash-in-india/; Bérénice Magistretti, "How Social Entrepreneurship Is Making a Difference in the World," *TechCrunch.com,* April 25, 2016, https://techcrunch.com/2016/04/25/how-social-entrepreneurship-is-making-a-difference-in-the-world/.

12. M. E. Porter, *Competitive Strategy* (New York: Free Press, 1980).

13. C. M. Christensen, S. D. Anthony, and E. A. Roth, *Seeing What's Next* (Boston: Harvard Business Publishing, 2004); Clayton Christensen, "Key Concepts: Disruptive Innovation," http://www.claytonchristensen.com; Innosight, "Expertise: Driving New Growth through Disruptive Innovation," http://www.innosight.com; Matthew Yglesias, "Stop 'Disrupting' Everything," *Slate,* May 1, 2013, http://www.slate.com.

14. R. Koch, "How Uber Used a Simplified Business Model to Disrupt the Taxi Industry," *Entrepreneur,* January 3, 2017, www.entrepreneur.com.

15. S. A. Zahra, S. Nash, and D. J. Bickford, "Transforming Technological Pioneering in Competitive Advantage," *Academy of Management Executive* 9, no. 1 (1995), pp. 17–31; and M. Sadowski and A. Roth, "Technology Leadership Can Pay Off," *Research Technology Management* 42, no. 6 (November/December 1999), pp. 32–33.

16. L. Luk, "Apple Plans Force of Touch Technology for New iPhones," *The Wall Street Journal* (online), March 11, 2015, http://www.wsj.com.

17. Company website, "3M: 2017 Sustainability Report," www.3m.com.

18. C. Andrew, "Drug Competition, the Patent Game, and Generic Cialis," *Canadian Pharmacy World,* March 6, 2017, www.canadianpharmacyworld.com; "Can't Buy Love? Sex Drug Prices Put Medicines out of Reach for Some," CBS News, December 5, 2016, www.cbsnews.com.

19. C. Trudell, Y. Hagiwara, and J. Ma, "Humans Replacing Robots Herald Toyota's Vision of Future," *Bloomberg Business* (online), April 7, 2014, http://www.bloomberg.com; M. Imai and G. Kaizen, *A Commonsense, Low-Cost Approach to Management* (New York: McGraw-Hill,

1997); and M. Imai and G. Kaizen, *The Key to Japan's Competitive Success* (New York: McGraw-Hill, 1986).

20. Press release, "Tufts CSDD Assessment of Cost to Develop and Win Marketing Approval for a New Drug," Tufts Center for the Study of Drug Development, March 10, 2016, www.csdd.tufts.edu; "2015 Profile: Biopharmaceutical Research Industry," www.phrma-docs.org, accessed May 14, 2017; D. Lazarus, "An Insider's View of Generic-Drug Pricing," *Los Angeles Times* (online), March 25, 2013, http://www.latimes.com.

21. See Matthew Semadeni and Brian S. Anderson, "The Follower's Dilemma: Innovation and Imitation in the Professional Services Industry," *Academy of Management Journal* 53 (October 2010), pp. 1175–1193.

22. Company website, "VitalPatch: Shattering the Paradigm of Patient Care," www.vitalconnect.com, accessed May 14, 2017.

23. D. Kawamoto, "10 Medical-Device Wearables to Improve Patients' Lives," *InformationWeek,* January 12, 2016, www.informationweek.com.

24. P. A. Geroski, "Models of Technology Diffusion," *Research Policy* 29, no. 4/5 (April 2000), pp. 603–25; and L. A. Thomas, "Adoption Order of New Technologies in Evolving Markets," *Journal of Economic Behavior & Organization* 38, no. 4 (April 1999), pp. 453–82.

25. Company website, "Healthcare's Most Overlooked Opportunity," Accenture, www.accenture.com, accessed May 14, 2017.

26. "78% of Americans Support This Revolutionary Healthcare Technology, but Only 21% Have Tried It," Fox Business News, March 2, 2017, www.foxbusiness.com.

27. R. E. Oligney and M. I. Economides, "Technology as an Asset," *Hart's Petroleum Engineer International* 71, no. 9 (September 1998), p. 27; C. MacKechnie, "What Are the Types of Business Techology," *Chron* (online), http://smallbusiness.chron.com, accessed on June 15, 2014; and J. Manyika, M. Chul, J. Bughin, R. Dobbs, P. Bisson, and A. Marrs, "Disruptive Technologies: Advances That Will Transform Life, Business, and the Global Economy," *McKinsey & Company Report,* May 2013, http://www.mckinsey.com.

28. B. Meyerson, "Top 10 Emerging Technologies of 2015," *World Economic Forum,* March 4, 2015, https://agenda.weforum.org/2015/03/top-10-emerging-technologies-of-2015-2/.

29. A. Rosenblum, "Air Force Tests IBM's Brain-Inspired Chip as an Aerial Tank Spotter," *Technology Review,* January 11, 2017, www.technologyreview.com.

30. Ameet Sachdev, "Bewitched by Baxter: Robot Draws Admirers," *Chicago Tribune,* January 22, 2013, sec. 2, pp. 1–3.

31. A. Szal, "Rethink Robotics Reaches Agreement for Distribution in Spain," *Manufacturing Net,* February 28, 2017, www.manufacturingnet.com.

32. "Quarterly Retail E-Commerce Sales 4th Quarter 2016," Census Report press release, February 17, 2017. www.census.gov.

33. "These 5 Retail Innovations Could Actually Make You Want to Shop in a Store Again," *Entrepreneur,* May 23, 2016, www.entrepreneur.com.

34. Ibid.

35. S. Elavia, "Why Department Stores Are Embracing Custom Fashion," Fox Business News, January 19, 2016, www.foxbusinessnews.com.

36. Ibid.

37. J. Cino, "How Does Facial Recognition Technology Work?" *Newsweek,* April 30, 2017, www.newsweek.com.

38. P. Grother, G. Quinn, and M. Ngan, "Face In Video Evaluation (FIVE) Face Recognition on Non-Cooperative Subjects," National Institute of Standards and Technology, March 2017, http://www.nist.gov.

39. J. Langston, "How Well Do Facial Recognition Algorithms Cope with a Million Strangers?" University of Washington, June 23, 2016, www.washington.edu.

40. Company website, "NEC's Video Face Recognition Technology Ranks First in NIST Testing," NEC, March 16, 2017, www.nec.com; Grother et al., "Face In Video Evaluation (FIVE) Face Recognition of Non-Cooperative Subjects.

41. General Electric, "GE's Dual Peizoelectric Cooling Jets (DCJ) Are Cool and Quiet," www.geglobalresearch.com, accessed May 15, 2017.

42. Clint Boulton, "Printing Out Barbies and Ford Cylinders," *The Wall Street Journal,* June 5, 2013, http://online.wsj.com; Elizabeth Royte, "The Printed World," *Smithsonian,* May 2013, pp. 50–57.

43. A. Frakt, "Blame Technology, Not Longer Life Spans, for Health Spending Increases," *The New York Times,* January 23, 2017, www.nytimes.com.

44. Ibid.

45. "CBP, ICE HSI Report $1.2 Billion in Counterfeit Seizures in 2014," U.S. Customs and Border Protection, April 2, 2015, http://www.cbd.gov.

46. R. Klara, "Counterfeit Goods Are a $460 Billion Industry, and Most Are Bought and Sold Online," *Adweek,* February 13, 2017, www.adweek.com.

47. M. Baccardax, "Merck Posts In-Line Fourth-Quarter Earnings, Issues Cautious 2017 Sales Outlook," *The Street,* February 2, 2017, www.thestreet.com.

48. Ibid.

49. T. Smith, "Lidl Opening First U.S. Stores This Summer; Earlier Than Expected," *Richmond Times-Dispatch,* February 15, 2017, www.richmond.com.

50. B. Tuttle, "7 Emerging Low-Cost Supermarkets That'll Save You Big Money on Groceries," *Time,* September 14, 2015, www.time.com.

51. H. Peterson, "A German Grocery Chain with the Power to Cripple Aldi, Whole Foods, and Trader Joe's Is about to Invade

America," *Business Insider,* February 15, 2017, www.businessinsider.com.

52. R. Reinhardt and S. Gurtner, "Differences between Early Adopters of Disruptive and Sustaining Innovations," *Journal of Business Research* 68 (2015), pp. 137–45; R. Dewan, B. Jing, and A. Seidmann, "Adoption of Internet-Based Product Customization and Pricing Strategies," *Journal of Management Information Systems* 17, no. 2 (Fall 2000), pp. 9–28; P. A. Geroski, "Models of Technology Diffusion," *Research Policy* 29, no. 4/5 (April 2000), pp. 603–25; Rogers, *Diffusion of Innovations.*

53. J. Stoll and M. Ramsey, "Tesla First-Quarter Car Deliveries Rise above 10,000," *The Wall Street Journal* (online), April 3, 2015, http://www.wsj.com; J. Lippert, "Will Tesla Ever Make Money?" Bloomberg Business (online), March 3, 2015, http://www.bloombergbusiness.com; Michael Levi, "How Tesla Pulled ahead of the Electric-Car Pack," *The Wall Street Journal,* June 20, 2013, http://online.wsj. com; Ashlee Vance, "Elon Musk, Man of Tomorrow," *Bloomberg Businessweek,* September 17, 2012, EBSCOhost, http:// web.ebscohost.com; George Blankenship, "Inside Tesla," *Tesla Motors blog,* March 21, 2013, http:// www.teslamotors.com; "General Electric Motors," *The Economist,* April 20, 2013, http://www.economist. com; Angus MacKenzie, "2013 Motor Trend Car of the Year: Tesla Model S," *Motor Trend,* January 2013, http://www. motortrend. com; Jason Cammisa, "Return to Power: The 2013 Tesla Model S," *Road & Track,* February 25, 2013, http://www.roadandtrack.com; Peter Valdes-Dapena, "Tesla: Consumer Reports' Best Car Ever Tested," *CNNMoney,* May 9, 2013, http://money.cnn.com; Mike Ramsey, "Tesla Motors Approaches Crossroad," *The Wall Street Journal,* February 10, 2013, http:// online.wsj.com; Tesla Motors, "Supercharger," http://www.teslamotors. com; Ina Fried, "Musk: Mainstream Tesla Model 3-4 Years Out, Will Be 20 Percent Smaller Than Model S," *All Things D,* May 29, 2013, http://allthingsd. com; Mike Ramsey and Tess Stynes, "Tesla Sees First-Ever Quarterly Profit," *The Wall Street Journal,* April 1, 2013, http://online.wsj.com; Mike Ramsey and Valerie Bauerlein, "Tesla Clashes with Car Dealers," *The Wall Street Journal,* June 18, 2013, http://online.wsj.com; Joseph B. White, "Tesla Has a Fresh $1 Billion—and Lots of Ways to Spend It," *The Wall Street Journal,* May 17, 2013, http://blogs.wsj.com; Loren McDonald, "Predicting When US Federal EV Tax Credit Will Expire for Tesla Buyers," *Cleantechnica.com,* January 20, 2017, https://cleantechnica.com/2017/01/20/predicting-us-federal-ev-tax-credit-will-expire-tesla-buyers/; Katie Fehrenbacher, "7 Reasons Why Tesla Insists on Selling Its Own Cars," *Fortune,* January 19, 2016, http://fortune.com/2016/01/19/why-tesla-sells-directly/; company website, https://www.tesla.com/charging, accessed April 30, 2017; Jordan Golson, "Tesla Is Doubling the Number of Supercharger Locations in North America," *The Verge. com,* February 22, 2017, https://www.theverge.com/2017/2/22/14703712/tesla-supercharger-growth-model-usa-canada-mexico; Bill Vlasic, "Tesla Reports Wide Loss with Critical Test Ahead," *New York Times,* May 4, 2017, https://www.nytimes.com/2017/05/03/business/tesla-quarterly-earnings-elon-musk.html.

54. "From AT&T to Xerox: 52 Corporate Innovative Labs," *CBI Insights,* August 25, 2016, www.cbiinsights.com.

55. E. Von Hippel, *The Sources of Innovation* (Oxford, UK: Oxford University Press, 1994); D. Leonard, *Wellsprings of Knowledge: Building and Sustaining the Sources of Innovation* (Cambridge, MA: Harvard Business School Press, 1998); and Melissa E. Graebner, Kathleen M. Eisenhardt, and Philip T. Roundy, "Success and Failure in Technology Acquisitions: Lessons for Buyers and Sellers," *Academy of Management Perspectives* 24, no. 3 (August 2010), pp. 73–92.

56. N. Clayton, "Israel at Center of Intel Empire," *The Wall Street Journal Tech Europe* (online), March 19, 2012, http:// blogs.wsj.com; T. Krazit, "Intel R&D on Slow Boat to China," *CNet News,* April 16, 2007, http://news.com.

57. "How the Unreal Engine Became a Real Gaming Powerhouse," *Popular Mechanics* (online), June 24, 2014, http://www.popularmechanics.com; "Online Gaming's Netscape Moment?" *The Economist,* June 9, 2007, http://find.galegroup.com.

58. B. Austen, "Bringing the Coffin Industry Back from the Dead," *The Atlantic,* December 2010, www.theatlantic.com.

59. Von Hippel, *The Sources of Innovation;* and Leonard, *Wellsprings of Knowledge.*

60. N. Tajitsu and M. Shiraki, "Toyota Unlocks Its Engine Technology, Could Sell to Rivals," Reuters, December 15, 2016, www.reuters.com.

61. J. Hagedoorn, A. N. Link, and N. S. Vonortas, "Research Partnerships," *Research Policy* 29, no. 4/5 (April 2000), pp. 567–86; S.-S. Yi, "Entry, Licensing and Research Joint Ventures," *International Journal of Industrial Organization* 17, no. 1 (January 1999), pp. 1–24; Satish Nambisan and Mohanbir Sawhney, "Orchestration Processes in Network-Centric Innovation: Evidence from the Field," *Academy of Management Perspectives* 25 (August 2011), pp. 40–57; Ulrich Lichtenthaler, "Open Innovation: Past Research, Current Debates, and Future Directions," *Academy of Management Perspectives* 25 (February 2011), pp. 75–93; Esteve Almirall and Ramon Casadesus-Masanell, "Open versus Closed Innovation: A Model of Discovery and Divergence," *Academy of Management Review* 35 (January 2010), pp. 27–47; Corey C. Phelps, "A Longitudinal Study of the Influence of Alliance Network Structure and Composition on Firm Exploratory Innovation," *Academy of Management Journal* 53 (August 2010), pp. 890–913.

62. Company website, "Key Investments," Nestlé Health Science, www.nestlehealthscience.com, accessed May 16, 2017; A. Ward and P. Waldmeir, "Chi-Med Draws on the Past for the Future," *Financial Times* (online), August 25, 2014, http://www.ft.com; Nestlé website, "New Partnership Gives Nestlé Health Science Access to One of the World's Leading Traditional Chinese Medicine Libraries," press release, November 28, 2012, http://www.nestle.com.

63. A. Heath, "Mark Zuckerberg Explains Facebook's Secrets for Acquiring Companies," *Business Insider,* January 18, 2017, www.businessinsider.com; K. Yeung, "Facebook Bought a Face-tracking Startup to Help It Take On Snapchat," *Business Insider,* November 16, 2016, www.businessinsider.com.

64. C. Pellerin, "CIO Priorities Include Cybersecurity, Innovation, Retaining IT Workforce," U.S. Department of Defense, March 23, 2016, www.defense.gov; P. Arandjelovic, L. Bulin, and N. Khan, "Why CIOs Should Be Business-Strategy Partners," *McKinsey Insights and Publications* (online), February 2015, http://www.mckinsey.com.

65. "Information Resources: The Evolution of R&D," *Research-Technology Management,* May–June 2011, pp. 65–66; and J. C. Spender and B. Strong, "Who Has Innovative Ideas? Employees," *The Wall Street Journal,* August 23, 2010, http://online.wsj.com.

66. D. L. Day, "Raising Radicals: Different Processes for Championing Innovative Corporate Ventures," *Organization Science* 5, no. 2 (May 1994), pp. 148–72; C. Siporin, "Want Speedy FDA Approval? Hire a 'Product Champion,'" *Medical Marketing & Media,* October 1993, pp. 22–28; C. Siporin, "How You Can Capitalize on Phase 3B," *Medical Marketing & Media,* October 1994, pp. 72–72; and E. H. Kessler, "Tightening the Belt: Methods for Reducing Development Costs Associated with New Product Innovation," *Journal of Engineering and Technology Management* 17, no. 1 (March 2000), pp. 59–92.

67. M. Ringel, A. Taylor, and H. Zablit, "The Most Innovative Companies 2016," Boston Consulting Group, January 2017, www.bcg.com.

68. J. G. March, "Exploration and Exploitation in Organizational Learning," *Organization Science* 2, no. 1 (1991), pp. 71–87; and S. C. Kang and S. A. Snell, "Intellectual Capital Architectures and Ambidextrous Learning: A Framework for Human Resource Management," *Journal of Management Studies* 46, no. 1 (2009), pp. 65–92.

69. Jeff DeGraff, "Why the 'Most Innovative Companies' Aren't," *Fortune,* March 13, 2013, http://management.fortune.com; Henry Chesbrough, "Why Bad Things Happen to Good Technology," *The Wall Street Journal,* June 19, 2012, http://online.wsj.com; Steven Levy, "Google's Larry Page on Why Moon Shots Matter," *Wired,* January 17, 2013, http://www.wired.com.

70. D. A. Fields, "How to Stop the Dumbing Down of Your Company," *Industry Week,* March 7, 2007, http://www.industryweek.com; L. K. Gundry, J. R. Kickul, and C. W. Prather, "Building the Creative Organization," *Organizational Dynamics* 22, no. 2 (Spring 1994), pp. 22–36; and T. Kuczmarski, "Inspiring and Implementing the Innovation Mind-Set," *Planning Review,* September–October 1994, pp. 37–48.

71. Steve Minter, "Priming the Supply Chain of Ideas," *Industry Week,* February 2013, Business Insights: Essentials, http://bi.galegroup.com.

72. Talent Management Exchange, "Speaker Information," http://www.talentmanagementexchange.com, accessed June 18, 2015.

73. Intuit Labs, "How We Do It," http://www.intuitlabs.com/about/, accessed June 18, 2015; D. Tsuruoka, "Intuit Innovation Lab, 'Idea Jams' Aim to Spur Creativity," *Investor's Business Daily,* April 14, 2009, Business & Company Resource Center, http://galenet.galegroup.com.

74. Leonard, *Wellsprings of Knowledge;* D. Leonard-Barton, "The Factory as a Learning Laboratory," *Sloan Management Review,* Fall 1992, pp. 23–38; and A. K. Gupta and V. Govindarajan, "Knowledge Management's Social Dimension: Lessons from Nucor Steel," *Sloan Management Review* 42, no. 1 (Fall 2000), pp. 71–80.

75. T. Brown, "Design Thinking" *Harvard Business Review* 86, no. 6 (June 2008), pp. 84–92.

76. M. Korn and R. Silverman, "Business Education: Forget B-School, D-School Is Hot," *The Wall Street Journal* (online), June 7, 2012, http://www.wsj.com.

77. IDEO website, "About Ideo," http://www.ideo.com, accessed July 5, 2015.

78. Korn and Silverman, "Business Education."

79. Brown, "Design Thinking."

80. J. Liedtka and T. Ogilvie, *Designing for Growth: A Design Thinking Tool Kit for Managers* (New York: Columbia Business School Publishing, 2011).

81. Brown, "Design Thinking".

82. H. K. Bowen, K. B. Clark, C. A. Holloway, and S. C. Wheelwright, "Development Projects: The Engine of Renewal," *Harvard Business Review,* September–October 1994, pp. 110–20; C. Eden, T. Williams, and F. Ackermann, "Dismantling the Learning Curve: The Role of Disruptions on the Planning of Development Projects," *International Journal of Project Management* 16, no. 3 (June 1998), pp. 131–38; and M. V. Tatikonda and S. R. Rosenthal, "Technology Novelty, Project Complexity, and Product Development Project Execution Success: A Deeper Look at Task Uncertainty in Product Innovation," *IEEE Transactions on Engineering Management* 47, no. 1 (February 2000), pp. 74–87.

83. E. Trist, "The Evolution of Sociotechnical Systems as a Conceptual Framework and as an Action Research Program," in *Perspectives on Organizational Design and Behavior,* ed. A. Van de Ven and W. F. Joyce (New York: John Wiley & Sons, 1981), pp. 19–75; and A. Molina, "Insights into the Nature of Technology Diffusion and Implementation: The Perspective of Sociotechnical Alignment," *Technovation* 17, nos. 11/12 (November/December 1997), pp. 601–26.

84. Company website, http://www.spacex.com, accessed May 1, 2017; Nicky Woolf, "SpaceX Founder Elon Musk Plans to Get Humans to Mars in Six Year," *The Guardian,* September 28, 2016, https://www.theguardian.com/technology/2016/sep/27/elon-musk-spacex-mars-colony; Mike Wall, "SpaceX's Elon Musk Unveils Interplanetary Spaceship to Colonize Mars," *Space.com,* September 27, 2016, http://www.space.com/34210-elon-musk-unveils-spacex-mars-colony-ship.html; Kenneth Chang, "Elon Musks's Plan: Get Humans to Mars—and Beyond," *The New York Times,* September 27, 2016, https://www.nytimes.com/2016/09/28/science/elon-musk-spacex-mars-exploration.html?_r=0.

85. Wayne F. Cascio and R. Montealegre, "How Technology Is Changing Work and Organizations," *Annual Review of Organizational Psychology and Organizational Behavior* 3 (2016), pp. 349–75; Lynda Aiman-Smith and Stephen G. Green, "Implementing New Manufacturing Technology: The Related Effects of Technology Characteristics and User Learning Activities," *Academy of Management Journal* 45 (April 2002), pp. 421–30; and Terri L. Griffith, "Technology Features as Triggers for Sensemaking," *Academy of Management Review* 24 (July 1999), pp. 472–88.

Chapter 18

1. D. Joling, "Shell Heads for Alaska While Awaiting Final Drilling Permits Anchorage, Alaska," *ABC News* (online), June 26, 2015, http://www.abcnews.com; United Nations Conference on Climate Change website, "What Is a Cop?" http://www.cop21.gouv.fr/en/cop21-cmp11/what-cop, accessed June 25, 2015; "Shell Can't Afford to Wait Until 2050 to Adapt Its Business to Climate Change," *The Conversation* (online), May 26, 2015, http://www.theconversation.com; S. Farrell, "Climate Change Dominates Marathon Shell Annual General Meeting," *The Guardian* (online), May 19, 2015, http://www.theguardian.com; "The Elephant in the Atmosphere," *The Economist* (online), July 19, 2014, http://www.economist.com; Terry Macalister, "Shell Creates Green Energy Division to Invest in Wind Power," *The Guardian,* May 15, 2016, https://www.theguardian.com/business/2016/may/15/shell-creates-green-energy-division-to-invest-in-wind-power; company website, http://reports.shell.com/sustainability-report/2016/, accessed May 5, 2017; Rakteem Katakey, "Shell Heads for Cleaner Future with Sale of Polluting Oil Sands," *Bloomberg.com,* March 9, 2017, https://www.bloomberg.com/news/articles/2017-03-09/shell-becomes-gas-company-with-7-25-billion-oil-sands-sale.

2. V. Bruno and H. Shin, "Globalization of Corporate Risk Taking," *Journal of International Business Studies* 45 (2014), pp. 800–20; M. Reeves and M. Deimler, "Adaptability: The New Competitive Advantage," *Harvard Business Review,* July–August 2011, pp. 135–41.

3. J. Bower, H. Leonard, and L. Paine, "Global Capitalism at Risk: What Are You Doing about It?" *Harvard Business Review,* September 2011, pp. 105–12.

4. Ibid.

5. T. Schooley, "Manufacturing Leader Optimistic for Industry's Future," *Business Times,* February 28, 2017, www.bizjournals.com.

6. J. Drogus, "Manufacturers' Optimism at 20-Year High, According to New NAM Survey," National Manufacturers Association, March 31, 2017, www.nam.org.

7. T. A. Judge, C. J. Thoresen, V. Pucik, and T. M. Welbourne, "Managerial Coping with Organizational Change: A Dispositional Perspective," *Journal of Applied Psychology* 84 (1999), pp. 107–22.

8. M. Fugate, A. Kinicki, and G. Prussia, "Employee Coping with Organizational Change: An Examination of Alternative Theoretical Perspectives and Models," *Personnel Psychology* 61 (2008), pp. 1–36.

9. C. Giffi, A. Roth, and G. Seal, *Competing in World-Class Manufacturing: America's 21st Century Challenge* (Homewood, IL: Business One Irwin, 1990).

10. R. M. Kanter, *World Class: Thriving Locally in the Global Economy* (New York: Touchstone, 1995).

11. R. M. Kanter, "How Great Companies Think Differently," *Harvard Business Review,* November 2011, pp. 66–78.

12. Giffi et al., *Competing in World-Class Manufacturing.*

13. J. Collins and J. Porras, *Built to Last* (London: Century, 1996).

14. Ibid.

15. Ming-Jer Chen, "Becoming Ambicultural: A Personal Quest, and Aspiration for Organizations" *Academy of Management Review* 39 (2014), pp. 119–37; D. Waldman and D. Bowen, "Learning to Be a Paradox-Savvy Leader" *Academy of Management Perspectives* 30 (2016), pp. 316–27; P. Junni, R. Sarala, V. Taras, and S. Tarba, "Organizational Ambidexterity and Performance: A Meta-Analysis," *Academy of Management Perspectives* 27, no. 4 (2013), pp. 299–312; C. Gibson and J. Birkinshaw, "The Antecedents, Consequences, and Mediating Role of Organizational Ambidexterity," *Academy of Management Journal* 47 (2004), pp. 209–26.

16. Collins and Porras, *Built to Last.*
17. N. Nohria, W. Joyce, and B. Roberson, "What Really Works," *Harvard Business Review,* July 2003, pp. 42–52.
18. G. Colvin, "Why Sears Failed," *Fortune,* December 6, 2016, www.fortune.com.
19. Ibid.
20. R. M. Kanter, "Thriving Locally in the Global Economy," *Harvard Business Review,* August 2003, pp. 119–27.
21. "Global Cities 2016," A.T. Kearney, accessed May 7, 2017, www.atkearney.com.
22. Kanter, "Thriving Locally in the Global Economy" Kanter, "How Great Companies Think Differently."
23. B. Burnes and B. Cooke, "The Past, Present and Future of Organization Development: Taking the Long View," *Human Relations* 65 (2012), pp. 1395–1429.
24. T. Cummings and C. Worley, *Organization Development and Change,* 8th ed. (Mason, OH: Thomson/South-Western, 2005); J. Bartunek, J. Balogun, and B. Do, "Considering Planned Change Anew: Stretching Large Group Interventions Strategically, Emotionally, and Meaningfully," *The Academy of Management Annals* 5 (2011), pp. 1–52.
25. Ibid.
26. Cummings and Worley, *Organization Development and Change.*
27. J. Fairest, "Leading Employees through Major Organizational Change," *Ivey Business Journal Online* 1 (July/August 2014); D. R. Conner, *Managing at the Speed of Change* (New York: Random House, 2006); and R. Teerlink, "Harley's Leadership U-Turn," *Harvard Business Review,* July–August 2000, pp. 43–48.
28. E. E. Lawler III, *Treat People Right!* (San Francisco: Jossey-Bass, 2003).
29. P. Zigarmi and J. Hoekstra, "Leadership Strategies for Making Change Stick," *Perspectives* (Ken Blanchard Companies, 2008), http://www.kenblanchard.com; D. Erwin and Garman, "Resistance to Organizational Change: Linking Research and Practice," *Leadership & Organization Development Journal* 31 (2010), pp. 39–56.
30. Kevin Wack, "Reinventing the Branch Employee: A How-to Guide," *American Banker,* June 2013, Business Insights: Global, http://bi.galegroup.com.
31. S. Fuchs and R. Prouska, "Creating Positive Employee Change Evaluation: The Role of Different Levels of Organizational Support and Change Participation," *Journal of Change Management* 14 (2014), pp. 361–83; S. Oreg and N. Sverdlik, "Ambivalence toward Imposed Change: The Conflict between Dispositional Resistance to Change and the Orientation toward the Change Agent," *Journal of Applied Psychology* 96 (2011), pp. 337–49; A. Rafferty and S. L. Restubog, "The Impact of Change Process and Context on Change Reactions and Turnover during a Merger," *Journal of Management* 36 (2010), pp. 1309–38; A. Rafferty, N. Jimmieson, and A. Armenakis, "Change Readiness: A Multilevel Review," *Journal of Management* 39 (2013), pp. 110–35.

32. J. Stanislao and B. C. Stanislao, "Dealing with Resistance to Change," *Business Horizons,* July–August 1983, pp. 74–78; J. D. Ford and L. W. Ford, "Decoding Resistance to Change," *Harvard Business Review,* April 2009, pp. 99–103; J. P. Kotter and L. A. Schlesinger, "Choosing Strategies for Change," *Harvard Business Review,* March–April 1979, pp. 106–14; and Zigarmi and Hoekstra, "Leadership Strategies for Making Change Stick."
33. M. Rendell, "The Future of Work: A Journey to 2022," PricewaterhouseCoopers (online), http://www.pwc.com/humancapital, accessed June 25, 2015.
34. "HR Best Practices during Organizational Change," American Management Association (online), June 19, 2014, http://www.amanet.org; D. Zell, "Overcoming Barriers to Work Innovations: Lessons Learned at Hewlett-Packard," *Organizational Dynamics,* Summer 2001, pp. 77–85.
35. E. B. Dent and S. Galloway Goldberg, "Challenging Resistance to Change," *Journal of Applied Behavioral Science,* March 1999, pp. 25–41; Ford and Ford, "Decoding Resistance to Change"; Zigarmi and Hoekstra, "Leadership Strategies"; and J. Ford, L. Ford, and A. D'Amelio, "Resistance to Change: The Rest of the Story," *Academy of Management Review* 33 (2008), pp. 362–77.
36. S. Cummings, T. Bridgman, and K. Brown, "Unfreezing Change as Three Steps: Rethinking Kurt Lewin's Legacy for Change Management," *Human Relations* 69 (2016), pp. 33–60; G. Johnson, *Strategic Change and the Management Process* (New York: Basil Blackwell, 1987); and K. Lewin, "Frontiers in Group Dynamics," *Human Relations* 1 (1947), pp. 5–41.
37. E. H. Schein, "Organizational Culture: What It Is and How to Change It," in *Human Resource Management in International Firms,* ed. P. Evans, Y. Doz, and A. Laurent (New York: St. Martin's Press, 1990).
38. M. Beer, R. Eisenstat, and B. Spector, *The Critical Path to Corporate Renewal* (Cambridge, MA: Harvard Business School Press, 1990).
39. D. Rigby, J. Sutherland, and H. Takeuchi, "Embracing Agile," *Harvard Business Review,* May 2016, www.hbr.org.
40. E. E. Lawler III, "Transformation from Control to Involvement," in *Corporate Transformation,* ed. R. Kilmann and T. Covin (San Francisco: Jossey-Bass, 1988).
41. D. Hellriegel and J. W. Slocum Jr., *Management,* 4th ed. (Reading, MA: Addison-Wesley, 1986).
42. F. Vermeulen, P. Puranam, and R. Gulate, "Change for Change's Sake," *Harvard Business Review* 88 (June 2010), pp. 70–76.
43. C. Aiken and S. Keller, "The Irrational Side of Change Management," *McKinsey Quarterly,* April 2009, http://www.mckinseyquarterly.com.
44. Lewin, "Frontiers in Group Dynamics."

45. Cummings et al., "Unfreezing Change as Three Steps."
46. Schein, "Organizational Culture."
47. E. E. Lawler III, *From the Ground Up* (San Francisco: Jossey-Bass, 1995).
48. Q. Nguyen Huy, "Time, Temporal Capability, and Planned Change," *Academy of Management Review* 26 (2001), pp. 601–23.
49. J. Shin, M. Taylor, and M. Seo, "Resources for Change: The Relationships of Organizational Inducements and Psychological Resilience to Employees' Attitudes and Behaviors Toward Organizational Change," *Academy of Management Journal* 55 (2012), pp. 727–48; B. Sugarman, "A Learning-Based Approach to Organizational Change: Some Results and Guidelines," *Organizational Dynamics,* Summer 2001, pp. 62–75.
50. Kotter and Schlesinger, "Choosing Strategies for Change."
51. R. H. Miles, "Beyond the Age of Dilbert: Accelerating Corporate Transformations by Rapidly Engaging all Employees," *Organizational Dynamics,* Spring 2001, pp. 313–21; D. Aguirre and M. Alpern, "10 Principles of Leading Change Management," Strategy1Business (online), June 26, 2014, http://www.strategy-business.com.
52. D. A. Nadler, "Managing Organizational Change: An Integrative Approach," *Journal of Applied Behavioral Science* 17 (1981), pp. 191–211; T. Laffoley, "Making Change Work," UNC Executive Development 2013, http://www.kenan-flagler.unc.edu.
53. D. Rousseau and S. A. Tijoriwala, "What's a Good Reason to Change? Motivated Reasoning and Social Accounts in Promoting Organizational Change," *Journal of Applied Psychology* 84 (1999), pp. 514–28.
54. "About Us," Envision, www.envisionco.org, accessed May 8, 2017, www.enisionco.org.
55. Dori Meinert, "Wings of Change," *HR Magazine,* November 2012, Business Insights: Global, http://bi.galegroup.com.
56. C. F. Leana and B. Barry, "Stability and Change as Simultaneous Experiences in Organizational Life," *Academy of Management Review* 25 (2000), pp. 753–59; A. Muller and R. Kräussl, "The Value of Corporate Philanthropy During Times of Crisis: The Sensegiving Effect of Employee Involvement," *Journal of Business Ethics* 103 (2011), pp. 203–20.
57. O. Gadiesh and J. Gilbert, "Transforming Corner-Office Strategy into Frontline Action," *Harvard Business Review,* May 2001, pp. 72–79.
58. Bartunek et al., "Considering Planned Change Anew."
59. B. Schneider, A. Brief, and R. Guzzo, "Creating a Climate and Culture for Sustainable Organizational Change," *Organizational Dynamics,* Spring 1996, pp. 7–19.
60. The Price Waterhouse Change Integration Team, *Better Change: Best Practices for Transforming Your Organization* (Burr Ridge, IL: Irwin, 1995).

61. M. Beer and N. Nohria, "Cracking the Code of Change," *Harvard Business Review,* May–June 2000, pp. 133–41; A. Spaulding, L. Gamm, J. Kim, and T. Menser, "Multiproject Interdependencies in Health Systems Management: A Longitudinal Qualitative Study," *Health Care Management Review* 39 (2014), p. 31.

62. N. Nohria and J. Berkley, "Whatever Happened to the Take-Charge Manager?" *Harvard Business Review,* January–February 1994, pp. 128–37.

63. D. Miller, J. Hartwick, and I. Le Breton-Miller, "How to Detect a Management Fad—and Distinguish It from a Classic," *Business Horizons,* July–August 2004, pp. 7–16.

64. "The Elephant in the Atmosphere"; Shell website, "New Lens Scenarios: A Shift in Perspective for a World in Transition," http://www.shell.com, accessed June 25, 2015; The White House, "Fact Sheet: U.S. Reports Its 2025 Emissions Target to the UNFCCC," press release, March 31, 2015; L. Foderaro and M. Flegenheimer, "Building toward a Goal of Reducing Emissions in New York City by 80 Percent," *The New York Times* (online), December 19, 2014, http://www.nytimes.com; company website, http://www.shell.com/sustainability/environment/climate-change.html, accessed May 5, 2017; Jess Shankelman, "Big Oil Replaces Rigs with Wind Turbines," *Bloomberg.com,* March 22, 2017, https://www.bloomberg.com/news/articles/2017-03-23/oil-majors-take-a-plunge-in-industry-that-may-hurt-fossil-fuel; Terry Macalister, "Shell Creates Green Energy Division to Invest in Wind Power."

65. The Price Waterhouse Change Integration Team, *Better Change.*

66. Ibid.

67. John P. Kotter, "Accelerate!" *Harvard Business Review,* November 2012, pp. 46–58; Kotter International, "Our Principles Urgency," http://www.kotterinternational.com.

68. Lawler, *From the Ground Up.*

69. J. Kotter, *Leading Change* (Boston: Harvard Business School Press, 1996).

70. Schneider, et al., "Creating a Climate and Culture."

71. R. Beckhard and R. Harris, *Organizational Transitions* (Reading, MA: Addison-Wesley, 1977); A. Carton, C. Murphy, and J. Clark, "A (Blurry) Vision of the Future: How Leader Rhetoric about Ultimate Goals Influences Performance," *Academy of Management Journal* 57 (2014), pp. 1544–70.

72. Kotter, *Leading Change.*

73. G. Hamel, "Waking Up IBM," *Harvard Business Review,* July–August 2000, pp. 137–46; and Deutschman, *Change or Die.*

74. Kotter, *Leading Change.*

75. D. Smith, *Taking Charge of Change* (Reading, MA: Addison-Wesley, 1996).

76. Kotter, "Accelerate!."

77. G. Hamel, "Killer Strategies That Make Shareholders Rich," *Fortune,* June 23, 1997, pp. 22–34.

78. G. Hamel and C. K. Prahalad, *Competing for the Future* (Boston: Harvard Business School Press, 1994).

79. "How Artificial Intelligence is Shaping the Future of Energy," *Open Energi,* February 9, 2017, www.openenergi.com.

80. T. Reddy, "Have You Seen the Future? Top 5 Predictions from the 2017 Tech Trends Report," IBM, January 23, 2017, www.ibm.com.

81. U. Saiidi, "How Smart Cities Are Building the Future," CNBC, Thursday 9, Feb 2017, www.cnbc.com.

82. "Smart Cities to Ease Traffic Congestion, Saving 4.2 Billion Man-Hours per Year by 2021," Juniper Research, June 27, 2016, www.juniperresearch.com.

83. Ibid.

84. G. Bell, "2017: Industrial IOT to Accelerate a Bright Future for Renewables," *Renewable Energy World,* February 16, 2017, www.renewableenergyworld.com.

85. E. Beinhocker, I. Davis, and L. Mendenca, "The 10 Trends You Have to Watch," *Harvard Business Review* 87 (July/August 2009), pp. 5–60.

86. S. Zuboff and J. Maxim, *The Support Economy* (New York: Penguin, 2004); R. M. Kanter, "How Great Companies Think Differently," *Harvard Business Review,* November 2011, pp. 66–78.

87. H. Courtney, J. Kirkland, and P. Viguerie, "Strategy under Uncertainty," *Harvard Business Review,* November–December 1997, pp. 66–79.

88. Courtney et al., "Strategy under Uncertainty."

89. N. Resnick, "How One Company Is Disrupting the $600 Billion Dollar Manufacturing Industry," *Huffington Post,* June 20, 2016, www.huffpost.com.

90. "The March of Financial Services Giants into Bitcoin and Blockchain Startups in One Chart," *CBInsights,* February 19, 2017, www.cbinsights.com.

91. "Seven Industries That Blockchain Will Disrupt in 2017," *Bitcoin Magazine,* January 17, 2017, www.nasdaq.com.

92. F. Gouillart and T. Hallett, "Co-Creation in Government," *Stanford Social Innovation Review* (online), Spring 2015, http://www.ssireview.org; "Why Co-Creation Is the Future of All of Us," *Forbes* (online), February 3, 2014, http://www.forbes.com; Ashoka website, https://www.ashoka.org, accessed June 22, 2015.

93. C. Krauss, and D. Cardwell, "Policy Shift Helps Coal, but Other Forces May Limit Effect," *The New York Times,* March 28, 2017, www.nytimes.com; C. Sweet, "Despite Trump Move on Climate Change, Utilities' Shift from Coal Is Set to Continue," *The Wall Street Journal,* March 28, 2017, www.wsj.com.

94. S. Condon, "Facebook Ramps Up Ecommerce Offerings," *ZDNet,* October 19, 2016, www.zdnet.com.

95. D. Brodwin, "Unsustainable America: Consumers in India and China Are Ready to Live Sustainably," *U.S. News & World Reports,* March 23, 2015, www.usnews.com;

A. Scott, "Sustainability: Building Better Practices," *Chemical Week,* October 11, 2010, pp. 24–27.

96. "Proof That Materials Behave Differently at the Nanoscale," *Nanowerk* (University of Cambridge), September 30, 2016, www.nonowerk.com; "Nanotechnology: The Promises and Pitfalls of Science at the Nanoscale," American Chemical Society, 2016, www.acs.org.

97. "Nanotechnology and You: Benefits and Applications," National Nanotechnology Initiative, www.nano.gov, accessed May "Global Nanotechnology Market Outlook 2016–2024 Featuring Altair, Nanophase Tech & Nanosys," Research and Markets press release, March 1, 2017, www.researchandmarkets.com.

98. "Nanotechnology and You"; May 11, 2017; "Global Nanotechnology Market Outlook 2016–2024."

99. National Science Foundation, "Market Report on Emerging Nanotechnology Now Available," Media Advisory 14-004, February 25, 2014, http://www.nsf.gov.

100. BCC Research, "Nanotechnology Sees Big Growth in Products and Applications," news release, *Globe Newswire,* January 17, 2017, www.globenewswire.com.

101. Julie Deardorff, "Scientists: Nanotech-Based Products Offer Great Potential but Unknown Risks," *Chicago Tribune,* July 10, 2012, http://articles.chicagotribune.com; Laura Walter, "Sizing Up Nanotechnology Safety," *EHS Today,* April 18, 2013, http://ehstoday.com; "Nanotechnology-Related Safety and Ethics Problem Emerging," *Science Daily,* April 28, 2012, http://www.sciencedaily.com.

102. "Nanotechnology," Centers for Disease Control," January 5, 2017, www.cdc.gov; Walter, "Sizing Up Nanotechnology Safety"; "News in Nanotechnology," *EHS Today,* December 2012, p. 20.

103. Hamel and Prahalad, *Competing for the Future.*

104. J. Kotter, *The New Rules: How to Succeed in Today's Post-Corporate World* (New York: Free Press, 1995).

105. T. Bateman and B. Barry, "Masters of the Long Haul: Pursuing Long-Term Work Goals," *Journal of Organizational Behavior,* 2012.

106. Kotter, *The New Rules.*

107. T. Bateman and C. Porath, "Transcendent Behavior," in *Positive Organizational Scholarship,* ed. K. Cameron, J. Dutton, and R. Quinn (San Francisco: Barrett-Koehler, 2003).

108. L. A. Hill, "New Manager Development for the 21st Century," *Academy of Management Executive,* August 2004, pp. 121–26; and D. A. Ready, J. A. Conger, and L. A. Hill, "Are You a High Potential?" *Harvard Business Review* 88 (June 2010), pp. 78–84.

109. Lawler, *From the Ground Up* and Kotter, *The New Rules.*

110. Lawler, *Treat People Right!.*

111. M. Peiperl and Y. Baruck, "Back to Square Zero: The Post-Corporate Career," *Organizational Dynamics,* Spring 1997, pp. 7–22.

112. Ibid.

113. D. R. Conner, *Managing at the Speed of Change* (New York: Random House, 2006), pp. 235–45.

114. J. W. Slocum Jr., M. McGill, and D. Lei, "The New Learning Strategy Anytime, Anything, Anywhere," *Organizational Dynamics,* Autumn 1994, pp. 33–37.

115. Kotter, *The New Rules.*

116. J. Collins, *From Good to Great* (New York: HarperBusiness, 2001).

117. "The Elephant in the Atmosphere"; Farrell, "Climate Change Dominates Marathon Annual General Meeting"; company website, "Our History," Shell.com, accessed June 25, 2015; G. Naik, "Scientists Back Pope Francis on Global Warming," *The Wall Street Journal* (online), June 18, 2015, http://www.wsj.com; E. Howard and J. Parsons, "Keep It in the Ground Climate Campaign," *The Guardian* (online), May 29, 2015, http://www.theguardian.com; C. Davenport and L. Goodstein, "Pope Francis Steps Up on Climate Change, to Conservatives' Alarm," *The New York Times* (online), April 27, 2015, http://www.nytimes.com; E. Howard, "The Biggest Story in the World: Inside *The Guardian*'s Climate Change Campaign," *The Guardian* (online), March 20, 2015, http://theguardian.com; company website, http://www.shell.com/energy-and-innovation/the-energy-future/scenarios/a-better-life-with-a-healthy-planet.html, accessed May 5, 2017; "How Shell Is Preparing for the Energy Sector's 'New Normal,'" March 29, 2016, http://knowledge.wharton.upenn.edu/article/how-shell-is-preparing-for-the-energy-sectors-new-normal/.

118. L. A. Hill, "New Manager Development for the 21st Century," *Academy of Management Executive,* August 2004, p. 125.

119. J. A. Raelin, "Don't Bother Putting Leadership into People," *Academy of Management Executive,* August 2004, pp. 131–35.

120. G. Binney and C. Williams, *Leaning into the Future* (London: Nicholas Brealey, 1997).

121. P. Omidyar, "How Great Companies Think Differently: eBay's Founder on Innovating the Business Model of Social Change," *Harvard Business Review,* September 2011, pp. 41–44; M. Porter and M. Kramer, "Creating Shared Value," *Harvard Business Review,* January–February 2011, pp. 62–77; H. Sabeti, "The For-Benefit Enterprise," *Harvard Business Review,* November 2011, pp. 99–104.

122. P. Adler, "Alternative Economic Futures: A Research Agenda for Progressive Management Scholarship," *Academy of Management Perspectives* 30 (2016), pp. 123–38; R. Gulati, F. Wohlgezogen, and P. Zhelyazkov "The Two Facets of Collaboration: Cooperation and Coordination in Strategic Alliances," *Academy of Management Annals* 6 (2012), pp. 531–83.

123. Adler, "Alternative Economic Futures"; Gulati et al., "The Two Facets of Collaboration."

A

ABC. *See* Activity-based costing (ABC)
ABC Supply, 201
Abercrombie & Fitch, 262
Absenteeism, 376
Accenture, 118

Accommodation A style of dealing with conflict involving cooperation on behalf of the other party but not being assertive about one's own interest, **419**

Accountability The expectation that employees will perform a job, take corrective action when necessary, and report upward on the status and quality of their performance, **229**, 412

Accounting audits Procedures used to verify accounting reports and statements, **470**

Accurid Pest Solutions, 464
Achievement-oriented leadership, 356

Acquisition One firm buying another, **55**, 59, 60

Activision Blizzard, 117

Activity-based costing (ABC) A method of cost accounting designed to identify streams of activity and then to allocate costs across particular business processes according to the amount of time employees devote to particular activities, **470**–471

ADAAA. *See* Americans with Disabilities Act Amendments Act (ADAAA)
Adafruit Industries, 194

Adapters Companies that take the current industry structure and its evolution as givens, and choose where to compete, **532**–533

Adapting at the boundaries, 57
Adapting at the core, 58
Adapting to the environment, 56–57
Adidas, 11

Administrative management A classical management approach that attempted to identify major principles and functions that managers could use to achieve superior organizational performance, **31**

Adobe, 467
Adopter categories, 492–494
Advanced Energy Technology, Inc., 220

Adverse impact When a seemingly neutral employment practice has a disproportionately negative effect on a protected group, **288**

Advertising support model Charging fees to advertise on a site, **196**

Advisory board, 208
Advisory relationships, 418
Aerospace industry, 238

Affective conflict Emotional disagreement directed toward other people, **88**

Affiliate model Charging fees to direct site visitors to other companies' sites, **196**

Affinity groups, 330

Affirmative action Special efforts to recruit and hire qualified members of groups that have been discriminated against in the past, **321**

Africa, 168

After-action review A frank and open-minded discussion of four basic questions aimed at continuous improvement, **464**

Age Discrimination in Employment Act, 289
Agile software development, 271
Agroelectric System of Appropriate Technology (STA), 197
Airbnb, 502

Alderfer's ERG theory A human needs theory postulating that people have three basic sets of needs that can operate simultaneously, **383**–384

Alexa, 491
Alibaba, 159, 172, 182
Alphabet, 281
Alternative work arrangements, 329
Amazon, 6, 39, 52, 53, 61, 116–117, 134, 164, 192, 196, 404, 416, 495
Amazon Chime, 433
Amazon's Lab 126, 504

Ambidextrous organization An organization that is simultaneously good at exploitation and exploration, **252**

America. *See* United States
American Express, 319, 518
American-Made Index, 161
American Red Cross, 262
American Training Resources, 329
Americans with Disabilities Act, 141
Americans with Disabilities Act Amendments Act (ADAAA), 289, 320, 331
Amtrak, 285

Analyzer firm, 502
AngelList, 205
Anytime Fitness, 174
AOL, 259
A&P, 120
APEC. *See* Asia-Pacific Economic Cooperation (APEC)
AppIt Ventures, 161
Apple, 56, 161, 164, 192, 311, 325, 330, 331, 332, 495, 501, 508
Apple Music, 492
Applications and résumés, 283
Applied Materials, 448

Arbitration The use of a neutral third party to resolve a labor dispute, **302**

Archer Daniels Midland, 50
Arm & Hammer, 120, 150
Armstrong Flight Research Center, 113
ASEAN. *See* Association of Southeast Asian Nations (ASEAN)
Ashoka, 13
Asia, 165–166
Asia-Pacific Economic Cooperation (APEC), 166

Assessment center A managerial performance test in which candidates participate in a variety of exercises and situations, **286**

Assets The values of the various items the corporation owns, **471**

Assimilation The absorption into the cultural tradition of a population or group, **313**

Assistant manager, 16
Association of Southeast Asian Nations (ASEAN), 166
AstraZeneca, 48
Astroturfing, 134
AT Kearney, 317
Atos, 435
AT&T, 175, 317
AT&T purchase of Time Warner, 55, 122
Audit relationships, 418
Augmented reality, 42

Authentic leadership A style in which the leader is true to himself or herself while leading, **360**–361

Authoritarianism, 356

Authority The legitimate right to make decisions and to tell other people what to do, **226**, 229

Authority compliance, 352

Autocratic leadership A form of leadership in which the leader makes decisions on his or her own and then announces those decisions to the group, **351**

Automation, 162
Automative firms, 225
Automattic, 436

Autonomous work groups   Groups that control decisions about and execution of a complete range of tasks, **406**–407

Autonomy, 388

Avoidance   A reaction to conflict that involves ignoring the problem by doing nothing at all or deemphasizing the disagreement, **419**

Avon, 326
AXA Canada, 118

B

B impact assessment (BIA), 463
B-Lab, 463
B2B. *See* Business-to-business (B2B)
Baby Boomers, 7, 120, 209
Baccarat, 462
Background checks, 284–285

Balance sheet   A report that shows the financial picture of a company at a given time and itemizes assets, liabilities, and stockholders' equity, **471**, 472

Balanced scorecard   Control system combining four sets of performance measures: financial, customer satisfaction, business processes, and learning and growth, **478**, 479

Bank Boston, 144
Bank of America, 56, 459
Barclays, 459
Barefoot College, 148
Barrier Break, 198

Barriers to entry   Conditions that prevent new companies from entering an industry, **48**

BARS. *See* Behaviorally anchored rating scale (BARS)
Base technologies, 498
Basecamp, 60
BASF Agricultural Solutions, 534
Basic Needs, 197
Batesville Casket Company, 505
BCG matrix, 121–122
Beats, 56
Bechtel, 177, 238
Bee Healthy, 167
Behavior, consequences, and effects, 375, 376
Behavioral appraisals, 293

Behavioral approach   A leadership perspective that attempts to identify what good leaders do—that is, what behaviors they exhibit, **349**

Behavioral description interview, 284
Behaviorally anchored rating scale (BARS), 293
Being different worksheet, 334–335
Bell Canada, 134

Benchmarking   The process of comparing an organization's practices and technologies with those of other companies, **54**, 117–118, 499

Best-case scenario, 54
Best Trust Bank, 454–455
Big Bison Resorts, 399–400
Big data, 532
Bigelow Aerospace, 196
Blake and Mouton's Leadership Grid, 352
Blockbuster, 8, 48
Blockchain technology, 533
Blogs, 134
Bloomin' Brands, 123
Blue Cross/Blue Shield, 433
BMW, 4, 8, 117
Board of directors, 226–227
Bob's Red Mill baking soda, 150
Body language, 441
Boeing, 196, 238
Bonuses, 297

Bootlegging   Informal work on projects, other than those officially assigned, of employees' own choosing and initiative, **210**

Booz & Company, 282
Borrow-use-return approach, 149
Boston (City), 326
Boston Consulting Group, 121

Boundary-spanning   Interacting with people in other groups, thus creating linkages between groups, **417**

Boundaryless organization   Organization in which there are no barriers to information flow, **449**

Boundarylessness, 449–450

Bounded rationality   A less-than-perfect form of rationality in which decision makers cannot be perfectly rational because decisions are complex and complete information is unavailable or cannot be fully processed, **92**

BP, 161
BP Deepwater Horizon oil spill, 46, 460
BPAmoco, 177

Brainstorming   A process in which group members generate as many ideas

about a problem as they can; criticism is withheld until all ideas have been proposed, **90**

Brainwriting, 90
Brazil, 166
Breitt, Starr & Diamond LLC, 368–369
Brexit, 164
Bribery, 181–182
Bribery and kickbacks, 43, 137, 138
Bricklin, Dan, 190
Bricks 4 Kidz, 174
Bring your own app (BYOA), 436
Bring your own device to work (BYOD), 436

Broker   A person who assembles and coordinates participants in a network, **241**

Brown v. Board of Education, 313
Budget, 125
Budgetary controlling, 469
Budgetary controls, 469–471

Budgeting   The process of investigating what is being done and comparing the results with the corresponding budget data to verify accomplishments or remedy differences; also called *budgetary controlling,* **469**

Buffering   Creating supplies of excess resources in case of unpredictable needs, **57**

Build Change, 362
Built to Last (Collins/Porras), 519
Built-to-last companies, 519

Bureaucracy   A classical management approach emphasizing a structured, formal network of relationships among specialized positions in the organization, **32**–33

Bureaucracy busting, 509

Bureaucratic control   The use of rules, regulations, and authority to guide performance, **460**, 461. *See also* Managerial control

Burger King, 328
Burt's Bees, 144

Business accelerator   Organization that provides support and advice to help young businesses grow, **201**–202

Business-as-usual philosophy, 533, 534

Business ethics   The moral principles and standards that guide behavior in the world of business, **135**, 137. *See also* Ethics

Business incubators   Protected environments for new, small businesses, **201**

Business model innovation, 490, 491

Business plan   A formal planning step that focuses on the entire venture and describes all the elements involved in starting it, **205**–208

Business school organization chart, 247–248

Business strategy   The major actions by which a business competes in a particular industry or market, **122**–123

Business-to-business (B2B), 50
Buy42.com, 198
Buzzwords, 440
BYOA. *See* Bring your own app (BYOA)
BYOD. *See* Bring your own device to work (BYOD)

C

C. F. Martin, 121
C-suite, 15, 227
CafePress, 196

Cafeteria benefit program   An employee benefit program in which employees choose from a menu of options to create a benefit package tailored to their needs, **299**

CAFTA-DR. *See* Central America–Dominican Republic–United States Free Trade Agreement (CAFTA-DR)
Calamities, 195
Campus recruiting, 283
Candor, 433
Capital budget, 470
Capital One, 261, 491
Capterra, 77, 78, 80, 81, 82

Carbon footprint   The output of carbon dioxide and other greenhouse gases, **149**

Career academy model, 533
Career development
   career advice from experts, 19
   common practices of successful managers, 21–22
   connecting with people, 20
   emotional intelligence (EQ), 18–19
   managing relationship with corporation, 20–21
   self-reliance, 19–20
   specialist and generalist, 19
Career development worksheet, 26
CareerBuilder, 282, 283
Carmike Cinemas, 233

Carrying capacity   The ability of a finite resource to sustain a population, **69**

Case incidents
   effective management, 100–101

employee raiding, 100
   implementing strategic change, 545–546
   robot repercussion, 544
Case Western Reserve University Medical School, 42
Cases
   Best Trust Bank, 454–455
   Big Bison Resorts, 399–400
   Breitt, Starr & Diamond LLC, 368–369
   DIY Stores, 274–275
   Dollar General, 543–544
   EatWell Technologies, 542–543
   Excel Pro Drilling Systems, 425–426
   Foxconn, 217–218
   Grizzly Bear Lodge, 487
   Invincibility Systems, 308–309
   Ma Earth Skin Care, 155–156
   Magna Exteriors and Interiors Corporation, 455–456
   Net-Work Docs, 186
   Niche Hotel Group, 336–337
   ScrollCo, 217
   Soaring Eagle Skate Company, 98–99
   Stanley Lynch Investment Group, 249
   Tata Motors, 67
   USA Hospital Supply, 27
   Wish You Wood Toy Store, 129
   Woody Manufacturing Company, 273–274
   Worldwide Games, 514–515
   Zappos, 99–100, 337–338
Cash budget, 470
Cash cows, 122
Cassini Imaging Science Team, 414
Caterpillar, 319

Caux Principles   Ethical principles established by international executives based in Caux, Switzerland, in collaboration with business leaders from Japan, Europe, and the United States, **136**

Cement companies, 225
CEMEX, 166
Central America–Dominican Republic–United States Free Trade Agreement (CAFTA-DR), 166

Centralized organization   An organization in which high-level executives make most decisions and pass them down to lower levels for implementation, **230**

CEO. *See* Chief executive officer (CEO)
CEO pay, 138, 298–299
CERES Roadmap for Sustainability, 69

Certainty   The state that exists when decision makers have accurate and comprehensive information, **75**

CFO. *See* Chief financial officer (CFO)
Change management, 522–531. *See also* Shaping the future

anchoring new approaches in the culture, 531
   case incident, 545–546
   communicating the change vision, 531
   consolidating gains and producing more change, 531
   education and communication, 526, 527
   empowering broad-based action, 531
   enlisting cooperation, 526, 527
   explicit and implicit coercion, 527, 528
   facilitation and support, 526–527
   force-field analysis, 525
   general model for managing resistance, 523–525
   guiding coalition, 531
   harmonizing multiple changes, 528–529
   leading change, 529–531
   manipulation and cooptation, 527, 528
   motivating people to change, 522
   negotiation and rewards, 527
   participation and involvement, 526, 527
   question to ask, 528–529
   reactive/proactive change, 532
   sense of urgency, 530–531
   short-term wins, 531
   total organization change, 528
   unfreezing/moving/refreezing model, 523–525
   vision and strategy, 531
   why people resist change?, 522–523
Change.org, 327
Chaparral Steel, 509

Charismatic leader   A person who is dominant, self-confident, convinced of the moral righteousness of his or her beliefs, and able to arouse a sense of excitement and adventure in followers, **358**

Charismatic leadership, 358–359
Cheer laundry detergent, 171
Chemical companies, 174
Chevron, 177
Chevy Volt electric car, 165
Chi-Med, 505
Chick-fil-A, 117, 373
Chief executive officer (CEO), 15, 227, 481
Chief financial officer (CFO), 470

Chief information officer (CIO)   Executive in charge of information technology strategy and development, 15, **506**–507

Chief innovation officer, 506
Chief knowledge officer, 15
Chief operating officer (COO), 15
Chief technology officer (CTO), 15, 560–507
Child care, onsite, 329
China
   economic growth, 165
   education hub, 175
   environmental problems, 70, 148

Environmental Protection Act, 70
GE Healthcare, 388
local executives, 177
Panasonic, 172
socializing with the boss, 444
state-owned enterprises (SOEs), 175
transformational leadership, 360
China National Petroleum, 4, 161
Chipotle Mexican Grill, 109–110, 265, 317, 468
Chrysler, 265
Church & Dwight Company, 120
Cialis, 496
CIM. *See* Computer-integrated manufacturing (CIM)
CIO. *See* Chief information officer (CIO)
Circle Internet Financial, 533
Cisco Foundation, 259
Cisco Systems, 59, 238, 404, 406, 413, 532
Citibank, 53
Citigroup, 286
Citizen scientists, 242
City of Boston, 326
City of Redmond, 114
Civil aspiration, 145
Civil Rights Act of 1991, 289

Clan control Control based on the norms, values, shared goals, and trust among group members, **461**, 482

Cleveland Clinic, 42, 491
Climate change, 150
Clínicas del Azúcar, 198
Clorox purchase of Burt's Bees, 150
Cloud computing companies, 9
Co-creation, 534
Co-working, 413

Coaching Dialogue with a goal of helping another be more effective and achieve his or her full potential on the job, 291, **446**

Coal mining, 300
Coalition, 57

Coalition model Model of organizational decision making in which groups with differing preferences use power and negotiation to influence decisions, **92**

Coca-Cola, 9, 47, 48, 50, 146, 170, 177, 255, 262, 446
Codes of ethics, 139–140, 141
Coercive power, 347
Cognitive ability tests, 286

Cognitive conflict Issue-based differences in perspectives or judgments, **88**

Cohesiveness The degree to which a group is attractive to its members,

members are motivated to remain in the group, and members influence one another, **414**–417

Coinbase, 533
Cold Stone Creamery, 174, 290
Colgate-Palmolive purchase of Tom's of Maine, 150

Collaboration A style of dealing with conflict emphasizing both cooperation and assertiveness to maximize both parties' satisfaction, **420**, 539

Collaboration across boundaries, 6, 7
Collective bargaining, 302–303
Columbus, Ohio, 150
Combating climate change, 46
Comcast, 262
Communicating, 428–456
   boundarylessness, 449–450
   coaching, 446
   communication pitfalls, 431–432
   digital communication, 433–437
   downward communication, 445–447
   general model of communication, 430
   grapevine, 448–449
   horizontal communication, 448
   informal communication, 448–449
   interpersonal communication, 430–437
   language skills, 440–441
   listening, 442–444, 452–453
   media richness, 437
   mixed signals and misperception, 432
   nonverbal skills, 441–442, 452
   observing, 444
   one-way/two-way communication, 430–431
   open-book management, 446–447
   oral and written channels, 433
   organizational communication, 444–449
   overseas business (local language/ customs), 440–441
   personal smartphones/devices at work, 436
   persuasion skills, 439–440
   presentation skills, 439
   reading, 444
   receiver skills, 442–444
   sender skills, 438–442
   social media, 433–435
   upward communication, 447–448
   virtual office, 435–437
   writing skills, 440

Communication The transmission of information and meaning from one party to another through the use of shared symbols, **430**. *See also* Communicating

Communication pitfalls, 431–432
Communities, 51
Company Pages, 51
Company president, 15

Comparable worth Principle of equal pay for different jobs of equal worth, **300**

Comparative balance sheet, 472
Comparative statement of profit and loss, 473
Compassion, 183

Competing A style of dealing with conflict involving strong focus on one's own goals and little or no concern for the other person's goals, **420**

Competitive advantage
   cost competitiveness, 10
   innovation, 8
   natural environment, 68
   quality, 8–9
   service, 9
   speed, 9–10
   sustainability, 11
Competitive aggression, 56

Competitive environment The immediate environment surrounding a firm; includes suppliers, customers, rivals, and the like, **40**, 46–52

   competitors, 47–48
   customers, 50–52
   new entrants, 48
   substitutes and complements, 49
   suppliers, 50

Competitive intelligence Information that helps managers determine how to compete better, **53**

Competitive pacification, 56
Competitor analysis, 115
Competitors, 47–48, 53
Complacency, 530
Complement, 49

Compliance-based ethics programs Company mechanisms typically designed by corporate counsel to prevent, detect, and punish legal violations, **140**

Compromise A style of dealing with conflict involving moderate attention to both parties' concerns, **419**

Computer-integrated manufacturing (CIM) The use of computer-aided design and computer-aided manufacturing to sequence and optimize a number of production processes, **266**

Concentration A strategy employed for an organization that operates a single business and competes in a single industry, **120**

Concentric diversification A strategy used to add new businesses that produce related products or are involved in related markets and activities, **121**

Conceptual and decision skills Skills pertaining to abilities that help to identify and resolve problems for the benefit of the organization and its members, **18**

Concluding cases. *See* Cases

Concurrent control The control process used while plans are being carried out, including directing, monitoring, and fine-tuning activities as they are performed, **465**–466

Concurrent engineering A design approach in which all relevant functions cooperate jointly and continually in a maximum effort aimed at producing high-quality products that meet customers' needs, **270**

Conflict Opposing pressures from different sources, occurring on the level of psychological conflict or conflict between individuals or groups, **76**

    constructive, 87–88, 418
    destructive, 418
    joint venture, 175
    managerial decision making, 76
    teams, 418–421
Conflict management strategies, 419, 420
Conflict style worksheet, 425
Conflict styles, 419–420

Conglomerate diversification A strategy used to add new businesses that produce unrelated products or are involved in unrelated markets and activities, **121**

Connecting with people, 20

Conservation An environmental philosophy that seeks to avoid waste, promote the rational and efficient use of natural resources, and maximize long-term yields, especially of renewable resources, **69**

Conservation movement, 69
Constructive conflict, 87–88, 418
Container Store, 361
Content validity, 286

Contingencies Factors that determine the appropriateness of managerial actions, **34**

Contingency perspective An approach to the study of management proposing that the managerial strategies, structures, and processes that result in high performance depend on the characteristics, or important contingencies, of the situation in which they are applied, **34**

Contingency plans Alternative courses of action that can be implemented based on how the future unfolds, **79**, 106

Contingent workers, 57
Continuous learning, 536

Continuous process A process that is highly automated and has a continuous production flow, **266**

Contracted development, 504
Contraction, 57

Control Any process that directs the activities of individuals toward the achievement of organizational goals, **460**

Control culture, 66
Control cycle, 461–464
Control systems. *See* Managerial control

Controlling The management function of monitoring performance and making needed changes, **14**

COO. *See* Chief operating officer (COO)
Cooperative action, 56, 57

Cooperative strategies Strategies used by two or more organizations working together to manage the external environment, **56**

Cooptation, 57

Coordination The procedures that link the various parts of an organization for the purpose of achieving the organization's overall mission, **225**

Coordination by mutual adjustment Units interact with one another to make accommodations to achieve flexible coordination, **243**

Coordination by plan Interdependent units are required to meet deadlines and objectives that contribute to a common goal, **242**–243

Coordination by standardization, 242
Copyright, 501
CopyShark.net, 203

Core capability A unique skill and/or knowledge an organization possesses that gives it an edge over competitors, **117**, 118, 254–255

Core values, 183
Corporate culture preference scale, 65–67
Corporate entrepreneurship, 209–211
Corporate ethical standards, 139

Corporate governance The role of a corporation's executive staff and board of directors in ensuring that the firm's activities meet the goals of the firm's stakeholders, **228**

Corporate mission statement, 60
Corporate scandals, 132, 137

Corporate social responsibility (CSR) Obligation toward society assumed by business, **144**–147. *See also* Ethics

    economic responsibilities, 144
    ethical responsibilities, 145
    legal responsibilities, 145
    philanthropic responsibilities, 145
    profit maximization perspective, 146
    social entrepreneurship, contrasted, 198
    social responsibility perspective, 146
    stewardship, 144
    transcendent education, 145
    triple bottom line, 144

Corporate strategy The set of businesses, markets, or industries in which an organization competes and the distribution of resources among those entities, **120**–122

Cost budget, 470

Cost competitiveness Keeping costs low to achieve profits and be able to offer prices that are attractive to consumers, **10**

Cost-effectiveness, 68
Counterfeit goods, 501
Country club management, 352
Courage, 142–143, 362–363
Creativity, 89–90, 508–509
Crestor, 48
Crises, 92–94
Crisis management, 93
Crisis plans, 106
Criterion-related validity, 286
Critical incident technique, 293
CRM. *See* Customer relationship
    management (CRM)
Cross-functional coordination, 234
Cross-selling, 132
Crowdfunding, 205, 207
Crowdsourcing, 7, 91
CTO. *See* Chief technology
    officer (CTO)
Cultural control, 461

Culture shock The disorientation and stress associated with being in a foreign environment, **179**

Current ratio A liquidity ratio that indicates the extent to which short-term assets can decline and still be adequate to pay short-term liabilities, **474**

Custom-made solutions New, creative solutions designed specifically for the problem, **78**

Customer divisions, 236
Customer feedback management software, 6

Customer relationship management (CRM) A multifaceted process focusing on creating two-way exchanges with customers to foster intimate knowledge of their needs, wants, and buying patterns, **260–262**

Customer service, 51
Customers, 50–52, 53
Cutting-edge technologies, 535

D

Dabble time, 210
Dannon, 46
Days Inn, 328

Debt–equity ratio A leverage ratio that indicates the company's ability to meet its long-term financial obligations, **474**

Decentralization, 230–232

Decentralized organization An organization in which lower-level managers make important decisions, **230**

Deceptive blogs, 134
Decision making. *See* Managerial decision making
Decision making worksheet, 97
Deep-discount retailers (dollar stores), 543
Deep-neural networks, 532
Deepwater Horizon oil spill, 46, 460
Defender firms, 502

Defenders Companies that stay within a stable product domain as a strategic maneuver, **55**

Delaware North Companies, 285

Delegation The assignment of new or additional responsibilities to a subordinate, 203, **229–230**, 231

Delivering strategic value, 12
Delivery.com, 535

Dell Computer, 50, 51, 266
Deloitte Consulting, 163
Deloitte LLP, 45, 281, 317, 331, 435
Deloitte Millennial Survey 2017, 134
Demand forecasts, 280
Deming's 14 points of quality, 263

Democratic leadership A form of leadership in which the leader solicits input from subordinates, **351**

Demographic changes, 194–195

Demographics Measures of various characteristics of the people who make up groups or other social units, **44–45**

Department of Homeland Security (DHS), 373

Departmentalization Subdividing an organization into smaller subunits, **232**

Deregulation, 195

Design thinking A human-centered approach to problem solving and solution finding that is based on nonlinear iterations of inspiration, ideation, and implementation, **509–510**

Destructive conflict, 418
Detroit Institute of Arts, 9
Developing countries, 148

Development Helping managers and professional employees learn the broad skills needed for their present and future jobs, **290**

Development project A focused organizational effort to create a new product or process via technological advances, **510–511**

Devil's advocate A person who has the job of criticizing ideas to ensure that their downsides are fully explored, **88**

Dialectic A structured debate comparing two conflicting courses of action, **88**

Differentiation An aspect of the organization's internal environment created by job specialization and the division of labor, **224–225**

Differentiation strategy A strategy an organization uses to build competitive advantage by being unique in its industry or market segment along one or more dimensions, **123**

Digital communication, 433–437

Digital monitoring tools, 140
Digital World boxes
    acknowledging employees' accomplishments, 393
    checking social media presence of prospective hires, 284
    citizen scientists, 242
    collaboration across boundaries, 7
    customer relations, 262
    digital monitoring tools, 140
    diversity in the workplace, 330
    entrepreneurs and funding, 202
    Ford NGL, 533
    innovation, 505
    internal communication apps, 60
    leaders and technology, 364
    loss of control, 482
    online companies, 116
    teamwork, 410
    time pressures and real-time data, 85
    video call, 437
Directive leadership, 349, 356
Disabilities, employees with, 319–320
Disciplinary procedures, 287

Discounting the future A bias weighting short-term costs and benefits more heavily than longer-term costs and benefits, **83**, 84

Diseconomies of scale, 258
Disney. *See* Walt Disney Company
Disney Interactive, 112
Dispute resolution, 420–421

Disruptive innovation A process by which a product, service, or business model takes root initially in simple applications at the bottom of a market and then moves "up market," eventually displacing established competitors, **495**

Diverse workforce One in which there are both similarities and differences among employees in terms of age, cultural background, physical abilities and disabilities, race, religion, sex, and sexual orientation, 310–338

    accommodating work and family needs, 328–329
    accountability, 331
    advantage through diversity and inclusion, 321–322
    affirmative action, 321
    age of workforce, 320–321
    alternative work arrangements, 329
    attracting employees, 328–330
    awareness building, 329
    being different worksheet, 334–335
    career development and promotions, 331
    challenges of diversity and inclusion, 322–324
    communication problems, 323

components of diversified workforce, 314
defined, **312**
diversity assumptions and implications, 326
education levels, 320
gender issues, 315–318
glass ceiling, 315
group cohesiveness, 323
he works, she works worksheet, 336
historical overview, 312–313
LBGT employees, 318
leveraging differences, 324
mental and physical disabilities, 319–320
mentoring, 331
minorities and immigrants, 318–319
mistrust and tension, 323
multicultural organization, 326
organizational assessment, 327–328
race and ethnicity, 318–319
recruitment, 328
retaining employees, 329–331
sexual harassment, 316–317, 318
skill building, 329
stereotyping, 323–324
support groups, 330–331
systems accommodations, 331
top management, 326–327
training employees, 329, 330

Diversification   A firm's investment in a different product, business, or geographic area, **55**

Diversity   A broad term used to refer to all kinds of differences, These differences include education, political belief, religion, and income in addition to gender, race, ethnicity, and nationality, **313**

Diversity training   Programs that focus on identifying and reducing hidden biases against people with differences and developing the skills needed to manage a diversified workforce, 291, 329, 330

Divestiture   A firm selling one or more businesses, **55**

Division of labor   The assignment of different tasks to different people or groups, **224**

Divisional organization Departmentalization that groups units around products, customers, or geographic regions, **234–236**

DIY Stores, 274–275
Do It Right Framework, 478

Dodd-Frank Wall Street Reform and
    Consumer Protection Act, 390
Dogs, 122
Dollar General, 543–544
Dollar stores, 543

Domain selection   Entering a new market or industry using an existing expertise, **55**

Don Chalmers Ford, 264
DonorsChoose.org, 202
DoSomething.org, 442
Dow Chemical, 117, 150, 177
Dow Corning, 238
Dow Jones Industrial Average, 41

Downsizing   The planned elimination of positions or jobs, **258**–259, 287

Downward communication
Information that flows from higher to lower levels in the organization's hierarchy, **445**–447

Dr Pepper Snapple Group, 255
Drive, 348–349
Dropbox, 406
Drug-Free Workplace Act, 285
Drug testing, 285–286
Dual-career couples, 177, 329
Duke Kunshan University (DKU), 175
Dumping, 174
Dunkin' Donuts, 164

Dynamic capabilities   Higher-level strategic capabilities (compared with ordinary capabilities) that aid rapid adaptation, **254**

Dynamic network   Temporary arrangements among partners that can be assembled and reassembled to adapt to the environment, **240**

Dynamic Organization (Follet), 31

E
E-mail, 180, 182, 433
Early adopters, 492, 493, 501, 502
Early majority, 493–494
Eastman Chemical, 412
Eastman Kodak, 175
Eaton, 11
EatWell Technologies, 542–543
eBay, 46

Ecocentric management   Its goal is the creation of sustainable economic development and improvement of quality of life worldwide for all organizational stakeholders, **149**

Economic cycles, 201

Economic dislocations, 195
Economic Outlook, 54

Economic responsibilities   To produce goods and services that society wants at a price that perpetuates the business and satisfies its obligations to investors, **144**

Economic strike, 302

Economies of scale   Reductions in the average cost of a unit of production as the total volume produced increases, **28**

Economies of scope   Economies in which materials and processes employed in one product can be used to make other related products, **257**

Economist's Global Forecasting Service, 54
Economy, 41–42
EDGAR database, 219
Edelman Trust Barometer, 143
Edom Nutritional Solutions, 198
EEOC. *See* Equal Employment Opportunity Commission (EEOC)
Effort-to-performance link, 379
Ego needs, 382

Egoism   An ethical system defining acceptable behavior as that which maximizes consequences for the individual, 135, **136**

Electronic lab notebook (ELN) app, 505
ELIXIR Strings, 210
Ellison, Lawrence, 526
EMC Insurance, 363
Emerging technologies, 498
Emerson Electric, 477

Emotional intelligence   Skills of understanding yourself, managing yourself, and dealing effectively with others, **18**–19

Empathy, 145
Employee benefits, 299
Employee compensation, 296–300
Employee health, 459, 475, 483
Employee raiding, 100
Employee Retirement Income Security Act (ERISA), 300
Employee satisfaction and well-being, 392–395
Employee self-management, 99
Employee termination, 287–288

Employment-at-will   The legal concept that an employer can terminate an employee for any reason, **287**

Employment interview, 283–284, 307
Empowering, 414

Empowerment The process of sharing power with employees, thereby enhancing their confidence in their ability to perform their jobs and their belief that they are influential contributors to the organization, **57, 388**–389

Enron, 137

Entrepreneur Individual who establishes a new organization without the benefit of corporate sponsorship, **191**

Entrepreneur.com and magazine, 219

Entrepreneurial orientation The tendency of an organization to identify and capitalize successfully on opportunities to launch new ventures by entering new or established markets with new or existing goods or services, **211**

Entrepreneurial strategy matrix, 199–200

Entrepreneurial venture A new business having growth and high profitability as primary objectives, **190**

Entrepreneurship The pursuit of lucrative opportunities by enterprising individuals, 188–220

advisory board, 208
business incubators/accelerators, 201–202
business plan, 205–208
controls, 203–204
corporate, 209–211
defined, **190**
delegation, 203
economic environment, 200–202
entrepreneurial strategy matrix, 199–200
franchising, 195
funding, 202, 205, 207
going public (IPO), 204
idea, 194
information/resources, 219–220
Internet, 196–197
intrapreneurs, 191, 210
legitimacy, 208
liabilities (newness/smallness), 200
management challenges, 202–204
misuse of funds, 203
myths, 190, 191
networking, 208
new business start-up worksheet, 216–217
next frontiers, 196
opportunity, 194–195
opportunity analysis, 205
partners, 209
planning, 204–208
risk, 199, 200
social, 197–199, 202
successful young entrepreneurs, 192
succession planning, 204
top management, 208
what does it take to succeed?, 193–194, 199–200

Entry barriers, 48
Environment. *See* Natural environment and sustainability
Environmental analysis, 52–54, 114
attractive/unattractive environments, 53
benchmarking, 54
competitor analysis, 115
environmental scanning, 53
forecasting, 54
human resources analysis, 115
industry and market analysis, 115
macroeconomic analysis, 115
political and regulatory analysis, 115
scenario development, 53–54
social analysis, 115
technological analysis, 115
Environmental complexity, 53
Environmental dynamism, 53

Environmental movement An environmental philosophy postulating that the unintended negative effects of human economic activities on the environment are often greater than the benefits, and that nature should be preserved, **69**

Environmental Protection Agency (EPA), 43, 116

Environmental scanning Searching for and sorting through information about the environment, **53**

Environmental uncertainty When managers do not have enough information about the environment to understand or predict the future, **52**, 53

Envision, 527
EPA. *See* Environmental Protection Agency (EPA)
Epic Games, 504
Equal employment opportunity, 288–289
Equal Employment Opportunity Commission (EEOC), 43, 317
Equal Pay Act, 289, 299, 300
Equal pay for equal work, 299–300
Equitable Life Assurance Society, 327

Equity theory A theory stating that people assess how fairly they have been treated according to two key factors: outcomes and inputs, **390**, 391

ERG theory, 383–384
ERISA. *See* Employee Retirement Income Security Act (ERISA)
Ernst & Young. *See* EY
Ethical behavior worksheet, 154–155

Ethical climate In an organization, the processes by which decisions are evaluated and made on the basis of right and wrong, **138**

Ethical decision making, 141–142

Ethical issue Situation, problem, or opportunity in which an individual must choose among several actions that must be evaluated as morally right or wrong, **135**

Ethical leader One who is both a moral person and a moral manager influencing others to behave ethically, **139**

Ethical responsibilities Meeting other social expectations, not written as law, **145**

Ethical systems, 135–137

Ethics The system of rules that governs the ordering of values, **132**. *See also* Corporate social responsibility (CSR)

aim, 134
business, 137
Caux Principles, 136
corporate ethical standards, 139
corporate scandals, 132, 137
courage, 142–143
current ethical issues, 138
danger signs, 139
deceptive blogs, 134
egoism, 135, 136
ethical climate, 138
ethical decision making, 141–142
ethical systems, 135–137
ethics codes, 139–140, 141
ethics programs, 140–141
excuses, 142
goal for ethical managers, 144
international management, 181–183
Kohlberg's model of moral development, 137
lying/truth-telling, 133
monitoring employees to ensure ethical behavior, 140
relativism, 135, 136
Sarbanes-Oxley Act. *See* Sarbanes-Oxley Act
underlying values, 134–135
universalism, 135
utilitarianism, 135, 136
virtual, 135, 136–137
whistleblowing, 143
Ethics codes, 139–140, 141
Ethics environment, 137–141
Ethics programs, 140–141
Ethics Resource Center, 140

Ethnocentrism The tendency to judge others by the standards of one's own group or culture, which are seen as superior, **179**

Etsy, 279, 328
European Union (EU), 164
Evolution of management
administrative management, 31
bureaucracy, 32–33
classical approaches, 28–33
contemporary approaches, 33–34
contingency perspective, 34
current events/eye on the future, 34
earliest university programs, 28
early concepts and influences, 28
Fayol's 14 principles of management, 31
human relations, 31–32
quantitative management, 33
scientific management, 29–30
systematic management, 29
systems theory, 33–34
timeline, 28
Excel Pro Drilling Systems, 425–426
Excuses, 142

Executive champion An executive who supports a new technology and protects the product champion, **507**

Executive order 11246, 289
Executive order 11375, 289
Executive pay, 298–299
Exelon, 440
Existence needs, 383

Expatriates Parent-company nationals who are sent to work at a foreign subsidiary, **176**–177

Expectancy Employees' perception of the likelihood that their efforts will enable them to attain their performance goals, **379**

Expectancy theory A theory proposing that people will behave based on their perceived likelihood that their effort will lead to a certain outcome and on how highly they value that outcome, **378**–380

Experiential exercises
active listening, 453–454
being different worksheet, 334–335
business school organization chart, 247–248
business strategies, 128–129
career development worksheet, 26
conflict style worksheet, 425
corporate culture preference scale, 65–67
cross-cultural anthropologist, 185
decentralized organization structure, 248–249
decision-making worksheet, 97

ethical behavior worksheet, 154–155
ethical stance, 155
external environment worksheet, 64–65
five sources of power worksheet, 367–368
gender stereotypes, 335
global integration–local responsiveness worksheet, 185
group problem solving at a social enterprise, 97–98
he works, she works worksheet, 336
innovation for the future, 514
legal interview worksheet, 307
listening feedback form, 454
listening skills survey, 453
managerial behaviors worksheet, 26
mechanistic and organic worksheet, 273
networking scenarios, 541–542
new business start-up worksheet, 216–217
nonverbal communication interpretation worksheet, 452
pay rise worksheet, 308
personal goal setting, 398
personal network, 25
preliminary, concurrent, and feedback control worksheet, 486–487
resistance to change worksheet, 540–541
safety program, 485–486
self-assessment worksheet, 397
student-run organization providing consulting services, 248
subject project group processes worksheet, 424
take an entrepreneur to dinner, 214–215
technology life cycle, 514
university system analysis worksheet, 36
What I Want from My Job worksheet, 399
Expert power, 347–348
Exporting, 173–174
Extended enterprise, 50

External audit An evaluation conducted by one organization, such as a CPA firm, on another, **468**

External environment All relevant forces outside a firm's boundaries, such as competitors, customers, the government, and the economy, **40**, 55–58

adapting at the boundaries, 57
adapting at the core, 58
adapting to the environment, 56–57
changing environment you are in, 55
changing the organization, 56–57
choosing an approach, 58
influencing your environment, 55–56
External environment worksheet, 64–65
External locus of control, 356
External opportunities and threats, 114–116
External recruiting, 283

Extinction Withdrawing or failing to provide a reinforcing consequence, **376**

Extrinsic reward Reward given to a person by the boss, the company, or some other person, **385**

Extroversion, 349
ExxonMobil, 42, 161
EY, 120, 219, 281, 313, 317, 331
Eye contact, 439, 441, 442, 444

F

FAA. *See* Federal Aviation Administration (FAA)
Facebook, 3, 4, 6, 15, 20, 22, 164, 192, 283, 285, 316, 321, 433, 434, 506, 534–535
FaceNet, 500
Facial expression, 441
FacioMetrics, 506
Failed global assignments, 177, 178

Failure rate The number of expatriate managers of an overseas operation who come home early, **177**

Fair Labor Standards Act, 289, 299
Fair pay, 390
Fairness, 183, 390–392
Fake pharmaceuticals, 501
False reporting of performance data, 475
Family and Medical Leave Act, 289
Farmhouse Delivery, 280
Fast Company, 219
Fast food companies, 225
Fayol's 14 principles of management, 31
FDA. *See* Food & Drug Administration (FDA)
FDI. *See* Foreign direct investment (FDI)
Federal Aviation Administration (FAA), 43
Federal government, 41
Federal Trade Commission, 195
FedEx, 51, 319, 414, 464
Feedback
decision evaluation, 82
Hackman and Oldman model, 388
international management, 180–181
performance appraisal, 295
reinforcing performance, 378

Feedback control Control that focuses on the use of information about previous results to correct deviations from the acceptable standard, **465**, 466

Feedforward control The control process used before operations begin, including policies, procedures, and rules designed to ensure that planned activities are carried out properly, **465**

Fictional blogs, 134
Fidelity Investments, 316

Fiedler's contingency model of leadership effectiveness A situational approach to leadership postulating that effectiveness depends on the personal style of the leader and the degree to which the situation gives the leader power, control, and influence over the situation, **354**–355

Filtering The process of withholding, ignoring, or distorting information, **431**

Final consumer A customer who purchases products in their finished form, **50**

Financial analysis, 117
Financial controls, 471–474
Financial ratios, 473–474
Financial service firms, 533
Financial statements, 471–473
Fitbit, 459
Fitness trackers, 459
Five sources of power worksheet, 367–368
FLEXcon, 404

Flexible benefit programs Benefit programs in which employees are given credits to spend on benefits that fit their unique needs, **299**

Flexible factories Manufacturing plants that have short production runs, are organized around products, and use decentralized scheduling, **267**

Flexible manufacturing, 266

Flexible processes Methods for adapting the technical core to changes in the environment **58**

Flexible work arrangements, 254, 316
Followership, 346, 497
Food & Drug Administration (FDA), 43, 48

Force-field analysis An approach to implementing the unfreezing/moving/refreezing model by identifying the forces that prevent people from changing and those that will drive people toward change, **525**

Ford Focus, 171
Ford Motor Company, 55, 144, 171, 175, 265, 294, 322, 360, 510–511
Ford Next Generation Learning (Ford NGL), 533

Forecast Method for predicting how variables will change the future, **54**

Forecasting, 54, 114
Foreign Corrupt Practices Act, 138
Foreign direct investment (FDI), 160
Forever 21, 319

Formalization The presence of rules and regulations governing how people in the organization interact, **242**

40K Plus Education, 198
Forward-looking companies, 534–535
Foxconn, 166, 217–218
Fracking, 42

Framing effects A decision bias influenced by the way in which a problem or decision alternative is phrased or presented, **83**

Franchise Chat, 195

Franchising An entrepreneurial alliance between a franchisor (an innovator who has created at least one successful store and wants to grow) and a franchisee (a partner who manages a new store of the same type in a new location), 173, 174–175, **195**

Friendster, 497
Frivolity, 477

Front-line managers Lower-level managers who supervise the operational activities of the organization, **16**

Fujitsu, 238
Functional manager, 239

Functional organization Departmentalization around specialized activities such as production, marketing, and human resources, **232**–234, 235

Functional strategies Strategies implemented by each functional area of the organization to support the organization's business strategy, **123**

Functions of the Executive, The (Barnard), 31
FundersClub, 205

G

Gainsharing plan, 298
Game theory, 410
Gametheory.net, 410
Gap, 46, 467

Garbage can model Model of organizational decision making depicting a chaotic process and seemingly random decisions, **92**

Gatekeeper A team member who keeps abreast of current developments and provides the team with relevant information, **417**

GE. *See* General Electric (GE)
GE Global Research, 501
Gender issues, 315–318. *See also* Women
General Dynamics, 316
General Electric (GE), 138, 139, 147, 160, 196, 228, 251, 260, 263, 271, 363, 449–450, 470, 518
General Electric Aviation, 329

General Mills, 46, 322
General Motors (GM), 105–106, 108, 161, 165, 175, 223, 232, 237, 245, 257, 265, 316, 509
Generation X, 7, 120
Generational tipping point, 241
Generativity, 145
Generic drug makers, 497
Genetically modified foods, 70

Genius of the *and* Ability to achieve multiple objectives simultaneously, **520**

Geographic divisions, 236
Geonetric, 412
Ghana, 182
Giveforward, 202

Glass ceiling An invisible barrier that makes it difficult for women and minorities to move beyond a certain hierarchical level, **315**

Glassdoor.com, 283, 297, 434
GlaxoSmithKline (GSK), 7, 505
Global Business Institute program, 5
Global Environment Fund, 150
Global Ethics Summit (2017), 134
Global Hyatt, 177
Global integration–local responsiveness worksheet, 185

Global model An organizational model consisting of a company's overseas subsidiaries and characterized by centralized decision making and tight control by the parent company over most aspects of worldwide operations; typically adopted by organizations that base their global competitive strategy on cost considerations, 168, **171**

Global Reporting Initiative (GRI) list of sustainability performance indicators, 150
Global virtual teamwork, 406
Globalization, 4–5, 138, 501. *See also* International management
GM. *See* General Motors (GM)
Go-it-alone approach, 536

Goal A target or end that management desires to reach, **105**

Goal displacement A decision-making group loses sight of its original goal and a new, less important goal emerges, **86**

Goal setting, 373–375

Goal-setting theory A motivation theory stating that people have conscious goals that energize them and direct their thoughts and behaviors toward a particular end, **373**

gofundme, 202
Going public (IPO), 204
Goldman Sachs, 140
Good to Great (Collins), 536, 537
Google, 56, 150, 164, 192, 255, 256, 448, 491, 497, 508
Google Docs, 406
Google Plus, 433
Google+, 51
Google+ Hangouts, 436
Gore & Associates, 99
Gossip, 448
Government regulators, 43
Grameen Bank, 197
Grameen Foundation, 463

Grapevine Informal communication network, **448**–449

Graystone Industries, 435
Greatest management principle in the world, 377
Greenling, 280
Greyball, 94
GRI list. *See* Global Reporting Initiative (GRI) list of sustainability performance indicators
Grid training, 352
Grievance procedure, 303
Grizzly Bear Lodge, 487
Group Danone purchase of Stonyfields, 150
Group incentive plans, 298

Group maintenance behaviors Actions taken to ensure the satisfaction of group members, develop and maintain harmonious work relationships, and preserve the social stability of the group, **350**

Groupon, 433

Groupthink A phenomenon that occurs in decision making when group members avoid disagreement as they strive for consensus, **86**, 415

Growth need strength The degree to which individuals want personal and psychological development, **388**

Growth needs, 384

H
H-1B visa, 281
H-E-B, 282
Habitat for Humanity, 113
Hackman and Oldham model of job enrichment, 387–388
Hai (yes), 441
Hammer's seven deadly sins of performance Measurement, 477
Harley-Davidson, 160
Harpo, 319
Havenly, 91

Hawthorne effect People's reactions to being observed or studied resulting in superficial rather than meaningful changes in behavior, **32**

Hawthorne studies, 31
He works, she works worksheet, 336
Health and safety, 300
Health care organizations, 194
Health care providers, 196
Healthy-TX, 198
Heineken, 170
Heinz, 170
Hermès International, 11

Hersey and Blanchard's situational theory A life-cycle theory of leadership postulating that a manager should consider an employee's psychological and job maturity before deciding whether task performance or maintenance behaviors are more important, **355**

Hershey Company, 141
Hertz, 466
Herzberg's two-factor theory, 387
Hewlett-Packard, 50, 194, 316, 328, 434, 470

Hierarchy The authority levels of the organizational pyramid, **227**

High information-processing demands, 243–244

High-involvement organization A type of organization in which top management ensures that there is consensus about the direction in which the business is heading, **256**–257

High school career academy, 533
Hilcorp, 447
Hilton, 142–143
Hitachi Data Systems, 363
Hofstede's four types of differences between country cultures, 179, 181
Holacracy, 99
HoloLens, 42
Hon Hai, 166
Honda, 170, 294
Honesty, 183
Honeywell, 327, 331
Hoovers.com, 219

Horizontal communication Information shared among people on the same hierarchical level, **448**

Horizontal structure, 232–241

Host-country nationals Natives of the country where an overseas subsidiary is located, **176**

Hostile work environment, 317
HR planning process, 279–282

HRM. *See* Human resources management (HRM)
Hult Prize Foundation, 167
Hulu, 48

Human capital The knowledge, skills, and abilities of employees that have economic value, **279**

Human dignity, 135
Human process intervention, 521

Human relations A classical management approach that attempted to understand and explain how human psychological and social processes interact with the formal aspects of the work situation to influence performance, **31**–32

Human resource management intervention, 521
Human resources analysis, 115
Human resources assessment, 117

Human resources management (HRM) Formal systems for the management of people within an organization, 276–309

  collective bargaining, 302–303
  defined, **278**
  demand forecasts, 280
  disciplinary procedures, 287
  drug testing, 285–286
  employee benefits, 299
  employment interview, 283–284, 307
  equal employment opportunity, 288–289
  equal pay for equal work, 299–300
  executive pay, 298–299
  grievance procedure, 303
  health and safety, 300
  incentive systems and variable pay, 297–298
  job analysis, 282
  labor relations, 300–303
  labor supply forecasts, 280–281
  layoffs, 286–287
  legislation, 289, 300, 301
  online tools to screen job applicants, 285
  pay decisions, 296–297, 307–308
  performance appraisal (PA), 292–296
  planning process, 279–282
  recruitment, 282–283
  reward systems, 296–300
  selection, 283–286
  staffing, 282–289
  stock options, 298–299
  strategic impact of human resources, 278
  termination, 287–288
  training and development, 290–291
  underperforming employee, 296
  unionization, 300–303
  workforce reductions, 286–288
Humanitarian organizations, 7
Huntsman Corporation, 373

Hygiene factors Characteristics of the workplace, such as company policies, working conditions, pay, and supervision, that can make people dissatisfied, **387**

I

IBM, 53, 131, 143, 151, 168, 170, 194, 238, 257, 286, 316, 317, 322, 363, 433, 459, 467, 491, 499, 508, 532
IdeaStorm, 51
IDEO, 59, 78, 89, 256, 510
Illinois Tool Works, 342
Illiteracy, 444

Illusion of control People's belief that they can influence events even when they have no control over what will happen, **83**

Immigrant labor, 281, 300, 318–319
Immigration, 45
Impact value chain (IVC), 463
Implementation agenda, 124
Impoverished management, 352
Inanity, 477
Inbound logistics, 261
Inc. magazine, 219
Incentive systems and variable pay, 297–298

Incremental model Model of organizational decision making in which major solutions arise through a series of smaller decisions, **92**

Indeed, 283
Independent action, 56

Independent strategies Strategies that an organization acting on its own uses to change some aspect of its current environment, 56

India, 165, 177
Indian University Health Center, 459
Indiegogo, 202, 205
inDinero, 192
Inditex, 11
Individual incentive system, 297
Individual pay decisions, 297
Individualism/collectivism, 179, 181
Indonesia, 182
Industrial pollution, 147
Industry and market analysis, 115
Informal authority, 226
Informal communication, 448–449
Information-processing capability, 243–244

Informing A team strategy that entails making decisions with the team and then informing outsiders of its intentions, **417**

Infosys, 165

Initial public offering (IPO) Sale to the public, for the first time, of federally registered and underwritten shares of stock in the company, **204**

Innovation The introduction of new goods and services; a change in method or technology; a positive, useful departure from previous ways of doing things, **8**, **490**. *See also* Managing technology and innovation

Innovation Lab, 509
Innovation types, 490, 491
InnovationXchange Lab, 509
Innovators, 492, 493

Inpatriate A foreign national brought in to work at the parent company, **179**

Inputs Goods and services organizations take in and use to create products or services, **40**

Inshoring Moving work from other countries back to the headquarters country. Work may be done by a domestic provider or in-house, **163**

Inside directors, 226
Insider trading, 137

Insourcing Producing in-house one or more of an organization's goods or services, **163**

Instagram, 192, 321, 433, 497

Instrumentality The perceived likelihood that performance will be followed by a particular outcome, **379**

Integration The degree to which differentiated work units work together and coordinate their efforts, **224**, 225–226

Integrity, 349

Integrity-based ethics programs Company mechanisms designed to instill in people a personal responsibility for ethical behavior, **140**

Integrity tests, 286
Intel, 46, 50, 91, 117, 255, 501, 504
Intellectual capital, 279

Intergroup leader A leader who leads collaborative performance between groups or organizations, **361**

Intermediary model Charging fees to bring buyers and sellers together, **196**

Intermediate customer A customer who purchases raw materials or wholesale products before selling them to final customers, **50–51**

Internal audit A periodic assessment of a company's own planning, organizing, leading, and controlling processes, **468**

Internal communication apps, 60
Internal environment, 58–62
Internal locus of control, 356
Internal recruiting, 282–283
Internal resource analysis, 116, 117
Internal Revenue Service, 236
Internal strengths and weaknesses, 116–118
International Franchise Association, 195
International Harvester, 351
International management, 158–186
  Africa, 168
  the Americas, 166–167
  Asia, 165–166
  bribery, 181–182
  China, 165
  cultural issues, 177–181
  culture shock, 179
  dual-career couples, 177
  e-mail, 180, 182
  entry modes, 173–176
  ethical issues, 181–183
  ethnocentrism, 179
  European Union (EU), 164
  expatriates, 176–177
  exporting, 173–174
  failed global assignments, 177, 178
  fast-trackers, 180
  feedback, 180–181
  foreign direct investment (FDI), 160
  franchising, 173, 174–175
  global integration, 168–169
  global model, 168, 171
  Hofstede's four types of differences between country cultures, 179, 181
  identifying international executives, 178
  India, 165
  inpatriates, 179
  inshoring/insourcing, 163
  international model, 168, 170
  joint venture, 173, 175
  key aspects of global environment, 164
  language skills (local language/customs), 440–441
  licensing, 173, 174
  local responsiveness, 170–171
  meetings, 179–180
  Middle East, 167
  multinational model, 168, 170–171
  organizational models, 168, 170–173
  outsourcing/offshoring, 162
  regional trade agreements, 166–167
  shared values, 183
  skills of global manager, 177
  tariffs, 169–170, 174

time zone differences, 182
top 10 global firms, 161
transnational model, 168, 171–173
Western Europe, 164
wholly owned subsidiary, 173, 175–176
work schedules, 180
working overseas, 176–177

International model An organizational model that is composed of a company's overseas subsidiaries and characterized by greater control by the parent company over local product and marketing strategies than is the case in the multinational model, 168, **170**

International Paper, 266
International Space Station, 196
Internet, 196–197
Internet of Things, 5, 532

Interpersonal and communication skills People skills; the ability to lead, motivate, and communicate effectively with others, **18**

Interpersonal communication, 430–437
Intolerance of inhumanity, 145

Intrapreneurs New venture creators working inside big companies, **191**, 210

Intrinsic reward Reward a worker derives directly from performing the job itself, **385**

Intuit, 258, 509
Investtext.com, 219
Invincibility Systems, 308–309
IPO. *See* Initial public offering (IPO)

ISO 9001 A series of quality standards developed by a committee working under the International Organization for Standardization to improve total quality in all businesses for the benefit of producers and consumers, **264**

Issue advertising, 56
IT-related crises, 93

J

J. M. Huber Corporation, 464
Jack and Jake's, 198
Japan
    apologizing, 441
    Cheer laundry detergent, 171
    hai (yes), 441
    high-quality co-workers, 385
    kaizen, 261, 496
    silence, 442
Jazzercise, 195
JCPenney, 319

JimmyJohn's, 195
JIT. *See* Just-in-time (JIT)

Job analysis A tool for determining what is done on a given job and what should be done on that job, **282**

Job dissatisfaction, 392

Job enlargement Giving people additional tasks at the same time to alleviate boredom, **386**

Job enrichment Changing a task to make it inherently more rewarding, motivating, and satisfying, **386**

Job hopping, 254
Job interview, 283–284, 307

Job maturity The level of the employee's skills and technical knowledge relative to the task being performed, **355**

Job posting system, 283

Job rotation Changing from one task to another to alleviate boredom, **385**–386

Job satisfaction, 392–393
Job shop, 265
Job specification, 282
JOBS Act. *See* Jumpstart Our Business Startups Act (JOBS Act)
John Deere, 281
Johnson Controls, 363
Johnson & Johnson, 56, 117, 194, 235, 317, 478
Johnson & Johnson Medical Devices, 319
Joint venture, 60, 173, 175, 505
Jumpstart Our Business Startups Act (JOBS Act), 207

Just-in-time (JIT) A system that calls for subassemblies and components to be manufactured in very small lots and delivered to the next stage of the production process just as they are needed, **269**–270

K

Kaiser Permanente, 317, 510
Kaizen, 261, 496
Kalundborg, Denmark, 150
Kauffman Center for Entrepreneurial Leadership, 219
Kawasaki Heavy Industries, 175
Kellogg Company, 46, 56, 170
Kenya, 182
Key employee behaviors, 372–373
Key technologies, 498
Kickbacks, 43, 137
Kickboard, 144

Kickstarter, 202, 205
Kindred Nursing and Rehabilitation Center, 264
Kiva, 202, 234

Knowledge management Practices aimed at discovering and harnessing an organization's intellectual resources, **6**

Knowledge workers
Kobold Watch, 258

Kohlberg's model of cognitive moral development Classification of people based on their level of moral judgment, **137**

Komatsu, 170
KPMG, 413
Kroger, 120, 322, 502
Kweli, 198
Kyosei, 135

L

Labor laws, 301
Labor-Management Relations Act, 301
Labor-Management Reporting and Disclosure Act, 301

Labor relations The system of relations between workers and management, **300**–303

Labor supply forecasts, 280–281
Laggards, 493, 494

Laissez-faire A leadership philosophy characterized by an absence of managerial decision making, **351**

Landrum-Griffin Act, 301
Language skills, 440–441

Large batch Technologies that produce goods and services in high volume, **265**

Large global corporations, 524

Large group interventions Introducing and sustaining multiple policies, practices, and procedures across multiple units and levels, **528**

Late majority, 493, 494

Lateral leadership Style in which colleagues at the same hierarchical level are invited to collaborate and facilitate joint problem solving, **361**

Lateral role relationships, 418
Latin America, 177
Latina entrepreneurs, 197

Law of effect   A law formulated by Edward Thorndike in 1911 stating that behavior that is followed by positive consequences will likely be repeated, **375**, 376

Laws and regulations, 43–44
Layoffs, 259, 286–287
Laziness, 477
LBGT employees, 318
LCA. *See* Life-cycle analysis (LCA)

Leader–member exchange (LMX) theory   Highlights the importance of leader behaviors not just toward the group as a whole but toward individuals on a personal basis, **350**

Leadership, 340–369
   authenticity, 360–361
   change management, 529–531
   charismatic, 358–359
   courage, 362–363
   decision making, 351
   developing leadership skills, 363–364
   entrepreneurship, 199
   Fiedler's contingency model, 354–355
   followers, 346
   group decision making, 87
   group maintenance behaviors, 350
   Hersey and Blanchard's situational theory, 355
   leader behaviors, 342, 343, 349–351
   leader traits, 348–349
   leadership grid, 352
   learning and leading, 536–538
   Level 5, 360
   LMX theory, 350
   management, distinguished, 345
   Millennials, 343
   opportunity for leaders, 361
   path-goal theory, 355–357
   performance and maintenance behaviors, 351–352
   power, 346–348, 367–368
   situational approach, 353
   substitutes for leadership, 357–358
   supervisory/strategic, 345–346
   task-motivated/relationship-motivated, 355
   technology, 495–497
   transformational, 359–360
   vision, 343–344, 345
   Vroom model, 353–354
Leadership grid, 352
Leadership motivation, 349

Leading   The management function that involves the manager's efforts to stimulate high performance by employees, **13**–14

Lean manufacturing   An operation that strives to achieve the highest possible productivity and total quality, cost-effectively, by eliminating unnecessary steps in the production process and continually striving for improvement, **267**–268, 271

Lean six sigma, 263
Leaning into the Future, 538

Learning organization   An organization skilled at creating, acquiring, and transferring knowledge, and at modifying its behavior to reflect new knowledge and insights, 256

Least preferred co-worker (LPC), 355
Legal action, 56
Legal interview worksheet, 307

Legal responsibilities   To obey local, state, federal, and relevant international laws, **145**

Legitimacy   People's judgment of a company's acceptance, appropriateness, and desirability, generally stemming from company goals and methods that are consistent with societal values, **208**

Legitimate power, 347
Lehman Brothers, 83
Lending Club, 205
Lenovo, 50
Lesbian, gay, bisexual, or transgender (LGBT) employees, 318
Level 5 hierarchy, 536–537

Level 5 leadership   A combination of strong professional will (determination) and humility that builds enduring greatness, **360**

Leverage ratios, 474
Leveraging differences, 324
Levi Strauss, 177
LG, 174

Liabilities   The amounts a corporation owes to various creditors, **471**

Liaison relationships, 418
Liaison roles, 244
Liberty Kitchen, 442
Licensing, 173, 174, 504
Lidl, 502
Lie detector test, 286
Life, 45

Life-cycle analysis (LCA)   A process of analyzing all inputs and outputs, through the entire "cradle-to-grave" life of a product, to determine total environmental impact, **149**

Lifeguards, 388
Lifelong learning, 536
Lifestyle and taste changes, 195

Line departments   Units that deal directly with the organization's primary goods and services, **232**

LinkedIn, 20, 51, 283, 285, 321, 433, 434
Linksys, 59
Liquidity ratios, 473–474
Listening, 442–444, 452–453
Listening feedback form, 454
Listening skills survey, 453
Litson Cotton Yarn Manufacturing Company, 100
Living Goods, 259
L.L.Bean, 6
LMX theory. *See* Leader–member exchange (LMX) theory
Lobbyists, 132
Lockheed Martin, 196, 316, 319, 407, 408
Locus of control, 356

Logistics   The movement of the right goods in the right amount to the right place at the right time, **269**

L'Oréal purchase of The Body Shop, 150
Love contract, 465

Low-cost strategy   A strategy an organization uses to build competitive advantage by being efficient and offering a standard, no-frills product, **122**

LPC. *See* Least preferred co-worker (LPC)
Lyft, 108
Lying/truth-telling, 133

M

Ma Earth Skin Care, 155–156
Maastricht Treaty, 164
Macroeconomic analysis, 115

Macroenvironment   The general environment; includes governments, economic conditions, and other fundamental factors that generally affect all organizations, **41**

   demographics, 44–45
   economy, 41–42
   laws and regulations, 43–44
   social issues, 45
   sustainability and natural environment, 45–46
   technology, 42–43
Macy's, 4, 236, 269, 500
Magic Bus, 167

Make-or-buy decision   The question an organization asks itself about whether to acquire new technology from an outside source or develop it itself, **504**

Malcolm Baldrige National Quality Award, 264

Management The process of working with people and resources to accomplish organizational goals, **12**

decision making. *See* Managerial decision making
functions, 12–14
greatest management principle in the world, 377
historical overview. *See* Evolution of management
leadership, distinguished, 345

Management audit An evaluation of the effectiveness and efficiency of various systems within an organization, **468**–469

Management bonus, 297

Management by objectives (MBO) A process in which objectives set by a subordinate and a supervisor must be reached within a given time period, **294**

Management by wandering around (MBWA), 447
Management functions, 12–14
Management in Action boxes
  Alibaba, 159, 172, 182
  Amazon, 39, 52, 61
  Apple, 311, 325, 332
  Facebook, 3, 15, 22
  General Electric, 251, 260, 271
  General Motors, 223, 237, 245
  Google, 277–278, 292, 304
  IBM, 131, 143, 151
  monitoring employee health, 459, 475, 483
  Musk, Elon, 489, 503, 511
  PepsiCo, 341, 357, 364
  SAS, 371, 381, 394
  Shell Oil Company, 517, 529, 538
  Starbucks, 189, 201, 212
  Uber, 71, 81, 94
  Walt Disney Company, 103–104, 112, 125
  Whole Foods Market, 403, 407, 422
Management information system (MIS), 42
Management levels and skills, 15–18

Management myopia Focusing on short-term earnings and profits at the expense of longer-term strategic obligations, **474**

Management teams Teams that coordinate and provide direction to the subunits under their jurisdiction and integrate work among subunits, **405**

Management training, 291
Manager
  decisional roles, 17
  front-line, 16
  informational roles, 17
  interpersonal roles, 17

middle-level, 16
skills, 17–18
top-level, 15–16
Managerial behaviors worksheet, 26
Managerial control, 458–487
  activity-based costing (ABC), 470–471
  balanced scorecard, 478, 479
  budgetary controls, 469–471
  bureaucratic control systems, 461–480
  characteristics of controls, 461
  clan control, 482
  concurrent control, 465–466
  control cycle, 461–464
  corrective action, 464
  designing effective systems, 476–480
  employee acceptance of controls, 478
  feedback control, 466
  feedforward control, 465
  financial controls, 471–474
  financial ratios, 473–474
  financial statements, 471–473
  Hammer's seven deadly sins of performance measurement, 477
  management audit, 468–469
  market control, 480–482
  open communication, 478
  out-of-control company, 460
  performance measurement, 462–463, 477
  performance standards, 461–462, 476–477
  principle of exception, 464
  resistance to control, 476
  rigid bureaucratic behavior, 474–475
  six sigma, 466–468
  strategy map, 478, 479
  tactical behavior, 475–476
Managerial decision making, 72–101
  barriers to overcome, 83–85
  best decision?, 82
  characteristics of managerial decisions, 74–76
  conflict, 76
  crises, 92–94
  decision making worksheet, 97
  evaluating alternatives, 78–79
  evaluating the decision, 82
  generating alternative solutions, 77–78
  implementing the decision, 80–82
  lack of structure, 74–75
  making the choice, 80
  organizational decision making, 91–94
  phases of decision making (exhibit 3.3), 77
  problem identification and diagnosis, 77
  programmed/nonprogrammed decisions, 74, 75
  psychological biases, 83–84
  social realities, 85–90
  time pressures, 84
  uncertainty and risk, 75–76
Managerial roles, 17

Managing diversity Managing a culturally diverse workforce by

recognizing the characteristics common to specific groups of employees while dealing with employees as individuals and supporting, nurturing, and utilizing their differences to the organization's advantage, **312**. *See also* Diverse workforce

Managing technology and innovation, 488–515
  adopter categories, 492–494
  assessing technology needs, 498–499
  bureaucracy busting, 509
  capability development, 501–502, 503
  creativity, 508–509
  decision making, 499–503
  design thinking, 509–510
  development project, 510–511
  diffusion of technological innovations, 492
  disruptive innovation, 495
  driving forces of technological development, 491
  economic viability, 501, 503
  elements essential to innovation, 509
  external technological trends, 499
  job design, 511
  make-or-buy decision, 504
  managerial roles, 506–507
  market receptiveness, 499–500, 503
  organizational suitability, 502, 503
  requirements for innovation, 508
  technological feasibility, 500–501, 503
  technology acquisition options, 504–506
  technology audit, 498
  technology followership, 497–498
  technology leadership, 495–497
  technology life cycle, 491–492
  types of innovation, 490, 491
Marijuana, 285–286

Market control Control based on the use of pricing mechanisms and economic information to regulate activities within organizations, **461**, 480–482

Marketing and sales, 262
Marketing audit, 117
Marriott, 150
Mars, 46
Mary Kay Cosmetics, 385
M&As. *See* Mergers and acquisitions (M&As)
Masculinity/femininity, 179

Maslow's need hierarchy A conception of human needs organizing needs into a hierarchy of five major types, **381**–383

Mass customization The production of varied, individually customized products at the low cost of standardized, mass-produced products, **266**, 267

Massey mine disaster, 300
Master budget, 470
MasterCard, 233, 317, 319
Matrix diamond, 239

Matrix organization An organization composed of dual reporting relationships in which some employees report to two superiors—a functional manager and a divisional manager, **236**–239

Mattel, 177

Maximizing A decision realizing the best possible outcome, **80**

MBO. *See* Management by objectives (MBO)
MBWA. *See* Management by wandering around (MBWA)
McClelland's needs, 384
McDonald's, 56, 145, 169, 174, 301, 464
McKinsey & Company, 6, 90, 317
Mechanistic and organic worksheet, 273

Mechanistic organization A form of organization that seeks to maximize internal efficiency, **252**

Media richness The degree to which a communication channel conveys information, **437**

Mediator A third party who intervenes to help others manage their conflict, **420**

Memorial Hermann Hospital, 264
Menlo Innovations, 377
Mental and physical disabilities, 319–320

Mentors Higher-level managers who help ensure that high-potential people are introduced to top management and socialized into the norms and values of the organization, **331**

Merck, 319, 495, 501–502

Merger One or more companies combining with another, **55**, 59, 60

Mergers and acquisitions (M&As), 122, 150
Michael Kors, 74
Microsoft, 192, 227, 281, 319, 374, 496, 497, 502, 532
Microsoft's Research Lab, 504
Middle East, 167

Middle-level managers Managers located in the middle layers of the organizational hierarchy, reporting to top-level executives, **16**

Middle-of-the-road management, 352
Millennial Generation, 7, 44, 91, 120, 180. *See also* Multiple Generations at Work boxes
MillerCoors Brewing Company, 412
Mining safety, 300
Ministry of Supply, 203
Minority internships, 319

Mission An organization's basic purpose and scope of operations, **113**

Mission statement, 60
Mistakes, 378
Mixed signals and misperception, 432
Model T, 30
Modern slavery, 137
Modular corporation, 240
Moment of truth, 61
Mondelez International, 315, 316
Monitoring employee health, 459, 475, 483
Monitoring employees to ensure ethical behavior, 140

Monolithic organization An organization that has a low degree of structural integration—employing few women, minorities, or other groups that differ from the majority—and thus has a highly homogeneous employee population, **325**

Monsanto, 46, 177
Monster, 283
Monster Strike, 55
Moral awareness, 141, 142
Moral character, 141
Moral judgment, 141

Moral philosophy Principles, rules, and values people use in deciding what is right or wrong, **135**

Motivating for performance, 370–400
Alderfer's ERG theory, 383–384
designing motivating jobs, 385–389
employee satisfaction and well-being, 392–395
empowerment, 388–389
equity theory, 390, 391
expectancy theory, 378–380
extrinsic/intrinsic rewards, 385
fairness, 390–392
feedback, 378
goal setting, 373–375
Hackman and Oldham model of job enrichment, 387–388
Herzberg's two-factor theory, 387
job rotation, enlargement, and enrichment, 385–386
job satisfaction, 392–393
key employee behaviors, 372–373
law of effect, 375, 376
Maslow's need hierarchy, 381–383
McClelland's needs, 384
mistakes, 378

need theories, 381–385
performance-related beliefs, 378–380
procedural justice, 392
psychological contract, 394–395
quality of work life, 393
reinforcing performance, 375–378
rewards and punishments, 376–377
teams, 412

Motivation Forces that energize, direct, and sustain a person's efforts, **372**

Motivators Factors that make a job more motivating, such as additional job responsibilities, opportunities for personal growth and recognition, and feelings of achievement, **387**

Motorola, 177, 263
Motorola Mobility, 177

Moving Instituting the change, **525**

MTV, 510

Multicultural organization An organization that values cultural diversity and seeks to utilize and encourage it, **326**

Multidomestic model, 170

Multinational model An organizational model that consists of the subsidiaries in each country in which a company does business, and provides a great deal of discretion to those subsidiaries to respond to local conditions, 168, **170**–171

Multiple Generations at Work boxes
bring your own device to work (BYOD), 436
crowdsourcing, 91
flexible workplace, 254
Gen Xers/Millennial generation, 7
global virtual teamwork, 406
higher-order needs, 383
job hunting, 524
leadership, 343
Millennial entrepreneurs, 209
Millennials and international work experience, 180
online social networks, 241
performance reviews, 467
portfolio career, 44
soft skills, 291
SoundCloud, 429, 438, 450
strengths and weaknesses of different generational cohorts, 120
trust in the workplace, 134
work–life balance, 316
Multitasking, 377
Mutuality, 145
MySpace, 497

N

NAACP, 313
Nabisco, 136
NAFTA. *See* North American Free Trade Agreement (NAFTA)
Nano-based technologies, 535
NanoHealth, 167
Nanometer, 535
Narcissism, 477
NASA, 196, 238
NASDAQ Composite, 41
National Counterterrorism Center, 243
National Geographic, 76
National Industries for the Blind (NIB), 320
National Labor Relations Act, 301
National Labor Relations Board (NLRB), 43, 301
National Marrow Donor Program (NMDP), 478, 480
National Restaurant Association, 317
National Retail Federation, 317
National Venture Capital Association, 204
Natura, 373
Natural disasters, 195
Natural environment and sustainability, 45–46, 147–150
    borrow-use-return approach, 149
    carbon footprint, 149
    collaborating on common ecological vision, 150
    competitive advantage, 68
    conservation, 69
    cost–benefit analysis, 70
    cost-effectiveness, 68
    developing countries, 148
    ecocentric management, 149
    economic arguments, 68–69
    economics and the environment, 69
    environmental movement, 69
    future directions, 150
    GRI list of sustainability performance indicators, 150
    industrial pollution, 147
    legal compliance, 68
    life-cycle analysis (LCA), 149
    long-term thinking, 150
    public opinion, 68
    science and the environment, 69
    sustainable growth, 149
    take-make-waste approach, 147
    tragedy of the commons, 69
NEC, 500
Need for achievement, 384
Need for affiliation, 384
Need for power, 384
Need theories, 381–385

Needs assessment An analysis identifying the jobs, people, and departments for which training is necessary, **290**

Negative reinforcement Removing or withholding an undesirable consequence, **376**

Nestlé, 4, 150, 232
Nestlé Health Sciences, 505
Nestlé Waters North America, 288
Net-Work Docs, 186
Net working capital ratio, 474
Netflix, 8, 48, 174
Network architect, 241
Network co-operator, 241
Network developer, 241
Network for Good, 259

Network organization A collection of independent, mostly single-function firms that collaborate on a good or service, **239**–241

Networking, 208
New Belgium Brewery, 373
New business start-up worksheet, 216–217
New Day Flyers, 119
New York City Board of Health, 45
NIB. *See* National Industries for the Blind (NIB)
Niche Hotel Group, 336–337
Nike, 46, 56, 262, 495
NikeID, 9
Nissan, 8
NLRB. *See* National Labor Relations Board (NLRB)
Noël, David, 429, 438, 450

Nonprogrammed decisions New, novel, complex decisions having no proven answers, **74**, 75

Nonverbal communication, 441–442, 452
Nonverbal communication interpretation worksheet, 452
Nordstrom, 58, 59, 500

Norms Shared beliefs about how people should think and behave, **413**–414

North American Free Trade Agreement (NAFTA) An economic pact that combined the economies of the United States, Canada, and Mexico into one of the world's largest trading blocs, 47, **166**

Not Mass Produced, 198
Novo Nordisk, 107
Nucor Steel, 404, 509
Nutrition Science Partners, 505

O

OB mod. *See* Organizational behavior modification (OB mod)
Obesity epidemic, 138
Observing, 444
Occidental Chemicals, 266
Occidental Petroleum, 42
Occupational Safety and Health Administration (OSHA), 43, 300

Ocean Renewable Power Company (ORPC), 115
Oculus, 506
OD. *See* Organizational development (OD)
OFCCP. *See* Office of Federal Contract Compliance Programs (OFCCP)
Office of Federal Contract Compliance Programs (OFCCP), 43

Offshoring Moving work to other countries, **162**

Ohio State studies, 351
Oil of Olay, 108
Omnica, 405

One-way communication A process in which information flows in only one direction—from the sender to the receiver, with no feedback loop, **430**

Online collaboration, 7
Online privacy, 138
Online social networks, 241
Onsite child care, 329

Open-book management Practice of sharing with employees at all levels of the organization vital information previously meant for management's eyes only, 446–**447**

Open source drug discovery (OSDD) database, 505
Open-system perspective of organization, 34

Open systems Organizations that are affected by, and that affect, their environment, **40**

Operational budget, 125
Operational manager, 16

Operational planning The process of identifying the specific procedures and processes required at lower levels of the organization, **109**

Operations analysis, 117, 262

Opportunity analysis A description of the good or service, an assessment of the opportunity, an assessment of the entrepreneur, specification of activities and resources needed to translate your idea into a viable business, and your source(s) of capital, **205**

Optimizing Achieving the best possible balance among several goals, **80**

Oracle, 316
Oral communication, 433
Orbital Sciences Corporation, 196

Ordinary capabilities Capabilities pertaining to basic administrative and operational functions, **254**

Organic structure An organizational form that emphasizes flexibility, **252**

Organization chart The reporting structure and division of labor in an organization, **224**, 225

Organization culture The set of important assumptions about the organization and its goals and practices that members of the company share, **58**–61

Organization development (OD) The systemwide application of behavioral science knowledge to develop, improve, and reinforce the strategies, structures, and processes that lead to organizational effectiveness, **521**

Organization structure, 222–249
  board of directors, 226–227
  decentralization, 230–232
  delegation, 229–230, 231
  departmentalization, 232
  differentiation, 224–225
  divisional organization, 234–236
  functional organization, 232–234, 235
  hierarchical levels, 227–228
  horizontal structure, 232–241
  informal/formal structures, 253
  integration, 225–226
  line/staff departments, 232
  matrix organization, 236–239
  network organization, 239–241
  organization chart, 224, 225
  organizational integration, 241–244
  span of control, 228
  vertical structure, 226–232
Organizational agility, 250–275
  ambidextrous organization, 252
  computer-integrated manufacturing (CIM), 266
  concurrent engineering, 270
  continually improving operations, 271
  core capabilities, 254–255
  customer relationship management (CRM), 260–262
  downsizing, 258–259
  flexible factories, 267
  flexible manufacturing, 266
  formal/informal organization structures, 253
  high-involvement organization, 256–257
  ISO 9001, 264
  just-in-time (JIT), 269–270
  lean manufacturing, 267–268, 271
  learning organization, 256
  logistics, 269
  mechanistic and organic worksheet, 273
  mechanistic organization, 252
  organic structure, 252
  quality initiatives, 262–264

  reengineering, 264–265
  six sigma quality, 263
  size of the organization, 257–259
  speed, 268–270
  strategic alliance, 255, 256
  technology configurations, 265–266
  time-based competition (TBC), 268–269
  total quality management (TQM), 262

Organizational ambidexterity Ability to achieve multiple objectives simultaneously, **520**

Organizational behavior A contemporary management approach that studies and identifies management activities that promote employee effectiveness by examining the complex and dynamic nature of individual, group, and organizational processes, **33**

Organizational behavior modification (OB mod) The application of reinforcement theory in organizational settings, **375**

Organizational climate The patterns of attitudes and behavior that shape people's experience of an organization, **61**–62

Organizational communication, 444–449
Organizational decision making, 91–94
Organizational integration, 241–244
Organizational size, 257–259
Organizational structure. *See* Organization structure

Organizing The management function of assembling and coordinating human, financial, physical, informational, and other resources needed to achieve goals, **12**–13

Orientation training Training designed to introduce new employees to the company and familiarize them with policies, procedures, culture, and the like, **290**

OSHA. *See* Occupational Safety and Health Administration (OSHA)
OshKosh, 139
Out-of-control company, 460
Outbound logistics, 262

Outcome A consequence a person receives for his or her performance, **379**

Outer space, 196

Outplacement The process of helping people who have been dismissed from the company regain employment elsewhere, **287**

Outputs The products and services organizations create, **40**

Outsourcing Contracting with an outside provider to produce one or more of an organization's goods or services, **162**

P

PA. *See* Performance appraisal (PA)
Pacing technologies, 498
Panasonic, 172
Pandora, 492
Panera Bread, 9, 195

Parading A team strategy that entails simultaneously emphasizing internal team building and achieving external visibility, **417**

Parallel teams Teams that operate separately from the regular work structure and are temporary, **405**

Parasole restaurant group, 388
Parents Network, 45
Paris Agreement, 46, 529
Part-ending cases. *See* Cases

Participation in decision making Leader behaviors that managers perform in involving their employees in making decisions, **351**

Participative leadership, 356
PartPic, 192
Patagonia, 46, 149
Patagonia Sur, 11
Patent, 501

Path–goal theory A theory that concerns how leaders influence subordinates' perceptions of their work goals and the paths they follow toward attainment of those goals, **355**–357

Patient Protection and Affordable Care Act, 43
Pay decisions, 296–297, 307–308
Pay level, 296
Pay rise worksheet, 308
Pay structure, 296
Payless ShoeSource, 286
Pedigree dog food, 144
Peer advisory groups, 227
Peer-to-peer loans, 205
People skills, 18
Pepsi True, 45
PepsiCo, 5, 47, 48, 49, 50, 55, 91, 255, 295, 316, 331

Perception   The process of receiving and interpreting information, **431**

Performance appraisal (PA)   Assessment of an employee's job performance, **292–296**

Performance culture, 67
Performance Food Group, 55

Performance gap   The difference between actual performance and desired performance, **525**

Performance measurement, 462–463, 477
Performance-related beliefs, 378–380
Performance reviews, 467
Performance standards, 461–462, 476–477
Performance tests, 286
Performance-to-outcome link, 379
Personality tests, 285
Personalized power, 384
Persuading, 414
Persuasion skills, 439–440
Pettiness, 477
PEURegen, 198
P&G. *See* Procter & Gamble (P&G)
Pharmaceutical companies, 137, 496, 505

Philanthropic responsibilities   Additional behaviors and activities that society finds desirable and that the values of the business support, **145**

Philippines, 162
Philips, 171, 262
Physical and mental disabilities, 319–320
Physiological needs, 382
PillPack, 78
Pinterest, 192
Piramal Sarvajal, 494

Planning   The management function of systematically making decisions about the goals and activities that an individual, a group, a work unit, or the overall organization will pursue; *see also* Strategic planning, **12**

    alternative goals and plans, 105–106
    entrepreneurship, 204–208
    goal and plan evaluation, 106
    goal and plan selection, 106
    hierarchy of goals and plans, 109
    human resources management (HRM), 279–282
    implementation, 107–108
    monitor and control, 108
    operational, 109
    situational analysis, 104–105
    steps in planning process (Exhibit 4.1), 105
    strategic, 108–109
    strategy map, 110, 111
    tactical, 109

Plans   The actions or means managers intend to use to achieve organizational goals, **105**

Plant closings, 259
Plante Moran, 393

Pluralistic organization   An organization that has a relatively diverse employee population and makes an effort to involve employees from different gender, racial, or cultural backgrounds, **325**

PNC Financial, 319
Pokemon Go, 55
Political action, 56
Political and regulatory analysis, 115
Polycast Technology, 328
Polygraph, 286
Popeyes Louisiana Kitchen, 361
Portfolio, 121
Portfolio career, 44
Porto Alegre, Brazil, 534

Positive reinforcement   Applying consequences that increase the likelihood that a person will repeat the behavior that led to it, **375**

Power   The ability to influence others, **346–348, 367–368**

Power distance, 179, 181
PowerPoint, 439
Practical Computer Applications, 203
Pregnancy Discrimination Act, 300
Preliminary, concurrent, and feedback control worksheet, 486–487
Preliminary control, 465
Presentation skills, 439
Priceline purchase of Momondo, 164
PricewaterhouseCoopers. *See* PwC

Principle of exception   A managerial principle stating that control is enhanced by concentrating on the exceptions to or significant deviations from the expected result or standard, **464**

Proactive change   A response that is initiated before a performance gap has occurred, **532**

Probing   A team strategy that requires team members to interact frequently with outsiders, diagnose their needs, and experiment with solutions, **417**

Problem identification and diagnosis, 77

Procedural justice   Using fair processes in decision making and making sure others know that the process was as fair as possible, **392**

Process innovation, 490, 491
Procter & Gamble (P&G), 68, 108–109, 170, 171, 194, 238, 264, 322, 518

Product champion   A person who promotes a new technology throughout the organization in an effort to obtain acceptance of and support for it, **507**

Product divisions, 235
Product innovation, 490, 491
Product manager, 239
Product Red, 56
Production budget, 470

Profit and loss statement   An itemized financial statement of the income and expenses of a company's operations, **473**

Profit maximization perspective, 146
Profit-sharing plan, 298
Profitability ratios, 474

Programmed decisions   Decisions encountered and made before, having objectively correct answers, and solvable by using simple rules, policies, or numerical computations, **74**, 75

Progress out of poverty index (PPI), 463

Project and development teams   Teams that work on long-term projects but disband once the work is completed, **405**

ProQuest.com, 219
Prospector firms, 502

Prospectors   Companies that continuously change the boundaries for their task environments by seeking new products and markets, diversifying and merging, or acquiring new enterprises, **55**

Prosper, 205
Provincialism, 477
Prudential Insurance, 317

Pseudotransformational leaders   Leaders who talk about positive change but allow their self-interest to take precedence over followers' needs, **361**

Psychological biases, 83–84

Psychological contract   A set of perceptions of what employees owe their employers, and what their employers owe them, **394–395**

Psychological maturity   An employee's self-confidence and self-respect, **355**

Psychological safety When employees feel they can speak up honestly and freely without fear, 410

Public opinion, 68
Public relations, 56
Punctuality, 441

Punishment Administering an aversive consequence, **376**

Purple, 533
PwC, 180, 317, 342

Q

Qualcomm, 322

Quality The excellence of your product (goods or services), **8–9**

Quality initiatives, 262–264

Quality of work life (QWL) programs Programs designed to create a workplace that enhances employee well-being, **393**

Quantitative management A contemporary management approach that emphasizes the application of quantitative analysis to managerial decisions and problems, **33**

Question marks, 121, 122
Quick Lane Tire & Auto Center, 373
Quicken Loans, 10, 258
Quid pro quo harassment, 317
Quotas, 170
QWL. *See* Quality of work life (QWL) programs

R

R. A. Jones & Co., 270
Race and ethnicity, 318–319. *See also* Diverse workforce
Radio frequency identification (RFID) tags, 269
Rapid Plant Assessment, 444
RCA Corporation, 171, 174

Reactive change A response that occurs under pressure; problem-driven change, **532**

Reading, 444

Ready-made solutions Ideas that have been seen or tried before, **78**

Recruitment The development of a pool of applicants for jobs in an organization, **282–283**, 328

Red Cross, 7
Redmond (City), 114

Reduced-calorie sodas, 45
Reengineering, 264–265
Referent power, 347

Reflection Process by which a person states what he or she believes the other person is saying, **443**

Refreezing Strengthening the new behaviors that support the change, **526**

Regional trade agreements, 166–167

Reinforcers Positive consequences that motivate behavior, **375**

Reinforcing performance, 375–378
Relatedness needs, 383
Relating, 414
Relationship culture, 67

Relationship-motivated leadership Leadership that places primary emphasis on maintaining good interpersonal relationships, **355**

Relativism Philosophy that bases ethical behavior on the opinions and behaviors of relevant other people, 135, **136**

Reliable PSD, 435

Reliability The consistency of test scores over time and across alternative measurements, **286**

Research and development, 261
Research partnership, 505
Resistance to change worksheet, 540–541

Resources Inputs to a system that can enhance performance, **116**–117

Respect for others, 183

Responsibility The assignment of a task that an employee is supposed to carry out, 183, **229**

Responsive culture, 67
Responsiveness to customers, 264
Results appraisals, 294
Résumés, 283
Rethink Robotics, 499
Retirees, 320

Return on investment (ROI) A ratio of profit to capital used, or a rate of return from capital, **474**

Reverse engineering, 220
Reward power, 347
Rewards
  change management, 527
  extrinsic/intrinsic, 385
  motivating for performance, 376–377
  teams, 412, 416

RFID tags. *See* Radio frequency identification (RFID) tags

Right-to-work Legislation that allows employees to work without having to join a union, **302**

Right-to-work states, 302–303

Rightsizing A successful effort to achieve an appropriate size at which the company performs most effectively, **259**

Ripple, 533

Risk The state that exists when the probability of success is less than 100 percent and losses may occur, **75**, 199, 200

Robots, 42
Rock, Arthur@, 207
Rocket mortgage, 10
ROI. *See* Return on investment (ROI)

Roles Different sets of expectations for how different individuals should behave, **414**

Root Capital, 463
Royal Dutch Shell, 4, 42, 54, 161, 295, 319, 468–469, 517
Rumors, 449
Russell Reynolds, 177
Ryan LLC, 377
Ryanair, 10

S

Safety or security needs, 382
Safeway, 120, 145, 502
Salary.com, 434
Sales budget, 470
Sales expense budget, 469
Salesforce.com, 56, 262
Sam's Club, 319
Samsung Galaxy Note 7 battery debacle, 132, 174
San Antonio, Texas, 150
Sanofi, 227
SAP, 233, 467

Sarbanes-Oxley Act An act passed into law by Congress to establish strict accounting and reporting rules in order to make senior managers more accountable and to improve and maintain investor confidence, **137**

  code of ethics, 139
  corporate governance rules, 228
  impact, 137

Satisficing Choosing an option that is acceptable, although not necessarily the best or perfect, **80**

Sautil, 259

Scandals, 132, 137
Scanning, 499

Scenario A narrative that describes a particular set of future conditions, **53, 106**

Scenario development, 53–54
Science and Survival (Commoner), 69

Scientific management A classical management approach that applied scientific methods to analyze and determine the one best way to complete production tasks, **29–30**

Scouting, 414
Sears, 257, 286, 520
Securities and Exchange Commission (SEC), 43, 207, 228
Selco Solar, 259

Selection Choosing from among qualified applicants to hire, **283–286**

Self-actualization, 382
Self-assessment worksheet, 397
Self-confidence, 349
Self-contained tasks, 243

Self-designing teams Teams with the responsibilities of autonomous work groups, plus control over hiring, firing, and deciding what tasks members perform, **407**

Self-managed teams Autonomous work groups in which workers are trained to do all or most of the jobs in a unit, have no immediate supervisor, and make decisions previously made by frontline supervisors, **406–407**

Self-reliance, 19–20, 199
Semco Partners, 99
Senegal, 182
Senior vice president (SVP), 15
Sense of urgency, 530–531

Servant-leader A leader who serves others' needs while strengthening the organization, **361**

Servatii Pastry Shop and Deli, 203–204

Service The speed and dependability with which an organization delivers what customers want, **9**, 262

Service Cloud, 262
Service relationships, 418
ServiceMaster, 373
Setting goals, 373–375
Seventh Generation, 68

Sexual harassment Unwelcome sexual conduct that is a term or condition of employment **316–317**, 318

Shake Shack, 227

Shapers Companies that try to change the structure of their industries, creating a future competitive landscape of their own design, **533**

Shaping the future, 532–539
    actions to take, 535
    adapters/shapers, 532–533
    collaboration, 539
    creating the future, 532–535
    cutting-edge technologies, 535
    growth opportunities based on customer needs, 533–535
    learning and leading, 536–538
    level 5 hierarchy, 536–537
    shaping your own future (career development), 535–536
    thinking about the future, 532
    world-class companies, 535

Shared leadership Rotating leadership, in which people rotate through the leadership role based on which person has the most relevant skills at a particular time, **361**

SharePoint, 433
Shell Oil Company, 517, 529, 538. *See also* Royal Dutch Shell
"Shoot the messenger" management, 460
Siemens, 175
Silence, 442
Silent Spring (Carson), 69
SimplyHired, 283
Singapore Airlines, 4, 10
Sinopec Group, 4, 161

Situational analysis A process planners use, within time and resource constraints, to gather, interpret, and summarize all information relevant to the planning issue under consideration, **104**–105

Situational approach Leadership perspective proposing that universally important traits and behaviors do not exist and that effective leadership behavior varies from situation to situation, **353**

Situational interview, 283

Six sigma quality A method of systematically analyzing work processes to identify and eliminate virtually all causes of defects, standardizing the processes to reach the lowest practicable level of any cause of customer dissatisfaction, **263**, 271, 466–468

Skill variety, 388
Skills shortage, 281

Skunkworks A project team designated to produce a new, innovative product, **210**

Skype, 436
Skype for Business, 433
Slack, 60, 406
Slack resources, 243
Small, agile companies, 524

Small batch Technologies that produce goods and services in low volume, **265**

Small business A business having fewer than 100 employees, independently owned and operated, not dominant in its field, and not characterized by many innovative practices, **190**

Small Business Administration, 195, 204, 220
Small Business Learning Center, 204
SMART goals, 374
Smarter Planet, 168
Smithfield Foods, 144, 145, 160

Smoothing Leveling normal fluctuations at the boundaries of the environment, **57**

Snagajob, 283
Snapchat, 192, 497, 506
Soaring Eagle Skate Company, 98–99
Social analysis, 115
Social and environmental enterprises, 524

Social capital Goodwill stemming from your social relationships; a competitive advantage in the form of relationships with other people and the image other people have of you, **20, 208**

Social Enterprise Alliance, 442
Social Enterprise boxes
    attracting business school graduates, 280
    Barefoot College, 148
    Build Change, 362
    Change.org, 327
    co-creation, 534
    co-working, 413
    combating climate change, 46
    Drayton, Bill (Ashoka), 13
    Kiva, 234
    Latina entrepreneurs, 197
    measuring social impact, 463
    Novo Nordisk, 107
    organizational size, 259
    social enterprise: nonprofit or for-profit?, 76
    storytelling, 442

student social entrepreneurs, 167
Team Rubicon, 386
water ATMs, 494

Social enterprise   Organization that applies business models and leverages resources in ways that address social problems, **197**

Social entrepreneurship   Leveraging resources to address social problems, **197**–199, 202

Social facilitation effect   Working harder when in a group than when working alone, **412**

Social Impact Stories, 442
Social issues, 45

Social loafing   Working less hard and being less productive when in a group, **412**

Social media, 433–435, 482
Social needs, 382
Social responsibility perspective, 146
Social Security, 299
Socialized power, 384
Socially responsible organizations, 146
Sociometric Solutions, 475

Sociotechnical systems   An approach to job design that attempts to redesign tasks to optimize operation of a new technology while preserving employees' interpersonal relationships and other human aspects of the work, **511**

SOEs. *See* State-owned enterprises (SOEs)
Soft drinks, 45
Soft skills, 291
Software piracy, 501
Solar power, 532
Solidarium, 198
Sony, 194, 518, 519
SoulCycle, 502
SoundCloud, 429, 438, 450
South America, 166
Southwest Airlines, 33, 56, 233
SpaceX, 114, 196
Spacious, 413

Span of control   The number of subordinates who report directly to an executive or supervisor, **228**

Specialization   A process in which different individuals and units perform different tasks, **224**

Speed   Fast and timely execution, response, and delivery of results, 9–**10**

Sport Clips, 208

Spotify, 192, 492
Spreadshirt.com, 196
Sprint, 434
Sproxil, 198
Stabilization relationships, 418

Staff departments   Units that support line departments, **232**

Staffing, 282–289

Stakeholders   Groups and individuals who affect and are affected by the achievement of the organization's mission, goals, and strategies, **114**

Stand by Task Force (SBTF), 7

Standard   Expected performance for a given goal: a target that establishes a desired performance level, motivates performance, and serves as a benchmark against which actual performance is assessed, **461**

Standard and Poor's 500, 41

Standardization   Establishing common routines and procedures that apply uniformly to everyone, **242**

Stanley Lynch Investment Group, 249
Staples, 46
Starbucks, 8, 9, 46, 53, 144, 189, 201, 212, 255, 386, 482
Stars, 121, 122
Start-Up Chile, 166
Startup Health, 196
Startupbootcamp, 202
Starwood Hotels, 160
State Farm Insurance, 388
State Grid, 4, 161
State-owned enterprises (SOEs), 175
Status symbols, 60
Steinway, 123
Stereotyping, 323–324

Stewardship   Contributing to the long-term welfare of others, **144**

Stock indexes, 41
Stock market, 41–42
Stock options, 298–299, 376

Stockholders' equity   The amount accruing to the corporation's owners, **471**

Stories, 60
Storytelling, 442

Strategic alliance   A formal relationship created among independent organizations with the purpose of joint pursuit of mutual goals, **255**, 256

Strategic budget, 125

Strategic control system   A system designed to support managers in evaluating the organization's progress regarding its strategy and, when discrepancies exist, taking corrective action, **124**–125

Strategic goals   Major targets or end results relating to the organization's long-term survival, value, and growth, **108**

Strategic human resources management, 278–282
Strategic intervention, 521

Strategic leadership   Behavior that gives purpose and meaning to organizations, envisioning and creating a positive future, **345**–346

Strategic management   A process that involves managers from all parts of the organization in the formulation and implementation of strategic goals and strategies, **112**

business strategy, 122–123
corporate strategy, 120–122
external opportunities and threats, 114–116
functional strategy, 123
internal strengths and weaknesses, 116–118
mission, vision, goals, 113–114
resources and core capabilities, 116–117, 118
steps in process, 112–113
strategic control, 124–125
strategy implementation, 123–124
SWOT analysis, 118–120
Strategic manager, 15

Strategic maneuvering   An organization's conscious efforts to change the boundaries of its task environment, **55**

Strategic planning   A set of procedures for making decisions about the organization's long-term goals and strategies, **108**–109, 111–112. *See also* Planning

Strategic triangle, 260

Strategic vision   The long-term direction and strategic intent of a company, **113**

Strategy   A pattern of actions and resource allocations designed to achieve the organization's goals, **108**, 109

Strategy implementation, 123–124

Strategy map A depiction of how an organization plans to convert its various assets into desired outcomes, 110, 111, **478**, 479

Streamed music, 492

Stretch goals Targets that are particularly demanding, sometimes even thought to be impossible, **374**

Strikes, 302
Strong organization culture, 59

Structured interview Selection technique that involves asking all applicants the same questions and comparing their responses to a standardized set of answers, **283**

Student Movement for Real Change (SMRC), 76
Student social entrepreneurs, 167
Subject project group processes worksheet, 424

Subscription model Charging fees for site visits, **196**

Substitute, 49, 53

Substitutes for leadership Factors in the workplace that can exert the same influence on employees as leaders would provide, **357**–358

Subunits Subdivisions of an organization, **228**

Subway, 174, 265
Suja Juice, 192
Sun Microsystems, 319
Super Mario Run, 55
Supercuts, 195

Superordinate goals Higher-level goals taking priority over specific individual or group goals, **420**

Superstorm Sandy, 93
Supervisor, 16

Supervisory leadership Behavior that provides guidance, support, and corrective feedback for day-to-day activities, **345**

Suppliers, 50, 53

Supply chain management The managing of the network of facilities and people that obtain materials from outside the organization, transform them into products, and distribute them to customers, **50**

Support groups, 330–331
Supportive leadership, 356

Sustainability Minimizing the use of resources, especially those that are polluting and nonrenewable, **11**. *See also* Natural environment and sustainability

Sustainability audit, 468–469

Sustainable growth Economic growth and development that meets present needs without harming the needs of future generations, **149**

Sweatshops, 137
Sweet Bites, 167

Switching costs Fixed costs buyers face when they change suppliers, **50**

SWOT analysis A comparison of strengths, weaknesses, opportunities, and threats that helps executives formulate strategy, **118**–120

Symbols, rites, and ceremonies, 60
Sysco, 55

Systematic management A classical management approach that attempted to build into operations the specific procedures and processes that would ensure coordination of effort to achieve established goals and plans, **29**

Systems accommodations, 331

Systems theory A theory stating that an organization is a managed system that changes inputs into outputs, **33**–34

T

T-shaped manager, 6
Tactical behavior, 475–476

Tactical planning A set of procedures for translating broad strategic goals and plans into specific goals and plans that are relevant to a distinct portion of the organization, such as a functional area like marketing, **109**

Taft-Hartley Act, 301
TAG Heuer, 255
Take-make-waste approach, 147
Target, 60, 110, 233, 285, 322, 459
Tariffs, 169–170, 174
Task force, 244
Task identity, 388

Task-motivated leadership Leadership that places primary emphasis on completing a task, **355**

Task performance behaviors Actions taken to ensure that the work group or organization reaches its goals, **349**

Task significance, 388

Task specialist role An individual who has more advanced job-related skills and abilities than other group members possess, **414**

Tata Consulting Services (TCS), 467
Tata Group, 165
Tata Motors, 67
TD Bank, 477

Team A small number of people with complementary skills who are committed to a common purpose, set of performance goals, and approach for which they hold themselves mutually accountable, **408**. *See also* Teamwork

Team leader, 16

Team maintenance role Individual who develops and maintains team harmony, **414**

Team management, 352
Team Rubicon, 386

Team training Training that provides employees with the skills and perspectives they need to collaborate with others, **291**

Teaming A strategy of teamwork on the fly, creating many temporary, changing teams, 405

Teamwork, 402–426
    accountability, 412
    cohesiveness, 414–417
    conflict, 418–421
    contributions of teams, 404
    critical periods, 409
    lateral role relationships, 418
    managing outward, 417
    member contributions, 412–413
    motivation, 412
    norms, 413–414
    performance focus, 411
    rewards, 412, 416
    roles, 414
    self-managed teams, 406–407
    size of team, 416
    stages of team development, 409
    team effectiveness, 411
    teaming, 405
    types of teams, 404–407
    why groups fail?, 410–411

Technical innovator A person who develops a new technology or has the key skills to install and operate the technology, **507**

Technical skill   The ability to perform a specialized task involving a particular method or process, **17**–18

Techno-structural intervention, 521
Technological analysis, 115
Technological change, 5–6
Technological discoveries, 194
Technological feasibility, 500–501, 503

Technology   The systematic application of scientific knowledge to a new product, process, or service, 42–43, **265**, 490. *See also* Managing technology and innovation

Technology acquisition options, 504–506

Technology audit   Process of clarifying the key technologies on which an organization depends, **498**

Technology champions, 502
Technology configurations, 265–266
Technology followership, 497–498
Technology leadership, 495–497

Technology life cycle   A predictable pattern followed by a technological innovation, from its inception and development to market saturation and replacement, **491**–492

Technology trading, 505
TechStars, 202
Teco Energy, 460
Termination-at-will, 287

Termination interview   A discussion between a manager and an employee about the employee's dismissal, **288**

Tesla Motors, 489, 503
Texas Instruments, 125
Texas Roadhouse, 288
The Alternative Board, 227
The Event Studio, 202
Theory of Moral Sentiments, The (Smith), 146
Theory of Social and Economic Organizations (Weber), 32
Theory X, 33
Theory Y, 33
ThinkImpact, 76

Third-country nationals   Natives of a country other than the home country or the host country of an overseas subsidiary, **176**

Thomson Venture Economics, 219
Threat of entry, 53
3D printing, 42, 116, 501
3M, 117, 344, 404, 474, 495, 496, 508, 518, 519

360-degree appraisal   Process of using multiple sources of appraisal to gain a comprehensive perspective on one's performance, **295**

Timberland, 149

Time-based competition (TBC)   Strategies aimed at reducing the total time needed to deliver a good or service, 268–**269**

Time Inc., 236, 238
Time pressures, 84
Time Warner Cable (TWC), 231, 459
Time zone differences, 182
Title VII of Civil Rights Act of 1964, 289, 317
TOMS, 463
Tone of voice, 441

Top-level managers   Senior executives responsible for the overall management and effectiveness of the organization, **15**–16

Top management team (TMT), 15, 227

Total organization change   Introducing and sustaining multiple policies, practices, and procedures across multiple units and levels, **528**

Total quality management (TQM)   An integrative approach to management that supports the attainment of customer satisfaction through a wide variety of tools and techniques that result in high-quality goods and services, **262**

Toxic Release Inventory (TRI), 68
Toyota, 6, 149, 161, 170, 256, 505
Toys "R" Us, 74
TQM. *See* Total quality management (TQM)

Tragedy of the commons   The environmental destruction that results as individuals and businesses consume finite resources (the commons) to serve their short-term interests without regard for the long-term consequences, **69**

Training   Teaching lower-level employees how to perform their present jobs, **290**

Training ABC, 329
Training and development, 290–291
Trait appraisals, 293

Trait approach   A leadership perspective that attempts to determine the personal characteristics that great leaders share, **348**

Transaction fee model   Charging fees for goods and services, **196**

Transactional leaders   Leaders who manage through transactions, using their legitimate, reward, and coercive powers to give commands and exchange rewards for services rendered, **359**

Transcendent education   An education with five higher goals that balance self-interest with responsibility to others, **145**

Transfer price   Price charged by one unit for a good or service provided to another unit within the organization, **481**

Transformational leader   A leader who motivates people to transcend their personal interests for the good of the group, **359**

Transnational model   An organizational model characterized by centralizing certain functions in locations that best achieve cost economies; basing other functions in the company's national subsidiaries to facilitate greater local responsiveness; and fostering communication among subsidiaries to permit transfer of technological expertise and skills, 168, **171**–173

Transnational teams   Teams composed of multinational members whose activities span multiple countries. Such teams differ from other work teams by being multicultural and by often being geographically dispersed, being psychologically distant, and working on highly complex projects having considerable impact on company objectives, **405**

Trendsetter Barometer Business Outlook, 54
TRI. *See* Toxic Release Inventory (TRI)
TripAdvisor, 6

Triple bottom line   Economic, social, and environmental performance, **144**

Trivago, 521
TrueNorth chip, 499
Truth-telling/lying, 133
TRW, 238
Tunisia, 182
Twitter, 6, 283, 285, 321, 433, 434
Two-boss employee, 239
Two-boss manager, 239

Two-factor theory   Herzberg's theory describing two factors affecting people's work motivation and satisfaction, **387**

Two-pizza rule, 416

Two-way communication   A process in which information flows in two directions—the receiver provides feedback, and the sender is receptive to the feedback, **430**–431

Two-way relationship, 21

Tyranny of the *or* The belief that things must be either A or B and cannot be both; that only one goal and not another can be attained, **519**

U

Uber, 71, 81, 94, 495
Ultra Mobile, 383

Uncertainty The state that exists when decision makers have insufficient information, **75**

Uncertainty avoidance, 179
Unemployment insurance, 299

Unfreezing Realizing that current practices are inappropriate and that new behavior is necessary, **525**

Unfreezing/moving/refreezing model, 523–525
Unilever, 144
Unilever purchase of Ben & Jerry's, 150
Union Pacific, 342

Union shop An organization with a union and a union security clause specifying that workers must join the union after a set period of time, **302**

Unionization, 300–303
Unisys, 434
United Airlines, 262
United Nations, 7
United States
    competitive health benefits, 385
    contingent workers, 57
    electricity, 532
    fast-trackers, 180
    federal government, 41
    foreign direct investment (FDI), 160
    foreign oil, 167
    generational tipping point, 241
    health care sector, 196
    illiteracy, 444
    manufacturing employment, 162
    meetings, 179
    melting pot, 313
    silence, 442
    skills shortage, 281
    sustainability, 11
    tariffs, 169

Unity-of-command principle A structure in which each worker reports to one boss, who in turn reports to one boss, **238**

Universalism The ethical system stating that all people should uphold

certain values that society needs to function, **135**

University of Michigan studies, 351
University system analysis worksheet, 36

Upward communication Information that flows from lower to higher levels in the organization's hierarchy, **447–448**

U.S. Air Force Research Lab, 499
U.S. Army, 464
U.S. Department of Veterans Affairs, 476
USA Hospital Supply, 27
USAA, 342

Utilitarianism An ethical system stating that the greatest good for the greatest number should be the overriding concern of decision makers, 135, **136**

V

Valence The value an outcome holds for the person contemplating it, **380**

Validity The degree to which a selection test predicts or correlates with job performance, **286**

Value The monetary amount associated with how well a job, task, good, or service meets users' needs, **12**

Value-added manufacturing, 270

Value chain The sequence of activities that flow from raw materials to the delivery of a good or service, with additional value created at each step, **261**–262

Vanity, 477
Veil of ignorance, 141
Venture capitalists, 208
Verizon, 83, 342

Vertical integration The acquisition or development of new businesses that produce parts or components of the organization's product, **121**

Vertical structure, 226–232
Viacom, 56
Viagra, 496
Video call, 437
Videoconferencing, 433

Vigilance A process in which a decision maker carefully executes all stages of decision making, **82**

Virginia Mason Medical Center, 466
Virtual corporation, 240
Virtual groups, 409

Virtual office A mobile office in which people can work anywhere, as long as they have the tools to communicate with customers and colleagues, **435–437**

Virtual teams Teams that are physically dispersed and communicate electronically more than face-to-face, **405**, 406

Virtue ethics Perspective that what is moral comes from what a mature person with "good" moral character would deem right, 135, **136**–137

Vision A mental image of a possible and desirable future state of the organization, **343**–344, 345

Vizio, 491
VMware, 436
Vocational Rehabilitation Act, 289
Volkswagen, 161
Voluntary action, 56

Vroom model A situational model that focuses on the participative dimension of leadership, **353**–354

VTOS, 94

W

Wage stagnation, 162
Wages, 296
Wagner Act, 301
Walgreens, 322
Walmart, 4, 106, 110, 145, 161, 194, 257, 258, 298, 518, 519, 520
Walt Disney Company, 59, 103–104, 112, 116, 125, 160, 194, 518, 519
Warner Music, 56
Water ATMs, 494
Water shortage, 150
Weak organization culture, 59
Wealth of Nations, The (Smith), 146
Web 2.0, 5
Web 3.0, 5
WebEx, 433
Wegmans Food Markets, 383
Welcyon, 195
Wellness programs, 459

Wells Fargo, 10, 132
Western Europe, 164
Weyerhaeuser Company, 56
What I Want from My Job worksheet, 399
WhatsApp, 60, 497
Whirlpool, 177
Whistleblowing, 143
Whole Foods Market, 110, 144, 361, 373,
    403, 407, 422
Whole Planet Foundation, 144
Wholly owned subsidiary, 173, 175–176
Wild Flavors, 50
Wildcat strike, 302
Wind farms, 532
Wipro, 165, 268
Wish You Wood Toy Store, 129
W.L. Gore, 117, 210, 383
Women
    excellent companies to work for, 317
    glass ceiling, 315
    sexual harassment, 316–317, 318
    ten most powerful women
        executives, 316
Woody Manufacturing Company, 273–274

Word choice, 440–441
Work–life balance, 316
Work-Out, 271

Work teams   Teams that make or do
things like manufacture, assemble, sell,
or provide service, **404**

Workers' compensation, 299
Workflow relationships, 418
Workforce reductions, 286–288
Working group, 408
Working overseas, 176–177
Workplace fatalities, 300
Worksheets. *See* Experiential exercises
World Bank, 150
World-class companies, 518–520, 535
World Trade Organization (WTO), 163
WorldCom, 137
Worldwide Games, 514–515
Worst-case scenario, 54
Writing skills, 440
Written communication, 433
WTO. *See* World Trade Organization
   (WTO)

X
Xerox, 53, 170, 319, 328

Y
Y Combinator, 202
Yahoo!, 83, 259
Yammer, 406
Yelp, 6
YouEarnedIt, 380
YouTube, 433
Yum! Brands, 4, 169

Z
Zappos, 6, 99–100, 117, 192, 207, 337–338,
   361
Zazzle.com, 196
Zenith, 171
Zero Waste Solutions, 192
Zipcar, 202
Zooniverse, 242
Zooppa, 91

A

Aaron, J. R., 571
Able, V., 67
Ableson, Mike, 108
Abood, Farif Ali, 116
Abrams, L., 586
Ackerman, T., 568
Ackermann, F., 591
Adams, J., 578
Adams, R. J., 191
Adams, S., 568, 579
Aditya, R., 573, 574
Adkins, A., 565, 577
Adler, N., 326, 552, 571, 577
Adler, P., 549, 565, 594
Agarwal, D., 564, 580
Aghili, S., 587
Agle, B., 574
Aguinis, H., 557
Aguirre, D., 592
Ahmed, M., 570
Ahmed, Umair, 588
Aiken, C., 592
Ailes, Roger, 132
Aiman-Smith, Lynda, 591
Aime, F., 580
Ainina, M. Fall, 572
Akerson, Daniel, 223, 237
Akhtar, Omar, 576
Alawadhi, N., 559
Albert, E., 557
Alderfer, C., 577
Aldrich, H., 561
Aldridge, J., 563
Alexander, E., 552, 583
Ali, A. J., 563
Ali, S., 584
Alic, M., 587
Allen, Paul, 192
Allen, S. J., 576
Allinson, R. E., 556
Almirall, Esteve, 590
Alpern, M., 592
Alsin, Arne, 556
Altaffer, A., 228
Amabile, T. M., 553, 578
Amano, Tomofumi, 559
Amason, A., 552
Anand, N., 566
Anand, V., 555, 556
Anatol, K., 585
Ancona, D. G., 417, 582
Anderson, Ariston, 583
Anderson, Brian S., 589
Anderson, D., 558
Anderson, K., 560
Anderson, R., 558
Anderson, R. C., 571
Andersson, M., 580
Andreason, A. W., 560
Andrew, C., 589
Ang, S., 574
Anner, J., 586
Ante, S., 586

Anthony, S. D., 588, 589
Antonakis, J., 548
Applebaum, R., 585
Applegate, M., 568
Aquila, F., 559
Aquino, K., 582
Arad, S., 586
Aragon-Correa, J. A., 557
Aral, S., 584
Aranda, E., 581
Arandjelovic, P., 590
Areddy, J., 558
Arena, Michael, 509
Arenas, A., 583
Arend, R., 561
Arends, L., 576, 581
Argenti, J., 563
Argyris, C., 578, 583
Armenakis, A., 592
Armstron-Stassen, M., 578
Arnold, Mason, 280
Arnoldy, B., 549
Arroniz, I., 588
Arther, M. B., 548
Arthur, J., 569
Arthur, W., Jr., 568
Aryee, S., 564
Ash, Mary Kay, 385
Ash, R. A., 568
Ashcroft, John, 370
Ashforth, B., 555, 556
Ashgar, R., 570
Ashkanasy, N., 548
Ashkenas, R., 288, 563, 586
Athos, A., 585
Atkins, P. W. B., 577
Attwood, Hannah, 205
Atwater, L., 574
Austen, B., 590
Austin, N., 578
Austin, Robert, 547
Autio, E., 563
Avalos, G., 571
Avolio, B., 555, 575
Axtell, C., 583

B

Baccardax, M., 589
Bacharach, S., 93, 553
Bachelder, Cheryl, 361
Bacher, J., 569
Badal, S., 573
Badorocco, J., 555
Baer, Drake, 588
Bahn, S., 564
Bailey, D., 580
Bailey, Sean, 103
Bailey, W., 555
Baird, L., 233
Bairn-Birch, N., 557
Balakrishnan, Anita, 558
Baldoni, John, 581
Baldwin, C. Y., 588

Baldwin, Timothy, 571
Bales, R. F., 582
Balkundi, P., 574
Ball, G., 577
Ball, J., 558
Ballam, D. A., 568
Balogun, J., 592, 593
Baltes, B., 584
Bamberger, P., 93, 553, 569
Banaji, M., 555, 556
Bandler, J., 569
Banga, Ajay, 319
Banjo, Shelly, 547
Banker, R., 580, 582
Bansal, P., 557
Bardes, M., 575
Barinka, A., 555
Barkema, H., 581
Barker, J., 564
Barling, J., 575, 579
Barnard, Chester, 31
Barnes, Brooks, 553, 554, 555
Barnes, C., 580, 581
Barnes, D., 580
Baron, R. A., 563
Barra, Mary, 237, 245, 316
Barratt-Pugh, L., 564
Barrett, Amy, 552
Barrick, M., 575
Barry, B., 592, 593
Barry, L., 587
Bartlett, C., 168, 548, 564, 576, 579
Bartol, K., 578, 581, 584
Barton, D., 552, 557
Barton, Dorothy Leonard, 508
Barton, M., 553
Bartunek, J., 556, 563, 592, 593
Baruck, Y., 594
Bass, B., 551, 552, 574, 575
Bateman, T., 354, 382, 548, 552, 563, 579, 593, 594
Battilan, J., 561, 564
Bauer, C., 584
Bauer, T., 547, 579
Bauerlein, Valerie, 590
Baughman, K., 568
Baum, J., 562, 573
Baysinger, R. A., 569
Bazerman, M., 551, 552, 555, 556
Bazigos, M., 238
Beal, Adam M., 568
Bear, M., 553
Beasley, R. C., 560
Beaudoin, C., 576
Beckhard, R., 593
Bedeian, Arthur G., 25, 26, 564
Bednarz, Ann, 555
Beer, M., 124, 592, 593
Beers, C., 584
Beersma, B., 580
Begin, Sherri, 547
Begley, T. M., 575
Behfar, K., 560
Behr, P., 574

Beinhocker, E., 593
Belanger, Lydia, 588
Belkin, L., 584
Bell, G., 593
Belogolovsky, E., 569
Benner, M., 548
Bennett, Jessica, 571
Bennett, Steve, 258
Bennis, W., 572, 573, 575, 582
Bensen, Connie, 550
Bentein, K., 575
Bergen, M. E., 552
Bergeson, L. L., 587
Berkley, J., 593
Berkley, R. A., 568
Berkowitz, L., 578
Berkowitz, M., 555
Berland, Edelman, 555
Berman-Gorvine, M., 586
Bernardin, H., 569
Bernasco, W., 564
Berra, Yogi, 444
Berson, Brett, 572
Bertolini, Mark, 18, 548
Bertrand, M., 571
Bezos, Jeff, 39, 52, 61, 359
Bezukova, Katerina, 572
Bian, Lin, 570
Bickford, D. J., 589
Bierce, Ambrose, 188
Bierly, P., 588
Bies, R., 556, 585
Bigelow, Robert, 196
Biley, W., 555
Bilimoria, D., 585
Billing, T., 580
Billington, C., 550
Binney, G., 537, 594
Birdwell, L., 577
Birkinshaw, J., 588, 591
Bishop, T., 555
Bisson, P., 589
Blackburn, R., 580
Bladt, Jeff, 585
Blake, Brock, 192
Blake, R., 574
Blake, Robert Rogers, 352
Blake, S., 571
Blancero, D., 570
Blanchard, K., 355, 574
Blankenship, Chip, 271
Blenko, M., 551
Block, P., 576
Blodget, H., 338
Bluestein, A., 554, 572
Blum, M., 421, 583
Blume, Brian, 571
Blumenthal, D., 581
Boal, K., 573
Bock, Laszlo, 277, 292
Boehm, R., 236
Boehm, S., 574
Boer, H., 564
Bohlander, G., 296, 297, 318, 570, 571

Boitnott, J., 588
Bolelovic, L., 562
Bonaparte, Napoleon, 228
Bonett, D., 579
Bono, J., 573, 575, 576
Boo, Michael, 478
Boone, Larry W., 575, 576
Bordia, P., 586
Borison, R., 192
Bornstein, D., 561
Borrelli, Christopher, 552
Bort, J., 555, 556
Bossidy, L., 584
Boulton, Clint, 589
Boulton, Guy, 567
Bourgeois, L. J., III, 553
Bowen, D., 574, 579, 591
Bowen, H. K., 591
Bower, J., 591
Bowie, Carol, 570
Boyatzis, R., 548, 577
Boyd, B., 584
Bozek, A., 567
Bozeman, David P., 319
Bracker, J., 553
Bradberry, T., 577
Bradley, B., 575
Bradley, T., 584
Bradshaw, T., 550
Branson, Richard, 343, 358, 360
Braun, M., 588
Brett, J., 560, 582, 585
Bricklin, D., 561
Bridgman, T., 592
Brief, A., 593
Bright, J. E. H., 577
Brin, Sergei, 192
Brockner, J., 578
Brodsky, Norm, 562
Brodt, S., 583
Brodwin, D., 593
Brodzinski, J., 572
Brookes, R., 555
Brown, A., 570
Brown, K., 592
Brown, Lester, 158
Brown, M., 556, 574
Brown, T., 591
Bruch, H., 574
Brueck, H., 555
Bruno, V., 591
Bruns, H., 582
Brush, C., 561
Brustein, J., 568
Bryan, L., 552, 573
Bryant, A., 569, 570
Buchanan, L., 562
Buchanan, Russ, 579
Buchholtz, A. K., 588
Buchko, A. A., 550
Buck, M. L., 572
Bucking, J. W., 569
Buckley, C., 559
Buckley, George, 344, 474

Buckley, M., 566
Bughin, J., 589
Bulin, L., 590
Buller, P., 560
Buluswar, M., 552
Bunch, John, 99
Bunge, J., 550
Burgelman, R. A., 588
Burgers, W. P., 551
Burkart, M., 572
Burke, L., 586
Burkemper, A., 561
Burks, Jewel, 192
Burkus, David, 580
Burnes, B., 591
Burnham, Kristin, 577
Burns, Janet, 551
Burns, M., 566
Burns, T., 252, 565
Burritt, C., 544
Busch, Elizabeth, 202
Butcher, V., 575
Butler, T., 585
Butterfield, K., 577
Butts, M. M., 578
Buyens, D., 553
Byham, W. C., 582
Bylund, Anders, 553
Bynum, L., 566
Byrd, M. J., 560
Byrnes, Brendan, 554
Byron, K., 571, 584

C

Caballero, J., 574
Cackowski, D., 564
Caesar, Julius, 340, 348
Cai, D., 551
Cain, Susan, 349
Caldicott, S., 576
Cameron, K., 551, 575, 594
Cameron, S., 578
Camp, R. C., 563
Campbell, Mikey, 570
Campion, M., 568, 578
Campisi, V., 552
Cancino, Alejandra, 573
Candee, D., 555
Cao, J., 568
Capell, P., 560
Cappelli, P., 573
Caprar, D., 580
Cardenal, A., 567
Cardon, M., 562
Cardwell, D., 593
Carey, G., 567
Carlson, J. R., 584
Caron, A., 582
Carr, A., 554, 587
Carr, L., 568
Carraher, S., 566
Carroll, A., 557
Carson, Biz, 553

Carson, J., 575, 582
Carson, Rachel, 69
Carstedt, G., 557
Carton, A., 573, 593
Cartwright, D., 573
Cartwright, Mary Jo, 505
Casadesus-Masanell, Ramon, 590
Cascio, Wayne F., 591
Case, D., 584
Case, J., 585
Casnocha, B., 579
Casselman, B., 560
Casserly, Meghan, 567
Catz, Safra, 316
Cendrowski, S., 547
Cerasoli, C., 578
Chafkin, C. Logorio, 572
Chakraborty, S., 580
Chakravorty, S., 587
Chambers, G. J., 564
Chambers, John, 360, 404, 440
Chamorro-Premuzic, T., 574
Champion, J., 100, 101, 544, 546
Champy, J., 566
Chandler, Alfred, 257, 566
Chang, Do Won, 319
Chang, Kenneth, 591
Charan, R., 574, 584
Chasan, Emily, 578
Chase, Robin, 202
Chatman, J., 582
Chau, Samantha L., 587
Chaykowski, Kathleen, 547, 548, 549
Chen, G., 580, 581
Chen, Ming-Jer, 591
Chen, N., 582, 586
Chen, T., 575, 582
Chen, Z. X., 564, 578
Chenault, Kenneth, 319
Cheney, G., 587
Cheramie, R., 577
Chesbrough, Henry, 590
Cheung, H., 572
Cheung, S., 553
Chew, Ian, 588
Chhabra, E., 551
Chilakapati, Rakesh, 77, 78, 80
Chiniara, M., 575
Chitre, S., 558
Cho, Y., 587
Choi, H., 581
Chon, G., 550
Chouinard, Y., 558
Chow, C. W., 587
Christensen, C., 495, 588, 589
Christensen, Tanner, 588
Christian, M. S., 581
Chrysostome, Elie, 560
Chu, C., 585
Chua, C. H., 583
Chugh, D., 555, 556
Chui, M., 558
Chul, M., 589
Chung, C. H., 567

Chung, Q. B., 564
Cianci, A., 576
Cianni, M., 580, 582
Cimilluca, D., 550
Cino, J., 589
Clark, Catherine, 463
Clark, J., 573, 593
Clark, K. B., 588, 591
Clayton, N., 590
Clifford, Catherine, 560, 563, 572
Clifton, J., 560
Cline, B. N., 571
Clinton, Bill, 167, 258
Clough, M. William, 575
Cobb, A., 583
Cober, A. B., 577
Cochran, P., 556
Coekly, E., 548
Cohen, S., 580
Cohler, Matt, 22
Colao, J. J., 561
Colbert, A., 575
Colbert, J. L., 587
Cole, S., 561
Colella, A., 569
Collins, D., 569
Collins, J., 458, 518–520, 536, 537, 561, 575, 586, 591, 594
Collis, D. J., 550, 554
Colony, G., 574
Colquitt, J., 575, 578
Coltrin, Sally A., 25, 26
Colvin, G., 548, 558, 565, 581, 591
Commoner, Barry, 69
Comstock, T. W., 583, 585
Condon, S., 593
Conerly, K., 582
Conger, J., 345, 569, 573, 584, 594
Conner, C., 561, 584
Conner, D. R., 592, 594
Connolly, T., 577
Conti, R., 578
Conway, R., 562
Cook, Tim, 311, 332, 360
Cooke, B., 591
Cooke, R. A., 556
Coon, H., 578
Coons, Rebecca, 587
Cooper, C., 176, 567, 576, 582
Cooper Procter, William, 32
Copeland, M., 562
Corbett, A., 567
Cordeiro, A., 562
Cording, M., 557
Corkery, M., 555
Cortada, J. W., 548
Cortina, J., 575, 582
Cory, K. D., 550
Cosier, R., 552
Cossin, D., 574
Cotton, R., 549
Courtney, H., 593
Courtright, S., 581
Cowell, J., 585

Cox, B., 553
Cox, T., 571
Coy, Peter, 566
Coyne, K., 553
Coyne, S., 553
Crabtree, S., 569
Cramton, C., 583
Crane, A., 555
Crant, J. M., 563
Crawford, E., 574, 578
Creech, B., 566
Cregan, C., 571
Creswell, J., 566
Crisp, C. B., 583
Crispin, G., 568
Cronin, B., 570
Crooks, Ed, 567
Cropanzano, R., 579
Crosby, F. J., 572
Cross, R., 233, 581, 583, 586
Crossan, M., 575
Crossley, C., 576
Crowley, Mark C., 576, 577, 5790
Crozier, Jen, 558
Cuban, Mark, 358
Culbertson, S., 574
Cullen, J., 555, 556, 565
Culpan, T., 218
Cumming, D., 571
Cummings, A., 578
Cummings, L., 553, 578
Cummings, S., 592
Cummings, T., 521, 582, 592
Curtin, M., 573

D

Dacin, M. T., 561
Dacin, P., 561
Daft, R., 550, 584
Dahl, D., 565
Dahl, M., 579
Dahlin, K., 582
Dahling, Jason J., 587
Daily, C. M., 563
Dalrymple, J., 218
Dalton, D. R., 563
D'Amelio, A., 592
Darcy, K., 555
Dasborough, M., 548
D'Aveni, R. A., 550
Davenport, C., 594
Davidson, M., 324, 571, 572
Davies, Alex, 565
Davila, A., 586
Davis, Andrea, 579
Davis, Edward W., 550
Davis, Grant, 587
Davis, I., 593
Davis, K., 586
Davis, Keith, 273
Davis, S., 552, 561, 564
Davison, S., 580
Day, D. L., 590

Day, D. V., 574
Day, G. S., 564
Day, Sudipto, 557
de Castro, A., 579
De Cremer, D., 578
De Dreu, C., 552
De George, R. T., 556
de Janasz, Suzanne, 25, 155, 397, 398, 542
de la Merced, M., 565
de Vise, Daniel, 571
De Vries, W., 582
de WeerdNederhof, P. C., 564
de Wit, F. R. C., 582
Dean, J., 551, 552, 553, 566
Deardorff, Julie, 593
DeChurch, L. A., 581, 583
Decker, C. D., 585
DeGraff, Jeff, 590
DeGroot, Christine, 314
Deimler, M., 591
DeJoy, D. M., 578
Dekas, K., 547
Delaney, Hollie, 338
della Cava, Marco, 572
Delmas, M., 557
DeMers, J., 584
Deming, W. Edwards, 9, 262, 263, 547
DeNisi, A., 567, 585
Denning, S., 100
Dent, E. B., 592
DeRue, D., 566, 576, 580, 581
Desai, A. B., 560
Dess, G. G., 563
DeStobbeleir, S. Ashford, 553
Deutsch, C., 583
Devine, C., 587
Dewan, R., 589
DeWitt, R.-L., 568
Dhillon, K., 559
Dhiraj, Amarendra Bhushan, 547, 548, 549
Diaz-Uda, A., 571
Dickson, M., 584
Diener, E., 579
Dienhart, J., 556
Difonzo, N., 586
D'Innocenzo, M. Lucian, 578
Dionne, S., 574
Do, B., 592, 593
Dobbs, R., 568, 589
Doerr, E., 566
Dollard, S., 547
Donahue, L., 580
D'Onfro, Jillian, 549, 567
Donnelly, J., Jr., 75
Donnelly, T., 583
Donovan, A., 570
Donovan, M. A., 586
Dooley, R., 552
Doppelt, B., 548, 557
Dorfman, J., 569
Dorfman, P., 574
Dou, E., 218
Douma, B., 576
Dowd, Karen O. 25, 155, 397, 398, 542

Doz, Y., 559, 592
Drach-Zahavy, A., 580
Dragija, Martina, 587
Drake, N., 554
Drayton, Bill, 13
Dreiling, Richard, 543
Driver, M., 562
Drnovsek, M., 562
Droge, C., 564
Drogus, J., 591
Drouin, M., 584
Drucker, Peter, 2, 21, 38, 204, 549, 562
Druskat, V. U., 582, 587
Dudley, Renee, 566
Duffy, M., 582
Duggan, Wayne, 565
Dulebohn, J., 567, 574
Dulski, Jen, 327
Dumaine, B., 548
Duncan, R., 233
Dunfee, T., 555
Dunnette, M. D., 419, 582
Dupre, Elyse, 551
Durham, C., 581
Dusumano, A., 550
Dutton, J., 548, 553, 575, 594
Dvir, T., 575
Dwertmann, D., 574
Dwoskin, E., 568
Dyer, L., 565

E

Early, P. C., 577, 580, 585
Eastman, L. J., 566
Economides, M. I., 589
Economy, P., 584
Eden, C., 591
Eden, D., 575
Edinger, S., 581
Edison, Thomas, 89, 492
Edmans, A., 579
Edmonson, A. C., 580
Edwards, Jim, 554
Edwards, M., 569
Edwards, Summer, 442
Egan, M., 549, 555, 559
Ehrnstein, Mark, 403
Einhorn, B., 218
Einstein, Albert, 89
Eisenberg, B., 570
Eisenhardt, K., 553, 579
Eisenhardt, M., 590
Eisenstat, R., 124, 555, 592
Ek, Daniel, 192
Ekegren, G., 577
Elahi, A., 568
Elavia, S., 589
Elliott, S., 559
Elliott-McCrea, Kellan, 572
Ellis, A. P. J., 564, 581
Ellis, K. M., 564
Ellison, J., 558
Ellison, Marvin, 319

Ells, Steve, 110
Ellwardt, L., 586
Ely, R. J., 572
Emerson, Ralph Waldo, 370, 439
England, Lucy, 583
Epitropaki, O., 575
Erdogan, B., 552, 579
Erez, A., 574
Erez, M., 581
Erhardt-Lewis, A., 587
Erickson, T., 551, 580
Ericsson, A., 548
Erlanger, S., 558
Ernst, H., 583
Ertug, G., 549
Erwin, D., 592
Esenhardt, K. M., 552
Esterl, M., 549
Etternson, R., 558
Ettkin, L. P., 567
Ettlie, J. E., 567
Etzion, D., 557
Eure, J., 586
Evans, J. R., 566
Evans, P., 550, 592
Evans, R., 552
Evanschitzky, Heiner, 579
Ewen, A. J., 569
Eyring, M., 67

F

Fahrbach, K., 588
Fairest, J., 592
Fairlie, R., 561
Falbe, C., 573
Faleye, O., 563
Fallon, N., 584
Fallow, N., 563
Fanelli, A., 574
Fang, M., 577
Farh, C., 582
Farh, J.-L., 582
Farmer, S., 553
Farnham, A., 556, 584
Farr, Christina, 586, 587
Farre-Mensa, J., 587
Farrell, C., 566
Farrell, D., 552
Farrell, S., 591, 594
Fay, C., 570
Fayol, Henri, 31
Feffer, M., 568, 587
Fehrenbacher, Katie, 590
Fellermanns, F., 553
Fellows, S., 553
Feloni, R., 100, 565, 570
Feng, J., 561, 562
Fenley, M., 574
Fenn, D., 561
Fenwick, M. S., 587
Ferguson, E., 568
Ferndale, Elaine, 559

Ferner, A., 564, 587
Ferrari, Bernard, 442, 585
Ferraro, G., 585
Ferrazzi, K., 584
Ferrell, O. C., 555, 556
Ferri-Reed, J., 580
Ferringer, M., 563
Ferris, T., 581
Fiedler, F. E., 354–355, 574
Field, A., 583, 586
Field, H., 569
Field, J., 580, 582
Fields, D. A., 590
Filbin, Bob, 585
Finegold, D., 577, 578
Finkelstein, S., 562, 564
Fisher, A., 569, 578
Fisher, L., 100
Fisher, R., 577
Fisher, S., 552
Flammer, C., 557
Flannery, John, 271
Flegenheimer, M., 592
Fleischauer, E., 580
Fleishman, E., 574
Fleming, P., 556
Flood, T., 585
Flores, N., 567
Florin, J., 563
Floyd, S., 554, 587
Flynn, B. B., 565
Flynn, F., 565, 577, 582, 583
Flynn, G., 570
Flynn, M., 570
Foderaro, L., 592
Foley, H., 562
Foley, R. T., 568
Folger, R., 578, 579
Folkman, Joseph, 572
Follet, Mary Parker, 31
Folz, C., 583
Fontein, D., 551
Forbes, D. P., 582
Forbes, M., 585
Ford, C. M., 578
Ford, Henry, 30, 58, 75, 121
Ford, J. D., 592
Ford, L., 572
Ford, L. W., 592
Ford, M., 578, 579
Ford, R. C., 564
Forelle, C., 569
Forrester, R., 564, 578
Fort, T., 556
Foti, R., 573
Fourne, J., 565
Fouts, P., 557
Fowler, Susan, 81, 552
Fowler, Tom, 586
Fraedrich, J., 555, 556
Frakt, A., 589
Francis, Pope, 538
Francis, S. C., 563
Francis, T., 576
Francoeur, C., 571

Frangos, Alex, 559
Frank, K. A., 588
Frankel, Todd C., 570
Frauenheim, E., 568
Frazier, Kenneth, 319, 502
Fredrickson, J. W., 554
Freeman, M., 578
Freeman, R. Edward, 554
Freeman, S. J., 566
French, J. R. P., 347, 573
Freshley, D. L., 443, 585
Frey-Mott, Anne, 202
Fried, Ina, 590
Fried, Limor, 194
Friedman, Milton, 146
Friedman, T., 569
Frier, Sarah, 559
Fritz, B., 558
Fritz, S. F., 335
Frost, P., 553
Fry, Erika, 579
Fry, R., 547
Fuchs, P. H., 588
Fuchs, S., 592
Fugate, M., 591
Fuld, Richard, 83
Fulk, J., 584
Fuller, J., 549
Fuller, T., 585
Fulmer, R. M., 586
Furst, S., 580
Fyxell, G., 552

G

Gabarro, J., 585
Gadiesh, O., 592
Gagnon, R., 586
Gaines, A., 576
Galan, Nely, 197
Galbraith, J., 488, 564, 565, 580
Galinsky, A., 555
Gallagher, M., 570
Gallo, A., 555
Galunic, C., 549
Galvin, B., 574
Gambhir, Ashish, 578
Gamer, D., 562
Gamm, L., 593
Gan, N., 559
Gandel, S., 558
Gandhi, Mahatma, 349
Gannon, M., 568
Gantt, Henry, 30
Garay, M., 550
Garbers, Y., 581
Garcia, A., 319
Gardner, H. K., 566
Gardner, J., 573, 585
Gardner, M., 584
Gardner, N., 567
Gargiuli, M., 549
Garlick, Saul, 76
Garr, S., 587

Garvin, D. A., 552, 565, 566
Garza, A. S., 564
Gates, Bill, 192
Gatewood, R., 569
Gebert, Diether, 571
Gee, G., 579
Gehlen, F. L., 551
Geiger, Daniel, 559
Gelles, D., 100, 548
Gellman, L., 567
Gennette, Jeff, 4
George, Bill, 555, 556
George, G., 563
George, J., 552
George, William, 19, 548
Gerbelli, L., 559
Gerhardt, M., 573
Gerhart, B., 569, 577
Germain, R., 564
Geroski, P. A., 589, 590
Gersick, C. J. G., 581
Gerstner, C. R., 574
Gerstner, Louis, 360
Gerwitz, J. L., 555
Gettys, C., 552
Ghoshal, S., 168, 564, 576, 579
Giacalone, R., 557
Giang, V., 554
Giard, Y., 587
Gibbs, M., 563
Gibson, C., 580, 581, 591
Gibson, J., 75
Gibson, L., 581
Giffi, C., 591
Gilbert, C., 30
Gilbert, J., 572, 592
Gilbreth, Frank and Lillian, 30
Gilchrist, K., 559
Gillett, R., 582, 585
Gillette, F., 547
Gilliland, S., 579
Gilmont, E. R., 565
Gilmore, J. H., 567
Gilson, L., 578, 581
Gino, F., 556, 573, 585
Gioia, D., 555, 573
Giorgi, S., 551
Glader, P., 555, 560
Gladstone, R., 570
Gladwell, Malcolm, 241
Glassberg, B., 584
Glater, J. D., 569, 587
Glavas, A., 557
Glickman, David, 383
Globe, D., 572
Glover, S., 556
Glueck, William F., 25, 26
Glunk, U., 548
Glynn, M., 551
Godrey, P., 557
Gold, M., 218
Goldapple, Lisa, 588
Goldberg, S. Galloway, 592
Goldenberg, Suzanne, 550
Goldman, D., 572

Goleman, D., 548, 573
Golson, Jordan, 590
Gomez-Mejia, 569
Gong, Y., 553
González, Angel, 550
González-Navarro, P., 584
Goodheim, L., 575
Goodnight, James, 371, 381, 394
Goodson, E., 585
Goodstein, L., 594
Goomas, David T., 587
Gopalakrishnan, S., 588
Gordon, J. A., 36
Gordon, Judith R., 26, 98
Goshal, S., 548, 550
Gottenbusch, Gary, 203–204
Goudreau, J., 569, 575, 584
Gouillart, F., 593
Gover, S. L., 133
Govindarajan, V., 578, 591
Gowan, J. A., Jr., 587
Gowdridge, A., 565
Gradwhol Smith, W., 574
Graebner, Melissa E., 590
Graen, G., 573
Grafton, L., 580
Graham, G., 585
Graham, K., 547
Grant, A., 573, 575, 581
Grant, S., 581
Gratton, L., 580
Gray, C., 569
Greathouse, J., 554
Green, Maria, 342
Green, S., 547, 591
Greenbaum, R., 575
Greenberg, E., 578, 579
Greenfield, R., 338, 583
Greening, D., 557
Greenwald, M., 547
Greer, L., 582
Griffin, Justine, 561
Griffith, Terri L., 591
Grimes, M., 561
Grisales, Claudia, 568
Groden, C., 559
Groening, Christopher, 579
Groscurth, C., 551
Gross, S., 569
Grosser, T., 586
Grote, D., 569
Grote, G., 579
Grother, P., 589
Grover, S. L., 555
Groysberg, Boris, 583, 585
Grunberg, L., 579
Grynbaum, Michael M., 549
Gryta, T., 550, 576
Guarraia, P., 567
Guerci, M., 571
Guest, D., 579
Guilhon, B., 588
Guion, Kathleen, 543
Gulate, R., 592
Gulati, R., 565, 594

Gundry, L. K., 590
Gunia, B., 556
Gunn, Dwyer, 570, 572
Gunther, M., 557
Guo, C., 548
Gupta, A., 552, 565, 591
Gurchiek, K., 338
Gurtner, S., 589
Gustafson, K., 547
Gustke, C., 553
Gutknecht, J., 585
Gutman, M., 585
Guy, M. E., 555
Guzzo, R., 593

H

Ha, A., 552
Haanaes, K., 557
Hackman, J. Richard, 387, 578, 579, 580,
    581, 582
Haden, Jeff, 288
Hadley, C., 553
Hagan, C., 569
Hagedoorn, J., 590
Hagen, A. F., 550
Hagey, K., 550
Hagiwara, Y., 589
Haidt, J., 579
Hale, J., 555
Hall, D. T., 585
Hall, E., 556
Hall, F., 556
Hall-Merenda, K. E., 575
Hallen, B., 562
Hallett, T., 593
Hallowel, E., 584
Halverson, K. C., 574
Hambrick, D., 554, 580
Hamel, G., 565, 588, 593
Hamermesh, R., 554
Hamilton, Lynn, 439
Hammer, M., 477, 566, 587
Handmaker, David, 119
Handy, C., 556, 557
Haney, W. V., 583
Hanna, J., 567
Hannah, S., 555
Hansen, F., 568
Hansen, Morten T., 547, 548
Hanson, Angela, 549
Hara, K., 564
Harbert, T., 586
Hardin, Garrett, 69
Hardy, K., 554
Harkins, S., 552
Harmans, Avery, 551
Harmon, S., 581
Harper, Stephen C., 586
Harrington, B., 585
Harris, E., 574
Harris, R., 593
Harrison, D., 556, 570
Harrison, J. S., 554

Hart, S. L., 548, 557, 558
Harter, J., 238, 579
Hartley, D. E., 568
Hartman, N. S., 576
Hartung, A., 552
Hartwick, J., 593
Harvey, S., 553
Harzing, A. W., 168, 559
Haspeslagh, P., 554
Hassan, F., 547
Hasson, R., 582
Hastings, Reed, 8, 443
Hathaway, I., 562
Hauenstein, N. M. A., 573
Hausler, Elizabeth, 362
Hay, B., 565
Hayek, M., 566
Hayes, T., 579
He, L., 586
Heaphy, E., 548
Heath, A., 192, 590
Hecht, J., 560
Hedlund, Marc, 328
Heffernan, Margaret, 563
Heijltjes, U., 548
Heimer, M., 555
Heineman, B. W., Jr., 556
Hellenbeck, J., 580, 581
Hellofs, L. L., 566
Hellriegel, D., 592
Helms, M. M., 567
Hendricks, Ken, 201
Heneman, H. G., III, 568
Henne, D., 579
Henning, E., 554
Henning, Peter, 94
Henshaw, Todd, 586
Henwood, C., 583
Herbert, Theodore T., 486
Hernandez, E., 584
Hernandez, M., 556
Herrmann, Pol, 559
Herron, M., 578
Hersey, P., 355, 574
Hertz-Lazarowitz, R., 573
Herzberg, Frederick, 387, 578
Hesketh, B., 568
Hess, A., 548
Hewlett, Bill, 194
Hewson, Marillyn, 316
Hickey, K., 203, 562
Higgins, E. T., 581
Hill, G. W., 552
Hill, L. A., 548, 594
Hill, N., 584
Hille, K., 560
Hiltrop, J.-M., 568
Hinchcliffe, D., 547
Hinds, P., 582, 583
Hipskind, M., 580
Hira, N. A., 571
Hisrich, R., 205, 562
Hitt, M. A., 554, 560, 561, 565, 573
Ho, Renyung, 585
Hodgetts, R. M., 586

Hoegl, M., 580, 583
Hoekstra, J., 592
Hoever, I., 581
Hoffher, Justine, 587, 588
Hoffman, Andrea, 311
Hoffman, R., 569, 579
Hofmann, D., 573
Hofstede, Geert, 179, 181
Hogg, M., 575, 582
Hoitash, R., 563
Hoitash, U., 563
Holder, Eric, 81
Hollenbeck, G. P., 585
Hollenbeck, J., 564, 566, 567, 580, 581
Holliday, C., 557
Holloway, C. A., 591
Holt, M., 582
Holusha, J., 93, 553
Hong, H., 559
Hope, K., 579
Hopkins, M., 585
Hoque, Z., 588
Horng, E., 584
Horowitz, E., 570
Horowitz, S., 549
Hosmer, L. T., 142, 152
Houghland, B., 547
House, Robert, 355, 573, 574
Hout, T. M., 567
Hovland, Kjetil Malkenes, 586
Howard, C., 192
Howard, E., 566, 594
Howell, J., 574, 575
Howell, L., 586
Howland, Daphne, 549
Hsieh, Tony, 99, 192, 207, 337, 343, 561
Huang, J., 553
Huang, L., 556, 562
Huang, Ryan, 587
Huber, V. L., 569
Huddleston, T., Jr., 555
Huffington, Ariana, 81
Hughes, J., 256
Hulett, Matt, 209
Hummel, E., 565
Humphrey, S., 564, 580, 581
Hunt, J. G., 574
Hunter, J. E., 570
Huntley, C., 569
Hurtado-Torres, N., 557
Huseman, R. C., 443, 585
Hutton, A., 586
Huy, Q. Nguyen, 548, 592

I

Ibarra, Herminia, 548
Ibuka, Masaru, 194
Ilgaz, Z., 575
Ilgen, D., 564, 566, 574, 581
Ilies, R., 573
Illmer, A., 559
Ilyashov, A., 551
Imai, M., 589

Immelt, J., 139, 251, 260, 271, 547, 578
Ingols, C., 563
Inkson, K., 548
Internicola, D., 561
Inverso, E., 192
Ireland, R. D., 554, 560, 561, 565, 566, 573
Isaac, Mike, 551, 552, 553
Isdell, Neville, 146
Isenberg, D. J., 560
Ishikawa, K., 566
Isidore, Chris, 564
Isumi, H., 580
Ivancevich, J., 75, 572
Iverson, R., 579

J

Jackman, J., 577
Jackson, D., 557
Jackson, Jesse, 332
Jackson, T., 578
Jacobs, D., 568
Jacobson, R., 566
Jahiel, P., 228
James, David, 413
James, J., 100, 101, 544, 546
James, L., 574
James, T., 555
Jamieson, B., 567
Janis, I., 552
Jankiewicz, Beckie, 202
Jannarone, J., 544
Jansen, J., 565
Janson, R., 578
Jao, J., 209, 563
Jargon, Julie, 586
Jarilowski, Chaire Stephen, 560
Jarvenpaa, S., 583
Jarzemsky, M., 544
Jassawalla, A., 581
Jauch, Lawrence R., 25, 26, 452
Jehn, K., 572, 582
Jena, A., 581
Jennings, J., 561
Jennings, P., 585
Jensen, J., 573
Jensen, M. C., 549
Jernigan, I. E., 583
Jervis, J., 583
Jesella, K., 571
Jick, T., 586
Jimmieson, N., 592
Jing, B., 589
Jobs, Steve, 192, 358
Johns, T., 563, 580
Johnson, Abigail, 316
Johnson, D. E., 574
Johnson, G., 592
Johnson, H., 547
Johnson, J., 555, 565
Johnson, L. K., 569
Johnson, M., 566, 580, 581, 588
Johnson, Madeleine, 551
Johnson, R., 585

Joling, D., 591
Jones, D., 585
Jones, K., 572, 578
Jones, T., 557
Jordan, Michael, 327
Josefy, M., 556, 566
Joshi, A., 570, 571
Joshi, M., 555, 556
Joyce, W., 564, 591
Judge, T., 568, 573, 575, 576, 577, 585, 591
Jundt, D., 566, 580, 581
Jung, D. I., 575
Junni, P., 548, 591
Juran, J. M., 9
Jurevicius, Ovidijus, 550
Jurgens, J., 557
Jusko, J., 567, 580

K

Kacperczyk, A. J., 563
Kadlec, Dan, 19
Kagermann, H., 588
Kahn, L., 570
Kahn, R. L., 576
Kahn, W., 553
Kahneman, D., 579
Kahwajy, J., 553
Kaizen, G., 589
Kalanick, Travis, 73
Kalb, I., 564
Kale, P., 565
Kammeyer-Mueller, J., 555, 568
Kan, M., 218
Kaneshige, T., 584
Kang, Cecilia, 570
Kang, S. C., 566, 590
Kannan, S., 559
Kanov, J., 553
Kanter, L., 562
Kanter, R. M., 563, 565, 591
Kaplan, Gary S., 586
Kaplan, J., 550
Kaplan, R., 111, 479, 551, 552, 553, 554, 586, 587
Karam, D., 580
Karam, E., 581
Karu, Z., 552
Kasperkevic, J., 569
Kastrenakes, Jacob, 551
Katakey, Rakteem, 591
Kato, Y., 587
Katz, D., 576
Katz, I., 551
Katz, Lee Michael, 588
Katz, R., 548
Katzanek, J., 556
Katzenbach, J., 580, 581, 582
Kavalanz, Parija, 559
Kawamoto, D., 589
Kearney, A. T., 567
Kearney, Eric, 571
Kearns, E. C., 570

Kell, J., 563, 574
Keller, R. T., 582
Keller, S., 592
Kellerman, B., 575
Kello, John, 586
Kelloway, E. K., 579
Kelly, Aidan, 560
Kelly, H., 571
Kelly, R. E., 573
Kemper, A., 557
Kennedy, John F., 358
Kennedy, Joyce Lain, 19
Kenny, D., 573
Kern, M. C., 560
Kerr, S., 574, 576, 577, 586
Kerschberg, B., 566
Kessler, E. H., 588, 590
Kessler, Sarah, 572
Kethley, R. B., 568
Kettering, Charles, 516
Kettinger, W., 584
Keyes, C. L. M., 579
Keys, J. B., 585
Keyton, J., 585
Kezar, C., 319
Khan, N., 590
Kharpal, Arjun, 560
Kickul, J. R., 590
Kiechell, W., III, 548
Kilduff, G., 555
Kilmann, H., 551
Kim, Eugene, 549
Kim, J., 583, 593
Kim, Peter H., 585
Kim, Susanna, 583
Kim, T., 582
Kim, Tae-Yeol, 570
Kim, W. C., 579
King, A. Wilcox, 554
King, Martin Luther, Jr., 358
Kinicki, A., 35, 591
Kircher, Madison Malone, 552
Kirkeby, S., 580
Kirkland, J., 593
Kirkman, B., 580, 581, 582
Kirkpatrick, S., 573
Klara, R., 589
Klassen, R. D., 558
Klein, Ezra, 547, 548, 549
Klein, K., 565, 570
Kleingeld, A., 576, 581
Klimoski, R., 580
Kline, Daniel B., 560, 562, 563
Kline Harrison, J., 575
Kneece, R., 563
Knight, A., 562
Knight, D., 581
Knight, J. M., 186
Kobold, Michael, 258
Koch, R., 589
Koehler, J., 585, 586
Koepfer, C., 558
Koerner, M. M., 576
Kohlberg, L., 555

Kohls, J., 560
Kohls, L. R., 186
Kolodny, H., 564
Kolodny, Lora, 562
Kondo, M., 582
Konopaske, R., 75, 569
Konradt, U., 581
Koo, Mee-Hyoe, 548
Koob, J., 551
Kopeikina, Luda, 551
Kopytoff, Verne, 558, 584
Korda, M., 585
Korn, M., 288, 591
Korten, D. C., 557
Kotler, P., 51
Kotter, J. P., 527, 530, 573, 592, 593, 594
Kouzes, James, 342, 343, 573, 576, 578, 585
Kowitt, Beth, 566
Kownatzki, M., 587
Kramer, M., 562, 594
Kramer, S., 553
Krantz, Gene, 94
Krauss, C., 593
Kräussl, R., 592
Krazit, T., 590
Kreeger, D., 548
Kreissl, B., 571
Kreitner, R., 576
Krell, E., 238
Krietner, R., 35
Kristof-Brown, A., 575
Kroeger, A., 548
Kroos, H., 30
Kross, E., 548
Kryscynski, D., 567
Kuban, S., 566
Kucera, Danielle, 550
Kuczmarski, T., 590
Kuenzi, M., 575
Kulik, C., 571
Kurland, N. B., 586
Kurtines, W. M., 555
Kurtzberg, T., 584
Kurylko, D., 547
Kuvaas, Baard, 587
Kwon, S., 549
Kynighou, A., 566

L

Labelle, R., 571
Labianca, G., 586
Laczniak, G., 555
Ladd, Julie, 203
Laffoley, T., 592
Lafley, A. G., 108, 554
LaFrance, Adrienne, 547, 548, 549
LaGanke, J., 584
Lagerstrom, K., 580
Lagges, J., 564
Lahiri, S., 580
Lai, Y., 567
Lam, S. S. K., 583
Lamont, B. T., 564

Lando, M. A., 588
Lane, P. J., 554
Lang, Derrik, J., 554
Langa, G., 584
Lange, J. E., 561, 562
Langfred, C., 580
Langston, J., 589
Lansing, Sherry, 197
Lanzolla, G., 554
LaPlante, J., 568
LaPort, K., 575, 582
Larcker, D., 585
LaReau, J., 576
Larkey, L. K., 583
Larrick, R., 585
Larson, L. L., 574
Lash, R., 238
Lashinsky, Adam, 547, 575
Latane, B., 552
Latham, G., 569, 576, 577
Latham, S., 588
Lau, James B., 274, 335
Lau, R., 583
Laubacher, R., 563
Laundauer, S., 576
Laurent, A., 592
Lavin, Frank, 558, 559, 560
Lawler, E. E., III, 564, 565, 566, 572, 576, 577, 578, 579, 580, 581, 585, 587, 592, 593, 594
Lawless, Annie, 192
Lawrence, P., 563, 564
Lazarova, Mila, 560
Lazarus, D., 589
Lazenby, J., 578
Le Breton-Miller, I., 593
Leana, C. F., 592
Leavitt, K., 555
LeBoeuf, Michael, 377
Lebowitz, S., 564
Lechner, C., 553, 587
Ledford, G. E., 566
Lee, C., 582
Lee, E., 561
Lee, H. L., 550
Lee, Jeong-Yeon, 570
Lee, Karen, 577
Lee, M., 564, 572
Lee, T., 578
Lee, Y., 218
Leggett, Jeremy, 538
Lei, D., 551, 594
Leifer, R., 588
Lencioni, P., 582
Lengel, R., 584
Lengnick-Hall, C., 547
Lengnick-Hall, M., 547, 572
Leon-Perez, J., 583
Leonard, D., 590, 591
Leonard, H., 591
Leonard-Barton, D., 591
Leopold, Aldo, 69
Lepak, D., 548
Lepine, J., 578

LePine, M. A., 574
Leske, Nicola, 576
Lesser, E., 586
Leung, T. Y., 571
Levin, D., 586
Levine, J. M., 581
Levine, R., 588
Levinson, Marc, 549
Levit, Alexandra, 561
Levitin, D., 577
Levitt, T., 553
Levy, Steven, 590
Lewin, D., 570
Lewin, Kurt, 525–526
Li, C., 560, 575
Li, Ming, 560
Liakopoulos, A., 587
Liao, C., 575
Lichtenhaler, Ulrich, 590
Liden, R., 552, 575, 578
Lieberman, D., 568
Liechti, S., 574
Liedtka, J., 510, 591
Liedtke, M., 567, 570
Lifei, Z., 218
Light, J., 568, 569, 570
Liker, J. K., 567
Likert, R., 574
Lilius, J., 553
Limpaphayom, W., 568
Lindner, S., 549
Lindorff, D., 584
Lindsay, W. M., 566
Linebaugh, Kate, 566
Ling, Y., 563, 575
Lingle, J., 566
Link, A. N., 590
Liodice, B., 556
Lipman, V., 555
Lippitt, R., 574
Litchfield, R. C., 577
Liu, Ansel, 581
Liu, D., 578
Liu, L. A., 583
Liveris, Andrew, 150
Livne-Tarandach, R., 549
Ljung, Alexander, 429
Lloyd, S., 564
Locke, E., 562, 573, 576, 579, 581
Lockwood, C., 551
Lockwood, N. R., 577
Logan, Gordon, 208
Logan, J., 584
Logue, C. M., 443, 585
Lohr, S., 555, 577, 587, 588
Loizos, Connie, 572
Lombardi, C., 558
Lombardo, M., 584
Longenecker, C. O., 583
Lopez, M., 570
Lopez-Kidwell, V., 586
Lord, R. G., 574
Lorinkova, N., 581
Lorsch, J., 563

Loten, A., 554
Lott, A., 582
Lott, B., 582
Low, M., 562
Lowes, P., 558
Lubatkin, M., 563, 575
Lublin, Joann S., 552, 560, 577
Luccocck, Halford E., 402
Ludwig, Timothy D., 587
Luk, L., 589
Lukas, B. A., 560
Lumpkin, G., 561, 563
Lungren, Terry, 4
Lussier, R., 199, 562
Luthans, F., 575, 576, 577
Lutilsky, Ivana Drazic, 587

M

Ma, J., 159, 172, 182, 589
Maak, Thomas, 560
Macadam, S., 585
Macalister, Terry, 591, 593
MacArthur, A., 558
MacDermid, S. M., 572
Macdonald, A., 558, 559
Macdonell, Robby, 584
Mace, M., 580
MacKechnie, C., 589
Mackey, J., 403, 407, 422, 579, 580, 583
Mackintosh, T., 584
Macy, B., 580
Maddux, William W., 585
Madison, Adam, 577
Madjar, N., 578
Magali, M., 557
Magasin, M., 551
Magistretti, Bérénice, 588
Mah, Jessica, 192
Mahendra, A., 67
Maher, K., 573
Mahoney, J. D., 178, 560, 564
Maidique, M. A., 588
Maier, N. R. F., 552
Maignan, I., 560
Mair, J., 561
Maishe, A., 581
Makhani, Sanya, 575
Makridakis, S., 550
Maldegen, R., 568
Malone, T., 563
Mancher, M., 558
Mandela, Nelson, 348
Mangalindan, J. P., 572
Manjoo, Farhad, 551, 552, 567, 570
Mankins, M., 551
Mann, Jennifer, 394, 579
Mann, L., 552
Mann, T., 554
Manning, R. L., 551
Manning, T., 573
Mannix, E., 582
Manyika, J., 558, 568, 589

Manz, C., 573
March, J., 551, 562, 563, 565, 566, 590
Marchington, M., 566
Marcus, A., 557
Markman, G. D., 563
Marks, M., 547, 581
Marler, J., 567
Marriott, Bill, 447
Marriott, J. Willard, 194
Marrone, J., 575, 582
Marrs, A., 589
Marsh, George Perkins, 69
Marsick, V. J., 565, 566
Marte, J., 570
Marti, L., 561
Martin, J., 579
Martin, K., 555
Martin, Melanie J., 579
Martin, R., 557, 573
Martin, Roger, 108, 554
Martinez-Moreno, E., 584
Martiott, William, 121
Marx, G., 557
Mas, A., 581
Maslow, Abraham, 32, 577
Mason, A., 547
Massey, A., 583
Mastroianni, B., 588
Matear, M., 561
Mathews, C., 555
Mathieu, J., 578, 581
Mathieu, R. G., 587
Matson, E., 573
Matten, D., 557
Matthews, Christopher M., 556
Matthews, G., 564
Mattioli, D., 573
Matusak, L. R., 575
Matuson, Roberta, 579
Mauborgne, R., 579
Maxim, J., 593
May, D., 555
May, M., 577
Mayer, D. M., 575
Mayer, Marissa, 83
Maynard, M. T., 578, 581
Mayo, Elton, 31
Mays, K., 558
McAlone, Nathan, 551
McCall, M., 178, 551, 552, 553, 560, 576, 584
McCann, Joel, 101
McCauley, C. D., 576
McClain, S., 67
McClaskey, M. B., 585
McClelland, D., 577, 578
McClendon, J. A., 570
McClesky, J., 548
McCnase, Anne Adams, 352
McCollum, J. K., 564
McCormack, M., 583
McCracken, M., 467, 587
McCullen, P., 567
McDermott, C. M., 588

McDonald, John, 72
McDonald, Loren, 590
McDowell, T., 564, 580
McFadden, Leah, 422
McFarland, L. A., 568
McGee, J. E., 551
McGill, M., 594
McGinnis, L. F., 567
McGirt, Ellen, 569
McGranahan, D., 567
McGrath, B., 550
McGrath, R. R., Jr., 129, 185, 249
McGregor, J., 547, 551, 568
McIlvaine, Andrew R., 564
McIntyre, K. Kung, 553
McIver, D., 547
McKay, B., 557
McKee, A., 548
McKinley, W., 588
McLernon, N., 558
McMillan-Capehart, A., 571
McMillion, Doug, 257
McNew, Bradley, Seth, 551
McPherson, S., 580
McShane, Steven L., 65, 66
McWilliams, A., 557
Meden, Scott, 500
Medina, C., 571
Medina, F., 583
Meek, T., 570
Megginson, L., 560
Megginson, W., 560
Mehler, M., 568
Mehrabian, A., 585
Meiland, D., 547
Meinert, D., 568, 584, 592
Meister, J., 584
Mellahi, K., 551
Mena, S., 556
Mendenca, L., 593
Mendoca, J., 559
Menser, T., 593
Menz, M., 548
Menza, J., 565
Meola, A., 547
Merchant, K., 586, 587
Merkin, R., 583
Mesmer-Magnus, J. R., 581, 583
Messick, D., 551, 552
Meuser, J., 575
Meyer, C., 577, 581
Meyer, E., 560
Meyer, K., 567
Meyers, G., 93, 553
Meyerson, B., 588, 589
Meznar, M. B., 551
Michael, D., 557
Michaels, Daniel, 552
Micou, Tripp, 203
Mifflin, K. E., 588
Miles, R. H., 592
Miles, Raymond E., 240, 550, 564, 565
Miles, S., 585
Milkovich, G., 569

Mille, D., 580
Miller, B., 586, 587
Miller, C., 559
Miller, Claire Cain, 567
Miller, D., 564, 584, 588, 593
Miller, T., 561
Milligan, S., 551
Milliken, F. J., 582
Mills, M., 574
Milner, C., 575
Milstein, M. B., 557
Minter, Steve, 580, 590
Mintz, H. K., 585
Mintzberg, H., 17, 548
Miremadi, M., 558
Misangyi, V. F., 574
Mishra, A. K., 566
Misumi, J., 350, 573, 574
Mitchell, T., 576
Mitroff, I. I., 553
Mittal, Vikas, 579
Mobley, William H., 560
Model, J., 561
Moeller, Sara B., 587
Mohammed, S., 583
Mohrman, S. A., 565, 566
Mol, Michael J., 588
Molina, A., 591
Mom, T., 565
Montealegre, R., 591
Montgomery, C. A., 550, 554
Montoya-Weiss, M., 583
Montrosse, J., 558
Moon, C. H., 559
Moon, J., 557
Moore, C., 556, 588
Moore, S., 553, 579
Moores, K., 588
Moran, Frank, 393
Moran, G., 573, 584
Moran, P., 579
Moretti, E., 581
Morgan, E., 563
Morgan, J. M., 567
Morgan, N., 585
Morgeson, F., 568, 581
Morris, S., 559, 571
Morris, Shad S., 559
Morris, T., 566
Morrison, A., 584
Morrison, E. W., 549
Mortensen, R., 560
Mosakowski, E., 585
Moss, S., 577
Moss, T., 561
Mount, I., 562
Mouton, J., 574
Moxley, R., 576
MucMullen, J., 561
Muczyk, J., 574
Muethel, M., 580
Muir, John, 69
Mukherjee, Ajoy, 467
Mukherjee, D., 580

Mukherjee, S., 550
Mula, J., 588
Mulally, Alan, 362
Mullainathan, S., 571
Mullen, B., 582
Mullen, J., 558
Muller, A., 592
Mullins, L., 580
Munduate, L., 583
Muoio, Danielle, 553
Murnighan, K., 556
Murphy, C., 573, 593
Murphy, R., 566
Murphy, S., 552
Murrell, A. J., 572
Musk, Elon, 114, 193, 489, 503, 511
Myatt, M., 582
Myers, Dave, 210
Myers, R., 119

N

Nadeau, Y., 587
Nadkarni, Sucheta, 559
Nadler, D., 580, 581, 592
Nagarajan, N., 574
Nahavandi, A., 581
Naik, G., 594
Nairn-Birch, N., 557
Najdawi, M. K., 564
Nakanishi, Leigh, 556
Nalick, M., 556
Nambisan, Satish, 590
Nanley, J., 571
Nanus, B., 572, 575
Naquin, C., 584
Nascimento, Barbara, 193
Nash, S., 589
Nazaryan, Alexander, 549, 551
Needleman, S. E., 562
Nefer, B., 564
Nelson, B., 564
Nelson, K. A., 560
Neubert, M., 583
Neuhaus, K., 567
Newcombe, R., 588
Newman, J., 569
Newstrom, John W., 273
Ng, S., 576
Ng-Mak, D., 572
Ngan, M., 589
Nichols, Ralph G., 443
Nicklin, J., 578
Nicolaides, V., 575, 582
Nicols, K., 586
Nidumolu, R., 557
Nigam, Roli, 560
Nilson, V., 552
Nisbett, R., 552
Noack, R., 558
Noguchi, Y., 100
Nohria, N., 564, 585, 591, 593

Nooyi, Indra, 5, 49, 58, 316, 341, 357, 360, 364
Norris, G., 555
Norton, D., 111, 479, 554, 587
Novakovic, Phebe, 316
Novicevic, M., 566
Nugent, P. S., 583
Nur, Y. A., 574
Nusca, A., 583
Nyberg, A., 567
Nystedt, D., 218

O

Obama, Barack, 70, 318
O'Boyle, I., 569
O'Brien, J. M., 338
Ochs, J., 583
O'Connor, G. C., 588
O'Connor, M., 567
Odum, Marvin, 538
Ogilvie, T., 510, 591
O'Hara, M., 580
Okamoto, T., 564, 580
Okhuysen, G., 552
Okie, Francis G., 508
Okumura, Tetsushi, 585
Oldham, G., 578
O'Leary, Michael, 10
Oligney, R. E., 589
Olsen, S., 586
O'Malley, Alison, 587
Omidyar, Pierre, 198, 562, 594
O'Neil, D., 585
O'Neill, E., 566
O'Neill, H. M., 588
Ones, D. S., 568
Orden, Erica, 555
Ordonez, L., 576
Oreg, S., 592
O'Reilly, C., 565
O'Reilly, Tim, 5
Organ, D., 354, 382, 579
Orlitzky, M., 557
Ortner, Michael, 77, 78, 80
Ortutay, B., 567, 570
Osborne, C., 583
Osman, M., 553
Oster, S., 560
Ostrower, Jon, 552
Otazo, K. L., 585
O'Toole, J., 557, 582
Ouchi, W. G., 461, 586
Overmyer Day, L. E., 572
Owen, R., 562

P

Paauwe, Jaap, 559
Pache, A. C., 561
Packard, David, 194
Paddock, Richard C., 553
Paetzold, R. L., 569

Page, Larry, 9, 192
Page, Scott E., 570
Page, T., 564, 580
Pagnamenta, R., 566
Pahnke, E. C., 562
Paine, L., 556, 591
Paisner, M., 567
Palazzo, G., 557
Pallotta, Frank, 553
Palmisano, Sam, 131, 143
Panzarino, Matthew, 555
Parboteeah, K., 555
Pardue, Nancy, 577
Parker, S., 563, 583
Parnell, D., 562
Parris, D., 575
Parsaei, H. R., 567
Parsons, J., 594
Pascual, Mig, 554
Pasztor, Andy, 561
Patel, P., 582, 585
Patel, Shivani Garg, 362
Patten, E., 570
Patterson, Anna, 292
Patterson, F., 568
Paulson, G., 584
Pawar, K. S., 563
Peachey, J., 575
Pearce, C. L., 564, 575
Pearsall, M., 578, 581
Pearse, R. F., 563
Pearson, C. M., 553
Pearson, J., 553
Peborde, M. S., 576
Peiperl, M., 594
Pelled, L. H., 582, 586
Pellerin, C., 590
Peloza, J., 557
Penley, L., 583
Pepitone, J., 568
Perera, S., 571
Perez, Pedro David, 559
Perez, S., 550
Perkins, Sam, 100, 101
Perkins, T., 563
Perlez, J., 559
Perlmutter, H., 565
Perlow, L., 552
Perrin, A., 554
Perry, James, 388
Perry, M. L., 564
Perry-Smith, J., 553
Peters, B. A., 567
Peters, L. S., 588
Peters, M., 205, 562
Peters, T., 549, 578
Petersen, Haley, 558
Petersen, L., 568
Peterson, H., 583, 589
Peterson, K., 580
Peterson, M., 350, 573, 574
Peterson, R. R., 550
Peterson, Richard B., 570
Petrick, J., 572

Petriglieri, G., 100
Petroff, A., 550, 572
Peyer, Urs, 548
Pfeffer, J., 548, 552, 563, 577
Pham, Sherisse, 559
Phelps, Corey C., 590
Phelps, S., 567
Philip, S., 67
Philips, M., 559
Phillips, R., 557
Phipps, C., 236
Phyrillis, R., 338
Piccolo, R., 573, 575, 577
Piet, Johan, 68
Pieterse, Anne Nederveen, 572
Pinchot, C., 563
Pinchot, E., 558, 563
Pinchot, G., 558
Pinder, C., 577
Pine, B. J., 567
Pineau, E., 558, 559
Pink, D. H., 576, 578
Pisano, G. P., 588
Pitaro, James A., 112
Pittinsky, T., 575
Plamondon, K. E., 586
Pless, Nicola M., 560
Ployhart, R. E., 568, 570
Podmolik, M. E., 578
Podsakoff, P., 574
Pogatchnik, S., 547
Pogson, C. E., 577
Poll, Jack, 371
Pollack, A., 550
Pollak, L., 573
Polzer, J., 583
Pond, Randy, 431
Porath, C., 594
Porras, Jerry, 458, 518–520, 561, 586, 591
Port, O., 547
Porter, Michael, 46, 261, 554, 562, 566, 589, 594
Posner, Barry, 342, 343, 573, 576, 578, 585
Post, C., 571
Post, J., 556
Potts, M., 574
Pounder, R. W., 588
Prahalad, C. K., 557, 565, 593
Pramuk, Jacob, 554
Prasad, S., 564
Prather, C. W., 590
Pratt, M. K., 585
Preidt, R., 581
Premack, S., 570
Prentice, C., 550
Preston, L., 556
Prestwood, D. C. L., 588
Price, M., 569
Priem, R. L., 554
Prietula, M., 548
Primack, D., 552
Procter, William, 32
Proctor, R. A., 554
Prouska, R., 592

Prussia, G., 591
Pruyn, A. T. H., 585
Pucik, V., 591
Pugh, A., 571
Pulakos, E. D., 574, 586
Pullin, J., 588
Puranam, P., 553, 574, 592
Purdy, K., 578

Q

Qi, Y., 567
Qian, C., 557
Qin, X., 585
Quast, L., 569
Quinn, D., 557
Quinn, G., 589
Quinn, J., 572
Quinn, R., 548, 551, 575, 594
Quittner, Jeremy, 562, 571

R

Raelin, J. A., 594
Raes, A., 548
Rafferty, A., 592
Rafflee, J., 561, 562
Rafter, M., 577
Rainee, L., 554
Rajacic, D., 578
Ramirez, G. G., 574
Ramoglou, S., 561
Ramsey, Mike, 590
Rancour, T., 467, 587
Randall, M., 554
Randall, R., 568
Randolph, W. A., 578
Rangan, S., 557
Rangaswami, M. R., 557
Ranil, D., 577
Rao, A. R., 552
Rao, K. S., 567
Rapier, R., 559
Rasmus, Daniel, 555
Rast, D., III, 575, 582
Raven, B., 347, 573
Rawls, John, 141
Ray, R., 565
Rayasam, R., 581
Ready, D. A., 594
Reagan, Ronald, 358
Rechheld, R., 578
Reddy, T., 593
Reeb, D. M., 571
Reed, J., 576
Reeves, M., 580, 591
Rehbein, K., 556
Reingold, Jennifer, 555
Reinhardt, R., 589
Reio, T., Jr., 572
Ren, C., 548
Ren, R., 585
Rendell, M., 592
Repenning, N., 552
Resnick, N., 593

Restubog, S. L., 592
Rhode, J., 587
Ricco, R., 571
Rice, M., 588
Rice, R., 584
Rich, B., 555, 574, 578
Richardson, H. A., 566
Richardson, N., 552
Richman, Alan, 549
Ridgeway, R., 558
Ridolfi, E., 579
Rigby, D., 592
Riggio, R., 573
Rigoni, B., 564, 577
Rijsdijk, Serge A., 588
Riley, C., 559
Ringel, M., 590
Ringseis, E., 583
Rinke, A., 558, 559
Rintamaki, J., 556
Ripoll, P., 584
Risher, H. W., 570
Rittenburg, T., 560
Robb, Walter, 403
Robbins, J., 579
Roberson, B., 564, 591
Roberto, M. A., 552
Roberts, L. M., 548, 549
Robertson, Brian, 99
Robertson, Jordan, 553
Robey, R. D., 461
Robinson, D. M., 572
Robinson, Marie, 74
Robinson, S., 555
Robinson, S. L., 579
Rockstuhl, T., 574
Rodriguez, G., 338
Rodriguez, R., 572
Rodriguez, Salvador, 570, 572
Roepe, L., 571
Roethlisberger, Fritz, 31
Rogers, Bruce, 579
Rogers, E. M., 588
Rogers, P., 551
Roh, H., 570, 571
Rohman, Jessica, 579
Rokos, B., 556
Romero, N., 571
Rometty, Ginni, 131, 316
Rosa, Fabio, 197
Rosedale, Philip, 240
Rosen, B., 572, 580, 581, 582
Rosen, R., 572
Rosenblatt, Z., 573
Rosenblum, A., 589
Rosenfeld, Irene, 136, 315, 316
Rosenthal, S. R., 591
Rosnow, R. L., 586
Ross, A., 588
Ross, L., 552
Roth, A., 589, 591
Roth, E. A., 588, 589
Roth, K., 557
Rotondo, D. M., 569

Rottig, D., 580
Roundy, Philip T., 590
Rousseau, D., 579, 592
Roy, Sanjit Bunker, 148
Roy, U., 567
Rubin, B., 555
Rubin, C., 568
Ruch, W. V., 585, 586
Ruddy, T., 581
Ruff, K., 586
Ruhe, G., 553
Rui, O., 571
Ruiz, Gisel, 319
Rupp, D., 578
Rusjan, B., 587
Russo, M., 557
Ruthrsdotter, M., 570
Ruvio, A., 573
Ryan, A. M., 568
Ryan, Katherine, 571
Rynes, S., 557, 572

S

Sabeti, H., 562, 594
Sachdev, Ameet, 589
Sachs, D., 566
Sadowski, M., 589
Safian, R., 550, 563, 572, 574
Sahin, F., 268, 567
Sahlman, W. A., 562
Saiidi, U., 593
Sakano, T., 565
Saleem, Fahad, 558
Sales, C. A., 461
Salvador, R., 575
Sambamurthy, V., 564
Sampson, R. C., 565
Sanborn, G., 578
Sanchez, J., 176, 577
Sanchez-Burks, J., 548
Sandberg, J., 559
Sandberg, Sheryl, 9, 22, 316
Sandino, T., 586
Santamaria, J. A., 581
Sapienza, H. J., 563
Sarala, R., 548, 580, 591
Saridakis, G., 567
Sarker, S., 580
Sarooghi, H., 561
Sashittal, H., 581
Sashkin, M., 578
Satell, G., 547, 575
Sauer, P. J., 561
Sawhney, M., 588, 590
Saxon, M. J., 551
Sayles, L., 235, 548, 582
Schaffer, B. S., 578
Schaubroeck, J, 583
Scheck, J., 555
Schein, E., 364, 592
Schere, R., 572
Schermerhorn, Jr, J., 556
Schill, B., 571

Schippers, M., 581
Schippmann, J. S., 568
Schisgall, O., 32
Schlesinger, Leonard A., 527, 592
Schmidt, F., 557, 568, 579
Schmidt, Stephanie, 534
Schmidt, W., 353, 574
Schmulen, M., 584
Schneider, B., 593
Schneider, Beth Z., 25, 155, 397, 398, 542
Schoemaker, P. J. H., 550
Schoenberger, Chana R., 581
Schonberger, Richard J., 567
Schooley, T., 591
Schouten, M., 580
Schrempf-Stirling, J., 556-557
Schroeder, R., 580, 582
Schuler, D., 557
Schuler, R. S., 569
Schultz, E., 550
Schultz, P., 573
Schulz, Howard, 189, 201, 212
Schulze, W., 563
Schumann, P. A., Jr., 588
Schumlen, M., 584
Schuneman, Pam, 471, 587
Schuster, J. R., 569
Schwab, K., 509
Schwabel, D., 565, 588
Schwarz, J. L., 571
Schwarz, N., 568, 579
Schweiger, D., 585
Schweitzer, M., 576
Schwenk, C., 552
Scorza, J., 565
Scott, A., 593
Scott, J., 568
Scott, K., 582
Scott, M., 559
Scott, S. R., Jr., 560
Scroxton, A., 547
Seager, C., 577
Seal, G., 591
Seals, A., 571
Seashore, S. E., 582
Sebastian, P., 565
Sedgwick, D., 456
Segaar, P., 553
Segal, J. A., 568
Seggerman, T. K., 563
Seibert, J., 566
Seibert, S., 578, 581
Seidmann, A., 589
Seijts, G., 577
Seitz, P., 588
Seligman, M. E. P., 549
Seligson, H., 585
Selingo, J., 568
Selko, Adrienne, 587
Semadeni, Matthew, 589
Senge, P. M., 557, 565
Sengul, M., 561
Seo, M., 592
Serpa, R., 551

Setty, Prasad, 278
Shafer, Scott M., 587
Shaffer, Margaret A., 560
Shah, Anand, 494
Shah, P. P., 568
Shalley, C., 553, 577, 581
Shamir, B., 574, 575
Shane, S., 560
Shani, A. B. (Rami), 274, 335
Shankelman, Jess, 592
Shao, R., 578
Shapiro, D., 580, 581
Shapiro, E. C., 573
Sharfman, M., 552, 553
Sharifi, S., 563
Sharma, A., 550
Sharma, P. N., 581
Sharp, A., 577
Sharp, Evan, 192
Shaw, G. B., 428
Shaw, J., 582
Shaw, K. N., 374, 576
Shehadi, R., 580
Shen, L., 554
Shen, Y., 549
Shergill, P., 571
Sheridan, K., 568
Sheridan, R., 577
Sheridan, Richard, 377
Sherisse, Pham, 558
Sherman, A., 297, 570
Sherman, M., 584
Shields, T., 550
Shih, H. A., 582
Shin, H., 591
Shin, J., 592
Shin, Shung J., 570
Shintaku, Junjiro, 559
Shipper, F., 569
Shippmann, J. S., 568
Shiraki, M., 590
Shirouzu, N., 560
Shore, L., 574
Short, J., 561
Shrivastava, P., 557
Shultz, S. F., 563
Sidebottom, P., 587
Siebdrat, F., 583
Siebold, D., 552
Siedle, E., 568
Siegel, D., 557
Sigala, R., 552
Sikka, P., 550
Sikora, P., 579
Silbermann, Ben, 192
Silver, S., 578
Silver, W., 576
Silverman, R., 100, 569, 584, 588, 591
Silverman, S. B., 577
Silversthorne, S., 567
Simha, A., 556
Simisek, Z., 575
Simmonds, P. G., 564
Simmons, Michael, 588

Simon, B., 576
Simon, Herbert, 92, 565
Simon, L., 555
Simon, S., 575
Simons, R., 586
Simons, T., 582
Sims, B, Jr., 577
Sims, H. P., Jr., 564, 578, 581
Simsek, Z., 563
Sinclair, R., 570
Sinclair-Desgangné, B., 571
Singh, A., 558
Singh, H., 565, 573
Singh, J., 562, 573
Singh, Nidhi, 581
Singh, Shavila, 192
Sinha, K., 580, 582
Siporin, C., 590
Sirmon, D. G., 554, 560, 561, 565
Sisodia, Raj, 579, 580, 583
Sitkin, S., 574
Skarlicki, D., 578
Slind, Michael, 583, 585
Sloan, Alfred, 104, 222
Sloane, A., 570
Slocum, J., 560, 592, 594
Slowinski, G., 565
Sluis, S., 566
Sluss, D., 555
Smidts, A., 585
Smith, Adam, 146
Smith, Brad, 360
Smith, C., 567
Smith, D., 580, 581, 582, 593
Smith, Ethan, 555
Smith, J., 556, 585
Smith, Jacquelyn, 583
Smith, Jake, 558
Smith, K., 548, 567, 582
Smith, N., 587
Smith, Stuart M., 587
Smith, T., 558, 578, 589
Smothers, J., 566
Snell, S., 296, 297, 318, 551, 559, 566, 567, 570, 571, 580, 590
Snow, C., 240, 550, 564, 565, 580
Snyder, Benjamin, 574, 576
Snyder, W. M., 579
Soda, G., 253, 565
Solomon, M., 561
Somech, A., 580
Son, J., 570
Sonenshein, S., 553
Sonfield, M., 199, 562
Song, M., 583
Song, Z., 581
Sonnenfeld, J., 574
Sonnentag, S., 579
Sook, Jin, 319
Sorkin, A., 565
Spangenburg, J., 575
Sparrowe, R. T., 578
Spaulding, A., 593
Spector, B., 592

Spector, P., 176
Spekman, Robert E., 550
Spell, Chester S., 572
Spender, J. C., 590
Spicer, A., 555
Spiegel, Evan, 192
Spinelli, S., Jr., 191, 193, 206, 213, 220, 560, 561, 562
Spitzer, Q., 552
Spreitzer, G., 178, 548, 560, 566, 575
Springsteen, Bruce, 258
Srinivasan, D., 574
Srivastava, A., 581
Stahl, G., 559, 560, 581
Stajkovic, A. D., 577
Stalk, G., 562, 567
Stalker, G., 252, 565
Stam, D., 583
Standifer, R., 583
Stanislao, B. C., 592
Stanislao, J., 592
Staples, D., 582
Staples, M., 564
Stark, Karl, 563
Stata, Ray, 250
Staw, B. M., 578
Steel, P., 583
Steel, R., 574
Steensma, H., 556
Steinfield, C., 584
Steinmetz, K., 568
Stevens, J., 556
Stevenson, N., 553
Stevenson, S., 585
Stevenson, W. B., 563
Stewart, Bill, 563
Stieglitz, N., 553
Stiles, Philip, 559
Stiller Rikleen, L., 573
Stillman, J., 562
Stinchcombe, A. L., 562, 563
Stogdill, R. M., 573
Stone, M., 192
Strauss, George, 235
Straw, B., 553
Strickland, A. J., III, 554
Strickland, O., 574
Strober, M., 577
Strom, S., 565
Strom, Stephanie, 549, 550
Strong, B., 590
Sturdevant, M., 581
Stynes, Tess, 590
Suarez, F. F., 554
Sugarman, B., 592
Sullivan, Eileen, 553
Sullivan, J., 572
Sullivan, W., 29
Sun, P., 551
Sunnucks, Mike, 583
Surdevant, D., 547
Susanto, E., 582
Sutherland, J., 592
Sutherland, Kiefer, 258

Suttle, J. L., 579
Sutton, R., 552, 577
Sverdlik, N., 592
Swaak, R. A., 560
Swartz, J., 552
Swedberg, C., 567
Sweeney, P., 556
Sweet, C., 593
Swiggett, Robert L., 343
Swinmurn, Nick, 192, 207
Swisher, Kara, 551
Symon, G., 564
Systrom, Kevin, 192
Szal, A., 589

T
Tajitsu, N., 590
Takeuchi, D., 579
Takeuchi, H., 592
Takla, M. G., 565
Talley, K., 554
Tangel, A., 560
Tannenbaum, A., 353, 574
Taras, V., 580, 583, 591
Tarba, S., 591
Tata, J., 564
Tatikonda, M. V., 591
Tausche, K., 584
Tayan, B., 585
Taylor, A., 590
Taylor, Alex, III, 551
Taylor, Frederick, 29, 30
Taylor, K., 550
Taylor, L., 563
Taylor, M., 548, 592
Taylor, P., 571
Taylor, Susan Johnston, 581
Team, T., 550
Teece, D. J., 565
Teerlink, R., 592
Tepper, B., 582
Terlep, S., 553, 564, 565
Terpstra, D. E., 568
Tesluk, P., 575, 578, 580, 581, 582, 584
Tetrick, L., 570, 579
Thatcher, Margaret, 348
Thatcher, S., 582
Thomas, B., 572
Thomas, G., 573
Thomas, K., 419
Thomas, K. W., 582
Thomas, L. A., 589
Thomas, R., 550
Thomas, T., 556
Thompson, A. A., 554
Thompson, B., 563, 575
Thompson, John, 319
Thompson, L., 553
Thompson, Scott, 284
Thomson, R., 550
Thoreau, Henry David, 130
Thoresen, C. J., 591
Thorn, R., 564
Thorndike, Edward, 375

Thorpe, D., 559
Thurgood, Barrick G., 578
Thurm, Scott, 570
Tierney, P., 553
Tijoriwala, S. A., 592
Tillema, H., 564
Timmons, Jeffry A., 155, 190, 193, 206, 213, 215, 220, 560, 561, 562
Tinsley, C., 582
Tita, B., 558
Tjosvold, D., 582, 586
Toegel, G., 569
Tolleson, Rob, 447
Tomassetti, A., 575, 582
Tome, George, 525
Torres, Denice, 319
Torsoli, A., 554
Tost, L., 585
Touryalai, H., 586
Towill, D. R., 567
Townsend, M., 544
Townsend, R., 346, 573
Toye, S., 585
Trahant, B., 578
Trahms, C., 560, 561
Trevino, L., 555, 556, 560, 574, 577
Trevor, Jonathan, 559
Trimble, C., 578
Tripathi, A., 582
Trist, E., 591
Troy, L., 570
Trudell, C., 589
Trump, Donald, 34, 137
Truxillo, D., 579
Tsakumis, G., 576–577
Tsang, E. W. K., 561
Tsuroka, D., 590
Tu, Janet I., 563
Tuckman, B. W., 409
Tulgan, Bruce, 321
Tullberg, Jan, 587
Tung, R., 560
Turban, D., 557
Turner, N., 575
Tushman, M., 548, 565
Tuttle, B., 589
Tweardy, J., 558
Tynan, D., 582

U
Uhl-Bien, M., 573
Ulrich, D., 567, 586
Unruh, G., 558
Unruh, J., 585
Upadhyay, A., 571
Upton, D., 585
Useem, M., 573
Usher, J. M., 567

V
Vaccaro, A., 577
van Agtmael, A., 559
Van Alphen, T., 456

van Beurden, Ben, 517
Van de Ven, A., 591
van den Ende, Jan, 588
Van der Vegt, G., 582
van Dierendonck, D., 572, 575
Van Fleet, D., 564
van Ginkel, W., 581
van Knippenberg, D., 572, 574, 575, 578, 581, 582, 583
van Mierlo, H., 576, 581
Van Nuys, K., 572
van Riel, C. B. M., 585
Van Velsor, E., 576
Vance, A., 566, 585
Vandebroek, Sophie, 507
Vandenberg, R. J., 566, 578
VanderHart, D., 558
Vanderkam, L., 584
VanderMey, Anne, 579
Vandlen, C., 551
Vas, T., 548
Vascellaro, J. E., 561
Vasel, K., 569
Vasilash, G. S., 268
Vater, D., 587
Veiga, J., 563, 575, 587
Venkataraman, S., 560, 562
Venus, M., 583
Vera, D., 575
Vermeulen, F., 592
Vernon, S., 571
Veryzer, R. W., 588
Vesper, K. H., 561
Vickery, S., 564
Viguerie, P., 593
Viswesvaran, C., 568
Vittorio, P., 553
Vlasic, Bill, 590
Voelpel, Sven, C., 571
Vogus, T., 561
Von Glinow, Mary Ann, 66
Von Hippel, E., 590
von Oetinger, Bolko, 547
Vonortas, N. S., 590
Vozza, S., 547, 584
Vroom, V. H., 574, 577

W

Waalewijn, P., 553
Wack, Kevin, 592
Waddock, S., 557, 587
Wadhwas, S., 567
Wageman, R., 581
Wagner, J., III, 574
Wagner, K., 549, 553
Wahba, P., 547, 566, 577
Wahlforss, Eric, 429
Wailgum, T., 566
Wakayama, Toshiro, 559
Waldinger, R., 561
Waldman, D., 574, 575, 591
Waldmeir, P., 590

Waldron, H., 571
Waldroop, J., 585
Walker, A., 588
Walker, Joseph, 569
Wall, J., 421, 574, 583
Wall, Mike, 591
Walsh, B., 558
Walter, F., 582
Walter, J., 553, 587
Walter, Laura, 593
Walters, J., 558
Walton, Mary Lu, 527
Walton, R. E., 579
Walton, Sam, 60
Wang, C., 582
Wang, D., 575
Wang, G., 581
Wang, H., 557
Wang, J., 556
Wang, L., 556, 578
Wang, M., 553
Wang, P., 571
Ward, A., 590
Ward, Marguerite, 576
Ward, R. D., 563
Warr, P. B., 579
Washington, George, 348
Waters, R., 567, 569
Watkins, K. E., 565, 566
Watrous, M., 550, 572, 574
Watson, Stephen T., 586
Watson, Thomas J., 276, 358
Wattles, Jackie, 572
Wayne, S., 552, 575, 578
Weaver, G. R., 556
Webb, A., 555
Webb, T., 550
Webber, R., 548
Weber, C., 548
Weber, J., 556
Weber, L., 568, 586
Weber, Lauren, 569
Weber, Max, 32, 252
Weekley, J. A., 568
Weeks, Linton, 584
Wehle, S., 584
Weingart, L., 552, 582
Weis, E., 575, 582
Weise, E., 549, 552, 584
Weisman, R., 562
Weiss, H., 574
Weiss, J., 256
Weiss, L., 573
Weiss, T., 578
Welbourne, T., 569, 591
Welch, D., 553
Welch, Jack, 102, 449
Well, B., 547
Wellins, R. S., 582
Wellman, N., 576
Welsh, D., 576
Welsh, T., 32
Wenger, E. C., 579

Wernsing, T., 576
Wesson, M. J., 569
Westerman-Behaylo, M., 556
Westman, Mina, 560
Weston, D., 554
Wexley, K., 569
Wheeler, J., 582
Wheelwright, S. C., 588, 591
White, B. Joseph, 378, 590
White, Martha C., 586
White, R., 574
Whitford, D., 558
Whitman, Meg, 316, 360
Whitney, J. O., 588
Whybark, D. Clay, 558
Whylly, L., 576
Wickelgren, I., 583
Wicks, A. C., 554
Wieczner, J., 554
Wilkie, D., 571
Williams, C., 537, 594
Williams, D., 561, 575
Williams, K., 552
Williams, T., 591
Willis, B., 551
Wilson, A., 576
Wilson, G., 578
Wiltermuth, S., 577, 583
Wincent, J., 562
Winfrey, Oprah, 319, 358
Wise, J. M., 586
Wise, S., 582
Wiseman, R. M., 569
Witney, F., 570
Witzel, M., 557
Wladaswasky-Berger, I., 547
Wnuck, D., 580, 582
Woehr, D. J., 568
Woetzel, J., 568
Wohl, J., 550
Wohlgezogen, F., 565, 594
Wolcott, R. C., 588
Wolf, W., 567
Wolfe, P., 570
Wong, A., 582, 586
Wood, Jake, 386
Wood, R. E., 577
Woodcock, Tony, 557
Woodward, Joan, 265, 566
Woolf, Nicky, 591
Worley, C., 521, 592
Worline, M., 553
Worthen, B., 551
Wozniak, Steve, 192
Wright, Aliah, 588
Wright, J., 549
Wright, M., 551, 561
Wright, P., 567
Wright, Patrick M., 559, 565, 567
Wright, T., 579
Wu, N., 570
Wunderlich, Maren, 579
Wysocki, M., 567

X

Xavier, Stephen, 548

Y

Yammarino, F., 574
Yang, Jenny, 332
Yang, W., 567
Yanouzas, J., 587
Yasai-Ardekani, M., 550
Ybarra, O., 548
Yeatts, D., 580
Yen, C., 579
Yerak, Becky, 562
Yeung, K., 590
Yglesias, Matthew, 589
Yi, S.-S., 590
Yorges, S., 574
Young, E., 550
Youngblood, S. A., 569
Yuhas, A., 554
Yukl, G., 573, 574
Yunus, Muhammad, 167, 197, 463

Z

Zablit, H., 590
Zablow, R. J., 556
Zaccaro, S., 573, 575, 581, 582
Zaheer, A., 253, 565
Zahra, S., 561, 563, 589
Zakaria, N., 580
Zakrzewski, C., 586
Zald, M., 556
Zardkoohi, A., 556, 569
Zaslow, J., 577
Zeidel, M., 562
Zeidner, R., 568
Zeithaml, C., 56, 57, 550, 552
Zeithaml, V., 56, 57, 550
Zeitz, G., 562
Zell, D., 592
Zenger, Jack, 572
Zezima, K., 587
Zhang, M., 567
Zhang, S., 578
Zhang, X., 578
Zhang, Y., 559, 574

Zhang, Z., 575, 585
Zhao, F., 580
Zhao, H., 575
Zhao, L., 582
Zhao, W., 571
Zhao, X., 567
Zhelyazkov, P., 565, 594
Zhu, J., 582
Zieminski, Nick, 558
Zigarmi, P., 592
Zillman, C., 587
Zimmerman, A., 544, 551
Zimmerman, M., 562
Zingheim, P. K., 569
Ziobro, P., 544
Zipay, K., 578
Zmud, R. W., 584
Zoellik, Robert, 150
Zornoza, A., 584
Zuboff, S., 593
Zuckerberg, Mark, 3, 4, 15, 22, 192